北京大学中国语言学研究中心

早期北京话珍稀文献集成

主编 刘云

——西人北京话教科书汇编

分卷主编 翟赟 郭利霞 陈颖

语言自迩集（第二版）

[英] 威妥玛 编著

卷二

北京大学出版社
PEKING UNIVERSITY PRESS

国家出版基金项目
NATIONAL PUBLICATION FOUNDATION

語言自邇集

(YÜ YEN TZŬ ÊRH CHI).

A

PROGRESSIVE COURSE

DESIGNED TO ASSIST THE STUDENT OF

COLLOQUIAL CHINESE

AS SPOKEN IN THE CAPITAL AND THE METROPOLITAN DEPARTMENT.

IN THREE VOLUMES.

SECOND EDITION.

PREPARED BY

THOMAS FRANCIS WADE,
Sometime H.B.M.'s Minister in China.

AND

WALTER CAINE HILLIER,
Chinese Secretary to H.B.M.'s Legation, Peking.

VOL. II.

SHANGHAI:
PUBLISHED AT THE STATISTICAL DEPARTMENT OF THE INSPECTORATE GENERAL OF CUSTOMS,
AND SOLD BY
KELLY & WALSH, LIMITED, SHANGHAI, YOKOHAMA, AND HONGKONG.
LONDON: W. H. ALLEN & Co., WATERLOO PLACE.
1886.

CONTENTS.

	PAGE.
PART III.—THE FORTY EXERCISES	1
Chinese Weights and Measures	213
PART IV.—THE TEN DIALOGUES	215
PART V.—THE HUNDRED LESSONS	249
PART VI.—THE GRADUATE'S WOOING, or THE STORY OF A PROMISE THAT WAS KEPT	351
PART VII.—THE TONE EXERCISES	419
Notes on the Tone Rules affecting the Finals	423
Exercises in the Tones	427
PART VIII.—THE PARTS OF SPEECH:—	
Introductory Observations	481
The Noun and the Article	484
The Chinese Numerative Noun	486
Number, Singular and Plural	493
Case	495
Gender	497
The Adjective and its Degrees of Comparison	497
The Pronoun (Personal, Relative, Possessive, Demonstrative, Distributive, Indefinite)	498
The Verb as modified by Mood, Tense, and Voice	504
The Adverb, of Time, Place, Number, Degree, etc.	511
The Preposition	517
The Conjunction	518
The Interjection	518
ERRATA AND ADDENDA	521

PART III.

THE FORTY EXERCISES.

PART III.
THE FORTY EXERCISES.

1. The Cardinal Numbers.—The Cardinal Numbers from 1 to 10 are these:—

1, 一 yi^1.   6, 六 liu^4.
2, 二 erh^4.   7, 七 $ch‘i^1$.
3, 三 san^1.   8, 八 pa^1.
4, 四 $ssŭ^4$.   9, 九 $chiu^3$.
5, 五 wu^3.   10, 十 $shih^2$.

Of these, 1, 2, 8, and 10 are found in the Radical Table.

兩 $liang^3$, a couple, dual, is often used as the cardinal number *two*, but under special circumstances, as will be seen presently.

倆 lia^3, a colloquial form of $liang$, has the same meaning, but is used with even greater restriction. See Exercise I.

2. From 11 to 19 inclusive, $shih^2$, ten, precedes the lesser number. Thus, $shih^2\text{-}yi^1$, 11; $shih^2\text{-}pa^1$, 18; etc.

3. From 20 to 99 the numbers are formed much as in English:—

20, $erh^4\text{-}shih^2$.   67, $liu^4\text{-}shih^2\text{-}ch‘i^1$.
21, $erh^4\text{-}shih^2\text{-}yi^1$.   78, $ch‘i^1\text{-}shih^2\text{-}pa^1$.
34, $san^1\text{-}shih^2\text{-}ssŭ^4$.   89, $pa^1\text{-}shih^2\text{-}chiu^3$.
45, $ssŭ^4\text{-}shih^2\text{-}wu^3$.   92, $chiu^3\text{-}shih^2\text{-}erh^4$.
56, $wu^3\text{-}shih^2\text{-}liu^4$.   93, $chiu^3\text{-}shih^2\text{-}san^1$.

4. For the rest, the Chinese count by the hundred, the thousand, and the myriad:—

100, 百 pai^3.   1,000, 千 $ch‘ien^1$.   10,000, 萬 wan^4.

Between 100 and 1,000 the hundreds are reckoned as with us; but 1,100 is one thousand one hundred; 11,000 is one myriad one thousand. No Chinese would speak of eleven hundred, eleven thousand, etc.

5. 零 $ling^2$, fractional. Whenever in counting above 100 a break in the series occurs such as obliges us to insert a zero, the Chinese introduce the word $ling$. Thus,

303, $san^1\ pai^3\ ling^2\ san^1$.   2,005, $erh^4\ ch‘ien^1\ ling^2\ wu^3$.

It may be used with the verb yu^3 (see **8**), to be, as *odd*, after myriads, thousands, hundreds; or, if the number spoken of be more than thirty, after tens. Thus, $yi^1\ pai^3\ yu^3\ ling^2$, one hundred and odd.

6. 第 ti^4, order, series.

The Ordinal Numbers.—Any cardinal number or group of cardinal numbers becomes Ordinal when ti^4 is prefixed to it. Thus,

liu^4, 6; ti^4 liu^4, 6th. san^1 pai^3 $ling^2$ $êrh^4$, 302; ti^4 san^1 pai^3 $ling^2$ $êrh^4$, 302nd.

7. For purposes of numeration the following words will be constantly required:—

幾 chi^3, some; how many?
數 shu^4, number; several; some; but
　　shu^3, to count.
些 $hsieh^1$, few; some.

多 to^1, many; more.
少 $shao^3$, few; less.
to^1-$shao^3$, how many? also, a good number.

When not interrogative more emphasis is laid on *to* than on *shao*, but the tone is held to be the same.

8. In Exercise I, given below to illustrate the method of numeration, words are used which the student has already learned in the Radical Table. The following are new:—

有 yu^3, to be; to have.
來 lai^2, to come; adverbially, in numeration, to approach a total, but under, not in excess.

不 pu^4, not; the tone varies before different characters.
好 hao^3, good; adverbially, very; verbally, to recover.

個, 箇, ko^4, one, or ones, of persons or things; the commonest numerative of a large number of nouns substantive; the second is the correct form of the character. The term numerative is explained below.

The Numeratives.—Chinese nouns substantive have commonly associated with them certain other nouns substantive, here styled Numeratives, between the meaning of which and their own there is an affinity. This may be generic, specific, formal, qualitative, and is sometimes so vaguely defined that nouns, being names of things in categories widely different, may have the same numerative. The latter, in virtue of this affinity, acts as the unit of the class, body, or other plurality that may be indicated by the noun on which it is dependent; and it should be borne in mind that a large number of numeratives are never used independently of those nouns to which they are related. We have in English nouns that do somewhat the same duty. We say so many *head* of oxen; so many *stand* of arms; a crew of so many *hands*; a fleet of so many *sail*. These are all plurals or collectives. If we were speaking of oxen, we might also say that there was not a *head* left; or if of arms, that every *stand* was destroyed. The Chinese numerative will be found to play both the parts here illustrated; but it also plays a part of its own. Where it comes between a number, one or more, and its substantive, it cannot be translated. For yi^2 ko^4 $jên^2$, one man, san^1 ko^4 $jên^2$, three men, the Cantonese, in the broken English which is the *lingua franca* of the open ports of China, would say, "one piece man," "three piece man." We have nothing analogous to this in our language.

There are many substantives which have no numerative, such in particular as are applied to the measure of time, space, quantity, etc.

As stated above, the numerative is itself a substantive, but in construction it will often represent our *one* or *ones*, the pronominal adjective indefinite.

A list of the numeratives is given in Part VIII.

Obs.—Yi^1, one, changes its tone before ko^4 and other numeratives.

PART III.—THE FORTY EXERCISES.

EXERCISE I.

八十。 六十七。 四十五。 三十。 二十九。 十六。 1. Sixteen. Nineteen. Twenty. Thirty-four. Fifty-seven. Sixty-eight.

百個人。 個五六。 個三五。 千三兩。 千兩三。 百二三。 個二三。 第十七。 2. The seventeenth person (or thing). Two or three hundred. Two or three thousand. Two or three thousand. Two or three persons or things. Three or five persons or things. Five or six hundred persons.

Obs.—The Chinese do also say three or four, four or five.

十五。 百六。 千八。 第一。 十七。 第二。 第一。 3. Number one; the first; also, figuratively, the best. Number twenty-seven; the twenty-seventh. Number one thousand eight hundred and sixty-five; or, the one thousand eight hundred and sixty-fifth.

二十。 十萬零七。 一十六百。 零六萬。 十七萬五。 百個三。 萬零三。 第一百。 4. The one million and three hundredth person (or thing). Five hundred and seventy thousand six hundred and ten. Seven hundred thousand and twenty.

Obs.—Six hundred and ten; the *yi*, one, before *shih* cannot be omitted. In reckoning myriads it is equally correct to use *yi* or to omit it. You may say *shih wan, shih pa wan*, or *yi shih wan, yi shih pa wan*.

七十萬。 五百萬零。 六萬零零。 萬零一。 萬五百。 三十五。 一百萬。 5. A million. Three hundred and fifty thousand. Five million and one. Sixty thousand five hundred and seven. One hundred thousand.

一千。 六萬。 四十萬。 千一。 十九。 百零一。 零一萬。 七萬 6. Seventy thousand one hundred and ninety-one. Ten millions; or, figuratively, any number; in any (or the utmost) degree; also, above all things. Four hundred and sixty-one thousand.

TZŬ ÊRH CHI.—COLLOQUIAL SERIES.

7. 五萬零八十八。九萬八千四百零二。一千零五。四千零七十二。八千三百六十七。一萬零六。一百零三。

7. Fifty thousand and eighty-eight. Ninety-eight thousand four hundred and two. One thousand and five. Four thousand and seventy-two. Eight thousand three hundred and sixty-seven. Ten thousand and six. One hundred and three.

8. 一百一十八。二百五十四。九百九十九萬三千。

8. One hundred and eighteen. Two hundred and fifty-four. Nine million nine hundred and ninety-three thousand.

9. 有幾個人來。有些個人。有好些個人。來多少人。多三萬人。

9. A number of people are come; or, How many people are come? There are some people. There are a good number of people. How many people are come? Upwards of thirty thousand.

10. 數十個。十幾個。幾個。個幾個不止兩。十來個。十個九個。九個。二百多。五千多。

10. Several score (*lit.*, tens); some score. Some score; or, How many score? Ten and more persons or things; or, How many over ten? Two persons or things. Some persons or things; or, How many? There are more than ten; *lit.*, [the number] does not stop at ten ones. Eight or nine. Near ten persons or things. Nine or ten persons or things. Two hundred and more. Five thousand and more.

Obs. 1.—Score: the Chinese have no word for score, but it is un-English to say some tens. Note that ten odd are supposed not to exceed fifteen.

Obs. 2.—Near ten, but below it: *lai* is only used with ten or a multiple of ten.

11. 長三寸四分。一口身。一口人。有幾口人。五斤牛肉。六斤羊肉。幾斤魚。

11. Three inches four-tenths long. A single individual. There are some persons; or, How many persons are there? Five catties of beef. Six catties of mutton. Some catties of fish; or, How many catties of fish?

Obs. 1.—Four-tenths: understand the word *fên*, part (emphatically, tenth part), after *ssŭ*, four.
Obs. 2.—*K'ou* refers to individuals, male or female.

12. 七斗麥子。九斗米。一斗黍子。

12. Seven measures of wheat. Nine measures of rice. One measure of millet.

幾13　長　里。四　有　高　里。斤
幾個　至　萬　二　三　有
萬牙。多　里。足　百　百　零。

13. Some teeth; or, How many teeth? Several myriads of *li* in length; some tens of thousands of miles long; or, How many myriads of miles long? At the most forty thousand *li*. There is a mountain (or there are mountains) full two hundred *li* high. Three hundred catties odd.

Obs.—Full: *see* Radical 157. The Chinese idea is rather to measure the heights of mountains by the length of the road by which they are ascended.

Turn the following into Chinese. (KEY, EXERCISE I.*)

1. Twelve. Fourteen. Ninety. Seventy-three. Forty-five. One hundred and ninety-nine.

2. Forty thousand one hundred and sixty-eight. Three million twelve hundred and twenty-four. Eight hundred and twenty-nine. Two hundred and ninety-two.

3. The twenty-first. The three hundred and forty-second. The eightieth. Number sixty-seven. Eight or nine men are coming.

4. The nine hundred and ninety-ninth. The seven million six thousand five hundred and forty-third. The three million four thousand five hundred and sixty-seventh.

5. Five million two hundred and one. Three million and twenty-seven. Six thousand and forty. Nine hundred and ninety-nine thousand nine hundred and ninety-nine.

6. There are a good many horses. How many oxen are there? There are fifty-six oxen and horses.

7. How many catties of fish are there? Seven catties and some ounces. Six measures of small millet. There are eighteen measures of rice. Fourteen measures of beans.

8. More than ten persons are coming. More than fifty persons are coming. A hundred odd persons are coming. A single individual.

9. There are about (but less than) ten catties of fish. Nineteen catties of beef. Seventeen catties of venison. Fourteen measures of rice. Eighteen measures of beans. Ten measures of small millet.

10. How many miles long? A good many. Full seventeen hundred *li*. Full nine hundred *li*. There are mountains fully eight *li* high.

9. The Article.—As will have been seen from Example 11 in the foregoing exercise, our Indefinite Article may be represented by *yi*¹, one, without any numerative. But if the substantive be one of those to which a numerative is assignable, that numerative will be commonly found between the *yi*¹ and the substantive. Sometimes the numerative will stand without the *yi*¹, as in *yu³ ko⁴ jên² lai²*, for *yu³ yi² ko⁴ jên² lai²*, there is a person come (or coming).

10. The Definite Article *the* is not uncommonly rendered by the demonstrative pronouns

這 *ché*⁴, this; and 那 *na*⁴, that;

* The Chinese text of this and all similar exercises will be found in vol. i.

but chiefly, if not always, when the thing or person indicated is for certain known to the hearer or has been recently referred to. But these are not the only equivalents.

11. The Noun Substantive.—One peculiarity of the Chinese Substantive has already been noticed—the employment, namely, of a large staff of words, themselves substantives, in close relation with other substantives, which from their most conspicuous function have been denominated Numeratives. By others they have also been styled Classifiers, as possessing in general a meaning in affinity with that of the nouns to which they are attached as adjuncts, or which, when detached from these, they represent.

Independently of these adjuncts, the Chinese substantive may be simple or compound.

Of the simple form, any substantive in the Radical Table is as good a specimen as another; such as *jên^2*, man; *shên^1*, body; *ma^3*, horse; etc.

Of the compound form, there are instances of more kinds than one in the Exercises in the Colloquial Radicals (vol. i, p. 34); such as *shih^1-shou^3*, a corpse (lit., corpse-head); *k'ou^3-shê^2*, altercation (lit., mouth and tongue); *kan^1-ko^1*, war (lit., shield and spear). These suffice to show that the words combined may be of like or of very different meaning. In the same Exercise will be found *ch'ên^2-tzŭ^3*, a minister of state; *shih^4-tzŭ^3*, a lettered man. The word *tzŭ^3*, son, is largely added to other substantives.

兒 *êrh^2*, also meaning son, is used in the same way as frequently as *tzŭ^3*; in Pekingese, more frequently. But neither of them can be appended *ad libitum*. Some substantives that take the one may at times take the other; and many do not take either.

Obs.—This *êrh* also sometimes plays a part in the formation of adverbs, especially of time and place.

Combinations of words, such as with us shipwright, horse-boy, landlord, etc., are common enough in Chinese; but, the independent individuality of almost every Chinese word considered, it is in most instances safer to speak of the relation of the first word to the second as attributive, rather than as part of a compound substantive.

Some English substantives, it will soon be seen, require for the reproduction of their meaning a string of words. Thus *carter* is the driving-cart-one, or the one who drives the cart; neither of which combinations, however, would it be convenient to designate a compound substantive.

12. Number.—The plural of substantives may be effected by the reduplication of the simple word, but this not without limitation; or by the addition of a noun of multitude, sometimes preceding, sometimes following, the simple word; or, in certain cases, by the addition of the particle *mên^1*, explained below (13).

13. 們 *mên^1*, a word used colloquially to indicate the plural of personal substantives or pronouns, and apparently for no other purpose. Thus,

ta^4 jên^2, your excellency, his excellency (*lit.*, great man).
ta^4 jên^2 mên, your excellencies, their excellencies.

Experience will show that its use even with personal substantives is limited.

Note.—When the tone mark is omitted it must be understood that the character is so little emphasised as to carry no tone.

PART III.—THE FORTY EXERCISES.

14. The Noun Adjective.—The Adjective, like the substantive, may be either a single word, such as *hao*³, good, in Exercise I, or a combination of words of like or different significations.

15. The Personal Pronoun.—The Personal Pronouns singular are—

我 *wo*³, the 1st person; 你 *ni*³, the 2nd; 他 *t'a*¹, the 3rd.

16. Their plural is formed by the addition of the particle *mén*¹, just noticed (13). Thus, *wo*³-*mén*, we, us; *ni*³-*mén*, ye, you; *t'a*¹-*mén*, they, them.

Obs.—*Ni*³-*mên* is often used politely to a single individual.

17. 偺, 咱, *tsa*², properly *tsan*, is a pronoun of the first person peculiar to northern Chinese, but never used in the singular. In the plural, *tsa*²-*mén* means you and I, or you and we, when the persons spoken of are present; parties in the same undertaking or concern. The second form of *tsa*² is but an abbreviation of the first.

18. When animate beings are in question, any male or female, man or beast, may be indicated by *t'a*¹, he or she; *t'a*¹-*mén*, they. But in speaking of inanimate things *t'a*¹ is used very sparingly.

In the constructions of the verb which we describe as impersonal, the pronoun *it* cannot be said to be visibly represented in Chinese.

19. 的 *ti*¹. This word, which is properly a substantive meaning a bright spot, the blot on a target, has come to perform various duties. Appended enclitically to substantives and pronouns, it forms, as we should say, the genitive or possessive case. Appended to adjectives or adjective constructions, it adverbialises them. It is sometimes a relative pronoun; sometimes an indefinite pronoun, such as one, some, etc.

In all these cases it has presumably usurped the place of other words, notably that of the verb *té*², noticed immediately below (21).

20. Attention is here directed to *ti*¹ as forming the **Possessive** of substantives or pronouns. Thus,

*tzŭ*⁴-*chi*³-*ti*, of or belonging to oneself.   *ta*⁴-*jén*²-*ti*, his excellency's.
*wo*³-*ti*, mine.   *wo*³-*mén*-*ti*, ours.
*ni*³-*ti*, thine.   *ni*³-*mén*-*ti*, yours.
*t'a*¹-*ti*, his.   *t'a*¹-*mén*-*ti*, theirs.

21. The following brief examples will help to confirm the student in his knowledge of the words just learned (10–19):—

巳 *chi*³	的 *ti*	咱 *tsa*²	人 *jén*²	咱 *tsa*²	的 *ti*	你 *ni*³	這 *ché*⁴	這 *ché*⁴
的 *ti*	馬 *ma*³	們 *mén*	咱 *tsa*²	們 *mén*	他 *t'a*¹	我 *wo*³	兒 *'rh*	個 *ko*⁴
馬 *ma*³	我 *wo*³	這 *ché*⁴	們 *mén*	兩 *liang*³	們 *mén*	他 *t'a*¹	那 *na*⁴	那 *na*⁴
	自 *tzŭ*⁴	兒 *'rh*	倆 *lia*³	個 *ko*⁴	的 *ti*	你 *ni*³	兒 *'rh*	個 *ko*⁴

This one. That one. This place here. That place there.
Thou, I, he; we three. Thine. Theirs.
We two persons here. We two.
A horse (or horses) of our place here.
My own horse (*lit.*, myself's horse).

Note.—There is nothing to show whether *ma*, horse, in the 4th example, is singular or plural.

22. The Relative Pronoun.—It has just been observed (19) that ti^1 acts sometimes as a Relative Pronoun. In constructions such as The person who did, The thing which was done, ti may be allowed to be so characterised. But for caution's sake it should be borne in mind that the Chinese may not unfrequently be rendered by our participle, past or present, if not in other ways.

23. The Interrogative Pronoun *who, which, what*, which has been described by some grammarian as a relative in search of an antecedent, is in general rendered colloquially as below. There are other forms of higher style.

誰 *shui²*, who, is never used but of persons.

甚 *shên²* 麽 *mo¹*, 嗎 *ma¹*. The combination *shên²-mo¹*, pronounced *shên²-mo¹*, used alone, signifies *what*, but may stand before a personal noun, as in *shên²-mo¹ jên²*, what person? The character *shên* signifies extreme, but is then read *shên⁴*, and it may be surmised that it has come to be corruptly employed in this combination. Its adjunct *mo* is a negative interrogative particle; it is sometimes also used as a conjunction, as in *na⁴ mo¹ to¹*, as much as that; *chê⁴ mo¹ hsiao³*, as small as this. *Ma* is a strictly colloquial interrogative.

什 *shih³*, a tithe, is sometimes written instead of *shên²*, but the compound is none the less pronounced *shên²-mo*, or *shê²-mo*.

那 *na³*, with *ko⁴* or other numerative (*yi¹*, one, intervening or not), is interrogative, What person? What thing?

Obs.—It is *na³*, not *na⁴*, which we have met with above (10) as a demonstrative pronoun.

24. Thus, for Who? Whom? What person? we may have *shui²* or *shên²-mo jên²* or *na³ yi² ko⁴ jên²* or *na³ ko⁴ jên²*.

For the interrogative *what*, *shên²-mo* may stand alone; or the substantive representing the thing spoken of may be expressed, and without its numerative.

But *which*, if referring to one of many objects, animate or inanimate, will be rendered by *na³*, as above, followed by *yi¹* and the numerative, or by the numerative without *yi¹*.

25. The Verb.—It will suffice for the moment to observe that in Chinese the Verb may be simple or compound—the compound verb being made up sometimes of the same verb reduplicated, sometimes of verbs of like or different meanings, sometimes of a verb and its object.

These remarks apply rather to verbs that we should designate Active or Neuter. The equivalent of our Passive formation is effected by prefixing to the verb concerned other verbs signifying to suffer, to receive, to perceive, etc., as the case may be.

Some verbs incontestably active are reinforced by other verbs, which, like the French *faire*, signify either to do or to cause to be done.

26. We have met above (8) two simple verbs: *yu³*, which means, as an active verb, to have, and as a verb substantive, to be; and *lai²*, to come. The latter has something of this sense even when used as an auxiliary, which it often is. The verb yu^3 has also, though limitedly, auxiliary functions.

27. With these and the following verbs, although also possessing all of them independent powers, there may be effected, as auxiliaries, a fair proportion of the equivalents of our verb's inflections.

28. 在 $tsai^4$, to be; to be at; at; in the act of; in.

29. 是 $shih^4$, to be; to be what ought to be, that is, right. Hence, in answer to a question, $shih^4$ means *yes*, and pu^2 $shih^4$, *no*; interrogatively, $shih^4$ pu $shih^4$, is it so or not? is it right or not? The combination pu^2 $shih$, not right, constantly occurs as a substantive meaning error, fault; or as an adjective or adverb, wrong, erroneously. It is well to remember, however, that the negative or affirmative in answer to a question is more frequently expressed in Chinese by the repetition, or partial repetition, of the question with the negative or affirmative prefixed than by the negative or affirmative alone. Thus,

$t'a^1$ lai^2 pu lai^2, is he coming? $t'a^1$ pu^4 lai^2, he is not coming.
$shih^4$ $t'a^1$ pu $shih^4$, it is he, is it not? $shih^4$ $t'a^1$, it is he.

We could not say, without being guilty of a vulgarity, pu^4 simply, in answer to the first question, and the simple affirmative $shih^4$ would rarely be used in answer to the second. *See* Exercise III, 10.

30. 得 $t\hat{e}^2$, to get; to have; to possess; to accomplish. See ti^1, above **(19)**. As an auxiliary, $t\hat{e}^2$ follows the verb to which it is attached, indicating sometimes that the action of the first verb is completed, but oftener the possibility of its completion. It discharges, perhaps more than any other verb in Chinese, what we regard as the functions of our verb *can* and *cannot*. Of this more directly.

31. 了 $liao^3$, 咯 lo^1, to end, or be ended, when following a verb, indicates the completion of an act, the occurrence of an event. It may often fairly be called a sign of the past tense. It is also freely used as a final expletive. *Lo* is much used as a colloquial termination.

When the negative pu^4 **(8)** intervenes between the other verb and $liao^3$, the construction is almost, if not quite, that represented by our potential auxiliaries.

Thus lai^2 pu $liao^3$, it is not possible that [he] should come. This is said, however, when the speaker merely holds a strong opinion as to the impossibility. Were he to say lai^2 pu $t\hat{e}$, he would affirm it more positively.

It should be remembered that, elsewhere as here, $t\hat{e}^2$ and $liao^3$, though both signify completion or achievement, are by no means identical in their functions as auxiliaries.

In the combinations $t\hat{e}^2$ $liao$, it is finished or achieved, $liao^3$ is the auxiliary of $t\hat{e}^2$; as we should say, it puts $t\hat{e}^2$ in the past tense.

32. 要 yao^4, to want; to desire; to be about to. It is used, but by no means invariably, to indicate future time. The tense of the verb is as often as not shown by the context alone. But from its meaning of "to want," yao^4 comes to represent our auxiliary *must*, both singly and in various combinations.

With one of these the student of Pekingese cannot too soon become acquainted. Out of $té^2$ and yao^4, a corrupt monosyllable, $téi^3$, has been formed, which is one of the most useful auxiliaries in the Peking colloquial. It is of course not recognised by native lexicographers, and has been represented in this course by the character $té^2$, distinguished by a Chinese tone mark attached to it on the right side.

Another corrupt combination is $pieh^2$ for $pu^2\ yao^4$, the imperative *do not*.

33. 沒 mo^4 or mu^4, not, is much less common than pu^4, but is used in a few cases where pu^4 is not used. While, for instance, pu^4 is never used with yu^3, to have or to be, mo^4 or mu^4 is never used with $shih^4$, to be.

With yu^3 it has formed the corrupt monosyllable mei^2, which will be found, however, before the verb yu^3 itself, standing as a simple negative. Thus,

$mei^2\ yu^3\ hao^3\ ti$, there are not any good ones.

When mo^4 or mei^2 stands before another verb, that verb is generally in the past tense. Thus,

$t'a^1\ lai^2\ liao\ mei^2\ yu^3$, is he come or not?
$t'a^1\ mei^2\ lai^2$, he is not (has not) come.

If your question were, Is he coming or not? you would ask $t'a^1\ lai^2\ pu\ lai^2$, and the answer in the negative would be $t'a^1\ pu^4\ lai^2$, he will not come (is not coming).

34. To recapitulate, the words just learned (21–33) are as follows:—

在 $tsai^4$, to be; to be at; at.
是 $shih^4$, to be; to be right.
得 $té^2$, to possess; to obtain; to achieve.
要 yao^4, to want; to will.
得 tei^3 ($té^2\ yao^4$), must.
了 $liao^3$, to end; ended.
沒 mo^4, mu^4, not; mei^2 (= $mo^4\ yu^3$), not to be.

誰 $shui^2$, who?
那 na^3, what?
甚 $shén^4$, extreme; but with mo^1, interrogative, and intoned $shén^2$.
什 $shih^2$, a tithe; but, like $shén^2$, used phonetically with the following mo^1, to express *what*? also *any*.
麼 mo^1, a negative interrogative particle.

35. Learn also the following:—

很, 狠 $hén^3$, an intensive; as in $hén^3\ hao^3$, very good. The second is a corrupt form.

東 $tung^1$, east; 西 hsi^1, west (*see* Radical 146). The combination $tung^1$-hsi^1 means a thing. Thus,

$hén^3\ hao^3\ ti\ tung^1$-hsi^1, very good thing (or things).

買 mai^3, to buy; 賣 mai^4, to sell. The combination mai^3-mai^4 means trade, business. Thus,

$ta^4\ mai^3$-mai^4, trade on a large scale.

PART III.—THE FORTY EXERCISES. 13

EXERCISE II.

小。那 麼 倆。偺 倆 我 1
麼 大。這 們 人。們

1. We two (men or women). You and I. As large as this. As small as that.

Obs.—In *chê-mo, na-mo*, the *mo* has no interrogative power. The syllable is sometimes represented by *mên* (13), which, however, is then pronounced *mo*.

.西 東 麼 甚。人 麼 甚 2

2. What man? What thing?

Obs.—Thing: *tung-hsi*, east and west; *q.d.*, everything between east and west.

些 麼 賣 他 是 誰 那 3
個 的。人 是 個 那 個
東 賣 賣 個 好 個 人
西。好 甚 買 人。人 是

3. Who is that man? That man is a good man. He is a trader. What does he sell? He sells a good many things.

Obs.—What does he sell? (*lit.*, he is a seller of what?) It would be equally correct to say *t'a mai ti shih shên mo.*

好。個 人 不 很 有 有 我 4
人 很 好。好 了。沒 要
很 好.這 那 這 有 好
不 那 個 個 個 沒 的

4. I want good ones; have [you] any? (or, are there any?) There are none; or, I have none left. This is very good; that is bad (or, this is a very good one; that one is bad). This man is very good; that man is very bad.

Obs.—I have none left: *liao* implies that there were some originally, but that they have gone.

的 不 兒 了。來 來 有 有。他 5
人。是 的 他 有 沒 甚 他 來
這 人。是 人 有 麼 沒 了
兒 他 那‘ 來 人 人 來 沒

5. Is he come? He is not come. Who is it that is come? There is no one come. A person is come; or, there is someone come. What place is he from? He is not of this place.

Obs. 1.—In the last two examples *chê êrh, na êrh* are pronounced *chê 'rh, na 'rh.*
Obs. 2.—It is simplest to construe *ti* as the sign of the possessive case; *q.d.*, he is what place's man?

幾 兒。人 有 些 來 人。了 他 6
個 有 在 多 個 了 他 們
人。十 那 少 人。好 們 少 來

6. How many people is it that are come? A good number. How many people are there there? Ten people and more.

Obs.—It would be equally correct in the answer to the first question to omit *t'a mên.*

7. This is ours. That is theirs. Whose is this thing? Whose is this thing? It is ours. How many have you of this article? Not many of them.

這個是我們的。那個是他們的。這個是誰的。那個是甚麽人的。這東西我們的。個東西你們有多少。不多的。

8. I do not want this one; they want it. Theirs is not very good. Have you got any good ones there? None good. Unless you have some very good ones, we do not want any. Have you got this thing? We do not want it. I cannot buy so many as that.

我不要這個。他們要這個。他們的不大好。你們那兒有好的沒有。沒好的。你們沒有很好的東西。我們不要這個東西。有沒有這個東西。我們不要這個東西。我買不了那麽些個。

Obs. 1.—We do not want any: note the use of *liao* as a final expletive.
Obs. 2.—In the last example, *na-mo*, that, those; *hsieh ko*, indefinitely numerous ones.
Obs. 3.—I cannot buy, etc.: *liao*³, a potential auxiliary.

9. This will never do; or, this is a bad business. That is not to be done; or, that cannot be accomplished.

這個了不得。那個了不了。

Obs.—The first *liao* is the verb to finish, to accomplish; the second *liao*, though literally possessing the same meaning, does the duty of the verb *can*, or, with *pu*, cannot.

10. This thing is very good.

這個東西很好。這個東西好得很。

Obs.—*Hao tê hên* in the second example: there is no perceptible difference in the meaning of the two sentences.

11. If you want to buy a horse you should (or, ought to) buy a good one. It won't do to buy that horse (*lit.*, that horse cannot be (=ought not to be) bought); he has a bad coat (*lit.*, the hair, *chang*³ *tê*², has grown, not good, or, not well).

你要買馬。個好的買。那馬買不得。長得毛不好。長得不好。

Obs.—*Chang*³, to grow, not *ch'ang*², long (Radical 168); *see* next example. *Tê* is here an auxiliary completing the action of the verb *chang*³; *see* 30.

PART III.—THE FORTY EXERCISES.

走。你來長。得子那12
得‘了他很長竹

12. Those bamboos have grown greatly. When he comes you must go; or, he is come and you must go.

Obs. 1.—*Chu* (Radical 118), the bamboo; *tzŭ* (Radical 39).
Obs. 2.—*Chang³ tê hên ch'ang²*, have lengthened very long.

人。十我幾你八兒比那13
來們口們寸子我個
口是人。是多。高的人

13. That man is upwards of eight inches taller than my son. How many in family are you? We are under ten.

Obs. 1.—*Lit.*, that man compared with my son [is] high eight inches [and] more.
Obs. 2.—See *k'ou* in the Colloquial Radicals; *lai* above in 8.

Turn the following into Chinese. (KEY, EXERCISE II.)

1. Thy horse. My sheep. His cart. Your rice. Our handkerchief. Their knife.

2. You buy, we sell. They want to buy things. What things do they want to buy? Good things. We here sell very good things.

3. As small as this; as large as that. This mountain is not as high as that (*q.d.*, as the height the other person declares it to be).

4. Have you any good horses? No. We sell good carts here; we do not sell horses. This cart is not a good one.

5. Whose is this horse? It is mine. How many horses have you? Three. How many carts are there here? Not very many.

6. What place are you from? I am of this place. What place is that trader from? He is not of this place. Does he sell good things? Not very good. The traders here have not very good things. We two traders sell good things.

Obs.—Trader: *lit.*, a buying selling man.

7. I want to buy things; are there any traders (sellers) here? Not very many. How many are there? Five. I want to buy a good many things; do you want to sell? (or, do you sell them?) What things do you want? Good things.

8. How many sons and daughters has he? Four daughters and five sons. His five sons are here; his daughters are there (in that place). I have walked a hundred *li*. He sells earthenware. What I want to buy is some bushels of wheat.

Obs.—Earthenware (Radical 98).

9. How many days do you require? I want three months. Do you use wheat or millet? What are these things? They are black beans. There are many fish in this place (*lit.*, here the fish are not few).

10. Is that thing gold? No; it is clay. His nose is very small. Venison (deer flesh) is very good. Is the antelope (yellow sheep) found here? Yes. The scenery (Radical Exercises, 10, 6) here is very fine.

Obs.—Clay: *lit.*, yellow earth (*see* Radical 201).

11. That man has grown very tall; or, he *is* very tall. That insect (or reptile) is more than three inches long. When he comes I must see him.

36. To return to verbs and verbal constructions. Note the following:—

拿 *na²*, simply, to lay hold of a person or thing. Thus,

na² jên², to arrest a person.   *na² ch'ê⁴ ko⁴ tung¹-hsi¹*, lay hold of this thing.

37. 去 *ch'ü⁴*, simply, to go, as opposed to *lai²*, to come. Thus,

wo³ lai², I come.   *ni³ ch'ü⁴*, you go.

38. From combination of the above we get *na² lai²*, to bring, and *na² ch'ü⁴*, to take away—an object, of course, being expressed or understood. When expressed, the object, in the simpler phrases, is placed between *na²* and its adjunct *lai²* or *ch'ü⁴*. Thus,

na² shui³ lai², bring water here.

na² ché¹ ko⁴ tung¹-hsi¹ ch'ü⁴, take this thing away (*lit.*, laying hold of this thing go). There are exceptions to this rule of construction which will be noticed in their place.

39. Referring to Sections **30** and **31**, write out the following in Chinese:—

na² té², can be laid hold of.   *na² pu⁴ té²*, cannot be, etc.
na² té² lai², can be brought.   *na² pu⁴ lai²*, cannot be, etc.
na² té² ch'ü⁴, can be taken away.   *na² pu⁴ ch'ü⁴*, cannot be, etc.

Observe *na² té² liao³*, can be laid hold of; *na² pu⁴ liao³*, cannot be, etc. In these two the first differs nothing from *na² té²*; but *na² pu⁴ liao³* will be found to have more force and scope than *na² pu⁴ té²*.

40. With the following verbs, *lai²* and *ch'ü⁴* may discharge much the same function as when attached to *na²*:—

進 *chin⁴*, to enter (as a door).   過 *kuo⁴*, to pass over (as a river, hill, street).
出 *ch'u¹*, to go out of (as a door).   往 *wang³*, to move towards, or in the direction of.

41. Thus, for instance:—

過 *kuo⁴*   來。*lai²*   往 *wang³*   過 *kuo⁴*   出 *ch'u¹*   進 *chin⁴*
去 *ch'ü⁴*   過 *kuo⁴*   這 *ché⁴*   山 *shan¹*   門 *mên²*   門 *mên²*
來 *lai²*   兒 *'rh*   去。*ch'ü⁴*   去。*ch'ü⁴*   來。*lai²*

To come in at the door.   To go out of the door.
To go over (across) the hills.
To be coming in this direction (or, come here).
To pass backwards and forwards.

42. 過 *kuo⁴*, to pass, is much used as an auxiliary in verbal constructions of past time.

43. 起 *ch'i³*, to rise, followed by *lai²*, may mean simply to rise from a lower position; to get up. But the combination *ch'i³-lai²*, it will be seen, has a separate function.

It has been mentioned above (**26**) that *lai²* is frequently used as an auxiliary. This it is as indicating progressive action. The combination *ch'i³-lai²*, itself an auxiliary, must be rendered variously according to circumstances.

44. 到 *tao¹*, to arrive; as *t'a¹ tao¹ liao³*, he has arrived; *t'a¹ mei² tao⁴*, he has not arrived. It is used as an auxiliary with certain verbs implying movement, but with greater freedom in the southern than in the northern mandarin.

45. 著, 着, *cho¹*, also *chao²*, written in the two forms here given. The first of these, however, is used in positions where the second would not be. Besides other parts, the word plays that of a most important auxiliary verb.

PART III.—THE FORTY EXERCISES.

As *cho*¹, attached to several verbs it produces a participial inflection. Under other conditions, hereafter explained, *cho* is read *cho*². Thus,

*tsou*³-*cho*, walking, going on foot.

But it must not be applied indiscriminately.

As *chao*², it resembles in power the verbs *tê*² and *liao*³, and often means to meet with unexpectedly, or to catch, as a cold, etc. *See* Note at the end of Exercise XL.

We may say *na*² *pu*⁴ *tê*², *na*² *pu*⁴ *liao*³, or *na*² *pu*⁴ *chao*². But here again the selection of the auxiliary must depend on circumstances.

46. Learn the following substantives:—

房 *fang*², a house.   屋 *u*¹, or *wu*¹, a room.   舖 *p'u*⁴, a shop.

These as often as not take *tzŭ*³ after them. Thus, *fang*²-*tzŭ*, *wu*¹-*tzŭ*, *p'u*⁴-*tzŭ*.

47. 間 *chien*¹, a division or space; the numerative of rooms and houses. (*See* Exercise XL, 3, Obs. 2.) Thus,

*yi*⁴ *chien*¹ *fang*²-*tzŭ*, a house.   *liang*³ *chien*¹ *wu*¹-*tzŭ*, two rooms.

Obs.—*Yi*⁴, properly *yi*¹; *tzŭ*, properly *tzŭ*³. The latter, when used thus enclitically, atonic.

But observe, *san*¹ *ko*⁴ *p'u*⁴-*tzŭ*, three shops.

間 *chien*¹ will also be found to act as a preposition of time or space; in which case it follows its object.

48. Learn the following:—

家 *chia*¹, house, home; also, family.
城 *ch'êng*², city wall; city.
街 *chieh*¹, street.
道 *tao*⁴, road, way; also, to say (as will be seen later).
裏 *li*³, inside of.

外 *wai*⁴, outside of.
上 *shang*⁴, above; towards; to ascend.
下 *hsia*⁴, below; to descend.
頭 *t'ou*², head; end; side.
住 *chu*⁴, to stop oneself; to stand firm; to reside at.

49. The following are examples of some of the simplest uses of these words:—

道 *tao*⁴	家 *chia*¹	下 *hsia*⁴	上 *shang*⁴	外 *wai*⁴	外 *wai*⁴	家 *chia*¹
兒 *'rh*	兒 *'rh*	雨 *yü*³	上 *shang*⁴	頭 *t'ou*²	裏 *li*³	裏 *li*³
上。 *shang*⁴	的。 *ti*	住 *chu*⁴	街。 *chieh*¹	街 *chieh*¹	頭。 *t'ou*²	城 *ch'êng*²

In the house; or, at home.
Outside the wall or city.
Inside. Outside.
Up (or, in) the street. To go up the street.
It rains (*lit.*, there descends rain).
Householders, as opposed to shopkeepers.
On the road.

Observe that *shang*⁴, *li*³, *wai*⁴, used as prepositions, follow the object. So would *hsia*⁴ as a preposition; it is here used only as a verb.

50. Add these words:—

做 *tso*⁴, to do; as *tso*⁴ *shih*⁴ (252), to do business.

開 *k'ai*¹, to open; hence, in composition, implying removal to greater or less distance. As *k'ai*¹ *mên*², to open the door.

EXERCISE III.

有 人 來 了。
人 來 要 拏 有 東
那 東 西 去。
那 東 西 很 多。
一 個 人 拏 不 了 去。

1. There is a man here with things; or, a man is come with things; a man has brought things. A man is come to take away that thing (i.e., with the wish or intention to take). Those things are too many for one man to take.

Obs. 1.—*Lit.*, there is a man [who] holding things is come.

Obs. 2.—If there were no *liao* at the end, it could mean that a man was come for the things; q.d., *na*, to lay hands on, the things.

Obs. 3.—That thing: *na* or *na ko*.

Obs. 4.—*Lit.*, those things [are] very many; one man cannot take [them] away.

Obs. 5.—Notice the *pu liao*, implying impossibility, between *na* and *ch'ü*. It might run, one man *na pu liao na tung-hsi ch'ü*.

2. That man must not be seized (e.g., because of his rank or other circumstance that makes it wrong to seize him). That man cannot be seized (there is no getting hold of him). That man is not to be seized, will never be seized (he is too powerful, too far off, etc).

那 人 不 是。
那 人 拏 不 得。
拏 不 著。
的 那 人 拏 不
是 的。拏 不 人
了 的。

3. In a room. To come into the room. No one lives in this room.

屋 裏。
進 屋 裏 來。
這 個 屋 子。
沒 有 人 住。

4. To live in a house. This house is a great deal better than that one of his.

住 屋 子。
這 個 房 子。
他 那 個 房 子。
比 那 個 房 子 好。
多 了。

Obs. 1.—The *liao* at the end is merely expletive.

Obs. 2.—*T'a = t'a ti*, his that house.

5. How many buildings have you over there? Thirty-five *chien*. Is the house you live in large or small? I live in a small room of three *chien*.

你 們 那 兒。
有 多 少 房 子。
五 間 房 子。
你 住 的 房 子。
是 大 小。
我 住 的 是 三
間 小 屋 子。

Obs. 1.—*Chien:* see Exercise XL, 3, *Obs.* 2.

Obs. 2.—Construe:—You reside(ing-*ti*) that house, [is it] large, [is it] small?

PART III.—THE FORTY EXERCISES.

6. What is he doing at home? He is not at home. Where is he gone? He is gone for a turn (*lit.*, up the street). Walking in the street. There is a great number of people in the street. There is a great deal of dust outside.

Obs.—*Shang*, verb and preposition.

7. Where do you live? I live in the city. (or, in Peking, in the Tartar city). Is it better to live in the eastern or in the western division of the city? Where is that man's shop, and what business does he do?

Obs. 1.—If *hao* were omitted, this would continue the conversation, [Are you] *chu cho*, living, in the eastern city or in the western?

Obs. 2.—*Lit.*, that man's shop that he opens is where?

8. His shops are three in the east division of the city, and four in the west; we have no business so large here. That shop is mine. There is a large number of people buying things in that shop; or, the number of people, etc., is large.

Obs. 1.—His shops, *lit.*, his those shops.
Obs. 2.—We, *wo-mên*, the person addressed being an outsider.
Obs. 3.—*Ti* has probably no more than a rhythmical function.

9. Has he come? He has come. He did not come in; he went past, westwards. He is gone up the street to buy something. Has he ever been over here?

10. Can you (or, one) get through by that way? You cannot get through (or, there is no thoroughfare). Where are you going? I am not going anywhere. Have you ever been there? No; I have never been there.

Obs.—The *na 'rh* in the first clause interrogative; in the second, indefinite—anywhere.

11 你 來 起 個 西 來 了 風
做 着 來 得 人 了 拿 起
甚 他 你 起 那 不 風 了
麼 沒 這 起 東 起 來 大

11. What have you been doing? or, What were you doing (at the time)? He is not up (out of bed). *You* must get up. That thing cannot be lifted (it is too heavy). The wind has risen (is beginning, or has begun, to rise). It has come on to blow hard.

Obs. 1.—Observe the auxiliaries *lai* and *cho*, signifying past time.

Obs. 2.—You this man: *chê ko jên* may be added in anger or not; it merely emphasises the personal pronoun, first, second, or third. *Liao* has here no more than a rhythmical function.

12 要 了 麼 了 個 得 拿
下 大 雨 東 不 住 住
雨 雨 住 西 拿 你 了
了 了 不 拿 得 小
下 這 住 了 這 心
過 這 不

12. It is going to rain. It has rained heavily. Rain as heavy as this won't stop. The rain has stopped. Can [one] get a firm hold of this thing or not? [One] can get a firm hold of it. Be careful to keep a firm hold of it (to hold it fast).

Obs. 1.—In the construction of possibility or impossibility, the *tê* and *pu* come between the *na* and *chu*. But you say *na chu tung-hsi*; you must not say *na tung-hsi chu*.

Obs. 2.—Be careful: *lit.*, little heart, little being here used in the sense of fine, minute; *q.d.*, pay minute attention.

13 他 門 得 開 不
那 開 開 開 開
不 開

13. Will his door open? (or, can that door of his be opened?) It won't open.

Obs.—*Lit.*, his that door open can open? open not [can] open? Open not [can] open. If the answer were *k'ai pu liao*, the impossibility would be more strongly affirmed than by *k'ai pu k'ai*.

Turn the following into Chinese. (KEY, EXERCISE III.)

1. You live inside the city. I live outside the city. I live in a house of six *chien*. Where do you keep a shop, and where do you live?

2. This house is much larger than that one. It has ten *chien*; that one has four. In the large streets there are not many dwelling-houses; [but] there are many shops there.

3. Where is his residence? He lives in a very small house in the west of the city. He keeps a shop there, does he not? He is not in trade.

Obs.—An intensive is often formed by the repetition of the adjective. Thus, *hsiao hsiao êrh ti*, very small.

4. Come into the room; it is dusty in the street. The door of that room is open. How many shops has he? Three or four. Where are they? They are in the east of the city. Does he do a large business? Not very large.

5. What is he doing at home? He has nothing to do; or, he does nothing (*lit.*, has not what to do). He has gone out of the city. Where has he gone? Towards the west. What does he want to do? He wants to buy horses and carts.

6. Where has that trader I wanted to buy things from gone? Does he know where I live? He does not know; he has not been into your room.

Obs.—To know: *see* 51.

7. That man's house is a much better one than mine or yours. How many *chien* has it got? Eight; mine has six, and yours has four. His house has a large frontage ($k'ou^3$ $mien^4$).

51. 知 $chih^1$, to know; commonly joined with tao^4, to say (48). Thus,
wo^3 pu^4 $chih^1$ tao^4, I cannot tell; *lit.*, I do not know to say.

52. 愛 ai^4 or $ngai^4$, to love or like. Thus,
ni^3 pu^2 ai^4 $t'a^1$ mo^1, do you not like him?

53. 話 hua^4, spoken language, what one says, as opposed to $wén^2$, language of books (Radical 67). Thus,
$t'a^1$ ti^1 hua^4 hao^3, his [style of] speaking is good.

54. 說 $shuo^1$, to say; as in wo^3 $shuo^1$, I say = this is my opinion. Also to speak; as $shuo^1$ hua^4, to speak language; or, the language spoken, as opposed to $wén^2$. But followed by a personal pronoun, $shuo^1$ means to blame; as $t'a^1$ $shuo^1$ wo^3, he blamed me.

55. Examples:—

他 $t'a^1$	他 $t'a^1$	那 na^4	他 $t'a^1$	你 ni^3	道 tao^4	你 ni^3
說 $shuo^1$	說 $shuo^1$	人 $jén^2$	不 pu^2	愛 ai^4	我 wo^3	知 $chih^1$
的 ti	的 ti	說 $shuo^1$	大 ta^4	他 $t'a^1$	不 pu^4	道 tao^4
話 hua^4	很 $hén^3$	甚 $shé^n2$	愛 ai^4	不 pu^2	知 $chih^1$	不 pu^4
好 hao^3	是 $shih^4$	麼 mo^1	他 $t'a^1$	愛 ai^4	道 tao^4	知 $chih^1$

Do you know? [I] do not.
Do you like him? Not much.

Obs.—*Ta*, great, used adverbially.

What is that man saying? What he says $hén^3$ $shih^4$, is quite (or, very) right (or, correct). He speaks very well (good accent, form, sense).

56. 叫, 叫, $chiao^4$, to call; to bid. As $chiao^4$ $t'a^1$ lai^2, bid him come; call him here. The first is the form more commonly used. As will be seen later, it sometimes means to cause, and, as an auxiliary, can render an active verb passive.

57. 回 hui^2, to return; as $t'a^1$ hui^2 lai^2 $liao$, he is come back. Also, an occasion; as $liang^3$ hui^2, on two occasions.

58. 乏 fa^2, to be tired; as wo^3 $shén^1$-$tzŭ$ fa^2 $liao$, I am (*lit.*, my person is) tired.

59. 站 *chan*⁴, to stand upright, as distinguished from sitting, or lying down.

60. 躺 *t'ang*³, to recline; to lie down.

61. 坐 *tso*⁴, to sit.

62. Examples:—

坐 *tso*⁴	起 *ch'i*³	乏 *fa*²	來 *lai*²	了 *liao*	他 *t'a*¹
着。*cho*	來。*lai*²	了。*liao*	走 *tsou*³	叫 *chiao*⁴	走 *tsou*³
躺 *t'ang*³	站 *chan*⁴	你 *ni*³	道 *tao*⁴	他 *t'a*¹	回 *hui*²
着。*cho*	着。*cho*	站 *chan*⁴	兒 *'rh*	回 *hui*²	去 *ch'ü*⁴

He is gone back on foot.
Obs.—Tsou here, on foot.
Call him back; or, bid him return.
Tired with one's journey.
Obs.—Tsou tao, to go the road: probably, but not necessarily, on foot.
You stand up!
Standing up. Sitting. Lying down.
Obs.—Cho inflecting these verbs participially.

63. 關 *kuan*¹, to close, to shut; as *kuan*¹ *mên*², shut the door. Also, a barrier or military frontier station; also, an important point; hence (as will be seen later), to bear upon, to concern.

64. 牕 *ch'uang*¹, a window; colloquially, always followed by *hu*⁴ (Radical 63). Thus, *kuan*¹ *ch'uang*¹-*hu*⁴, shut the window.

65. 樓 *lou*², an upper story; also a storied building; as *lou*² *shang*⁴, upstairs.
*Obs.—*Its numerative in the latter case is not *chien*, but *tso*. *See* Part VIII.

66. 衙 *ya*², a bureau or official residence; colloquially, not used alone, but with *mên*². Thus,

shang⁴ ya²-mên², to go to office.

67. 地 *ti*⁴, the ground; as *ti*⁴ *hsia*⁴, on the ground.

68. Examples:—

在 *tsai*⁴	人 *jên*²	在 *tsai*⁴	我 *wo*³	有 *yu*³	樓 *lou*²	關 *kuan*¹
樓 *lou*²	躺 *t'ang*³	地 *ti*⁴	要 *yao*⁴	人 *jên*²	上 *shang*⁴	門 *mên*²
上 *shang*⁴	在 *tsai*⁴	下 *hsia*⁴	上 *shang*⁴	上 *shang*⁴	坐 *tso*⁴	開 *k'ai*¹
坐 *tso*⁴	地 *ti*⁴	躺 *t'ang*³	衙 *ya*²	樓 *lou*²	着 *cho*	牕 *ch'uang*¹
着。*cho*	下。*hsia*⁴	着。*cho*	門。*mên*²	去。*ch'ü*⁴	人。*jên*²	戶。*hu*⁴

Shut the door and open the window.
There is a person (or, persons) sitting upstairs.
Obs.—Cho marking present time.

PART III.—THE FORTY EXERCISES.

Someone is gone upstairs (*lit.*, ascending the story is gone).
I want to go to office (to the *ya²-mên²*).
Obs.—*Shang*, going towards or to.
A person (or persons) stretched on the ground.
Sitting upstairs.

69. 步 *pu⁴*, a pace. As *pu⁴ hsia⁴* (**48**), on foot; *pu⁴ hsia⁴ tsou³*, to go on foot. Also, with *hsing²* (Radical 144); as *pu⁴ hsing²*, to walk; *pu⁴ hsing² tsou³*, to go on foot.

70. 騎 *ch'i²*, to bestride; as *ch'i² ma³*, to ride on horseback.

71. 轎 *chiao⁴*, a sedan-chair; as *tso⁴ chiao⁴*, to sit in a sedan-chair.

72. 頂 *ting³*, the numerative of *chiao⁴*, sedan-chair; as *san¹ ting² chiao⁴-tzŭ*, three sedans. Also the numerative of caps. It means as well the crown of the head, as will be seen later.

73. 車 *ch'ê¹* (Radical 159), cart or carriage; as *tso⁴ ch'ê¹*, to sit in a cart.

74. 輛 *liang⁴*, the numerative of *ch'ê¹*, cart; as *ssŭ⁴ wu³ liang⁴ ch'ê¹*, four or five carts.

75. 馬 *ma³* (Radical 187), a horse.

76. 匹 *p'i¹ ² ³*, numerative of *ma³*; as *pa¹ p'i² ma³*, eight horses.

77. 騾 *lo²*, a mule. Its numerative is *t'ou²* (**48**); as *san¹ t'ou² lo²-tzŭ*, three mules. *Ko* (**8**) can also be used.

78. 驢 *lü²*, a donkey. Its numerative is *p'i²* (**76**); as *liang³ p'i² lü²*, two donkeys. Mules and donkeys are spoken of collectively as *lo²-tzŭ lü²*. *Ko* (**8**) can also be used as the numerative of donkeys.

79. Examples:—

買 *mai³*	騎 *ch'i²*	是 *shih⁴*	他 *t'a¹*	我 *wo³*	他 *t'a¹*	我 *wo³*
了 *liao*	騾 *lo²*	騎 *ch'i²*	賣 *mai⁴*	要 *yao⁴*	是 *shih⁴*	是 *shih⁴*
兩 *liang³*	子 *tzŭ*	馬 *ma³*	騾 *lo²*	買 *mai³*	步 *pu⁴*	坐 *tso⁴*
輛 *liang⁴*	來 *lai²*	來 *lai²*	子 *tzŭ*	頂 *ting³*	下 *hsia⁴*	車 *ch'ê¹*
車。 *ch'ê¹*	的 *ti*	的 *ti*	驢。*lü²*	轎 *chiao⁴*	走 *tsou³*	來 *lai²*
	我 *wo³*	是 *shih⁴*	他 *t'a¹*	子。*tzŭ*	的 *ti*	的。*ti*

I came in a cart; *lit.*, I am seated in a cart come.
He goes (or, is or was going) on foot.
I want to buy a chair.
Obs.—*Ting=yi ting*, one piece.
He sells (or, is selling) mules and donkeys.
Did he ride here on a horse or on a mule? *q.d.*, he, was he riding a horse hither, was he riding a mule hither?
I have bought two carts.
Obs.—Not *êrh liang*.

80. 快 *k'uai*⁴, quick; as *na*⁴ *p'i*² *ma*³ *k'uai*⁴, that horse [is] quick.

81. 慢 *man*⁴, slow; as *na*⁴ *lo*²-*tzŭ* *man*⁴, that mule [is] slow.

82. 前 *ch'ien*², before, in time or place.

83. 後 *hou*⁴, behind, in time or place.

84. 都 *tou*¹ (properly *tu*¹), all, plurality; as *na*⁴ *hsieh*¹ *jén*² *tou*¹ *hao*³, those people are all good. Also, under some circumstances, both or either.

85. Examples:—

頭	*t'ou*²	不	*pu*²	慢	*man*⁴	走	*tsou*³	騾	*lo*²	頭	*t'ou*²	我	*wo*³
裏	*li*³	是	*shih*⁴	前	*ch'ien*²	得	*té*²	子	*tzŭ*	騾	*lo*²	那	*na*⁴
好	*hao*³	他	*t'a*¹	頭	*t'ou*²	快	*k'uai*⁴	驢	*lü*²	子	*tzŭ*	匹	*p'i*²
後	*hou*⁴	後	*hou*⁴	他	*t'a*¹	都	*tou*¹	慢	*man*⁴	馬	*ma*³
來	*lai*²	頭	*t'ou*²	走	*tsou*³	好	*hao*³	那	*na*⁴	快	*k'uai*⁴
比	*pi*³	都	*tou*¹	得	*té*²	我	*wo*³	些	*hsieh*¹	那	*na*⁴

That horse of mine is fast.

That mule is slow.

Those mules and donkeys are all good.

Obs.—Were the *hsieh* omitted, *lo* and *lü* would be singular, and *tou*=both.

I walk fast; *q.d.*, I walking achieve speed. He walks slow.

Front and rear both wrong; *lit.*, not what [the thing] should be, before or behind.

Obs.—*Tou pu*, all not, in such a context=neither.

He was better subsequently than he had been at first.

Obs. 1.—*Hou lai* may mean (as here) after a date already past, or hereafter. The combination *ch'ien lai* is not colloquial, nor is it analogous to *hou lai* in construction. In writing it means to proceed to or towards. It has also auxiliary power.

Obs. 2.—*T'ou li*: *q.d.*, within the beginning=at first. Also, in front; see Exercise IV, 1, English (p. 27). There are many other combinations signifying *before*, in some of which, as will be seen, *ch'ien* plays a part.

86. 把 *pa*³, to hold; to take hold of. Frequently prefixed to what we call the object of the transitive verb. Thus,

*pa*³ *na*⁴ *mén*² *kuan*¹ *shang*⁴, shut to that door.

As a substantive, *pa*³ has various uses; amongst others, that of a numerative.

87. 給 *kei*³ (properly *chi*³), to give; as in *ni*³ *kei*³ *wo*³ *yi*² *ko*⁴, you give me one. Hence it often acts as *to* or *for*; as we should say, it forms the dative case. Thus,

*ni*³ *kei*³ *wo*³ *na*² *yi*² *ko*⁴ *lai*², bring one for me.

88. 跑 *p'ao*³, to run, as a man; to gallop, as a horse. As *p'ao*³ *ch'ü*⁴ *liao*, ran off, or galloped away.

PART III.—THE FORTY EXERCISES.

EXERCISE IV.

兒	的。| 是	誰	不	方	那	有 1
知	你	我	說	得。| 兒	個	人
道	那'	說	的。| 是	住	地	說

1. They say, or, some say (*lit.*, there is a man, or there are men, who say), that that place is uninhabitable. Who is that says so? I (*lit.*, it is I that) say so. How do you know?

了	少	他	說	不	知	的 2
一	回。	做	不	出	道。	房 是
回。	他	過	出	來。	我	子 誰
	做	多	來。| 他	做	誰 家

2. Whose house is this? (what family does it belong to?) Who knows? I can't do it. He can't tell. How many times has he done (or, made) it? He has done it once; *q.d.*, one turn.

Obs. 1.—*Ch'u-lai*, as an auxiliary completing the action of the verbs *tso* and *shuo*.
Obs. 2.—*Chi*³ *hui*² would be equally correct.

知	我	麼	是	個	五	來	外 3
道。	不	人。	甚	人。	六	了	頭

3. There are five or six people outside that have come. Who are they? I cannot say.

躺	是	坐	在	起	都	來	大 4
著,	地	著,	樓	來。	得'	你	人
下	他		上	我	站	們	進

4. When His Excellency comes in you must all stand up. I was (or am) sitting upstairs; he was or is lying on the ground.

Obs. 1.—Do not construe *ti hsia*, below. We shall come presently to *ti*³ *hsia*, below.
Obs. 2.—Were *liao*³ placed after the first *lai*, the sentence would run, His Excellency has come in, etc.
N.B.—A *ta-jên* is not necessarily His Excellency, the title being applied to any official above a certain rank.

大	我	不	這	你 5
愛。	不	愛。	個	愛

5. Do you like this? Not very much.

了。| 乏	了	你	門	兒	你 6
	我	家	回	一	走、| 快
走	身	了。| 不	關	城	些
不	子					

6. Walk a little faster; when once the city gate is shut you won't get home. I am too tired to walk any more.

Obs.—*Lit.*, my body is tired, walk [I] cannot.

關	上	牕	牕	了。| 開	把 7
上	牕	戶	戶。| 關	門	門
了。| 戶	關	把	上	開	開

7. Open the door. The door is open. Shut the window. Shut the window. The window is shut.

Obs.—Shut; the *shang*⁴ as an auxiliary completing the action of the verb *kuan*.

上。門來。他著。上道他 8
關把起叫躺兒在

8. He is lying down in the road; tell him to get up. Shut the door.

Obs.—With verbs of motion *tao-'rh shang* means, on the way, on the road, while one is travelling.

慢走。他的。的。走走 9
兒快在我他著。著
的走後在是他他
走。了。頭前步坐走
　　慢走頭行車了。的
　　快走來來來步
　　　　　　下

9. Walking here. Walking; or, to come or to go on foot; going on foot. He walked here; I came in a cart. He came on foot. I was walking in front; he was behind. Go fast; or, make haste and go (imperative). I am going shortly or soon. Go gently.

Obs. 1.—*Ti* at the end of the first clause is probably used corruptly for *tê*, as auxiliary completing the act of *tsou lai*.

Obs. 2.—In the second clause, if *ti* be not used for *tê*, a word signifying manner must be understood after *ti*; *q.d.*, my [manner of coming] *shih*, was, sit-in-cart-coming's manner.

Obs. 3.—There is a difference between *k'uai tsou* used imperatively and otherwise.

Obs. 4.—Note *liao* indicating future action.

轎愛小轎門上沒他 10
子坐轎子去那'有那
好。車去是了。兒他個
　是的、坐他去沒人
　他他車。去是了。回
　那不坐坐上回來
　頂大頂　衙來了
　　　　　門他

10. Is that man come back or not? He is not back. Where did he go (is he gone to)? To the *ya²-mên²* (office). Did he go in a chair or in a carriage? In a small chair; he does not much like being in a carriage. That chair of his is good; or, his is the better chair.

Obs.—*Yi*, one, colloquially omitted before *ting*, the numerative noun.

騾兒那兒的子是 11
子的騾兒騾好這
驢慢子的子是兒
都那比好沒那的
快。兒那這有。兒騾

11. Which are the better, the mules from this place or from that? The mules here are not so good as those there; *q.d.*, this place's mules are not (or, have not) that place's good. The mules here are slower than what you get there. Both the mules and donkeys from that place are fast.

　子了子買　他 12
　七三頭多驢。麽買
　個頭少少。的是的
　驢。騾買他是不是
　　　　買騾。是

12. Is it horses that he is buying? No, he is buying (or, what he has bought are) mules and donkeys. How many has he bought? Three mules and seven donkeys. (*See* **78**.)

PART III.—THE FORTY EXERCISES.

你 來 是 馬 的。快。
是 的 騎 我 跑
步 是 馬 那 得
騎 我 的。匹 很
行 騎 來 來

13. 你來是步行，是騎馬來的。是我騎那匹馬來的。我那匹馬跑得很快。

13. Did you come on foot or on horseback? I rode here. That horse of mine gallops very fast.

Turn the following into Chinese. (KEY, EXERCISE IV.)

1. He is sitting upstairs; tell him to come here quickly. He won't come fast; he is coming very slowly. I went in front in a cart; he followed in a sedan-chair.

Obs.—In front, *t'ou² li³. See* 85, Obs. 2.

2. Tell him to buy two carts and four horses. He says there are no horses here. He says mules are better than horses. Has he bought mules? Yes. How many has he bought? Four. Has he bought any donkeys? No; you did not tell him to buy donkeys.

3. Has he gone to the *ya-mên* in a sedan-chair or in a cart? He has gone on foot; he says he does not like carts or sedans. He will not come back soon. He is lying on the ground; he can't get up.

4. That horse is faster than this one. Horses are faster than mules; mules are faster than donkeys. Has he arrived? No. What is he doing? He is walking slowly. Tell him to come quickly.

5. How many sedan-chairs have you? Two. How many mules, horses, and donkeys? Four horses, three mules, five donkeys. Have you any carts? No; I have sold all my carts. Why are you standing up? For no reason (*lit.*, I am not doing anything); you like sitting down; I like standing up.

Obs.—Why: *lit.*, to do what?

89. 請 *ch'ing³*, to pray; to request. Hence, please; as in *ch'ing³ tso⁴*, please be seated.

90. 教 *chiao¹*, to teach; as *t'a¹ chiao¹ wo³ shuo¹ hua⁴*, he is teaching me to speak the language.

91. 看 *k'an⁴*, to behold; to regard. As *wo³ k'an⁴ t'a¹ hao³*, I think him good. *K'an¹*, to watch (*see* 526).

見 *chien⁴* (Radical 147), to see; to perceive. Often combined with *k'an⁴*; as *wo³ mei² k'an⁴ chien⁴*, I have not seen him (or it).

92. 書 *shu¹*, a book; writings. As *k'an⁴ shu¹*, to read or study.

93. 找 *chao³*, to seek; to search for. As *chao³ p'i³ hao³ ma³*, to look out for a good horse.

94. 字 *tzŭ⁴*, written words; Chinese characters.

95. 典 *tien³*, a rule; a canon. With *tzŭ⁴* (94), a dictionary; *q.d.*, a word-canon. Thus, *na² tzŭ⁴ tien³ chao³ tzŭ⁴*, with (*lit.*, taking hold of) a dictionary to look out words.

Obs.—*Na* before the instrumental case.

96. 學 hsiao², also read hsio², hsüeh², hsüo², to learn. Also, to imitate; to follow, as an example. When combined with 生 shêng¹ (Radical 100), to be born, hsio²-shêng¹ or hsüeh²-shêng¹, a pupil.

97. 認 jên⁴, to recognise. With tzŭ (94), to be able to read; as t'a¹ pu⁴ jên⁴ tê tzŭ⁴, he cannot read (lit., is not able to recognise characters).

98. Examples :—

生 shêng¹	是 shih⁴	找 chao³	拏 na²	我 wo³	他 t'a¹	他 t'a¹
認 jên⁴	學 hsio²	找。chao³	字 tzŭ⁴	不 pu⁴	看 k'an⁴	要 yao⁴
得 tê²	字。tzŭ⁴	這 ché⁴	典 tien³	認 jên⁴	書。shu¹	請 ch'ing³
字 tzŭ⁴	那 na⁴	個 ko⁴	給 kei³	得 tê²	有 yu³	人 jên²
多。to¹	學 hsio²	字 tzŭ⁴	我 wo³	請 ch'ing³	字 tzŭ⁴	教 chiao¹

He wants to engage (lit., request) someone to read with him (lit., to teach to read books). There is a character (or, there are characters) which I do not know; please look [it] out in the dictionary for me.

Obs.—Kei wo, for me, chao chao (short for chao yi chao; lit., seek a seek).

This character is the character hsio², to learn.

That pupil (or student) knows a number of characters.

99. 先 hsien¹, before (in time); as hsien¹-shêng¹ (Radical 100), a teacher; lit., elder-born. (Compare our senior, signor, sir.) Thus,

ch'ing³ hsien¹-shêng¹, to engage (lit., request, or, to invite, send for) a teacher.

100. 抄 ch'ao¹, to copy; as ch'ao¹ shu¹, to copy writings or books. Often coupled with the following hsieh³.

101. 寫 hsieh³, to write; as hsieh³ tzŭ⁴, to write (lit., write the character).

102. 真 chên¹, true, truly; as ché⁴ shih⁴ chên¹ hua⁴, this is true (lit., true statement).

103. 正 chêng⁴, upright, correct; as k'ou³ yin¹ chêng⁴, mouth sounds correct = accurate pronunciation.

104. 肯 k'ên³, to wish, to choose to; as t'a¹ pu⁴ k'ên³ lai², he won't (does not choose to) come.

105. 還 properly huan², to return. Colloquially, han², hai², yet, still; as wo³ hai² yu³ yi² ko⁴, I have still got one; I have got no more than one.

106. Examples :—

肯 k'ên³	還 hai²	你 ni³	說 shuo¹	他 t'a¹	先 hsien¹	請 ch'ing³
不 pu⁴	有 yu³	口 k'ou³	的 ti¹	不 pu⁴	生 shêng¹	先 hsien¹
肯 k'ên³	比 pi³	音 yin¹	是 shih⁴	肯 k'ên³	還 hai²	生 shêng¹
都 tou¹	他 t'a¹	不 pu²	真 chên¹	抄 ch'ao¹	沒 mei²	進 chin⁴
好。hao³	好。hao³	正。chêng⁴	話。hua⁴	寫。hsieh³	來。lai²	來。lai²

Ask the teacher to come in.

Obs.—If the ch'ing were placed after hsien-shêng, this would mean, Please walk in, sir.

PART III.—THE FORTY EXERCISES. 29

The teacher is not come yet.
He won't (does not want to) copy.
What is said is the truth.
Your pronunciation is incorrect; you have a bad pronunciation.
There is another (or, there are others) better than he.
Whether [I, you, he] choose or not, it makes no difference (q.d., assent or not assent), both are good. See *tou*¹ (**84**).

107. 瞧 *ch'iao*², to look at; to see. As in *mei*² *ch'iao*² *kuo*⁴, not to have seen [him, it]. Like *k'an*⁴ (**91**), it is very commonly joined with *chien*⁴ (Radical 147); as in *ch'iao*² *pu*² *chien*⁴, unable to see. The forms *k'an*⁴-*chien*⁴ and *ch'iao*²-*chien*⁴ differ little in sense, but the latter seems to be used rather when the object is small enough to escape attention.

108. 告 *kao*⁴, to announce; colloquially, most often coupled with *su*⁴ (**109**). With *shih* (Radical 113), *kao*⁴-*shih*⁴, a proclamation.

109. 訴 *su*⁴ or *sung*⁴, to tell to; to complain that. *Kao*⁴-*su*⁴, also pronounced *kao*⁴-*sung*⁴, to tell to; as in *ni*³ *kao*⁴-*su*⁴ *wo*³, you tell me.

110. 問 *wên*⁴, to ask; to inquire. As in *wo*³ *wên*⁴ *t'a*¹ *ni*³ *shih*⁴ *shui*², I asked him, who are you?

111. 記 *chi*⁴, to record in writing; but, colloquially, to remember. As *wo*³ *pu*² *chi*⁴ *tê*², I do not remember.

112. 呢 *ni*¹, a particle, generally, but not always, interrogative.

113. Examples:—

那 *na*³	甚 *shen*²	大 *ta*⁴	記 *chi*⁴	瞧 *ch'iao*²	還 *hai*²	請 *ch'ing*³
個 *ko*⁴	麼 *mo*¹	很 *hên*³	得 *tê*²	瞧 *ch'iao*²	沒 *mei*²	你 *ni*³
好 *hao*³	話 *hua*⁴	記 *chi*⁴	不 *pu*²	好 *hao*³	看 *k'an*⁴	告 *kao*⁴
呢 *ni*¹	呢 *ni*¹	得 *tê*²	記 *chi*⁴	不 *pu*⁴	見 *chien*⁴	訴 *su*⁴
	請 *ch'ing*³	這 *chê*⁴	得 *tê*²	好 *hao*³	過 *kuo*⁴	他 *t'a*¹
	問 *wên*⁴	是 *shih*⁴	不 *pu*²	你 *ni*³	你 *ni*³	我 *wo*³

Please tell him.
I have not seen [him or it].
Obs.—*Hai*: merely intensive; strictly, not yet seen, etc.
You look [at it and] see whether it is good or not.
Do you remember?
[I] do not very well remember.
Obs.—Note the double intensive *ta*³ *hên*³.
What is this that you are saying? (what is the meaning of such language?)
I beg to ask [you] which is the better (or best)?
Obs.—*Ch'ing*³ preceding *wên*⁴ : a respectful form of question; sometimes also sarcastic.

EXERCISE V.

1 我書先了學請字
要你生他生來教
請給沒不那請這
先我有來麼生是
生找他多請甚
教著了說不坐麼

1. I want to engage a teacher to teach me to read (*lit.*, books); have you found a teacher for me? [I] have found one, [but] he is not coming; he says that he won't come to so large a number of students. Teacher, please be seated. Be so good as to tell me what this character is.

Obs. 1.—*Lit.*, he says students being that many, he does not choose (refuses) to come.

Obs. 2.—Be so good: *ch'ing chiao* is a polite form of asking for information of an equal or superior on any subject.

2 叫那拿先出字找字找
人字來生來甚呢瞧字
把典請找麼要字
來個 要

2. Tell someone to bring that dictionary here. Teacher, please look out that character. What character do you want looked out? The character *ch'iao*² (to see).

3 請認個見你那有沒
問得字過個字個看看
這不過個字你看見見
個認呢我字還見過過
字得。還還沒過麼。
你這沒沒有。
字看這

3. Do you know this character, sir? I have not met with (*lit.*, seen) this character. Have you met with this character? Have you never met with that character either? No, indeed; never.

Obs. 1.—Sir gives the force of the *ch'ing wên*, I beg to inquire.

Obs. 2.—The object *chê ko tzŭ* precedes the verb only for emphasis sake.

Obs. 3.—The two questions are different. In the first the speaker is in doubt; in the second he assumes a fact.

Obs. 4.—Either: *hai* or *han*, also, still.

Obs. 5.—Indeed: *chên*, truly, have [I] not seen [it or them].

4 你那音沒音好字的
告個有有不他比多
訴人你的大我我
我的的口甚認認
他口好 麼得得

4. Tell me is that man's pronunciation as good as yours? My pronunciation is not particularly good; he knows more characters than I.

Obs.—You might say equally well *mei shên mo hên hao*.

PART III.—THE FORTY EXERCISES.   31

多。得麼還不訴見這 5
的那有記我過個
少兒不記是。字
不沒不得甚見你
記有記那個過見
得呢得字麼了。過
的記的字字。你沒
的字了。我告

5. Have you [ever] met with (*lit.*, seen) this character? I have. Tell me what character it is. I do not remember the character. Are there any other characters that you do not remember? Of course there are; I remember but few compared with the number I forget.

Obs.—Of course there are: *lit.*, how, *na 'rh* [can it be that there should] not be, eh? This interrogative form of affirmation is very common.

Turn the following into Chinese. (KEY, EXERCISE V.)

1. I have asked a teacher to come and teach me to talk. Do you want to learn to write as well? Teacher, please tell me is my pronunciation correct? Not very correct; besides you do not know many characters.

Obs.—Besides: *lit.*, you recognised characters yet not many.

2. Where is that dictionary? It is in the teacher's room; he is looking out characters there. Ask him to copy them for me. The teacher does not wish to come. He tells me that your pronunciation is very far from good and that your diction is also incorrect.

Obs.—Also (Radical 29).

3. Have you seen my teacher? I saw him riding on horseback; the horse was galloping very fast, he did not see me. Please look out the character *chi* in the dictionary. I have found it. Do you recognise that character? I have never seen it.

4. What are these pupils learning? They are learning to write and to read. Who is their teacher? I do not know who he is. Have you ever seen him? Yes, he is here teaching the pupils. Have you copied those characters yet? Not yet, but I will copy them soon.

5. Do you like riding? If a horse gallops fast, I do not like to ride him. Is this horse a good one? Not very good; he does not gallop fast. Sit tight (on your horse).

Obs.—Sit tight: *lit.*, ride firm (**48**).

114. 紙 *chih*^{3}, paper.

115. 張 *chang*^{1}, properly to open, to spread out; hence when used as the numerative of *chih*^{3}, paper, a sheet. Also, the numerative of tables, chairs, etc.; also, a common surname.

116. 筆 *pi*^{3}, a Chinese pencil; as *na*^{2} *pi*^{3} *hsieh*^{3} *tzŭ*^{4}, take a pen and write characters (*sc.*, to write *with* a pen).

117. 管 *kuan*^{3}, a tube; the numerative of pencils. As *liang*^{3} *kuan*^{3} *pi*^{3}, two pencils. Also, to superintend; to look after. *See* Exercise XV, 6, Obs. 2.

118. 墨 *mê⁴*, *mo⁴*, ink; as *pi³ mo⁴*, pen and ink (*fig.* for composition).

119. 塊 *k'uai⁴*, a bit; a piece; the numerative of Chinese ink, which is in small cakes. As *san¹ k'uai⁴ mo⁴*, three cakes of ink.

120. 本 *pên³*, the numerative of books; as *san¹ pên³ shu¹*, three volumes, or, a three-volume book. Properly, *pên³* is the trunk of a tree, its root above ground; hence, primary, original; hence, under certain circumstances, the pronoun *this*, *self*.

121. Examples :—

筆 *pi³*	抄 *ch'ao¹*	這 *ché⁴*	筆 *pi³*	張 *chang¹*	買 *mai³*
都 *tou¹*	字 *tzŭ⁴*	書 *shu¹*	兩 *liang³*	白 *pai²*	的 *ti*
說 *shuo¹*	用 *yung⁴*	多 *to¹*	塊 *k'uai⁴*	紙 *chih³*	是 *shih⁴*
得 *tê²*	筆 *pi³*	少 *shao³*	香 *hsiang¹*	十 *shih²*	三 *san¹*
拿 *na²*	本 *pên³*	墨 *mo⁴*	管 *kuan³*	十 *shih²*	

The purchase (that which is bought) is thirty sheets of white paper, ten pencils, and two pieces of scented ink.

Obs.—Scented; *hsiang¹* (Radical 186).

How many volumes does this book consist of?

[When speaking of] copying [with a pencil], it is as correct to say *yung pi* (use the pencil) as *na pi* (take the pencil).

Obs. 1.—*Lit.*, [as to] copying characters, use pencil, take pencil, *tou*, all = both, may be said.

Obs. 2.—Use, *yung⁴* (Radical 101), here, like *na²*, forms with its object our instrumental case; *sc.*, with a pencil.

122. 念 *nien⁴*, to think of; to commit to memory; to repeat aloud; to study. Thus,

nien⁴ shu¹, to recite, as Chinese beginners do their books.

123. 完 *wan²*, to end; hence sometimes used as an auxiliary to imply completion of an act, as *k'an⁴ wan²*, to have read [it] all (*lit.*, read ended).

124. 可 *k'o³*, to be right; to be able. *K'o³* is also used idiomatically as an adverb or a disjunctive, in abatement of affirmation; and otherwise. Thus,

k'o pu shih, can it not be? (It certainly is; indeed it is.)

k'o shih, it may be; but.

125. 以 *i³*, properly, to use; hence employed as an instrumental preposition. With the preceding word *k'o³*, it answers a question affirmatively, sometimes with reserve, sometimes not; or it may simply mean can, is able to, or, may possibly. With certain verbs it has an adverbial sense; as in *shih⁴ i³* (**34**), therefore, accordingly.

PART III.—THE FORTY EXERCISES.

126. Examples:—

用 yung⁴	話 hua⁴	以 i³	的 ti	書 shu¹	月 yüeh⁴	他 t'a¹
我 wo³	可 k'o³	那 na⁴	筆 pi³	沒 mei²	的 ti	念 nien⁴
不 pu⁴	用 yung⁴	可 k'o³	墨 mo⁴	看 k'an⁴	書 shu¹	過 kuo⁴
好 hao³	不 pu⁴	是 shih⁴	還 hai²	完 wan²	那 na⁴	三 san¹
說 shuo¹	可 k'o³	眞 chên¹	可 k'o³	他 t'a¹	本 pên³	個 ko⁴

He has been studying three months; *lit.*, he has recited three months' books.
[I have] not read through that book; *lit.*, have not completed reading it.
His composition is pretty fair.

Obs.—Note the power of *hai*, still, notwithstanding; it modifies the abatement of *k'o i*.
That is the truth, no doubt.
Obs.—Without *k'o* the affirmation would be stronger.
Whether available or not, it is not for me to say.
Obs.—Construe thus:—[Whether man] *k'o yung*, can rightly, possibly, use [it or] not, I cannot well (or properly) say.

127. 官 *kuan¹*, an official. As an attributive, that which belongs to government; as in *kuan¹ hua⁴*, the government spoken language, commonly styled the mandarin dialect.

128. 民 *min²*, the people; as *kuan¹ min²*, the government (or officials) and people.

129. 會 *hui⁴*, as a verb, to meet, to come together; also, to be competent to, to know how to, to understand. As *hui⁴ shuo¹*, to be able to speak.
As a substantive, it means a conjuncture; also, a period of time. As *yi⁴ hui³-tzǔ* or *yi⁴ hui³-'rh*, a while. Note the change of tone. It is not to be confounded with *hui²* (57).

130. 分 *fên¹*, to divide; a fraction; specially, a tenth. As *shih² fên¹*, ten-tenths, a whole; hence, adverbially, much, very; as *shih² fên¹ hao³*, very good. *Fên⁴*, a set (*see* 153).

131. 聽 *t'ing¹*, to hear; as *t'ing¹ hua⁴*, to hear what is said = to obey. Also, to submit to, to comply with.

132. 明 *ming²*, plain to the sight; also, clear-seeing. As *ming² pai²* (*lit.*, clear white), intelligent; intelligible.

133. Examples:—

明 ming²	不 pu⁴	說 shuo¹	不 pu²	房 fang²	民 min²	官 kuan¹
白 pai²	出 ch'u¹	的 ti	會 hui⁴	那 na⁴	人 jên²	住 chu⁴
	來 lai²	官 kuan¹	說 shuo¹	人 jên²	住 chu⁴	的 ti
	都 tou¹	話 hua⁴	官 kuan¹	十 shih²	的 ti	是 shih⁴
	說 shuo¹	我 wo³	話 hua⁴	分 fên¹	是 shih⁴	衙 ya²
	不 pu⁴	聽 t'ing¹	他 t'a¹	好 hao³	民 min²	門 mên²

[The building] that an official lives in is a *ya-mên*.

Obs.—This would be said in answer to the question, What is a yamên? There are numbers of men in office who have no yamên.

What the people live in are *min² fang²* (houses of the people).

Obs.—In both these examples either *fang* or some similar word is understood after *chu ti*.

That is a very good man.

He cannot speak mandarin.

When he speaks mandarin (or, the mandarin that he speaks) I do not understand.

Obs 1.—*Ch'u lai* is here more than auxiliary of time; it affects the meaning of *t'ing¹*.

Obs. 2.—Here also the speaker may be unintelligible on account of either the sound or the sense.

He cannot speak intelligibly at all.

Obs.—This might be because of lack of intelligence or of error in form.

134. 也 *yeh³*, also; even. As *ché⁴ ko⁴ yeh³ hao³*, this one also is good; or, this one will do as well.

135. 懂 *tung³*, to understand; as *tung³ pu⁴ tung³*, do you understand or not?

136. 聲 *shéng¹*, sound; specially, the tones. As *ssŭ⁴ shéng¹*, the four tones.

137. 平 *p'ing²*, even; level; at peace; also (as will be seen later), ordinary, common.

138. 忘 *wang⁴*, to forget. As *wang⁴ pu⁴ liao³*, never can forget.

139. 錯 *ts'o⁴*, to err; wrong. As *t'ing¹ ts'o⁴ liao*, to mistake what is said; *lit.*, to hear wrong. When following active verbs in general, *ts'o⁴* affects them like our syllable *mis* prefixed; but generally, if not always, where the error is unintentional.

140. Examples:—

眞 *chén¹*	這 *ché⁴*	去 *ch'ü⁴*	平 *p'ing²*	那 *na⁴*	土 *t'u³*	那 *na⁴*
是 *shih⁴*	字 *tzŭ⁴*	聲 *shéng¹*	下 *hsia⁴*	四 *ssŭ⁴*	話 *hua⁴*	管 *kuan³*
不 *pu²*	我 *wo³*	那 *na⁴*	平 *p'ing²*	聲 *shéng¹*	也 *yeh³*	筆 *pi³*
記 *chi⁴*	忘 *wang⁴*	不 *pu²*	上 *shang³*	是 *shih⁴*	懂 *tung³*	也 *yeh³*
得。*té*	了 *liao³*	錯。*ts'o⁴*	聲 *shéng¹*	上 *shang⁴*	得。*té*	好。*hao³*

That pencil is also a good one (or, will do as well).

[He] also understands the local dialect.

Obs.—*T'u* (Radical 32): *see* Radical Exercises, 10, 18.

The four tones are the *shang-p'ing* (upper even), the *hsia-p'ing* (lower even), the *shang* (ascending), the *ch'ü* (departing).

Obs.—*Shang⁴* when applied to the third tone is *shang³*.

That is quite right; *lit.*, that is not wrong.

Obs.—*Pu* changes its tone before *ts'o*, *shih*, and other words.

This character I have forgotten; I really do not remember it.

EXERCISE VI.

<table>
<tr><td>他
說
的
官
話
還
可</td><td>好。
他
說
的
官
話
你
還</td><td>有
可
是
沒
有
你
還</td><td>以
可
是
沒
有
你
還
的</td><td>得
土
音。
聽
見
說
你</td><td>完
了
幾
本
書、
是
得</td><td>了、
了
沒
有。
得
是
得</td><td>本。
看
了
不
過
一
兩</td><td>1</td></tr>
</table>

1. His speaking [of] mandarin is passable, but not so good as yours. His mandarin has a certain local accent. I hear (or, one hears) that you have got some books; have you read them all through yet? I *have* got them, but I have not read more than one or two volumes.

Obs. 1.—In both sentences *hai* or *han* diminishes the force of the affirmation.
Obs. 2.—*K'o shih*, but.
Obs. 3.—Passable, *k'o i*; *lit.*, one can use, is tolerably available.
Obs. 4.—Local accent: *t'u yin*, sound of the locality or country. (*See* 140, Obs.)
Obs. 5.—I *have* got: *tê shih tê liao*, as to possessing, *shih*, it is a fact that [I] am in possession.

<table>
<tr><td>我
聽
見
說</td><td>你
學
著
官</td><td>話
呢、
學
那
四</td><td>很
好。
你
分
得</td><td>聲
你
分
不
得</td><td>出
分
不
出。</td><td>都
還
可
以</td><td>分
得
開。</td><td>2</td></tr>
</table>

2. I hear it said that you are learning mandarin, and getting on very well; can you distinguish the four tones? I can distinguish them all.

Obs.—I can distinguish: *lit.*, all still can [I] distinguish. Note the force of *han* or *hai*, still; *q.d.* [obstacles or difficulties notwithstanding], still can I, etc.

<table>
<tr><td>那
一
本
書
你</td><td>看
完
了
沒
有。</td><td>十
分
裏
看
了</td><td>有
七
八
分
明</td><td>白
不
不
明
白。</td><td>幾
分
不
大
明</td><td>白
也
有
幾
個</td><td>字
不
認
得。</td><td>3</td></tr>
</table>

3. Have you done reading that book yet? (or, have you finished that book?) I have read about four-fifths of it; *lit.*, seven or eight tenths. Do you understand it? There are portions of it that I do not well understand; there are also some characters [in it] that I do not know.

<table>
<tr><td>你
念
了
多
少
日</td><td>子
的
書。
我
念
了</td><td>十
個
月
的
書。</td><td>書
上
的
字
都
記</td><td>得
麼。
記
不
了
那</td><td>麼
多。
忘
了
好
些</td><td>個
了。
還
有
記</td><td>了
的
還
有
記
錯</td><td>4</td></tr>
</table>

4. How long have you been reading (studying)? I have been studying ten months. Do you remember all the characters in the book (or books) you have been studying? I cannot remember so many as that. I have forgotten a good number altogether, and there are some that I do not remember accurately (*lit.*, remember wrong).

5. Does he understand mandarin? I have heard people say that he does not. Does he know the written character? That he does; he has learned four or five thousand characters. How do you know? We read together last month. If I tell him to copy will he be able to? There is no reason why he should not.

他那個人懂得官話不
懂。我聽見人說他不認
得字。懂得字不認得。
他認得認得過四五千字。
你那兒知道呢。上月我叫
他們在一塊兒看書。沒有
甚麼抄寫他行不行。的。

Obs. 1.—Read together: *tsai yi k'uai-'rh*; *lit.*, in one piece (or, forming one piece).
Obs. 2.—Last month: *lit.*, the upper month. "Next month" is *hsia yüeh*, the lower month.
Obs. 3.—Will he be able to: *hsing pu hsing*, can he do or not? (*Hsing*, Radical 144.)

6. Tell me, do you understand him when he speaks?

你告訴我。他的話你聽得來聽不來。出得來。很是。

7. You must on no account forget the books you read. Certainly not (you are quite right).

你念過的書千萬不可忘了。錯不了。說得你很是。

Obs.—On no account: *ch'ien wan* (thousand myriad), with a negative, *pu k'o* (must you not).

8. Can you use our dictionary? Yes, I can use it, but when I look out words I have to go slowly.

你會用這兒的字典會用。我們會用。可是用‘找字得慢些兒。

Obs. 1.—Our: *lit.*, our this place's.
Obs. 2.—*K'o* qualifies *tei*, must.

Turn the following into Chinese. (KEY, EXERCISE VI.)

1. Bring me that pencil. This pencil is not a good one; have you (*lit.*, is there) not another good one? Not a good one; I have two or three bad ones.

2. Take a sheet of paper, a cake of ink, and a pencil, and write some characters. What characters do you want me to write? All the characters you do not know in this book.

3. I hear that you are learning mandarin; do you understand it? Not very well; I have not been studying it long.

4. Can you distinguish the four tones? I can distinguish them all. What tone is *k'ên* in? The third. Right. Write that character on this sheet of paper. You have written it wrong.

Obs.—Can: *hui* (129).

5. Have you finished that book yet? Yes, and I understand it perfectly. Are there any characters in it you do not recognise? Of course there are; the characters I know are few compared with those I do not know.

6. Do you understand me when I speak? Your pronunciation is so correct that I understand you very well.

7. Can you buy me a sheet of paper and a pencil? I can. Do you want ink too? No, I want five sheets of paper and two pencils; do you understand? Perfectly.

141. 炕 *k'ang*⁴, the stove-bed, built of bricks.

142. 鋪 *p'u*¹, properly, to spread out, as a cloth. The numerative of *k'ang*⁴, stove-bed; as *yi*⁴ *p'u*¹ *k'ang*⁴.

Obs.—Not to be confounded with the same character in a corrupt form (46), *p'u*⁴, a shop.

143. 蓋 *kai*⁴, to cover; a cover. With *p'u*¹ (142), as in *p'u*¹-*kai*⁴, bedding; *q.d.*, that which is spread and that which covers. As a verb, in its sense of to cover, it is used as to build; as *kai*⁴ *fang*²-*tzŭ*, to build a house.

144. 蓆 *hsi*², a mat, such as is spread on a bed, on the floor, etc.; as *p'u*¹ *hsi*²-*tzŭ*, to spread a mat (or mats).

145. 牀 *ch'uang*², a bedstead; one's bed. Its numerative is *chang*¹ (115) or may be *ko*⁴; as *yi*¹ *chang*¹ *ch'uang*² or *yi*² *ko*⁴ *ch'uang*².

146. 帳 *chang*⁴, a curtain; as *chang*⁴-*tzŭ*. Also an account, or accounts, as will be seen presently.

147. Examples:—

下 *hsia*⁴	兒 *'rh*	帳 *chang*¹	上 *shang*⁴	把 *pa*³	鋪 *p'u*¹	那 *na*⁴
鋪 *p'u*¹	蓋 *kai*⁴	子 *tzŭ*	牀 *ch'uang*²	鋪 *p'u*¹	着 *cho*	鋪 *p'u*¹
蓆 *hsi*²	上 *shang*⁴	把 *pa*³	上 *shang*⁴	蓋 *kai*⁴	蓆 *hsi*²	炕 *k'ang*⁴
子 *tzŭ*	地 *ti*⁴	蓋 *kai*⁴	沒 *mei*²	鋪 *p'u*¹	子 *tzŭ*	上 *shang*⁴

There are mats spread on that stove-bed.
Spread the bedding; *q.d.*, on the *k'ang*.
There are no curtains to the bed.
Put on the cover; *lit.*, taking the cover, cover to; *shang* completing the action of the verb.
Spread mats (or, the mat) on the ground.

148. 桌, 卓 *cho*¹, *cho*², a table. Its numerative is *chang*¹ (115); as *san*¹ *chang*¹ *cho*¹-*tzŭ*, three tables. The character *cho*² is the ancient form.

149. 椅 *i*³, a chair; its numerative is also *chang*¹.

150. 燈 *têng*¹, a lamp; a candlestick. Not a lantern unless joined with *lung*², of which more in its place.

151. 盞 *chan*³, the numerative of *têng*¹, a lamp; as *liu*⁴ *chan*³ *têng*¹, six lamps.

152. 蠟 *la*⁴, wax or tallow, animal or vegetable. The latter, made from the berry of the *Croton sebiferum*, is spoken of as *pai*² *la*⁴, white wax; *huang*² *la*⁴, beeswax.

153. Examples:—

坐 tso⁴	那 na⁴	都 tou¹	上 shang⁴	四 ssŭ⁴	是 shih⁴	那 na⁴
的 ti	張 chang¹	是 shih⁴	那 na⁴	張 chang¹	一 yi¹	一 yi¹
是 shih⁴	椅 i³	蠟 la⁴	兩 liang³	椅 i³	張 chang¹	分 fên⁴
誰 shui²	子 tzŭ	燈 têng¹	盞 chan³	子 tzŭ	桌 cho¹	桌 cho¹
上 shang⁴	在 tsai⁴	燈 têng¹	桌 cho¹	子 tzŭ	椅 i³	

That set consists of one table and four chairs.

Obs.—*Yi² fên⁴*, one division. (*See* 130.)

The two *têng* on the table are *la têng* (candlesticks).

Who is it that is sitting on that chair?

154. 酒 *chiu³*, Chinese wine; distilled spirit.

155. 盃 *pei¹*, a cup in which wine is drunk; as *chiu³ pei¹*, a wine-cup.

156. 盅 *chung¹*, a cup, which may hold either tea or wine. Its numerative is *ko⁴*. The word *chung¹* is said to be less used in the South than in the North.

157. 茶 *ch'a²*, tea.

158. 碗 *wan³*, a bowl or cup, which may hold tea or rice; *ch'a² wan³*, a tea-cup.

159. 飯 *fan⁴*, properly cooked rice; generally, any cooked victuals; one's meals.

160. 喫 or 吃 *ch'ih¹*, to eat; *ch'ih¹ fan⁴*, to eat a meal.

161. 喝 *ho¹*, to drink.

162. Examples:—

好 hao³	喝 ho¹	兩 liang³	拿 na²	喝 ho¹	喫 ch'ih¹	他 t'a¹
喫 ch'ih¹	過 kuo⁴	個 ko⁴	個 ko⁴	過 kuo⁴	過 kuo⁴	喫 ch'ih¹
不 pu⁴	三 san¹	酒 chiu³	茶 ch'a²	三 san¹	三 san¹	飯 fan⁴
好 hao³	盃 pei¹	盅 chung¹	碗 wan³	碗 wan³	碗 wan³	去 ch'ü⁴
喫 ch'ih¹	酒 chiu³	兒 'rh	來 lai²	茶 ch'a²	飯 fan⁴	了 liao³

He has gone to get his meal; *lit.*, to eat rice.

To have eaten three bowls of rice.

To have drunk three cups of tea.

Bring a tea-cup here.

Two wine-cups.

To have drunk three cups of wine.

[Is it] fit to eat (good for food)? (or, is it nice?)

163. 弄 *nung⁴*, properly *lung*, to play tricks with. Colloquially used of numerous processes, moral or material; as with the following word *ts'ai⁴*. It is often used also to represent the sound *lung²* in the Pekingese expression *lung² huo³*, to light the fire; there is another *lung* (198) which appears equally admissible.

164. 菜 *ts'ai⁴*, originally vegetable, but used generally of eatables; as *nung⁴ ts'ai⁴*, to prepare food.

165. 厨 *ch'u²*, to cook; but, colloquially, oftenest found forming part of substantives. As *ch'u²-fang²*, the cook-house, *ch'u²-tzŭ*, a cook.

166. 煎 *chien¹*, to fry; as *chien¹ yü²* (Radical 195), to fry fish.

167. 炒 *ch'ao³*, to fry or broil; a drier process than *chien¹*. So, *ch'ao³ jou⁴*, to broil meat.

PART III.—THE FORTY EXERCISES.

168. 煮 chu^3, to boil, actively; as chu^3 $ts'ai^4$, to boil vegetables, or eatables generally.

169. 燒 $shao^1$, to burn; in cooking, to roast. As $shao^1$ jou^4, to roast meat, or meat roasted.

170. 壞 $huai^4$, to spoil, morally or materially; combined with various other verbs as indicative of ill result.

171. Examples:—

飯 fan^4	飯 fan^4	子 $tzŭ$	都 tou^1	分 $fên^1$	都 tou^1	那 na^4
都 tou^1	得 $té^2$	很 $hên^3$	壞 $huai^4$	燒 $shao^1$	弄 $nung^4$	厨 $ch'u^2$
弄 $nung^4$	了 $liao$	會 hui^4	了。$liao^3$	肉 jou^4	壞 $huai^4$	子 $tzŭ$
好 hao^3	是 $shih^4$	煎 $chien^1$	這 $ché^4$	煮 chu^3	了 $liao$	把 pa^3
了。$liao$	菜 $ts'ai^4$	炒。$ch'ao^3$	厨 $ch'u^2$	肉 jou^4	不 pu^4	菜 $ts'ai^4$

The cook has spoiled all the dishes; roast meat and boiled are spoiled alike.

Obs. 1.—The cook pa, taking the $ts'ai$, eatables, tou, all, has he $nung$, in his treatment, preparation, $huai$, spoiled. The phrase $nung$ $huai$ may be applied to failure in the conduct of various operations.

Obs. 2.—Alike, pu $fên$, not distinguishing roast meat and boiled meat, all [has he] spoiled. The subject of $huai$ is throughout $ch'u^2$-$tzŭ$, the cook.

This cook is very skilful (*lit.*, is very competent in frying); but $chien^1$ $ch'ao^3$ is here used of cooking in general.

[The expression] fan^4 $té^2$ means that the meal is ready; *lit.*, that the victuals are cooked.

Obs. 1.—$Ts'ai$, the other eatables, and fan, the rice.

Obs. 2.—Hao here completes the action of $nung$; the food is *fully* prepared. But $nung$ pu hao, said of anything, differs little from $nung$ $huai$ except in intensity. It may be applied to cooking, negotiation, building, a campaign, etc.

172. 鍋 kuo^1, the large pan in which things are cooked, notably rice; as fan^4-kuo^1, the rice-pan.

173. 刀 tao^1 (Radical 18), a knife; as tao^1-$tzŭ$.

174. 鏟 $ch'a^1$, a fork; as $ch'a^1$-$tzŭ$. The numerative of tao and $ch'a$ is pa^3 (**86**).

175. 勺 $shao^2$, properly, a pan not so large as kuo^1 (**172**). As $shao^2$-$tzŭ$, a spoon; fan^4 $shao^2$-'rh, a spoon to ladle out rice with from the pan.

176. 匙 $ch'ih^2$, a smaller kind of spoon than $shao^2$. The difference is explained below in Exercise VII.

177. 傢 $chia^1$. The character is not found in the native dictionaries.

178. 伙 huo^3, nor is this character; combined, they include every variety of utensil. Familiarly, small arms may also be spoken of as $chia^1$-huo^3; spears, muskets, or any paraphernalia.

179. Examples:—

勺 $shao^2$	一 yi^4	的 ti	西 hsi^1	的。ti	飯 fan^4
子 $tzŭ$	把 pa^3	是 $shih^4$	都 tou^1	家 $chia^1$	鍋 kuo^1
兩 $liang^3$	鏟 $ch'a^1$	一 yi^4	是 $shih^4$	裏 li^3	是 $shih^4$
把 pa^3	子 $tzŭ$	把 pa^3	傢 $chia^1$	用 $yung^4$	煮 chu^3
匙 $ch'ih^2$	三 san^1	刀 tao^1	伙 huo^3	的 ti	飯 fan^4
子。$tzŭ$	把 pa^3	子 $tzŭ$	買 mai^3	東 $tung^1$	用 $yung^4$

The fan^4-kuo^1 (rice-pan) is used to boil rice.

All things used in a house are $chia^1$-huo^3.

[The things] that have been bought are one knife, one fork, three large spoons, and two small spoons.

Obs. 1.—Note the numeratives.

Obs. 2.—In Tientsin spoons should be called $t'iao^2$-$kêng^1$ or $kêng^1$-$ch'ih^2$.

EXERCISE VII.

個一碗鍋個一子廚 1
酒個一蓋飯個一房
盅酒個一鍋炒把一
子杯茶個一勺鏟把
　盅茶個一子刀

1. Kitchen. A knife. A fork. A frying-pan. A cooking-pan; a pan to cook rice. A cooking-pan lid. A tea-cup. A tea-cup. A wine-cup. A wine-cup. (*See* below, Example 6.)

牀人上鋪你上我炕他 2
了快那蓋快躺在躺要
　上個鋪把著牀著上

2. He will (or, wants to) lie down on the stove-bed. I shall (or, am going to) lie (or, am lying) down on the bed. Be quick and make the bed; *lit.*, spread the bedding. That man will soon be laid out (is sick unto death).

Obs.—We may say *ch'uang shang* of lying down on the bed; but in *shang ch'uang* the *shang* is a verb, and has in this phrase only the special meaning assigned it in the translation. We may say *shang k'ang*, to ascend the stove-bed, of a person who is going to sleep upon one.

上在躺在沒有那 3
坐椅著牀有帳牀
著子我上他子上

3. Are there curtains to that bed? He is (or was) lying on the bed; I am (or was) sitting on a chair.

呢弄了廚去燈子快這 4
　上廚子了是上拿屋
　還房拏是誰的燈裏
　沒的過我拏那來黑
　著火去給了蠟桌了

4. It is very dark in this room; bring a lamp here quick. Who took away the candlestick that was on the table? It was I that took it for the cook (or, took it over to give to the cook). The kitchen fire has been lighted, but is not well alight yet.

Obs. 1.—*Lung*²: see 163.

Obs. 2.—The last word, read *chao*², is not here an auxiliary as in Exercise V, 1, but an independent verb signifying to throw out light.

的有盅茶的是鍋煮飯 5
蓋也碗蓋飯蓋飯鍋
兒有茶兒鍋就的是

5. A rice-pan (*fan*⁴-*kuo*¹) is a pan for boiling rice; the *kuo*¹-*kai*⁴ is the cover of the rice-pan. Tea-cups, whether *ch'a*² *wan*³ or *ch'a*² *chung*¹, [may] both have *kai-'rh*, covers.

Obs.—May both: *yeh yu*, also are there, *yu kai-'rh ti*, possessing cover ones—ones that have covers.

PART III.—THE FORTY EXERCISES.

6. 酒杯 酒盅兩個不大可也分得出來。本是酒盅比酒杯分分很東西

6. There is no great difference between a *chiu³ pei¹* and a *chiu chung¹-tzŭ* (wine-cups of chinaware or metal), and yet they may be distinguished (they are distinguishable); the fact is that the *chiu pei* is larger than the *chiu chung*.

Obs. 1.—And yet: these two things [one can] not very much distinguish. [Although this be so] *k'o*, but, [one can] *yeh*, also, *fên tê ch'u lai*, succeed in distinguishing; [for] *pên*, in reality, *shih*, it is a fact that, the *chiu pei* compared with the *chiu chung* is large.

Obs. 2.—The words *fên tê ch'u lai* may be rendered by the verb *distinguished* or the verbal adjective *distinguishable*; the mood and tense of the verb being entirely dependent on the context. In answer to the question, Can (or do) you distinguish or not? *fên tê ch'u lai*, I can (or do) distinguish, would be, as we say, in the present tense of the indicative mood.

Obs. 3.—*Pên*: see above (120). It forms part of various adverbial constructions in this sense.

7. 那屋裏那些桌子椅子都壞了。說桌椅分是兩張桌兩八張椅子。

7. The chairs and tables in that room are all spoiled. [When one] speaks of two sets of chairs and tables, [what is meant] is two tables and eight chairs.

8. 那個勺子匙子比勺子小。還說小勺子比匙子大。一把勺子一把匙子是用京話這麽都

8. The *shao²* is properly a large spoon. The *shao²-tzŭ* is smaller than the *shao²*. The *ch'ih²-tzŭ* is still smaller than the *shao²-tzŭ*. One says *yi² pa³ shao²-tzŭ* and *yi² pa³ ch'ih²-tzŭ*; these are Pekingese idioms.

Obs.—*Lit.*, these all are in Peking spoken language thus used.

9. 你們屋裏有蓆。我們炕上都有蓆子。

9. Have you mats in your apartment (or apartments)? There are mats on all the stove-beds in our apartments.

10. 你們那兒用蠟燈麽我們也用蠟燈。是下也黑

10. Do you also use candles in your part of the world? We also use candles at night in our part of the world.

Obs. 1.—*Lit.*, *la têng*, candlesticks; *ni mên na 'rh*, that place of yours.
Obs. 2.—At night, when darkness (blackness) has fallen: *hei* (Radical 203).

看 都 用 用。都 作 麼 你 11
書 是 麼。是 是 甚 些 買
用 黑 不 廚 家 麼 蠟 了
的。下。是。房 裏 用。是 那

11. What have you been buying such a quantity of wax for? For household use. Is it for kitchen use? No; it is for reading at night.

Obs. 1.—Construe the first question as two sentences, or with the first clause treated as the subject of the verb *shih*; *q.d.*, your purchase of that much wax is to make what use of? *Na mo: see* 23.

Obs. 2.—*Tso shên mo* is very common as Why? For what reason? Here with *yung* it is, For what purpose?

Obs. 3.—*Tou* in the last two replies is used rather for emphasis sake. We do not translate it necessarily in English.

Obs. 4.—In the last answer understand *la*, wax, after the *ti* at the close; *lit.*, it is all in the dark to read books use's [wax].

Turn the following into Chinese. (KEY, EXERCISE VII.)

1. He has taken away the mat that was on the stove-bed. Tell him to bring it to me. Where is the bedding belonging to this bed? He has taken it away too, and sold it all.

2. Where is the candlestick? On the chair. Take it away, and bring a lamp. Have you found the lamp? The room is so dark I cannot see where the lamp is. Give me the candlestick, and I will go and look for it.

3. A *chiu³ chung¹-tzŭ* (wine-cup) is smaller than a *chiu³ pei¹*. You may say either *ch'a² wan³* or *ch'a² chung¹* (tea-cup). *Kai⁴* (covers) are both large and small; the cover of a cooking-pan is larger than that of a tea-cup.

4. The curtains and mats in that room are all spoiled. Go at once and buy curtains and bedding, and make the bed.

5. Give me a knife and fork and spoon. There are knives and forks on the table, [but] no spoon. Tell the cook to give you a spoon.

6. That man has taken away the pan which the cook used for boiling rice; the cook says he can't boil the rice. I asked that man who had taken away the pan; he said he did not know who it was.

7. Your statement is not correct. I did not say I saw him do it; what I did say was that you told me he had done it. You didn't understand what I said. Whether I did or whether I didn't, why should you want to find fault with me? Who is finding fault with you? you do your [business] and I'll do mine.

Obs. 1.—Whether, etc.: *lit.*, I did or did not [there's] no use saying.

Obs. 2.—Find fault with me: *lit.*, find (or, look for) my faults.

8. I want to divide this piece of paper amongst those five men, but I must give that one a larger piece than the other four. Go and ask him to return (**105**) those two books of mine that he took away.

Obs.—I want to divide, etc.: translate—I want to divide this piece of paper [and] give it to those five men; give[n] to him that one, however, must [be] compared with those four men's share, large.

180. 櫈 *têng⁴*, a stool; a bench. Its numerative is the following substantive *t'iao²*; as *liang³ t'iao² têng⁴-tzŭ*, a couple of stools. You may equally well say *liang³ ko⁴ têng⁴-tzŭ*.

181. 條 *t'iao²*, a branch; a twig; the numerative of stools and many dissimilar things that are long and narrow, also of other articles.

PART III.—THE FORTY EXERCISES.   43

182. 倒 tao^1, to pour, actively; as tao^4 $ch'a^2$, to pour tea. (*See* below, Exercise VIII.) Also, on the reverse, or to reverse; as, tao^4 pu^2 $shih^4$, on the contrary, it is not so; tao^4 kuo^4 lai^2, to turn end for end. Read tao^3, to upset, or to be upset.

183. 壺 hu^2, a pot or kettle in which tea may be made, wine heated, etc.; as $ch'a^2$ hu^2, a tea-pot. Its numerative is either pa^3 or ko^4.

184. 花 hua^1, flowers; also, to spend, to squander, or to dissipate, as will be seen later on.

185. 瓶 $p'ing^2$, a bottle or vase; as hua^1 $p'ing^2$, a flower-vase.

186. 破 $p'o^4$, to crack; to break. As $p'o^4$ $huai^4$, to ruin (or, be ruined) by breaking.

187. 收 $shou^1$, to receive; to recover; to put away. Both singly and in combination it has other meanings.

188. 拾 $shih^2$, to pick up; to put in order; with the preceding $shou^1$, to mend. The combination $shou^1$ $shih^2$ has various other uses.

189. Examples:—

會 hui^4	都 tou^1	倒 tao^4	壺 hu^2	水 $shui^3$	花 hua^1	三 san^1
收 $shou^1$	破 $p'o^4$	了。$liao$	裏 li^3	壺 hu^2	瓶 $p'ing^2$	條 $t'iao^2$
拾 $shih^2$	了 $liao$	這 $ché^4$	的 ti	拿 na^2	倒 tao^3	長 $ch'ang^2$
沒 mei^2	有 yu^3	傢 $chia^1$	水 $shui^3$	來。lai^2	了。$liao$	橙 $téng^4$
有。yu^3	人 $jén^2$	伙 huo^3	給 kei^3	把 pa^3	把 pa^3	那 na^4

Three long benches.
That flower-vase has been upset.
Bring the water-kettle here.
Pour the water out of that pot.
Obs.—The $liao$, pronounced lo, merely expletive. Note kei, for [me].
All these articles are (or, all this furniture is) broken; is there anyone that can repair them?

190. 盤 $p'an^2$, dishes. The numerative is ko^4; as yi^2 ko^4 $p'an^2$-$tzŭ$.

191. 碟 $tieh^2$, plates, saucers, smaller than $p'an^2$. The numerative is ko^4; as $ssŭ^4$ ko^4 $tieh^2$-$tzŭ$, four plates.

192. 點 $tien^3$, a point, a particle; to punctuate; to light, as a candle. Thus,
   $tien^3$ $téng^1$, to light a lamp (or lamps).
As a particle, yi^4 $tien^3$-$'rh$, a minute point; used adverbially, a little, slightly.

193. 吹 $ch'ui^1$, to blow; as $ch'ui^1$ $téng^1$, to blow out a lamp or candle.

194. 滅 $mieh^4$, to extinguish, as a light, a fire; with the foregoing, $ch'ui^1$ $mieh^4$, to blow out.

195. 使 $shih^3$, to employ. As $shih^3$ $té^2$, available, capable of being used; $shih^3$ pu^4 $té^2$, cannot be used.

196. Examples:—

些 hsieh¹	房 fang²	誰 shui²	點 tien³	幾 chi³	小 hsiao³	盤 p'an²
話 hua⁴	火 huo³	給 kei³	燈 têng¹	個 ko⁴	幾 chi³	子 tzŭ
都 tou¹	滅 mieh⁴	滅 mieh⁴	那 na⁴	碟 tieh²	個 ko⁴	大 ta⁴
使 shih³	了 liao	了 liao	燈 têng¹	子 tzŭ	盤 p'an²	碟 tieh²
得 tê²	這 chê⁴	厨 ch'u²	是 shih⁴	快 k'uai⁴	子 tzŭ	子 tzŭ

P'an²-tzŭ are larger than tieh²-tzŭ.
Some p'an-tzŭ (dishes) and some tieh-tzŭ (plates or saucers).
Make haste and light the lamp.
Who put that lamp out?
The fire is gone out in the kitchen.
All these expressions may be employed.

197. 爐 lu², a stove. Its numerative is ko⁴; as yi² ko⁴ lu²-tzŭ, a stove.

198. 籠 lung², properly, a cage; hence, joined with têng¹, a Chinese lantern; used **verbally** with huo³, fire, as to light   See **163**.

199. 空 k'ung¹, empty; hence, k'ung⁴, leisure.
_{Observe the change of tone.}

200. 滿 man³, full.

201. 同 t'ung², same; with. As chê⁴ liang³ ko⁴ t'ung² pu⁴ t'ung², are these two the same or different?   t'a¹ t'ung² wo³ ch'ü⁴, he is going (or, he went) with me.

202. 算 suan⁴, to reckon, arithmetically; also, to consider as.   Thus,
chê⁴ suan⁴ hao³, this one may regard as good.

203. 碎 sui⁴, in fragments; in tatters.   Hence, ling² sui⁴ (5), fragmentary; odds and ends.

204. Examples:—

碎 sui⁴	算 suan⁴	是 shih⁴	的 ti	爐 lu²	的 ti	爐 lu²
東 tung¹	數 shu⁴	同 t'ung²	這 chê⁴	子 tzŭ	快 k'uai⁴	子 tzŭ
西 hsi¹	目 mu⁴	我 wo³	壺 hu²	那 na⁴	燒 shao¹	是 shih⁴
沒 mei²	那 na⁴	來 lai²	倒 tao⁴	壺 hu²	火 huo³	燒 shao¹
空 k'ung⁴	是 shih⁴	的 ti	滿 man³	是 shih⁴	快 k'uai⁴	火 huo³
兒 'rh	零 ling²	算 suan⁴	他 t'a¹	空 k'ung¹	籠 lung²	用 yung⁴

A lu²-tzŭ (stove or fireplace) is used for lighting a fire in.
Make haste and light a fire.   Make haste and light the fire; lit., the stove.
_{Obs.—Shao huo can only be used with reference to a furnace in which wood or millet stalks, etc., are used for fuel.}

That pot is empty, but this one is full (this pot, on the other hand (**182**), is full).
He came with me.
To count up.
That is a thing (or, those are things) of small account.
I have no leisure; q.d., to do what you ask me.

EXERCISE VIII.

學話的多的都一　1
話條多說是說個條
用子說條長得撬撬
的。是個。方的分子子

1. A stool or bench; you may also use *ko*⁴ as the numerative of *têng*⁴. If a distinction is to be made, it is (or, the difference is) that *t'iao*² is oftener said of [benches that are] long, and *ko*⁴ oftener of [stools that are] square. *Hua*⁴ *t'iao*²-*tzŭ* (*lit.*, slips of oral language) are what are used in learning a spoken language.

碟盤茶酒酒花　2
子。子。壺。壺。瓶。瓶。

Obs.—The Chinese drink their wine warm.

2. Flower-vase. Wine-bottle. Wine-kettle. Tea-pot. Dishes. Plates.

火滅火燒燈吹燈點　3
。　　。　。　。　。

3. Light the lamp. Blow out the lamp. Light the fire. Put out the fire.

壞倒西茶水倒這倒　4
了。下站來。去了。個水。
　來不這了。他水你
　了。住。東倒倒給把

Obs. 1.—*Lai*: *q.d.*, bring tea *in* and pour it out.
Obs. 2.—Overturned *tao*³.

4. To pour water. You pour out this water (= throw it away). He is gone to pour out (throw away) water. Pour tea here (= Serve tea). This thing would not stand up; it has overturned, and is spoiled.

空的那了。倒滿手西空　5
的。是酒酒滿。了。也在是
　滿壺壺茶　是裏沒
　的。是滿把　得頭有
　是空了。空壺　壺空東

5. *K'ung*¹ means that there is nothing inside; you may also say *k'ung*¹ *shou*³, empty-handed. [The words] *hu*² *man*³ mean that something has been poured into the *hu*² (pot) until it was full. The tea-pot has been emptied. The wine-kettle has been filled. Has that wine-kettle anything in it? It is empty.

Obs. 1.—Construe:—*Hu man*, pot filled, is = means [that someone] taking the pot, *tao man*, has by pouring filled it.
Obs. 2.—Note the force of *liao*.

6. 那花瓶是甚麼人弄破的那是我弄破了的還可以收拾收拾可以使得那傢伙壞了使不得。

6. Who is it that has broken the (or that) flower-vase? I broke it, but it is not utterly spoiled; it can be mended, and (or, if it be mended) then some use can be made of it. That article is so badly injured that no use can be made of it.

Obs. 1.—Mend, mend, still can [one] use it. The reduplication of verbs and attributives is very colloquial. It has no special significance.
Obs. 2.—Construe:—That article [by some agency] breaking has been spoiled, or ruined; [one] cannot use it.
Obs. 3.—As a rule, even in what we consider passive or impersonal constructions, construe the verb as governed by a cause or personal agent.

7. 那刀子叉子勺子碟子盤子碗酒杯這些個都是喫飯的傢伙

7. Knives, forks, spoons, dishes, plates, bowls, and wine-cups, are all table utensils (*chia*¹ *huo*³ for eating one's meals).

8. 花瓶也是傢伙麼也可以是算傢伙

8. Are flower-vases also considered *chia*¹ *huo*³? They may be so considered.

9. 爐子有大小不同廚房裏做飯是燒爐子炕裏燒的是爐子屋裏用的也是爐子。

9. Stoves (*lu*²-*tzŭ*) are of different sizes, some larger, some smaller. The stove for cooking things in the kitchen is a *lu*²-*tzŭ*; so is the stove which is lit in the stove-bed; so also is the stove which is lit in one's room.

10. 叫人倒茶是叫人把茶拿來在茶碗裏倒。點燈沒有我點了他給吹滅了。

10. When you tell a man to *tao*⁴ *ch'a*² (pour tea), you mean, pour tea into the tea-cups. Have you lit the lamp? I lit it, but he blew it out.

Obs. 1.—The action of *tien* is completed by *shang*.
Obs. 2.—But he blew: *kei* (to give) before *ch'ui mieh* implies, idiomatically, that the act of the person in question was not to be expected. Were it omitted, the two acts would be simply distinguished: I lit it; he blew it out.

11. 吹燈是人吹燈把燈吹滅了燈滅了火滅了自己滅了。

11. *Ch'ui*¹ *têng*¹ (*lit.*, to blow lamp) means that someone is blowing it out (or, has done so). [The expressions] *têng*¹ *mieh*⁴ *liao*, *huo*³ *mieh*⁴ *liao*, mean that the lamp (or fire) has gone out of itself.

12. 那倆水壺裏有水沒有一個空一個滿是的你把那空的滿了水。

12. Is there water in those two kettles? One is empty, the other is full. Fill the empty one with water.

PART III.—THE FORTY EXERCISES.   47

Turn the following into Chinese.   (KEY, EXERCISE VIII.)

1. I really don't know what you want so many chairs for.

2. Now just count, you have asked twenty-five people to dinner, and do you think that those few chairs of ours will seat five-and-twenty people?

3. If they won't seat twenty-five people, the benches in the kitchen will do very well.

4. With the benches we can seat them, [but] allow me to ask if benches would look well in the dining-room? Then there are the plates and rice-bowls; I must find some, but I don't know where to look for them.

Obs.—Seat them: *lit.*, [they] can sit open, *i.e.*, not too close.

5. We have thirty rice-bowls here.

6. They won't do; besides, six are broken.

7. I don't care whether they are broken or not, just send for someone to mend them.

8. I have bought a dinner set (*lit.*, table of utensils) of him, also some odds and ends for kitchen use, with some fire-irons (*lit.*, things used for lighting the fire); just add all this up for me and see if his account is correct.

Obs.—Just add up: *lit.*, he opened that account you for me reckon one reckon, wrong not wrong.

9. I can't do accounts; *lit.*, reckon bills. (*See* 146.) What do you mean by that; has not the teacher taught you the numerals (字目數)?

10. I know the numerals in their abbreviated form, but these are all written in the full (*lit.*, large) form, and I am not acquainted [with that] yet.

205. 今 *chin*^{1}, now; the present.

206. 年 *nien*^{2}, the year.

207. 時 *shih*^{2}, time.

208. 令 *ling*^{4}, to command; a command; also, honourable. When combined with the foregoing, as *shih*^{2}-*ling*^{4}, the weather that prevails; the state of weather that the season demands.

209. 暖 *nuan*^{3}, also *nan*^{3}, warm.

210. 和 *ho*^{2}, *huo*^{2}, *hai*^{4}, peace; together with; also, soft or gentle. Combined with *nuan*^{3} or *nan*^{3}, warm; as the temperature in-doors or out-of-doors. Read *huo*^{4}, to mix, as powder, flour, etc., with water.

211. 昨 *tso*^{2}, of yesterday.

212. 天 *t'ien*^{1}, heaven; a day.

213. Examples:—

都 *tou*^{1}	日 *jih*^{4}	天。*t'ien*^{1}	昨 *tso*^{2}	的 *ti*	年。*nien*^{2}	今 *chin*^{1}
可 *k'o*^{3}	子 *tzŭ*	前 *ch'ien*^{2}	天。*t'ien*^{1}	時 *shih*^{2}	去 *ch'ü*^{4}	年。*nien*^{2}
以 *i*^{3}	多 *to*^{1}	兒。'*rh*	昨 *tso*^{2}	令 *ling*^{4}	年。*nien*^{2}	明 *ming*^{2}
說。*shuo*^{1}	少 *shao*^{3}	多 *to*^{1}	兒。'*rh*	暖 *nan*^{3}	前 *ch'ien*^{2}	年。*nien*^{2}
	天 *t'ien*^{1}	少 *shao*^{3}	前 *ch'ien*^{2}	和。*huo*^{2}	年 *nien*^{2}	後 *hou*^{4}

This year. Next year. The year after next. Last year; *sc.*, the year that is gone. The year before last the weather was warm.

Obs.—Note the special use of *ch'ien*, before, and *hou*, after, in these phrases.

Yesterday. Yesterday.

The day before yesterday. The day before yesterday.

[In how many days?] you may say *to shao jih-tzŭ* or *to shao t'ien*.

214. 就 *chiu⁴*, to follow as a consequence; consequently; then, in time or argument.
215. 定 *ting⁴*, to fix, make firm; hence, certain. As *yi² ting⁴*, entirely certain.
216. 晝 *chou⁴*, daytime.
217. 夜 *yeh⁴*, night.
218. 晴 *ch'ing²*, fine; clear.
219. 亮 *liang⁴*, light as day.
220. Examples:—

夜 *yeh⁴*	天 *t'ien¹*	起 *ch'i³*	道 *tao⁴*	晝 *chou⁴*	沒 *mei²*	我 *wo³*
裏 *li³*	今 *chin¹*	來 *lai²*	兒 *'rh²*	夜 *yeh⁴*	有 *yu³*	來 *lai²*
可 *k'o³*	兒 *'rh*	昨 *tso²*	天 *t'ien¹*	的 *ti*	定 *ting⁴*	他 *t'a¹*
以 *i³*	下 *hsia⁴*	兒 *'rh*	亮 *liang⁴*	都 *tou¹*	日 *jih⁴*	就 *chiu⁴*
到 *tao⁴*	雨 *yü³*	晴 *ch'ing²*	就 *chiu⁴*	走 *tsou³*	子 *tzŭ*	走 *tsou³*

As soon as I come (or came) he goes (or went); *lit.*, then he goes.
There is no day fixed.
To travel both by day and night.
To rise at dawn; *lit.*, as soon as the heavens are bright, to rise.
It was fine yesterday; to-day it rains.
May arrive in the course of the night.

221. 鐘 *chung¹*, a bell; also, in modern Chinese, a clock.
222. 表 *piao³*, the outside as opposed to the inside; hence, manifestation. In modern Chinese, a watch.
223. 刻 *k'ê⁴*, to engrave; a short time; in modern Chinese, a quarter of an hour. Also, to oppress, as will be seen later.
224. 候 *hou⁴*, to await; hence, when combined with *shih²*, time, a time, the time.
225. Examples:—

刻 *k'ê⁴*	說 *shuo¹*	鐘 *chung¹*	時 *shih²*	辰 *ch'ên²*	了 *liao*	看 *k'an⁴*	是 *shih⁴*
得 *tê²*	三 *san¹*	辰 *ch'ên²*	鐘 *chung¹*	這 *chê⁴*	鐘 *chung¹*	甚 *shên²*
四 *ssŭ⁴*	下 *hsia⁴*	表 *piao³*	那 *na⁴*	鐘 *chung¹*	就 *chiu⁴*	麼 *mo²*
點 *tien³*	鐘 *chung¹*	三 *san¹*	表 *piao³*	是 *shih⁴*	知 *chih¹*	時 *shih²*
三 *san¹*	都 *tou¹*	點 *tien³*	是 *shih⁴*	時 *shih²*	道 *tao⁴*	候 *hou⁴*

What o'clock is it?
Look at the clock and you will see (*lit.*, know).
This is a clock; *lit.*, a bell of *shih² ch'ên²* (Radical 162), hour periods.
That is a watch; *lit.*, an indicator of hour periods.
You may say [for three o'clock] *san tien chung* or *san hsia chung*, three points or three blows of the bell.
Obs.—Hsia, blows.
Three quarters past four.

226. 冷 *lêng³*, cold; as in *chin¹ t'ien¹ lêng³*, it is cold to-day.

PART III.—THE FORTY EXERCISES.

227. 熱 *jé*⁴, hot; as *pu*⁴ *léng*³ *pu*² *jé*⁴, neither hot nor cold.

228. 雪 *hsüeh*³, snow; as *hsia*⁴ *hsüeh*³, it is snowing.

229. 涼 *liang*², cool; cold. As *liang*² *shui*³, cold water. Often used with *k'uai*⁴ (**80**), brisk or fresh; as *liang*² *k'uai*, cool (not cold).

230. 刮 *kua*¹, to rasp; to cut; to shave.

231. 颳 *kua*¹ (said to be a vulgar form of the above), to blow, as the wind.

232. 氣 *ch'i*⁴, breath, air; the material influences of nature; morally, temper, anger; also (under certain circumstances, and in combination), aspect, appearance, taste, and smell. As *t'ien*¹ *ch'i*⁴, weather; temperature.

233. Examples :—

話。*hua*⁴	我 *wo*³	兒 *'rh*	了 *liao*	風 *féng*¹	颳 *kua*¹	天 *t'ien*¹
說 *shuo*¹	天 *t'ien*¹	半 *pan*⁴	住 *chu*⁴	起 *ch'i*³	氣 *ch'i*⁴
了 *liao*	涼 *liang*²	夜 *yeh*⁴	了 *liao*	大 *ta*⁴	冷。*léng*³
半 *pan*⁴	快 *k'uai*⁴	的 *ti*	下 *hsia*⁴	風 *féng*¹	天 *t'ien*¹
天 *t'ien*¹	他 *t'a*¹	雪 *hsüeh*³	雪 *hsüeh*³	來 *lai*²	氣 *ch'i*⁴
的 *ti*	和 *hai*⁴	今 *chin*¹	下 *hsia*⁴	了。*liao*	熱。*jé*⁴

The weather is cold. The weather is hot.
A high wind has got up.
When the wind stopped, it snowed.
It snowed half the night. *Pan*⁴: see **236**.
To-day it is cool.
He had a long talk with me; *lit.*, half a day's talk.

234. 初 *ch'u*¹, the first; when first. As *ch'i*³ *ch'u*¹, in the beginning. *Ch'i*³, to rise: see **43**.

235. 次 *tz'ǔ*⁴, a time or turn; as *ch'u*¹ *tz'ǔ*⁴, the first time. In a series, any place but the first.

236. 半 *pan*⁴, half.

237. Examples :—

二。*érh*⁴	月。*yüeh*⁴	半 *pan*⁴	上 *shang*⁴	上 *shang*⁴	他 *t'a*¹	兩 *liang*³
兩 *liang*³	正 *chéng*¹	個 *ko*⁴	半 *pan*⁴	月。*yüeh*⁴	們 *mên*²	個 *ko*⁴
點 *tien*³	月 *yüeh*⁴	月。*yüeh*⁴	月。*yüeh*⁴	本 *pên*³	初 *ch'u*¹	人 *jên*²
半 *pan*⁴	初 *ch'u*¹	一 *yi*¹	下 *hsia*⁴	月。*yüeh*⁴	次 *tz'ǔ*⁴	初 *ch'u*¹
鐘。*chung*¹	一 *yi*	個 *ko*⁴	半 *pan*⁴	下 *hsia*⁴	見 *chien*⁴	見 *chien*⁴
	初 *ch'u*¹	半 *pan*⁴	月。*yüeh*⁴	月。*yüeh*⁴	面。*mien*⁴	是 *shih*⁴

When [it is said that] two people *ch'u*¹ *chien*⁴, it means that they have seen each other for the first time.

Last moon. This moon. Next moon.
In the first half of the moon. In the last half of the moon.
A half moon. A month and a half.
The first and second days of the first moon.

Obs.—First moon: *chêng* (see **103**); *q.d.*, the right or chief moon, to which all the rest are subordinate. Note the change of tone.

Half-past two o'clock.

EXERCISE IX.

那 後 明 今 昨 前 1
麼 天 天 天 天 兒
著 都 後 明 今 昨
。 是 兒 兒 兒 兒
　　　　　　　就
　　　　　　　是

1. *Ch'ien-'rh²* is simply *ch'ien² t'ien¹* (the day before yesterday); [and the combinations meaning] yesterday, to-day, to-morrow, and the day after to-morrow, all follow the same rule.

都 下 晴 暖 熱 是 天 2
在 雪 天 和 天 天 氣
裏 這 下 颳 涼 冷 分
頭 些 雨 風 天 天 得
。

2. The weather (*lit.*, air of the sky) is distinguished as cold, hot, cool, warm, windy, clear, rainy, snowy.

Obs.—The last clause is not translated; *chê hsieh*, these some, or many, all are inside, are all included.

鐘 是 下 兩 一 一 3
。 一 鐘 刻 點 點
　 點 就 一 鐘 半
　　　 是 鐘 就

3. An hour and a half is the same as an hour and two quarters. Both the following expressions, *yi¹ hsia⁴ chung¹* and *yi¹ tien³ chung¹*, mean an hour.

看 馬 人 的 了 過 他 4
書 黑 白 先 五 二 那
。 下 日 生 六 十 個
　 回 愛 這 不 多 人
　 家 騎 個 過 年 念

Obs. 1.—Habit: *ai* (52) to love=to be used to.
Obs. 2.—By day: *pai jih* precedes the verb.

起 鐘 兒 個 來 可 走 我 5
來 還 八 人 你 以 下 今
麼 沒 下 今 這 回 月 兒
。

Obs.—You: *lit.*, you this man! reproachfully.

雪 天 候 天 很 後 說 前 6
。 冷 兒 熱 說 月 得 年
　 就 下 的 這 不 前
　 下 雨 時 兒 大 後
　　　　　　 月 年

5. I am going to-day, and may be back next moon. What! were you not up at eight o'clock to-day?

4. That man there has studied upwards of twenty years; he has been a teacher only five or six months. It is this man's habit to ride in the day and to study in the evening when he comes home.

6. You may say both *ch'ien² nien²* for the year before last and *hou⁴ nien²* for the year after next, but *ch'ien² yüeh⁴* and *hou⁴ yüeh⁴* are not much used. At this place it rains in the hot weather and snows in the cold.

PART III.—THE FORTY EXERCISES. 51

7 前 北 天 冷。下 裡
四 風 天 昨 下 住
天 第 氣 兒 雨 了。
颱 二 很 黑 夜 今
　 　 　 　 　 兒
　 　 　 　 　 天
　 　 　 　 　 晴
　 　 　 　 　 了。

7. Four days ago it blew from the north, and the day following it was very cold. It rained last evening, but it stopped in the night, and it was fine this morning.

8 今 去 今 不 誰 裡
和 年 年 正 見 還
得 的 這 過 下
很 那 幾 四 雪
天 麼 時 月 呢。
氣 冷。令
暖 　 有

8. The weather is very mild this year; not so cold as it was last year. The weather is not seasonable this year; nobody has seen snow in the fourth moon for some years.

Obs.—Not seasonable: *pu chêng*, not correct.

9 我 這 去 我 倆 到 過
倆 兒 年 是 的 去 了。
到 好 他 上 他 年
些 是 來 月 們 來

9. We two have been here a good many years; or, it is many years since we came here. He came last year; I arrived last moon; they two came here last year.

Obs.—Not *tsa mên* (see 17) unless the person addressed is present.

Turn the following into Chinese. (KEY, EXERCISE IX.)

1. In what year did you arrive in Peking?

2. I came this year. I have not been here long; only half a year.

3. But you speak mandarin very correctly.

4. That is all owing to my having learned Chinese in the South (*lit.*, southern quarter). (Radical 70.)

5. That accounts for it. Do you find the climate here agree with you (good)?

Obs.—Climate: *lit.*, water and earth.

6. There is nothing the matter with it; the seasons are very regular, and the heat is nothing to speak of; but not having passed a winter here, I cannot say what the cold is like.

Obs. 1.—Regular: *ho² p'ing²* (210, 137).
Obs. 2.—Passed a winter: *lit.*, passed the [new] year.

7. It is warm enough in one's room, but it's pretty cold all the same if you go on a few days' trip.

Obs. 1.—All the same: *lit.*, but [though] it is thus said.
Obs. 2.—If: this is commonly expressed by the characters *yao⁴ shih⁴* (32, 29), the former being corruptly used for *jo*, of which more presently.

8. The snow, I am told, is very heavy here.

9. No, that is not the case; on the contrary, there is little snow,—only an inch or so falls during the year. What I referred to were the winds, which blow so cold.

Obs.—Only: *pu² kuo⁴*; *lit.*, not exceeding.

10. What do you do every day?

11. I rise every morning at 7.30 and have my breakfast, then I send for my teacher and read for three hours and a half, after which I dine and go out for a ride.

Obs. 1.—Breakfast, lunch, or any minor meal, is called in Peking "little heart," said to be short for four words (以點饑心) which, literally translated, mean "in order to satisfy slightly the hungry craving." Puddings are also called *tien hsin*.

Obs. 2.—" After which" or "afterwards" is often rendered by the words *hui² t'ou²*, to turn the head; *hui lai*, to return, has the same force.

12. In that case come for a ride with me after your dinner to-day, will you?

13. Look at the weather; [it has turned] cold and is going to rain; I do not think it can possibly clear up.

14. So it is; in that case we had better go to-morrow. What time to-morrow shall we fix?

Obs. 1.—So it is: *see* **124**.
Obs. 2.—Fix: **215**.

15. Say daylight. The cold is nothing; after a short gallop we shall be all right.

238. 更 *ching¹*, properly *kêng¹*, to change; the watches of the night, of which there are five. When read *kêng⁴* it is an adjective of comparison; as *na⁴ kêng⁴ hao³*, that is better still.

239. 夫 *fu¹*, a man, especially a husband; commonly, any working man. As *chiao¹-fu¹*, a chair-bearer; *ma³-fu¹*, a groom. Joined with *kung¹* (Radical 48), work. *See* Exercise X, 1.

240. 每 *mei³*, every; as in *mei³ yi² ko⁴*, every individual one.

241. 打 *ta³*, to strike; as *t'a¹ ta³ wo³*, he is striking (or, has struck) me; also, idiomatically combined with many verbs of action. It is also used as a preposition. Thus,

ta³ tso² t'ien¹ tao⁴ chin¹ tien¹, from yesterday until to-day.
ta³ na⁴ 'rh kuo⁴, to go by there.

242. 罷 *pa⁴*, to end; to cause to cease. At the end of a sentence, "there's an end of it;" but sometimes used to imply doubt, like our Eh? or a command.

243. Examples:—

你 *ni³*	打。*ta³*	甚 *shên²*	回 *hui²*	的。*ti*	更 *ching¹*	夜 *yeh⁴*
說 *shuo¹*	他 *t'a¹*	麼。*mo¹*	更。*ching¹*	每 *mei³*	夫 *fu¹*	裏 *li³*
他 *t'a¹*	有 *yu³*	不 *pu⁴*	打 *ta³*	夜 *yeh⁴*	是 *shih⁴*	分 *fên¹*
罷 *pa⁴*	不 *pu²*	能 *nêng²*	他 *t'a¹*	打 *ta³*	打 *ta³*	五 *wu³*
了。*liao*	是 *shih⁴*	不 *pu⁴*	做 *tso⁴*	五 *wu³*	更 *ching¹*	更。*ching¹*

The night is divided into five watches.
The *ching-fu* are the men who beat the watches (strike the changes).
A watch is struck five times every night.
What are you beating him for? I cannot do otherwise; or, he must be beaten.
If he has done wrong, reprove him and have done with it.
Obs.—Wrong: *pu shih*.

244. 早 *tsao³*, early. As in *tsao³ fan⁴*, early rice; *sc.*, breakfast.

245. 晚 *wan³*, late. As in *wan³ fan⁴*, the evening meal; dinner or supper.

PART III.—THE FORTY EXERCISES.

246. 晌 *shang*³, noon; coupled, colloquially, with the following *wu*³, and often pronounced *shang*² *hu*⁴. *Pan*⁴ *shang*³, half the day, or a long while; *wan*³ *shang*¹, evening. Note the change of tone.

247. 午 *wu*³, noon. See *ch'ên*², Radical Exercise XII, 7. The 24 hours of the day are divided by the Chinese into 12 *shih*²-*ch'ên*². Of these, *wu*³ represents the two hours from 11 A.M. to 1 P.M.

248. 嗜 *tsan*¹, length of time; popular contraction of *tsao*³ *wan*³. As in *to*¹ *tsan*¹, the common phrase for When? *q.d.*, how soon, how early?

249. Examples:—

你 *ni*³	我 *wo*³	不 *pu*²	嗜 *tsan*¹	沒 *mei*²	午 *wu*³	他 *t'a*¹
的 *ti*	來 *lai*²	定 *ting*⁴	喫 *ch'ih*¹	回 *hui*²	出 *ch'u*¹	早 *tsao*³
罷。*pa*⁴	的 *ti*	他 *t'a*¹	的 *ti*	家。*chia*¹	門 *mên*²	起 *ch'i*³
	晚。*wan*³	來 *lai*²	早 *tsao*³	晚 *wan*³	去 *ch'ü*⁴	起 *ch'i*³
	你 *ni*³	的 *ti*	晚 *wan*³	飯 *fan*⁴	下 *hsia*⁴	來 *lai*²
	走 *tsou*³	早 *tsao*³	都 *tou*¹	多 *to*¹	午 *wu*³	晌 *shang*³

He got up early, went out at noon, and had not returned in the afternoon.
Obs.—The afternoon is often spoken of as *hou pan t'ien*, the latter half of the day.
What is the dinner hour? It is uncertain.
Obs. 1.—Late (or evening) meal when can be eaten; *ti*=*tê*.
Obs. 2.—Early late both not fixed.
He came early; I came late (or, he came before me).
Go your own ways; or, mind your own business.
Obs.—Note *pa*, a command. See 242.

250. 件 *chien*⁴, properly, to distinguish; a distinction; but best known as a numerative; amongst other substantives, numerative of *shih*⁴, affairs (252).

251. 情 *ch'ing*², feelings; circumstances; very commonly combined with

252. 事 *shih*⁴, affairs; a matter. See **257**.

253. 擱 *ko*¹, a character of doubtful authority; primarily, to delay; but colloquially, to put; to place. As *ko*¹ *tsai*⁴ *chê*⁴ *'rh*, put it here.

254. 各 *ko*⁴, each; every.

255. 樣 *yang*⁴, kind; fashion. As *ko*⁴ *yang*⁴, every sort or kind.

256. 短 *tuan*³, short. As *ch'ang*² *tuan*³, long and short; hence, the length of.

257. Examples:—

那 *na*⁴	各 *ko*⁴	各 *ko*⁴	把 *pa*³	那 *na*⁴	那 *na*⁴	這 *chê*⁴
東 *tung*¹	樣 *yang*⁴	樣 *yang*⁴	那 *na*⁴	椅 *i*³	件 *chien*⁴	件 *chien*⁴
西 *hsi*¹	的 *ti*	各 *ko*⁴	桌 *cho*¹	子 *tzŭ*	事 *shih*⁴	事 *shih*⁴
長 *ch'ang*²	事 *shih*⁴	樣 *yang*⁴	子 *tzŭ*	擱 *ko*¹	情 *ch'ing*²	我 *wo*³
短 *tuan*³	都 *tou*¹	的 *ti*	擱 *ko*¹	在 *tsai*⁴	不 *pu*⁴	不 *pu*⁴
不 *pu*⁴	懂 *tung*³	都 *tou*¹	開 *k'ai*¹	那 *na*³	好 *hao*³	明 *ming*²
同。*t'ung*²	得 *tê*²	有。*yu*³	些。*hsieh*¹	兒。*'rh*	說。*shuo*¹	白。*pai*²

I don't understand this thing (affair, matter).
That thing should not be spoken of. (It is not good to speak of that thing.)
Where shall that chair be put (or placed).
Move away (*lit.*, place apart) that table a little.
There are some of every kind.
[He] understands every kind of thing.
Those things are of different lengths.

258. 雲 *yün²*, cloud; commonly coupled with *ts'ai³*. As *yün² ts'ai³*, clouds; *lit.*, cloud colour.

259. 彩 *ts'ai³*, colours. As in *wu³ ts'ai³*, the five colours; *sc.*, blue, yellow, red, white, and black. It may also mean luck, as will be seen later.

260. 陰 *yin¹*, the female of the dual powers of nature; darkness; dark. *T'ai⁴ yin¹* (264), the moon, but not colloquially.

261. 陽 *yang²*, the male power of nature; brightness; light. *T'ai⁴ yang²* (264), the sun.

262. 霧 *wu⁴*, mist. As in *hsia⁴ wu⁴*, a fog, or mist, has come on; *lit.*, there has descended a fog or mist.

263. 怕 *p'a⁴*, to fear; hence, to doubt; hence used as perhaps.

264. 太 *t'ai⁴*, properly the superlative of *ta⁴*, great; used both as an adjective and an adverb.

265. Examples:—

大	*ta⁴*	太	*t'ai⁴*	陰	*yin¹*	的	*ti*	颳	*kua¹*	滿 *man³*
太	*t'ai⁴*	陽。	*yung²*	天	*t'ien¹*	時	*shih²*	風。	*fêng¹*	天 *t'ien¹*
陽	*yang²*	下	*hsia⁴*	是	*shih⁴*	候。	*hou⁴*	太	*t'ai⁴*	的 *ti*
看	*k'an⁴*	的	*ti*	看	*k'an⁴*	白	*pai²*	陽	*yang²*	雲 *yün²*
不	*pu⁴*	霧	*wu⁴*	不	*pu²*	日	*jih⁴*	平	*p'ing²*	彩 *ts'ai³*
出。	*ch'u¹*	很	*hên³*	見	*chien⁴*	說	*shuo¹*	西	*hsi¹*	怕 *p'a⁴*

With a sky so overcast, it will probably blow.

Obs. 1.—The first clause is pendent; [there being] a full heaven's clouds.

Obs. 2.—Probably: one fears that there will blow wind.

When the sun is nearly set.

Obs.—Nearly: *lit.*, is even with the west; but sunset is otherwise described.

When *yin t'ien* is used of the day in the daytime, it means that the sun is not visible; *lit.*, the sun [one] cannot discern.

There is a very thick mist; the sun is not visible.

Obs.—There is: *hsia ti*, there has descended; *ti=tê*.

PART III.—THE FORTY EXERCISES.

EXERCISE X.

那麼樣。日還是。每天每月。是月就每年麼。年年不是每 工夫。 **1**

1. Work. Every year *(mei³ nien²)* is the same as year after year *(nien² nien²)*, is it not? *Mei³ yüeh⁴* is moon after moon (monthly); so with the phrases *mei³ t'ien¹*, *mei³ jih⁴* (daily).

Obs. 1.—Hence, time at man's disposal for work; hence, leisure; time taken up by anything. The *fu* in *kung-fu* cannot be explained.

Obs. 2.—Is it not? interrogative affirmative, common in Chinese.

Obs. 3.—So with: *lit.*, also is it so fashion.

都是這麼樣。上躺著。天天更天就在炕書到夜裏看晚晌回家街上來晌午他是早起起 **2**

2. He rises early, goes for a walk (*lit.*, up the street) at noon, comes home in the evening and reads, and in the third watch of the night he goes to bed. He does the same every day.

Obs.—Goes to bed: not *shang ch'uang²*, which means to take to one's bed in mortal sickness. See Exercise VII, 2, Obs.

各兒住著。就是他各房自子各兒去。得你各自事情人是自己一個各自兒就 **3**

3. The expression *ko⁴ tzŭ⁴ ko³-'rh* means simply one's individual self. In this matter it is essential that you should go yourself. He lives by himself in that house.

Obs. 1.—Essential: *tei* (see 30, 32).

Obs. 2.—By himself: either he is master or senior, or no outsiders live there.

Obs. 3.—Note the tone of the second *ko*.

就是半夜。冷。三更天和後半夜半夜還暖天晴了。了雨下半上半天下 **4**

4. It rained in the forenoon, but the afternoon was fine. It was warm before midnight but cold after. The third watch is midnight.

Obs.—*Ch'ien pan t'ien* and *hou pan t'ien* would be equally correct.

定更。更就是更頭一夜有五打更一打更的夜裏那 **5**

5. As regards the watches which a watchman strikes during the night, the night is divided into five, the beginning of the first of which is the watch-setting.

6. 天事夫短空情著
　長的多沒兒得罷。
　做工天有事擱

6. When the days are long there is more time to do things; when they are short, one has not leisure for them, and they must just wait (be put aside).

Obs. 1.—Leisure: *k'ung*⁴-*'rh*. Note the change of tone. *See* 199.
Obs. 2.—Must just wait : *lit.*, affairs [one] *tei*, must, *ko cho*, put, or be putting [aside], *pa*, and that's all about it.
Obs. 3.—It is difficult to define the precise power of *cho* here. The Chinese seem to treat it as a mere expletive.

7. 他來回茶那在子
　多明來壺兒屋上
　咱。罷。擱了。裏了。
　回那在擱桌

7. When will he be back? Probably to-morrow. Where is the tea-pot put? On the table in the room.

Obs.—Where put, etc. Construe:—That teapot [man has] put in what place?

8. 天彩是兒的那山見
　上滿陰早霧麼都了。
　就了。天起很大看
　雲今下大的不

8. When the sky is overcast the day is said to be *yin*¹ (dull, obscured). There was a thick mist this morning; even those big mountains were invisible.

Obs.—Overcast: *lit.*, the clouds in (*lit.*, on) the sky fill [the sky].

9. 你那站做麼去
　在兒著甚快罷。

9. What are you standing there for? be off at once.

10. 那10沒了一呢偺上一
　飯罷。會子那們街走
　得還麼還走罷。
　得

10. I suppose dinner is ready? No, it is not ready, and it will be some time yet before it is. In that case let us have another turn up the street.

Obs. 1.—I suppose: *pa* here=eh? *See* 243.
Obs. 2.—A time: *see* 129.

Turn the following into Chinese. (KEY, EXERCISE X.)

1. I heard a lot of noises in the street yesterday evening. What sort of noises did you hear?

2. [A sound like] someone striking wood outside the door.

Obs.—Outside the door : *mên k'ou-'rh* ; *lit.*, the mouth of, or entrance to, the door.

3. That was the watchman striking the watches. The night is divided into five watches, the first of which is the watch-setting and the third is midnight. The watchman has nothing to do in the daytime, but he has not a moment's leisure at night. He lives quite by himself in that small house yonder, and has neither wife nor child. He has to be out in all weathers, wet or fine (*lit.*, not regarding fine days nor cloudy days); and he never can say, "I'll put aside my work to-day." From year's end to year's end (*lit.*, one year up to the head, *i.e.*, the end), it is always the same.

PART III.—THE FORTY EXERCISES.

4. The sky has been completely overcast to-day, and so dull that one could see nothing at all.

5. Hasn't it been dull! There was a thick fog in the morning, but it lifted (*lit.*, cleared) for a while at noon. It may be fine towards dark, but that is uncertain.

Obs.—Towards dark: *lit.*, arriving at dark coming up.

6. The days are now getting shorter and shorter; whenever (*to^1 tsao^3 wan^3*, **248**) shall you and I commence our night studies? (*lit.*, our night book is from whenever reading commenced?)

7. We've no time at present; let it be for a bit. I propose to talk about that a day or two hence.

Obs.—Propose: *ta^3 suan^4*. *See* **241**.

266. 衣 *i^1* (Radical 145), clothes; classically, upper garments.

267. 裳 *shang^1*, classically, a skirt; colloquially appended to *i^1*, clothes in general.

268. 腌 *a^1*, *^{n}ga^1*, *ang^1*, *^{n}gang^1*, dirty; not used colloquially except in combination with the following.

269. 臢 *tsa^1*, *tsang^1*, dirty; used with the preceding *ang^1* or *a^1*, but also without it. The combination is as often pronounced *a^1-tsa^1* as *ang^1-tsang^1*.

270. 換 *huan^4*, to exchange.

271. 乾 *kan^1*, dry.

272. 淨 *ching^4*, clean. The compound *kan^1-ching^4*, however, means simply, clean; as dirty things are washed *kan^1-ching^4*, clean.

327. Examples:—

把 *pa^3*	手 *shou^3*	我 *wo^3*	弄 *nung^4*	乾 *kan^1*	了 *liao^3*	你 *ni^3*
他 *t'a^1*	巾 *chin^1*	換 *huan^4*	飯 *fan^4*	淨 *ching^4*	不 *pu^4*	的 *ti*
倒 *tao^4*	來。 *lai^2*	一 *i^4*	弄 *nung^4*	的。 *ti*	得 *tê^2*	衣 *i^1*
出 *ch'u^1*	水 *shui^3*	條 *t'iao^2*	的 *ti*	這 *chê^4*	你 *ni^3*	裳 *shang^1*
去 *ch'ü^4*	腌 *ang^1*	乾 *kan^1*	乾 *kan^1*	個 *ko^4*	快 *k'uai^4*	腌 *ang^1*
罷。 *pa^4*	臢 *tsang^1*	淨 *ching^4*	淨 *ching^4*	廚 *ch'u^2*	去 *ch'ü^4*	臢 *tsang^1*
	了 *liao*	的 *ti*	給 *kei^3*	子 *tzŭ*	換 *huan^4*	的 *ti*

Your clothes are dreadfully dirty.

Obs.—*Liao pu tê*: *lit.*, in a manner that will never do. *See* Exercise II, 9.

Go and change them at once.

Obs.—*Lit.*, change clean [ones for them].

This cook cooks cleanly.

Obs.—*Lit.*, this cook, preparing rice, prepares it clean. Note *ti* for *tê*.

Bring me a clean handkerchief.

Obs.—Towels are also called *shou-chin*; but there is a special term for silk handkerchiefs.

The water is dirty; pour it away.

Obs.—Note the employment of *t'a* in referring to an inanimate object.

274. 刷 shua¹, to brush, as a hat or clothes. In brushing boots, shoes, furniture, etc., water is used.

275. 洗 hsi³, to wash, as clothes, the hands, the face; coupled with the following tsao³, to bathe.

276. 澡 tsao³, with the foregoing, to bathe.

277. 臉 lien³, the face.

278. 盆 p'ên², a basin; as hsi³-tsao³ p'ên², a bath-tub.

279. 胰 i², soap made from hogs' lard; it always takes tzŭ after it. Coarse soap made from the bean is called fei²-tsao⁴, and a mixture of the two, i²-tsao⁴. The new characters will be met with later.

280. 最 tsui⁴, much; very.

281. 溫 wên¹, warm; often combined with ho² (210), but pronounced huo¹.

282. 梳 shu¹, a comb; to comb. When used as a noun it either takes mu⁴, wood, before it, or is followed by tzŭ. Thus,

        mu⁴ shu¹ or shu¹-tzŭ, a comb.

N.B.—A woman's comb is called lung³-tzŭ, with which she shu¹ t'ou², combs her hair (*lit.*, head).

283. 髮 fa³, the hair; colloquially, it takes the prefix t'ou², the head, as t'ou² fa³. Emphasis must be laid on the first character.

284. Examples:—

澡 tsao³	梳 shu¹	臉 lien³	最 tsui⁴	得 tê²	洗 hsi³	臉 lien³
最 tsui⁴	梳 shu¹	給 kei³	熱 jê⁴	乾 kan¹	手 shou³	盆 p'ên²
好。hao³	頭 t'ou²	我 wo³	我 wo³	淨 ching⁴	用 yung⁴	是 shih⁴
刷 shua¹	髮 fa³	一 i⁴	洗 hsi³	了 liao	胰 i²	洗 hsi³
子。tzŭ	早 tsao³	把 pa³	了 liao	前 ch'ien²	子 tzŭ	臉 lien³
	起 ch'i³	木 mu⁴	六 liu⁴	兒 'rh	就 chiu⁴	用 yung⁴
	洗 hsi³	梳 shu¹	回 hui²	個 ko⁴	洗 hsi³	的。ti

A basin is used for washing the face.

In washing the hands, if you use soap you can wash them clean.

Obs.—Mark the force of *chiu*; *lit.*, washing the hands, using soap, you *then* washing obtain clean [ones].

The day before yesterday was the hottest [we have had]; I washed my face six times.

Obs.—The *ko* after *ch'ien-'rh* must be regarded as a simple colloquial expletive peculiar to Peking; the *êrh* is probably a corruption of *jih*, day.

Bring me a comb to comb my hair.

Obs.—Note the reduplication of the verb; *shu shu*, short for *shu i shu*, to comb a comb, or have a comb at.

It is best to bathe early.

A brush.

285. 針 chên¹, a needle.

PART III.—THE FORTY EXERCISES.

286. 線 hsien⁴, thread; the numerative is t'iao². Chén¹-hsien⁴ in combination means needlework.

287. 縫 féng², to stitch together; read féng⁴, a seam or crack. See **737**.

288. 補 pu³, to patch; hence, to fill up a vacancy, make good a deficiency.

289. Examples:—

很 hén³	的 ti	都 tou¹	兒 'rh	線。hsien⁴	一 i²
得 tei³	衣 i¹	學 hsio²	太 t'ai⁴	這 ché⁴	個 ko⁴
縫 féng²	裳 shang¹	針 chén¹	小 hsiao³	個 ko⁴	針 chén¹
補 pu³	破 p'o⁴	線。hsien⁴	女 nü³	針 chén¹	一 i⁴
了。liao	得 té²	你 ni³	人 jén²	眼 yen³	條 t'iao²

A needle. A thread.
The eye of this needle is too small.

Obs.—The eye of a needle is also called chén pi²-'rh, the needle's nose; chén yen, without the érh, means a stye in the eye, but chén must be emphasised.

Women all learn sewing.
Your clothes are very tattered; they must be mended.

Obs.—Féng pu, to mend: lit., stitch and patch.

290. 穿 ch'uan¹, to bore through; to put on clothes.

291. 鞋 hsieh², shoes.

292. 脫 t'o¹, to take off or away. Often used with hsia⁴, below; as t'o¹ hsia⁴, to take off.

293. 靴 hsüeh¹, boots; it takes tzǔ after it.

294. 雙 shuang¹, a pair.

295. 襪, 韈, wa⁴, stockings; it takes tzǔ after it. The character is found under both radicals.

296. Examples:—

雨 yü³	穿 ch'uan¹	脫 t'o¹	不 pu⁴	麼 mo¹	脫 t'o¹	一 i⁴	
就 chiu⁴	雨 yü¹	一 i⁴	了 liao³	大 ta⁴	靴 hsüeh¹	雙 shuang¹	
不 pu²	靴 hsüeh¹	身 shén¹	一 i⁴	的 ti	子。tzǔ	襪 wa⁴	
怕 p'a⁴	雨 yü³	的 ti	百 pai³	靴 hsüeh¹	你 ni³	子。tzǔ	
了。liao	衣 i¹	衣 i¹	步 pu⁴	子 tzǔ	穿 ch'uan¹	穿 ch'uan¹	
	下 hsia⁴	裳。shang¹	了。liao	走 tsou³	那 na⁴	鞋。hsieh²	

One pair of stockings.
To put on shoes.
To take off boots.
If you put on boots as big as that you won't be able to walk a hundred paces.
To take off all one's clothes.
With rain boots and rain clothes on, rain need not be dreaded.

Obs.—Rain boots are more commonly called yu² hsüeh, oil (or oiled) boots; the character for yu will be met with later.

EXERCISE XI.

腌
臢。
乾
淨。

衣
裳。
靴
子。

鞋
襪
子
穿
上。

把
靴
子
脫

下
來。

靴
子
一
雙

1. Dirty. Clean. Clothes. Boots. Shoes. Stockings. Put on your clothes. Take off your boots. A pair of boots.

那
一
雙
靴
子

得
補
上
皮
子

兒
十
雙
襪
子

買
一
條
手
巾
那

了
也
不
算
多。

靴
子
温
和
水
洗

使
不
得。

2. You must patch that pair of boots with a little leather. He has bought ten pairs of stockings and one handkerchief. That is not very many after all. Warm water will not do to wash boots in.

Obs.—After all : note the force of *yeh* ; *lit.*, that also not reckoned many.

這
盆
水
腌
臢

臢
了、
換
乾
淨

淨
的
臉
那

我
洗
臉
臢

衣
裳
腌
臢

給
刷
一
刷。

3. The water in this basin is dirty; change it and bring me some clean water instead to wash my face. Those clothes are dirty; take a brush and brush them.

這
件
衣
裳

破
了、
給
補
補

來
縫
不
用
補

罷。
縫
一
縫

衣
裳
腌
臢
罷、

個
臉
盆。

4. This garment is torn; call someone here to patch it. There is no occasion, I think, to patch it; it will do as well if it is sewn up. A wash-basin.

Obs.—The second *pa* implying doubt.

你
快
起
來

裳、
他
脫
了
衣

衣
裳
一
件

那
一
件
穿
了

好
些
日
子

沒
換
呢。

5. Get up quickly and dress. He is (or was) lying down undressed (or, has taken off his clothes and is lying down). He has had that garment on for a number of days without changing it.

今
兒
個
天

穿
一
件
多

裳、
你
見
他

他
的
時
候

子、
他
是
穿
靴

呢。
是
穿
鞋

6. It is cold to-day; you must put on something more. When you saw him had he got on boots or shoes?

Obs.—*Lit.*, when you saw him's time, he wore, etc. Note *ni*, the sign of the interrogative.

PART III.—THE FORTY EXERCISES.

7. 這條手巾不乾淨、擱在臉盆裏洗罷。你愛穿的是靴子。那麼都看我是做甚麼。裏沒事我就穿鞋。上衙門的時候兒可得穿靴子。

7. This handkerchief is not clean; put it in the wash-hand basin and wash it. Do you prefer to wear boots or shoes? That all depends upon what I am doing; when I am at home with nothing to do I wear shoes, but when I go to the yamên I am obliged to wear boots.

Obs.—That all depends: *lit.*, that [is] all to be seen.

8. 你那一雙皮靴子這麼些日子擱在那兒老不刷、一刷罷。錯。你給刷罷。

8. Those leather boots of yours which have been lying by all this time ought to be brushed, surely. You are quite right; suppose you brush them for me.

9. 你洗手是愛涼水是愛開水、兩樣裏都不好、涼水太涼開水太熱、最好的溫和水。

9. Do you prefer cold water or boiling water to wash your hands in? Both are bad; cold water is too cold, boiling water is too hot. Warm water is the best.

10. 你快把這水倒在鍋裏溫一溫罷。那火要滅了。這水老開不了了半天。

10. Be quick and pour this water into the pan and warm it. The fire is going out. The water has been on a long while and will not boil.

Turn the following into Chinese. (KEY, EXERCISE XI.)

1. Your mother tells me you did not get up very early to-day.

Obs. 1.—Your mother, 老太太: *lit.*, the old lady or dame. *T'ai-t'ai* is a term of respect applied to the wives of officials and aged women; it is of comparatively modern origin, but nothing seems to be known about its derivation.

Obs. 2.—*Shuo*, to speak, generally follows *kao-su* when the latter is in the past tense.

2. Quite true; I was dining out yesterday evening, and came back late. The roads were really in a bad state, and, not to speak of my boots and clothes, which were all dirtied, my face even was not fit to be seen for grime. When I got home I called for warm water to wash it, and, taking off my clothes and boots, I saw at once that my stockings were in holes

and would have to be mended. I ordered the servants (men) to bring me a pair of shoes, and to put them on the stove of the *k'ang*, and had a change of clean clothes all over. *Ai ya!* when these boots of mine get wet with rain they are not easy to take off; in my opinion it is better to wear shoes. After I had taken a cup of tea I felt better (*lit.*, in the heart then good a little). But the way the rain came down in the night was enough to frighten one. Did you go out, too?

Obs. 1.—Get wet: *chao*² *yü*³. See **45**.
Obs. 2.—In my opinion: *lit.*, in my saying. See **28**.

3. I had on a suit of good clothes which I did not want to get spoilt, [so] I did not cross (go out of) the door.

4. Please have some tea. Don't let us talk about this.

5. Is this water for the tea boiling?

6. The water has been on the fire for ever so long (half the day); of course it is boiling.

Obs.—Of course: *k'o pu shih*. See **124**.

297. 儘 *chin*³, to the greatest extent; prefixed adverbially.

298. 摘 *chai*¹, to pluck off, as fruit, etc. (but not flowers).

299. 戴 *tai*⁴, to wear on the head.

300. 撢 *tan*³, to tap; to dust. With *tzŭ*, a duster.

301. 帽 *mao*⁴, a cap; generally takes *tzŭ* after it.

302. 中 *chung*¹, middle; midst. Often used with *chien*¹, a division or space (**47**); as *chung*¹ *chien*⁴-*'rh*, in the middle; or, the middle. Note the change of tone. It can also be used as a verb, to fulfil or accomplish, as will be seen later. Read *chung*⁴, to pass an examination.

303. Examples:—

了 *liao*	帽 *mao*⁴	帽 *mao*⁴	土 *t'u*³	帽 *mao*⁴	中 *chung*¹	儘 *chin*³
子 *tzŭ*	子 *tzŭ*	子 *tzŭ*	你 *ni*³	子 *tzŭ*	間 *chien*⁴	裏 *li*³
叫 *chiao*⁴	摘 *chai*¹	一 *i*²	拏 *na*²	兒 *'rh*	頭 *t'ou*²
風 *fêng*¹	下 *hsia*⁴	進 *chin*⁴	撢 *tan*³	戴 *tai*⁴	儘 *chin*³
颳 *kua*⁴	來 *lai*²	屋 *wu*¹	子 *tzŭ*	帽 *mao*⁴	前 *ch'ien*²
下 *hsia*⁴	我 *wo*³	裏 *li*³	撢 *tan*³	子 *tzŭ*	頭 *t'ou*²
去 *ch'ü*⁴	的 *ti*	把 *pa*³	撢 *tan*³	摘 *chai*¹	正 *chêng*⁴

At the very inside. At the very front. Right in the middle.
To wear a cap. To take off the cap.
Tap the dust off with a duster.
The moment you enter a room take your hat off.
My cap was blown off by the wind.

Obs.—Note the use of *chiao*, to call or cause, as an auxiliary, by means of which *kua*, to blow, becomes passive. There are other verbs which perform the same function, but of these more hereafter. See **56**.

304. 砍, 坎, *k'an*³, to chop; to strike with a sword or like weapon (not with a stick, a spear, the hand, etc.). The second is the correct form, but the first is often used.

PART III.—THE FORTY EXERCISES.

305. 肩 $chien^1$, shoulders; when linked with the foregoing, it means a waistcoat, *q.d.*, a garment that divides, or lies between, the shoulders.

306. 汗 han^4, sweat.

307. 衫 $shan^1$, a shirt; a shift. Generally used with the preceding.

308. 單 tan^1, single; a term applied to many kinds of documents. It also means only.

309. 夾 $chia^2$, double; read $chia^1$, to place between two objects. *See Examples.*

310. Examples:—

裡。li^3	單 tan^1	收 $shou^1$	一 i^4	衣 i^1	汗 han^4 一 i^2
子。$tzŭ$	單 tan^1	天 $t'ien^1$	裳。$shang^1$	衫 $shan^1$ 個 ko^4
把 pa^3	給 kei^3	的 ti	昨 tso^2	兒。'rh 欵 $k'an^3$
紙 $chih^3$	他 $t'a^1$	汗 han^4	天 $t'ien^1$	單 tan^1 肩 $chien^1$
夾 $chia^1$	開 $k'ai^1$	寫 $hsieh^3$	我 wo^3	衣 i^1 兒。'rh
在 $tsai^4$	一 i^2	一 i^2	出 $ch'u^1$	裳。$shang^1$ 一 i^2
書 shu^1	個 ko^4	個 ko^4	了 $liao$	夾 $chia^2$ 件 $chien^4$

A waistcoat. A shirt.
Clothes without lining. Lined clothes.
I perspired all day yesterday.
Write a receipt and give it him.
Make a list.
Place the paper between [the leaves of] the book.

311. 棉 $mien^2$, the cotton plant; as $mien^2$ hua^4, raw cotton.

312. 褲 $k'u^4$, trousers, of which the numerative is $t'iao^2$ **(181)**; it takes $tzŭ$ after it.

313. 裁 $ts'ai^2$, to cut, as a tailor when shaping clothes; hence, $ts'ai^2$-$fêng^2$, a tailor, one who cuts and stitches.

N.B.—Emphasise $ts'ai$.

314. 褂 kua^4, an outer coat; as ma^3 kua^4-$tzŭ$, or ma^3 kua^4-'rh, a riding jacket, or short coat.

315. 袖 $hsiu^4$, a sleeve; it takes $tzŭ$ after it.

316. Examples:—

衣 i^1	褂 kua^4	是 $shih^4$	褲 $k'u^4$	褲 $k'u^4$	棉 $mien^2$
裳。$shang^1$	子。$tzŭ^4$	夾 $chia^2$	子 $tzŭ$	子。$tzŭ$	衣 i^1
裁 $ts'ai^2$	袖 $hsiu^4$	的。ti	是 $shih^4$	這 $ché^4$	裳。$shang^1$
縫。$fêng^2$	子。$tzŭ$	一 i^2	單 tan^1	一 i^4	一 i^4
	裁 $ts'ai^2$	件 $chien^4$	的 ti	條 $t'iao^2$	條 $t'iao^2$

Wadded clothes.
A pair of trousers. Is this pair of trousers single or lined?
A coat. Sleeves.
To cut out clothes. A tailor.

EXERCISE XII.

1. 女人們小的時候兒學針線．他們多半兒不認得字．帽子不是說一頂．裁縫裁衣裳縫衣裳都行．

1. Women in their childhood learn needlework; the majority of them cannot read. The numerative of caps is *ting*[3]. A tailor can both cut out and make up clothes.

Obs.—The majority: *lit.*, the excess half; *ta pan* would be equally correct.

2. 你洗澡的時候兒不要把頭髮擱在水裏．頭髮一着水老乾不了．

2. When you bathe, do not put your hair in the water; when once the hair gets wet, it takes a long time to dry.

Obs.—*Chao*[2], to come in contact with. See 45.

3. 單衣裳是就有一面兒沒有裏兒的夾衣裳是有面兒有裏兒的那一件衣裳儘裏頭穿的．棉衣裳是夾衣裳中間有棉花的．出汗．

3. Clothes, *tan*[1] (not lined), are such as have an outside with nothing inside it; clothes, *chia*[2] (lined), are such as have both a lining and an outside. Wadded garments are *chia*[2] (lined) with cotton in between. To perspire.

4. 砍肩兒是有前後沒有袖子的衣裳．汗衫兒就叫馬褂兒官帽兒兩樣兒官帽兒

4. A *k'an*[3]-*chien*[1] is the article of dress which has a back and front and no sleeves. The *han*[4]-*shan*[1] is the garment without lining worn innermost of all.

5. 袿子是儘外頭穿的小帽兒

5. The *kua*[4]-*tzŭ* is the garment worn outermost of all; when short it is called a *ma*[3] *kua*[4] (or riding jacket). Is this pair of trousers wadded or is it lined?

6. 帽子有小帽兒官帽兒官帽兒兩樣兒分涼帽暖帽．

6. Caps are distinguished as small caps and official hats; while official hats are of two kinds, the cool (summer) cap and the warm (winter) cap.

PART III.—THE FORTY EXERCISES.

7 你會做針線不會那麼我就叫一個裁縫來把我那一件汗衫補了。

7. Do you know how to sew? I do not. In that case I will call a tailor here to mend (patch) my shirt.

8 那一件砍肩縫裁了還沒縫呢那一件破馬褂子撣得撣一撣了撣衣裳上的土。

8. The waistcoat is cut out but not put together yet. That torn riding coat should be mended. Tap the dust off the clothes with a duster.

9 那一把木梳梳頭是誰的一洗澡一身都洗天兒洗澡很好。

9. Who is it that combs his hair with that (or the) wooden comb? The expression hsi^3-$tsao^3$ means to bathe the whole body. It is a good thing to bathe every day.

Obs.—Shu t'ou, to comb the hair; fa can be omitted.

10 你老先生頭髮短得很頂兒上就沒有了我也五十多了沒頭髮的時候兒了。

10. Your hair, sir, is very short, and you have already become bald on the top of your head. I am more than fifty; it is time for one to lose one's hair.

Obs. 1.—Sir: lit., old elder born; a polite term of address to an elderly person.
Obs. 2.—Note $ting^3$, the crown of the head; t'ou being understood. See 72.
Obs. 3.—More than fifty: it would be better to add the character sui^4 (952), but it has been omitted as it has not yet been introduced.

11 今年棉花多不多多少是多少可不少沒有去年那麼多。

11. Is raw cotton plentiful this year? It is not, so to speak, scarce, but it is not so abundant as it was last year.

Turn the following into Chinese. (KEY, EXERCISE XII.)

1. The tailor has come.
2. Tell him to come in.
3. What clothes do you want made, sir?

Obs.—Nin² (您) is a polite form of the personal pronoun ni³. See 648.

4. Coats, trousers, and waistcoats; and, besides, I want you to make those what-do-you-call-'ems that one wears next the skin.

Obs.—What-do-you-call-'em: lit., that what (with the possessive appended).

5. You mean under-shirts, don't you, sir?
Obs.—Under-shirts: *lit.*, little coats.

6. That's it; and I want a good many shirts too.

7. Do you want that coat wadded, sir, or lined?

8. I don't want it either way; the weather is too hot. If you make a single one that will do.

9. In what style are the sleeves to be made?

10. I want them a little longer than this [coat] of mine.
Obs.—Longer: *lit.*, compared with (Radical 81) this one, etc., long.

11. Be a little careful about these clothes; I want them all cut to [the shape of] my body, so that when worn they may have a style about them. And, I must tell you, I don't want them to wear out as soon as they are put on.
Obs. 1.—Cut to the shape of: *lit.*, comparing body cut.
Obs. 2.—Have a style: *lit.*, have kind or fashion (*yang*⁴).

12. If you brush your clothes clean every evening, sir, they will not spoil for a long time.

13. In how many days will these clothes be ready?

14. I am very good at needlework; they will not be many days before they are ready.

15. This tailor is so dirty he isn't [fit] to be seen; he looks somewhat as if he had not used soap for a long time; his hair, too, is not combed.
Obs.—Dirty: *tsang* is often used without *ang*.

16. Possibly because he has not got a comb.

317. 金 $chin^1$ (Radical 167), metal, especially gold; gold is also termed $huang^2\ chin^1$ (Radical 201), the yellow metal.

318. 銀 yin^2, silver.

319. 銅 $t'ung^2$, copper.

320. 鐵 $t'ieh^3$, iron.

321. 錢 $ch'ien^2$, coin, especially cash.

322. 吊 $tiao^4$, in Peking, a 500-cash note; elsewhere, a string of 1,000 copper cash. Also, to hang or suspend.

323. 票 $p'iao^4$, a printed note or written order for money; also, a police warrant.

324. Examples:—

是 $shih^4$	是 $shih^4$	我 wo^3	百 pai^3	銀 yin^2	子 $tzŭ$	三 san^1
鐵 $t'ieh^3$	銅 $t'ung^2$	分 $fên^1$	個 ko^4	子 $tzŭ$	三 san^1	十 $shih^2$
做 tso^4	做 tso^4	不 pu^4	錢 $ch'ien^2$	的 ti	吊 $tiao^4$	兩 $liang^3$
的 ti	的 ti	出 $ch'u^1$	兒 $'rh$	票 $p'iao^4$	錢 $ch'ien^2$	銀 yin^2
	那 na^3	那 na^3	裏 li^3	這 $ché^4$	三 san^1	子 $tzŭ$
	個 ko^4	個 ko^4	頭 $t'ou^2$	一 i^1	兩 $liang^3$	金 $chin^1$

Thirty taels.

Obs.—*Liang*, two, is a measure of weight, commonly called a tael; 10 *liang* go to the *chin* or catty.

Gold.

Three *tiao* (elsewhere than in Peking, 3,000, or three strings of, cash).

A bank-note for three taels.

Obs.—In Peking, notes for silver are called *p'iao*, and notes for cash are called *p'iao-tzŭ*.

Amongst these hundred cash I cannot distinguish which are made of copper and which of iron.

PART III.—THE FORTY EXERCISES.

325. 桿 *kan*³, properly, any straight pole or rod of wood; the numerative of spears, muskets, etc.

326. 秤 *ch'êng*⁴, a balance; a weighing beam. Scales are called 天平 (*t'ien*¹-*p'ing*²); a small steelyard has another name.

327. 稱 *ch'êng*¹, to weigh; hence, to esteem. In certain combinations, to speak of; to designate; to speak. *Ch'êng*¹ is to weigh with a *ch'êng*⁴; *p'ing*² *i p'ing*² is to weigh with a *t'ien*¹-*p'ing*². There is another term for weighing with a steelyard.

328. Examples:—

麼 *mo*	小 *hsiao*³	這 *chê*⁴	天 *t'ien*¹	麼 *mo*	桿 *kan*³	稱 *ch'êng*¹
多 *to*¹	稱 *ch'êng*¹	一 *i*⁴	買 *mai*³	稱 *ch'êng*¹	秤 *ch'êng*⁴	東 *tung*¹
的 *ti*	不 *pu*⁴	桿 *kan*³	來 *lai*²	一 *i*⁴	來 *lai*²	西 *hsi*¹
米 *mi*³	了 *liao*³	秤 *ch'êng*⁴	的 *ti*	稱 *ch'êng*¹	做 *tso*⁴	拏 *na*²
	那 *na*⁴	太 *t'ai*⁴	米 *mi*³	昨 *tso*²	甚 *shên*²	一 *i*⁴

To weigh things.

Obs.—*Yao*⁴ *i yao*⁴ (32) is also permissible and perhaps more popular.

Bring me a balance. What for? To weigh the rice we bought yesterday.

This balance is too small; it will not weigh so much rice as that.

329. 價 *chia*⁴, price; value.

330. 值 *chih*², to be worth. As *chia*⁴-*chih*², the price anything is worth or is valued at; *chia*⁴-*ch'ien*² (321) is more common.

331. 貴 *kuei*⁴, dear; valuable; honourable; esteemed.

332. 賤 *chien*⁴, cheap.

333. 便 *p'ien*², a popular pronunciation of *p'ien*⁴, convenient. Read *p'ien*² only when followed by *i*²; see below. *Fang*¹-*pien*⁴ (Radical 70), convenient; handy.

334. 宜 *i*², to be befitting; morally, essential. As *p'ien*²-*i*², cheap; advantageous; advantage.

335. 輕 *ch'ing*¹, light.

336. 重 *chung*⁴, heavy. Read *ch'ung*², to repeat; twice over (*see* Part IV, Dialogue IX, 29).

337. Examples:—

不 *pu*⁴	賤 *chien*⁴	個 *ko*⁴	木 *mu*⁴	便 *p'ien*²	兩 *liang*³	這 *chê*⁴
值 *chih*²	得 *tê*	銅 *t'ung*²	頭 *t'ou*²	宜 *i*²	銀 *yin*²	一 *i*⁴
錢 *ch'ien*²	很 *hên*³	壺 *hu*²	是 *shih*⁴	鐵 *t'ieh*³	子 *tzŭ*	匹 *p'i*¹
	酒 *chiu*³	的 *ti*	輕 *ch'ing*¹	是 *shih*⁴	不 *pu*²	馬 *ma*³
	瓶 *p'ing*²	價 *chia*⁴	的 *ti*	重 *chung*⁴	貴 *kuei*⁴	值 *chih*²
	子 *tzŭ*	錢 *ch'ien*²	那 *na*⁴	的 *ti*	很 *hên*³	幾 *chi*³

How many taels is this horse worth? It is not dear; it is very cheap.

Iron is heavy; wood is light.

That copper kettle is very cheap.

Wine bottles are valueless.

Obs.—*Pu chih ch'ien* may also mean to cost a trifle.

338. 借 *chieh*⁴, to lend; to borrow.

339. 賬 *chang*⁴, a bill; an account. This is a corrupt form of *chang*⁴ (**146**); it is not recognised by the dictionaries, but is so universally used that it demands notice.

340. 該 *kai*¹, to owe anything; morally, to owe duty; ought. Often combined with *tang*¹ (**342**).

341. 費 *fei*⁴, to expend money, pains, etc.

342. 當 *tang*⁴, to represent; to stand for. *Tang*¹, to act as; suitable; proper; that which ought to be done. *Tang*⁴, to pawn or pledge. *Tang*¹ or *tang*⁴, an adverb of time.

343. 於 *yü*², in; in the case or matter of; proceeding out of. Used only in certain combinations.

344. 好 *hao*⁴, to like much; to be fond of. To be distinguished from *hao*³, good.

345. Examples:—

當 *tang*⁴	做 *tso*⁴	他 *t'a*¹	錢 *ch'ien*²	他 *t'a*¹	這 *chê*⁴	我 *wo*³
天 *t'ien*¹	是 *shih*⁴	好 *hao*⁴	費 *fei*⁴	該 *kai*¹	一 *i*⁴	的 *ti*
兒 *'rh*	他 *t'a*¹	看 *k'an*⁴	心 *hsin*¹	了 *liao*	本 *pên*³	錢 *ch'ien*²
去 *ch'ü*⁴	該 *kai*¹	書 *shu*¹	費 *fei*⁴	好 *hao*³	書 *shu*¹	都 *tou*¹
的 *ti*	當 *tang*¹	這 *chê*⁴	心 *hsin*¹	多 *to*¹	是 *shih*⁴	借 *chieh*⁴
他 *t'a*¹	做 *tso*⁴	件 *chien*⁴	當 *tang*¹	帳 *chang*⁴	借 *chieh*⁴	出 *ch'u*¹
當 *tang*¹	的 *ti*	事 *shih*⁴	鋪 *p'u*⁴	過 *kuo*⁴	了 *liao*	去 *ch'ü*⁴
厨 *ch'u*²	我 *wo*³	該 *kai*¹	當 *tang*⁴	於 *yü*²	來 *lai*²	了 *liao*
子 *tzŭ*	是 *shih*⁴	誰 *shui*²	票 *p'iao*⁴	費 *fei*⁴	的 *ti*	他 *t'a*¹

My money is all lent out.
This book of his is borrowed.
He owes a great many debts.
To spend too much money.
Much obliged to you.

Obs.—This expression is generally confined to thanks for favours which entail the exercise of mind rather than of body (*lit.*, I have spent your heart; or, you have expended your mind or brain on me). The heart, according to the Chinese theory, is the seat of the intellect.

A pawnshop. A pawn-ticket.
He is very fond of reading.
Who ought to undertake this affair? It is he that ought to do it.
I went on the same day (*q.d.*, the day on which it happened).
He acts as cook.

Obs.—*Tang* here implies either that his previous occupation was something different, or that cooking is only one of other crafts with which he is acquainted.

PART III.—THE FORTY EXERCISES.

EXERCISE XIII.

秤 輕 個 不 錢 賬 1
稱 重 東 知 花 目
一 得 西 道 費 四
稱。拏 的 那 票 花
　　　　　子。錢。
　　　　　吊

1. Accounts. To spend money (184). Expenses; expenditure. A four-*tiao* note. You must weigh it in the balance if you do not know its weight.

Obs.—The word *chang*⁴, as already explained, is not authorised by the native dictionaries; it is, however, a very common substitute for the correct form (146), and means, says a teacher, a memorandum of expenditure. *Mu*, the eye, combined with *chang* has something of the force of our word *heads*, in a discourse: sections, or other subdivisions.

麼 還 兩 不 他 他 2
些 不 銀 下 賬 欠
個 了 子。一 目 人
罷。那 他 千 不 的
　　　　　賬 少。

2. He owes different people a great deal of money. He has bills outstanding to the extent of at least (not below) one thousand taels. I don't suppose he can pay that amount.

拏 把 給 我 的 我 3
給 我 人 使。錢 把
人 的 錢 我 拏 借
使。錢 是 借 來 錢
　　　 是

3. The expression *wo*³ *chieh*⁴ *ch'ien*² means that I am getting money of people for my use. *Wo*³ *chieh*⁴ *kei*³ *jên*² *ch'ien*² means that I am letting another have my money for his use.

Obs. 1.—The expression: *lit.*, [the words] *wo chieh ch'ien* are=mean [that] I holding people's money bring it [to me] for my own use. *Chieh kei jên ch'ien* means [that I] holding my money take it [to people] for people's use.

Obs. 2.—People: *jên-chia*. The *chia* generalises *jên*, and has something of the force of our word *kind*, though *jên-chia* cannot bear so wide a meaning as mankind; *folks* would be a nearer rendering.

快 錢。個 都 花 不 天 我 4
完 他 人 說 錢 很 兒 們
了 的 過 得 好 多 的 家
罷。本 於 他 花 他 花 裡
　 錢 花 那 錢 愛 費 天

4. Our daily domestic expenditure is not large. It is equally correct to say *t'a ai*⁴ (he loves to spend) or *hao*⁴ (is fond of spending) money. That man spends too much; his capital must be nearly at an end.

Obs. 1.—Too much: *lit.*, is excessive, or exceeds, *yü*, in the matter of, spending money.

Obs. 2.—Capital or principal: *lit.*, root or stock of money.

5. 那個房子不貴這一件皮襖價錢。宜子那個花瓶不值價。值錢那個花瓶不便宜。花錢今年他家裏棉花很賤。一個很賤。有一個大錢都沒。

5. That is not a dear house. The price asked (or paid) for this fur cloak is very small. That flower-vase is worth nothing. Cotton is very low this year. He has not got a cash to live on.

Obs.—Not a cash: *lit.*, he in his house one large cash even has not got. This might mean equally that his family were all in as great distress; but were it an object to isolate the individual, *shou³ li³*, in his hand, might be used instead of *chia li*.

6. 那大錢當十的裏頭有七分是銅的有三分是鐵的。分是鐵比銀的。黃金比鐵的。銀子重。子輕。

6. Seven-tenths of those ten-cash pieces are copper, and three-tenths iron. Gold is heavier than silver; iron is lighter than silver.

Obs.—Ten-cash pieces: *lit.*, representing ten's large cash (342). The second *ti* is simplest construed as *ones*; *q.d.*, there are seven-tenths being copper ones, there are three-tenths being iron ones. Were it meant that each cash contained seven-tenths copper to three-tenths iron, the text might be variously modified: you might omit the *li-t'ou*, and then proceed, *tou shih ch'i fên t'ung san fên t'ieh*; or, retaining the *li-t'ou*, proceed, *yu ch'i fên t'ung san fên t'ieh*.

7. 票子是一張紙上頭寫著錢數兒買東西同銀子錢一樣兒。他當了十吊子錢的票子。掛一個他當了。

7. A *p'iao⁴-tzŭ* is a paper note on which is written the number of cash it is worth; for buying things it is the same as coin. He has pawned that coat for notes to the value of ten *tiao* (or, for a ten-*tiao* note).

Obs.—A paper note: *lit.*, a *p'iao-tzŭ* is a strip of paper upon [which one] writes a number (or amount) of cash; [in] buying things [it is] with money [of] one and the same fashion. Instead of *i ko yang-'rh*, you may read *shih i ko yang*.

8. 那花瓶兒他不賣。他賣是賣你要一定得賣他花錢兒可是賤買的。

8. Will he sell that flower-vase? He is sure to sell, but if you want it you will have to pay pretty well for it; he didn't buy it cheap.

Obs. 1.—*Hua lia chien-'rh*: *lit.*, spend a couple of cash; a Pekingese expression for putting one's hand in one's pocket.

Obs. 2.—*Ti* here stands for *tê*.

PART III.—THE FORTY EXERCISES. 71

該 9 誰 一 這 開 十 的
當 的 怕 個 口、 兩 話。
花 時 花 二 人 就
錢 候 兒、 兩、 一 是
個 你 個 兩
花 你 八

9. No one minds spending a tael or two when they have (or ought) to be spent, but it's nine or ten taels with you directly you open your mouth (you are too large in your ideas altogether).

Obs.—Ought : note the use of the two verbs with a similar meaning. *Kai* alone would be equally correct, but perhaps slightly less forcible; *tang* could also be used alone.

Turn the following into Chinese. (KEY, EXERCISE XIII.)

1. I am thinking of going beyond the frontier, [where] I hear that notes are not handy (*lit.*, not good to use)—silver being more convenient to use,—and that one will want some small copper cash too.

Obs. 1.—Am thinking: where this is used in the sense of proposing to carry out a project, the word *suan*, to reckon, is commonly employed, preceded by the auxiliary *ta*³ (**241**).

Obs. 2.—The frontier: *k'ou* (Radical 30), a mouth or pass; *k'ou wai*, outside a pass or gateway on the Chinese frontier. In Peking, *k'ou wai* is understood to mean the region beyond the Great Wall.

2. You will certainly want some; but the cash they use [there] is not, I fancy, the cash used in the capital.

3. Quite right; the cash used in the capital are large cash, each representing ten [small ones]. When one gets beyond the frontier, changing silver gives a deal of trouble. Not only (*lit.*, there's no use saying) does the price of silver vary, but its amount when weighed varies too (*lit.*, the large and small of the *p'ing*, or scale, is also not the same).

4. I have heard that when one goes beyond the barrier living is much cheaper.

Obs. 1.—A barrier (**63**).

Obs. 2.—Living: *lit.*, fire and food (Radical 184).

5. Living is cheap, certainly; but if you reckon up the cart hire (*lit.*, money) and inn (*lit.*, house) money, expenses are by no means small. When you get back I fear you will owe many bills.

Obs.—If: *yao shih*, if it be that; *yao* (**32**) being corruptly used for another word, *jo*⁴, if, which will be met with later.

6. If I owe bills they must certainly be paid. If I cannot pay them I shall just ask you to lend me a little money.

Obs.—I shall just, etc.: *lit.*, [I will] request you to lend to me a little money, *chiu shih liao*, and that's all.

7. So you are thinking of borrowing again, eh? you owed me long ago a good many taels which you have not paid me back all this time; another loan would be a little too much, surely.

Obs. 1.—You owed: *lit.*, were short [to] me.

Obs. 2.—Too much: *t'ai kuo yü i tien-'rh*, a little too excessive.

8. Well, well; let's say no more about it. What is the exchange for silver to-day?

Obs. 1.—Well, well, etc.: *lit.*, that then ended, *na chiu pa liao*.

Obs. 2.—Exchange: *lit.*, how many cash does silver (*i.e.*, the ounce of silver) change for?

9. To-day the tael changes for over seventeen *tiao*.

10. In that case weigh [out] for me twenty taels.

Obs.—Weigh: *p'ing* (**327**).

11. Here they are, weighed; take them. A prosperous journey to you.

Obs.—Prosperous journey: *lit.*, you on this road a great great, tranquility tranquility one. The reduplication is merely employed for the sake of euphony.

346. 煤 mei², coal.

347. 炭 t'an⁴, charcoal.

348. 柴 ch'ai², fuel; when used with huo³, fire, it means straw or reed fuel, shavings, etc.

349. 論 lun⁴, to discuss. As pu² lun⁴, never mind; no matter.

350. 石 tan⁴, a corrupt form of shih², stone (Radical 112); 100 catties are ordinarily called a tan⁴ or picul.

351. Examples :—

少 shao³	賣 mai⁴	的 ti	炭 t'an⁴	山 shan¹	一 i²	煤 mei²
不 pu²	的 ti	米 mi³	是 shih⁴	裡 li³	塊 k'uai⁴	炭 t'an⁴
論 lun⁴	不 pu²	是 shih⁴	過 kuo⁴	柴 ch'ai²	兒 'rh	出 ch'u¹
輕 ch'ing¹	論 lun⁴	論 lun⁴	秤 ch'êng⁴	火 huo³	出 ch'u¹	在 tsai⁴
重 chung⁴	多 to¹	石 tan⁴	賣 mai⁴	煤 mei²	在 tsai⁴	那 na³

Where do coal and charcoal come from? From the hills.
Obs.—Lit., coal, charcoal come out in what one piece, bit, or spot. Na³ 'rh would be equally correct, but not perhaps so definite. Note na i k'uai-'rh pronounced na³ k'uérh.
Fuel.
Coal and charcoal are sold by weight.
Obs.—Lit., passing the beam sold.
Rice is sold by the picul.
Obs.—Lit., reckoning the picul sold.
No matter whether many or few. No matter whether light or heavy.

352. 麵 mien⁴, flour.

353. 油 yu², oil.

354. 芝 chih¹, properly, the plant of immortality; used with ma², the following character, it means sesame, and is pronounced chih¹-ma², the chih¹ being emphasised.

355. 麻 ma² (Radical 200), hemp.

356. 糖 t'ang², sugar.

357. 鹽 yen², salt.

358. 粗 ts'u¹, coarse.

359. 細 hsi⁴, fine.

360. Examples :—

細 hsi⁴	麻 ma²	糖 t'ang²	你 ni³	的 ti	麵 mien⁴	菜 ts'ai⁴
線 hsien⁴	是 shih⁴	們 mên²	鹽 yen²	我 wo³	油 yu²
粗 ts'u¹	好 hao³	的 ti	粗 ts'u¹	們 mên²	芝 chih¹
棉 mien²	吃 ch'ih¹	細 hsi⁴	沒 mei²	這 ché⁴	麻 ma²
線 hsien⁴	的 ti	白 pai²	有 yu³	兒 'rh	乾 kan¹

PART III.—THE FORTY EXERCISES.

Vegetable oil, made from the seeds of certain vegetables. It is also used to denote foreign salad oil.

Sesame. Flour.

Obs.—Note that *mien* used alone colloquially often means vermicelli.

Our salt here is coarse, not so fine as yours.

White sugar is nice to eat.

Twine is coarse; cotton thread is fine.

361. 湯 *t'ang*¹, broth.

362. 雞 *chi*¹, chicken; as *chi*¹-*tzŭ*³ *'rh*, fowls' eggs.
N.B.—Emphasise *tzŭ*.

363. 奶 *nai*³, milk.

364. 果 *kuo*³, fruit. Also, in certain combinations, a strong affirmative; certainly; if indeed.

365. 饅 *man*², a dumpling. Commonly used with *t'ou*², a head; as *man*²-*t'ou*, Chinese bread, or steamed dumplings. Foreign bread is generally called *mien*⁴-*pao*⁴, flour balls, or rolls. The term *man*²-*t'ou* has its origin in an incident in Chinese history, a certain general having caused paste effigies to be substituted for the human heads it was customary to offer as a propitiatory sacrifice when crossing a river in the country of the southern savages, in which he was operating.

366. 熟 *shu*², ripe; cooked. Hence, accustomed; familiar. Vulgarly, *shou*².

367. 端 *tuan*¹, in combination, morally upright; to place properly.

368. 撤 *ch'ê*⁴, to remove.

369. Examples:—

子 *tzŭ*	個 *ko*⁴	果 *kuo*³	麼 *mo*	也 *yeh*³	了 *liao*	雞 *chi*¹
糖 *t'ang*²	來 *lai*²	子 *tzŭ*	的 *ti*	可 *k'o*³	端 *tuan*¹	湯 *t'ang*¹
果 *kuo*³	水 *shui*³	熟 *shou*²	都 *tou*¹	以 *i*³	進 *chin*⁴	山 *shan*¹
子 *tzŭ*	果 *kuo*³	了 *liao*	撤 *ch'ê*⁴	說 *shuo*¹	來 *lai*²	羊 *yang*²
	子 *tzŭ*	摘 *chai*¹	下 *hsia*⁴	這 *ché*⁴	開 *k'ai*¹	奶 *nai*³
	乾 *kan*¹	下 *hsia*⁴	去 *ch'ü*⁴	書 *shu*¹	飯 *fan*⁴	飯 *fan*⁴
	果 *kuo*³	幾 *chi*³	那 *na*⁴	甚 *shé*ⁿ²	來 *lai*²	好 *hao*³

Chicken soup. Goat's milk.

When the food is ready, serve *(tuan)* it up. You can also say *k'ai* (serve it up).

Obs.—*T'uan fan* is, strictly speaking, to "serve up," and *k'ai fan* to "dish up." In the second sentence, *lai* implies the act of bringing to the table as well.

Take away these books and things.

Obs.—And things : *lit.*, and what ones.

That fruit is ripe; pluck some.

Obs.—*Chai*¹, to pluck (298).

Fresh fruit. Dry fruit. Jam.

Obs.—In Peking the term *shui kuo-tzŭ* is applied only to plums.

EXERCISE XIV.

雞子兒。牛奶。燈
油。香油。這菜弄
得吃不得快撤
了去罷。燈油是
豆子做的。香油
是芝蔴做的。火
油出在地裏。

1. Fowls' eggs. Cows' milk. Lamp oil. Sweet oil. The food is cooked [so badly] that it is uneatable; take it away at once. Lamp oil is made from the bean; sweet oil from sesame; mineral oils come out of the ground.

我昨兒買了
炕爐子是
有熟的在
的
三百斤煤五
十斤炭八十
斤柴火四石
米二百斤麵。
天冷的時候
煤炭用的
多。

2. I bought yesterday three hundred catties of coal, fifty catties of charcoal, eighty catties of fuel, four piculs of rice, and two hundred catties of flour. When the weather is cold the consumption of coal and charcoal is larger.

炕爐子是
燒煤的多。
火盆是用
炭。火盆是
屋裏用的。
不是做飯
做水的。

3. Most stoves of stove-beds burn coal; in a chafing-dish one uses charcoal. A chafing-dish is for use in a room; it is not meant [for] cooking food or heating water with.

菜有生
有熟的
的在
都是熟
生菜在地
下長出來
就可以吃
得。

4. Things to be eaten are either *shêng*[1] (raw) or *shou*[2] (cooked); all that are prepared over a fire are *shou*[3] (cooked); the *shêng*[1] *ts'ai*[4] are vegetables that may be eaten in their natural state.

Obs.—Natural state: *lit.*, the *shêng ts'ai* are [these; such as] growing out of the ground [man] thereon (or immediately) can eat. In Peking the term *shêng ts'ai* is confined to such vegetables as are never cooked.

你去給我買一個
小雞子兒。還要三四個
雞子兒。還要牛奶就
不便宜我們這兒
要幾斤。牛奶不論斤
買牛奶不論碗論
瓶。兒都是論

5. You go and buy me a chicken and three or four eggs. Do you want any milk as well? I should like a few catties of milk if it is cheap. In this part of the world we do not buy milk by the catty, but by the cup or bottle.

Obs.—Milk by the catty: *lit.*, you do not consider (or reckon) the catties' number.

PART III.—THE FORTY EXERCISES.

6 買 是 你 飯 得 端
果 論 兒 去, 了 上
子 多 的 飯 就 來。
箇 弄 快,

6. Fruit is generally bought by the piece. Go and get the food ready directly, and as soon as it is ready put it on the table.

Obs.—Food ready: *tê*, having achieved that which is in course of preparation. The expression *tê liao* is used of several other operations completed.

7 你 頭 兩 喝 什 肉 都
愛 愛 樣 湯。 麼 湯 好
吃 吃 兒 不 愛 雞
饅 飯。 都 愛 我 湯
愛 喝 呢。 湯

7. Do you prefer bread or rice? Neither; I like broth. What kind of broth? Either meat soup or chicken broth suits me.

Obs.—Prefer: *ai* might also be rendered, what are you in the *habit* of eating?

8 我 人 不 不 都 家
明 吃 們 論 是 的
天 飯 什 甚 偹 人。
要 給 麼 麼 他
請 他 茶 茶 們
好。 本

8. I purpose asking some people to dinner to-morrow; what had I better give them to eat? Anything will do for them; they are all our own immediate belongings (*lit.*, people of our own family stock).

Obs.—*Pên chia* is only used of blood relations.

Turn the following into Chinese. (KEY, EXERCISE XIV.)

1. This year I have spent no little money on coal and fuel. The price of coal keeps getting dearer every day, and, besides, there is not much "kindling" in the market (*lit.*, produced, *ch'u*¹); my monthly expenditure must be at the very least thirteen dollars.

Obs. 1.—I have spent, etc.: *lit.*, my this year's coal fire money spent not little. *Huo*, short for *ch'ai huo*.

Obs. 2.—Note *yu* (Radical 29), also, besides.

Obs. 3.—At the very least: *chih*⁴ *shao*³ (Radical 133).

2. That is because you burn the best coal, which all comes from beyond the frontier. I burn charcoal, which is much cheaper; it can be used in the kitchen too.

Obs.—Much cheaper: *chien to cho ni*. It is difficult to explain the use of *cho* in this connexion; it appears to act as an intensive, and is said by the teachers to be a corruption of *cho shih*³, in very truth, an expression that will be met with later. *See* Note on *cho* at the close of Exercise XL.

3. I hear your cook cooks by no means badly.

Obs.—By no means badly: *lit.*, on the reverse (*tao*⁴, 182) not wrong. This use of *tao* is perhaps a colloquialism peculiar to Peking, but, like many idiomatic expressions of a similar nature, it is considered by northerners as indispensable to fluency of diction; it would not be incorrect to omit the *tao*, but the sentence would have an unfinished sound. It is the judicious use of these little auxiliaries that just makes the difference between a fluent and an awkward speaker.

4. Yes, he does; the soup and butter puddings he makes are very good indeed. Suppose you dine here at my place to-day. Here *(to the servant)!* Bring the [dinner] things. Tell the cook to make a chicken salad (*lit.*, raw vegetable chicken), with a mixture of eggs and sweet oil; tell him to use fine salt, not coarse. I want also every kind

of fruit, and tell him to be careful to buy them ripe.

Obs. 1.—Butter puddings: *lit.*, milk oil pudding (*tien³ hsin¹*, Exercise IX, Eng., 11, Obs. 1; p. 52).

Obs. 2.—With a mixture: *lit.*, using eggs and sweet oil mix (*huo⁴*, 210) together (*i k'uai-'rh*, in one place or piece).

Obs. 3.—Ripe: *shou² fên⁴*; *lit.*, the ripe distinction one's. This is a localism.

5. This dinner I must say is excellent. Now my cook is no use; he has not the least bit of a turn for cooking.

Obs.—A turn for: *pên³ shih⁴*; *lit.*, root matter. This does not mean, as might be supposed from its formation, inborn qualities, but acquired ones.

6. That is because he learnt badly. Please take some wine; I remember that you don't like to drink water.

Obs.—Wine: *huang² chiu³*, yellow wine, is the name given to a light wine that the Chinese commonly drink at their principal meal.

7. We have eaten a very good dinner to-day and drunk lots of wine; the fire, too, burns with plenty of warmth; what more can we two want?

Obs.—Lots: *lit.*, very enough (Radical 157).

370. 京 *ching¹*, the capital of a state, ancient or modern.

371. 遠 *yüan³*, far.

372. 近 *chin⁴*, near. *Yüan³-chin⁴*, in combination, means distance; *to¹ yüan³*, how far.

373. 路 *lu⁴*, a road; a way.

374. 直 *chih²*, straight.

375. 繞 *jao⁴*, winding.

376. Examples:—

這	*ché⁴*	來	*lai²*	遠,	*yüan³*	京,	*ching¹*	路,	*lu⁴*	兒,	*'rh*	到	*tao⁴*
麼	*mo*	告	*kao⁴*	叫	*chiao⁴*	近	*chin⁴*	北	*pei³*	有	*yu³*	京	*ching¹*
繞	*jao⁴*	訴	*su⁴*	他	*t'a¹*	得	*té²*	京	*ching¹*	八	*pa¹*	城	*ch'êng²*
着	*cho*	我,	*wo³*	一	*i⁴*	很,	*hén³*	南	*nan²*	十	*shih²*	有	*yu³*
走	*tsou³*	惜	*tsa²*	直	*chih²*	遠	*yüan³*	京	*ching¹*	多	*to¹*	多	*to¹*
罷。	*pa⁴*	們	*mén²*	進	*chin⁴*	不	*pu²*	東	*tung¹*	里	*li³*	遠	*yüan³*

How far is it to the capital?

Obs.—How far? *lit.*, [how] many far? When speaking of short distances, *yu³ to¹ shao³ lu⁴* is often used, or *chi³ li³ lu⁴*, how many *li* of road, whether by land or water.

More than eighty *li*.

Peking, Nanking, Tokio.

Very near. Is it far?

PART III.—THE FORTY EXERCISES.

Tell him to come straight in and tell me.
Obs.—Had the sentence run, he *came* straight in and told me, *su* should be followed by *shuo*, to speak.
Suppose we take a roundabout in this direction.
Obs.—The *pa* at the close of this sentence has the force of "what do you think?" *i.e.*, expresses a doubt as to the willingness of the person addressed to comply with the suggestion.

377. 河 *ho²*, a river.

378. 海 *hai³*, the sea.

379. 邊 *pien¹*, side.

380. 深 *shên¹*, deep; morally, profound.

381. 淺 *ch'ien³*, shallow. Morally, commonplace; not profound.

382. 隻 *chih¹*, numerative of ships, also of many other things, such as oxen, sheep, and chickens.

383. 船 *ch'uan²*, a ship or boat.

384. Examples:—

多 *to¹*	地 *ti⁴*	的 *ti*	那 *na⁴*	兒 *'rh*	隻 *chih¹*	海 *hai³*
少 *shao³*	方。*fang¹*	地 *ti⁴*	一 *i⁴*	上 *shang⁴*	船。*ch'uan²*	面 *mien⁴*
樣 *yang¹*	海 *hai³*	方 *fang¹*	條 *t'iao²*	就 *chiu⁴*	我 *wo³*	兒 *'rh*
兒 *'rh*	裏 *li³*	有 *yu³*	河 *ho²*	看 *k'an⁴*	在 *tsai⁴*	上 *shang⁴*
的 *ti*	頭 *t'ou²*	深 *shên¹*	有 *yu³*	見 *chien⁴*	海 *hai³*	有 *yu³*
魚。*yü²*	有 *yu³*	的 *ti*	淺 *ch'ien³*	了。*liao*	邊 *pien¹*	三 *san¹*

There are three ships on the sea.
Obs.—*Hai mien-'rh* implies distance.
I was on the shore and saw them; or, I saw them from the shore.
In that river there are shallow places and deep.
How many kinds of fish are there in the sea?

385. 客 *k'ê⁴*, *k'o⁴*, a stranger. Also, a guest; a passenger; a traveller. *Mai³ k'o*, a customer.

386. 店 *tien⁴*, a large shop; an inn.

387. 掌 *chang³*, the palm of the hand; to superintend.

388. 櫃 *kuei⁴*, the counter; a till; a cupboard; a wardrobe.

389. 計 *chi⁴*, to reckon; to count.

390. Examples:—

算 *suan⁴*	手 *shou³*	櫃。*kuei⁴*	店。*tien⁴*	人。*jên²*	來 *lai²*
計 *chi⁴*	掌 *chang³*	掌 *chang³*	衣 *i¹*	飯 *fan⁴*	往 *wang³*
帳 *chang⁴*	手 *shou³*	櫃 *kuei⁴*	櫃。*kuei⁴*	店 *tien⁴*	的 *ti*
目。*mu⁴*	心。*hsin¹*	的 *ti*	錢 *ch'ien²*	茶 *ch'a²*	客 *k'o⁴*

Passing strangers.
A restaurant. A tea-shop.
Obs.—Ch'a-tien is not a "tea-house."
A wardrobe. A till.
An inn manager, or cashier of a shop; *q.d.*, the person who holds or superintends *(chang)* the till *(kuei)*.
The palm of the hand. The centre of the palm.
To do accounts.
Obs.—You can also say *suan chang*.

391. 能 *nêng^2*, to be able.

392. 南 *nan^2*, south.

393. 北 *pei^3*, north.

394. 受 *shou^4*, to receive; to suffer; hence used in many passive formations.

395. 累 *lei^4*, entanglement; to entangle; to trouble.

396. 苦 *k'u^3*, bitterness; bitter; grief; mental or physical suffering.

397. 歇 *hsieh^1*, to rest.

398. 連 *lien^2*, to join; to connect; even. Often employed as the conjunction *and*.

399. Examples:—

雨。*yü^3* 一 *i^4* 一 *i^2* 連 *lien^2* 辛 *hsing^1* 累 *lei^4* 你 *ni^3*
連 *lien^2* 個 *ko^4* 茶 *ch'a^2* 苦 *k'u^3* 了 *liao* 去 *ch'ü^4*
下 *hsia^4* 人 *jên^2* 也 *yeh^3* 歇 *hsieh^1* 麼 *mo* 年 *nien^2*
了 *liao* 也 *yeh^3* 不 *pu^4* 歇 *hsieh^1* 一 *i^2* 走 *tsou^3*
三 *san^1* 看 *k'an^4* 能 *nêng^2* 乏 *fa^2* 路 *lu^4* 海 *hai^3*
天 *t'ien^1* 不 *pu* 喝。*ho^1* 兒 *'rh* 真 *chên^1* 受 *shou^4*
的 *ti* 見 *chien^4* 連 *lien^2* 罷。*pa^4* 是 *shih^4* 了 *liao*

When you went to sea last year did you suffer any hardship?
Obs.—Went to sea: *lit.*, walked or travelled the sea.
It was truly misery the whole voyage.
Obs.—*Hsin^1* or *hsing^1* (Radical 160).
Rest a bit.
Obs.—*Pa* is here an invitation; *hsieh hsieh* alone or *hsieh cho* is equally admissible.
I cannot even drink tea.
There was (or is) not even a single man to be seen.
Rain fell for three days consecutively.
Obs.—Consecutively: *lit.*, one connexion; *i.e.*, without a break.

EXERCISE XV.

1. 算計道路的遠近,走遠路繞着走,走近道直。南北東西。坐船。過河。那船上的客不少。

   1. A straight road is the shortest; a winding road is longer (or, as to distance, the straight road there is the shortest). North, south, east, and west. To be on board a ship. To cross a river. There are a good many passengers on board that ship (or boat).

Obs. 1.—A straight road, etc.: *lit.*, if you reckon *(suan-chi)* the distance *(yüan-chin)* of a road, it is nearer to walk straight than to go by a circuitous route.
Obs. 2.—Note the order in which the Chinese enumerate the points of the compass.

2. 我們明天一早開船往南邊去。河裏的水沒有海水深。他是南邊人。

   2. We set sail the first thing to-morrow morning for the South. The water in the rivers is shallower than that of the sea. He is a southerner.

Obs. 1.—Set sail: *lit.*, open the boat; *q.d.*, let her loose from her moorings.
Obs. 2.—The first thing: *lit.*, the first early; the moment it is early.

3. 你去年進京的時候住在那兒。我住著一個客店。聽見說城外頭那客店有的好住的不好。那都看掌櫃的好不好。我看都好。乏了那兒都好。裏不過歇着罷了。

   3. When you went to Peking last year where did you live? I stopped at an inn. I have heard it said that the inns outside the city are some of them not very good to stay at. That is all according as the inn-keeper is a good or a bad one; in my opinion, when one is tired any place is good; all you go to an inn for is to rest yourself.

Obs.—All you go, etc.: *lit.*, [the object of] going to an inn [is] not more than to rest [or resting], and there an end.

4. 你愛走路愛坐車那是愛坐船那是看地方兒南邊沒有車走道兒的客人都是坐船走河路的都是小船兒走海的船大。

   4. Do you prefer travelling by cart or in a boat? That depends upon the country I am in; there are no carts in the South, and travellers all go by water. The vessels used in river-travelling are small; sea-going vessels are larger.

5 你　海　錯　船　邊　淺　人　不
　老　船　了　在　兒　我　辛
　前　不　累　是　上　們　苦
　年　是　不　大　擱　那　的
　坐　受　風、海、了　些　了。

5. In the voyage you made by sea, sir, the year before last, you had a hard time of it, hadn't you? I had; it blew hard, and the ship got ashore on the coast of Shantung; all of us who were on board suffered terribly.

Obs. 1.—Sir: *ni lao*, short for *ni lao hsien-shêng*. This abridged form is slightly less courteous than the longer address, but it is very commonly used. The student should bear in mind that the simple pronoun *ni³* is only used when addressing inferiors, or persons with whom the speaker is on intimate terms; *nin* is more frequently used in Peking than *ni lao*.

Obs. 2.—Hard time: *lit.*, you *shou*, were the recipient of, suffered, trouble.

Obs. 3.—Got ashore: *lit.*, [the wind, or some accident] put the ship on a shoal [place].

Obs. 4.—Dreadfully: *lit.*, we, those persons = I and the others there, were troubled infinitely. The adjective *hsing k'u* is verbalised by *ti*.

6 船　是　管　的　管　南　老
　上　甚　船　家　船　邊　大
　吃　麽　頭　管。兒　就
　飯　人　兒　也　的。叫
　　　叫　是

6. Who looks after the messing on board ship? The people of the ship look after it. The head man in a boat is called *kuan³-ch'uan²-'rh-ti*; in the South he is called *lao³-ta⁴* (*Anglicè*, lowdah).

Obs. 1.—The people of the ship: *ch'uan chia*; those who make *ch'uan*, the boat, *chia*, their home. *Yeh* implies that it is their business to look after the meals as well as other things.

Obs. 2.—Note *kuan³*, to look after (117).

7 你　車　錢　車　不　在　坐　幾　店
　算　貴。多。價　知　車　車　個　的
　計　坐　沒　比　道　店　那　錢　盤
　是　車　有　船　北　裏　攔　還　費
　坐　貴　車　價　邊　擱　着　有　沒
　船　那　比　還　的　着　的　天　算
　貴　兒　坐　貴　車　你　車　也
　花　有　船　呢。多　要　錢　要
　的　坐　貴　　是　　天　使
　　　　　　　　　　　兒
　　　　　　　　　　　住

7. Which do you consider costs most, travelling by water or travelling in a cart? One spends more travelling in a cart. Nonsense; how can a cart be dearer than a boat? You don't understand; most of the carts in the North are put up in the cart inns, and if you want to employ carts the inn-keeper must also make his squeeze; then there are the daily inn expenses *en route* which you have not taken into account.

Obs. 1.—One spends: *hua ti*, though commonly so pronounced, should be written *hua tê*, the construction being, literally, sitting in a cart compared with sitting in a ship, [one] *hua tê*, succeeds in expending (comes to spend), more money.

Obs. 2.—Nonsense: *lit.*, not existing talk; you talk about what does not exist.

Obs. 3.—Squeeze: the word *shih*, properly, to use, when placed as here means to use another's money, of course unfairly.

Obs. 4.—Travelling expenses: *p'an² fei¹*. *P'an* is, properly, a circular dish, bowl, or plate; it also means to travel backwards and forwards; to go to and fro, as when loading or unloading a vessel. *P'an fei* are therefore the expenses when travelling to and from a place; hence, travelling expenses generally.

PART III.—THE FORTY EXERCISES. 81

Turn the following into Chinese. (KEY, EXERCISE XV.)

1. At the present moment the capital is in the North and is called Peking. Several hundred years ago there was also a capital in the South; it was the city now called Nanking.

Obs. 1.—Present moment: *k'ê⁴ hsia⁴* (223).

Obs. 2.—Now: *lit.*, under the eye (Radical 109).

2. I went into the city with him. The road I went by was straight and very short; he went by a winding road, which was consequently very long.

Obs.—Consequently: *chiu*.

3. Rivers are of different sizes. The sea is bigger than a river. Rivers are not so deep as the sea.

4. *Ho² pie-'rh¹* (the bank of a river), *hai³ pie-'rh¹* (the sea-shore), both refer to the ground at the side of a river or of the sea. The water at the side is shallow, but everywhere in the middle it is very deep.

5. People who journey by water must go by boat. The ships one goes by on the sea are large; the boats which sail on rivers are all small.

6. In a journey by boat there is no necessity for putting up at an inn, but going by cart one must put up at an inn every day, which costs a lot of money. Estimating the cost of the two, one spends less money travelling by boat; the price of a boat, too, is less than that of a cart.

7. The *chang³-kuei⁴-ti* is the manager of a shop. In an inn there is also a *chang³-kuei⁴-ti*.

Obs.—Manager: *lit.*, the man who superintends or controls matters.

8. In my opinion, to go by boat and by cart are both good [ways of travelling]. In a boat the one thing one has to fear is a high wind; in a cart, heavy rain; in either case one will have a bad time of it. One year we were travelling in a cart, and while we were on the road the rain began to fall. During the whole journey we did not fall in with (*lit.*, there was not) even one man selling food; we were very distressed and dreadfully fatigued. Eventually we came to an inn, where we rested a night and recovered.

Obs.—The one thing, etc.: *chiu shih p'a*. Note this fresh use of *chiu*.

400. 李 *li³*, plums; but in the phrase *hsing²-li³*, baggage, corruptly used for some other character.

401. 箱 *hsiang¹*, a trunk; a box. Alone, it takes *tzŭ* after it.

402. 包 *pao¹*, a bundle *(pao¹-'rh)*. To make into a bundle, *pao¹ shang⁴ pao¹-'rh*, *pao¹ shang⁴*, or *pao¹ ch'i³ lai²*.

403. 袋 *tai⁴*, a bag; a purse. Commonly used with *k'ou³*, a mouth.

404. 氈, 毡, *chan¹*, felt or similar fabrics.

405. 毯 *t'an³*, a carpet or rug; as *mao² t'an³-tzŭ*, a woollen or hair carpet.

11

406. 布 *pu*⁴, cotton fabrics. Also, as will be seen later, to spread out; to arrange; to distribute.

407. Examples :—

毯	*t'an*³	口	*k'ou*³	地	*ti*⁴	來	*lai*²	包	*pao*¹	李	*li*³
子	*tzŭ*	袋	*tai*⁴	布	*pu*⁴	毡	*chan*¹	起	*ch'i*³	子	*tzŭ*
鋪	*p'u*¹	小	*hsiao*³	是	*shih*⁴	帽	*mao*⁴	這	*ché*⁴	皮	*p'i*²
在	*tsai*⁴	米	*mi*³	粗	*ts'u*¹	便	*p'ien*²	個	*ko*⁴	箱	*hsiang*¹
炕	*k'ang*⁴	兒	*'rh*	的	*ti*	宜	*i*²	衣	*i*¹	行	*hsing*²
上	*shang*⁴	把	*pa*³	三	*san*¹	本	*pén*³	裳	*shang*¹	李	*li*³

Plums.
A leathern box (portmanteau). Baggage.
Wrap up these clothes.
Obs.—Note *ché ko* with a plural word.
Felt caps are cheap.
Native cotton fabrics are coarse.
Obs.—Native: *lit.*, original, proper, or indigenous to, the locality.
Three bags of millet.
Spread the carpet on the *k'ang*.

408. 餧 *wei*⁴, to feed animals.

409. 駱 *lo*⁴, described in native dictionaries as a white horse with a black mane; conversationally, only used with the following.

410. 駝 *t'o*², the camel with two humps, known to us as the Bactrian camel, and commonly called *lo*⁴-*t'o*²; to carry on the back, as a beast a burden.
N.B.—Emphasise *lo*⁴.

411. 牲 *shéng*¹, cattle; beasts. Rarely used alone, and generally with *k'ou*, a mouth.

412. Examples :—

一	*i*⁴	他	*t'a*¹	得	*tei*³	牲	*shéng*¹	着	*cho*	那	*na*⁴	叫	*chiao*⁴
回	*hui*²	駱	*lo*⁴	好	*hao*³	口	*k'ou*	四	*ssŭ*⁴	一	*i*²	馬	*ma*³
毛	*mao*²	駝	*t'o*	好	*hao*¹	是	*shih*⁴	百	*pai*³	個	*ko*⁴	夫	*fu*¹
兒	*'rh*	一	*i*⁴	兒	*'rh*	長	*ch'ang*²	斤	*chin*¹	駱	*lo*⁴	來	*lai*²
		年	*nien*²	的	*ti*	騎	*ch'i*²	煤	*mei*²	駝	*t'o*	餧	*wei*⁴
		脫	*t'o*¹	餧	*wei*⁴	的	*ti*	這	*ché*⁴	駝	*t'o*²	馬	*ma*³

Tell the *ma-fu* to come and feed the horse.
Obs.—*Ma-fu*: *lit.*, horse man (239).
That camel has a load of 400 catties of coal.
This beast is constantly ridden; he must be well fed.
Camels cast their coats once a year.
Obs.—*Lit.*, camels one year put off one time wool.

PART III.—THE FORTY EXERCISES.

413. 跟 *kên*¹, the heel; hence, to follow, to accompany. It often takes the place of the preposition *with*; as *kên*¹ *wo*³ *ch'ü*⁴, go with me.

414. 班 *pan*¹, properly, any set of persons organised to act together, as a troop of players, a set of chair-bearers, a guard, etc. *Kên*¹-*pan*¹-*ti* or *kên*¹-*pa*¹-*'rh*-*ti*, the servant or servants of an official of rank; a general servant or valet is also called *hsia*⁴ *jên*² (*lit.*, under man). By common usage, *kên*¹-*pa*¹-*'rh*-*ti* is the term applied to the servants of foreigners in Peking; there are other terms for domestics, which will be met with later.

415. 裝 *chuang*¹, to put into; to contain.

416. 帶 *tai*⁴, a girdle (with *tzŭ*); to lead; to bring; also, as will be seen later, a stretch or strip of country, etc.

417. 馱 *to*⁴, a beast's load.

418. Examples:—

沒 *mei*²	那 *na*⁴	下 *hsia*⁴	去。*ch'ü*⁴	來。*lai*²	外 *wai*⁴	我 *wo*³
有。*yu*³	一 *i*⁴	那 *na*⁴	這 *chê*⁴	你 *ni*³	帶 *tai*⁴	的 *ti*
一 *i*⁴	隻 *chih*¹	麼 *mo*	個 *ko*⁴	跟 *kên*¹	了 *liao*	跟 *kên*¹
船 *ch'uan*²	多 *to*¹	箱 *hsiang*¹	我 *wo*³	一 *i*⁴	班 *pan*¹
裝 *chuang*¹	的 *ti*	子 *tzŭ*	上 *shang*⁴	匹 *p'i*¹	的 *ti*
好 *hao*³	東 *tung*¹	裝 *chuang*¹	衙 *ya*²	馬 *ma*³	打 *ta*³
了 *liao*	西。*hsi*¹	不 *pu*²	門 *mên*²	回 *hui*²	口 *k'ou*³

My servant has come back from beyond the frontier with a horse.
Obs.—*Ta*, here a preposition, from.
Go with me to the yamên.
This box won't hold all these things.
Obs.—Won't hold: *lit.*, put into not down.
Is that ship loaded yet? (Is the loading of it completed *(hao liao)*?)

419. 追 *chui*¹, to pursue; to follow up; to prosecute, as a claim or an inquiry. *Chui*¹ *shang*⁴, to overtake.

420. 趕 *kan*³, also to pursue. It appears to have much the same sense as the preceding, but also means to drive; as *kan*³ *ch'ê*¹, to drive a cart; *kan*³ *lü*², to drive a donkey.

421. 喚 *huan*⁴, to call aloud; commonly combined with *chiao*⁴, to call.

422. 無 *wu*², not to be; not to have. The opposite of *yu*³, to be; to have.

423. 利 li^4, commonly, profit; advantage. Properly, sharp-edged; hence, with the following character, hai^4, terrible, terribly.

424. 害 hai^4, harm; hurt. Also, to receive or suffer injury, etc.; as hai^4 $ping^4$, to get ill, to catch an illness; hai^4 $p'a^4$, to be afraid.

425. Examples:—

里 li^3	錯 $ts'o^4$	熱 $jé^4$	在 $tsai^4$	們 $mén^2$	車 $ch'é^1$	你 ni^3
無 wu^2	是 $shih^4$	得 $té$	那 na^4	趕 kan^3	的。ti	快 $k'uai^4$
雲。$yün^2$	無 wu^2	利 li^4	兒。'rh	快 $k'uai^4$	趕 kan^3	去 $ch'ü^4$
	心 $hsin^1$	害。hai^4	叫 $chiao^4$	些 $hsieh^1$	牛 niu^2	追 $chui^1$
	的。ti	他 $t'a^1$	喚。$huan^4$	兒。'rh	的。ti	他 $t'a^1$
	萬 wan^4	這 $ché^4$	天 $t'ien^1$	誰 $shui^2$	惜 tsa^2	趕 kan^3

Go after him quickly.
A carter. A herd-boy.
Let us get on quicker.
Who is calling (or crying) out there?
The day is terribly hot.
His error was unintentional.
Not a cloud all round.

426. Learn also the following:—

春 $ch'un^1$, spring.　　　　　　秋 $ch'iu^1$, autumn.

夏 $hsia^4$, summer.　　　　　　冬 $tung^1$, winter.

427. Examples:—

明 $ming^2$	去 $ch'ü^4$	來。lai^2	颳 kua^1	天 $t'ien^1$	夏 $hsia^4$	春 $ch'un^1$
年 $nien^2$	年 $nien^2$	冬 $tung^1$	起 $ch'i^3$	的 ti	天 $t'ien^1$	天 $t'ien^1$
冬 $tung^1$	夏 $hsia^4$	天 $t'ien^1$	涼 $liang^2$	時 $shih^2$	熱。$jé^4$	暖 $nuan^3$
天。$t'ien^1$	天。$t'ien^1$	冷。$léng^3$	風 $féng^1$	候 hou^4	秋 $ch'iu^1$	和。huo

Spring is warm.
Summer is hot.
In autumn cool breezes begin to blow.
Winter is cold.
Last summer.
Next winter.

PART III.—THE FORTY EXERCISES.   85

EXERCISE XVI.

那馱子太重
一個牲口駄
不了。這些東
西不好帶。這
人帶的東西
箱子做的有
皮子做的
拏氈子把
他是甚麼
零碎東西
装
道兒上
那口袋
帶了來你
做甚麼装

好帶了。
在箱子裏就
是甚麼話裝
西不好帶
行李是走
包上包兒
包起來了
得餵牲口。
到店裏就

1

2

3

4

1. That is too heavy a load; one animal cannot carry it. It will be difficult to carry all these things. What are you talking about? pack them in a box and you can carry them easily enough.

2. The expression *hsing-li* comprises whatever a traveller carries with him. Trunks are made, some of leather, some of wood, and will hold all sorts of things.

3. *Pao¹ shang pao¹-'rh* (to make a bundle) is to wrap up things in anything. He has wrapped up that small box in a rug.

4. What have you brought that bag for? To put odds and ends into. On a journey the beasts have to be fed as soon as one arrives at an inn.

Obs.—Note the force of *chiu*, as soon as; *lit.*, arriving at an inn one must then and there *(chiu)* feed the animals.

不了城了。
兒起身怕趕
走。要不齊快點就
子都行李駄
心着來的
外來的你小
駱駝都是口
5

5. Camels all come from beyond the frontier. Take care of the baggage; when the packages are all there, we will start. If we don't get off quickly, I am afraid we sha'n't save the gates.

Obs. 1.—All there: *lit.*, if the baggage be all *ch'i*, complete (Radical 210).
Obs. 2.—Get off, start: *lit.*, raise the body; *q.d.*, to be on the move.
Obs. 3.—Save the gates: *lit.*, shall not catch up the city wall; *i.e.*, shall not reach the city in time to get in before the gates are shut.

6. 跟 使 他 的 裝 車 趕
班 喚 叫 把 在 走 不
的 的 跟 箱 車 了。上
是 人。班 子 上、他 了。

6. The *kên¹-pan¹* are they who take orders (your servants). He ordered a servant to put his box (or boxes) into the cart (or carts), but the cart had started and he could not catch it up.

Obs. 1.—In southern "mandarin" an individual servant is spoken of as a *kên-pan*; in Peking as *kên-pan-ti*, or oftener, *kên-pa-'rh-ti*.

Obs. 2.—Take orders: *lit.*, are those whom [one] sends and calls.

7. 性 駝 西 騾 子 說。
口 着 就 驢 說 子
身 的 叫 馱 得 可
上 東 子、子 馬 不
馱 都 馱 大

7. The things which a beast bears on its back are called a *to⁴-tzŭ*. One may speak of an ass or a mule *to⁴-tzŭ*, but seldom of a horse *to⁴-tzŭ*.

8. 我 的 後 了 趕 的 可 是
出 跟 頭 半 上 看 不 追
門 班 道 天 我 見 知 我
去、的 我 也 老 他 道 呢。
他 在 追 沒 遠 跑、他

8. After I had gone out his servant came after me, but though he pursued me for a good while he did not overtake me; I did see him at a great distance running, but I did not know he was after me.

Obs. 1.—A good while: *lit.*, half the day.

Obs. 2.—A great distance: *lao*, old, is sometimes used as an adverb of intensity; you can say also *lao³ tsao³ ti*, very early.

9. 那 呢。快 怕 論 上、他
個 他 跑 趕 你 就
人 可 他 不 快 是
在 以 早 上 跑 了。
那 走 罷。趕 着
兒 得 無 不 追

9. Where is that man? He has gone out; if you run fast [enough] you will be able to overtake him. He is gone some time (*lit.*, early); I fear it will not be possible to overtake him. Whether he is to be overtaken or not, you just run after him as hard as you can.

Obs. 1.—Fast enough: *lit.*, running quickly you will be able to achieve coming up with him.

Obs. 2.—As hard as you can: *lit.*, quick running pursue [him], then it will be right (or well).

PART III.—THE FORTY EXERCISES. 87

Turn the following into Chinese. (KEY, EXERCISE XVI.)

1. Everyone, no matter who, when going on a journey must take baggage with him.

2. The cart will soon be here; get your luggage and boxes ready. The bundle of clothes and the bag have still to be made up.

Obs.—Get ready: ta^3 $tien^3$ (*lit.*, beat and point); to arrange and check off. $Tien^3$, short for $tien^3$ shu-$'rh$, to count or check the number.

3. The carpet on the floor of this room is dusty, it must be taken out and beaten; the table-cloth is very dirty, too, and will have to be washed.

Obs.—Is dusty: *yu liao t'u liao*. Note the repetition of the particle *liao*, which does not here mark the past tense, but is simply a final expletive.

4. Tell the *ma-fu* to feed the animals. I am going out in a little while, and I don't want anybody with me; tell my boy to pack up the things I am taking with me.

Obs. 1.—Feed the beasts: *pa shêng-k'ou wei shang*; *shang* signifying the completion of the act. *Wei shêng-k'ou* would be equally correct.

Obs. 2.—With: *kên*.

5. For carrying things about with one animals are always used in the North; they are called to^4-$tzŭ$. There are donkey to^4-$tzŭ$ and mule to^4-$tzŭ$; a camel's [load] may also be called a to^4-$tzŭ$. $T'o^2$-$chiao^4$ (a litter) is a $chiao^4$-$tzŭ$ (sedan-chair) carried by mules.

6. You walk so quickly I cannot keep up with you.

Obs. 1.—So: *lit.*, this kind or fashion.

Obs. 2.—Not keep up: *lit.*, follow not up.

7. He has not been gone out long; hurry after him and tell him I have some more things to give him to take.

Obs.—Long: not a great *kung-fu*, while.

8. I have a small matter I want to employ you on: go to him and borrow a little money for me; no matter whether he says he has or has not got any, you must positively get a small loan for me.

Obs. 1.—A little money: *lia ch'ien-'rh*; *lit.*, two cash.

Obs. 2.—For me: this is indicated here by the verb *lai*, to come.

9. He is a dreadful fellow.

Obs.—*Hao*, good, is often used as a substitute for *hên*, very.

10. Summer is dreadfully hot; winter is terribly cold; these are expressions for great heat and great cold. The seasons when it is neither hot nor cold are spring and autumn.

Obs.—Expressions: *hua t'ou-'rh*; *lit.*, heads of talk.

428. 腦 nao^3, the brains, when used with $tzŭ$; when followed by tai^4, a bag, it means the head, but, with the exception of the human head, the term nao^3 tai^4 is only used for the heads of animals whose names are composed of more than one word, as lao^2 hu^3, a tiger, etc.

429. 辮 $pien^4$, the pigtail or queue worn by the Chinese.

430. 朵 to^3, a bud; the lobe of the ear.

431. 眼 yen^3, the eye; often used with the following; the numerative of wells.

432. 睛 $ching^1$, the pupil of the eye.

433. 嘴 $tsui^3$, the mouth.

434. 脣 $ch'un^2$, the lips.

435. 鬍 hu^2, the beard or moustache.

436. Examples:—

的 ti	嘴 tsui³	唇 ch'un²	隻 chih¹	的 ti	髮 fa	大 ta⁴
飯 fan⁴	裡 li³	上 shang⁴	眼 yen³	耳 êrh³	打 ta³	腦 nao³
不 pu⁴	說 shuo¹	的 ti	睛 ching¹	朵 to³	一 i⁴	袋 tai⁴
要 yao⁴	好 hao³	鬍 hu²	打 ta³	聽 t'ing¹	條 t'iao²	梳 shu¹
說 shuo¹	話 hua⁴	子 tzŭ	辮 pien⁴	不 pu⁴	辮 pien⁴	好 hao³
話 hua⁴	滿 man³	短 tuan³	子 tzŭ	真 chên¹	子 tzŭ	了 liao
	嘴 tsui³	他 t'a¹	嘴 tsui³	一 i⁴	他 t'a¹	頭 t'ou²

A big head.
When you have combed your hair well, do it into a pigtail. *See* **241**.
His ear is incorrect; or, he does not hear distinctly.
One eye.
To plait the queue.
The hair on the lip is short.
He speaks fair.
Don't speak with your mouth full.

437. 胳 ko¹, kê¹, properly, the armpit; not used alone.

438. 臂 pei⁴, the arm in general.

439. 指 chih³, the finger; to point to; to point out; to point at. *Chih²-t'ou*, the finger or toe. Note the change of tone.

440. 甲 chia³, the nails. *Chih¹-chia³*, the nails, whether of the hand or foot. Note the tone of *chih*, which must be emphasised.

441. 腰 yao¹, the loins; the waist.

442. 腿 t'ui³, the thigh; the legs.

443. Examples:—

短 tuan³	乏 fa²	有 yu³	看 k'an⁴	用 yung⁴	粗 ts'u¹	那 na⁴
拿 na²	了 liao	兩 liang³	腰 yao¹	指 chih²	你 ni³	個 ko⁴
不 pu⁴	我 wo³	條 t'iao²	裡 li³	頭 t'ou²	的 ti	人 jên²
著 chao²	的 ti	腿 t'ui³	有 yu³	指 chih³	指 chih¹	的 ti
他 t'a¹	胳 ko¹	都 tou¹	錢 ch'ien²	給 kei³	甲 chia³	胳 ko¹
	臂 pei⁴	走 tsou³	沒 mei²	我 wo³	快 k'uai⁴	臂 pei⁴

That man's arm is thick.
Your nails are sharp.
Point it out to me with your finger.
Have you any money in your waistbelt?
Obs.—Lit., in your waist; a Chinaman's purse is attached to his girdle.
Both my legs are tired out with walking.
My arm is short; I cannot get hold of him.

444. 結 chieh², to knot, bind, or collect together; hence, to conclude, to finish. When used with the following as an adjective, it means substantial, strong, or vigorous, and is pronounced *chieh¹-shih¹*.

N.B.—The *chieh* must be emphasised.

445. 實 *shih*[2], true; sound; solid, as opposed to hollow. *Shih*[2] *tsai*[4], in reality; truly; really.

446. 輭 *juan*[3], soft.

447. 弱 *jo*[4], weak.

448. 抓 *chua*[1], to catch or claw hold of, as a man with his hand, or a bird with its talons; to clutch.

449. 拉 *la*[1], to pull; to drag.

450. 搋 *chuai*[4], to haul at. The dictionaries give a different sound to this character, but the colloquial pronunciation is as above.

451. Examples:—

住	*chu*[4]	拉	*la*[1]	過	*kuo*[4]	拽	*chuai*[4]	結	*chieh*[1]	弱	*jo*[4]	我	*wo*[3]
我	*wo*[3]	破	*p'o*[4]	來	*lai*[2]	住	*chu*[4]	實	*shih*	沒	*mei*[2]	的	*ti*
的	*ti*	了	*liao*	不	*pu*[2]	罷	*pa*[4]	馬	*ma*[3]	有	*yu*[3]	身	*shên*[1]
手	*shou*[3]	衣	*i*[1]	要	*yao*[4]	把	*pa*[3]	要	*yao*[4]	去	*ch'ü*[4]	子	*tzŭ*
了	*liao*	裳	*shang*[1]	拉	*la*[1]	桌	*cho*[1]	跑	*p'ao*[3]	年	*nien*[2]	今	*chin*[1]
		他	*t'a*[1]	他	*t'a*[1]	子	*tzŭ*	把	*pa*[3]	那	*na*[4]	年	*nien*[2]
		抓	*chua*[1]	怕	*p'a*[4]	拉	*la*[1]	他	*t'a*[1]	麽	*mo*	輭	*juan*[3]

I am weak this year; not so strong as I was last year.
The horse is going to bolt; hold on to him.
Haul that table over.
Don't drag him, or you may tear his clothes.
He grasped me by the hand.

452. 病 *ping*[4], illness; disease.

453. 疼 *t'êng*[2], pain, whether from wound or sickness; intensity of kindly feeling. *T'êng ai*[4], tender love, or to love tenderly.

454. 奇 *ch'i*[2], strange (in a good sense).

455. 怪 *kuai*[4], monstrous; strange (in a bad sense). Often used with the foregoing. *Kuai*[4] can also be used verbally; to take offence at; to be astonished at.

456. 怎 *tsên*[3], how? what? In Peking never met with colloquially except when followed by *mo*[1] (23), and then the final *n* is not heard, the dissyllable being pronounced *tsêm*[3]-*mo*, with the emphasis on the first syllable.

457. Examples:—

這	*chê*[4]	奇	*ch'i*[2]	疼	*t'êng*[2]	怪	*kuai*[4]	疼	*t'êng*[2]	我	*wo*[3]
是	*shih*[4]	怪	*kuai*[4]	嘴	*tsui*[3]	不	*pu*[4]	的	*ti*	病	*ping*[4]
怎	*tsên*[3]	不	*pu*[4]	乾	*kan*[1]	得	*tê*[2]	了	*liao*[3]	得	*tê*
麽	*mo*	奇	*ch'i*[2]	你	*ni*[3]	你	*ni*[3]	不	*pu*[4]	利	*li*[4]
了	*liao*	怪	*kuai*[4]	說	*shuo*[1]	頭	*t'ou*[2]	得	*tê*[2]	害	*hai*[4]

I am terribly ill.
I am in awful pain.
No wonder your head is sore and your mouth dry.
Obs.—No wonder: *lit.*, [you] astonished not can [be] that, etc.
Don't you think it strange?
How is this? or, how did this come about?

EXERCISE XVII.

看聽人辮腦有 1
不不老子袋人
真真了得你的
。。耳梳這頭
　　朵了個裏
　　　　。　頭

1. A man's *t'ou*[2] has *nao*[3]-*tzŭ* (brains) inside it, and is accordingly called *nao*[3]-*tai*[4] (his brain bag). Your queue must be combed. When a man is old he can neither hear well (*lit.*, truly) with his ears nor see clearly (distinctly) with his eyes.

2. That man has a very odd-looking countenance. I am too fond of this horse to let him tire himself.

Obs.—Countenance: *lit.*, that man's nose and eyes=his face, growing has attained to singularity. In this and similar combinations, *chang*[3], to grow, must generally be construed *is*; much as we say is turning out, or, has turned out.

3. This man is very strong (sound); that man is very feeble. Native cloth is very strong. This seat is very soft (or comfortable).

Obs. 1.—Strong: note that *chieh*[1] must be strongly emphasised.
Obs. 2.—Note *tso*[4]-*'rh*, a seat; there is another form of the character.
Obs. 3.—*Juan*[3]-*huo*[4]: *lit.*, soft and comfortable. Cf. *nuan*[3]-*huo*[4], warm.

4. Have you anything the matter with you? No, I am not ill; only weak. I really cannot manage (or, look after) this matter. How can I possibly look after (or control) so many men?

5. This horse is very quiet; won't you buy him? (or, you had better buy him). He looks quiet enough, but you feed him up for a few days, and then see; were you to ride him I doubt if you could hold him.

Obs.—Quiet: *lit.*, old and sound, sincere, or honest; the term is applied to men as well as animals.

6. 佾們這五六年沒有見你的鬍子都白了。是我這幾年病得利害。連家裏的人都不認得我。

7. 道兒上躺着的那個人，兩腿都破了。腰上有病，直不起來。我的指頭疼。

8. 你這麼慢有病麼。身上不是，是人老了。腰腿都輭了。這個麼事我實在做不來。

9. 他的舌頭有病連嘴唇子都破了。那女人的指甲那麼長把他的胳臂抓破了。

10. 你這麼拽着我，是有甚麼事麼。要沒事這麼拉拉拽拽的是甚麼樣子呢。有話直說就是了。

6. In these five or six years that you and I have not met your beard has turned quite white. That's because I have been sadly ailing for some years; even my own family don't recognise me.

7. That man who is lying on the road has both his legs injured (or ulcerated). To have something the matter with the back (loins) that makes it impossible to stand upright (or, straighten oneself). My finger is sore (or, pains me).

8 Do you walk so slowly because you have something the matter with you? No, it is age which makes me weak both in the back and limbs. I really cannot do this.

9. There is something the matter with his tongue, and both it and his lips have broken out. That woman's nails were so long that when she clutched hold of his arm they tore it.

10. Why do you drag at me like that? it is not seemly (*lit.*, what fashion is it?) to claw me so for no reason. [If] you have anything to say, just say it out straight.

Obs.—For no reason: *lit.*, if (*yao* for *jo*) you have no business, thus to drag drag, clutch clutch, is what fashion? There being talk straight speak, then it will do.

Turn the following into Chinese. (Key, Exercise XVII.)

1. How can anyone go and speak to him about this matter? Why are you so weak? After all the man has only one head (*i.e.*, is much the same as anyone else), what are you afraid of him for?

Obs. 1.—How can, etc.: *lit.*, this matter cause men how go with him speak.

Obs. 2.—After all: *lit.*, also not more.

Obs. 3.—What for: *tso shên-mo*.

2. When a man comes to be old, he breaks down in every way; his ears do not hear distinctly, his eyes do not see true, and in speaking his lips even are of no use.

Obs.—Breaks down in every way: *yang yang-'rh tou pu hsing*; *lit.*, kind kind all not work, move, or act. Note the plurality obtained by repetition: *yang yang-'rh*, each or every kind; *jên jên-'rh*, each or every man. It must be remembered, however, that only certain substantives form the adjective pronoun *each* or *every* by duplication. We could not say, for instance, *cho cho*, every table; *i i*, every chair.

Obs. 2.—No use: *pu chung yung*, do not fulfil, or accomplish, use. *See* 303.

3. In spring the weather is too dry; my lips are liable to chap.

Obs. 1.—Weather: *see* 232.

Obs. 2.—Liable: this is frequently rendered by *ai*, to love, to be prone to.

4. With so little hair as this to make a pigtail! why! it appears to me it isn't so long as a man's beard.

5. Look what a long beard he has!

6. Don't pull me about like that, your nails are long; to spoil them would be a misfortune, and to scratch my arm would be equally so.

7. There is something the matter with his legs; in walking he drags them after him in great pain.

8. He appears to me to be just at the age when a man is strong; how is it that he is so weak?

Obs.—When a man is strong: *lit.*, the time when he has strength (*li*⁴) and breath (*ch'i*⁴).

9. Do you mean to say that if you haul and pull at a man in such a weak condition as this you can't pull him over on his back?

Obs.—*Lit.*, this kind of weak man; *lien*, together with, hauling, *tai*, and, clutching do you still fear not to pull him recumbent? Note the use of *lien* and *tai* as conjunctions.

10. I saw a man to-day with a very queer countenance.

Obs.—Countenance: *lit.*, face (*mien*) and eyes (*mu*).

458. 眉 *mei*², eyebrows.

459. 鬢 *pin*⁴, the hair on the temples.

460. 顋 *sai*¹, the jaws; probably, inside the cheek. Generally combined with the following.

461. 頰 *chia*⁴, *chieh*⁴, the jaws; probably, the cheek on the outside.

462. 巴 *pa*¹, the name of a place; used corruptly as part of the combination *hsia*⁴-*pa*¹, the chin.

463. 頦 *k'o*¹, the lower part of the face; colloquially, only used with the foregoing, with which it is identical.

464. Examples:—

喝 *ho*¹	顋 *sai*¹	得 *tê*	鬍 *hu*²	巴 *pa*¹	顋 *sai*¹	眉 *mei*²
了 *liao*	就 *chiu*⁴	很 *hên*³	子 *tzŭ*	頦 *k'o*¹	頰 *chieh*⁴	毛 *mao*²
酒 *chiu*³	知 *chih*¹	看 *k'an*⁴	眉 *mei*²	兒 *'rh*	下 *hsia*⁴	鬢 *pin*⁴
了。*liao*	道 *tao*⁴	他 *t'a*¹	毛 *mao*²	連 *lien*²	巴。*pa*¹	角 *chiao*³
	他 *t'a*¹	兩 *liang*³	長 *ch'ang*²	鬢 *pin*⁴	下 *hsia*⁴	兒 *'rh*

PART III.—THE FORTY EXERCISES. 93

Eyebrows. The hair on the temples.
The cheeks. The chin. The chin.
Whiskers. Very long eyebrows.
Look at his cheeks and you will see that he has been drinking.

465. 脖 po^2, the neck.

466. 嗓 $sang^3$, the throat, within and without.

467. 節 $chieh^2$, joints, of the bones, the bamboo, etc.

468. 剃 $t'i^4$, to shave; used only of shaving the head.

469. 刮 kua^1, to scrape with a knife; to scrape the hair off an animal's skin. Kua^1 $lien^3$, to shave the face.

470. Examples:—

幾 chi^3	兒。$'rh$	竹 chu^2	頭 $t'ou^2$	不 pu^2	子 $tzŭ$	他 $t'a^1$
回 hui^2	你 ni^3	子 $tzŭ$	節 $chieh^2$	要 yao^4	疼。$t'êng^2$	的 ti
頭。$t'ou^2$	一 i^2	有 yu^3	兒。$'rh$	這 $ch\acute{e}^4$	說 $shuo^1$	脖 po^2
刮 kua^1	個 ko^4	多 to^1	這 $ch\acute{e}^4$	麼 mo	話 hua^4	子 $tzŭ$
臉。$lien^3$	月 $y\ddot{u}eh^4$	少 $shao^3$	一 i^4	大。ta^4	嗓 $sang^3$	長。$ch'ang^2$
	剃 $t'i^4$	節 $chieh^2$	桿 kan^3	骨 ku^2	子 $tzŭ$	嗓 $sang^3$

His neck is long.
My throat is sore.
Don't speak so loudly.
Obs.—*Pu yao chê mo ta sang-tzŭ shuo hua* would be equally correct.
Joints of the bones.
How many joints has this bamboo?
Obs.—*Chu* has another numerative, *kên*¹, which will be met with later.
How many times a month do you shave your head?
Obs.—Note that $t'i^4$ can only be used of shaving the head.
To shave the face.

471. 胸 $hsiung^1$, the breast; in Peking, commonly called $hsiung^1$ $p'u^2$-$tz\check{u}$. There is no recognised character for $p'u$, but the following is generally used, though its proper pronunciation is fu^3.

472. 脯 fu^3, $p'u^2$.

473. 背 pei^4, the back. Pei^1, to carry on the back.

474. 脊 chi^3, the spine.

475. 梁 $niang^2$, the spine; properly read $liang^2$, a horizontal beam. Note, chi^2-$niang^2$, the backbone, emphasising chi^2.

476. 膀 $pang^3$, the shoulders; seldom used alone.

477. 肚 tu^4, the belly. Tu^3, the entrails; used only of the entrails of animals.

478. Examples:—

肚 tu⁴	肩 chien¹	脊 chi²	麼 mo	你 ni³	站 chan⁴	胸 hsiung¹
子。tzŭ	膀 pang³	梁。niang²	東 tung¹	背 pei⁴	在 tsai⁴	脯 p'u²
指 chih²	兒。'rh	脊 chi²	西 hsi¹	上 shang⁴	我 wo³	子 tzŭ
頭 t'ou²	肚 tu⁴	梁 niang²	椅 i³	背 pei¹	的 ti	疼 t'êng²
肚 tu⁴	子。tzŭ	背 pei⁴	背 pei⁴	著 cho¹	背 pei¹	不 pu²
兒。'rh	腿 t'ui³	兒。'rh	兒。'rh	甚 shên²	後。hou⁴	要 yao⁴

My chest is sore.
Don't stand behind my back.
What are you carrying on your back?
The back of a chair.
The spine. The back between and below the shoulders.
The shoulders   The belly.
The calf of the leg.   The fleshy tip of the finger.
Obs.—The thigh is ta⁴-t'ui³.

479. 波 po¹, waves. Shui³ po¹, a ripple on the water.

480. 棱, 楞, lêng², an edge; both forms are admissible.

481. 脚, 腳, chiao³, the feet; the first form is the commoner.

482. 踝 huai², the ankle; colloquially, used only in the combination huai²-tzŭ ku³, ankle-bone (or ankle).

483. 體 t'i³, the body. With mien⁴, the face (Radical 176), the combination means respectable; very commonly also, of persons and things, nice-looking.

484. 斬 chan³, to behead.

485. 賊 tsei², robbers; rebels; any malefactors.

486. 級 chi², a step in gradation; the heads of criminals when cut off.

487. Examples:—

袋。tai⁴	斬 chan³	面 mien⁴	了。liao	骨 ku³	波 po¹
長 ch'ang²	下 hsia⁴	的 ti	他 t'a¹	兩 liang³	棱 lêng²
毛 mao²	來 lai²	人。jên²	是 shih⁴	脚 chiao³	蓋 kai⁴
賊 tsei²	的 ti	首 shou³	個 ko⁴	都 tou¹	兒。'rh
老 lao³	賊 tsei²	級 chi²	很 hên³	走 tsou³	踝 huai²
賊。tsei²	腦 nao³	是 shih⁴	體 t'i³	疼 t'êng²	子 tzŭ

The knee-cap.   The ankle-bone (or ankle).
I have walked till both my feet are sore.
He is a most respectable man.
Shou³-chi² is the head of a malefactor when cut off.
The long-haired rebels.   An old thief.

PART III.—THE FORTY EXERCISES. 95

EXERCISE XVIII.

女 我 個 有 了 愛 年 1
人 要 剃 鬍 四 刮 輕
們 打 頭 子 十 臉、 的
梳 辮 的 了。 多 人 人
頭 子。 來、 叫 就 到 多

1. Most young men are in the habit of shaving their faces; when men get to forty or upwards they have beards. Send for a barber; I want my hair dressed. Women comb (or dress) the hair.

Obs. 1.—Most: note that *to* does not mean all, but the greater part.
Obs. 2.—*Shu t'ou* is only applied to the female *coiffure*.

叫 的 年 頭 以 是 剃 2
長 那 不 髮 外 那 頭、
髮 賊 剃 前 的 辮 剃
賊 就 頭 些 子 的
短

2. In the [Chinese] tonsure, what is shaved off is the short hair growing outside the pigtail. Some years ago the outlaws who did not shave the head were called long-haired rebels.

Obs.—Outside: *i wai.* One of the senses of *i* is to follow, hence with words indicating place it means in the direction of; thus, *i tung,* to the east of; *i wai,* outside of. The sentence literally construed is, shaving the head, that which is shaved is the queue towards outside short hair.

剃 長 面 他 個 是 說 3
頭 得 是 長 好 說 人
鋪。 好 說 得 人, 他 體
看。 他 體 說 是 面
體 是

3. When you say a man is *t'i³-mien⁴* you mean that he is a person of good character; when you say that such a person is *chang³ té t'i³-mien⁴* you mean that he is good-looking. A barber's shop.

剃 都 頭 說 體 子 他 4
頭 是 刮 得 面 蓋 那
刀。 用 臉 剃 也 得 屋

4. You can also say that that house of so-and-so's is *t'i³-mien⁴* (that it is erected, *kai⁴,* in a respectable way). The *t'i⁴-t'ou²-tao⁴* (razor) is used both for shaving the head and the face.

Obs.—You cannot say *kua-lien-tao.*

吊 學 他 了 用 和 剃 我 5
了。 問 肚 我 胰 水 頭 們
他 子 背 子 兒 不 本
上 裏 你 你 也 使 地
了 有 罷。 乏 不 溫 人

5. We natives use neither warm water nor soap in shaving the head. If you are tired I'll carry you on my back. He is a man of learning. He has hanged himself.

Obs. 1.—Note *hsio²-wên,* learning; the *hsio²* must be emphasised. The stomach is held by the Chinese to be the seat of intelligence.
Obs. 2.—*Shang tiao* (322) can only be used of suicide by hanging.

明 幾 方 6
天 個 官
那 斬 要
地 賊 斬
斬 聽 賊

見 的 刀 不 是
說 那 不 過 了。
斬 一 很 重
賊 把 快、 就

你 兒 黃。 叫 打 下
鼻 上 麼 我 了 兒。
梁 怎 這 昨 人 一
麼 是 兒 家

四 東 四 個 刀 可
方 西 楞 角 楞 不
的 有 有 兒、 兒。 說。
楞 四 個 兒。

6. The local authorities are going to behead several rebels (or malefactors) tomorrow; I am told that the sword with which criminals are beheaded is not very sharp, only heavy.

7. How is it that the bridge of your nose is so yellow? Because someone hit me [there] yesterday.

Obs.—Hit: *lit.*, was hit by someone one blow. *Hsia: lit.*, a fall; *sc.*, a fall of the hand.

8. Square things have four edges (*lêng²*) and four corners (*chiao³*); but [you can] not say *tao¹ lêng²-'rh* (the edge of a knife).

Turn the following into Chinese. (KEY, EXERCISE XVIII.)

1. How pretty that little girl belonging to the LI family has grown up to be; have you seen her?

Obs.—Girls are often called *ch'ien chin* (thousand [pieces of] gold), especially when speaking of them to their own parents.

2. Yes, I have seen her. She has heavy eyebrows, big eyes, and a high bridge to her nose; her hair on either temple is both black and bright; she has a fine skin, too, on her cheeks, a small chin, long neck, and slender waist, while she speaks out very distinctly; her foot also are not large, nor her figure clumsy; she is indeed [pretty], and no mistake.

Obs. 1.—Both : *yü* (Radical 29).
Obs. 2.—Figure : *lit.*, body and form, *shên¹ t'i³*.
Obs. 3.—Is indeed : *kuo³ chên¹*, in very truth.

3. Is it because he is ill that every bone in his body aches? No; it is because he is old and has not sufficient vitality.

Obs. 1.—Body: *man³ shên*; *lit.*, full body of *ku-t'ou*, bones, *t'êng*, that ache.
Obs. 2.—Vitality : *lit.*, breath and blood, *ch'i hsüeh*.

4. To get the head or the face shaved one must send for a barber.

5. For a man's *hsiung¹-ch'ien²* (breast) and *pei⁴-hou⁴* (back) the expressions *ch'ien²-hsin¹* and *hou⁴-hsin¹* may be used.

6. The bag contains heavy articles and will have to be carried on the back, or it may be placed on the shoulders.

7. What is the matter with you? your face has a bad colour. Are you lying down there because you have a stomach-ache?

Obs. 1.—What is the matter : *lit.*, you how? *ni tsêm³-mo liao*.
Obs. 2.—Colour; *lit.*, aspect colour, *ch'i sê⁴*. See **232**.

8. It is not my stomach that aches; it is the ankle-bone of this foot, which a boy hit with a stone. Both it and my knee are dreadfully painful.

Obs.—Boy: *lit.*, small man. There is another expression for a boy or child, which will be met with later.

9. There are a whole lot of men's heads hanging up outside the city gate. A man told me they were, every one of them, the heads of criminals who had been decapitated.

Obs.—Hanging : *tiao⁴; see* **322**. There is another expression for to hang.

PART III.—THE FORTY EXERCISES.

488. 君 *chün*¹, the Sovereign.

489. 民 *min*², the people, as distinguished from their governors.

490. 主 *chu*³, a master. *Chün*¹ *chu*³, the term adopted in the British Treaty to designate Her Majesty the Queen.

491. 爵 *chio*², *chüeh*², *chiao*², high rank, whether official or hereditary.

492. 位 *wei*⁴, properly, the position of a person, the place where he stands or sits. Specially, high position; hence, the numerative of gentlemen, scholars, and officials, also of cannon.

493. 參 *ts'an*¹, to counsel. When combined with *jên*², a man, read *shên*¹; as *jên*²-*shên*¹, ginseng. Also read *ts'ên*¹ (see **576**).

494. 贊 *tsan*⁴, to assist; as *ts'an*¹-*tsan*⁴, to aid with counsel and advice. Also, an official title. See Examples.

495. 尊 *tsun*¹, honoured.

496. Examples :—

這 *chê*⁴	贊 *tsan*⁴	是 *shih*⁴	他 *t'a*¹	主 *chu*³	民 *min*²	君 *chün*¹
一 *i*²	他 *t'a*¹	個 *ko*⁴	的 *ti*¹	子 *tzŭ*	人 *jên*²	上 *shang*⁴
位 *wei*⁴	是 *shih*⁴	甚 *shên*²	爵 *chio*²	家 *chia*¹	那 *na*⁴	小 *hsiao*³
是 *shih*⁴	個 *ko*⁴	麽 *mo*	位 *wei*⁴	主 *chu*³	是 *shih*⁴	民 *min*²
誰 *shui*²	尊 *tsun*¹	爵 *chio*²	尊 *tsun*¹	兒 *'rh*	個 *ko*⁴	他 *t'a*¹
	重 *chung*⁴	位 *wei*⁴	貴 *kuei*⁴	船 *ch'uan*²	民 *min*²	是 *shih*⁴
	人 *jên*²	參 *ts'an*¹	他 *t'a*¹	主 *chu*³	房 *fang*²	個 *ko*⁴

The Sovereign. The people.

He is a man of the people.

Obs.—*Min jên* in general conversation is the designation applied to Chinese as distinguished from Tartars. In places in the provinces where there is no Tartar colony *min jên* may mean a private individual with no official rank or status; in Peking he is called *pai*² *jên*²-*'rh*, *lit.*, a white man.

That is an ordinary dwelling-house.

Obs.—*Min fang*, in Peking, is a house which is the property of a private individual, as opposed to *kuan fang*, Government property.

The lord or master. The master of the house.

The captain of a ship.

His official position is honourable.

What rank has he?

Obs.—If *wei* were omitted the question would be understood of hereditary rank only.

The Assistant Resident in certain Chinese colonies. (Used by us as the term for diplomatic secretaries.)

He is an honourable man.

Obs.—*Lit.*, honourable and important.

Who is this gentleman?

497. 文 wén² (Radical 67), civilian, as opposed to the following.

498. 武 wu³, military.

499. 兵 ping¹, soldier.

500. 缺 ch'üeh¹, to vacate; a vacancy; hence, in certain contexts, any official post. It also means short, or deficient.

501. 額 ngê², ngo², properly, the forehead; colloquially, as well as in writing, a fixed number.

502. 捐 chüan¹, to subscribe for a public purpose.

503. 充 ch'ung¹, to stand for; to stand in the place of; to act as; to play the part of. Often used with tang¹ (**342**). Also, to make up, as a number.

504. Examples:—

額 ngo²	開 k'ai¹	過 kuo⁴	出 ch'u¹	當 tang¹	文 wén²
數。shu⁴	缺 ch'üeh¹	兵 ping¹	兵。ping¹	兵。ping¹	官 kuan¹
捐 chüan¹	補 pu³	沒 mei²	你 ni³	充 ch'ung¹	武 wu³
官。kuan¹	缺 ch'üeh¹	有。yu³	出 ch'u¹	兵。ping¹	官 kuan¹

Civil officials. Military officials.
To be a soldier. To be a soldier.
To go on a military expedition.
Have you been on active service?
To remove from office for sickness or misconduct; or, to vacate a post.
To fill, or succeed to, a vacancy.
A given number.
To purchase a grade of rank by subscribing to the State's necessities.

505. 殺 sha¹, to kill; also, adverbially, an intensive.

506. 退 t'ui⁴, to retire; to drive back.

507. 勒 lo⁴, to bind; to coerce. In combination read lê², as lê²-so³, to squeeze; to extort money. Lei¹, to hold in, as a horse; also, in combination, to strangle, as will be seen later.

508. 索 so³, to demand; to extort.

509. Examples:—

把 pa³	捐 chüan¹	子。tzŭ	人 jên²	退 t'ui⁴	人 jên²	店 tien⁴
馬 ma³	出 ch'u¹	那 na⁴	勒 lê²	出 ch'u¹	賊 tsei²	主 chu³
勒 lei¹	銀 yin²	個 ko⁴	索 so³	城 ch'êng²	都 tou¹	兒 'rh
著 cho	子 tzŭ	官 kuan¹	了 liao	去。ch'ü⁴	殺 sha¹	殺 sha¹
點 tien³	來。lai²	勒 lê²	我 wo³	那 na⁴	退 t'ui⁴	了 liao
兒。'rh	勒 lei¹	令 ling⁴	五 wu³	關 kuan¹	了。liao	兩 liang³
	住 chu⁴	人 jên²	兩 liang³	上 shang⁴	把 pa³	個 ko⁴
	馬 ma³	家 chia¹	銀 yin²	的 ti	賊 tsei²	客 k'o⁴

PART III.—THE FORTY EXERCISES.

The innkeeper killed two guests.

The rebels were repulsed with loss.

Drive the rebels out of the city.

Obs.—*T'ui* cannot be used promiscuously; you could not, for instance, use it in speaking of driving a dog away.

The Custom House people squeezed me out of five taels.

That official compels people to subscribe money.

Obs.—*Ch'üan* is not generally used of subscriptions to a *private* object.

Pull the horse up.

Obs.—Up: *chu*, to a standstill.

Hold in your horse a bit.

510. 底 *ti*³, the bottom; below.

511. 全 *ch'üan*², all; entire.

512. 姓 *hsing*⁴, surname of family or tribe.

513. 名 *ming*², name, or cognomen, as distinguished from the surname.

514. Examples:—

兒 'rh	麼。mo	不 pu⁴	辛 hsing¹	石 shih²	事 shih⁴		樓 lou²
地 ti⁴	貴 kuei⁴	好 hao³	苦 k'u⁴	頭 t'ou²	的。ti	底 ti³	
名 ming²	姓 hsing⁴	百 po²	全 ch'üan²	桌 cho¹	河 ho²	下 hsia⁴	
叫 chiao⁴	名 ming²	姓 hsing⁴	是 shih⁴	子 tzŭ	底 ti³	底 ti³	
甚 shên²	子。tzŭ	你 ni³	用 yung⁴	底 ti³	下 hsia⁴	下 hsia⁴	
麼。mo	這 chê⁴	姓 hsing⁴	的 ti¹	下 hsia⁴	全 ch'üan²	人。jên²	
	塊 k'uai⁴	甚 shên²	人 jên²	他 t'a¹	是 shih⁴	管 kuan³	

Downstairs.

Servants. A head servant or butler. *See* 414.

The bottom of the river is all stones.

Below the table; or, underneath the table.

Obs.—This might also mean on the under face of the table; but in that case it would be more accurate to say *cho*¹ *mien*⁴-*'rh ti*³ *hsia*⁴.

His troubles are all owing to the inefficiency (worthlessness) of the people in his employ.

The people.

Obs.—*Lit.*, hundred surnames. Note the change in sound and tone of *pai*³, a hundred.

What is your name (to inferiors)?

What is your name (to equals and superiors)?

A name.

What is the name of this place?

EXERCISE XIX.

這一匹馬走的這麼慢是沒你買全不下人生的兒女足餒的兒。 1. The reason this horse goes so slowly is all because you have not given him enough to eat.

君上是百官萬民的家主子兒子買的下人生的兒女。 2. The *chün¹-shang⁴* (Sovereign) is lord over all his subjects, official and unofficial. *Chia¹ shêng¹-tzŭ³-'rh* are the children born to bond-servants (while in a state of bondage).

Obs.—All subjects, etc.: *lit.*, lord over the hundred officials and myriad non-officials. *Wan* is often used to denote an infinite quantity or number. The Manchus more particularly speak of the Emperor as their *chu-tzŭ*, master.

爵位尊是說人的官大小官不算了有爵位。 3. When you say that a man's position is honourable you mean that his office is considerable; a petty official is not considered to have "position."

管民的是文官帶兵的是武官。 4. Officials who have charge of the people are *wên² kuan¹* (civilians); those who command troops are *wu³ kuan¹* (military officers).

文武官的衣裳怎麼不大好分不分是他們的補帶的是子不同。 5. What is the difference between the dress of civil and military officials? It is not very easy to distinguish between them; the only difference is that the *pu³-tzŭ* (or insignia) that they wear are not identical.

Obs.—*Pu³-tzŭ* is the name given to the square embroidered patch worn by officials on the breast and back of the court robe: on the civil "patch" birds are represented, each grade having a distinctive bird; on the military patch animals are depicted. The *pu-tzŭ* of princes and nobles of the highest grades are round.

各地方的兵額數是一定的不過有官候兒多趕到月底要點些名就找一個人充數兒。 6. The strength of the army in different places is fixed, but it is at most times under the proper complement; [so] when a muster is called at the end of the month some men are found to make up the number.

Obs. 1.—When: *lit.*, pursuing, arrive at, etc.; *i.e.*, when the end of the month is arrived at. Note *yüeh ti*, the end of the month.

Obs. 2.—Call the muster: *tien ming*; *lit.*, prick, or check, the names.

PART III.—THE FORTY EXERCISES.

7 山 塊 了 缺 道 得 着 是
　東 兒 個 不 是 誰 補 誰
　那 出 好 知 誰 該 就

7. A good vacancy has occurred over in Shantung; I don't know who will get it. The person whose turn it is will get it.

Obs.—Whose turn it is: *lit.*, who, owing to fill it, will then fill it. *Kai-cho* is frequently used in the above sense; were the *cho* omitted, *kai* would simply mean ought.

8 拿 捐 官 捐 麼 的 得
　銀 官 是 官 不 是 的
　錢 就 捐 出 是
　買 叫 的 捐 兵

8. When an office or rank is obtained by payment of money, that is called *chüan*¹ *kuan*¹ (to obtain an office by subscription). Was his office purchased? No; it was obtained by active military service.

9 那 一 沒 那 裏 了 他
　帶 點 有 頭 他 們 們
　兵 兒 前 賊 很 殺
　的 本 跑 都 要 退
　大 事 到 沒 當 可 了
　官 都 山 吃 時 以
　　　 子 的 追 把

9. The high officer at the head of the troops has no ability whatever; some days ago the rebels escaped into the mountains, where they had nothing to eat; if he had pursued them at the time he could perfectly well have driven them back with loss.

Obs. 1.—*Ta kuan* might be either singular or plural.
Obs. 2.—Nothing to eat: *mei*, had not (*yu*, understood), *ch'ih ti*, eatables.

10 貴 姓 賤 姓 馬

10. May I ask your name? My name is MA.

Obs.—*Lit.*, your honourable name? My common name, MA.

Turn the following into Chinese. (KEY, EXERCISE XIX.)

1. The greatest person in the Empire is the Sovereign; the most numerous body are the *min² jên²* (people). The Sovereign is also called the master, and the people, *po² hsing⁴* (the hundred surnames).

Obs. 1.—Empire: *t'ien¹ hsia⁴* (*lit.*, under Heaven); the idea being that the Emperor of China exercises sway over everything under Heaven.

2. A schoolfellow of mine is a *ts'an¹-tsan⁴* down West; I hear that the position of such officers is very honourable.

Obs. 1.—Schoolfellow: *t'ung² hsiio²*; *lit.*, same learning. *Hsuo²*, short for *hsiio²-fang²*, a school.

Obs. 2.—Down west: *hsi¹ hsia⁴*; this is the general name given to Thibet and the portion of Chinese territory to the north-west of the Great Wall.

3. He thoroughly understands [the management of] affairs; is he likely to employ you to assist him?

Obs.—Employ: *ts'an-tsan* (**494**); emphasise *tsan*.

4. Most military officers rise from the ranks.

Obs.—Rise from the ranks: *lit.*, are from serving as soldiers risen (got up) most.

5. The number of officers in command of troops is fixed. Whenever there is a vacancy

it must be filled up. When there is a vacancy and nobody [to fill it up], it is a *k'ung*¹ (empty) vacancy.

6. Supernumerary officials are those in excess of the regular establishment.

Obs. 1.—Supernumerary: *ngo*² *wai*⁴, outside the fixed number.

Obs. 2.—Regular: *chêng*⁴ (103).

7. I have been casting about to find a bit of a job, but I have not been able to do so; so I have come to ask you to find some opening for me.

Obs. 1.—Have come, etc.: *ch'ing ni lai* may be read in two ways.

Obs. 2.—Opening: *mên*² *lu*⁴; *lit.*, door and way; *i.e.*, a way of access to employment.

8. To insist on having money from a person whether he possesses it or not is to squeeze.

Obs.—To insist on having, etc.: *i*² *ting*⁴ *han*² *jên*² *chia*¹ *yao*⁴, positively from persons wanting.

9. When I fixed on the things, I insisted that I wanted all of them good; why have you put in a quantity of bad ones just to make up the number? If you don't exchange them for good ones, I shall throw the whole lot back on you.

Obs. 1.—Fixed on: *ting*⁴.

Obs. 2.—Insisted: *shuo*¹ *chu*⁴ *liao*, stood firm at the statement. *See* 48.

Obs. 3.—Throw back: *t'ui*⁴ *hui*² *ch'u*⁴.

10. I told you to put the table in the middle of the room; why have you put it on one side? In future, when I tell you anything you must remember it.

Obs.—In future: *ti*³ *hsia*⁴, which can be applied to time as well as to material objects.

11. Are all the surnames of the people in the volume of the "*Po Chia Hsing?*"

12. How could they all be? [it] only [contains] those which one is familiar with, that's all.

Obs.—Familiar: *lit.*, have heard ripe.

13. Kill a fowl for me.

515. 國 *kuo*², a nation; a State; a Government.
516. 章 *chang*¹, a rule; a law. Often used with *ch'êng*² (519).
517. 律 *lü*⁴, statutes.
518. 例 *li*⁴, laws; amendments.
519. 程 *ch'êng*², a stage in a journey.
520. Examples:—

例 *li*⁴	程 *ch'êng*²	中 *chung*¹	程 *ch'êng*²	一 *i*²	出 *ch'u*¹	那 *na*⁴
不 *pu*⁴	不 *pu*⁴	國 *kuo*²	你 *ni*³	定 *ting*⁴	來 *lai*²	律 *lü*⁴
同。*t'ung*²	行。*hsing*²	律 *lü*⁴	知 *chih*¹	的 *ti*	的。*ti*	例 *li*⁴
各 *ko*⁴	例。*li*⁴	道 *tao*⁴	章 *chang*¹	各 *ko*⁴	是 *shih*⁴
國 *kuo*²	這 *ché*⁴	不 *pu*⁴	程。*ch'êng*²	關 *kuan*¹	國 *kuo*²
的 *ti*	些 *hsieh*¹	知 *chih*¹	這 *ché*⁴	都 *tou*¹	家 *chia*¹
律 *lü*⁴	章 *chang*¹	道。*tao*⁴	路 *lu*⁴	有 *yu*³	定 *ting*⁴

Laws are made by the State.

Obs.—It would be equally correct, but perhaps more indefinite, to say simply *lü li shih kuo chia ting ti*. *Ch'u lai* in this connexion signifies completion of an act; made and promulgated.

Every Custom House has fixed regulations.

Do you know the road?

Obs.—*Lu ch'êng*: *lit.*, stages of a road. *Lu ch'êng* can only be applied to long distances divided into stages.

The penal code of China.

These regulations won't do.

The laws of different countries are not identical.

PART III.—THE FORTY EXERCISES.

521. 巡 *hsün²*, to go the rounds.

522. 察 *ch'a²*, to inquire into.

523. 搜 *sou¹*, to search, as the person, baggage, etc.

524. 動 *tung⁴*, to move; and, less frequently, to be moved.

525. 種 *chung⁴*, to sow; to cultivate. Read *chung³ 'rh*, seeds. *Chung³* (colloquially, *tsung¹*), a kind or class.

526. Examples :—

東	*tung¹*	不	*pu²*	的	*ti*	幾	*chi³*	不	*pu²*	方	*fang¹*	看	*k'an¹*
西	*hsi¹*	要	*yao⁴*	種	*chung⁴*	點	*tien³*	要	*yao⁴*	的	*ti*	街	*chieh¹*
這	*ché⁴*	菜	*ts'ai⁴*	鐘	*chung¹*	動	*tung⁴*	人	*jén²*	的	*ti*
種	*tsung¹*	種	*chung⁴*	動	*tung⁴*	那	*na⁴*	搜	*sou¹*	是	*shih⁴*
樣	*yang⁴*	種	*chung³*	身	*shén¹*	東	*tung¹*	察	*ch'a²*	巡	*hsün²*
兒	*'rh*	兒	*'rh*	種	*chung⁴*	西	*hsi¹*	行	*hsing²*	察	*ch'a²*
的	*ti*	我	*wo³*	地	*ti⁴*	你	*ni³*	李	*li³*	地	*ti⁴*

The *k'an¹-chieh¹-ti* is the man who goes the round of the locality and sees (q.d., that order is kept).

Obs.—Note that *k'an¹* means here to watch or keep guard over, and is in the first tone. *See* 91.

To search baggage.

Do not touch those things.

What time do you start?

A farmer (or farm labourer).

To grow vegetables.

To sow seeds.

Obs.—Also called *tzŭ³ 'rh*.

I don't want this kind of thing.

527. 治 *chih⁴*, to regulate; to reform; to restore order; good government as distinguished from disorder. Also, to treat medically; as *chih⁴ hao³*, to cure.

528. 理 *li³*, regulating principle or force. Also, to manage; to regulate. Read *lii³*, to arrange; to set in order. *Li³ hui⁴* (129), to pay attention; to observe; to notice.

529. 暴 *pao⁴*, passionate; fierce. The opposite of *ho²*, soft; gentle; accommodating (210).

530. 亂 *lan⁴, luan⁴*, disorder.

531. 急 *chi²*, quick in movement or temper.

532. 性 *hsing⁴*, nature; natural disposition.

533. Examples :—

急	*chih²*	那	*na⁴*	官	*kuan¹*	道	*tao⁴*	治	*chih⁴*	方	*fang¹*	百	*po²*
不	*pu²*	個	*ko⁴*	性	*hsing⁴*	理	*li³*	理	*li³*	官	*kuan¹*	姓	*hsing⁴*
用	*yung⁴*	人	*jén²*	子	*tzŭ*	不	*pu²*	治	*chih⁴*	一	*i⁴*	亂	*luan⁴*
著	*chao²*	說	*shuo¹*	過	*kuo⁴*	錯	*ts'o⁴*	亂	*luan⁴*	點	*tien³*	得	*té*
急	*chi²*	話	*hua⁴*	於	*yü²*	這	*ché⁴*	這	*ché⁴*	兒	*'rh*	很	*hén³*
		太	*t'ai⁴*	暴	*pao⁴*	個	*ko⁴*	個	*ko⁴*	不	*pu²*	地	*ti⁴*

The people are very disorderly (or turbulent); the local officials do not keep them in the slightest order.

Order and disorder; or, to restore order.

This reasoning (or principle) is perfectly correct.

Obs.—*Tao*, morally, the right road; *li*, the principle imparted to man, if he conform to which he will keep the right road. *Tao-li* is, hence, right principle; next, any principle conformity to which produces the normal estate of men or things, the rationale or logical condition of anything. It is against *tao-li*, in the first sense, to steal; but the *tao-li* of a thief is to steal, for he would not be a thief if he did not steal: a Chinese would say *mei chê ko tao-li*, it is not logical, there is no sense in such a proposition as that a man should be a thief and not steal. Lastly, the term *tao-li* is used as the principles collectively, the philosophic system, of any teacher. Confucianism is the *tao-li* of Confucius.

This official is too passionate.

That man talks too impetuously.

Do not get excited; or, there is no occasion to excite yourself.

Obs.—Note the peculiar use of *chao*, which here means to put forth or give out; not as in the expression *chao²-liang²*, to catch, or meet with unexpectedly.

534. 普 *p'u³*, universal.

535. 羣 *ch'ün²*, a flock; a drove; a multitude.

536. 耕 *kêng¹*, to till; also read *ching¹*, as *ching¹ ti⁴*, to plough.

537. 總 *tsung³*, to collect; collectively. Hence, in any case; never; positively; always.

538. 之 *chih¹*, used in books as the pronoun of the third person and the sign of the possessive; also, in some instances, comparatively rare, in the spoken language.

539. Examples:—

去	*ch'ü⁴*	那	*na⁴*	言	*yên²*	國	*kuo²*	地	*ti⁴*	多	*to¹*	普	*p'u³*
把	*pa³*	一	*i⁴*	之	*chih¹*	人	*jên²*	我	*wo³*	要	*yao⁴*	天	*t'ien¹*
書	*shu¹*	羣	*ch'ün²*	國	*kuo²*	你	*ni³*	總	*tsung³*	種	*chung³*	下	*hsia⁴*
理	*lii³*	羊	*yang²*	家	*chia¹*	沒	*mei²*	種	*chung³*	的	*ti*
一	*i⁴*	趕	*kan³*	之	*chih¹*	得	*tei³*	看	*k'an⁴*	兒	*'rh*	人	*jên²*
理	*lii³*	到	*tao⁴*	大	*ta⁴*	去	*ch'ü⁴*	見	*chien⁴*	先	*hsien¹*	種	*chung⁴*
		山	*shan¹*	官	*kuan¹*	總	*tsung³*	過	*kuo⁴*	得	*tei³*	地	*ti⁴*
		上	*shang⁴*	把	*pa³*	而	*êrh²*	外	*wai⁴*	耕	*ching¹*	的	*ti*

The population of the world is mostly agricultural.

If you want to sow seeds you must first plough the land.

I have never seen a foreigner (or foreigners).

You will have to (must positively) go.

In a word; speaking collectively.

Obs.—This is, strictly speaking, not colloquial, though the phrase is constantly used in conversation; *chih* is here a final particle of no particular value.

The high officials of the State.

Obs.—*Ti* would here be more colloquial than *chih*, but the latter character is introduced to show its use in a possessive construction.

Drive that flock of sheep on to the hills.

Put the books in order.

PART III.—THE FORTY EXERCISES.

EXERCISE XX.

城門上的官兵是查盤出入的人。 1	1. The guards on the city gates are [there] for [the purpose of] searching [the baggage of] persons entering and leaving the city.
國家定的律例是治理百姓的。 2	2. The laws passed by the State are for the administration of the people.
種地是小民的本分夏天人人種地。 3	3. Farming is the proper business of the humbler classes; in the summer everyone is tilling the ground.

Obs.—Proper business: *pên*, that which is originally, *fên*⁴, the lot or share, *hsiao min*, of the humbler classes.

秋天種的麥子就叫秋麥春天種的麥就叫春麥。 4	4. Wheat sown in the autumn, which is gathered in the summer, is called *ch'iu¹ mai⁴* (autumn wheat); wheat sown in the spring and gathered in the summer is called spring wheat.
那麼着秋麥和春麥是一樣的麼。不能一樣。秋麥收的多。 5	5. In that case are autumn wheat and spring wheat identical? They cannot be considered so; the autumn wheat gives always a better yield.
近年天下大亂是官長治理的不好普天下百姓都知道。 6	6. That the great disorder which has everywhere [prevailed] of late years is due to the maladministration of the authorities is a fact known to the people of the whole Empire.

Obs. 1.—Late : *chin ; lit.,* near.

Obs. 2.—Authorities: *kuan chang*³, the officials who *chang*³, are superior ; the expression is only used in speaking of the whole official class, in contradistinction to the *hsiao min*.

Obs. 3.—Maladministration : *chih-li*, in governing, *ti*=*tê*, attained to, *pu hao*, badness.

Obs. 4.—Notice the construction of the whole sentence : [the fact that of] late years the Empire's great disorder is [the result of] the authorities' maladministration the entire Empire's people all know.

你那個兒子太不講理告訴他說甚麼話也不理會甚麼事總不論甚麼事全愛說嘴。 7	7. That son of yours is altogether too unreasonable; he never pays attention to anything he is told, and has an opinion to offer on every subject going.

Obs. 1.—Unreasonable : *lit.,* does not speak reason.

Obs. 2.—Opinion to offer : *shuo tsui* often means boasting or self-glorification.

都呢人那子那一去 8
跑他怎住都一羣年
了麼着燒片賊來
們樣的了房把了
一了數馬叫塊人好 9
羣也兒牛一兒些
說多羊羣那一
話去本晚告他名你 10
說見人半訴那把
他兒晌他片我
有過兒我去拏的
到

8. A horde of rebels came over there last year and burnt that whole lot of buildings. How about the occupants? They decamped long before the rebels came.

9. A large number assembled together is said to be a *ch'ün*²; the same term may be applied to horses, oxen, and sheep in any number.

10. Take my card to his place and tell him that I shall go over myself in the latter part of the afternoon to see him, as I have something to say to him

Obs.—Note *ming-p'ien*, a visiting card (Radical 91). See 1,025.

Turn the following into Chinese. (KEY, EXERCISE XX.)

1. There are Chinamen all over the world. Every country has a penal code. The penal code was fixed by the State for the government of the people. Regulations are drawn up by the officials.
Obs.—Draw up: *li* (Radical 117).

2. A man yesterday drove a flock of sheep on to my ground, and they ate up all the wheat I had sown there.

3. The *k'an*¹-*chieh*¹-*ti* are official underlings who go the rounds and inspect every place.

4. Somebody, I don't know who, has been putting all my books into confusion; arrange them for me.
Obs.—Put into confusion: *la luan; lit.*, drag into confusion.

5. That man is dreadfully passionate; why do you pay any attention to him?
Obs.—Pay attention to: *li*³ (528).

6. The Great Wall (10,000 *li* long wall) is the first of the seven great wonders of the world. I have heard that it was a king who compelled his people to build it.

7. Quite right. That Sovereign was utterly without principle; he governed his people in an exceedingly oppressive way. Within a few years from the completion of the wall the whole Empire was in great disorder.
Obs. 1.—Utterly without, etc.: *lit.*, not principle to the utmost (Radical 133). This phrase is not strictly colloquial, though quite admissible in conversation. It has been introduced to show the use of the possessive *chih*.
Obs. 2.—Oppressive: *k'ê*¹ *k'u*³. See 223.

8. It is necessary to put on the official dress when receiving a visitor who is a stranger.
Obs.—Stranger: *shêng k'o; lit.*, raw stranger (Radical 100).

PART III.—THE FORTY EXERCISES.   107

540. 搶 *ch'iang³*, to take by violence.

541. 奪 *to²*, to snatch away.

542. 偷 *t'ou¹*, to steal; to filch. Also, secretly; stealthily.

543. 股 *ku³*, classically, the leg or thigh. Colloquially, used of banditti, etc.; a gang or band.

544. 逃 *t'ao²*, to fly, as a fugitive.

545. 竄 *ts'uan⁴*, to escape or scuttle off, as rats or mice; applied also to the escape of rebels or banditti.

546. 散 *san³ ⁴*, to disperse. *San³*, a medicinal powder.

547. 混 *hun³ ⁴*, mingled in confusion, like the water of torrents. Read *hun²*, stupid; idiotic; reckless. It also means muddy when applied to water, though, strictly speaking, another character of the same sound should be used.

548. Examples :—

個 *ko⁴*　混 *hun⁴*　個 *ko⁴*　四 *ssŭ⁴*　西 *hsi¹*　把 *pa³*　他 *t'a¹*
混 *hun²*　說。*shuo¹*　兒 *'rh*　川 *ch'uan¹*　偷 *t'ou¹*　我 *wo³*　們 *mên*
小 *hsiao³*　混 *hun³*　竄 *ts'uan⁴*　那 *na⁴*　偷 *t'ou¹*　的 *ti*　把 *pa³*
子。*tzŭ*　和 *ho²*　到 *tao⁴*　一 *i⁴*　兒 *'rh*　筆 *pi³*　行 *hsing²*
一 *tsai⁴*　雲 *yün²*　股 *ku³*　的 *ti*　奪 *to²*　李 *li³*
塊 *k'uai⁴*　南 *nan²*　賊 *tsei²*　走。*tsou³*　了 *liao*　搶 *ch'iang³*
兒。*'rh*　去 *ch'ü⁴*　散 *san⁴*　他 *t'a¹*　去 *ch'ü⁴*　了 *liao*
他 *t'a¹*　了。*liao*　了 *liao*　逃 *t'ao²*　了。*liao*　去 *ch'ü⁴*
是 *shih⁴*　混 *hun²*　一 *i²*　走 *tsou³*　偷 *t'ou¹*　了。*liao*
　　　水。*shui³*　個 *ko⁴*　了。*liao*　東 *tung¹*　他 *t'a¹*

They seized the baggage and went off with it.
He snatched my pen away from me.
To steal things.
To walk stealthily (*i.e.*, that no one shall know).
He has run away.
That band of robbers from Ssŭch'uan (Szechwan) has dispersed, and skulked off one by one into Yünnan.
Muddy water.
To talk wildly.
Jumbled together.
He is a reckless (or rowdy) youngster.

549. 懶 *lan³*, idle; commonly used with the following.

550. 惰 *to⁴*. *Lan³-to⁴*, idle.

551. 棍 *kun⁴*, a staff.

552. 扔 *jéng¹*, to cast; to throw. Also read *jéng³*.

553. 放 *fang⁴*, to release; to let go.

554. 槍 ch'iang¹, a spear; a musket. The numerative of the second is kan³ (**325**) or kên¹; and of the first, kan³, kên¹ (**644**), or t'iao².

555. Examples:—

放 fang⁴	邊 pien¹	用 yung⁴	鳥 niao³	槍 ch'iang¹	上 shang⁴	那 na⁴
他 t'a¹	兒 'rh	不 pu²	兒 'rh	就 chiu⁴	街 ya²	個 ko⁴
麼 mo	罷 pa⁴	着 chao²	那 na⁴	打 ta³	門 mên²	人 jên²
放 fang⁴	放 fang⁴	了 liao	一 i⁴	着 chao²	他 t'a¹	懶 lan³
他 t'a¹	了 liao	扔 jêng¹³	條 t'iao²	了 liao	放 fang⁴	惰 to⁴
罷。pa⁴	他 t'a¹	在 tsai⁴	棍 kun⁴	一 i²	了 liao	不 pu²
	罷。pa⁴	一 i⁴	子 tzŭ	個 ko⁴	一 i⁴	愛 ai⁴

That man is lazy; he does not like going to the yamên.
He fired a shot and hit a bird
Obs.—Note *chao*; its special force will be seen later.
You have (or, will have) no use for that stick; you had better throw it aside.
Obs.—*Pa*, as before, may also be rendered imperatively.
Let him go.
Obs.—Note that *liao* is only an expletive, and might be omitted, though it has a certain force, as will be seen from the following sentences.
Let him go? Yes, let him go.

556. 恰 ch'ia⁴, to coincide with exactly.

557. 巧 ch'iao³, cunning; also, opportune, with or without the preceding.

558. 特 t'ê⁴, special; particular.

559. 意 i⁴, meaning; purpose.

560. 偶 ou³, ⁿyou³, accidental.

561. 然 jan², thus by nature; as it were; positively. Affixed to many words and combinations with an adverbial force; as jan² êrh² (Radical 126), and yet; nevertheless.

562. Examples:—

個 ko⁴	那 na⁴	不 pu²	偶 ou³	意 i⁴	來 lai²	他 t'a¹
人 jên²	是 shih⁴	是 shih⁴	然 jan²	的 ti	的 ti	恰 ch'ia⁴
巧 ch'iao³	自 tzŭ⁴	特 t'ê⁴	錯 ts'o⁴	來 lai²	狠 hên³	巧 ch'iao³
得 tê	然 jan²	意 i⁴	了 liao	看 k'an⁴	巧 ch'iao³	來 lai²
很。hên³	的 ti	做 tso⁴	自 tzŭ⁴	你。ni³	我 wo³	了。liao
	這 chê⁴	的 ti	然 jan²	我 wo³	特 t'ê⁴	你 ni³

He came in the nick of time.
You have arrived most opportunely.
I came here purposely to see you.
Obs.—*T'ê i*, with special intent.
My mistake was accidental; of course it was not done intentionally.
Obs.—Of course: *tzŭ jan*, of itself thus.
That is a matter of course.
This man is very ingenious.

EXERCISE XXI.

你 意 好 不 呢 是 1
的 是 樣 去 自 去
主 怎 還 好 然 好
意 麼 是 好。 。
去

Obs.—Opinion: *lit.*, leading or dominant idea.

1. What is your opinion, should I go or not? Of course you had better go.

把 小 我 裝 鳥 打 2
我 棍 要 那 兒 的
那 兒 出 一 可 着
一 拿 門 桿 不 打
個 來 。 把 要 不
。 槍 打 定

2. Bring me that small cane (or stick) of mine; I am going out. Load my gun; I want to shoot some birds, though I am not certain that I shall hit any.

Obs.—Note *ta*, to fire or shoot at; *ta chuo* or *ta liao*, to hit what is fired at. *Fang* (see next paragraph), to fire a gun.

我 槍 道 偶 人 誰 可 3
昨 拿 是 然 恰 要 了
兒 起 裝 放 巧 是 不
把 來 得 了 沒 打 得
那 了 不 一 打 着 了
桿 知 的 下 有 。 。

Obs.—All round: *lit.*, on four sides.

3. I picked up that gun yesterday without knowing it was loaded, and accidentally let it off. There were people all round me, but luckily I did not hit anyone; if I had, it would have been no end of a business.

背 不 東 是 夜 槍 拿 4
地 叫 西 奪 裏 刀 東
裏 人 偷 。 明 到 西
拿 知 。 好 火 人 就
東 道 硬 些 拿 家 是
西 就 拿 個 着 硬 搶
的 人 賊 。
家 去
。

4. When a person takes a thing unobserved without letting anyone know, that is *t'ou*[1] (to steal or pilfer). To take away anything from a person by force is *to*[2] (to snatch or seize violently). When a number of robbers armed with spears (or muskets) and swords go at night by the light of torches to a man's house and forcibly take his property, that is *ch'iang*[3] (robbery with violence).

Obs. 1.—Unobserved: *lit.*, in (or on) the ground behind the back; *i.e.*, where one cannot be seen.
Obs. 2.—Torchlight: *lit.*, the light or brightness of fire; burglary is often referred to as *ming-huo* simply, and the combined characters are never used in any other sense.

說 沒 理 算 混 5
話 有 那 是 說
。

5. To talk without reference to reason (or, the right) is what is considered *hun*[4] *shuo*[1] (talking wildly).

110　TZŬ ÊRH CHI.—COLLOQUIAL SERIES.

我的洗澡水怎麼混這麼打了不大工夫一會兒就好了。 6

6. How is it that my bath water is so muddy? It hasn't been drawn very long; it will be all right after a little while.

我那個學生過於懶惰不愛用功。打他兩下看看罷兒。 7

7. That pupil of mine is too idle altogether; he won't study. Give him a thrashing, and then see how he does.

那一天有倆賊、一個拏着一條長槍一個拏着一根大棍子、四下裏混打着人拏着槍的恰巧來了槍打見了那倆賊呢那拏混槍的趕着拐下裝上桿就跑打了那賊棍子的叫槍子兒打著腿跑不了拏棍子放槍的那個人是特意來的還是偶然來的那怕是偶然來的可也不定。 8

8. The other day two robbers, the one armed with a long spear, the other with a large staff, were assaulting people right and left, when it fortunately happened that someone with a musket came along. Seeing the robbers so engaged, he hurriedly loaded and fired. And what did the robbers do? The one with the spear threw it down and ran away; the one with the stick was struck by the bullet in the leg, so he couldn't run. Did the man who fired make his appearance designedly or by accident? Probably by accident, but I am not sure.

Obs. 1.—Note the numerative of *ch'iang*. Spears may be spoken of as *kan*, *kên*, or *t'iao*, but muskets are always *kan* or *kên* (644).

Obs. 2.—Right and left: *hsia li*, in the sense of direction. *Ssŭ hsia*, the four directions; properly, the four points of the compass. Cf. also *ssŭ mien-'rh* in paragraph 3.

Obs. 3.—Note *ch'iang-tzŭ*³, a bullet.

Turn the following into Chinese. (KEY, EXERCISE XXI.)

1. Last year over ten robbers armed with spears and knives came into the city and made a clean sweep of everything in my shop. An hour before this happened that lazy servant of mine had gone to his home, and when he went he did not shut the door. I am afraid this was done intentionally, too.

Obs. 1.—Clean sweep: *lit.*, took the things in my shop and robbed it clean; the word "clean" is repeated for euphony's sake, though it would be quite correct to say, simply, *kan-ching*.

Obs. 2.—Gone home: this may be rendered by *chia ch'ü liao*, *hui chia ch'ü liao*, or *shang chia ch'ü liao*.

2. One of the robbers gave me a cut, and I called in a foreign doctor, who cured me.

PART III.—THE FORTY EXERCISES. 111

Another, seeing a fowling-piece of mine that was loaded, let it off by accident.

Obs. 1.—Cut (**304**).

Obs. 2.—Doctor: commonly called *tai-fu* (太夫), though there is a more literary term. Note *tai*⁴, not *t'ai*⁴.

Obs. 3.—Cure (**527**).

3. The *k'an*¹-*chieh*¹-*ti*, hearing the report of the gun, came to see what was the matter. On seeing the robbers he was frightened, and ran straight away. On the road he saw an official, and told him some confused story or other, I don't know what.

Obs. 1.—*K'an*¹-*chieh-ti*, the local constable. Note *k'an*¹, to watch (**91**).

Obs. 2.—Frightened: *hai liao p'a liao*. See **424**.

Obs. 3.—Straight off: *lit.*, one straight ran. See **374**.

4. The officer said, "That will do with that story. I will take my soldiers to the place forthwith, and arrest the robbers." When the robbers heard that the soldiers were coming directly, they all dispersed in different directions.

Obs.—That will do, etc.: *lit.*, you need not say all this.

5. By this time my servant had come back, saying that the business which had taken him out was finished. The official said to him, "I suspect you and they had an understanding." His rejoinder was so full of untruths that orders were given for him to get a few blows with a stick

Obs. 1.—Understanding: *lit.*, I fear you with them were one breath; were in collusion.

Obs. 2.—Rejoinder: *lit.*, the talk he returned all not true.

6. If you are to be so idle when you are young, and dislike study, how will you succeed in life when you grow up? If you do not make a man of yourself, you will have no means of livelihood, and, without that, you will naturally have to seek your bread by thieving. Yesterday you threw away your book and went out shooting with the visitors. Even after they had gone you did not study.

Obs. 1.—Young: *lit.*, your years' light time.

Obs. 2.—Means of livelihood: *lit.*, a road of passing the days; a means of subsisting from one day to another.

563. 凡 *fan*², all whatsoever. Also, as will be seen later, vulgar; common.

564. 揣 *ch'uai*³, to feel, or feel for, by thrusting in the hand; hence, in combination with the following word, to guess.

565. 摩 *mo*¹, to feel with the fingers.

566. 約 *yo*¹, *yüeh*¹, primarily, to bind; an agreement. *T'iao*² *yo*¹ (**181**) is the expression for treaty (*i.e.*, *yo*¹, an agreement; *t'iao*², in strips, sections, or clauses).

567. 准 *chun*³, to authorise; true to a course.

568. 否 *fou*³, if not; or, not. Rarely used colloquially.

569. Examples:—

同	*t'ung*²	不	*pu*⁴	准	*chun*³	不	*pu*⁴	准	*chun*³	揣	*ch'uai*³	凡	*fan*²
他	*t'a*¹	大	*ta*⁴	不	*pu*⁴	着	*chao*²	不	*pu*⁴	摩	*mo*¹	事	*shih*⁴
去	*ch'ü*⁴	長	*ch'ang*²	准	*chun*³	准	*chun*³	准	*chun*³	不	*pu*⁴	總	*tsung*³
大	*ta*⁴	說	*shuo*¹	話	*hua*⁴	否	*fou*³	我	*wo*³	知	*chih*¹	要	*yao*⁴
約	*yo*¹	約	*yo*¹	裡	*li*³	就	*chiu*⁴	揣	*ch'uai*³	道	*tao*⁴	小	*hsiao*³
		我	*wo*³	可	*k'o*³	是	*shih*⁴	摩	*mo*¹	他	*t'a*¹	心	*hsin*¹

In all things great care should be taken.
To guess.
I do not know whether he will give his sanction or not.
I cannot guess.
Chun³ fou³ (to authorise or to negative) is the same as *chun³ pu⁴ chun³*, but it is not often used in conversation.
He invited me to go with him.
Most probably.

570. 更 *kêng¹*, to change; but *kêng⁴*, more, the sign of the comparative (*see* 238).

571. 改 *kai³*, to change.

572. 妥 *t'o³*, secure; satisfactory. Often used with *tang¹* (342).

573. 專 *chuan¹*, single; special.

574. 失 *shih¹*, to lose; to miss.

575. 神 *shên²*, spirits, divine or human; animal spirits.

576. 參 *ts'ên¹*, with the following *tz'ŭ¹*, irregular; uneven (*e.g.*, like foliage). Read also *ts'an¹* and *shên¹* (*see* 493).

577. 差 *tz'ŭ¹*, with *ts'ên¹*, irregular.

578. Examples:—

西 *hsi¹*	駱 *lo⁴*	神 *shên²*	念 *nien⁴*	用 *yung⁴*	逭 *chê⁴*
的。*ti*	駝 *t'o*	就。*chiu⁴*	書。*shu¹*	更 *kêng¹*	章 *chang¹*
那 *na¹*	是 *shih⁴*	有 *yu³*	做 *tso⁴*	改。*kai³*	程 *ch'êng²*
更 *kêng⁴*	專 *chuan¹*	參 *ts'ên¹*	事 *shih⁴*	他 *t'a¹*	妥 *t'o³*
不 *pu⁴*	駝 *t'o²*	差 *tz'ŭ¹*	一 *i⁴*	專 *chuan¹*	當 *tang¹*
行。*hsing²*	東 *tung¹*	了。*liao*	失 *shih¹*	心 *hsin¹*	不 *pu²*

These regulations are satisfactory; they need not be amended.
He gives his whole attention to study.
In the transaction of business absent-mindedness at once leads to irregularity.
Camels are specially employed as beasts of burden.
That will answer still worse.

579. 忙 *mang²*, to haste; busy.

580. 向 *hsiang⁴*, to face towards; towards; direction.

581. 規 *kuei¹*, a rule; custom.

582. 幹 *kan⁴*, to attend to business; business. It often takes the place of *tso⁴*, to do.

583. 辦 *pan⁴*, to administer; colloquially it has many meanings, as to purchase, to punish, etc. *Pan⁴-tsui³* (433), to squabble.

584. 法 *fa²⁻³*, method; fashion. Read *fa³*, law or laws. *Fa⁴ kuo²*, France; note the tone.

PART III.—THE FORTY EXERCISES.

585. Examples:—

會 hui⁴	辦 pan⁴	了。liao	你 ni³	明 ming²	很 hén³	我 wo³
辦 pan⁴	不 pu⁴	這 ché	們 mén	年 nien²	忙。mang²	們 mén
事。shih⁴	來 lai²	個 ko⁴	幹 kan⁴	出 ch'u¹	我 wo³	向 hsiang⁴
忙 mang²	的。ti	法 fa²	甚 shén²	遠 yüan³	定 ting⁴	來 lai²
甚 shén²	他 t'a¹	子 tzŭ	麼 mo	門 mén²	規 kuei¹	不 pu²
麼。mo	真 chén¹	是 shih⁴	來 lai²	兒。'rh	了 liao	大 ta⁴

Hitherto we have never been very busy.
Obs.—Hitherto: *lit.*, towards [the time that has now] come; *hsiang lai* with a negative can generally be rendered *never*.

I have decided to make a long journey next year.
Obs.—Decided: *lit.*, *ting*, have determined or laid down, *kuei*, as a definite line of action.

What have you come for?

This plan is impracticable.

He is really an able administrator.

What's your hurry?

586. 胡 *hu²*, wildly; blindly.

587. 鬧 *nao⁴*, to be in a rage; of events, to occur when they should not occur.

588. 掄 *lun¹, lün¹*, to whirl about, as a mace, etc.; to brandish, as the fist, etc.

589. 催 *ts'ui¹*, to urge.

590. Examples:—

兒。'rh	裡 li³	忙 mang²	槍 ch'iang¹	成 ch'êng²	姓 hsing⁴	不 pu²
鬧 nao⁴	鬧 nao⁴	去 ch'ü⁴	混 hun⁴	天 t'ien¹	鬧 nao⁴	要 yao⁴
了 liao	嗓 sang³	辦。pan⁴	掄 lun¹	家 chia¹	了 liao	胡 hu²
個 ko⁴	子 tzŭ	他 t'a¹	催 ts'ui¹	擎 na²	大 ta⁴	鬧 nao⁴
亂 lan⁴	了。liao	們 mén	他 t'a¹	着 cho	亂 lan⁴	了。liao
兒。'rh	今 chin¹	家 chia¹	趕 kan³	桿 kan³	子。tzŭ	百 po²

Don't be disorderly.

There was a great outbreak of the people.
Obs.—Note that *lan⁴-tzŭ* is a disturbance; *luan⁴*, a state of disturbance. *Nao* can be used of the outbreak of an epidemic (see below).

To brandish a spear the whole day.
Obs.—The whole day: *lit.*, a complete day. The teachers can give no explanation of the use of *chia* in this connexion. We find the same sound in the expression *pu¹ chia*, it is not so; no.

Urge him to go and attend to it with all despatch.

Diphtheria has broken out in their house.

I have had a misfortune to-day.

EXERCISE XXII.

那 1　不　事、　背　人　不　好
人　叫　不　人、　家　背、　話。
幹　人　然　可　常　人
的　知　他　不　說　背
事　道　怎　是　好　人
總　好　麼　麼　話　沒

1. That man never lets anyone know what he is about. Probably it is nothing very reputable, otherwise why should he be so secret about it? Yes, indeed; there is a common saying that "Good advice is not given in secret; secret advice is never good."

Obs. 1.—Otherwise: *pu*, were it not, *jan*, thus.

Obs. 2.—Secret: *pei⁴ jên*, behind people's backs. Cf. *pei ti li*.

還 2　當'　得'　知　人　大　麼
沒　了、　改　道　准　約　更
一　章　可　李　不　沒　改
件　程　不　大　准　甚　的。
事　辦　人
要　安

2. That matter is not satisfactorily disposed of yet. The regulations require alteration, but I do not know whether LI *ta-jên* will approve or not. Most probably no important alteration will take place.

Obs.—*Ta-jên*: this might be translated His Excellency, but it must be remembered that the title *ta-jên* is given to any officer of the third or higher grades of official rank.

要 3　甚　事　得'　規　准　意。
幹　麼　先　定　個　主

3. If one wants to engage in any affair one must first settle on a definite line of action.

幹 4　時　心　在　那　失
事　候　不　事　就　神。
的　兒　擱　上、　叫

4. When one is engaged in any transaction and one's attention is not devoted to the matter [in hand], that is what is called *shih¹ shên²* (to be absent-minded).

Obs.—Attention devoted to: *lit.*, heart placed in or upon.

定 5　事　法　總　他　上。
安　的　子　在　身
辦　了

5. The final determination of the way in which the thing is to be done rests entirely with him.

Obs.—Rests with him: *lit.*, is on his body; he bears the responsibility.

PART III.—THE FORTY EXERCISES.

肯些催不他得一那 6
聽。兒他忙，一趕件個
　　他快同點着要人
　　不着人兒辦事有

6. That man had a matter of importance in hand which it was necessary he should dispose of promptly; but he would not hurry himself a bit, and when someone who was acting with him urged him to make a little more speed he would not listen.

Obs. 1.—Matter of importance: *yao*, short for *yao chin*³, a combination which will be met with later.
Obs. 2.—Acting with him: *t'ung jên*, short for *t'ung shih*⁴ *ti jên*.

喝是什掄胳兒他 7
多喝麽。是臂摜在
了。酒怕幹混倆那
　　的裏定中各條 8
　　章往兩國國約
　　程。來下立和是

7. What is he swinging his arms about there for? I suspect he has had too much to drink.

8. *T'iao²-yo¹* (treaties) are the regulations for intercourse between their respective countries drawn up by different nations with China.

Obs.—*Lit.*, *t'iao-yo* are each nation's with China drawn up both sides going and coming regulations. *Wang lai*, going and coming; hence, interchange, whether of courtesies, correspondence, trade, or otherwise.

不你弄給子是兒這 9
吃。倒的你專廚茶樣
　　差全這麼條一目大 10
　　不是寫開。的條都凡
　　齊。參的你那一是帳

9. This dish was specially prepared for you by the cook, and yet you won't eat it.

10. Most accounts are drawn up item by item. These that you have written out are irregular and incomplete.

Obs. 1.—Most: *ta fan*; *lit.*, the great whole; hence, the majority.

Obs. 2.—Irregular: *ts'ên-tzŭ*; *lit.*, jaggedness. The irregularity here referred to is unevenness in the writing; *pu ch'i* may also mean uneven, though the context in this case rather indicates incompleteness than unevenness, which is already provided for by *ts'ên-tzŭ*. We can say that a certain number of persons *lai ch'i liao*, have all arrived, or that a hedge has been trimmed *pu ch'i*, unevenly.

Turn the following into Chinese. (KEY, EXERCISE XXII.)

1. Whenever you are studying and happen to meet an expression you do not understand, if you try diligently to get at it (*lit.*, guess) you will most probably understand its meaning.

2. Yesterday I invited him to go to the Western Hills; he said he must first go home to ask leave. I fear he will not be allowed to go any distance.

3. In writing letters and despatches, should there be any part written wrongly, a piece of paper must be put over the characters that are mis-written; this [operation] is called *ta³ pu³-tzŭ* (to put in a correction).

4. If you are absent-minded in this way, you will do nothing satisfactorily.

5. I brought that flower-pot purposely and specially for you. If you decline it, it shows (this is) you look down upon me.

Obs. 1.—Purposely and specially: *lit.*, with special heart and special intent.

Obs. 2.—Look down upon: *ch'iao pu ch'i*; *lit.*, you regard not elevated; *i.e.*, you don't look up to me. The converse is *ch'iao tê ch'i*.

6. This is indeed nonsensical talk! I decline it because I do not feel at liberty to accept your things without having done anything to deserve them.

Obs. 1.—Nonsensical talk: *lit.*, this talk spoken is truly wild extravagance. I do not want is [because] I [could] not [with] good intent for nothing at all (*pai²*) want your things.

Obs. 2.—Note *pai*, white; hence, a synonym for nothing at all, in vain, etc. Cf. *pai jên-'rh*, a private individual (p. 97).

7. The furniture of this room is all in disorder; put it to rights.

Obs. 1.—Disorder: *ts'ên-tz'ŭ pu ch'i*.

Obs. 2.—Put to rights: *see* 528.

8. What is your hurry? it will be a little time yet before the guests come.

9. What did you go away for? Directly I took my eyes off you, away you ran. I'll have to take a stick again and lay it about you a few times.

Obs. 1.—Took my eyes off: *lit.*, I, one erring (or straying) of the eyes *(i ts'o yên-'rh)*, you then ran.

Obs. 2.—Lay it about you: *lun* (588).

10. The mode of action they have always (hitherto) laid down cannot well be altered or modified.

591. 語 *yü³*, language; sayings.

592. 句 *chü⁴*, a clause; a sentence.

593. 吵 *ch'ao¹*, *ch'ao³*, to wrangle (of two or many).

594. 嚷 *jang³*, to talk too loud. *Jang¹*, to chatter in a loud tone; also, to talk about matters that should be kept quiet; to let out a secret.

595. Examples:—

你 *ni³* 起 *ch'i³* 兩 *liang³* 俩 *lia³* 同 *t'ung²* 各 *ko⁴*
嚷 *jang³* 來 *lai²* 句 *chü⁴* 不 *pu⁴* 一 *i²* 國 *kuo²*
甚 *shên²* 了 *liao* 話 *hua⁴* 和 *ho²* 句 *chü⁴* 的 *ti*
麼 *mo* 少 *shao³* 就 *chiu⁴* 說 *shuo¹* 話 *hua⁴* 言 *yen²*
嚷 *jang¹* 嚷 *jang³* 吵 *ch'ao³* 不 *pu⁴* 他 *t'a¹* 語 *yü³*
嚷 *jang¹* 些 *hsieh¹* 鬧 *nao⁴* 到 *tao⁴* 們 *mên* 不 *pu⁴*

The languages spoken in different countries vary.

A sentence; also, once and for all.

Those two are not on good terms; before they have spoken two sentences they begin to quarrel.

Obs.—Note that *ch'ao nao* is verbal altercation (*see also* 583).

Make less noise.

What are you making such a noise about?

To chatter; also, to let out a secret; or, to talk about a matter which should be kept quiet.

596. 阿 *a¹*, an ejaculation; sometimes interrogative.

PART III.—THE FORTY EXERCISES.

597. 訛 *ngé²*, *ngo²*, wrong; untrue. Colloquially, generally to defraud by false representation; to extort money under false pretences; to accuse wrongfully.

598. 笑 *hsiao⁴*, to laugh; laughter.

599. Examples:—

就 *chiu⁴*	不 *pu⁴*	和 *han²*	笑 *hsiao⁴*	有 *yu³*	你 *ni³*
是 *shih⁴*	該 *kai⁴*	人 *jén²*	的 *ti*	甚 *shén²*	笑 *hsiao⁴*
訛 *ngo²*	的 *ti*	家 *chia¹*	阿 *a¹*	麼 *mo*	甚 *shén²*
人 *jén²*	錢 *ch'ien²*	要 *yao⁴*	硬 *ying⁴*	可 *k'o³*	麼 *mo*

What are you laughing at?
What is there to laugh at?
To insist upon payment of money that is not owed is extortion.

600. 衰 *shuai¹*, decayed; worn out.

601. 困 *k'un⁴*, *k'uen⁴*, surrounded; embarrassed; fatigued.

602. 極 *chi²*, extreme; excess.

603. 夢 *méng⁴*, a dream.

604. Examples:—

笑 *hsiao⁴*	見 *chien⁴*	話 *hua⁴*	說 *shuo¹*	極 *chi²*	夢 *méng⁴*	他 *t'a¹*
極 *chi²*	一 *i¹*	熱 *jé⁴*	了 *liao*	了 *liao*	他 *t'a¹*	氣 *ch'i⁴*
好 *hao³*	件 *chien⁴*	極 *chi²*	一 *i²*	躺 *t'ang³*	那 *na⁴*	血 *hsüeh³*
的 *ti*	奇 *ch'i²*	了 *liao*	夜 *yeh⁴*	在 *tsai⁴*	個 *ko⁴*	衰 *shuai¹*
事 *shih⁴*	事 *shih⁴*	我 *wo³*	的 *ti*	炕 *k'ang⁴*	人 *jén²*	了 *liao*
	冷 *léng³*	夢 *méng⁴*	夢 *méng⁴*	上 *shang⁴*	困 *k'un⁴*	做 *tso⁴*

His constitution is worn out.
To dream.
Being extremely tired (sleepy) he lay down on the *k'ang⁴*, and talked in his sleep all through the night.
Extremely hot.
I dreamt a strange dream.
Obs.—Dreamt: *lit.*, saw in my dreams a strange thing.
A chuckle; or, ironical laugh.
A most excellent undertaking (or arrangement).

605. 貌 *mao⁴*, personal appearance.

606. 相 *hsiang⁴*, the physiognomy. This character will be met with later in a different tone.

607. 醜 *ch'ou³*, ugly (morally or physically).

608. 摔 *shuai¹*, *shuai³*, to throw; to dash down.

609. 掉 *tiao⁴*, to hang (neuter); to fall down.

610. 擉 ch'o¹, ch'uo¹, to jar by a fall.

611. 揝 tsuan⁴, to grasp in the hand.

612. Examples:—

揝	tsuan⁴	了	liao	笑	hsiao⁴	到	tao⁴	下	hsia⁴	得	tê	相	hsiang⁴
住	chu⁴	把	pa³	他	t'a¹	河	ho²	來	lai²	醜	ch'ou³	貌	mao⁴
我	wo³	胳	ko¹	把	pa³	裏	li³	掉	tiao⁴	一	i²	長	chang³
的	ti	臂	pei⁴	瓶	p'ing²	去	ch'ü⁴	下	hsia⁴	件	chien⁴	得	tê
手	shou³	擉	ch'o¹	子	tzŭ	了	liao	去	ch'ü⁴	醜	ch'ou³	好	hao³
了。	liao	了。	liao	摔	shuai¹	很	hên³	他	t'a¹	事。	shih⁴	看	k'an⁴
		他	t'a¹	破	p'o⁴	可	k'o³	掉	tiao⁴	掉	tiao⁴	長	chang³

Good-looking. Ugly.

Obs.—Lit., appearance grown to, etc. *Hsiung mao* might equally well be placed before *ch'ou*; in either case *chang tê* is best not translated.

A disgraceful (or scandalous) business.

To fall down. To fall down.

Obs.—The use of *lai* and *ch'ü* will vary according to the position of the speaker with reference to the object fallen. Thus, were the speaker on foot he would say of a man on horseback, *t'a tiao hsia lai liao*, he has fallen off; if the speaker were on horseback too, he would say *t'a tiao hsia ch'ü liao*.

He fell into the river; such a joke!

Obs.—We could say also *tiao tsai ho li.*

He dashed the bottle down and broke it.

To give a shock to one's arm.

He grasped me tightly by the hand.

613. 窄 chai³, narrow.

614. 則 tsê², then; in consequence.

615. 況 k'uang⁴, besides.

616. 且 ch'ieh³, also; in the next place. Also, under certain circumstances, temporarily.

617. Examples:—

件	chien¹	地	ti⁴	況	k'uang⁴	兒	'rh	不	pu⁴	那	na⁴	一	i¹
事	shih⁴	方	fang¹	且	ch'ieh	窄	chai³	穿	ch'uan¹	一	i²	則	tsê²
我	wo³	兒	'rh	又	yu⁴	二	êrh⁴	一	i¹	件	chien⁴	二	êrh⁴
且	ch'ieh³	窄	chai³	弄	nung⁴	則	tsê²	則	tsê²	袷	kua	則	tsê²
不	pu²	那	na⁴	臟	tsang¹	太	t'ai⁴	袖	hsiu⁴	子	tzŭ	況	k'uang⁴
問。	wên⁴	一	i²	了。	liao	長	ch'ang²	口	k'ou³	我	wo³	且	ch'ieh³

In the first place. In the second place.

Moreover; besides.

I won't put on that coat: in the first place, the sleeves are too narrow; in the second, it is too long; and, moreover, it has been dirtied.

The place is narrow; there is not much space.

I won't inquire into that matter for the moment (temporarily).

EXERCISE XXIII.

多。車往窄方的口城 1
馬的來兒地兒門

1. There is but little space at the city gates for the number of carts and horses that are moving through them in opposite directions.

Obs.—*Lit.*, the city gates' mouth place narrow; coming and going carts and horses many.

鬧不去兒和人外 2
出要告吵趕嚷頭
事嚷訴呢車底是
來。嚷他你的下甚
　看們出那人麽

2. Who is it that is making such a noise outside? The servants and carters are wrangling about something. Go out and tell them not to make such a row, or they may get into trouble.

Obs. 1.—Note *jang¹ jang¹*, the noise of several people talking loudly; it cannot be used of the noise made by one person.

Obs. 2.—Get into trouble: *lit.*, *k'an*, [or they may] find trouble *(shih)* break out *(nao ch'u lai)*.

醜。長看個人兩你 3
　的一很兒個看
　真個好一小那

3. Look at those two little fellows; one of them is good-looking, the other very much the reverse.

下就他人茶醜那那 4
去說害說碗的長好
的。茶起了摔生的看
　碗怕碎了氣的的
　是來兩了。有笑
　掉了、句。　把那話
　　　　　　那

4. The good-looking one was making fun of the ugly one, and the latter, getting into a rage, smashed a tea-cup. Someone found fault with him for this, when he was frightened and said the tea-cup had fallen down.

Obs. 1.—Rage: *lit.*, begot, or generated, breath. *Ch'i*, air, breath: in Chinese physiology often untranslatable; it is best rendered matter; in this instance, wrath matter; the boy begot wrath matter; *i.e.*, got into a rage.

Obs. 2.—Found fault: *shuo*, to speak, followed by a personal noun or pronoun, means to blame; but when the same nouns or pronouns are so circumstanced as to be in what we call the dative case, *shuo* means to speak to.

臂下躺他要的揪 5
摑把在去拉辮住
了。胳地他了子他

5. They took hold of his pigtail and were trying to drag him off, when he lay down and jarred his arm in doing so.

6　晚　吃　裏　做　他　馬　了。
　　飯　多　夜　夢。叫　摔

6. If you eat too heavy a late dinner you are liable to dream at night. He was thrown from his horse.

7　我　笑　困　了　兒　我
　　告　話　的　子　同　都
　　訴　兒。利　上　人　不
　　你　昨　害。坐　把　知
　　一　兒　　　着　嘴　道。
　　個　我　　　就　墨
　　　　　　　　着　水

7. I will tell you a comical story. Yesterday I was dreadfully tired, and went off to sleep as I sat in my chair. The people that were with me poured some liquid ink into my mouth without my knowing anything about it.

Obs.—Went off to sleep: *chao² liao*, short for *shui³-chao² liao*, to go off to sleep; this character will be met with later.

8　街　兒　那　大　車　不　去。
　　道　窄，麼　的　拉　過

8. The street is too narrow for so large a cart to be taken through it.

Turn the following into Chinese. (KEY, EXERCISE XXIII.)

1. There were two men yesterday having an altercation in that narrow space on the top of the city wall, one a good-looking individual, the other very ugly. The good-looking one said to the ugly one, "There is only one of two answers, are you going to do this or are you not?"

Obs. 1.—One of two answers: *lit.*, there are not two sentences or two words about it.

Obs. 2.—Are you going to do this, etc.: *lit.*, this matter you, *tao ti, au fond* (or eventually), do or not; *tao ti* is best not translated. Cf. also *tao liao³ 'rh.*

2. The ugly one replied, "In the first place, I am afraid of what people will say; and in the second, I am terribly tired. Go and do it yourself; if you don't do it, how can I?"

Obs.—What people will say: *lit.*, I fear remarks (*yen-yü*). Note that *yen-yü* may mean to tell in the sense of to blab; also, to mention; *e.g.*, when you want me *yen-yü i shêng-'rh*, let me know. In Peking *yen-yü* is pronounced nearly *yüan-i*.

3. The other burst out into a loud laugh and said, "You are wrong there; why are you afraid of what people will say? I expect you can't do it. If you don't go at once, it is very plain that I must pitch you down." The ugly fellow ran off before [the other] had finished what he was saying.

Obs. 1.—Very plain: *ming² ming²-'rh ti.*

Obs. 2.—Must pitch you down: *lit.*, this is evidently causing me (*chiao wo*) to take you and throw you down. Note *shuai³*, not *shuai¹*; *hsia ch'ü*, not *hsia lai*, the speaker being also on the wall.

4. You surely must have been dreaming; there was no one on the wall yesterday.

5. I was riding along the main street of the *ch'ien² mên²* the day before yesterday, when an altercation between some men behind me, I don't know who, sent my horse off at full speed. After a little I fell off, and gave a jar to my ankle. Luckily, the shock was not a

heavy one; I rested a bit and got all right. I don't know where the horse galloped to; he has not been found yet.

Obs. 1.—Full speed: *lit.*, caused my horse to spread his legs (*k'ai t'ui*) and run off.

Obs. 2.—Luckily: *hai hao*, it was yet good (or fortunate).

Obs. 3.—Yet: *lit.*, this while. *See* 129.

6. I have walked all day to-day and am extremely sleepy. There is no help for it; the best thing you can do is to rest for a night; you will have got over your fatigue by to-morrow.

Obs.—Got over your fatigue: *lit.*, rested over your fatigue (*hsieh kuo fa-'rh lai liao*).

618. 兆 *chao*⁴, a presage; an omen.

619. 吉 *chi*², auspicious.

620. 凶 *hsiung*¹, inauspicious. Also, cruel; malevolent; hence applied to acts of violence or murder.

621. 祥 *hsiang*², good fortune; that which bodes good fortune.

622. 瑞 *jui*⁴, the same as the foregoing *hsiang*².

623. Examples :—

情 *ch'ing*²	祥 *hsiang*²	出 *ch'u*¹	吉 *chi*²	出 *ch'u*¹	我 *wo*³	吉 *chi*²
凶 *hsiung*¹	祥 *hsiang*²	兵 *ping*¹	兆。*chao*⁴	了 *liao*	們 *mên*	兆。*chao*⁴
暴 *pao*⁴	瑞。*jui*⁴	很 *hên*³	去 *ch'ü*⁴	一 *i*²	家 *chia*¹	凶 *hsiung*¹
性 *hsing*⁴	吉 *chi*²	年 *nien*²	個 *ko*⁴	裏 *li*³	兆。*chao*⁴

A good omen. An ill omen.
A good omen has occurred in our family.
Last year's campaign was most successful.
Prosperity.

Obs.—This phrase is seldom met with in conversation. The characters are constantly seen on shop signs.

A cruel and violent disposition.

624. 安 *ngan*¹, repose.

625. 寧 寗 *ning*², tranquility; the second form is now always used, the original character being tabooed, as it formed the *ming*², or personal designation, of the Emperor whose reign is styled Tao Kuang. When read *ning*⁴, and followed by a negative, it becomes a term of comparison.

626. 順 *shun*⁴, obedient; hence, following.

627. 寬 *k'uan*¹, broad; liberal.

628. 綽 *ch'o*⁴, of exceeding extent (said of place, fortune, etc.); inseparable in the spoken language from *k'uan*¹.

629. Examples:—

事 shih⁴	綽 ch'o⁴	他 t'a¹	順 shun⁴	不 pu⁴	亂 luan⁴	安 ngan¹
都 tou¹	他 t'a¹	家 chia¹	水 shui³	安 ngan¹	百 po²	寧 ning²
順 shun⁴	們 mén	裡 li³	順 shun⁴	寧 ning²	姓 hsing⁴	天 t'ien¹
當 tang¹	的 ti	寬 k'uan¹	風 féng¹	了 liao	就 chiu⁴	下 hsia⁴

Peace and quietness (state of freedom from danger).
When the Empire is in disorder the people are not tranquil.
A fair wind and tide (or stream).
His family is in easy circumstances.
Everything goes smoothly with them.

630. 貧 p'in², poor.

631. 窮 ch'iung², extremity; hence, poverty.

632. 窘 chiung³, straitened (of space or fortune); not often used colloquially out of Peking.

633. 產 ch'an³, to produce, as the earth its fruits; productions; property.

634. 業 yeh⁴, a calling; an occupation; hence, acquired property. It is also a sign of the past tense.

635. Examples:—

有 yu³	也 yeh³	一 i⁴	家 chia¹	貧 p'in²	他 t'a¹
甚 shên²	沒 mei²	點 tien³	裏 li³	窮 ch'iung²	真 chén¹
麼 mo	有 yu³	兒 'rh	很 hén³	的 ti	不 pu²
出 ch'u¹	這 ché⁴	產 ch'an³	窘 chiung³	人 jén²	是 shih⁴
產 ch'an³	兒 'rh	業 yeh⁴	連 lien²	他 t'a¹	個 ko⁴

He is by no means a poor man.
His family is in very straitened circumstances.
They have absolutely no property.
What are the natural products of this place?

636. 朋 p'éng², a friend or companion; a person with whom one is in constant contact. Never used alone colloquially.

637. 友 yu³, a friend; a person of kindred tastes or sentiments.

638. 賞 shang³, to bestow on; also, under certain circumstances, to take pleasure in, as a pretty sight.

639. 相 hsiang¹, mutual; reciprocal; but it also indicates the unreciprocated relation of one person or thing to another. See 606.

640. 幫 pang¹, to assist.

PART III.—THE FORTY EXERCISES.

641. Examples:—

多 to^1	幫 $pang^1$	姓 $hsing^4$	地 ti^4	一 i^2	這 $ch\check{e}^4$
年 $nien^2$	著 cho^1	銀 yin^2	方 $fang^1$	個 ko^4	些 $hsieh^1$
的 ti	我。wo^3	子。$tz\check{u}$	官 $kuan^1$	朋 $p'\acute{e}ng^2$	花 hua^1
相 $hsiang^1$	我 wo^3	請 $ch'ing^3$	賞 $shang^3$	友 yu^3	盆 $p'\hat{e}n^2$
好。hao^3	們 $m\acute{e}n$	你 ni^3	給 kei^3	賞 $shang^3$	是 $shih^4$
	倆 lia^3	來 lai^2	百 po^2	的 ti	我 wo^3

These flower-pots were presented to me by a friend.
The local officials rewarded the people.
Obs.—Note that in most instances *shang* is used of the gift of a superior to an inferior; in the preceding example it is used politely.
Please come and assist me.
We two have been good friends for many years.

642. 留 liu^2, to keep; to detain.

643. 丟 tiu^1, to lose.

644. 根 $k\acute{e}n^1$, the root of a tree; the numerative of sticks, spears, ropes, etc.

645. 現 $hsien^4$, now; present time.

646. 別 $pieh^2$, do not; a contraction of the characters pu^2 yao^4. It will be met with presently in its proper signification.

647. Examples:—

能 $n\acute{e}ng^2$	了。$liao^3$	底 ti^4	根 $k\acute{e}n^1$	能 $n\acute{e}ng^2$	費 fei^4	留 liu^2
寫 $hsieh^3$	手 $shou^3$	根 $k\acute{e}n^1$	棍 kun^4	別 $pieh^2$	心 $hsin^1$	他 $t'a^1$
字。$tz\check{u}^4$	疼 $t'\acute{e}ng^2$	兒。'rh	子。$tz\check{u}$	給 kei^3	今 $chin^1$	吃 $ch'ih^1$
現 $hsien^4$	到 tao^4	丟 tiu^1	丟 tiu^1	天 $t'ien^1$	飯。fan^4
在 $tsai^4$	底 ti^3	不 pu^4	那 na^4	怕 $p'a^4$	費 fei^4
不 pu^4	丟 tiu^1	了。$liao^3$	一 i^4	不 pu^4	心 $hsin^1$

Keep him to dinner.
Much obliged; I am afraid I cannot to-day.
Obs.—Obliged: *lit.*, you have expended your thoughts; one of many expressions of thanks.
Don't lose that stick.
Obs.—We might also say *pieh tiu na kén kun-tzǔ*, but in southern *kuan hua* this would mean don't throw it away.
It can't be lost.
At the root; originally.
Obs.—Note ti^4, not ti^3.
Eventually (or, after all) it was lost.
My hand is sore; I cannot write at present.
Obs.—At present: *lit.*, the now that is.

EXERCISE XXIV.

1. 昨兒晚上有人行兇。兇手拏住了。怕是要正法的。正法就地正法。

   1. A murder was committed there last night. The murderer has been seized, and will, I expect, eventually be executed. Execution at the scene of the crime.

   Obs. 1.—Murder: *lit.*, a man there did a cruel action. Note that *hsing hsiung* may not mean to commit a murder, though it generally does.

   Obs. 2.—Murderer: *hsiung shou*; *lit.*, murdering hand. *Shou*, the hand, is not unfrequently used in place of *jên*, the individual.

   Obs. 3.—Executed: *chêng*, in legal phraseology, means to punish; *chêng fa*, to punish by the law, or as the law directs, is, however, limited to capital punishment.

2. 事情沒來先看見甚麼能知道日後祥瑞那就叫吉兆。

   2. When before a thing comes to pass there is something seen by which one can tell that there will be prosperity at some future date, that is called *chi² chao⁴* (an auspicious omen).

   Obs.—When before: *lit.*, things not come's before; the word *chih* here, like *ti*, forming a number of words preceding it into a predicate of the word following it.

3. 家裏日用的錢足了過日子有錢用足了太寬綽。日子不過足就是貧窮。

   3. When there is money enough in a house for daily use, that is called *k'uan¹-ch'o¹* (comfort). When there is not enough for daily need, that is *p'in²-ch'iung²* (poverty).

4. 過日子有准進錢的那就叫產業。

   4. When there is a regular income to provide for daily subsistence, that is called *ch'an³-yeh⁴* (property producing a regular income).

   Obs.—Regular income: *lit.*, certain incoming's money.

5. 那時候兒我甚麼都沒了就找了一個朋友說你們這些年的相好他們幾個錢幫我說沒有甚麼不肯不肯真有是他你們不能我們底根兒本現在產業也沒了連弄一個大錢都很費事。

   5. I lost everything at that time, so I looked up a certain friend of mine and said to him, "We have been good friends these ever so many years; will you help me with a little money?" He said, "It is not that I will not, but really that I cannot. We had a little money originally, as you know, but now our income has disappeared and we find very great difficulty in making a single cash."

PART III.—THE FORTY EXERCISES.

酒錢。	賞多去 你兒我 們的多 了。要動 一們身 路這那 平就分 安那手 罷。麼着	趕進城這三五天可就	當天兒要沒丟那銀子	車，要是多喀起身。	你們這你們6 7

6. If you can get your cart into the city in the one day I will give you a large *pour-boire*.

7. When do you start? If I had not lost that silver I should have been off to-day, but I shall certainly start within the next three or four days. In that case we will say good-bye now. May you have a prosperous journey!

Obs.—Good-bye: *fên shou*; *lit.*, separate the hands. It is the custom amongst Chinese to shake hands, though not quite in the European fashion, when taking leave of each other for a long period; and the drawing away of the hands after such a leavetaking is *fên shou*.

分去了。麼鋪你8 手年我不子們 了。就們開怎那

8. How is it that your shop is no longer open? We dissolved partnership last year.

Obs.—Note another meaning of *fên shou*.

月。好節中十八9 賞正秋五月

9. The 15th of the 8th moon, the Festival of Mid-autumn, is just the right time for viewing the moon.

Obs.—Festival: the Chinese year is divided into three principal periods or festivals (*chieh*; *lit.*, joints), exclusive of New Year's Day, to each of which a specific name is given; the first is on the 15th of the 1st moon (the Feast of Lanterns), the second on the 5th of the 5th moon, and the third as above.

不兒件不個請10 了。個事然忙你 完今這兒，幫

10. Please come and lend me a hand, otherwise I sha'n't get through with this business to-day.

Obs.—Lend a hand: *lit.*, aid a haste; *q.d.*, a person who is in haste or busy.

Turn the following into Chinese. (KEY, EXERCISE XXIV.)

1. That man's affairs are certainly not prosperous.

2. Originally he had a regular income, and was in easy circumstances as regarded his daily needs. There came a year when there was no rain for months in succession, so he got no crops off his land, and his family affairs did not go smoothly. He spent all his capital by degrees, and now he is very poor. His intimate friends now and again (accidentally) help him along with a little money.

Obs.—Capital: *lit.*, root money.

3. Did he alone lose his money, or did he involve others in his misfortune?

Obs.—Involve : *lit.*, to connect *(lien)* in misfortune or trouble *(lei)*; in combination they form the verb to involve. The sentence, literally translated, runs : was it he one man lost money, yet was it [that he] involved other persons?

4. The greater part of the farmers thereabouts lost their money also, so the district has been far from quiet of late; I, however, did not suffer much inconvenience. [You ask me] why (*lit.*, how)? It was in this wise. In my opinion, things, whether good or evil, give always a presage of their advent. One day I dreamt a dream. I dreamt I saw a man come and burn all the wheat in my fields; so I sold the whole of it unripe [as it stood]. Afterwards we were short of rain, but I had got hold of my money long beforehand.

Obs. 1.—Of late : *lit.*, near coming *(chin lai).*
Obs. 2.—However : *tao*. See 182.

Obs. 3.—Give a presage, etc.: *lit.*, all have a previous omen.

5. Please keep this jar, sir *(ta-jên)*; I am very poor. My friends won't assist me, so I have sold or pawned all my household furniture, and this one jar is all I've got [left].

Obs.—Note *p'ing*, a jar ; *p'ing-tzŭ*, a bottle, or small jar.

6. Isn't your name CHANG? How have you become so poor as this? I remember two or three years back you had a regular income and could manage to live well enough.

Obs.—So poor: *lit.*, you how straitened *chiung*^{3}) into *(ch'êng*^{2}) this kind?

7. What you say, sir, is quite true; I lost my money after that, and at present am a beggar.

Obs.—Beggar: *lit.*, wanting rice's man; the "man" may be omitted.

648. 您 *nin*^{2}, more commonly pronounced *ni-na*, which, again, is short for *ni lao jên chia*; politely, you my elder, you, sir, or madam.

649. 喳 *cha*^{1} (rather *dja*^{1}), a sound taken from the Manchu; yes, sir, or madam.

650. 親 *ch'in*^{1}, intimate relationship.

651. 旁 *p'ang*^{2}, the sides.

652. 母 *mu*^{3}, a mother.

653. Examples:—

的	*ti*	走	*tsou*^{3}	車	*ch'ê*^{1}	大	*ta*^{4}	兒	*'rh*	父	*fu*^{4}	來	*lai*^{2}
我	*wo*^{3}	人	*jên*^{2}	輛	*liang*^{4}	道	*tao*^{4}	的	*ti*	親	*ch'in*^{1}	喳	*cha*^{1}
親	*ch'in*^{1}	我	*wo*^{3}	兩	*liang*^{3}	中	*chung*^{1}	人	*jên*^{2}	母	*mu*^{3}	您	*nin*^{2}
筆	*pi*^{3}	親	*ch'in*^{1}	旁	*p'ang*^{2}	間	*chien*^{4}	那	*na*^{4}	親	*ch'in*^{1}	要	*yao*^{4}
寫	*hsieh*^{3}	自	*tzŭ*^{4}	邊	*pien*^{1}	兒	*'rh*	一	*i*^{4}	旁	*p'ang*^{2}	甚	*shên*^{2}
的	*ti*	做	*tso*^{4}	兒	*'rh*	走	*tsou*^{3}	條	*t'iao*^{2}	邊	*pien*^{1}	麼	*mo*

Boy! Sir. What do you want, sir?
Father (Radical 88). Mother. Bystanders.
On that high road the middle is for carts and the two sides for people on foot.

Obs.—Note that *ch'ê* is generalised by the numerative following instead of preceding it.

I did it myself. I wrote it myself.

Obs.—We might also say *wo pên*^{3} *jên-'rh*, my individual self.

654. 祖 *tsu*^{3}, ancestors.

655. 翁 wêng¹, an old man. Generally employed with the first character of a person's hao⁴, or literary appellation; thus, a man whose name was WANG, and his hao⁴ YA³-T'ING², could be spoken of or addressed as YA³ wêng¹.

656. 兄 hsiung¹, an elder brother.

657. 孫 sun¹, a grandchild.

658. 舍 shê⁴, a cottage.

659. 弟 ti⁴, a younger brother.

660. Examples:—

孫。sun¹	您 nin²	兒 êrh²	七 ch'i²	老 lao³	父。fu⁴	我 wo³
有 yu³	跟 kên¹	子 tzŭ	個 ko⁴	翁。wêng¹	家 chia¹	的 ti
五 wu³	前 ch'ien²	孫 sun¹	家 chia¹	我 wo³	祖 tsu³	祖 tsu³
個 ko⁴	幾 chi³	子 tzŭ	兄。hsiung¹	們 mên	母。mu³	上。shang⁴
小 hsiao³	位 wei⁴	孫 sun¹	舍。shê⁴	弟 ti⁴	這 chê⁴	家 chia¹
孫。sun¹	令 ling⁴	女。nü³	弟。ti⁴	兄 hsiung¹	位 wei⁴	祖 tsu³

My ancestors. My grandfather. My grandmother.

Obs. 1.—My is implied by the use of *chia*, which is used only in referring to one's own relations.

Obs. 2.—We can also say *chia tsu*, my grandfather.

This old gentleman.

We are seven brothers.

Obs.—Note that *ti* precedes *hsiung* when the word is plural, but that *hsiung ti* means a younger brother.

My elder brother. My younger brother (*see* Exercise XXV, 4).

A son. A grandson. A granddaughter.

How many grandsons have you, sir?

Obs. 1.—Note *ling sun* when speaking of others; *hsiao sun* of one's own grandchildren. See 208.

Obs. 2.—Have you: *kên ch'ien*; lit., in your presence.

I have five grandsons.

661. 奴 nu², a slave; but also used disparagingly of inferiors not slaves.

662. 才 ts'ai², talent; but when coupled with nu², the foregoing, it does not appear to affect its sense.

663. 迎 ying², to go out to meet an equal or superior.

664. 接 chieh¹, to receive a present; to greet a guest. Can be used with the foregoing.

665. Examples:—

迎 ying²	道 tao⁴	才 ts'ai²	那 nu⁴	得 tei³	父 fu¹	奴 nu²
接 chieh¹	兒 'rh	們 mên	壞 huai⁴	去 ch'ü⁴	快 k'uai⁴	才。ts'ai²
您。nin²	趕 kan³	走 tsou³	心 hsin¹	迎 ying²	回 hui⁴	迎 ying²
	不 pu²	錯 ts'o⁴	的 ti	接。chieh¹	來 lai²	接。chieh¹
	上 shang⁴	了 liao	奴 nu²	我 wo³	我 wo³	家 chia¹

Slaves.

To receive; to go to meet, as a parent, visitor, etc.

My father will be back directly; I must go and receive him.

Those rascally servants of mine lost their way, and were not in time to receive you.

666. 葬, 塟, *tsang*⁴, to bury; the first form appears to be more frequently used.

667. 絲 *ssŭ*¹, silk (spinning or winding) not yet made into a fabric.

668. 團 *t'uan*², a ball, a lump, as of silk, cotton, etc.

669. 絨 *jung*², woollen cloth; velvet; worsted; very coarse silk.

670. 尺 *ch'ih*³, the Chinese foot, of 10 inches.

671. Examples:—

五 *wu*³		長 *ch'ang*²		是 *shih*⁴		一 *i*⁴		那 *na*⁴		下 *hsia*⁴				
尺 *ch'ih*²		三 *san*¹		論 *lun*⁴		根 *kên*¹		絨 *jung*²		葬 *tsang*⁴				
寸 *ts'un*⁴		尺 *ch'ih*³		尺 *ch'ih*³		絲 *ssŭ*¹		三 *san*¹		一 *i*⁴				
過 *kuo*⁴		二 *êrh*⁴		賣 *mai*⁴		線 *hsien*⁴		尺 *ch'ih*³		團 *t'uan*²				
長 *ch'ang*²		寸 *ts'un*⁴		的 *ti*		絨 *jung*²		寬 *k'uan*¹		絲 *ssŭ*¹				

To bury.
A ball of silk.
That velvet is three feet wide.
A silken thread.
Velvet is sold by the foot.
Three feet two inches and a half in length.
Too long; *lit.*, feet and inches excessive length.
Obs.—Note *ch'ih*² *ts'un*⁴ in combination, not *ch'ih*³.

672. 貨 *huo*⁴, goods; merchandise.

673. 昂 *ang*², rising; risen. Seldom used alone.

674. 替 *t'i*⁴, to supply the place of; for; instead of.

675. 挑 *t'iao*,¹ to carry on the shoulder; to select.

676. Examples:—

菜 *ts'ai*⁴		挑 *t'iao*¹		打 *ta*³		長 *chang*³		現 *hsien*⁴		貴 *kuei*⁴		買 *mai*³		
挑 *t'iao*¹		一 *i*²		算 *suan*⁴		了 *liao*		在 *tsai*⁴		絲 *ssŭ*¹		土 *t'u*³		
了 *liao*		個 *ko*⁴		請 *ch'ing*³		都 *tou*¹		昂 *ang*²		貨 *huo*⁴		貨 *huo*⁴		
來 *lai*²		好 *huo*³		您 *nin*²		說 *shuo*¹		貴 *kuei*⁴		的 *ti*		出 *ch'u*¹		
		的 *ti*		替 *t'i*⁴		得 *tê*		現 *hsien*⁴		價 *chia*⁴		口 *k'ou*³		
				我 *wo*³		我 *wo*³		在 *tsai*⁴		錢 *ch'ien*²		昂 *ang*²		

To buy goods for export.
Obs.—Note *k'ou*, a port, sea or riverine; also, a pass, frontier or otherwise.
High price; rising in price.
The price of silk goods is *ang*²-*kuei*⁴ (high) just now, or *chang*³ (has risen); you may say either.
I propose to ask you to choose me a good one.
Bring (carry with a pole) those vegetables here.

EXERCISE XXV.

思意。的人 重人 兒尊 有點 您是 稱人 1

1. To address a person as *nin²* (you, sir) conveys a certain idea of doing honour to the person addressed.

Obs.—*Lit.*, when one accosts anyone as *nin*, it is that there is a particle of honouring the person's intention.

家老翁 就稱人 的父親 子。旁人 親是我老父 是家祖就 2

2. *Chia¹ tsu³* (my grandfather) is my father's father. The father of a third person is called his *lao³ wêng¹*.

Obs. 1.—Third person : *lit.*, side person. Though *lao wêng* is a term of respect, you do not use it when speaking to a man of his own father.

Obs. 2.—*Ch'êng*, here, to speak of ; translated in Example 1 by *addressing*, because its object is there in the second person.

的安。 家父。 的祖人。 問人家 好阿是 阿令尊 令祖好 3

3. Is the honoured grandfather well? is the honoured worshipful one well? are inquiries after the well-being of the grandfather or father of the person addressed.

Obs.—Note the interrogative *a*.

兄令弟。 兄是說的 人家的弟 兄舍的稱家 說的弟 已的令兄 向人說自 4

4. In speaking to anyone of one's own brothers, the form used is *chia¹ hsiung¹* (the elder brother of my family), *shê⁴ ti⁴* (the younger brother of my cottage). In speaking to anyone else of his brother, the form is the honoured elder brother, or the honoured younger brother.

多人。 下說的。 是買的 買不還 有人是 是使的 的才有喚就 奴 5

5. The term *nu²-ts'ai²* means, simply, servants, some are property (slaves), some are not; but the more common phrase is *ti³ hsia⁴ jên²* (inferiors).

Obs.—But the more common : *lit.*, [but] still is [it the fact that] saying *ti hsia jên's* [fashion is the] more frequent ; or, the saying *ti hsia jên's* [people] predominate.

他們去。 去幫葬, 幫老得 我翁兒 兒他下 迎們後 接去 得'回 我來, 祖家 今 6

6. My grandfather returns to-day, and I must go to meet him. Their father is to be buried the day after to-morrow, and I shall have to go and lend a hand at the funeral.

Obs. 1.—Buried, etc.: *lit.*, the day after to-morrow their father [they] bury ; I must to help them go. *Hsia tsang* are two verbs compounded, not a verb and its object.

Obs. 2.—Here, as in many places, the object *(lao wêng)* preceding the verb may be made in our idiom the subject of a passive verb.

130   TZŬ ÊRH CHI.—COLLOQUIAL SERIES.

7. 生絲不是你們這兒的土貨麼。可不是麼。那可絨不是土貨，請您替我挑一點兒好的。

7. Is not raw silk a product of your country here? To be sure it is; but velvet is not, and I shall be obliged to you to choose me some that is good.

Obs.—To be sure: *lit.*, can it not be?

8. 我兄弟給大人請安他說他怕明兒不能來了找個替工兒替他幾天。

8. My younger brother presents his respects to you, sir; he says he is afraid he cannot come to-morrow, so he has found a substitute to act in his stead for a few days.

Obs. 1.—Note that *hsiung-ti*, in combination, means a younger brother or brothers, and *ti hsiung*, brothers, elder and younger.
Obs. 2.—Present respects: *ch'ing an*; *lit.*, requests [to be informed of your] comfort or well-being.
Obs. 3.—Substitute: *lit.*, an instead-of workman.

9. 我挑出來的那瓦盆總得挑着擱在車上不行。

9. You will have to carry those earthenware basins that I have chosen with a carrying pole; it won't do to put them in a cart.

Obs.—Note *t'iao*, to choose; *t'iao cho*, to carry with a pole.

10. 他把紙弄成團兒往我臉上扔。

10. He rolled some paper into a ball and threw it in my face.

Obs.—*Lit.*, he took paper, worked it [till it] formed a ball, towards my face threw it; *ch'êng* is often an auxiliary simply denoting completion of an action.

11. 性口馱的東西叫駝子，人肩髈上挑的東西叫挑子，人背上背的東西叫背子。

11. The load carried on the backs of animals is called a *to⁴-tzŭ*, as has been before explained; that carried by men with a pole over the shoulder is called a *t'iao¹-tzŭ*; and that carried by men on the back is called a *pei¹-tzŭ*.

Obs.—髈 and 膀 are identical.

Turn the following into Chinese. (KEY, EXERCISE XXV.)

1. Three days ago our elder brother returned home, bringing with him some 200 balls odd of silk and 50 bales of velvet. My father told me to go and meet him, and, while I was about it, to assist him in carrying in the goods.

Obs. 1.—Three days ago: *lit.*, the great day before yesterday.

Obs. 2.—While I was about it: *lit.*, following with the hand; *i.e.*, taking advantage of one job to do another (to take the opportunity).

2. Is your elder brother a draper, then?

3. To be sure. Father and an ancestor of his were also in that line of business. What object have you in asking?

Obs.—What object: *lit.*, you ask this talk have what lofty vision (or idea)?

4. My younger brother wants to buy some fine raw silk, [and I wish to] ask your brother to pick out a little good [stuff] for him; can it be done?

5. It can be done, of course; he will certainly select some silk for your brother; but there is one thing, I am afraid the price has gone up; it is very dear at present.

6. Good-bye, sir! *Au revoir!*

Obs. 1.—Good-bye: *lit.*, you please; *q.d.*, please do not remain on my account, or, please do not let me detain you.

Obs. 2.—*Au revoir: lit.*, returning see; we shall meet when you or I return, or by-and-by. These are two of the most common salutations in use; *nin ch'ing* may be also used for, that will do, thank you.

7. Their grandfather was buried yesterday. I told my servants to go and lend them a hand, but the rascals wouldn't listen to me, and never went at all. Some bystander had said there was a ghost over there, and they were so frightened that they refused to go. My grandson eventually called one of them to him. He gave a *cha* and came slowly across, whereupon my grandson gave him a few strokes with a stick.

Obs. 1.—Never: *tao liao³-'rh*; *lit.*, to the finish.

Obs. 2.—A ghost: *kuei³* (Radical 194).

8. What your servants say has some little truth in it. I passed the place the other night, and I saw a ghost running about in a wild sort of way. His hair was red, his face yellow, and the moment I saw him it frightened me terribly.

Obs. 1.—By: this is rendered by *ta³* (**241**).

Obs. 2.—Frightened me terribly: *p'a ti wo liao pu tê*. Note *p'a* as an active verb.

9. What nonsense! You certainly must have had too much to drink again.

677. 想 *hsiang³*, to think; to think of.

678. 却 *ch'io⁴*, *ch'üeh⁴*, properly, to reject a present; a strong disjunctive, to be rendered sometimes by *but*, sometimes by emphasis only.

679. 睡 *shui⁴*, to sleep.

680. 覺 *chiao⁴*, *chio²*, *chüeh²*. *Chiao⁴* is properly to perceive, to feel, in which sense it is sometimes pronounced *chio²* and *chüeh²*; when joined with *shui⁴*, to sleep (**679**), it is pronounced *chiao⁴*; it does not seem to affect the sense of that word in any way.

681. Examples:—

著 *chao²* 睡 *shui⁴* 說 *shuo¹* 他 *t'a¹* 你 *ni³* 到 *tao⁴* 我 *wo³*
身 *shên¹* 覺 *chiao⁴* 我 *wo³* 昨 *tso²* 你 *ni³* 我 *wo³* 想 *hsiang³*
上 *shang⁴* 來 *lai²* 沒 *mei²* 兒 *'rh* 想 *hsiang³* 常 *ch'ang²* 他 *t'a¹*
覺 *chio²* 著 *cho* 在 *tsai⁴* 來 *lai²* 他 *t'a¹* 常 *ch'ang²* 明 *ming²*
著 *cho* 我 *wo³* 家 *chia¹* 過 *kuo⁴* 怎 *tsên³* 兒 *'rh* 兒 *'rh*
冷 *lêng³* 睡 *shui⁴* 我 *wo³* 他 *t'a¹* 麼 *mo¹* 的 *ti* 可 *k'o³*
　 　 不 *pu⁴* 却 *ch'io⁴* 們 *mên* 樣 *yang⁴* 想 *hsiang³* 以 *i³*

I think he can arrive to-morrow.
I am continually thinking about you.

Obs.—For *ch'ang*, see **688**.

What do you think of him?
He came yesterday, and they said I wasn't at home, but I was asleep.
Obs.—*Shui-chiao* does not necessarily imply sleep, but it does imply the attempt to sleep; *see* next example.
I cannot sleep; I feel cold.

682. 對 *tui*⁴, opposite to; to agree with; a pair. It also sometimes takes the place of the preposition *to*, or marks the sign of the dative.

683. 賽 *sai*⁴, to compete with.

684. 嗇 *sê*⁴, niggardly; never used alone.

685. 吞 *t'un*¹, to swallow; to bolt down. Oftener used figuratively of peculation or avarice.

686. 疊 *tieh*², in folds or layers; to fold; repeatedly.

687. 增 *tsêng*¹, to add to.

688. 常 *ch'ang*², constant; continual.

689. Examples:—

是 *shih*⁴	裳 *shang*¹	吞 *t'un*¹	嗇 *sê*⁴	馬 *ma*³	面 *mien*⁴	對 *tui*⁴
平 *p'ing*²	疊 *tieh*²	人 *jên*²	刻 *k'ê*⁴	那 *na*⁴	我 *wo*³	面 *mien*⁴
常 *ch'ang*²	起 *ch'i*³	家 *chia*¹	人 *jên*²	青 *ch'ing*¹	們 *mên*	頓 *juan*³
的 *ti*	來 *lai*²	的 *ti*	不 *pu*²	馬 *ma*³	賽 *sai*⁴	是 *shih*⁴
事 *shih*⁴	增 *tsêng*¹	錢 *ch'ien*²	好 *hao*⁴	跑 *p'ao*³	過 *kuo*⁴	硬 *ying*
	多 *to*¹	把 *pa*³	花 *hua*¹	得 *tê*²	兩 *liang*³	的 *ti*
	却 *ch'io*⁴	衣 *i*¹	錢 *ch'ien*²	快 *k'uai*⁴	回 *hui*²	對 *tui*⁴

The opposite; the reverse side; also, in front of.
Soft is the opposite of hard.
We tried the horses twice; the grey gallops the faster.
Niggardly men do not like to spend money.
Obs.—*Hao*⁴.
To pocket (*lit.*, swallow) people's money.
Fold up the clothes.
Obs.—*Ch'i lai*, the auxiliary verb of *tieh*, does not necessarily imply movement upwards.
Many added.
It is nevertheless a matter of common occurrence.
Obs.—*P'ing-ch'ang* may also mean indifferent, as a person's reputation.

690. 葱 *ts'ung*¹, onions.

691. 苗 *miao*², sprouts; the first appearance of any vegetation above the ground belonging to the category of grasses.

PART III.—THE FORTY EXERCISES.

692. 嫩 *nên*⁴, *nun*⁴, tender, fresh, or young, as opposed to tough, stale, or old.

693. 桑 *sang*¹, the mulberry tree.

694. 樹 *shu*⁴, a tree.

695. 林 *lin*², a grove; a wood; a forest.

696. Examples:—

兒 'rh	我 wo³	有 yu³	桑 sang¹	來 lai²	兒 'rh	一 i⁴
不 pu²	要 yao⁴	桑 sang¹	樹 shu⁴	了 liao	豆 tou⁴	斤 chin¹
要 yao⁴	嫩 nên⁴	樹 shu⁴	山 shan¹	樹 shu⁴	苗 miao²	蔥 ts'ung¹
老 lao³	雞 chi¹	林 lin²	背 pei⁴	林 lin²	兒 'rh	嫩 nên⁴
的 ti	子 tzŭ³	子 tzŭ	後 hou⁴	子 tzŭ	上 shang⁴	苗 miao²

A catty of onions.
Tender sprouts.
The beans have sprouted.
Obs.—Emphasise *shang*: note that *shang* verbalises *miao*.
A grove of trees; or, a wood.
The mulberry tree.
At the back of the hill there is a mulberry grove.
I want soft-boiled eggs, not hard-boiled ones.

697. 森 *sên*¹, density, as of foliage.

698. 綠 *lü*⁴, green; the literary pronunciation is *lu*⁴.

699. 草 *ts'ao*³, grass; plants not being trees.

700. 濕, 溼, *shih*¹, wet; damp. The first form is the commoner.

701. 曬, 晒, *shai*⁴, a verb describing the action of the sun's rays; not necessarily to scorch. The second is a vulgar form.

702. Examples:—

出 ch'u¹	裳 shang¹	我 wo³	草 ts'ao³	子 tzŭ	的 ti	蔥 ts'ung¹
去 ch'ü⁴	都 tou¹	一 i⁴	鞋 hsieh²	綠 lü⁴	那 na⁴	苗 miao²
曬 shai⁴	濕 shih¹	身 shên¹	草 ts'ao³	森 sên¹	個 ko⁴	兒 'rh
一 i⁴	了 liao	的 ti	帽 mao⁴	森 sên¹	竹 chu²	是 shih⁴
晒 shai⁴	拏 na²	衣 i¹	兒 'rh	的 ti	林 lin²	綠 lü⁴

Onion sprouts are green.
How green that bamboo grove is!
Straw shoes. Straw hats.
All my clothes are wet; take them out and dry them in the sun.

EXERCISE XXVI.

好你說好。 土。涼快又沒 又草地裏坐着 樹林子在 那兒就找個 西山去罷。 我們明兒上 1

1. Let's go to the Western Hills to-morrow. When we get there we will look for a grove of trees and sit down on the green grass, where we shall be both cool and free from dust. What do you say?

Obs.—Green grass: the word *ch'ing* applies to many other colours besides green; it may also mean glossy black, grey, or blue, and further qualifies the shades of certain primary colours.

對呢。 時候兒還不 樹林子坐着 裏曬暖兒好 是在太陽地 我却想着還 去倒沒有甚 麼不能去的 2

2. There is nothing to prevent our going, but I think it would be better to bask in the sun; it is not the time of year to sit in the woods.

Obs.—*Lit.*, go, there is not, on the contrary, any not being able to go's [reason]; I, however, think, still it is in the sun's place to warm better; in a wood sitting the time [is] not apposite.

過你。 長却怕比我的 心正對你的 賽着我跑罷 偺們倆人 3

3. Let's have a race. It's just what I should like, but your legs are longer than mine, and I fear I can't beat you.

Obs.—Just what I should like: *lit.*, correctly agrees with my wishes (or feelings).

增的多。 天比一天 們的錢他 肯於花錢 很都是過 弟都利害得 他那倆兄 4

4. Those two brothers of his are terrible fellows, they are both too niggardly; they won't spend anything, and their money increases every day.

一斤。 二百錢 嫩都不分老 兩天貴 那葱這 5

5. Onions have been dear these last two days; old and young alike, they are all 200 cash the catty.

PART III.—THE FORTY EXERCISES.

6. 草 花 木 名 出 兒 苗 說
   木 的 總 了 了 兒 得
   是 樹 草 子 苗 火 也。

Obs.—Generic: *lit.*, all-including name.

6. The term $ts'ao^3$ mu^4 is generic of flowers, plants, and trees. The wheat has sprouted. You can also say huo^3 $miao^2$-'rh (the flame of a fire).

7. 苗 是 川 南 人 生 熟
   子 四 東 的 分 的 的。

Obs.—Wild, etc.: *lit.*, unripe and ripe; reclaimed and unreclaimed.

7. The Miaotzŭ are people to the south-east of Szechwan; they are divided into wild and reclaimed.

8. 樹 叫 林 那 樹 子 森 的。
   多 樹 子。桑 林 綠 森

8. A number of trees is called a shu^4 lin^2-$tz\breve{u}$. How deep (or dense) the green of that mulberry grove is!

9. 要 裳 頭 一 了 來。
   把 鋪 地 曬 就
   溼 在 裏 曬。曡
   衣 乾 日 曬 起
   了、曬 乾 乾

Obs. 1.—To dry: *nung*, here, and often elsewhere, pronounced *nou*, verbalises the adjective *kan*, dry.
Obs. 2.—Sunny: *lit.*, you must spread them in a sun place; note *jih-t'ou*, the sun.

9. If you want to dry damp clothes you should spread them out in a sunny place for the sun to shine upon them. When the sun has dried them they should be folded up.

10. 聽 兒 人 銀 下 兒 了。
    見 住 曡 子。鐘 們
    說、的 好 天 了 該
    對 那 些 有 小 睡
    過 個 吞 八 人 覺

Obs. 1.—Over the way: *lit.*, fronting over (or across).
Obs. 2.—Over and over: *lit.*, on repeated occasions.

10. I hear that the man who lives over the way has pocketed people's money over and over again. It's 8 o'clock; youngsters should be in bed.

Turn the following into Chinese. (KEY, EXERCISE XXVI.)

1. The other day we two were having an archery match in the grove. The weather was excellent, the sun's rays were warm, and that stretch of wood was of a lovely deep green. When we had finished our archery I told him a funny story.

Obs. 1.—Archery: *la kung* (Radical 57), to draw the bow.
Obs. 2.—A stretch: *i tai*. See 416.

2. I proceeded to say that once upon a time there was a man of the name of MA, who sold onions. He was sleeping one day on the ground in a mulberry grove, and when he got up he saw a man standing before him roaring with laughter.

Obs. 1.—Once upon a time: *lit.*, formerly.
Obs. 2.—Roaring with laughter: *lit.*, [with] great sound laugh[ing].

3. "What is there to laugh at here?" he asked in a rage. The man said to him, "The ground here is very damp; look at your clothes, they are all wet, and must be spread out in the sun to dry; besides, you have lost the merchandise you brought with you."

Obs. 1.—Asked in a rage: *lit.*, he begot rage, then said, here is what laughing head (or item)?

Obs. 2.—Said to him: *tui t'a shuo*; note *tui* as a preposition.

4. The old man gave a look, and, true enough, his bags were empty. "Then," said he, "if it isn't you who has eaten my young onions, who has?" "I've not eaten them for nothing," the other replied; "there's the money;" and as he spoke he threw some large cash into the grass

Obs. 1.—Old man: *lit.*, old head; a common expression, but not often addressed to the individual.

Obs. 2.—There's the money: *lit.*, the price I have given is there; *kei ti* for *kei tê* (have given).

5. The man MA, thinking this really was money, went forward to get it, but the moment he took his eyes off the other, he was gone. The money, too, could not be found, so MA knew that it was not a man but a sprite.

6. That man is fearfully stingy. He comes from that place Yünnan. I think that by origin he is a Miaotzŭ, who, several years since, did a business in straw (dry grass). His money increases largely month by month; he has repeatedly pocketed other people's money, but he is not fond of spending it himself.

Obs.—Business: *shêng*¹ *i*⁴; *lit.*, growing (or life) intention; a metaphorical synonym for trade, which a person engages in with, *i*, the intention, *shêng*, of growing (*q.d.*, rich), or of living. The metaphor was originally applied to the revival of vegetation in early spring.

703. 某 *mou*³, certain; as, a certain man.

704. 乍 *cha*⁴, suddenly; unexpectedly.

705. 和 *hai*⁴, *ho*², together with; in relations with. *See also* **210**.

706. 別 *pieh*², to distinguish; to separate; hence, another. *See also* **646**.

707. 素 *su*⁴, of uniform plainness; hence, uninterruptedly through past time; heretofore. Also, vegetable diet, as opposed to meat diet.

708. Examples:—

來 *lai*²	平 *p'ing*²	我 *wo*³	都 *tou*¹	別 *pieh*²	開 *k'ai*¹	某 *mou*³
的 *ti*	素 *su*⁴	分 *fên*⁴	不 *pu*⁴	告 *kao*⁴	起 *ch'i*³	人 *jên*²
意 *i*⁴	素 *su*⁴	別 *pieh*²	知 *chih*¹	訴 *su*⁴	當 *tang*⁴	我 *wo*³
思 *ssŭ*¹	常 *ch'ang*²	不 *pu*⁴	道 *tao*⁴	人 *jên*²	鋪 *p'u*⁴	和 *hai*⁴
	是 *shih*⁴	出 *ch'u*¹	乍 *cha*⁴	別 *pieh*²	來 *lai*²	某 *mou*³
	向 *hsiang*⁴	來 *lai*²	見 *chien*⁴	人 *jên*²	你 *ni*³	人 *jên*²

A certain person.
I have opened a pawnshop with So-and-so (or, a certain individual).
Don't tell anybody. Nobody else knows.
On suddenly seeing [them] I can't distinguish [which is which].
*P'ing*² *su*⁴ and *su*⁴ *ch'ang*² have the meaning of *hsiang*⁴ *lai*² (heretofore, in all past time).

709. 原 yüan², origin; beginning; in fact.

710. 待 tai⁴, towards; to await; to treat, or behave to.

711. 厚 hou⁴, thick; staunch; liberal.

712. 薄 pao², po², thin.

713. Examples:—

兒 'rh	薄 pao²	人 jén²	他 t'a¹	毛 mao²	熱 jé⁴	我 wo³
的 ti	我 wo³	這 ché⁴	原 yüan²	病 ping⁴	那 na⁴	們 mén
要 yao⁴	一 i⁴	是 shih⁴	他 t'a¹	是 shih⁴	倆 lia³
厚 hou⁴	張 chang¹	個 ko⁴	待 tai⁴	原 yüan²	原 yüan²
一 i⁴	紙 chih³	厚 hou⁴	我 wo³	來 lai²	來 lai²
點 tien³	太 t'ai⁴	道 tao⁴	好 hao³	的 ti	親 ch'in¹

We were hot friends at first.
Obs.—Lit., intimate and hot.
That is an original flaw (or defect); one that has always been there.
Obs.—Note *mao-ping*, a flaw or defect: *mao*, a hair, hence a synonym for anything minute; the term may be applied to moral, physical, or material blemishes.
He treats me well.
At bottom he is a staunch (liberal-minded) man.
Obs.—Staunch: *hou tao*; *lit.*, of stout or staunch principles.
This sheet of paper is too thin; I want a little thicker one.

714. 傲 ngao⁴, proud.

715. 嫉 chi⁴, not used in speaking without the following tu⁴, with which it is identical in meaning.

716. 妒 tu⁴, envious; jealous.

717. 慚 ts'an², to be ashamed; generally used with the following.

718. 愧 k'uei⁴, to be ashamed; shame.

719. Examples:—

心 hsin¹	眞 chén¹	待 tai⁴	地 ti⁴	做 tso⁴	他 t'a¹
裏 li³	是 shih⁴	人 jén²	裏 li³	了 liao	嫉 chi⁴
慚 ts'an²	叫 chiao⁴	傲 ngao⁴	說 shuo¹	官 kuan¹	妒 tu⁴
愧 k'uei⁴	我 wo³	慢 man⁴	我 wo³	背 pei⁴	我 wo³

He is jealous of my being an official.
Obs.—*Chi-tu* cannot be used of jealousy of the affections, the term for which is, literally, to eat vinegar (*ch'ih ts'u⁴*).
Behind my back [he] says I treat people arrogantly.
Obs.—One of the primary meanings of *man⁴*, slow, is indifferent or rude.
This really makes me feel ashamed.

720. 絶 *chüeh²*, to cut off, to interrupt, as a stream, supplies, intercourse; to be so cut off.

721. 交 *chiao¹*, to interchange; intercourse; to hand over. *Chiao¹-ch'ing²*, friendship.

722. 憑 *p'ing²*, to lean upon; to depend on. Also, to let; to allow. It will be met with later in the sense of proof or evidence.

723. Examples:—

交 *chiao¹*	交 *chiao¹*	交 *chiao¹*	們 *mên*	話 *hua⁴*	麼 *mo*	憑 *p'ing²*
給 *kei³*	逭 *ché⁴*	情 *ch'ing²*	是 *shih⁴*	也 *yeh³*	連 *lien²*	他 *t'a¹*
我 *wo³*	件 *chien⁴*	總 *tsung³*	多 *to¹*	沒 *mei²*	一 *i²*	們 *mên*
辦 *pan⁴*	事 *shih⁴*	沒 *mei²*	年 *nien²*	有 *yu³*	句 *chü⁴*	說 *shuo¹*
罷 *pa*	情 *ch'ing²*	絕 *chüeh²*	的 *ti*	我 *wo³*	實 *shih²*	甚 *shên²*

Let them say what they like (or, no matter what they say), there is not a word (*lit.*, sentence) of truth in it.

Ours is a friendship of long standing, which has never been interrupted.

Obs.—Friendship: *lit.*, interchange of feelings.

You had better leave the settlement of this matter to me; or, hand that matter over to me to deal with.

724. 賓 *pin¹*, guest, stranger, as opposed to *chu³*, in the sense of host.

725. 拜 *pai⁴*, to salute; to visit; to pay respects to.

726. 應 *ying¹*, to conform to what is right; ought.

727. 陪 *p'ei²*, to play second to, as a candidate in reserve; to bear one's guest company.

728. Examples:—

喝 *ho¹*	茶 *ch'a²*	陪 *p'ei²*	來 *lai²*	應 *ying¹*	會 *hui⁴*	有 *yu³*
一 *i⁴*	你 *ni³*	客 *k'o⁴*	得 *té*	該 *kai¹*	那 *na⁴*	賓 *pin¹*
杯 *pei¹*	陪 *p'ei²*	我 *wo³*	巧 *ch'iao³*	見 *chien⁴*	麼 *mo*	客 *k'o⁴*
兒 *'rh*	著 *cho*	要 *yao⁴*	請 *ch'ing³*	他 *t'a¹*	著 *cho²*	來 *lai²*
罷 *pa⁴*	我 *wo³*	喝 *ho¹*	你 *ni³*	你 *ni³*	我 *wo³*	拜 *pai⁴*

A visitor has come to call. In that case I must see him.

Obs.—*Pai* is simply to leave a card; *pai hui*, to call with the intention of seeing the host.

You have come in the very nick of time; please keep the guests company.

I am going to have a cup of tea; will you join me?

EXERCISE XXVII.

我們倆人
起初很親
後來他
熱待我傲慢
這麼着我
就和他絕
了交了。

1. We were warm friends at first, but he afterwards behaved in an arrogant way, so I broke off relations with him.

我昨兒到你
那兒去拜會、
怎麼不見。
這話有點兒
不可憑罷
是你留下名
片就走了。

2. When I went to your place to call yesterday, how was it you wouldn't see me? I'm afraid your statement can't be altogether depended upon; I expect you just left your card and went away.

你這麼待我這
來傲慢回
父親告訴你
愛告訴誰
就告訴誰。
我都不怕。

3. If you treat me in this arrogant manner, I'll tell your father by-and-by. You may tell whom you please; I'm not afraid of anyone.

Obs.—You please: *lit.*, it depends on your liking to tell whom, then tell whom; I all not fear.

某人告
訴我說、
你那一
筆賬的
銀子還
沒交出
來,你不
慚愧麼。

4. A certain person tells me that you have not yet handed over the money for that bill of yours; aren't you ashamed of your-self?

Obs.—Note *pi*, the numerative of bills or of items in a bill.

那倆
見的
好相
兒對是
細兒
細的一
尺寸就
瞧一
不一樣。

5. When I first glanced at those two jars they appeared very like a pair, but directly I had a careful look at them, I found that their dimensions were not the same.

Obs.—Directly: note the force of *i*; *lit.*, minutely one look, feet and inches then not the same. *Ch'ih ts'un* may be used with reference to small articles as well as large.

6. 有我兒也常且應
   人這然是的且當
   嫉個而件事也得
   妒好這平。是的。

   6. Some people envy me this good fortune of mine, yet it is a matter of very ordinary occurrence, and, what is more, it was my turn to get it.

   Obs.—Turn: note that *ying tang* might equally mean, deserve to get it. *See* Exercise XIX, 7, Obs.

   7. 應的有麼子上知
   當意分別總道
   倆思別的得了。
   怎。沒法看就
   字　　　上下文

   7. How can you distinguish the meaning of the two characters *ying tang?* The only way we can tell is to look at the context.

   Obs.—Context: *lit.*, upper and lower text (literature, Radical 67). The sentence, literally translated, runs, there is no other way only (altogether) must look at upper and lower text (what goes before and after), then know.

   8. 會主坐兒在不屋
   客人賓下對子
   的在客邊那的
   時東陪兒總方
   候西著坐是向
   兒邊的人對看
   　兒　　　的。

   8. In entertaining (receiving) guests, the host sits on the eastern side and the guest on the western side, [while] those who help to entertain sit below; isn't that correct? That depends entirely upon the direction (*fang—lit.*, place) in which the room faces (*hsiang*).

   Obs. 1.—Correct: does it agree or not (*q.d.*, with the facts)?
   Obs. 2.—Note *fang hsiang*, the direction in which anything faces.

   9. 不我
   客。愛
   冬拜
   天
   得穿
   穿夏
   衣薄
   裳
   的。
   素
   常

   9. As a general rule, I am not fond of paying visits. In winter thick clothes must be worn; in summer, thin.

   10. 寬厚是刻薄的對面兒。

   10. *K'uan¹-hou⁴* (generous, liberal-minded) is the opposite of *k'ê¹-po²* (illiberal, unhandsome in conduct).

   Turn the following into Chinese. (KEY, EXERCISE XXVII.)

   1. Have you seen So-and-so before? No, we have not. We also have seen him to-day for the first time. He is a very good fellow, and I was very intimate with him from the first moment I met him.

   Obs.—Seen: *chien kuo mien*, met face to face; it implies something more than seeing a person without being acquainted with him.

   2. I have heard from other people that he is at bottom a staunch, liberal man; one who has all along treated people well, and who does his business without any meanness.

   Obs.—Does his business, or business: *hsing shih*.

   3. If I were to institute a comparison between him and the man I know, the latter

PART III.—THE FORTY EXERCISES.

(the man I know) is by no means a fellow of this kind.

Obs.—By no means: this is implied by the word *k'o*³.

4. He is arrogant to everybody, no matter who. Whenever anyone is in luck, he is envious. He takes people's things without understanding that they have to be returned; and when one asks him [for them], he feels no shame. How can one help breaking with a man of this kind?

Obs.—*Lit.*, how can [one] be able not with him to cut off relations?

5. I have really no time to do this; go and do it yourself if you like (or, manage it how you please).

6. To *ch'ing*³ *k'o*⁴ is to ask guests to a meal. Guests ought to be seated at the upper end, and the host should keep them company at the side.

7. What do you want that small bird of yours for? hand it over to me. There, there! Why do you want people's things whenever you see them?

Obs. 1.—Why? what for? *kan shên-mo.*

Obs. 2.—There (or, that will do)! *tê liao* (*lit.*, finished).

8. If you don't want to go by yourself, I will accompany you; what do you say?

729. 裱 *piao*³, to paste two sheets of paper together; to mount a picture.

730. 糊 *hu*², to paste paper, cloth, etc., against another substance.

731. 匠 *chiang*⁴, workman; artificer.

732. 染 *jan*³, to dye.

733. 顏 *yen*², colours.

734. 紅 *hung*², red.

735. 藍 *lan*², blue.

736. 畫 *hua*⁴, to draw or paint; a drawing or painting.

737. Examples:—

布	*pu*⁴	藍	*lan*²	上	*shang*⁴	裱	*piao*³	兒	*'rh*	裱	*piao*³
染	*jan*³	顏	*yen*²	染	*jan*³	門	*mén*²	你	*ni*³	糊	*hu*²
不	*pu*⁴	色	*sé*⁴	店	*tien*⁴	縫	*féng*⁴	給	*kei*³	匠	*chiang*⁴
上	*shang*⁴	這	*ché*⁴	紅	*hung*²	兒	*'rh*	我	*wo*³	這	*ché*⁴
紅	*hung*²	一	*i*²	顏	*yen*²	得	*tei*³	裱	*piao*³	張	*chang*¹
的	*ti*	塊	*k'uai*⁴	色	*sé*⁴	糊	*hu*²	一	*i*²	畫	*hua*⁴

A paper-hanger.
Mount this picture for me.
The cracks in the door must be pasted up.

Obs.—Note *féng*⁴-*'rh*, a crack. See 287.

A dyer's shop.
Red colour. Blue colour.
Obs.—*Sĕ* (Radical 139): also read *shai*³ or *shê*⁴.
This piece of cloth won't take a red colour.
Obs.—We might also say *jan pu ch'u hung ti lai.*

738. 淡 *tan*⁴, weak (as of tea); pale (as of colours).

739. 新 *hsin*¹, new.

740. 舊 *chiu*⁴, old.

741. 紗 *sha*¹, crape.

742. Examples :—

淡 *tan*⁴	氈 *t'an*³	這 *ché*⁴	是 *shih*⁴	是 *shih*⁴	這 *ché*⁴
了。 *liao*	顏 *yen*²	個 *ko*⁴	舊 *chiu*⁴	新 *hsin*¹	疋 *p'i*³
	色 *sĕ*⁴	地 *ti*⁴	的。 *ti*	的 *ti*	紗 *sha*¹

Is this piece of crape new or old?
The colour of this carpet is faded.

743. 必 *pi*⁴, necessarily; must.

744. 須 *hsü*¹, must.

745. 光 *kuang*¹, brightness.

746. 潤 *jun*⁴, moist; to moisten.

747. 玻 *po*¹ }
748. 璃 *li*² } (said to be derived from a Sanskrit word), glass of all kinds.

749. 料 *liao*⁴, materials; often specially applied to vitreous ware. Also, to estimate; to measure. *See* Part V, Lesson III, Note 8; Part V, Lesson L, Note 4.

750. Examples :—

好 *hao*³	蓋 *kai*⁴	摔 *shuai*³	把 *pa*³	兒。 *'rh*	潤 *jun*⁴	這 *ché*⁴
木 *mu*⁴	房 *fang*²	出 *ch'u*¹	玻 *po*¹	日 *jih*⁴	必 *pi*⁴	顏 *yen*²
料。 *liao*⁴	子 *tzŭ*	去 *ch'ü*⁴	璃 *li*²	光 *kuang*¹	須 *hsü*¹	色 *shĕ*⁴
料 *liao*⁴	必 *pi*⁴	做 *tso*⁴	瓶 *p'ing*²	很 *hén*³	染 *jan*³	不 *pu*⁴
貨。 *huo*⁴	得 *tei*³	甚 *shén*²	的 *ti*	大。 *ta*⁴	深 *shén*¹	很 *hén*³
	用 *yung*⁴	麼。 *mo*	冰 *shui*³	你 *ni*³	些 *hsieh*¹	光 *kuang*¹

PART III.—THE FORTY EXERCISES.

The colour is not very glossy; it will have to be dyed a little deeper colour.

Obs.—Note that *pi*, followed by *hsü* or *tei*, is more emphatic than either of the latter words used singly.

The sunlight is very strong.

Obs.—The sun's disc is called *jih kuang-'rh*, as are also the sun's rays.

Why do you throw away the water in the glass bottle?

In building a house one must use good wood.

Vitreous ware (also a slang term for a person who is a fraud, spurious imitations of jade or agate being made of this vitreous ware).

751. 擦 *ts'a*¹, to rub with the hand or a cloth, etc.

752. 碰 *p'êng*⁴, to run against; to come violently in contact with.

753. 裂 *lieh*⁴, to crack of itself, as wood or paper.

754. 行 *hang*², a vulgar modification of *hsing*² or *hang*² (Radical 144); a trade or calling; a place of business; a hong. Also, a column of characters.

755. Examples:—

不 *pu*²	裡 *li*³	一 *i*⁴	紙 *chih*³	碰 *p'êng*⁴	擦 *ts'a*¹
在 *tsai*¹	幾 *chi*³	行 *hang*²	都 *tou*¹	人 *jên*²	一 *i*¹
行 *hang*²	位 *wei*⁴	字 *tzŭ*⁴	裂 *lieh*⁴	那 *na*⁴	擦 *ts'a*¹
問 *wên*⁴	東 *tung*¹	你 *ni*³	了 *liao*	窗 *ch'uang*¹	小 *hsiao*³
別 *pieh*²	家 *chia*¹	們 *mên*	開 *k'ai*¹	戶 *hu*⁴	心 *hsin*¹
人 *jên*²	我 *wo*³	行 *hang*²	行 *hang*²	的 *ti*	別 *pieh*²

To give a thing a rub.

Take care; don't bump against people.

The paper in that window is all cracked.

To carry on a wholesale (or mercantile) business; or, to start a business.

A column (or row) of characters.

How many partners are there in your hong (or firm)?

Obs.—Partners: *tung*, the east, is a synonym for a master or host, the east being by ancient custom the position occupied by the master of the house, and the west that by the guests; hence, *tung-chia*, a master or proprietor, *chia* having much the same force as in *jên-chia*. It should be noticed that *tung-chia* is the term generally used by Chinese servants in Peking to denote their foreign masters, though native heads of households are seldom so spoken of. Cf. also *fang-tung*, the owner of a house.

I am not an expert; ask someone else.

Obs.—Note *expert*: I am not in that line of business. It can be used with reference to any subject with which the speaker is unfamiliar.

EXERCISE XXVIII.

那 面 不 光 把 擦 擦 1
桌 兒 很 潤 他 一 罷。
兒。   。

1. The top of that table is not very bright; give it a rub.

玻 來 是 國 做 璃 別。
璃 的 當 貨, 料 有
是 東 初 這 貨 點
外 西 是 兒 和 兒
國 不 我 也 玻 分

2. Glass is a foreign article, isn't it? In the first instance it was a foreign product, but of late we have been able to make it here too. There is a slight difference between $liao^4$-huo^4 (vitreous ware) and po^1-li^2 (glass).

Obs.—In the first instance: *lit.*, at the time of *(tang)* commencement *(ch'u)*.

那 瓶 不 破 是 時 就
玻 子 是 破 燒 候 裂
璃 怎 碰 了 的 兒。 了。
麼 了。 的,

3. How did that glass bottle get broken (or cracked)? It was not broken by a blow (collision); it cracked of its own accord in baking.

Obs.—Note the distinction: *p'o*, a break or crack from collision, etc.; *lieh*, spontaneous cracking. *Lieh* is never applied to glass except under the above conditions.

牕 叫 糊 上 張 一
戶 糊 上。 頭 兒 塊
紙 匠 單 是 紙 兒
裂 來 張 糊 是 糊
了, 糊 兒 在 雙 裱。

4. The paper of the window is cracked; tell a paper-hanger to come and paste it up. To paste a single piece of paper upon anything is hu^2; two sheets of paper pasted together are $piao^3$.

Obs. 1.—Paper-hanger: *lit.*, pasting artisan.
Obs. 2.—Paste it up: *shang* indicates completion of the act, not upward movement.

各 手 的 匠 鐵 說 5
行 工 叫 多 匠, 得
的 人 匠 木 瓦 都
人 人 匠, 匠

5. The term $chiang^4$ is applied to handicraftsmen in most trades; you may say mu^4 $chiang^4$ (a carpenter), wa^3-$chiang^4$ (a bricklayer), $t'ieh^3$-$chiang^4$ (a blacksmith).

Obs.—The character *hang* is not recognised by the dictionaries; from the original meaning of the character without the dot (namely, to move, the way or course of movement, the order of proceeding), it comes to mean class, calling, etc.

PART III.—THE FORTY EXERCISES.

布是棉花做的紗是絲做的。

6. Shirtings are made of cotton; crape is made of silk.

那一塊紗顏色舊了必須染。紅的顏色還可以別的顏色也可以染藍的。

7. The colour of that piece of crape is faded; it must be dyed some other colour. The original colour was red, and it can be dyed red again; if you prefer some other colour, sir, it can be dyed blue.

Obs.—Original colour: *lit.*, original old colour.

你瞧那一疋紅紗顏色怎麼樣原來是光潤的那紗新的染的好光潤又是好看。這光潤的顏色不止於說紗說別的也行。

8. Look at that piece of red crape and tell me if it is not *kuang*[1] *jun*[4]. What does *kuang*[1] *jun*[4] mean? That in the first place the crape is good crape; then that it is new; and, besides, that it is dyed a good colour. The expression *kuang*[1] *jun*[4] is not used only of crape; it is equally applicable to other things.

Obs. 1.—In the first place, etc.: *lit.*, that the crape in the first instance was good; again [that it] is new; the colour [men] dyeing it achieved = the colour that it is dyed, also is good to see.

Obs. 2.—Not used only: *lit.*, does not halt in (or at) the speaking of crapes; to speak of other things also it does.

我拿那玻璃瓶要擦一擦碰在桌子上碰破了。收拾收拾不必收拾了。

9. I was bringing that glass bottle here to give it a rub, when I bumped it against the table and cracked it; shall it be mended? It need not be mended.

他是甚麼行當。必是當廚子。你們行幾。兄弟五個。我行二。

10. What is his craft (or, line of business)? He must be a cook. Where do you come in the family? We are five brothers, and I come second.

Obs. 1.—Craft: *lit.*, the trade or calling (*hang*) that he performs (*tang*).

Obs. 2.—*Hang*, a list: hence, to be on a list; I am second in the list (or column) [of my generation]. Note that sisters do not count; *e.g.*, a man with two elder sisters and an elder brother would *hang êrh*; a girl, however, reckons her position in the family *quoad* her sisters in the same way.

Turn the following into Chinese. (KEY, EXERCISE XXVIII.)

1. The paper hung (pasted) in this room is dirty; call a paper-hanger to paper it afresh (*lit.*, paste new).

2. Find a man to mount this picture for me; but do not let the mounting be too thick.

3. The window is in holes (broken) and lets in the wind; get a sheet of paper and paste it up.

Obs.—Lets in : *chin*, to enter. Note that in this construction *chin* precedes its object.

4. Why have you dyed this piece of crape this colour? Didn't I tell you to dye it blue, and yet you have dyed it red? The colour is pale, too, and not glossy.

Obs.—Yet : *tao*, on the other hand.

5. This coat of mine is too old; it is unwearable.

6. There is dust on the glass in (on) the window; you must give it a rub with a piece of cloth, and the room will not be so dark.

7. Where can one buy the colours for dyeing things? They are sold in the colour (colour material) shops.

8. Take care how you carry that tumbler; don't bump it against anything.

9. There has been absolutely no rain; the weather has been terribly dry. Just look at this table top, it is all cracked with dryness.

10. Businesses are divided into hongs. Of the different hongs in the capital, the biggest are the silver (banks), wine, tea, and cloth hongs.

756. 剛 *kang*^{1}, properly, hard, which meaning in certain combinations it retains; with the following character it has an intensive force.

757. 纔 *ts'ai*^{2}, just now; but a moment ago. Also, only just; then; thereupon.

758. 再 *tsai*^{4}, again; the second time; then.

759. 等 *têng*^{3}, a class or grade; also, to wait.

760. Examples :—

剛	*kang*^{2}	打	*ta*^{3}	等	*têng*^{3}	等	*têng*^{3}	再	*tsai*^{4}	了	*liao*	他	*t'a*^{1}
兒	*'rh*	我	*wo*^{3}	了	*liao*	我	*wo*^{3}	說	*shuo*^{1}	等	*têng*^{3}	剛	*kang*^{1}
裝	*chuang*^{1}	來	*lai*^{2}	他	*t'a*^{1}	再	*tsai*^{4}	罷	*pa*^{4}	一	*i*^{4}	纔	*ts'ai*^{2}
得	*tê*^{2}	著	*cho*	纔	*ts'ai*^{2}	不	*pu*^{4}	等	*têng*^{3}	會	*hui*^{3}	回	*hui*^{2}
下	*hsia*^{4}	剛	*kang*^{1}	剛	*kang*^{1}	能	*nêng*^{2}	一	*i*^{4}	兒	*'rh*	來	*lai*^{2}

He came back a moment ago.

Wait a bit and we will see about it.

Obs.—*Tsai shuo* may also be translated literally.

Wait a bit. I can wait no longer.

He hit me just now.

Obs.—Note that *ts'ai-kang* and *kang-ts'ai* are interchangeable, but that the latter perhaps places the time in the more immediate present.

It will just (exactly) fit (pack in).

Obs.—Note the tone of the second *kang*.

PART III.—THE FORTY EXERCISES.

761. 取 *ch'ü³*, to fetch; to bring; to take for oneself.

762. 送 *sung⁴*, to carry to; to present; to accompany.

763. 落 *la⁴*, *lao⁴*, *lo⁴*, down; to descend; to leave behind one; to leave out.

764. 永 *yung³*, eternal.

765. Examples:—

回 *hui²*	沒 *mei²*	不 *pu⁴*	落 *la⁴*	去。*ch'ü⁴*	一 *i⁴*	順 *shun⁴*	
來。*lai²*	落 *lao⁴*	知 *chih¹*	下。*hsia⁴*	一 *i²*	本 *pên³*	便 *pien⁴*	
不 *pu²*	兒 *'rh*	道 *tao⁴*	鳥 *niao³*	個 *ko⁴*	書 *shu¹*	取 *ch'ü³*	
送 *sung⁴*	了。*liao*	他 *t'a¹*	兒 *'rh*	大 *ta⁴*	我 *wo³*	幾 *chi³*	
不 *pu²*	他 *t'a¹*	的 *ti*	落 *lao⁴*	錢 *ch'ien²*	給 *kei³*	吊 *tiao⁴*	
送。*sung⁴*	永 *yung³*	下 *hsia⁴*	在 *tsai⁴*	都 *tou¹*	你 *ni³*	錢 *ch'ien²*	
	遠 *yüan³*	落。*lo⁴*	樹 *shu⁴*	沒 *mei²*	送 *sung⁴*	來。*lai²*	
	不 *pu⁴*	他 *t'a¹*	上。*shang⁴*	有 *yu³*	回 *hui²*	這 *ché⁴*	

Fetch me a few strings of cash at the same time (while you are about it).

Obs.—At the same time: *shun pien*; *lit.*, following the convenience (*i.e.*, opportunity). Cf. *chiu shou-'rh* (Exercise XXV, Eng., 1, Obs. 2; p. 130).

I will send this book back for you.

I have not omitted (left out) a single cash.

The bird has lighted on the tree.

I don't know his whereabouts (the place in which he has lighted).

He has no home (or, no person or place to whom or which he can go for help or shelter); to be thrown upon the world.

He will never come back.

Obs.—Never: *lit.*, in the infinite, or eternal, distance.

Don't [I pray] accompany me [to the door].

Obs.—This is a parting salutation in very common use, and it is polite so to address one's host when seeing one to the door. Another form is *liu² pu⁴*; *lit.*, detain your footsteps.

766. 湊 *ts'ou⁴*, to add to a body or number; to assemble, of men or things; active or neuter.

767. 挪 *no²*, to move a thing from one place to another.

768. 拴 *shuan¹*, to tie up animals or things.

769. 套 *t'ao⁴*, generally, a closely-fitting case or envelope. The numerative of *i-shang* clothes generally; as *i t'ao i-shang*, a suit of clothes.

770. Examples:—

馬 ma³	上 shang⁴	一 i²	書 shu¹	兒 'rh	子 tzŭ	我 wo³
一 i²	今 chin¹	個 ko⁴	是 shih⁴	把 pa³	把 pa³	們 mên
套 t'ao⁴	兒 'rh	書 shu¹	四 ssŭ⁴	馬 ma³	牀 ch'uang²	湊 ts'ou⁴
套 t'ao⁴	套 t'ao⁴	套 t'ao⁴	套 t'ao⁴	拴 shuan¹	挪 no²	了 liao
杯 pei¹	騾 lo²	把 pa³	一 i²	上 shang⁴	在 tsai⁴	五 wu³
	子 tzŭ	車 ch'ê¹	套 t'ao⁴	這 chê⁴	那 na⁴	兩 liang³
	套 t'ao⁴	套 t'ao⁴	書 shu¹	個 ko⁴	邊 pien¹	銀 yin²

We have got together (subscribed) five taels.
Remove the bed to that side.
Tie up the horses (or horse).
This book is in four covers.

Obs.—*T'ao* is the cover or wrapper in which the *pên* or volumes are encased.

A book within a cover. A book cover.
Get the cart ready.

Obs.—*Lit.*, harness the cart. The Chinese do not as a rule say *t'ao* of the horse or mule, but it would be correct to do so in the following sentence.

Will you harness the mule or the horse to-day?

Obs.—Note that there is another word for to saddle a horse, which will be come to in due course.

A set of cups that fit one within the other.

771. 商 *shang*¹, a trader; to consult.

772. 量 *liang*², *liang*⁴, to calculate; to measure.

773. 彀, 够 *kou*⁴, enough; the second form is the correct one.

774. 斟 *chên*¹, properly, to pour out wine; colloquially, it has not this sense, but is joined with *cho*² (see next word).

775. 酌 *cho*², combined with the foregoing *chên*¹, means to deliberate, whether with another or oneself; it also means to pour out wine, but not colloquially.

776. Examples:—

米 mi³	罷 pa⁴	你 ni³	能 nêng²	賽 sai⁴	商 shang¹	那 na⁴
分 fên⁴	彀 kou⁴	們 mên	彀 kou⁴	馬 ma³	量 liang⁴	一 i⁴
量 liang⁴	不 pu²	去 ch'ü⁴	去 ch'ü⁴	去 ch'ü⁴	著 cho	天 t'ien¹
不 pu⁴	彀 kou⁴	斟 chên¹	不 pu⁴	今 chin¹	出 ch'u¹	我 wo³
輕 ch'ing¹	量 liang²	酌 cho²	能 nêng²	兒 'rh	城 ch'êng²	們 mên

The other day we were discussing the question of having races outside the city.
Can you go to-day or not?

Obs.—*Kou* here does not seem to affect the force of *nêng*.

PART III.—THE FORTY EXERCISES.

Go and talk the matter over (or, consider it).
Is it enough? have you enough? enough?
To measure rice.
The weight is not light.

Obs.—*Fên⁴ liang⁴*; *lit.*, the share or portion (*fên⁴*) contained in the *liang⁴*, cubic capacity: note that *liang⁴* is a measure of capacity. We may say of a box that it has not *liang⁴-'rh*, capacity, to contain a certain quantity; also that a man's *chiu³ liang⁴*, capacity for wine, is great or small.

777. 疑 *i²*, doubts; to doubt.

778. 惑 *huo⁴*, to doubt; to bewilder. Not used alone in the spoken language.

779. 喊 *han³*, to cry aloud; to halloo.

780. 答 *ta¹*, to reply.

781. 應 *ying⁴*, echo; to echo; to respond to. Not to be confounded with *ying¹* (726).

782. 從 *ts'ung²*, proceeding from; forth from.

783. 末 *mo⁴*, the end; *lit.*, the tip of anything that runs to a point. Read *mo-'rh*, a time or occasion; as *san¹ mo⁴-'rh*, three times.

784. Examples:—

的 *ti*	末 *mo⁴*	前 *ch'ien²*	答 *ta¹*	天 *t'ien¹*	是 *shih⁴*	你 *ni³*
了 *liao³*	在 *tsai⁴*	應 *ying⁴*	他 *t'a¹*	眞 *chên¹*	這 *chê⁴*
兒 *'rh*	外 *wai⁴*	了 *liao*	也 *yeh³*	的 *ti*	話 *hua⁴*
告 *kao⁴*	頭 *t'ou*	沒 *mei²*	不 *pu⁴*	我 *wo³*	我 *wo³*
病 *ping⁴*	做 *tso⁴*	有。*yu³*	答 *ta¹*	喊 *han³*	疑 *i²*
回 *hui²*	官 *kuan¹*	我 *wo³*	應。*ying⁴*	他 *t'a¹*	惑 *huo⁴*
來 *lai²*	末 *mo⁴*	從 *ts'ung²*	你 *ni³*	半 *pan⁴*	不 *pu²*

I have my doubts about the truth of what you say.

I hallooed for him ever so long, and yet he wouldn't answer (or, though I shouted to him, etc.).

Obs. 1.—The *yeh* implies that the result was contrary to expectation or the natural order of things.

Obs. 2.—*Ta ying*: emphasise *ta*.

Did you agree (consent)?

Obs.—Agree: *lit.*, answer [in the affirmative].

I was formerly an official in the provinces, [but] I eventually (finally) reported myself as ailing (retired on the ground of ill-health), and came back.

Obs. 1.—Another expression for to retire from office is *kao t'ui* (506).

Obs. 2.—Note that *wai-t'ou*, as a general rule, when employed by a person in Peking, means anywhere in the Empire outside the capital.

Obs. 3.—Eventually; at the very last: *lit.*, at the tip of the finish. The reduplication of *mo* is perhaps slightly emphatic; we could also say *mo liao-'rh* or *mo hou⁴*.

EXERCISE XXIX.

剛
纔
我
們
在
這
兒
商
量
這
件
事
情
他
過
來
等
了
半
天
他
不
答
應
我
疑
惑
他
沒
聽
見
。

1. We were discussing this affair here just now, and we called to him again and again to come; but after waiting ever so long he made no answer. I suspect he did not hear.

Obs.—Again and again: the *ti*, adverbial, standing for fashion; *q.d.*, three times' fashion.

再
三
再
四
的
請
他
把
那
個
舊
書
套
送
給
我
他
總
不
答
應
末
了
兒
還
是
我
買
了
個
新
的
。

2. I asked him again and again to make me a present of that old book cover, but he refused every time, and after all I had to buy a new one.

Obs.—After all: *lit.*, at the very end, still (*hai*) was it I bought a new one.

我
們
前
定
得
十
個
人
湊
錢
做
買
賣
後
來
還
有
落
下
了
兩
個
人
還
有
取
回
去
的
把
本
錢
取
回
去
我
瞧
這
個
也
不
肯
再
往
裏
入
錢
了
。

3. Ten of us agreed, some time ago, to put some money into a business. Two afterwards withdrew, and others took out their capital; when I saw this I did not choose to put any more money in either.

Obs. 1.—Agreed: *ting tê*; most Pekingese would write and say *ti*.

Obs. 2.—To put money: *ts'ou*, properly written with Radical 159, means to converge, as the spokes to the nave of a wheel; here, *lit.*, to contribute money to do trade.

Obs. 3.—Withdrew: *lit.*, there dropped out two men.

Obs. 4.—And others, etc.: *lit.*, yet more there were laying-hand-on-capital took [it] back ones.

Obs. 5.—Did not choose: *pu k'ên* translates very well as decline or refuse, where there is evidence that a proposal has been made. Note *ju*, to enter, as an active verb.

我
兄
弟
送
我
的
那
個
箱
子
叫
你
挪
開
兒
挪
那
麽
怎
麽
遠
。

4. Because I told you to move the box away which my younger brother gave me, why should you have moved it so far?

Obs.—*Lit.*, [I] tell you to move apart my younger brother gave me's that box; [this being so] why move it thus far. *Ti* can often be translated which.

PART III.—THE FORTY EXERCISES.   151

了。足套一穀量這 5
拉兒個五了米
的車單石不我

5. According to my measurement, this rice does not amount to five piculs, and a one-horse cart will draw it perfectly well.

Obs. 1.—One-horse cart: *lit.*, single-harness cart.

Obs. 2.—Perfectly well: *lit.*, enough dragging accomplish; note *liao*, here and below, to be able, *la tê liao, la pu liao*. The *tsu* is emphatic.

不車是五個這在 6
了怕二石不麼我
罷。拉套不止些說

6. In my opinion this quantity is not so little as five piculs, and I don't think that less than two beasts will draw it.

Obs.—*Lit.*, quantity (*hsieh*) as this (*chê-mo*) does not stop at five piculs; if it is not a two-harness cart, [I] fear dragging not accomplish.

兒理著就店過來我 7
再叫從要裏車的是
來他來錢。那我從
罷。等沒我趕們南
一這疑車一沒邊
等個惑的到坐兒

7. I come from the South; I have never travelled by cart before, and the moment we got to the inn the carter asked for his money. I suspected that this was not the rule, so I told him to wait a while and come again.

Obs. 1.—The moment: *lit.*, we once arrived in the inn, the carter thereon wanted money; *na*, that carter belonging to the cart just spoken of.

Obs. 2.—Not the rule: *lit.*, I suspected that hitherto there was not this *li*, a principle or rule that should obtain because it was just. The carter would plead that to pay at once was *li*, justice; the traveller suspects that this had never been the principle in accordance with which action ought to be taken.

意氣一酌話了到我 8
了。就會斟說。這他永
改兒酌你是那遠
了沒罷再怎兒再
主了等斟麼去不

8. I will never go to his place again. What a remark to make! Think the matter over again; wait a while till your anger has gone, and you will have changed your mind (or decision).

Obs. 1.—What a remark! *lit.*, this is how talk to say! A vulgarism in frequent use in Peking; it is not necessarily a comment on a remark made, but is used under many conditions as an ejaculation of regret, surprise, or indignation; *e.g.*, the servant lets fall a glass and breaks it, upon which the master would ejaculate *chê shih tsêmmo hua shuo*.

Obs. 2.—Wait a while till; or, by-and-by when.

Obs. 3.—Note *mei liao ch'i liao*, not *mei liao ch'i-'rh liao*, which means dead; hence, care must be taken to omit the *êrh*.

152   TZŬ ÊRH CHI.—COLLOQUIAL SERIES.

9. 那馬還拴不好。他把門兒碰壞了。那倒沒甚麼。叫個木匠來收拾。就收拾得了。

9. Why won't you tie that horse up properly? Look! he has bumped against the door and broken it. That doesn't signify; call a carpenter to mend it, and that matter will be settled.

Obs. 1.—Why won't you? *lit.*, you still (in spite of my orders or consequences) do not efficiently tie up that horse.

Obs. 2.—Doesn't signify: *lit.*, that, on the other hand, not what (= anything); call a carpenter to come and mend it, and there an end.

10. 昨兒我叫他們上山買一百雞子兒。誰想他們連丟帶碰。趕到了山上。就沒甚麼了。

10. I told them yesterday to buy a hundred eggs and bring them to the Hills. Can you imagine it? what with what they broke and lost on the road, by the time they reached the Hills there were hardly any left.

Obs. 1.—Bring them: note that *lai* shows the speaker to be at the Hills himself.

Obs. 2.—Can you imagine, etc.? *lit.*, who would have thought? in connexion with *(lien)* lost, together with *(tai)* bumping, coming up with arrival at the Hills [time] there was not anything [appreciable left]; *mei shêmmo* does not mean that there were none at all, but that the quantity was unappreciable. Note the conjunctions *lien* and *tai*; the Chinese seldom make use of the same conjunction twice running in the same sentence, whether conversationally or in writing.

Turn the following into Chinese. (KEY, EXERCISE XXIX.)

1. I had just got out of the door and was on the point of starting (walking) when a man came looking for you. I said you were not at home, and told him to come again by-and-by (later on).

2. To borrow people's furniture (or, utensils, tools, etc), and not send it back when you have finished with it, but even wait till they come to fetch it, is that right?

Obs.—Is that right? *shih tê*, will [such conduct] do?

3. Since I came here, I have never seen the price of things fall.

4. This money is terribly short [of the amount]. I have been everywhere to [try and] get it together, and this trifle is all I have managed to raise (*ts'ou*). It's not enough for my purpose; I'll give it to you, if you like.

Obs. 1.—Short: *ch'üeh shao* (see **500**).

Obs. 2.—Is all: *ts'ai ts'ou liao chê-mo i tien-'rh*, I have only collected as little as this.

Obs. 3.—Not enough, etc.: *pu kou wo yung ti*, not enough my use's [purpose]; the use to which I want to put it.

5. With him it's a never-ending get-from-here and scrape-together-there for a livelihood; never enough for his expenses.

Obs.—*Lit.*, he, passing his days (getting his livelihood), eternally is east removing, west scraping together; ever *(lao)* not enough for spending's [purpose].

6. Tie up the beasts; I shall want to (or, am going to) put them in the cart shortly.

7. I have bought a book in a cover. I have not enough money with me, and I want

to ask you (*lit.*, consult with you) if you have any about you (*lit.*, on your body) to lend me a little; can you?

Obs.—Can you? *hsing pu hsing.*

8. I doubt whether what he says is true; inquire for me when you get there.

Obs. 1.—I doubt, etc.: *lit.*, I doubt (suspect) what he says is not true.

Obs. 2.—Inquire: *ta t'ing*, to beat about for information. *See* 241.

9. If you do things behind my back so that I shan't know, you just look out! If I find you out in future, I shall have some objections to make.

Obs.—*Lit.*, you, backing me, do things not causing me to know, you then (*k'o*, hypothetical particle) take care; a day hereafter if it is causing me to inquire out (*ch'u lai*, if the inquiry elicits the fact), then (*k'o*) I shall not agree. Note that the second *chiao* makes *ta t'ing* passive: if [your doings] are found out by me. *Ta ying* means here something stronger than mere objection, and implies that the matter will not be passed by with a mere protest.

10. There is a man calling out outside; answer, and go out and see who it is.

Obs.—Answer: *lit.*, answer a sound.

11. Ah! and so it's he that has come again, is it? He has never been here since the day I gave him a blowing up.

Obs. 1.—And so: *yüan lai*, which cannot here be rendered by its ordinary meaning.

Obs. 2.—"Never" must not here be rendered by *yung yuan* and the negative, as this refers to the future.

12. He came twice, and on both occasions caught me at home; unlucky, wasn't it?

Obs. 1.—Twice: *liang mo-'rh*; though *hui²* would do as well.

Obs. 2.—Caught me at home: *kan shang wo tsai chia*, caught me up at home.

Obs. 3.—Unlucky: *ch'iao³*, which can be used in a bad as well as a good sense.

13. We have thought out two plans for managing this affair, and would ask you to consider which we had better employ.

785. 臺 *t'ai²*, a terrace.

786. 灣 *wan¹*, curving; to curve; a bay or indentation.

787. 江 *chiang¹*, a river; see *ho²* (**377**). *Chiang¹* is never used of a small stream, though *ho²* may be applied to large ones.

788. 湖 *hu²*, a lake.

789. 流 *liu²*, to flow; not to be confounded with *liu⁴*, a current.

790. 浪 *lang⁴*, waves, larger than *po¹* (**479**).

791. 闊, 濶, *k'uo⁴*, spacious; hence, wealthy. Both forms are admissible.

792. Examples:—

得 *tê*	沒 *mei²*	浪 *lang⁴*	濶 *k'uo⁴*	兒 *'rh*	一 *i⁴*	臺 *t'ai²*	
快 *k'uai⁴*	有 *yu³*	就 *chiu⁴*	風 *fêng¹*	就 *chiu⁴*	灣 *wan¹*	灣 *wan¹*	
順 *shun⁴*	甚 *shê²*	起 *ch'i³*	大 *ta⁴*	到 *tao⁴*	再 *tsai⁴*	一 *i²*	
流 *liu²*	麼 *mo²*	來 *lai²*	海 *hai³*	了 *liao*	繞 *jao⁴*	個 *ko⁴*	
頂 *ting³*	波 *po¹*	太 *t'ai⁴*	裡 *li³*	大 *ta⁴*	一 *i²*	灣 *wan¹*	
流 *liu²*	浪 *lang⁴*	湖 *hu²*	的 *ti*	江 *chiang¹*	個 *ko⁴*	子 *tzŭ*.	
	流 *liu²*	裡 *li³*	波 *po¹*	寬 *k'uan¹*	灣 *wan¹*	灣 *wan¹*	

Formosa.

A curve; a bay.

To bend, as a bow, one's back in bowing, etc.

Round one turn more, and there we are.

Large rivers are wide.

When the wind is high the waves in the sea rise.

There are no great waves on the T'ai-hu (lake).

It flows quickly; glides quickly.

To float with the current.

Obs.—*Shun*⁴ *liu*, with the emphasis on *shun*, means smooth, as the hair of a dog or cat brushed the right way. It should be borne in mind that *shun liu* does not mean going with the stream when propelling power is used, nor does it mean a fair or favourable current; the character for this is *liu*⁴, which will be met with later. *Cf.* also *shun fêng*, *ting fêng* (*see* 72).

793. 浮 *fou*², *fu*², floating; movable. *Fu*⁴ *shui*³, to swim.

794. 橋 *ch'iao*², a bridge.

795. 井 *ching*³, a well.

796. 坑 *k'êng*¹, a pit, natural or artificial; also, to cheat or swindle (*see* Part IV, Dialogue III, 113).

797. 衚 *hu*²
798. 衕 *t'ung*² } a small street; an alley. Generally pronounced *hu*²-*t'ung*⁴-'*rh*.

799. 巷 *hsiang*⁴, a small street; an alley. Not so common as the above.

800. Examples:—

颳 *kua*¹	裡 *li*³	那 *na*⁴	頭 *t'ou*²	那 *na*⁴	水 *shui*³
風 *fêng*¹	頭 *t'ou*²	一 *i*⁴	橋 *ch'iao*²	邊 *pien*¹	面 *mien*⁴
走 *tsou*³	有 *yu*³	條 *t'iao*²	井 *ching*³	兒 '*rh*	兒 '*rh*
小 *hsiao*³	個 *ko*⁴	衚 *hu*²	水 *shui*³	有 *yu*³	上 *shang*⁴
巷 *hsiang*⁴	深 *shên*¹	衕 *t'ung*⁴	好 *hao*³	個 *ko*⁴	浮 *fou*²
好。*hao*³	坑 *k'êng*¹	兒 '*rh*	喝。*ho*¹	石 *shih*²	著。*cho*

Floating on the water.

There's a stone bridge there.

Well water is good to drink.

In that lane there is a deep hole.

When the wind blows it is best to walk along the small alleys.

PART III.—THE FORTY EXERCISES.

801. 野 *yeh*³, properly, uninhabited ground, but often country as opposed to town. Hence, wild; savage.

802. 鄉 *hsiang*¹, a village; a region. Often used with the following.

803. 村 *ts'un*¹, a village; a hamlet. Smaller than *hsiang*¹.

804. 墳 *fên*², a grave; a tomb; the mound or monument above a grave, but not a headstone or tablet.

805. 墓 *mu*⁴, a grave; a tomb. Rarely used without the preceding word *fên*².

806. 峯 *fêng*¹, the peak of a hill.

807. 嶺 *ling*³, a height not peaked.

808. 尖 *chien*¹, a projecting point, of a knife, hill, etc.

809. Examples :—

的。	*ti*	鄉	*hsiang*¹	兒	'*rh*	嶺	*ling*³	野	*yeh*³	墓	*mu*⁴	那	*na*⁴
那	*na*⁴	下	*hsia*⁴	的	*ti*	冬	*tung*¹	草。	*ts'ao*³	這	*chê*⁴	一	*i*²
是	*shih*⁴	人	*jên*²	山	*shan*¹	天	*t'ien*¹	鄉	*hsiang*¹	兒	'*rh*	片	*p'ien*⁴
個	*ko*⁴	從	*ts'ung*²	峯	*fêng*¹	過	*kuo*⁴	村	*ts'un*¹	沒	*mei*²	野	*yeh*³
墳	*fên*²	門	*mên*²	很	*hên*³	不	*pu*²	兒	'*rh*	野	*yeh*³	地	*ti*⁴
地。	*ti*⁴	頭	*t'ou*²	尖	*chien*¹	去。	*ch'ü*⁴	這	*chê*⁴	雞。	*chi*¹	全	*ch'üan*²
		村	*ts'un*¹	他	*t'a*¹	前	*ch'ien*²	個	*ko*⁴	野	*yeh*³	是	*shih*⁴
		來	*lai*²	是	*shih*⁴	邊	*pien*¹	山	*shan*¹	花	*hua*¹	墳	*fên*²

The whole of that waste ground is occupied by graves.

Obs. 1.—*P'ien*, the numerative of spaces of ground, generally large; the word "whole" is rendered by *i*.

Obs. 2.—Waste: *yeh* can only be properly applied to places at a distance from human habitations.

There are no pheasants here.

Wild flowers. Wild grasses.

A village.

Obs.—The term can be applied to any collection of houses, large or small, where there is no resident official.

This mountain pass is impassable in winter.

The peak ahead of us is very sharp pointed.

He is a countryman, and comes from Mên-t'ou Ts'un.

Obs.—Mên-t'ou Ts'un, the village of Mên-t'ou.

That is a cemetery.

EXERCISE XXX.

也很好看得。那山峯長大。兒又多，又長嶺。兩頭兒山南北。地方兒南。東南海裏。臺灣是中國

1. Taiwan (Formosa) is a place in the sea, south-east of China, the northern and southern extremities of which are very mountainous, the heights being of considerable elevation; the mountain scenery is at the same time very picturesque.

Obs.—Very mountainous: the mountain heights are both numerous and large. Were they not lofty as well as extensive, their *tao-'rh*, or extent (48), would be *ch'ang*, long, or *k'uan*, broad; but not *ta*, great.

兒。總名。水的大。下天海。是湖河。江河

2. The phrase *chiang¹ ho² hu² hai³* (rivers, streams, lakes, and seas) designates in general terms the greater waters of the Empire.

裏和湖相同。地方兒寬下。江的過江面有長。以過去。那就可窄。有浮橋兒。小河兒很。俗們這兒的

3. Our small rivers here are so narrow that they can be crossed by movable bridges. The Great River (the Yangtze) is as broad as a lake in many places.

Obs. 1.—The Great River: the *ch'ang mien*, surface, of the Great (*lit.*, long) River in its breadth with a lake [is] mutually (639) the same.

Obs. 2.—Breadth: *hsia li*, in the direction of, *k'uan*, its breadth. Cf. *ssŭ hsia li*, in every direction. We may also invert the expression, as *ch'ang li hsia*, *k'uan li hsia*, but the meaning is precisely the same.

以。山水也可了。江西那兒都是順流。江西去的一路。北西來的到東到湖。那長江之流

4. The course of the Great River is from west to east; vessels from Hupeh to Kiangsi go with the stream the whole way. The scenery when you get to Kiangsi is rather fine.

Obs.—Rather fine: *lit.*, will do; is tolerably good.

的樣子。沒有那就是尖。也高，的山嶺。尖的是高而。峯個不同。個山。那兒山峯是的

5. The mountain peaks in a *shan¹-fêng¹* are no two alike. A *shan-fêng* is lofty and pointed; a *shan¹-ling³* is also a height, but not of peaked form.

Obs.—Also a height: the construction is somewhat elliptical; *q.d.*, a *shan-ling* is also high [like a *shan-fêng*, but when it is a *shan-ling*] *chiu*, then, there is not that pointed form.

PART III.—THE FORTY EXERCISES.

都說得。 筆尖兒。 刀尖尖兒。 兒甚麼 個字眼 尖兒那 6

6. The term *chien*[1]-'*rh* may be equally applied to the point of a knife, a pencil, or the like.

Obs. 1.—Term: *lit.*, character eye. It is extremely difficult to analyse this expression with any success, but its force can be seen at once by illustration; thus, of *hung*, red, one would say that the *tzŭ*, character, was *hung*, and that it was a *tzŭ-yen-'rh*, term, for a particular *yen-shé*, colour.

Obs. 2.—The like: understand *chê tsung* (525) *yang-tzŭ ti*, this kind of ones, after *pi chien*. Were *tao chien* and *pi chien* omitted, the sentence would run—can be applied to anything. Note *shên-mo*, any, anything.

水井多。 是都喝的 水河麼甚 有甚沒裏 京城 7

7. There is no river water to speak of in the capital; what is drunk is well water.

住家兒的 小巷都是 鋪子衙衛 大街上半開 賣大京城的買 8

8. Trade in the capital is for the most part conducted in shops on the great streets; the houses in the lanes and small streets are principally dwelling-houses.

的也算。 有墳墓 野地連 方就叫地 兒的人家 麼沒有甚 城外頭 9

9. The country outside the city walls where there are comparatively few habitations is called *yeh*[3] *ti*[4]; even when there are graves in it it is so regarded.

Obs. 1.—Where: *lit.*, outside the walls a not-having-men's-houses' place [men] consequently (*chiu*) call *yeh ti*.

Obs. 2.—Regarded: *lit.*, together with having grave's [place men] also reckon *yeh ti*.

家兒的。 是闊人 很大必 那墳地害。 的利野 的人鄉村兒 他是個 10

10. He is a yokel (villager), and dreadfully raw. That cemetery is very large, and must belong to a wealthy family.

浮不過去。 河面兒太寬 去浮不過去。 道河浮的過 了可是不行 會是會浮水麼。 你會 11

11. Can you swim? I can swim, but I can't swim very far. Could you swim across this river? It is too wide for me to swim across.

Obs.—It is contended by purists that *fu*[4], to swim, should be written 鳬.

Turn the following into Chinese. (KEY, EXERCISE XXX.)

1. Formosa has been Chinese territory for more than two hundred years. There are mountain ranges in the north and south in which are several very lofty peaks. The country (place) is not very extensive, but [in it] there are some small rivers the fields on the banks of which produce many things. It contains both villages and towns, the inhabitants of which are of the same type as the Chinese (min^2 $jên^2$, common people). I am told that there are several places inhabited by savages, most of whom make their living by thieving. They are (live) scattered about, and do not form village [communities]. Some people, too, say that these savages are cannibals. The people who do business there deal (do it) for the most part with Chinese; of late, however *(ch'iu)*, ships from the various European countries have frequented the place, and there are foreigners who have taken up their residence there in order to carry on business.

Obs. 1.—Has been: *lit.*, Formosa *is* Chinese territory *there are* two hundred years.

Obs. 2.—In the north and south; cf. Exercise XXX, 3, Obs. 2.

Obs. 3.—Fields: *t'ien ti* (Radical 102).

Obs. 4.—Produce: *ch'u ch'an* (see 635), with the possessive; the produced things many.

Obs. 5.—Same type as: *t'ung min jên* (Chinese subjects) *i ko yang.*

Obs. 6.—Savages: *yeh jên*, men of the wilds.

Obs. 7.—They live scattered about: *t'a mên san³ cho chu*, they scattered live, and do not form *(ch'êng)* villages.

Obs. 8.—Frequented: *lit.*, of late, however, there are (have been) extreme-west *(tai hsi)* various-nation's vessels [that] come [and] go. *T'ai hsi kuo* is a common term for foreign countries in general.

2. China has several rivers, both large and deep, which are perfectly navigable for large vessels. When the water rises (grows), [the current] flows very rapidly, and upward-bound junks find it very slow [work]. The downward current, as seen from a boat [proceeding against the stream], appears to flow with even greater rapidity [than it does]. The smaller rivers are narrow and winding, and are navigated only by river boats; travellers by road may cross them by floating bridges.

Obs. 1.—Perfectly navigable: *lit.*, very much can walking accomplish large vessels.

Obs. 2.—Downward current: *lit.*, the water that flows downwards.

3. That country possesses *(yu)* several large lakes, which (the surfaces of which) are very extensive and resemble the sea in size. In the lakes, too, there are mountain peaks; they are navigable for both large and small vessels. The moment there is a high wind the waves are really terrible.

Obs.—Size: *ta li hsia.* See Exercise XXX, 3, Obs. 2.

4. There are some places where the making of wells is a matter of great labour; the ground is too hard.

Obs.—Labour: *hên fei shih*; *lit.*, much expends effort (matter).

5. I have a friend who lives in a small street. I went to look him up the other day, but I got into the wrong lane and did not find his house.

810. 男 nan^2, male.

811. 爺 yeh^2, properly, a father; but forming part of certain appellations of honour, also of other words.

812. 娘 $niang^2$, properly, a mother; but in certain combinations, any woman.

813. 幼 yu^4, of tender years.

814. 輩 pei⁴, a class; an order; a generation.

815. Examples:—

比 pi³	子 tzŭ	老 lao³	們 mên	你 ni³	我 wo³	男 nan²
他 t'a¹	比 pi³	幼 yu⁴	娘 niang²	們 mên	的 ti	女 nü³
長 chang³	我 wo³	老 lao³	兒 'rh	少 shao⁴	男 nan²	女 nü³
一 i²	晚 wan³	少 shao⁴	們 mên	爺 yeh²	人 jên²	人 jên²
輩 pei⁴	一 i²	一 i²	娘 niang²	好 hao³	老 lao³	那 na⁴
	輩 pei⁴	輩 pei⁴	家 chia¹	爺 yeh²	爺 yeh²	是 shih⁴

Man and woman.
One's wife; a woman.
Obs.—*Nü jên* could only be used of the speaker's own wife.
That is my husband.
Your worship; or, a gentleman; the title Mr.
Obs.—*Lao-yeh* was originally the title given to *chü jên*, or graduates of the second grade, but it is now universally applied to any officials below the rank of District Magistrate, or indeed any person of education and social standing; it answers very much to our Esquire.
Is your son well?
Obs.—*Shao⁴*, not *shao³*. Note that in polite language *ni mên* is either singular or plural.
Men.   Women.
Obs.—Pronounce *nia²-'rh mên*.
A wife's family.
Old and young.   Old and young.
Obs.—Note *shao⁴*.
A generation.
Of a generation later than I.
Of a generation earlier than he.

816. 玩 wan², to trifle; to play.

817. 耍 shua³, to flourish, as a weapon in fencing; to play.

818. 蠢 ch'un³, loutish in form or mind, or both.

819. 笨 pên⁴, of things, unwieldy; of persons, stupid.

820. 獃 tai¹, silly; idiotic; abstracted; abstractedly.

821. Examples:—

耍 shua³	的 ti	這 ché⁴	笨 pên⁴	法 fa²	他 t'a¹	年 nien²
錢 ch'ien²	他 t'a¹	事 shih⁴	人 jên²	子 tzŭ	鬧 nao⁴	輕 ch'ing¹
別 pieh²	是 shih⁴	情 ch'ing²	獃 tai¹	笨 pên⁴	著 cho	的 ti
耍 shua³	個 ko⁴	不 pu²	頭 t'ou²	他 t'a¹	玩 wan²	人 jên²
笑 hsiao⁴	書 shu¹	是 shih⁴	獃 tai¹	是 shih⁴	兒 'rh	好 hao⁴
我 wo³	獃 tai¹	玩 wan²	腦 nao³	個 ko	這 ché⁴	玩 wan²
	子 tzŭ	兒 'rh	的 ti	蠢 ch'un³	個 ko⁴	耍 shua³

Young people are fond of play (or, practical joking).
He is playing (or joking).
This method is rude, clumsy.
He is a loutish fellow.
A silly creature.
This business (or matter) is no joke (or, child's play).
He is dazed with study; a bookworm absorbed in his books.
To gamble.
Don't [try and] fool me.

822. 冒 *mao*⁴, properly, a covering for the head; a word descriptive of obtrusiveness, of doing that which one ought to let alone, of things that happen inopportunely; out of place.

823. 爽 *shuang*³, of weather, bright, cheery; of persons, lively, free from care. Also, to break, as a promise; or to fail in, as an engagement. It also means to be in error.

824. 靜 *ching*⁴, at rest, as opposed to unquiet.

825. 舒 *shu*¹, properly, open; unrolled. Often combined with the following.

826. 服 *fu*², complying; obedient. It has many meanings besides.

827. 艱 *chien*¹, very difficult; but used in combination with the following *nan*² without intensifying its meaning.

828. 難 *nan*², difficult. *Nan*⁴, difficulties or misfortunes.

829. 哈 *ha*¹, the sound of loud laughter.

830. Examples:—

大	*ta*⁴	舒	*shu*	兒	*'rh*	舒	*shu*¹	爽	*shuang*³	身	*shên*¹	冒	*mao*⁴
笑	*hsiao*⁴	服	*fu*	都	*tou*¹	服	*fu*	快	*k'uai*⁴	子	*tzŭ*	著	*cho*²
你	*ni*³	他	*t'a*¹	是	*shih*⁴	你	*ni*³	人	*jên*²	爽	*shuang*³	雨	*yü*³
別	*pieh*²	爽	*shuang*³	艱	*chien*¹	這	*ché*⁴	安	*an*¹	快	*k'uai*⁴	兒	*'rh*
打	*ta*³	了	*liao*	難	*nan*	話	*hua*⁴	靜	*ching*⁴	天	*t'ien*¹	走	*tsou*³
哈	*ha*¹	約	*yo*¹	的	*ti*	我	*wo*³	人	*jên*²	氣	*ch'i*⁴	他	*t'a*¹
哈	*ha*¹	了	*liao*	難	*nan*²	不	*pu*⁴	這	*ché*⁴	爽	*shuang*³	是	*shih*⁴
		他	*t'a*¹	道	*tao*⁴	服	*fu*²	房	*fang*²	快	*k'uai*⁴	個	*ko*⁴
		哈	*ha*¹	說	*shuo*¹	連	*lien*²	子	*tzŭ*	他	*t'a*¹	冒	*mao*⁴
		哈	*ha*¹	你	*ni*³	走	*tsou*³	住	*chu*⁴	是	*shih*⁴	失	*shih*¹
				的	*ti*	不	*pu*⁴	道	*tao*⁴	著	*cho*	個	*ko*⁴	鬼	*kuei*³

To walk in the rain.
He is a blundering fool (a person who says and does the wrong thing at the wrong time).
In brisk health.
Bracing, cheerful weather.
He is a smart, energetic fellow; also, a man who speaks to the point and acts with promptitude.

PART III.—THE FORTY EXERCISES.   161

A quiet, steady man.
This is a comfortable house to live in.
Obs.—It would not be incorrect to say *chê shih ko shu fu fang-tzŭ*, but the first rendering is preferable, as there are many cases in which *shu fu* cannot be used as a simple qualifying adjective; thus, we could not say *shu fu ma*, a comfortable horse, or *shu fu i-tzŭ*, a comfortable chair, but would have to insert the verbs to ride and to sit on respectively, as in the example above.

I am not satisfied with this statement of yours; or, I object to or protest against what you say.

[He] finds difficulty even in walking.

You don't mean to say (*lit.*, it is hard to say, you cannot say with truth) that you are not comfortable.

Obs.—*Tao*, to say (*see* 48). *Shuo* may be omitted.

He has broken his compact.
He roared with laughter.
Don't humbug me; or, don't "stuff me up."

831. 耐 *nai*⁴, to endure, either in the sense of to put up with or to last.

832. 羞 *hsiu*¹, shame; to be ashamed.

833. 辱 *ju*⁴, *ju*³, to insult.

834. 討 *t'ao*³, to exact; to demand; to provoke.

835. 嫌 *hsien*², to dislike.

836. Examples:—

飯 *fan*⁴	賬 *chang*⁴	他 *t'a*¹	懶 *lan*³	也 *yeh*³	這 *chê*⁴	耐 *nai*⁴	
的。*ti*	的 *ti*	不 *pu*⁴	做 *tso*⁴	沒 *mei*²	個 *ko*⁴	過 *kuo*	
他 *t'a*¹	你 *ni*³	乾 *kan*¹	的 *ti*	羞 *hsiu*¹	不 *pu*²	這 *chê*⁴	
嫌 *hsien*²	不 *pu*²	淨 *ching*⁴	討 *t'ao*³	辱 *ju*⁴	耐 *nai*⁴	兩 *liang*³	
少 *shao*³	害 *hai*⁴	他 *t'a*¹	人 *jên*²	他 *t'a*¹	長 *ch'ang*²	天 *t'ien*¹	
了。*liao*	羞 *hsiu*¹	是 *shih*⁴	嫌 *hsien*²	們 *mên*	那 *na*⁴	就 *chiu*⁴	
	麼。*mo*	來 *lai*²	我 *wo*³	好 *hao*⁴	個 *ko*⁴	好 *hao*⁴	
	討 *t'ao*³	討 *t'ao*³	嫌 *hsien*²	吃 *ch'ih*¹	人 *jên*²	了。*liao*	

Get over the next two days (or, few days) and you will be all right.
This won't last long (or, wear well).
And yet that man did not insult them.
[Men who are] fond of eating and lazy at work (people who like to live at another person's expense) provoke people's dislike.
I object to his want of cleanliness.
He has come for payment of his bill (or, to dun for debts).
Are you not ashamed? Have you no shame?
Obs.—*See* 424.
A beggar.
He objects that it is not enough; he is not satisfied with what he has got.

EXERCISE XXXI.

耐不得的手脚他，那麼重的兄弟年幼，罷別你太粗了總得，一下兒腦袋上打棍子鬧，在我玩兒他把棍子鬧，我們倆人剛 1

1. We two were skylarking together just now, and he hit me over the head with a stick. Be a little more quiet; don't be too rough: you must remember that your brother is of tender years and cannot stand such rough treatment.

Obs.—Rough treatment: *lit.*, cannot endure such rough hands and feet [as you lay upon him].

不舒服。有點兒過身上甚麼。安沒有欠老爺說聽見 2

2. I hear, sir, that you are a little indisposed. It's nothing at all to speak of; I am only a little out of sorts.

Obs. 1.—Indisposed: *lit.*, deficient in repose (624); this is a polite form of address reserved for equals or superiors.

Obs. 2.—Out of sorts: *lit.*, on (or in) my body not comfortable.

歇兒。歇一的快。雨自然穿着常冒壞可難得說要袿子怕那耐我這件新 3

3. This new coat of mine won't last long, I am afraid. It's difficult to say; if you wear it continually in the rain of course it will soon be spoilt. To take a spell.

Obs.—Spell: *tai*, to abstract oneself; *q.d.*, from work that is engaging one's attention.

人嫌。真討樣子人的羞辱他那 4

4. That insulting manner of his is really most annoying.

都殺了。女老少賊把男兒們。娘們。是男爺們就 5

5. The words *nan²*, *nü³* mean simply men and women. The rebels slew all, without distinction of age or sex.

不舒服。輕的全年高年不分了，都老幼，他一家 6

6. Were you to say his whole family, *lao³* and *yu⁴*, were sick alike, you would mean that both those who were of respectable age and those who were of tender years were all indisposed without distinction.

Obs.—Respectable age: *lit.*, years high; *q.d.*, piled up, as opposed to the lesser burden of years, which is *ch'ing*, light

PART III.—THE FORTY EXERCISES. 163

和 7
祖
父

一
輩
兒

的
是
長

孫
一
兒

兒
和
孫

晚
輩。
的
一
輩
是
輩。

7. The generation which is the contemporary of your father and your grandfather is the *chang³ pei⁴* (senior generation); that which is the contemporary of your son and grandson is the *wan³ pei⁴* (junior (or later) generation).

Obs. 1.—Contemporary: *lit.*, the with [a man's] grandfather and father one and the same generation's ones are the senior generation, etc.

Obs. 2.—Grandfather: *see* 660, where *tsu fu* combined make one word; they are here separate.

你 8
怎
麼
這

麼
冒
失。
碰

着
了
我
了.

真
是
討
人

我
嫌。
錯
了、
實

神。
在
是
沒
留

8. Why are you so careless? You have bumped up against me; it is really most annoying. I beg your pardon.

Obs.—I beg your pardon: *lit.*, I am wrong, I am wrong; I really did not pay attention. There are other forms of apology, such as *yu tsui* (852), etc.

你 9
過
於

的
利
害、

快
些
兒

罷。
管
我

你
這
麼
呢、

頭
獸
腦
的

還
要
說
人。

獸
獸

9. You are too dreadfully awkward; be a little more smart. Mind your own business; an idiot like yourself to attempt (want) to find fault with other people!

Obs.—Mind your own business (or, what is that to you?): *lit.*, do you take charge of (or mind) me? Great emphasis must be laid on *kuan*, which, preceding a character in the third tone, is of course in the second. The expression must be used with discretion, as it is not very polite. Emphasise the final *jên*.

我 10
們
過

日
子
真

耐
着
些
兒

罷、
你
這
麼

能
耐
人、

道
一
輩
子
難

不
出
頭
麼。
艱
難。

10. It is indeed a hard task for us to live from day to day. Be a little patient; such an able man as you will surely not remain in obscurity all his life.

Obs. 1.—Able: *nêng nai*, ability; *lit.*, the ability that is acquired by patient application. The term, however, is not confined to skill acquired by practice. Cf. also *nêng kan*, capable, able, or capability (582).

Obs. 2.—Obscurity: *lit.*, not put out the head; come to the front; make oneself prominent; also, to take the lead.

TZŬ ÊRH CHI.—COLLOQUIAL SERIES.

Turn the following into Chinese. (KEY, EXERCISE XXXI.)

1. In the street yonder there is a fellow going through some performance. A whole lot of people, men and women, old and young, are looking at him. Have you heard of it?

Obs.—Performing: *shua wan i êrh*; *lit.*, brandishing playthings. The term is used of any performance, such as juggling, performing with a dancing bear, etc.

2. You've just found that out, have you? When I was out in the street a little while ago I saw a lot of men and women standing there; I thought there must be some performance or other going on, otherwise what would a lot of people be gaping at? I was just going to have a look, when, at the very moment, a man in a blundering manner put a question to me; said he, "You haven't been very well, have you quite recovered?" I gave one glance, and saw it was no other than a certain member of our family of the same generation as myself; he had grown loutish and awkward, and I have no idea what his conversation was all about. He is certainly a disagreeable creature.

Obs. 1.—You've just found that out: *ni hai shuo ni*, you still (or just) speak of it, is an idiomatic colloquialism something equivalent to "that's stale news; other people knew all about it long ago, and talked the matter out, but you are still talking about it."

Obs. 2.—Otherwise: *pu jan*, were it not thus.

Obs. 3.—Gaping at: *tai-cho lien-'rh k'an*, looking with abstracted faces. Note the participial force of *cho*.

3. Isn't the man you speak of So-and-so? I know his father; a very steady man, exceedingly brisk, both in action and speech. Several years ago he was not very well off, but I judge from his appearance of late that he is now very comfortable. Times, I imagine, are somewhat easier with him than they used to be in the early days.

Obs. 1.—In action: *hsing shih*, in the putting through (causing to progress) of business.

Obs. 2.—Judge from: *lit.*, of late looking at his that fashion (appearance), on the other hand *(tao)* very comfortable.

Obs. 3.—Times are somewhat easier, etc.: *lit.*, [I] think it is days compared with original *(yüan)* before *(hsien)* good to pass a little.

4. If you are insulted by people it is not very hard to bear with them a little; why get into a rage?

837. 皇 *huang*², august; imperial.

838. 宮 *kung*¹, an imperial palace.

839. 朝 *ch'ao*², properly, to see the Emperor, as at Court; any dynasty of China. Read *chao*¹, the morning; not used colloquially.

840. 廷 *t'ing*², properly, a hall of assembly; specially, the Emperor's Court.

841. Examples:—

朝 *ch'ao*²	朝 *ch'ao*²	時 *shih*²	皇 *huang*²	方 *fang*¹	皇 *huang*²
衣 *i*¹	去 *ch'ü*⁴	候 *hou*⁴	城 *ch'êng*²	就 *chiu*⁴	上 *shang*⁴
戴 *tai*⁴	應 *ying*¹	朝 *ch'ao*²	明 *ming*²	是 *shih*⁴	住 *chu*⁴
朝 *ch'ao*²	該 *kai*¹	廷 *t'ing*²	朝 *ch'ao*²	皇 *huang*²	的 *ti*
帽。*mao*⁴	穿 *ch'uan*¹	上 *shang*⁴	的 *ti*	宮。*kung*¹	地 *ti*⁴

The place where the Emperor lives is the Imperial Palace.

Obs.—The Emperor: *lit.*, the august [one] above.

The Imperial city.

PART III.—THE FORTY EXERCISES.

In the time of the Ming dynasty.
The Court.
When one goes to Court one ought to put on a Court dress and hat.

842. 建 *chien*⁴, to set up; to establish.

843. 臨 *lin*², to descend; to approach to. Colloquially, rarely, except in time.

844. 強 *ch'iang*², energetic. Often, over-energetic; violent; also, superior to. *Ch'iang*³, to insist on against a person's will or inclination. *Chiang*⁴, obstinate; self-willed.

845. 良 *liang*², virtuous; good.

846. 禁 *chin*⁴, to prohibit.

847. Examples:—

良 *liang*²	嘴 *tsui*³	利 *li*⁴	比 *pi*³	候 *hou*⁴	立 *li*⁴	各 *ko*⁴
民 *min*²	耍 *shua*³	害 *hai*⁴	別 *pieh*²	強 *ch'iang*³	的 *ti*	衙 *ya*²
臨 *lin*²	錢 *ch'ien*²	沒 *mei*²	人 *jên*²	要 *yao*⁴	他 *t'a*¹	門 *mên*²
民 *min*²	是 *shih*⁴	有 *yu*³	強 *ch'iang*²	我 *wo*³	臨 *lin*²	是 *shih*⁴
的 *ti*	禁 *chin*⁴	良 *liang*²	強 *ch'iang*²	的 *ti*	走 *tsou*³	朝 *ch'ao*²
官 *kuan*¹	止 *chih*³	心 *hsin*¹	暴 *pao*⁴	錢 *ch'ien*²	的 *ti*	廷 *t'ing*²
	的 *ti*		強 *chiang*⁴	的 *ti*	他 *t'a*¹	時 *shih*²	建 *chien*⁴

Yamêns are established by the Court.
When he was on the point of starting he insisted on having my money.
He is superior to other people.
He is terribly violent.
Devoid of moral sense (or conscience).

Obs.—Liang hsin, lit., virtuous heart, is the innate goodness of man, who, according to Chinese ethics, is born virtuous.

To answer (argue with) a superior.
Gambling is prohibited.
Honest (law-abiding) subjects.
The official in direct relations with the people (the Chih-hsien, commonly called the District Magistrate).

848. 為 *wei*², to do; to be.

849. 匪 *fei*³, wrongdoing, in a grave sense; wrongdoer.

850. 反 *fan*³, to turn upside down; on the contrary; hence, to rebel.

851. 犯 *fan*⁴, to stumble against; to offend; to incur a penalty.

852. 罪 *tsui*⁴, properly, punishment; also, offences, great or small. See Exercise XXXI, 8, Obs.

853. 死 *ssŭ*³, to die.

854. 黨 *tang*³, a gang; a band; a political party; a class.

855. Examples:—

他 $t'a^1$	麼 mo	是 $shih^4$	死 $ssŭ^3$	法 fa^3	了 $liao$	那 na^4
叫 $chiao^4$	罪 $tsui^4$	一 i^4	了 $liao$	的 ti	難 nan^2	地 ti^4
人 $jên^2$	名 $ming^2$	黨 $tang^3$	這 $ché^4$	人 $jên^2$	爲 wei^2	方 $fang^1$
勒 lei^1	應 $ying^1$	的 ti	些 $hsieh^1$	總 $tsung^3$	你 ni^3	的 ti
死 $ssŭ^3$	該 kai^1	應 $ying^1$	賊 $tsei^2$	得 tei^3	們 $mên$	土 $t'u^3$
了 $liao$	死 $ssŭ^3$	該 kai^1	匪 fei^3	治 $chih^4$	了 $liao$	匪 fei^3
	罪 $tsui^4$	甚 $shén^2$	都 tou^1	罪 $tsui^4$	犯 fan^4	反 fan^3

The bad characters of that place have rebelled.

Obs.—*T'u fei* must be natives of the locality. *Fei* can be applied to any individual who is guilty of grave misdemeanours, but it is generally understood to refer to banditti or rebels.

Sorry to have troubled you; much obliged.

Obs.—*Nan wei* is constantly used courteously, "May I trouble you to," "Much obliged," both as a request for a favour and as an acknowledgment of one. Distinguish *wei² nan²*, to be in difficulties, difficult.

It is essential that those who break the laws be punished.

Obs.—*Chih tsui*, to treat an offence; *q.d.*, with punishment. *Chih ping*, to treat a complaint; *q.d.*, with medicine.

Dead.

Obs.—Of persons it is common to use the euphemism *kuo ch'ü liao*, he has passed away; or *pu tsai liao*, he is no more.

These bandits are all of one gang.

Obs.—*Tsei fei* must be bandits or rebels.

What penalty ought they to receive?

Obs.—*Tsui ming*: what is the name of the punishment (what particular penalty) [they] ought [to receive]?

It should be death.

He was strangled. *See* 507.

Obs.—Note that there is another term for the punishment of death by strangulation.

856. 爭 $chêng^1$, to emulate; to wrangle; to fight with.

857. 鬬 tou^4, to fight, with or without arms; but not used of war.

858. 號 hao^4, a signal, visible, as a flag; audible, as a bugle call; a verbal order; a sign, style, or number. Also, to call, or the name by which a person is called by his friends, in contradistinction to his *ming²*, or cognomen by which he is known to his family.

859. 靖 $ching^4$, quiet, as a country free from disorder.

860. Examples:—

頭 $t'ou^2$	靖 $ching^4$	字 $tzŭ^4$	了 $liao$	下 $hsia^4$	土 $t'u^3$
兒 $'rh$	年 $nien^2$	號 hao^4	貴 $kuei^4$	裡 li^3	匪 fei^3
口 $k'ou^3$	號 hao^4	地 ti^4	行 $hang^2$	爭 $chêng^1$	同 $t'ung^2$
號 hao^4	甚 $shén^2$	方 $fang^1$	是 $shih^4$	鬬 tou^4	百 po^2
號 hao^4	麼 mo	不 pu^4	甚 $shén^2$	起 $ch'i^3$	姓 $hsing^4$
衣 i^1	號 hao^4	安 an^1	麼 mo	來 lai^2	兩 $liang^3$

PART III.—THE FORTY EXERCISES.   167

The local rowdies and the people began (or, have begun) to fight with each other.
What is the style of your hong?
The country is disturbed.
The style of a reign, *i.e.*, that by which its years are called; thus, TAO KUANG *wu nien*, the fifth year of TAO KUANG.
What is the number (*sc.*, of a despatch, house in a street, etc.)
Obs.—*Hao t'ou-'rh*; *lit.*, the number or distinguishing mark on the head, front, or top.
A password.
A soldier's uniform.
Obs.—So called from the *hao*, the distinctive number or name of regiment, marked on the circular patch which is sewn on the breast and back of most soldiers' jackets.

861. 恩 *ngén*^{1}, grace; goodness shown to an inferior.

862. 赦 *shé*^{4}, pardon; amnesty. Used only of Imperial pardons.

863. 免 *mien*^{3}, to avoid; to cause to avoid; to dispense with; to forgo. Hence also, under certain circumstances, to let off; to pardon.

864. 隨 *sui*^{2}, following after; according to.

865. Examples:—

隨 *sui*^{2} 錢 *ch'ien*^{2} 口 *k'ou*^{3} 下 *hsia*^{4} 回 *hui*^{2} 是 *shih*^{4} 皇 *huang*^{2}
事 *shih*^{4} 隨 *sui*^{2} 亂 *luan*^{4} 免 *mien*^{3} 來 *lai*^{2} 打 *ta*^{3} 上 *shang*^{4}
隨 *sui*^{2} 時 *shih*^{2} 說 *shuo*^{1} 得 *tê*^{2} 的 *ti* 黑 *hei*^{1} 的 *ti*
你 *ni*^{3} 來 *lai*^{2} 難 *nan*^{2} 費 *fei*^{4} 隨 *sui*^{2} 龍 *lung*^{2} 恩 *ngén*^{1}
的 *ti* 隨 *sui*^{2} 免 *mien*^{3} 事 *shih*^{4} 便 *pien*^{4} 江 *chiang*^{1} 典 *tien*^{3}
便 *pien*^{4} 時 *shih*^{2} 費 *fei*^{4} 隨 *sui*^{2} 坐 *tso*^{4} 赦 *shé*^{4} 他 *t'a*^{1}

The Emperor's bounty or goodness.
Obs.—*ngén tien*: *tien*, the standard, canon, or law of bounty or favour. The term, though now universally applied to acts of kindness shown by superiors to inferiors, was originally confined to Imperial acts of grace, which were a *tien*, canon, standard, or law for others to follow.
He came back pardoned from the Black Dragon River (the Amoor).
Obs.—The Amoor region is a common place of banishment for officials and soldiers guilty of crimes.
Sit down as you like, to save bother.
To talk recklessly; to let one's tongue run away with one.
Expenditure of money is hardly avoidable.
Obs.—*Nan* has here almost the sense of a negative; unavoidable. It is often thus used courteously.
Come from time to time.
To be guided by circumstances.
Obs.—*Lit.*, according to time following after (or up) matters; to deal with a matter as [the conditions of] the moment require.
As you please; or, at your convenience.
Obs.—This may be used either courteously or otherwise.

EXERCISE XXXII.

他臨死的時候兒他的兒孫們都爭起家產來咯。 1. As his end approached his sons and grandsons began to wrangle about the property.

良民是不犯國法的人。 2. Liang² min² (good subjects; or, virtuous people) are those who do not offend against the laws.

大臣上朝進皇宮不是進皇宮麼兒。不是住的皇宮地方兒就是禁地向例連大臣們都不准到的。 3. When high officers go to Court, do they not enter the huang² kung¹? No; the huang² kung¹ is the place in which the Emperor lives, and is forbidden ground, which even high officials have never been allowed to visit.

Obs.—Never: *lit.*, [by] heretofore [existing] law are not permitted to go to.

你把這幾件文書給打上號頭裏日子號起。 4. Number these despatches for me, commencing the numbers with the earliest date.

Obs.—Commencing, etc.: *lit.*, from the very front days numbering commence.

我們大人出了號令禁止底下要錢犯了禁是必要治罪的。 5. Our chief (or master) has issued an order forbidding the servants to gamble; if the prohibition is disregarded, [the offender] will certainly be punished.

Obs.—Ti: *lit.*, the *fan chin*, disregard of the prohibition, certainly will be (*yao*) a punished one.

幹這沒心的事難免犯法爲匪比良民強反倒不愛做眞是怪事。 6. You will hardly escape a breach of the laws if you pursue this unprincipled business. Would it not be better to behave as an honest citizen than to act in an illegal manner? and yet you won't behave like one; it is really most strange.

Obs.—Note that *wei fei* may mean to play the robber, or become a rebel, though the title can be earned by the commission of any act of an intentionally illegal nature; thus, smuggling, brawling, gambling, etc., come within the category of *wei fei*.

PART III.—THE FORTY EXERCISES.

隨7 人 就 起 打 可 意
你 關 是 來. 起 不 兒。
們 嘴 別 要 來. 是
倆 兒. 打 是 那 玩

7. You two may squabble as much as you please, only don't come to blows, for that would be beyond a joke.

Obs.—As much as you please : *sui*, short for *sui pien*, according to your convenience or inclination.

大8 下. 犯 罪 出 上 典。
赦 寬 人 名 於 的
天 的 總 皇 恩
免 恩

8. A general amnesty. The pardon of criminals always proceeds from the Emperor's bounty.

Obs. 1.—Note that *shê* can only be applied to Imperial pardons or the diminution of sentences by Imperial command. An offence against a private individual can be *k'uan mien*, condoned (*lit.*, liberal remission; q.d., of penalties remitted); a more common expression is *jao²*.
Obs. 2.—Criminal : *fan jên*, a man who offends ; q.d., against the laws.

你9 陽 他 隨 治 是
別 地 免 那 早 要
在 裏 得 怎 晚 死
太 走. 受 麼 總 的.
 熱。 病

9. Don't walk in the sun, and you won't get sunstroke. It doesn't matter how you treat his complaint, he must die sooner or later.

Obs. 1.—Sunstroke : *shou jê* can be used of any complaint caused by the action of the sun, whether directly or indirectly.
Obs. 2.—Doesn't matter : *lit.*, you may treat his complaint according to how [you please].

朝10 酌 地 臨 地 然 靖
廷 情 方 民 方 就 了。
隨 建 官 的 官 的 能
地 立 治. 官。 好, 方 安
爲 自

10. The Sovereign is guided by places and circumstances in his establishment of local authorities to be in near relations with the people. If the local authorities govern wisely (well), quiet naturally prevails.

Obs.—Is guided : *lit.*, following (acting according to) place, considering circumstances establishes officers [for the government of] the locality. *Ti-fang kuan* does not include exclusively judicial, fiscal, or educational authorities, nor, in the capital, the departments of the central government, unless these be executive. *Ching* (859) must not be confounded with *ching* (824) ; the former applies to conditions of place, and the latter to the character or state of the individual.

Turn the following into Chinese. (KEY, EXERCISE XXXII.)

1. A great many years ago there was a man called LIN who wanted to be Emperor. Before he rebelled he distributed his sworn confederates here and there [till] they were [posted] everywhere; his men were even [to be found] in the forbidden ground of the Imperial Palace. His arrangements (the affair) subsequently got known (*lit.*, was broken), and he himself was arrested. His sworn followers continued in rebellion for very many months in Shantung and Honan.

Obs. 1.—Sworn confederates : *ssŭ³ tang³*, confederates to the death.
Obs. 2.—Distributed : *pu san* (406), arranged and distributed.

2. When the people rebel the Emperor sends (orders) a high official to pacify the disturbed country. When the high official is about to start he has to go to Court to see the Emperor.

Obs.—Pacify: *p'ing ting*; *lit.*, to level and fix.

3. What is the number of that despatch? It has not yet been numbered.

4. The date of the establishment of the northern capital (the city of Peking) is not far back *(yüan³)*. The Court was formerly established in the South; the place where the Emperor resides is called *ching¹* (the capital), and so that city was called *Nan-ching* (the "southern capital").

Obs.—Date: *nien fên*; *lit.*, year distribution, the place it occupies in the cyclical distribution of time.

5. Cockfighting is a pastime in which virtuous people do not indulge. It is a most disreputable amusement (matter), and ought to be prohibited by law.

6. I hear that that fellow LI has committed a grave crime; some people say that he is certain to be sentenced to death. He deserves it, for when men become burglars they cannot escape capital punishment. If men of that stamp are not put to death, how can honest people gain a quiet livelihood?

Obs.—Burglars: *see* Exercise XXI, 4, Obs. 2.

7. What you say is quite correct; still, who would have thought that the man LI would have become a robber?

8. Come and see me from time to time. Although I am not a rich man, I am always able to give you a bowl of rice to eat and a cup of tea to drink.

9. Then you will be my true friend, for what I particularly dread is giving people trouble. If you will really let me come to see you in this way, you will see whether I shall come often or not.

Obs. 1.—True friend: *lit.*, good friend.
Obs. 2.—Let me, etc.: *chiao wo*.

866. 古 *ku³*, ancient.

867. 世 *shih⁴*, an age; a generation.

868. 孔 *k'ung³*, properly, a hole; the surname of Confucius.

869. 聖 *shêng⁴*, virtuous as heaven; sainted; canonised.

870. 儒 *ju²*, generally, a scholar; specially, a Confucianist, as opposed to the Taoist and Buddhist.

871. Examples:—

夫 *fu¹*	儒 *ju²*	稱 *ch'êng¹*	稱 *ch'êng¹*	是 *shih⁴*	從 *ts'ung²*
子 *tzŭ³*	教 *chiao⁴*	他 *t'a¹*	他 *t'a¹*	尊 *tsun¹*	古 *ku³*
古 *ku³*	後 *hou⁴*	的 *ti*	為 *wei²*	重 *chung⁴*	至 *chih⁴*
玩 *wan²*	世 *shih⁴*	教 *chiao⁴*	聖 *shêng⁴*	孔 *k'ung³*	今 *chin¹*
鋪 *p'u⁴*	孔 *k'ung³*	為 *wei²*	人 *jên²*	子 *tzŭ³*	都 *tou¹*

In all ages Confucius has been honoured and styled the Sacred Man, and his doctrine has been styled Confucianism.

Obs.—*Lit.*, from of old till now all have (are) honoured Confucius.

PART III.—THE FORTY EXERCISES.   171

Future generations; posterity.
K'ung Fu-tzŭ (Confucius).
Obs.—The great master Confucius; *fu-tzŭ*, a sage, a master, a distinguished man. Emphasise *tzŭ*.
A " curio " shop.
Obs.—*Ku wan*: lit., ancient gems; applied to any objects of *vertu* that are not absolutely new.

872. 佛 *fo*², Buddha.

873. 廟 *miao*⁴, a temple.

874. 座 *tso*⁴, properly, a seat or throne; also, the numerative of cities, temples, etc.

875. 僧 *sêng*¹, a Buddhist priest.

876. 俗 *su*², properly, common; in vulgar use; but under certain conditions, a layman. Also, with *chia*¹, Confucian.

877. 尚 *shang*⁴, properly, eminent; but most commonly a conjunction, not in frequent use colloquially. When linked to *ho*² (**210**), it is merely phonetic; as *ho*²-*shang*⁴, a Buddhist priest.
N.B.—Emphasise *ho*².

878. Examples:—

古。*ku*³	有 *yu*³	方 *fang*¹	人 *jên*²	位 *wei*⁴	這 *ché*⁴	拜 *pai*⁴
尚 *shang*⁴	文 *wên*²	的 *ti*	一 *i*²	和 *ho*²	一 *i*²	佛 *fo*²
且。*ch'ieh*³	廟。*miao*⁴	風 *fêng*¹	個 *ko*⁴	尚。*shang*⁴	座 *tso*⁴	爺。*yeh*
回 *hui*²	俗 *su*²	俗。*su*²	老 *lao*³	三 *san*¹	廟 *miao*⁴	和 *ho*²
敎。*chiao*⁴	家。*chia*¹	各 *ko*⁴	道。*tao*⁴	個 *ko*⁴	有 *yu*³	尚 *shang*⁴
	尚。*shang*⁴	城 *ch'êng*²	地 *ti*⁴	僧 *sêng*¹	幾 *chi*³	廟。*miao*⁴

To worship Buddha.
A Buddhist temple.
How many priests are there in this temple?
Three priests and a servant (or, temple coolie).
Obs.—A temple servant is *lao*³-*tao*⁴, but the character of the latter sound is merely phonetic; indeed, both may be. Note that Taoist priests are also styled *lao-tao*.
The customs, or morality, of a district (or locality).
Obs.—In addition to its original meaning. wind, *fêng*, also means manner, deportment, or style; as *fêng su*, the manner that is common or in vulgar use.
Every city has a Confucian temple (or temples).
Obs.—*Wên miao*: lit., temples of literature, as opposed to *wu miao*, lit., military temples, temples to *Kuan Ti*, or *Lao-yeh*, the God of War.
A layman, as opposed to *ho*²-*shang*⁴, a priest.
Obs.—When priests renounce their vows and become laymen they are said to *huan su* (**105**), return to laymen.
Early antiquity.

Besides; moreover.
The Mahomedan faith.
Obs.—A Mussulman is called a *hui-hui* or *hui-tzŭ*, though the latter is slightly opprobrious. The term *hui-hui* is said to be a reproduction of Turkish sounds.

879. 傳 *ch'uan*², to communicate by tradition; to propagate by preaching; to convey a message; to be a medium of communication. *Chuan*⁴, a record or chronicle.

880. 經 *ching*¹, a canonical book or Buddhist *sutra*; also, to pass through or by. In composition, a sign of the past tense.

881. 楷 *ch'iai*³, *k'ai*³, properly, the stalk of grain; applied to a clerkly kind of Chinese writing somewhat corresponding to our round text.

882. 率 *shuai*⁴, to follow one's nature; properly, in a good sense, but in the example given below, careless.

883. 更 *kêng*⁴, before adjectives, more. Distinguish *kêng*¹, to change (**570**).

884. 濃 *nung*², thick, of fluids.

885. Examples:—

淡	*tan*⁴	兒。	*'rh*	楷 { *ch'iai*³ / *k'ai*³	好	*hao*³	話。	*hua*⁴	時	*shih*²	傳 *ch'uan*²
的	*ti*	更	*kêng*⁴	書	*shu*¹	些	*hsieh*¹	名	*ming*²	傳	*ch'uan*²	敎 *chiao*⁴
對	*tui*⁴	不	*pu*⁴	寫	*hsieh*³	難。	*nan*⁴	臣	*ch'ên*²	流	*liu*²	的。 *ti*
面	*mien*⁴	好	*hao*³	得	*tê*	他	*t'a*¹	傳。	*chuan*⁴	下	*hsia*⁴	五 *wu*³
兒。	*'rh*	了	*liao*	草	*ts'ao*³	昨	*tso*²	他	*t'a*¹	來	*lai*²	經 *ching*¹
		濃	*nung*²	率	*shuai*⁴	兒。	*'rh*	經	*ching*¹	的	*ti*	是 *shih*⁴
		是	*shih*⁴	今	*chin*¹	寫	*hsieh*³	過	*kuo*⁴	傳	*ch'uan*²	古 *ku*³

Missionaries.
The Five Classics (or Canons) have been handed down by tradition from ancient times.
Obs.—*Lit.*, ancient times transmitted flowing down come.
To convey a message.
A biography (or record) of illustrious officials.
Obs.—Illustrious: *ming*, short for *ch'u ming*, to make a name.
He has been through a deal of trouble.
He wrote his round text yesterday carelessly, and to-day even worse.
Obs.—*Ts'ao*, grass, amongst other meanings, has that of "hasty;" hence its combination with *shuai*.
*Nung*² (thick, glutinous) is the opposite of *tan*⁴ (**733**) (weak, watery).

886. 貼 *t'ieh*¹, to stick; to be sticking to, as a placard on a wall.

887. 牆 *ch'iang*², a wall.

PART III.—THE FORTY EXERCISES.

888. 層 ts'êng², layers or sections of various things, from front to rear, side to side, top to bottom.

889. 掛 kua⁴, to hang up; to be hung up.

890. 示 shih⁴ (Radical 113), to proclaim; a proclamation.

891. Examples:—

一	i⁴	兩	liang³	上	shang⁴	個	ko⁴	有	yu³	各	ko⁴
層	ts'êng²	層	ts'êng²	這	ché⁴	套	t'ao⁴	告	kao⁴	城	ch'êng²
的	ti	道	tao⁴	事	shih⁴	兒	'rh	示	shih⁴	的	ti.
擱	ko¹	理	li³	裡	li³	掛	kua⁴	貼	t'ieh¹	門	mên²
起	ch'i³	一	i⁴	頭	t'ou²	在	tsai⁴	著	cho	口	k'ou³
來	lai²	層	ts'êng²	有	yu³	牆	ch'iang²	弄	nung⁴	兒	'rh

At the gates of every city there are proclamations posted.

Obs.—Proclamations: *lit.,* informing proclamations. *Shih* is not used alone colloquially.

Make a loop and hang it up on the wall.

In this matter there is a two-fold principle.

Place it (or them) in layers, one above the other.

Obs.—One above the other: this is indicated by *ch'i lai*.

892. 唱 ch'ang⁴, to sing.

893. 曲 ch'ü³, one kind of songs. Also, crooked; tortuous.

894. 抽 ch'ou¹, to draw one out of many, as a stick from a faggot.

895. Examples:—

灣	wan¹	抽	ch'ou¹	他	t'a¹	把	pa³	唱	ch'ang⁴	唱	ch'ang⁴	他 t'a¹
的	ti	身	shên¹	有	yu³	線	hsien⁴	罷	pa⁴	曲	ch'ü³	唱 ch'ang⁴
往	wang³	曲	ch'ü¹	事	shih⁴	抽	ch'ou¹	我	wo³	兒	'rh	得 té
東	tung¹	曲	ch'ü¹	不	pu⁴	出	ch'u¹	們	mên	唱	ch'ang⁴	好 hao³
流	liu²	灣	wan¹	能	néng²	來	lai²	聽	t'ing¹	一	i²	聽 t'ing¹

He sings pleasantly.

To sing ballads.

Give us a song; let's hear you.

Draw out the thread.

He is occupied and cannot get away (*lit.*, draw himself out; *q.d.*, from his work).

[The river] takes a winding course to the east.

Obs.—We can also say *wan¹ wan¹ ch'ü³ ch'ü³*. *N.B.*—*Wan wan ch'ü³ ch'ü³*, but *ch'ü¹ ch'ü¹ wan wan*.

EXERCISE XXXIII.

1. 那座廟門口兒貼着告示禁止娘兒們上廟燒香。

1. There is a proclamation posted (pasted) on the wall at the gate of that temple prohibiting women from going there to burn incense.

2. 他們令祖死了、今兒個去念經。和尚吃素。

2. Their grandfather is dead, and to-day the Buddhist priests are going there to hold a service (recite canons). Priests eat maigre (or, are vegetarians). (*See* **707**.)

3. 俗語兒說、今日飯今日吃明天有事明天辨。剛剛你的性情相對。

3. The proverb says, "Just eat the rice you've got to-day; deal to-morrow with what comes to-morrow (don't look ahead; live for the moment)." This exactly corresponds with your disposition.

Obs. 1.—Just: *ch'ieh*; *lit.*, temporarily (616).
Obs. 2.—Exactly: *kang-kang²-'rh*. *See* 760.

4. 老爺廟是和尚廟麼不錯。是關夫子俗叫老爺。關夫子是文話俗話就是老爺。

4. Are *Lao³-yeh¹ miao⁴* (temples to *Lao-yeh*, the God of War) Buddhist temples? Yes. *Kuan¹ Fu¹-tzŭ³* is commonly called *Lao-yeh*. *Kuan Fu-tzŭ* is *wén² hua⁴* (the literary style); in colloquial parlance he is *Lao-yeh*.

5. 這文書得寫楷書行書草字都不行墨又得濃。

5. This *wén²-shu¹* (despatch) must be written in round (clerkly) characters; neither running hand nor "grass characters" (the much abbreviated form) will do. The ink, too, must be thick.

6. 那山上廟裏頭的房子一層比一層高。

6. Each tier of buildings in that temple on the hill is higher than the other (the one below it).

7. 你抽一張兒給我畫一張兒行不行畫兒早已過時候兒就是往古。

7. Can you find time to draw me a picture? *Wang³ ku³* (past antiquity) is time long gone by.

Obs.—Find time: *lit.*, pull out [a portion of] leisure.

PART III.—THE FORTY EXERCISES.

8. 古來有位聖人姓孔。他的教後世叫做聖教爲中國最尊重的。同時還有老子的教叫做道教。佛教是西方僧家傳來的說就叫做尊佛教。爺出家的是僧家俗說就叫道士。尚尊老子出家的是僧家的人叫俗家。又名儒教、儒教的人叫俗家。教的總名就叫僧道儒。三教和

8. In ancient times there was a sainted man called (whose surname was) K'UNG. His doctrine was entitled by subsequent generations the *shêng*⁴ *chiao*¹ (the doctrine of the Sainted Man). It is that most honoured in China. There was also contemporaneous with this the doctrine of *Lao*³-*tzŭ*, which is called the doctrine of *tao*⁴ (reason or right). The doctrine of Buddha was propagated (or preached) by the *sêng*¹-*chia*¹ (priests) from the West. Those who leave their homes for the honour of Buddha are *sêng-chia*; in common parlance they are called *ho*²-*shang*⁴. Those who leave their homes for the honour of *Lao*³-*tzŭ* are *tao*⁴-*shih*⁴ (priests of *tao*). The *shêng*⁴ *chiao*¹ (doctrine of Confucius) is also called *ju*² *chiao*¹. Persons belonging to the *ju*² *chiao*¹ are called *su*²-*chia*¹ (members of the ordinary persuasion). The three sects (or persuasions) are spoken of collectively as *sêng*¹ *tao*⁴ *ju*² (Buddhism, Taoism, and Confucianism).

Obs. 1.—Most honoured: *ti* representing *chiao*; it is the China most honours one.
Obs. 2.—Also called: *lit.*, other name.
Obs. 3.—Collectively: *lit.*, the three doctrines all-including term is *sêng tao ju.* Notice the *chiu* after the subject *tsung ming*; it emphasises, but is untranslatable in English.

9. 京城的廟多、有的是和尚廟。有的是道士廟。念經的聲兒。和人家唱曲兒一個樣。

9. There are many temples in the capital; some are temples of Buddhist priests, some are temples of Taoist priests. The recital of the books in these sounds as if people were singing songs.

Obs.—Sounds as if: *lit.*, the in that place reciting book's sound is with men singing songs one (or, the same) fashion. *Nien*, to recite: *see* 122.

10. 我屋裏牆上掛張古畫兒那今兒拿新紙裱上一層。

10. I pasted a fresh piece of paper to-day under (or, at the back of) that old picture that hangs on the wall of my room.

Obs. 1.—*Hua*, a picture, may also mean a scroll with characters written on it.
Obs. 2.—Under: *lit.*, on, but it must have been under, or at the back of, the picture.

Turn the following into Chinese. (Key, Exercise XXXIII.)

1. In ancient days, more than 2,430 years ago, there lived (was) in China a man named K'UNG, who is styled by everybody the Sacred Man. A book has been compiled (made up) from his everyday conversations, by reading which men [can] know how to follow after the right. How it is followed after is in this wise. As an official, in conducting affairs as the agent (on behalf) of one's Sovereign, one must be circumspect (use attention); at home, one must also honour one's father and mother, be tenderly affectionate towards one's brothers, and even *(chiu shih)* one's wife should be treated with amiability, while one's friendships must be genuine. If [you] can act in this manner [you] are a good Confucianist (*lit.*, a good man in the middle of the Confucian sect).

Obs. 1.—Everyday conversation: *lit.*, of his ordinary (*p'ing*, 137) days spoken talk [men] have formed (*ch'êng liao*) a book.

Obs. 2.—Follow after: *lit.*, imitate, *hsiao*² (96).

Obs. 3.—In this wise, etc.: the sentence is interrogative; how is the right imitated? it is thus.

Obs. 4.—Amiable, amiability: *ho ch'i*; *lit.*, harmonious breath. It is here reduplicated for the sake of euphony.

Obs. 5.—Genuine friendship: *lit.*, the interchange (*chiao*, 721) [of relations with] friends must positively [be] *shih tsai*, true; *pi hsu*, there must, *shih*, truth, *tsai*, be present.

2. Written characters are distinguished as *chên*¹ (the proper character) and *ts'ao*³ ("grass," or running, character). The proper (or round) text is also called *ch'iai*³ (or *k'ai*³) *shu*¹. When one is writing the ordinary character the ink must be thick for it to look well. The "grass character" is also called *ts'ao*³ *shu*¹.

Obs.—Written characters: *lit.*, [in] writing characters there is the *chên tzŭ* and *ts'ao tzŭ's* (*chih*) distinction (*fên*).

3. Why are they called "grass characters"? Some people say they are so called [because] when written the characters are just like grass, but I don't know whether this statement is correct or not.

Obs.—They are so called: *lit.*, there are men say it is the character written out with grass one and the same, then (therefore) called *ts'ao tzŭ*. The origin of the term is more generally supposed to be derived from *ts'ao*, in its meaning of careless, hasty.

4. Recitation and writing require undivided (special) attention; one ought not to recite without thinking (*lit.*, empty, or emptily, recite), as if one were singing a ballad.

5. Buddha is the Sacred Man of the West. The books which propagate his faith are called the Buddhistic books (or *sutras*). The principle of the Buddhistic canon is simply to give men tranquility of mind, that is all. [This] the common people do not know, [for] they talk of being able to escape retribution for their sins by reciting these canonical books, which is really nonsense.

Obs. 1.—Simply to give, etc.: *lit.*, not exceeding (*pu kuo*) cause (*chiao*) men to tranquilise [their] hearts, and there an end.

Obs. 2.—Escape retribution for sins: *mien tsui*. *Mien tsui*, forgiveness of sins in a religious sense.

6. *Ho²-shang*⁴ are the men who recite the books of Buddha. Another name for them is *sêng*¹ *jên*².

7. The day before yesterday I saw a proclamation posted on the wall, the writing on the upper portion of which I could not see distinctly, while the lower portion was rubbed and torn in places, so I don't know what it was about.

Obs.—The writing on the upper portion: *lit.*, the upper side's characters pen strokes [I] saw not distinctly (true).

PART III.—THE FORTY EXERCISES.

896. 倉 ts'ang¹, a granary.
897. 庫 k'u⁴, a store-room.
898. 宗 tsung¹, a sort; also used as a collective, pluralising the noun that precedes it.
899. 考 k'ao³, to compare; to examine competitively.
900. Examples:—

回 hui²	是 shih⁴	我 wo³	不 pu⁴	宗 tsung¹	沒 mei²	管 kuan³
的。ti	一 i⁴	們 mén	能 néng²	事 shih⁴	有 yu³	倉 ts'ang¹
	年 nien²	的 ti	做 tso⁴	情 ch'ing²	銀 yin²	的。ti
	考 k'ao³	學 hsio²	祖 tsu³	我 wo³	子。tzŭ	庫 k'u⁴
	五 san¹	生 shéng¹	宗。tsung¹	萬 wan⁴	這 ché⁴	裡 li³

The custodian of a granary.
There is no silver in the treasury.
I cannot on any account do things of this kind.
Ancestors.
Our pupils are examined three times a year.

901. 如 ju², if; as.
902. 若 jo⁴, if.
903. 雜 tsa², miscellaneous; not uniform.
904. 另 ling⁴, additional.
905. 派 p'ai⁴, properly, the branches or ramifications of a stream. Hence, to distribute; to allot; to send on a mission.
906. Examples:—

如 ju²	另 ling⁴	雜 tsa²	倒 tao⁴	了 liao	派 p'ai⁴	這 ché⁴
同。t'ung²	外 wai⁴	貨 huo⁴	有 yu³	若 jo⁴	人 jén²	件 chien⁴
如 ju²	的。ti	鋪 p'u⁴	一 i⁴	是 shih⁴	辦 pan⁴	事 shih⁴
今。chin¹	另 ling⁴	那 na⁴	點 tien³	另 ling⁴	理 li³	情 ch'ing²
外 wai⁴	飯 fan⁴	兒。'rh	派 p'ai⁴	就 chiu⁴	如 ju²
還 hai²	錢 ch'ien²	邊 pien¹	人 jén²	雜 tsa²	果 kuo³
有。yu³	是 shih⁴	兒。'rh	我 wo³	亂 luan⁴	不 pu²

If someone is not sent to attend to it, this affair will all be in a mess.
Obs.—*Ju kuo*: *lit.*, if indeed (see 364). *Ju jo* would not be incorrect.
If somebody else is sent instead, I shall then have a slight chance.
Obs. 1.—*Jo shih*, commonly pronounced *yao shih*, and often so written.
Obs. 2.—Chance: *lit.*, margin or verge; *q.d.*, of hope.
A grocer's shop. (Not much used in Peking.)
The allowance (money) for food is not included.
Besides that there are.
Like; similar to.
Now.
Obs.—*Lit.*, as now. The origin of this expression is obscure.

907. 盼 p'an⁴, to look for anxiously.

908. 望 wang⁴, to expect; to hope; to look towards; towards.

909. 列 lieh⁴, separated in due order.

910. 衆 chung⁴, a number of persons; all; everyone.

911. 渴 k'o³, thirsty; to thirst for.

912. Examples:—

雜 tsa²	別 pieh²	兒 'rh	好 hao³	來 lai²	著 cho	他 t'a¹
兒 'rh	喝 ho¹	去 ch'ü⁴	沒 mei²	了 liao	你 ni³	們 mên
的 ti	涼 liang²	望 wang⁴	有 yu³	衆 chung⁴	來 lai²	列 lieh⁴
	水 shui³	看 k'an⁴	指 chih³	位 wei⁴	可 k'o³	位 wei⁴
	一 i²	你 ni³	望 wang⁴	老 lao³	巧 ch'iao³	正 chêng⁴
	個 ko⁴	渴 k'o³	了 liao	爺 yeh²	你 ni³	盼 p'an⁴
	打 ta³	了 liao	明 ming²	們 mên	就 chiu⁴	望 wang⁴

These gentlemen were just hoping you would come, and, most opportunely, here you are.

Are your honours all well?

There is no hope.

Obs.—Lit., there is no indication, nothing to point to (nothing on which to base) hope.

I'll look you up to-morrow.

Obs.—Wang k'an is more familiar than *pai*, or *pai hui*, and can only be reciprocally used by equals on intimate terms, or by superiors to inferiors.

When you are thirsty don't drink cold water.

A coolie.

Obs.—Lit., one who does (*ta*, verb of action) *tsa*, miscellaneous [jobs]. The word "coolie" (? k'u³ li⁴, hard labour) is not known in Peking except as an Anglo-Chinese term.

913. 依 i¹, to lean against; closely following. Hence, according to; to accede to; to comply with. Hence, pu⁴ i¹, to object; I won't stand it. *See* Part IV, Dialogue VII, 37.

914. 戀 lien⁴, lüan⁴, to be warmly attached to a person or place.

915. 跨 k'ua⁴, to bestride; to be seated with one leg hanging.

916. 轅 yüan², the shaft of a cart; the side gates leading into the outer court of a yamên.

917. 捨 shê³, to let go; to part with; not to detain.

918. 礙, 碍 ngai⁴, to obstruct; to interfere with. The second character is only an abbreviation of the first. In Peking the *ng* is hardly sounded, if at all.

919. Examples:—

兒 'rh	去 ch'ü⁴	怕 p'a⁴	捨 shê³	轅 yên²	依 i¹	人 jên²
的 ti	罷 pa⁴	不 pu²	不 pu⁴	兒 'rh	戀 lien⁴	出 ch'u¹
依 i¹	碍 ai⁴	礙 ai⁴	得 tê²	轅 yüan²	父 fu⁴	遠 yüan³
我 wo³	手 shou³	不 pu²	銀 yin²	門 mên²	母 mu³	門 mên²
說 shuo¹	碍 ai⁴	碍 ai⁴	子 tzŭ	他 t'a¹	跨 k'ua⁴	難 nan²
	脚 chiao³	你 ni³	別 pieh²	是 shih⁴	車 ch'ê¹	免 mien³

When a man goes on a long journey he can hardly help feeling unwilling to leave his father and mother.

Obs.—*I lien* is generally used in connexion with love for parents or elders, not of love for children, which is *lien* alone, or *shê pu tê*. *Lien* can also be used of addiction to a vice; *e.g.*, a man *lien*, clings to, his opium pipe.

To sit on the shafts of a cart.

Obs.—Note *yê-'rh²*, not *yüa-'rh²*.

The outer gates of a yamên.

He cannot part with (is loth to part with) his money.

Don't be afraid; its nothing (or, there is no harm done; there is no harm in it; it doesn't matter).

Be off with you! you're in my way.

I should say *(lit., according to my statement)*.

920. 彼 *pi³*, that, as opposed to this.

921. 此 *tz'ŭ³*, this.

922. 處 *ch'u⁴*, a place; but *ch'u³*, in composition, to live in a place. Also, to manage; to punish. Hence, *ch'u³ fên⁴*, official penalties (see *infra*).

923. 偏 *p'ien¹*, to lean towards. Hence, partial; specially; particularly.

924. 或 *huo⁴*, expressive of uncertainty; if; perhaps; either; or.

925. Examples:—

我 *wo³*	甚 *shên²*	兄 *hsiung¹*	這 *ché⁴*	相 *hsiang¹*	分 *fên¹*	彼 *pi³*
偏 *p'ien¹*	麼 *mo*	弟 *ti⁴*	有 *yu³*	待 *tai⁴*	彼 *pi³*	此 *tz'ŭ³*
不 *pu²*	偏 *p'ien¹*	或 *huo⁴*	甚 *shên²*	各 *ko⁴*	此 *tz'ŭ³*	總 *tsung³*
去 *ch'ü⁴*	向 *hsiang⁴*	待 *tai⁴*	麼 *mo*	處 *ch'u³*	總 *tsung³*	要 *yao⁴*
處 *ch'u³*	的 *ti*	朋 *p'êng²*	好 *hao³*	處 *ch'u³*	是 *shih⁴*	商 *shang¹*
分 *fên⁴*	地 *ti⁴*	友 *yu³*	處 *ch'u⁴*	處 *ch'u⁴*	一 *i²*	量 *liang⁴*
	方 *fang¹*	他 *t'a¹*	或 *huo⁴*	到 *tao¹*	樣 *yang⁴*	他 *t'a¹*
	兒 *'rh*	沒 *mei²*	待 *tai⁴*	處 *ch'u⁴*	兒 *'rh*	不 *pu⁴*

We must each consult the other; or, both parties will have to consult each the other.

He treats all alike without distinction.

Obs.—Lit., he, not distinguishing this one or that, collectively is one fashion treating [people].

Everywhere. Everywhere. Everywhere.

What advantage is there in this? or, what advantage (or, good points) has this?

Neither to his brothers nor to his friends does he show any marks of partiality.

I just won't go.

Obs.—It is difficult to give the exact force of *p'ien* in this combination; I should do so and so (or, you want me to), but I will *p'ien*, diverging from the proper path, do something quite the contrary.

Official penalties (the penalties, heavy or light, imposed upon officials for dereliction of duty).

EXERCISE XXXIV.

彼彼渴渴回子些這 1
此。此。想。想。來，儘日麼

1. What a time you have been away! I have been longing to see you. The feeling is mutual.

Obs.—Lit., these many days only then return! [I have] thirstily thought [of you]. We two, we two (in the relation of reciprocity). *K'o hsiang* is a common salutation amongst friends meeting after a separation.

是兒到一兒打 2
水。上。天望。往這
都　邊直東塊

2. Looking from this spot in an easterly direction one can see nothing but water right up to the horizon.

Obs.—Lit., from this spot towards the east, one look [in] one [unbroken] straightness as far as the edge of heaven, all is water.

的來要米考專衆 3
事。不得兒倉派人
　來處有對了都
　碍分。短不一說
　不依少對。位皇
　着我列或大上
　偺說。位銀官新
　們他怕或米察近
　　　銀的

3. Everybody says that the Emperor has recently specially deputed a high official to examine the amounts of silver and rice in the treasury and granary [and see if] they are correct. If either the rice or silver are short [of the proper amount], all you gentlemen will receive (get) penalties I expect. I should say that it can't matter to us whether he comes or not.

Obs. 1.—Recently: *hsin chin*; *lit.*, in the new (fresh) proximity, *q.d.*, of time.

Obs. 2.—Correct: *tui pu tui*; if it agrees [with the registered amount] or not.

Obs. 3.—It won't matter to us: *ai pu chao*; *lit.*, interfering not succeed in our matter, *chao* being a particle indicating successful completion of an action (*see* 45; also Note at the close of Exercise XL).

捨戀你麼的打這 4
的。戀這好有雜一
　不麼處。甚兒個

4. What good points (or qualities) does this coolie possess that you should be so loth to part with him?

業下祖兒是錢中你 5
阿。的宗就大甚進們
　產留是宗麼的年

5. In what does the chief portion of your yearly income consist? In the property left us by our ancestors.

PART III.—THE FORTY EXERCISES. 181

老 6 鄉 昨 點 偏 又 散
不　的 兒 兒 偏 叫 了。
下　下 剛 雲 兒 兒
雨、 人 長 彩、 的 風
　　 盼 害。 　　 　　 颳

6. There has been no rain for ever so long, and the country-folk are longing (hoping dreadfully) for it to come. Yesterday, just as a few clouds had made their appearance (grown), the wind most provokingly again blew them all away.

Obs.—Most provokingly : *p'ien p'ien* could here be fairly rendered "I'll be hanged if the wind," etc.

另 7 輛 若 着 必 一
找 車 是 轅 要 身
一 罷。 跨 兒 弄 土。
　　 　　 兒 　　 　　

7. You had better get (find) another cart; if you sit on the shafts [of this one] you are sure to get covered with dust.

Obs.—Get covered with dust : *lit.*, make (163) one body's dust (*ti*, understood).

京 8 是 方 處 地 兒。
城 五 雜 的 方
　　 雜 　　 　　

8. The capital is a place with a miscellaneous population.

Obs.—*Lit.*, the capital is a five-quarters-miscellaneous-residing's place. Note *ch'u*^{3}, not *ch'u*^{4}. The fifth quarter is the centre.

Turn the following into Chinese. (KEY, EXERCISE XXXIV.)

1. In every city of China there are granaries and treasuries. Granaries are for holding (containing) rice; treasuries for putting silver into. These granaries and treasuries all have official underlings in charge of them, and when rice or money is lost, these official underlings are in all cases responsible. The money and rice contained in the treasuries and granaries have to be inspected once every year. Some years ago (that year) I had a friend who was in charge of a treasury; some robbers came in the night, broke (beat) open the door, and carried off the whole of the treasure. The high officials thereupon called upon my friend to make good the silver stolen, but of course he had no such sum in ready money, and after deliberating for some days, [he could think of] no plan, so he ran away.

Obs. 1.—Note *kuan jên*, official underlings; *kuan*, officials.

Obs. 2.—Are responsible: *lit.*, *wei*, it is, *kuan jên*, the official underlings, *shih*, that are, *wên*, asked.

Obs. 3.—To make good: *lit.*, according to the original quantity patching return.

Obs. 4.—Of course, etc.: *lit.*, my friend, where had [he] so much now (=ready) money as that?

2. What was the use of that? Even if he had run to the ends of the earth (the horizon), couldn't the police have got hold of him? and even if they could not manage to arrest him, he would be unable to return to his home; supposing he did return, he could not live there permanently.

Obs.—The police, etc.: *lit.*, the official underlings yet seizing not arrive [at success]?

3. As I regard it, it would have been far better for him to have waited and submitted to his penalty than to have run all over the country.

Obs.—Waited and submitted to, etc.: lit., *têng cho*, waiting, *ti'ng*, to have accepted or submitted to (131), his *ch'u fên*; *tao*, on the contrary, compared with the whole (full) place running superior (*ch'iang*) much.

4. Carter! look, there's a man sitting behind the cart! why don't you whip behind?

Obs.—Whip behind: *wang hou ch'ou* (**894**); a Pekingese idiom.

5. You wouldn't part with that woollen carpet when I asked you for it last year; if you were to make me a present of it now I just wouldn't take it (want it).

926. 揑 *nieh*[1], to hold between the fingers, as a flower; to work up, as clay.

927. 灑 洒 *sa*[3], to sprinkle water; the second character being an abbreviation of the first.

928. 掃 *sao*[3], to sweep; when combined with the following it is pronounced *sao*[4], and means a large broom.

929. 帚 *chou*[3], a broom.

930. 砌 *ch'i*[4], to raise in courses or layers, as a wall.

931. 硋 夯 *hang*[1], to beat the ground for building, before bricks or stones are laid. This character, according to some authorities, should be written in the second form.

932. Examples:—

再 *tsai*[4]	房 *fang*[2]	出 *ch'u*[1]	拏 *na*[2]	灑 *sa*[3]	小 *hsiao*[3]	揑 *nieh*[1]
砌 *ch'i*[4]	子 *tzŭ*	個 *ko*[4]	個 *ko*[4]	了 *liao*	牛 *niu*[2]	着 *cho*[2]
牆。*ch'iang*[2]	先 *hsien*[1]	道 *tao*[4]	掃 *sao*[4]	滿 *man*[3]	兒 *'rh*	筆。*pi*[3]
	得 *tei*[3]	兒 *'rh*	帚 *chou*[3]	地 *ti*[4]	當 *tang*[4]	揑 *nieh*[1]
	打 *ta*[3]	來。*lai*[2]	掃 *sao*[3]	下 *hsia*[4]	玩 *wan*[2]	了 *liao*
	硋 *hang*[1]	要 *yao*[4]	雪 *hsüeh*[3]	的 *ti*	意 *i*[4]	一 *i*[2]
	後 *hou*[4]	蓋 *kai*[4]	掃 *sao*[3]	水。*shui*[3]	兒。*'rh*	個 *ko*[4]

Holding a pencil in the fingers.

He moulded a small cow (out of clay) for a plaything.

He sprinkled the whole ground (or, the whole floor) with water; or, he spilt the water all over the floor.

Sweep the snow away with a broom and make a path.

In building a house the ground has to be prepared first, and the walls then raised.

PART III.—THE FORTY EXERCISES.

933. 狗 kou³, a dog.

934. 修 hsiu¹, to put or keep in order; to repair; to revise.

935. 圓 yüan², round.

936. 扁 pien³, flat and thin; also, a tablet hung over the door of a room or house. Note that p'ing **(137)** is used of a flat surface without reference to thickness.

937. 幌 huang³, a shop sign, whether of wood or any design indicating the nature of the goods sold or business done.

938. 表 piao³, properly, the outside. Hence, to manifest; hence, a watch.

939. Examples:—

幌 huang³	扁 pien³	有 yu³	兒 'rh	表｡piao³	一 i⁴
子 tzŭ	了｡liao	扁 pien³	的 ti	修 hsiu¹	條 t'iao²
是 shih⁴	酒 chiu³	的｡ti	尺 ch'ih³	房 fang²	狗｡kou³
布 pu⁴	鋪 p'u⁴	大 tai⁴	有 yu³	子｡tzŭ	修 hsiu¹
做 tso⁴	子 tzŭ	夫 fu¹	圓 yüan²	畫 hua⁴	理 li³
的｡ti	的 ti	掛 kua⁴	的 ti	道 tao⁴	鐘 chung¹

A dog.

Obs.—Note the numerative.

To mend clocks and watches.

Obs.—*Lit.*, to mend and regulate.

To repair a house.

Rulers are round or flat.

Obs.—Rulers: *lit.*, drawing lines's feet. *Ch'ih* is also a foot measure or rule.

The doctor has started in practice.

Obs.—*Lit.*, has hung up his signboard. Note that a *pien* can only be placed over the door, or horizontally; there are exceptions to this rule, but in such cases the *pien* is called *li pien* (Radical 117), an upright tablet.

Wine-shop signs are made of cotton cloth.

940. 冤 yüan¹, to be aggrieved.

941. 枉 wang³, properly, not straight; hence, injustice.

942. 迸 pêng⁴, to jump off the ground with both legs; to bound. This rendering is not recognised by the dictionaries.

943. 跳 t'iao⁴, to jump off the ground; generally, with one leg.

944. 嚇 hsia⁴, to frighten; to scare. In composition, read ho⁴.

945. Examples:—

了 liao	井 ching³	有 yu³	進 péng⁴	枉 wang³	那 na⁴
我 wo³	去 ch'ü⁴	人 jén²	上 shang⁴	他 t'a¹	不 pu²
一 i²	了 liao	跳 t'iao⁴	牆 ch'iang²	麼。mo	是 shih⁴
跳。t'iao⁴	嚇 hsia⁴	下 hsia⁴	去。ch'ü⁴	你 ni³	寃 yüan¹

Is not that doing him an injustice (or, accusing him wrongfully)?
Jump up on the wall.
A man has jumped into the well.
Gave me a fright; or, made me jump.

Obs.—Lit., frightened me a jump; t'iao, however, refers to the action of the heart, not of the body.

946. 造 tsao⁴, to make.

947. 報 pao⁴, to announce; to give notice of. Hence, a newspaper; a gazette; to recompense.

948. 彷 fang³, to resemble.

949. 彿 fu², only used with the foregoing fang³. As fang³-fu², to resemble; to seem; seemingly.

950. 笤 t'iao², with chou³ (929), a small broom.

951. Examples:—

樣 yang⁴	彿 fu	著 cho	票。p'iao⁴	造 tsao⁴	得‘ tei³	要 yao⁴
子。tzŭ	要 yao⁴	把 pa³	有 yu³	了 liao	報 pao⁴	造 tsao⁴
京 ching¹	掃 sao³	笤 t'iao²	個 ko⁴	一 i⁴	官。kuan¹	房 fang²
報。pao⁴	地 ti⁴	帚 chou³	人 jén²	張 chang¹	他 t'a¹	子 tzŭ
	的 ti	彷 fang³	拏 na²	銀 yin²	担 nieh¹	先 hsien¹

Before building a house you must give notice to the authorities.
Obs.—Tsao is not the common word for building a house, which is *kai⁴*.
He forged a cheque (or, bank note).
A man is holding a broom as if he were going to sweep the ground.
Obs.—Lit., there is a man holding a broom [with a] seemingly wanting-to-sweep-the-ground's appearance.
The "Peking Gazette."

PART III.—THE FORTY EXERCISES.

EXERCISE XXXV.

1. 我那個時辰表叫他舖裏送去修，給他們修理。他們就手兒那個風雨表收拾了沒有。

   1. Send that watch of mine to the watchmakers' and tell them to repair it for me. You can take the opportunity to ask them whether the repairs to my barometer are finished.

Obs. 1.—Watch: *lit.*, an indicator of *shih ch'ên*, time, or periods of time; there are 12 *shih ch'ên* in the 24 hours. A watch can also be called *piao* simply, but special care must be taken not to append the common affix *tzŭ*.

Obs. 2.—Barometer: *lit.*, wind and rain indicator; the term is naturally a modern one. Cf. also *han² shu³ piao*, an indicator of cold and heat; *q.d.*, a thermometer.

2. 他手裏拿着筆彷彿要寫甚麼。瓦盆是瓦盆匠拿的。

   2. He has hold of a pencil in his fingers, as if he wanted to write something. Earthenware bowls are made by the hand of the potter.

3. 那賊造假告示，作為官出的。

   3. The rebels forged a proclamation which was to pass as one issued by the authorities.

Obs. 1.—To pass as: *tso wei*, both verbs, and both here meaning to play a part, to act as.

Obs. 2.—Issued: *ch'u*, to issue, here an active verb, of which *kuan*, officer, or the government, is the subject; *lit.*, to act as an authorities-issue-one = one that is issued by the authorities.

4. 他帶的貨物是李行挐上關叫查出全入了官了。

   4. He returned the merchandise he had with him as baggage, which being detected at the Customs station, the whole was confiscated.

Obs. 1.—Being detected: *chiao*, *lit.*, to cause; *q.d.*, [some agent or incident] caused [the inspector] at (*shang*) the Customs station to find out [the truth]=[the truth] was discovered by the Customs. There is not in Chinese any verb properly passive, but the passive construction is effected by a verb like *shou*, to receive, *pei*, to suffer, or by statement of the action that caused what was received or suffered; the action being indicated by one active verb, the subject of which, whether agent or incident, is understood.

Obs. 2.—Confiscated: *lit.*, all entered into the official [custody].

5. 先灑水後掃地不然土就飛起來咯。

   5. Sprinkle water before you sweep the floor, otherwise the dust will fly about.

6. 你那個狗兒真好，毛兒長，腿兒短，耳朶也不小，就是嘴頭兒尖點兒。

   6. That is certainly a very nice-looking little dog of yours. His coat is long, his legs are short, and his ears are not small; only his muzzle is a little [too] pointed.

7. 他們那打別是蓋子
   打那兒碎就要房罷。

7. They must be going to build a house there that they are preparing the ground.

Obs.—They must be, etc.: *pieh chiu shih*; *lit.*, it is not then other than [to] build a house, I expect. *Pieh*, to distinguish, has here the force of deciding between two alternatives; [it can't be] other than to build. The *chiu* may be dispensed with.

8. 若不論圓扁，瓜是圓的，扁豆就是扁的，錢是又圓又扁的。

8. As regards the difference between *yüan*² (round) and *pien*³ (flat), a water melon is round and a broad bean is flat; a cash is both the one and the other.

Obs.—As regards, etc.: *lit.*, if [one would] discuss *yüan* and *pien's* unsameness.

9. 我沒犯法，人告我做賊，那不是枉了我麼。

9. If I have not broken the law and I am accused of being a thief, that is an injustice to me, is it not?

Obs.—Note *tso tsei*, to be a thief.

10. 他近來的事情不好，是他實在的自己想不出甚麼法子來報答他。我的報答不應。

10. That his affairs of late have not gone well is entirely the reward of his own misdeeds. I really can't think of any way of repaying his goodness to me.

Obs.—Reward of misdeeds: *pao ying*, answering recompense, can only be applied to the reward of evil-doing.

Turn the following into Chinese. (KEY, EXERCISE XXXV.)

1. I notice that the coolie you have there is a very good one; he does things very promptly, and keeps the rooms extremely clean; whenever I go [to your house] I always see him there with a broom sweeping up. That servant of mine is a terrible boor; with that tall figure of his, when he walks he is constantly jumping about in one direction or another. The whole day long, if he is not driving (beating) the fowls he is worrying (*tou*) the dogs, for all the world like a youngster.

Obs. 1.—Promptly: *k'uai*⁴ *tang*¹ (342), *lit.*, quickly and properly; but *tang*, it is maintained, has no force at all in this connexion. Cf. *shun tang* (626), favourable, free from obstruction; *pien tang* (333), convenient.

Obs. 2.—Keeps clean, etc.: *lit.*, in the room sprinkles and sweeps (*ti* for *tê*) very clean.

Obs. 3.—Tall figure, etc.: *lit.*, as great body measurement (*shên liang*, stature) as that. *Shên liang* refers to height only, not girth.

Obs. 4.—Jumping about, etc.: *lit.*, a forward jumping (*pêng*) backward bounding (*t'iao*) one.

2. Another thing [about him is that he] is quite inexperienced. One day, my watch being out of order (spoilt), I had put it on

PART III.—THE FORTY EXERCISES.   187

the table intending to look for a man to mend it. He saw it, and, taking it in his hand, said, "What sort of a thing is this? it's both round and flat." He was not holding it tightly, so it slipped from his hand and fell to the ground. I asked him why he threw my watch down, and he concocted a story (falsely reported) that the dog had jumped on the table, and in jumping off had knocked the watch down. He went on to say that if I falsely asserted (**597**) that he had damaged the watch, he would be the victim of an injustice. How can I employ a man of this kind?

Obs. 1.—Inexperienced: *lit.*, has not opened his eyes; has never seen anything.

Obs. 2.—Hold tightly: he had not *nieh chu*, pinched it to.

Obs. 3.—Slipped from his hand, etc.: *lit.*, one losing of the hand (*shih shou*, **574**), it fell to the ground.

3. It seems to me that your servant is good enough (*lit.*, also not wrong). He is a rustic by origin, and, though a little rough and careless, that kind of man is sure to be strong (muscular), and if you should be building a wall by-and-by, you can get him to help in beating the ground (pile-driving), or in helping the masons; for that he will do well enough.

Obs. 1.—And though, etc.: *lit.*, rough and careless a little, also there is (*shih yu*) of it (*ti*).

Obs. 2.—Helping the masons: *tso hsiao kung-'rh*, *lit.*, to do little jobs, refers especially to the work done by a bricklayer's assistant, who is called *hsiao kung-tzŭ*; the bricklayer, or master mason, being a *ta kung-tzŭ*.

952. 歲, 嵗 *sui*⁴, the year; but used more limitedly than *nien*². The second is the correct form.

953. 紀 *chi*⁴, anciently, a period of twelve years; hence, any period of years. Verbally, to reckon a period.

954. 壽 *shou*⁴, old age.

955. Examples:—

壽 *shou*⁴ 人 *jên*² 年 *nien*² 紀 *chi*⁴ 多 *to*² 萬 *wan*⁴ 歲 *sui*⁴
您 *nin*² 紀 *chi*⁴ 有 *yu*³ 大 *ta*⁴ 歲 *sui*⁴ 數 *shu*⁴
高 *kao*¹ 的 *ti* 了 *liao* 年 *nien*² 爺 *yeh*² 兒 *'rh*

One's age.
The Emperor; *lit.*, the lord of 10,000 years.
How old are you?

Obs.—This is not a very polite form, the ordinary one being *kuei*⁴ *kêng*¹, which will be met with later.

A man of mature years; well advanced in life. Not applied to persons under sixty.
What is your age, sir?

Obs.—This form is only used to men over forty years of age, the limit being generally indicated by the moustache, which is seldom allowed to grow before that age, unless in the case of officials of a certain rank.

956. 因 *yin*¹, a cause; because of.

957. 爲 *wei*⁴, because of. Not to be confounded with *wei*² (**848**).

958. 緣 *yüan*², origin; clue; cause.

959. 故 *ku*⁴, ancient; a cause of.

960. 耽, 躭 *tan*¹, to loiter; to delay. The second is the commoner form.

961. Examples:—

那 na^4	爲 wei^4	會 hui^4	你 ni^3	有 yu^3	爲 wei^4
緣 $yüan^2$	甚 $shên^2$	兒 'rh	就 tan^1	病 $ping^4$	甚 $shên^2$
故 ku^4	麼 mo^1	縂 $ts'ai^2$	擱 ko^1	不 pu^4	麼 mo
難 nan^2	緣 $yüan^2$	來 lai^2	到 tao^4	能 $nêng^2$	因 yin^1
說 $shuo^1$	故 ku^4	因 yin^1	這 $ché^4$	去 $ch'ü^4$	爲 wei^4

Why?
I cannot go because I am unwell.
What is the reason for delaying your arrival until now?

Obs.—Lit., you delay put [on one side] until this while, only then come is because of what cause? *Tan* is never used alone colloquially, being generally combined with *ko*, as above, or with *wu* (962).

The reasons are hard to give (or, difficult to explain).

962. 悮, 誤 wu^4, to leave undone; to fail in doing; to be in error; to hinder. Both forms are used.

963. 容 $jung^2$, $yung^2$, alone, to receive; to contain; to tolerate; to allow; also, the countenance. But with the following i^4, easy.

964. 易 yi^4, i^4, alone, to change; but with $jung^2$, easy.

965. Examples:—

從 $ts'ung^1$	討 $t'ao^3$	屋 wu^1	辦 pan^4	就 tan^1	悮 wu^4	怎 $tsên^3$
從 $ts'ung^1$	人 $jên^2$	裡 li^3	這 $ché^4$	悮 wu^4	會 hui^4	麼 mo
容 $jung^2$	嫌 $hsien^2$	容 $jung^2$	桌 cho^1	工 $kung^1$	他 $t'a^1$	就 tan^1
容 $jung^2$	沒 mei^2	不 pu^4	子 $tzŭ$	夫 fu^1	的 ti	悮 wu^4
兒 'rh	人 $jên^2$	下 $hsia^4$	尺 $ch'ih^2$	那 na^4	意 i^4	了 $liao$
的 ti	能 $nêng^2$	他 $t'a^1$	寸 $ts'un^4$	不 pu^4	思 $ssŭ^1$	半 pan^4
	容 $jung^2$	過 kuo^4	太 $t'ai^4$	容 $jung^2$	了 $liao$	天 $t'ieh^1$
	他 $t'a^1$	於 $yü^2$	大 ta^4	易 i^4	別 $pieh^2$	我 wo^3

How is it you have delayed so long?
I have mistaken his meaning (or intention).
Obs.—Lit., I have mistakenly understood. *See* 129.
Don't delay.
It is not easy to manage (or, deal with).
This table is (the dimensions of this table are) too large; there is not space for it in the room.
He is too aggravating; no one can tolerate him.
In a leisurely (or deliberate) manner.

966. 勁 $chin^4$, muscular strength; also, in combination, inclination.

967. 塗 $t'u^2$, tu^4, properly, mud; but in hu^2-tu^4, stupid, read tu^4.

968. 喜 hsi^3, joy; to be pleased; to like.

PART III.—THE FORTY EXERCISES.   189

969. 歡 *huan*¹, to rejoice; to show pleasure.

970. 惜 *hsi*¹, to pity; to feel for; to like; to spare; to save (economically).

971. Examples:—

倆 *mên*	可 *k'o*³	你 *ni*³	喜 *hsi*³	塗 *tu*⁴	勁 *chin*⁴	這 *chê*⁴
倆 *lia*³	惜 *hsi*¹	道 *tao*⁴	歡 *huan*¹	極 *chi*²	兒 。*'rh*	兩 *liang*³
很 *hên*³	得 *tê*	喜。*hsi*³	他 *t'a*¹	了 *liao*	他 *t'a*¹	天 *t'ien*¹
對 *tui*⁴	很。*hên*³	他 *t'a*¹	喜 *hsi*³	我 *wo*³	那 *na*⁴	身 *shên*¹
勁 *chin*⁴	愛 *ai*⁴	的 *ti*	事。*shih*⁴	實 *shih*²	個 *ko*⁴	上 *shang*⁴
兒。*'rh*	惜。*hsi*¹	少 *shao*⁴	我 *wo*³	在 *tsai*⁴	人 *jên*²	沒 *mei*²
	他 *t'a*¹	爺 *yeh*²	給 *kei*³	不 *pu*⁴	糊 *hu*²	有 *yu*³

These two days past I have had no strength in my body (I have felt limp).
That man is utterly stupid; I certainly do not like him.
A wedding (generally); a birth, etc.; any event which is the subject of congratulation.
I congratulate you.
His son is much to be pitied.
Obs.—Lit., his son is a [men] ought to (may) pity one (*tê*=*ti*) very.
To be fond of.
Those two hit it off (get on together, suit each other) very well.
Obs.—Lit., their muscle corresponds. The origin of this expression is said to be found in the explanation that as their muscular strength corresponds, is equal, each would be careful not to come to blows with the other.

972. 欺 *ch'i*¹, to deceive.

973. 哄 *hung*³, to beguile.

974. 誆, 誑 *k'uang*¹, to attempt to gain one's end by lies, false promises, etc.

975. 騙 *p'ien*⁴, to defraud one of.

976. 屜 *t'i*⁴, a drawer; a tray.

977. Examples:—

把 *pa*³	個 *ko*⁴	誆 *k'uang*¹	他 *t'a*¹	方 *fang*¹	有 *yu*³	那 *na*⁴
那 *na*⁴	抽 *ch'ou*¹	騙 *p'ien*⁴	把 *pa*³	兒。*'rh*	欺 *ch'i*¹	個 *ko*⁴
個 *ko*⁴	屜 *t'i*⁴	了 *liao*	人 *jên*²	你 *ni*³	哄 *hung*³	人 *jên*²
關 *kuan*¹	抽 *ch'ou*¹	去。*ch'ü*⁴	家 *chia*¹	別 *pieh*²	人 *jên*²	老 *lao*³
上 *shang*⁴	出 *ch'u*¹	把 *pa*³	的 *ti*	哄 *hung*³	的 *ti*	實 *shih*²
罷。*pa*⁴	來 *lai*²	這 *chê*⁴	表 *piao*³	我。*wo*³	地 *ti*⁴	沒 *mei*²

That man is honest, and does not cheat in any way.
Obs.—Lit., has not cheating men's places.
Don't deceive me.
He did a man out of his watch.
Pull this drawer out and shut that one to.

EXERCISE XXXVI.

1. The drawer in this wardrobe (or, chest of drawers) won't come (pull) out. Give it a good hard pull and you will get it out.

Obs.—Good hard pull, etc.: *lit.*, you use muscle one pull out, and you will drag it out.

2. What is the reason why that affair has not succeeded (or, has lagged)? There are a great many reasons; too many to make it easy to tell them.

3. What is the age of this son of yours, sir? My son is eighteen; his birthday is on the 8th of the 6th moon; next year we are going to marry him. When the wedding day comes I shall be sure to go and offer my congratulations.

Obs.—Marry: *lit.*, we want to arrange matters for him; *yao* being a sign of the future tense. Note that the father speaks of his son's marriage as *pan shih* simply, not *hsi shih*.

4. Don't try and deceive me, for [allow] me to tell you, it is not an easy matter. I am quite a match for you, and if you come to (discuss) cheating, you are not up to my form.

Obs.—Up to my form: *pu shih ko-'rh*; *lit.*, are not a piece, *q.d.*, of a piece with me. The expression is a slang one.

5. What a pity it is that that man is so exceedingly stupid that he cannot make himself intelligible. He has taken up ever so much of my time.

Obs.—Exceedingly: exceeds in the matter of stupidity. See **343**.

PART III.—THE FORTY EXERCISES.   191

6. 我們倆彼此很對勁。可惜他那個兄弟很哄人、去年還欺誆騙了我幾兩銀子呢。

6. He and I suit each other very well. Unfortunately, his brother is a great cheat; he did me out of some taels last year.

Obs.—Great cheat: is very competent (well knows how) to cheat people.

7. 我最不喜歡他待人的那個樣子、你那時候都是小兒老家兒不管他的緣故。

7. I particularly object to his manner towards elderly people. I'll tell you the reason [of his behaviour]; it's all because his elders did not keep him in order in his childhood.

Obs. 1.—I'll tell you the reason, etc.: *lit.*, I tell you that all is in childhood elders not control him's cause. It would not be incorrect were *yuan ku* to precede the cause, as in the translation.

Obs. 2.—Elders: *lao chia-'rh*, the elders of his family, inclusive of relations, such as uncles, aunts, etc.

8. 他是個人、安靜、不論甚麼事從從容容兒的辦。

8. He is a steady fellow, and does everything, no matter what, in a quiet, methodical way.

Turn the following into Chinese. (KEY, EXERCISE XXXVI.)

1. After the new year you will be a year older.

Obs.—The Chinese reckon age by the year, commencing with the 1st of the 1st moon, the fraction of the year counting in favour of the child; thus, a child born in the 10th moon would be two years old on the 1st of the following 1st moon.

2. How old is your father? My father is now eighty-two. A person of his years may be considered an aged man.

Obs.—A person of his years, etc.: *lit.*, [with] this kind of age he also can be considered to be a possessing longevity number's man.

3. Yesterday I waited the whole day for you; why did you not go and look me up? There was a reason for it. I was just going to start, when at the moment, as luck would have it, a distant relation turned up (came); there was nothing for it but to sit down and talk with him, and there I was kept. He only left after a long time, and as it was then getting late, I did not go and look you up.

Obs. 1.—I sat with him, etc.: *lit.*, there being no plan I accompanied (entertained, *p'ei*) him sitting down [and] talked, being delayed to the spot (*tan wu chu liao*); the *chu* indicating the impossibility of getting away.

Obs. 2.—He only left, etc.: *lit.*, after half a day had passed he only then (*ts'ai*) left.

4. It is quite near for you to get into the main street where you live, which is very convenient indeed for buying anything [one wants]. The little lane in which we live is most inconvenient; it is by no means easy to buy anything, however small.

Obs.—By no means easy: *lit.*, to buy a little of anything truly not easy.

5. That man has not an atom of muscle about him, and yet he thinks of learning

military [exercises] (studying for the army). How foolish he is!

Obs.—How foolish : *lit.*, in his heart there is how much stupidity!

6. You like this vegetable, don't you? Unfortunately (it's a pity), there isn't any more.

7. Don't deceive me; just now I saw there was a whole lot in that drawer.

8. You are not cheated when you buy things in shops, but when you buy them in the street you have to look out; they mostly sell you bad things and cheat you out of your money.

Obs. 1.—You are not cheated : *lit.*, in the shops buy things [they] do not cheat people.

Obs. 2.—Mostly : *to* (7).

978. 屢 *lü³*, frequent.

979. 公 *kung¹*, public ; just ; disinterested. Also, as will be seen later, a gentleman.

980. 私 *ssŭ¹*, private ; illicit ; interested.

981. 務 *wu⁴*, business ; the verb *must*.

982. Examples :—

道 tao¹	私。ssŭ¹	賣 mai⁴	私 ssŭ¹	事 shih⁴	的 ti	屢 lü³
人。jên²	他 t'a¹	人 jên²	事。shih⁴	務 wu⁴	說 shuo¹	次。tz'ŭ⁴
私 ssŭ¹	是 shih⁴	不 pu⁴	家 chia¹	必 pi²⁴	他。t'a¹	我 wo³
情。ch'ing²	個 ko⁴	准 chun³	務。wu⁴	用 yung⁴	辦 pan⁴	屢 lü³
	公 kung¹	走 tsou³	買 mai³	心。hsin¹	公 kung¹	次 tz'ŭ⁴

Many times.

I have reprimanded him time after time.

In transacting public business there must positively be attention (attention is essential).

Obs.—Note that *wu pi* is stronger than either *pi* or *tei* alone. We can either say *wu pi²* or *wu pi⁴*.

Private affairs.

Household affairs.

Merchants are not authorised (forbidden) to smuggle.

Obs.—Smuggle : *lit.*, walk secretly.

He is a just man (a man of just principles).

A private understanding; or, private relations, in a good or a bad sense. Where one of the parties is a woman, always in a bad sense.

983. 閒 *hsien²*, empty ; without occupation ; leisure.

984. 悶 *mên⁴*, sad ; in low spirits.

985. 慌 *huang¹*, an intensive of adjectives describing disagreeable sensations. Also, scared ; agitated.

986. 樂 *lê⁴, lo⁴*, joy in the heart ; gladness in the countenance. Also, to laugh.

987. 煩 *fan²*, to put, or be put to, trouble.

PART III.—THE FORTY EXERCISES.

988. 急 chi^2, quick in movement or temper; rushing of water. With $chao^2$ **(45)**, anxious; eager; impatient.

989. Examples:—

他 $t'a^1$	的。 ti	帶 tai^4	散 san^4	要 yao^4	的 ti	我 wo^3
那 na^4	別 $pieh^2$	了 $liao$	悶, $mên^4$	請 $ch'ing^3$	慌 $huang^1$	沒 mei^2
話 hua^4	著 $chao^2$	去。 $ch'ü^4$	逭 $ché^4$	客 $k'o^4$	我 wo^3	有 yu^3
他 $t'a^1$	急。 chi^2	慌 $huang^1$	包 pao^1	樂 lo^4	悶 $mên^4$	閑 $hsien^2$
樂 lo^4	我 wo^3	慌 $huang^1$	兒 $'rh$	一 i^1	死 $ssŭ^3$	空 $k'ung^4$
了。 $liao$	告 kao^4	忙 $mang^2$	煩 fan^2	樂 lo^4	了。 $liao$	兒。 $'rh$
	訴 su^4	忙 $mang^2$	你 ni^3	散 san^4	我 wo^3	悶 $mên^4$

I have no leisure. *See* **199**.
Much bored; intensely dull.
I am bored to death.
I want to ask some guests to have a good time, and dispel my melancholy (cheer me up a bit).
May I trouble you to take this parcel with you?
Flurried; flustered.
Don't be anxious (get excited; or, be impatient).
When I told him that (or, gave him that message), he laughed.

990. 奉 $fêng^4$, properly, to raise the hands, as when presenting anything; to receive, as orders, an appointment, etc.

991. 求 $ch'iu^2$, to request; to crave; to seek.

992. 託 $t'o^1$, to commission; to request one to act as agent.

993. 發 fa^1, to issue forth; to cause to issue; to send.

994. 信 $hsin^4$, good faith; to believe; a letter. Also, to follow, as one's inclination.

995. Examples:—

不 pu^4	的 ti	個 ko^4	託 $t'o^1$	您。 nin^2	我 wo^3	
得 $tê^2$	話 hua^4	人 $jên^2$	您 nin^2	求 $ch'iu^2$	有 yu^3	
的 ti	我 wo^3	送 $sung^4$	替 $t'i^4$	老 lao^3	件 $chien^4$	
信 $hsin^4$	不 pu^2	信 $hsin^4$	我 wo^3	爺 yeh^2	事 $shih^4$	
口 $k'ou^3$	信。 $hsin^4$	去。 $ch'ü^4$	打 ta^3	的 ti	奉 $fêng^4$	
說。 $shuo^1$	信 $hsin^4$	你 ni^3	發 fa^1	恩。 $ngên^1$	求 $ch'iu^2$	

I have a favour to ask of you.
I crave Your Honour's clemency (or favour). Would you (I would commission you to) send a man for me with a letter (or, to take a letter)?

Obs.—Note *sung hsin*, to send a letter; *sung hsin-'rh*, to send a message.

I do not believe what you say.
It is incredible.
To be free with one's tongue; to say what comes into one's head.
Obs.—Note *hsin* in the sense of to follow one's inclination.

996. 雇 *ku*⁴, to hire, as a servant, horse, conveyance; not said of a house, furniture, etc.

997. 孩 *hai*², a child.

998. 撒 *sa*¹, to scatter from the hand, as seed, etc.

999. 謊 *huang*³, falsehood.

1000. 賺 *chuan*⁴, to gain, as money.

1001. 星 *hsing*¹, a star.

1002. 所 *so*³, properly, a place; the relative pronoun *that which*. With the verb *yu*³, to be, it means all. With *i*³ (**125**), it means therefore, consequently (see **125**).

1003. Examples:—

所	*so*³	本	*pên*³	帶	*chou*³	沒	*mei*²	去	*ch'ü*⁴	雇	*ku*⁴	雇	*ku*⁴
有	*yu*³	事	*shih*⁴	星	*hsing*¹	人	*jên*²	罷	*pa*⁴	船	*ch'uan*²	一	*i*²
的	*ti*	大	*ta*⁴	流	*liu*²	信	*hsin*⁴	他	*t'a*¹	好	*hao*³	個	*ko*⁴
書	*shu*¹	也	*yeh*³	星	*hsing*¹	他	*t'a*¹	常	*ch'ang*²	孩	*hai*²	小	*hsiao*³
全	*ch'üan*²	不	*pu*⁴	雖	*sui*¹	說	*shuo*¹	撒	*sa*¹	子	*tzŭ*	孩	*hai*²
好	*hao*³	能	*nêng*²	然	*jan*²	謊	*huang*³	謊	*huang*³	去	*ch'ü*⁴	子	*tzŭ*
		賺	*chuan*⁴	他	*t'a*¹	話	*hua*⁴	所	*so*³	玩	*wan*²	送	*sung*⁴
		錢	*ch'ien*²	的	*ti*	掃	*sao*⁴	以	*i*³	兒	*'rh*	信	*hsin*⁴

To hire a small boy to carry a letter.
Obs.—Note that *hai-tzŭ* may mean a boy or a girl.
To hire (or charter) a boat or ship.
Go and play, that's a good child.
He constantly tells lies, so nobody believes him.
To say what is not the truth; to tell a falsehood.
A comet. A meteor.
Although his ability is great, he cannot make money.
Obs.—It would be equally correct to say *t'a ti pên shih sui jan ta*.
All the books that there are are good.
Obs.—All that there are: *lit.*, that which there are of (*ti*) books are all good. Note that *so yu* must be followed by some word signifying all, such as *tou* or *ch'üan*, the *so yu* being only intensive.

EXERCISE XXXVII.

您₁ 忙 很 有 的 兒。
公 不 忙 天 閒 時
事 忙。 兒 兒 着 候
　　 算 總
　　 天

1. Do your public duties keep you busy, sir? I cannot be considered to be very busy, as I always have some leisure time during each day.

我₂ 我 兒 人 不 閒 要
有 奉 屢 去 總 着 一
一 求 次 說 不 託 要
件 那 他 沒 見 您 纔
事 李 們 空 我 替 好_c
情 老 那 兒 多 我
　 爺 賬 的 儹

2. I have a favour to ask of you. I have been time after time to Lɪ lao-yeh's place to ask for payment of that account which he owes me, but his people always say that he is not at leisure, and he won't see me. Would you, when you have nothing to do, ask him for payment on my behalf?

Obs.—The final *ts‘ai hao*, then it will be all right, is omitted in the translation, as it seems unnecessary to the completion of the sentence.

昨₃ 爲 託 信 他 來、 他
兒 孩 我 去 說 他
我 子 發 雇 沒 是
一 病 信 替 到 撒
個 心 到 他 了 謊
相 裏 鄉 雇 後 所
好 煩 下 一 半 以
的、 悶 問 個 天 我
因 的、 一 人 他 不
急 問 送 打 知 肯
　 　 發 　 道

給
他
錢。

3. Yesterday a friend of mine who was in great distress about a child of his in the country that is ill, wanted to send a note off at once to inquire how he was, and asked me to hire someone to take it. I did hire a man, and sent him off, but he came back in the afternoon and said that he had not been able to find the place. I knew he was not telling the truth, so I would not give him any money.

Obs. 1.—In the afternoon: *tao*, when the time came to be afternoon.
Obs. 2.—Find the place: see Note on *chao* at the end of Exercise XL.

小₄ 的、 貨 子 還 子 不
大 價 就 一 是 賣 能
價 錢 是 斤 一 的 賺
錢 兒 一 買 斤 所 錢。
買 賺 兩 的 兩 以
來 錢。 賣 銀 買

4. To buy cheap and sell dear is *chuan*⁴ *ch‘ien*² (to make money). The goods cost a tael a catty and were sold at a tael a catty; there is consequently nothing made on the transaction.

Obs.—To buy: *ti* representing the goods, or any like word; *lit.*, [when men] at a great price sell [they] at a small price bought *ti*, goods, articles=the goods bought by them, *na chiu*, that then=such a transaction, is making money.

5.

他帶着一車子私
貨進城門上的官
人過來查問他慌
忙忙的說是行李
官慌忙人不信把箱子
李官打開一看果然
子的都是私貨所
裝以全入了官了

5. He brought a barrow-load of smuggled goods into the city, [and when] the official underlings at the gate came forward to ask what they were (*lit.*, to search and inquire), he said in a flurried sort of way that it was personal baggage. They didn't believe him, and when they opened the boxes they saw at once that, sure enough, the boxes contained nothing but contraband articles, which were consequently all confiscated.

Obs. 1.—Note *ch'ē-tzŭ*, or *hsiao ch'ē-tzŭ*, a barrow.

Obs. 2.—Sure enough: *kuo jan*; *lit.*, indeed, in very truth, thus, they were, etc.

6.

天上星星多
的星宿彗星
可不常見

6. Although there are plenty of stars in the sky, comets are not often seen.

7.

我鄉下買
了個所在那兒
趕到夏天住
着、小孩子
們必是樂
極了。

7. I have bought a place in the country, and when we come to live there in the summer the children are sure to be as happy as possible (happy in the extreme).

Obs.—Place: *so tsai*; *lit.*, where [one] is. It is difficult to account for the use of *tsai* in this connexion, though colloquially *so* is seldom used without it in its meaning of place.

Turn the following into Chinese. (KEY, EXERCISE XXXVII.)

1. What do you generally occupy yourself with? How is it that on the repeated occasions that I have been to your place your servants always answer me that you are not at home. Just think! what spare time have I got? If it is not public business [that occupies me], it is private, and my household affairs, too, are numerous. Nothing of any kind can be done without me, so I have never any leisure time.

Obs. 1.—Spare time: *kung fu*, short for *hsien² kung fu*.

Obs. 2.—Nothing of any kind, etc.: *lit.*, what one kind not must I manage?

Obs. 3.—So: see 1002.

2. If a man is out of spirits, the best thing he can do is to take a walk in the streets. When he sees some trifle that amuses him (in which he can find pleasure), his mind of course is no longer troubled. If one chances on a rainy day, so that one cannot go out, it makes one very impatient.

Obs.—Chances on: *lit.*, runs against.

3. I have a pressing matter [in hand], and must trouble somebody to take a message to him. You are at leisure and have nothing to do, so I beg you to take him the message. I cannot (it won't do), I have no time to spare; please ask somebody else. In my

PART III.—THE FORTY EXERCISES.   197

opinion it will be all the same (all will do) no matter whom you send.

4. That child is given to lying. I sent him to hire a cart, and he came back and told me there were no carts on the street. I didn't believe him, and sent another person to hire one. It came in a short time, [so] I knew that the boy wanted to make a squeeze (make money), and that the bargain was not concluded because the carter wouldn't follow suit in the lie (*lit.*, follow him in lying).

Obs. 1.—It came in a short time: *lit.*, in not a great while, then it hired came.

Obs. 2.—The bargain, etc.: *lit.*, therefore the hiring was not completed.

5. His business pays well; he sells miscellaneous articles of every kind, so he cannot but make money. Although it's a grocer's shop, the business is a first rate one.

1004. 承 *ch'êng²*, to receive or undertake on commission; to be the recipient of, as favours.

1005. 差 *ch'ai¹*, to send, whether as an envoy or, on ordinary occasions, as an official messenger. Read *ch'a¹*, different; to differ: *ch'a⁴*, to be out; wrong.

1006. 任 *jên⁴*, to hold an office; the office so held. Also, a trust or burden; to allow, in the sense of *p'ing²* (722).

1007. 署 *shu³*, an official bureau. *Shu⁴*, provisional tenure of office.

1008. 習 *hsi²*, to practise when learning.

1009. Examples:—

不 *pu⁴*	署 *shu⁴*	不 *pu⁴*	使 *shih³*	差 *ch'ai¹*	承 *ch'êng²*	這 *ché⁴*
多 *to¹*	理 *li³*	是 *shih⁴*	三 *san¹*	差 *ch'ai¹*	了 *liao*	事 *shih⁴*
不 *pu⁴*	學 *hsio²*	實 *shih²*	年 *nien²*	人 *jên²*	承 *ch'êng²*	情 *ch'ing²*
差 *ch'a¹*	習 *hsi²*	任 *jên⁴*	任 *jên⁴*	都 *tou¹*	情 *ch'ing²*	沒 *mei²*
甚 *shên²*	一 *i⁴*	不 *pu²*	滿 *man³*	說 *shuo¹*	承 *ch'êng²*	有 *yu³*
麼 *mo*	年 *nien²*	過 *kuo⁴*	了 *liao*	有 *yu³*	問 *wên⁴*	人 *jên²*
	差 *ch'a¹*	是 *shih⁴*	他 *t'a¹*	差 *ch'ai¹*	聽 *t'ing¹*	應 *ying¹*

Nobody has undertaken this business (*lit.*, consented to undertake).

Obs.—*Ying²*, although in the 1st tone, has the force of *ying⁴* (781), not of *ying¹* (726).

To be the recipient of favours or good offices; I am obliged to you for your good offices.

Thanks for your kind inquiries.

An office servant or messenger (*lit.*, one who waits to be sent on an errand).

A yamên "runner"; or, to send a person, *q.d.*, on an errand.

They all say they have official business.

Obs.—*Ch'ai shih*: *lit.*, official sending employment; employment in an official capacity.

The time for which the post is held expires in three years.

His is not the substantive (actual) appointment; he is only acting.

To learn for a year; a year's novitiate.

Almost; very nearly the same.

Little difference.

Obs.—This and the foregoing phrase, which are in constant use, may be varied to *ch'a pu yüan³ liao* (371), *ch'a pu liao to shao*, etc.

1010. 部 *pu⁴*, any great category; a tribunal or board; the numerative of books.

1011. 堂 *t'ang²*, a large hall; in certain departments of State, collective of the chiefs of the establishment.

1012. 司 *ssŭ¹*, to manage; to direct; to manage one of the departments in a great office; the department so managed.

1013. 委 *wei³*, to depute, as a higher officer a lower.

1014. 員 *yüan²*, any officer of civil or military service.

1015. 吏 *li⁴*, properly, to exercise authority over others, is used with reference to the civil service in various ways; also, to mean clerks.

1016. 役 *i⁴*, *yi⁴*, properly, any employé; but especially such people as constables, etc.

1017. 皂 *tsao⁴*, properly, black; the *tsao* of *fei-tsao*, soap (see **279**).

1018. 隸 *li⁴*, properly, one under the authority of another.

1019. Examples:—

幾 *chi³*	麼。*mo*	書 *shu¹*	極 *chi²*	那 *na⁴*	上 *shang⁴*	六 *liu⁴*
位 *wei⁴*	一 *i⁴*	辦 *pan¹*	了。*liao*	些 *hsieh¹*	司 *ssŭ¹*	部 *pu⁴*
官。*kuan¹*	班 *pan¹*	不 *pu⁴*	書 *shu¹*	衙 *ya²*	派 *p'ai⁴*	的 *ti*
員。*yüan²*	皂 *tsao⁴*	差 *ch'a¹*	吏 *li⁴*	役 *yi⁴*	委 *wei³*	堂 *t'ang²*
	隸。*li⁴*	甚 *shên²*	同 *t'ung²*	壞 *huai⁴*	員。*yüan²*	官。*kuan¹*

The chiefs of the Six Boards in the capital.
Obs.—Both Presidents and Vice-Presidents of Boards are so called, as also chiefs of other departments.
The high authorities (or, chief of the department) are sending a weiyuan (or deputy).
Obs.—The word *wei-yuan* has become anglicised in China.
Those yamên runners are utterly corrupt (or depraved).
Shu li are almost the same as *shu pan* (yamên clerks) (there is no appreciable difference).
Obs.—*Shu li* are clerks in a provincial yamên; *shu pan* are clerks in a metropolitan Board. Note the tone.
A body of runners (or lictors).
Obs.—They are probably so called from the colour of the dress they wear; in Peking the black coat is not insisted on. For *pan*, see **414**.
Several officials (or, how many?)

1020. 供 *kung⁴*, properly, to supply for use. *Kung¹*, to accuse; evidence.

1021. 禀 *ping³*, to represent to a superior; the petition or document in which the representation is made. The original form took the 115th Radical, under which it will be found in the dictionary.

1022. 帖 *t'ieh³*, a slip of silk or paper with writing on it; also, under certain circumstances, read *t'ieh⁴*.

PART III.—THE FORTY EXERCISES.

1023. 存 ts'un², to preserve; to retain.

1024. 稿 kao³, the rough draft of a document.

1025. Examples :—

屈	t'i¹	把	pa³	地	ti⁴	說	shuo¹	帖	t'ieh³	我	wo³
稟	li³	稿	kao³	方	fang¹	得	té	告	kao⁴	寫	hsieh³
上	shang⁴	子	tzŭ	官	kuan¹	口	k'ou³	他	t'a¹	了	liao
供	kung⁴	存	ts'un²	起	ch'i³	供	kung¹	供	kung¹	一	i²
名	ming²	在	tsai⁴	稿	kao³	稟	ping³	他	t'a¹	個	ko⁴
帖	t'ieh³	抽	ch'ou¹	子	tzŭ	報	pao⁴	也	yeh³	稟	ping³

I have written a petition accusing him (I have brought an action against him).
One can also say *kung* (implicating him).
Oral evidence.
To petition (report to) the local authorities.
To draw out (to prepare) a draft.
Keep the draft in the drawer.
To make offerings to an idol (or, before the tablets of ancestors).
A visiting card.

Obs.—Also called *ming-p'ien* (see Exercise XX, 10, Obs.). The difference is technical; any teacher will explain it.

1026. 陳 ch'ên², to spread out; hence, to state. Here, and very commonly, stale; used.

1027. 案 ngan⁴, in legal or official language, a case or question. Also, the correspondence regarding a case; hence, records.

1028. 照 chao⁴, properly, to reflect light; hence, according to.

1029. 式 shih⁴, a fashion; the fashion.

1030. Examples :—

沒	mei³	式	shih⁴	辨	pan⁴	陳	ch'ên²	辨	pan⁴	都	tou¹	不	pu²
了	liao³	樣	yang⁴	照	chao⁴	米	mi³	的	ti	是	shih⁴	論	lun⁴
咯	lo	這	ché⁴	着	cho	按	ngan⁴	我	wo³	照	chao⁴	誰	shui²
照	chao⁴	一	i²	現	hsien⁴	照	chao⁴	喜	hsi³	着	cho	起	ch'i³
會	hui⁴	案	ngan⁴	在	tsai⁴	公	kung¹	歡	huan¹	陳	ch'ên²	稿	kao³
		還	hui²	的	ti	道	tao⁴	吃	ch'ih¹	案	ngan⁴	子	tzŭ

No matter who prepares the draft, it is always done according to the precedents on record.
Obs.—Precedents: *lit.*, old cases.
I like to eat old rice.
To act (or, deal with a matter) in accordance with justice.
According to the present style (or fashion).
This case is not yet finished (or closed).
An official communication; or, to write officially.
Obs.—The term is almost exclusively confined to correspondence between foreign and Chinese officials.

EXERCISE XXXVIII.

小兒得了部裏寫的差使都是承您的情。 1. I am entirely indebted to your good offices for my son's [success in] obtaining the post of copyist in the Board of Works.

Obs.—The post of copyist: *lit.*, slip-writing employment. Note *t'ieh*⁴, not *t'ieh*³; *t'ieh*⁴ (886) can also be used, but the tone is as above.

現任的官出了缺,司裏就派署理,署理的新派實趕任到那,使就完了差。 2. The present incumbent of the post is dead, and the chief has sent an officer to act; when the newly appointed substantive incumbent arrives, the acting man's duties will be at an end.

Obs.—Dead: *lit.*, has created a vacancy; the term used in official reports for announcing the decease of an official in active employment.

六部的堂上官、司官都稱堂官、司官。下官就是新到衙門、候補的官。爲學習行走。 3. The superior officers of the Six Boards are called the *t'ang*² *kuan*¹; those under them are the *ssŭ*¹ *kuan*¹ (sub-chiefs, or chiefs of departments). An expectant *ssŭ kuan* newly come to any yamên serves a novitiate.

Obs. 1.—Expectant: *lit.*, waiting to fill; *hou* being here the verb to wait.
Obs. 2.—Novitiate: *lit.*, is, or acts as, [one who] to learn by practice moves [therein].

京城的衙門辦稿、不是書辦。官就是有頂戴的供事的差使可就、書辦和書辦一樣。 4. The drafts of public documents in the yamêns in the capital, when not prepared by sub-chiefs of departments, are prepared by the *shu*¹ *pan*¹ (clerks). *Kung*⁴ *shih*⁴ are clerks with an official button; their duties are, however, of the same nature as those of the *shu*¹ *pan*¹.

文書發了之後、存起來的稿子就叫陳案。 5. When a despatch has been sent off, the draft that is placed in the archives is called a *ch'ên*² *ngan*⁴ (a case or correspondence of the past no longer in hand).

PART III.—THE FORTY EXERCISES.

他 6
偷
了
我
們
墳
上
的

樹，
上
我
寫
了
一
個
稟
帖
的

役
衙
們
不
給
送
進
去，
說
衙

先
們
得
不
給
他
們
多
少
錢。

你
的
還
習
氣
麼
就
那
衙
門

人
的
子
去
打
官
司，
也
是
他

一
樣
兒
的
要
錢。

6. He stole some trees from our cemetery, so I wrote a petition and went to the yamên to bring an action against him. The *ya yi* would not send it in for me, however, and said I must first give them so much money. Don't you yet know the ways of those yamên people? even if the father of one of them were to go to law, they would want money just the same.

Obs. 1.—Ways: *hsi-ch'i*, habit or manner; *ch'i*, the aspect, air, or temper, *hsi*, acquired by practice. Used only in a bad sense.

Obs. 2.—Go to law: *ta*, verb of motion, to undertake, *kuan ssŭ*, an action at law. The derivation of the term is obscure.

供。 案 問 來 是 做 位 新 7
兒 那 的 上 甚 官 來
的 明 委 司 麼 員 的
口 火 員 派 的。 是 那

7. What has the official that is newly arrived come to do? He is a *wei-yüan* sent by the chief to take evidence in that burglary case.

Turn the following into Chinese. (KEY, EXERCISE XXXVIII.)

1. If a man makes a mistake in anything he does (*lit.*, manages a matter wrongly), and is in fault, he must *ch'êng² tang¹* (abide the consequences; *lit.*, accept what he ought to get). Who undertakes this business?

2. In official business, whether great or small, one ought in all cases to serve one's country with zeal; and it is all one whether the appointment be substantive or acting.

Obs.—Serve with zeal: *lit.*, for (*kei*) the State put forth strength.

3. *Tang¹ kuan¹ ch'ai¹* is the same as *tang¹ ch'ai¹ shih³* (to have official duties). The management of private affairs cannot be termed *ch'ai¹ shih³*.

4. Expectant officials must first serve a novitiate, that is, learn their official duties when they first come to a public office. When a vacancy occurs they may be sent to act.

5. The largest public offices are the Six Boards, and the highest officials in these are the *t'ang² kuan¹* (chiefs); they are also called *shang⁴ ssŭ¹*. A Board is divided into so many *ssŭ¹* (departments), and the officials in charge of the departments are called *ssŭ¹ kuan¹* (chiefs of departments) or *ssŭ¹ yüan²*. The drafts are prepared by them, but there are some handed over to the *shu¹ pan¹* (clerks) to do.

6. *Shu¹ pan¹* is the common name for *shu¹ li⁴*. When a matter is duly transacted and the draft finished, it is given to the chiefs of the Board to read. That is called *hui² t'ang² hua⁴ kao³* (to lay before; *lit.*, to report) to the chiefs for signature.

7. When any public office has outside business, an official must be deputed to transact it.

8. *Ya² yi⁴* and *tsao⁴ li⁴* are the underlings employed in every yamên to perform miscellaneous duties.

9. *Kung⁴ shih⁴* get their appointments by examination; when they pass they get a button. It is a more honourable appointment than that of *shu¹ pan¹* (*lit.*, they are more honourable, etc.).

Obs.—To pass an examination: *chung⁴* (302).

10. The correspondence in official matters that are concluded is stowed away and called *ts'un² kao³* (archived drafts). Of the archived drafts some have been sanctioned and others not, but they are all archives.

1031. 脾 *p'i²*, the part of the stomach that produces digestion.

1032. 禍 *huo⁴*, adversity; calamity.

1033. 福 *fu²*, prosperity.

1034. 命 *ming⁴*, decree, of fate or of a superior; with *hsing⁴* (532), and sometimes without, existence.

1035. 運 *yün⁴*, to convey; to bring to pass.

1036. Examples:—

氣 *ch'i⁴*	禍 *huo⁴*	氣 *ch'i⁴*	急 *chi²*	太 *t'ai⁴*	脾 *p'i²*
好 *hao³*	麼 *mo*	逗 *chê⁴*	他 *t'a¹*	暴 *pao⁴*	氣 *ch'i⁴*
運 *yün⁴*	天 *t'ien¹*	不 *pu²*	很 *hên³*	性 *hsing⁴*	他 *t'a¹*
貨 *huo⁴*	命 *ming⁴*	是 *shih⁴*	有 *yu³*	兒 *'rh*	脾 *p'i²*
	運 *yün⁴*	大 *ta⁴*	福 *fu²*	又 *yu⁴*	氣 *ch'i⁴*

Temper; also, eccentricity of character.
Obs.—For *ch'i*, see Exercise XXXVIII, 6, Obs. 1.
His temper is too passionate.
He is also of a quick (or impatient) temperament.
He has a very prosperous air; or, he is a prosperous (or happy) man.
Is not this a great calamity?
The decrees of Heaven.
Good fortune.
Obs.—Lit., the *ch'i* [that the revolutions of fate bring] round.
To convey merchandise.

1037. 志 *chih⁴*, resolution.

1038. 益 *yi²*, *yi⁴*, addition; advantage. Colloquially, far oftener *yi²* than *yi⁴*.

1039. 活 *huo²*, alive; living.

1040. 聰 *ts'ung¹*, quick to apprehend what one hears.

PART III.—THE FORTY EXERCISES.

1041. 願 *yüan*⁴, to wish; to be willing.

1042. 功 *kung*¹, exertion in a good cause.

1043. Examples:—

用	*yung*⁴	聽	*ts'ung*¹	看	*k'an*⁴	在	*tsai*⁴	志	*chih*⁴	他	*t'a*¹
功。	*kung*¹	明。	*ming*²	他	*t'a*¹	沒	*mei*²	空	*k'ung*¹	很	*hên*³
怕	*p'a*⁴	他	*t'a*¹	外	*wai*⁴	有	*yu*³	活	*huo*²	有	*yu*³
活	*huo*²	不	*pu*²	面	*mien*⁴	益	*yi*²	百	*pai*³	志	*chih*⁴
不	*pu*⁴	願	*yüan*⁴	兒	*'rh*	處。	*ch'u*⁴	歲。	*sui*⁴	氣	*ch'i*⁴
了。	*liao*³	意。	*i*⁴	很	*hên*³	我	*wo*³	實	*shih*²	無	*wu*²

He is a man of great resolution.
"Without resolution one may live a hundred years in vain."
Really there is no advantage.
Obs.—*Yi ch'u*: *lit.*, places of advantage.
His appearance, to my eye, is that of a very intelligent man.
He is unwilling to exert himself.
I fear he can't live.

1044. 虧 *k'uei*¹, to be deficient.

1045. 辜 *ku*¹, properly, fault; specially, ingratitude; to be ungrateful for.

1046. 負 *fu*⁴, to turn the back on; to bear on the back.

1047. 抱 *pao*⁴, to hold in the bosom or the arms; hence, to cherish.

1048. 怨 *yüan*⁴, resentment.

1049. Examples:—

把	*pa*³	負	*fu*⁴	願	*yüan*⁴	要	*yao*⁴	辦。	*pan*⁴	虧。	*k'uei*¹	他	*t'a*¹
孩	*hai*²	了	*liao*	意	*i*⁴	叫	*chiao*⁴	結	*chieh*²	這	*chê*⁴	本	*pên*³
子	*tzŭ*	我	*wo*³	抱	*pao*⁴	他	*t'a*¹	了。	*liao*	件	*chien*⁴	錢	*ch'ien*²
抱	*pao*⁴	的	*ti*	怨	*yüan*⁴	念	*nien*⁴	從	*ts'ung*²	事	*shih*⁴	虧	*k'uei*¹
進	*chin*⁴	好	*hao*³	着	*cho*	書	*shu*¹	前	*ch'ien*²	多	*to*¹	空	*k'ung*¹
來。	*lai*²	心	*hsin*¹	我	*wo*³	他	*t'a*¹	我	*wo*³	虧	*k'uei*¹	了。	*liao*
		了。	*liao*	辜	*ku*¹	不	*pu*²	很	*hên*³	你	*ni*³	吃	*ch'ih*¹

His capital was encroached upon; he lost some of his capital.
To suffer loss; to get the worst of an encounter; to have a bad time.
Obs.—*Lit.*, to eat (=suffer) loss.
It is almost entirely owing to you that this matter has been settled.
Obs.—Owing to you: *lit.*, this matter, for the most part, if you had not been there (if your aid had been wanting), would [not] have been settled. *Chieh*, completed; *lit.*, to knot (*see* **444**). To *k'uei* may be freely rendered, I am greatly indebted to you.

Formerly I wanted him very much to study; he was unwilling, and felt resentment against me, being ungrateful to me for my good intentions.

Obs.—Ungrateful: *k'uei* (1044) *fu* is as often used in Peking as *ku fu*.

Bring the child in

1050. 寒 *han²*, cold.

1051. 悔 *hui³*, to repent, of good or evil.

1052. 善 *shan⁴*, virtuous.

1053. 惡 *ngo⁴*, *ngǎ*, vicious.

1054. Examples:—

不 *pu⁴*	不 *pu⁴*	了 *liao*	了 *liao*	了 *liao*	他 *t'a¹*
能 *nêng²*	能 *nêng²*	善 *shan⁴*	錢 *ch'ien²*	我 *wo³*	們 *mên*
都 *tou¹*	都 *tou¹*	人 *jên²*	如 *ju²*	當 *tang¹*	如 *ju²*
算 *suan⁴*	算 *suan⁴*	惡 *ngo⁴*	今 *chin¹*	初 *ch'u¹*	今 *chin¹*
是 *shih⁴*	善 *shan⁴*	人 *jên²*	後 *hou⁴*	多 *to¹*	寒 *han²*
惡 *ngo⁴*	也 *yeh³*	人 *jên²*	悔 *hui³*	花 *hua¹*	苦 *k'u³*

They are now in bitter poverty.
I spent too much to begin with (at first), and now I regret it.

Obs.—Regret: *lit.*, after regrets. When verbalised, to repent or regret.

Good men and bad men.
Men cannot all be accounted good, and yet they cannot all be accounted bad.

1055. 其 *ch'i²*, used in particular locutions as the definite article: *the* person or thing.

1056. 餘 *yü²*, surplus; remainder.

1057. 靈 *ling²*, spiritual; intelligent.

1058. Examples:—

得 *tê*	玩 *wan²*	很 *hên³*	上 *shang⁴*	其 *ch'i²*	那 *na⁴*
起 *ch'i³*	意 *i⁴*	靈 *ling²*	他 *t'a¹*	餘 *yü²*	孩 *hai²*
來 *lai²*	兒 *'rh*	便 *pien⁴*	他 *t'a¹*	的 *ti*	子 *tzǔ*
	都 *tou¹*	甚 *shên²*	心 *hsin¹*	比 *pi³*	很 *hên³*
	拏 *na²*	麼 *mo*	裡 *li³*	不 *pu*	靈 *ling²*

That child is very intelligent; the others cannot be compared with him.

Obs.—Others: *lit.*, the (*ch'i*) remaining ones all compare not up to (or above) him.

He is very quick, and can pick up any accomplishment.

Obs.—Note *wan-i-'rh*, accomplishments, such as music, archery, etc.

EXERCISE XXXIX.

處。用有氣說運是事他 1
功志都不好。他情那
的氣是關在的成一
好肯他運我命了。件

1. That success of his is due to his luck. I do not attribute it to his luck; I think it was all due to his own merits, his determination and industry.

Obs. 1.—Not attribute: *lit.*, in my saying=opinion, it is not connected with luck. See *kuan* (63), to concern.

Obs. 2.—All due: *lit.*, wholly is it that he has resolution-and-willingness-to-use-exertion's good points, or advantage.

理。自命都得禍作 2
然所是禍作善
之定天這惡得

2. That good deeds bring happiness and evil deeds misfortune is a natural principle ordained by the laws of Heaven.

虧本賺的隸他 3
空兒錢米運打
了。都連沒來直

3. He has not made anything on the consignment of rice that he brought from Chihli, and has even lost some of his capital.

Obs. 1.—Consignment: *lit.*, the from Chihli conveyed coming (*ti*) rice.

Obs. 2.—Note that *tou* does not here mean all, but both: both the profits were absorbed, and some of the capital as well.

抱麼憑氣明人可 4
怨。好待不到雖惜
總他行。底然那
是怎任脾聰個

4. What a pity it is that although that man is intelligent, he has an impossible temper. No matter how well one treats him, he is sure to grumble (*lit.*, feel resentment).

Obs. 1.—No matter how: *jên p'ing*, you may as you please treat him well, etc.

Obs. 2.—His temper: note that one can speak of a man's *p'i-ch'i* being good, or of his having no *p'i-ch'i*, eccentricities of character or temper, at all.

悔了不纔活人的天 5
不病。然不動得時氣
來就趕吃身活候寒
了。後有虧子動兒冷

5. When the weather is cold, people must move about, and then their bodily health will not suffer; otherwise, when they get ill, they will repent in vain.

Obs. 1.—Note *kan*³, when, short for *kan tao*, when they arrive at.

Obs. 2.—Repent in vain: *hou hui pu lai*; *lit.*, repentance won't come, there will be no result from repentance. *Lai* must here be treated as *hsing*, to succeed, to have good results, or some similar word.

6. 你專在這不相干的事情上用功，老人家給你銀子經當賁經老正貢，差使這不是官，捐了若干的，人家兒的恩典是辜負，命家寒心阿疼的要叫

6. What do you gain by devoting your energies to these undertakings which do not concern you? Your father spent all that money in buying you an official post, and yet you won't carry out your official duties as you should. Isn't this ingratitude for the goodness of your parents to you? You really estrange people [by your conduct]. The pain is unendurable (*lit.*, killing).

Obs. 1.—All that money: *jo kan*; *lit.*, as these ones. *Kan* (Radical 51) is explained in the native dictionaries to be equivalent in this combination to *ko*, one or ones; and by a process of amplification which it is not necessary here to go through, the two characters can be shown to mean as many as these or this. The expression is in common use colloquially, and may be positive as well as comparative, as *jo kan jên*, a whole lot of people.

Obs. 2.—As you should, properly: *chêng ching*; *lit.*, the straight length. Hence, the proper or direct route; morally, properly, respectably. Cf. *chêng ching jên*, a respectable person.

Obs. 3.—To estrange: *lit.*, cause people's hearts to be cold. *Han hsin*, a cold heart, refers to the coldness engendered by ingratitude.

7. 這個學生極靈，又願意用功。其餘那些孩子真是個中用不。

7. This student is most intelligent, and, besides, is willing to exert himself. The rest of the children are really no good at all. (*See* **302**.)

8. 你臉上發了福了。這個時候兒看那個樣兒，你就活不了。

8. You are quite fat in the face. This time last year, to judge from your appearance, you could not live.

Obs. 1.—Fat in the face: *lit.*, your face has put forth happiness.
Obs. 2.—Last year: *lit.*, the old year; *chiu* often taking the place of *ch'u*.

9. 把那個窗戶開開罷。那個窗戶不活，是開不開的。

9. Open that window. The window is a fixture; it won't open.

Obs.—Fixture: *huo* can be used of anything that can be moved or taken to pieces; as, for instance, the stock of a gun, which is *huo ti*, can be taken off. The converse is *ssŭ ti*; *lit.*, dead, a fixture, or a dummy.

Turn the following into Chinese. (KEY, EXERCISE XXXIX.)

1. He has a very good disposition, and has not a grain of temper; how can any calamity befall him? Besides, he looks a prosperous man.

Obs.—He looks prosperous: *lit.*, growing has attained a very-much-possessing-prosperity's manner.

2. The *ming*⁴ (fortune) of a man at his birth may be good or evil; and even *yün*⁴ *ch'i*⁴ (luck) is not all of one kind.

3. No matter what one does, one must have resolution, and then success is a matter of course. If a man has not the slightest

resolution, he need not think to make any way all his life.

Obs.—Way, progress: *chin yi⁴*; *lit.*, advancement [on the path of] gain, advantage. Note the tone.

4. Don't you make any mistake about that man. In speech and action he has plenty of "go," and is not in the least a "stick." He is exceedingly intelligent withal, and has lots of resolution. He is always at home, and won't go anywhere, being so very fond of work.

Obs. 1.—Don't make a mistake: *lit.*, him that man do not you wrongly regard (*ch'iao*).

Obs. 2.—"Go:" *huo tung*, lively movement; the converse of which is *ssŭ yang*, inanimate, *lit.*, dead fashion.

5. You borrow other people's money, and he, fearing the payment of interest may cause you loss, pays it back for you. This is an advantage to you, and yet you resent his interference. Isn't this ingratitude for a well-intentioned [act] on his part, and won't it disgust people with you (estrange them)? If he finds it out (knows) by-and-by, and duns you for the money, you will certainly repent it.

Obs. 1.—Interference: *to shih*; *lit.*, many matters, a term applied to a busybody or a person who interferes in matters with which he has no concern.

Obs. 2.—Certainly repent: *chun shih hou hui ti*, it is assuredly a to-be-a-hereafter repented of *ti*, action, or some similar word; hereafter being rendered by *yao*, the sign of the future.

6. The doing of good or the doing of evil depends entirely on a man himself. An evil-doer who repents and reforms (*hui³ kai³*) is equally a good man.

Obs.—Depends on: *tsai*, is in, or rests with.

7. These different sorts are all good. Leave them. You can take the rest away; I don't want them.

8. This little dog is very quick; whatever I say he understands.

Obs.—Very quick: *hên yu ling hsing*; *lit.*, very much has an intelligent disposition or nature.

1059. 緊 *chin³*, tight; pressing. Also, extreme; hence, when used with *yao⁴*, to want, which may precede or follow it, important.

1060. 預 *yü⁴*, beforehand. When so used it is generally coupled with *hsien¹*, before; it is also found in combination with the next character.

1061. 備 *pei⁴*, to prepare; ready.

1062. 通 *t'ung¹*, passing from one point to another without hindrance; to understand.

1063. 共 *kung⁴*, collectively; together with.

1064. 合 *ho²*, united; agreeing with.

1065. Examples:—

很	*hên³*	不	*pu⁴*	個	*ko⁴*	備	*pei⁴*	沒	*mei²*	去	*ch'ü⁴*	不	*pu³*
合	*ho²*	通	*t'ung¹*	道	*tao⁴*	馬	*ma³*	有	*yu³*	屋	*wu¹*	要	*yao⁴*
意	*i⁴*	通	*t'ung¹*	兒	*'rh*	預	*yü⁴*	預	*yü⁴*	子	*tzŭ*	緊	*chin³*
正	*chêng⁴*	共	*kung⁴*	通	*t'ung¹*	備	*pei⁴*	先	*hsien¹*	預	*yü⁴*	趕	*kan³*
合	*ho²*	三	*san¹*	不	*pu⁴*	下	*hsia*	告	*kao⁴*	備	*pei⁴*	緊	*chin³*
式	*shih⁴*	十	*shih²*	通	*t'ung¹*	馬	*ma³*	訴	*su⁴*	好	*hao³*	送	*sung⁴*
		個	*ko⁴*	路	*lu⁴*	這	*ché⁴*	我	*wo³*	了	*liao*	信	*hsin⁴*

It does not matter; it is not important.
Send the letter as quickly as possible.
Is the room prepared?
Tell me beforehand.
Get the horse ready; saddle the horse (not harness him, for which see **770**.)
Have the horse ready.
Obs.—Note the difference; *hsia* has here the force of to be in waiting.
Can one get through by this road?
No thoroughfare.
Altogether thirty.
Very much to my liking.
Obs.—We can say also *ho wo ti i*.
It just suits.
Obs.—*Lit.*, exactly agrees with the pattern.

1066. 除 *ch'u*², to take away; to subtract from. With *fei*¹ (Radical 175), except.

1067. 剩, 賸 *shêng*⁴, to remain, as the balance of a sum. The second is the correct character, though the first form is generally used.

1068. 盈 *ying*², excess; overplus.

1069. 像 *hsiang*⁴, properly, a figure resembling; to resemble; to seem like.

1070. 似 *ssŭ*⁴, *shih*⁴ (differently pronounced under different circumstances), resembling.

1071. Examples:—

非 *fei*¹	的 *ti*	子 *tzŭ*	流 *liu*²	盈 *ying*²	一 *i*⁴	除 *ch'u*²
他 *t'a*¹	老 *lao*³	長 *chang*³	水 *shui*³	餘。*yü*²	千 *ch'ien*¹	了 *liao*
去 *ch'ü*⁴	子。*tzŭ*	得 *tê*	似 *shih*⁴	花 *hua*¹	銀 *yin*²	花 *hua*¹
不 *pu*⁴	照 *chao*⁴	很 *hên*³	的。*ti*	錢 *ch'ien*²	子。*tzŭ*	費 *fei*⁴
行。*hsing*²	像。*hsiang*⁴	像 *hsiang*⁴	這 *chê*⁴	好 *hao*³	沒 *mei*²	下 *hsia*⁴
	除 *ch'u*²	他 *t'a*¹	孩 *hai*²	像 *hsiang*⁴	有 *yu*³	剩 *shêng*⁴

After deducting the expenditure there remains a balance of 兌. 1,000.
There is no surplus (nothing over).
To spend money as fast as water flows; money goes as water flows.
Obs.—Note that *ssŭ* is always pronounced *shih* when followed by *ti*.
This child is very like his father.
To photograph.
Except he goes, it won't do.

1072. 橫 *hêng*², horizontal, as opposed to perpendicular.

PART III.—THE FORTY EXERCISES.

1073. 豎, 竪 *shu⁴*, perpendicular, as opposed to horizontal.

1074. 傷 *shang¹*, of a man's person or feelings, to wound; to injure. Also of many things beside, animate and inanimate.

1075. 棚 *p'êng²*, a mat-shed; a pent-house; an awning.

1076. 搭 *ta¹*, to place on; to pile up; to put up. Also, to join, as a party of people; to add.

1077. Examples :—

個 *ko*	傷 *shang¹*	的 *ti*	去 *ch'ü⁴*	兒 *'rh*	豎 *shu⁴*	把 *pa³*
涼 *liang²*	心 *hsin¹*	牛 *niu²*	我 *wo³*	上 *shang⁴*	起 *ch'i³*	這 *ché⁴*
棚 *p'êng²*	夏 *hsia⁴*	受 *shou⁴*	打 *ta³*	人 *jén²*	來 *lai²*	一 *i⁴*
好 *hao³*	天 *t'ien¹*	傷 *shang¹*	傷 *shang¹*	家 *chia¹*	橫 *héng²*	根 *kên¹*
搭 *ta¹*	搭 *ta¹*	我 *wo³*	了 *liao*	過 *kuo⁴*	在 *tsai⁴*	木 *mu⁴*
船 *ch'uan²*	一 *i²*	很 *hên³*	他 *t'a¹*	不 *pu²*	道 *tao⁴*	頭 *t'ou²*

Set that log of wood upright; people can't pass when it is lying across the road.
I have wounded his cow.
To suffer injury (of persons or things).
I am very distressed in mind.
In summer it is a good thing to put up an awning.
To take passage on board a ship.

1078. 準 *chun³*, to adjust; to equalise. Hence, a rule; accurate; accuracy; certain; sure. The character is interchangeable with *chun³* (**567**), but the latter is the form in more common use.

1079. 勢 *shih⁴*, property; power; authority; hence, power to change. Also, appearance of power; aspect; condition.

1080. Examples :—

派 *p'ai⁴*	一 *i²*	二 *érh⁴*	兩 *liang³*	有 *yu³*	他 *t'a¹*
兒 *'rh*	座 *tso⁴*	分 *fên¹*	銀 *yin²*	我 *wo³*	的 *ti*
不 *pu⁴*	廟 *miao⁴*	隨 *sui²*	子 *tzŭ*	的 *ti*	天 *t'ien¹*
小 *hsiao³*	的 *ti*	勢 *shih⁴*	總 *tsung³*	準 *chun³*	平 *p'ing²*
呢 *ni*	勢 *shih⁴*	這 *ché⁴*	差 *ch'a⁴*	一 *i⁴*	沒 *mei²*

His balance is not so true as mine; it is invariably two candareens out on every tael.
Obs.—*T'ien-p'ing*, a balance for weighing silver (*see* **326**). Note *ch'a⁴* (*see* **1005**).
According to circumstances.
This is an imposing looking temple.
Obs.—*Lit.*, this temple's *shih p'ai-'rh*, distributed appearance (=the way in which it is laid out), is not small. The term can be applied to persons, also to any pageant or procession, such as a funeral *cortége*, a wedding, etc.

EXERCISE XL.

你1 兒 來 要 有 的 橫 叫
天 來 緊 緊 事 竪 你
天 不 若 急, 情, 得' 去。
都
不

1. Whether you come every day or not is of no consequence. If there be anything of pressing importance you will have to be sent for in any case.

Obs. 1.—In any case: *hêng shu* (here read *hêng² shih*); *lit.*, horizontally or perpendicularly, whichever way you take it.

Obs. 2.—Note the force of *lai* and *ch'ü*, showing that the person addressed is at the moment at the place to which he will have to come when sent for. Emphasise *chiao*.

可2 的 不 的 像 不
惜 那 像 式 馬 的
他 房 樣。 棚 住
蓋 子 好 似 着
房 子 很 兒。
樣

2. It is a pity that he has built that house so unlike what a house ought to be. It looks just like a stable, and is by no means a seemly place for him to live in.

Obs. 1.—Looks just like: *hao*=*hên*. Note the object resembled between *hsiang* and *shih*, the two words which combine to produce our verb resemble; the latter had better be translated as a noun, *q.d.*, much like a horse-shed's likeness.

Obs. 2.— A stable is commonly called *ma hao* (858), *ma p'êng* being, strictly speaking, a lean-to without doors or windows.

Obs. 3.—Seemly or suitable: not like the appearance, *q.d.*, that a house in which he lives should have.

那3 房 有 通 百 下 四
一 子, 多 共 多 謄 五
所 少 有 間 人 十
兒 通 一 除 住 間。
共 間。 的 還
有

3. How many *chien*[1] are there in that house (or, block of buildings)? There are altogether more than a hundred; some forty or fifty over and above what people are living in.

Obs. 1.—House: note that *i so fang-tzŭ* means the whole of the rooms or separate buildings forming one block, courtyard, or set of courtyards comprising one establishment; *i tso fang-tzŭ* would be one building, as, for instance, that on one side of a courtyard, but the expression is not common.

Obs. 2.—*Chien* is not, strictly speaking, the numerative of rooms or houses, but is a noun indicating a certain space measurement. Chinese houses are not spoken of as containing so many rooms, but so many *chien*, the *chien* being the space between any four of the pillars that support the roof: thus, if we spoke of a *ssŭ chien wu-tzŭ* or *ssŭ chien fang-tzŭ*, we should mean that there were four such spaces in the room or house, or, in other words, that the roof was supported by ten pillars, five on a side; a house of 100 *chien* would be a house that contained 100 such spaces, irrespective of the number of rooms. The student is requested to modify the rendering given of *chien* in **47** in accordance with the above explanation: *yi chien fang-tzŭ* is not a house irrespective of the number of *chien* it contains (which is *yi tso fang-tzŭ*), but a house of one *chien*.

Obs. 3.—Over and above: *lit.*, having excluded the persons inhabiting ones, below remaining still are there **40 or 50** *chien*.

PART III.—THE FORTY EXERCISES.

4. 我合一算起來有一萬兩銀子的外欠除還賬還有一二千兩銀子的盈餘。

4. I put the total of what is due to me at ten thousand taels, and after paying my own debts I shall have a credit balance of one or two thousand taels.

Obs. 1.—What is due to me: *wai ch'ien*; *lit.*, outside owings, the converse of which is *ch'ien wai*.

Obs. 2.—After paying: read *huan*², not *han* or *hai*.

5. 我的月月兒進的錢總不敷的沒有盈餘反倒賒下些個賬目不能還。過這種樣兒的日子真叫我傷心。

5. My monthly income is never sufficient, I have nothing left from it; on the contrary, I have some debts remaining that I cannot pay. I am sorely distressed at having to live in this way.

6. 有人放槍把他小孩子打着了頭傷的很重。

6. A man let a gun off and hit his little child, which he hurt very badly.

7. 門旁邊兒的頭是竪的門上下的頭是橫的木。

7. The doorposts of a door are perpendicular; the [beams of] wood above and below the door are horizontal.

8. 在地下平擱的東西都是說橫說竪那情都活動隨勢着若倒目前直面着的是在竪旁面的人就以為是橫。

8. The direction of things laid flat will be said to be perpendicular or horizontal conditionally; if [the direction of] a thing lying end on to a person be held to be perpendicular, it will be regarded as horizontal by anyone whose face is turned at right angles to that of the first person.

Obs. 1.—Conditionally: *lit.*, of a thing laid flat on the ground the saying *hêng* and the saying *shu* are according-to-the-case-and-considering-the-circumstances' *huo tung hua*, movable expressions.

Obs. 2.—End on: *lit.*, if that before [one's] face *chih*, in a right line, confronting, be *shu*, [whoever] *tsai*, may be, a side-facing man, then will regard it as *hêng*.

Obs. 3.—Held to be: *wei*², to make of, as in *tso wei*.

Obs. 4.—Regarded: the same verb *wei* preceded by *i*, to use, here acting as the sign of the objective case of a noun, the object of *wei*, understood; *q.d.*, of the direction specified, the side-facing man makes horizontal=he regards it as horizontal. Treat *i wei* as the verb to regard, remembering that the object may either precede the combination or come between its two parts. It is equally correct to say *chê ko i wei shih hêng* and *i chê ko wei hêng*.

Turn the following into Chinese. (KEY, EXERCISE XL.)

1. I told you just now I had a very important matter to attend to, and that you were to get the horse ready saddled in waiting for me; and even at this hour you have not got it ready. If I don't scold you, you will put me in a temper, and if I do, it will look as if my temper was bad.

2. Our accounts must be gone into from end to end. Putting together what I have borrowed from you at different times, what does the total amount to? After deducting what I have repaid you, I estimate that I have a small sum over to the good.

Obs.—From end to end: *t'ung ch'ang*, the complete length (**1062**).

3. You have borrowed more than you have repaid. How can you have any balance to the good?

4. From your appearance I should say you were a very intelligent man, and yet (how) you don't know horizontal from perpendicular. I told you to hang up the drawings; the perpendicular ones to be hung at the two sides of the door, and the horizontal one over the top. You have hung them all wrong.

5. You hand this matter over to me to deal with. In any case I will manage it all right for you.

6. Say nothing about it. You managed that other affair in a way that distressed me very much. The last time I thought of putting up an awning (sky awning) I asked you to buy mats for me. To my surprise (who would think?), you were not in the least to be depended on (had not a grain of accuracy). You did not buy the articles, and I couldn't even catch a sight of your face.

NOTE.—*Cho²* or *chao²* is written in the two different forms given in **45**, but the second is that more commonly employed, except when *cho* signifies to command. It is especially used in this latter sense in Imperial Decrees, to express the "We will" of the Emperor. When preceding adjectives or adverbs, it is read both *cho* and *chao*. We have, for instance, *cho shih*, of that which is real and true, *bonâ fide*; *cho lo*, of the settlement of a doubt, claim, inquiry, etc.; but *chao chi*, anxious, duly eager, or over-eager, and from the latter, impatient. After verbs, when nothing intervenes, it is most commonly, almost universally, *cho*, as in *tsou cho*, going, *p'ao cho*, running; but if the auxiliary *tê*, or *pu* representing *pu tê*, come between it and the verb, it is invariably *chao*, as in *chao tê chao*, has found or can find, *chao pu chao*, cannot find. In either case, whether *chao* or *cho*, after a verb its meaning is almost identical with that of *tê*, which, again, as has been before observed, is often corruptly supplanted by *ti*. The probability is that the *ti* used now to produce what we call the inflection of the possessive case was originally *tê*, and it is reducible to an equivalent of *tê* in almost every construction in which we find it, except perhaps those which we should term adverbial; those, that is, where *ti* may be rendered by our terminations *like* as in *sailorlike*, or *wise* in *crosswise*. Even in these *tê* would do their duty, but as the parallel constructions in classical written Chinese are formed by *jan*, thus, and there is between the primitive meaning of *jan* and that of *ti* a certain affinity, it may be safer to infer that in these *ti* figures in its earlier and uncorrupted sense. This was brightness, manifestness, like the white part of a target; hence, that which is evident. The word *jan*, originally the flashing of fire, came to mean *thus* by apparently a similar process.

CHINESE WEIGHTS AND MEASURES.*

LENGTH.—As in England we commence with barleycorns, so in China have the natives started with a certain number of kernels of grain; whether disposed lengthwise or crosswise is disputed. One grain is held to make a *fên*¹ (分); 10 *fên* a *ts'un*⁴ (寸), the Chinese inch; 10 *ts'un* a *ch'ih*³ (尺), the Chinese cubit, covid, or foot; and 10 *ch'ih* a *chang*⁴ (丈). The *ch'ih*, says the Chrestomathy, fixed by the Mathematical Board at Peking is 13.125 English inches, that used by tradesmen in Canton varies from 14.625 inches to 14.81 inches, and that employed by the engineers of public works is 12.7 inches, while that by which distance is usually measured is 12.1 inches nearly. The *li*³ (里), or mile, is 1,897½ English feet; and 192½ *li* used to be reckoned for a degree of latitude or longitude. But the European mathematicians at the capital, deviating from their predecessors, divided the degree into 250 *li*, reducing it to 1,826 English feet, or the tenth part of a French league; and this, at present, is the established measure. Accordingly, the *li* is a little *more* than one-third of an English mile.

The *fên* may be taken as equivalent to a line in rough calculations; it is (calling the *ch'ih* 14.625 inches) exactly 1.015625 of the twelfth of an inch. The *ts'un* in Canton is equal to 1.21875 of an inch, or one inch and one-fifth. The *chang* is frequently used by carpenters and other artizans in measuring their work; its length of course depends on that of the *ch'ih* employed, but it is usually about 14.35 feet.

N.B.—The *chang* of the Foreign Trade Tariff of 1858 is 141 English inches; the *ch'ih*, 14.1 English inches.

LAND MEASURE.—Five *ch'ih*, Chinese feet, make one *pu*⁴ (步), pace; 240 *pu*⁴ one *mou*³ (畝) or *mu*³ = about one-sixth of an English acre; and 100 *mou* one *ch'ing*³ (頃).

WEIGHT.—It must be borne in mind that, except copper cash, the Chinese have no current coin, and that, except where foreign coin is employed, all payments in silver are calculated with reference to weight. The maximum money weight is the *liang*³ (兩), say ounce, commonly known as the *tael*, the subordinate divisions of which are the *ch'ien*² (錢) or mace, *fên*¹ (分), candarin, *li*² (釐), cash; the three last-named denominations respectively equalling the one-tenth, one-hundredth, and one-thousandth of the *liang*. The cash of the copper currency, which should properly be worth a tael a thousand, are spoken of as *t'ung*² (銅) *ch'ien*² or *ch'ien*, the latter term being moreover generic of money, like our word cash.

In what we should call avoirdupois, the weights to be remembered, in addition to the above, are the *chin*¹ (斤 or 觔) catty, or Chinese pound of 16 *liang* or ounces, the ounce being subdivided, as in money weight. The *chin* is equal to about 1⅓ ℔. English, and 100 *chin* make the *tan*⁴ (擔), or *shih*² (石), known by us as the picul = 133⅓ ℔. English. The characters *tan* and *shih* are used interchangeably at Peking, but the latter is never used with its proper sound, being called *tan*⁴, and almost invariably written 否.

* Condensed from the "Chinese Chrestomathy," the highly valuable work compiled by the late Dr. BRIDGMAN.

PART IV.

THE TEN DIALOGUES.

PART IV.
THE TEN DIALOGUES.

DIALOGUE I.

1. What part of the country are you from, sir?
2. I am a T'ien-ching (Tientsin) man; may I ask your country?
3. I am a Chihli man too.
4. Ah! we are fellow-provincials, then.
5. Who is that gentleman?
6. He is a foreigner.
7. Do you know what brings him here?
8. I do not; you had better ask him himself.
9. May I ask what brings you to our country, sir?
10. I am in business.
11. What have you brought with you, sir?
12. Small things in the Japanese lacquerware way.

13. Oh! you are from Japan, sir?
14. Yes; I am a Japanese.
15. Indeed! I had been told that no one could get into Japan or out of it.
16. That difficulty did exist once, but of late the restrictions have been removed, and intercourse is an easier matter than it used to be.
17. Have any of our merchants gone over there yet?
18. There are some Chinese merchants and subjects there.
19. From what province of China do the majority of them go?
20. The greater part are from the provinces of Kwangtung and Fukien.
21. Do they do a large business?
22. Not very large, I should imagine.

2. 敝 pi^4 2. 領 $ling^3$ 12. 洋 $yang^2$ 19. 省 $shêng^3$ 22. 只 $chih^3$
2. 津 $chin^1$, $ching^1$ 9. 駕 $chia^4$ 12. 漆 $ch‘i^1$, $ch‘u^4$ 20. 廣 $kuang^3$

1. *Obs.*—What part: *kuei*, honourable, for the possessive pronoun of the second person.
2. *Obs.* 1.—I am: *pi*, vile, in ill condition, for the possessive of the first pronoun; my humble place is T'ien-chin or T'ien-ching. *Obs.* 2.—May I ask: *lit.*, I have not *ling*, received your instruction; you have not said whence you come.
4. *Obs.*—Fellow-provincials: *hsiang*, properly, village; both the speakers are men of the province of Chihli.
8. *Obs.*—Himself: *lit.*, him, the individual man.
9. *Obs.*—Sir: *tsun chia*; *lit.*, honoured chariot.
12. *Obs.* 1.—Japanese: *tung yang*; *lit.*, the eastern sea; the sea or ocean; hence, foreign. *Obs.* 2.—Lacquerware: *ch‘i*, the gum with which lacquerware is covered.
15. *Obs.*—No one: *nan*, difficult, is as often as not used for impossible.
16. *Obs.* 1.—Did exist: *t‘ou li*, in the beginning, formerly, *ch‘io*, notwithstanding, [however easy now, it was] nevertheless difficult. *Obs.* 2.—Removed: *k‘ai*, to open, *chin*, the prohibitions; hence, the state of things is *hao hsieh-'rh*, somewhat better.
19. *Obs.*—Province: *shêng*, of which there are 18 in China.
20. *Obs.*—Kwangtung: *kuang*, broad.
22. *Obs.*—I should imagine: *chih p‘a*; *lit.*, I only fear.

PART IV.—THE TEN DIALOGUES.

23. Why not? haven't they money?
24. Well, I should say not much.
25. Why do they go to Japan, then, if they haven't money?
26. Most of them have accompanied Europeans.
27. What do Europeans carry them with them for?

28. It is to take charge of their hongs and to act as brokers for them.
29. Do they get on well with the Japanese?
30. Neither has much confidence in the other, I imagine.

28. 作 tso⁴   30. 異 i⁴

28. *Obs.* 1.—Act as: *tso* is but another form of *tso* (see Part III, 50). *Obs.* 2.—Brokers: *ching*, in the sense of to pass through, *shou*, the hand.

30. *Obs.*—Confidence: *hsiang hsin*, reciprocal trust, faith, or belief in each other (*pi tzʻŭ*).

DIALOGUE II.

1. Is not the horse you are riding, sir, a horse of our country here?
2. Yes; it was bought in your country.
3. Who bought it for you?
4. The people in the horse-yard chose it for me.
5. How much did they ask you for him?
6. They asked thirty taels.
7. Did you give it?
8. I did not; I thought they asked too much.
9. And how much did you give?
10. I closed with them for twenty-two taels.
11. The horse was mine once.
12. Was he really? why did you sell him?

13. I sold him because I wanted money.
14. It was not on account of any defect, was it?
15. Not at all; he had no defect whatever.
16. What did you pay for him in the first instance?
17. A good deal; I had money then.
18. Ah! you had something in the public service, had you not?
19. I was in a public office until my father died; I gave up my employment then, and returned home to look after my family affairs.
20. Dear me! was your father long ill?
21. Oh yes; pretty near ten years.
22. And during his illness who took charge of his family?

1. 納 na⁴   20. 哎 ai¹   20. 呀 ya¹   20. 久 chiu³

1. *Obs.*—Sir: *ni-na*. See *nin*, above (Part III, 648).
9. *Obs.*—And how much? [though you did not give what they asked] *tao ti*, in the end, etc.
19. *Obs.* 1.—Father died: *hsien fu*, my late father, *cʻŭ*, departed from, *shih*, the world. *Obs.* 2.—Gave up: *ko hsia*, laid down, the appointment. *Obs.* 3.—Look after: *liao li*; the first word signifying here the calculation, the second the administration, required in *chia wu*, household business.
20. *Obs.* 1.—Dear me! *ai ya*. *Obs.* 2.—Your father: *ling tsun*; both words signifying honourable. *Obs.* 3.—Long: *jih-tzŭ chiu*, days long enduring.
22. *Obs.* 1.—His illness: *tʻa-na*, like *ni-na*, a respectful form; pronounced *tʻan-na*. *Obs.* 2.—Took charge: *chao ying*, looked to everything, and met every requirement.

23. He was able to attend to his affairs in-doors, though he could not go out.

24. Should you have remained in office had you not lost your father?

25. I might have remained or I might not; I am not sure.

26. How not sure?

27. I would have staid in the place if there had been more to be made out of it.

28. Did your salary in it not cover your expenses?

29. Well, it did; still a little addition was required to make one comfortable.

30. Don't think it odd if I say that you were wrong to give up your place.

31. Why, what do you think I ought to have done?

32. Is not His Excellency WANG your connexion by marriage?

33. More; he is my blood relation.

34. Better still; was not he made Governor of a province the other day?

35. He was; Governor of Honan. But what do you imply by your question, sir?

36. My idea is that were you still in public employ His Excellency WANG would beyond doubt be willing to give you a lift.

37. You are wrong; he never liked me.

38. That's all imagination; what evidence have you that he did not?

39. The last time he left home I asked him to take me with him.

40. And what answer did he make?

41. He said, "If there were not another man in the world, I wouldn't have you."

27. 項 *hsiang*⁴ 28. 墊 *tien*⁴ 32. 王 *wang*² 34. 撫 *fu*³ 36. 拔 *pa*²
28. 賠 *p'ei*² 31. 依 *i*¹ 32. 戚 *ch'i*⁴ 36. 提 *t'i*² 38. 證 *cheng*⁴

23. *Obs.*—He: note that a son cannot speak of his *fat her* as *t'a*.
24. *Obs.*—Remained in office: *tang*¹, here to perform.
25. *Obs.*—*To-shao ch'ien:* in Peking as often pronounced *to-'rh ch'ien.*
27. *Obs.*—More to be made: *hsiang*, properly, he neck; items; subdivisions. *Tê hsiang*, the items, sums, obtained; specially used of the profits or pickings of an office.
28. *Obs.*—Cover expenses: *p'ei*, to make up a deficiency, but, popularly, to lose money; *tien*, to advance money. *P'ei tien*, to lose the advances made.
29. *Obs.*—Well: [though I could have wished more] *tao*, yet, I had not to *p'ei tien.*
30. *Obs.* 1.—Think it odd: *kuai*, to be angry with. *Obs.* 2.—Were wrong: in laying down your office you were *pu tang*¹, not right.
31. *Obs.*—You think: *i*, to follow, to lean against, according to; *lit.*, in that case, according to your idea, [you would have] *chiao*, caused me to do what?
32. *Obs.* 1.—His Excellency: WANG *ta-jên*; the two last words make an honourable appellative proper to a large number of officials whom, however, we should not style Excellency. *Obs.* 2.—Connexion: *ch'in ch'i*, related by marriage. Emphasise *ch'in.*
34. *Obs.*—Made governor: *fang*, to let go (in the higher grades of office, to appoint), *hsun fu*, the former character signifying to go rounds, as a watch; the latter, to soothe, to conciliate. Under the present dynasty, the chief authority over a single province, with a few exceptions.
35. *Obs.*—Imply by your question: *lit.*, what is your lofty view, the view of your superior intelligence?
36. *Obs.*—Give you a lift: *t'i*, to lift or pick up, *pa*, to pluck or pull up; *t'i* also means to mention or allude to (*see* Dialogue IV, 81). *T'i pa*, to help on anyone in preference to others; to show preference to.
37. *Obs.*—Never liked: he heretofore has not *hsi huan*, rejoiced in, me.
38. *Obs.*—Evidence: *lit.*, what is a *tui chêng*? the latter word (*chêng*) signifying witness, that *tui*, accords with, what you advance.
39. *Obs.* 1.—Last time: *shang tz'ŭ*, the time, or turn, last above the present. *Obs.* 2.—Left home: *lit.*, went outside; said of anyone going to some distance to trade, on duty, etc.

PART IV.—THE TEN DIALOGUES.

42. Dear me! was there any reason for such sternness?

43. He can't bear me because I was idle and extravagant when I was young.

44. Oh! be easy about that. Bygones are bygones. His Excellency surely doesn't continue to bear you such illwill now.

45. You don't know; he said more than what I have told you

46. But not that he would never forgive you?

47. He said that no matter what luck he might have, he would never show me any favour again.

48. What a pity that with such an opportunity as this you shouldn't be able to avail yourself of it.

49. There is no help for it; it's no one's fault but my own that I did not make better use of my time long ago.

50. Did your father's property all come to you, or was it divided?

51. Not all to me; my two brothers, elder and younger, have each a share.

52. Has your elder brother a larger share than the rest?

53. No: it is equally divided amongst the three of us.

54. What sort of property was it, money?

55. There was some ready money and some house property, and business as well.

56. How came the house to you when you were not the eldest son?

57. While my father was alive my eldest brother always looked after the shop.

58. Oh! and you live in the house to take care of your mother?

59. Exactly, my younger brother being also away from home; he has got a private secretary's place somewhere or other.

43. 恨 $hên^4$	44. 唉 ai^1	46. 宥 yu^1	50. 歸 $kuei^1$	58. 伺 $tz^cŭ^1$
43. 勤 $ch'in^2$	44. 既 chi^4	48. 機 chi^1	53. 均 $chün^1$	59. 幕 mu^4
43. 儉 $chien^3$	44. 咎 $chiu^{1\,4}$	49. 息 $hsi^{1\,2}$	54. 哪 na^1	

43. *Obs.* 1.—Can't bear: *hên*, to hate, to be wrath with. *Obs.* 2.—Idle: was not *ch'in*, diligent, and *chien*, economical.

44. *Obs.* 1.—Oh! *ai*, an interjection. *Obs.* 2.—Bygones: *chi*, of time that is past; since. *Chi wang*, as to what is past, or, since the thing is past, *yu chiu*, there is no fault [imputed].

46. *Obs.*—Forgive: *yu*, to forgive; *k'uan yu*, to have the liberality to forgive.

47. *Obs.*—Luck: *lit.*, no matter what share of promotion, wealth, etc., he might reach.

48. *Obs.*—Opportunity: *chi*, motive power, *hui*, to meet, to come across; the meeting with the motive power that will accomplish a certain object in view.

49. *Obs.*—Better use: *hsi*, properly, rest; the profit, interest, accruing on money put out. *Ch'u hsi*, to make profit, or the profit made; colloquially, seldom used except in a moral sense. Emphasise *ch'u*.

50. *Obs.*—All come: *chuan*, exclusively, *kuei*, to revert to.

53. *Obs.*—Equally: *chün*, in even shares.

54. *Obs.* 1.—Was it: *na*, an interrogative particle. *Obs.* 2.—Property: *ch'an yeh* may mean land, house, or business.

56. *Obs.* 1.—The house: *lit.*, the dwelling-house below your person. *Obs.* 2.—Eldest: *chang³*; cf. *chang pei*, an elder generation.

57. *Obs.*—Alive: *tsai*, existing.

58. *Obs.* 1.—Take care of: *tz'ŭ hou*, to wait on; both words meaning to wait, to wait for. *Obs.* 2.—Your mother: *ling t'ang*; the latter word, properly a hall, being elliptically used for *hsüan t'ang*, a poetical term for mother.

59. *Obs.*—Private secretary: *mu*, properly, a curtain or screen, behind which the secretary would sit, his employer being in court. The term has a classical origin.

DIALOGUE III.

1. Come here, somebody!
2. Here, sir! what did you want, sir?
3. Who are you?
4. My name is LAI-FU.
5. What is your surname?
6. My surname is CHANG.
7. What do you do here?
8. I came to do my elder brother's work.
9. Who is your elder brother?
10. My brother's name is LAI-SHUN.
11. What, the LAI-SHUN who looks after the library?
12. Yes; the same.
13. How came he to go away without asking leave?
14. He thought he oughtn't to trouble you about leave, sir, when you were unwell.
15. Why couldn't he wait till I was well again?
16. He was wanted at home on very particular business.
17. What particular business?
18. His mother was very ill.
19. If so, why should you and he have changed places?
20. He went because father desired it, and I came for fear your work might not be done, sir.
21. Well, be all that as it may, servants should never leave the house without asking leave.
22. Don't be hard on my brother, sir, pray; he will be back soon.
23. Is your house far from this?
24. I should not call it very far.
25. What do you mean by not very far?
26. It's not more than four *li* at the most; it's in the Eastern Division too.
27. Well, in the meanwhile you can go home.
28. Must my brother come back directly?
29. It will do if he is here by to-night.
30. Oh, here is LAI-SHUN himself!
31. Ah! tell him to come here. You can go.
32. You have no further orders for me, sir?
33. None whatever; you go. Here, LAI-SHUN!
34. I have made a sad mistake, sir, but I hope you will forgive me.

8. 哥 *ko¹*	21. 勿 *wu²⁴*	23. 離 *li²*
13. 假 *chia⁴*	22. 饒 *jao²*	34. 恕 *shu⁴*

4. *Obs.*—My name: *hsiao ti*, the little one; servants so style themselves to their masters; in a court, prisoners and witnesses do the same. Differently used farther on, in Part V, Lesson LXXXVII.
8. *Obs.*—Elder brother: *ko-ko*; borrowed from the Manchu language. Notice *t'i* first as the preposition instead of, and then as the verb to replace, or to do instead of.
13. *Obs.*—Ask leave: *chia*, to rest, to take a holiday; not to be confounded with *chia*, false. *Kao chia*, to give notice of leave.
14. *Obs.*—He oughtn't: *pu pien*, it was not expedient, convenient, befitting, that he should.
19. *Obs.*—If so: since it is *chê-mo cho*, thus.
21. *Obs.*—Be all that: *wu⁴*, a negative imperative particle; *lit.*, of other matters, before [I speak of this most essential matter] do not speak. Colloquially, *wu²*.
22. *Obs.*—Don't be hard: *jao*, to forbear, to pardon, to excuse. See Part III, Exercise XXXII, 8, *Obs.* 1.
23. *Obs.*—Far from: *li*, to separate; hence, from; is your house from this far or near?
27. *Obs.*—In the meanwhile: *hsien*, before your brother comes.
28. *Obs.*—Directly: *chiu*, now.
34. *Obs.*—Forgive me: *k'uan shu*. *Shu*, properly, to forbear doing to others what one does not wish done to oneself; hence, to show mercy.

PART IV.—THE TEN DIALOGUES.   221

35. It was a mistake indeed; why did you go out without saying a word to me?

36. You were not well, sir, and they were pressing me for the money.

37. Who were *they*, and what was *the* money?

38. The shop, sir, where I bought the table for you the other day wanted to be paid for it.

39. Isn't that shop in the Western Division?

40. No, sir; outside the walls.

41. Outside the walls! near which gate?

42. I don't know much about the town outside the walls, sir.

43. But you know whether the shop was north or south of this, don't you?

44. Oh! I remember; it's outside the An-ting Gate.

45. There's something I don't quite understand in all this.

46. What is it you don't understand, sir?

47. You have got to speak the truth, mind.

48. I shouldn't venture to tell you a lie, sir.

49. Halloo! who is it that's making such a noise in the court?

50. Shall I go out and see, sir?

51. No, you needn't go. Shut (let down) the window.

52. Dear me! what can the matter be? there's someone coming rushing into the house.

53. Why, you are a waggoner, are you not? what do you mean by rushing in in this way?

54. Oh, sir! my humble service to you; I want you to stand my friend, sir.

55. What do you mean?

56. Oh, sir! justice, if you please; I've been thrashed and I've lost my money.

57. And what have I to do with your thrashing or your losses?

58. If you have nothing to do with it, sir, your servant has, at any rate.

59. Which servant? what, LAI-SHUN here, perhaps?

60. Ah! yes, indeed; that is the man; I didn't notice him before.

61. What has he had to do with you?

62. He hasn't paid me my fare.

63. Your fare from the Northern Division?

64. Northern Division? I belong to an inn at Foal's Bridge.

65. Dear, dear! this really requires explanation; take care what you say.

48. 敢 *kan*³	54. 噯 *ai*¹	56. 伸 *shên*¹	64. 駒 *chü*¹
49. 院 *yüan*⁴	54. 磕 *k'o*¹	57. 與 *yü*³	65. 咳 *hai*¹
52. 闖 *ch'uang*³ ⁴	56. 挨 *ai*², ⁿ*ai*²	57. 何 *ho*²	65. 詳 *hsiang*²

36. *Obs.*—Pressing: *lit.*, they were impatient in the matter of *(yü)* from me wanting money.

48. *Obs.*—Venture: *kan*, to dare.

49. *Obs.*—Court: *yüan*, an enclosure surrounded by walls; the open spaces between the buildings in a Chinese house are so called.

52. *Obs.* 1.—Dear me! *ai*¹, here an interjection indicative of surprise or regret. *Obs.* 2.—Rushing in : *ch'uang*³, to burst a way into; said of man or beast. In Peking, *ch'uang*⁴.

54. *Obs.* 1.—Oh, sir! *ai*, a mere exclamation. *Obs.* 2.—Humble service: *k'o*, to knock, *t'ou*, the head; perform a kotow. *Obs.* 3.—Stand my friend: *lit.*, I pray you, sir, to *tso chu*, to play the master, to manage my business for me.

56. *Obs.* 1.—Have been thrashed: ⁿ*ai*; originally, to beat; more commonly, side by side with. In northern mandarin, to suffer, to be the recipient of; hence, when with other verbs, what we should call a sign of the passive. *Obs.* 2.—Justice: *lit.*, I pray you, sir, *shên*, stretch out so as to straighten, *yüan*, my wrong.

57. *Obs.*—To do with: *yü*, with; your loss of money, etc., has with me, *ho kan*, what connexion or concern?

64. *Obs.*—Foal's Bridge: *chü*, a horse, an ass, or a mule, not full grown. Ma-chü Ch'iao is a village a few miles east of Peking.

65. *Obs.* 1.—Dear, dear! *hai*, an interjection. *Obs.* 2.—Explanation: *lit.*, this *hai*, still, requires *hsiang hsi*, explicit and minute explanation.

66. You may take my leg off, sir, if I say a word that's not true.

67. What time did you start this morning?

68. The cart was put to at cock-crow.

69. Had you one beast or two?

70. A pair; we were to go quick.

71. Had you no passenger but LAI-SHUN here?

72. There was a companion of his as well.

73. And which of the two was it that proposed to go so fast?

74. LAI-SHUN hired the cart, and when he came to hire it he said that if I made haste he would pay me something extra.

75. What did you and he agree should be the fare?

76. It was settled that I was to have five *tiao*.

77. Including the extra charge for speed?

78. Yes, the extra fare included; I never take in anybody.

79. Oh! the fare is fair enough; was it about this you came to blows?

80. We didn't come to blows at all.

81. What! didn't you say just now that you had a thrashing?

82. Yes; but it was not LAI-SHUN that thrashed me.

83. Who then?

84. A number of people; I don't know any one of them.

85. What, a lot of people headed by LAI-SHUN?

86. No, no; LAI-SHUN did not bring anyone.

87. They were thieves then?

88. No, not thieves either. Oh dear! it's a long story to tell.

89. Well, but you have got to tell it, whether it be long or short.

90. Oh, sir! please pay me the fare that's due to me and I'll go about my business.

91. Not so fast; I want to clear up this business.

92. It's not worth taking up your time, sir.

93. Don't you trouble yourself about that; all you've got to do is to answer my questions.

94. Well, sir, what do you want me to tell you?

95. Is CHANG LAI-SHUN here a Foal's Bridge man?

96. His father is a market-gardener outside the village.

97. Oh! then of course LAI-SHUN is an old acquaintance of yours?

98. I used to see him when he was quite a little fellow playing about the streets.

72. 伴 *pan*⁴   79. 架 *chia*⁴   91. 晰 *hsi*¹
74. 加 *chia*¹   88. 呦 *yo*¹   96. 園 *yüan*²

70. *Obs.*—*Wei*⁴, for, going quickly.

72. *Obs.*—Companion: *pan*, a partner, an associate.

74. *Obs.*—Extra: *chia*, to add to; *lit.*, he said if I made haste he could add some cash.

78. *Obs.*—Take in: *ngo* (see Part III, 597).

79. *Obs.*—Came to blows: *chia*, properly, a frame; to ward off blows; with *ta*, to fight, with arms or without.

88. *Obs.*—Oh dear: *ai yo*, an interjection.

91. *Obs.*—To understand: *hsi*, bright, clear; I must *fên hsi*, distinguish one part from another, *ming-pai*, clearly.

93. *Obs.*—All you have to do: *chih*, only; I only require that when I ask you something you say that something.

96. *Obs.*—Gardener: *yüan*, a garden; his father keeps (*lit.*, opens) a *ts'ai yüan*, vegetable garden, as distinct from *hua yüan*, a flower garden, *kuo mu yüan*, an orchard.

99. Was he honest as a boy, or the reverse?

100. Sir, I had rather not tell tales of anybody.

101. But I don't want you specially to tell tales; you can tell me any good you know of him, can't you?

102. Sir! please pay me my fare and let me go about my business.

103. Well, tell me; where did the people come from who fell upon you?

104. They belonged to a tea-house on the road.

105. How far from the city?

106. Not far; just outside the Sha-wo Gate.

107. And LAI-SHUN had some tea there?

108. No, no tea; some spirits and something to eat besides.

109. Did you breakfast with him?

110. No; I was away getting my whip mended.

111. Well, and when it was mended you came back to the house?

112. Yes, I came back; and when I got back I found that they were off.

113. Off! having done you out of your fare?

114. Yes, and not only me but the tea-house as well.

115. Oh! that was it; and the tea-shop wanted you to pay your passengers' bill?

116. That *was* it; and when I wouldn't pay they set upon me.

117. Well, so far as the beating you got at the tea-house goes, I don't see that I can do anything for you, eh?

118. Oh! the beating doesn't signify; but please, sir, pay me my fare, and let me go about my business.

119. There is no difficulty about the fare; I shall stop it out of LAI-SHUN's wages for you.

120. Could you give it me at once, sir, if you please, and let me go home?

121. Don't disturb yourself about the fare; but have you nothing to say to him about what took place at the tea-shop?

| 103. 毆 ou^1 | 106. 沙 sha^1 | 110. 鞭 pien^1 | 119. 折 ché^2 |
| 104. 舘 kuan^3 | 106. 窩 wo^1 | 114. 但 tan^4 | |

99. *Obs.*—Reverse: *liu li*, slippery, evasive, dishonest, not to be depended upon. *Liu li* is, lit., glassware (see Dialogue VII, 72); hence, metaphorical for a slippery customer, commonly called *liu li ch'iu²-'rh*, "a glass marble."

100. *Obs.*—Tell tales: to tell people's *tuan ch'u*, short places, demerits; *ch'ang ch'u* is a man's special merit.

103. *Obs.*—Fell upon: *ngou*, to beat, with or without a weapon.

104. *Obs.*—Tea-house: *kuan*, a term to be differently translated according to circumstances; a school, an hotel, the temporary residence of an official travelling on duty, etc.

106. *Obs.*—Gate: *Sha-wo*, popularly pronounced *Sha-hou*; lit., dust, or sand, nest. *Wo* is the nest or lair of bird or beast.

110. *Obs.*—Whip: *pien*; mended, *shuan*, as before, to tie to, or round.

112. *Obs.* 1.—When: *kan*, as before, to overtake, to come up to. *Obs.* 2.—They were off: they had, before the time so described, run away.

113. *Obs.*—Done you out of: *k'êng* (see Part III, **796**).

114. *Obs.*—Not only: *tan*, only; not only the waggon fare, *lien*, also, etc.

117. *Obs.*—So far as: *ts'êng*; lit., a layer; hence, a stage in proceedings, an incident.

119. *Obs.*—Stop it: *ché*, properly, to snap off; here, as elsewhere, to deduct from one account in favour of another. Also read *shê*² (see Part V, Lesson XXVII, 13)

122. No, no; nothing whatever. Please pay me my fare, sir, and let me go home.

123. Well, you are a right good fellow to put up with your neighbour's wrongdoing in this way; but when you get back to your village, you may tell LAI-SHUN'S father that neither of his sons is any good, and that I will have nothing whatever to do with such servants.

123. 忠 *chung*¹ 123. 擔 *tan*¹ 123. 材 *ts'ai*² 123. 決 *chüeh*²

123. *Obs.* 1.—Right good: *chung*, honest, loyal; *hou*, thick (morally, sound, liberal, the opposite of mean). *Obs.* 2.—Put up with: *tan*¹, to bear on the shoulder, but read *tan*⁴ when used materially; *tan tai* to behave towards men as one bearing their *pu shih*, faults, on one's own shoulder. *Obs.* 3.—But when: *ching*, a strong disjunctive. *Obs.* 4.—Any good: *ts'ai liao*, *lit.*, materials; neither of them is of the material that makes a good, useful, or honest man. *Obs.* 5.—Nothing whatever: *chüeh*; *lit.*, to cut; positively, decidedly.

DIALOGUE IV.

1. LUNG-T'IEN!
2. Sir!
3. Who is that in the court?
4. His name is HSÜ.
5. Oh! a man you know, is it?
6. Yes, sir; an old acquaintance.
7. Where did you meet?
8. We met at Shanghai.
9. When was that?
10. Many years ago.
11. Were you intimate?
12. Pretty well, sir; we are distantly connected.
13. Oh, you're connected? Do you know what he has come for?
14. No, sir, but I can ask him; shall I?
15. Do; I have no objection.
16. He says he is come to see Your Excellency.
17. Come to see me! what about?
18. His father has sent him to pay his respects, he says.
19. His father! what is his father?
20. He was in business once; at present he has no occupation.
21. I don't remember the man at all; what line of business was he in?
22. Surely you remember the large draper's shop in the Western Division, sir?
23. Oh! HSÜ FU-CH'ING; I do remember him. It's *his* son, is it?
24. His son, sir.

4. 徐 *hsü*² 6. 識 *shih*²·⁴ 7. 遇 *yü*⁴ 23. 慶 *ch'ing*⁴

1. *Obs.*—LUNG-T'IEN! the name of the person addressed, not the surname; this, in familiar intercourse, especially with a junior, is omitted. Were the surname expressed, it would precede the name as above in Dialogue III, 95.

4. *Obs.*—Hsü: a surname. There are in all China but some 540 single-syllabled surnames, with perhaps 30 of two syllables.

5. *Obs.*—Know: *shih*, to know, to recognise.

6. *Obs.*—Old acquaintances: *ch'ên*, old, of things long in use; also, stale (*see* Part III, **1026**).

7. *Obs.*—Meet: *yü*, to meet by accident.

18. *Obs.*—Respects: sent to *ch'ing*, for *ch'ing wên*, to beg to be allowed to inquire after your *an*, health, comfort.

21. *Obs.*—The man: *q.d.*, this man is one *so*, whom, I do not remember; the addition of the *so* is held to emphasise the affirmation.

23. *Obs.*—HSÜ FU-CH'ING: *ch'ing*, prosperity, congratulations upon prosperity; here, part of a man's name.

PART IV.—THE TEN DIALOGUES.

25. Ask him to step in.
26. His Excellency begs you will walk in.
27. I hope Your Excellency is well.
28. Take a seat! take a seat!
29. When Your Excellency is seated.
30. Take a seat! take a seat! Here, somebody!
31. *Dja!*
32. Some tea! Your name is Hsü, sir?
33. Hsü, at your service, sir.
34. The son of Hsü Fu-ch'ing?
35. Hsü Fu-ch'ing is my father.
36. I used to know him years ago; I hope he is well.
37. Very well, thank you, sir; he sent me to inquire after Your Excellency's health.
38. It was very good of him to think of me, I am sure, and very good of you to take so much trouble.
39. Oh, sir, it was no more than my simple duty.

40. Your father used to suffer from his eyes, if I remember rightly; are they any better now?
41. His eyesight *is* pretty good, thank you, considering his age.
42. Age! why, he is much the same age as I am!
43. He is sixty-nine, sir.
44. Then I beat him by two years, for I am seventy-one.
45. I should be well satisfied if he looked as hearty as Your Excellency.
46. Well, I don't understand why he should not; he has not gone through what I have.
47. As a public man Your Excellency has had great cares no doubt; but my poor father has had his domestic financial anxieties.
48. But they are over now that he has retired from business.
49. Yes, sir, he *has* retired, but that was because he could not help himself.

25. 讓 *jang*⁴	37. 托 *t'o*¹	38. 勞 *lao*²	45. 朗 *lang*² ⁴
32. 沏 *ch'i*¹	38. 惦 *tien*⁴	40. 糢 *mo*¹	49 奈 *nai*⁴

25. *Obs.*—Ask him: *jang*, properly, to concede to; hence, to offer to, to invite to benefit by. Very commonly used of invitations to eat, to drink, to smoke, etc.

32. *Obs.*—Some tea: *ch'i*, to pour boiling water on tea.

33. *Obs.*—Your service: *chien*, cheap, lowly; like *pi* (see Dialogue I, 2), for the pronoun of the first person.

37. *Obs.*—Thank you: *t'o*, the same as *t'o* (see Part III, 992), to be beholden to, *fu*, the prosperity, of the person addressed; *q.d.*, goodness, which Heaven rewards by making him prosper, has a beneficial influence on the speaker.

38. *Obs.* 1.—Good of him: *chiao*, to cause, as elsewhere, puts the verb in the passive; *tien*, to be anxious about persons or things; not recognised by the dictionaries. *Obs.* 2.—I am sure: *chao shih*, in very truth. *Obs.* 3.—Take trouble: *lao*, trouble, to trouble. *Lao chia*, to trouble the chariot, politely for to trouble you; it is also frequently used in the sense of "thank you."

40. *Obs.*—If I remember: *mo*, a word not used separately from *hu*; the combination implying dimness of sight or sense; dimly remember. The character *mo* is not recognised by the native dictionaries, and is probably a corruption of *mo*, to feel, or the same phonetic with the 72nd or 109th Radical.

42. *Obs.*—Much the same: *ch'a*¹, properly, diverging; not to be confounded with the same character read *ch'ai*¹ (see Part III, 1005), or *tx'a*¹ (see Part III, 577). *Ch'a pu to*, differing not much, nearly the same as.

45. *Obs.* 1.—As hearty: *ying*, hard; *lang*⁴, properly *lang*², tall. There is, strictly speaking, no character to represent this latter sound. *Obs.* 2.—Well satisfied: *lit.*, if my father could be like Your Excellency that hearty, that [would be a thing that though] one asked for it, one could not obtain it; too good a thing to be got.

49. *Obs.*—Not help: *nai*, properly, a certain fruit, but as used in this phrase, untranslatable. *Wu nai ho* and *wu k'o nai ho* both mean that the case is without any remedy; there is no help for it.

50. Oh, indeed! he was unfortunate in business?

51. Not exactly, sir.

52. No? then was he robbed?

53. Far worse, sir; he was cheated out of almost all the money he had made.

54. Dear me! I'm sorry to hear that; how was it? did someone who owed him money make off with it?

55. No, sir, a friend he went security for—

56. Absconded! how abominable! and the loss has told on your father's health, has it?

57. Naturally, sir; he has a large family and nothing to give them.

58. How many are there of you?

59. Four sons and three daughters.

60. But not all at home?

61. Every one at home, sir.

62. I thought your father's daughters were all married?

63. Two of them were married to officers of the army, but their husbands were killed in that last campaign in the West.

64. And their widows are come home again?

65. Yes, sir; one with her two children, and the other with six.

66. That is a large family to keep, indeed; and there is another lady unmarried?

67. She is quite a young thing, and always ailing.

68. Ah! what does she suffer from?

69. My mother died while she was a baby at the breast, and she never throve afterwards.

51. 竟 *ching*⁴	53. 惡 *wu*⁴	56. 精 *ching*¹	60. 未 *wei*⁴	63. 亡 *wang*²
52. 莫 *mo*⁴	53. 掙 *chêng*⁴	57. 養 *yang*³	62. 姑 *ku*¹	64. 孀 *shuang*¹
52. 被 *pei*⁴	54. 繃 *pêng*¹	59. 姐 *chieh*³	62. 嫁 *chia*⁴	64. 婦 *fu*⁴
52. 竊 *ch'ieh*⁴	55. 保 *pao*³	59. 妹 *mei*⁴	63. 陣 *chên*⁴	

51. Obs.—*Ching*, a strong disjunctive; then, but then, only, nothing but; when followed by a negative, never.

52. Obs. 1.—No? *mo*, generally, negative imperative; *mo pu*, if it were not; was it not then that he was robbed? Obs. 2.—Robbed: *pei*, to cover (hence, to suffer; hence, sign of the passive); *ch'ieh*, to steal, to pilfer.

53. Obs. 1.—Worse: *wu*, to hate; *k'o wu*, deserving hate, detestable, abominable. Obs. 2.—Made: *chêng*, to make an effort, as when trying to extricate oneself from bonds; *chêng ch'ien*, to make money by exertion.

54. Obs.—Make off with: did the *ch'ien chu*, debtor, *pêng*, flick it, the money, away? *Pêng*, which is not a recognised character, is used of the action of a bowstring, or of a piece of wood so set as to propel anything, upon the missile propelled.

55. Obs.—Security: *pao*, to secure, to ensure, in any sense.

56. Obs.—Health: *ching*, properly, minute, subtle; *ching*, the spirit within one, as distinguished from *shên*, its external manifestation; *ching shên*, animal spirits, health.

57. Obs.—Nothing to give: *lit.*, he has not *li liang*, resources wherewith to, *yang huo*, to keep them alive; *yang*, to feed, to rear, man or beast.

59. Obs.—Daughters: *chieh*, elder sisters of the speaker; *mei*, his younger sisters.

60. Obs.—But not: *wei*, not, not yet; *wei pi*, it does not necessarily follow.

61. Obs.—All: *ko ho-'rh*, every individual.

62. Obs. 1.—Daughters: *ku-niang*, a spinster. Obs. 2.—Married: *chia*, of the woman married, to leave home.

63. Obs. 1.—Married: those they were given to were military officers. Obs. 2.—Killed: *chên*, a rank, the ranks of a force; *wang*, to die; *chên wang*, died in battle; were killed the last time that in the West, *lit.*, on the western road (beyond the frontier) there was a *ch'u ping*, going forth to war.

64. Obs.—Widows: *shuang*¹, widowed (in Peking, *shuang*⁴); *fu*, a wife. *Fu-jên* is used of any woman.

67. Obs.—Always ailing: *ai*, to love; here and often, in the sense of "to be used to."

69. Obs. 1.—While: *ta*, proceeding from; hence, at the time when. Obs. 2.—At the breast: *ch'üeh nai*, she wanted, was deficient in, milk. Obs. 3.—Throve: *tsu chuang*, sufficiently vigorous.

PART IV.—THE TEN DIALOGUES. 227

70. This is very sad, really; but you and your brothers are doing something for the family, I suppose.

71. I should be very glad to do anything, but unfortunately I can get nothing to do.

72. Are you the eldest son?

73. The eldest but one, sir.

74. Well, but what is your eldest brother about?

75. He is a cripple and quite unfit for anything.

76. Well, this is a terrible case; and your younger brothers?

77. They were quite children when my father gave up business, and as he couldn't pay for their schooling they have been very imperfectly educated.

78. Well, I suppose the long and the short of it is that you want me to find you a place, eh?

79. Oh, Your Excellency, I should be inexpressibly grateful if you would take so much interest in me.

80. And that was the real object of your visit to-day, wasn't it?

81. Indeed, I shouldn't have presumed to mention the subject, sir, if you had not alluded to it.

82. Well, I'll see what I can do for you: be so good as to call again about ten days hence.

83. I am greatly indebted to you for the preference you are showing me, sir; I will wait on Your Excellency again in a few days.

84. Good-bye, then, for the present.

85. Good-bye to Your Excellency.

| 70. 憐 *lien*² | 75. 殘 *ts'an*² | 76. 景 *ching*³ | 77. 培 *p'ei*· | 79. 激 *chi*· |
| 73. 排 *p'ai*² | 75. 疾 *chi*² | 77. 栽 *tsai*· | 79. 感 *kan*· | 79. 盡 *chin*⁴ |

70. *Obs.* 1.—Very sad: *lien*, to compassionate; *k'o lien*, that rightly may be, deserves to be, pitied; but it is used simply as to pity. *Obs.* 2.—For *liang*, see Part III, 772.

71. *Obs.*—But: *lit.*, I, *ch'üeh*, for all that may be argued to the contrary, am very willing; *k'o hsi*, lamentably, there is no *tao-lu*, road.

72. *Obs.*—Eldest son: *chang³ fang*; *lit.*, the chamber first in order. The sons, while children, are all in one apartment; as each one marries, he has a room to himself; the eldest will be first married.

73. *Obs.*—Eldest but one: *p'ai*, to arrange in order. *P'ai êrh*, I stand second among the sons; a daughter might say it of her place among her sisters. Cf. also *hang*, Part III, Exercise XXVIII, 10.

75. *Obs.*—Cripple: *ts'an chi*, dreadfully ailing in the legs and feet. *Ts'an*, to destroy, to seriously injure (hence, cruel); *chi*, ailments in general.

76. *Obs.* 1.—Terrible case: *kuang ching*, circumstance; the latter word, alone, being more strictly applicable to scenery, features of a landscape. *Obs.* 2.—*K'o*, is properly, may properly be said to be, *liao pu tê*, infinite, sc., in its badness.

77. *Obs.* 1.—Gave up: *shou*, here in the sense of to pack up, as a huckster his wares. *Obs.* 2.—Pay for schooling: *tsai p'ei*, properly, of trees; *tsai*, to plant; *p'ei*, to pile earth round the roots; could not take care of them [so as to enable them] to read. *Obs.* 3.—Imperfectly: *lit.*, their learning [though they have some] *hai*, or *han*, for all that, cannot either be considered deep.

79. *Obs.* 1.—Interest: *t'êng ai*, to tenderly love. *Obs.* 2.—Grateful: *kan chi*; the character *kan* meaning to move the heart, or to have the heart moved; *chi*, the outbursting of the heart moved. *Obs.* 3.—Inexpressibly: *chin*, to exhaust, words will hardly exhaust.

81. *Obs.*—Allude to: *t'i*, properly, to pick up (see Dialogue II, 36).

83. *Obs.*—Preference: *t'i pa*; the first word as in 81; the second means, to draw one out of a bundle. *T'i pa*, to help on anyone in preference to others (*see* Dialogue II, 36).

DIALOGUE V.

1. LUNG-T'IEN! when Hsü Yung calls again, you tell him I've left town.
2. Poor fellow! he'll be sadly disappointed; what has he done to offend Your Excellency?
3. Offend! his whole story was a tissue of falsehoods from beginning to end.
4. Why, isn't he the son of Hsü Fu-ch'ing?
5. Oh, yes; he's Hsü Fu-ch'ing's son.
6. And didn't his father fail as he said?
7. He did fail; but not as he said.
8. How did he fail then?
9. It was his own extravagance and folly that broke him; nothing else.
10. Still he has an immense family to support.
11. Nothing of the sort. In the first place, Hsü Fu-ch'ing himself has been dead some years.
12. Dead some years! and who maintains all those sons and daughters of his?
13. His daughters all died before him, and he never had any son but this impostor.
14. Sir, I think Your Excellency must be misinformed on that point.
15. Not in the least; I've been making very careful inquiries. Didn't you say that you were connected with these people by marriage?
16. I did.
17. But you have seen nothing of them for four or five years?
18. Oh, more than that; nine or ten years.
19. Just so. Now, when old Hsü kept the draper's shop, what was his character?
20. They used to say he was a very proud man; I never heard anything else against him.
21. Wasn't he very much given to smoking opium?
22. He did smoke, certainly; and he was a little fond of his glass too.
23. Exactly. Now, when you met his son at Shanghai, what was he doing there?
24. He said he had been commissioned to buy produce for exportation.
25. What produce, tea or silk?

| 9. 抛 p'ao¹ | 20. 狂 k'uang² | 22. 貪 t'an¹ |
| 15. 查 ch'a² | 21. 烟 yen¹ | 25. 葉 yeh⁴ |

1. *Obs.*—Hsü Yung: *yung*, eternal; here the name of the man surnamed Hsu.
2. *Obs.* 1.—Disappointed: *pai hsi huan*, lit., to rejoice in vain; the literary equivalent is *shih wang* (失望).
Obs. 2.—Offend: *tê tsui*, to get blame of you; before *ta-jên* understand *yü* (see Part III, 343), in the sense of "from" or "of."
3. *Obs.*—Beginning to end: *t'ung shên*, entire body.
9. *Obs.*—Extravagance: *p'ao*, to let go suddenly of what is held in the hand; *p'ao fei*, to spend without restraint.
15. *Obs.*—Careful inquiries: *kao ch'a*, the latter character being identical in the colloquial language with *ch'a* (see Part III, 522).
20. *Obs.*—Proud: *k'uang*, of unbridled temper or passions; *k'uang ao*, ungovernably proud, contemptuous.
21. *Obs.*—Smoking: *yen*, smoke of any kind. *Ch'ih yen*, to eat smoke, to smoke; nowadays more particularly used of opium-smoking, at least in conversation with foreigners. Opium is often particularised as *ta yen*.
22. *Obs.*—Fond of his glass: *t'an*, to covet, to desire immoderately.
24. *Obs.*—Produce: *t'u huo*, merchandise of the place or country.
25. *Obs.*—Tea: *yeh*, a leaf; *ch'a yeh*, tea leaves, tea in the market.

26. Tea and silk and medicines.

27. And where were they to have been carried?

28. I forget whether he said north or south.

29. And did he say nothing about purchasing imports?

30. He may possibly have done so, but I don't remember.

31. Nothing about opium?

32. Yes, yes; now you mention it, I recollect that he had some little difficulty about his opium.

33. There wasn't as much as he wanted in the market, I suppose.

34. Oh yes. The price of the drug was rising every day, but there was plenty of it to be bought.

35. What publicly?

36. Not exactly; it was stowed away in the receiving ships or in warehouses.

37. And had it to be smoked on foreign premises?

38. No; the divan Hsü Yung used to frequent was in the back of a small house up a narrow street.

39. Oh, he used to frequent a divan, did he? Like father, like son.

40. Well, he didn't smoke so much after all.

41. Only purchased it for others, eh? And what was the difficulty he got into about it?

42. The prohibitions against the trade were still in force, and after he had purchased what he wanted, he couldn't get it away for a long time.

43. And how did he succeed at last?

44. He shipped it in a boat freighted with firewood, and smuggled it out of port.

45. I thought firewood all came *to* Shanghai; where could it be going to *from* the port?

46. Probably to some place in the neighbourhood. The junk, you may be sure, had more opium than firewood on board.

47. And so he got into a scrape?

48. Yes; his junk was dropping down the tide when a revenue cruiser pounced upon her.

26. 湖 hu^2 26. 材 $ts'ai^2$ 36. 躉 tun^3 36. 藏 $ts'ang^2$
26. 藥 yao^4 32. 微 wei^1 36. 棧 $chan^4$

26. *Obs.* 1.—Silk: $Hu\ ss\ddot{u}$, properly, silk of Hu-chou Fu, in the province of Chê-chiang (Chêkiang), but used generically of the finer silk. *Obs.* 2.—Medicines: yao, drug; ts'ai, materials; the latter word used particularly of timber.

27. *Obs.*—Carried: yun, to convey (see Part III, 1035).

29. *Obs.*—Imports: yang huo, foreign commodities (see Dialogue I, 12).

30. *Obs.*—May possibly have: ch'iao lai, lit., coming by chance; ch'iao is short for p'êng ch'iao (see Part III, 752), casually, by chance.

31. *Obs.* 1.—Nothing about: lit., did he not mention that he was pan, managing, engaged in, an operation of (that is, as it is very commonly used, buying). *Obs.* 2.—Opium: yang yao, foreign drug, drug from the seas; hence, abroad.

32. *Obs.*—Some little: wei, minute; hsieh wei i tien, a very common diminutive.

35. *Obs.*—Publicly: kung jan; the latter word as in Part III, 561.

36. *Obs.* 1.—Receiving ships: tun ch'uan; the first character meaning to buy wholesale. *Obs.* 2.—Warehouses: chan fang. *Obs.* 3.—Stored: ts'ang, to conceal, to put out of sight.

44. *Obs.*—Smuggled it out: t'ou, to steal; t'ou-cho, stealthily, went out of port.

48. *Obs.*—Pounced: ch'ou lêng-tzŭ, an expression indicating unlooked-for occurrences; on a sudden chua chu, clapped the paw, or claw, upon, and held or stopped the boat. The word lêng, cold, may refer to the shock of any occurrence unlooked for, but ch'ou, to draw, is scarcely explicable.

49. And put the cargo under seal?

50. No; but the tidewaiters threatened to search her if Hsü Yung didn't behave liberally.

51. How much did they ask?

52. They named no sum; they only said he must be liberal.

53. And what did he offer?

54. Well, like a fool, he offered a hundred taels.

55. That was pretty liberal; didn't the Custom House people think so?

56. They thought it much too liberal for a boat loaded with fuel, and they said that unless he paid down three hundred taels they would seize the whole cargo.

57. And did he pay three hundred taels?

58. He hadn't got it to pay.

59. Then how did he manage?

60. He gave them an order on a foreign house in Shanghai.

61. I wonder they took it. He was in great luck to get away at all.

62. But he didn't get away immediately, that was the best of it.

63. What, did the Customs people repent of their bargain after they had got the order for the money?

64. No; but while all this negotiation had been going on the Customs boat and the junk had been dropping down the tide side by side, and they ran foul of two other boats that were lying at anchor.

65. What, two other cruisers?

66. No, not cruisers; two boats belonging to the Imperial Commissioner LIU; one for himself and the other for his suite.

67. Capital! Was it very late at night?

68. Not very late; about nine o'clock.

69. Still, the Commissioner and his people were all asleep, I suppose?

70. The Commissioner, I should think, was at his rooms in the city; but his people were laughing and singing and keeping it up on board.

71. But his people had no concern with a Customs question?

49. 封 *fêng*¹ 61. 虎 *hu*³ 65. 哨 *shao*⁴ 66. 劉 *liu*²
52. 豐 *fêng*¹ 64. 撞 *chuang*⁴ 66. 欽 *ch'in*¹

49. *Obs.*—Under seal: *fêng*, properly, to stop up an orifice; here, to close by pasting certain official papers over a door, hatch, etc.

50. *Obs.*—Tidewaiter: there is another term for the tidewaiters in the employ of the Foreign Customs.

52. *Obs.*—Handsome: *fêng*, abounding, plenteous; *ts'ung fêng*, in an abounding manner, in the most abounding manner.

60. *Obs.* 1.—An order: *lit.*, he wrote *ko tzŭ-'rh*, a [paper of] characters; applicable to any note, memorandum, etc. *Obs.* 2.—On a house: *kên*, commonly, following, in the presence of; here, of or from; of the foreign house *ch'ü ch'ien*, to take the money.

61. *Obs.*—Get away: *hu*, the tiger; that he got out of the tiger's mouth was his *p'ien i*, advantage.

62. *Obs.*—But he didn't, etc.: *lit.*, but there was more [to come]; this wasn't yet to be considered entirely (so) getting out of the tiger's mouth.

64. *Obs.* 1.—Ran foul: *chuang*, to run up against; collision of persons or things. *Obs.* 2.—At anchor: *wan* (see Part III, 786); there, a bay; but here and often, to be at anchor.

65. *Obs.*—Cruisers: *shao*, properly, to whistle, or to make the like sound; hence, to make it as a signal; *hsün shao ch'uan*, circulating signal-making vessels.

66. *Obs.* 1.—Not cruisers: *kuan*, here short for *hai kuan*, Maritime Customs establishment. *Obs.* 2.—Commissioner: *ch'in*, imperial; *ch'ai*, envoy. *Obs.* 3.—LIU, a surname.

PART IV.—THE TEN DIALOGUES.   231

72. True; but when his boat ran bump up against them, it frightened them, and then, when they had recovered from their alarm, they came down on him for compensation.

73. Compensation for what?

74. For the fright, and damage done to the Imperial Commissioner's boats, and anything else you please.

75. I wonder Hsü Yung didn't show fight.

76. They were too many for him, and, besides, he had a guilty conscience.

77. As well he might have. But how did it all end?

78. The Customs boat had hauled off, but his experience in her case had taught him not to be too liberal this time, so he offered the Commissioner's people ten taels only.

79. And they were satisfied?

80. Oh yes; they would have taken anything; they were much too far gone to overhaul his junk.

72. 驚 ching¹   76. 寡 kua³   76. 膽 tan³   78. 躲 to³
74. 損 sun³   76. 敵 ti²   76. 虛 hsü¹   80. 醉 tsui⁴

72. *Obs.*—Frightened: *ching*, a word indicating surprise, but also terror.
74. *Obs.*—Damage: *sun*, to injure; *sun huai*, to injure seriously.
76. *Obs.* 1.—Too many: *kua*, the few, could not *ti*, stand before, as equal to, *chung*, the many. *Obs.* 2.—Guilty conscience: *tan*, the liver, was *hsü*, the opposite of *shih*, true, sound, solid. With the Chinese the liver is the seat of courage. Compare our term white-livered.
78. *Obs.* 1.—Had hauled off: *tsao*, early, some time before; *to*, to withdraw; *to k'ai*, to get out of the way. *Obs.* 2.—Experience: he *ching kuo*, having passed through that [other affair], *chang*, had added a piece of *chien shih*, seeing and knowing.
80. *Obs.* 1.—Oh yes: *lit.*, how should they not consent? *Obs.* 2.—Too far gone: they had all drunk to a state of *pan tsui*, semi-intoxication.

DIALOGUE VI.

1. Well, to return to his fabrications. Did he tell you whom he was buying opium for?

2. I forget.

3. He didn't tell you it was for his father?

4. I don't remember, really.

5. It *was* for his father, however, and his father's bankruptcy was due to this very transaction.

6. It was a bad speculation?

7. In one sense, yes; the opium was shipped for Tientsin.

8. What, and seized there?

9. It never arrived; the junk it was on board of was taken by pirates off the Shantung coast.

10. And old Hsü lost all the money he had invested in it?

1. 岔 ch'a⁴   9. 始 shih³   9. 終 chung¹   9. 扣 k'ou⁴   10. 資 tzŭ¹

1. *Obs.*—To return: *lit.*, that digression let us consider ended; *ch'a*, a forked road: *p'ang-ch'a*, branching off from one side; *chieh*, to tie a knot, to close an affair or a conversation.
5. *Obs.*—Bankruptcy: *kuan pi*, *lit.*, to close (a business), is used only of failure: for to retire from business, see Dialogue IV, 77.
9. *Obs.* 1.—Never: *shih*, beginning, *chung*, end; *shih chung*, from first to last. *Obs.* 2.—Taken by pirates: *lit.*, was by sea robbers *k'ou chu*, kept fast; *k'ou* is properly to strike, as one knocking at a door.
10. *Obs.*—Invested: *tzŭ*, properly, goods; here, money; *tzŭ pên*, capital.

11. Yes, and not only that, but his button to boot.

12. But I didn't know that he had any rank.

13. He had purchased a grade the year before.

14. Purchased a grade! But how could the piracy affect his rank? it is not alleged that he was in relations with the pirates, surely?

15. The piracy did not affect it, but the smuggling did.

16. What, did the smuggling come to the knowledge of the authorities?

17. Do you suppose large sums are ever extorted without the knowledge of the authorities?

18. Three hundred taels was not so very large a sum.

19. Quite large enough to be divided; and the cruiser's people not only kept more than their share, but fought about what they kept.

20. And then one told on the rest?

21. Precisely; and once the authorities got wind of it, the whole operation was traced to its source, and old Hsü had to pay the heaviest fine that could be inflicted, and was stripped of his rank as well.

22. Well, one can't wonder at Hsü Yung's desire to keep his father's disgrace quiet.

23. Certainly not, he wasn't obliged to publish such a thing; but that is no reason why he should come here with a long invention about his father being the victim of misplaced confidence.

24. That was too bad, I admit.

14. 涉 shê⁴   21. 究 chiu¹   22. 遮 chê¹   23. 揚 yang²   24. 逾 yü⁴
16. 場 ch'ang³   21. 罰 fa²   22. 掩 yen³   23. 編 pien¹   24. 詐 cha⁴

11. *Obs.*—Button: *ting tai*; *lit.*, that which is borne on the crown of the head; but it means, generally, the insignia of office.

12. *Obs.*—Rank: *kung ming*, elliptically, for the credit one has gained, the name one is leaving; commonly used for official rank, whether obtained by merit or purchase.

14. *Obs.* 1.—But: *jan êrh*, often pronounced *jan 'rh*; the case being *jan*, thus, *êrh*, yet,——. *Obs.* 2.—Could affect: *shê*, properly, to ford; *kan shê*, to be affected by prejudicially; *q.d.*, the thing *kan*, strikes me, I am *shê*, implicated in it; as a man fording a stream is wet by the water. *Obs.* 3.—Not alleged: *nan tao* (see Part III, **830**). *Obs.* 4.—In relations: *t'ung*, to penetrate; here, to be in communication with, to be in league with.

15. *Obs.*—Smuggling: *tsou ssŭ*; the *ssŭ* is applied to any act unauthorised by law; a Chinese here understands *huo*, goods, after it, and treats *tsou*, to go, as an active verb. Compare our phrase to *run goods*.

16. *Obs.*—Authorities: *ch'ang*, an arena; *kuan ch'ang chung*, in the official arena, amongst the authorities.

19. *Obs.*—Divided: with their *t'ung shih*, fellows in the business, *chün fên*, in equal parts shared; *t'ung shih* is equally applicable to associates in a lawful undertaking, those one acts with.

21. *Obs.* 1.—Traced: *chiu*, to investigate; they carefully investigated [in such wise that there was] a water-descending-stone-appearing, a discovery of the truth. *Obs.* 2.—Heaviest: *ts'ung chung* (see *ts'ung fêng*, Dialogue V, 52). *Obs.* 3.—Fine: *fa*, properly, to punish; but, colloquially, to fine. *Obs.* 4.—Stripped: *ko* (Radical 177); *lit.*, to skin.

22. *Obs.* 1.—Father's disgrace: *tiu lien*, to lose, to throw away, face. *Obs.* 2.—To keep quiet: *chê*, to screen wholly, *yen*, to half-screen; *chê yen* may be used literally, but is oftener figurative.

23. *Obs.* 1.—Publish: *chang yang*; the first word meaning to spread wide, the second, to raise high. *Obs.* 2.—Invention: *pien*, to weave; *pien tsao*, to fabricate a story.

24. *Obs.*—Too bad: *yü*, to overpass, to exceed, *cha*, falsehood; *kuo yü*, to exceed in, *hsü cha*, what is empty and false.

PART IV.—THE TEN DIALOGUES.

25. I half mistrusted him at the time, and I resolved to ask Li Yung-ch'êng about him; I knew that he used to be very intimate with his father.

26. And his account of him was not satisfactory, I suppose?

27. Not at all. He knows Hsü Yung very well; he was weak enough to recommend him for a place once without examining him.

28. As what?

29. As an office copyist; but he didn't keep the place a month.

30. Why not? was he ill-conducted or incompetent?

31. Both; he could not write round hand at all, so he was of no use as a copyist; and they never could believe a word that he said.

32. I wonder how he contrives to dress as well as he does, with nothing to live on.

33. The coat he had on the other day was no great things, I am sure.

34. Great things or not, it was a coat that must have cost something; and so must that mule he was on.

35. I thought he came in a cart.

36. No, he rode here; on a stout mule in very good case.

37. And yet, with all you know of his dishonesty and extravagance, you seem inclined to take his part.

38. I can't help pitying people that have known better days, when I see them in extremity.

39. Pity him as much as you will; but don't ask me to get him employment, for I won't do it.

40. He'll be on the streets before long, poor fellow.

25. 概 kai⁴ 31. 靠 k'ao⁴ 35. 摸 mo¹ 36. 壯 chuang⁴ 38. 享 hsiang³
27. 舉 chü³ 35. 估 ku¹ ³ 36. 臕 piao¹ 37. 護 hu⁴ 38. 恤 hsü¹

25. *Obs.* 1.—Intimate: *shou ho*; *ho*, short for *ho p'ing*. *Obs.* 2.—Resolved: *tu-cho*. *Obs.* 3.—To ask: *ta t'ing*, to inquire.

26. *Obs.* 1.—I suppose: *ta kai*, in all probability. *Obs.* 2.—Account: *shuo*, not here to blame, but to talk of.

27. *Obs.*—Recommend: *chü*, classically, to raise; *pao chü*, to recommend, to guarantee the goodness of, a person. That man formerly besought him *kei chao*, for him to seek, something; he being in heart *juan*, soft, consented; not having examined him, *chin*, yet proceeded, to recommend him.

29. *Obs.*—Office copyist: *t'ieh hsieh*; *lit.*, to write memoranda that are *t'ieh*, appended, to the document. *See* Part III, Exercise XXXVIII, 1, Obs., for another form of the same character.

30. *Obs.*—Ill-conducted: *hsing chih*, moving and being stationary (=conduct under all conditions), not good.

31. *Obs.* 1.—Not write round hand at all: *lit.*, as to *ch'iai shu*, round hand, *so*, it was what, he could not write; the *so*, as before observed, is sometimes regarded by a Chinese, however, as intensive or emphasising, not as a relative pronoun. *Obs.* 2.—Believe: *k'ao*, to lean against, to rely upon; *kao pu chu*, not to be relied on.

32. *Obs.*—Wonder: *lit.*, that man is strange; being without money, how is it that what he wears is so respectable.

33. *Obs.*—No great things: also not anything.

35. *Obs.*—I thought: *ku¹ mo*, from *ku* (in Peking, *ku³*), to estimate, as number or value; *mo*, to feel with the fingers.

36. *Obs.*—Good case: *piao chuang*, sleek and stout; *piao* not used except of beasts.

37. *Obs.*—Take his part: *hu*, to protect.

38. *Obs.* 1.—Better days: having formerly *hsiang*, enjoyed, *fu*, happiness. *Obs.* 2.—Pitying: *lien*, to pity (*see* Dialogue IV, 70); *hsü* means the same as *lien*.

40. *Obs.* 1.—Poor fellow: *k'o-hsi-liao-'rh-ti*, one deserving of pity. *Obs.* 2.—Pitying: *yen k'an-cho*, while the eye is beholding. *Obs.* 3.—On the streets: he will, or is about to, want rice.

41. Well, when he comes to want a meal I'll give it him; but recommend him for any place I will not.

42. He was to be here the day after tomorrow.

43. Then tell him what I told you.

44. That you will have nothing to say to him, sir?

45. No; that I am gone out of town.

46. And if he asks when you are likely to be back?

47. You can't say; you don't know how long I shall be away.

48. But if he should be calling every day to find out?

49. Let him call as often as he likes, he is not to be admitted.

50. Wouldn't it be better to tell him plainly that he mustn't count on Your Excellency's support?

51. No, no; that will involve explanations into which I am still less inclined to enter with him.

52. If I don't mistake, I hear his voice in the yard.

53. Then you may just put him off in the best way you can, for see him I won't.

54. I was only joking; it's the block-cutter come for his money.

55. Let him come at the end of the month.

56. The man has been here twice already, sir.

57. So he has, and I promised to pay him; so he must be paid.

58. I'll pay him, sir; don't trouble yourself.

41. 頓 tun⁴	50. 簡 chien³	50. 倚 i³	53. 推 t'ui¹
49. 許 hsü³	50. 轉 chuan³	52. 哼 hêng¹	53. 辭 tz'ŭ²

41. *Obs.* 1.—A meal: *tun*, originally, to bow the head a time or turn; hence, one time of eating. *Obs.* 2.—Recommend: *pao*, to guarantee (see above, 27, *pao chü*).

42. *Obs.*—Was to be here: according to what was that day agreed to, you *yo*, engaged, him to come the day after to-morrow.

43. *Obs.*—What I told you: *ch'i hsien*, at the beginning.

49. *Obs.*—He is not to be: *hsü*, to permit; I do not permit him to come in.

50. *Obs.* 1.—Better: *pu ju*, nothing so good as; interrogatively, would it not be best? *Obs.* 2.—Plainly: *chien chih*, from *chien*, concise, summary, and *chih*, straight. *Obs.* 3.—Mustn't count: *lit.*, if you are *ta suan*, speculating on anything, do you *chuan*, turning round, commission someone else; *chuan*, as here, constantly used as a disjunctive; *q.d.*, so far from commissioning you, *chuan*, on the contrary, commission someone else. *Obs.* 4.—Your Excellency's support: it is of no use *i k'ao*, to lean against Your Excellency; *i* and *k'ao* are nearly identical in meaning.

51. *Obs.* 1.—No, no: note the force of *ch'io* as above. *Obs.* 2.—Explanations: *lit.*, it will be necessary to tell him minutely and plainly *so i jan ti hua*, words stating the *so i jan*, wherefore thus; the reason why.

52. *Obs.*—If I don't mistake: *hêng*, here, an interrogative word, ah? what? also, an ejaculation or grunt.

53. *Obs.* 1.—Put him off: *t'ui tz'ŭ*, to push or put forward excuses; the latter word meaning originally language. *Kao tz'ŭ*, to make one's excuses, is to take leave. As a verb, *tz'ŭ* means to decline; also, to dismiss from one's employ. *Obs.* 2.—See him I won't: *chüeh*, positively, decidedly; a strong affirmative.

54. *Obs.*—Block-cutter: *k'o*¹, to engrave; not to be confounded with the same character read *k'o*⁴ (see Part III, 223); *k'o-tzŭ chiang*, a type-cutter.

57. *Obs.*—Promised: *ying hsü*; both words in the sense of responding favourably to what is proposed, promising to perform.

58. *Obs.*—I'll pay him: *lit.*, I for you, sir, will *k'ai fa*, distributingly issue; *k'ai fa* in strictness applying to the settlement of a number of accounts.

DIALOGUE VII.

1. Was it you who were knocking at the door?
2. It was I.
3. Where are you from?
4. I am from outside the city.
5. Who are you looking for?
6. A person named MÊNG.
7. Well, that's my name.
8. Oh! you are Mr. MÊNG?
9. Yes, I am MÊNG; what do you want of me?
10. I was sent from the Kuang Wên Chai.
11. Is not the Kuang Wên Chai a bookseller's?
12. Yes, a bookseller's.
13. What book is it you were told to bring?
14. I have not brought any book.
15. What, isn't that a book you have in your hand?
16. No; it's a book cover, not a book.
17. If you have no books, why bring an empty book cover?
18. The book cover is not empty.
19. If it isn't, what has it got inside?
20. A few drawings.
21. Drawings! you've come to the wrong house, I suspect.
22. No, it's all right; I was to bring them here.
23. How so? I've bought no drawings.
24. No; I know that it was not you who bought them.
25. Well, then, why bring them to me?
26. Someone bought them for your house.
27. What could anyone have meant by buying drawings for me?
28. Oh, sir, you needn't ask what his motive was.
29. Well, but who was it that bought them for me?
30. Do you know Mr. CHANG who lives in the T'ang-tzŭ Hu-t'ung?
31. I do know him; and it was he, was it?
32. No, it was not he.
33. Not he! then why mention him?
34. I have a reason for mentioning him.
35. If you have, why don't you state it?
36. You're in a great hurry, sir; you will understand more about it presently.
37. Come, I won't stand this; you're quizzing me.
38. Quizzing! I shouldn't think of such a thing.
39. But why not speak, if you have got anything serious to say?

6. 孟 *mêng*⁴   10. 齋 *chai*¹   37. 戲 *hsi*⁴

1. *Obs.*—Knocking: *lit.*, calling, *sc.*, someone to come out.
6. *Obs.*—MÊNG: a family name; the surname of the philosopher known to us as Mencius.
10. *Obs.*—Kuang Wên Chai: *chai*, properly, a swallow's nest; a pavilion in which to repose; elegantly used of certain shops (*see* below, Part V, Lesson LXXX, 2).
16. *Obs.*—Book cover: *t'ao* (*see* Part III, **769**); here, the cover of pasteboard and cloth in which Chinese volumes are wrapped.
30. *Obs.*—T'ang-tzŭ Hu-t'ung: *see* Part III, **797**; *t'ang*, properly, a hall; *t'ang-tzŭ* may also mean a bathing establishment, but is specially the name of the chapel in which the Emperor sacrifices to his ancestors.
36. *Obs.*—Presently: *hui lai*, in a turn of time; not, when you return.
37. *Obs.*—Quizzing: *hsi*, to play, dramatically or otherwise; this is *shua hsi*, joking language; I *pu i*, will not submit to it (*see* Part III, **913**).
39. *Obs.*—Serious: *chêng ching*, *lit.*, upright and straight; often used as we vulgarly use the word regular; here, the opposite of *shua hsi*, fun.

40. It's a long story to tell.
41. Well, if you can't tell it me, I'll go in; be off with you!
42. Stop, stop! don't be in such a hurry; I've got something more to say.
43. Be quick about it then; I've no time to waste.
44. You say you know Mr. CHANG, sir?
45. Yes, I told you so before.
46. Do you know his nephew, sir?
47. Not well; I've seen him once.
48. Well, it is he that ordered these drawings to be sent to you.
49. He ordered them? When did he return?
50. Return? has he been absent?
51. Wasn't he away with some officer?
52. I don't know; what year was it?
53. I recollect his going to Kiangsi the year before last.
54. Indeed! I've seen him in Peking ever since last year.
55. Never mind; what did he send me the drawings for?
56. It was not for you that he bought them.
57. Then what have you brought them here for? I am not going to buy them, I can assure you.
58. Buy them! no; he has paid for them.
59. Well, I do not understand one word of all these contradictions.

60. But you will if you let me say a few words more.
61. Quick, then; don't keep me here all day.
62. Isn't your son employed in the Board of Revenue?
63. You do nothing but ask questions; my son *is* under the Board of Revenue.
64. He doesn't live with you, does he?
65. He has a separate establishment at present.
66. May I ask where his house is?
67. He lives at the west end of Chiao Min Hsiang, on the north side of the way.
68. Lives in Chiao Min Hsiang?
69. To be sure he does; what makes you doubt it?
70. I thought he lived in the Chinese town.
71. What, all that way from the Board's office? that would never do; what made you think he lived in the Chinese town?
72. I met his cart yesterday at sunset in the Liu-li Ch'ang.
73. How could that be? he was here with me last night.
74. The cart was his, but he wasn't in it.
75. How did you know, then, that the cart was his?
76. An old woman in the cart said that it was Mr. MÊNG's cart.

46. 姪 *chih²* 65. 搬 *pan¹* 72. 琉 *liu²* 72. 廠 *ch'ang³* 76. 婆 *p'o²*

46. *Obs.*—Nephew: *chih*, the son of a brother, not of a sister.
61. *Obs.*—All day: *chin-cho*, completely, utterly.
62. *Obs.* 1.—Your son: see *shao*, Part III, 815; his junior worship. *Obs.* 2.—Board of Revenue: Hu Pu; *lit.*, the Department of the Population = of the Census.
64. *Obs.*—Does not live with you: *tan chu*, to live alone, apart from parents or brothers.
65. *Obs.*—Separate establishment: *pan*, to remove from one place to another; not used of small things; specially used of a change of residence; he at this time has in singleness removed [his establishment] out, *sc.*, of his father's house.
72. *Obs.* 1.—Sunset: *jih-t'ou lao*. *Obs.* 2.—Liu-li Ch'ang: *lit.*, glassware manufactory; the name of a street in the outer, or Chinese, city. *Liu*, glassware; *li*, as in *po-li*; *ch'ang*, properly, a large booth.
76. *Obs.*—Old woman: *p'o*, any married woman.

PART IV.—THE TEN DIALOGUES.

77. An old woman with a child in her arms?

78. Exactly; a child some seven or eight years old.

79. Dear me! it must have been my grandson; where could he have been going so late?

80. Don't be alarmed, sir; they had met with a little accident.

81. What was it, pray? had the mule taken fright?

82. No; the fact is that the roads were in a bad state.

83. Oh! and the cart had been upset?

84. No, not that either; it and another cart had run against each other.

85. Well, and were they still discussing the collision at that hour?

86. It wasn't that any discussion they might have had wasn't over.

87. Then the little boy was hurt?

88. Not severely; he jumped out of the cart, and in jumping out he sprained his leg.

89. Confound that other cart! do you know whose it was?

90. It belonged to Mr. CHANG'S nephew.

91. Mr. CHANG'S nephew! and the drawings that he has sent——?

92. Are for your grandson, sir.

93. But why should he buy drawings, of all things in the world, to pacify the child?

94. He had bought the drawings; he didn't buy them on purpose for the child.

95. And he had them with him in his hand, I suppose, when the carts came into collision?

96. Yes, he had; he had just bought them at our shop.

97. And did the child ask him for them?

98. No; your grandson cried, and he said, "Don't cry, and I'll send you something to play with."

99. Oh! and these drawings are for him to play with; but why didn't you take them to my son's house instead of bringing them here?

100. Mr. CHANG'S nephew came to our shop this morning to find out where your son lived, sir. We said we couldn't say, but that we knew your house; and then he told us to bring the drawings here; he'll call himself in a day or two.

83. 翻 *fan*^{1} 93. 壓 *ya*^{1} 98. 哭 *k'u*^{1} 100. 府 *fu*^{3}
88. 扭 *niu*^{3} 94. 並 *ping*^{4} 100. 郎 *lang*^{2}

79. *Obs.*—So late: *na tsao wan*=such a time of day.

83. *Obs.*—Upset: *fan*; originally, flight or other movement backwards and forwards.

84. *Obs.*—Run against each other: the cart had with a *tui-t'ou-'rh ch'ê*, an opposing cart, made collision.

85. *Obs.*—Still discussing: *lit.*, the collision having taken place, had they *lao*, in so long a time, not *shuo k'ai*, talked it out, thoroughly explained it.

88. *Obs.*—Sprained: *niu*, to twist; here, twisted, or sprained, the leg.

93. *Obs.*—To pacify: *ya*, properly, to press down, to suppress; *ching*, fright.

94. *Obs.*—*Ping* is a copulative particle meaning with; also; moreover; when followed by a negative it intensifies the negation.

98. *Obs.*—Cried: *k'u*, to cry, as a human being.

100. *Obs.* 1.—Your son: *lang*, properly, a male, a man; *ling lung*, your son's, *chu ch'u*, abiding place. *Obs.* 2.—The word *sir* is introduced here in the translation to give the force of *ling*, honoured. *Obs.* 3.—Here: *fu*, properly, a treasury, a palace; politely, *fu shang*, your residence; the *shang* also indicating the superiority of the person addressed. *Obs.* 4.—Himself: *ch'in tzŭ*, his own self.

DIALOGUE VIII.

1. Your servant, sir.
2. How do you do? Who are you?
3. I have been sent by the Ying Shun Hong to show you the way to Peking, sir. When do you propose going, sir?
4. I want to be off to-morrow.
5. Do you intend to go by land or by water, sir?
6. Which is the better way?
7. I should say by land; the river will be so high with the heavy rains we have had these last few days that it will be hard work tracking the boat up stream, and if you were to come in for a northerly wind, I don't think you could fetch T'ung Chou in five or six days.
8. Dear me! it won't do to go by water, then. How about going by land?
9. If you were off to-morrow morning, sir, and pushed on, you ought to be at Peking by the following evening; if you took your time, you would be well able to reach it on the third day.
10. Do you know the land road well?
11. Know it well? I should think I did; I've been travelling it back and forward for these ten years and more.

12. Then can you tell me enough about it to enable me to dispense with a guide, supposing I don't take one?
13. Yes; there is no difficulty about that. Do you know the floating bridge to the east as you leave this city, sir?
14. Yes, I know the bridge.
15. When you are on the other side of it, sir, you will be in a street where there is a good deal going on; you must inquire there for another bridge, and when you are across the second bridge, you will be in a road going north-west, which is the high road to Peking.
16. I have heard that one has to cross a river somewhere; is there one?
17. You mean the ferry, I suppose. There is a ferry.
18. There is a ferry! and how do the carts and horses manage?
19. There is no trouble with them; they can be ferried over.
20. Well, and after the ferry, what then?
21. When you leave the ferry station, you keep along the high road for thirty odd *li* from Tientsin, when you come to a market town called P'u-k'ou; that is the first stage.

3. 英 *ying*¹   9. 州 *chou*¹   17. 渡 *tu*⁴   21. 叚 *tuan*⁴
5. 旱 *han*⁴   17. 擺 *pai*³   21. 浦 *p'u*³

3. *Obs.*—Ying Shun Hong: *ying*, properly, bursting into flower; hence, gallant, heroic; *shun*, obedient, that flows without check. *Ying shun* might translate as the Prosperous; the hong, mercantile firm, whose sign is Prosperity. *Ying* is the character employed to denote England, commonly called *ying kuo*.
5. *Obs.*—By land: *han*, dry.
7. *Obs.*—T'ung Chou: *chou*, one of the minor jurisdictions into which a *fu*, prefecture, is ordinarily divided. See *hsien*, Dialogue IX, 47.
9. *Obs.*—Were off: *tung shên*, to move the person; specially, to start on a journey.
13. *Obs.*—Floating bridge: *fou ch'iao* or *fu ch'iao*.
15. *Obs.*—Good deal going on: *jê nao chieh-'rh*, a bustling street.
17. *Obs.*—Ferry: *pai-tu*; from *pai*, to shake, as the ferryman must the boat, and *tu*, to cross water.
21. *Obs.* 1.—Ferry station: *k'ou*, the mouth; on the sea-coast, a port; here, specially, of the hollow in the banks where they are touched by the ferry boat going and returning. *Obs.* 2.—P'u-k'ou: *p'u*³, a bend in the bank of a river; here read *p'u*². *Obs.* 3.—Stage: *tuan*; properly, a piece, a section.

PART IV.—THE TEN DIALOGUES. 239

22. What, isn't the first stage Ho-si Wu?

23. No, sir; Ho-si Wu is a long way on; it's the end of the first day's journey. When you have passed through P'u-k'ou, you come next to Yang Ts'un, and after that to Nan-ts'ai Ts'un, and you may then reach Ho-si Wu towards nightfall. These places are all something over thirty *li* from each other.

24. And how much of the road to Peking are you supposed to have done when you get to Ho-si Wu?

25. It's about half way. You spend the night there, and you may be in Peking next day.

26. And where does one pass the night?

27. Some of your countrymen stop at the inns, sir; some in the temples.

28. Which are the better, the inns or the temples?

29. I think the inns more convenient myself. At the temples strangers are taken in only now and then, and it is not certain, in the first place, whether there is accommodation to be had in them or not; then, if there is a large number of carters, the priests do not like it; and, besides, if anything is missing there is no one to make responsible.

30. Ah! then the innkeeper has to look to it if things are lost at an inn, has he?

31. Yes, sir; that's the way of it. And there is another consideration, the inns can get you what you want to eat or drink; in the temples there is not even a kitchen.

32. No kitchen! then where do the people cook?

33. The people in the temples cook nothing but maigre; they may not cook meat.

34. Humph! one will be best off in an inn then. Which is the best inn in Ho-si Wu?

35. There is the Fu Hsing and the Shun Lai, both of them large inns; one stands at the south end of the street, and the other at the north.

36. And which will it suit me best to go to?

37. It must be for you to decide, sir, whether it suits you best to stop at a south end inn or an inn at the north end; the fare and accommodation are pretty much the same at both.

38. What does it signify whether I stop at the inns north or the inns south? are they a great way apart?

39. No great way apart; Ho-si Wu is not a large place like our city here; it is only a market town, one long street with some shops and so forth on either side of it.

23. 楊 *yang²*   23. 隔 *ko²*   33. 葷 *hun¹*   35. 興 *hsing¹*
23. 蔡 *ts'ai⁴*   29. 格 *ko²*   35. 富 *fu⁴*   39. 鎮 *chên⁴*

23. *Obs.* 1.—Yang Ts'un: *lit.*, the village of the family of Yang. *Obs.* 2.—Nan Ts'ai Ts'un: the southern village of the family of Ts'ai. *Obs.* 3.—From each other: *hsiang kê*, or *ko*, mutually separated.

24. *Obs.*—Much of the road: *lit.*, speaking according to, with reference to, the length of the road.

25. *Obs.*—About half way: *lit.*, it may be reckoned to be *chung chien*, in the middle.

29. *Obs.*—Now and then: *kê*, or *ko*, from various other meanings comes to signify a bound or rule; *ko wai*, beyond rule; in the temples *liu k'o*, the keeping strangers, is an extraordinary thing, a thing not usual.

33. *Obs.*—Maigre: *su* (*see* Part III, 707), but here used of food which is not meat; *hun*, properly, that which has a relish, but simply meat or fish when opposed to *su*, maigre.

35. *Obs.* 1.—Fu Hsing: *fu*, rich; *fu hsing*, wealth and prosperity; say, the sign of the Well-to-do. *Obs.* 2.—Shun Lai: the inn to which guests come *shun*, in an uninterrupted stream; say, the Ever-going.

37. *Obs.*—Fare: *ch'ih shih.*

39. *Obs.* 1.—Market town: *chên*, properly, to control; amongst other meanings it has that of a town, less in importance than a district city. *Obs.* 2.—Some shops: *p'u-tzŭ*, shops, *shên-mo ti*, and anything you like.

40. Very well; then what difference is there between the north end and the south?

41. There is no difference; but the gentlemen I have shown the road to have in most instances put up at the inn nearest at hand after they had got into the town

42. You mean, put up at the south end if they were going from Tientsin, and at the north coming from Peking, don't you?

43. Exactly so, sir.

44. All right. Now, when I get to my inn, what had I best tell them to get ready for me?

45. I don't suppose you have tried our Chinese fare, have you, sir?

46. No, I have not.

47. Well, if you have not, sir, you had best have something that will carry got ready at Tientsin, and take it with you.

48. Take it with me! but if I don't feed at the inn, they won't like it, will they?

49. It doesn't signify; the inn people will charge you for your accommodation.

50. Is there any fixed sum that one pays for one's lodging?

51. We pay much the same under any circumstances, but the man in charge will probably make a foreign traveller pay a little more than we do.

52. Is the man in charge the proprietor of the inn?

53. There is no rule; in some cases the proprietor takes charge himself, sometimes he engages a man in charge to look after the business for him.

54. I understand. And how much is it likely that I shall be asked to pay for my lodging?

55. I can hardly tell, but you speak Chinese, sir, and so you can have a talk with them about that before you take your rooms; if their charge is too high, there's no harm in objecting to it and offering something less.

56. Yes, that will do very well. Now, to get to Peking next day, which way am I to go?

57. After leaving Ho-si Wu in the morning, you still keep north-west, and, at twenty odd *li* on, you come to An-p'ing, and at some twenty *li* more, to Ma-t'ou; and then, twenty *li* from Ma-t'ou, you come to the old walled town of Chang-chia Wan.

58. Isn't there a small stream somewhere before you reach Chang-chia Wan?

59. No, sir; the town is on the river, part north of it, and part south. You will go in at the south gate, up the main street. across the river, and out by the north gate. Outside the gate there is a forked road; the road north takes you to T'ung Chou; the other, which bears west, takes you to Peking.

60. How far is it from that to Peking?

61. That depends on the gate you go in by, sir. If you stop at an inn in the Chinese city, you will go in by the Sha-wo Gate, and that is some fifty *li* from Chang-chia Wan; if you are going into the city by the East Wicket, you must keep north two or three *li*; no great distance farther.

55. 妨 *fang*¹

55. 駁 *po*²

41. *Obs.*—Nearest at hand: *i chin chieh*, once they entered the street.

47. *Obs.*—With you: *pu ju*, there is nothing so good as that, *ts'ung*, at, Tientsin [the place *from* which you are moving], you should *tso*, having prepared, a little good-to-carry victuals, *tai-cho*, carry them with you.

55. *Obs.* 1.—No harm: *pu fang*, no hurt, no objection. *Obs.* 2.—Objecting: *po*, properly, to turn sharp round; to contradict.

59. *Obs.* 1.—On the river: *ch'i-cho*, bestriding the river face. *Obs.* 2.—Forked road: two *ku*, *lit.*, limbs, of a diverging road. *Obs.* 3.—Bears west: *p'ien*, swerving from a right line, leaning off the perpendicular, which in this case is north.

60. *Obs.*—From that: *chieh* is here used in the same sense as *ta*, from.

PART IV.—THE TEN DIALOGUES.   241

62. Which gate should one go in by to get to the Foreign Legations?

63. They are all inside the Ha-ta Gate, in the neighbourhood of the Imperial Canal Bridge; I should say the best way would be by the East Wicket.

64. Very good; I understand perfectly. There is another question I want to ask, if I am to go so fast, what am I to do with my baggage?

65. How much baggage have you, sir?

66. Those things lying outside the door.

67. What, are all those large cases yours too, sir?

68. To be sure they are.

69. If you intend to be in Peking in two days, I am afraid you must leave some of the baggage behind, sir; you would have to pay a good deal for the hire of so many large carts, and, not only that, it would be impossible for you to go any pace.

70. Well, then, what do you recommend me to do?

71. I think, sir, you might hire a small cart to carry your bedding and all that sort of thing with you, and ship the rest of the baggage by T'ung Chou.

72. In that case do I ride in the cart with the baggage I take with me?

73. Better hire another small cart to ride in, sir; don't you think so?

74. Will they be carts with one beast or two?

75. If you want to get on, sir, you must have two beasts; indeed, you might well have three, for there will be a good deal of water on the roads after the rain, and they will be heavy.

76. Ah! but if the roads are so heavy I don't much fancy riding in a cart; can I hire a horse here?

77. Yes, sir, or a mule; but I am afraid our saddles will not do for you.

78. I've got English saddlery and all that sort of thing with me.

79. I don't think that will do all the same; the saddle might be put on one of our horses, but I don't think he would stand the $chiao^2$-mao^4-$tzŭ$.

80. What is the $chiao$-mao-$tzŭ$ (headpiece)?

81. It is the gear on a horse's head for attaching the bit and reins to. What I am afraid of is that as the horse is not used to carrying the like he might be restive. I should say you would do better to buy a foreign horse.

63. 岱 tai^4 69. 恐 $k\text{'}ung^3$ 79. 嚼 $chiao^2$ 81. 慣 $kuan^4$
63. 御 $yü^4$ 77. 鞍 an^1 81. 扯 $ch\text{'}ê^3$

63. *Obs.* 1.—Ha-ta Gate: properly, Hai Tai; the name given the gate by the late dynasty; tai, classically, a hill. *Obs.* 2.—Imperial Canal Bridge: $yü$, properly, to drive a chariot; when prefixed to certain words, imperial.

69. *Obs.*—Afraid: $k\text{'}ung$, the same in meaning as $p\text{'}a$, with which it is joined.

73. *Obs.*—Small cart: $chiao$ $ch\text{'}ê$, a passenger cart; with a top, as opposed to ta $ch\text{'}ê$, or $ch\text{'}ang^3$ $ch\text{'}ê$, a large or open cart (*see* Dialogue VII, 72); $hsiao$ $ch\text{'}ê$, also a passenger cart; $hsiao$ $ch\text{'}ê$-$tzŭ$, a wheel-barrow.

77. *Obs.* 1.—Afraid: $chih$ $p\text{'}a$, I only fear. *Obs.* 2.—Saddles: an.

79. *Obs.* 1.—Be put on: *lit.*, our horses hai, after all, can pei, take on the back. *Obs.* 2.—Chiao: properly, to bite, whether of man or beast; here, short for $chiao$-$tzŭ$, a bit (*see* 81).

81. *Obs.* 1.—Reins: $ch\text{'}ê$, to draw; $ch\text{'}ê^2$ $shou$, the bridle used by a rider. *Obs.* 2.—Not used: $kuan$, accustomed to. *Obs.* 3.—Restive: nao $hsing$-$tzŭ$, to let his temper break out, to give way to temper.

82. But how am I to buy a foreign horse here at Tientsin?

83. There's a horse in our hong that one of the gentlemen wants to sell; he is a very good horse, quiet and fast, and he has been to Peking and back three or four times.

84. Good; I'll go to the hong and have a talk about it. And now, when these boxes go up to T'ung Chou, whom can I hire to go with them to Peking?

85. Would it do to hire me, sir?

86. It would do very well, but I doubt whether the house will let you go; I don't think they could spare you for so many days.

87. They can spare me, sir; what did they send me here to-day for but to take your orders?

83. 夥 *huo*³   87. 吩 *fên*¹   87. 附 *fu*⁴

83. *Obs.* 1.—Gentlemen: *huo*, originally, a number of persons or things; thence, the same with, associated with; *huo chi*, one who is associated with one in a place, sometimes as a partner, but more generally as a paid *employé*. *Obs.* 2.—Quiet: *lao-shih*, honest; hence, simple; when applied to animals, inoffensive.

86. *Obs.*—Let you go: *jung*², the same character as that read *yung* in Part III, 963, but here meaning to allow, to tolerate; I fear [the people] in your *hong li pu k'ai*, unable to separate from you, will not let you go.

87. *Obs.*—Orders: *fên fu*, to give orders to; the combination is not well explained by the dictionaries. By some teachers the two words are said to mean no more than they would without the Radical *k'ou*, namely, to allot to different persons their several functions.

DIALOGUE IX.

1. [*Servant.*] There's a teacher who wishes to see you, sir.

2. [*Master.*] Ask him to walk in.

3. The teacher, sir.

4. [*Master, to the Teacher.*] Take a seat, please.

5. [*Teacher.*] Thank you, sir; pray be seated.

6. May I ask your name, sir?

7. My name is Su.

8. And your business with me is———?

9. I heard that you wanted to engage a teacher, sir; a friend of mine mentioned it yesterday.

10. Ah! it must have been CHANG *hsien-shêng* who was speaking of it.

11. It was CHANG *hsien-shêng*.

12. Did he tell you that I was looking out for a teacher for myself or for someone else?

13. He did not specify whether it was for yourself or not, sir; is it not for yourself?

14. It is not; I do not want a teacher myself, but a friend of mine has commissioned me to engage one for him.

15. Is your friend a countryman of your own, sir?

16. He is; he has not been in China long.

7. 蘇 *su*¹   9. 閣 *ko*²

7. *Obs.*—Su: *su*, properly, reviving; here, a surname.

9. *Obs.*—Sir: *ko*, properly, an upper story; *ko-hsia* in ancient times applied only to certain ministers; now, as used in the text, sir.

13. *Obs.*—Specify: he did not tell me *hsiang hsi*, explicitly.

PART IV.—THE TEN DIALOGUES.   243

17. Then he does not understand Chinese, I suppose?

18. He does not speak a word of Chinese, nor does he know a character.

19. How am I to read with him then?

20. You will have to teach him to talk first. When he begins to speak, we shall see what can be done in the written language.

21. But how am I to begin if he doesn't know a character?

22. Oh, sir, a teacher of your experience, who has had so many pupils among your own countrymen, will not find it impossible to teach him, surely?

23 Teaching as we are taught is another affair. We become able to speak Chinese without learning it, and we acquire the written language by learning books off by heart when we are very young; but I don't think it likely that your friend will put himself to the trouble of keeping to the same order of proceeding as our Chinese boys.

24. That of course not; still we may hit upon something. How old were you when you began to read, may I ask?

25. I began at seven.

26. Did you begin with the Three-character Classic and the Poem in a Thousand Characters?

27. Yes; they were my first studies.

28. The Chinese all begin with those little books; what is the real advantage of their so doing?

29. The Three-character Classic is in sentences of three characters each, and this makes it easy for little children to commit it to memory; the Poem in a Thousand Characters has no character twice repeated, and therefore, when they have learned this, they know a thousand characters.

30. And what do they learn after these?

31. As a rule, the Four Books, and, after these, the Five Canons.

32. How many years did it take you, sir, to learn them all, from the time you began the Four Books until you knew the Five Canons?

33. Some six or seven years from the beginning of the course to the end of it.

34. Ah! then by the time you had learned the Five Canons you were fourteen?

35. Yes, in my fourteenth year.

36. And how old were you when you began to have them explained to you?

37. I was twelve years of age.

38. Did you study the commentary, or did you have the text explained to you orally by your teacher?

18. 漢 han⁴   36. 講 chiang³   38. 註 chu⁴

18. *Obs.*—Chinese: *han*, the name of the dynasty which commenced about B.C. 200; now applied generally to all men and things Chinese.

19. *Obs.*—Read with: *chiao kei*; the *kei* being untranslatable in English; grammatically, we should say that it puts *t'a* in the dative case.

22. *Obs.* 1.—Experience: *lao shou*, an old hand. *Obs.* 2.—Pupils: *mên-shêng*; the word *shêng* being construed as man; those who come to the *mên*, gate or door, of the *hsien-shêng*, teacher.

23. *Obs.* 1.—Without learning: *êrh*, and yet; we do not learn, and yet we are able. *Obs.* 2.—Learn by heart: *pei nien*, *lit.*, backing recite; *pei*, short for *pei-cho shu*, with one's back to the book, *i.e.*, without looking at it.

29. *Obs.*—Twice repeated: *ch'ung²* (*see* Part III, **336**).

31. *Obs.*—Five Canons: *ching* (*see* Part III, **885**); here specially of the five great classical books of China.

36. *Obs.*—Explained: *chiang*, properly, to tell; specially, to explain the meaning of a character or a text; *k'ai chiang*, to begin explaining.

38. *Obs.*—Commentary: *chu*, properly, to make a note of; thence, to annotate.

39. At first, by my teacher; but after listening to his explanations a year or so, I began to read the commentary myself. Then I worked at prose and verse composition some two years or more, and then I graduated.

40. At sixteen! that was early; you must be a first-rate man.

41. Nothing of the kind, indeed; it was all luck. I had to stand several examinations for my licentiate's degree, and I didn't get it for seven or eight years after.

42. May I ask your age?

43. I am thirty.

44. And what has been your occupation in the six years since you took your licentiate's degree?

45. I have been doing nothing to speak of; I took pupils at home for the first two years, and for some time after that I acted as private secretary to a friend.

46. What office did your friend hold?

47. He was magistrate of a district in Shantung; he died last year, and I came home again.

48. Your having acted as a private secretary is an additional recommendation.

49. How an additional recommendation?

50. In this respect: my friend, who wishes to engage you, will want to study official correspondence when he has learned the spoken language.

51. It's a pity that one can't see one's way to beginning the spoken language.

52. I have a plan, but I am too busy to-day to explain it; could you come and see me to-morrow and talk it over with me?

53. By all means; I'll wait on you to-morrow as you desire, sir; at what o'clock?

54. Shall we say between three and four?

55. Very good, sir; then I take my leave.

56. Good-day.

57. Good-day.

39. 詩 shih¹	41. 黴 chiao³	42. 庚 kêng¹	51. 緒 hsü⁴
40. 中 chung⁴	41. 倖 hsing⁴	46. 榮 jung²	53. 遵 tsun¹
40. 秀 hsiu⁴	41. 試 shih⁴	47. 縣 hsien⁴	54. 申 shên¹

39. Obs. 1.—Prose composition: wên chang; lit., forms of literature, literature which conforms to the rules of composition; shih, poetry, is not included in the term. Obs. 2.—Graduated: chin hsio, to enter hsio, the colleges, or literary establishments, of which the graduates who have taken the first degree are members.

40. Obs. 1.—Early: what, at sixteen, chung⁴ (not to be confounded with the same character read chung¹), you obtained the degree of hsiu ts'ai, fine talent, your B.A. Obs. 2.—Chung⁴: properly, to hit a mark; hsiu, fair, elegant. Obs. 3.—First-rate man: your t'ien fên, share of ability assigned you by Heaven, is kao, of high degree.

41. Obs. 1.—All luck: chiao, amongst many meanings, has that of a byway; hsing, properly, fortunate; chiao hsing, generally, of success beyond merit. Obs. 2.—Licentiate: hsiang shih, lit., village trial; an allusion to ancient competitive examination in one's native district, but now technically signifying the examination for the second degree held in the capital of the province.

42. Obs.—Your age: kêng, one of the characters used in the Chinese time cycle; colloquially, as here, the years of one's age.

46. Obs.—What office: jung, properly, of vegetation, flourishing; used as here, complimentarily; jung jên, your post.

47. Obs.—District: hsien, one of the minor jurisdictions into which a prefecture is divided; somewhat less important than a chou; the magistrate governing it is called a chih-hsien, as in the chou, a chih-chou.

50. Obs.—Correspondence: wên-shu, generic of all official documents.

51. Obs.—See one's way: hsü, a skein of silk; t'ou hsü, the clue to unravel a skein.

53. Obs.—As you desire: tsun, to obey; I will just obey your commands.

54. Obs.—Three and four: shên, the ninth of the 12 two-hour periods into which the 24 hours are divided; it extends from 3 to 5 P.M.; shên ch'u, the first part of the period shên.

55. Obs.—Take leave: shih (see Part III, 574), to lose, to deprive oneself of [the pleasure of] p'ei, bearing you company.

PART IV.—THE TEN DIALOGUES.   245

DIALOGUE X.

1. This morning a friend of mine sent me an invitation to dinner at a restaurant; I am in two minds about going, because it seems to me that as I am not very well up in any of your forms of social etiquette, I should raise a laugh at my expense if I were to omit any of the usual formalities.

2. Don't imagine that; when I have told you what the ordinary formalities are, you will understand what to do. Let me have a look at your invitation. Oh! I see; its CHANG ta lao-yeh, who asks you to dine at the Ch'ing Hui T'ang; that's a capital restaurant; it is roomy, and the apartments are very cool; I often go there myself. They are very particular there about the cooking, and everything is palatable; there is no establishment that comes up to it; you'd better go; you'll be glad to have a chat with them all, and wake yourself up a bit.

3. I have heard that the time stated on Chinese invitations cannot be considered absolute; for instance, when noon is the hour given, one should go at about 2 P.M. to be in order.

4. That depends on how the invitation is worded; if the character *chun*³ (precisely) occurs, one must go at the hour named. The character *chun* does not occur in CHANG ta lao-yeh's invitation, which names four o'clock simply, so if you go at six you won't be late. If you go too early, not only will the other guests not have all assembled, but it may chance even that your host has not arrived.

1. 莊 *chuang*¹	1. 豫 *yü*⁴	1. 禮 *li*³	2. 究 *chiu*⁴	3. 未 *wei*⁴
1. 猶 *yu*²	1. 酬 *ch'ou*²	1. 倘 *t'ang*³	2. 味 *wei*⁴	

1. *Obs.* 1.—Invitation: *t'ie-'rh*, a slip of paper in the form of a memorandum; anything extending over one sheet is not generally included in the term (see Part III, 1022). Cf. *shuo t'ie-'rh*, a memorandum generally; *ch'ing t'ie-'rh*, an invitation. *Obs.* 2.—Restaurant: *chuang*, *lit.*, a large place of business, also a village, is only applied in this connexion to a restaurant which does not supply lodging accommodation. *Obs.* 3.—In two minds: *yu yü*, or *yu yi*⁴, indecision; *yu*, *lit.*, a monkey; *yü*, an elephant; both supposed to be suspicious animals, and hence typical of doubt or indecision. *Obs.* 4.—Etiquette: *ying ch'ou ti li chieh*, *lit.*, the items (*chieh*) of *li*, observances (ritual or ceremonial), belonging to (*ti*) *ying ch'ou*, social requirements; *ying* and *ch'ou* both mean to return, as a compliment, though the latter in certain combinations means also to recompense. *Ying ch'ou* is applied only to the amenities of society; we can say *t'a ti ying ch'ou ta*, or *to*, his social duties are numerous, or he has a large circle of friends. *Obs.* 5.—If: *t'ang*; seldom used without *jo* in conversation. *Obs.* 6.—Omit: *la* (see Part III, 763). *Obs.* 7.—Formalities, observances: *kuo chieh*; *chieh* (short for *li chieh*, as above), the formalities, *kuo*, that pass.

2. *Obs.* 1.—Ordinary formalities: *su t'ao-tzŭ*, *lit.*, common casing, suit, or set; *t'ao*, an envelope or casing (see Part III, 769), is here, as in the phrase *i t'ao i-shang*, a suit of clothes, a numerative of some such word as ceremony, form, etc., understood, of which it takes the place; hence, the affix *tzŭ*. *See* observations on the numeratives, Part III, 8. *Obs.* 2.—Ch'ing Hui T'ang: this might be rendered the Hall of Happy Meetings; for *ch'ing*, see Dialogue IV, 23. *Obs.* 3.—Particular: *chiang chiu*, *lit.*, in the dishes they prepare they very much explain and inquire; they give particular directions [as to how the food should be cooked], and inform themselves [as to the manner in which these directions are carried out]; *chiu*, to inquire into, to examine; it will be found later in another combination. *Obs.* 4.—Palatable: *tê*, to obtain (=have), *wei-'rh* (pronounce *wê-'rh*⁴), a flavour; *wei*, taste, flavour, smell; *wê-'rh* may be used indiscriminately of either. *Obs.* 5.—Glad to: *lo tê*² (emphasise *tê*), *lit.*, gladly obtain: it is slightly intensive, only too glad. *Obs.* 6.—Wake yourself up: see Part III, 989.

3. *Obs.* 1.—Absolute: *ch'êng* has here no special force, *chun* being the important word, and therefore emphasised. *Obs.* 2.—Noon: *wu k'ê*, one of the eight *k'ê*, or divisions, in the *shih ch'ên*, or hour period, *wu* (see Part III, 225), which lasts from 11 A.M. to 1 P.M.; *wu k'ê* is indefinite, and may mean any quarter between 11 and 1. To make it precise, additional characters would be required; thus, *wu ch'u* (see Dialogue IX, 54) *êrh k'ê* would be the second division in the *ch'u*, or commencing half, of the *wu* period; in other words, half-past 11. *Wei* is the next period to *wu*.

5. There is another point upon which I want the benefit of your advice: if I accept his hospitality, it seems to me that I ought to send him an answer.

6. There is no occasion; your retention of the invitation is a proof of your positive intention to go.

7. When I go I shall have to give up the invitation, sha'n't I?

8. Yes; the custom is this. When you go, you should, on arrival at the door of the restaurant, tell your servant to hand in your card. The people in attendance at the door will take your card, and, showing you the way in, will invite you to enter whatever room the host may be in. When you see your host, I need not remind you that you should in the first place salute him, after which you should take the letter of invitation and present it to him with both hands, saying as you do so, "Here I am bothering you again; I am as ashamed of myself as I can be; I am not worthy of the terms you have applied to me in your invitation." The host, as he takes the invitation from you, will also make some depreciatory remark about himself, and everybody will then sit down and take tea. When all the guests have arrived, you will be invited to take your places, and dinner will be put on the table.

9. It sometimes happens that all the guests cannot come; and if only one is wanting, you do not keep on waiting for him. When he does turn up, he is invited to take the vacant seat. The seats that the different guests shall take have all been determined beforehand by the host, so when you come to table, although you are bound to protest, he is certain not to allow you to sit as you please. A vacant seat is thus reserved for a guest who comes late, and when he does arrive he can sit down without much formality.

[*The guest is now supposed to have met his host, and made his bow and speech.*]

10. [*Host.*] Here you are, sir! I have been remiss in not going to meet you; pray forgive me.

| 5. 領 *ling*¹ | 6. 據 *chü*⁴ | 8. 矩 *chü*⁴ | 8. 揖 *i*¹ | 8. 謙 *ch'ien*¹ |
| 5. 乎 *hu* | 7. 繳 *chiao*³ | 8. 遞 *ti*⁴ | 8. 擾 *jao*³ | |

5. *Obs.* 1.—Accept his hospitality: *ling*, here, to receive, to accept; if I receive his *ch'ing*, politenesses (tokens of friendly sentiment). *Ling* can also be applied to the drawing of pay, etc.; it further means the neck; hence, *ling-tzŭ*, a collar. See also Dialogue I, 2. *Obs.* 2.—It seems to me: *hu* is here a particle implying doubt; for *ssŭ*, see Part III, 1070.

6. *Obs.*—Proof: *p'ing*, to lean upon (see Part III, 722); *chü*, to lay hold of, the something reliable that one lays hold of; hence, proof, evidence.

7. *Obs.*—*Chiao*, to deliver up, to surrender.

8. *Obs.* 1.—Custom: *kuei* (see Part III, 581), *lit.*, a pair of compasses, a rule, custom; *chü*⁴, a carpenter's square; hence also, a rule or custom; the two are never used apart in the above sense. *Obs.* 2.—When you go: *ming-'rh* is often used indefinitely of some future date not very far remote. *Obs.* 3.—*Ti*, to hand in or over to; for *jang*, to invite, see Dialogue IV, 25. *Obs.* 4.—Salute: *tso i*, to make the Chinese bow with the hands folded. *Obs.* 5.—Bothering: *jao*, to bother, to give trouble to, to incommode; for *t'ao*, see Part III, 834 and 836. *Obs.* 6.—Ashamed: *pao k'uei, lit.*, carry shame in my bosom; see Part III, 718. *Obs.* 7.—Not worthy: *lit.*, I dare not act as (represent myself to be) the person you treat me as (see Part III, 342, *tang*¹); I cannot play the part you assign to me; a very common depreciatory expression applicable to almost any compliment or civility. There are of course many other forms of saluting a host than the one here given. *Obs.* 8.—Depreciatory: *ch'ien*, humble, modest; *hsü*, empty, in the sense of deficiency (see Dialogue V, 76). *Obs.* 9.—One: note *i pan wei*; this is a pure colloquialism. The *pan* must not be emphasised.

9. *Obs.*—Formality: *jang*, to invite; in the present instance, in the sense of to yield, to give way to others in which sense it is frequently used.

10. *Obs.*—Remiss, etc.: *shih ying*, failed to meet you.

PART IV.—THE TEN DIALOGUES.   247

11. [*Guest.*] Not at all; I'm late, I'm afraid, and have kept all you gentlemen waiting.

12. [*Host.*] No, no; they've only just arrived; let's get to dinner.

13. [*Guest.*] I'm guilty of great assumption in taking this place.

14. [*Host.*] It's yours by right. Pray take wine all of you; we'll begin with a bumper.

15. [*To host.*] Your health.

16. [*Host.*] Please begin. I won't help you; we're all intimates here, and each one must help himself.

17. [*Guest.*] That's the best way; if we all begin to press each other to eat, it will look too formal; we'd much better go as we please. There you are! we've just agreed to dispense with formalities, and you are commencing them. We shall have to return the compliment to make it right.

18. [*Host.*] No, I am not. I sent a man a day or two ago to the manager's office to tell him to beg them in the kitchen to pay particular attention to the cooking of the dishes, and they seem to me rather better than those not made to order. I notice you gentlemen won't get your chopsticks to work, so I am obliged to help you. You might taste them.

* * * * *

19. [*Host.*] Don't put your chopsticks down; you must all make a good meal.

20. [*Guest.*] We've all had as much as we can eat, and more wine than we can carry, and are very much obliged to you for your excellent dinner.

21. [*Host.*] There has been nothing fit for you to eat to-day, and the wine is so bad that you have not done justice to your drinking powers.

22. [*Guest.*] What are you talking about? I'll say no more to-day, as my cart has come, and it's no longer early, so I must be getting home. I shall call shortly at your house to offer my thanks.

11. 諸 *chu*^{1}		17. 顯 *hsien*^{3}		17. 敬 *ching*^{4}		18. 嚐 *ch'ang*^{2}		21. 屈 *ch'u*^{1}	
12. 席 *hsi*^{2}		17. 拘 *chü*^{1}		18. 竈 *tsao*^{4}		19. 飽 *pao*^{3}		22. 謝 *hsieh*^{4}	
13. 僭 *chien*^{4}		17. 泥 *ni*^{4,2}		18. 筷 *k'uai*^{4}		20. 盛 *shêng*^{4}			

11. *Obs.* 1.—All you gentlemen: *chu*, all; for *kung*, see Part III, 979. *Obs.* 2.—Kept you waiting: *lit.*, caused you *shou*, to endure [the trouble of], *têng*, waiting.

12. *Obs.*—Get to dinner: *hsi*, a repast or banquet; let's enter upon our repast.

13. *Obs.*—Assumption: *chien*, to usurp, to assume what does not belong to one; [in taking] this seat I am indeed guilty of much assumption.

14. *Obs.*—A bumper: *lit.*, let us all drain a cup.

16. *Obs.*—Help you: *pu*, to distribute (see Part III, 406).

17. *Obs.* 1.—Look: *hsien*, manifest, apparent; *hsien-cho*, apparently; hence, to appear to be, to look as. *Obs.* 2.—Formal, conventional: *chü*, to grasp, to adhere to; *ni*^{4}, bigoted, opinionated; *chü ni*, a grasping at what one conceives to be the proper thing; *ni*^{2}, mud. *Obs.* 3.—Return the compliment: *ching*, to honour, to show respect to.

18. *Obs.* 1.—Manager's office: *kuei shang*; *lit.*, in, or at, the counter. *Obs.* 2.—Kitchen: *tsao*, a furnace, or cooking range, of a large establishment; *shang*, as above. *Obs.* 3.—*K'uai*, a chopstick; also called *k'uai-tzŭ*. *Obs.* 4.—*Ch'ang*, to taste: properly written without the radical "mouth."

19. *Obs.*—Make a good dinner: *ch'ih pao*, eat till you are full, or satisfied.

20. *Obs.*—Excellent dinner: *shêng*, superlative, excellent, fine, etc.; *shê*, to spread, to lay out, to arrange; hence, what is so laid out, *q.d.*, a dinner. Cf. our slang word "spread."

21. *Obs.*—Not done justice, etc.: *ch'ü*, *lit.*, crooked, or bent awry; also, a wrong or grievance, to do wrong to; *liang*, capacity (see Part III, 776, *Obs.*); here, capacity for drink.

22. *Obs.*—Offer my thanks: *tao*, to say, to give expression to, *hsieh*, thanks; *hsieh hsieh nin*, thank you, sir.

23. [*Host.*] I couldn't think of such a thing. Please yourself about going, I beg; I won't venture to detain you.

24. [*Guest.*] Are you gentlemen going to sit a while? in that case I must take my leave before you? Good-bye, good-bye; don't see me to the door. pray; stop where you are.

there's no occasion for our host either to see me out; now, please, return and see to your other guests.

25. [*Host.*] I'll come no further; I'll see you into your cart.

26. [*Guest.*] Thanks, many thanks.

27. [*Host.*] *Au revoir.*

23. 豈 *ch'i*³   25. 乘 *ch'êng*²

23. *Obs.* 1.—Couldn't think of: *lit.*, how could I venture (to trouble you, or some such phrase, understood); *ch'i* is the interrogative particle how or what, but only used in certain set phrases. The above is one of the commonest of polite phrases, and is used with as much frequency as *pu kan tang* (see above, 8, Obs. 7). *Obs.* 2.—Detain: *fêng liu*. It is difficult to give the exact force of *fêng* in this phrase; it means, properly, to raise the hands when presenting anything (see Part III, 990); to do an act of homage or respect; hence, the respect that such an act implies.

24. *Obs.*—Stop where you are: *liu pu*, *lit.*, detain your footsteps; only used politely.

25. *Obs.*—Get into your cart: *ch'êng shang*, to mount, as a horse or a chariot; not used colloquially except in polite conversation.

26. *Obs.*—Many thanks: *k'o t'ou* is a common expression for thanks, but not to an inferior.

PART V.

THE HUNDRED LESSONS.

PART V.
THE HUNDRED LESSONS.

LESSON I.

1. [*Senior.*] So I hear you are studying Manchu,¹ eh? That's right. Manchu is with us Manchus the first and foremost of essentials; it is to us, in short, what the language spoken² in his own part of the country is to a Chinese; so it would never do to be without a knowledge of Manchu, would it?

2. [*Junior.*] To be sure not; and I have an additional reason for wishing to acquire it. I've been studying Chinese for the last ten years, but I am still as far as ever from seeing my way in it. I've now begun Manchu, but if I can't master enough of it to pass for a translatorship,³ ⁴ I shall have broken down at both ends of the line. So I am come to-day, sir,⁵ in the first place, to pay my respects to you, and, in the next, to ask a favour of you. I find it not so easy⁶ to open the subject, however.

3. [*Senior.*] What's your difficulty? pray say what you have got to say. If it's anything that I can do for you, do you suppose that, with the relations existing between us, I shall try to back out?⁷

4. [*Junior.*] What I have to ask, then, is this: that you will so far take an interest in me as to put yourself to a little trouble on my account; I will tell you how. Find time, if you can, to compose a few phrases for me to study, and if I manage⁸ to succeed at all, I shall regard it entirely as your work.⁹ Sir, I shall never forget your kindness, and shall not fail to repay it handsomely.

5. [*Senior.*] What are you talking about? You are one of us, are you not? My only fear would have been that you were not anxious to learn; but, since you are willing, I shall be only too glad¹⁰ to contribute to your success. Talk of handsome return, indeed! people as intimate as you and I are should never use such language to one another.

6. [*Junior.*] Well, sir, if that's the way of it, I am sure I feel extremely obliged. I have only to make you my best bow, and I shall say no more.

1. 洲 *chou*¹, properly, a river shoal; also, an island; not used colloquially; here merely as a sound to represent the second syllable of the word Manchu, the name of the original territory of the present dynasty.
2. 鄉談 *hsiang t'an*, *lit.*, country chat: *t'an*, to chat or talk with another.
3. 繙 *fan*¹, to translate.
4. 譯 *yi*⁴, to explain, to interpret: *fan yi*, to translate or interpret; *fan yi kuan*, an official interpreter.
5. 兄台 *hsiung-t'ai*, my elder brother's worship; you, sir.
6. 怪難 *kuai nan*, monstrously difficult.
7. 辭 *tz'ŭ*², a plea, an argument, an apology; also, to resign: *t'ui tz'ŭ*, to put forward excuses.
8. 能彀 *nêng kou*, power sufficing.
9. 賜 *tz'ŭ*⁴, to confer on an inferior.
10. 巴不得 *pa*¹ *pu tê*, may it be that: *pa* is probably used for *pa* (*see* Part III, 86); *q.d.*, not to be laid hands on, too good to get, or too good to be caught.

LESSON II.

1. [*Senior.*] Well, I hear that you have made such way in Manchu that you are beginning to speak it quite correctly.[1]

2. [*Junior.*] Nonsense! I understand it, certainly, when I hear it spoken, but it will be some time yet before I can speak it myself. It is not only that I can't go right through with a piece of conversation of any length like other people, but I can't even string[2] half a dozen sentences together. Then there is another odd thing I do: whenever I am going to begin, without being the least able to say why, I become so alarmed about mistakes that I dare not go on without hesitating;[3] now, so long as this continues to be the case, how am I to make a speaker?[4] Indeed, so far from considering myself one, I quite despair[5] of ever learning to speak. I say to myself that if with all my studying I have not got farther than this, I shall certainly never be a proficient.

3. [*Senior.*] This is all mere want of practice. Listen to me. Whenever you meet a man,[6] no matter who, that can talk Manchu, at him at once, and talk away with him. You must[8] go and take lessons of competent professors[7] of the language as well, you know; and if you have any friends who are good Manchu scholars, you should be for ever talking with them. Read some Manchu every day, commit phrases to memory, and talk incessantly, until the habit of speaking comes quite naturally to your mouth. If you follow this rule, in a year or two at the farthest you will speak it without an effort; so now don't despair[9] any more.

1. 規模 *kuei mo²*, compasses mould, a mould or form on which anything should be fashioned; only figuratively used; colloquially, *mu²-tzŭ*, a mould.

2. 接不上 *chieh pu shang*, do not become connected: *chieh*, specially of connexion between what is above and what is below; *shang*, an auxiliary verb, to a certain extent in affinity with *chieh*.

3. 簡簡決決 *chien-chien-chüeh-chüeh-ti*, summarily and decidedly.

4. 可叫 *k'o chiao*, [the causes specified above] properly make me how speaking; that is, not speaking, unable to speak.

5. 灰 *hui²*, ashes; here verbally used; my heart is made ashes, it despairs.

6. 但凡 *tan fan*, whether singly or universally, all whatsoever.

7. 師傅 *shih¹-fu⁴*, any master of a craft: *shih*, among other meanings, means a model, hence a teacher; *fu*, originally, to aid by counsels.

8. 要 *yao*, here imperative.

9. 愁 *ch'ou²*, to grieve: [after what I have said] *yu*, still, do you lament what inability?

LESSON III.

1. [*Senior.*] Why, when did you find time to learn all the Manchu you know, sir? Your pronunciation is good, and you speak quite intelligibly.

2. [*Junior.*] Oh, sir, you are too complimentary.[1] My Manchu does not amount to a great deal. There's a friend of mine who really does talk well; he is thoroughly at home in the language—intelligible,[2] fluent, and speaks without a particle of Chinese accent; he is quite proficient.[3] Then, besides this, he has such a stock of words and phrases. Now, that is what one may call a good scholar, if you please.

3. [*Senior.*] How does he compare with you?

4. [*Junior.*] Me! I should never venture to compare myself with him; I am as far[4] from being his match as the heavens are from the earth.

5. [*Senior.*] What is the reason of that?

6. [*Junior.*] Oh, he has been much longer at it, and knows a great deal more. Then he is very studious;[5] he has been committing to memory steadily ever since he began, without stopping; the book is never out of his hand. I should have trouble enough to come up with him.

7. [*Senior.*] Nay, my young friend, I think you are making a slight mistake. Don't you remember what the proverb says, "Be resolved and the thing is done"?[6] What he knows he knows only because he has learnt it;[7] it has not come to him by intuition. And are we in any way otherwise constituted? not at all! Well, then, no matter how exact or practised a speaker he may be, all we have to do is to make up our minds and apply ourselves to the language; and if we don't quite reach the point he has attained, we shall not be very far behind him, I suspect.[8]

1. 獎 *chiang*³, to praise: I, *ch'êng*, am the recipient of, my worthy elder brother's too great praise.

2. 清楚 *ch'ing-ch'u*³. distinct. clear; applied also to transaction of business, settlement of accounts, etc.

3. 練 *lien*⁴, originally, to boil silk until it is soft; hence, to practise: *shou lien*, proficient.

4. 懸隔 *hsüan² ko²*, separated by space, the division caused by space: *hsüan* is properly to hang, q.d., the vacuum in which the heavens are hung; *ko*, a partition, something that divides off; *ko k'ai*, to separate, to keep apart.

5. 頗 *p'o*¹, a strong intensive; only used with certain adjectives: *hao*⁴, to be fond of.

6. 竟 *ching*, after all, in any contingency: to him who has *chih*, resolution, an affair [he commences will be] *ching*, happen what may, completed.

7. 咧 *lieh*⁴, a final particle expressing certainty.

8. 料想 *liao hsiang*, I suspect. *See* Part III, **749**.

LESSON IV.

1. The chief thing that every man who comes into this world has to do is to study, and the great object[1] of his reading is the understanding of the rights of things *(tao-li)*. Such an understanding once arrived at, a man will do his duty[2] by his parents while he is at home; he must do his best for the State when he enters the public service; and he will be certain to succeed[3] in whatever he undertakes.

2. Once you have really acquired the knowledge you ought to have, you are respected wherever you go. I don't mean only by other people; you have yourself a sense[4] of your own title to be respected.

3. There is a class[5] of persons who do not read, and who take no pains to be well conducted,[6] relying exclusively on their attainments, as they regard them, in the arts of intrigue[7] and adulation.[8] For my part, I can't comprehend what their minds can be like, but I know I feel sorely ashamed[9] for them.

4. Such men not only bring discredit and disrepute on themselves, but they make people execrate[10] the parents that could have had such children.

5. Now, my young friend, just[11] reflect a moment and tell me whether the obligation a man is under to his parents[12] for their goodness to him can ever be repaid in the very smallest degree?[13] Well, then, the least a child can do is to behave himself. If he cannot make his family illustrious, and bring glory[14] to his line by great achievements, that can't be helped; but, on the other hand, what can be more utterly good-for-nothing[15] than so to conduct oneself as to bring down curses on one's father and mother?

6. A careful consideration of the subject, then, satisfies us, does it not, that no man can with propriety neglect the study of books and the regulation of his moral conduct?

1. 特爲的 *t'ê wei ti*, the special wherefore: *wei*⁴, because of; *ti*, as a relative, representing the word cause understood.
2. 孝 *hsiao*⁴, pious to parents: *hsiao shun*, filially obedient; here construed verbally.
3. 成就 *ch'êng chiu*, to accomplish satisfactorily, to make a good job of; *chiu* here differing little from *tê*.
4. 覺 *chio*, to perceive, to be sensible of.
5. 種 *chung*³ (to be distinguished from *chung*⁴, to plant), a kind or sort.
6. 品 *p'in*³, properly, a kind or class; hence, select: *p'in hsing*, each man's peculiar nature; *hsiu p'in*, to study, to take care of one's moral nature.
7. 鑽 *tsuan*¹, to pierce as with a *tsuan*⁴, a centre-bit; to make way through a small aperture: *tsuan kan* is elliptical for a longer phrase, *tsuan ying mou kan*, to study the accomplishment of business by intrigue; *mou kan* may be used of a good object as well.
8. 逢 *fêng*², to meet; *ying*, to go to meet, to welcome: *fêng ying*, to play up obsequiously to what you know to be a superior's wish, to endeavour to ingratiate oneself with a superior.
9. 害羞 *hai hsiu*, sorely ashamed: *hai* as in *hai p'a*, *hai sao*, etc.
10. 咒 *chou*⁴, to curse; 罵 *ma*⁴, to revile.
11. 白 *pai*, white, blank. in vain; *q d.*, whether there be such a case or not, just think, etc.
12. A man, etc., *wei jên-tzŭ-ti: wei*, he who is, *jên-tzŭ-ti*, a man's son; *q.d.*, a son in his relation to his parents.
13. 萬一 *wan i*, here 1 part in 10,000; also used elsewhere as 10,000 chances to 1.
14. 耀 *yao*⁴, *yo*⁴, brightness, glory; here to glorify: *tsung*, for *tsu tsung*, ancestral plurality, one's ancestors; illustrate one's house, make glorious one's ancestors.
15. 出息 *ch'u hsi*, to make profit, interest: to cause one's parents to be reviled by people is to be unprofitable up to what *fên*, in what degree?

LESSON V.

1. [*Senior.*] I observe you pass this way every day, sir; what place is it that you go to?

2. [*Junior.*] I go to my studies.

3. [*Senior.*] To read Manchu, isn't it?

4. [*Junior.*] It is.

5. [*Senior.*] What are you reading in Manchu?

6. [*Junior.*] Oh, no new books; nothing but the two old things, detached sentences on common subjects,[1] and the "Ch'ing Hua Chih Yao" (Guide to the Essential in Manchu).

7. [*Senior.*] Are they teaching you to write Manchu round hand yet?

8. [*Junior.*] The days are too short at present to leave any time for writing; but presently, when they begin to lengthen, we shall be taught to write and to translate too.

9. [*Senior.*] Well, sir, I have been wanting to study Manchu myself, and I have looked, I assure you, in every hole and corner[2] for a school; I have tried every imaginable means of procuring instruction; left no place unexamined; but in our neighbourhood,[3] I am sorry to say, there is no school for Manchu. I was thinking that the one you go to would do for me well enough, and that one of these days I might commence my attendance. Will you be so good as to say a word for me to the master beforehand?

10. [*Junior.*] Ah! I see you think[4] that it is a regular professor that teaches us; but that is not the case. Our instructor is one of the elders of our clan,[5] and he has scarcely any pupils but our own near cousins;[6] any others[7] that may attend are relations by marriage; there is not an outsider among them. But the fact is that our elder is too busy to give regular lessons; for, besides teaching us, he has to go to the yamên every day. It is only because we are so idle that we don't work by ourselves that he feels obliged[8] to find time[9] to play the tutor. Under these circumstances I fear I cannot help you, sir; were the case otherwise, your desire to study Manchu is a thing commendable in itself, and as for the trouble of speaking in your behalf, I should not have thought it any trouble[10] at all.

1. 眼面前兒 *yen mien ch'ien*, before the face and eyes; things of constant occurrence.

2. 覓縫 *mi*⁴, to seek for; *fêng*⁴, a seam, a crevice, to be distinguished from *fêng*², to stitch (see Part III, Exercise XI, 4): *tsuan t'ou*, boring with the head; *mi fêng*, searching for a crevice, trying every approach to a question.

3. 左近 *tso*³-*chin*, neighbouring: *tso*, properly, the left side or hand.

4. 打量 *ta-liang*, to reckon, sc., the merits or chances of anything; not used of numbers or amounts.

5. 族 *tsu*², properly, class, species; colloquially, clan or tribe of men: *tsu hsiung*, an elder brother of the tribe.

6. 子弟 *tzŭ ti*, sons and younger brothers, sc., of the clan; the speaker's near cousins.

7. 再者 *tsai cho*, here those who [may come] in addition, sc., to the blood relations aforesaid; but in argument *tsai cho* constantly means in the second place, or furthermore.

8. 萬不得已 *wan pu tê i*, feels obliged: *i* is properly to stop; 10,000 times can he not stop, he cannot in any way help himself.

9. 勻著 *yün*²-*cho*, properly, dividing into even shares; here simply apportioning a part of *k'ung-'rh*, his leisure.

10. 費 *fei*, as in *fei-shih* (see Part IV, Dialogue VI, 58).

LESSON VI.

1. This morning when I went to hear[1] those lads their lessons I found one less prepared[2] than another. There they stood, humming and hawing, gaping and staring,[3] and nothing else could they do.

2. I saw how the land lay, so I said to them, "There![4] stop and listen to me! it's your business, now that you are studying Manchu, to give your whole mind[5] to your work; but when will it be accomplished[7] if you go on in this fashion, making believe that you are students, and endeavouring to get credit[6] that you are not entitled to? It is not only that you are wasting[8] day after day and month after month, but I am expending my energies to no purpose either; you are the sufferers, but the harm done you is your own doing, not mine, remember."

3. "Really, it shows a want of all shame,"[9] I said, "that grown-up lads like you should pay so little attention to what is said to them; you treat[10] the lecturing that I give you for your good just as if it was so much wind in your ears."

4. "I don't go out of my way to find fault[11] with you, don't say that; there are plenty of arguments against such an hypothesis. With the little leisure that is left me, don't you think[12] that when I come home from my business I should be glad enough to repose myself, for instance? Why don't I? why, instead of sitting down to rest, do I set to work to find one fault after another[13] with you? Simply because, being my flesh and blood, I want you to turn to some account; I want to make men of you."

5. "I am really quite at my wit's end. I can only throw my whole soul into the advice I give you, and so acquit myself of my responsibility.[14] You may listen to me or not, as you please; I've done all that I can do."

1. Heard their lessons: by an elliptical process *pei* is here to *hear* lessons repeated, not to repeat them.
2. 生 *shêng*, raw; here, unprepared with a lesson.
3. 瞪 *têng*⁴, to open the eyes wide.
4. 且住 *ch'ieh chu*, there! stop: *ch'ieh*, for *chan ch'ieh*, temporarily, for the time being.
5. 撲 *p'u*¹, colloquially, of the forward movement one would make with one's arm to catch a bird, an insect, etc.: i, undividedly, *p'u*, making such a forward movement, *na hsin*, tender your mind.
6. 沽 *ku*¹, properly, to buy wine: *ku hsü ming*, to buy an empty name, false credit.
7. 了手 *liao shou*, to bring one's work, *lit.*, hand, to an end.
8. 度 *tu*⁴, to pass; *hsü tu*, to pass to no purpose; also, a rule, a measurement, a plan.
9. 皮臉 *p'i lien*, a skin face, a face with too thick a skin to blush.
10. 當成 *tang ch'êng*: you *tang*, let it represent, make it, *ch'êng*, to be, wind by the side of the ear.
11. 錯縫 *ts'o fêng*, fault crevices, holes in one's coat.
12. 譬 *p'i*⁴, to compare with: *p'i ju*, for instance; used in argument, as we say, do you suppose, etc.
13. 這個那個的 *chê ko na ko ti*, this and that; *shuo*, to speak, must be understood.
14. 責 *tsê*², originally, amongst other meanings, a fault; to punish for a fault; hence, responsibility: I desire *wan*, to complete, what my *tsê-jên*, responsibility, requires; then will it be right.

LESSON VII.

1. [*Senior.*] As to becoming a translator of Manchu, you are a Chinese scholar, and you can have no difficulty in learning to translate. All you need is an exclusive devotion of your mind to the one subject. Don't let anything interfere [1] with your studies, and let these be progressive; [2] and in two or three years, as a matter of course, you will be well on your way. If you go to work like the fisherman, who fishes for three days and then is two days drying his nets,[3] you may read for twenty years, but it will come to nothing.[4]

2. [*Junior.*] Will you do me the favour to look over these translations, sir, and make a few corrections?

3. [*Senior, examining them.*] Oh, come, you really have made very great progress; every sentence runs as it should; every word is clear; I have not a fault [5] to find. If you go up for your examination, success is in your own hands.[6] Have you returned [8] yourself as a candidate at these examinations [7] that are coming off now?

4. [*Junior.*] I should be glad enough to stand, but I am afraid that, being a *hsiu-ts'ai*, I am not qualified.

5. [*Senior.*] What? when any Bannerman [9] can go up, do you mean to say that a man of your attainments would not be allowed to? [10] Nonsense! why, even the *i-hsio* [11] *shêng* may stand; and if so, how should a *hsiu-ts'ai* not be qualified? But the *hsiu-ts'ai* are entitled to stand, I can assure you, and it is for this reason that my son [12] is now working as hard as he can at Manchu for the little time that remains before he has to go up. Don't you throw away the opportunity.[14] Add your name [13] to the list at once.

1. 隔斷 *ko tuan*, to interrupt: *ko*, by interposition, *tuan*, to cut.
2. 挨 *ai*, in the sense of side by side, *ai-cho tz'ŭ-'rh*, in proper order, seriatim.
3. 網 *wang*³, a net.
4. 枉然 *wang jan*, in vain: for *wang*, as crooked, unjust, *see* Part III, 941; here useless.
5. 肒 *ko*¹, a pimple; *hsing*¹, a star: *ko-hsing*, any spot on paper, wood, porcelain, etc; hence, figuratively, defect, blemish.
6. 操 *ts'ao*¹, to grasp in the hand: you will be able to grasp, *ch'üan* (權), the balance, power, of *pi shêng*, certain success; *shêng*¹ (勝). to overcome; *shêng*¹, to sustain, to be equal to sustaining.
7. 筆帖式 *pi-t'ieh-shih*, three words used to produce the Manchu word *bitgheshi*, a lettered man, a clerk.
8. 遞 *ti*⁴, to tender, to hand up: have you returned your name?
9. 旗 *ch'i*², a flag, a banner: *pa ch'i*, the Eight Banner Corps, of mixed civil and military organisation, in which the Manchus are enrolled. There are also eight Mongol Banner Corps, and eight of Chinese descended from those who sided with the Manchus when they invaded China.
10. 獨 *tu*, only: the *li*, justice of exceptionally not permitting you to be examined, can there be?
11. 義學 *i-hsio*: a *hsio*, school. whether Chinese or Manchu, founded by one or more persons of *i*, public spirit, where boys are taught to read gratis. The *i-hsio shêng* of the Banner Corps are distinguished from the *kuan-hsio shêng*, candidates from the Government establishments.
12. 姪 *chih*², nephew; here the son of the speaker who addresses the other person as his brother.
13. 補名字 *pu ming-tzŭ*, add your name, *lit.*, supplementarily, as you have not yet returned it.
14. 機會 *chi hui*, opportunity: *chi*, as elsewhere, the motive spring; *hui*, a conjuncture, the right moment.

PART V.—THE HUNDRED LESSONS.

LESSON VIII.

1. Never read novels.[1] If you read anything, read the Mirror of History;[2] that will extend the range of your scholarship for you, and if you keep the events of the past in your memory, making the good your pattern and taking warning[3] by the bad, you will find yourself all the better for it, body and mind.

2. As to[4] novels and old tales,[5] fictions without a shadow[6] of truth[7] that different people have composed, it will do you no good if you read a thousand volumes of them.[8]

3. There are people who have got no sense of decency, who will go on reading to their audience how that once upon a time, in such-and-such a state, so-and-so fought ever so many fights[9] with so-and-so; how that this one made a cut with his sword, which the other one guarded[11] with his axe;[10] how that this one made a thrust[12] with his spear, which the other one parried[13] with a staff. If either of the parties is supposed to be defeated,[14] the auxiliaries he invokes are spirits and fairies,[15] who come on clouds and go in mist; grass that, when cut,[16] makes horses, or beans that he scatters,[17] on which they become fighting men.

4. All this is evidently false, yet the stupid people it is told to receive it as gospel; there they stand like idiots, taking it in with a positive gusto.[18] Men of sense[19] not only ridicule[20] works of the sort, but have a certain distaste[21] for them. So don't you bestow any pains on such trash.

1. 小說 *hsiao shuo*, tales, romances.
2. 鑑 *chien*[4], a mirror: the *t'ung chien*, universal mirror, is a famous historical work.
3. 戒 *chieh*[4], to beware of.
4. 至於 *chih yü*, to come to; very common where a new proposition is introduced.
5. 詞 *tz'u*[2], talk expressions: *ku-êrh tz'ŭ*, talk about the men of old; *êrh* for *jên*, man.
6. 影 *ying*[3], shadow.
7. 瞎 *hsia*[1], properly, blind: *hsia hua*, falsehood.
8. 整 *chêng*[3], becoming, made up to.
9. 仗 *chang*[4], to fight, as armies; properly, and very commonly, to lean against, to depend upon.
10. 斧 *fu*[3], an axe, carpenter's or other.
11. 架 *chia*[4], to ward off, to guard; also, a frame, a stand, a staging.
12. 扎 *cha*[1], to thrust at with the point of a stick or weapon.
13. 搪 *t'ang*[2], to parry a thrust.
14. 敗 *pai*[4], originally, damaged, destroyed; here, and commonly, defeated.
15. 神 *shên*[2], spirits in general; 仙 *hsien*[1], fairies: *shên-hsien*, a collection of such beings.
16. 剪 *chien*[3], to cut with scissors, to cut with a knife, etc.: *chien-tzŭ*, scissors.
17. 撒 *sa*[3], to scatter. See *sa*[1], Part III, 998.
18. 滋 *tzŭ*[1], a pleasant flavour; 味 *wei*[4], any flavour: *tzŭ-wei*, a pleasant flavour, a relish.
19. 見識 *chien-shih*, experience; the sense derived from it.
20. 笑話 *hsiao hua*, to laugh at.
21. 怠 *tai*[4], slow, taking no interest in: *lan-tai*, lazy; not eager *ch'iao*, to read such books.

LESSON IX.

1. [*Senior.*] Has that book come yet?

2. [*Junior.*] It has been sent for, but it is not come yet.

3. [*Senior.*] Not come yet! Who was sent for it?

4. [*Junior.*] The young lad, sir. When we first told him to go, he wouldn't stir for us, but kept loitering here ever so long, as if it didn't matter[1] whether he went or not. At last I told him it was you who had desired that the book should be brought, and then he started off post haste. But when he came back he brought only three *t'ao*, and, as you know, sir, the book is in four. So we asked him, "What made you leave[2] a *t'ao*? you had better make all the haste you can, and get it," we said, "or when your master comes in he won't be best pleased[3] with you." However, he would not plead guilty; on the contrary, he tried to put us in the wrong. We had bungled the directions we gave him, he said; and so he went off in a huff, and he is not back yet. Someone might be sent to meet him, but then he would be most likely returning by one road while the messenger was going another.

5. [*Senior.*] Was there ever such a slippery[4] article in this world? Of course, he is off to some place where there is something going on, to amuse himself. The right thing, beyond all doubt,[6] is to correct him severely;[5] so, as soon as he returns, I shall tie him up[7] and give him a very sound thrashing.[8] Otherwise this kind of thing will grow into a habit, and he will become a greater good-for-nothing[9] than he is now.

1. 沒緊 *mei chin*: some such word as attitude must here be understood; *yu*, he had a, *yao*, importance, *mei chin*, not pressing [manner]; the word in brackets being represented by *ti*.

2. 漏 *lou⁴*, to leak, as anything holding fluid; to leak out, as the fluid itself; frequently used, as here, of things left out, omissions in writing, business, etc. *La* (see Part III, 763) is more common.

3. 依 *i¹*, to lean against; hence, to incline to, to assent to: *pu i*, not to assent to, to be dissatisfied with.

4. 滑 *hua²*, slippery, to slip.

5. 嚴 *yen²*, severe: *kuan chiao*, to keep in order and teach; here, much as we often use the word correction.

6. 斷斷 *tuan⁴-tuan*, decidedly, positively, beyond doubt.

7. 捆 *k'un³*, to bind with cords, things or persons.

8. 頓 *tun⁴*, in the sense of turn or time: *i tun fan*, a meal.

9. 堪 *k'an²*, to have strength to bear; to be equal to duty, responsibility, etc.: *pu k'an*, here, unequal to doing what he ought; elsewhere it may mean that more is laid on a person than he can bear.

LESSON X.

1. [*Senior.*] Foot archery[1][2] is with us Manchus a most important consideration. Easy as it seems, it is so much the reverse in practice that notwithstanding the number of archers who shoot[3] from morning till night, ay, take their very bows to bed with them, there are but a small number who come to shoot so well[4][5] as to distinguish themselves[6] above their competitors.

2. [*Junior.*] What is the difficulty?

3. [*Senior.*] The body must be kept quite upright, the shoulders of the same height, the attitude of the whole person perfectly[8] unconstrained;[7] then[9] the bow should be so stiff withal that when the arrow leaves it it goes with force; and then if every arrow hits the mark, the shooting may be pronounced good.

4. [*Junior.*] Well, look at my shooting, sir, and see if I have improved. If there is anything to find fault with, please correct me.[10]

5. [*Senior.*] No, there is nothing to be said against your shooting as a foot archer. Trust to your thumb,[11] and sooner or later you will wear the peacock's feather.[12] Your style is good, you show training, and you shoot clean. If everyone shot like you, there would be no fault to find with anyone. The only thing to remark is that your bow is not quite stiff enough, and that the bow hand is slightly[13] unsteady. Reform in these few particulars, and, no matter where you go to shoot, you are certain to shoot better than the majority; no one will be able to keep you under him.[14]

1. 射 *shih²*, in books *shê⁴*, to shoot arrows.
2. 箭 *chien⁴*, an arrow: *pu chien*, foot archery.
3. 長拉 *ch'ang la*, continually to draw the bow.
4. 類 *lei⁴*, a class or category.
5. 萃 *ts'ui⁴*, reeds or grass growing in tufts: *pa ts'ui*, to draw out one stem or blade from such a tuft, thereby giving it pre-eminence; if there be any whose *la*, shooting, come to be so good as to *ch'u lei*, excel their class, [and as such] to be extracted from the bunch. *See below, ch'u chung.*
6. 出名 *ch'u ming*, to put forth a name, to become famous: of those who have done so, there are how many?
7. 自然 *tzŭ jan*, as of itself, unconstrained.
8. 毛病 *mao-ping*, evil or fault even so large as a hair.
9. 搭著 *ta-cho*, additionally; it may be used with *yu* preceding it, as here, or without *yu*.
10. 撥 *po²*, in books *po¹*; properly, to move apart with the hand: *po chêng*, to set right; not used of moving material things.
11. 拇 *mu³*, a finger; not used alone: *chang-cho*, relying on; *ta mu-chih-t'ou*, the great finger—great in the sense of first in the series,—the forefinger being *êrh mu-chih-t'ou*. The middle finger is *chung chih*; the next, *ssŭ mu-chih-t'ou*, but also, politely, *wu-ming chih*, the finger without a name. The little finger is *hsiao mu-chih-t'ou*.
12. 翎 *ling²*, feathers; here, a feather from the tail of the pheasant or the peacock, the latter being much more honourable than the former; *tai ling*, to wear such a feather in the cap.
13. 略 *liao⁴* or *lio⁴*, to diminish, to abridge, a digest, a sketch, a *résumé*; hence, slightly. The first reading is more common. *See also Lesson XXIII, 4.*
14. 壓 *ya¹*, to press down, as anything laid on another presses that which is below it. Observe *ni*, the object of *ya*, between its auxiliaries *hsia* and *ch'u*.

LESSON XI.

1. [*Junior, entering.*] A happy new year[1] to you, sir!
2. [*Senior.*] You are very good; a happy new year to both of us.
3. [*Junior*] Please take your seat, sir.
4. [*Senior.*] What for?
5. [*Junior.*] That I may make my new-year salaam to you.
6. [*Senior.*] No, no! I won't hear of such a thing.
7. [*Junior.*] Indeed, sir, I must make you a kotow; it's my bounden duty, as you are my elder.
8. [*Senior.*] Get up, get up, I beg of you. There! may you have promotion![2] may you have posterity! may you pass your life in wealth and honour![3] now please get up off your knees, and sit down on the upper seat. Let me give you a few of these dumplings[4] I have here.
9. [*Junior.*] Not any, thank you; I ate some at home, before I came out.
10. [*Senior.*] Well, but you did not eat so much that you can't eat any more, surely? At your time of life a man has no sooner done eating than he is hungry again. Do eat some, or I shall certainly think that your abstemiousness is all pretence.[5]
11. [*Junior.*] I am in earnest, I assure you, sir. You don't suppose, do you, that in your house I should do otherwise than make myself at home? I should never think of telling you an untruth, depend on it.
12. [*Senior.*] Here, then, make some tea for this gentleman.
13. [*Junior.*] No tea for me, thank you, sir.
14. [*Senior.*] But why not?
15. [*Junior.*] I must be off elsewhere; I have a number of places to go to, and if I don't pay my visits in good time, it will set people wondering.[6] Now don't get up from table, sir; let me find my way out by myself;[7] you'll spoil your dinner if you come away from it.[8]
16. [*Senior.*] What, not see you out? A likely story! Dear me! to think that you have had the trouble of coming for nothing;[9] not even a cup of tea! Well, good-bye till we meet again.[10] Make my compliments to all your people, will you?

1. 新喜 *hsin hsi*, new [year's] congratulations.
2. 陞 *shêng*[1], properly, to rise: *shêng kuan*, to obtain promotion.
3. 富貴 *fu*[4] *kuei*, rich and honourable.
4. 餃 *chiao*[3], flour dumplings with or without meat inside.
5. 粧假 *chuang*[1] *chia*[3], pretending; specially, pretending to have no appetite: *chia chuang* is used of any other kind of pretence; *chuang*, to adorn oneself, to dress up; also, to pretend. Note *chia*[3], not *chia*[4], as in Part IV, Dialogue III, 13.
6. 犯思量 *fan ssŭ liang:* I shall *fan*, offend, run foul of, people's *ssŭ liang*, speculations as to the cause of my not coming to see them. Construe: people will all be [by me] *fan ssŭ liang*.
7. 別送 *pieh sung*, do not accompany me, *sc.*, to the door.
8. 看 *k'an*, lest: look to it that you do not carry away the *wei*, relish of your dinner.
9. 空空 *k'ung-k'ung-'rh-ti*, emptily, specially where a visitor has had nothing to eat, or nothing presented to him.
10. 改日 *kai jih*, another day; *tsai chien*, we shall see each other again.

LESSON XII.

1. [*Junior.*] I congratulate you, sir. They say you have been selected for a *chang-ching*-ship.[1]

2. [*Senior.*] Yes; at the selection [2] yesterday they decided on proposing [3] me as the effective nominee.

3. [*Junior.*] On whom did they decide as nominee in waiting?

4. [*Senior.*] A man you don't know; a subaltern of the Vanguard.[4]

5. [*Junior.*] Has he seen any service?[5]

6. [*Senior.*] Only with the Hunting Camp;[6] he has never served a campaign.

7. [*Junior.*] Well, I feel satisfied that you will be wearing the peacock's feather [7] presently.

8. [*Senior.*] Don't flatter me, pray; I have no particular merits of my own, and there are too many better men than I in the field to admit of my counting on [8] the appointment as a certainty. I may have the luck to lay hold [10] of it, but if I do, it will be by the virtue of those who have gone before me and have found favour with Heaven;[9] and I can't be sure about getting it at all.

9. [*Junior.*] You underrate yourself, sir. Why, think of the number of years you have been in the service! You're a man of good standing; all your friends of the same date, if you come to that, are now *ta-jên*, and those who entered the army later than you did have all been promoted. Then, as to your services, you have been in the wars, you have been wounded, and you are now one of the Picked Archers.[11] Who is there, therefore, in your Banner Corps [12] that is a better man than you are? I know what you are thinking of; you are afraid, I suppose, that I am come to get a glass of wine [13] out of you in honour of the occasion.

10. [*Senior.*] Wine, indeed! I can only tell you that if the news is true,[14] it's not to say wine, but anything you like I shall be happy to offer you.

---

1. 章京 *chang-ching*: the words are supposed to give nearly the sound of the Manchu word *chanyin*, signifying an "assistant."

2. 選 *hsüan*³, to choose; 擇 *chien*³, to select: *chien-hsüan*, colloquially used only of choosing officers, not in their turn, but by merit; *shang* is an auxiliary verb, but indicating at the same time the *superior* merit of the person chosen.

3. 擬 *ni*³, commonly, to suggest; here, of submitting a name to the Throne.

4. 前鋒校 *ch'ien fêng*¹ *hsiao*⁴: the *hsiao* are military officers in Manchu corps, of the sixth grade; *fêng*, the point of a weapon; the *Ch'ien Fêng* is one of the grand divisions of the Manchu army; the point in advance, or vanguard.

5. 有兵 *yu ping*, to have seen military service.

6. 圍 *wei*², to surround; hence applied to hunting as carried on with a corps of beaters: *kua*³, only, has he done *wei*, Hunting Camp service; *ta wei*, to go shooting or hunting.

7. 孔雀 *k'ung ch'io*⁴, the peacock: *ch'iao*³ is the common reading of the second character.

8. 指望 *chih wang*, to point to and look towards; to hope.

9. 蔭 *yin*⁴, the shade cast by trees, plants, etc.: *fu yin*, the overshadowing of prosperity [due to the virtues] of *tsu tsung*, one's ancestors.

10. 撈 *lao*¹, to take up out of water, with the hand or otherwise.

11. 善射 *shan shê*, Manchu soldiers and petty officers selected for proficiency in three branches of archery, five successful shots being fired in each way.

12. 旗下 *ch'i hsia*: serving under the chiefs of your *ch'i*, Banner Corps, who is *ch'iang*, more able, than you?

13. 喜酒 *hsi chiu*, congratulation wine.

14. 果然 *kuo jan*, in very deed.

LESSON XIII.

1. [*Senior.*] Success in the public service all depends on the opportunities of the individual. If you have no more than ordinary luck, nothing will go well with you. Your object, whatever it be, may seem on the point of attainment, and some *contretemps*[1] will present itself expressly to foil you. There are people who hold such hands, who have such a run of luck,[2] that there really is nothing that does not turn out as they desire and expect. They have their own way without let or hindrance,[3] and, in the twinkling of an eye,[4] there they are in the highest places they can fill.[5]

2. [*Junior.*] Well, sir, I am of an entirely different opinion; I think it is all a question of exertion or no exertion.[6] If an *employé* idles the year away, showing no sign of life,[7] and spending his pay without doing any duty for it, how can he possibly expect to be promoted? why, he ought to be dismissed from the service.[8] The foremost duties of an *employé* are diligence and attentiveness.[9] He must also keep on good terms with his friends; not taking a line of his own, nor refusing to do as others do; never bringing in [10] his comrades for a share of trouble that belongs only to him; and when any duty, no matter what, devolves upon him, it behoves him to give his whole mind to the discharge of it, and to push gallantly [11] to the front. Let a man take this line, and he is certain to rise; how can he fail of success?

1. 杈 *ch'a*⁴, stumps or lesser boughs branching out from the stem of a tree; figuratively for an occurrence out of the plain course one would pursue.

2. 彩頭 *ts'ai t'ou*, colour end; the right colour side of the dice: you might say that the *ts'ai t'ou* is bad; but this is rare; *tsou yün*, to follow in the track of luck.

3. 爽利 *shuang-shuang-li-li-ti*, quickly and without hindrance: *shuang*, as in Part III, 823, free as the morning air, untrammelled, as a sky without clouds; *li*, sharp, quick.

4. 瞅 *ch'ou*³, to see, to look at.

5. 優 *yu*¹, excellent: *yu têng*, highest degree of *kao shêng*, rising to high place.

6. 巴結 *pa chieh*, in a good sense, as here, to exert oneself; in a bad sense, to intrigue for patronage. The expression is purely colloquial, and *pa* evidently stands for some other character.

7. 餐 *ts'an*¹, what is eaten, to eat: *su*, properly, white; here used like *pai*, vainly; *su ts'an*, vainly eating, doing no work for one's wages; *shih wei*, a corpse personage, a dead person; but rarely used except in this combination, the upper and lower parts of which are sometimes transposed.

8. 革退 *ko t'ui*, to strip off [office and compel] to retire.

9. 勤 *ch'in*², diligent; 謹 *chin*³, attention; properly, solemn attentiveness, as in a place of worship.

10. 攀 *p'an*¹, to drag towards one with the hand; here, of pulling in others to do one's own work.

11. 勇 *yung*³, brave; also, a "brave," or irregular soldier.

LESSON XIV.

1. This CHANG is anything but cordial[1] to his acquaintance; not like an old gentleman that I know, who is quite another style of old man; very friendly[2] with everybody; delights in a long literary conversation; will sit talking history a whole day, and never tire.

2. He is very amiable,[3] too, with any young people he happens to meet; tries to win them[4] to the right road; reproves what there is to reprove,[5] and gives them good advice[6] when it is needed.

3. Then he is so kind-hearted[7] and charitable;[8] as eager to help anyone he finds in distress as if he were the party concerned; sure to leave nothing undone that may relieve[9] the sufferer. He really is an old man who has to thank his virtues for all the blessings he enjoys,[10] and I feel this so strongly that[11] I am quite dissatisfied[12] with myself when I let any great length of time pass without paying him a visit.

4. He brings luck on all belonging to him; as the proverb says, "The man who is blest himself, brings blessings on his whole house."[13] And there is the old man with an ample fortune,[14] and sons and grandsons in plenty;[15] all the reward[16] of his own well-doing.

1. 冷淡 *lêng tan*, cold and thin, tasteless, not cordial.

2. 親熱 *ch'in jo*, the opposite of *lêng tan*.

3. 悅 *yüeh*⁴, to rejoice : *ho yen*, with friendly colour, and *yüeh shê*, gladsome tint.

4. 引 *yin*³, to lead, to guide ; 誘 *yu*⁴, to tempt, to draw on, in a good or bad sense ; here, *yin yu*, to draw on to *hao ch'u*, good ways.

5. 指撥 *chih po*², to point to and set right. See above, *po*¹ in *po*² *chêng* (Lesson X, Note 10).

6. 教導 *chiao tao*⁴, to give good advice : *tao*⁴, properly *tao*³, to guide.

7. 仁 *jên*², benevolence, humanity, disinterestedness, Christian charity : *jên ai*, kind-hearted.

8. 護 *hu*⁴, to assist : *hu chung*, charitable, philanthropic.

9. 救 *chiu*⁴, to save : *ta*² *chiu*, to come to the rescue of (*q.d.*, adding one's own hand or person) ; *ta*², properly *ta*¹ (*see* Part III, 1076).

10. 積 *chi*², to accumulate : his *fu*, blessings. accumulate ; thanks to his *tao*, way of life, the characteristic of which is *hou*, that is, *chung hou*, sincerity and unselfishness.

11. 故此 *ku tz'ŭ*, accordingly, for this cause.

12. 不過意 *pu kuo i*, not to be able to get over the thought. Observe the emphasis given by *chih shih*, it is simply the fact that, etc.

13. 托帶 *t'o tai*, not used except in this proverb : the whole house *t'o*, being beholden to his *fu*, blessings (which prove the greatness of his virtues), *tai*, are drawn, follow him, and share these blessings.

14. 充足 *ch'ung tsu*, amply sufficing : *ch'ung* in the sense of filling to the full.

15. 旺 *wang*⁴, brilliancy, great success : *hsing wang*, flourishing, either as here, or of commerce, harvests, etc.; *hsing* (*see* Part IV, Dialogue VIII, 35).

16. 報應 *pao ying*, Heaven's reward of good or retribution of evil.

LESSON XV.

1. [*Junior.*] You must mind what you are about, gentlemen, before His Excellency here. He is very quick and decided,[1] and whatever comes to his hand is certain to be turned out shipshape.[2] Then he is very clear-sighted: he knows what people are worth. He is not to be humbugged[3] as to any man's real qualities. With all this he is very kind-hearted, and when the young fellows belonging to those about him are diligent and respectable, he will never fail to bring them forward, and support their claims to appointments or promotion at the fitting season. But if he comes across fellows who shirk duty, eye-servants who try to make their game[5] by a show[4] of diligence, they may as well look out. They can't escape him, and once they fall into his hands they will not get away very easily.

2. [*Senior.*] You young gentlemen may say what you please on the subject; what else can I do? When you are watching me day after day with all your eyes,[6] in the hope that I shall make a career for you, how would your respective merits be done justice to[8] if I did not recommend those who deserve to be recommended, and pull up those who deserve to be pulled up?[7] As to coming down on delinquents, it is my nature to say out what I feel. Still, my conduct and my language are pretty much what they ought to be,[9] I suspect; and this is the reason why people obey me, and are ready to exert themselves when I require it.

---

1. 敏 *min*³, quick intelligence; 捷 *chieh*², quick in movement, active: his *ts'ai-ch'ing*, abilities, are, in character, those of a man clear-seeing and prompt.

2. 有條有理 *yu t'iao yu li*, a figure taken from thread duly sorted, not in confusion, *li* representing the word *order*.

3. 瞞 *man*², to hoodwink.

4. 獻 *hsien*⁴, to make offer to a superior of a present or of a suggestion; here, to make a show of tendering diligence.

5. 占 *chan*⁴, so pronounced, to take without right: *chan p'ien i*, to gain advantage unduly.

6. 巴巴兒 *pa¹-pa-'rh*, of the eye fixed on a mark; not to be explained etymologically, unless *pa¹* is taken as corrupt for the same character written with the 177th Radical, *pa*³, a target.

7. 束 *shu*⁴, to tie up, as a bundle of sticks; *yo*, also, properly, to bind: *yo shu*, to control, to enforce discipline upon.

8. 賞 *shang*³, to confer on an inferior; hence, to reward; *kung*, exertion, hence well-doing, merit.

9. 正派 *chêng p'ai*⁴, right course, correctness: *p'ai*, in the sense of divergent courses of water poured out.

LESSON XVI.

1. Children are reared to be the prop[1] of age, and a son should remember all the trouble[2] he has given his parents; how kind it was of them to bring him up as they did; and this should make him show his sense of filial duty[4] now, while[3] they are alive, by finding them good food to eat and good clothes to put on, and by rejoicing the heart of the old folks with his amiability and cheerfulness.

2. If a son neglects to feed and clothe his parents, if he does not trouble himself about what they may suffer from want[5] or from weather, and so, by treating[6] them as if they did not belong to him, pains and vexes the old people while they are yet with him, he may weep and wail[7] as he will a hundred years later, but what good will that do? Supposing his grief to be sincere,[8] no one will believe in it. It will be put down as a sham, got up because he is afraid of people's contempt. And as for sacrifices, you may set[9] any dainties[10] you please before the dead, but who ever knew the spirits[11] enjoy[12] these dishes? They are all gobbled up[13] by the living; the dead don't gain anything by them.

3. There are some children who are worse than neglectful; children who will tell you that their parents are so old that there is no making them understand anything they ought to do;[14] and who go on clamour, clamour, in the house, until at last they insist on having a separate establishment. Language such as this[15] makes one distressed and angry in spite of oneself.[16] Such persons revolt[17] the powers of nature, and the spirits abhor them. How[18] is it possible, one asks, that they should die in their beds?[19]

4. Just observe these undutiful[20] people, and, in the twinkling of an eye,[21] you will see their children and their children's children as undutiful as they have been.[22]

1. 防 *fang*², to guard against: *fang pei*, to make preparation against possible evil.
2. 勞 *lao*², labour, pains, trouble.
3. 趁 *ch'ên*⁴, properly, to avail oneself of an opportunity.
4. 孝敬 *hsiao*⁴ *ching*⁴, filially, to respect, to pay that honour which filial piety demands; it is also used of an offering made by an inferior to a superior, or of gratuitous labour given under similar conditions.
5. 饑 *chi*¹, to hunger, to starve.
6. 看待 *k'an tai* is explained by the clause preceding it, without which *tang tai* or *tai*, alone, would be used; it must be construed as if *k'an* were detached from *tai* and linked with the words preceding it.
7. 慟哭 *t'ung*⁴ *k'u*¹, to cry bitterly: *t'ung*, the excitement of strong emotion.
8. 誠 *ch'êng*², true, sincere, real.
9. 供 *kung*, here, to set out for sacrifice.
10. 珍 *chên*¹, jewels; 饈 *hsiu*¹, dainty fare: *chên hsiu*, dainty fare; *mei*³ (美) *wei*, goodly taste.
11. 魂 *hun*², the spirit of life which leaves man when he dies; not his *ch'i*, the breath: *hun ling*, this same spirit belonging to men dead or dreaming; in abeyance when a man is half-drowned; in ordinary men, not immortal.
12. 享 *hsiang*³, to enjoy, as happiness: *shou hsiang*, the same.
13. 囊 *nang*³, to eat; 搡 *sang*¹, properly, to push back with the hand: *nang sang*, filling the mouth with food like a glutton.
14. 晦 *hui*⁴, of the sight darkened: *lao pei hui*, so old that they turn the back on what is right and go in darkness; are drivelling, doting.
15. 塲處 *ch'ang*² *ch'u*, arena-place, this length.
16. 不由的 *pu yu ti*, without one's permission, whether one will or no: *yu*, from, out of; also, of one's own accord.
17. 不容 *pu jung*, not to tolerate: heaven and earth, the powers of nature, cannot bear them.
18. 焉 *yen*¹, a classical interrogative; how can they, etc.?
19. 終 *chung*¹, the end; here, to die: *shan chung*, comfortably to die; *shan*, as in the phrase *shan fa*, good, commendable, methods; not virtuous, righteous, etc.
20. 靜 *ching*⁴, still, tranquil: *ching-ching-ti*, silently.
21. 眨 *chan*³, also colloquially read *cha*³, and in books, *pien*³; to wink the eye.
22. 學 *hsiao*², to imitate.

LESSON XVII.

1. Touching quarrels in families: brothers are borne in the one mother's womb, and while they are little they eat together, play together, and each one will love the other as much as himself. Up to a certain time they will be as affectionate as possible;[1] and if later in life they become less intimate, it is in most cases because they are egged on[3] by their wives[2] to fight[4] about property, or because they listen to persons not connected with them, who tell them things calculated to produce estrangement;[5] the result of which cause is, in very many instances, a state of selfish indifference[6][7] on the part of each to the interest of the other.

2. And so, when their senses have become so affected[9] by daily calumnies[8] that they can think of nothing else, some fine day they lose all patience,[11] and then come[10] blows and altercations,[12] and, in fine, there is a feud[13] between them.

3. But they should remember that if they lose goods or property, they can buy[14] more; that if the wife were to die, they could marry[15] again; but that injury done to a brother is like injury done to a hand or foot; if you snap[16] it off, it cannot be reproduced.

4. They should remember also that there is no ally like a brother; who else, if you are in any serious difficulty, will feel to you like the brother who is bone of your bone and flesh of your flesh—will risk[17] his life in his efforts to help you? Will any outsider make such an effort? not a bit of it; he will sheer off for fear of being compromised;[18] he won't be able to get out of the way fast enough.[19]

5. All this proves that there is no friend so near one as a brother. Why can't people bear these facts somewhat more particularly in mind?

1. 何等 ho² têng, what degree? a form of the superlative; in the highest degree.
2. 妻 ch'i¹, the wife, who is espoused; 妾 ch'ieh⁴, the concubine, who is purchased: a man cannot legally have two ch'i.
3. 挑 t'iao², to set trouble going privily; not to be confounded with t'iao¹, to carry on the shoulder; 唆 so¹, to make mischief: t'iao so, to incite to contention.
4. 爭 chêng¹, to quarrel, to quarrel about.
5. 間 chien⁴, to divide; not to be confounded with chien¹ (see Part III, 47): language that li chien, separates.
6 懷 huai², the breast, to carry in the breast or heart.
7. 異 i⁴, strange; here, estranged.
8. 譖 ts'an², to criticise ill-naturedly, to backbite.
9. 濡 ju², thoroughly saturated, as a thing steeped in water: the ear saturated, mu jan, the eye dyed.
10. 致 chih⁴, to cause: i, using [the means above described] chih, they cause, what follows; yü, classically, governing the object of chih.
11. 忍 jên³, to endure, to bear patiently.
12. 辨 pan⁴ (properly, and often, pien⁴), to distinguish in discussion: pronounced pan only in this phrase; pan-tsui, altercation.
13. 讎 ch'ou², hate, feud.
14. 置 chih⁴, to make, to provide; hence, as here, to buy.
15. 娶 ch'ü³, to take a woman to wife.
16. 折 chê², to snap off; also read shê².
17. 捨 shê³, to fling away: shê ming, to fling away life.
18. 連累 lien lei, entanglement, complication.
19. 迭 tieh², here, in the sense of achieving satisfactorily: to pu tieh, cannot succeed in escaping.

LESSON XVIII.

1. As to friendship, men should imitate KUAN CHUNG[1] and PAO SHU[2] of the olden time.

2. These two were walking[4] together one day out in the country,[3] when they saw an ingot[5] of gold lying by the roadside.

3. Each wanted the other to take it, but as neither would pick it up[6] to keep for himself, they left it[7][8] and walked on

4. Until they fell in with a labouring man.[9] "There's an ingot of gold over there," said they to him; "you go and take it up now."

5. Away went the labourer as hard as he could to look for the gold, but no gold could he see, and all he did see was a snake[10] with two heads.

6. This startled[11] him considerably. Without further loss of time he cut the snake in two[13] with his hoe,[12] and then gave chase to his two informants. "Here, I say!" shouted he, when he had caught them up, "what bad blood is there between you and me that you should have told me a two-headed snake was an ingot of gold? You have pretty near cost me my life, let me tell you."

7. Not believing what he said, they went back to the spot to take a look, and there they found the lump of gold lying where they had first seen it, but cut in two pieces.

8. KUAN CHUNG took one half, and PAO SHU the other, and off they went, while the labourer had to go his way empty-handed.

9. Such was friendship as it subsisted between friends of the olden time. This story comes out of a story-book, it is true; still the conduct of these two men, as here related, undoubtedly reads a lesson[15] to the profit-at-any-price[14] folks of our own day.

1. 仲 *chung*[4], properly, the second son in a family; here, a name.

2. 鮑 *pao*[1], 叔 *shu*[2]: the first character always a surname; the second, here a name, means the younger brother of one's father; colloquially, *shu-shu*.

3. 郊 *chiao*[1], originally, the land at a radius of 10 *li* round a capital city; 荒 *huang*[1], barren, waste, deserted: *huang chiao*, the country, as opposed to ground that is built over; *yeh wai*, nearly the same.

4. 逛 *kuang*[4], to stroll, to walk for pleasure; to visit, as a temple or other place of interest.

5. 元 *yüan*[2], properly, original; here, in the sense of great; 寶 *pao*[3], a jewel, here in the sense of something precious: *chin yüan pao* means simply a large lump of gold fashioned into the shape in which the Government silver is usually cast.

6. 揀 *chien*[3], to pick up.

7. 仍 *jêng*[2], still as ever, still as before.

8. 撂 *liao*[4], properly, to throw down; here, to leave on the ground, *jêng*, where it was.

9. 莊稼漢 *chuang*[1] *chia*[1] *Han*, a Chinese who has to do with *chuang chia*, grain crops; an agricultural labourer.

10. 蛇 *shê*[2], a serpent: a snake is commonly called *ch'ang ch'ung*; lit., long reptile.

11. 嚇 *hsia*[4], in books read *ho*[4]; to frighten: [the sight] frightened him a great start.

12. 鋤 *ch'u*[2], a hoe.

13. 兩截 *liang chieh*[2], two fragments: observe the construction; *pa* before the object *shê*, snake; *k'an*, struck, [so that the snake] *ch'êng*, became two *chieh*, fragments; the verb *chieh* meaning to cut off.

14. 忘 *wang*[2], here so intoned, but identical with *wang*[4], to forget: the phrase *chien li wang i*, to forget justice at the sight of gain, is classical.

15. 榜樣 *pang*[3] *yang*, a lesson, an example: *pang*, amongst other meanings, the list posted up to show the order in which successful graduates stand.

LESSON XIX.

1. You mean that young friend of ours, don't you?
2. I do.
3. Ah! he's a regular awl[2] in a bag.[1] He is certain to make his way before long.[3]
4. How is this?
5. He is naturally very steady; highly educated,[4] uncommonly well conducted, and well looking;[5] and so diligent in the discharge of his public duties. When he has none to discharge, and he is living[6] quietly with his family, he gives himself up entirely to the management of household affairs and to the care of home expenditure. He is dutiful to his parents and affectionate to his brothers; he really has not a single fault. Then, again, he is such a friend to have if you want his assistance. If a man apply to him he will help if he can, or he will tell him plainly if he can't, be the applicant who he may. If he does not promise his aid, that's all about it; if he gives you to understand[7] that you shall have it, he will not fail to do all he can for you, and till the question is settled he won't take his hand off it. Everyone, consequently, respects him, and entertains an affection for him.

6. No doubt; and such a man as this will never[8] go through life empty-handed. "Heaven," says the proverb, "stands by[9] the good man," and Heaven will not fail to bless[10] him.

1. 囊 *nang*², a purse, a bag.

2. 錐 *chui*¹, an awl.

3. 久 *chiu*³, long in duration.

4. 淵 *yüan*¹, a deep place with water in it, an abyss; only used in certain set phrases; 博 *po*², of learning, extensive: his *hsio-wên*, learning, is deep and wide.

5. 漢仗 *han-chang-'rh*, a fine fellow: *han*, as in Lesson XVIII, Note 9, a fellow; *chang*, probably a corruption of 丈 (*chang*), an elder, a senior, one worthy of respect.

6. 居 *chü*¹, to dwell in, to inhabit: *chü chia*, to live at home, not elsewhere on business or pleasure.

7. 點頭 *tien t'ou*, to nod the head in token of assent: if he do not *ying*, promise, enough; if he assent, then, etc.

8. 豈 *ch'i*³, how; *ch'i yu*, how can there be? is a common form of negation: how can there be *li*, a rational, just possibility, that he should go *k'ung*, without advantage, through life?

9. 相 *hsiang*⁴ (not *hsiang*¹), to aid, to stand by; hence, anciently, a minister or counsellor.

10. 降 *chiang*⁴ (not *hsiang*²), to descend, or, as here, to cause to descend. Observe *chi jên*, the fortunate, or prosperous, man, identical with the good man.

LESSON XX.

1. [*Senior.*] That young fellow is our old neighbour,[1] you know; the lad we have seen grow up here. He has not been away from us so very long,[2] and now one hears that he is doing very well; that he has got an appointment. I only half believed the report when I first heard it,[3] until on inquiring of friends I find it really is the case. It shows the truth of the proverb, "If a man but resolve, the thing he wants to do is done;" and of the other proverb, "No man is too young to make a resolution."

2. [*Junior.*] That is all very well, sir; still, his father's virtues must have had claims known to Heaven[4] to[5] enable him to beget a son of such promise; a young man so plain[6] and honest, so well conducted; spending any spare time his archery drill may leave him at home, and there always at his studies; never moving in the direction of a dissolute[7] life. Then he is so careful in the discharge of his public duties; so diligent; and as to looking out for himself, or turning a penny underhand, he is perfectly spotless.[8] It's quite a case[9] in which one may observe that "The house where virtue accumulates from generation to generation will not fail to have more than an ordinary share of happiness."

---

1. 坊 *fang*[1], properly, in past times, a region or quarter of a city: *chieh-fang*, neighbours, a neighbour.

2. 能有 *nêng yu*, can it be how many days? *q.d.*, it is but a few days, *ko liao*, that he has been separated from us.

3. 來著 *lai-cho* implies the continuance of the action of the verbs *hsin* and *i* until the time indicated by *hou lai*, by-and-by.

4. 陰功 *yin*[1] *kung*, secret desert, merit known to Heaven only.

5. 緩 *ts'ai*: [his father's claims being known to Heaven] *ts'ai*, then, or thereon, was he enabled; his claims must have been known before he could, etc.

6. 樸 *p'u*[2], properly, wood as yet untouched by tools, paint, etc.; *q.d.*, in primitive simplicity: *p'u shih*, plain and true, guileless.

7. 唐 *t'ang*[2], a Chinese surname, taken as its style by a celebrated dynasty; here, most likely, corruptly used for some other character: *huang-t'ang*, wild, dissolute in conduct.

8. 沾染 *chan*[1] *jan*, dipped and dyed; only used morally, as here.

9. 合了 *ho liao*, that agrees with: [the case] is indeed one that agrees with that *chü hua*, **saying.**

LESSON XXI.

1. [*Host.*] But you're not a stranger here, surely. If you wanted to see me, you should have walked straight in; what occasion was there for you to have yourself announced[1] at all? And once you had got to the door, why turn back without coming in? The fact is that you were put out, I suppose, because my people said I was not at home, eh? Well, you won't see why they should have said so unless I explain; so listen.

2. For some time past[2] our young fellows have had a gambling club going, and they had just been here vowing and protesting[3] that I must attend too. Now, in the first place, as you very well know, I haven't time to play; I never can tell from one moment to another but I may be wanted on duty; and, in the next place, even if I had the time, the laws[4] against gaming are extremely severe, and if[5] anything were to go wrong, I should lose my character.

3. So I resolved, *coûte que coûte*, not to go to the club, let them take it as they pleased,[6] and I told the servants to deny me to all visitors, without distinction of persons. Well, *you* call, and the stupid beggars make the same answer to you as to A or B, and send you about your business before they come in to say a word to me. I did send after you post haste, but, to my great annoyance, my messenger came back and reported that he had not been able to catch you up. Now, don't, pray, think[7] that I am to blame in this matter; I do assure you that you were denied without my knowledge.

---

1. 通報 *t'ung pao*, announced: *t'ung*, passing through (*sc.*, from the door to the rooms within).

2. 一向 *i hsiang*, for some time past: *i*, unity unbroken, continuity; *hsiang*, as in *hsiang lai*, of time towards this point coming; heretofore.

3. 誓 *shih*[4], an oath; *ch'i shih*, to make oath, *fa yüan*, to utter a vow: the words *ch'i shih* are used without *fa yüan*, but the latter seldom, if ever, without the former.

4. 王 *wang*[2], a king or prince, the title in ancient times of the ruler; now only applied to princes or tributary rulers, *e.g.*, the King of Corea: *wang fa*, the laws of the State.

5. 儻 *t'ang*[3], if, but if; 倘 is the abridged form.

6. 到底 *tao ti*, *lit.*, to the bottom; used in various ways; here, happen what might.

7. 較 *chiao*[4], properly, to compare two sides: *chi chiao*, to reckon and compare, to think over a wrong.

LESSON XXII.

1. He and I were friends a long time back,[1] and then we became connected by various intermarriages; and as we had not met for years, when I came home from[2] the wars I wanted to hunt him up and have a chat[3] with him. However, one thing or another prevented[4] my going to see him, and I never could find time until yesterday, when, as I was passing that way, I took the opportunity[5] of calling at the house he used to live in. When I got there I asked for my friend, but they said he had long removed[6] elsewhere, and was now residing round a corner[7] at the west end of a certain small street.

2. I went in search of the house according to their directions, and up a blind alley,[9] at the farthest end[8] of the street, I found it; but the door was fast, and no one made answer, though I called and called for half an hour. At last, when I had been knocking[10] and shouting ever so long, there appeared an old woman[11] who could not put one foot before the other, and she said that her master was not at home; he was gone somewhere or other. "Then," said I, "when he comes home, tell him I called, will you?"

3. But, in addition to her other infirmities, the old woman was so deaf[12] that she could hear nothing, and I was obliged to borrow a pen and ink[14] of a small shop next door[13] and write a note,[15] which I left, to tell my friend that I had been to see him.

1. 底根 *ti⁴ kên¹*, in the root, at the beginning.

2. 打 *ta*, as often elsewhere, from.

3. 叙 *hsü⁴*, written sometimes with the 29th, sometimes with the 66th, Radical; properly, to state in order; not used alone colloquially: *hsü t'an*, to converse, to chat.

4. 絆住 *pan⁴ chu*, prevented, detained: *pan*, to entangle, to hamper.

5. 順便 *shun pien*, following convenience; the opportunity presenting itself.

6. 搬 *pan¹*, here, for *pan chia*, to shift one's home: *pan*, to remove from one place to another.

7. 拐 *kuai³*, to gull, to deceive, to kidnap; but probably in the combination before us confounded with the same character written with the 75th Radical, meaning a crutch: *kuai wan*, crutch-like bending, round a corner.

8. 儘溜頭兒 *chin liu t'ou-'rh*, the farthest end: *liu*, properly, to fall, as water after running down a rock, a roof, etc.; *q.d.*, the extreme point before the fall commences; *liu⁴*, a current (*see* Part III, 789).

9. 閘 *ka¹* has no meaning alone: *ka-la-'rh* in Manchu means the opening of a seam in wood; in Peking, it is used of a *cul-de-sac* round a corner.

10. 敲 *ch'iao¹*, to strike.

11. 媽 *ma¹*, properly, an old woman; children call their mothers *ma* or *ma-ma: lao ma-'rh*, a nurse.

12. 聾 *lung²*, deaf.

13. 隔壁 *ko² pi⁴*; in this connexion commonly read *chieh² pi³-'rh*, the first word meaning to divide, the second, a partition wall.

14. 硯 *yen⁴*, the stone upon which the Chinese rub their ink; commonly called *yen-t'ai* (硯台), the latter character being an abbreviation of Part III, 785.

15. 字兒 *tzŭ-'rh*, a short letter or note.

LESSON XXIII.

1. [*Junior.*] Keep on your horse, sir, pray! I ought to have got out of your sight.¹ Now, why should you go through the form of dismounting when you are so tired?

2. [*Senior.*] Not dismount, indeed! If I had not seen you, well and good; but when I did see you ever so far off,² you wouldn't have had me keep on my horse, would you?

3. [*Junior.*] Well, sir, won't you step in and sit down?

4. [*Senior.*] Oh, yes, I'll step in and sit down a moment;⁴ it's so long³ since we met. But, dear me! what a show of flowers you have, and what a stock of gold fish! And your rockery,⁵ so ingeniously⁶ conceived; every tier of it has a character of it's own! And what a tidy library! everything in it looks so nice;⁷ it's quite the place for reading men like us.

5. [*Junior.*] It's nice enough, no doubt; the misfortune is that I have no friend to study with, and studying all alone is tame⁸ work.

6. [*Senior.*] Well, there needn't be much difficulty on that score. I'll be your fellow-student, provided that I don't bore⁹ you; what say you?¹⁰

7. [*Junior.*] Bore, indeed! it will be a real blessing¹¹ if you will. I never asked you to come, because I feared you would refuse; but if you really are coming I shall be the most fortunate¹² of men.

1. 躲避 to³ pi⁴, to get out of the way: I *shih*, failed, to *to pi*.
2. 老遠 *lao yüan*, very far off: *lao*, intensive of *yüan*; has no reference to time.
3. 許久 *hsü chiu*, very long time: *hsü*, purely intensive.
4. 暑 *liao*⁴, diminutive of time, as here, or of quantity. See Sound Table (Vol. I, p. 13), *lio*, *lieh*, *hio*.
5. 堆 *tui*¹, a pile, to pile up: *shan-tzŭ shih-'rh*, stones making a hill; *tui-tê*, piled up, very nicely.
6. 心思 *hsin ssŭ*, hearts' thoughts, one's fancy, has been employed *hên ch'iao*, very ingeniously.
7. 入眼 *ju yen*, to enter the eye; said of a sight that causes pleasure.
8. 冷清 *lêng ch'ing*, cold and clear, no warmth in the thing, dull work.
9. 厭煩 *yen⁴ fan²*, disgust and trouble; to regard as a bore, the object being *wo*, me, understood.
10. 何如 *ho² ju²*, what say you? *lit.*, how if [I do]?
11. 造化 *tsao⁴ hua⁴*, properly, to create; often, as here, the good fortune bestowed on one by Heaven when one was created: *hua*, to change, the operation of nature.
12. 幸 *hsing⁴*, good fortune: *wan hsing*, immense felicity.

LESSON XXIV.

1. When first I met that man I thought his manner very frank and hearty. Then he looked so like a gentleman that, with his fine handsome person[1] and his powers of conversation,[2] he took my fancy[3] greatly. I used to ask myself how I should best cultivate his acquaintance, and never ceased singing his praises.[4]

2. But, by-and-by, as we grew better acquainted[5] and we came to be constantly thrown together,[6] I had occasion to observe[7] his conduct more carefully, and then began to see that he was not at all what he ought to be.[8] There was display enough in him, but no solid qualities.[9] A dark and dangerous[10] man withal; always setting people wrong,[11] and, however fair he might be to your face, doing you serious damage behind the scenes. Let a man drop into his net,[12] and he is laid on his back at once.[13] He has been the ruin[14] of I can't say how many people; more than you could count on your fingers.[15]

3. His acquaintances, consequently, never speak of him without remarking that he is a man to be afraid of. There is not one of them that he has not made smart.

1. 魁 k'uei², properly, the head; eminent; a hero; 偉 wei³, great, remarkable: k'uei wei, of large stature; han chang, as to stature, a fine person.

2. 伶牙俐齒 ling² ya li⁴ ch'ih, ready of speech: ling li is used of any kind of cleverness; ling, classically, is an actor or musician; li is not used without ling.

3. 羨慕 hsien⁴ mu⁴, took my fancy: hsien, to admire as superior to oneself; mu, to feel devotion to as superior to oneself.

4. 誇 k'ua¹, to boast: k'ua chiang, to praise.

5. 交上 chiao shang, as intercourse began or proceeded.

6. 混混 hun⁴-hun, properly, the mingling of water.

7. 考較 k'ao chiao, to examine and compare, to observe.

8. 正經 chêng ching, of persons, rightly going, well-conducted; of things, right and proper.

9. 弄空 nou⁴ k'ung, the first character commonly read nung⁴; working out hollowness; without, an empty frame; in his heart, an impostor.

10. 陰險 yin hsien³, dark and dangerous, treacherous.

11. 好道 hao tao, not letting men go the right way: observe pu kei and various analogous constructions mean, in Chinese, to prevent.

12. 圈套 ch'uan¹ t'ao, a ring, circular enclosure, and a trap; a figure from hunting.

13. 觔 chin¹, properly, the same as the 69th Radical, a catty; here read kên¹: why kên tou should mean a somersault, or fall, is not explained; it is so used whether of man or beast; 仰面 yang³, to look upwards; yang mien, face upwards, on one's back; yang also means to admire.

14. 坑害 k'êng¹ hai, injured by falling into a pit; not used except figuratively.

15. 屈着指頭 ch'ü¹-cho chih-t'ou, lit., crooking the fingers: suan, to reckon; ch'ü, to crook, crooked; hence, often, bent by oppression.

4. He is just one of those men, in fact, to whom the proverb applies exactly, "The heart is concealed by the coat of the stomach; you may see a man's face, but you don't see his mind."

5. I have had wonderful luck in escaping him. He would have had me in his grip [16] for certain, like other men, if I hadn't taken great care to give him a wide berth.

16. 籠絡 $lung^3$ lo^4: lo, netted cords, a small net; $lung^3$, properly $lung^2$, a cage; $lung$ lo, only used as here, figuratively.

LESSON XXV.

1. No, really, you take things too easy.[1] If you can't do what you are asked to do, there's an end of it; but when you have undertaken[2] a thing, what do you mean by keeping people waiting, instead of making all the haste in your power? What confidence[3] will your friends ever place in your promises if this is the way you get through your business?

2. And you don't seem to think you are to blame either? Well, *I* feel ashamed for you, I can assure you. It would have been far better,[6] instead of[4] dawdling[5] along in this way, to have told the man the truth[7] plump and plain in the first instance; his mind would have been set at ease, so far as you were concerned, and he might have turned his attention to some other means of attaining his end.

1. 疲 $p'i^2$, properly, wearied, exhausted; here, callous, not paying due attention to.

2. 應承 $ying$ $ch'êng$, to promise, to undertake a commission.

3. 信 $hsin$, earlier used as a letter, news; here, in its proper sense of *to believe*.

4. 與其 $yü^3$ $ch'i$, as compared with......, the proposition following $ch'i$.

5. 顢頇 man^1-han^1, dawdling, not exerting oneself as one should. Neither character in this dissyllable is found apart from the other.

6. 索性 so^2 $hsing$: so^3, here so^2, properly, a cord; in combination with various words, to draw, to extort; also, to tie up; hence, to curb or force; *so hsing*, to do violence to, or curb, the natural bent of one's will, to stretch a point; *e.g.*, although you prefer dawdling, *so hsing*, make an effort, stretch a point, and tell him the real truth; in some instances it may be fairly rendered "nevertheless," or "in spite of the fact that" (*see* Part VI, Chapter XXI, Note 6).

7. 景 $ching^3$, properly, the light of the sun: $kuang$-$ching$, circumstances.

LESSON XXVI.

1. What is all this about? The affair has not even assumed shape[1] yet, and if it had, a little delay[2] would make no difference. Besides,[3] the party principally interested is in no hurry whatever about it, so why on earth should you take the initiative in pressing one[4] so violently on the subject?

2. The grand essential is that a question should be carefully considered again and again, and that one should give out nothing until one's mind is made up as to the proper solution of it. It does not do to begin talking in the headlong random[5] fashion you would have me talk.

3. But, however, I am so constituted that in anything I undertake I must be left unfettered.[6] If people try to make me act prematurely,[7] by getting my head into chancery, it's my nature to decline all action whatever.[8] If our friend has confidence in me, let him bide my time; if[9] he has not, let him apply to someone else to do his business; who would prevent him?[10]

1. 有影 *yu ying*, to have a shadow, which a thing cannot have till it has form or shape.

2. 遲 *ch'ih²*, late.

3. 尚且 *shang ch'ieh*, a strong affirmative; *q.d.*, the *chêng ching*, rightful principal in the affair, even he is in no hurry.

4. 催 *ts'ui¹*, to urge on; 逼 *pi¹*, to press, to constrain: that you should *hsien*, moving before he does, urgently press, is what reasonableness?

5. 糊裏麻裏的 *hu²-li-ma²-li-ti*, in a wild, irregular fashion.

6. 纏 *ch'an²*, to tie a cord about persons or things.

7. 得實 *tê shih*, to get or become solid, as the fruit after the blossom has fallen.

8. 斷不 *tuan⁴ pu*, a strong dissent; on no account, under no circumstances.

9. 倘 *t'ang³*, if, but if; not used colloquially without *jo*, and then, as a general rule, disjunctively. This character is used interchangeably with 儻 in Lesson XXI, Note 5.

10. 攔 *lan²*, properly, to stop with the hand; to hinder.

LESSON XXVII.

1. Ah! you don't know yet [that there are other men as able as you are]; this fondness for feats of strength is all along of your youth; the heyday[1] is in the blood; but when you have met with a few reverses, naturally, you won't be so full of heart.

2. I'll tell you my own case: I was once very fond of martial exercises,[2] and I used to practise[3] them every day; but after a time I gave them up,[4] and for this reason. My elder brother was equally fond of these gymnastics;[5] his weapon was the lance, and he was so handy with it that not one in a score could get within his guard.[6]

3. One day, however, at my uncle's,[7] he fell in with a lame[9] man who had come in from the country[8] and who was a swordsman, and they proposed, one to the other, that they should have a trial of skill; each man to use the weapon[10] he was accustomed to.

4. Well, my brother made nothing of[11] an antagonist like this. He took his lance in his hand and made a thrust straight at the lame man's heart. But the lame man, without hurrying himself the least in the world, deliberately parried the thrust with his sword; the lance was snapped[12] straight across, and the piece broke off[13] at the joint. My brother made all haste to draw the lance in, but before he could recover it the lame man's blade was upon his neck, and as he tried to dodge, he was caught[14] by his foe under the throat and jerked[15] to a considerable distance.

5. This gave him a great distaste[16] for the thing, and I left off learning too. But this shows, doesn't it, that I am right in maintaining that there is no dearth of powerful men in the empire?

1. 旺 *wang*⁴, properly, bright; colloquially, of anything that is succeeding, or at its best; here, of the *hsieh ch'i*, blood and breath, the constitution, which is *wang*, in its prime. See above, Lesson XIV, Note 15.

2. 打把勢 *ta pa³-shih*, to do feats of strength or of arms; a good authority explains *pa* to be the hand or arm; *pa-shih*, the condition, or circumstances, in which the arm is placed while performing martial exercises (?).

3. 演習 *yen³ hsi*, to practise in order to proficiency.

4. 歇手 *hsieh shou*, to rest the hand, to give up some practice or habit.

5. 動勁 *tung chin*, to move the muscles.

6. 跟前 *kên ch'ien*, here, of getting at the person of the opponent; *kên ch'ien³-'rh*, not *ch'ien²-'rh*.

7. 舅 *chiu*⁴, one's maternal uncle.

8. 屯 *t'un²*, a village; originally, allotments of land granted to soldiers.

9. 瘸 *ch'üeh²*, lame, whether of a person or an animal.

10. 器 *ch'i*⁴, a weapon, an implement, a utensil.

11. 那兒有他 *na³-'rh yu t'a*, in his mind where had he him? he held him cheap.

12. 镲 *ch'a*¹, a character not recognised by the dictionaries; a crack or split. Observe the idiom, *ch'i*, even; *ko*, individual; *ch'a*, crack: *ch'i-ko-ch'a-'rh-ti*, in the manner of cracks evenly separating. The tone of *ch'a* varies.

13. 折 *shê²*, not *chê²*, as in Part IV, Dialogue III, 119.

14. 夾 *chia*¹, not to be confounded with *chia²* (Part III, 309); to keep fast hold of, as between the fingers, under the arm, in the leaves of a book, etc.

15. 撂出 *liao ch'u*, to jerk away: *liao*, properly, to put down, to let fall.

16. 趣 *ch'ü*⁴, pleasing savour, taste.

PART V.—THE HUNDRED LESSONS.   277

LESSON XXVIII.

1. No, really, you are too extravagant;[1] I can't help taking you to task for your wastefulness: if a man wants to live, he must accustom himself to economy[2] in everything. Instead of throwing the rice you don't eat into the kennel,[3] wouldn't it be better to give it to your servants? I wonder the very thought of such waste doesn't make you uneasy.

2. The fact is that all you trouble yourself about, my friend, is *eating* the rice. You ignore altogether the trouble people have had growing it, and tracking[4] it up the canal, before it arrives here; such trouble that even to get a single grain[5] is no easy matter.

3. Besides, men like you and myself can't go on like your millionaires, who have plenty of money at their command, who eat this and fancy that. If you habituate yourself to your present way of living, eating for ever[6] and without limit[7] to the variety of your dishes, you'll not only have no luck,[8] but you'll beggar yourself to boot.

4. Old men tell us, "Waste not want not,"[9] and be your luck[10] as good as you please, if you don't become a better manager,[11] look to it[12] that you don't starve[13] in the long run; it will be too late to repent when that day comes.

1. 奢 *shê*[1], extravagance; 侈 *ch'ih*[1 3], extravagance, also pretentiousness: *shê-ch'ih*, wastefulness.

2. 省儉 *shêng-chien*[3], or *chien-shêng*, economy.

3. 溝 *kou*[1], a ditch, a sewer, a kennel: *kou yen*, a kitchen sink, the head of a drain.

4. 縴 *ch'ien*[4], the tow rope by which the crew *la*, drag the vessel.

5. 粒 *li*[4], a grain of rice.

6. 捆 *k'un*[3], or *k'uên*[3], properly, to tie up persons or things; here, q.d., put a stopper on the mouth to prevent eating.

7. 盡頭 *chin t'ou*, extreme end, farthest limit.

8. 折 *chê*, as in Lesson XVII, Note 16, to snap off: *chê fu*, to do a damage to the happiness which Heaven meant one to enjoy.

9. 惜衣 *hsi i*, to be fond of one's clothes; hence, to save or spare them.

10. 福田 *fu t'ien*, the field of your blessings, the region of your luck; a Buddhistic expression.

11. 會過 *hui kuo*, to know how to get through *jih-tzŭ*, one's days, understood; to take proper care of one's money.

12. 隄 *ti*[1], an embankment: *ti fang cho*, be on your guard.

13. 捱 *ai*[2], to suffer: the *shang* auxiliary, and marking progress of time; you will come to suffer hunger.

LESSON XXIX.

1. [*Neighbour.*] What is the use of stowing your money away so safe and never spending any? a hundred years, if a man live so long, are past in the twinkling of an eye. How few days, I say to myself, will this vagrant dream-stuff[1] body of mine have any enjoyment? in the space of a flash of light[2] we become fit for nothing. We had best make use of our time, then, and occupy ourselves a little with the table and the toilet before we grow old. When our bones and sinews are become stiff, dress don't become us, we have no great relish for what we eat, and we have to do our children's bidding;[3] what pleasure is there in life under such circumstances? No; all that is incumbent on a man is to avoid excess, and then, when we know what we have got to spend,[4] it is quite proper that we should enjoy ourselves to a certain extent.

2. [*Host.*] Are you speaking with any knowledge of my affairs, pray, or is it all mere speculation? Were I indeed the man of money you make me out, with enough and to spare, it would be quite right that I should enjoy myself like other people; but how if I have not the money and estate that other people have? Would you have me run in debt[5] for dress, or eat myself out of house and home? Supposing that I did what you recommend, what would become of me when all my gear was gone and I was left bemoaning[6] my lot in such misery that death would be a blessing? And if, which is most likely, I did not die, but was to drag on existence with just enough breath left to live, how should I support myself? If I turned to you, would you listen to my application?

1. 浮生 *fou shêng*, life, as if on waves, *ju mêng*, like to a dream.
2. 晃 *huang*³, to dazzle; the action of any strong light upon the eyes.
3. 瞅著 *ch'ou*³-*cho*, regarding our children's chins, watching what they say, we pass our days.
4. 所得 *so tê*: the *fên*, portion, that we have got.
5. 債 *chai*⁴, debt; hence, *chai-chu*, debt-proprietor, a creditor.
6. 嘆 *t'an*⁴, to sigh; *k'ou ch'i*, a breath of the mouth: to heave a sigh and then to die, that would be well; [but] 10,000 to 1 not dying, still having breath I should live; rightly, possibly, how should I live?

LESSON XXX.

1. [*Senior.*] Who has been here to-day?
2. [*Junior.*] Two visitors came just after you left the house, sir; they came to congratulate[1] you, they said, on your promotion.
3. [*Senior.*] Who went out to speak to them?
4. [*Junior.*] I was standing[2] at the door at the time; I told them you were out, and I said, "Gentlemen, will you walk in and sit down?" but they declined and went away again.
5. [*Senior.*] What were they like?
6. [*Junior.*] One was a stout[3] man, sir, a little taller than you; he had a square face, with a beard[5] up to his temples,[4] prominent[6] eyes, and a dark, ruddy complexion.[7] The other was quite a figure of fun; shockingly dirty; but one eye, and he squinted[8] with that; his face was densely pitted[9] [10] with pock-marks,[11] too; he had a curly[12] beard that covered his whole chin, and he talked as if his tongue was too short.[13] He said something to me, and I was within an ace of bursting[14] out laughing.
7. [*Senior.*] The stout man I know, but who can the other be?
8. [*Junior.*] I asked them their names, and they each left a card.[15] Wait, and I will bring you the cards to look at, sir.
9. [*Senior.*] Dear me! that monkey,[16] eh? where is he from, I wonder? You fellows must not look down on him, though. His form may be as crooked[17] as you please, but he is very able with his pen, and he has all his wits about him;[18] he has long had a reputation, that man; you can name him to no one that has not heard of him.

1. 道喜 *tao hsi*, to offer congratulations.
2. 來著 *lai-cho*, auxiliary of *chan-cho*; so below, after *wên*, to ask.
3. 胖 *p'ang*⁴, fleshy, corpulent.
4. 鬢 *pin*⁴, the temples: *lien pin*, connected with the temples.
5. 鬍 *hu*², the beard.
6. 豹子 *pao*⁴-*tzŭ*, properly, a leopard; applied to prominent eyes, not in the sense of ferociousness.
7. 紫 *tzŭ*³, purple; 棠 *t'ang*², a species of crab tree, the wood of which is mahogany coloured.
8. 斜 *hsieh*², slanting; diverging from the right line, whether perpendicular or horizontal.
9. 糡 *chiang*⁴, flour paste.
10. 稠 *ch'ou*², standing thick together.
11. 麻子 *ma*²-*tzŭ*, a man pitted with small-pox, the marks of which were *chiang ch'ou*, close together, like the grains of over-boiled rice.
12. 捲毛 *chüan*³ *mao*, curly-haired: *chüan*, to curl, to roll up.
13. 咬著舌兒 *yao*³-*cho shê-'rh*; *lit.*, biting his tongue, unable to speak out, clipping sounds, especially the sound *êrh*.
14. 噗嗤 *p'u*¹ *ch'ih*¹, the sound of laughing; the first character is not found in dictionaries.
15. 職 *chih*², properly, office, department: *chih*⁴ *ming* (note the tone), properly, one's official title, but used now of one's card, whether it bear one's title or not. See also *ming-p'ien*.
16. 猴 *hou*², a monkey.
17. 歪 *wai*¹, deflected, crooked; the opposite of *chêng*, upright: *wai-wai niu-niu*, turning and twisting.
18. 韜 *t'ao*¹, properly, the case for a bow; to put the bow in its case; it would then be concealed; *lüeh*, in the sense of to ponder, to devise: *t'ao lüeh*, concealed devices; specially stratagems in war.

LESSON XXXI.

1. [*Senior.*] What! are you not off[1] yet?

2. [*Junior.*] Oh! I shall be off by-and-by. My travelling baggage and other traps are all packed[2] right enough; what I am a little short of is money to pay my travelling expenses.[3] I believe to-day in the truth of the saying that it's easier to go up a hill after[4] a tiger than it is to begin speaking about a thing one wants. I have been begging with the greatest effrontery in every direction, but to no purpose; I couldn't get anyone to lend me the money. So in my extremity, sir, I'm come to look for you, to beg you to oblige me with a slight loan either of money or of some article to pawn.[5] As soon as I return I shall do myself the honour of repaying you both[6] principal and interest.

3. [*Senior.*] It is lucky[7] you came to me when you did; if you had been a little later you would not have been in time. I happen to have in hand a few ounces that have just[8] been brought in from the country; you take the half of them for your use. When you have drunk your tea, I'll weigh them out to you. By the way, tell me, are you not leaving home now for the first time?

4. [*Junior.*] I am.

5. [*Senior.*] Well, then, a word in your ear; the right line to take when you are going to a distance from home[9] is this. Let your first care be to keep on good terms with the friends you live amongst;[10] show kindness to all the common *employés* who serve under you, without distinguishing between those who are in more immediate contact with you and the rest. If you get on ground where you may turn a penny, never forget that reputation is the grand essential, and hold your hand.[11] Ill-gotten gain will seriously compromise[12] a good name.

6. [*Junior.*] I fully appreciate the value of your advice, sir, and to the end of my days I shall never forget it.

1. 起身 *ch'i shên*, to be in movement for a journey.

2. 整理 *chêng³ li*, to put in proper order: for *to-tzŭ*, see Part III, 417.

3. 盤纏 *p'an ch'an²*, travelling expenses: *p'an*, see *p'an fei*, Part III, Exercise XV, 7, Obs. 4; *ch'an*, to tie; *q.d.*, tied in your girdle, about your waist.

4. 擒 *ch'in²*, to lay hands on, to make prisoners of, evil-doers, wild beasts; 虎 *hu³*, a tiger, commonly called *lao hu* (老虎).

5. 當頭 *tang⁴-t'ou*, a something that will stand for money at the *tang-p'u*, pawnshop.

6. 併 *ping⁴*, collected together: *pên li*, principal and interest, *i ping*, entirely and together, will I *fêng huan*, tender back (*see* Part III, 990, 995).

7. 幸 *hsing⁴*, fortunate, auspicious; *k'uei*, to be deficient, has not here any translatable meaning: *hsing-k'uei*, luckily.

8. 方纔 *fang ts'ai*, just now: *fang* (Radical 70), then.

9. 遠門 *yuan mên*, as if it were *li mên yüan*, far from your own door.

10. 處 *ch'u³*, to dwell in or amongst; not to be confounded with *ch'u⁴*, a place.

11. 手長 *shou ch'ang*, the hand long, too far reaching; let not this be.

12. 係 *hsi¹*, properly, to connect as by threads; very commonly in books, the verb *to be*, the participle *being*; but not so here: *kuan hsi*, to have relation to, to affect, to concern; but always of *evil consequences*.

LESSON XXXII.

1. [*Senior.*] When[1] did you come in from the country, sir?
2. [*Junior.*] I've been here some days.
3. [*Senior.*] I never heard a word about your return, sir, or I should have called on you long ago.
4. [*Junior.*] It was not likely you should hear, sir; we live so far[2] from one another; and, besides, you have your official duties to attend to.
5. [*Senior.*] Will you allow me to ask whereabouts your military allotment is?
6. [*Junior.*] It's a place in the jurisdiction of Pa[3] Chou.
7. [*Senior.*] By the Liu-li River, is it?
8. [*Junior.*] No; by the Hun[4] River.
9. [*Senior.*] And how have the crops turned out there this year?
10. [*Junior.*] Very well indeed; the harvest has been perfect.[5]
11. [*Senior.*] How odd! Wasn't there a talk of floods[6] there first, and then of drought?
12. [*Junior*] All mere report;[7] no truth in it. Take black pulse alone: it is down to ten cash or so a *shêng*;[8] it has not been so low this many years.
13. [*Senior.*] You don't say so!
14. [*Junior.*] But I do say so.
15. [*Senior*] Well, in that case, the next time you send there, please buy a few piculs of pulse for me; and when you have made out the account, if you'll tell me, I'll pay you whatever it cost you.
16. [*Junior.*] Aye; you are right. I see you have a number of horses standing in your stables,[9] which, of course, you must have pulse to feed; and it will be much better to have it brought in from down yonder at half-price[10] than to be paying for it at the rates they are charging us here

1. 幾兒 *chi êrh*, properly speaking, what day of the moon?

2. 窵 *tiao⁴*, properly, the nest of a large bird; deep; not used alone colloquially: *tiao yuan*, far off.

3. 霸 *pa⁴*, properly, to domineer; hence, 霸道, domineering; here, the name of a district in the province of Chihli. 屬 *shu³*, belonging to, under the authority of.

4. 渾 *hun²*, properly, confused, like pure and turbid water mingling; here, the name of a river.

5. 收成 *shou ch'êng*, in-gathered in a state of completeness, used only of crops, whether of fruit or grain.

6. 潦 *lao⁴*, to flood with rain; *han*, dry (see Part IV, Dialogue VIII, Note 5).

7. 謠 *yao²*, properly, to sing as one works: *yao yen*, gossip, idle report.

8. 升 *shêng¹*, a measure; the tenth of the *tou*.

9. 槽 *ts'ao²*, a trough, whether for water or forage: *ts'ao shang*, in the stable, speaking of any cattle; *ma ts'ao*, a horse trough; but it is incorrect to put the name of any other animal before *ts'ao*.

10. 減 *chien³*, to diminish.

LESSON XXXIII.

1. [*Senior.*] If you buy a horse at all, buy a good one, and then it will be a pleasure to see it in the stable; but why waste forage on the keep of a such a screw[1] as this?

2. [*Junior.*] You don't know his points, sir, but I do; for when they brought[2] the horse home yesterday I took him outside the walls and tried him, and I found that he would do well enough to ride; his amble was even;[3] his gallop was fast; at the archery practice he didn't swerve[4] a hair's breadth off the course or within it; he has a good mouth, and he is sure-footed.

3. [*Senior.*] From what you say on the subject it's quite clear to me that you don't know a horse when you see one. A good horse must have his legs[5] sound, must be equal to hard work; he should know the drill of the hunting field, and he should be well-shaped and handy. That's the sort of horse that one of your fine young fellows[6] will mount, with his quiver[8] on his back,[7] and away he flies like[10] the hawk;[9] a sight worth looking at.[11] But what manner of horse is this beast of yours? He's old in the teeth, with his lower jaw drooping,[12] and so gone in the legs that they are always coming down with him.[13] Besides, with a figure as unwieldy[14] as yours, he is not at all a suitable[15] horse for you.

4. [*Junior.*] Well, but what am I to do? The horse is bought and paid for, and so there is nothing for it[16] but to see to his keep, such as he is. I have no business of much importance to take me out, nor any that sends me a great way from home. There's one point in his favour, he has no vice;[17] so he'll answer my purpose. It's better to be on him than on foot, at any rate.[18]

1. 傪 *ts'an*⁴, a word disparaging appearance: *ts'an-t'ou*, speaking of men, a blockhead; here, simply poor-looking, good-for-nothing.

2. 牽 *ch'ien*¹, to drag, or to lead along, animals.

3. 顛 *tien*¹, here, to amble, like a horse or mule: *tien tê wên*, his amble is secure, even; 穩 *wên*³, stable, not to be shaken.

4. 裹 *kuo*³, properly, to wrap round with cord or cloth: in the Chinese riding-school the horse gallops along a trench; if he swerve outwards, he is said to *chang*, if inwards, to *kuo*.

5. 骽子 *t'ui*³-*tzŭ* can only be applied to beasts, or the legs of tables, chairs, etc.; for the common form of *t'ui*, see Part III, 442.

6. 英雄 *ying*¹ *hsiung*², a hero, a fine fellow.

7. 繫 *chi*⁴, to bind on, to tie; also pronounced, but more rarely, *hsi*⁴.

8. 撒袋 *sa-tai*, a quiver.

9. 鷹 *ying*¹, a falcon.

10. 一般 *i pan*; *lit.*, one sort, like.

11. 觀 *kuan*¹, to look at, to attend to; but *kuan*⁴, a Taoist temple.

12. 搭拉 *ta la*, hanging down; both characters used corruptly.

13. 前失 *ch'ien shih*, to miss the footing forward: this horse *k'ên*, is in the habit of, tripping.

14. 笨 *pên*, of the body, clumsy.

15. 相宜 *hsiang i*², suited.

16. 將就 *chiang chiu*, here means, by an effort to make a thing suit; *chiang* being corruptly used for another word that means to move from one place to another.

17. 老實 *lao-shih*, honest; of horses and like animals, quiet, harmless.

18. 究竟 *chiu ching*, seeking to the end; after all.

LESSON XXXIV.

1. [*Senior.*] Where did you buy that cloak of sable;[1] in a shop?

2. [*Junior.*] No; I bought it at one of the fairs.[2]

3. [*Senior.*] How much did you give for it?

4. [*Junior.*] Guess.[3]

5. [*Senior.*] It's worth at least[4] three hundred ounces.

6. [*Junior.*] I began with an offer of two hundred, and went up,[5] and when I got to two hundred and fifty, the man let me have it.

7. [*Senior.*] What could have made it so cheap? I remember some time ago the common price of such a cloak as this was as much as five hundred ounces. Why, just look at it; how deep the colour is, and the fur[6] so thick and smooth; then the hair along the edges[7] is quite even; the lining is a piece of thick satin,[8] the figure on that is of a new pattern, and, to add to all this, the cloak itself is of the latest fashion. As to fitting you, it couldn't have fitted you better if it had been made for you.

8. [*Junior.*] If I don't forget, sir, you used to have one.

9. [*Senior.*] Mine! that's worth nothing. You can call it a cloak by courtesy, but that's all one can say for it. The hair[9] is coming out, and the colour is faded; I can't wear it with the fur outside.

10. [*Junior.*] Well, well, if that's the case, you must get yourself a good one next pay-day.[10]

11. [*Senior.*] Oh! I'm too much a man of the past to be nice about dress; all I require is something to keep me warm. You are one of the younger fellows just commencing a career.[11] It's quite right for you to put on good clothes and turn out smart on a levée[12] day; but if I were to dress[13] in that way, we won't say how I should look; I should be so uncomfortable as well. Besides, we who have got military duty to do have no occasion for fine clothes. We just put on anything; it may be old, or it may want mending, but we are quite satisfied with it all the same.[14]

1. 貂 *tiao*[1], the marten or sable.

2. 廟上 *miao shang*, in the temple; one of two temples in Peking where fairs are held on certain days every month.

3. 猜 *ts'ai*[1], to guess.

4. 至不濟 *chih pu chi*[4], most not complete, farthest from completeness, at the very least: *chi*, to complete, to come up to.

5. 添 *t'ien*[1], to add.

6. 毛道兒 *mao tao-'rh*, the fur: *tao*, not translatable by any of the meanings ordinarily assigned it.

7. 風毛 *fêng mao*, the fur edge that projects beyond the silk or satin lining on which the fur is laid: *ch'i chieh*, even and regular, as if cut with a knife; it also means complete, or in a state of readiness.

8. 緞 *tuan*[4], satin.

9. 稍 *shao*[1], the tip of anything; also used in the sense of to carry, as a note or a message, but in excess of one's proper business or errand.

10. 俸 *fêng*[4], official salary; *kuan*, probably in its original sense of to bar, to bolt; when the *fêng*, official salary to which you are limited, is assigned to you: *kuan fêng* is now used to mean simply drawing one's allotted pay or rations.

11. 巴結 *pa chieh*, here, to make an effort to get on in one's career.

12. 朝會 *ch'ao hui*, a levée at court.

13. 扮 *pan*[4], to dress.

14. 倒 *tao*, notwithstanding, all the same.

LESSON XXXV.

1. I've a friend who is a man of great nerve. He was lying one summer's night with the window propped open,[1] and in the midst of his slumbers he became sensible that something was making a noise.[2] He opened his eyes[3] to see what it was, and there, in the bright moonlight, was an elfin thing[4] hopping towards him, with a face the colour of yellow paper, blood running out of its eyes, its whole body[5] white as snow, and its hair all in confusion.[6]

2. Such an apparition suddenly[8] presenting itself to my friend as he was startled out of his sleep[7] made him jump considerably. "Dear me!" said he, "it's a ghost; let us watch him quietly[9] and see what line he takes."

3. Well, for a time the ghost went hopping about, but before very long he began to open the doors of a standing-press;[10] out of this he took a large quantity of clothes, clapped[11] them under his arm,[12] [13] hopped out of the window, and away he went.

4. Come, thought my friend to himself,[14] if this were a *bonâ fide* ghost he would not be taking clothes, I should think; and he was discussing this phenomenon with himself when the gallows-bird came in again. My friend jumped up at once[15] and gave the creature a blow with a sword,[16] on which it fell to the ground with a loud *ai-ya*.

5. The servants were called, and the lamp being lit,[17] it turned out that the ghost—a good joke, really—was a thief, who, intending[18] to rob the house, had disguised himself as a ghost in order to frighten[19] anyone he might come across.

1. 撐 *chih¹*, to prop up, to keep from falling by putting a stick under.
2. 響 *hsiang³*, sound of any kind; it may be used alone, or as here, in composition.
3. 睜 *chêng¹*, to open the eyes.
4. 物 *wu⁴*, things, animate or inanimate; affairs, business.
5. 渾身 *hun² shên*, the entire person; see *hun*, Lesson XXXII, Note 4, of streams mingling in confusion, undistinguishable; *q.d.*, all parts of the person without distinction.
6. 蓬 *p'êng²*, here *p'êng¹*, a kind of flag; in disorder like the foliage of such plants; should probably be written with the same radical as the following character, 鬆 (*sung¹*), dishevelled hair, tumbled, confused.
7. 醒 *hsing³*, to wake: *ching hsing*, to be startled out of one's sleep.
8. 忽然 *hu¹ jan*, suddenly, abruptly, unexpectedly.
9. 悄 *ch'iao⁴*, still, quiet; generally pronounced *ch'iao¹* or *ch'iao³*.
10. 立櫃 *li kuei*, a standing-press.
11. 挾 *chia¹*, to put under the arm; read *hsia²*, to put pressure on a superior.
12. 肢 *chih⁴*, the upper part of the arm; not used alone, nor without the characters here immediately preceding and following.
13. 窩 *wo¹*, a nest or den of bird or beast: *ko-chih wo*, the armpit.
14. 暗 *an⁴*, secret: *an hsiang*, thought to himself.
15. 猛 *mêng³*, fierce, courageous: *mêng jan*, moving rapidly, *q.d.*, without fear; it also means suddenly, or savagely.
16. 腰刀 *yao¹-tao*, a sword, not a dagger.
17. 一照 *i chao*, the moment [the light] shone on him.
18. 故意 *ku i*, with intent, designedly.
19. 唬 *hu³*, to intimidate; with *hsia*, to frighten; *hu* must not be intonated.

LESSON XXXVI.

1. Well, gentlemen, as ghosts have been your subject of conversation, I'll tell you a curious thing now. Your stories are all out of story-books; mine is an adventure[1] of my own.

2. Some years ago I and some friends had been outside the city for a walk, and we were on our way home again when we came to a large cemetery[2] that was by the road-side; it was in a very tumble-down condition; walls[3] and buildings in a state of utter dilapidation; but inside the enclosure there was a fine thick[4] growth of trees of every kind.

3. "So," said we, "this is a nice cool place; let us go in and rest awhile;" and we put out the fruit and other eatables we had brought with us, and sat ourselves down in front of the tomb, and began to eat and drink.

While we were so engaged, all of a sudden the wine we had in our cups[5] blazed up of itself, with a purring sound, like a thing on fire.[6]

4. Everyone was aghast[7] at the sight, and we were all for getting out of the way, when an uncle[8] of mine shook his hand[9] and stopped us before we had time to move. "Stand up,[10] and don't be frightened," said he; "there used to be a saying, 'Leave a thank-offering[12][13] for the spirit on the boundary[11] of his jurisdiction;' and the spirit of this spot has now alighted here." So saying, he hastily filled[14] a cup with wine and poured a libation,[16] praying[15] to the spirit at the same time; and the flame of the wine that had been in a blaze went out immediately.

5. This was a thing I saw myself; curious, wasn't it?

1. 經過 *ching kuo*, to have passed through.
2. 墳院 *fên yüan*, a grave enclosure, a cemetery. Observe the numerative *tso*.
3. 垣 *yüan²*, properly, a large wall: *ch'iang-yüan*, a wall, not necessarily large.
4. 密 *mi⁴*, close together; also, secret.
5. 鍾 *chung¹*, a cup; the same as *chung*, Part III, 221; this is larger than that, and probably distinguished as being made of metal.
6. 烙 *hu¹*, the sound of fire as it catches anything.
7. 愣 *lêng⁴*, stupefied; not recognised by the dictionaries.
8. 叔叔 *shu-shu*, my father's younger brother.
9. 擺手 *pai shou*, to wave the hand.
10. 站住 *chan chu*, literally, stand and stop; don't go.
11. 鄂 *ao⁴*, here, a sound to express that the first syllable in *aopo*, or *obo*, a Mongolian word for boundary line. The spirit disturbed was the god Terminus.
12. 謝 *hsieh⁴*, to thank.
13. 儀 *i²* has many meanings; here, a ceremony: *hsieh-i*, a thank-offering.
14. 掛了 *chên¹ liao* (see Part III, 774): *chên* here, to pour out.
15. 禱 *tao³*, properly, to pray for happiness.
16. 祭 *chi⁴*, properly, to make an offering of meat; 奠 *tien⁴*, to pour a libation: *chi tien*, to offer a meat and drink offering, or either without the other.

LESSON XXXVII.

1. [*Junior.*] What sort of house[1] is that opposite yours?

2. [*Senior.*] Why do you inquire?

3. [*Junior.*] A friend of mine wants to buy it.

4. [*Senior.*] The house is uninhabitable; it's haunted. An elder brother of mine did live there once on a time, and a fine spacious[2] house it is; seven rooms in front,[3] and five rows of buildings from front to rear, all distributed as they ought to be in a dwelling-house, and in good order. But after his death, when the place came into my nephew's hands, according to his account, the side buildings[4] got out of repair,[5] and though he had them rebuilt, all of a sudden ghosts and hobgoblins commenced their antics[6] there. They were not so bad at first, but as time went on sounds came to be heard in broad daylight; these were followed by apparitions;[7] and the women in the family were so scared by their constant[8] encounters[9] with these horrors that some of them actually died of fright. The wise women called in only wasted their arts[10] on the spirits; the other exorcists[11] were of no use either, and so there was nothing for it but to let the house go for anything it would fetch.

5. [*Junior.*] Well, you know, sir, this is all because the owner was not in luck's way. When a man has luck with him, these evil spirits,[12] if there be any by, keep out of sight, and have no power to hurt. On the other hand, he is a very timorous subject, that friend of mine; I shall tell him the truth as I have heard it, and then I shall have done my duty; it will be for him to buy the house or not, as he sees fit.

---

1. 所 *so*, originally, a place; here, a collective numerative of *fang-tzŭ*; all the buildings in the house being included in the question.

2. 地勢 *ti shih*, the circumstances of the ground, its dimension, condition, etc.

3. 門面 *mên mien*, not the face of the gate, but the gate-face, the face in which the gate stands.

4. 廂 *hsiang¹*, the lesser buildings that commonly flank the central building at right angles to it; not used colloquially without *fang*.

5. 動 *ts'ao²*, colloquially, in disrepair; 爛 *lan⁴*, tattered, dilapidated, worn out: *ts'ao lan*, all in ruins.

6. 祟 *sui⁴*, properly, evil done spontaneously by spirits: *tso-ch'i sui lai*, [the spirits] began their pranks.

7. 形 *hsing²*, the outer, or visible, form.

8. 動不動 *tung pu tung*, on every occasion; used only in speaking of unpleasant occurrences.

9. 撞磕 *chuang k'o*, to run up against.

10. 跳神 *t'iao shên*, the act of female exorcists; they stand on a table and affect by *t'iao*, posture-making, moving the limbs, to attract the spirits to themselves.

11. 送祟 *sung sui*, to see the *sui*, the evil influence, to the door; also the act of exorcists, male or female.

12. 邪 *hsieh²*, deflected, sloping; hence, moral depravity, depraved.

LESSON XXXVIII.

1. [*Junior.*] That string¹ of beads² of yours, sir, that I said I would take away I have never taken.

2. [*Senior.*] Why haven't you?

3. [*Junior.*] I have been here several times,³ but you were not at home, and I couldn't think of taking your things without saying a word to you;⁴ and that was impossible, as you were not to be found. So I came to-day for the express purpose of seeing you and telling you what I was going to do, after which I could take the beads with a clear conscience.⁵ I'll buy anything you fancy in return for your liberality, and if it's something that is not to be got in the shops, I shall do my best to hit upon a means of procuring it for you somewhere or other; what do you say?

4. [*Senior.*] If you had just carried off the beads whether I was at home or not, it would have been better, I can tell you.

5. [*Junior.*] How do you mean?

6. [*Senior.*] They're lost.

7. [*Junior.*] Oh,⁶ what a pity! There are p'u-t'i⁷ beads enough in the world, but⁸ it's seldom one sees any like those. From being carried about daily, they had become saturated¹⁰ with the sweat⁹ of the hand, and it had made them quite bright and smooth.¹¹ You ought to have put them away in the press when you hadn't them in your hand.

8. [*Senior.*] Ah! they were doomed to be lost. I was going into the garden one day last month, and they were hanging against the wainscoting of the stove-bed,¹² and I forgot to put them by. When I came in I went to look for them, and where were they? not a sign¹³ of them to be seen; I don't know who stole them.¹⁴

---

1. 盤 p'an¹, not as in Part III, 190; snakes p'an, coil themselves; p'an is here a coil or set of beads.

2. 誦 su⁴, properly, sung⁴; pronounced su, it means to recite, as the Buddhists do their books; 珠 chu¹, a pearl or bead: su-chu, properly, the Buddhist chaplet. The character for su given in this note is the correct one.

3. 遭遭 tsao¹ tsao, every time; *lit.*, every rencounter.

4. 含糊 han² hu², to be reticent: han, to hold in the mouth; hu, in the sense of mystery, confused.

5. 好 hao: having told you, I could then without wrong take them away.

6. 嗐 hai¹, an exclamation.

7. 菩 p'u², merely gives the sound of the first syllable of p'u-t'i, a Thibetan word.

8. 却 ch'üeh or ch'io: observe its relation to sui, although, and its place after the subject of the verb it immediately precedes.

9. 汗 han⁴, sweat of man or beast.

10. 漚 ou⁴, to saturate; 透 t'ou, to penetrate thoroughly.

11. 光滑 kuang hua², bright, glossy: hua, properly, to slip, slippery.

12. 牉 ch'a⁴, properly, ch'a¹, the planking at the end of the stove bed, when but one end of this rests against a wall; not used except as in the combination p'ai-ch'a.

13. 踪 tsung¹, man's footprint: tsung ying, footprint and shadow.

14. 叫 chiao: by whom they were stolen.

LESSON XXXIX.

1. [*Junior.*] Perhaps you've heard, sir, have you, of the new [1] arrival in the suburb? an astrologer that they say is as sharp as if he had come back from the other world.[2] He makes out one's past history as truly [3] and tells it as correctly [4] as if someone had told it him. People of our acquaintance are going to him in such numbers the whole day long that his booth is quite crowded.[5] If he is so first rate, why shouldn't you and I go too, and make him tell us our fortunes?

2. [*Senior.*] I heard of him some time ago. All my friends have been going to him for some days past, and I went there myself the day before yesterday and had my nativity [6] calculated by him. He made out my father's and mother's age,[7] the number of my brothers, my wife's family name, and the date of my admission into the service, without a mistake in the minutest particular;[8] but, thought I to myself, although he was quite right about all that *has* happened, it's not quite so certain that things that *have not* will turn out as he predicts.

3. [*Junior.*] Well, that may be all true enough; still, what is there that you and I wouldn't spend the few hundred cash he asks upon? so, come along. It is better for us to be out walking than sitting at home here with our hands before us; it's only [9] to cheer [10] one up a bit, and there is nothing improper [11] in going there either.

1. 新近 *hsin chin*, near in time, lately.
2. 轉世 *chuan shih*, returned to the world.
3. 極 *chi²*, properly, the ridge of a roof; extremest, most.
4. 準對 *chun tui* (see Part III, 1078), exactly corresponding.
5. 擠 *chi³*, to crowd, to shoulder as in a crowd; also, to squeeze, to press out.
6. 八字 *pa tzŭ*, the eight characters, taken from the Chinese cyclic system of 60 combinations of the 10 stem and 12 branch characters; the first combination marks the year, the second the month, the third the day, the fourth the hour, in which the person was born, and on the eight his fortune is calculated.
7. 屬 *shu*, to belong to; here, to belong to a certain year.
8. 毫 *hao²*, a small hair: *ssŭ hao*, anything small, as a thread of silk or a single hair; the minutest degree.
9. 只當 *chih tang* (observe *tang⁴*, not *tang¹*), it only represents, it only amounts to.
10. 解悶 *chieh mên*, to relax, to dissipate, sadness.
11. 不可 *pu k'o*, impropriety. Observe the force of *yu* at the beginning of the clause, followed as it is by the negative; *q.d.*, when all is said, *yu*, on the other part, what impropriety is there?

LESSON XL.

1. I'll give you something to laugh at. I was sitting here all alone just now when I saw that a bird had lit on the window-frame.[1] The sun cast his shadow against the window as he hopped about.

2. So I stole over very softly[2] to the place where he was, and made a grab at him through the window paper, tearing a large hole[3] in it; but I made a good shot,[4] and got him safe in my hand, when I saw directly that he was a sparrow.[5]

3. I was in the act of passing[6] him from one hand to the other, when P-r-r-rh![7] away he flew. I made haste and shut the door, but just as I had got hold of him a second time he freed himself again,[8] and I was chasing him all round the room, when the boys, hearing that a bird had been caught, came in in a body, and we all chased and chevied, until one little fellow popped[9] his cap over him and secured him.

4. Well, then I interceded for the bird: "Why," I said, "some people even buy birds to give them liberty.[10] What can you do with this one? let him go, can't you?" But he would not hear of it, and he held out with such stubbornness [11] [12] that I was obliged to let him have the bird. This made him quite happy, and away he went, hopping and skipping,[13] as pleased as could be.

1. 檔 *tang*[1], also pronounced *têng*[4], properly, a wooden framework; also, a cross-piece or bar of such a frame (*têng*), the rungs of a ladder, etc.; read *tang*[4], the open spaces between the rungs of a ladder or of lattice-work; it also means a trap or snare.

2. 捻 *nieh*[1], also read *nien*[4], to nip in the fingers: *nieh-shou-nieh-chiao-'rh-ti*, used of moving mincingly, softly, so that one may not be heard.

3. 窟窿 *k'u*[1]-*lung*[2], a hole; the two words are colloquially inseparable.

4. 抓住 *chua*[1] *chu*, the first verb indicating the motion of the hand, the dash made at the object; the second, its success: *ch'ia hao*, by good fortune, the issue being just what I desired, I made the dash and got hold of the bird.

5. 家雀 *chia ch'iao*[3], a house sparrow.

6. 倒 *tao*[3], to fall down, as a man, a wall, etc.; here, to pass from one hand to another; used in this sense of transferring a shop, business in trade; not to be confounded with *tao*[4], to pour (*see* Part III, 182).

7. 嗜嚕 *p'u*[1]-*lu*[1], of no meaning but to express the sound of a bird's wings in motion, or the like.

8. 掙 *chêng*[4]. *See* Part IV, Dialogue IV, Note 53.

9. 扣住 *k'ou chu*, the first word signifying to cover over either with the hand, a cap, a cup, or the like.

10. 放生 *fang shêng*, to let go alive; in conformity with the doctrine of Buddhism, which teaches to spare life.

11. 墜 *chui*[4], to be kept hanging by a weight.

12. 轂 *ku*[1], an axle-tree; 轤 *lu*[4], a roller or pulley: *ku-lu*, properly, the wheel of a cart; but *chui-ku-lu*[3] is a circular stone weight hung to awnings or curtains to keep them from shifting in the wind. Note the tones.

13. 跳 *t'iao*, to jump; 鑽 *tsuan*, properly, to bore; here, indicating the action of the head as the child skips away.

LESSON XLI.

1. [*Junior.*] Was there ever such a brat, sir, as that boy there!¹ Other people have given him all sorts of advice,² only for his good, and to keep him from learning what is bad for him. For all men are alike in that regard; they find it just as hard to acquire what is right and proper as it is easy to pick up what is vicious.

2. As for this boy, I have blown him up till my mouth is quite sore with talking, but he pays no attention to what I say; on the reverse, it makes him sullen,³ and he pouts⁴ and looks black.⁵ I could stand it no longer, and just now I lost my temper and gave him a very severe thrashing.

3. He coloured up, and, says he, "Why can't they do something else besides picking holes in my coat?" and he went off with his eyes full⁷ of tears.⁶ Blockhead that he is; he's born to do no good.

4. The proverb says, "Good medicine is bitter to the taste, and honest⁸ advice grates⁹ on the ear." If he didn't belong to me, I should be glad enough, I'm sure, to speak in a way that would be pleasanter to him to listen to.¹⁰ Why should I be doing what is certain to disgust him if it wasn't for this reason?

---

1. 壞孩子 *huai hai-tzŭ*, not spoiled in our sense of the term, but so bad that he will do no good.
2. 勸 *ch'üan⁴*, to advise, to admonish.
3. 無精打彩 *wu ching ta ts'ai* (see *ts'ai t'ou*, Lesson XIII, Note 2), *q.d.*, he has no spirit to play; though gambling be a pleasant thing, yet has he no soul for it. This is one explanation; another is, that *ta ts'ai* means any enjoyment. It is not used in either way except with *wu ching*, the latter character being the *ching* in *ching shên*, animal spirits.
4. 噘 *chüeh¹*, to protrude the lips, to pout.
5. 撂臉 *liao lien*; *lit.*, to let down the face.
6. 淚 *lei⁴*, to weep.
7. 汪 *wang¹*, properly, wide and deep; of a wide expanse of water.
8. 忠 *chung¹*, faithful, loyal, as a minister to his sovereign, as a friend to a friend.
9. 逆 *ni⁴*, the opposite of *shun*, obedient, compliant; rebellious, opposed to.
10. 哄著 *hung³-cho*; *lit.*, would that humbugging him I might make him glad.

LESSON XLII.

1. Just see what a miserable creature[1] that is; he is not a man at all; he is a beast; the very counterpart of his father;[2] the more one sees of him the more he disgusts one.

2. Wherever he goes he gets into the same scrape; his eyes are so closed up[3] that he can't see, and he runs against everything; and when he talks he stammers and stutters,[4] like a real lout[5] as he is.

3. As for doing anything that he ought to do, he's of no use whatever. He's ready enough for any tomfoolery[6] If you allow him no leisure, and keep him constantly attending[7] upon you, he does a little better; but otherwise he is all play without ceasing; and such a fidget[8] as he is, up with one thing and down with another, like a monkey; trouble, trouble,[9] never quiet for an instant.

4. When I am angry I feel as if nothing short of his life would satisfy me; then I cool down, and I say to myself, no; even if he didn't belong to the family, I could never[12] seriously[10] set about killing[11] him; and then he does belong to the family,[13] and whatever his shortcomings, he is of more use in the house than no one at all. A poker[14] may not be the length it ought to be, but it's better than one's hand to stir the fire with. And when I'm in this vein I am so far from wishing him any harm that if any money comes in, or if I've anything nice to eat or drink, I give him a little for love's sake.[15]

1. 賤貨 *chien huo*, commodity of small value: *ching*, [though he seems to be a man] yet he is not at all a man.

2. 活脫 *huo t'o*, while living to put off the skin: he has grown up so that he resembles his father as if his father, without dying, had thrown off his skin.

3. 擠顧 *chi*[3]-*ku*[4], to gaze with the eyelids closed together: *ku*, properly, to look over the shoulder, to look; also, to attend to, to look after.

4. 磕磕巴巴 *k'o-k'o pa-pa*, stammering.

5. 漚人 *ou jên*, a booby that people dislike and ridicule.

6. 陶氣 *t'ao*[2] *ch'i*, tomfoolery, mischief, high spirits.

7. 侍 *shih*[4], amongst other meanings, to attend upon: *fu shih* is used of the personal attendance of the wife on the husband, or of the other women of the harem upon husband and wife, or of the children upon both parents, in helping them to dress and undress, etc.

8. 鬧事精 *nao-shih ching*: the *ching* is here elliptically used for 精靈 (*ching-ling*) or 妖精 (*yao*[1]-*ching*), an imp, impish, devilish; *q.d.*, clever as an imp in *nao shih*, making trouble; how, is explained in the words that follow.

9. 唧叮咕咚 *chi*[1] *ting*[1] *ku*[1] *tung*[1]: the combination does not admit of analysis; no character in it is intended to do more than express a sound; the whole means a jumble of sounds.

10. 當眞 *tang chên*: observe *tang*[4], in the sense of to stand for, to represent.

11. 打殺 *ta sha* differs somewhat from *sha*, alone, which would imply that death was inflicted by a lethal weapon.

12. 忍 *jên*[3], the pain felt by the heart; to bear to do, to bear to see: *kuai*, devilishly, that is, exceedingly not can I bear.

13. 家生子 *chia-shêng-tzŭ*, one born in the house, the son of a slave.

14. 火棍 *huo kun*, a poker, whether of wood or metal, though short, is *ch'iang*, better, than *shou pa*[1], stirring with the hand. See *po*, Lesson X, Note 10.

15. 偏疼 *p'ien t'êng*, specially tender, to show special kindness to.

LESSON XLIII.

1. Yesterday, while I was out, those rascally servants of mine began to wrangle and make a row as if the house belonged to them, and by the time I came home there was a fine uproar. Pack of monkeys! I gave a cough¹ and walked in, and they all became dumb together, and then they sneaked out² one by one, looking at each other³ as guilty and frightened as possible.

2. This morning, just as I was out of bed, in came the villains and dropped down on their knees⁵ as stiff as posts,⁴ and began, "Oh! we deserve to die," and so on; and they kept on praying and kotowing and begging pardon⁶ so dolefully that my wrath began to cool a little, and I said to them, "Do you feel as if you wanted the stick, that you can't be quiet?⁷ if you oblige me to give you a thrashing, what good will it do you, pray? Now, if this happens again,⁸ look out for your skins, for I'll thrash you very soundly, I promise you. You won't mind unless I do."

3. And when I had done, they took themselves off, all *dja*-ing as they went.

1. 咳嗽 *k'é²-sou⁴*, to cough; the first word, which is also read *hai¹* (see Part IV, Dialogue III, Note 65), representing the "hacking" sound of coughing.

2. 賊眉鼠眼 *tsei mei shu yen*, eyebrows of wrong-doers, eyes of mice; the *ti* adverbialising the phrase.

3. 使眼色兒 *shih yen-shai-'rh*, using colour of the eyes, with an expression of the eyes, to wit, such as is described in the foregoing clause; *q.d.*, thief and mice-like glancing at each other, took themselves off one by one; also, to tip a wink, to make signs with the eyes.

4. 橛 *chüeh²*, a short wooden post, straight-post-like.

5. 跪 *kuei⁴*, to kneel down.

6. 哀 *ai¹*, painful feeling: *ai ch'iu*, to implore.

7. 好好兒的 *hao³-hao¹-'rh-ti*, of things, satisfactorily, arranged as they ought to be; of persons, quiet, orderly: your disorderliness [is it because] your flesh 癢 (*yang³*), itches? *sc.*, for the stick.

8. 再要 *tsai yao*, if on another occasion you are so minded, are set on like doings.

LESSON XLIV.

1. [*Senior.*] Just look at him, sir; there he is, drunk again to-day; dead drunk,[1] so that he can't keep his legs. I asked him if he had given the orders I desired, and he stared straight at me, heeling and lurching to and fro,[2] without answering a word. Why couldn't he answer; he is neither deaf nor dumb?[3] I'll give the scoundrel a very severe[4] correction[5] to-day; if I don't, I vow[6] I wish something may happen to me.

2. [*Junior.*] Come, come, sir, I daresay he forgot to go; and then, as he knew he was to blame, he became frightened, and this was the reason why he did not answer you. As[7] I happen to be by to-day, forgive him this once in consideration of that circumstance;[8] and warn him from this time forth to make up his mind[9] to beware[10] of drink. You know what the proverb says, "The stocking is a sure find inside the boot, and the slave has as little chance of giving his master the slip." You can always get at him. If he reforms, so much the better; if he does not, and if he gets drunk in this way any more, thrash him as much as you please; and if I chance to be a witness, I shall not say a word for him.

3. [*Senior.*] Ah! you don't know, sir, what a hopeless[11] thing he is, and always has been; and as for drink, he'll give his life for it; it's dearer to him than his father's blood. I may let him off to-day, but I'll answer for it he won't reform. He'll not abstain for more than a couple of days at the longest, and then he'll be drinking again as hard as ever.

1. 成泥 *ch'êng ni*, has become as mud, lies unable to rise; used only of persons lying senseless from drink, or who have been beaten till they were insensible.

2. 前仰, the strictly correct expression is *ch'ien hou yang ho*; *hou* referring to *yang³*, to look up; *ch'ien* to *ho*, the forward movement of the body.

3. 啞吧 *ya³-pa¹*, a dumb person: *ya*, interchangeable with 瘂, which also means hoarse.

4. 痛快 *t'ung k'uai*, indicating a combination of promptitude and completeness; it may be applied to the despatch of any business.

5. 責罰 *tsê-fa*, to punish, but specially of corporal punishment.

6. 起誓 *ch'i shih*, to make oath: observe the idiom; *q.d.*, if I don't beat him [may I incur the penalty of breaking] the oath I swear to beat him.

7. 既然 *chi jan*, since it is so that I am present.

8. 面上 *mien shang*, having regard for my face, not to put me to shame.

9. 狠狠心 *hên hên hsin*, harden his heart: *hên* here in the sense of cruel, hard-hearted.

10. 戒 *chieh⁴*, to beware of; also read *chi⁴*.

11. 成器 *ch'êng ch'i*, to make a utensil, to be of some use or other.

LESSON XLV.

1. [*Junior.*] Why, what's the matter, sir? Your face is as pale as if you had whitened[1] it; and since I saw you[2] a short time ago you have quite fallen away.[3]

2. [*Senior.*] Yes, but you don't know what has happened since then, sir. These last few days they have been cleaning the drains,[4] and the stench was very bad; and besides this, the weather has been so variable, cool one moment and hot the next, that a man couldn't say how he was to take care of himself. As for me, the day before yesterday it had been very *cool up to breakfast time*, but soon after it became so hot that no one could stand it; a violent perspiration[5] broke out all over me, and I took off my long dress[6] to cool myself, and drank a cup of cold tea, on which I was seized with a violent pain in the head, my nose began to run,[8] I had a cold in my head, a hoarseness came on in my throat, and I felt as sick and dizzy[7][9] as if I was in the clouds.

3. [*Junior.*] You're not the only person in the same condition. I am *out of sorts* myself, and not moving about more than I can help. However, yesterday I had the luck to throw up[10] all there was in my stomach; if I had not, I should not have been able to hold myself up[11] to-day even as well as I am doing.

4. [*Senior.*] I'll give you a rule to follow—a simple one: when you are hungry, eat sparingly. If you will do this, a little cold won't do you any harm.[12]

---

1. 刷 *shua*[4], not different in meaning from *shua*[1], to brush.

2. 冷孤丁 *lêng*[3] *ku*[1] *ting*[1], all of a sudden; the expression is incapable of analysis: *lêng*, cold, here, a shock; *ku*, solitary, properly, fatherless, but also used of one who has lost both parents; *ting*, a person, an individual; but it has other meanings.

3. 瘦 *shou*[4], thin.

4. 淘 *t'ao*[2], to cleanse out a well or a ditch: *t'ao kou*, to clean the drains.

5. 炮 *p'ao*[4], properly, the action of fire upon meat; here read *p'ao*[2]; 燥 *tsao*[4], dried by fire heat: *p'ao-tsao-ti*, as if I had been roasted, my whole person *t'ou han*, throughout perspired.

6. 袍 *p'ao*[2], properly, the long dress, open in front below, worn by officials under the *kua-tzŭ*; in hot weather the latter is dispensed with. The common people erroneously apply *p'ao-tzŭ* to other long robes.

7. 暈 *yün*[4], dizzy.

8. 鼻涕 *pi ting*[1], the mucous discharge from the nose: *ting*[1], properly, *t'i*[4]; *shang fêng*, to catch or have a cold; *shang*, short for *shou shang*, to suffer injury from, *fêng*, the wind.

9. 忽 *hu*[1], properly, to forget; hence, not to attend to: *hu-hu*, wool-gathering.

10. 吐 *t'u*[4], vulgarly *t'u*[3], to spit out: *ch'üan t'u*, to throw up everything.

11. 扎掙 *cha*[2] *chêng*, to hold oneself up by an effort; q.d., *cha*, planted in the ground, *chêng*, struggling. Observe the construction: [having done what I did I am able to-day to hold myself up by an effort;] had it not been thus, *yeh chiu*, then, even though I made the effort, I could not succeed. Note *cha*[2], not *cha*[1], as in Lesson VIII, Note 12.

12. 妨 *fang*[1], to injure, to interfere with: though you *chao liang*, encounter cold, even so it will not hurt you.

LESSON XLVI.

1. [*Senior.*] Dear, dear! what does this mean, sir? It was only the other day that we met, and here you are with your beard grown grey, and your whole appearance[1] that of an old man? Now, don't be angry with me for speaking out; but I do hear that you play, and that you have a number of debts unpaid. This is no joke, if it's true; you had best give up the habit.

2. [*Junior.*] This is all the merest gossip, not a shadow of truth in it. Inquire carefully, if you don't believe me, and then you'll see.

3. [*Senior.*] No, no; why should I inquire of anyone else? No man is ignorant of his own doings. I could not but think there must be some truth in the charge when I found all our friends making it.[2] Now, gambling is an evil without bounds—a bottomless pit to any victim that falls into it.[3] If he does not get foul of the law, he plays away till he hasn't a cash left, and he is cleaned[4] out of house and land before he gives over. I won't say that a hundred is a very large number, but I have seen or heard of more than a hundred cases of the kind. You and I are very intimate; and what would our friendship be worth if I knew of such a thing as this and did not try to dissuade you from it? One word for all, don't gamble;[5] that's all I have to say; you needn't insist on my "inquiring."

---

1. 露 lu^4, the dew; lou^4, to become manifest, to allow to be seen.

2. 議論 i^4 lun, to discuss, to talk about a thing: *i*, to deliberate in council, to debate.

3. 陷進 $hsien^4$ $chin$, to fall into: if it be that you fall into [gambling], na^3, in what [place], is there a bottom? *chiu shih*, we may proceed hence to say that, etc.; *hsien* also means to collapse, to fall in.

4. 精光 *ching kuang*, clean and bright. Observe the construction: *ti* representing the noun, of which *ching kuang* is the attributive; *q.d.*, in every case is it that the family estate is *nung*, worked to, a clean bright [condition]; then (=before that) [the player] will let go his hold.

5. 賭 tu^3, to play, to gamble, to bet.

LESSON XLVII.

1. You drink very hard, I observe; you're never away from the wine; you're too fond of it, really. And when[1] you drink, you will get so drunk; you never think you have had enough[2] till you can't stand on your legs. This is not as it ought to be; wouldn't it be better if you were to drink a little less than you do?

2. If one is dining out,[3] or at a wedding,[4] a little excess doesn't matter much; but what good can come of it if, with special reason or without special reason, you have always the cup to your lips? You simply excite the disgust of your wife and children, and you get blown up[5] by your elders, when they see you in this state. The least[6] penalty you will pay will be the ruin of some business or other of importance; and you may do far worse, you may bring[7] very serious calamity upon yourself. On the other hand, as for any man making[8] wine the means of acquiring any particular accomplishment or developing any faculty, so as to be able to do what is right and proper in such wise as to make people respect[9] one, that, I should say, is a thing that very rarely comes to pass.

3. In a word, wine is a poison[10] as injurious to the mind as it is harmful to the body, and a man should on no account give way to indulgence in it. Look in the glass,[11] if you don't believe me, and you'll see how thoroughly the wine has stained[12] your nose and face. What makes it worse in you, too, is that you are a man of a certain class, and to drink night and day as you do is an act of suicide so far as your career is concerned.

1. 每逢 *mei fêng*, every time you meet with, every time it happens.

2. 算了 *suan liao*; the latter is here the verb to finish: you then, when you can't stand, consider you have finished; not before.

3. 赴 *fu⁴*, to repair to; *hsi*, see Part IV, Dialogue X, Note 12: *fu hsi*, to go to a great dinner.

4. 喜事 *hsi shih*, a joyful affair, a wedding.

5. 不是 *pu²-shih*, a fault; here, the blame for it: *tê pu-shih*, to be found fault with.

6. 輕著 *ch'ing-cho*: observe the antithesis of *ch'ing* and *chung*, and our corresponding idiom; also that *cho* is here equal to *ti*, or to the classical relative *cho* so often used to isolate the thesis.

7. 惹 *jê³*, or *jo³*, to draw down, as evil things.

8. 藉 *chieh⁴*, to be beholden to.

9. 敬 *ching⁴*, reverence, reverential: *ching chung*, to respect.

10. 毒 *tu²*, poison: *tu yao*, a poisonous drug.

11. 鏡 *ching⁴*, a mirror.

12. 糟 *tsao¹*, properly, the dregs left after distilling spirit; hence, a soft, broken condition such as that of grain so used; hence, thoroughly saturated, as grain must be so to break: *tsao t'ou*, thoroughly saturated, the spirit within showing itself in the face.

LESSON XLVIII.

1. I have had a great deal to do the last few days, and after sitting up for two nights[1] in succession, my whole frame was so exhausted that I had no spring left in me.

2. So last night I thought I would be in bed early, but it wasn't to be. There was a rendezvous[3] of the whole family[2] at my house, and how was I to go to bed and leave them to take care of themselves? Well, though it was a great effort, I did contrive to stay up and keep them company; but oh! it was sore work for the eyes; my eyelids drooped, and I was quite stupid; however, there was no help for it till my guests departed. The moment they did, I clutched a pillow[4] and lay down, all dressed as I was, and slept till about two o'clock, when I woke rather chilly; what had made me so I can't say; my stomach[5] was puffed out and uncomfortable;[6] I was burning[7] from head to foot as if I had been over a fire;[8] and, to add to[9] all this, I had a pain in the ears which was so severe that it inflamed the whole jowl; I had no appetite left,[10] and I was equally uncomfortable lying down[11] or sitting up.

3. I thought the best thing I could do would be to abstain from eating altogether,[12] and to take a purgative.[13] This I did, and when it had carried away everything inside[14] me, good, bad, and indifferent, I began to feel a little more at ease[15] than I had been.

1. 熬夜 ao^2 yeh, to burn the night, to sit up all night working by lamplight: ao means also to cook or prepare by stewing or simmering.

2. 普裏普兒 $p'u^3$-li $p'u^3$-$'rh$, all, the whole tribe; said of persons or things.

3. 會齊 hui $ch'i$, all met together: observe here, hui $ch'i$-$'rh$, as if it were hui ko $ch'i$-$'rh$, meeting made a full number.

4. 枕 $chên^3$, a pillow for the head.

5. 腹 $fu^{2\ 3\ 4}$, the bowels.

6. 膨 $p'êng^2$, puffed out; used only of the stomach: $p'êng$ $mên$, puffed out and uncomfortable.

7. 發燒 fa $shao$, burning hot: fa jo, to be feverish.

8. 烤 $k'ao^3$, to roast.

9. 搭上 ta $shang$, to add to. Observe the construction: also add to this [there was that which] hurt the inside (lit., bottom) of the ear; the pain was such that also the whole cheek 腫 ($chung^3$), swelled.

10. 飲 yin^3, to drink; not so used colloquially alone.

11. 臥 wo^4, to recline, to lie down; not used colloquially alone; also written 卧.

12. 停 $t'ing^2$, to stop, to cause to stop: I thought that the case was one for $t'ing$ chu $shih$, stopping eating.

13. 服 fu, not differing in sound or tone from the same character in Part III, 826; but here, to swallow a dose: i chi ta yao, a dose of purging medicine; 劑 chi^4, a dose, a mixture; we cannot, however, say that a bottle contains so many chi, doses; the expression for this is 一服藥.

14. 內 nei^4, inside, as opposed to wai, outside.

15. 鬆快 $sung$ $k'uai$, the opposite of $p'êng$ $mên$, the comfort derived from getting rid of the latter; $sung$ $k'uai$ may also be applied to the mind.

LESSON XLIX.

1. He had not much strength to begin with, and he never knew how to take proper care of himself. He was too fond of wine and women, and now his constitution is paying the penalty.[1]

2. His present illness has been a long affair,[2] but yesterday, when we went to see him, he managed to bring himself into the drawing-room to speak to us: "Really, gentlemen," he said, "you do me too much honour,[4] putting yourselves to the trouble[3] of coming to call on me so often this hot weather, and I am sure I can't thank you enough[5] for the different things you are so good as to send me; there is always something coming from you. Of course, I attribute the interest you take in me to our relationship. If you had no connexion with me,[6] I could not reasonably expect you to take such an interest[7] in me. I don't say much, but I sha'n't forget your attention, and when I am well again I shall make you the fullest acknowledgments."

3. He went on in this strain, but it was evident[8] at the same time what an effort it was to him to hold himself up.

4. We merely observed, "You are too sensible a man, sir, to make it needful for us to say more to you than that you must take good care of yourself and you will soon be well. We'll come and see you again when we have time." When we had said this we came home.

1. 損 *sun³*, to injure: his *ch'i hsüeh*, breath and blood, his constitution, *k'uei sun*, is deficient and injured, fails him.

2. 延 *yen²*, properly, to go to a distance, to go on for a long time: *yen ch'an*, as of a long cord wrapped round.

3. 勞動 *lao tung*, I with fatigue stir you, I give you the trouble of moving.

4. 不敢當 *pu kan tang*, I do not venture to bear, to be the recipient of, so much kindness; I am not worthy.

5. 感情 *kan ch'ing*: my *kan*, feeling in my heart, your *ch'ing*, kindly disposition, my gratitude for it, is *pu chin*, inexhaustible.

6. 相干 *hsiang kan*, to be concerned with: if you were *p'ang*, bystanding persons with no concern in me.

7. 惦 *tien⁴*, to think kindly of: *tien chi*, to remember one with kindness. The character *tien* is not in the dictionaries.

8. 可露出 *k'o lou ch'u*; the *k'o* has a certain disjunctive power, in answer to the *sui jan* in the preceding clause: although such words were in his mouth, his person, to say the truth, *lou ch'u*, allowed to escape, the appearance of one who could not hold himself up. Observe *lai liao* at the close, auxiliary of *lou ch'u*, the object intervening between the verb and its auxiliary.

LESSON L.

1. Last summer he did contrive to walk, but he has grown much worse in the last few days; so much so, indeed, that he has taken to his bed altogether. His people[1] have no idea what to do for him; they are all confusion and racket;[2] and the old folks are in such affliction that they have quite fallen away.

2. I went to see him the other day, and found him lying on the stove-bed gasping[3] for breath, and so thin that he was no longer the same man. I went up to him very gently and I said, "Are you any better than you were?"

3. He opened his eyes wide, and when he saw it was I, he grasped my hand in his own very tight, and he said, "Ah! sir, no doubt I deserve my fate; I don't suppose[4] that after sinking so low I can possibly recover. Of course, I know it's my lot. Since[5] I first fell ill I've been treated by every physician[6] there is here, and I have taken every description of medicine, and again and again, just as I was beginning to improve, I have had a relapse.[7] It's my destiny. I've done myself no injustice.[8] But what moves me is the thought of my father and mother, who are now well on in years, and of brothers who are still children; and then all my nearest relations are here too, and I can't bear to tear myself from anyone belonging to me."

4. Before he had done speaking, his eyes were streaming with tears. It was a most distressing scene; had one been iron and stone, one must have been quite upset[9] at hearing him talk in this way.

---

1. 閤 *ho²*, properly, a folding door; to close it; hence, all within it; hence, of persons, all: *ho chia-tzŭ*, the whole family.

2. 烘 *hung¹*, properly, the flickering or flaring of flames: *hung-hung-ti*, of restless, anxious, movement.

3. 倒 *tao²* (not *tao³*, Lesson XI, Note 6, nor *tao⁴*, Part III, 182), especially of the breath when it is short; to gasp.

4. 大料 *ta liao*, most likely: *ta*, on the whole; *liao*, I imagine. See Lesson III, Note 8.

5. 自從 *tzŭ ts'ung*, both words meaning *from* in time; ever since.

6. 大 *tai⁴*, only so read in *tai-fu*, physician.

7. 重落 *ch'ung lo*, of sickness only; to go down a second time, to relapse.

8. 委曲 *wei-ch'ü*, injustice, oppression: *wei* means truly; *ch'ü*, as before, to bend; no injustice; *q.d.*, had I not taken all the pains I have to get well, I should have been unjust to myself.

9. 慘 *ts'an³*, to be moved in the heart: *tê huang*, as in Part III, 989.

LESSON LI.

1. If a man is not to be killed it must be because it is his destiny to be saved.[1] That night I was with our friend he was very bad;[2] he lost all consciousness,[3] and didn't come to his senses again[4] for a long time; and though I tried to quiet[5] his parents by begging them not to be alarmed and assuring them that there was no danger, in my own mind, I must confess, I thought the case desperate.

2. However, the sick man and his parents had better luck than one gave them credit for. The day after I was there a fresh physician was called in, and from the time he began to treat him the patient improved visibly from day to day.

3. I paid him a visit the day before yesterday, and though he is not quite himself[6] yet, he has got back his colour[7] and he has picked up a little flesh. He was leaning against his pillow, eating. "Well," I said to him, "are you all right again? I congratulate you most sincerely on your escape. Your attack was a pretty severe one; you were at death's door,[8] I can tell you."

4. He chuckled[9] as I spoke, and, said he, "It's no merit of mine; it's heaven's love for you and the rest of my friends; as to danger,[10] I am out of it now; it's a most providential recovery,[11] I take it."

1. 救星 *chiu hsing*, a redeeming star, a spirit that will save one.

2. 沉 *ch'ên*², to sink in water; hence, in some phrases, weighty: *ch'ên chung*, heavy, of things; grave, of affairs.

3. 昏 *hun*¹, properly, dusk, twilight; hence, to be mentally obscured, to faint away.

4. 甦 *su*¹, to revive from apparent death or from a swoon: *su hsing*, reviving, to wake up, to come to life again.

5. 慰 *wei*⁴, sense of comfort in the mind; to cause it; to console: *an wei*, to comfort, to console.

6. 還元 *huan yüan*, to restore the original *ch'i*, breath, animation.

7. 氣色 *ch'i sê*, the colour due to his reanimation. Observe the *k'o* for *k'o wei*, may be said to. Note *chuan*⁴, not *chuan*³.

8. 脫皮 *t'o p'i*, you put off one layer of skin, *sc.*, before you could get through your difficulty; you had a very narrow escape.

9. 嘻 *hsi*¹, to smile; in conversation, always doubled as here.

10. 災 *tsai*¹, any misfortune inflicted by Heaven.

11. 大好 *ta hao*, as opposed to *hao i tien*, a slight improvement. Observe *k'o*, which does not here modify the affirmation, but indicates the attainment of something that was almost despaired of. Cf. *k'o tê*² *liao*, I've got it at last; *k'o wan liao*, at last it is done, meaning I began to despair of finishing it.

PART V.—THE HUNDRED LESSONS.

LESSON LII.

1. It's all very well¹ your recommending me to take physic, but I have an idea of my own on the subject. If it was really necessary that I should take physic, I am not too stingy² to buy some; one isn't such a fool as to love money better than life. But the reason why I object to medicine is that the year before last I took the wrong dose, and very nearly³ killed myself;⁴ it makes my heart beat to think of it even now.

2. And then as to the doctors⁵ of the present day, there may be some good ones among them, but not more than one per cent. All the rest care for is to get in the money as hard as they can; what does it signify to them whether a patient lives or dies?

3. Call one in, if you don't believe me, and try him. He may understand medicine or he may not; but if he doesn't, he won't flinch from undertaking the case. He comes bustling into the house, and, as he calls it, feels your pulse,⁶ that is to say, he puts his finger somewhere or other for a moment; then he dashes off⁷ a prescription,⁸ pockets his fee,⁹ and away he goes. If the case turns out well, then it's all the skill of the doctor; if it does not, he says it was your destiny; it doesn't concern him the least in the world.

4. In the present instance I know very well what I'm about Instead of swallowing every variety of medicine, all to do me no good,¹⁰ I shall keep quiet and take care of myself; I shall get well enough.¹¹

1. 曾 ts'êng², properly, an adverb of past time; here it in no way affects the sense of ho.

2. 看 k'an¹, to take care of; to be distinguished from k'an⁴, to see (see Part III, 91).

3. 幾 chi¹, nearly; to be distinguished from chi³ (see Part III, 7): chi-chi-hu, nearly; the hu being here merely an adverbial termination. Observe the idiom; ours would require yu, not mei yu, before sang liao ming.

4. 喪 sang⁴, properly, to die; here, to cause to die: sang ming, to do mortal injury to one's own life; not used of injury to another's; sang¹, mourning, or matters pertaining to death.

5. 醫 i¹, to treat, as a medical man: i-shêng, a physician.

6. 診 chên¹ ³, properly, to regard, to scrutinise; here, specially to feel the pulse; 脈 mo⁴, properly, any artery; here, specially the pulse.

7. 胡哩嗎哩 hu²-li⁴-ma¹-li³, bustling; the sentence is incapable of analysis; hu-li-ma³-'rh-ti is as often used.

8. 藥方 yao-fang, a prescription; fang being used in the sense of fang-fa, a way or means.

9. 馬錢 ma ch'ien, horse money, the doctor's fee.

10. 效 hsiao⁴, to succeed, to result favourably: pu chien hsiao, to be sensible of no favourable result. Observe the yü ch'i, as compared with [the first proposition], pu ju, there is nothing so good as [the second proposition].

11. 倒好 tao hao; this reinforces the pu ju: the second proposition, whatever the merits of the first, tao, notwithstanding, is better.

LESSON LIII.

1. [*Senior.*] What does it signify to you if other people find fault with him? And then when I try to mollify you, why get more and more angry? Oh! you are too hot,[1] really. Wait till they're gone and then speak if you like; why must you argue[2] the whole case this very minute?

2. [*Junior.*] Come, sir, 1 cannot stand this sort of language from you. We are both in the same boat. You yourself have a certain interest in this question; you don't mean to maintain, do you, that it doesn't concern[3] you at all? Well, when they discuss him it brings you and me more or less under review,[4] and it is your place to stop them; but instead of this, you take the same side as they do; this I don't understand, and I certainly do feel somewhat dissatisfied.

3. [*Senior.*] No, no; I did nothing of the sort. All I meant was that if a man has anything to say he should be gentle and quiet about it; but to fly into such a passion as you did, to be actually bursting with rage,[5] is surely not the way to settle the matter, is it? All these people who are sitting[6] here are come on your account; and what must you do but boil up[7][8] in such style that one might suppose you wanted to turn everybody out of doors.[9] They were so scandalised that they were all thinking of going away, and the reason that they did not go was that they didn't want to cause you the mortification you would have felt if they had gone; but if you keep on raving and storming[10] in this way you'll make it as unpleasant for them to stay as to go; and then the next thing will be that you'll be cut by all your acquaintance.

1. 躁 *tsao*⁴, properly written with this, the 157th, radical; of the heart, easily moved: *chi-tsao*, impetuous.

2. 辨 *pien*⁴, to distinguish in the mind: *fén pien*, to argue a point, not necessarily with vehemence.

3. 罣 *kua*⁴, properly, to hook on to; *ai*, generally, to impede: *kua-ŋai*, to affect, more or less prejudicially.

4. 稍上 *shao shang* (see Lesson XXXIV, Note 9), *q.d.*, the matter with its extreme end touches us; it more or less regards us; it carries us along.

5. 綳 *pêng*¹, properly, to tie up: *pêng-pêng-ti*, tied tight; as, for instance, a drum head.

6. 在座 *tsai tso*, occupying the seats; *i.e.*, sitting here.

7. 怒 *nu*⁴, rage, furious anger.

8. 冲 *ch'ung*¹, also written 沖, of water bursting embankments; or, to carry away with a rush, as water an object in its way: your only concern is rage boiling over.

9. 攆 *nien*³, to drive out. Observe the construction: [instead of being calm,] *tao*, on the contrary, you are *hsiang-shih ti*, one seeming, to want to drive away [everyone, no matter] whom.

10. 山嚷 *shan*¹ *jang*³, clamour as within a mountain: *kuai chiao*, devilishly crying out.

LESSON LIV.

1. [*Senior.*] Well, now, from what I have seen of you in this affair, I should say that, however well you may talk,[1] you haven't the sense[2] that, to look at you, one would suppose you had. If he chose to leave you alone,[3] so much the better for you; why[4] should you go and provoke him? I advised you not to do it, but instead of listening to me, you tore away[6] as if you were possessed;[5] and now here you are again having got the worst of it.[7]

2. [*Junior.*] Oh! you don't half know him, the villain.[8] Everyone says he's a terrible fellow. He never shows mercy[9] to anyone that comes in his way; so long as he is not interfered with, it's all right; but if anyone, no matter who, crosses him ever so little, he sets to work, might and main,[10] to make his own side win,[11] and he never stays his hand till he has carried the day.

3. [*Senior.*] Exactly so; but then, why not let a sleeping tiger lie?[12] What is the fun[13] of going out of your way to look for trouble? Remember what the proverb says, "Take a staff in your hand when you walk, and you won't tumble down;[14] take counsel in action, and you'll make no false moves."[15] Well, you had best lean on me now; your own experience, unaided,[16] won't carry you very far; I'm some years ahead of you anyway; and if the course you preferred had been the right course, so far from offering opposition, which would have been unjustifiable on my part, I should have felt it my duty to remind[17] you that it *was* the right course; aye, and to urge you to follow it, had you been of another way of thinking.[18]

1. 就是 *chiu shih*: observe that *chiu* is connected with *shih*, and not with the *chih* which precedes it.

2. 燎 *liao³*, originally, a torch; hence, to illumine: *liao² liang*, of intellectual brightness; *liao³* also means to singe or scorch.

3. 嗔 *ch'ên¹*, also written with other radicals; to be angry with, to show anger by speech or looks: *hsün ch'ên*, to provoke by anger or censure.

4. 你可 *ni k'o*, that you must provoke him, that you should think it right to provoke him. The Chinese, however, here assign *k'o* something of the power of the disjunctives *ch'io, tao*, etc.

5. 指使 *chih¹ shih*, to give direction to and make to act; here, impelled by, *shên-kuei*, demons.

6. 拗 *niu⁴*, also read *ning³*, to twist, as a cord, a wire, etc.

7. 釘 *ting¹*, a nail; *p'êng liao ting-tzŭ*, to run foul of a nail, to kick against the pricks, to come back with a flea in your ear.

8. 該死 *kai ssŭ*. Construe thus: that one deserving death, tell me [if you can] what is he? There is no end to [his viciousness]; he is a notoriously terrible man.

9. 留分 *liu fên*; *lit.*, to leave a portion, *sc.*, of consideration for; *fên* being *ch'ing fên*, the apportionment of the feelings, of which more would be shown to one man and less to another.

10. 疊著 *tieh²-cho*, reiterating, redoubling; *ching-'rh*, muscle, muscular effort.

11. 站住 *chan-chu*, to stand fast; here, to effect a position, that is, if *chan* be written with the 117th Radical; if written without it, it means to usurp; but so written it is not found with *chu*.

12. 哄 *hung¹*, to rouse to motion by a cry; not *hung³*, to deceive.

13. 趣兒 *ch'ü⁴-'rh*, pleasure from seeing or hearing.

14. 跤 *chiao¹*, by itself, vulgarly, to struggle hard together like wrestlers, both with hand and foot: if you have *kuai-kun-'rh*, a staff such as old men lean on, you will not *tieh chiao*, get a fall; 跌 *tieh¹*, to slip or fall.

15. 失著 *shih¹ chao¹*, to err in your move; a figure taken from chess or draughts; *chao* is to move a piece in the one, or to put one down in the other: *chao-'rh*, a plan or move.

16. 光 *kuang¹*, often vulgarly used, as here, for only, alone: is it only your *chien-shih*, experience.

17. 提撥 *t'i² po¹*, to bring to the recollection, to remind of.

18. 豈有 *ch'i yu*, how should there be *tao*, on the contrary, *ch'ing-li*, justice, in stopping you.

LESSON LV.

1. [*Elder Brother, to younger.*] Why can't you behave[1] yourself in society? People won't set you down as having nothing in you[2][3][4] because you sit still, as a decent, orderly person should. If you never say a word no one will accuse you of not having the use of your tongue. And what pleasure can there be in going on as you do whenever you find yourself in society; irritating[6] this person or the other person by talking as if you wanted to raise a laugh[5] against him. You don't perceive how ill it looks, but it makes all the rest of the company uncomfortable, and one of these days you will fall in with someone who is not to be trifled with, and when you come to grief, you'll understand the risk you run by this sort of conduct.

2. [*Friend, addressing the younger Brother.*] What your brother says is very true, sir. Quizzing leads to warm words, and, in the long run, to no good. You should mind what he says, for no one not connected with you would take the same interest[7] in you; and though you are so tall for your years, you are still young; you really must make a serious effort to break yourself of this habit.

3. [*Continuing, to the elder Brother.*] You and I have been young, you know, and in youth one is all for play. I should recommend you, without loss of time, to get him some man of good repute as a tutor, and let him read with him. He'll add by degrees[8] to his stock of information, and as soon as he knows more of the world, he'll mend of himself. Don't distress yourself with the notion that he'll go to the bad.

---

1. 穩重 *wên³-chung*, of gravity, decorum, opposed to 輕佻 *(ch'ing-t'iao)*, levity, want of manners.

2. 雕 *tiao¹*, to carve wood.

3. 塑 *su⁴*, to model the human figure out of clay.

4. 廢物 *fei¹ wu*, a thing to throw aside: who would say you were a thing to throw aside, a worthless article, carved of wood, or fashioned of mud?

5. 鬭笑 *tou¹ hsiao*, to provoke a laugh: *tou*, to fight, to set by the ears; it is maintained by some that 逗 is the proper character to be used in this phrase.

6. 招 *chao¹*, to beckon; also, to annoy or excite.

7. 關切 *kuan ch'ieh⁴*, affectionately interested in: *kuan*, to connect; *ch'ieh*, to cut deep into, to chop up.

8. 漸 *chien⁴*, gradual, beginning from the spring or source.

LESSON LVI.

1. [*Friend.*] What odd behaviour[1] to be sure! He stammers[2] so when he is with anyone that it's impossible either to make out what he wants when he speaks to you, or to get an intelligible answer out of him; and he's in such a state of trepidation[3] all the time that he never knows when he ought to come forward or when to go back. He always seems asleep; a perfect apology for a man, really. How can anyone be such a booby as he is at his time of life. You and his other friends ought to take him to task[4] a little; it might do him good, perhaps.

2. [*Host.*] Ah! you haven't been long enough acquainted with him to know him thoroughly. He has many an absurd trick besides those you have been enumerating. You may be sitting with him talking, and just as you have got upon one subject, some other comes into his head, and he'll make a remark about that; or he'll be staring at you with his eyes[5] fixed and his mouth open, and all of a sudden he'll blurt out some piece of incoherent nonsense, and make people split their sides with laughing. He came to pay me a visit the day before yesterday, and when he got up to go away, instead of walking straight on, he turned himself half round and moved backwards. I called out to him, "Take care of the door-sill,[6] sir!" but before the words were out of my mouth he had caught his foot against it, and over he tumbled on his back. I ran to help him up[7] in such a hurry that I was very near[8] getting a fall myself. As to taking him to task, I have spoken to him often enough before now, but I found he was the kind of good-for-nothing that advice won't improve; so I don't see the use of wasting my breath on him any longer.

---

1. 動作 *tung-tso*, behaviour, whether as regards speech or action.

2. 結巴 *chieh¹ pa*, to stammer; as if, says one Chinese, *hsia-pa*, the chin, were *chieh*, tied to something. Note *chieh¹*.

3. 畏 *wei⁴*, to fear: *wei-shou-wei-wei-ti*, fearing the head, fearing the tail; extremely nervous; 尾 *wei³*, the tail or end, colloquially, 尾把 (*i³ pa*).

4. 指教 *chih chiao*, to point out a man's errors for his edification, to pull him up.

5. 眼珠 *yen chu-'rh*, the pupil of the eye.

6. 檻 *k'an³*, a door-sill; when read *chien⁴*, it has other meanings.

7. 扶住 *fu² chu*, properly, to support by holding under the arm: *fu chu* may be used with persons or things.

8. 幾幾乎, or *chi¹ hu*, nearly. Note *chi*, an adverb meaning nearly.

LESSON LVII.

1. Did you observe, sir, how ill-natured he was all the time about my old clothes?[1]

2. I don't want to boast of my superiority,[2] but really, for his years, *he* knows nothing. As for this question of dress, neither he nor any of them understands it at all. New clothes are intended to be worn on extraordinary occasions. What does it matter if my home suit here, the clothes that I put on every day, be a little the worse for wear? If a man is an ignoramus he has something to be ashamed of; but what can it signify how he dresses? Take myself;[3] I am not a dressy man I admit, but I am a great deal better off than people that are.

3. How so? Why, because I contrive to keep out of debt without applying to any man for help,[4] and therefore I have nothing to feel shame about.[5] As for our young friends there, I've something less than contempt for them.[6] All they are good for is to dress themselves out in fine new clothes,[7] and to swagger jauntily about, as if *that* made them respectable; they learn nothing that makes a man useful. And what is there wonderful in being swathed[9] in silk and satin[8] from head to foot as they are?

4. Your thoroughly low fellows, who have not eyes to distinguish a lout from a gentleman, may mistake them for gentlemen, and make up to them accordingly; but I regard them simply as so many clothes-horses.

---

1. 糟 ts'ao², the same as ts'ao (see Lesson XXXVII, Note 5); ts'ao chiu, worn out.

2. 誇 k'ua¹, to praise another, to boast of oneself.

3. 卽 chi², a word as common in the written language as chiu in the spoken, and used much as chiu is: chi ju is more elegant than chiu pi fang, well, for instance.

4. 求告 ch'iu kao, praying and appealing to.

5. 恥 ch'ih³, to be ashamed of; also written 耻.

6. 眼角 yen chiao³, the corner of the eye: not even in the corner of my eye do I hold them.

7. 鮮 hsien¹, fresh, just killed, as meat; hsien³, seldom, rare.

8. 綢 ch'ou², silk; 緞 tuan⁴, satin.

9. 裹 kuo³, to wrap about, as a cord or bandage: swathed in silks and satins tao ti, down to the bottom, sc., the feet.

LESSON LVIII.

1. [*Senior.*] You have no right to be taking him in in this way. When people ask you for an opinion in the most respectful manner,[1] if you know the thing, good; if you don't know it, you should say you don't; but it makes you look as if you wanted to do them a mischief when you set them wrong by telling them what isn't the case. If the man were some scoundrel that one ought to have no love for, I shouldn't pull you up; but I can see that he's a very simple fellow. A single glance shows one that he is too slow[2] to do any great harm. Supposing it was any-one else that was humbugging him, it would be our place to remonstrate; and that you, instead of taking his part, should be using him so ill is really more than I can put up with.[3]

2. [*Junior.*] You don't understand him, sir. He'd get round you soon enough if you had anything to say to him. He's just that sort of being that *seems* to have no sense,[4] while in reality he's extremely mischievous. You couldn't form an idea of his viciousness[5] without some experience of it. He's full of shifts, and he'll circumvent anybody. His way is to make sure[6] of the line you are going to take. He'll lead you on[7] till he has wormed your views out of you, and then he'll stand off and watch his opportunity. The moment he sees an opening,[8] no matter how small, he'll follow it up and he'll checkmate you then and there.[9] Now, with the risk I run in the case he was speaking of, do you think, sir, it would have done for me to put him in full possession[10] of my intentions? Admit that you have been censuring me unjustly.

1. 恭 *kung¹*, reverential, respectful.

2. 慢性子 *man hsing-tzŭ*, a slow-natured fellow, no great quickness either for good or for evil.

3. 過不去 *kuo pu ch'ü*, not to be able to pass; said of places through which there is no way; here, of the feelings, unable to pass by, unable to put up with, the objectionable matter in question.

4. 愚 *yü*¹ ², stupid, inwardly; 蠢 *ch'un³*, loutish, outwardly; both are used separately: *yü ch'un* may be used of either stupidity within or loutishness without.

5. 陰惡 *hsien ngo*, treacherous and evil; vicious, malevolent.

6. 據 *chü⁴*, properly, to lay hold of: *p'ing-chü*, proof.

7. 勾 *kou¹*, to hook: *kou yin*, to lead on.

8. 破綻 *p'o chan⁴*, a rent and opening seam, a hole in one's coat.

9. 兜屁股將 *tou¹-p'i⁴-ku³-chiang¹*, to checkmate: *tou*, to carry, as a napkin having something in it that one does not wish spilt; also, to take in the rear; *p'i-ku*, the buttocks; *chiang*, in the sense of a general; *q.d.*, a general who takes his adversary in the rear. The king in Chinese chess is called *chiang*.

10. 徹 *ch'ê⁴*, properly written with the 85th Radical, to clear, as water of its sediment; *ch'ê ti-tzŭ*, cleared to the bottom. *See* Lesson LXI, Note 9.

LESSON LIX.

1. What has befallen our friend So-and-so? There he has been for the last few days with a face full of woe,¹ looking as if he cared for nothing² and had nobody to care for him;³ what is it all about?

2. I can't tell you. He used to be always out of doors; never at home, except on a wet day. If it wasn't snowing or raining, he was sure to be off in some direction or other. They never could get him to sit in the house with his hands before him. For some time past, however, he hasn't shown at all, so yesterday I paid him a visit.

3. Yes? and didn't you find him changed?

4. He's grown very thin, and he seems worn; in fact, he looks as if he got no rest, night or day. His appearance disquieted me a good deal, and I was just going to ask him a question when, as luck would have it, a relation of his came in, and I said no more.

5. Dear me! from what you say I should infer that it's the difficulty he finds himself in about that business, you know, that is disturbing him so. Still,⁴ a man that has lived through hard trials, as the proverb says, is not to be frightened by the lesser ills of life; and seeing that What's-his-name has always come very well out of any serious difficulty he may have had on his hands in times past, I don't see why he should attach so much importance to a trifle like this; it's not worth so much distress of mind,⁵ surely.

1. 愁容 *ch'ou jung*, sorrowful appearance, *man mien*, all over his face: *jung*, the same character as *yung* (see Part III, 963), but with a different meaning.

2. 聊 *liao²*, properly, to lean against, to depend upon.

3. 賴 *lai⁴*, much the same as *liao*, and more in use: *wu-liao-wu-lai-ti*, in a listless, apathetic manner: *lai* also means to repudiate, as a just debt, or to deny a true accusation.

4. 然而 *jan-êrh*, read *jan-'rh*, nevertheless: *jan*, thus, this being so, *êrh*, yet, notwithstanding.

5. 值得 *chih tê*, is it indeed worth that 憂愁 (*yu¹ ch'ou*), sadness and dissatisfaction.

PART V.—THE HUNDRED LESSONS.   309

LESSON LX.

1. You can have seen nothing of life to be in such a state of nervousness as this.¹ If you have anything to say to him, why keep it on your mind when by going to him and telling him plainly what you think you could bring the thing to a conclusion? He is only a man like yourself; he's not a beast; and, of course, he must act like a reasonable being; why should he not? What you have to do is, first, to state how all this came about, and then to go over the whole ground step by step, arguing each point separately. Do you suppose that he will take your life in some way or other? that he'll murder you or devour you, which?

2. Besides, when everyone else interested is perfectly at his ease,² is it manly³ in you to be in this state of chronic alarm, and taking all these precautions?

3. Follow my advice, and keep your mind easy like the rest of them. If he doesn't intend to let you have your way in the matter, if he's going to try a fall with you,⁴ he'll give you no law; and don't suppose that the state of terror you are in at this moment will bring you through without scathe, for it will do nothing of the kind. I have observed that so far⁵ no one has hinted that he does intend hostility, and my own idea is that the thing has long passed out of his recollection. If you think otherwise, set to work quietly and try and get some information;⁶ but I believe he has forgotten it, and I'll engage⁷ that you have no trouble at all.

1. 怯 *ch'ieh⁴*, timidity; not so strong a word as *p'a*: *fa ch'ieh*, *lit.*, to put forth timidity; to be nervous.

2. 動靜 *tung ching*; *lit.*, to stir what is still: *mei tung ching*, not to move, to give no sign of concern; *lai pu lai ti*, whether anything is happening or not.

3. 味兒 *wei⁴-êrh*, read *wê-'rh*, the odour, that by which the true quality is known of *han-tzŭ*, a Chinese; that is, a man.

4. 低 *ti¹*, low; *kao ti*, the height of anything, but here, the keeping up or falling down: if [like a wrestler] he is about to see with you who is to be *kao* and who *ti*; to try a fall.

5. 而今 *êrh chin*, up to the present time. So says a Pekingese, but to judge from another dialect, *êrh* has simply the sense of *ju* (*see* Part III, 906); *q.d.*, as at this time.

6. 探 *t'an⁴*, properly, to reach to oneself from a distance; to spy out: *t'an-tzŭ*, a spy; *t'an t'ing*, to look out for information.

7. 管保 *kuan pao*, to warrant; the first character adds nothing to the force of the second.

LESSON LXI.

1. [*Senior.*] You two used to be such friends, and now he never crosses[1] your threshold; what's the reason?

2. [*Junior.*] I don't profess to understand him. I suppose some of our people here must have offended him. If not, I can only account for it in one other way, and that is that he took offence at something I said myself; it was only a few words,[3] and nothing that, considering the terms we had been on,[2] need have put him out so that he couldn't forget it;[4] but it did, and he gave up coming to see me. Not that that would have mattered so much, but what I don't understand is, why he should never be saying anything but evil of me behind my back; making me out so bad and so dangerous; never meeting any of my acquaintances without introducing[5] my name and disparaging me. A short time ago I was marrying my son,[6] and feeling that it would be a shame[7] not to ask an old friend like that to the wedding, I did write him an invitation, and he didn't send so much as a dog to acknowledge it. I may as well make no more acquaintances,[8] really; everyone I have met has treated me with just the same want of regard.

3. [*Senior.*] Didn't I tell you you couldn't trust him either for word or for deed? and you wouldn't even go into such a question: indeed, you were far from satisfied with me for saying what I did.

4. [*Junior.*] True enough; as the proverb says, "You may know a man's face, but you can't tell what his heart's like." I couldn't see into his so as to know all[9] that was in it of good or evil. All one can do is to be more careful in future.

5. [*Senior.*] That's the right thing, undoubtedly. It won't do to call every man you meet your very good friend, indiscriminately.[10]

1. 登 *têng*[1], to mount, as a ladder; to ascend, as a height.

2. 好好端端 *hao-hao-tuan-tuan*, well and rightly: we indeed were in the habit of going on [with one another well and rightly].

3. 上 *shang*, on, or in: it was because of [what was] on, or in, a half sentence of talk.

4. 不犯 *pu fan*, here, not to regard or concern; not worth remembering. *Cf.* also *fan pu shang*, not worth the trouble, or inconsistent with dignity.

5. 當作 *tang tso*, to treat as, to make of: treating me as *hua pa*[4]*-'rh*, a handle of discourse; *tsao t'a*, to injure me, this is what *hsin-i*, intention? 蹧塌 *tsao*[1] *t'a*, to injure, to spoil: *tsao*, to tread under foot; *t'a*, to fall down in ruins, to subside. Note *pa*[4], not *pu*[3]; the character should properly be written 掱.

6. 媳婦 *hsi*[2] *fu*[4]*-'rh*, properly, a son's wife, but vulgarly, anyone's wife.

7. 臉上 *lien shang* must be construed as a noun, the subject of *hsia pu lai*, to be unable to lower, to let pass away, *sc.*, not the face, but the regard it would show to a friend.

8. 往後 *wang hou*, in after time, hereafter; *chieh chiao*, to knit intercourse, to make acquaintance.

9. 透徹 *t'ou*[4] *ch'ê*[4], thoroughly, to the bottom.

10. 一概 *i*[2] *kai*[4], the whole collectively, of men or things.

LESSON LXII.

1. [*Senior.*] He began it; who was finding fault with him, I should like to know? It was he who forced me to speak by what he said. You are the last man I should think of trying to deceive,¹ and I tell you that since² New Year's day he has never once been to the office;³ and now to-day he comes in, after having been drinking somewhere or other, and the moment he sees me he calls out, "Hallo! how is it I only now find you here?" In other words, instead of being grateful to me for working double tides,⁴ and doing his duty for him a whole month, he attacked me as if I had been neglecting my own duty. I certainly felt very angry.⁵ However, I didn't think it necessary to argue the point with him to-day; we'll see about it to-morrow.

2. [*Junior.*] I wouldn't join issue with him on the subject, sir. Why should you be contentious?⁷ That's the very thing that he is;⁶ talking at people⁸ is just the one thing he loves, as you must know. I expect he was drunk again. All you have got to do is to go on just as if⁹ you had heard nothing and seen nothing, and there will be an end of it. You are not obliged to take notice of him, are you?

3. [*Senior.*] Yes; but I can tell you, sir, that forbearance to a bully like this, who is as insolent as he is cowardly,¹⁰ merely makes him more cock-a-hoop.¹¹ If he had said, "I was only in joke; what I said slipped out unintentionally; I apologise for the rudeness¹² of my remark," one might have forgiven him;¹³ but it wasn't so at all; he was flushed with anger when he spoke to me. Now, who is going to be afraid of him? I am sure I'm not.¹⁴

1. 瞞 *man*², to blind, to deceive.

2. 自從 *tzŭ ts'ung*, from, a certain time; the combination has no greater force than either of its parts separately.

3. 走了 *tsou liao*: on what *ch'ai shih*, official duty, has he gone? You could not, however, say *tsou liao ch'ai shih* for having been on duty.

4. 脫空 *t'o³ k'ung*, withdraw [the person in order to enjoy] leisure. Construe: if it were as he says, I, [though I] without allowing myself leisure, for a whole month have been bearing his office for him [instead of having done well], on the reverse, am in the wrong, am I? Note the tone of *t'o*.

5. 頸 *kêng³*, the back of the neck: *po-kêng-tzŭ*, the back of the neck, which, say the Chinese, stiffens as one's choler rises.

6. 配 *p'ei⁴*, the mate of, to match with: *i pan*, of the same sort; *i p'ei*, a match with; *i pan i p'ei*, to put oneself on the same level as; *pu p'ei*, the converse of *fan pu shang* (see Lesson LXI, Note 4), not good enough, not of sufficiently exalted position. See "fit company," Lesson LXIII, 1.

7. 競 *ching⁴*, to strive, to wrangle; not used colloquially alone, or otherwise than as here, in *chêng ching*.

8. 耍嘴皮子 *shua tsui p'i-tzŭ*; *lit.*, to fence with the lips, to bandy words with, in fun or in earnest.

9. 只當 *chih tang*, only to represent, to bear oneself just as if.

10. 跟前 *kên ch'ien*, in the presence of: when you stand before this sort of *tung-hsi*, who insults the soft and fears the hard, etc.

11. 長價 *chang chia*, to increase in price or value of; said of things, or, as here, of self-esteem.

12. 冒失 *mao shih*: by my abruptness, or inconsiderateness, I erred; a common form of apology.

13. 諒 *liang⁴*, originally, faith, confidence; hence, to assume as fact: in *yüan liang* it signifies forgiveness, this combination being an elliptical form of 原情諒事 *yüan ch'ing liang shih*, bethinking you of the matter; *sc.*, my fault, forgive that matter.

14. 不成 *pu ch'êng*, a common form of ending a sentence interrogatively, especially when *nan tao* has preceded it.

4. [*Junior.*] Don't let him put you in a rage, sir; I'll get in a rage for you.¹⁷ The drunken villain! I'll take him to some quiet corner, out of the way,¹⁵ and I'll shake my finger in his face and call him all sorts of names.¹⁶

15. 僻 *pi*⁴, properly *p'i*⁴, unfrequented by man, out of the way and quiet.
16. 罵 *ma*⁴, to revile, to curse; *chih-cho*, pointing with the finger at his face.
17. 出出氣 *ch'u ch'u ch'i*, to vent rage; here, for another.

LESSON LXIII.

1. You false-hearted villain, you!¹ to be showing these airs to *me!* am I not fit company for *you*, I should like to know? What do you take yourself for, pray, that, right or wrong, you must always be laughing in your sleeve at me?² If I were disposed to talk, we have been long enough in daily contact to enable me to do so; but I don't, because if I were to go back on the past, the next thing you would accuse me of³ would be of trying to show you up.⁴

2. I know as much about you in your home as you know about me in mine; it is not so very long ago that you used to catch it from everybody,⁵ and now, forsooth, you miserable wretch! you affect superiority over me;⁶ what do you mean by it? If you had said, "I had no business to say what I did," one might have forgiven you;⁷ but no, not a bit of it;⁸ nothing will make you give in;⁹ you are determined not to admit you were in the wrong, and enrage one more than ever.

3. What it is that you consider entitles you to conduct yourself¹⁰ with such impertinence to me I cannot understand. We're too fairly matched, remember, for either to be afraid of the other. If you want to try a fall, I'm ready. If I hang fire,¹¹ I'm no true man.

1. 壞了 *huai liao*, here, attributive of 腸子 (*ch'ang²-tzŭ*), *lit.*, the bowels (figuratively, for the inner man): ruined, or corrupted, heart.
2. 譏誚 *chi¹ ch'iao⁴*, to criticise covertly; the first character used alone; the second not without the first. The combination may be used of criticism either to a man's face or behind his back, the critic not speaking plainly, but employing *ch'iao hua*, cunning talk, clever innuendoes; the *ch'iao* of *ch'iao hua*, or *ch'iao p'i hua* is not as above, but 俏.
3. 免 *mien³*, to avoid: *wei mien*, inevitably, *yu*, in the next place, you would say.
4. 揭 *chieh¹*, to open, to disclose: *chieh tuan*, to show up the shortcomings of.
5. 揉 *jou²*, to rub between the hands; used by itself of things; of persons, as here, with 挫 (*ts'o⁴*), a verb of the same meaning, used only with the first: *jou-ts'o*, to bully. Observe the construction: [since] you have ceased *shou*, to be subject to, people's bullying, then how many days is it?
6. 作足 *tso tsu*, to play the part of a self-sufficient man. Observe the place occupied by the auxiliary verbs *ch'i* and *lai*.
7. 恕 *shu⁴*, to pardon.
8. 死扭 *ssŭ niu*; *lit.*, determined to twist something held in the hand: you were in the wrong, yet you *p'ien*, specially, were ready to die rather than not twist; determined to have your way.
9. 一口 *i k'ou*, holding one language unchanged; *yao³ ting*, biting fast, not yielding.
10. 舉動 *chü tung*, rising and moving; conduct, behaviour.
11. 磴 *têng⁴*, properly, stairs, steps, of stone: *ta i ko têng-'rh* (pronounced *tê'rrh*) is used of a halting advance, as if the person were mounting steps, not walking on a smooth level.

LESSON LXIV.

1. He's no good, that fellow; how came you to take a fancy to him? He may be a man in form, but he's a beast by nature. Keep clear of him, whatever you do.

2. Mind what I'm saying to you. He's a mischief-making[1] scoundrel;[2] a dark and dangerous man.[3] According to him there's always a storm brewing somewhere. He'll get hold of some small trifle about a man, and blab, blab,[4] he'll publish all over the place in a way that's intolerable;[5] or he'll go and tell[7] So-and-so something about you, and he'll come and tell you something about So-and-so, in order that he may set you both by the ears, and then step in between you as mediator.[6]

3. If you think I'm not telling you the truth, observe this fact; not only has he no friend, but he's in great luck if he's spoken of without being abused.

4. Ah! his father and mother must have been a bad lot[8] to have been the parents of a fellow so odious and contemptible.

1. 混帳 *hun chang*; *lit.*, an account in confusion; a strong term of abuse implying certain mischievousness.
2. 行子 *hang-tzŭ*; *lit.*, one of a class; a fellow; but used always in a bad sense.
3. 心眼 *hsin yen*, the eyes of the heart or mind, by which its intelligence is emitted; the heart should be red.
4. 嚼說 *chiao² shuo*, to chatter, to babble; intensified by *hun*, preceding it. See Part IV, Dialogue VIII, 79.
5. 不堪 *pu k'an¹*, not to tolerate, intolerable. Construe: he *chang yang*, promulges it to a degree, that I *pu k'an².*
6. 從中作好人 *ts'ung-chung tso hao jên*, to act as mediator; 說合 (*shuo ho*) is equally admissible.
7. 傳 *ch'uan²*, to propagate reports; when read *chuan⁴*, a story.
8. 德 *tê²*, virtue: *tê hsing*, virtuous conduct.

LESSON LXV.

1. [*Senior*] I was coming home from the office just now, when, at some distance from me, I heard the noise¹ of a large party on horseback. I looked hard as they came up to me, and I saw it was What's-his-name, our old neighbour, you know. Such a toilet and such a team, quite a case of "the sleek steed and the costly cloak,"² and the man himself well filled out both in face and person. He saw me, but he took no notice of me whatever; screwed his head back and looked up to the sky. At first I was going to call out to him to stop, and I would have made him well ashamed of himself;³ but on second thoughts I said to myself, "Pooh! what's the use? it isn't his recognition of me that would make me respectable; who has got leisure to go into such a question with him? I am sure I've not."

2. Dear me! you must remember well enough, sir, how he used to go on when he lived down in our neighbourhood three years ago. He was wretchedly poor; so poor that as soon as he had his breakfast he had to set to work to secure a dinner. Day after day he'd be roaming about as restless as a spirit;⁴ when he had nothing to eat, doing without; but trying everyone for a meal; very lucky⁵ if he managed to pick up any trifle of the commonest description. He'd come to my house at least two or three times a day, and if he didn't ask⁶ for one thing he would for another. I should like to know what there was belonging to me that he didn't taste; he made my chopsticks shine again,⁷ he ate with them so often. Well, one fine day⁹ he becomes a new man, with means of his own,⁸ and his antecedents¹⁰ all pass out of his head. Really, without presumption,¹¹ I think we can afford to be quite indifferent about the bearing of such a beggar on horseback.

1. 轟 *hung*¹, originally, a clatter of wheels; roar of thunder or of cannon, any loud clamour. Construe: there was a noise that came to be, was such, as if there were a large body of men, etc.

2. 裘 *ch'iu*², a certain long dress lined with fur, more commonly called *p'i-ʰgao*³: the words *fei ma ch'ing ch'iu*, sleek steed and light fur cloak (the light fur being expensive), are a classical passage, somewhat shorn of its proportions, signifying a wealthy condition.

3. 來 著 *lai-cho* is auxiliary, observe, of *yao*, to be about to, not of *hsiu ju*, to insult: *pi shih*, at the time I was going to call, etc.

4. 游 *yu*², to roam: *yu hun*, a wandering spirit.

5. 希 罕 *hsi¹-han*³, rare: *shih-cho*, if he picked up one straw, even that, a straw, was esteemed a rarity.

6. 尋 *hsin*², to want, to look for; *hsin*², to try and get something for nothing.

7. 咂 *tsa*¹, to put in the mouth, to taste with the tongue.

8. 求 不 著 人 *ch'iu pu chao jên*, he no longer requests people, *sc.*, to assist him; here, with money; it might mean with their talents; he is become independent.

9. 旦 *tan*⁴, properly, sunrise: *yi tan*, one day.

10. 景 況 *ching k'uang*, circumstances: *k'uang* amongst other meanings has, classically, that of to bestow; hence, the condition of things bestowed by Heaven.

11. 擡 *t'ai*², to carry; properly, as two men carry anything on a pole between them: *t'ai chü*, only figurative of extolling another or oneself.

LESSON LXVI.

1. [*Senior.*] Well, of all bad memories in the world, I do think yours is the worst. What did I tell you[1] the day before yesterday? on no account to let any mortal know anything about this business; notwithstanding which you have let it out.[2] All the arrangements you and I have been privately concerting have been made public, and at this moment they are the talk of the town. If they get to the ears of these people, they'll feel shame first,[3] then shame will turn to anger; and if in their disgust at our proceedings they commence operations against us,[4] a nice mess we shall be in. There's a good scheme brought to nothing, and all your doing.

2. [*Junior.*] You're blaming me unjustly, sir, I assure you. It's of no use entering into particulars, for under existing circumstances[5] you wouldn't believe me if I made my innocence as plain as words could make it; but God sees my heart, and time will show whether I have been talking or not. In the meantime I should say that, instead of feeling unkindly towards me before you know whether I am to blame or not, you had best pretend to be entirely ignorant of the publicity of this affair, and keep your eye on the movements of the other party. If they are not going to quarrel, they are not; if they are, you'll have time enough to reorganise your plans[6] and be prepared for them.

1. 囑 *chu*³, to enjoin on another (one's equal or inferior): *chu-fu*, not so imperative as *fên-fu*, which is to command, as a superior.

2. 洩漏 *hsieh*⁴-*lou*⁴, both characters mean to leak, and serve, singly, in their literal sense; the combination is only used figuratively.

3. 羞惱 *hsiu-nao*, not used except with the rest of the phrase; *hsiu* will become *nao*, and both be turned into *nu*, rage.

4. 動起 *tung ch'i*, with *lai* as an auxiliary, to set going, *e.g.*, mischief; here, the hand and foot, to act against aggressively.

5. 縱然 *tsung*⁴ *jan*, admitting that: although I were *fên pien*, to argue, [until there was] a teeth-clean-mouth-plain's [state of things]. Observe that the word *ya*, teeth, is used for talk, as *ch'ih* in Lesson LXIX, Note 4. *Ch'ing pai*, plain and clear: were I to argue till my talk fully explained this case.

6. 道理 *tao-li*, here in the sense of theory, system; again make a theory, devise some other order of proceeding.

LESSON LXVII.

1. [*Senior*.] You are an excellent fellow, I know, with the best heart possible;[1] but you are too blunt. When you know a man's faults, you give him no law at all; you will tell him plainly what you think. It is an act of friendship to correct one's friends' faults,[2] but one should study the person to see whether advice will do good, before one gives it. It isn't right, surely, to tender advice to everyone that comes under the denomination of friend, without reference to degrees of intimacy.[3] Now, in what you said to So-and-so, you meant well, I am sure, but it put him out very much. He stared with astonishment: "Ho, ho," thought he, "I must mind what I am about; he may mean mischief."

2. [*Junior*.] This is very salutary counsel of yours, sir; it's no doubt the right medicine for my complaint. I have full faith in the prescription. I know as well as anyone that this bluntness has always been a fault in my character. Something like this to-day turns up, my lips burn to speak,[4] and out it comes. It's an old saying that words addressed to a man who is not worthy of them[5] are words thrown away. I'll reform in earnest[6] at once; and if[7] from this time forth, sir, I commit myself by speaking when I ought to be silent, I'll give you leave[10] to spit[8][9] in my face.

1. 渣 *cha³*, dregs, lees; here, impurity, unsoundness; properly, *cha¹*.

2. 規過 *kuei kuo*, to correct the fault of another: *kuei*, properly, a compass; *kuo*, transgression.

3. 親疏 *ch'in su¹*, near and far.

4. 不由的 *pu yu ti*, without one's allowing it, involuntarily; abbreviated from *pu chin pu yu ti*, not restraining, not allowing; independently of one's pleasure in the matter.

5. 與言 *yü yen*, to a person to speak: *pu k'o*, if it be not right to [such a person] to speak, *êrh*, and yet, one does speak to him, etc.

6. 痛改 *t'ung⁴ kai*, thoroughly reform; *ch'ien fei*, my former errors: *t'ung*, sore, suffering; morally used as an intensive of feelings.

7. 縱使 *tsung shih*, although; in no way differing from *tsung jan* (see Lesson LXVI, Note 5).

8. 啐 *ts'ui⁴*, to spit.

9. 沫 *mo⁴*, properly, scum; *t'u*, to spit: *t'u-mo*, spittle; also read *t'u-mi*.

10. 領 *ling³*, properly, the neck; hence, to lead; from inclination of the head (probably), to receive: *ling shou*, to receive, specially, if not solely, an injury.

LESSON LXVIII.

1. There is no better fellow than yourself, but it's too simple of you to keep on praising[1] that friend of yours in the way you do. A scoundrel like that! what is there so wonderful about him? why, you ought never to mention his name.

2. He's the kind of man that will agree to do anything so long as he has a favour to ask of you, but the moment his business is settled he turns on his heel and forgets there is such a person as you in the world.

3. He was hard up last year, and he came to beg me to help him. No one asked him if he had anything to put down, but of his own accord he told me that he had got a nice book, "which," says he, "I'll send you to look at, if you like."

4. This was the promise he made me, but when the loan was raised, not a word more did he say about the book. I waited a considerable time without any news of it, until one day we met, and then I asked him, "What about that book you promised me?" but instead of giving me any good reason for not sending it, on my putting the question to him in this way, face to face, he turned first red and then pale, and put me off[2] with all sorts of excuses.

5. As for his book, a book is nothing so very curious.[3] It didn't signify much whether he gave it me or not; but his gratuitous deception of one is simply disgusting in the extreme.

---

1. 稱讚 ch'êng tsan⁴, to praise: tsan, properly meaning to aid, to support, should be distinguished from another tsan of the same sense, which is simply this character written without the 149th Radical.

2. 吾 wu², a classical form of the pronoun of the first person: chih wu¹, more properly written with the 75th Radical to the left of both characters, to make a defence, in speech or action, where none ought to be made.

3. 稀罕 hsi¹-han³, rare: the phrase is identical with that in Lesson LXV, Note 5, this hsi also meaning rare, in the sense of widely scattered; it is also applied to thin or watery paste, in opposition to ch'ou² (see Lesson XXX, Note 10), thick, glutinous.

LESSON LXIX.

1. [*Junior.*] What motive you can have for so positively refusing[1] to keep the present I have brought you, sir, I really cannot make out. Do you treat me in this way because I came so late, or on some other ground?

2. As to the first, I have been in the habit[2] of visiting here constantly, and I couldn't have done so unfriendly an act as to omit calling on your father's or mother's birthday. What really made me late was this, that I did not know in time that it was a birthday; if I had known it, I should, of course, have been here long ago.

3. I don't mean to say that my presence or absence would have made any material difference, still, had I been in time I might have been of use in helping you to do the honours; and as to my present, sir, and though no doubt your other friends and relations have brought things in such quantities[3] that it is, of course, impossible to get through them all, and the trifles I have brought are not worth mention,[4] still they were brought to show that I have a certain sense of affectionate regard for your parents.

4. I don't presume to press your parents to eat my presents, but if they were just to taste them[5] it would show a kindly feeling towards me, and this would make me quite contented; whereas a positive refusal[6] to receive them places me in a very disagreeable dilemma; it becomes as unpleasant for me[7] to sit here as to go away.

---

1. 固 *ku*[4], originally, fortified; hence, adequately fortified; hence, secure, impregnable: *ku tz'ŭ*, positively to decline; *ku jan*, it follows as a necessary consequence, of course.

2. 尚且 *shang ch'ieh*, a strong affirmative: *su ch'ang*, all along, I in very deed have constantly come; [and this being so] on your parents' birthday notwithstanding not to have come, etc.

3. 還少麼 *hai shao mo*, are they indeed few? [No.]

4. 掛齒 *kua ch'ih*, to hang on the teeth; *sc.*, to speak of.

5. 嚐 *ch'ang*[2], to taste by eating or drinking.

6. 決 *chüeh*[2], another form of 决 (*see* Part IV, Dialogue III, 123).

7. 倒爲了難 *tao wei liao nan:* [whichever I might do, my intention either way being good,] you nevertheless make me a difficult course.

LESSON LXX.

1. [*Junior.*] Have you heard what they say, sir? That *gourmand*[1] of ours is utterly ruined,[2] and in the greatest distress; all in rags,[3] like a mere beggar,[4] and shivering away there[5][6] under a quilt that is all in pieces.[7]

2. [*Senior.*] I said he'd come to no good, the gallows-bird![8] Last year he underwent every species of suffering, and if he had had any strength of mind,[9] he would have turned over a new leaf. We know what the proverb says, "If the poor man chooses to be the rich man's mate, the mate[10] will have no breeches to wear." This is quite true, and, accordingly, it behoved our friend to revise his tastes.[11] What business[12] had he to be fancying this wine or that dish, and to gad about[13] precisely as if he was a rich man and a grand seigneur? I said at the time, "Wait till the winter,[14] and then we shall see how he gets on." And now there he is, in the mess I predicted he would be.

3. [*Junior.*] Yes, sir, you may be quite right in what you say; still, now that he is in this wretched condition, it won't do[15] to look on and see him die outright, will it? The right thing, it appears to me, would be for us each to give a trifle, and make a subscription[16] for him.

4. [*Senior.*] That is, you would give him pecuniary aid; I don't think that's a good suggestion. I'll tell you why. He is so constituted, as you must know, that the

---

1. 饞 *ch'an²*, to be an epicure: *ch'an tsui*, to gluttonise, to be always eating; *t'a ch'an²*, he is fond of good eating.

2. 破敗 *p'o pai*, to be ruined; of persons, without funds; not otherwise used.

3. 襤褸 *lan² lü³⁴*, tattered and torn; the two characters are not used apart from each other.

4. 花子 *hua-tzŭ*, a beggar; explained by some to be short for *hao⁴ hua ch'ien chih-tzŭ*, a fellow who has been fond of spending money.

5. 戰 *chan⁴*, properly, to fight in battle; here, and often, to tremble as from cold or fear: *ta lêng³ chan-'rh*, to shiver from cold; *hsia⁴ ti ta³ chan-'rh*, to tremble with fear. The character 顫 (*ch'an⁴*) is also used in the same sense; *e.g.*, *t'a ch'an⁴ ch'i lai liao*, he commenced to shiver.

6. 抖 *tou³*, to shake, as you would any material to get the dust off it; here read *tou¹*.

7. 披 *p'ei¹*, also *p'i¹*, to throw over one's person, to carry over one: carrying over his person a *p'o pei*, ragged coverlid.

8. 趁愿 *ch'ên yüan⁴*, to come in for the wishes, *sc.*, the bad wishes, of someone; *kai-ssŭ-ti*, the deserving to die; the two epithets are entirely separate: *yuan* is simply another form of 願.

9. 志氣 *chih-ch'i*, resolution: had there only been to his share a fraction of resolution.

10. 伴的 *pan-ti*, an associate; used verbally in the foregoing clause.

11. 回過味兒 *hui kuo we-'rh*, to profit by experience: the Chinese olive is said not to be tasted until after it is swallowed; its *wei*, flavour, then *hui kuo lai*, comes back.

12. 心腸 *hsin ch'ang*, heart and bowels; here, for the mind; a man in sorrow may be said to have no *hsin ch'ang*, heart to do this or that.

13. 游玩 *yu wan*, roaming about and amusing himself.

14. 上冬 *shang tung*, the beginning of winter; *shang ch'iu*, the beginning of autumn; but *shang* is not so used with spring or summer.

15. 可當 *k'o tang*: the *k'o* would not be used here if the position that he ought to die were affirmative.

16. 攢 *ts'uan²*, to pile up together: *ts'uan ts'ou*, to make up a heap or amount by contribution.

moment he got hold of the money there would be an end to it; not a fraction would he keep in hand; he'd spend the whole of it.

No; I should say that if we were to buy him a suit of clothes,[17] that would be of some use.

17. 一套 *i t'ao*, of good clothes, would mean no more than a *p'ao-tzŭ* and a *kua-tzŭ*; here, a whole suit of common garments.

LESSON LXXI.

1. [*Senior.*] How is it I have been so long without a sight of you; and where have you been off to all this time?[1] Why can't you come to my house when you have a little time to spare?

2. [*Junior.*] I have been coming to pay you a visit for some time past, but I became mixed up in an affair that didn't concern me in the least, and I got so entangled in it that latterly I have never had a moment to myself from morning to night. I should not have got away[2] even to-day if I hadn't adopted a ruse; I said I had business of importance, which was an untruth, and they have just let me go[3] in consequence.

3. [*Senior.*] Well, you have come at the right moment; I was just feeling very low. You'll be able to give me a little of your company, I hope, so as to let us have a day's chat together. We'll have a quiet pot-luck dinner, and then you can go; I'll not order anything additional.

4. [*Junior.*] But, really, it makes me uncomfortable to be turning the house upside down gratuitously[4] whenever I come here; that's the reason I'm afraid to come often.

5. [*Senior.*] Don't talk as if you were such a stranger,[5] pray. When did the coolness commence between us? If a few more days had elapsed without a visit from you, I should have got something ready and sent you a formal invitation; but this very ordinary meal is not worth talking about, so don't refuse it. Besides, I have eaten everything that you had to give me at your house, and if you are going to act so disloyally[6] by me, it will be a plain proof that you want me not to go there any more.

1. 奔 *pên¹*, to run; when read *pên⁴* it may stand alone, colloquially, for to go: *pên⁴ na³ 'rh*, where are you off to? as *pên¹* it forms part of various combinations.

2. 摘 *chai³*, so read only in this combination; properly, *chai¹* (*see* Part III, 298), to take off, as one's cap, fruit on a tree, etc.: *chai-t'o*, to take oneself off, to withdraw oneself.

3. 放了 *fang liao*, let me go, released me.

4. 騷 *sao¹*, originally, to stir, to set in motion; to fidget actively or passively; here read *tsao¹*: *tsao¹ jao³*, to fidget a person, to put him to trouble; *sao jên*, a man of troubles; elegantly, a poet; *q.d.*, one who vents his *sao*, sorrows, in verse.

5. 外道 *wai tao*, reasoning on the basis of one's being an outsider: why should you thus regard yourself as an outsider?

6. 實誠 *shih-ch'êng*, truthful, reliable: *pu shih-ch'êng* is the falsehood of politeness; it might here almost be rendered *ceremoniously*.

LESSON LXXII.

1. [*Junior.*] Oh! here you are at last, sir; I have been waiting for you a long time; a few minutes more and I would have been in bed.

2. [*Senior.*] Well, what made us so late was this: we were just starting for your house when, to our horror, a fellow, who is the greatest bore in the world,¹ presented himself and set to work talking;² ³ din, din, on he went without stopping; all about nothing, too; first one trifle and then another; there was no end to it. If I had had nothing else to attend to, I shouldn't have objected to more or less of a yarn;⁴ ⁵ I should have let him spin it out; but I feared that you would begin to feel uncomfortable at our non-appearance,⁶ so I was obliged to stop him by telling him that we were busy to-day and must put off the rest of it till to-morrow. If it hadn't been for him we should have been seated here ever so long ago.⁷

3. [*Junior.*] Oh! don't imagine that you are late; you have arrived in the very nick of time. Here! who is outside there? Be quick and set the table;⁸ the gentlemen must be hungry; and look sharp with whatever you have got to bring in.

4. [*Senior.*] No, no, sir; pray don't give any such orders. A slice of meat, quite plain,⁹ will do very well; there is no occasion for all these dishes.¹⁰ You are not going to treat us as if we were strangers,¹¹ surely?

5. [*Junior.*] Nay, what little there is here is only by way of showing my desire to be hospitable; there's nothing much worth offering you; but do eat something¹² with your rice, gentlemen.

6. [*Senior*] We don't require pressing with such a display before us,¹³ ¹⁴ I can assure you. We are not waiting to be asked, and we sha'n't lay down our chopsticks till we can eat no more.

7. [*Junior.*] In that case I've nothing more to say; that's treating me as if you really loved me.¹⁵

1. 死肉 *ssŭ jou*, dead flesh, a fellow without animation: unexpectedly there happened to present himself a certain *ssŭ-jou*, who provokes people's disgust.

2 刺 *tz'ŭ⁴*, properly, to prick with a point; here read *la¹*; *la²*, to cut with a knife.

3. 休 *hsiu¹*, to rest, to cease: *la la pu hsiu*, the worry of incessant talking.

4. 絮 *hsu⁴*, gossamer, the down of the willow; the quality of cotton, etc., which may be drawn out to an indefinite length.

5. 叨 *tao¹*, colloquially, to talk; properly read *t'ao¹*, to receive, to be the subject of, as kindness, mercy: *hsü t'ao¹*, much talk, a long yarn; *tao tao*, to find fault with.

6. 等急 *tĕng chi*, to be made impatient by waiting.

7. 坐煩 *tso fan*, seated a long time: *fan* not here indicating fatigue either in oneself or one's host.

8. 放桌子 *fang cho-tzŭ*, set the table in the middle of the room, or on the *k'ang*; not lay the table.

9. 副 *p'ien⁴*, to slice; *pai jou*, meat boiled without salt or seasoning.

10. 蔬 *su¹*, or *shu¹*, properly, wild vegetables: *ts'ai su*, food, dishes, in general, when a compliment to the *cuisine* is intended.

11. 當客 *tang⁴ k'o*, representing strangers: do you taking us act towards us as strangers? or, merging *pa* in *wo-mĕn*, as the object of the verb *tai*, do you treat us as strangers?

12. 就著 *chiu-cho*; *lit.*, moving on to, proceeding to: adding something to the plain rice which they are already eating.

13. 盛 *shĕng⁴*, a state of prosperity or affluence.

14. 設 *shê⁴*, properly, to place in order, to array; *shĕng shê*, to put out in great abundance; used only, as here, of dishes: there is no occasion *kuo jang*, to exceed in invitations to eat and drink; there is an over-display of dishes, etc.

15. 我兄弟 *wo hsiung-ti*, me, your younger brother.

LESSON LXXIII.

1. [*Junior.*] Where are you from,[1] sir, may I ask?

2. [*Senior.*] I have been to visit a relation of mine who lives down yonder. Won't you step in and sit down on your way,[2] sir?

3. [*Junior.*] Do you reside in this neighbourhood, sir?

4. [*Senior.*] Yes, in this house; I moved into this house not long ago.

5. [*Junior.*] Oh! indeed, sir; then we are not so very far from each other. If I had been aware that you lived here, I should have called before. Go on, sir, pray; I'll follow you, if you please.

6. [*Senior.*] What, in my own house? who ever heard of such a thing? Now, please take the upper seat.[3]

7. [*Junior*] Thank you, I am very well where I am.

8. [*Senior.*] But if you sit where you are sitting, what place am I to take?

9. [*Junior*] I have got a seat, thank you; and a seat with a back to it.[4]

10. [*Senior.*] Here! bring a light.

11. [*Junior.*] Not for me, thank you, sir; I can't smoke; I have a sore mouth.[5]

12. [*Senior.*] Well, then, bring some tea.

13. [*Junior.*] Drink first, then, pray.

14. [*Senior.*] After you, sir. Boy, go and see what there is in the kitchen, and bring whatever is ready first.

15. [*Junior.*] No, indeed, sir; do not put yourself to so much trouble. I have still got to go somewhere else.

16. [*Senior.*] But it's only whatever is ready; nothing is being prepared for you. Do try[6] and eat a little of anything you please.

17. [*Junior.*] Not just now, thank you, sir; but we are old acquaintances, you know; and now that I have found out where you live, I'll come another time and spend the day with you; to-day I really have not the time, so I'll say good-bye.

1. 來著 *lai-cho*, coming: having been to what place are you coming?

2. 順便 *shun pien*, elliptical for *shun-cho ni-ti pien tao*, your halt being an incident *shun*, in accordance with *pien tao*, the way most convenient to you.

3. 上坐 *shang tso*, sit in the upper seat; generally to the left of the host, though in some cases the arrangement of the room makes the right seat, as farthest from the door, or from the outer wall, the place of honour.

4. 靠頭 *k'ao t'ou*, something to lean against when one is seated; not necessarily the back of a chair.

5. 瘡 *ch'uang¹*, generally, a large boil or ulcer: a *k'ou ch'uang* may be any pimple in the mouth; a boil is commonly called 疙瘩 (*ko¹ ta¹*), which also means a knot.

6. 將就 *chiang chiu*, make an effort; *sc.*, although the food is not good, to eat it.

LESSON LXXIV.

1. [*Senior.*] You were out very late yesterday; whose house were you at?

2. [*Junior.*] I went to pay a visit to a friend of ours; he lives close to the west wall of the city, an immense way from this; and then he made me stay and eat a bit of dinner with him; so that, altogether, it was rather late before I got home.

3. [*Senior.*] I had something of importance that I wanted to talk to you about, and I sent several times to ask you to look in, but your servants said you had left home in the cart, without saying where you were going to. "Well," I said, "he doesn't visit a great deal; he'll only have gone to see someone in our small circle,[1] and he'll be certain to come here afterwards;" but no such thing. I waited till the sun was well down, but you never came, and, thought I to myself, I might just as well not have waited at all.

4. [*Junior.*] I was out, sir; I had started long before your messenger came to look for me, and when I got home, and my servants[2] told me you had been sending for me two or three times, I would have come to you at once, but it was very late to be disturbing you, and, besides, I was afraid the street gates[3] would be shut; so I waited till to-day, and here I am.

---

1. 圈兒內 *ch'üan¹-'rh nei*, within the circle, *sc.*, of our friends: a circle, mathematically speaking, is called *yuan²-ch'üan-'rh*.

2. 小子們 *hsiao-tzŭ-mên*, here, the servants, not the sons of the house.

3. 柵欄 *cha⁴-lan²*, a wooden barrier or gateway at the end of a street, closed at night: *cha* is properly the upright poles which form this; *lan*, the transverse beams that connect the poles; *lan-tzŭ* is becoming the term for an outlaw's stockade. Cf. also 欄杆, a railing, a balustrade; *kan¹* being a pole or mast.

LESSON LXXV.

1. Wasn't it to visit your cemetery that you left town¹ the day before yesterday?

2. It was.

3. How is it that you only got back to-day?

4. Our cemetery is so far off that you can't go and return in a day;² besides, I stayed there a couple of nights. I started the day before yesterday, the moment the city gates were open,³ and I travelled all day; but it was night before I reached the place. I offered⁴ my meat and drink offerings yesterday, passed the second night there, and commenced my journey home with the dawn this morning; but though I didn't venture to halt, except for a mouthful of lunch,⁵ I only got back here just as the gates were being closed for the night.

5. Ay, they may say what they like about the preferableness of cemeteries that lie a good way off, but if one's posterity have not wherewithal, they won't find it so easy to pay their visits there at the proper seasons.

6. They will not, indeed. We had a cemetery⁶ very near the city, but as there was no room for any more graves in it,⁷ we engaged the geomancers⁸ to look at some ground for us, and we laid out ours where it now is, because they said it was a good spot for one. It *is* a long way off, to be sure; still, the long and the short of it is that we must manage to get to our cemetery somehow or other; like rich people, if we have money, or like poor people, if we have none; and supposing our circumstances were so narrow as to put a cart beyond our means, we could always reach the cemetery and pour our cup of wine to the dead if we would but walk there. As to what a man's descendants will do by him, that depends entirely upon their own dispositions; if they are good-for-nothing fellows, whose regard for their ancestors is so slight that they can't pay the usual visits to their tombs because they lie some distance off, it by no means follows that they would burn a piece of paper money⁹ to him were the family grave-yard ever so near.

1. 莊子 *chuang-tzŭ*, a small village; as we say, the country: observe *lai-cho*, as in Lesson LXXIII, 1, showing that the person addressed is returning.

2. 當天 *tang⁴ t'ien*, in one day. Note that we cannot say *tang⁴ t'ien* under any circumstances, but *tang¹ jih* and *tang⁴ jih* are both employed, though in different ways, *e.g.*, 當日上通州去遇見大風 and 上通州當⁴ 日回不來; *tang¹ jih* meaning "on the day that," *tang⁴ jih* meaning "within the day" or "on one and the same day." Cf. also the following: 當¹日上通州,當¹日回不來.

3. 頂城門兒 *ting ch'êng mên-'rh*, as though I had *ting*, run my head, against the gate before it was opened.

4. 供 *kung⁴* (see Part III, 1020); here in the sense of laying out a sacrifice; read *kung¹*, it means the evidence or admission of a criminal or a witness.

5. 打尖 *ta chien*, to eat any short meal when travelling. See *chien*, Part III, 808; its employment here cannot be explained.

6. 塋 *ying²*, a grave-yard.

7. 埋 *mai²*, to bury anything; *tsang*, to bury the dead.

8. 風水 *fêng-shui*, wind and water; a term for the condition of a locality geomantically considered: *k'an-fêng-shui-ti*, a geomancer.

9. 紙錢 *chih ch'ien*, the paper money, shaped like ingots, which is burned to the dead.

LESSON LXXVI.

1. Which of their family is it that is dead?[1] I was passing their house three days ago, and I observed that they were all in mourning.[2] It was my day at the office,[3] so I hadn't time to make any inquiries; but I have just heard that a younger brother, or cousin of their father, is dead; is it his brother?

2. It is; his own brother.

3. Have you paid your visit of condolence?[4]

4. Yes; they were reading the service of the dead yesterday, and I was there the whole day.

5. Do you know when he is to be buried?[5]

6. I hear about the end of the moon.

7. Whereabouts is their cemetery?

8. Close by ours.

9. Oh, dear! that's a long way off; I should say at least forty *li*, if not fifty. The next time you call, you can tell our friend for me how sorry I am to hear of his loss,[6] and that I shall pay him a visit in company with you to condole with him in person as soon as I am off duty. And pray, whatever you do, let me know[7] when they are going to bury his uncle; for if it is not in my power to accompany the coffin to the cemetery, I shall certainly go with it outside the city. There has never been much intercourse between the nephew and myself, but whenever we do meet we are very cordial; and, besides, all the world should be friends; so if I do go the whole length in testifying my sympathy with him on the occasion of so serious a loss, I don't apprehend that people will say that I am running after him.[8]

---

1. 不在 *pu tsai*, not to be, to be dead; not so used in the South, where it means not at home.

2. 穿孝 *ch'uan hsiao*, to be in mourning; to be wearing clothes in token of *hsiao*, filial piety, or, in a more extended sense, family affection.

3. 該班 *kai pan*, to come to one's turn of duty according to the roster. See *pan*, Part III, **414.**

4. 喪 *sang*¹, to die, death; to be distinguished from *sang*⁴, to do mortal, or irreparable, damage to (see Lesson LII, Note 4); *tiao*, lit., to hang up, *sc.*, one's contribution of paper money (*see* above, Lesson LXXV, Note 9): *tiao sang*, to mourn with the bereaved; in Peking, *t'an sang* is more common; for *t'an*, see Lesson LX, Note 6.

5. 殯 *pin*⁴, to carry a coffin to the grave: *ch'u pin* is the funeral as the act of the family; *sung pin* may be the same, or it may be the attendance of friends at the funeral.

6. 道惱 *tao nao*, condolence in case of death: *tao*, to tell, *sc.*, my sympathy with your *nao*, trouble, sorrow. See below, *fan nao*, in the same sense.

7. 信兒 *hsin-'rh*, as we say, a word of intimation; whether in writing or verbally.

8. 走動 *tsou tung*, of any ordinary movement, going about; *tsou pu tung*, unable to move. Caution must be exercised in the use of *tsou tung*, which has another meaning.

LESSON LXXVII.

1. I was at home when he came, and lying down. All of a sudden something woke me; I listened and heard a strange voice in the drawing-room. Who can this be, thought I, talking so loud? Oh! of course, it's that bore What's-his-name. I went into the room, and at the first glance I saw it was he, sure enough. And there he sat as stiff as a post,[1] and talked and talked, first of this and then of that; his tongue never stopped from the moment he came in; and he staid such a time; two dinners might have been served while he was there; it was getting dark[2] before he went away.

2. It really is too bad that a man should come to your house and sit there talking the whole day, whether he has got anything to say or not. And it is not only that this fellow makes your head ache[5] with his exhaustive chatter about all manner of dirty trifles[3] that have been talked of till they are stale,[4] but he has got another detestable[6] trick of laying hands on everything; when he is coming to call, everything, good, bad, or indifferent, has to be put out of his sight. You mustn't let him set eyes on anything; if you do, he asks no questions, but he just snaps it up,[7] and away he goes with it.

3. No one has ever been able to say a good word[8] for him since he was born; and is it to be pretended that such men, who are but beasts within,[9] in whom all principle is annihilated, are to have the monopoly of whatever it strikes them will be to their advantage?

---

1. 挺 *t'ing*³, of persons or things, to stick up stiffly.

2. 黃昏 *huang-hun*, twilight, of the evening only.

3. 穀 *ku*³, properly, any kind of grain; *ku-tzŭ*, used generally of rice with the husk on; *ch'ên*, that is stale, and, here, spoiling; *lan chih-ma*, damaged sesame.

4. 餿 *sou*¹, rotten rice, to rot like rice: things, that were as stale rice and damaged sesame, that people have *chiang chiu*, discussed, until they were *sou*. Observe that all between *pa* and *shih-ch'ing* is attributive of the latter.

5. 聽得 *t'ing tê:* [a person] listening arrives at the condition of a person whose head is quite aching, etc.

6. 惡 *wu*⁴, to hate; to be distinguished from the same character read *o* or ᵑ*go* (*see* Part III, 1053): *k'o-wu*, odious, detestable.

7. 撈摸 *lao mo*, properly, of taking things out of the water; generally, of picking up things.

8. 說頭 *shuo t'ou*, a point, or trait, of which one can speak favourably: he, *chê i pei-tzŭ*, this whole lifetime of his, has never had that merit.

9. 雜碎 *tsa sui*, properly, miscellaneous fragments; the offal of sheep, pigs, etc.

LESSON LXXVIII.

1. What is the meaning of this? Don't you perceive what a bore[1] you must be, always asking for anything out of the common way that you happen to see in people's possession? It's positively disreputable. After one has let you have things, too, ever so many times, because one didn't know how to refuse; why can't you be satisfied? Why must you go on insisting on having everything that belongs to a man?

2. But worse than this, to be angry because you can't get it! presents are a matter of favour; if people won't make presents, they commit no sin;[2] and what right have you, therefore, to lose your temper[3] with those that don't give what they want? Suppose that it was something of yours that someone or other took a liking to, mightn't you have a liking for it as well? And how would you feel if your wishes were not consulted at all, and the whole concern was carried off bodily?

3. I bore with you yesterday because I knew what an ill-tempered fellow[4] you are; but no one else would have given way. Now, ponder my words well, and mend your ways without loss of time.

4. If you were a man of no capacity, it would be another affair; but that is not your case; and when you have wherewithal to feed and clothe yourself, what can make you so eager to lay hands on every small thing going? I wonder you are not afraid of being talked about as a man that can't see a thing belonging to another without begging for it.[5]

---

1. 絮煩 *hsü fan*, the annoyance occasioned by trouble repeatedly given.

2. 本分 *pên fên*, one's proper duty.

3. 摔搭 *shuai ta*, to fling things about: *shih hsing-tzŭ*, giving vent to temper; *shuai ta jên*, to show one's anger against a person by throwing things about; *shou shuai ta*, to go through a course of rough treatment with a view to being hardened.

4. 行子 *hang-tzŭ*, slightly abusive, as above, in Lesson LXIV, Note 2.

5. 眼皮子淺 *yen-p'i-tzŭ ch'ien*, the eyelid of no thickness; so that whatever is seen is thought worth having.

LESSON LXXIX.

1. "If you don't study in your youth," says the ancient proverb, "what will you do when you grow old?" the moral of which is that all men ought to study with diligence, and that no man should be idle. But of all people it behoves the Bannerman to be diligent; for whereas any man, no matter who, that achieves by application the power of doing something, however small, for himself, may be looked on as provided for, to those who study so hard as to rise to the highest standard of qualifications an official career is à fortiori a certainty.

2. Now, to attain this point is more the duty of the Bannerman than of anyone else, because he has to trouble himself neither about his food nor his clothing; he is exempt from agricultural labour, coolie labour, and mechanical labour;[1] he has nothing to do but eat the rations given him by the State, without stirring from his place. And if with all these privileges he does not set to work in his youth to study hard,[2] what qualities will he acquire that will enable him to exert[3] himself in the service of his lord and master; or what return will he make to Heaven for bringing him into the world and keeping him in it?

1. 藝 i⁴, properly, ability: shou-i, handicraft.

2. 努 nu³, to exert oneself: nu li, with all one's might, ch'in hsio, to be diligent in learning.

3. 以著 i-cho: the i in the sense of to employ.

LESSON LXXX.

1. What is properly meant by the expression "well-doing" is the observance of those principles in conformity with which it is man's duty to live, namely, duteousness, subordination, loyalty,[1] and truth. It is not only those who go sacrificing to spirits and Buddhas, or giving alms[2] to the priests of Tao or Fo, that are to be accounted well-doers. A man may be a vicious man, and if so, he may repair bridges or mend roads as much as he pleases, but will that give him absolution?[3] Not at all; neither is it in the power of the very Buddhas and spirits themselves to bestow happiness upon him.

2. All that going to heaven if you fast,[4] and going somewhere else[5] if you eat meat, is mere talk got up by the priests of the Buddhist and Taoist sects to enable them[6] to put bread in their mouths;[7] it is not all to be taken for gospel. If they did not terrify[8] people with this tremendous story and that tremendous story, how would they swindle them out of their money? And if they were obliged to confine themselves strictly to what Buddhism enjoins, to shut the gates of the temples and stay quietly within doors, devoutly fasting[9] and reading out their sacred books, never going abroad to convert the elect of Buddha,[10] they would have neither food to eat nor clothes to put on; and then what would they do? Could they live upon air?

1. 悌 t'i⁴, duty to elder brothers and seniors, as *hsiao* is to parents.

2. 齋 chai, reverent, respectful; here, to show respect to Buddha by subsidising his priests. See Part IV, Dialogue VII, Note 10; also below, Notes 4 and 8.

3. 解了 chieh liao, loosen, absolve him of his *tsui-ngo*, iniquities.

4. 喫齋 ch'ih chai, to fast; the same as ch'ih su (see Part IV, Dialogue VIII, 33), the opposite of *hun ts'ai*.

5. 獄 yu⁴, classically, a prison: *ti yü*, the hell of the Buddhists; *t'ien t'ang*, their paradise.

6. 借端 chieh tuan, to borrow a kind or form of things, to make something a plea for.

7. 餬 hu¹ ², only used in *hu k'ou*, to plaster the mouth, sc., with a little food, not more than will enable one to live.

8. 諕 hu¹, to frighten; identical with hu³ (see Lesson XXXV, Note 19).

9. 持 ch'ih², to grasp in the hand: *ch'ih chai*, to maintain a reverent heart and bearing, to be devout.

10. 化緣 hua yüan, the begging of Buddhist priests, whose ostensible avocation is to *hua*, convert, those who *yu yüan*, those whose lot it is, sc., to repay the kindness done them by the priest now asking alms when both were in a former existence.

LESSON LXXXI.

1. [*Junior.*] I've come for the express purpose of asking your advice, sir, in a matter that interests me. It's a thing that might be attended with certain consequences to myself, perhaps, were I to do it; but, on the other hand, it would be a great pity, now that I've gone as far as I have gone, to leave it undone. It's not in reason to let an advantage that is ready to drop into your mouth go away to other people who have no claim to it; but what with objections to doing it and objections to not doing it, I am fairly in a dilemma, and I want you to tell me what line you think will preserve me perfectly harmless in the transaction.

2. [*Senior.*] Your course is clear enough.[1] There's nothing to prevent you making your mind up, surely. Let the thing alone, and it will be all the better for you. How are you to keep people's mouths shut[2] if you don't? And it's when[3] the thing comes to be well talked about that you will find yourself in a difficulty. It's but little good you'll get out of it, and that little is neither more nor less than the first growth of future trouble. Whatever advantage may belong to it, there is, without doubt, disadvantage; and it will be too late to repent when you come to grief. My advice to you is not to hesitate; make up your mind positively *not* to do the thing, and have no more to say to it. If you continue undecided, if you can't give up the idea,[4] you'll be like the man who not only gets no rice into his sack, but loses his sack to boot. You'll incur all the disgrace[5] that attaches to a discreditable affair.

---

1. 顯 *hsien*³, brightness, visibility: this thing is plainly visible and easy to be seen.

2. 堵 *tu*³, to stop a hole, to close a passage.

3. 那纔 *na ts'ai*, elliptical for *na ko shih-hou*, at that time; *ts'ai*, then, etc.

4. 拉扯住了 *la ch'ê chu liao*, to keep back from moving onward, where circumstances are the cause; were the cause a person, the verb would be *la chu*. The construction is here passive; *q.d.*, if, delaying and doubting without intermission, you let yourself be held fast.

5. 醜 *ch'ou*³, ugliness of the face; here, figuratively, of moral deformity.

PART V.—THE HUNDRED LESSONS. 331

LESSON LXXXII.

1. [*Junior.*] There is something I want to ask you to do for me, sir, but I feel some delicacy in addressing you on the subject; I have asked so many favours of you. Still, if I don't apply to you, there is no one else who can manage the matter for me, and I am therefore come to trouble[1] you once more.

2. [*Senior.*] Isn't it that affair in which you want CHANG's assistance?

3. [*Junior.*] It is. How came you to know that, sir?

4. [*Senior.*] Your son was speaking to me about it this morning, and I went over there at breakfast-time, but, as luck would have it, CHANG was out. Towards noon[2] I went again; but as I entered the court I heard a noise of talking and laughing in the drawing-room; so I went up the steps,[3] and quietly put my tongue[4] to the window-paper, and on looking through the hole I had made, I saw a room full of people, one helping the other to wine, and the other returning the compliment; and the whole company[5] eating and drinking, and as merry as possible. At first I thought I would go in; but there were a great number of the guests who were strangers to me, and it struck me that they would be dreadfully put out[7] at my obliging them all to get up[6] from their wine to receive me; so I withdrew. The servants saw me and wanted to announce me, but I made signs to them not to do so. Don't you disturb yourself, however; I'll arrange it all with him comfortably the first thing to-morrow morning.

---

1. 瑣 *so*[3], properly, fragments of precious stones; hence, things small, trifles: *fan so*, to give trouble to.

2. 纔交晌午 *ts'ai chiao shang wu:* just as [the *ssŭ* period, nine to eleven,] was joining the *wu* period [eleven to one].

3. 階 *chieh*[1], a flight of stone or brick steps: in *t'ai chieh* the word *t'ai*, terrace, does not modify the meaning.

4. 舔 *t'ien*[3], to lick, to wet with the tongue.

5. 攪在一處 *chiao*[3] *tsai i ch'u; lit.,* stirred up together.

6. 冲散 *ch'ung san:* if I by *ch'ung*, breaking in, were to make them *san*, disperse, quit their places.

7. 得人意兒 *tê jên i-'rh*, to please people; *kuai*, as before, an intensive; monstrously to displease.

LESSON LXXXIII.

1. It wasn't of my own motion that I took charge of the affair for him, I am sure. I am a quiet, stay-at-home sort of man, and I don't know where he found out that I knew the person he wanted; but he came to me again and again about him. "I rely entirely upon you, sir," said he, and begged that I would be so good as to say a word for him. He never let me out of his sight, in short.

2. Well, as you very well know, I've always been a soft-hearted fellow, and when I saw a man in this kind of strait, imploring me on his knees[1] to assist him, I hadn't the face to send him home discontented; and as nothing I advanced would induce him to leave me alone,[2] I undertook the commission for him.

3. So I spoke to my friend So-and-so about his affair, but I found that he was not, as I had hoped,[3] alone in the case, and he declined to engage himself to me, as he said there were too many parties to be consulted.[4] At first I was going to enter into particulars, and press the matter farther, but I thought to myself I had best say no more about it. To judge from appearances, the thing is not to be brought about,[5] and what right have I to insist[6] on anyone's undertaking it,[7] *nolens volens?*

4. So I went back and told my principal what had occurred, and instead of thanking me for the trouble I had taken, he turned round and abused me as a marplot, and scowled[8] at me so that I really felt as if I had no hope left. If I had known what was to come of it, I certainly should not have spoken at all. What object[9] could I have had in speaking?

1. 跪 *kuei*⁴, to kneel.

2. 推脫不開 *t'ui t'o pu k'ai:* though I *t'ui,* put forward excuses, *t'o pu k'ai,* I could not get myself away from him.

3. 不承望 *pu ch'êng wang,* contrary to the hope I had entertained: *man ch'êng wang,* to entertain the strongest hopes.

4. 掣 *ch'ê*⁴, to pull towards one; 肘 *chou*³, the elbow: *ch'ê chou,* to hold back by the arm.

5. 挽 *wan*³, colloquially, to force round, as the ends of a bow: *wan hui,* to force back from a direction already taken, to retrieve a false step.

6. 壓派 *ya p'ai; lit.,* with pressure to require; *p'ai* being used in the sense of official requisition.

7. 允 *yün*³, to sanction, to give assent to: *ying yün,* to promise assent, to agree to a proposition.

8. 撩 *liao*¹, to let down; a hanging screen, for instance: *liao*² *ch'i lai,* to trice or close up such a screen; it is here, of course, *liao*⁴.

9. 圖 *t'u*², a map, a plan; here, a verb; to contemplate, to plan.

PART V.—THE HUNDRED LESSONS. 333

LESSON LXXXIV.

1. I did think that I should have had no difficulty in arranging that affair of yours with him; but instead of that, he proved so utterly impracticable, the wretch, that it gave me a great deal of trouble before I could manage it.

2. When I told him[1] what had passed between you and me in conversation on the subject, his countenance fell at once, and he told me I was talking nonsense. This made my blood rise directly. If that's to be the order of the day, thought I, so be it; and I felt every inclination to say something sharp to him in return.[2]

3. But then I reflected and reasoned with myself. It would be a mistake, I said, to lose my temper with him; I am here about[3] the business of friends, not on my own account; and if he and I fall out, it will be to the loss of other people's time and pains; besides which, after all, what will it cost me to give in to him[4] a little?

4. So I let him run on[5] finding fault till he was tired, taking all he had to give, without allowing a syllable to escape me; and I sat on and on, watching him and humouring him, until by degrees I got so far as to press my request on him earnestly, and he then at last assented.

5. Now, if I had been a little hasty, you see, your affair would never have been settled.

---

1. 一遍 *i pien*, one time; here untranslatable in our idiom.

2. 惹他 *jê t'a*, to provoke him a provocation.

3. 爲的 *wei ti*, the cause; that which is the *wei*[4], because of.

4. 容讓 *jung jang*, to give way to: *jung*, properly, capable of containing; used singly as to allow, to let, a person speak or act.

5. 數落 *shu³ lo; lit.*, to run down the whole score; used only, as here, of moderate vituperation: *wo shu lo t'a i tun*, as we say, I told him all I thought about his conduct.

LESSON LXXXV.

1. [*Host.*] May I ask to what I am indebted[2] for the pleasure of this visit, sir?[1]

2. [*Visitor.*] Well, as our good luck has brought you and myself together in this world,[3] we are come to beg you to let us have your daughter in marriage.[4] My son here is not at all superior,[5] I admit, to the rest of his kind, either in mind or person, nor does he possess any extraordinary accomplishments; but, on the other hand, he neither drinks nor plays, nor does he ever visit those haunts of dissipation[6] where men lose their wits; he has never been astray. And now, gentlemen, if you don't consider him unworthy your goodwill,[7] I shall ask you to be so kind as to tell him so. [*To his son.*] Step forward, and let us prefer our request with our heads to the ground.[8]

3. [*Host.*] Stop, gentlemen! [*To all the company.*] Pray be seated, everybody, and hear what I have got to say. We are all kinsmen here, it is true; be our degree what it may, all of the same flesh and blood; there is no one present who is not known to every-one else. But what I have to say is this: Marriages, we know, are made in heaven quite independently of man; and parents, however great the affection with which they regard their children, can do no more than hope they may be matched in a manner that will satisfy their own anxiety to do their utmost for their offspring.[9] Still, as my old people have never seen your son, I had better present him; and, on the other part, your ladies can have my little girl brought out for them to see.

4. [*Visitor.*] Certainly, sir, you are quite right. Please go in and inform your ladies, and take my boy in for them to see. It will not be too late for him to make his *kotow* when all parties are agreed.

1. 吾兄 *wu hsiung*, my brother. See above, Lesson LXVIII, Note 2.

2. 見敎 *chien chiao*, to bestow instruction; the word *chien* is found in the sense of conferring, bestowing, in various complimentary phrases used in letters.

3. 有緣 *yu yüan*. See Lesson LXXX, Note 10.

4. 求親 *ch'iu ch'in*, to ask for [the daughter of the person addressed] as a wife for one's son, younger brother, or other junior.

5. 超 *ch'ao*[1]; *lit.*, to overleap: *ch'ao ch'ün*, to rise above the crowd.

6. 迷 *mi*[2], to lose, to stray off, the road: *mi hu*, or *mi huo*, to cause to stray and make unsteady; used specially of libertinism. The expression *ch'u-ch'u-'rh*, places one goes to, can be used in any connexion.

7. 棄 *ch'i*[4], to abandon: *ch'i hsien*, to leave a person unnoticed because he is not to one's taste.

8. 叩 *k'ou*[4], to knock the head: *k'ou ch'iu*, to ask a favour on one's knees.

9. 掖 *yeh*[4], properly, to hold up by the arm: *k'u pa*, anxiously drawing out; *k'u yeh*, anxiously helping along, *sc.*, the incidents that shall conduce to the children's happiness.

NOTE.—It should be observed that the above is not the prevailing method of arranging marriages.

LESSON LXXXVI.

1. [*Visitor.*] Are not these clothes being made for your daughter's intended?[1]
2. [*Host.*] Yes.
3. [*Visitor.*] And what are all these people about?
4. [*Host.*] They are tailors that have been called in for the job.
5. [*Visitor.*] Dear! dear! but have you forgotten our old ways then? Why, in former days all the girls in the house could make clothes. If the question was[2] the making up of a cotton *ao*, for instance, all hands took a part in laying the wadding and fitting the lining; and when this had been turned, one would be stitching the overlap,[3] another would be laying the chalk line,[4] and another closing the seam[5] of the arm-hole, and another putting on the collar.[6] If there was a cuff to bind,[7] it would be bound; if there was a button[8] to be put on, it was put on; and in a day or two, at the most, the work was done. Even the caps were made in the house. People would have sneered[9] at you if you had hired a tailor to make one, or if you had gone to the expense of buying one.
6. [*Host.*] What you say is quite correct, sir. Still, you only know one part of the story, and not the other. In the first place, is there no difference between the style of the past time and that of the present? In the next, the wedding-day is well in sight; we have but ten days left, all told;[10] and though we are not giving ourselves a moment's rest, and the tailors are working night and day, it's a question now whether the clothes will be ready in time or not. If we were to hold on, *coûte que coûte*, to the old usage, why we should be like the soldier who comes on the parade-ground[11] all in good time, and contrives notwithstanding to be late for parade. It would never do[12] for us to let things be behindhand, surely, when we knew right well how time was flying.

1. 壻 *hsü*[4], the husband of one's daughter; colloquially, he is always So-and-so's *nü hsü*, but when asking the wife's parents about him, you call him *ling hsü*; 婿 is another form of the same character.

2. 以 *i*, a somewhat classical construction; *i* being used pretty much as *pa* before the object of *lun*; 襖 *ao*[3], a jacket worn under the *ma-kua*, though it can be worn without it.

3. 襟 *chin*[1], the overlap of the Chinese dress, which buttons on the right breast and side.

4. 盪 *t'ang*[4], the line made on the dress in chalk or ink, to guide the tailor in stitching.

5. 煞 *sha*[1], properly, the same as *sha*, to kill; sometimes used as *hên*, very; here, to close the seam of the *ko-chih-wo*, the armpit; not used of any other part of the dress; in Peking the expression *sha k'ên*[4] (根) is more common.

6. 領條 *ling t'iao*, the strip of stuff that binds the neck of a garment.

7. 緣 *yen*[2], also read *yuan*[2], a binding on a garment; here, of binding the edge of the cuff.

8. 鈕 *niu*[3], the clothes' button, made of cloth, metal, etc.; 襻 *p'an*[4], a cord loop or "becket" that secures one side of the dress to the button on the other side, which is not sewn on to the stuff, but passed through a similar loop sewn down to the garment.

9. 見笑 *chien hsiao*, to laugh at (see *chien*, Lesson LXXXV, Note 2); people might *chien hsiao* in their hearts; here, without laughing outright, they laugh through the nose, sneer.

10. 招 *ch'ia*[1], to nip between finger and thumb: *ch'ia-cho chih-t'ou* is explained as meaning "to measure to a nicety."

11. 旗杆 *ch'i-kan*, flagstaff, staff of the colours: to be on the drill-ground and miss drill, sc., by falling asleep there, after being at the trouble of rising early in order to attend. The *ch'i* here is another form of *ch'i* (see Lesson VII, Note 9).

12. 成事 *ch'êng shih*, to complete the matter in hand, sc., as it ought to be completed: *ch'êng shên-mo shih*, how far would it be right, if *ta chêng-cho*, widely opening the eyes, we were *tan wu*, to make a mess of the business.

LESSON LXXXVII.

1. [*Junior.*] Where does this son stand in the family, sir?
2. [*Senior.*] He is the Benjamin of the party; the child of my old age.
3. [*Junior.*] Has he had the small-pox?[1]
4. [*Senior.*] He had it last year.
5. [*Junior.*] And do all these boys come one after the other?[2]
6. [*Senior.*] One after the other, without a break. There were nine born, and there are nine there alive.[3]
7. [*Junior.*] Is it possible? Well, sir, in sober earnest I must say that your good lady[4] is a clever mother and an experienced nurse; quite a *tzŭ-sun niang-niang*. You're a fortunate man, indeed.
8. [*Senior.*] Fortunate! I must have sinned in a previous existence, I think. The elder children are a little more bearable, but the chatter of these younger ones makes a din[5] that gives me the headache.
9. [*Junior.*] Well, we're all alike in this world. Folks that have plenty of children and grandchildren are always discontented because the number is so large, while others, like myself, who have but few, are always wishing to have more, without being able to have them. It's a hard matter for Heaven[6] to satisfy both parties.
10. [*Senior.*] If your little girl[7] had lived,[8] how far would she have got in her teens?
11. [*Junior.*] She was in her seventh year when she died;[9] she would be ten years old if she was alive now.
12. [*Senior.*] Ah! that was a nice child. The mention of her name even now makes me feel for you. She looked so different and talked so differently from other children. If she was brought in to see anyone she stood so erect, and her manner was so quiet;[10] and when she came forward to ask you how you were, it quite touched one to look at her.[11] That little tongue of hers, too, could talk of anything. If she was asked a question on any subject, she would come out with a long story, just as if someone had taught it her, and not omit a word. A child like that is as good as any ten.[12] Mine here are not worth the trouble of bringing up.

1. 出花 *ch'u hua*, to have the small-pox; *lit.*, to put forth flowers, to blossom.
2. 挨肩 *ngai chien*, standing shoulder to shoulder; in which sense it may be used literally; here, figuratively, in consecutive order.
3. 存了 *ts'un liao*, there are preserved, there are alive.
4. 嫂 *sao*³, the wife of one's elder brother: *ta sao-tzŭ*, wife of one's eldest brother; the person addressed being complimentarily assumed to be this relative.
5. 吃 *chih*¹, with *cha*, a sound of chattering.
6. 老天爺 *lao t'ien-yeh*, the old lord of heaven, providence.
7. 妞 *niu*¹, a girl; the character is said to have been introduced from Corea, where it is used as a surname.
8. 扔 *jêng*¹, used only in this sense of the loss of a child.
9. 沒得 *mei tê*, she died; *lit.*, was not, came to be not; generally read *mei ti*.
10. 安詳 *ngan-hsiang*, may be used of demeanour that is *ngan-ching*, quiet, and *hsiang-hsi*, careful.
11. 可憐 *k'o lien*. Observe the construction: the *êrh* makes a substantive of *k'o lien chien*, with tender feeling beholding, *q.d.*, touched one as soon as one beheld her; *êrh*, a person, to look on whom moved one directly; *ti*, of that class was she.
12. 頂十個 *ting shih ko*, would be a substitute for ten: *ting*, in the sense of *tang*⁴, to serve for.

PART V.—THE HUNDRED LESSONS. 337

LESSON LXXXVIII.

1. [*Visitor*.] It was really too good of you, when I had eaten of your morning sacrifice[1] yesterday, to send your evening[1] sacrifice to-day; why did you?

2. [*Host*.] My dear sir, not a word. It was my duty to present it, and I was just going to send to you to invite you to come over; but you know how all my people here are occupied; the pigs have to be killed[2] and their insides made up, and all these things keep their hands so busy that I had no one I could make a messenger of.

3. [*Visitor*] Oh! I didn't wait for an invitation, for I know well enough that you have to attend to everything yourself, and that is why I engaged our friends here to come along with me and eat your *ta jou*.[3] We did fear that we should be late; however, here we are in the nick of time. Now, gentlemen, we won't put our host to the trouble of attending to us individually; let us just sit down in a row,[5] *seniores priores*,[4] and begin.

4. [*Host*.] Let me beg you to eat, gentlemen. Put[6] a little broth over the meat.

5. [*Visitor*.] Eh, sir? What? formalities on an occasion like this? Never was such a thing heard of amongst us Manchus before. The meat is your ancestors' dole,[7] remember, and it is not in reason that your guests should require pressing to eat it. Friends and relatives who come for the purpose should not either be received with ceremony when they arrive, nor accompanied to the door when they depart. This fashion you are introducing of pressing your visitors on such an occasion is quite out of order.

1. 背燈 *pei têng*; *lit.*, behind the lamps, in the dark; used only with reference to Manchu sacrifices (prepared by women) after removing the lights. They *chi shên*, offer [pork] to the spirits, *sc.*, of their ancestors, shortly after midnight. The *pei têng* sacrifice. also of pork, is offered about 8 on the evening of the same day. It should be observed that 鐙 (*têng*⁴), a stirrup, is interchangeable with *têng*, a lamp, but in the latter case is read *têng¹*.

2. 宰 *tsai*³, to kill with a knife any beast or bird good for eating, though an exception should perhaps be made in the case of game.

3. 大肉 *ta jou* is the meat which has been offered in the *chi shên* sacrifice, and which on the following day friends are invited to eat. There are two *chi shên* sacrifices on successive days, followed by one *pei têng* sacrifice.

4. 序齒 *hsü*⁴ *ch'ih*, in order of our teeth, that is, our ages.

5. 一溜 *i liu*, as a stream uninterrupted, the seniors not ceremoniously declining the upper seats.

6. 泡 *p'ao*⁴, properly, a bubble; here and elsewhere, to pour, or to soak in liquid, as bread in milk, etc.

7. 克 *k'o*¹, classically *k'o*⁴, to be able; here, without meaning, *k'o-shih* being simply used to represent a Manchu word signifying bounty. More politely these sacrificial viands are called 神餘 (*shên yü*), the leavings of the ancestral spirits.

LESSON LXXXIX.

1. When we were in Manchuria[1] we used to go out after game regularly every day, and one day that I was out a roe-deer[2] sprang out of the grass before me. I laid on with the whip immediately, and then I let fly an arrow at him. It fell a little short, and by the time I got my hand behind me to draw out another, I could only just see his tail bobbing, and, in the twinkling of an eye, he was over the crest of the hill[3] and breasting the hill next to it. I gave chase with all the speed I could muster, but he topped the next hill and was off down the far slope of it.

2. Well, I kept my horse at it, and the moment I got well up with the roe-deer, I let fly another arrow, but this time over his head. Strange to say, a deer[4] that was coming cantering over the brow of the hill in my direction stood right into my shot, and down he fell.

3. Such a throw is too good a joke, really; but, as they say, you get a thing always when you least expect it. I may as well keep the story to myself, however, for if I were to tell it people would think it was only a traveller's tale.

1. 關東 *kuan-tung*, the country east of the Shan-hai Kuan, the barrier which divides Manchuria from China Proper.

2. 麅 *p'ao²*, a small deer, which WILLIAMS surmises may be the nylghau, but other authorities declare to be a roebuck.

3. 山前 *shan ch'ien*, the front, the opposite side, of the hill I was ascending; having passed this, the animal was *wang shang*, ascending, the next hill.

4. 鹿 *lu*, evidently not the same as the *p'ao*, though what other species of deer there is nothing to show.

PART V.—THE HUNDRED LESSONS. 339

LESSON XC.

1. [*Senior.*] I find it very dull this spring weather sitting at home all day idle; and I have nothing to do.

2. [*Junior.*] It is dull, indeed. I went out yesterday with a young brother of mine. He came in and invited me to go outside the walls with him for a stroll, and we went on till we came to a place that was all country,[1] with a distant spring prospect that was really charming.[2] Along the river banks[3] the red peach[4] blossoms were looking so fresh, and the willow[5] branches so green;[6] all kinds of birds were calling pleasantly in the trees, and a gentle breeze blew the scent of the meadows against one's nostrils. Small craft were moving to and fro without ceasing on the water, and on both sides[7] of it people were strolling about in parties of four or five. My brother and I followed a narrow winding path till we reached a spot where the wood was thick, and there, all in one *tableau*, we saw before us a group of people, some playing the guitar,[8] some singing, some selling tea and wine; and then for refreshments there were live fish and live shrimps[9] to be had, and very cheap. We spent a full day enjoying ourselves. Don't take it ill of me, sir, that I didn't ask you to accompany us: it wasn't that I wished to conceal our trip from you, but I feared that we might fall in with someone that would be disagreeable to you, so I didn't come to look for you.

1. 曠 *k'uang*⁴, properly, empty, vacant; hence, disused: *k'uang yeh*, properly, desert and wild, but used of the country in general as distinct from the town.

2. 可愛 *k'o ngai*. Observe the construction: the prospect truly caused people *k'o*, to be justly able, *ngai*, to love it.

3. 沿 *yen*⁴, properly *yen*², the shore of a sea or river; *yen*², along the edge of.

4. 桃 *t'ao*², the peach tree.

5. 柳 *liu*³, the willow tree.

6. 碧 *pi*⁴, green jadestone; hence, the colour of this stone, which may be bluish green or greenish blue.

7. 岸 *an*⁴, a beach or shore; it differs from *yen* (see Note 3, above) in that it can be used alone; *e.g.*, we say *shang an*, not *shang yen*, to go ashore.

8. 彈 *t'an*², to touch the strings of an instrument with the finger, to play on a stringed instrument; also, to fillip with the finger.

9. 蝦 *hsia*¹, shrimps.

LESSON XCI.

1. The day before yesterday we made an excursion to the Western Hills, and I really may say that it was impossible to enjoy anything more.[1] A ramble by day is pleasant enough we know, but it is even more delightful[2] by night.

2. When we had had our dinners, we got into a boat, and before very long the moon rose as bright as day. We punted[3] gently down the stream, and as we came round a point in the hills there lay a broad sheet[4] of silver before us; sky and water so blended together that there was no saying which was which; hill and stream, too, in perfect repose.

3. We had punted the boat on to a spot where the reeds[5] were thick, when, all of a sudden, the sound of a temple bell was heard, and as it came booming[6] down the wind, one's heart felt as free as if all[8] its cares[7] had been washed away; in short, we were in such a state of contentment that I defy the gods[9] themselves to be happier than we were. There we sat enjoying the thing more and more, and we drank the whole night long without either getting drunk or feeling sleepy.

4. It is but seldom in the course of one's life that one lights on such a moon[10] and such weather;[11] and when one does, it is a pity not to turn[12] them to good account,[13] is it not?

1. 盡興 *chin hsing*, exhaustively pleasurable: *chin*, to exhaust; *hsing*, for *kao hsing*, elevation of spirit. See *kao-liao hsing*, towards the end of the third paragraph of this Lesson.

2. 暢 *ch'ang⁴*, properly, to penetrate; to grow, to increase: *ch'ang³ k'uai*, the sensation of happiness belonging to freedom from care; note the tone.

3. 撐 *ch'êng¹*, to keep off an assailant with the hand; with a boat, as here, to push with a pole, to punt: *ch'êng p'o*, to burst, as a box over-full.

4. 浩 *hao⁴*, like a large sheet of water: *hao-hao*, sheet-like, *ju yin*, as silver.

5. 蘆葦 *lu²-wei³*, reeds, rushes; both may be used independently, as in *lu hua*, *wei hua*, the flower of such reeds; a reed is *i kên wei-tzŭ*.

6. 悠 *yu¹*, properly, mournful; also, distant: *yu-yu yang-yang*, used of distant sounds borne upon the air.

7. 慮 *lü⁴*, to bethink one, more especially of what is to come; to be anxious about, forethoughtful; hence, care, anxiety, forethought.

8. 皆 *chieh¹*, all; only used colloquially in some few combinations.

9. 出世 *ch'u shih*, not who have died, but who have left this world and become spirits.

10. 朗 *lang³*, bright.

11. 致 *chih⁴*, a word of many meanings; in books, most commonly to cause, in which sense it occurs colloquially in the combination *i chih*, whereby was occasioned, the result of which was; hence, the cause, the occasion; but here its sense is form, or appearance; *ching*, see Lesson LXV, Note 10: *ching-chih*, scenery, landscape.

12. 徒 *t'u²*, originally, to walk on foot; hence, a tramp, a rowdy; also, empty; hence, *t'u jan*, in vain, to no purpose; with *ti*, a younger brother, it means an apprentice, pupil, or neophyte.

13. 度 *tu⁴*, to cross over, to pass through: *hsü tu*, vainly to pass; used humbly, elsewhere, in stating one's age; I have vainly passed so many years; here, *t'u jan hsü tu* means to have passed by without availing oneself of.

LESSON XCII.

1. The day before yesterday we went out, a few of us, for a stroll, though it was not worthy of the name, for, turn which way we would, we got into difficulty.[1] First of all, as we left the city we got off[2] the proper road, and made a round, I can't tell you where. However, by dint of asking here and inquiring there as we went along, we did hit the canal lock.[3] There we seated ourselves in a boat, and chatted and hobnobbed until we had dropped down to Tung-hua Yüan; here we turned back, but by the time we reached the lock the sun was well down.

2. So as soon as dinner was over I said to them all, "Gentlemen, we had better be off; the servants have all got to walk, and its a long way home." Not a bit of it; nobody would stir; and there they sat on,[4] talking and laughing, until, by-and-by, they saw that it was close to sunset, and then they got on their horses and began to ride back as hard as they could.

3. By the time they reached the suburb there was a slight glimmer of moonlight,[5] and the people coming out of the city were all crying out, "Make haste!" and telling us that one leaf[6] of the gate was shut to already. This made us more anxious than ever, and we laid on[7] with the whip and pressed our horses up to the wall; but the rear[8] of the party was shut out all the same.

4. It was certainly an expedition with a merry beginning[9] and a sorrowful termination.

1. 受罪 *shou tsui*; *lit.*, to receive punishment; here, to come to grief, to have a bad time of it.

2. 放著 *fang-cho*, we let go our hold of *chêng-ching tao*, the proper or regular road.

3. 閘 *cha*², a lock in a canal, a sluice: *cha-k'ou*, the points on the river bank at which the locks lie; *q.d.*, their ports. See Part IV, Dialogue VIII, Note 21.

4. 儘自 *chin*³ *tzŭ*, not of the persons' will, but of their act; they sat on and on.

5. 恍惚 *huang*³ *hu*¹, properly, of indecision of mind, or forgetfulness, of which it is frequently used; but often, as here, of the struggling light of the sun and moon.

6. 扇 *shan*¹, to fan: *shan*⁴-*tzŭ*, a fan; *shan*⁴, the leaf of a door, one half of a hinge.

7. 加 *chia*¹, properly, to add to; but often employed, as here, for the verb *to use*.

8. 末尾 *mo wei*³, the tail end. Note *wei*³, not *i*³.

9. 乘 *ch'êng*⁴, properly *ch'êng*² (see Part IV, Dialogue X, Note 25); *lit.*, riding on; *hsing*, a merry, exalted state of mind: *sao*⁴ *hsing*, having swept that state away; note the tone of *sao*.

LESSON XCIII.

1. [*Visitor.*] It's dreadfully hot. I suspect[2] it's the very hottest[3] day we have had this summer;[1] there is not a breath of wind stirring. Everything in the house is so burning it scorches[4] one's hand to touch it, and the more[5] cold water one drinks the thirstier one feels. I could see nothing else for it, so I took a bath, and after cooling myself a little while in the shade of the trees, I felt somewhat more at my ease. But you; what are you about? on a fiery day like this, when everyone else is sitting stripped[6] to the middle and even then in dread of the heat,[7] there you are seated writing, with your head down to the table. What sin did you commit before you were born?[8] Do you intend to kill yourself?

2. [*Host.*] This is all very fine talk for idlers like you, who have no official business to do, and who just take your ease from one year's end to the other. But what do you say to the pedlars, for instance, who, in order to earn a hundred cash or so to keep them alive, have to run about in all directions carrying great loads, with their backs bending under their weight and their necks stretched out, crying their wares[9] till the perspiration runs off them like rain? Are they as well off as I am here, writing at any pace that suits me, and with wherewithal to live upon? Besides, it is the rule,[10] and it always has been, that the summer should be hot and the winter should be cold. Let it be as hot as it will, put up with it quietly, and perhaps you may light on a cool moment. As the proverb says, "It will be cool if you only determine it shall be." But you won't escape[11] the heat if you let it put you out at all, remember.

---

1. 立夏 *li hsia*, the commencement of summer, one of the 24 fortnightly terms into which the Chinese year is divided.

2. 說得起 *shuo tê ch'i*, we may say, we can afford to say. Cf. *mai pu ch'i*, I can't afford to buy.

3. 頭一 *t'ou i*. Construe: the number one hot of days, the hottest of days. Had the speaker meant the first hot day we have had, he would have said *chin t'ien ts'ai² jê* (emphasising *ts'ai*).

4. 燙 *t'ang*[4], to scald, to scorch; the action of fire or hot water.

5. 越 *yüeh*[4], to overstep, to exceed, to pass over; hence, still more, the more.

6. 光著 *kuang-cho*, bare, naked.

7. 暑 *shu*[3], sun-heat; *chung*, to hit, as a mark: *chung shu*, to get a fever, to suffer from heat.

8. 孽 *nieh*[4], the earliest sprouts of any vegetation: *tsui nieh*, the punishment incurred, according to the Buddhists, for sin in a previous state of existence.

9. 吆喝 *yao¹ ho¹*, not used apart; to cry wares, etc., in the street; also, to call to a person to desist or to go away; in carter's parlance, *yao ho* means "drive on."

10. 易 *yi*, or *i*, used in Part III, 964, as easy; here, to change.

11. 還能脫了麼 *hai nêng t'o³ liao*. Note the tone of *t'o*.

PART V.—THE HUNDRED LESSONS.   343

LESSON XCIV.

1. [*Host.*] Hallo! where have you been to in such a rain as this? Come in directly.

2. [*Traveller.*] I have been attending the funeral of a friend. The morning was dull; still, though it looked rather like rain at that time, the day was perfectly fine[1] at noon; so I went. But as we were on our way back I saw the clouds begin little by little to gather,[2] and in no time the whole sky was overcast; so I said to my people, "I don't like the look of the weather; get on with you, or we shall be caught in the rain." Well, as I was speaking, down it came steadily,[3] sir. There wasn't much chance of shelter, as you may suppose, out there in the open[4] country, and as I couldn't get on my felt[5] coat or my waterproof quick enough, I was wet through from head to foot.

3. [*Host.*] Never mind; change your clothes; I will give you some of mine to put on, and as it's so late you had better not go into the city till to-morrow. I have nothing much worth eating in this out-of-the-way corner; still, I have got some little pigs[6] and chickens of our own rearing, and we'll kill one or two for your supper.

4 [*Traveller.*] Oh! no excuses, pray, on the score of my fare, sir; I'm lucky enough, I'm sure, to have found so snug a billet to rest in.[7] I don't see how I could have helped facing[8] the rain otherwise.

---

1. 響 *hsiang*³, brightness; also, sound, in which sense, according to some authorities, it is here used with reference to the sound of the ground on a clear day; whether as bright or ringing, it is intensive of *ch'ing*, clear, fine.

2. 稠 *ch'ou*², thick, as grain growing close together.

3. 刷 *shua*¹, the sound of falling rain; it has no other meaning; *shua* cannot be used of a very heavy downpour.

4. 漫 *man*⁴, an expanse or overflow of water; hence, any waste or expanse.

5. 氈 *chan*¹, felt, or any like fabric.

6. 猪 *chu*¹, a pig; also written 豬.

7. 棲 *ch'i*¹, to roost like birds: *ch'i shên*, to rest the body, to set oneself down.

8. 冒著 *mao-cho*, running the head against: *hai p'a*, is it indeed probable that I could have gone on without facing the rain?

LESSON XCV.

1. I got an awful frightening last night. I had had quite enough[1] of this succession of dismal days; what with a leak here and damp there, there was not a place in the whole house one could lie down in to sleep.

2. And then the mosquitoes,[2] the bugs,[2] and the fleas[3] bit[4] me beyond endurance. There I lay tumbling and tossing about[5] without having slept a wink until after morning bells; I then closed[6] my eyes deliberately, and after lying patiently[7] for a time I was dropping off, when, just as I was half asleep, I was roused[10] by a tremendous crash to the north-west of the house that sounded[9] as if a mountain had collapsed[8] or the earth been rent asunder. I lay ever so long trembling with fear and my heart going pit-a-pat,[11] until at last I opened my eyes, and seeing that nothing in the room had been injured, I sent out to ascertain what was the matter, and was told that it was the end wall[12] of a neighbour's house that had come down, undermined[13] by the rain.

3. Dear me! it's something beyond a sleeping man's powers of endurance, an uproar[14] like that.

1. 心熟 $hsin\ shou$, it was no longer a novelty: observe $hsia\ tê$, raining it had attained to, had rained until, etc.

2. 蚊 $wên^2$, mosquitoes, gnats; $ch‘ou\ ch‘ung$, stinking insects, sc., bugs.

3. 虼蚤 $ko^4\text{-}tsao^3$, or $tsao^1$, fleas: ko is a character not recognised by the dictionaries; $tsao$, in books, is used alone.

4. 叮 $ting^1$, properly, of talk that bores one; colloquially, to sting: stung me, $tê$, to such a degree that, it was really hard to bear them. Yao^3 can also be applied to the bite of insects.

5. 翻覆 $fan^1\ fu^4$, backwards and forwards: fan, to turn over; fu, to come back to the original position.

6. 閉 pi^4, to close; often used with $kuan$ (see Part III, 63), with which it is almost identical in meaning.

7. 忍了 $jên\ liao$, I bore it: perforce I closed my eyes and bore the annoyance a little while.

8. 崩 $pêng^1$, the sound of a landslip; used classically of the death of an Emperor.

9. 响 $hsiang^3$, to sound; properly written as in Lesson XCIV, Note 1.

10. 陡 tou^3, colloquially, of heights, precipitous, descending abruptly: $tou\text{-}jan$, suddenly.

11. 突 $t‘u^1$, properly, to come upon unawares; to butt against: $t‘u\ t‘u\ ti$, knock, knock, as water bubbling up from a spring; here, of one's heart.

12. 山牆 $shan\ ch‘iang$, the hill-shaped wall, the gable of a house.

13. 淋 lin^2, vulgarly $lün^2$, to soak or moisten with dropping water; also used passively.

14. 震 $chên^4$, the shock of a clap of thunder, or to shock like one: how $ching\ tê\ ch‘i$, could a man go through, the shock of such a sound?

LESSON XCVI.

1. Yesterday morning when I got up it was so dark I thought the sun could not have risen yet. I stepped out into the court to look, and I saw that it was daylight, but that the sky was as black as pitch. However, I gave my face a wash, and I was going to start for the yamên, when it began to spit, and soon after I heard it coming down steadily; so I sat down again, and I might have been seated time enough to drink a cup of tea, when there was a clap[1] of thunder,[2] and the rain came down in a perfect torrent.[3] I thought it was too violent to last very long, and that I would wait a little, and start when it held up. But I was quite out; it rained all day and all night without stopping; nor was it till after breakfast this morning that the sun began to show himself a little. It's fine seasonable rain though, for all that. I should think the ground is well saturated everywhere. The autumn crops are certain to be fair.

1. 霹 $p'i^1$, the sound of a clap of thunder; not used alone.

2. 雷 lei^2, thunder: $p'i$-lei combines the ideas of the suddenness and loudness of a clap of thunder.

3. 傾 $ch'ing^1$, to turn out the contents of anything by upsetting it: $ch'ing$ $p'ên$, a bowl upset.

LESSON XCVII.

1. It was so cold the night before last that it¹ woke me up, and I lay awake till morning. The moment it was light I jumped out of bed, and on opening the door to take a look, I found the whole place glittering white² with snow.

2. About eleven o'clock, after I had breakfasted, it began to snow harder;⁵ the flakes grew larger and larger, and came fluttering wavily³ ⁴ down. Said I to myself, "I've nothing to do; I wish a friend would drop in for a chat; how is this to be managed?"

3. To my great delight, just at that very moment in came the servants and announced some visitors. I told them to put out something to eat and drink, and to light⁶ a pan of charcoal. Then I made haste and asked my friends to walk in, which they did. The wine and other things that were ready were brought in, and we sat sipping our liquor without hurrying ourselves, until by-and-by we had the door-curtain⁷ rolled well up to see how things looked, and there before us was a superb⁸ snow scene that beat anything one had ever beheld. The snow was falling thick in all directions;⁹ hill, stream, and woods, all white with it. The sight made us jollier than ever. We got out the chess-board¹⁰ and played two games, and after dinner, just as it was dusk, our party broke up.

1. 凍 *tung*⁴, to freeze: *yeh li shang tung*, it freezes at night.

2. 白亮亮 *pai liang*¹ *liang*¹, glittering white. Note the tone of *liang*.

3. 飄 *p'iao*¹, to whirl round as wind.

4. 飆 *yao*², the same as *p'iao*, unless combined with which it is not found.

5. 越發 *yüeh fa*, more than ever. *See* Lesson XCIII, Note 5.

6. 爖 *lung*², to prepare a stove, to make a fire. *See also* Part III, **198**. The dictionaries do not recognise this term.

7. 簾 *lien*², a curtain, a screen, properly of split bamboo, but also used of those composed of other materials.

8. 雅 *ya*³, of anything that is nice, refined; *ch'ing ya* may be said of scenery, of the interior of a house, etc.: the snow scene, as compared with anything, was fine.

9. 紛 *fên*¹, in numbers and in confusion; can be used of rain as well as snow. Note *hsüeh*⁴ *pai*, not *hsüeh*³.

10. 棋盤 *ch'i*²-*p'an* is a chess-board; *i p'an ch'i*, a set of chess-men and board; *ch'i-tzŭ*³-*'rh*, chess-men: *hsia liao i p'an*, played one game. There are two other ways of writing *ch'i*².

LESSON XCVIII.

1. Yesterday we were all at the yamên, and it was a fine clear day, without a breath of wind. All of a sudden, the sun began to look gloomy,[1] and I said to the rest of them, "I don't like the look of the weather; we are going to have a blow, and we had best be off." They all thought so too, and we broke up accordingly.

2. I had just reached home when the storm began in earnest. The way in which the blast roared through the trees was something awful, and this continued until after midnight, when the wind lulled a little.

3. But as I was coming here this morning I remarked that everyone I met was doubled up with the cold. People were all hissing[2] and blowing, and running to keep themselves warm.

4. As for me, I got on pretty well at first, for I had my back to the wind; but when I came to breast it, the cold set my cheeks and my whole face tingling as if they had been pricked with needles. My fingers grew so stiff[3] that I couldn't hold my whip; and my very spittle became ice before it could reach the ground, and broke in pieces as it fell.[4]

5. Never did anybody in all his life see such cold.

1. 惨淡 ts'an³ tan⁴, of weather, gloomy : ts'an, of the sky, sad ; generally, cruel, inhuman, or, adjectively, pitiful, heart-rending ; tan, of the sun's rays, weak.

2. 吸 hsi¹, the sound of drawing the breath in ; ha, here, the sound of the breath emitted.

3. 攣 lien⁴, of the fingers stiffening : chü lien, so stiff that they could not chü, keep their hold of anything.

4. 摔碎 shuai sui, broke in pieces as it fell.

LESSON XCIX.

1. Man stands highest of all created beings, as being possessed of reason. If he did not know good from evil, if he could not understand the rule of right, wherein would he differ from the beasts?[1]

2. Well, in the relations of friends the right rule is that each should treat the other with proper respect, is it not; that I should show a certain deference to you, and you to me?

3. Now, this fellow, ever since he has arrived this time, has been bullying[3] and over-bearing[2] on all occasions, giving people whatever bad language came into his head.[4] Whether he thinks this clever, or what else may be the meaning of his conduct, I can't say; but just look at the man, with that ill-favoured phiz[5] of his and his large paunch;[6] and to think that a genius[7] like that has the pretension to imagine himself a man of education is enough to make one's flesh creep.[8] Then his voice is more like a dog's bark than anything else; it disgusts people so that they can't bear to hear him speak.

4. If he had any of the proper sentiments a man ought to have, he would feel how unpopular his way of talking makes him; but no, not a bit of it;[9] he bears himself as if it made everybody like him, and he was all the more contented[10] in consequence. I can't understand it.

5. His father was always a good enough kind of man when he was alive. What sin could he have committed before he was born, to breed such a good-for-nothing as this? However, there's nothing before him now; his father expended all the luck[11] of the family. He has come to the end of his tether,[12] and as for rising[13] any higher, as he expects, I should like to know how he is to compass it.

---

1. 畜 *ch'u*[4], also read *hsü*[4]; originally, to breed, to rear; domestic animals: *ch'u-shêng*, animals, not being wild animals; here, the beasts of the field.

2. 豪 *hao*[2], among other meanings, eminent by prowess, heroic; here, in a bad sense.

3. 橫 *hêng*[4] (see *hêng*[2], Part III, 1072), here, morally what *hêng* is materially: *hao hêng*, the qualities of a bully.

4. 信著 *hsin-cho*, trusting to; *q.d.*, leaving it to his mouth, *hun ma*, at random to abuse, people.

5. 嘴巴 *tsui-pa*, properly, the cheeks: *tsui-pa ku-tzŭ*, the jaw-bones; here used for the whole face, that face being ill-looking. Note: *tsui-pa-tzŭ*, the lower half of the face; *tsui pa*, a slap on the face, a box on the ears.

6. 骰 *ku*[3], to bulge out, as paper, a wall, etc.; here, of the person.

7. 傻 *sha*[3], properly, a sharp fellow; but colloquially, always the reverse.

8. 肉麻 *jou ma*, the flesh creeping: *ma*, elliptically representing *ma mu*, hemp-seed and wood, used for inanimate matter; hence, the affection of a foot asleep, or a palsied limb, which is *ma mu*.

9. 腆 *t'ien*[3], thick, substantial; here, of the skin of the face: brazening it out, he *pu chih ch'ih*, is insensible to shame.

10. 興頭 *hsing-t'ou*, happiness, contentedness: *hsing*, as in *kao hsing* (*see* Lesson XCI, Note 1); a man's *hsing-t'ou* may be *hao* or *pu hao*; that is, he may be contented or discontented.

11. 福分 *fu fên*, the amount of happiness allotted [his family], his father *hsiang chin*, enjoyed to exhaustion.

12. 結果 *chieh kuo*, he has formed into fruit; *q.d.*, he has done blooming, he has come to the end of his career.

13. 陞騰 *shêng t'êng*[2], to rise; *sc.*, as an official.

LESSON C.

1. What do you mean by leading such a life as this? All you do of a day is to fill your belly, and then to take up your guitar[1] or your lute[2] and go on strumming upon it for no purpose that I can make out. Do you propose to make yourself famous by your guitar-playing, or are you going to get your bread by it?

2. We have the luck to be Manchus, and as such we have Government rice to eat and Government money monthly to spend. Our quarters, from the roof[3] that covers our families to the ground that is under our feet, are all our master's. We owe him some return, then; and when a man, while he neglects the acquisition of things right and proper for him to learn, and displays no zeal in the discharge of his duty, devotes himself[4] heart and soul to such an accomplishment as this guitar-playing, he is a disgrace[5] to the name of Manchu. Surely it would be better worth your while to be studying[6] than expending all the best powers of your mind on a useless subject of this sort.

3. Recollect that the proverb says, "It is as much the mission of man to rise as it is the property of water to descend;" and remember that, however great proficiency you may achieve on the guitar, you won't escape the repute of being a dirty, low-caste[7] individual. Will your ability to play the guitar avail you as a qualification in your regular official career, pray?

4. Certainly not; and if I am not speaking the truth, perhaps you'll name someone high in rank or office who owes his first appointment[8] to his skill on the guitar, will you?

---

1. 琵琶 *p'i²-pa¹*, a certain stringed instrument.
2. 絃 *hsien²*, also a musical instrument; *t'an*, to play, either on it or on the *p'i-p'a*. See Lesson XC, Note 8.
3. 頭頂 *t'ou ting*, what my head rises to, *sc.*, my roof; *chiao tz'ŭ³*, or *ts'ai³*, what my foot treads, *sc.*, my floor.
4. 鑽著 *tsuan-cho*, burrowing with, *sc.*, the mind.
5. 玷 *tien⁴*, a blemish, as on a jewel.
6. 讀書 *tu² shu*, to study.
7. 卑污 *pei¹ wu¹*, mean and dirty: *pei*, low, lowly; *wu*, foul.
8. 出身 *ch'u shên*, to commence an official career.

PART VI.

THE GRADUATE'S WOOING.

PART VI.
THE GRADUATE'S WOOING
OR
THE STORY OF A PROMISE THAT WAS KEPT.

CHAPTER I.

1. Once upon a time,³ under the T'ang dynasty, there was a man high in office named Ts'UI² CHIO, who, having retired into private life,¹ built a temple at P'u Chou,⁴ which was called the P'u-chiu Ssŭ.

2. He died some years after, and his wife, Madame Ts'UI, whose maiden name⁶ was CHÊNG,⁵ then moved into the temple, where she lived apart in some buildings on the west side.

3. She had one son and one daughter. The son's name was HUAN LANG; the daughter's, YING YING.⁷ She also brought with her a serving maid⁸ named HUNG NIANG; she was in close attendance upon YING YING, who never stirred without her.

4. YING YING was just of the charming age;⁹ her eyebrows were well defined, her eye was clear, and her air of high breeding¹⁰ and gravity gave great promise of future happiness.

5. She was, besides, as clever as she was pretty.¹¹ She knew all history, ancient and modern, and she could write in all the four

---

1. 退 歸 林 下, to retire into private life; used only of retirement from office; *kuei*, to return to an original condition of things.

2. 崔 *ts'ui*¹, a surname; 珏 *chio*⁴ is also used only as a name.

3. 曾. Note the use of *ts'êng* as an adverb of past time, supplying the "once upon a time" with which the story opens.

4. 蒲 州 *p'u*² *chou*, the name of a prefecture in Shansi.

5. 鄭 *chêng*¹, a surname; also the name of a feudal state in the Chou dynasty (B.C. 774–500); *chêng chung*, to be in earnest, to attach importance to.

6. 氏 *shih*¹ after two proper names indicates that the latter is the maiden name of a married woman; thus, Madame Ts'UI, *née* CHÊNG.

7. 鶯 *ying*¹, the oriole; commonly called *huang*² *ying* or *huang li*² (黃 鸝).

8. 丫 頭 *ya*¹ *t'ou*, a serving maid: *ya*, a fork or crotch; *ya t'ou*, lit., forked head, referring to the two tufts or knots into which the hair of a young girl is tied; a father can speak of his own daughters as *ya t'ou*.

9. 妙 齡 *miao*⁴ *ling*², charming age: *miao*, good, excellent; *ling*, the years of one's life, an elegant synonym of *nien*.

10. 典 雅, high breeding: her *ya*³, excellence, *tien*³, was of an orthodox kind, was regulated by the *tien*, canon or standard, of education.

11. 雙 全: her *mao*, personal appearance, and *ts'ai*, ability, [were] *shuang*, equally (a pair), *ch'üan*, complete [in their excellence].

CHAP. I.]   PART VI.—THE GRADUATE'S WOOING.   353

styles of handwriting—round hand, running hand, the *li* character, and the seal character.[12]

6. While still quite a child she had been promised in marriage to CHÊNG HÊNG, a nephew [13] of Madame TS'UI's. This CHÊNG HÊNG, unfortunately, was an especially worthless person. His livelong day was passed in playing the man of means and consequence;[14] nothing could exceed his affectation of position. Another bad habit he had was this, that whatever he saw people doing, eating choice fare or wearing fine clothes, he must needs be following their example. There was positively nothing to be made of him.

7. The upshot was that a fortune [15] he had had of over ten thousand taels was all squandered [16] clean away, and foraging [17] for supplies became the sole purpose of his life—discovery of someone who might have money to lend. Whoever had, he would borrow of him for his need; and seeing that to the end of time he never paid his debts, the interest of these ran on from month to month and from year to year,[18] until, in fact, it exceeded the original loan. Added to this [19] he was very dangerous. He would speak you fair, and be tripping you up,[20] so that you came to grief when you least expected it. And then he was so greedy,[21] always after some small advantage. Any man he found with money he would cheat [22] if he could not bully him. He certainly was an out-and-out rascal.

8. For these reasons he was despised by everybody, and, little by little, he had to subsist himself as best he might, empty handed,[23] without a fraction of income of any sort—to such a degree of distress was he reduced.

12. 眞草隸篆 *chên ts'ao li*⁴ *chuan*⁴, the four kinds of Chinese text: *chên*, the true, fairly formed; *ts'ao*, the running hand; *li*, a style introduced shortly before the Christian era; *chuan*, ordinarily known as the seal character.

13. 內姪, a wife's brother's son. A wife's relations are distinguished as *nei* when they belong to the males of her family, and as *wai* when they belong to the females; thus, Madame TS'UI's brother's children were her *nei chih-'rh* and *nei chih nü-'rh*, her sister's children were her *wai shêng*¹ (外甥) and *wai shêng nu-'rh*; her brothers stood in the relation of *nei hsiung* and *nei ti* to her husband, whose own sister's children were both her and his *wai shêng* and *wai shêng nü*; his brothers, elder and younger, being Madame TS'UI's *ta po*² (大伯) and *hsiao shu* (小叔) respectively, or, in Peking, *ta pai*³-*tzŭ* and *hsiao shu-tzŭ*; Madame TS'UI's sisters, elder and younger, standing in the relation to her husband of *ta i*² (大姨) and *hsiao i* respectively. 恆, *lit.*, constant, regular.

14. 耍排子 *p'ai*², to arrange in order, to set out; hence, *p'ai-tzŭ*, ostentation, display; *pai*³ *chia-tzŭ*, to set out a stall (*sc.*, of wares) is used in much the same sense. Note that 盡 when used in the sense of only is read *ching*⁴.

15. 家當兒, fortune: *tang-'rh*, that would serve [to maintain], *chia*, a family or home.

16. 拋費, squandered. See Part IV, Dialogue V, Note 9.

17. 搜羅 *sou*¹ *lo*², to forage, to "cadge": *lo*, a net; looked about, *sou*, for what he could net, *lo*.

18. 積年累月, ran on from month to month and year to year: both *chi*² and *lei*³ (note the tone) mean to accumulate.

19. 又搭著, in addition; see Part III, 1076. Note that *yu*, or some similar adverb, must precede *ta*.

20. 使絆子, trip you up: *pan-tzŭ* (see Part V, Lesson XXII, Note 4) are properly hobbles; 使上絆子, to put the hobbles on.

21. 眼皮子淺, greedy; strictly speaking, "shallowness under the skin of the eyes" is applied to a person who has seen little and has no experience, but the expression is generally used to indicate the childish greediness that covets every new object.

22. 骈 *pêng*¹, to cheat, to do out of; properly, to pull a bow; *pêng-kung-'rh*, the bow attached by the Chinese to doors to make them shut of themselves.

23. 拳頭 *ch'üan*²-*t'ou*, the fist: *tsuan ch'üan-t'ou*, to close the fist.

CHAPTER II.

1. It was his destiny,[1] however, that he should be rescued from his difficulties. He suddenly remembered that there was still one friend to whom he might apply for assistance[2]—a man named T'IEN ÊRH,[3] whose sole occupation it had been to do jobs for other people.[4] He had, as a fact, begun with nothing, but had succeeded in establishing himself, and at the time we are speaking of he was worth a good deal of money. At the commencement of his career his conduct had not been by any means correct, but he was now a reformed character.[5]

2. CHÊNG HÊNG, having no abilities of his own, had in earlier times associated himself as a partner with T'IEN ÊRH, and the two had been closely linked together[6] in various shady transactions.

3. On the day in question it occurred to CHÊNG HÊNG that he ought to look this friend up, and borrow a little money of him. Without loss of time he slipped on an old doublet that was of something between a green and a blue, and so worn that it made a terrible show. As soon as it was on, he saw at a glance that, as if on purpose,[7] there were also two button-loops off, which he had to stitch on, and then he perceived that his cap had no throat-lash either. But he had no time to mend this, as he was afraid of missing his chance; so away he went with his cap in this condition, wagging his head from side to side[8] pretentiously, till he got to T'IEN ÊRH'S, when he knocked at the door.

1. 合該, read huo^2 kai, it was his destiny: ho, lit., to correspond to, to meet; kai, what ought to happen. Note that huo kai does not mean "served him right," but that the bad or good fortune, as the case may be, was foreordained.

2. 幫助 $pang^1$ chu^4, to assist; both characters are identical in meaning.

3. 行二 $hang^2$ $êrh$, the second in the family: $hang$, a row, a list, a line, a series; second in the list (q.d., of sons). See Part III, Exercise XXVIII, 10; Part IV, Dialogue IV, Note 73.

4. 拉篷扯縴 la^1 $p'êng^2$ $ch'ê^3$ $ch'ien^4$, to do odd jobs for other people; lit., to hoist the sail ($p'êng$) and drag the tow rope. La $ch'ien$ is often used with the object placed between the two characters; thus, 拉房縴, a house agent. Note that to hoist a sail is properly 打篷.

5. 都收歛了 $shou^1$ $lien^4$, was a reformed character: $lien$, to gather together, as a number of scattered articles; some such word as "wild oats," bad propensities, etc., must be understood. $Lien^4$ is also read $lien^3$, as 歛錢, to get in subscriptions; 歛帳, to collect debts.

6. 勾搭連環 kou^1 ta^1 $lien^2$ $huan^2$, closely linked together; lit., added together and linked: $huan$, a ring; $lien$ $huan$, a ring of two links; cf. 九連環, the Chinese ring puzzle. The above expression is only applied to transactions of a questionable nature. 放一個連環, to fire a volley.

7. 偏偏兒的, as if on purpose. See Part III, 925.

8. 搖頭提腦的 yao^2 $t'ou$ $huang^4$ nao ti, wagging his head from side to side: both yao and $huang$ mean to shake, to vibrate, or to move from side to side; the latter character, which is not recognised by the dictionaries, indicates a more violent action; the two are often used together as a single verb.

CHAPTER III.

1. T'IEN ÊRH came to the door, and as soon as he had looked[1] at him and seen who it was, he asked him to walk in; "And pray," said he, "where do you come from?"

2. "I come from my house, sir," replied CHÊNG HÊNG; "I have not a cash[2] in the world, and how to get a mouthful[3] I don't know. A relative of mine, a journeyman, once wanted me to learn his craft of him. But now, in your opinion, sir, was this possible?"

3. "You are right there," said T'IEN ÊRH; "for men of our class a handicraft is quite out of the question."

4. "True indeed, sir," said CHÊNG HÊNG; "I that am used to my comforts,[4] how should I engage in handicraft? much less[5] could you, worthy sir, so full of years and good actions; better off than the gods themselves. Your position inspires me with infinite respect.[6] "

5. This was a happy hit on the part of CHÊNG HÊNG, for the man T'IEN was very fond of being complimented. He was accordingly much pleased to hear CHÊNG HÊNG speak in this way.

6. "As you are well aware, sir," continued CHÊNG HÊNG, "I have a good deal of pride[7] about me; but a fine fellow [as they say] may be ruined[8] for want of a single cash. That is precisely my case, and there remains but one way out of it, a very narrow way, to which I betake me in utter despair.[9] I am here to-day, sir, to ask you to help me; it is for you to do so or not as it suits you."

7. Now this T'IEN was a fellow who always had an eye to the main chance,[10] and he did not at all like to lose anything. So as soon as he heard such words as these he bounced out before he had time to stop himself,[11] "Your idea is to get something

1. 抬頭 t'ai² t'ou, to raise or lift the head: t'ai, to raise or lift, means also to carry between two or more men on a pole; 抬轎子的, chair-bearers.

2. 分文 fên¹ wên: fên is the one-hundredth part of a tael; wên is the numerative of cash.

3. 餬口. See Part V, Lesson LXXX, Note 7.

4. 受用慣了的, accustomed to comforts: shou yung, comfortable, is elliptical; shou, in the matter of what one enjoys or gets, yung, in what one makes use of [there is sufficiency]; a sufficiency in the requirements of daily life; in other words, comfortable surroundings as compared with 舒服, bodily comfort.

5. 何況 ho k'uang, how much less? lit., how much more?

6. 羨慕 hsien⁴ mu⁴, to admire; the first word meaning to admire as superior to oneself; the second, to feel devotion to as superior to oneself.

7. 揚氣 yang² ch'i, pride; lit., to hold up one's spirit; not to be overridden; proper pride, or self-respect, is 自愛.

8. 癟倒 pieh¹ tao³, to crush: pieh in its original sense is an ulcer or abscess which has not yet burst; hence it is a synonym for suppression, sc., of feelings, etc., as 癟氣, to hold one's breath, 癟著一肚子氣, to keep down one's indignation; pieh tao in the present instance means to crush under the weight, q.d., of poverty; [the want of] a single cash may ruin a man.

9. 無可奈何. See Part IV, Dialogue IV, Note 49.

10. 佔便宜 chan⁴ p'ien i, to get an advantage out of anything: chan, lit., to encroach upon; he only looked to (chih ku; see Part V, Lesson XLII, Note 3) tzŭ-chi chan p'ien i, getting a personal advantage, the main chance; he was a shou-'rh, hand, that would positively (chüeh) not suffer loss.

11. 不由得, involuntarily, in spite of himself.

for nothing;¹² what is it?" "Whatever you please," answered CHÊNG HÊNG; "it matters not what."

8. T'IEN's countenance changed at once: "You have come at an unfortunate¹³ time, I assure you," said he; "I have lost money in business; my stock of goods is low, and the question is no longer what can be made on them; they have to be sold off cheap for what ready money they will fetch,¹⁴ and just now business is at a standstill. I owe money, besides, that I have not paid off in full,¹⁵ and in addition to all this, the crops have been swamped by the floods;¹⁶ I have a little money, but not more than just enough¹⁷ to pay my own way. And then there is another matter; I had some idea¹⁸ of purchasing myself a grade, and of buying some land as well. I can't make both ends meet¹⁹ myself; just think, now, how is it possible I should be lending money to anyone else?"

12. 尋 *hsin*², to want something for nothing (*see* Part V, Lesson LXV, Note 6); read *hsün*², to look for.

13. 湊巧 *ts'ou*⁴ *ch'iao*, opportune; *lit.*, a combination of fortuitous [circumstances].

14. 賤賣不賒 *chien*⁴ *mai pu shê*¹, to sell cheap without giving credit: *shê*, to buy or sell on credit; *wo shê kei ni*, I'll let you have it on credit; *wo shê cho*, I'll take it on credit.

15. 清楚. *See* Part V, Lesson III, Note 2.

16. 淹 *yên*¹, to swamp, to drown; used of persons or things, but with the former in combination with 死, as *yên ssŭ*, drowned.

17. 僅殼 *chin*³ *kou*, only just enough: *chin*, only, scarcely, exactly, with nothing to spare.

18. 打着, short for 打算着.

19. 週轉不開 *chou*¹ *chuan pu k'ai*, can't make both ends meet: both *chou* and *chuan* mean to revolve; *chou chuan*, a complete revolution; *k'ai* must be here used in the sense of clearing a passage, as in *tsou k'ai*, to get out of the way, *fên pu k'ai*, undistinguishable. *K'ai* has often the force of the adverbial termination *able*, which is the property of many other words in Chinese, such as 着, 得, 完, etc. *Chou chuan pu k'ai*, the circle or revolution (*q.d.*, of my daily expenditure) is uncomplete-*able*; there is a block in it that cannot be *k'ai*, cleared away.

CHAPTER IV.

1. "That purchasing of grades," said CHÊNG HÊNG, when he had heard what the other had to say, "is simply a trap for the unwary;¹ purchase of land is right enough.² How many acres³ are you now farming, sir, may I ask?"

2. "Are you my keeper?" abruptly asked T'IEN; "mind your own business, and don't be playing the dog after the mice,⁴ meddling with what doesn't concern you." CHÊNG HÊNG was too great a coward ever to put himself in the way of a collision, and finding his

1. 上檔 *shang tang*⁴, to fall into a trap. *See* Part V, Lesson XL, Note 1.

2. 倒罷了 will do, is good enough; a qualified approval. Note that *pa liao* without the prefix *tao*⁴ means "that will do," "that's enough of the matter."

3. 畝 *mu*³, a Chinese measure of land; 6 *mu* and upwards are equivalent to an English acre.

4. 狗拏耗子多管閒事 *kou*³ *na hao*⁴-*tzŭ*; *hao-tzŭ*, a rat, a mouse; distinguished as *ta* or *hsiao*: to meddle with what does not concern one, the catching of rats and mice being the business of a cat, not a dog; 閒 is merely another form of 閑 (*see* Part III, 983). Rats and mice are also called 老鼠 (Radical 208), being distinguished as *ta* and *hsiao*.

friend, whose tone had been pleasant enough, suddenly changing his front, he made equal haste to say, "Dear me! I only wanted to borrow a little money of you; if there was anything to be done, good; if nothing, nothing; I don't see what occasion there was for this sort of thing." And thereupon he rose up to go.

3. T'IEN was a piece of gristle that always turned the edge of the knife [5] (a man who was ready to face any conditions). When he saw that CHÊNG HÊNG was going away, he came round at once, and said with a smile, "I was only joking. The proverb says well, 'Money is but dirt:[6] one's reputation is worth any sum' [and mine is engaged in this matter]. We two were as great friends once upon a time as it was possible for us to be, and it would be to ignore all our past claims [7] on each other, wouldn't it, if I were to let you tell me the story you have told me to no purpose?

4. Then after a short pause [8] he went on, "That's a worn-out old thing you have on; are you still up to mending your own clothes?" CHÊNG HÊNG blushed up to the ears and over; "Every man," said he, "is bound to know how to stitch and patch; [9] you needn't be making fun of people."

5. "Don't talk like that," said T'IEN, "will you let me make you a present of something new?"

6. Saying which he brought out a cloth wrapper [10] more or less the worse for wear, containing a number of articles of dress, and having opened it out on the stove-bed, "Now, sir," said he, "how many things do you want?"

7. "You don't mean to say that you are ready to give me any number," said CHÊNG HÊNG. "So far as I am concerned, the more the better."

8. "I shall give you but one article," said T'IEN. "Take the first that comes to hand; there is no occasion for you to be picking and choosing."

9. CHÊNG HÊNG took no notice whatever of this illiberal speech, but while T'IEN was talking his eye lit upon [11] a brand new [12] cloak, which he drew out, taking care to observe at the same time, "This is no great things."

5. 滾刀筋 kun³ tao chin¹, gristle that turns the edge of the knife, a tough customer, one on whom it is not easy to make an impression; also, a man who is ready to face any emergency: kun, to turn, to roll over; 打滾兒, to roll, as a dog or a mule, in the dust; kun also means to bubble, to boil, as kun shui, boiling water, but k'ai shui is more common.

6. 糞 fên⁴, dung: fên t'u, earth used for manure, as the sweepings of streets, etc.

7. 前功盡棄 ch'ien kung¹ chin ch'i⁴, the merit of past service utterly thrown away: ch'i, to fling away, to abandon; for kung, see Part III, 1042.

8. 獃了一會兒 after a pause. See Part III, Exercise XXXI, 3.

9. 縫縺補綻: fêng², to stitch a seam; lien², a seam, but it is not found apart from fêng; chan⁴, an opened seam, generally applied to hard articles, as a division between the "uppers" and the sole of a boot, an open seam in the timbers of a boat, and so forth; pên fên shih, a matter which it is one's proper share or lot to perform.

10. 包袱 pao¹-fu⁴, a wrapper: fu, a square cloth, properly read fu².

11. 冷眼看見, his eye lit upon: lêng yen, an unprejudiced eye; an eye that looks upon a thing for the first time, or that is not influenced by familiarity with the object contemplated; e.g., a person is ill, and he invites a friend with whom he is not in constant contact to look at him with a lêng yen and tell him whether he appears worse than he did some time previously; as the people in constant contact with him regard him with an accustomed eye (看熟了), they are not able to appreciate the difference in his appearance.

12. 斬新 chan³ hsin¹, brand new, just cut off [from the original piece]: the character 湛 (chan⁴) appears in the first edition of this work and is also given in WILLIAMS's Dictionary, but native dictionaries support the first reading.

10. "Chut!" said T'IEN ÊRH, with a sneer, "Try and put up with [13] it; you will disgust people if you show that you are never satisfied. Take the thing and go your ways; but once out of this house, mind, I won't undertake to change it."

11. "Might it be changed for something else now?" asked CHÊNG HÊNG, smiling.

12. "I should say," said T'IEN, "that you had best make up your mind at once; if you take this you'll have done very well."

13. "And what," said CHÊNG HÊNG, as he thanked him, "what little thing shall I have the honour of presenting you with in return?"

14. "Keep what you have for yourself," said T'IEN ÊRH; "I want for nothing; and now I think of it, here is a sack of rice with fifty catties in it; you might take it along with you as well."

15. "You are too thoughtful, really," said CHÊNG HÊNG; "but it's out of my power to lift [14] such a weight; what shall I do?"

16. "I've a stout she-ass [15] here that I will lend you to put it on," said T'IEN; "there now, don't go and play the spendthrift any more."

17. CHÊNG HÊNG promised most emphatically [16] that he would not, and bidding his friend good-bye, away he went.

13. 包含 *pao¹ han²*, put up with, keep one's opinion to oneself; used generally with reference to presents given, or as an apology for a blunder, etc.: 他沒見過世面您包含着點兒罷, he is inexperienced, make due allowance for him. *N.B.—Shih²*, not *shih⁴*.

14. 提溜 *ti¹ liu¹*, to carry in the hand, to carry by one's side or lift from the ground: the value of *liu* in this phrase is difficult to discover; it is a colloquialism probably peculiar to the North. *N.B.—Ti¹*, not *t'i²*, as in Part IV, Dialogue II, 36.

15. 騍驢 *ts'ao³ lü*, a she-ass: *ts'ao*, the female of equine animals, but colloquially only applied to asses and, for some reason or other, to domestic fowls, though generally without the radical "horse."

16. 切切實實的 emphatically, decisively: *ch'ieh⁴*, to chop up (see Part V, Lesson LV, Note 7); also, a particle expressive of earnestness, emphasis, or sincerity.

CHAPTER V.

1. For all his promises, unfortunately the old man remained unchanged in him, and he went straight to a gambling house that he had been used to frequent. The people at play there were men whose experience of the outside world was limited.¹ They were aware that CHÊNG HÊNG had of late been without means of any kind, and they were quite surprised to see him all of a sudden with such a coat as this. Up comes one of them to him, accordingly, and says he, "What is this made of? [let's have a look;] I'm a near-sighted [2] man, you know, and I don't see well." "What does it signify to you?" said [3] CHÊNG HÊNG; "don't be chaffing; [4] I want something to eat; dispose [5] of this for me, some of you, and let us get some meat and drink with the money; what say you?"

1. 沒見過世面. *See* above, Chapter IV, Note 13.
2. 近視眼 *chin-shih⁴-yen*, short-sighted: *shih*, to regard, to behold; 花眼 long sight.
3. 嗊. *See* Part V, Lesson LIV, Note 3.
4. 俏皮話 *ch'iao⁴ p'i hua*: *ch'iao p'i* is, strictly speaking, pretty, winsome, attractive, and is often used in that sense; but when applied to speech it means to chaff, to give a person credit for attractions he does not possess.
5. 出脫, to get rid of, either by pawning or selling.

2. This suited his hearers well;⁶ they were greatly pleased; and in no time the coat had been sold and a lot of things bought and brought in.

3. Some of the party stewed down the meat till it was all in shreds⁷ and smelt fragrantly;⁸ others kneaded⁹ dough as fast as they could; and others baked the scons. And just as all this was being got ready, there were still some who had a fancy for savoury dumplings.¹⁰ It was every man to his liking, without a doubt.

4. Now observe, when CHÊNG HÊNG had no money, these men would all keep out of his way. The moment that he had got meat and wine to give them, their friendly demeanour¹¹ returned, and they ate his meat and drank his wine and made merry¹² with him. True indeed is the proverb: "Friends may be friends only when there is meat and wine going; man and wife will remain man and wife where there is nothing to cook but plain rice." [There is no bond that holds in adversity but the matrimonial.]

5. Now, amongst these gamblers there was one bald-headed fellow,¹³ well known for as crafty a schemer¹⁴ as any man. He was tempted by the sight of the rice that CHÊNG HÊNG had got with him, and taking two or three of the party aside, he entered into consultation with them on the subject.

6. "I learned the ways of a certain craft a long time ago," said he; "I see nothing to prevent my trying my hand to-day, except that what I want to do can't exactly be done by me all alone. You help me to get hold of the thing, and then we can divide it amongst us, share and share alike;¹⁵ what do you say?"

7. The men objected to his proposition; "It will never do to break the law like that," said they; "you must be set on your own destruction." So far from minding what they said, however, the bald man threatened them; "If you won't join me in the business," said he, "well and good; but if I get into trouble¹⁶ and am taken up for it, may I

6. 正中下懷, just suited their ideas or wishes; *lit.*, exactly hit [the wish that was] at the bottom of (or beneath) [each man's] bosom. See Part III, 302.

7. 燉 *tun*⁴, stewed (or boiled) a long time until it was 稀 (*hsi*¹), watery, and 爛 (*lan*⁴), done to a shred.

8. 噴香 *p'ên*⁴ *hsiang*, gave forth a fragrant odour: *p'ên*, to puff out, as from the mouth.

9. 搋麪 *ch'nai*¹, to thump or knead the dough preparatory to making scons, these scons or cakes 餅 (*ping*³) being baked on an iron, 烙 (*lao*⁴).

10. 餑餑 *po*¹-*po*¹, dumplings; also, small cakes of various kinds.

11. 情面, friendly demeanour: *mien*, the face of *ch'ing* (short for 交情), friendship, *tiao kuo lai*, was turned round to him.

12. 開懷暢飲 *k'ai huai*² *ch'ang*⁴ *yin*³; *lit.*, opened their hearts (cast care to the winds) and joyously (*ch'ang*) drank (*yin*). Cf. 暢快, happy, free from care.

13. 禿子 *t'u*¹-*tzŭ*, a bald-headed person: *t'u* is also applied to the point of a Chinese pencil or writing brush which from much use has opened out.

14. 刁鑽 *tiao tsuan*, unscrupulous and scheming to a degree that *pu kuo*, could not be surpassed: *tiao* is an adjective expressive of general depravity.

15. 均攤勻散 *chün*¹ *t'an*¹ *yün*² *san*⁴, share and share alike: *chün* and *yün*, or *chün yün*, mean in even parts; *t'an*, properly, to contribute to, but here merging its sense into that of *san*, to distribute. Cf. 均背拉一算, to strike an average.

16. 犯了事, get into trouble; not to break the law, but to get into trouble in consequence of breaking the law; just so 犯人 is a criminal under arrest, not a law-breaker who has not been caught out.

never die in my bed if I don't drag you in for it too."[17]

8. The men reflected a little. This was no child's play: "When a thief bites," 'thought they, "he bites right into the bone. If we don't do as he wants, we shall only sacrifice ourselves for nothing."[18] And so back they came to CHÊNG HÊNG, and said they, "There's still such a lot of liquor here; what say you to a drinking match to see who has got the hardest head?" CHÊNG HÊNG tried to excuse himself; "I can't carry[19] much," said he, "and I have already had my fill." "Nonsense!" cried the bald man, "force the wine into his mouth,[20] and see whether he will drink or not."

9. CHÊNG HÊNG was by nature as much afraid of bad people as he was ready to bully the gentle, and when he found his companions using strong language,[21] he became afraid that there would be a general row.[22] So he had no alternative but to turn to and drink with them as hard as he could. The drinking went on till the day began to break[23] in the fifth watch, when they had all drank so much that they were staggering and stumbling from side to side; not one could stand on his legs.

10. CHÊNG HÊNG, however, was not so far gone; he was still half sober; and having had his suspicions from the first, when he saw what was now taking place, he pretty nearly guessed the truth. So he watched his opportunity, and when the rest were not minding him, he stole away home with the donkey behind him, reeling and lurching backwards and forwards as he went.

11. It was broad daylight when he got to his house, and at the same moment a man that had been sent by T'IEN ÊRH for the ass presented himself, and led her off home.

12. CHÊNG HÊNG went in, and having put down his rice and bolted the door, he sat down to rest a while on the stove-bed; presently he stretched himself upon it and fell fast asleep. While he was unconscious of every mortal thing, the bald man, coming stealthily to his door, wrenched it open[24] with a poker, and carried off his rice.

13. It was well past noon when he woke, and the very first thing he did was to look for the rice; but not a grain of rice was there there, and the door, he observed, had been forced as well. "What?" cried he, as he turned himself over and got off the stove-bed, "Robbery in broad day! Ah! it's like my

17. 把你們攀出來: *p'an¹*, drag you in for it; *lit.*, drag you out. See Part V, Lesson XIII, Note 10.

18. 白饒 *pai jao²*, for nothing; *jao* is here used in the sense of to throw something extra into a bargain; 把這個饒給我, throw this in as well: *pai jao* is to throw in something for nothing, to give absolutely away.

19. 量 *liang⁴*. See Part III, 776, Obs. (p. 149).

20. 灌 *kuan⁴*, here, to pour forcibly down the throat, to compel to drink: *kuan yao⁴*, to administer medicine.

21. 出言不遜 *hsün⁴*, using strong language; *hsün*, properly, docile, modest, humble; the humility of demeanour which courtesy requires.

22. 大家夥兒跟他鬧糟糕: *tsao¹ kao¹*, there would be a general row: *ta chia huo-'rh*, the whole of the parties associated would with him *nao*, get angry to the making of a *tsao kao*; the first word is used of anything so rotten or saturated as to have lost its consistency (see Part V, Lesson XLVII, Note 12); the second signifies a cake of a certain kind. Cf. *tsao kao*, here's a mess; used of any disastrous combination of circumstances.

23. 濛濛亮兒的時候兒: *mêng¹ mêng¹ liang⁴-'rh*, the break of day; *mêng*, properly, misty or foggy.

24. 撬 *ch'iao⁴*, to prize, to burst open: poker, *t'ung-t'iao*; *lit.*, penetrating rod.

luck; the worse I am off, the worse my misfortunes be."[25] And so he went on, crying and howling ever so long, making a great noise, and to no purpose either.

14. The explanation of all this is that CHÊNG HÊNG came primarily of a bad stock.[26] His father, who had held a provincial appointment, confined his attention to taking bribes.[27] He had no feeling for the troubles of the people; the aged and lonely, widows, orphans, or childless parents,[28] all alike, he would have something out of them;[29] whenever a chance presented itself he would turn the public interest to his own account;[30] then he had no capacity except for bad ends, and being at last denounced to the Emperor,[31] His Majesty launched a most dreadful decree[32] at him, directing him to shut himself up and meditate upon his wrong-doing. He had a stroke of paralysis[33] in his house some time after, and this not yielding to treatment, he died of it.

15. CHÊNG HÊNG, his favourite[34] son, had been allowed to run riot[35] in his childhood, and the family, as we have just shown, being thus unsound at the root, it was not possible, was it, that he, CHÊNG HÊNG, should be any good himself? So true is it that no cloth can be drawn out of the indigo vat[36] unstained. In the ruin that had at this time befallen his whole family[37] is seen the perfect unerringness of Heaven's justice.[38]

25. 遭殃 tsao¹ yang¹, to meet with misfortune or mishap. Cf. 越渴越吃鹽.

26. 根基 kên¹-chi², stock: chi, a foundation, a basis.

27. 受賄賂 shou hui⁴ lu⁴, to take bribes; the first sometimes used without the second; 行賄, to offer or give bribes.

28. 鰥寡孤獨 kuan¹ kua³ ku¹ tu² : kuan, an aged widower; kua, lone, alone; here, a widow (commonly called 寡婦); ku, properly, fatherless, but here used of one without either parent; tu, properly, single, but used of men in years who have no son.

29. 勒掯 lo² k'ên³, to levy black mail, to extort money from; k'ên also means to detain by force.

30. 假公濟私 chia³ kung¹ chi⁴ ssŭ¹, turned the public interest to his own account; chia is here used in its secondary sense of to borrow: he borrowed the public [opportunities his position afforded him], chi, to further, ssŭ, his private interests.

31. 參 ts'an¹, also read ts'ên (see Part III, 493 and 576), to impeach or denounce to the Emperor.

32. 雷霆 lei² t'ing², both meaning thunder, are applied to the anger of the Emperor.

33. 癱瘓 t'an¹-huan⁴, paralytic, paralysis: t'an, paralysis; huan, a word of the same meaning never separated from t'an.

34. 疼 t'êng², short for t'êng ai (see Part III, 453).

35. 縱他撒野 tsung⁴ t'a sa¹ yeh³, allowed him to run riot: tsung, to loosen, to let go; hence, to allow; sa, to scatter; hence, to be unrestrained, to let go (cf. sa shou³, let go); yeh, in a wild manner.

36. 靛缸 tien⁴ kang¹, an indigo vat: kang, an earthenware jar or vessel.

37. 全家敗盡 ch'üan chia pai⁴ chin, his whole family utterly ruined : pai, damaged or destroyed, also defeated (see Part V, Lesson VIII, Note 14).

38. 天理昭彰: chao¹ chang¹, the manifestation, t'ien li, of Heaven's justice, ssŭ hao², in the minutest degree (see Part V, Lesson XXXIX, Note 8), pu shuang, is not incorrect; chao¹, bright light; chang, manifestation of light; shuang³, to be wrong (see Part III, 823).

CHAPTER VI.

1. And now [leaving CHÊNG HÊNG for a while] let us confine[1] our attention to YING YING and her maid HUNG NIANG (Miss ROSE), who, although nominally the servant of her mistress,[2] was in their private relations quite like a sister.[3] She was, to say the truth, nice-looking, a very handy[4] servant, and ready of speech.

2. "I don't know what can be the matter with me," says YING YING to her one day in the work-room;[5] "for the last few days, I don't know why, I've had a bad headache, and it has made me feel so low that I have hardly been able to bear it."

3. "Mayn't it be that you have something on your mind, miss?" answered HUNG NIANG. "If I might give a guess, whether it's right or not, I should say that that CHÊNG HÊNG was the cause of it, eh? Well, when I think that he is no longer a youth, and yet there he is, not only with half his life spent in doing nothing, but getting himself ill spoken of by everybody, I can't help detesting him. We were nicely taken in indeed when we were told he was so good. My idea is that it is the thought of him that keeps you from taking pleasure in anything you are about." "There, there," said YING YING with a sigh; "don't begin talking nonsense the first thing in the morning." "Very good, miss," said HUNG NIANG; "if you'll please tell me what you think it best you should do, I'll wait upon you." "Those trees you planted in the garden one day," said YING YING, "are budding[6] by this time, I daresay; what do you say to going with me to see?"

---

1. 單 tan^1, only. See Part III, 308.
2. 主僕 $chu\ p'u^2$, master and servant.
3. 弟足 can be used of the relationship of brothers as well as sisters.
4. 麻利 $ma^2\text{-}li$, sprightly, handy; 麻 probably corruptly used for 馬.
5. 繡房 $hsiu^4\ fang$, a boudoir or lady's work-room: $hsiu$, to embroider.
6. 芽 ya^2, buds; not sprouts, which are $miao^2$ (see Part III, 691). The bud of a flower is 骨朵兒.

CHAPTER VII.

1. While we leave them to take their walk, let us speak of a certain graduate at this time in Hsi-lo;[1] his name was CHANG KUNG,[2] and his style[3] was CHÜN JUI (the Jewel of his Sovereign).

2. His father likewise had held high office, but had retired, and, returning to his home, had died[4] long since. Our graduate, though small of stature, had a distinguished countenance; he was modest in manner and of a courteous and kindly disposition;[5] at the same time he possessed so much of accomplishment, whether as a man of letters or in the way of manly exercises, that everyone, in fact, put faith in[6] him. And now, most opportunely, while he was wishing to test the ability within him, the year of the metropolitan examinations[7] came round, and he determined to go up to the capital in time for them, taking with him a single servant called CH'IN T'UNG[8] (the lad CH'IN).

3. The day before they were to start the graduate said to CH'IN T'UNG, "We shall be off to-morrow the moment it is light; have you got everything ready[9] that you ought to have?"

4. "I have everything ready, sir," answered CH'IN T'UNG; and next morning, very early, master and man set out on their journey. They had been travelling some days when they came to a place at no great distance from which the graduate CHANG remembered that a man named TU[10] was living; the two had been friends in adversity,[11] and suited each other so perfectly[12] that they were just like brothers.

1. 洛 *lo*[4].
2. 珙 *kung*[1] [3], a jewel; not used colloquially.
3. 號 *hao*[4], a person's "style," or the name by which he is known to his friends. *See* Part III, 858.
4. 謝世 *hsieh*[4] *shih*[4], to die; *lit.*, withdraw from life. Note that *hsieh* is here used in its primary sense of to decline, to withdraw from. Cf. also 謝罪, to apologise.
5. 和靄 *ho ai*[3]; *lit.*, friendly and pleasing; in combination, courteous, friendly.
6. 佩服 *p'ei*[4] *fu*[2], to have regard or respect for, to have confidence in: *p'ei*, to carry on the person, as clothes; *fu p'ei*, to wear ornaments. The expression *p'ei fu* is derived from an ancient poem, in which the poet says that he will write the words of a certain philosopher upon his girdle and wear them constantly about him: 願言書諸紳可以爲佩服 (*see also* LEGGE's Classics, Vol. I, p. 160, 4).
7. 大比之年, *lit.*, the year of the great comparison; the metropolitan examination for the degree of *chin-shih* (the highest literary grade), which is held once in every three years. 來京趕考: note *lai*, indicating that the author of the story is in the capital; were he not, *lai* would be incorrect.
8. 琴童 *ch'in*[2] *t'ung*[2]: *ch'in*, the Chinese lute or harpsichord; *t'ung*, a lad under 15 years of age.
9. 齊截 *ch'i*[2] *chieh*[2], all ready; *yü pei ti*, prepared, *ch'i chieh*, to a state of completeness: *chieh*, to cut off; hence, bring to an end.
10. 杜 *tu*[4], properly, a species of crab apple, commonly called 杜黎兒; also, to shut out, as 杜門謝客, to deny oneself to visitors.
11. 患 *huan*[4], misfortune, calamity.
12. 情投意合, suited each other perfectly: their *ch'ing*, feelings, *t'ou*[2], accorded, and their *i*, opinions, *ho*, were in harmony. *T'ou* has various other meanings.

5. This man, who was now in the army, was quartered with a force under his command at the P'u Kuan, in charge [13] of that barrier. His extraordinary proficiency in martial exercises and his skill in the movement of troops [14] were such that he was known as the Pai Ma Chiang-chün.[15]

6. As the graduate called his friend to mind, it occurred to him that he could not do better than try and make time to pay him a passing visit before he went on to the capital; it would not interfere at all with the business he had in hand. So making a slight *détour* he arrived at the P'u Kuan, and alighted at an inn that he found in the suburb [of the town]. He was so fatigued [16] by his journey that before going out for a stroll [17] he proposed to rest for a little.

7. Accordingly, he did rest awhile, and then he asked one of the people of the inn if there was any place worth going to in the neighbourhood. "There's the P'u-chiu Ssŭ not far from this," said the man; "that's a very pleasant place."

8. "Ah!" said the graduate; "well, get me something to eat first, for I am exceedingly hungry."

9. The man immediately went out and bought a pickled chicken,[18] and when he had brought it in he set on with it two bowls of vermicelli prepared with sauce.

10. The graduate ate this, and after telling the people of the inn to feed his horse and to take good care of his odds and ends, he left the inn with CH'IN T'UNG behind him.

---

13. 守 *shou*³, to have in custody, to hold on guard; can be used alone, or, as here, with *fang*, for which, see Part V, Lesson XVI, Note 1.

14. 調度 *tiao*⁴ *tu*⁴; *lit.*, movement plans or arrangements; *tiao* referring here specially to the movement of troops (*tiao ping*); it has other meanings, and is sometimes read *t'iao*².

15. 將軍 *chiang*¹-*chün*¹, a general; properly, a Manchu General-in-chief, or, as he is commonly called, Tartar General; it is also the title given to certain military governors stationed beyond the Great Wall: *chün* in its original sense is a division or army corps; it is also a general term for "military," as 軍務, military affairs; 軍器, munitions of war.

16. 勞碌 *lao*² *lu*⁴, fatigued: *lao*², labour, trouble; *lu*, properly, the unevenness of stony ground. *Lao lu* may also be used of hard physical work.

17. 遊逛 *yu*² *kuang*⁴, to stroll: *yu*, to roam or saunter about; in Peking, more commonly 溜打 (*liu*¹ *ta*¹).

18. 滷牲口 *lu*³ *shêng*¹-*k'ou*³, a salted chicken: *lu*, brine, pickle; a chicken, which is generally called *hsiao chi-tzŭ* (or *êrh*), is not unfrequently spoken of as *shêng-k'ou*, an animal, to avoid the risk of making the mistake of giving the word *chi* an equivocal meaning by the addition of a common affix which is likely to slip out involuntarily.

CHAPTER VIII.

1. There was a temple gathering that day in the P'u Kuan, and there was such a constant flow of people that walking along the road was no easy matter.

2. "Out of the way, you," shouted CH'IN T'UNG; "don't block up[1] the road so." The crowd thereupon opened a passage for them, and the two, master and man, passed through, and made straight for the P'u-chiu Ssŭ. Before they got much farther the temple in question became visible in the distance; a lofty, imposing[2] edifice it was.

3. They went in, and had been wandering about here and there some time [without meeting anyone] when a young bonze made his appearance; he was called FA TS'UNG, and the graduate and he having communicated to each other their respective names, FA TS'UNG invited the stranger to come in and have some tea.

4. The tea was served by a young shabi,[3] when FA TS'UNG exclaimed, "This tea is too[4] pale in colour; it's just like so much hot water: quick, and make a fresh cup for us."

5. The young shabi changed the tea for some better immediately, and when they had drunk it they strolled all about the place until the graduate suddenly observed, inside the half-open door of a flower garden that lay to the west of the temple, a young lady who, with her servant behind her, was strolling about like himself.

6. The young lady's complexion was white as snow, and her lips were rosy red; her deep black hair was gathered behind[5] into a yüan-puo, and in the hair on the top of her head were[6] fresh, sweet-smelling roses;[7] she wore ear-rings of green jade in her ears; on her wrists,[8] a pair of bracelets[10] of deep[9] yellow gold; and her dress was a long robe of pale blue.[11] All this matched besides by a quantity of pearls and jewels and ornaments of jade, set[12] in gold; a unique and perfect toilet indeed it was.

7. At the sight of her the graduate CHANG was so taken by surprise that even physically he was no longer master of himself. And as for the young lady, when, as she looked through the door, she observed our

1. 攔 tang[3], to impede, to obstruct.
2. 威武 wei[1]-wu[3], imposing: wei, majestic, awe-inspiring; with wu, properly, martial grandeur, but it is generally applied to objects; 威嚴, personal dignity or majesty.
3. 沙彌 shami or shabi, a Buddhist novice; a reproduction of a Sanskrit word.
4. 忒 t'ê[4], here an adverb, equivalent to too, very.
5. 鑽 tsuan[3], a chignon, a top-knot.
6. 插 ch'a[1], to thrust or stick, as a sword into its sheath, flowers into the hair, etc.
7. 玫瑰 mei[2] kuei[1] [4], a species of rose, red and very fragrant; common monthly roses are called 月季花.
8. 手腕子 shou wan[4]-tzŭ, the wrist; 脚腕子, vulgarly 脚脖子, the ankle.
9. 焦 chiao[1], to scorch or burn with fire; in cooking, to scorch or burn the meat, etc., is 煳 (hu[2]).
10. 鐲子 cho[2], a bracelet.
11. 翠藍 ts'ui[4] lan[2], kingfisher blue: ts'ui can also be applied to green; 翠雀兒, the kingfisher.
12. 鑲 hsiang[1], to inlay, to frame, to put an edging round, to set.

graduate, with his lips so red and his teeth so white, his distinguished [13] air, his whole appearance that of no common [14] person, she experienced quite the same sort of feeling towards him. "Can you tell me who that young lady is?" asked the graduate of FA TS'UNG.

8. 'They are official [15] people," answered FA TS'UNG; "the family [16] of His Excellency TS'UI. When he died, Madame TS'UI came with the young lady to take up her quarters temporarily [17] in this neighbourhood. They are in very comfortable circumstances; really without a care in life." [18]

9. "Well, I've been all round [19] the empire," thought the graduate CHANG to himself, "and I have seen no small number of women, but never the superior of this one. What a pity it is that there should be any difficulty in my way: if I stay here some days longer, I shall inevitably miss the examinations; [20] and if I go up for the examinations, I may lose my opportunity here;

it really puts me in a sore dilemma." And so he kept on irresolute, with no decision taken, until he came round to the opinion that with so fair a young lady [to woo] it would be better [21] for him [to stay where he was] than to go up to the examinations.

10. This conclusion arrived at, he interrogated FA TS'UNG: "Can I have accommodation here," asked he; "I want to come and live in the temple too."

11. "The superior is not at home," said FA TS'UNG, "and I can't take upon me to speak; come to-morrow a little earlier, if you please, sir, [22] and you can talk the matter over with him."

12. The graduate CHANG had nothing for it but to return to his inn for the time being; he was too much out of spirits [23] to try his hand at anything; he didn't care for his tea, and as little about anything to eat; his thoughts were all about Miss TS'UI, and he got no sleep all night.

13. 不凡 *pu fan*², uncommon: *fan* here in the sense of common, vulgar. *See* Part III, 563.

14. 尋常 ordinary, common: *hsün* is an ancient measure of 8 *ch'ih* in length; a *ch'ang* was 2 *hsün*; there is nothing to show how it came to be used in the sense of common or ordinary.

15. 官宦 *kuan huan*⁴, official; the word *huan* is a somewhat classical equivalent of *kuan*.

16. 家眷 *chia chüan*⁴, the members of a family; the women and children, but generally, the women only; also, a wife: *chüan*, to regard, to care for, to love; hence, one's wife and children. 寶眷, your wife (politely).

17. 寄居 *chi*⁴ *chü*¹, to take up temporary quarters, to lodge: *chi*, to lodge; also, to deposit temporarily; cf. 寄放, to leave on deposit; *chi* also means to send, as a letter.

18. 逍遙快樂 *hsiao*¹ *yao*² *k'uai lo*, without a care, in easy circumstances; the native dictionaries explain that 逍遙 are identical with 消搖, which the dictionary of K'ANG HSI explains as follows: *hsiao*, to melt, as ice, which leaves the substance behind; *yao*, to shake, to vibrate, as a ship in motion without injury to its contents. Hence the two characters are synonymous of bodily comfort, of a condition of body that does not feel the waste of vital energy consequent upon a struggle for existence; *k'uai lo* applies more particularly to mental comfort.

19. 走偏了 *tsou pien*⁴ *liao*, have been right round, or everywhere: *pien*, everywhere, entire, to make a complete circuit. 找偏了, I've looked everywhere.

20. 期 *ch'i*² ⁴, a set time or period; hence, times or seasons.

21. 甯可不 better to. *See* Part III, 625.

22. 施主 *shih*⁴ *chu*³, a patron, a benefactor: *shih*¹, amongst other meanings, to dispense, to bestow, as charity. The common term by which priests address their visitors. Note the tone of *shih*.

23. 無精打彩的, dejected, out of spirits: *wu ching* (*see* Part IV, Dialogue IV, Note 56), without spirits, and luck (*ts'ai*, see Part III, 259) driven away, *ta*.

CHAPTER IX.

1. The following morning, getting up the moment it was day, the graduate CHANG went off to the temple and had an interview with the old bonze, whose name was FA PÊN.

2. After each had informed himself of the other's name, the graduate stated that he wanted to take[1] some rooms; on which, before going farther, FA PÊN inquired where his honoured visitor's mansion might be.

3. "I belong to another part of the country," said the graduate; "I am here about some business; but I find staying at the inn inconvenient, and the living there is very expensive, so I was thinking of shifting elsewhere. When I beheld this temple[2] of yours, and seeing what a fine place it was, I proposed to move into it; if I do, I should prefer being near the family on the west side there."

4. The fact is that the graduate CHANG was an ingenuous[3] man; it had always been his way to speak without reserve; what there was in his mind, therefore, he had said in so many words.

5. "Well, it does happen that there is just what will suit you," said FA PÊN; "there is a building in two divisions over there in the west wing; but then, what with the grime of the smoke and the heat of the fire,[4] the kitchen is in such a condition that I was thinking of doing it up myself; but I have not set about it yet." "It would be quite the right thing to make a collection for temple repairs,"[5] said the graduate CHANG; "who may the proprietor be?"

6. "The temple is the temple of the TS'UI family," said FA PÊN; "the buildings they occupy are on the other side of the wall. You see where the ground rises over there; beyond the wall of the court is their residence. They are not without means, but whether they would choose to find such a sum as this, I don't know."

7. The graduate CHANG thought to himself, "After all, it will only be risking[6] a little more money on the venture." "And so," said he, "you undertake the repairs; I'll be responsible if the funds run short, and come to your aid; what say you?"

8. FA PÊN thanked him; "Nothing could be better, sir," said he; "your charitable intentions lay me under great obligation to you."

---

1. 租 *tsu*[1], to hire or rent from; 租給, to rent to; 租子, rents on land; 房租, the rent of a house.

2. 刹 *ch'a*[4], a Buddhist temple; *pao*, as in Chapter VIII, Note 16.

3. 樸 *p'u*[2] *shih*., ingenuous, straightforward: *p'u*, lit., an unfinished (unpolished) vessel of wood.

4. 烟熏火燎 *yên*[1] *hsün*[1] *huo liao*[3], grimed with smoke and scorched by fire: *hsün*, sooty, stained by smoke; *liao*[4], properly, to burn; here, stained by scorching.

5. 募化重修 *mu*[4] *hua*[4] *ch'ung*[2] *hsiu*[1], to beg subscriptions for the repair [of Buddhist temples]: *mu*, to hire, to enrol; *hua*, to change, sc., men's hearts; to evoke their sympathies [and obtain money for] *ch'ung*, afresh, *hsiu*, repairing.

6. 劉著 *huo*[1]-*cho*, colloquially, to run a risk, as 劉著挨淋, I'll risk a wetting; 劉著碰釘子, I'll run the risk of a rebuff: *huo* is, literally, to rip up or open.

9. The graduate CHANG at once [7] begged him to send someone with him forthwith for the money, who could at the same time get a carpenter to make some things that might be ready [8] when he wanted them; and then he asked FA PÊN how many days it would take to complete the repairs. FA PÊN said that it would probably be quite done inside of ten days. This said, the two men took leave of each other, and FA PÊN went to look for workmen.

7. 登時 *têng¹ shih*, at once: *têng*, *lit.*, to mount, to ascend, is here identical with 當, q.v.

8. 應用 *ying⁴ yung*, ready for use. Note the tone.

CHAPTER X.

1. The lad CH'IN was by his master's side, and when he heard him talking in this fashion, "This habit of taking no thought for the morrow," said he to himself, "won't do at all;" and without farther ceremony, he said, "Sir, the money you have with you is not much; if you spend it all here, how will you manage when you get to the capital?"

2. "Is it any business of yours?" said the graduate in a rage; "what does it matter to you if I choose of my own goodwill to do the old superior a turn?"

3. The lad CH'IN did not speak, but he thought, "There's a proverb in two lines, 'Say what you know will be agreeable; plain speaking [1] provokes people:' let him go his own way; I don't see how I'm to make any hand of it."

4. A few days later and back came the graduate to the temple to ask FA PÊN if the rooms were ready yet. "The rooms," said FA PÊN, "will soon be done, but, unfortunately, the carpenter who was to have made the furniture, in his stupidity, has not turned out the things as they should be, and I have just desired him to make them all over again."

5. The prospect of this delay of several days made the graduate feel impatient, and he went off himself to look for the carpenter.

6. "No time must be lost about those tables and chairs," he told him; "you must do just as I desire you; you had best be careful if you want to please."

7. "How many articles do you want altogether, sir?" said the carpenter.

8. "Didn't I tell you long ago," said the graduate, "that I wanted two tables and five chairs, and don't two added to five [2] make seven?" And then turning to CH'IN T'UNG, he desired him to keep the people to their work, so that not a moment should be lost.

9. "How many days are they to do the work in?" asked the lad CH'IN.

10. "The things are not so very many," said the graduate CHANG; "they could all be finished in four or five days, I am sure."

1. 耿直 *kêng³-chih²*, outspokenness, generally in a good sense: *kêng* is here used in the sense of 介 (*vide* native dictionaries), which means alone, a single person; hence, one who stands firm to his principles; *chih*, straight.

2. 哇 *a¹*, properly *wa¹*, to vomit, is here a corruption of the numerative *ko*; it often follows the numerals 4, 5, 6, and 7.

11. The repairs of the buildings had been completed some time, and in less than five days the tables and chairs were quite ready.

12. The graduate having inspected them all, declared that they were not so bad: "The legs of the tables," said he, "are well turned,[3] and the chairs are solid; there is no fault to be found this time." And then he told the people of the temple where the things were to be put; this was to stand in this place, and in this other place that other thing was to stand; and they were to hang four scrolls[4] on the wall, and to be careful not to tear them. Then, as soon as all these preparations were ended, he told the lad CHʻIN to go over at once for the baggage, which he brought and duly distributed.

3. 鏇 *hsüan*[4], to turn in a lathe.

4. 幅 *fu*[2], a roll; a rather long and narrow slip of paper with either writing or a design upon it.

CHAPTER XI.

1. They had been installed, master and man, some days, when the graduate saw a young girl come out, followed by a little boy; she asked FA PÊN if any day had been fixed for the reading of a service for the late TSʻUI *ta-jên*. FA PÊN said yes, a day had been fixed; the fifteenth of that moon.

2. The graduate observed that the young girl was very nice-looking;[1] [and she was nicely dressed;] her hair ornaments[2] were silver gilt, and her coiffure was very trimly arranged. He nudged (*lit.*, pulled) FA PÊN, and asked him in a low voice, "What place does this person hold in Madame TSʻUI's house?"

3. "She is Miss TSʻUI's maid," said FA PÊN, "and her name is HUNG NIANG. Miss YING YING's own wit and beauty are such that HUNG NIANG from attending on her has insensibly taken the same colour.[3] Notwithstanding *(tao)* their difference in degree, they are just like twin sisters, and the young lady, finding that the maid has a clever tongue of her own, that she is equally ready whether in

1. 俊 *chün*[4], nice-looking, superior in mental and bodily qualifications; applicable only to young persons of either sex; classically, the cleverest man in a thousand.

2. 首飾 *shou*[3] *shih*[1], head ornaments: *shih*, to adorn, to embellish; *shou shih* can be used of a woman's ornaments in general. 鍍 *tu*[4], to gild.

3. 近硃者赤近墨者黑, one takes the colour of one's company: near vermilion (*chu*[1]) one is red, near ink one is black.

speech or action, and a girl of modest⁴ demeanour withal, trusts her with everything; she is her mistress's right hand.

4. The graduate, when he had heard all this,⁵ turned his head round and said out loud to FA PÊN, "I myself have been desiring to have a service read for my father ever since he died, and I shall be much obliged to you, sir, as superior of this establishment, if you will bring me in⁶ as well; will it be possible?"

5. Before FA PÊN could reply, HUNG NIANG, who was a kind-hearted body, and saw that the graduate was a well-mannered man, observed gently, "This gentleman⁷ can have a service read for him on the fifteenth at the same time as ourselves if he wants to; why should he not?"

6. The graduate was well pleased at this, and his countenance so beamed with smiles that the girl asked FA PÊN, "What is it that makes the gentleman smile so?"

7. Now FA PÊN was too experienced a veteran⁸ ever to be kept in the dark, and he pretty soon saw through the whole business. "Well, it doesn't mean anything," said he, "except that the gentleman is extremely delighted to learn that he can have his service performed on the fifteenth too." HUNG NIANG stepped into the waiting-room when she heard this, and sat down for a while, and while she was sitting there she whispered to one of the bonzes, "What is the name of the gentleman outside?" The bonze told her all about him, and as she came out again the graduate took occasion⁹ to ask her, "Whose business are you in charge of, miss?" "In the charge of the old lady's business," said HUNG NIANG, and as she spoke she turned away and went home.

4. 恬惔 *mien³ tien³*, coy, bashful, modest; both words mean embarrassed in manner.

5. 一番話 *fan¹*, a turn: *i fan*, once; here the numerative of *hua*.

6. 捎帶 *shao¹ tai⁴*, let me come in, bring me in, let me join you: *shao*, to take along with one, to carry; to send, as a message by a convenient opportunity.

7. 相公. *See* Chapter XII, Note 2.

8. 老江湖, short for 老走江湖的, an old traveller; hence, an experienced person.

9. 趁勢 *ch'ên⁴ shih⁴*, seized the occasion, took advantage of the circumstance.

CHAPTER XII.

1. From this day forward the graduate used to walk in the court every day, but though he met Hung Niang several times, he could never muster up courage enough to speak to her.

2. At last one day he could stand it no longer, and out he came with it, *coûte que coûte*, "I have a service to ask of you, miss," said he; "if you can perform it I shall feel unboundedly grateful, and should you ever have any trouble in the time to come, miss, I shall of course use all the wit I have to help you. As you know, miss, it is only necessary for two people to join heart and hand, and there is nothing, is there, that they cannot accomplish? Still, your old lady does keep such a very tight hand over the family that in trying to bring about the arrangement[1] I am committing to your hands, I want you to put yourself entirely on my side, and never to go against me."

3. "You are getting rather free with your remarks, aren't you," thought Hung Niang, as she listened; and then she went on, out loud, "Have you lost your senses, sir,[2] that you forget yourself so? have you no idea of what is right and wrong? fancy, when you were running on with nothing but wild, nonsensical talk, if any busybody by had heard you and told the old lady, where would it all have ended?"

4. "Dear me!" said the graduate Chang, "I am such a bungler,[3] I never can speak as I ought; pray bear with me a little, and I'll be more careful[4] in future." "Well, that's as it should be," said Hung Niang, and taking her leave of him, she went home.

5. As soon as she got home she said to Ying Ying, "You remember the graduate you saw the other day, miss, don't you? well, his name turns out[5] to be Chang, and I have just met him again." And then she

---

1. 周旋 *chou¹-hsüan²*: *chou*, to make a circuit, to environ; *see* Chapter III, Note 19, with which character it is identical; *hsuan*, to revolve, to come back to the same point; the two in combination mean to get round an object or enclosure, with a view of stopping a place of entry or attack. *Chou-hsüan* also means to pay attention to, as a host to a guest.

2. 懞憧 *mêng²-tung³*, to lose one's senses, to be oblivious to the proprieties: *mêng*, oblivious, stupid; *tung* has much the same sense; to "understand" appears to be a secondary meaning of *tung*, which is not recognised in native dictionaries. 相公 (*hsiang⁴*) was originally the title applied to Secretaries of State, but it is now used indiscriminately to denote "young gentlemen;" parents speak of their sons to the servants as *ta hsiang-kung, êrh hsiang-kung*, master one or two; *see also* Part V, Lesson XIX, Note 9.

3. 拙嘴笨顋 *cho² tsui³ pên⁴ sai¹*, a bungler, one with awkward lips and clumsy cheeks; used, not of the lips or cheeks, but figuratively of a man's lack of power to express himself: *cho pên* (also read *chuo²*) is awkward, clumsy in large things and small.

4. 謹愼 *chin³-shên⁴*, careful, attention: *chin*, properly of solemn attentiveness, as at worship; *shên*, also attentive.

5. 敢情 *kan³-ch'ing*: it is extremely difficult to find an exact equivalent for this phrase in English; it is generally expressive of surprise at the realisation of some fact in a manner different to expectation, though, as in the present instance, it does not seem to have a stronger force than our expression "turns out." Cf. the following: 我原想是某人，敢情是你呀, I thought it was So-and-So, but it turns out to be you instead.

went on and reproduced the whole of her conversation⁶ with him, word for word.

6. After a moment's thought, YING YING divined what was passing in the graduate's mind, and, to say the truth, she felt equally alarmed and gratified; "You needn't tell the old lady," she hastened to remark.

7. "That, of course," said HUNG NIANG; "it's one's business to speak of what ought to be spoken of; I know that very well."

6. 學說 *hsiao² shuo* implies a reproduction of the manner and gestures of the people speaking. *N.B.*—To mimic is 學舌.

CHAPTER XIII.

1. Meanwhile the graduate remained standing in the court, all alone, turning the thing over and over in his mind. "It was the headlong way I went at it,"¹ said he to himself; "no wonder the girl was so hard on me." The reflection became quite intolerable, and he sat there on a stone in a sad way² until it was nearly dark,³ when the lad CH'IN came over from the servants' quarter, and seeing how melancholy his master looked, he gave a start; "Oh, sir," said he, "don't you think you may get a chill sitting there on that very cold⁴ stone? And, dear me, there's a number of scorpions⁵ here too; if you don't mind you'll get stung."

2. "Yes; but its cooler sitting here in a shady place," said the graduate, with an air of annoyance; "what are you come about?" "I came to tell you that dinner was ready, sir," said the lad CH'IN.

3. "I can't swallow⁶ a mouthful," said the graduate; "you can go and get your own dinner." And he sat on without stirring⁷ till just at midnight, while the moon was shining as bright as if it was daylight, he heard, all of a sudden, female voices on the other side of the wall.

4. Moving on tiptoe⁸ to the wall, he climbed up⁹ it, and peeping over he saw that it was YING YING herself burning incense under the trees.

5. The cover was thick, still her face was to a certain extent visible, and to the eyes of the graduate it seemed more attractive than

1. 莽撞 *mang³ chuang⁴*, headlong, impulsive, abrupt: *mang*, properly, tangled, like brushwood, etc.; *chuang*, to run up against.

2. 納悶 *na⁴ mên⁴*, to be absorbed or involved in melancholy: *na*, to take in, to receive, has many meanings, the most common of which is to pay, as taxes or fees; *na mên* also means to be puzzled.

3. 傍晚 *pang⁴ wan*, nearly dark: *pang*, near.

4. 冰涼 *ping¹ liang*, icy cold: *ping*, ice.

5. 蠍子 *hsieh¹*, a scorpion. 螫 *chê¹*, to sting, of bees, wasps, scorpions; not of centipedes, serpents, etc., which bite.

6. 嚥 *yên⁴*, to swallow, to gulp down.

7. 沒動窩兒, never budged; *lit.*, did not move his *wo¹*, lair, form, or nest.

8. 躡手躡脚, to go on tiptoe, to walk stealthily: *nieh⁴*, to tread.

9. 爬 *p'a²*, to crawl, to creep, to climb; *pa¹*, as will be seen below, in 爬著牆, to *hang on* to the wall, by the elbows or hands; also, under certain circumstances, to get at, to get hold of (*see* Chapter XXXIV, paragraph 7).

at first; he could not help feeling more in love with her than ever.

6. When she had done burning her incense, HUNG NIANG pointed to the shrubs, observing that such a one had ripe fruit upon it, and that on such another the fruit was just forming; "It is such a pity," said she, "that the roots are all eaten into by the ants."[10]

7. As she rattled on in this strain, the graduate could hear every word, and he was just saying to himself that it would be best to have some of these shrubs plucked up, so that there might be less hindrance to the view, when the lad CH'IN happening to come out, and seeing his master with his arms on the wall and his feet unsupported, cried out, "Take care not to let go with your hands, sir; it would be no joke if you were to fall."

8. "What should you be making such a noise for?" said the graduate to him sharply; "do you want to give the alarm to everyone?"

10. 螞蟻 ma^3 i^3, an ant; 蛀 chu^4, to eat into, specially of the action of any insect on wood, paper, etc. The word ma is also applied to wasps or bees (see Chapter XIX, Note 3).

CHAPTER XIV.

1. In a short time YING YING went home, and the graduate returning to his chamber, the lad CH'IN put supper on the table. But the graduate's equilibrium was too disturbed[1] for anything to seem to be as it ought to be, and as he leaned against the side of the table he did nothing but try to put his people in the wrong.[2]

2. "The cook is a very dirty cook," he said; "the rice is full of grit; it hasn't been properly washed;[3] why wasn't it passed through the sieve?[4] And the wine is cold; why haven't you warmed it?" Then, when he had taken a mouthful of it, "And it's quite bitter too; pour it back into the flask directly."

3. The lad CH'IN obeyed, and put on the soup, but the first taste of this dissatisfied the graduate more than ever. "The dust has got into the soup," he cried; "skim[5] it

1. 七上八下的, his equilibrium was disturbed. The expression is a quotation from a common proverb indicative of mental disturbance or indecision: 十五個柳罐打水,七個上來,八個下去; liu^3 $kuan^4$, a well bucket or basket made of withes.

2. 找尋他們, found fault, tried to put them in the wrong, looked for [their faults].

3. 淘 $t'ao^2$, here, to wash or scour rice.

4. 篩子 $shai^1$, a sieve: kuo $shai$-$tzŭ$, to pass through a sieve; $shai$ i $shai$, to sift.

5. 撇 $p'ieh^1$, to skim off.

directly, and turn out the bottom of it as well."

4. "I've just bought a pomegranate,"[6] said the lad CH'IN, "but I am not sure whether it is in proper order;[7] will you try it, sir?"

5. It was brought in, but the graduate, having peeled[8] it, as soon as he put a piece of it in his mouth, exclaimed, "This is very bad; sour and rough."[9]

6. The lad CH'IN, finding that things gave as little satisfaction one way as another, was at his wit's end. Then, remembering that the cook had bought some soft beancurd,[10] he said to his master, "There's some soft beancurd; will you have any?" "Tell the cook to fry me a little of it," said the graduate, "and to boil the rest."

7. This was done, and the beancurd was brought in; but when the graduate had done eating it, he recommenced his animadversions[11] on the cooking: every dish had been so dreadfully salt[12] that day; nothing had been as well flavoured as it usually was. The lad CH'IN was to tell the cook that he positively must be more careful.

8. The lad CH'IN signified his obedience, and having cleared the dinner table,[13] brought in tea. The tea was so scalding hot that there was no putting it to one's lips, and while the graduate was waiting for it to cool, he kept on stretching out one leg or drawing up[14] the other, just out of[15] temper with everything. CH'IN was out of temper too, but he had to be patient and hold his peace; his hope was that his master would get over the worst of his temper, and then all would be well.

6. 石榴 $shih^2$-liu, the pomegranate.

7. 甜 $t'ien^2$, sweet, pleasant to the taste.

8. 剝 pao^1, to flay, to peel, to skin; not used of fruit which cannot be peeled with the fingers, as apples, etc.

9. 酸 $suan^1$, sour; 澀 $sê^4$, rough, that sets the teeth on edge.

10. 豆腐 tou^4-fu, beancurd: fu^3, properly, rotten; sloughing flesh.

11. 叨叨 tao^1. See Part V, Lesson LXXII, Note 5.

12. 鹹 $hsien^2$, salt in flavour.

13. 歛傢伙 $chien^3$ (or $lien^3$) $chia^1$-huo, cleared the table. Both readings of the first character are admissible.

14. 踡 $ch'üan^2$, to double up the arm or leg.

15. 左不過 tso^3 pu kuo, it was nothing more than, it was just (temper): tso, short for tso yu, right or left; i.e., any way you like to take it.

CHAPTER XV.

1. The next day, however, there was no change; but on the morning after, the graduate suddenly inquired, "Isn't this the fifteenth of the moon?" "Certainly," said CH'IN; "it is the fifteenth." Whereupon the graduate had his queue plaited without delay, and this done he went out to the front part of the temple and asked FA PÊN if everything was in order[1] for the reading of the service. "Not quite," said FA PÊN; "but it will be presently." The graduate drew[2] a lump of silver out of the breast of his dress, and presenting it with both his hands, he said to FA PÊN, "Please accept this as a contribution to your expenses;[5] it is a *ting*[4] of the highest touch."[3]

2. FA PÊN thanked him; "It is very good of you to think of it, sir," said he; "it's my duty to do my best without remuneration."[6]

3. "That would be out of the question," said the graduate; and they kept chatting in this way, saying one to the other whatever came uppermost, when Madame TS'UI and YING YING, having duly fasted and performed their ablutions,[7] came over together from their house into the front court of the temple. As they were making for the waiting-room FA PÊN stepped forward to meet them, and having saluted them with folded hands,[8] he pointed to the graduate CHANG, and informed the old lady that the graduate was a friend of his who was desirous of having a service read for his late father, like herself, on that same day.

4. The old lady observing from the graduate's style that he belonged to the lettered class, answered, "Very proper that he should; there is no objection to his having it read on the same day as ourselves." After which conversation the Buddhistic service began up in the chief chapel.[9] The people who had come to look on at the show, some of them old fellows and some youngsters, when

---

1. 停當 *t'ing*² *tang*¹, in order, satisfactory: *t'ing* is here equivalent to 定.

2. 掏出 *t'ao*¹ *ch'u*, drew out (from his jacket), "forked out."

3. 十足紋銀, pure silver: *shih tsu*, *lit.*, 10 parts complete; *wên*², *lit.*, streaks; specially the marks on the metal by which its quality may be known.

4. 錠 *ting*⁴, an ingot, bar, or shoe of bullion.

5. 香資. See Part IV, Dialogue VI, Note 10.

6. 効勞 *hsiao*⁴ *lao*², to exert oneself, to take pains: *hsiao*, to exert; *lao*, labour, pains; in combination the phrase means to work for nothing. Cf. the legal term 効力贖罪, to expiate a crime by gratuitous labour (*shu*²).

7. 齋戒沐浴 *chai*¹ *chieh*⁴ *mu*⁴ *yü*⁴, fasting (*chai*), abstinence (*chieh*), and purification: *mu*, to wash the hands and face; *yü*, to bathe the person.

8. 打個問訊 *ta*³ *ko wên*⁴ *hsün*⁴, made a salutation; Buddhist priests salute with the palms of the hands placed together (合掌): *hsün*⁴, to ask, *sc.*, after a person's health. Laymen 拱手 (*kung*³), fold the hands in salutation.

9. 殿 *tien*⁴, the main building of a temple; also, a palace, a hall.

they beheld YING YING, all declared that she was indeed fair to see. And what with the remarks of this one and of that one, they created such a stir that the bonzes became quite nervous, and made a sad jumble of what they had to do. FA PÊN observing that they were not minding what they were about, cried out loud, "Don't be so careless, you there; be a little more attentive, do."

5. There was a young bonze standing outside the chapel in a state of abstraction whom FA PÊN told to peel the fruit and cut it into slices. The young bonze obeyed, but, like the rest of them, he could not take his eyes off YING YING while he was cutting the fruit, and the consequence was that he cut [10] his finger with the knife; on which FA PÊN abused him for a useless good-for-nothing, that only cared to be fed and wouldn't work.

6. All this was due, beyond doubt, to the superior charms of Miss YING YING, nor was it the young bonze alone that lost his wits; there was another bonze in the kitchen, who was deaf and dumb from his birth; he was splitting wood [12] for fuel with a hatchet [11] in the court, when, in a moment of inattention, the head of his hatchet flew off, and another bonze, blind of an eye,[13] who was running over to have a look at YING YING, caught his foot against the head of the hatchet and came down sprawling on his face.[14]

7. The din from the roar of voices was really amusing, but it irritated and fidgeted FA PÊN; still, he could not help himself; so he just kept on telling his beads and muttering his incantations,[15] pretending not to observe what was going on.

8. The service ended, YING YING followed the old lady home. The graduate also, as soon as he had made his prostration, returned home, changed his dress, and drew off his boots.

9. He was too sad to enjoy anything; too restless to sit still or to lie down; he kept walking all over the place with his shoes down at heel.[16] In which condition we leave him for the present,[17] and confine ourselves to what was passing elsewhere.

10. 剌破 la^2 $p'o$. See Part V, Lesson LXXII, Note 2.

11. 斧子 fu^3, an axe.

12. 劈劈柴 $p'i^1$ $p'i^3$-$ch'ai^2$, to split firewood: $p'i^1$, to split, to cleave; $p'i^3$-$ch'ai$, firewood; note the change of tone. See Part III, 348.

13. 一隻虎, blind of one eye; a Peking vulgarism; 一隻眼的人 would be equally admissible.

14. 趴虎兒 $p'a^1$ hu-$'rh$; lit., sprawling or crouching tiger; a vulgarism for falling flat on one's face: $p'a$ is not recognised in native dictionaries.

15. 念咒 $nien$ $chou^4$, to mutter incantations: $chou$, a litany or incantation which priests recite; it also means to curse, to wish evil to.

16. 跋拉著鞋: $t'a^1$ or sa^1, with shoes down at heel.

17. 題 $t'i^2$, here, to discuss, to notice; the character 提 (see Part IV, Dialogue II, Note 36) is perhaps preferable. For convenience of arrangement, the last portion of paragraph 9, Chapter XV, English text, has been included in Chapter XVI of the Chinese text.

CHAPTER XVI.

1. At a short distance from the temple stood a mountain upon which a band of outlaws[1] had for years located[2] themselves. Their chief[3] was named SUN FEI-HU, and at the head of his gang,[4] which numbered a thousand or more, he robbed and plundered in every direction.

2. He had been at the temple the day that YING YING was sacrificing there, and had seen her; and when he returned to his stronghold he said to his followers, "That's a very fine girl I have just seen in the temple, and I have a mind to bring her home and make her my queen of the camp;[5] now which of all you fellows is equal to such a glorious enterprise[6] as this?"

3. "Well, sir, it's not so difficult," answered one of his mates, a captain whose name was CH'IEN; "but the thing must be done as I propose, if it's to succeed."

4. It was not SUN FEI-HU's nature to give ear to other people's counsel or to adopt their plans, and on hearing CH'IEN's observation he asked with a smile, "And pray, honoured sir, what may be the fine proposal that you are able to suggest?"

5. CH'IEN knew perfectly well that the remark was ironical; but he replied, with affected humility, "I have heard a report that a graduate named CHANG, who is from the same part of the country as myself, is living in the temple; let me go and see him, and I can take the opportunity to make inquiries."

6. SUN FEI-HU was overjoyed at a suggestion that marched so well with his own ideas. "Capital," said he; "when the thing is done you shall be rewarded handsomely."

7. The captain, CH'IEN, having got his orders, did not venture to lose any time, and so, having changed his dress and attired himself like any ordinary person he came straight to the P'u-chiu Ssŭ.

---

1. 强盗 $ch'iang^2\ tao^4$, a bandit, a robber: *tao*, one who robs openly, as opposed to 贼, a thief.

2. 佔踞 $chan^4\ chü^4$, had taken forcible possession: *chan*, to encroach (*see* Part V, Lesson XV, Note 5); *chü*, to squat down, to crouch.

3. 寨主 $chai^4\ chu$, the chief of the stronghold: *chai* is a stockade or "log fort," not necessarily the stronghold of rebels or banditti.

4. 偻儸 $lou^2\ lo^2$, the rank and file of a gang of rebels or banditti.

5. 壓寨夫人 is only applicable as in the text; it is a quotation.

6. 頭功; *lit.*, meritorious service (*kung*) of the first order (*t'ou*).

CHAPTER XVII.

1. He there called upon the graduate CHANG, and the two men having referred to their long separation,¹ and interchanged some phrases of compliment,² CH'IEN said, "May I inquire whether your honoured father has quite recovered from the malady that used to trouble him?"

2. "Thank you, thank you," answered the graduate; "it's very good of you to inquire, but my father has long departed this life."

3. "Ah!" exclaimed the captain with a sigh; "dead! how true it is that good men are short lived; it is very sad, really."

4. After a short pause he asked another question, "Do you live in this place by yourself, sir," said he, "or do you mess with the rest?"

5. "Well, I don't mess with them," said the graduate; "it's the custom in this temple for anyone staying here to have his cooking done separately."³

6. "Ah! so," answered the captain; "may I ask if it's true, as I have heard it said, that a family named TS'UI, who used to live in the village next down the road, have moved over to this place?"

7. His words rather startled⁴ the graduate; he fancied that he remembered this man as having been an ill-ordered person in his village, and the more he reflected the more suspicious he became that his visitor had not come for any good purpose; the one thing to be done was summarily to stop⁵ all talk on the subject: so he said, "I really cannot say; my way is not to trouble myself about what does not concern me; you had best ask some other gentleman, if you please, sir."

8. The man CH'IEN, seeing that this plan did not answer, felt that he must just bethink him of some other, and so he staid there two days without offering to stir.

9. The graduate CHANG, when he saw that he was not going, began to be angry with everything, and at meal-time he made CH'IN T'UNG the handle for a further outbreak [being unable to attack the real offender]: "The cookery has been getting worse and worse these last few days," said he; "neither the boiled meat nor the roast is properly done; less done one day than another; and to-day everything is more spoiled than ever."

10. "I cooked this myself," said CH'IN T'UNG. "And who desired you to cook at all?" said the graduate; "of course, the cook has been drunk again; call him here directly."

11. CH'IN T'UNG went out and presently⁶ came back; "The cook is here," said he. "Why are you always drinking; and why

---

1. 久違 *chiu wei*², long separation: *wei*, here, to leave, to relinquish; but 違背, to infringe, to disobey, to contravene, as regulations, treaties, etc. The word 犯 is more applicable to a breach of laws or prohibitions.

2. 客套話 *k'o t'ao⁴ hua*, complimentary or polite remarks, set phrases; *lit.*, talk that is confined to the *t'ao*, usages restrictions (*t'ao*, *lit.*, envelope or case; *see* Part III, 769), in force when treating with a stranger.

3. 同居各爨, living together but messing apart : *ts'uan*⁴, *lit.*, a furnace for cooking.

4. 怔了一怔 *lêng*⁴, was startled, taken aback : *lêng*⁴, properly read *chêng*⁴, restless, nervous, agitated ; *lêng*⁴ also means to be silent, to pause, as below in Chapter XVIII, paragraph 2.

5. 閘住 *cha³ chu*, put a stop to (the conversation). Note *cha³*, not *cha²*, a dam or sluice, as in Part V, Lesson XCII, Note 3.

6. 一遍 *t'ang*⁴, a turn, a time; but seldom so used except with verbs of motion, as 我家去了一遍, 去了三遍: *t'ang*, the numerative of times or rows, *sc.*, of figures, etc.

don't you pay proper attention to your cooking?" asked the graduate, his face red and his ears crimson with anger; "your wages will just have to be docked, and we'll see if you won't be more careful after that"

12. The cook certainly was a tippler, and when he saw what he had run foul of, he thought to himself, "Yes; I've put out my money to my own damage,[7] no doubt." He did not venture to exculpate himself, but bowed to the storm and went out without saying a word.

13. The graduate now shifted his displeasure to CHʻIN TʻUNG; "How is it," asked he, "when I have told you to look after everything in the room, that my knife is not to be seen, and that my inkstone is never forthcoming when I want it? what is it that you do attend to, pray?"

14. "It's really no fault of mine, sir," answered CHʻIN TʻUNG; "I put everything back into its proper place whenever it is done with."

[7]. 貼錢買罪受, put my money out to my own damage; *tʻieh*, *lit.*, to stick on, as a placard: I have applied my money to the purchase of *tsui*, retribution for [my own] use.

CHAPTER XVIII.

1. The captain observed the scene as a spectator, and divining that almost all that was passing was due to his presence there, he was greatly amused; he asked the graduate in a sheepish sort of way,[1] "Did not those polished shoes you have on, sir, come from Canton? they are very nice."

2. The graduate, who was as angry as he could be, did not answer a word. Then said CHʻIEN to CHʻIN TʻUNG, with a dry chuckle, "Your master's service does not give you overmuch trouble, I daresay; what wages may you be getting a month?" But CHʻIN TʻUNG, seeing how his master looked, did not venture to answer the question, and the whole party remained without making sign or sound until the graduate, turning to CHʻIN TʻUNG, called for his water-pipe.[2] CHʻIN TʻUNG could not lay his hand upon it immediately, and this put the graduate in a passion again, and he began to abuse the lad.

3. "You might just as well be blind at once," cried he; "why, there it is, and yet you can't see it." Then CHʻIN TʻUNG did see the pipe, and he brought it with all speed. The graduate smoked a couple of pipes, and

[1]. 踏趫著 *ta¹ shan¹-cho*, in a sheepish or diffident sort of way. There is considerable difference of opinion as to the meaning of this phrase, and also as to the characters that should be employed: one authority decides in favour of the above rendering; another prefers 搭訕, and says that it means to come up to the point in an indirect way; preference has been given to the first meaning in this case simply because the authority is more trustworthy, but it must be received with caution; in another instance it seems to mean a pretension of inadvertence (*see* Chapter XXVII, 1).

[2]. 烟袋 *yên¹-tai⁴*, a pipe: why *tai*, a bag, is introduced it is difficult to say.

then, without taking any notice of CH'IEN, he went out of the temple, followed by CH'IN T'UNG.

4. There happened to be a number of children outside the temple gate engaged in play; and very rough play.³ Some were setting on the dogs to worry⁴ the pigs; some were wrestling;⁵ others, again, were looking on at chickens fighting, and backing⁶ one chicken against another as the better of the two. And there were some very young children who were arguing as to the way to distinguish between cocks and hens; and there were others, older than they, explaining that hens laid eggs,⁷ and that cocks crew.⁸ But with this explanation the younger ones would not be satisfied.

5. Then, again, in the midst of all this bustle there was a very little child threading his way through the crowd, with no one to look after it; which the graduate observing as he passed along, he was much moved at the thought that it would be hustled by the crowd, and he told someone to take it home at once.

6. He had gone some steps farther when he saw a man carrying a small dog. It had fine drooping⁹ ears, and he wanted to buy it; but after a good deal of bargaining, no agreement could be come to regarding the price; so he continued his walk for some time longer, and then he thought he would go in.

7. The children were still outside the gate, and so taken up with their play that they did not get out of his way. The graduate, not being in the happiest of moods, got angry, and cried out:

8. "Get up and stand aside there, and let me by; put your playthings back a bit; you mustn't take up so much room with them."

9. The children were frightened and made way for him as fast as they could, and the graduate went into the temple, where finding the captain, CH'IEN, still making no move, he said to him, "Are you not going home to-day, sir?"

10. As a matter of fact, the man, having learned all about YING YING, was just about to start to make his report to his chief; so he answered, "Certainly, sir, I was just starting; I've been a great trouble to you for several days, and I feel I can't show my gratitude as I desire, but I shall make farther acknowledgment some other time."

3. 粗魯 ts'u¹ lu³, of play, etc., rough; of individuals, coarse, stupid-looking: lu not colloquially separated from ts'u.

4. 齩 yao³, to bite, is the correct form of yao in Part V, Lesson XXX, Note 13.

5. 摔跤 shuai¹ chiao¹, to wrestle: chiao, lit., the ankle-bone.

6. 輸贏 shu¹ ying², to lose and win respectively, whether in gambling or any contest: shêng⁴ and pai⁴ are the terms for victory and defeat in warfare.

7. 下蛋, to lay eggs: tan⁴, an egg. Ts'ao chi, a hen; see Chapter IV, Note 15.

8. 打鳴兒 ta ming²-'rh, to crow: ming, the sound made by any bird or animal; also applied to other sounds; ta makes a verb of it.

9. 耷拉著 ta¹ la-cho, hanging down: ta, to hang down; la, to drag; used of anything pendulous, such as a cord, a curtain, etc.

CHAPTER XIX.

1. This said, the two men parted. The captain, you may be sure, lost no time in returning to the hills and reporting to SUN FEI-HU every particular.

2. SUN FEI-HU was greatly delighted; his expedition, it seemed to him, could not fail to succeed. So he came on³ next day at the head of all the brigands in the hills,¹ blowing their horns;² they swarmed round the temple, investing it so closely that not a drop of water could get through, and the whole body kept on shouting that YING YING must come out and answer a question.

3. The news frightened FA PÊN out of his senses; he rushed into the old lady's court, crying out, "Do you hear, madame? there is a great band of brigands outside; their chief, SUN FEI-HU, is a murderous robber, quite impervious to any sentiment of humanity or justice, whose constant thought is of rapine and murder; and now here he is at the head of a thousand or ten thousand men, beating gongs and drums,⁴ and shouting as loud as they can bawl that Miss YING YING must go out and parley with them. Never in all my experience, I may say, have I met with anything so calamitous."

4. His story frightened the old lady in no ordinary degree;⁵ away she went to YING YING's room, and toddling⁶ in, she repeated it to her. YING YING burst into tears, crying loudly⁷ and bitterly, unable to get out a word. The old lady at her great age was very far from clear when she had anything to speak about; says she to the bonze, "Dear me! I haven't a relative in the world that I could rely on to help me except one, my own elder brother, and he is away at Su-chou (Soochow), where he has been promoted; couldn't someone fetch him back at once, eh?"

5. "Oh! it's of no use making such suggestions as that," said FA PÊN; "the only thing to be done is to try and find out for your ladyship if any of the people living here in the temple can suggest a means of getting this force to draw off; which is doubtful, after all." "So be it," said Madame TS'UI; "Heaven send you may find⁸ someone; go and ask at once."

---

1. 可山的僂儸, all the brigands in the hills. Note the peculiar use of *k'o*, which is here equivalent to *ch'üan*, all, or *man*, full. Cf. the following: 可著身上都不舒服, I feel uncomfortable all over; 可著京城的道兒都不好走, every road in the capital is bad; 可屋子全得‵糊, the whole room must be papered.

2. 喇叭 *la³-pa¹*, a trumpet, a long horn.

3. 蜂擁的來了 *fêng¹ yung³*, came on in a swarm: *fêng*, insects of the bee, wasp, or hornet tribe; 螞蜂, a wasp; 蜜蜂, a bee (*see* Chapter XIII, Note 10); *yung*, to crowd, throng, or push together.

4. 摋鑼擂鼓 *shai¹ lo² lei³ ku³*, gonging and drumming: *shai*, to strike, specially the gong (*lo*); *lei³*, properly *lei²*, to beat, specially the drum.

5. 非同小可, in no ordinary degree; *lit.*, [the fright] was not (*fei*) identical with (*t'ung*) a small *k'o*: *k'o*, which is here a noun, will not bear any of the meanings usually assigned to it, and must be treated as equivalent to 事 or some similar word.

6. 蹀蹀躞躞 *tieh² hsieh⁴*, tottered, trotted, toddled; generally applied to the shuffling gait of old age. Both characters mean to walk, but are not used separately.

7. 謑喓 *hao² t'ao²*, to cry aloud: *hao*, to cry out; *t'ao*, *lit.*, the prattle of a child; in combination the two characters are only applied to loud weeping.

8. 巴不能彀, short for 巴不得能彀. *See* Part V, Lesson I, Note 10.

6. She then turned and spoke to YING YING: "If," said she, "I send you out to them, I shall be disgraced [9] by so doing; if I don't send you, I jeopardise the lives of one and all of us. I am thinking of asking if there is anyone in the temple who can destroy these brigands and rescue us, and if there is, of promising to marry you to him; do you say yea or nay?"

7. YING YING felt how pressing was the emergency, but she was too bashful to speak; however, there was no alternative, so she nodded her head in token of acquiescence.

8. Whereupon FA PÊN went forth and repeated what had been said to all there assembled. No one moved but one person, the graduate CHANG; he came into Madame TS'UI's court, and, addressing the old lady, said he, "Don't be afraid; I am quite able to bring these brigands under;[10] all you have to do is to set your heart at rest."

9. The old lady was delighted; "How comes it," asked she, "that you, who are a man of letters, should also be skilled in war?"

10. "I have not myself, I admit, any knowledge of war," said the graduate, "but that's of no consequence; what I meant when I spoke was that I have a friend who is the *Pai Ma Chiang-chün*; he is stationed at [11] the P'u Kuan, and as soon as it was rumoured that these robbers were on their way I sent a messenger to let him know; he is certain to come to the rescue with some good plan [12] or other."

11. He only said this, however, to allay the old lady's fears for the moment. His words made her more than ever delighted; she could hardly contain herself;[13] what rejoices the heart is certain to be believed in; and this was quite her case: "When our difficulty is satisfactorily disposed of," said she, "I shall feel bound, you may be sure, to reward you handsomely." YING YING also felt a good deal more at her ease.

9. 丟人. Note, not "lose a man," but lose face, lose the attributes of a man, a manly character; hence, generally, to be disgraced.

10. 降伏 *hsiang² fu²*, to bring into subjection: *hsiang*, to submit, to cause to submit; *fu*, to prostrate oneself. See Part V, Lesson XIX, Note 10.

11. 駐劄 *chu⁴ cha²*, to reside at, to be stationed at; generally, of officials; but a vessel of war may *chu*, be stationed at, a given place.

12. 計策 *chi ts'ê⁴*, a plan, an expedient.

13. 樂的不可支, could not contain herself for joy: *chih*, here, to withstand, to bear up against, to sustain.

CHAP. XX.]   PART VI.—THE GRADUATE'S WOOING.   383

CHAPTER XX.

1. Notwithstanding all these consoling speeches of the graduate's, however, the brigands kept on bawling incessantly outside the temple; and after the brave words he had used he could do no less than turn his attention to the discovery of some expedient that might make them good;¹ hurrying out, he asked, "Which of you, as a first step, will carry a letter to SUN FEI-HU?" "SUN," said FA PÊN, "is a rude fellow; he is a man of no education; it's no use writing to him, and anyway it will be simpler to send him a message by word of mouth."

2. "Very good," said the graduate; "will you be able to go and say a word to him?" "I?" said FA PÊN; "I am not fit for such a mission,² and I don't know who would venture to undertake³ anything so serious."

3. "All you will have to do," said the graduate, "is to tell SUN FEI-HU that Miss YING YING is just now in a sad state of trepidation; but that if he will draw off his men a bowshot from the temple, and wait two or three days, so as to give her time to get somewhat composed, she shall be sent out to him; now, away with you, and don't be frightened."

4. FA PÊN was no hero, but after fighting off⁴ a long time he agreed to go, and he went accordingly with the message. SUN FEI-HU, though he refused at first, was at last prevailed upon by repeated entreaties to give a grudging consent to what was proposed; "But if," said he, "she be not sent out when the third day arrives, not a fowl nor a dog will I leave alive in the place."

---

1. 以踐其言, to make his words good: *chien*⁴, to tread on or in, *sc.*, the footsteps of another; hence, *chien yen*, to tread in the track of one's words, to fulfil one's promises. The expression is rather literary, but there is no exact equivalent in colloquial; the nearest is 應他所說的 (*ying*⁴), but that is rather the fulfilment of a prediction.

2. 不勝其任, I am not fit for the mission, task, or duty: for *shêng*¹, see Part V, Lesson VII, Note 6.

3. 承擔 *ch'êng*² *tan*¹, to undertake; *lit.*, to undertake the carrying of: *tan*¹, to carry on a pole; *tan*⁴-*tzŭ*, the thing so carried. *See* Part IV, Dialogue III, Note 123. The common expression is 擔戴不起.

4. 支吾. *See* Part V, Lesson LXVIII, Note 2.

CHAPTER XXI.

1. FA PÊN carried this message back to the graduate CHANG. "If that is it," said the graduate, as soon as he had heard it, "we must not waste any time. Which of you," he asked in a loud tone, "is man enough to start at once with a letter for the *Pai Ma Chiang-chün*, to hurry him here as fast¹ as he can come?"

2. Not one of the bonzes present ventured to say a word, but at the back of the temple there was an old one, named HUI² MING, who lit the fires, and who, though not possessed of much brains, was very handy with his fists and his feet; such a boxer that no one that he hit cared to return his blow. FA PÊN suddenly bethought himself of him, and said he to the graduate, "HUI MING is the very man to send, but there is this against it: he is so cross-grained³ that if one were to recommend⁴ him for the mission he would be certain to refuse it; the only way to succeed is to say something that will pique⁵ him."

3. The graduate thought a minute, and then, observing that he had something to try, he called out, "If there is anyone here except HUI MING that has the courage to take a letter to the *Pai Ma Chiang-chün*, let him come and speak to me directly." Up came HUI MING with all speed as soon as he heard this, in a great state of mind, and insisted upon going himself. But in order yet more to excite⁶ him, the graduate threw in another word or two: "It's no child's play," said he; "if others can't do the thing, how much less can you? supposing it breaks down, who is to bear the blame?"

4. "I have no meat⁷ for my dumplings," replied HUI MING, with the air of a man who was not to be gainsaid; "and very insipid they taste; when I have killed this chief I shall

---

1. 飛速 *fei¹ su²*; *lit.*, with flying haste: *su*, quick, quickly.

2. 惠 *hui⁴*, here, a proper name; properly, kindness, benevolence, compassion; seldom used alone.

3. 軟硬不喫, cross-grained, amenable neither to command nor persuasion, a man that must be humoured.

4. 舉薦 *chü² chien⁴*, to recommend; *lit.*, to select for recommendation: *chü*, to raise (*see* Part IV, Dialogue VI, Note 27); *chien*, to introduce, to recommend; 薦信, a letter of introduction. Note the tone of *chü* in this combination.

5. 激發 *chi fa*, to pique, to rouse to action: *chi¹*, to rouse, to excite to; *fa*, the putting forth, *q.d.*, of energy, temper, etc.

6. 逗 *tou⁴*, here, to excite, to irritate, to impel (*cf.* 逗孩子笑, to make a child laugh); the proper meaning of *tou* is to delay, to loiter, as 道兒上逗遛, to loiter on the road; *so hsing*, see Part V, Lesson XXV, Note 6: although HUI MING was already prepared to go, the graduate thought he would *nevertheless, in spite of that,* stir him up a little more.

7. 餡 *hsien⁴*, the meat or stuffing inside a dumpling; *man-t'ou*, properly, steamed bread, is occasionally made with a stuffing of chopped meat or sugar. *Cf.* 肉饅頭.

make mincemeat of him. Give me the letter, sir; that's all you need mind about; but now, if the *Pai Ma Chiang-chün* doesn't come, who is to be responsible, pray?"

5. "It won't affect you," said the graduate. And in order to put further pressure upon [8] him, FA PÊN put in his word: "There is an affair of mine," said he, "that you could dispose of for me at the same time." But HUI MING promptly rejoined that that could not be; two commissions were more than one person could charge himself with.[9]

6. "Well, if that's the way of it," said the graduate, who saw that his mind was so bent in the right direction that nothing could oppose him, "off with you at once."

7. HUI MING, striding along with light step and valourous air,[10] took leave of the graduate then and there, and rode out of the gate, a solitary horseman; and as he galloped along he shouted, "Which of you is coming to try his strength with me? do your best now, and let us see which is the stronger man."

8. Now, the temple stood on the high shoulder of a hill,[11] so that once out of the gate the horse found it easy going down the hill, and he set off at full gallop, plunging[12] and prancing as if he was frightened.

9. Even if the robbers had given chase, being on foot of course they could not come up with him. HUI MING never stopped once to draw breath, but galloped straight to the P'u Kuan, and taking the letter out of his breast, he presented[13] it to the *Pai Ma Chiang-chün*, and told him the whole state of the case exactly as it stood.

8. 擠對 *chi³ tui*, to put pressure upon : *tui* is said to be equivalent to 試, to try (cf. 對一對); *chi*, press him and, *tui*, try [whether he will yield to pressure].

9. 一身不能當二役; *lit.*, one [man in his own] person cannot perform two affairs.

10. 趾高氣揚, with light (or high) step and valourous air: *chih³*, the foot.

11. 趄坡子 *ch'ieh⁴ p'o-tzŭ*, the shoulder of a hill: *p'o*, a sloping bank; *ch'ieh*, here, deviating from the perpendicular; the dictionaries do not support this pronunciation of the character, which is properly read *tsu³* or *ch'ü¹*.

12. 竄 *ts'uan¹*, here apparently to plunge. See Part III, 545. Note the change of tone.

13. 呈 *ch'êng²*, to hand to a superior; *ch'êng-tzŭ*, a petition.

CHAPTER XXII.

1. The perusal of the letter startled the *Pai Ma Chiang-chün*; "Ah," exclaimed he, "this is a pretty business indeed!" Without more ado, he mustered a body of infantry and cavalry, and set it in motion, and with banners waving and loud shouts his force came straight down upon the P'u-chiu Ssŭ.

2. The graduate heard the noise made by the men and horses, a din as if the skies were falling and the earth was being rent;[1] and he knew that a rescue was at hand.

3. As for SUN FEI-HU, when he espied this great movement afar off, it made his heart beat:[2] there was only one course open to him; he sheathed[3] his sword, and stealing timidly along[4] to the general, he knelt down before him as he sat on his horse and implored his mercy.

4. The *Pai Ma Chiang-chün* knew what a notorious brigand he was, and how he had for years contrived to keep out of the meshes of the law; and to have let such a man go when he had fallen into his hands would have been throwing away a chance, would it not? so he gave orders that the chief himself should be put to death[5] then and there, but that mercy should be extended to his followers on condition that they abandoned their evil courses and, returning to honest ways, submitted to the disposition that might be made of them by the authorities.

1. 天塌地陷 $t'a^1$, to fall in ruins; $hsien^4$, vulgarly $hsüan^4$, to fall in. Note that $t'a$ can only be used of any building that falls down from the top; to collapse in consequence of the subsidence of the foundation is $t'an^1$ (坍).

2. 忐忑 $t'an^3 t'ê^4$, a term expressive of the palpitation of the heart.

3. 鞘 $ch'iao^4$, a sheath, a scabbard.

4. 蹭 $ts'êng^4$, to drag the feet along; generally used of the shuffling gait of old age; to walk hesitatingly or "delicately."

5. 正法 $chêng fa$, to put to death, to inflict the last penalty of the law: lit., $chêng$, to execute, to carry out in the proper manner; fa, the law.

CHAPTER XXIII.

1. And now, the work of suppression being completed, the graduate CHANG came out to visit the *Pai Ma Chiang-chün* and to thank him for his goodness in thus rescuing them all from death. The *chiang-chün* on his part complimented the graduate upon his ability,[1] and the two men having interchanged a few phrases, each declining the other's praise,[2] the general took off a deer's horn[3] thumb-ring[4] that he was wearing, and presented it to the graduate.

2. "We have not seen each other for many years," said he; "accept this in honour of our meeting to-day; don't refuse[5] it, sir, pray."

3. The graduate took the ring from him in both his hands, and, thanking him for his present, began to extol the fine workmanship of it; it had a pattern upon it, and the graduate asked if the design was artificial. The general said that it was natural. And so they went on conversing about one trifle or another,[6] more in number than one can recount.[7]

4. The graduate made his friend stay two days, but when the third day came the general said to him, "I have been trespassing greatly on your hospitality for the last two days, sir, and to-morrow being pay[9]-day at head-quarters,[8] the troops will be going up for their pay; so I must wish you good-bye."

5. The graduate did not venture to press him to stay longer, when he heard that he had public business upon his hands, but he again expressed his sincere thanks for what he had done; "I am really most concerned, sir," said he, "to think how your troops have been put about[10] by this *alerte*." With such words he conducted the general to the gate, and when the moment of parting came, he reiterated his thanks for his trouble.

6. The general modestly declined his compliments; "Don't mention it," said he; "may we meet again some day; accompany me no farther, I beg, sir." And so they took leave of one another.

---

1. 智畧 *chih*[4] *lio*[4], ability. See Part V, Lesson XXX, Note 18.
2. 謙虛. See Part IV, Dialogue X, Note 8, Obs. 8.
3. 觭角 *chi*[1] *chio*, the horn of any horn-bearing animal.
4. 搬指兒 *pan*[1] *chih-'rh*, a thumb-ring, the ring worn on the right thumb by archers: *chih* has here no tone, the emphasis being laid on *pan*.
5. 推却 to refuse, as a present. See Part III, 678.
6. 一席話 a desultory conversation, a talk on miscellaneous subjects. No satisfactory explanation of the origin of this phrase can be obtained.
7. 述 *shu*[4], to narrate.
8. 營 *ying*[2], a military cantonment, a camp, barracks; commonly called 營盤; also, a regiment.
9. 餉 *hsiang*[3], soldier's pay.
10. 驚師動衆: *chung shih*, your whole brigade, *ching tung*, have been disturbed; *shih*, not, as in Part V, Lesson II, Note 7, a teacher, but a legion or brigade, originally consisting of 2,500 men. Cf. the common polite expression 驚動您納, I apologise for disturbing you.

CHAPTER XXIV.

1. The graduate turned round and had re-entered the temple, when, behold! out of the inner gate came HUNG NIANG, hurrying along as if her mind was full of something.[1]

2. "What breeze blows you this way to-day?" asked the graduate, smiling. "Well, the fact is," said HUNG NIANG, "that my old mistress wishes to invite you to take up your quarters in the library, sir; but she hopes that you will breakfast with her first to-morrow morning."

3. "Oh! why should Madame TS'UI give herself this trouble," exclaimed the graduate; "I really ought not to regard myself as deserving her invitation, but as she commands me to go, I shall not fail to avail myself of it."

4. Accordingly, the following day he dressed himself with very great care. And he was just going to put on his cap when CH'IN T'UNG observed that the cap was somewhat old-fashioned;[2] wouldn't it be better to exchange it for such a cap as was then the mode, he asked.

5. The graduate changed the cap, and his whole toilette being now perfectly en règle,[3] away he went, quite the gentleman in his bearing,[4] to the other side of the temple.

6. The servants hastened to thrust back[5] the hanging screen of the library, and the graduate entering found a picture hung upon the wall; the person represented was YING YING, and the picture[6] was so finely and carefully executed that it was the living image of the lady herself.

7. The graduate had been feasting his eyes upon the portrait for some time, in rapt contemplation, when Madame TS'UI came over from her apartments. The moment she saw him she began to say how grateful she was, and so on, but the graduate, making a deep bow, modestly declined her acknowledgments:

8. "You are too complimentary, madam," said he; "what benefits others, as the proverb says, equally benefits oneself; the service I rendered was surely not so very meritorious."

1. 忙忙忉忉 *mang*, in a hurry; *tao*, lit., harassed, oppressed with care.

2. 與時, or *shih hsing*¹, in the fashion: *hsing*¹, to be in demand, to be fashionable; *e.g.*, 這會兒不興窄袖口兒, narrow sleeve openings are not fashionable now.

3. 衣冠齊楚, properly dressed: *kuan*¹, a cap, specially the ancient form of cap, which is now obsolete except amongst Taoist priests; *ch'i*, complete; *ch'u*, in due order; the praise is less of the clothes than of the way they are put on.

4. 斯文, gentlemanlike deportment. This expression is extremely difficult to analyse, and the student would do well to accept the fact that *ssŭ wên* means gentlemanly and dignified in bearing; any attempt to show how it came to have this meaning would involve a more elaborate explanation than the scope of these notes is intended to embrace. Cf. 他是個斯文人, he is a gentlemanly man; a man who is quiet, dignified, and patient.

5. 掀 *hsien*¹, to lift, to raise, as the cover of a dish, a hanging screen, or a sheet of paper lying flat: 掀一篇兒, to turn over a page.

6. 行樂圖, the portrait of a person drawn when he is alive: *t'u*, the picture of one who is *hsing lo*, enjoying pleasure, *i.e.*, who is engaged in some pursuit that interests or amuses him. The *hsing lo t'u* is generally a representation of the individual engaged in his favourite pursuit. A portrait drawn during life for use sacrificially after death is called a 喜容兒, and on the death of the individual it becomes a 影. The difference between a *hsing lo t'u* and the other two descriptions of portrait is that in the latter the person portrayed is generally sitting in a formal attitude and dressed in his official robes.

CHAPTER XXV.

1. The servants began forthwith to put the food on the table—a *recherché* repast;[1] wine, meats, and everything else equally good; dried fruits and fresh; and the service all of old porcelain[2][3] as thin as paper.

2. The book-cases which surrounded the room were piled up with volumes as high as the ceiling, and while the breakfast was being served the graduate kept on gazing at them incessantly in one direction or another. The books were first editions, printed in the South; the paper and type[4] both excellent.

3. Madame Ts'UI, observing that his eyes were never away from the book-shelves, asked him, "What kind of books is it, sir, that you esteem the most?" "Well," said the graduate, "the older an edition is, the better; but there is this objection to old books, that the book-worm[5] breeds in them so easily, and then of course they get honeycombed and destroyed."

4. "There is every sort of reading in these," said the old lady: "the canonical books, history, philosophy, and all other kinds of literature;[6] and at any time that you wish to read any of them, sir, all you have to do is to take out what you want."

5. They conversed in this way until the larger dishes were brought in, and the butler requested his mistress to do the honours. The old lady, with the aid of the chopsticks, helped the graduate to different viands, and this done she said to him, "Don't make a stranger of yourself, sir, pray; my teeth are too loose to allow of my eating these things. HUNG NIANG, go to the young lady and beg her to come and keep my visitor company."

6. YING YING, as a rule, was not an early riser, but this day, being aware that the graduate was invited to breakfast, she had been up the first thing in the morning, and having completed her toilette, she had been seated some time waiting, all forlorn, in the work-room when HUNG NIANG arrived.

7. "Your mamma begs that you'll come and keep the graduate CHANG company at breakfast, miss," said HUNG NIANG; "I do think that this way of managing a marriage shows a strong sense of economy on your mamma's part; she has always been in the habit of spending her money right and left, and now, on an occasion like this, to begin counting the cost with such care does really seem penny wise and pound foolish."

8. YING YING scolded her for talking in this way; "You are too fond of letting your tongue run on,"[7] said she; "if mamma were

---

1. 肴饌 *yao¹ chuan⁴*: *yao*, savoury meats; *chuan*, a banquet, a meal.

2. 窰 *yao²*, a kiln or furnace for firing porcelain; also, a pit, as 煤窰, a coal-mine; hence, *yao-tzŭ*, a brothel.

3. 瓷器 *tz'ǔ² ch'i⁴*, porcelain; *lit.*, porcelain utensils.

4. 板 *pan³*, a block on which type for printing is cut; also, a board, as 一塊板, or *pan-tzŭ*. Note that *pan-tzŭ* alone without the numerative is an instrument of flagellation.

5. 蠹魚子 *tu⁴-yü-tzŭ*, a bookworm: *tu*, an insect, somewhat like a fish in appearance, which destroys books.

6. 經史子集 *ching¹ shih³ tzŭ³ chi²*: *ching*, canonical works (the *wu ching*); *shih*, historical works; *tzŭ*, the works of philosophers, as LIEH-TZŬ, CHUANG-TZŬ, LAO-TZŬ, etc.; *chi*, miscellaneous works.

7. 敞 *ch'ang³*, wide, open, spacious; *shuo-hua ch'ang*, to give rein or latitude to one's tongue.

to hear you, do you suppose that you wouldn't catch it? you must keep a little more within bounds, if you please."

9. Saying which she crossed over, followed by HUNG NIANG. She saluted the graduate as soon as she saw him; he returned the salute, bowing low, with his arms extended; and the whole party sat down. The old lady looked intently at the pair, ability on the one side and beauty on the other, a couple truly formed by nature to be united,[8] and she thought sadly to herself how nice it would have been, had her daughter not been engaged, to have married her[9] to the graduate; but this was at present out of the question, and there was but one alternative. "My child," said she to YING YING, "you must not treat the graduate CHANG henceforward as a stranger; you must call him brother and he must call you sister, and your affection[10] for each other will be the comfort of my heart."

10. As YING YING listened to these words, which declared as plainly as could be that now the scar[11] was healed all past pain was forgotten, she said to herself, "This is not right; why is my mother shifting round in this way?"[12] And after sitting there a short time, knitting her brows in vexation,[13] she took leave of the graduate and departed.

11. "One's got to put one's head to it a bit now[14] [before anything can be done]," thought HUNG NIANG; "good things, as they say, are pretty sure to be hitched somehow;[15] what a pity it all is to be sure!"

12. And to the graduate likewise it seemed that the bridge had been broken down as soon as the river was crossed; he tried to speak, but he found he could not open his lips. The old lady guessed what was passing in his mind and anticipated him; "There is a difficulty in the way, sir," said she, "which you are not aware of; my girl has been engaged ever since her childhood to my nephew, CHÊNG HÊNG; your action in saving our whole family, sir, it would be hard indeed to repay; never so long as I live shall I forget your goodness, sir, and the way you sympathised with us."

13. "What the eye doesn't see," says the proverb, "the mouth has no craving for; when the ear does not hear, the heart is not troubled." The graduate was a disinterested

8. 佳偶 *chia*[1] *ou*[3], an admirable match: *ou*, a pair, a match: used specially of a married couple.

9. 成就婚姻, contract a marriage: *hun*[1], properly, a bridegroom; *yin*[1], properly, a bride; hence, *hun yin*, marriage.

10. 友愛 is used specially with reference to fraternal affection.

11. 疤瘌 *pa*[1]-*la*[1], a scar: the old lady had forgotten her promise to marry YING YING to her deliverer as soon as the danger was over.

12. 變了卦, changed her plans or arrangements, came round to another way of thinking: *pien*[4], to change, to transform; *kua*[4], certain symbolical groups of lines of classical origin which may be called the categorical indices of Chinese philosophy, but here spoken of with reference to divination; *q.d.*, the good *kua* originally selected has been changed; *fig.* for someone's change of purpose after passing his word. For a description of the eight *kua* the student is referred to MAYERS' "Chinese Reader's Manual," p. 333.

13. 愁眉不展, a fixed air of melancholy or vexation; *lit.*, sad eyebrows that will not *chan*[3], open.

14. 撓頭 *nao*[2] *t'ou*; *lit.*, to scratch the head; this is a scratch-head business, one that requires the exercise of thought.

15. 好事多磨; *lit.*, there are many annoyances attending the performance of good actions (or enjoyment of good things): *mo*[2], to grind; used of continuous annoyances.

man, and when he put himself forward in the time of danger, and exerted himself, it had not been in the least degree from any hope of reward; still, when he heard the old lady talk in this way, he could not help feeling greatly disappointed, and not a single word could he bring out in reply; he lost all his self-possession, and kept on fidgeting and rocking himself about,[16] looking at the good wine and the excellent[17] fare with which the table was covered without touching them; not a mouthful could he have eaten; and after a short interval he sadly and gravely took formal leave of Madame TS'UI and went his way.

16. 提離提盪 *huang⁴ li² huang⁴ tang⁴*, fidgeting and rocking himself about: *tang*, a condition of disturbance; see also Part V, Lesson LXXXVI, Note 4, where it has a different sound and meaning.

17. 嘉 *chia¹*, good, excellent, admirable; identical in meaning with 佳, *q.v.*, but the former cannot be applied to individuals.

CHAPTER XXVI.

1. HUNG NIANG accompanied him to his own room, and seeing how very much out of spirits he was, she asked him in a low voice, "What makes you so sad, sir?"

2. "I have drunk a cup or two too much," said the graduate.

3. "Where may have you been drinking?" said HUNG NIANG, repressing[1] a smile; "one's unsteadiness is to be laid on the wine![2] I am afraid this doesn't tally with the facts; you had better speak out now." "Well," said the graduate, "the truth is that I have been put to some trouble and all to no purpose; no good is come of it; of course it doesn't signify whether the old lady holds to her word or not so far as she is concerned, but how am I to get over it?"

4. "Ah!" said HUNG NIANG, "then I see I wasn't out in my guess; why didn't you come to me? I've a plan in my head."

5. "Indeed?" asked the graduate eagerly, "and what may your plan be,[3] when things are in such a mess as they are?"

6. "Some people are clever one way and some another," said HUNG NIANG, laughing; "when I tell you what it is, I'll guarantee it will please you. You play very well on the cithern, don't you, sir? well, the cithern is

1. 抿著嘴兒 *min³ cho tsui*, pursed up her mouth; the dictionaries do not recognise this meaning of *min*.

2. 沒酒三分醉, a proverb indicative of a person who feigns drunkenness or makes it a plea for indulging in vituperation or an outburst of temper, etc.

3. 著兒. See Part V, Lesson LIV, Note 15.

the instrument our young lady is fondest of hearing; you play on it this evening, and let us see what she says when she hears it."

7. The graduate sprang up; "Is it really the case?" said he; "that is a suggestion, I must say, quite in accordance with my ideas. Be it so then; this evening I'll play an air on the cithern, and you will watch and see how it affects her, and then come and tell me."

8. HUNG NIANG assented, and away she went; and in the evening, greatly to her surprise, YING YING heard all of a sudden the sound of a cithern.

9. After listening very attentively for some time, she asked HUNG NIANG, "Where is that cithern being played, and in such good cadence too?[4] I can't think who it can be that is playing it."

10. "It's most likely the graduate CHANG," said HUNG NIANG, "playing to relieve his feelings; I observed that when he got up from breakfast he looked very sad; I don't think he is going to stay here."

11. YING YING started as if she had sat down on a rug full of needles; then, making an effort, she said, "He can't be going off directly, surely; to-morrow, when you hear fruit cried in the street, buy some good fruit and take it to him."

12. HUNG NIANG promised to do as she was desired, and the next day she spoke to the graduate; "There's a faint sign of a beginning of things," she told him. "How does it show itself?" said the graduate.

13. "Last evening, when she heard the sound of the cithern, she looked all lost, bewildered, as if she had something on her mind; and then she told me to buy some fruit and bring it to you: now, just think, sir; to a clever gentleman like yourself there is no need to be more particular, is there?"

14. "Very good," said the graduate; "I really am greatly obliged to you." But as he was speaking a cold fit seized him, and he shivered so from head to foot that it frightened HUNG NIANG, and she asked with a start what was the matter.

15. "I've had ague[5] these two days," said the graduate. "Indeed!" said HUNG NIANG. "Then you should take something for it, and keep quiet and not trouble your head about anything."

16. She was moving towards the temple gate as she spoke, and as luck would have it, there was a man there with a load of watermelons for sale. HUNG NIANG asked him how he sold them. He told her his price, but she tried to beat him down, and the man, declaring that what she offered wouldn't cover the cost price, took his pole[6] in his hand [as if he was going to shoulder it]; still he did not move, but waited until HUNG NIANG rose her price a little, and then he let her have the water-melons.

17. HUNG NIANG took her melons in and presented them to the graduate CHANG, asking him if he felt any better.

18. "A little better," said he; "your present comes in very nice time, and the fruit looks pretty good; won't you eat a little of it yourself?"

19. HUNG NIANG thanked him, but declined; "Water-melon doesn't agree with

4. 琴韻悠揚: $yün^4$, here a musical chord or harmonious tone; yu^1, far-reaching, protracted; $yang^2$, to raise, as the voice (see Part V, Lesson XCI, Note 6).

5. 發瘧子, to have a fit of ague: yao^4, aguish fever.

6. 扁擔 $pien^3$ tan^4, a carrying pole; so called because the pole is flattened so as not to hurt the shoulder.

me,"[7] said she. So when the graduate had eaten a little of it, he told CH'IN T'UNG to put the rest away.

20. There were a great many mosquitoes in the room, and they kept the graduate so constantly scratching[8] himself that he could get no sleep at nights; and he was now leaning with his elbow upon the small table of the stove bed, half asleep and half awake,[9] when he suddenly noticed some peaches that he had bought, which were standing in a bowl on the cithern stand; they were very good, and he asked HUNG NIANG, "Is the young lady fond of peaches? if she is, I'll trouble you to take her a few with my respects, in return for her present."

21. HUNG NIANG said she was, and having selected some of the best, was just going away when the graduate called to her to wait a little; "I'll write something on a fan," said he, "and you can carry it with you at the same time."

22. "Don't write your name[10] on the fan," said HUNG NIANG, "for fear the old lady should see it; she is very suspicious."

23. This seemed to the graduate a sensible observation, and having rubbed his ink[11] and moistened[12] his pencil well, in the twinkling of an eye he had written a stanza[13] upon the fan, which, without putting his signature to it, he handed to HUNG NIANG, with the following injunction: "Whatever the young lady may say when she sees it," said he, "you can come and tell me, you know."

7. 喫怕了, I am afraid to eat them; my previous experience causes me to avoid them.

8. 抓癢癢 *chua¹ yang³ yang*, to scratch oneself; *lit.*, to scratch an itching [place]: *yang yang*, to itch; not *yang*; *chua*, to scratch or tear with the fingers; also, to clutch, as in Part III, 448.

9. 打盹兒 *ta tun³-'rh*, to nod with sleep.

10. 落欵 *lao k'uan³*, to put down a name: *k'uan*, a form, a section, an article, *q.d.*, of a treaty; when used as here with *lao* it means the name or surname either of the person presenting the fan or of the recipient (distinguished as *hsia* and *shang* respectively) or of both.

11. 研墨 *yén² mo⁴*, to rub ink on the *yên⁴-t'ai*, or ink-stone.

12. 蘸 *chan⁴*, to dip, as a pen in the ink, bread in sauce, etc.

13. 禿頭兒的詩; *lit.*, bald-headed poetry, *i.e.*, without a heading (題目) or a name (欵).

CHAPTER XXVII.

1. Home went Hung Niang accordingly, and presented the peaches to Ying Ying; as to the fan, she thought to herself it would not be so well to give it to her mistress direct, so she laid it on the table, as it were inadvertently,[1] and stepped aside without making any remark.

2. Ying Ying's eye caught sight of it, and taking it up she immediately exclaimed, "Where did this fan come from? who wrote what is on it? I don't recognise the handwriting;[2] ah! no doubt it's the graduate Chang's; now why should he choose deliberately to show his contempt for me in this way? of course, it's in consequence of something you said to him yesterday without my knowledge; a servant girl like you! and you weren't afraid that it would be discovered? we'll see what will become of you when I tell mamma.

3. "Now don't be angry, whatever you do, miss," replied Hung Niang, with all haste; "I am not the one to be blamed for what has happened, and I should never have ventured to suggest it; and if your mamma were to ask me how it came about, should I ever have the courage to say that I was sent to the graduate with a present from you, miss?"

4. This embarrassed Ying Ying, and finding it as much out of order to be indulgent as to be severe, she asked the girl, "Is the gentleman any better?"

5. "He is not very well," said Hung Niang; "and one might just as well hold one's tongue as recommend him to take medicine; then, again, if one asks him if there is anything that would be certain to put him to rights, he won't say a word."

6. Ying Ying pondered[3] what she heard, and turned it over in her mind ever so long without being able to speak; at last, with some show of shame, she came out with her idea, "I have a note here ready written," said she; "you take it to him immediately."

7. Such capriciousness as this there was no keeping in hand, and a smile involuntarily escaped Hung Niang as she observed it.

8. "Oh! miss," she cried, "but don't you think that it may perhaps upset him? wouldn't the sight of the note be sure to make him worse?"

9. Her words added to Ying Ying's confusion, and then from being displeased she became angry, and, flying into a passion,[4] she flung the note on the ground.

10. Hung Niang just picked it up;[5] though she felt indignant, she held her peace; but as she thought it all over, she asked herself, "Why should she fly in a rage about everything with me when I always do every-

---

1. 搭趁著. See Chapter XVIII, Note 1.

2. 筆跡 *pi-chi*[2], handwriting: *chi*, a trace, a footmark; also written 迹 and 蹟.

3. 忖度 *ts'un*[3] *to*[2], to reflect, to consider: *to*, elsewhere *tu*[4], short for *to liang*, also to consider, to calculate, to estimate.

4. 賭氣子 *tu*[3] *ch'i-tzŭ*, to get into a rage: *tu*, to gamble, to wager; ? to stake one's passion against that of the person giving offence.

5. 檢 *chien*[3], here, to pick up.

thing she bids me?⁶ here am I fetching and carrying letters for them, slaving away; and have I been looking to get anything by it?"

11. She thought on in this way for a while, but as nothing suggested itself to her, she stifled her wrath, and went straight over to the graduate CHANG's side of the buildings.

12. Now the graduate was looking out for HUNG NIANG, and as she did not appear, he had been walking up and down⁷ his room, trying hard to hit upon some excuse⁸ for getting her to come; and to this end he had just desired CH'IN T'UNG to go to HUNG NIANG and ask her for a needle and thread to stitch the leaves of a book together, when she arrived with the note, communing with herself as she came along.

13. She handed the note to the graduate; he opened it, and at the first glance he perceived that, like his own message, it was a stanza of poetry; this he had to con some little time before he guessed its purport; yes, YING YING was very anxious for an interview with him! overjoyed at news that went so far beyond his expectations, he addressed himself to HUNG NIANG.

14. "By these verses," said he to her, "it is plain that I am given a rendezvous for this evening; you advise me now as to how to go to her; had I not better jump over the garden wall?"

15. "What?" exclaimed HUNG NIANG, with simulated indignation; "what manner of talk is this? what do you mean by making up idle stories like these out of your own head? if I don't tell my old mistress so much the better for you; give you an inch and you take an ell; you are never to be satisfied."

16. "Why should I lie at all?" rejoined the graduate; "it's the strict truth;⁹ there is not the slightest mistake about it."

17. "Well now," said HUNG NIANG to herself, "what is one to say to this? that the young lady should have been making an appointment on the sly, of all things in the world! this is singular; to go on as she did when she knew the graduate was ill, seeming not to care about it, and then to set about such a piece of business as this! who would have thought it? it certainly does beat anything one could have fancied.'¹ This cogitation ended, she took leave of the graduate and went home.

6. 低三兒下四的伺候他, to perform all the most menial offices for, to wait upon in a slavish manner. Cf. 低三兒下四的奉承人, to pay slavish court or adulation to.

7. 踱來踱去, walking backwards and forwards : *tu*⁴, properly *to*², to step, to tread, to walk.

8. 想個杈兒 *hsiang ko ch'a²-'rh*, looked for an opportunity or excuse: *ch'a*², properly *ch'a*⁴, a branch of a tree (樹杈子), or an unexpected incident. Cf. the following: 那件事昨兒說停當了,今兒個又出了杈兒了 (*ch'a*⁴).

9. 的確 *ti*² *ch'io*⁴, in plain truth, in very truth: *ti*¹, a bright spot (*see* Part III, 19), hence, evident, manifest, clear; note the change of tone; *ch'io*, here, an adverb, really, certainly, indeed.

CHAPTER XXVIII.

1. The graduate took out the verses again, and tried their meaning this way and that way, and the more he considered them the more they fitted in with the guess he had made; "Oh that the evening were come," thought he. And he went out to see where the sun was; it was just past noon; by-and-by it got lower down in the west; he turned round and listened to the clock, but it made no sound; what? it had stopped! He fell foul of CH'IN T'UNG; why had he not wound up[1] the clock? CH'IN T'UNG, duly responding, wound it up as fast as he could. Then after a bit came the twilight, and then, to the graduate's delight, the lamps were brought in, whereupon he went and took a good look over the wall; not a sign was there, however, of anyone on the other side, so he had to return to his room, and there he waited on until, just as they were setting the night watch, he fancied he heard the tinkling of a lady's ornaments;[2] he hurried to the wall, and mounting it once more, he saw at a glance that it was indeed YING YING coming that way; whereon he leaped lightly and deftly down into the garden.

2. "Who is that?" asked YING YING when she saw someone in the garden; then, looking well[3] at him and perceiving that it was the graduate himself, she began with much gravity,[4] "Don't be under any false impression about me, sir; my conduct is always above-board and straightforward; you had conferred a favour upon us, and it was for this reason only that, after much reflection, I felt indisposed to show mamma that fan; so, too, my sending HUNG NIANG to make inquiries about your illness these last few days was simply to satisfy my feelings on the same ground; but I have something else to say to you that I feared if I entrusted it to HUNG NIANG she might fail to convey to you with perfect correctness, so I thought it would be safest for me to submit the recommendation I have to make to you in person. What I take the liberty of observing is this: the present Emperor,[5] as everyone knows, has the examinations for degree[6] in the highest esteem:

---

[1] 上弦, to wind up, sc., a clock: hsien², the string of a bow or musical instrument; the character 絃 (see Part V, Lesson C, Note 2) is often used, but erroneously; shang, to make to ascend, hsien, the string or spring of the clock.

[2] 環珮 huan² p'ei⁴, rings and girdle ornaments; hence, women's jewellery.

[3] 子細 tzŭ³ hsi, attentively, minutely. The dictionaries give no explanation of this use of tzŭ, which is sometimes written 仔.

[4] 正顏厲色 chêng yen li⁴ sê, gravely; lit., with correct (properly adjusted) countenance and severe looks: li, properly, a whetstone; hence, severe, harsh, stern.

[5] 當今的老佛爺, the reigning Emperor; a phrase specially used by people about the Palace; fo yeh alone is perhaps more common.

[6] 科甲 k'ê¹ chia³: chia, the class, first, second, or third, in the k'ê, or examinations for the degree of chin-shih or chü-jên, the two highest degrees. 他是科甲出身, he commenced his official career as a graduate in one of the classes of the first or second degree; i.e., he obtained official employment in virtue of the literary degree he held; not by purchase or for military service.

'It is to the dashing warrior that the jewelled sword is given,' says the proverb; 'to the beauty, the pearl powder.'[7] You are a fine scholar; why don't you aspire to the highest prize?[8] and then, after obtaining it, if you were to make a successful career, you would be honoured by everybody; whereas if you continue, as at present, unavailable for any useful purpose, you'll be nothing more than any other private individual,[9] and people will set you down as a mediocre person of no energy."[10]

3. Having concluded this severe oration, she turned round and departed.

4. The graduate was just about to speak when it occurred to him that it would be as well not to provoke her while she was excited; so, indignant though he was, he kept his feelings to himself, and jumping over the wall as he had jumped over it before, he returned to his room.

5. The lady's explosion he felt to be intolerable; still, he could not tear himself away from *the place, and with difficulties besetting him turn which way he would*, as great in shoal water as in deep, it came to pass that his malady attacked him again with increased violence; and on the following day FA PÊN, hearing that the visitor who had been *so good to him was ill*, went straight to Madame TS'UI in great tribulation and informed her.

6. The old lady was as much concerned as FA PÊN when she heard it; she gave orders immediately that the doctor should be called in, and she sent HUNG NIANG to see what was the matter with the graduate.

7. "Do you feel any better now, sir?" asked HUNG NIANG when she came into his room. "Ah," said the graduate, "I have no experience of suffering of any sort or kind,[11] and yesterday I had a wrong done me that beats everything; the road to the grave, they say, is as much for the young as the old,[12] and I don't suppose that I shall recover."

8. It cut[13] HUNG NIANG to the heart to hear him talk in this way, but she forced a smile as she said, "No, no, it's not so bad as all that; keep your mind easy and take care of yourself; I have brought a dose which the

7. 寶劍贈與烈士，紅粉贈與佳人: *pao³ chien⁴*, the jewelled sword (*chien*, properly a two-edged sword), *tsêng⁴*, is presented, *yü³*, to, *lieh⁴ shih*, the dashing (*lit.*, blazing) warrior; red *fên³*, powder, is given to the pretty woman; *chia¹*, good, fair, of persons or things, but used only in rather classical phrases.

8. 獨占鰲頭: (why don't you *li*, set up, a *chih hsiang*, resolution in the direction of) *tu chan*, standing forth alone on the *ao² t'ou*, head of the *ao*; *ao* is a sea monster on whose head stands a representation of the divinity who is the patron of candidates for literary honours.

9. 丁 *ting*, an individual; originally, a nail or pin, but not so used.

10. 稀鬆平常, a mediocre individual: *hsi*, watery; *sung*, dishevelled, as hair.

11. 酸鹹苦辣 *suan hsien k'u la*, things sour, salt, bitter, and pungent or acrid; hence, the vicissitudes or troubles of life.

12. 黃泉路上無老少, the road to the grave is for the young as well as the old; there is no distinction of age amongst the travellers on the road to the yellow spring: *ch'üan²*, a spring, commonly called 泉眼. The grave is likened to a hollow in the yellow clay where the springs lie.

13. 割 *ko¹*, to cut, to gash.

young lady gave me for you; take it, and I'll be bound it will make you well directly."

9. While she was speaking the doctor arrived, and having duly examined the patient, he said, "The weather is unseasonable; a number of people are affected with vomiting and purging;[14] but this gentleman has something else the matter with him; his stomach is as hard as a stone, and the saliva is running out of his mouth;[15] this is symptomatic[17] of fever, aggravated by suppressed excitement."[16]

10. "The gentleman has got a cough too," cut in CH'IN T'UNG, who was standing by; "and what is a deal worse, this morning, when he was drinking some water, he threw it all out again[18] without being able to swallow it."

11. This irritated the graduate; "Who told you to be making nonsensical replies?" he asked; "don't speak till you are spoken to."

12. The doctor felt his pulse,[19] and taking out a packet of medicine, "There are two medicines in this," said he, "which must be mixed together[20] when taken; you will take one dose in the morning and another in the evening, and in the course of a day or two you will be sure to find that it has done you some good."

13. HUNG NIANG looked carefully at the medicines for a while, and then she asked the doctor, "Is that black paste medicine too?" "Pills, powders, and pastes,"[21] said the doctor, "are all medicine; the art of medicine is a profound[22] study, and not so easy to acquire."

14. He then took leave of the graduate CHANG: "I shall call again to-morrow or next day, sir, to see how you are,"[23] said he; and with these words he went his way.

14. 上吐下瀉, vomiting and purging: *hsieh*[4], to purge, purging.

15. 嘴裏流黏涎子: *nien*[2], thick, glutinous, as paste; *hsien*[2], properly *yen*[2], the saliva of a sick man or animal.

16. 夾氣傷寒, a cold (*shang han ping*, influenza), aggravated or increased (*chia*, to place between or insert; see Part III, 309) by *ch'i*, excitement.

17. 來派 *lai p'ai*, symptomatic; *p'ai*, the branch of a stream: the *p'ai*, branch or direction to which his illness will tend (*lai*, comes from), is influenza; in other words, he is sickening for a feverish cold.

18. 喝嗆了 *ho ch'iang*[1] *liao*, choked in drinking: *ch'iang*, to eject anything that has gone down the windpipe.

19. 侯脈 *hou*[4] (commonly *hao*[4]) *mo*[4], to feel the pulse. See also Part V, Lesson LII, Note 6.

20. 攙和著吃 *ch'an*[1] *ho cho*, mixed together.

21. 丸散膏丹 *wan*[2] *san*[3] *kao*[1] *tan*[1], pills, powders, paste (or plaster) and globules. There is apparently little difference between *wan* and *tan*.

22. 深奧 *shên ao*[4], profound: *ao*, retired, deep, mysterious.

23. It may be well to note that a Chinese doctor never tells his patient that he will call again, as this is a presumptive indication that the patient is going to get worse.

CHAPTER XXIX.

1. HUNG NIANG waited until the doctor had got a certain distance, and then in a low voice she said, "My old mistress and the young lady are greatly distressed about your illness, sir, and they have vowed a vow[1] that the day you recover they will sacrifice an ox to heaven."

2. "What's the use of slaying an ox?" said the graduate; "taking life won't benefit me, will it? on the reverse, I shall only be so much the worse off for it."

3. HUNG NIANG was a person of a kindly and sympathising disposition; instead of taking any notice[2] of the graduate's angry words, she set to work to attend on him, prepared a drink[3] for him and heated his medicine, and she told CH'IN T'UNG to make some gruel,[4] and to keep stirring it rather briskly so as not to let it burn.

4. The graduate was not comfortable; he felt an incessant tickling or itching[5] all over him, and it occurred to him that a bath would set him more at ease, so he desired CH'IN T'UNG to warm some water for him. There was a well in the court all handy, with a windlass[6] on the stage over the well; CH'IN T'UNG rushed along to draw some water out of it, but he made such headlong haste as he ran that he nearly came down,[7] and HUNG NIANG, noticing in what a careless fashion he was going on, called out in alarm:

5. "Be a little more careful, pray; the well is very deep indeed; if you slip you'll find it no joke, I can tell you." CH'IN T'UNG answered her hail with a cheery laugh, and having drawn the water, he put it on the fire to get hot.

6. While he was waiting for the water the graduate began to chat with HUNG NIANG; "What is the young lady doing at home?" he asked. The question amused HUNG NIANG, but she didn't show it:

7. "When I came away," said she, designedly misleading him, "the young lady was fishing.[8] There is a small hill in our flower garden, with springs under it in all

---

1. 許愿 hsü[3] yüan[4], vowed a vow: hsu, to promise; yüan (or 願), hopes, expectations. The phrase is elliptical; promised something in return for a fulfilment of hopes or desires.

2. 饒不理會, instead of taking any notice. Note this new use of jao[2], which is not, as in Part IV, Dialogue III, 22, to pardon, or as in Chapter V, Note 18, to do something for nothing; it is here used in the sense of to forbear: forbearing and not heeding him, she, on the contrary.

3. 煎湯, prepared a drink; not necessarily soup.

4. 粥 chou[1], properly chu[1], a sort of gruel or thick soup made from rice, millet, etc. For 煳, see Chapter VIII, Note 9.

5. 莿 撓 tz'ŭ[4] nao[2], a tickling or tingling sensation: tz'ŭ, a thorn or prickle; nao, to scratch. Emphasise tz'ŭ.

6. 轆轤 lu[4] lu[2], a windlass; the wooden apparatus for lowering the bucket which stands on the ching t'ai, or level surrounding the well's mouth. Emphasise the first lu.

7. 跌勼斗 tsai kên tou. See Part V, Lesson XXIV, Note 13. Note tsai[1], not tieh[1], as in Part V, Lesson LIV, Note 14. For chi hu, see Part V, Lesson LVI, Note 8.

8. 釣魚竿, a fishing-rod: tiao[4], a hook, to hook; tiao[4]-yü[2] kan[1], a hook-fish rod; tiao yü, to angle.

directions, and the water from these runs into a pond,⁹ which is up to one's chin, and full of fish of all sorts; when you get well, sir, they might ask you in there to take a walk."

8. The graduate made no remark, but he thought to himself that it was hard that, under the circumstances, YING YING should find any pleasure in fishing; how was it that when he was thinking so of her she should be taking no interest in him?

9. HUNG NIANG, seeing that he was muttering [10] his reflections to himself, had turned to go, when all of a sudden she gave a start, and cried out, "I had as near as possible forgotten that I had another note which the young lady told me to give you, sir; please make haste and read it."

10. This information at once changed the graduate's sorrow into joy, and promptly stretching out his hand for the letter he took it and broke it open: "What!" exclaimed he, as soon as he saw what was inside it, "another piece of verse!" He had to study it attentively, but at length its meaning flashed[11] upon him; "She is probably[12] coming this evening to see how I am," said he.

11. "The young lady coming to see how you are," said HUNG NIANG; "how comes it that she never said a word about it to me? I don't think that's possible."

12. "It's the truth as plain as can be," said the graduate; "and what I take to be the case is this, that as the old lady bound us to one another as brother and sister, she is most likely coming to satisfy a feeling of sisterly affection."

13. While they were still talking CH'IN T'UNG reported that the water was hot and the bath ready; on which HUNG NIANG took her leave and went home. The graduate had his bath, and felt so much the better for it that he thought he would take a turn, but just as he was going out he heard a rustling kind of sound,[13] and looking round he saw the cat[14] had caught a rat; this reminded him that there were a good many rats in the room, and lest they should frighten YING YING when she came, he gave orders to have all the rats' holes stopped up. Then, again, out in the court he found the ground all uneven,[15] so he told CH'IN T'UNG to get some earth and make it level.[16]

9. 池子 *ch'ih²*, a pool, a pond, a tank; *hua-'rh ch'ih-tzŭ*, a flower-bed.

10. 沉吟 *ch'ên² yin²*, muttering, murmuring: *ch'ên*, to sink, hence deep down; *yin*, to hum or recite, as poetry.

11. 晃然大悟 *huang³ jan*, in a flash as it were, *ta wu⁴*, greatly comprehended it.

12. 光景是, the probabilities are, the circumstances point to.

13. 咧咧喳喳 *ch'i¹ ch'a¹*, two characters representing a scratching or rustling sound.

14. 貓 *mao¹*, a cat.

15. 坑坑窪窪, uneven, full of pits and depressions: *k'êng¹*, a pit; *wa¹*, a hollow.

16. 填平了, to make level by filling in, *sc.*, with earth: *t'ien²*, to fill in or up; *p'ing*, level.

CHAPTER XXX.

1. And there, quietly waiting for YING YING, for the time being we leave him, and discourse of HUNG NIANG, who, having returned to YING YING, informed her that though the graduate CHANG was taking medicine every day, he did not seem to improve, and that, according to the doctor, it was probably from something on his mind that he was ailing.

2. "Ah," said YING YING with a sigh, "I've thought the matter over a good deal, and I was going to visit him myself, but I feel greatly embarrassed about it?" "Really, miss," said HUNG NIANG, "there is nothing to be embarrassed about; when a person has saved all our lives, and you have engaged to honour him as your brother to boot, that you should pay him a visit now he's ill is but a proper satisfaction of affection that is due to him."

3. "Well, but," said YING YING, "though mamma did engage us to each other, it's true, as brother and sister, she watches every step I take, and if she came to learn that I had been to see how he was, there would be a nice piece of work, wouldn't there?" "So long as a thing isn't known to anybody dead or alive," said HUNG NIANG, "what is there to be afraid of? we've only got to work quietly."

4. This was quite YING YING'S view of the question,[1] and the same evening over she came to the graduate's quarters, attended by HUNG NIANG.

5. HUNG NIANG was a steady, respectable girl; so she left the young lady for the moment outside, while she went on a couple of paces by herself, for propriety's sake, and stepped into the room softly, so that the sick man's nerves might not be agitated. She knew better, of course, than to be winking or making any signs with her lips; she merely beckoned to the graduate with her hand, and he, knowing by this that YING YING was come, hurried forward to receive her; as he advanced he presented his compliments to her, but instead of acknowledging his salutation, YING YING, blushing exceedingly as she entered the door, hung down her head and took a seat.

6. The graduate began the conversation: "When the indisposition[2] of your unintelligent brother's insignificant person became comparatively serious," said he, "he is greatly indebted to his worthy[3] sister for sending someone to wait upon him in all things so assiduously;[4] and that his worthy sister should now have been put to the farther trouble of visiting him in person does indeed distress him."

7. "Why make so much of such a trifle,"[5] said YING YING, concealing her bashfulness; "when that great trouble came upon

---

1. 可心, after her own heart; suited her wishes or feelings. Cf. 可口兒, suited to one's taste; or, of tea, etc., just the right temperature for drinking; 可腦袋的帽子, a cap that fits the head.

2. 恙 yang⁴, a complaint, an ailment; used only in polite conversation: 貴恙, your complaint; chien yang, mine.

3. 賢 hsien², worthy, virtuous; a polite form of address to men or women.

4. 慇懃, assiduously: yin¹, careful, anxious; ch'in², earnest, zealous.

5. 些須小事何足掛齒: hsieh hsü, a trifling and, hsiao shih, small matter, ho, how, tsu, sufficient, kua ch'ih, to hang upon the teeth (i.e., to speak about). The phrase is not colloquial, but represents the affected style of conversation often adopted by people of polite manners and education.

our house, had we not been rescued[6] by my brother's energy unaided, how should we have been alive this day? this visit from your humble sister, expose her though it may to scorn and suspicion,[7] is but paid as an imperfect satisfaction of the feelings she should entertain towards a brother."

8. And so they talked on, these two, their respect and love for each other increasing, until HUNG NIANG, who was by all the while, seeing that the night was far spent, and fearful lest they should be discovered, said to the young lady, "Do come home, miss, please; it's getting rather late." YING YING knew that she was right, so she made an effort and rose, and HUNG NIANG gave her her arm home.

9. The graduate accompanied her into the court, and there he remained standing until she was a long way off, gazing vacantly, while his thoughts were going up and down like buckets in a well: it was nearly dawn before he went back to his room.

10. From this time onward the pair met constantly; they became quite inseparable;[8] and the graduate continued to improve until by degrees he perfectly recovered his health.

6. 援 yüan², to lead by the hand or pull out: *chiu yüan*, elegantly, to rescue.
7. 不避嫌疑; *lit.*, not shrinking from (avoiding) scornful (depreciatory, hostile) suspicion.
8. 膠 *chiao¹*, gum or glue; the latter is commonly called 鰾 (*piao⁴*), fish glue.

CHAPTER XXXI.

1. And now let us return to TS'UI HUAN LANG; he was in reality the son of other parents, and had been adopted[1] by the TS'UI family. He made no headway at all; his one characteristic was an insatiable curiosity. How he came to get wind of our friends' doings[2] it is impossible to say; but he did, and off he went to the old lady and gave her all the particulars.

2. Madame TS'UI was astonished[3] beyond measure at what he told her: "No wonder," said she, "that your sister and her maid have been so mysterious[4] about everything they said and did these last few days; I felt sure that there must be some reason for it all; you go and call HUNG NIANG here this minute."

3. HUAN LANG went and called HUNG NIANG, with whom, as it happened, YING YING was sitting at work.[5] It made them both jump to hear Madame TS'UI's message, but YING YING gave the girl a look of which

1. 過繼: *chi⁴*, unbroken succession; hence, a line of succession; *kuo chi*, to cross over to a line of succession, *i.e.*, to be adopted into another family; *kuo chi êrh-tzŭ*, to adopt a son; *t'a shih kuo chi ti*, he is an adopted son.
2. 瞧出楞縫兒來; *lit.*, to discover corners and chinks: *lêng²-fêng-'rh*, something that breaks the evenness of respectable conduct; peccadilloes.
3. 詫異 *ch'a⁴ i⁴*, to be astonished: the original meaning of *ch'a* seems to be to boast or talk big; *i*, different, extraordinary.
4. 鬼鬼祟祟, mysterious; like demons and elfs in their movements and actions.
5. 做活計, to do needlework: *huo chi*, *lit.*, plans for living, *i.e.*, for gaining a livelihood; *tso huo*, to work at any manual calling.

[PART VI.—THE GRADUATE'S WOOING.]

she perfectly understood the meaning, and away she went with HUAN LANG to the old lady.

4. "What is this that you two have been doing all this time [6] without my knowledge?" she burst out, with a face full of wrath, as soon as she saw HUNG NIANG; "what do you mean, I ask you, by not telling me of the young lady's going to the graduate CHANG'S rooms?"

5. "I really don't understand, ma'am, what it is you are asking me about," answered HUNG NIANG; "your slave [7] has not so much as seen the graduate for some days past."

6. This reply made the old lady still more furious: "When you have been guilty of conduct so immoral, have you the face to deny [8] it as well? HUAN LANG has told me all about your goings back and forward by night [and I know it's all your fault]; if you hadn't acted as their go-between they would never have dared to do such things; you have shown no regard for the good repute of the family, and here is a fine scandal in consequence; who is the chief offender [9] if it isn't you?"

7. HUNG NIANG turned towards HUAN LANG and said to him in a low voice, "Now, young gentleman, ain't you just one of those people who have got a nostril more than is natural to breathe through? [10] what you see in your dreams you must come out with; you chatter a great deal too much, and it's all made up of such nonsense as one hears from old women." [11]

8. "What are you muttering [12] to him there," said the old lady; "isn't it on purpose to provoke me, this, when you know how bad my hearing is?"

9. "You know, ma'am," said HUNG NIANG, speaking louder, "that the ear isn't to be trusted like the eye; the child catches up a thing here and a thing there, [13] and no one ought to pay the slightest attention to anything he says."

10. The old lady looked very stern as she said, "It was your doing and no one's else; the child is telling nothing but the truth; he saw [14] what happened with his own eyes, and yet you have the audacity to persist in denying the charge, eh? Now, I tell you, any more of this obstinacy will just get you a beating."

11. HUNG NIANG was never to be taken aback, [15] and as soon as she heard this awful outburst of wrath, which she was absolutely

---

6. 這陣子, all this time. Note *chên*, a period of time, generally a short interval; not as in Part IV, Dialogue IV, Note 63, a rank or file.

7. 奴婢 *nu pei*¹, your slave: *pei*, properly *pi*⁴, an unmarried slave girl; *nu pei* is the feminine of *hsiao*³ *ti*.

8. 賴 *lai*⁴, to repudiate, to deny. See Part V, Lesson LIX, Note 3.

9. 罪魁 *tsui k'uei*², the chief offender, the head of the offence. See Part V, Lesson XXIV, Note 1.

10. 三鼻子眼兒多出口氣兒, a proverb indicative of a busybody or officious person. Note *sa*¹, not *san*.

11. 盡拉些個老婆舌頭, given to tittle-tattle; *lit.*, only [caring to] drag [from one place to another] old wives babble (*lit.*, tongues).

12. 喃嚷 *tu*¹ *nang*¹, to mutter: *nang*, or *nung*, to utter sounds the purport of which cannot be made out; *tu* is not to be found in the dictionaries.

13. 東拉西扯, catches up a thing here and there; *lit.*, pulls east and hauls west.

14. 睹 *tu*³, to observe, to see.

15. 權變 *ch'üan*² *pien*, shifts or expedients, specially of a temporary nature: *ch'üan*, here, temporary; *pien*, to change, to modify.

powerless to avert or to stop the way of,[16] she knew that concealment was out of the question, and with a propitiatory smile she at once replied:

12. "I have something to say, but it mightn't be proper to speak so plain; if your ladyship won't be hard on me, I'll make bold to tell you what it is."

13. "Anything you've got to say that's true," said Madame Ts'UI, "you may say, and I sha'n't be angry; but if you tell any more fibs, positively I'll show you no mercy."

14. "Well, I should say, ma'am," began HUNG NIANG, still smiling, "that it is you who have been to blame all along: in the first place, you took the young lady with you that day that you went to have the service read; now, wasn't that exposing her to the public gaze?[17] and didn't you bring down trouble and invite misfortune, for it was this way that SUN FEI-HU came to know what an attractive looking[18] young lady she is? and then, when he brought his people here to carry her off, it was you, ma'am, wasn't it, that promised to marry the young lady to anyone that would get us out of our difficulty. And later, when we were all delivered from our perils by the graduate CHANG, didn't you change your mind and make him and the young lady brother and sister instead? now, surely, that was kicking the plank away as soon as you were across the stream, wasn't it? who is to blame if your promise hasn't been kept?"

15. "Then I must say this: although their meetings have been private, your slave can answer for it that there was never anything dishonourable[19] about them; your slave was always present, and if anything improper has taken place, punish her, do, and welcome."

16. "And, besides, it is good that people should marry: one strand of silk don't make a cord, as they say; nor one tree a forest; and in this case there's a providence in it, and a natural affinity combined. When they are both so willing, ma'am, why should you go out of your way to make them disgusted? it's as if you couldn't tell red from blue or black from white; and as to being angry with me, surely there is still less sense in that. One word for all; if I may make so free, I should say, while you keep one eye open, let the other eye be shut (don't take too much notice of what has happened)."

---

16. 塞 *sai*⁴, to stop up, as a hole: *sai-tzŭ*, a cork; *sai shang*, to cork up; *t'ang*², to ward off.

17. 拋頭露面 *p'ao*¹ *t'ou lu*⁴ (or *lou*) *mien*, of a woman, to exhibit herself to the world: *p'ao*, to cast, to throw; *lu* or *lou*, as a verb, to become manifest, to allow to be seen. A Chinese woman showing herself unnecessarily is said to throw her head [at the public], to disclose her countenance.

18. 標緻 *piao*¹ *chih*⁴, good looks, attractiveness: *piao*, amongst other meanings, to exhibit; *chih*, delicate, fine; *piao chih*, lit., exhibition of fineness; the expression generally refers to beauty of a refined and delicate sort.

19. 劣跡 *lieh*⁴ *chi*²; lit., discreditable traces.

CHAPTER XXXII.

1. After an interval of meditation, the old lady seemed as if she had been wakened up from a dream by what she had heard, and she sent off HUNG NIANG at once to call YING YING.

2. "What did mamma want with you?" asked YING YING, as soon as HUNG NIANG came in with the message. "We may just as well say no more about that," said HUNG NIANG; "my lady knows all that we have been doing so quietly."

3. "How came she to know?" asked YING YING in a great fright.

4. "Oh! for that matter," said HUNG NIANG, "there's but one way of keeping a thing from people, and that is not to do it; just think, miss, with HUAN LANG in the house, it would be a pity if the thing didn't get out, wouldn't it?"

5. YING YING was dreadfully agitated; "What is one to do then?" she asked hurriedly.

6. "Well, it doesn't signify now, miss," said HUNG NIANG; "all you have to do is to go to your mamma as she desires; she was angry at first, but after I had talked to her a bit she became quite cool[1] again, and now there is nothing whatever to be alarmed about."

7. YING YING stood up, and with fear and trembling she worked herself along, a step at a time, over to where the old lady was; but as soon as she saw her, without being able to help herself, she hung down her head and burst into tears; the fact was that, taken up as she was by the injustice[2] that had been done her, she could not bring herself to speak of it.

8. Old Madame Ts'UI had a tender[3] heart, and her face showed it; when she saw YING YING in this predicament, she felt such love and pity for her that, instead of saying anything harsh, she looked at her mildly and pleasantly, and did her best to soothe her:

9. "Don't cry, my child," said she; "it was all your mother's own fault; there now, don't vex yourself any more; let me try and see what can be done;[4] we shall hit on some plan that will work, you may be sure."

10. YING YING was delighted to see the sky that had been so overcast all clear again; with a single sound of acquiescence hurriedly uttered, she dried her tears, and taking leave of her mother, returned to her work-room.

11. Now, it was all very well for the old lady to comfort her daughter by talking in this way, but as a fact she felt it to be next to impossible to make any arrangement;[5] that earlier[6] engagement perplexed[7] her so that she could take no line one way or another.

---

1. 消 *hsiao*[1], to melt, to thaw, to disappear, to cause to disappear.

2. 委曲 *wei*[3] *ch'ü*[1], a wrong, an injustice; also, to do an injustice to: *wei*, here, to bear, to sustain; *ch'ü*, crooked, wrong, to wrong.

3. 慈 *tz'ŭ*[2], kind, as a mother to her offspring.

4. 思索, to reflect, to ponder: *so*, here, to search or look into.

5. 佈置 *pu chih*, to make arrangements, to put in place: *pu* is identical with 布, to distribute; *chih*[2] (not *chih*[4], as in Part V, Lesson XVII, Note 14), to establish, to place, to arrange.

6. 業已. *See* Part III, 634.

7. 躊躇 *ch'ou*[2] *ch'u*[2], perplexed, embarrassed, undecided; both characters have much the same meaning.

12. But for singular coincidences, however, no novel could ever be written; and the very next day she received a letter from her own brother, which on opening it she found, after the merely formal inquiries about health[8] and so on at the beginning, to be devoted to an account of her nephew CHÊNG HÊNG's finale.

8. 寒暄 *han² hsüan¹*, cold and warm: *hsüan*, the warmth of the sun's rays. The two characters in combination are used to indicate the formal inquiries in a letter after the health of the person addressed.

CHAPTER XXXIII.

1. The loss of his rice had left the fellow as destitute as he had been before he got it; there was no way open to him; he could no more go up to the sky than he could find a door into the earth. "Emergency," says the proverb, "will make a man climb to the house-top, or a dog leap a wall;" and one day he said to himself, "If I don't turn thief, I don't see how I am to live."

2. Accordingly, the same night he went out, sneaking stealthily along under the walls, and he had not gone a great distance before he came upon a gang of men; they looked at him, and although they saw that he was not an acquaintance, they surmised that he was in the same line as themselves, and they made him one of the company; from this time forth, lying *perdu*[1] by day and stirring at night, he did contrive to keep himself in meat and drink. And how should he remember that good luck will not last for ever; that in life no future is to be trusted save that of the scholar, the husbandman, the artificer, or the merchant; that no one certainly who plays the thief will have a long career? The gang committed themselves one day, and being carried, CHÊNG HÊNG and the rest, before the magistrate, were found guilty and sentenced, every one of them, to be tattooed and banished to a penal settlement;[2] they set out for their destination in charge of an escort,[4] every convict in chains;[3] but CHÊNG HÊNG's constitution was a feeble one, and before they reached the second halting place,[5] his strength failed him and he died from exhaustion.[6]

3. When she had perused the letter, Madame TS'UI could not help feeling distressed for a while; for, however worthless the fellow who had come to such grief, she remembered that he was none the less her own nephew; after a certain time, however, it was borne in upon her that in the midst of this misfortune there was, on the other part, the best of good fortune, so far as her daughter's union with the graduate CHANG was concerned; it was the very thing that was required, and without loss of time she sent to request the graduate's attendance.

1. 伏 *fu²*, to lie *perdu*; *lit.*, to prostrate oneself.
2. 充軍 *ch'ung chün¹*, to undergo penal servitude in a penal settlement; *lit.*, to serve as a soldier, but only applied to the enforced military service of penal offenders in distant garrisons, who are tattooed on the arms or face, as the case may be.
3. 鐐銬 *liao⁴ k'ao⁴*, fetters: *liao*, manacles, commonly called 手鐲; *k'ao*, a fetter for the feet, commonly called 脚鐐; the latter character is not recognised by the dictionaries.
4. 起解 *chieh⁴*, to forward, to conduct, to transmit: *chieh³*, to loosen, as a girdle; to dissipate, as melancholy.
5. 站 *chan⁴*, here, a stage in a journey.
6. 拖累死了, died from the fatigue or exhaustion he had to undergo: *t'o¹*, *lit.*, to drag behind one; *lei*, fatigue, hardship.

CHAPTER XXXIV.

1. The graduate was reading in his room; when he was told that Madame Ts'ui begged him to come to her, he did not know what to make of it; and, having likewise an unquiet conscience,[1] he was alarmed lest the proceedings of the last few days should have been brought to light.

2. He hastened over to the old lady, and as soon as they met and he had asked after her health, she began as follows:

3. "Chang hsiang-kung, it is quite true that I did say some time ago that I would give you my daughter, and the reason why the arrangement did not take place immediately was this, that in our house there has never been a son-in-law before that was no more than a simple graduate; they have all been doctors of the *Han-lin*[2] at the very least; if you were to succeed in getting a *Han-lin* degree, well, it would add something to the credit of our family."[3]

4. "Since my mother-in-law[4] so orders it," replied the graduate, "her humble son-in-law is of course bound to exert himself to carry out her wishes; the matter admits of no delay, and I shall start for the capital tomorrow morning." This said, he saluted her, and she him, and they separated.

5. In the evening Ying Ying, attended by Hung Niang, came over to pay him a farewell visit. Hung Niang stepped forward to lend a hand to help Ch'in T'ung to pack up, folding and smoothing out[5] the things, and laying them in the box; but there was a bundle that evidently could not be got into the box; in her opinion it wanted tightening up; so she told Ch'in T'ung to press it and make it a little more compact.

6. A large vessel of wine stood in one corner[6] of the room; Hung Niang told Ch'in T'ung to pour out half of its contents ready for drinking, and to put the other half into a smaller vessel, and to close its mouth well, and pack it in the trunk.

7. Then she noticed a pair of new shoes on the footstool by the bedside that Ch'in T'ung said were too small and might hurt when they were worn; so she went to get them stretched on the trees.[7] While she was away Ying Ying asked the graduate if he wouldn't like some biscuits; "There are some of every kind here," said she, "and after all they will be better than nothing when you come to one of those places where there is neither a village in one direction nor an inn in the other."

---

1. 懷著鬼胎, possessing an unquiet conscience: *t'ai*[1], properly, a fetus; *huai t'ai*, to be with young.

2. 翰林: *han*[4], a pencil; *Han-lin*, the Imperial College of Literature, or great Literary Academy of China.

3. 壯門風 *chuang*[4] *mên fêng*, add to the credit of the family: *chuang*, strong, robust (*see* Part IV, Dialogue VI, 36); hence, to strengthen; for *fêng, see* Part III, 878, Obs.

4. 岳母 *yo*[4]-*mu*, a mother-in-law; commonly called 丈母娘. *Yo-fu*, a father-in-law; commonly called 丈人.

5. 疊舒展了, folded and smoothed out (the things): *tieh,* see Part III, 686; *shu,* see Part III, 825.

6. 觭角兒 *chi*[1] *chiao*[3]-*'rh*, a corner: *chiao*, a corner, a point, an angle; *chi*, properly, a horn; also, single, solitary.

7. 楦頭 *hsüan*[4]-*t'ou*, boot-trees or lasts; *hsüan shang*, to place on trees; *hsüan* is, properly, anything put in to fill up a space.

8. The graduate thanked her; "Certainly," said he; "it was really very kind of you to think of it;" and he put a few into his luncheon-box.⁸

9. The man now brought the shoes back; and CH'IN T'UNG, observing that the box would have to be corded tighter, said to HUNG NIANG, "Will you please help me to bind this rope⁹ more tightly round, miss? we'll make a slip-knot,¹⁰ as it is untied more easily."

10. HUNG NIANG lent a hand, and between them they made it quite safe; and the graduate CHANG apologised for giving her so much trouble. And now, the things being all packed, YING YING asked the graduate how long he would be absent.

11. "I shall return the moment the examinations are over," said he; "how should one defer a thing that is all one could wish it?"

12. And so the two went on, the greater part of the night, about how sad it was to part and how pleasant it would be to meet again;¹¹ the same words over and over thousands of times, and yet they had not said all they had to say; as the poet says, "Of the world's myriad sorrows there is none like parting, whether in life or in death."

8. 盒子 *ho-tzŭ* or *ho-'rh*, a box with a cover, the two halves of which should, strictly speaking, be the same size.

9. 繩子 *shêng²*, a rope or cord, large or small.

10. 繫活扣兒 *chi huo k'ou⁴-'rh*, to tie a slip-knot: *chi*, see Part V, Lesson XXXIII, Note 7; *k'ou*, not to strike, as in Part IV, Dialogue VI, Note 9, but to buckle, to loop, to knot. *K'ou-'rh* is a knot made by tying two ends together; a knot in a single piece of cord, *e.g.*, a whip-lash, is *ko¹ ta¹* (疙瘩); see Part V, Lesson LXXIII, Note 5.

11. 悲歡離合: *pei¹*, the sadness or mournfulness, *li*, of separation, *huan*, the joy, *ho*, of union.

CHAPTER XXXV.

1. The moment the sun was up the following morning CH'IN T'UNG and the rest, with much confusion and bustle, shifted the baggage into the carts; the graduate got in, and they set off. Three light chairs were in readiness on Madame TS'UI's side of the house, and she now came over with YING YING and HUNG NIANG, and the three of them accompanied the graduate some miles on his way, until they came to a place by the river-side where there were vessels lying along the bank; here they all got out of their respective conveyances, and the old lady, addressing the graduate, "Take good care of yourself on the journey, sir," said she, "and may no harm befall you by land¹ or by water."

2. This speech ended,² she was for going on board with YING YING to see him off, but as neither lady was sufficiently strong on her legs to be able to walk alone, HUNG

1. 陸 *lu⁴*, dry land as opposed to water.

2. 畢 *pi⁴*, to finish, to bring to an end.

CHAP. XXXV.] PART VI.—THE GRADUATE'S WOOING. 409

NIANG had to hold them up,³ first one and then the other, by the arm, and in this way the mother and daughter contrived with some difficulty to cross into the vessel by the gangboard.

3. Some of the vessels had anchors⁴ down, some were made fast by ropes⁵ to the shore; the vessel the graduate chartered was a boat with a large stern sweep⁶ and three very tall masts.⁷

4. When the party got on board they found there was a tolerably large crew; the steersman⁹ was sitting abaft,⁸ and a number of trackers were squatting¹⁰ forward.

5. The graduate desired some of the crew to help CH'IN T'UNG with the baggage; one-half to be put in the cabin,¹¹ handy for use, and the other half, being things not constantly required, to be lowered¹² into the hold.

6. The two ladies remained seated a little while, and then the graduate asked how soon the vessel would start. "We shall get under way as soon as ever your things are all right, sir," answered the ship's people. When YING YING heard this she began to cry; "My lord must take special care of himself when he gets to the capital," said she, "in his eating and drinking, at all times and seasons; and he must not be thinking too much of what may be going on elsewhere."

7. To this expression of sympathetic¹³ interest on her part the graduate replied with like words of good counsel: "Pray be at ease about me," said he; "I shall take good care of myself in every way, you may be sure; and I needn't impress on you, my sister, that you too, living here at home, ought to be equally careful of your own health."

8. This said they parted, both in tears. YING YING, and HUNG NIANG with her, followed the old lady ashore, and they all returned in their chairs. On reaching home the young lady and her maid went to their room, after making the old lady comfortable; there YING YING's tears still continued to fall without ceasing, and she said, "Now that he's gone I cannot help thinking of him; it's such a length of time to be looking forward to; what is to be done?"

9. "You must not take on so, miss," said HUNG NIANG; "everything is hard at first; it will be all right after a few days."

3. 攙 *ch'an¹*, to support. *See also* Chapter XXVIII, Note 20.
4. 錨 *mao²*, an anchor; *ch'i³ mao*, to raise anchor.
5. 纜 *lan⁴*, a hawser.
6. 艪 *lu³*, a long oar worked over the stern or over the quarter.
7. 桅杆 *wei² kan¹*, a mast; also called *wei* simply.
8. 艄 *shao⁴*, the stern of a ship or boat.
9. 柁工 *to⁴ kung*, a steersman: *to*, the helm or rudder.
10. 蹲 *tun¹*, properly *tsun¹*, to squat on the heels.
11. 艙 *ts'ang¹*, the hold or cabin of a vessel.
12. 繫 *hsi⁴* (note the change of sound), to lower with a rope attached.
13. 關切 sympathy, sympathetic: *kuan*, to affect; *ch'ieh*, here, an intensive.

CHAPTER XXXVI.

1. And here, leaving YING YING at home, passing her days as if each was a year long, let us follow the graduate CHANG, who was seated on the vessel gazing with CH'IN T'UNG at the fine view along shore.

2. "When shall you anchor?" asked the graduate of the crew. "We shall anchor[1] rather early to-night," they said; "there is a whirlpool[2] in the stream some way on ahead, and as it's blowing very fresh, we must look out a little; Ts'ao Ch'iao is a good place to anchor."

3. While they were speaking the vessel arrived at Ts'ao Ch'iao, where a hawser was passed round a post[3] on the shore, and the anchor was let go. As evening drew near, the graduate had his dinner, and shortly after he turned in.

4. He was not quite asleep, just beginning to be unconscious, when, all of a sudden, he saw YING YING coming in; "It was so hot all day," said she, "that I couldn't get along as fast as I wanted, and though I tried hard to catch you up, I didn't succeed; then when I was about half-way here, there came on such a storm[4] of wind and rain that though I had an umbrella[5] up, I was wet through and through, and with the mud up to one's instep it is very bad walking indeed; the rain doesn't stop either, and what am I to do?"

5. The graduate sprang out of bed, and a single glance showed him that the cabin was indeed well wet; he himself was splashed[6] all over from head to foot; however, he could see nothing for it but to wait till the sun came out, and he was in the act of spreading out YING YING's clothes on the grass to dry, when a host of people came up making a prodigious uproar; the graduate was just going to tell them that he would not have such a noise, when he woke up with a start; it was only one of those dreams of the *Nan K'o*[7] after all. With a loud "ah!" he got on his feet, and stepping outside, he found that it was broad daylight.

6. Two days later, as he was gazing at the land for want of something better to do, a range of high hills suddenly presented itself, and the vessel came alongside a busy place of trade;[8] here a number of people, all talking

---

1. 站船 *chan³ ch'uan*, to anchor, to come to a stop. Note the tone of *chan*. The expression is probably peculiar to the North.

2. 漩窩 *hsüan⁴ wo¹*, a whirlpool; the first word meaning the whirling of water, the second a nest or lair of birds, beasts, or reptiles.

3. 椿子 *chuang¹*, a post or stake driven into the ground.

4. 暴 *pao⁴*, violent, tempestuous. *See* Part III, 529.

5. 傘 *san³*, an umbrella: *ta san*, to put an umbrella up.

6. 濺 *chien⁴*, to splash; the rebound upwards of water falling on the ground, etc.

7. 南柯一夢 *nan k'o¹ i mêng*, a dream, the "baseless fabric of a vision;" for an explanation of this quotation, *see* MAYERS' "Chinese Reader's Manual," p. 159, No. 513.

8. 馬頭, a place of trade; also, a wharf, a landing-place, a jetty. The origin of the term appears to be unknown.

at the same time, were carrying large cases on shore, which, to the graduate's eye, looked as if they contained foreign wares that were contraband; still, to judge from the covers of the cases, they did not seem to have been packed abroad, and this made him suspect that the goods in them were no doubt being smuggled from other provinces; he sighed as he said to himself, "It's evident that smuggling is not confined to the foreigner, our own people here in China are quite as sure to engage in it;[9] but in that case, when we complain so of others, are we not forgetting to look at home?"

7. While this was in his thoughts he suddenly observed at a certain distance in shore a number of singular looking people. As they came nearer the graduate heard them talking, but he could not understand what they said, and he asked CH'IN T'UNG, "What language are they speaking? they are dressed exactly like circus riders."[10]

8. "They are foreigners," said CH'IN T'UNG; and while he and his master were still gazing at them, one of the party came on board, made his bow to the graduate CHANG, and inquired after his health in Chinese. The graduate responded in due form, and the other then went on, "I have learned to speak your language a little, sir, but I regret to say that I don't understand the written character at all; I have a piece of writing here that I am going to ask you to tell me the meaning of, if you will be so good."

9. The graduate hastened to take the paper from him, and explained it all to him very carefully, sentence by sentence. The man thanked him for his trouble, and after some farther conversation he asked what characters those were that appear upon the copper currency of China?

10. "The Chinese characters on the one face of the cash," said the graduate, "are the style of the reign; those on the other face are seal characters, and these I do not understand very well myself."

11. As they talked on in this fashion of one thing or another, the man asked to have another thing explained to him:

12. "They said just now," said he, "that there were $t'u$[11] hu here; what is the business of a $t'u$ hu?"

13. "Properly," said the graduate, "the two words mean a man who kills pigs or sheep, but in common parlance anyone that sells meat is called a $t'u$ hu."

14. The man thanked him for the information and took his leave, and a few minutes after he sent over a basket[12] of eggs as a present. The graduate told CH'IN T'UNG to take out the eggs, to hand back the basket to the bearer, and to give him two hundred cash, and tell him to return with his, the graduate's, thanks to the donor.

15. The messenger departed, and the vessel got under way again, and they held on, sailing or tracking according to circumstances.

16. They were no great way from their second port when there appeared another

---

9. 在所不免; *lit.*, are among so, those which, cannot avoid [doing likewise].

10. 跑獬馬的打扮兒: *ta pan*, the dress of, *p'ao hsieh*[4] *ma ti*, circus riders; *hsieh*, a fabulous animal of the unicorn kind, supposed to be very fleet; mountebanks in a circus are said to be *p'ao hsieh ma ti* or *p'ao ma hsieh*, unicorn runners or riders.

11. 屠 $t'u^2$; *see* context.

12. 筐子: $k'uang^1$, an open basket with a handle.

batch of foreigners on the shore, with guns on their shoulders,¹³ as if they were going out shooting. "What are they after?" asked the graduate with some surprise of the ship's people. "There are musk deer and all other kinds of deer¹⁴ on the hills" was the answer; "this is an open port,¹⁵ and there are a number of foreign firms here, and whenever they can get away from their business the merchants go up the hills to shoot; people say that there are large bears¹⁶ in the woods up there, and tigers and leopards too."

13. 扛 k'ang², to carry on the shoulder.

14. 麇麕野鹿: chang¹, the musk deer; p'ao², the roe-buck; yeh lu, any and every kind of deer.

15. 通商口子, an open port, a port for commercial intercourse (t'ung shang); the term applied to the Treaty ports of China, where there is t'ung, through or direct, commerce between foreigners and Chinese. The reader will forgive the anachronism of Treaty ports in the T'ang dynasty.

16. 熊 hsiung², a bear.

CHAPTER XXXVII.

1. In the midst of this chat the skipper sang out, "Look out sharp, here's a ram's horn¹ upon us, if I don't mistake;" and in a moment the water in the river was being whirled round and round, and a regular cyclone was blowing, sure enough. The sails filled full with the wind, and the vessel was in great danger, she heeled over so; while the crew were all rushing here and bawling there as they let everything fly to bring the sails down; fortunately, the squall lasted but a few minutes, and as soon as it was over, all hands were laughing and talking again as usual, except the graduate CHANG, who sighed sadly to himself:

2. "This bodes no good, I fear; YING YING is dead, that's what it means; and her spirit is come after me."

3. CH'IN T'UNG divined what was passing in his master's mind, and he hit most happily upon the right thing to say to comfort him: "Don't let it distress you, sir," said he; "Heaven looks after the good man; in his case, as the saying is, bad fortune will be turned to good, and if trouble come across him, he'll prosper all the same; what does a puff of wind like that signify? And so no more on this subject."

4. When the vessel came to its destination, master and servant disembarked and travelled by cart several days, halting always at night, until they reached Peking.

5. As they came within the walls of the capital they heard a din of people's voices in the streets; there was a fire² in the great street leading to the Ch'ien Mên, and think-

1. 羊角風, a whirlwind, so called from its spiral movement; 颴 hsüan⁴, just below, is also applied to the spiral movement of wind.

2. 走了水, a euphemism for a conflagration, which is too great a disaster to be spoken of directly.

ing it likely that the inns in the outer city might object to receive strangers in consequence, they looked out for a place in the city proper, and put up at a temple.

6. There was an old schoolmaster next door who was also a Hsi-lo man, and had in fact been on the most intimate terms with the graduate CHANG; he well remembered their old friendship, and as soon as he learned that the graduate was in Peking and residing in the temple, of course he felt bound to pay him a visit; so says he to his pupils, "I am going to call on a friend, but I sha'n't be away long, and see that you know your lessons thoroughly by the time I come back; if you can't say them off, look out."

7. One of the pupils, a little fellow, who was a great pet of the schoolmaster's, wanted to go with him; "You'll let me go too, sir, won't you, please?" said he. "Well," said the schoolmaster, "You may; but mind I'm not going to allow any skylarking."[3] Which said, he and his pupil went round to the temple.

8. CH'IN T'UNG having announced the visit to his master, the graduate, as soon as he saw his old acquaintance, came forward and gave him a hearty welcome. "It's years since we met," said he; "is all going on well with you?" "Thanks to your well-doing, it is, sir," said the old teacher; "and is it equally well in the mansion of my elder brother?"

9. The conversation continued in this strain of compliment, the speaker always depreciating himself, until the old teacher observed, "I remember that in years gone by[4] my brother was a considerable scholar;[5] during the long interval that has separated us from each other, he is no doubt still more proficient; could he favour me with the sight of a specimen of his composition?"

10. It did so happen that the verses YING YING had sent by HUNG NIANG that time were lying on the table, and the old teacher, observing a paper with writing upon it, without thinking much of the matter, took it up in his hand[6] to read it; but his eyesight was not strong enough, the characters were so fine, no bigger than a fly's[7] head; so said he, "This room is rather dark, and my eyes are so dim that I fear I shall not be able to make this out; may I be allowed to open the window?"

11. The graduate propped open the window for him; he read the verses, and when he had finished them, his whole countenance beamed with delight; he praised them without ceasing; he read them over again and again; so pleased was he with them that he could not bring himself to let them out of[8] his hand; at last his eyes were so dazzled with the glare of the sun that he could not open them, and the window had to be shut again.

3. 淘氣 *t'ao² ch'i*, playful, skittish, mischievous : *t'ao*, here, to fidget, to play.

4. 昔年 *hsi² nien*, in years gone by : *hsi*, formerly, anciently, old.

5. 文才茂富, your literary talent was *mao⁴*, flourishing, or highly developed, and *fu⁴*, abundant.

6. 一手拏過來, took them up nonchalantly : *i shou*, short for *i shên shou*, a stretch out of the hand, implying that the act was casual and not done with set purpose.

7. 蠅 *ying²*, a fly ; commonly called *ts'ang¹ ying* (蒼蠅).

8. 釋 *shih⁴*, to free, to let go, to unloose.

12. "Seeing that the credit of the verses belongs to YING YING," thought the graduate to himself, "I feel quite ashamed at accepting the praise I am receiving;" he was just going to change the subject when the old fellow began a rambling discourse the sum of which was that the best thing a man could do was to give up all else and become a priest of Buddha. Talk of this kind suited the graduate even less[9] than his compliments; he forced out a few words in reply because he could not help himself, but only such as belonged to the part he was performing, that is, of a friend treating another friend with civility.[10]

13. They sat on together ever so long, the conversation never flagging, until the graduate began to lose all patience;[11] he had begun to think the man never would go. At last the old teacher took his leave; "I must go home now," said he; "I am wanted to-day at the house of one of my pupil's friends; but I shall wait upon you again some other time."

14. The graduate, much relieved, was accompanying him out, but as they came into the court, up rushed the little pupil in great grief:

15. "I've been stung by a wasp on the elbow," he bawled out, "and it's all swollen, and hurts dreadfully."

16. This brought the teacher down upon him[12] sharp; "Who told you to go tearing about this place as if you were mad?"[13] said he; "you never can keep quiet when one takes you anywhere; another time you'll just have to be left in the school-room." Which rebuke administered, they went their way.

9. 不投機 *pu t'ou² chi*, did not hit the mark, was beside the question; lit., [the talk] did not *t'ou*, when thrown, [hit] *chi*, the spring: *t'ou* (see Chapter VII, Note 12), used figuratively of tendering, making to be seen, allegiance, enmity, and much more.

10. 逢塲做戲應酬朋友罷咧. Construe thus: meeting an occasion to indulge in the amusement, he showed a kindness to his friend and that was all. *Fêng*, to meet; *ch'ang²*, properly an arena, the place where various things may be done; hence, the doing of those things, the occasion of their being done; *hsi⁴*, properly, to perform a play; *tso hsi*, to do anything that amuses; *t'ing¹ hsi*, to go to the play; 戲館子, a theatre; for *ying ch'ou*, see Part IV, Dialogue X, Note 1, Obs. 4.

11. 急躁 *chi² tsao⁴*, impetuous, impatient: *tsao*, hasty, to hurry.

12. 埋怨 *man yüan*, to grumble, to reproach, to rebuke mildly. Note *man²*, not *mai²*, as in Part V Lesson LXXV, Note 7.

13. 瘋跑 *fêng¹ p'ao*, running about like a lunatic: *fêng-tzŭ*, a lunatic; *fêng liao*, has gone mad, or is mad.

CHAPTER XXXVIII.

1. When they had got some distance from the gate, CH'IN T'UNG asked his master who the old man of letters¹ was? "Ah," said the graduate with a sigh, "that gentleman is a fellow-townsman of mine, a good deal my senior; in his earlier years he was reputed a man of promise, but he is old now, and he has run down² sadly; just like every other created thing, as time goes on;³ nothing escapes."

2. "Run down," said CH'IN T'UNG contemptuously, "that he is indeed; why, there's no more relish in that talk of his than in beancurd made out of plain water."

3. The lad would soon have been pulled up⁵ for his unmannerly⁴ speech on any ordinary occasion, but at the present moment the graduate was so full of sad thoughts that he paid no attention to it; and without going in-doors again, he went off to take a turn.

4. The streets were as busy as they could be with buyers and sellers moving in all directions; of the latter there were vendors of thread, inviting custom by shaking their bells;⁶ itinerant packmen, sounding their drums; men with articles in baskets slung under their arms;⁷ dealers of every sort and kind. The graduate walked on to a place where two streets crossed each other, and here the sight of some druggists' shops reminding him of his old complaint, he stepped into one and asked if they had any *ch'ang-shan?* the people in the shop said they had not; then he tried another shop, and then another; but there was none to be had; and after wasting ever so much time in inquiring here and there, he cursed them in his heart for a useless lot, and went back to his temple to rest himself.

---

1. 學究 *hsio chiu*, a man of letters; one who *chiu*, investigates, searches into (*see* Part IV, Dialogue X, Note 2, Obs. 3), objects of study.

2. 衰邁 *shuai¹ mai⁴*, run down, played out: *shuai*, decayed, worn out (*see* Part III, 600); *mai*, to wax old, to go beyond [the time of vigour], to lapse into senility.

3. 循環 *hsün² huan²*, to revolve in an orb, the revolution of time: *hsun*, to revolve; *huan*, to encircle, to go round.

4. 鹵莽 *lu³ mang³*, unmannerly, boorish: *lu*, properly, barren land impregnated with nitre; *mang*, jungle, thick grass; hence, synonymous of uncultivated manners.

5. 挨上說了, would have come in for a reprimand. *See* Part IV, Dialogue III, 56.

6. 搖鈴兒 *yao² ling²-'rh*, shaking bells: *ling*, a small bell; here, specially of one of those small plates of brass with knotted cords attached to it which the pedlar sounds by turning his wrist; a small bell is commonly called 鈴鐺 (*tang¹*). The drum mentioned below is also sounded by a turn of the wrist, and is used by vendors of miscellaneous articles.

7. 攔籃子 *k'uai³ lan²*, to pass the arm through the loop or handle of a basket, etc.: *lan* is commonly applied to a smaller kind of basket than 筐子, though the dictionaries state the opposite.

CHAPTER XXXIX.

1. And now let us see what YING YING was about at home; one day, having desired HUNG NIANG to bring her the looking-glass, she perceived that her complexion was growing sallow; "Ah," sighed she, "this is because I have been so many days without seeing his face; this strain at the heartstrings is indeed hard to bear." And so she went on sighing and sighing, day after day, without intermission.

2. It was the last quarter of the year,[1] and so cold that YING YING found that even with an additional wadded coat she could not keep herself warm.

3. "And my sweetheart," thought she, "in Peking there; who knows how he is getting through this inclement weather, when even the fire gives no heat?"

4. With these thoughts in her mind she went to take a look at the graduate's old quarters, HUNG NIANG accompanying her; the doors and windows were closed; within, the rooms were bare and desolate; spiders had hung their webs[3] from the eaves of the roof,[2] and looking through the window she saw that the floors were covered with dust.[4] YING YING gave orders to have them swept, but she still stood there ever so long, musing and melancholy.

5. "Let us go," said HUNG NIANG to her soothingly; "there is no use in our staying in this lonesome place."

6. YING YING was just turning to go when she observed a bird light on the branch of a tree, and as she paused to look at it, she heard the sound of a woman weeping hard by; "Who is that?" asked she. "It's our neighbour," said HUNG NIANG; "I have been told that her husband[5] has lately gone away about some business or other, and it's uncertain when he'll be home again."

7. "Ah!" said YING YING, "I can sympathise with her; when the hare dies the fox mourns! every creature feels for its kind."[6]

8. "Yes, indeed," continued HUNG NIANG, "and to think that this journey of the graduate's was all owing to the chatter of that child; it's he that was the cause of all this trouble." "There, there," said YING YING, rebuking her, "no more about that; let bygones be bygones."

9. They returned to their own room and sat sorrowfully talking together until it was dark, when it suddenly occurred to YING YING that she could not do better than write a letter to the graduate. HUNG NIANG brought her a pencil and the ink-stone; but

---

1. 十冬臘 shih tung la⁴, the names given to the tenth and two last moons of the year respectively; the twelfth moon is so called in consequence of the sacrifices, termed la, which are held in that month.

2. 房簷兒 fang yen²-'rh, the eaves of a house: yen, the edge of the 房頂, roof.

3. 蜘蛛網 chih¹ chu¹ wang, a spider's web; a spider is also called 蛛蛛.

4. 塵土 ch'ên² t'u, dust: ch'ên is not used alone colloquially.

5. 丈夫 chang fu, a husband: chang, an elder or senior (see Chapter XXXIV, Note 4).

6. 兎死狐悲物傷其類, when the t'u⁴, hare, dies the hu², fox, is mournful; wu⁴, created beings, shang, are wounded in the heart for, ch'i, their, lei⁴, kind, species. A hare is commonly called 野猫; a fox, 狐狸 (li²).

perceiving that the point of the pencil was worn, she got a new pencil instead.

10. "And now, don't you think, miss," said she, "that instead of sending the letter by itself, it would be better to put up some pretty present along with it?"

11. "Very good," said YING YING; "I think that I should like to send a set⁷ of buttons."

12. "Well, miss, if I may be allowed to speak," said HUNG NIANG, "I should say that red silk handkerchief⁸ you have there would be better than the buttons; don't you think so?"

13. No; in YING YING'S opinion, presents made up in pairs would be better still; she would send ¹⁴ both the things.

14. Saying which, she spread out her paper and took up her pencil to write. HUNG NIANG was leaning upon the table, looking on; the table shook, and her mistress attributing its unsteadiness to her, called out, "Don't jog so; put something under the leg of the table directly, to keep it steady." ⁹ This effected, she was just about to recommence when ¹⁰ one of those moths that will fly about a light ¹¹ flopped into the lamp and put it out; the lamp had to be lit again, and this caused so much delay that it was some time before the letter could be finished. Then it was put up in a cover with the presents, and this being sealed,¹² a man was despatched with it to the post office,¹³ who was to tell the people there to forward ¹⁴ it as fast as it could go to Peking; the faster the better.

15. It so happened that the letter arrived on the day before the graduate went in to the examinations; having opened ¹⁵ it and read it from beginning to end, he looked at the presents, and though the handkerchief seemed a little faded, still the kind motive that had prompted the person so dear to him to send it made it none the less precious, and he put it away in his trunk with more than ordinary care.¹⁶

7. 副 fu⁴, here, a set or suit.

8. 絹子 chüan⁴, a kerchief, whether for the throat or pocket; a pocket handkerchief is commonly called shou chüan-'rh.

9. 墊穩了 tien⁴ wên³, put something under to make it steady: tien, to put one thing under another to make the latter level or wên, steady.

10. 抽冷子, all of a sudden: lêng, in the sense of a shock (see Part V, Lesson XLV, Note 2).

11. 撲燈蛾兒, a moth; lit., the knocking-lamp moth; applied indiscriminately to all moths that appear at night. The reader must excuse the introduction of moths in mid-winter.

12. 圖書, commonly, a private seal, as opposed to yin⁴, an official seal.

13. 信局子 a post office: chü², an establishment, a committee, a manufactory, a depôt, an office; it has other meanings besides.

14. 寄 chi¹, to send. See Chapter VIII, Note 17.

15. 拆開 ch'ai¹ k'ai, to open: ch'ai, to open by the application of force.

16. 珍重, to set great store or value by: chung, to hold in esteem, chên, as a precious jewel (see Part V, Lesson XVI, Note 10); chên chung also means to take care of, as in the expression chên chung, chên chung, take care of yourself, addressed to a person starting on a journey.

CHAPTER XL.

1. And now, unfortunately, we have used up all the detached phrases in the original edition of the "Tzŭ Êrh Chi;" no slight addition has been made to these in the composition[1] of this narrative, but it is out of our power to prolong "The Story of the Promise that was kept" any farther.

2. There is no need[8] to tell how the graduate went in for his examinations the day after he got the letter; how, when he came out, he was congratulated upon the high degree he had taken; how office was quickly conferred[2] upon him; how, starting for his home in official costume,[3] he returned by way of the P'u-chiu Ssŭ; how YING YING's face lit up with delight when she saw how well he was looking; how Madame TS'UI, equally pleased, received her son-in-law most handsomely;[4] how she made preparations[5] for the happy event; and how, what with hanging lanterns and silk tapestry, and the noise[6] of the drums and other instruments, never was anything so gay; how the graduate CHANG, with his official cap on his head and his girdle round his waist, and YING YING with him, paid their homage to Heaven and Earth; how they pledged friends and relatives in the wedding cup; and how, when the company broke up, they, the husband and wife, went into their bridal chamber.[7]

3. Relation of all this would be like laying flowers over embroidery; utter superfluity. Nor is reference necessary either to the perfect harmony of their wedded life, the happiness of the entire family, or the prosperity that attended them in all things. These were a matter of course, and details of the kind will not fail to be understood by the reader, though not noted by the pen.

1. 撰 *chuan*⁴, to compose or compile, as a literary work.

2. 授 *shou*, to bestow, to confer, to give.

3. 衣錦 *chin*³, embroidery or brocade: *i*⁴, to wear, or dressed in (note the tone), *chin*, fine clothes.

4. 款待 *k'uan*³ *tai*⁴, to treat courteously or handsomely: *k'uan*, here, true, sincere. See also Chapter XXVI, Note 10.

5. 張羅, to make preparations, to arrange: *chang*, to spread, *lo*, the net (see Chapter I, Note 17).

6. 喧闐 *hsüan*¹ *t'ien*², a noise or din; applied only to the noise of musical instruments: *hsüan*, noise, clamour; *t'ien*, the sound of drums.

7. 洞房 *tung*⁴-*fang*, the bridal chamber: *tung*, a cave, a deep recess.

8. 不消, not necessary: *hsiao*¹, here in the sense of to need, to require (see also Chapter XXXII, Note 1).

PART VII.

THE TONE EXERCISES.

PART VII.

THE TONE EXERCISES.

The following Part, as described by its Chinese title (練習燕山平仄編), is *pien*, a compilation, *lien hsi*, for practice in, *p'ing tsé*, the tone system (*lit.*, the smooth and the deflected tones), in vogue in the metropolitan department of *Shun-tien Fu*, classically distinguished as *Yen Shan*. It will be seen that pages 286 and 287 of Volume I (Chinese text) repeat, in the same order, but, for practice sake, without the orthography, the table of characters given on pages 10–17 of Part I of that volume, as representing the sounds of the dialect. Let these be denominated, for the moment, Sound Index characters. In the succeeding pages of Part VII of Volume I will be found a Chinese text in columns headed each one by a Sound Index character, having immediately below it a note of its meaning in Chinese; below this note, a series of four places, some occupied by characters, some blank, which represent the Tone Classes, or changes of tone to which each Syllabic Sound is liable, and may therefore be called the Tone Scale; and below the Tone Scale, a corresponding series of short exercises in the tones. The Sound Indices are ranged from left to right in their original numerical order, but if the student be at any time at fault, his search will be farther guided by the numbers placed above each character, which refer him to the Sound Table in Part I.

The note explaining the sense of the Sound Index is composed in accordance with a Chinese method of illustration which cannot be too soon taken into account; I have enlarged upon its importance in the Preface. And now as regards the Tone Scale: where the *yin*, sound, represented by the Sound Index is common to *tzŭ*, written words, in all the four tones, the Tone Scale exhibits four characters, of which the Sound Index is one, placed in the order of the tones; the *shang-p'ing* taking the upper place in the series, the *hsia-p'ing*, the second, and so on. Where no *tzŭ* is to be found under a particular tone, the interruption of the series is marked by a circle. If the student listen carefully to the teacher reading the Tone Scale of one syllable after another, he will not be long, unless his ear is unusually defective, in catching the chime of the tones, and this once caught, he will soon habituate himself to determine the tone of any *tzŭ* that he may hear pronounced for the first time.

The short exercises which follow the Tone Scale are composed of the words given in the scale, combined each with one or more such words as they most ordinarily accompany. The text of these is repeated in the following pages, with orthography and tone marks, and a careful translation. As the combination given in the explanatory Chinese note appended to each Sound Index in Volume I is itself always one of the exercises, its meaning must be looked for amongst the translations of these.

PART VII.—THE TONE EXERCISES.

It is scarcely requisite that anything more should be said as to the manner of using these exercises or upon their utility. Different ears are differently accommodated, and it will appear to some that the law and practice of the tones is more satisfactorily understood from the study of examples of greater length, and unrestricted by the regular sequence here observed. Nothing can be simpler in such a case than to convert any number of short sentences out of Parts III or IV into tone exercises, with the aid of a native speaker. Without the assistance of the latter, acquisition of the tones is a pure impossibility.

The Tone Scale has been made to include the entire Sound Table within its limits, for the express purpose of enabling the student to test for himself the influence of tone upon the independent syllabic sound. From the notes in the order of the finals appended to these observations, he will perceive that this modification is often such as almost, if not fully, to justify us in representing the syllabic change effected by the tone as a distinct syllabic sound; but that our alphabet is hardly equal to the emergency, this distinction would have been attempted in the Peking Syllabary. It remains to direct attention to certain departures from the rule prescribed by the Tone Scale, to which the syllabic sound is subject when it is not independent, but connected with other sounds, whether as part of dissyllable or of a longer combination.

To take the last first. The student will recall the few words said about Rhythm in page 9 of Part I, Volume I. Now let him turn to the Chinese text of Part V (Volume I, page 229), and get his teacher to enunciate rapidly the words *t'ou i tsw^u-'rh-yao-chin-ti shih-ch'ing*, the first and foremost of essentials, at the foot of the first column, or the words *ko-ch'u-'rh-ko-ch'u-'rh-ti hsiang-t'an*, particular dialect, in the second column. He will see, if he watch the speaker's voice carefully, that, even though he may be unable to declare that this or that syllable has quite passed to a new place in the Tone Scale, the syllables first uttered are not uttered with the full tone belonging to them as independent syllables. This need not alarm him. Tone is to the Chinese monosyllable pretty much what quantity is to the individual syllable in Latin. As we shall presently see, its primitive or natural conditions are so affected by position that change of position will in some cases produce entire change of tone. But, rhythmically, in long combinations such as I have instanced, and especially in attributive and adverbial constructions, there is a modulation of the voice that is not to be defined by the Tone Scale, and which nothing but practice can teach; just as rules of prosody will carry us only a certain length in Latin. It is impossible that such words as *Constantīnŏpŏlītānus, mĕmŏrābĭlĭă, văgābŭndŭs* should have been articulated without a rhythmical emphasis more or less at variance with the apparent prescriptions of prosody. The prosody of our own vowels is the sport of circumstances; still, the fluctuation in the value of the vowels in *analysis* and *analytical, meteorology* and *meteorological*, is somewhat analogous to that which we are here considering.

In the matter of just accentuation, therefore, the memory will be greatly relieved if the language be treated, whenever construction will admit of it, as polysyllabic. The individual syllabic sound should be ticketed, so to speak, by its tone, as the syllable in a Latin word is by its quantity, and that it may not be forgotten, the Syllabary should be frequently consulted; but in speaking, the student may safely endeavour to reproduce any sound that forms part of a more than dissyllabic combination, rather with reference to correct rhythmical emphasis of the whole polysyllable than to strict accordance with the tone-quantity of its component parts.

A change of meaning in the *tzŭ*, monosyllabic word, in some cases involves a change of the *yin*, syllabic sound; in some, the *yin* is retained but the tone changes. In dissyllabic combinations, where the two words combined belong, as independent syllables, to the same tone class, the tone of the first or second is disturbed, in some cases slightly, in some so much as to authorise the relegation of the word to a tone class not properly its own. The following combinations read aloud will show to what extent the tone in different places of the scale will be affected under the conditions adverted to:—

1. 山西 shan¹ hsi¹   west of the hills (the province so named).
西山 hsi¹ shan¹   the western hills.
當差 tang¹ ch'ai¹   to be employed officially.
珍珠 chên¹ chu¹   pearls.

2. 湖南 hu² nan²   south of the lake (the province so named).
南湖 nan² hu²   the southern lake.
衙門 ya² mên²   a public office.
銀錢 yin² ch'ien²   money in general.

3. 早起 tsao³ ch'i³   early in the morning.
洗臉 hsi³ lien³   to wash the face.
小馬 hsiao³ ma³   a small horse.
馬小 ma³ hsiao³   the horse is small.

4. 日月 jih⁴ yüeh⁴   days and moons.
數目 shu⁴ mu⁴   a number.
算計 suan⁴ chi⁴   to reckon.
志向 chih⁴ hsiang⁴   ambition.

Under the 1st tone, I consider the voice to fall in the second syllable in *Shan-hsi*, but to be lower on *hsi* than on *shan* in *hsi shan*; to rise on the second syllable of *tang ch'ai*, and to fall on the second in *chên chu*. Under the 2nd tone, the abruptness with which the syllable closes is to me much more apparent in the last syllable than in the first. But the native teachers will not admit in either case that the tone is modified. Under the 3rd, the change is more remarkable: the first syllable is changed nearly, if not quite, to the 2nd tone; still, there is a manifest limitation proper to particular vowels. If you make a native repeat *hsiao³ ma³, ma³ hsiao³*, a certain number of times, you will perceive that the voice rises and falls as if the words were accented *hsiáo mā, mā hsiáo*. Where three words are joined, as in *wu³ tou³ mi³*, five bushels of rice, the last is the only one which is sounded with a full 3rd tone; in *tsao³ ch'i³ hsi³ lien³*, to wash the face in the morning, the tone of *ch'i* certainly differs from that of *tsao*, but *lien* is the only word of the four that preserves the full 3rd tone. Under the 4th tone, the voice descends in the second syllable, but not so pronouncedly as under the 3rd tone. Different examples will show that this inflexion, again, is more evident with some vowels than with others; but double the *suan⁴* in *suan-chi*, and you will still find the second *suan* in *suan-suan*, to reckon, lower in key than the first, although the difference detected does not transfer the syllable to any other of the four tones in the scale; and it is only of these four that a native speaker conceives our dialect capable.

The words *tzŭ, êrh*, appended to nouns, *ti*, following both nouns and verbs, and *liao*, corrupted to *la* and *lo*, also after verbs, but more frequently at the end of a sentence, cannot be allowed, while in this enclitic relation to other words, to belong to any class in the Tone Scale; but when not enclitics, they reassert their rights, as in *tzŭ³ sun¹*, posterity; *êrh² ma³*, a stallion; *ti² ch'io⁴*, positively; *liao³ shih⁴*, to finish an affair. The word *cho²* when enclitic becomes *cho⁴*.

NOTES ON THE TONE RULES AFFECTING THE FINALS.

a.—Under the 1st tone, the *shang-p'ing*, the *a* is sounded somewhat as in *a*nt, *ya*rn, *ma*st, very slowly pronounced. Under the 2nd, the *hsia-p'ing*, shorter and sharper, as in *a*rtful, *a*rchitect. Under the 3rd, the *shang*, the *a*, commencing as under the *shang-p'ing*, gradually descends and then suddenly rises; the vowels in the words a*h*a! pa*p*a, with the italicised consonants dropped, give some idea of the effect of this tone on the terminal *a*. Under the 4th tone, the *ch'ü*, the vowel sound begins on a higher key than under the *shang-p'ing*, and descends immediately, not protracted, but *diminuendo*; as it were, A-A-ʌ.

ai.—Under the 1st tone, the two vowels in *ai* are pronounced in nearly equal time; the latter if anything quicker than the other. Under the 2nd, the *i* prevails, as when a speaker ejaculates *ay?* implying surprise and doubt. In the 3rd, it is on *a* that the voice descends, and on *i* that it remounts; the vowel sound produced somewhat resembling that in car*ee*n. In the 4th tone, the voice dwells on the *a*; the latter part of the diphthong being, if I may use the expression, enclitic; as though it were written *áa-y*.

an.—The remarks on *a* are generally applicable to this final, except that in the 2nd tone the inflexion of the vowel is more apparent, if indeed the vowel itself does not become a diphthong.

ao.—In this final the *a* and *o* are uttered in the 1st tone, as in *ai*, with a slight degree more prolongation of the *a* than of the *o*. Under the 2nd tone, *ao* is almost *áu*, or *áoo*; indeed, in the words *ao* or *ngao*, it is nearly *ou* in l*ou*d. Under the 3rd tone, as the voice rises on the *o*, that vowel becomes nearly *au, aw*, in c*au*l, br*aw*l. Under the 4th tone, the *a* claims again the longer utterance, the *o* figuring but enclitically, as it were *aa* . . *ŏ*.

eh.—The only syllable in which this final is found is *yeh*. In the 1st tone, it might be written *ieh*, and, as in the case of *ai, ao*, the voice is evenly distributed over both parts of the diphthong; but in the 2nd, the *y* is an undoubted consonant, and the syllable, simply *ye* in *ye*t. In the 3rd, there is the double vowel sound noticed before, commencing as though the sound to be uttered were *yea*, but rising suddenly to the sound of the *e* in *ye*t. In the 4th tone, the sound is a prolonged declining *yea*. It might be otherwise expressed by Y-E-E-E.

ê or o.—It is under the 2nd tone that the *é* approaches the *o* in l*o*t, t*o*p. In the rest, it is nearer the vowel sound of l*ea*rn, s*i*r, *ea*rth, t*e*rse. In the 3rd and 4th tones, the reduplication of the vowel sound is apparent; as if *lé*, for instance, were written *léé, lé-é-é*.

ên.—The vowel is reduplicated in the 3rd and 4th tones. Try to intone the word *u*pp*er* in the key of the 3rd and 4th tones, and then drop the consonants; the *u-é* remaining give a fair idea of the vowel sound required.

êrh.—There is properly no *shang-p'ing* tone in this sound, but, as will be seen in many instances, the vowel sound of *êrh*, when placed in enclitic relation to a word preceding it, is absorbed more or less in the vowel sound of that word. The tone is also modified. It was called by the compiler of the Syllabary a *shang-p'ing*, in preference to any other tone, although he allowed that in strictness the *êrh*, with its new sound, did not belong to any one of the four classes. In my opinion, the fusion modifies the tone not only of the *êrh* itself but also of the word to which it is attached.

i.—The independent sound *i* is frequently also *yi*, but the *y* is not so apparent, if it appear at all, in the *shang-p'ing* as in the other tones. The student must beware of shortening the *i* of the *hsia-p'ing* into *ih*. The vowel preserves its length, the difference between its sound in the 1st and 2nd tones being faintly represented by that in *cheer* and *peep*. In the 3rd, the *i* is inflected, rising as if *ee-ih*; in the 4th, as if *ee . . e. e.*

ia.—In the 1st tone, the *i* is distinct, though not so prominent as the *a*. In the 2nd, the *a* is rather more prominent, *chia*² sounding *chya*. In the 3rd, *chia*³ sounds *cheeah*; in the *chia*⁴, is almost *chéyaa*.

iang.—The remarks on *ia* apply equally to *iang*; but in the syllables *liang*, *niang*, the *i* in the 1st, 3rd, and 4th tones is often much nearer *ey*. In the 2nd tone, it is almost *y* consonantal; *lyang*², *nyang*².

iao.—The remarks on *ao*, *ia*, and *iang* apply to the effect of tone on this final. In the 1st, 3rd, and 4th tones, especially in the syllables *liao*, *niao*, the *i* becomes almost *ey*; in the 2nd, it is *y*, the *ao* becoming a sound between *aoo* and *ow*.

ieh.—As in *ia*, in the 1st tone, the first vowel and the second are articulated distinctly one from the other, and with nearly equal stress. In the 2nd tone, the *i* becomes *y*, and in the 3rd and 4th, nearly *ey*. Thus, the changes in *ch'ieh* might be expressed thus :—*ch'iyeh*, *ch'yeh*, *ch'eyéh*, *ch'éyeh*. In *lieh*, *mieh*, *nieh*, in all except the 2nd tone, usage seems very capricious; the same native sounding *i* at one time as *ee*, and at another as *ey*.

ien.—The remarks regarding the vowel *i* in *ieh* apply equally to the *i* in *ien*. The *en* is nearly as uncertain as the *an* in *üan*, frequently becoming *an* under the 3rd, and yet more frequently under the 4th, tone.

ih.—The difference between the *i* in the 1st and that in the 2nd tone is faintly represented by that between the same vowels in *children* and *chip*. In the other two it is inflected as in *a, é*, etc.; beginning like the *ee* in *cheek*, and rising suddenly to the *i* in *ill*; then descending gradually in the 4th. Drop the consonants in the word *limit*, and prolong the utterance of the latter vowel, to form some idea of the sound of the final *ih*⁴.

in.—As in *ih*. Take the vowel sound in *thin*, *thick* as approaching those under the 1st and 2nd tones, and unite the vowel sounds in the first two syllables of *initial* for the 3rd, and of *incident* for the 4th, tone.

io.—When preceded by *hs* and *l*, this final is in Peking as often *üo* or *üeh* as *io*; after *n*, more rarely. Under the 3rd tone, *lio* is pronounced *li-ó*; under the 4th, *nio* is rather *nyó-ó-ó*.

iu.—In the 1st tone, the two sounds *ee* and *oo*, of which *iu* is compounded, are distinct and even, as in *ai*, *ao*, *ia*. In the 2nd, the *iu* is nearly *yew*, but shorter, as though written *yewh*. In the 3rd, the voice descends on the *ee*, to rise sharply on the *ooh;* and in the 4th, dwells on the *ee*, and breaks off on the *oo* in a lower key.

iung.—This syllable is only found in the 1st and 2nd tones. The vowel *i* is not so distinct as in *ia, ieh:* in the 1st tone and in the 2nd, *i* is nearly *y;* read *hsiung*², almost *syung*. The *u* or *oo* sound inclines to *ó* in *home* in the 1st, but is *oo* in the 2nd tone, and pronounced short, as if the final *g* were nearly a *k*, or a French nasal.

o.—In the 1st tone, the *o* is nearly as in *roll;* in the 2nd, it is shorter, as in *shot*, a slight reduplication of the vowel sound following, somewhat as if it were *oóh*. In the 3rd tone, a second vowel is also perceptible, but rather resembling *á*. In the 4th, the change of vowel is very slightly felt, the dominant sound being *o*, which is prolonged *diminuendo*. In the single *o*, or *ngo*, the nasal pronunciation of it, much as it modifies the vowel sound, does not affect the tone.

ou.—In the 1st tone, *ou* is much as in *round;* in the 2nd, shortened, as in *lout*, but with a certain inflexion, as though it were *owoo* or *owuh*. This is more clear in the 3rd and 4th tones, which might be expressed *où-óo*³, *oú-oo*⁴.

ü.—In the 1st tone, the *ü* as in the French *pureté;* in the second, as in the French *tut, salut*. In the 3rd and 4th, the reduplication and inflexion of the vowel noticed in *a, i, o* is perceptible, as though *ü*³ were *ü-üh*, and *ü*⁴, *ü - ü - - ü*.

uan.—This presents the same difficulties as *ien*, so far as the vowel *a* is concerned. The *a* of the 1st tone, pronounced sometimes broad, as in the syllables ending in *an*, is flattened sometimes to the *a* in *mat*, and sometimes modified so as to be nearly the *e* in *then: uen* is the orthography of MORRISON and others. The native who was my guide, whatever might be his pronunciation under the 1st, made little difference under the 2nd, uttering the *an* as in the English *can, mantle*. In the 3rd, the uncertainty between *a* and *e* is greater than in the 4th tone, which prefers the *a*. In both, the vowels are distinguished much as in *ia, ieh*, etc.; as it were *üan*³, *üaan*⁴.

üeh.—In the 1st tone, the voice pauses evenly on *ü* and *eh*, which last vowel is pronounced as in *sentry*. In the 2nd, *eh* is as in *set*, and is much clearer than the *ü*. In the 3rd, the *eh* of the 1st tone is prolonged, the *ü* shortened. In the 4th, the *ü* is more prominent to the ear, and the stress of the voice is laid upon it; but the *eh* is very prolonged.

ün.—The *ün*¹ is the French *une;* in *ün*², the vowel sound resembles that in *lutte*, slightly inflected, as if an *i*, very faint and rapidly pronounced, intervened between *ü* and *n*. In *ün*³ and *ün*⁴, there is the reduplication of the vowel before noticed.

u.—The *u*¹ resembles *oo* in *coon;* the *u*², *oo* in *cook*. In *u*³, *u*⁴, the vowel is reduplicated like *a, i, o*, above; *u*³, as if *ù-úh;* *u*⁴, as *ú-uh* or *oo-ooh*.

ua.—In the 1st tone, the *ua* is certainly nearly *ŏá;* in the 2nd, the *o* almost disappears, becoming *oo*, *u*, or *w;* in the 3rd, it is again apparent, prominence being given to the *a* or *ah*, which is very short. In the 4th, it seems to depend on the initial consonants which vowel shall be sounded; *shua*⁴ sounds *shóaa*, but *hua*⁴ is *húaa*.

uai.—What applies to *ua* is more or less true of *uai*, so far as the *u* is concerned; but in the 1st tone, the division is between *u* and the diphthong *ai*; in the 2nd, *u* is consonantal and *ai* shortened; in the 3rd, the voice descends on *u* and rises sharp on *a*, to which *i* is enclitic; in the 4th, the voice rises on the *u*, and dies away on the *ai*, dwelling more on the first vowel. In the 1st, 3rd, and 4th tones, *u* might often be *o*; and in the 2nd, *w*.

uan.—The division of the vowel sounds is as in *ua*. In the 3rd tone, the final is almost *ówán*; in the 4th, *óan*, like *awn* in *awning*, or *ohn* in the German *ohne*.

uei.—In the 1st tone, the vowel sounds are nearly *oowei*; in the 2nd, *wey*; in the 3rd, *oò-w.é.i*; in the 4th, *óo-w.e.i*, the *i* leaning enclitically on the *e*. The *u* in all four tones in *kuei* is nearer *w* than in *hui*.

uên, un.—The double vowel might be written for all four tones, but is more remarkable in the 3rd and 4th. In the 1st, the *u* or *oo* sound is dominant, prolonged as in *pool, moon*; in the 2nd, the *u* is nearly the vowel in *put, foot*; but in the 3rd tone, the vowel sounds are well divided, as if *oo-ún* or *ú-én*; and in the 4th, as if *óo-ŭn* or *ú-ên*, the latter part declining gradually as if *ū-é-n*.

ui.—As observed under *uei*, there is a difference between that final and *ui*. This is most perceptible in the syllable *hui*, and under the 2nd tone; in others, *ui* is nearly, if not quite, *uei*. The syllable *chui* might otherwise be written *chōō-ēy*[1], *chooy*[2], *choo-éy*[3], *chóo-ey*[4]. The same native will be found to pronounce this differently at different times.

un.—In the 1st tone, there is a perceptible inflexion of the vowel, but slighter than in *huên, kuên*. In the 2nd, it is nearly the *un* in the Italian *punto*, pronounced quickly, though a certain reduplication is still to be perceived. In the 3rd and 4th tones, this inflexion is acted on by the tones as in *an* and other finals noticed before.

ung.—The remarks on *un* apply generally to *ung*; but in the 2nd tone, the inflexion of the vowel is less apparent. The *g* final is faint in the same tone; indeed, *ung*[2] is something between the final sounds of the French *long* and *longue*. The sound is rather *u* than *ō* in *yung*.

uo.—The three syllables to which I have assigned this final in the Syllabary are *huo, kuo, shuo*. I must admit that it is only in the last that the *u* asserts itself as a vowel; in the rest, it has the power of *w*. In *shuo*, the tones might be expressed thus: *shūōh*[1], *shwŏh*[2], *shuó*[3], *shú-óh*[4].

ŭ.—The difficulty here is in representing the vowel sound; this determined, the inflexions of it by the tone resemble those in the other final vowels. The word *sy-rup*, with the italicised consonants struck out, might represent *szŭ*[1]; *such*, *szŭ*[2]; the 3rd and 4th might be otherwise written *szŭ-ŭh*, *szŭ-ŭ-h*; but our alphabet aids us less in this than in any sound in the Table.

There remain unnoticed a few finals, the tone rules affecting which do not differ from those already laid down for others. Those under *an* suffice for *ang* and *êng*, under *ai* for *ei*, under *eh* for *en*, under *ih* and *in* for *ing*, under *üeh* for *üo*, and under *ua* and *uan* for *uang*.

EXERCISES IN THE TONES.

The larger numbers and characters to the left of the page correspond with those in the Sound Table prefixed to the Tone Exercises in Volume I (pages 286 and 287), and are followed by a general explanation of their meaning. The examples in smaller type, which are, in fact, a repetition of the exercises, are literally translated.

1. 阿 *a*, a particle, sometimes affirmative, sometimes interjectional; as the last, partly interrogative.

    是 阿 *shih⁴ a¹* . . . . It is so indeed.
    阿 甚 麼 *a³ shên² mo²* . . . . . Ah! What?
    阿 哥 *a⁴ ko¹* . . . . (The Manchu *a-gê*) elder brother. The sons of a reigning Emperor are called *ako*; the eldest being *ta ako*, the second *êrh ako*, and so on.

2. 愛 *ai*, ⁿᵍ*ai*, to love.

    哀 求 *ai¹ ch'iu²* . . . . To implore; to cry to in tribulation.
    塵 埃 *ch'ên² ⁿᵍai²* . . . . . . Fine dust.
    高 矮 *kao¹ ⁿᵍai³* . . . . Tall and short; of things, high and low.
    愛 惜 *ai⁴ hsi⁴* . . . . To love.

3. 安 *an*, ⁿᵍ*an*, peace; comfort; health; well-being.

    平 安 *p'ing² an¹* . . . . . . Peace; freedom from trouble.
    俺 們 *an³ mên¹* . . . . . . A provincial form of the pronoun *we*.
    河 岸 *ho² ⁿᵍan⁴* . . . . . . The bank or shore of a river.

4. 昂 *ang*, ⁿᵍ*ang*, high; rising.

    腌 臢 *ang¹ tsang¹* . . . . . . Dirty.
    昂 貴 *ang² kuei⁴* . . . . . . High in price.

5. 熬 *ao*, ⁿᵍ*ao*, to boil (not used alone in speaking).

    熬 菜 *ao¹ ts'ai⁴* . . . . . . To boil meat, vegetables, etc.
    熬 夜 *ao² yeh⁴* . . . . To work at night; to burn midnight oil.
    綿 襖 *mien² ao³* . . . . . . A quilted (*lit.*, cotton) *ao* (an article of dress worn by both sexes; it may be long or short).
    狂 傲 *k'uang² ao⁴* . . . . . Conceited and supercilious; arrogant.

6. 乍 *cha*, suddenly; unexpectedly.

    渣 滓 *cha¹ tzŭ³* . . . . . . Dregs; leavings of things eaten or drunk.
    劄 文 *cha² wên²* . . . . . . A despatch to an inferior.
    一 拃 *yi⁴ cha³* . . . . A span.
    乍 見 *cha⁴ chien⁴* . . . . . To see, or meet, unexpectedly.

7. 茶 *ch'a*, tea.

    叉手 *ch'a¹ shou³* . . . . The two hands clasped together.
    茶酒 *ch'a² chiu³* . . . . Tea and wine; said of a meal prepared for guests.
    扠腰 *ch'a³ yao¹* . . . . To place the hands on the hips; to stand a-kimbo.
    樹枒 *shu⁴ ch'a⁴* . . . . The fork formed by a bough at the point it branches off from the stem.

8. 窄 *ch'ai*, narrow.

    齋戒 *chai¹ chieh⁴* . . . . Fasting and purification.
    住宅 *chu⁴ chai²* . . . . [Speaking of another's] a residence.
    寬窄 *k'uan¹ chai³* . . . . Broad and narrow; the breadth of.
    欠債 *ch'ien⁴ chai⁴* . . . . To be in debt.

9. 柴 *ch'ai*, fuel; being wood, weeds, or any similar firing.

    拆毀 *ch'ai¹ hui³* . . . . To demolish, as houses, furniture, etc.
    柴炭 *ch'ai² t'an⁴* . . . . Wood and charcoal.
    樣冊子 *yang⁴ ch'ai³ tzŭ* . . . . . A book of patterns, such as milliners use.

10. 斬 *chan*, to decapitate; the *chan* in *chan chiao*, [capital punishment by] beheading or strangling. Observe that *chan* standing by itself is read *chan³*, but being followed by *chiao³*, a word in the 3rd tone, becomes *chan²*. In the example of the 3rd tone, therefore, *chan³*, the numerative of lamps, has been substituted for it.

    沾染 *chan¹ jan³* . . . . Steeped in; saturated with; hence, morally, contaminated.
    一盞燈 *yi⁴ chan³ têng¹* . . . . . A lamp.
    驛站 *yi⁴ chan⁴* . . . . Government post stations; courier offices.

11. 產 *ch'an*, to produce, as females, the earth, etc.

    攙雜 *ch'an¹ tsa²* . . . . To mix up, so that the component parts are undistinguishable; said of fluids or solids; also used figuratively.
    嘴饞 *tsui³ ch'an²* . . . . Gluttonous.
    產業 *ch'an³ yeh⁴* . . . . An estate; property producing an income.
    懺悔 *ch'an⁴ hui³* . . . . To reform (*neut.*); *lit.*, to reform and see the error of one's ways.

12. 章 *chang*, a rule; a law.

    章程 *chang¹ ch'êng²* . . . . . . Regulations.
    生長 *shêng¹ chang³* . . . . . . To be born and to grow up.
    帳目 *chang⁴ mu⁴* . . . . Bills; debts. Both forms of this character are admissible.

13. 唱 *ch'ang*, to sing.

    娼妓 *ch'ang¹ chi⁴* . . . . A prostitute.
    長短 *ch'ang² tuan³* . . . . . . Long and short; length.
    木廠 *mu⁴ ch'ang³* . . . . A woodyard.
    歌唱 *ko¹ ch'ang⁴* . . . . To sing.

14. 兆 *chao*, a presage.
    招呼 *chao^1 hu^1* . . . . To hail; to call to.
    着急 *chao^2 chi^2* . . . . Eager, in a good sense; also, over-eager, impatient.
    察找 *ch'a^2 chao^3* . . . . To make search for.
    先兆 *hsien^1 chao^4* . . . . A presage; an omen.

15. 吵 *ch'ao*, the wrangle (of two or of more).
    吵嚷 *ch'ao^1 jang^3* . . . . Noise of loud voices; *jang* is here atonic.
    窩巢 *wo^1 ch'ao^2* . . . . Nest of birds; lair of beasts; den of thieves.
    煎炒 *chien^1 ch'ao^3* . . . . To fry in oil, fat, etc.
    錢鈔 *ch'ien^2 ch'ao^4* . . . . Cash and paper; or, a cash-note, but this is oftener called a *ch'ien-p'iao*.

16. 這 *ché*, the pronoun *this*.
    遮掩 *ché^1 yen^3* . . . . To screen, as another's faults.
    摺奏 *ché^2 tsou^4* . . . . To report to the Throne in a *ché*, memorial.
    再者 *tsai^4 ché^3* . . . . Again (in argument); farther; what is more, etc.
    這個 *ché^4 ko^4* . . . . This one.

17. 車 *ch'é*, a cart, a carriage, etc.
    車馬 *ch'é^1 ma^3* . . . . Carts and horses.
    拉扯 *la^1 ch'é^3* . . . . To drag; also, to implicate.
    裁撤 *ts'ai^2 ch'é^4* . . . . To do away with; to dismiss part of an establishment; to abrogate a law, etc.

18. 這 *chei*, this.
    這塊兒 *chei^4 k'uai^4 êrh* . . . . . Here, in this place; *chei* is simply short for *ché yi*, this one. Observe *k'uai-êrh*, pronounced *k'uairh^4*.

19. 眞 *chén*, true.
    眞假 *chén^1 chia^3* . . . . True and false; the truth of anything.
    枕頭 *chén^3 t'ou^2* . . . . A pillow; *lit.*, to pillow the head.
    地震 *ti^4 chén^4* . . . . An earthquake.

20. 臣 *ch'én*, a public servant in his relation to the Sovereign; not applied, except historically, to any but the higher officers of State.
    嗔怪 *ch'én^1 kuai^4* . . . . To rebuke sternly; to censure gravely, either to the face or behind the back.
    君臣 *chün^1 ch'én^2* . . . . Sovereign and minister.
    砢磣 *k'o^1 ch'én^3* . . . . Hideous; very unsightly; of persons or things.
    趁著 *ch'én^4 cho^4* . . . . Taking advantage of, *sc.*, circumstances, opportunity, etc.

21. 正 *chêng*, upright.
    正月 *chêng^1 yüeh^4* . . . . The first moon of the year (*chêng^1*).
    整齊 *chêng^3 ch'i^2* . . . . Regular; in symmetrical order.
    邪正 *hsieh^2 chêng^4* . . . . Of lines, roads, etc., straight and diverging; hence, figuratively, moral and depraved, orthodox and heterodox.

22. 成 ch'êng, accomplishment, as opposed to failure.

 稱呼 ch'êng¹ hu¹ . . . . To address a person, or speak of one (by such or such a term of respect).
 成敗 ch'êng² pai⁴ . . . . Accomplishment or failure.
 懲辦 ch'êng³ pan⁴ . . . . To punish, punishment of, crime.
 斗秤 tou³ ch'êng⁴ . . . . Measures and weights; *lit.*, pecks and steelyards.

23. 吉 chi, of good omen.

 雞犬 chi¹ ch'üan³ . . . . Poultry and dogs; *e.g.*, none left in a country that has been devastated; the place of them to be shunned by a compounder of certain medicines, because his operations should be conducted in quiet.
 吉凶 chi² hsiung¹ . . . . Auspicious and inauspicious.
 自己 tzŭ⁴ chi³ . . . . Oneself.
 記載 chi⁴ tsai⁴ . . . . To put on record in a history, essay, etc.

24. 奇 ch'i, strange.

 七八 ch'i¹ pa¹ . . . . Seven, eight.
 奇怪 ch'i² kuai⁴ . . . . Strange; curious; how strange.
 起初 ch'i³ ch'u¹ . . . . At the beginning.
 氣血 ch'i⁴ hsüeh³ ⁴ . . . . The constitution; *lit.*, breath and blood.

25. 家 chia, a house; a home; the family.

 住家 chu⁴ chia¹ . . . . To live at home.
 夾帶 chia² tai⁴ . . . . To carry privily; *lit.*, under the arm.
 盔甲 k'uei¹ chia³ . . . . Casque and coat of mail; armour.
 價錢 chia⁴ ch'ien² . . . . The price of.

26. 恰 ch'ia, to coincide with exactly.

 掐花 ch'ia¹ hua¹ . . . . To pick a flower off its stem.
 卡子 ch'ia³ tzŭ . . . . A Customs barrier; also, the clasp of a belt.
 恰巧 ch'ia⁴ ch'iao³ . . . . In the nick of time; in exact coincidence.

27. 楷 ch'iai (also k'ai), the stalk of grass.

 楷書 ch'iai³ shu¹ . . . . The written character in which despatches are copied; say, round hand.

28. 江 chiang, a river; rather of large streams than small.

 大江 ta⁴ chiang¹ . . . . The great river; *sc.*, the Yangtze.
 講究 chiang³ chiu¹ . . . . To look into curiously, minutely, fastidiously, particularly; hence, in some cases, the result of such care; *e.g.*, if one *chiang chiu*, is particular, about one's room, one's room is *chiang-chiu*.
 匠人 chiang⁴ jên² . . . . A workman; an artizan.

29. 搶 ch'iang, to carry off with violence.

 腔調 ch'iang¹ tiao⁴ . . . . Sound in accord; in tune, whether of speaking or singing; also, figuratively, of things.
 牆壁 ch'iang² pi⁴ . . . . Properly, a partition wall, but used of any wall of a house.
 搶奪 ch'iang³ to² . . . . To rob; to steal.
 戧木 ch'iang⁴ mu⁴ . . . . Wooden supports.

30. 交 chiao, to interchange.

 交代 chiao¹ tai⁴ . . . . To hand over to a successor in office; also, to give orders to a servant or subordinate.
 嚼過 chiao² kuo⁴ . . . . One's bread; lit., to eat, = the food, needed to enable one to pass one's days, = to live, or one's daily expenses of a necessary kind.
 手腳 shou³ chiao³ . . . . Hand and foot. Observe shou³ becomes nearly shou² before chiao³.
 叫喊 chiao⁴ han³ . . . . To call out loud; to call to a person.

31. 巧 ch'iao, cunning; but also, clever, of men; ingenious, of things.

 敲打 ch'iao¹ ta³ . . . . To beat, as drums, gongs, etc.; to knock at a door.
 橋梁 ch'iao² liang² . . . . A bridge; lit., bridge beams.
 巧妙 ch'iao³ miao⁴ . . . . Of men, clever; of inventions, ingenious.
 俏皮 ch'iao⁴ p'i² . . . . Of women only, well-looking; also, well-dressed; used fig. of fair words that cover censorious allusions.

32. 街 chieh, a street.

 街道 chieh¹ tao⁴ . . . . Public ways.
 完結 wan² chieh² . . . . To complete; completed.
 解開 chieh³ k'ai¹ . . . . To untie; to explain. Cf. solvere.
 借貸 chieh⁴ tai⁴ . . . . To borrow.

33. 且 ch'ieh, moreover.

 切肉 ch'ieh¹ jou⁴ . . . . To slice meat, cutting vertically.
 茄子 ch'ieh² tzŭ . . . . (Amongst other things) the brinjal, or egg-plant.
 況且 k'uang⁴ ch'ieh³ . . . . Moreover; farther.
 姬妾 chi¹ ch'ieh⁴ . . . . Concubines; in speaking of one alone, ch'ieh would be used without chi.

34. 見 chien, to perceive.

 奸臣 chien¹ ch'ên² . . . . A traitorous or disloyal minister.
 裁減 ts'ai² chien³ . . . . To diminish number or quantity.
 見面 chien⁴ mien⁴ . . . . To have an interview with; during a tête-à-tête.

35. 欠 ch'ien, to owe; to be deficient in.

 千萬 ch'ien¹ wan⁴ . . . . A thousand myriads = any number; with a negative, on no account.
 錢財 ch'ien² ts'ai² . . . . Money; wealth.
 深淺 shên¹ ch'ien³ . . . . Deep and shallow; the depth of.
 該欠 kai¹ ch'ien⁴ . . . . To owe.

36. 知 *chih*, to know.

    知道 *chih¹ tao⁴* . . . . To know.
    值班 *chih² pan¹* . . . . To be on duty in one's turn.
    指點 *chih³ tien³* . . . . To point out; to indicate.
    志向 *chih⁴ hsiang⁴* . . . . . . Ambition; *lit.*, direction or aim of one's resolution.

37. 尺 *ch'ih*, the Chinese foot,=about 14 inches English.

    紅赤赤 *hung² ch'ih¹ ch'ih¹* . . . . Red as red can be.
    涎誤 *ch'ih² wu⁴* . . . . To fail, or ruin, by unpunctuality.
    尺寸 *ch'ih³ ts'un⁴* . . . . Feet and inches; the length of; commonly pronounced *ch'ih² ts'un⁴*.
    翅膀 *ch'ih⁴ pang³* . . . . A bird's wings.

38. 斤 *chin*, the Chinese pound.

    斤兩 *chin¹ liang³* . . . . Pound and ounce; *see* "Chinese Weights and Measures," Part III, p. 213.
    錦繡 *chin³ hsiu⁴* . . . . Embroidery, in gold, silk, etc.
    遠近 *yuan³ chin⁴* . . . . Far and near; distance.

39. 親 *ch'in*, nearly related or allied.

    親戚 *ch'in¹ ch'i⁴* . . . . Connexions by marriage.
    勤儉 *ch'in² chien³* . . . . Industrious and frugal.
    寢食 *ch'in³ shih²* . . . . Sleep and food; part of a proverb in which anxiety of mind is said to interfere with both rest and appetite.
    狗唚 *kou³ ch'in⁴* . . . . The dog is vomiting; a dog's vomit.

40. 井 *ching*, a well.

    眼睛 *yen³ ching¹* . . . . The eyes; *lit.*, the pupil of the eye.
    井泉 *ching³ ch'üan²* . . . . . . Wells and springs; but with *shui*, the water of either or both, as distinguished from river water.
    安靜 *an¹ ching⁴* . . . . Quiet; tranquil; said of the mind, of a scene, of a state of things.

41. 輕 *ch'ing*, light, as opposed to heavy.

    輕重 *ch'ing¹ chung⁴* . . . . . . Light and heavy (morally or materially); also, the weight of things; value of character, counsels, etc.
    陰晴 *yin¹ ch'ing²* . . . . (Of the sky) clouded or fine; rainy or fine; the weather.
    請安 *ch'ing³ an¹* . . . . To inquire after the health of; hence, a form of salutation.
    慶弔 *ch'ing⁴ tiao⁴* . . . . Congratulations and condolences.

42. 角 *chio*, a horn.

    角色 *chio² sê⁴* . . . . The particular business in which a man is engaged; the class he belongs to. You ask, what is his *chio sê?* The word *sê* here meaning class, description.

43. 卻 *ch'io*, to stop abruptly. Observe the other form of this character in the example below.

    推却 *t'ui¹ ch'io⁴* . . . . To decline; to refuse.

[CHIU-CHÜ.] PART VII.—THE TONE EXERCISES. 433

44. 酒 *chiu*, Chinese wine or spirit in general.
    究辦 *chiu¹ pan⁴* . . . . To inquire into and punish an offence.
    酒肉 *chiu³ jou⁴* . . . . Wine and meat; the dinner one gives his friends. Such a man is a *chiu-jou* friend; *sc.*, not in one's intimacy, or, not a friend with whom one would be intimate.
    救護 *chiu⁴ hu⁴* . . . . To succour, as people in poverty, danger, etc.

45. 秋 *ch'iu*, autumn.
    春秋 *ch'un¹ ch'iu¹* . . . . Spring and autumn; the title of a certain historical work attributed to Confucius.
    央求 *yang¹ ch'iu²* . . . . To beseech; *yang* intensifies *ch'iu*, but is not so strong as *ai*, which see, above.
    飯糜了 *fan⁴ ch'iu³ liao* . . . . . The rice is [boiled to] gruel; the *liao* becomes in fact *lo*, nearly *lo⁴*.

46. 窘 *chiung*, straitened; of space or fortune.
    窘迫 *chiung³ p'o⁴* . . . . Hard pressed, by circumstances, want of means, etc.

47. 窮 *ch'iung*, extremity; the farthest verge.
    貧窮 *p'in² ch'iung²* . . . . Very poor; poverty.

48. 卓 *cho*, a table. *See* Part III, 148.
    桌凳 *cho¹ têng⁴* . . . . Tables and stools or benches.
    清濁 *ch'ing¹ cho²* . . . . Clear and muddy; hence, perspicuity and obscurity.

49. 綽 *ch'o*, roomy; hence, comfortable.
    撦碰 *ch'o¹ p'êng⁴* . . . . To poke and to bump against; hence, collision in general.
    寬綽 *k'uan¹ ch'o⁴* . . . . In easy circumstances.

50. 晝 *chou*, day, as distinguished from night.
    週圍 *chou¹ wei²* . . . . Surrounding; all round.
    車軸 *ch'ê¹ chou²* . . . . The axle-tree.
    臂肘 *pei⁴ chou³* . . . . The arm; *lit.*, the upper and lower parts of the arm.
    晝夜 *chou⁴ yeh⁴* . . . . Day and night.

51. 抽 *ch'ou*, to draw towards one.
    抽查 *ch'ou¹ ch'a²* . . . . To examine one article of a lot.
    綢緞 *ch'ou² tuan⁴* . . . . Silk and satin; silk manufactures.
    醜俊 *ch'ou³ chün⁴* . . . . Ugly and fair.
    香臭 *hsiang¹ ch'ou⁴* . . . . . . Good smells and bad.

52. 句 *chü*, a short clause.
    居處 *chü¹ ch'u³* . . . . A dwelling-place; one's abode. Note *ch'u*, in this sense, properly *ch'u⁴*. *See* under 62, below.
    賭局 *tu³ chü²* . . . . A gambling table or establishment.
    保舉 *pao³ chü³* . . . . To recommend for promotion. Note *pao³*, which becomes *pao²* before *chü³*.
    句段 *chü⁴ tuan⁴* . . . . Clauses and sentences; *q.d.*, such or such a piece of writing will not make them=is not constructed so as to make sense.

53. 取 *ch'ü*, to take, as opposed to presenting.

    冤 屈 *yüan¹ ch'ü¹* . . . . Wronged; oppressed.
    溝 渠 *kou¹ ch'ü²* . . . . Ditches and gutters; drains in general.
    取 送 *ch'ü³ sung⁴* . . . . To take and to present.
    來 去 *lai² ch'ü⁴* . . . . Coming and going.

54. 捐 *chüan*, to contribute in aid of the necessities of the Government.

    捐 納 *chüan¹ na⁴* . . . . To contribute in aid of Government necessities; *lit.*, to contribute and present.
    舒 捲 *shu¹ chüan³* . . . . Open, as the hand, and closed, as the fist; *chüan*, to roll up.
    家 眷 *chia¹ chüan⁴* . . . . One's family; said of one's wife alone, or of wife and children.

55. 全 *ch'üan*, complete.

    圈 點 *ch'üan¹ tien³* . . . . Circles and points; the former marking the sentence, the latter, the clauses in the sentence; or, to punctuate with circles.
    齊 全 *ch'i² ch'üan²* . . . . Completeness; *lit.*, in regular order and complete.
    犬 吠 *ch'üan³ fei⁴* . . . . A dog's bark; the dog barks.
    勸 戒 *ch'üan⁴ chieh⁴* . . . . To warn; *lit.*, to counsel and warn against, *sc.*, a vice or bad habit.

56. 絕 *chüeh*, to cut off.

    噘 嘴 *chüeh¹ tsui³* . . . . To protrude the lips; to pout.
    斷 絕 *tuan⁴ chüeh²* . . . . To cut off.
    馬 撩 蹶 子 *ma³ liao⁴ chüeh³ tzŭ* . . The horse kicks; *liao* meaning to lift.
    倔 喪 *chüeh⁴ sang⁴* . . . . Churlish.

57. 缺 *ch'üeh*, vacant; deficient.

    補 缺 *pu³ ch'üeh¹* . . . . To fill up a vacancy.
    瘸 腿 *ch'üeh² t'ui³* . . . . Lame.
    確 然 *ch'üeh⁴ jan²* . . . . Positively so.

58. 君 *chün*, the Sovereign.

    君 王 *chün¹ wang²* . . . . The Sovereign; *wang* being used in its ancient and classical sense.
    菌 子 *chün³ tzŭ* . . . . Rice with the husk on. The term is unknown in Peking.
    俊 秀 *chün⁴ hsiu⁴* . . . . Fine, of person or talents.

59. 羣 *ch'ün*, properly, a drove, a flock; also, a party of persons.

    成 羣 *ch'êng² ch'ün²* . . . . To make a group or party.

60. 爵 *chüo*, nobility; high position.

    爵 位 *chüo² wei⁴* . . . . Position, where the person spoken of is of somewhat high rank.

61. 郤 *ch'üo*. See above, 43, *ch'io*.

[CHU–CH'UAN.]   PART VII.—THE TONE EXERCISES.   435

62. 主 *chu*, lord; master; host.

     猪羊 *chu¹ yang²* . . . . Pigs and sheep; farming stock.
     竹子 *chu² tzŭ* . . . . The bamboo.
     賓主 *pin¹ chu³* . . . . Guest and host.
     住處 *chu⁴ ch'u⁴* . . . . One's abiding place; one's residence.

63. 出 *ch'u*, to go forth; to go out of.

     出外 *ch'u¹ wai⁴* . . . . To leave home for a place at a certain distance.
     廚房 *ch'u² fang²* . . . . A kitchen.
     處分 *ch'u³ fên⁴* . . . . The punishment of official delinquency; *ch'u³*, to regulate; hence, to punish an official, *sc.*, by fine or disgrace.
     住處 *chu⁴ ch'u⁴* . . . . One's abiding place.

64. 抓 *chua*, to clap the hand, paw, claw, upon.

     抓破 *chua¹ p'o⁴* . . . . To tear by clapping the hand, etc., upon.
     雞爪子 *chi¹ chua³ tzŭ* . . . . . . A fowl's claw.

65. 欻 *ch'ua*, any whistling sound produced by the rapid movement of something through the air.

     欻一聲 *ch'ua¹ i⁴ shêng¹* . . . . There was a whiz, a whir, or any sudden sound.

66. 拽 *chuai*, properly, to draw, or drag, towards one.

     拽泥 *chuai¹ ni²* . . . . To fling mud at; how *chuai¹* comes to mean *fling* is not explained.
     鴨踥 *ya¹ chuai³* . . . . A duck waddles; the waddle of a duck.
     拉拽 *la¹ chuai⁴* . . . . To drag or draw a person, thing, or animal.

67. 揣 *ch'uai*, to feel with the fingers.

     懷揣 *huai² ch'uai¹* . . . . . . To stick [a thing] in the breast of one's garment; [a thing] stuck in the breast.
     揣摩 *ch'uai³ mo²* . . . . To feel for, with the hand; or, *fig.*, of a person speculating, to guess.
     蹬踹 *têng¹ ch'uai⁴* . . . . . . To kick a succession of short kicks.

68. 專 *chuan*, special; individual.

     專門 *chuan¹ mên²* . . . . . . *Lit.*, the only entrance; one particular pursuit; devotion to one pursuit.
     轉移 *chuan³ yi²* . . . . Transfer of things from place to place; of cases, *sc.*, by correspondence between co-ordinate jurisdictions.
     經傳 *ching¹ chuan⁴* . . . . . . The ancient classics of China and the commentary, *lit.*, the tradition.

69. 穿 *ch'uan*, to bore through; hence, to get into one's clothes.

     穿戴 *ch'uan¹ tai⁴* . . . . . . What one wears on the body and carries on one's head; apparel.
     車船 *ch'ê¹ ch'uan²* . . . . . . Carts and junks; carriage by land and water.
     痰喘 *t'an² ch'uan³* . . . . . . An asthmatic affection; *t'an*, the phlegm, the effort to expectorate which produces the *ch'uan*.
     串通 *ch'uan⁴ t'ung¹* . . . . . . In collusion with.

70. 壯 *chuang*, stout; hearty.
 裝載 *chuang¹ tsai⁴* . . . . To load; to put into; to contain.
 粗奘 *ts'u¹ chuang³* . . . . . . Bulky; or, simply, of large dimensions.
 壯健 *chuang⁴ chien⁴* . . . . . . Robust.

71. 牀 *ch'uang*, a bed.
 牕戶 *ch'uang¹ hu⁴* . . . . . . A window. Observe that this *ch'uang¹* is written in several ways; the vulgar form is as here.
 牀鋪 *ch'uang² p'u⁴* . . . . . . Bed and bedding.
 闖入 *ch'uang³ ju⁴* . . . . . . To burst one's way into.
 創始 *ch'uang⁴ shih³* . . . . . . To found; to invent; to originate.

72. 追 *chui*, to pursue.
 追趕 *chui¹ kan³* . . . . To overtake.
 廢墜 *fei⁴ chui⁴* . . . . To go to rack and ruin.

73. 吹 *ch'ui*, to blow with the breath.
 吹打 *ch'ui¹ ta³* . . . . Beating drums and playing on wind instruments.
 垂手 *ch'ui² shou³* . . . . . . To let the hands hang down; hands so hanging.

74. 准 *chun*, to authorise.
 准駁 *chun³ po²* . . . . Approval and disapproval.

75. 春 *ch'un*, spring.
 春夏 *ch'un¹ hsia⁴* . . . . . . Spring and summer.
 純厚 *ch'un² hou⁴* . . . . . . Morally sound; sincere.
 蠢笨 *ch'un³ pên⁴* . . . . . . Loutish and stupid.

76. 中 *chung*, central; inner.
 中外 *chung¹ wai⁴* . . . . . . Within and without; in the capital and the provinces; native and foreigner.
 腫痛 *chung³ t'ung⁴* . . . . . . Swollen and painful.
 輕重 *ch'ing¹ chung⁴* . . . . . Light and heavy; the weight of.

77. 充 *ch'ung*, to represent; to act as.
 充當 *ch'ung¹ tang¹* . . . . . . Representing; filling the place of.
 虫蟻 *ch'ung² yi³* . . . . Creeping things; *lit.*, reptiles and ants.
 寵愛 *ch'ung³ ai⁴* . . . . To be specially fond of; to love fondly.
 鐵銃子 *t'ieh³ ch'ung⁴ tzŭ* . . . A petard; small iron ordnance without any carriage.

78. 擉 *ch'uo*, to strike with a point.
 擉撐 *ch'uo¹ p'êng⁴* . . . . . . Collision in general; *lit.*, blow with the point and laterally.

79. 額 *ê*, a limit, as of number or quantity.
 太阿 *t'ai⁴ ê¹* . . . . An obsolete official title; the name of a sword in history.
 額數 *ê² shu⁴* . . . . A fixed number.
 爾我 *êrh³ ê³* . . . . You and I (the ancient pronunciation of *wo*, I, being *ngo* or *ngê*).
 善惡 *shan⁴ ê⁴* . . . . Virtuous and vicious.

80. 恩 ên, ᵑgên, favour.
 恩典 ên¹ tien³ . . . . Grace; *lit.*, law or rule of grace; originally, grace of the Sovereign.
 揾倒 ên⁴ tao³ . . . . To keep [a man] down on the ground by force.

81. 哼 êng, a sound; humph!
 哼阿 êng¹ a¹ . . . . To hum and to haw.

82. 兒 êrh, a son.
 兒女 êrh² nü³ . . . . Sons and daughters.
 耳朶 êrh³ to⁴ . . . . The ear; *to⁴*, properly *to³*.
 二三 êrh⁴ san¹ . . . . Two or three.

83. 法 fa, a means.
 發遣 fa¹ ch'ien³ . . . . To send into exile.
 法子 fa² tzŭ . . . . Means; plans; resources.
 頭髮 t'ou² fa³ . . . . The hair of the head.
 法門 fa⁴ mên² . . . . The gate of a Buddhist temple.

84. 反 fan, to turn back or over.
 翻騰 fan¹ t'êng² . . . . To turn topsy-turvy.
 煩惱 fan² nao³ . . . . Distressed in mind.
 反倒 fan³ tao⁴ . . . . Upset; turned over; on the contrary.
 喫飯 ch'ih¹ fan⁴ . . . . To eat rice; generally, to eat any meal.

85. 方 fang, square.
 方圓 fang¹ yüan² . . . . . . Square and round.
 房屋 fang² wu¹ . . . . House and rooms; the house [is clean, is dirty, etc.].
 訪查 fang³ ch'a² . . . . To make inquiry into.
 放肆 fang⁴ ssŭ⁴ . . . . To give way to violence, evil passions; to commit disorderly acts.

86. 非 fei, the wrong, as opposed to the right.
 是非 shih⁴ fei¹ . . . . Right and wrong; also, tittle-tattle, scandal, mischief.
 肥瘦 fei² shou⁴ . . . . Fat and lean.
 賊匪 tsei² fei³ . . . . Banditti, rebels, etc.
 使費 shih³ fei⁴ . . . . Expenses; *sc.*, in the way of fees, etc.

87. 分 fên, to divide.
 分開 fên¹ k'ai¹ . . . . To divide into shares, portions, etc.
 墳墓 fên² mu⁴ . . . . A grave; a graveyard.
 脂粉 chih¹ fên³ . . . . Red pigment and white; cosmetics in general.
 職分 chih² fên⁴ . . . . The duties of one's office.

88. 風 fêng, wind.
 風雨 fêng¹ yü³ . . . . Wind and rain.
 裁縫 ts'ai² fêng² . . . . To cut and to sew. N.B.—*Ts'ai²-fêng⁴*, a tailor.
 供奉 kung⁴ fêng⁴ . . . . . . Make tender of [service], *sc.*, in the palace; said of the attendance of high officers on the Sovereign, or of worship to deities; anciently, and still politely, to offer, to present, a thing.

89. 佛 *fo*, Buddha.
    佛老 *fo² lao³* . . . . Buddha and LAO CHÜN; the latter, the founder of the Tao sect.

90. 否 *fou*, not so.
    浮沉 *fou² ch'ên²* . . . . . . Floating and sinking.
    然否 *jan² fou³* . . . . Whether so or not.
    埠口 *fou⁴ k'ou³* . . . . Any port on sea or river.

91. 夫 *fu*, a man; a husband.
    夫妻 *fu¹ ch'i¹* . . . . Husband and wife.
    扶持 *fu² ch'ih²* . . . . To hold oneself up by, *e.g.*, a staff: *fu*, to hold up, as by the arm; *ch'ih*, to grasp in the hand.
    斧鉞 *fu³ yüeh⁴* . . . . Axes; *yüeh*, a battle-axe.
    父母 *fu⁴ mu³* . . . . Father and mother.

92. 哈 *ha*, the sound *ha*.
    哈哈笑 *ha¹ ha¹ hsiao⁴* . . . . . To laugh heartily.
    蝦蟆 *ha² mo⁴* . . . . A frog; *mo*, commonly *ma*.
    哈吧狗 *ha³ pa¹ kou³* . . . . . A lap-dog.
    哈什馬 *ha⁴ shih² ma³* . . . . . Dried frogs, or some such eatable, brought from Manchuria.

93. 害 *hai*, grave injury, moral or material.
    咳聲 *hai¹ shêng¹* . . . . . . The exclamation *hai!*
    孩子 *hai² tzŭ* . . . . A child.
    江海 *chiang¹ hai³* . . . . . . The waters; *lit.*, rivers and seas.
    利害 *li⁴ hai⁴* . . . . A strong intensive, used more commonly of evil things than good; also, profit and damage.

94. 寒 *han*, cold.
    顢頇 *man¹ han¹* . . . . . . Dilatorily, undecidedly; the two characters are not used apart.
    寒涼 *han² liang²* . . . . . . Cold.
    叫喊 *chiao⁴ han³* . . . . . . To call to; to call out.
    滿漢 *man³ han⁴* . . . . . . Manchus and Chinese.

95. 硔 *hang*, to beat the ground preparatory to building a wall.
    打硔 *ta³ hang¹* . . . . To beat the ground preparatory to building a wall.
    各行 *ko⁴ hang²* . . . . Every trade.
    項圈 *hang⁴ ch'üan¹* . . . . . . A neck-ring worn by a child; *hang*, properly, the neck, but not colloquially used in northern mandarin.

96. 好 *hao*, good; to love; to be addicted to; to be in the habit of.
    蒿草 *hao¹ ts'ao³* . . . . . . Jungle; specially, aromatic weeds used for burning; *sc.*, artemisia.
    絲毫 *ssŭ¹ hao²* . . . . The floss of silk; a particle of any kind; very common with a negative; *q.d.*, not a particle.
    好不好 *hao³ pu⁴ hao³* . . . . . Is it well (or good) or not? (Commonly implying that it is.)
    好喜 *hao⁴ hsi* . . . . To be addicted to [any pursuit, good or evil]. N.B.—*Hsi* is atonic.

97. 黑 *hĕ, hei,* black.
    黑白 *hei¹ pai²* . . . . Black and white; used also figuratively as with us; *q.d.,* he can't tell black from white,=good from bad.
    黑豆 *hei³ tou⁴* . . . . Black beans; black pulse.

98. 很 *hĕn,* originally, wilful, litigious, but commonly a strong intensive; often written with the 94th Radical.
    傷痕 *shang¹ hên²* . . . . . . The scar of a wound.
    好得很 *hao³ tĕ² hên³* . . . . . Exceedingly good.
    恨怨 *hên⁴ yüan⁴* . . . . . . Animosity: *hên,* properly, wrath that one feels; *yüan,* that one vents.

99. 恆 *hêng,* constant; enduring.
    哼哈 *hêng¹ ha¹* or *êng¹ a¹* . . To hum and to haw; the guardians at the door of a temple.
    恆久 *hêng² chiu³* . . . . . . Enduring for a long time.
    兇橫 *hsiung¹ hêng⁴* . . . . . Ferocious; brutal.

100. 河 *ho,* a river.
    喫喝 *ch'ih¹ ho¹* . . . . To eat and drink.
    江河 *chiang¹ ho²* . . . . . . Rivers in general.
    賀喜 *ho⁴ hsi³* . . . . To congratulate.

101. 後 *hou,* after, in time or place.
    鮈鹹 *hou¹ hsien²* . . . . . . Briny salt; salt in the extreme.
    公侯 *kung¹ hou²* . . . . . . The two first titles of the ancient five orders of national, as distinct from imperial, nobility: *kung,* generally translated duke, belongs to both orders; *hou,* marquis.
    牛吼 *niu² hou³* . . . . The lowing of oxen; *hou,* also the roar of a lion.
    前後 *ch'ien² hou⁴* . . . . . . Before and behind, in time or place.

102. 戶 *hu,* a door.
    忽然 *hu¹ jan²* . . . . Of a sudden.
    茶壺 *ch'a² hu²* . . . . A tea-pot.
    龍虎榜 *lung² hu³ pang³* . . . . Dragon and tiger affiche; the list published of graduates who obtain degrees as licentiates or doctors. Note *hu³,* but *hu²* before *pang³.*
    戶口 *hu⁴ k'ou³* . . . . A family; population; *lit.,* the mouths in a house.

103. 花 *hua,* flowers.
    花草 *hua¹ ts'ao³* . . . . . . Flowers and grass, or herbs; vegetation.
    泥滑 *ni² hua²* . . . . The mud is slippery.
    話敗人 *hua³ pai⁴ jên²* . . . . To speak ill of a person behind his back, whether your censure be merited or not.
    說話 *shuo¹ hua⁴* . . . . . . To speak; to talk.

104. 壞 *huai,* to injure seriously; to destroy.
    懷想 *huai² hsiang³* . . . . . To think; to cherish a thought.
    損壞 *sun³ huai⁴* . . . . To spoil, be spoiled, more or less; said of things.

105. 換 *huan*, to exchange.

歡喜	*huan¹ hsi³*	To rejoice; to delight in.
連環	*lien² huan²*	Several rounds [of musketry or artillery]; also, of the involution of circles in a pattern; *q.d.*, ring on ring.
鬆緩	*sung¹ huan³*	Slackened, as zeal, industry.
更換	*kêng¹ huan⁴*	To change.

106. 黃 *huang*, yellow.

荒亂	*huang¹ luan⁴*	Wild disorder; *e.g.*, that occasioned by a bad year, by brigandage, etc.
青黃	*ch'ing¹ huang²*	Green and yellow; said of ripening corn.
撒謊	*sa¹ huang³*	To tell lies.
一晃兒	*yi² huang⁴ 'rh*	A flash; its duration,=a moment.

107. 回 *hui*, to turn back.

石灰	*shih² hui¹*	Lime.
回去	*hui² ch'ü⁴*	To go back. Note the two forms of *hui*.
後悔	*hou⁴ hui³*	To repent.
賄賂	*hui⁴ lu⁴*	Bribes.

108. 混 *huên, hun*, mingled in confusion.

昏暗	*hun¹ an⁴*	Dark, as a cloudy day; obscure, of a man's meaning.
鬼魂	*kuei³ hun²*	The spirit of man after death.
渾厚	*hun³ hou⁴*	Lit., stupidly honest; that *will* not see another's faults; not used in a bad sense.
混亂	*hun⁴ luan⁴*	In great confusion; of things tumbled together; also, *fig.* of the state of a country.

109. 紅 *hung*, red.

烘烤	*hung¹ k'ao³*	To heat before the fire.
紅綠	*hung² lü⁴*	Red and green, as trees in blossom; *lü⁴* also read *lu⁴*.
欺哄	*ch'i¹ hung³*	To deceive.
煉汞	*lien⁴ hung⁴*	To smelt quicksilver.

110. 火 *huo*, fire.

豁口子	*huo¹ k'ou³ tzŭ*	An indentation on the body, as a harelip; a gap in a wall; an opening at the end of a seam.
死活	*ssŭ³ huo²*	Dead or alive; whether he will live or not [one cannot tell].
水火	*shui³ huo³*	Water and fire; a poor man *has* these=these and nothing beside; they are said to be *wu² ch'ing²*, unnatural, unreasonable, in cases of flood or fire; *q.d.*, they make no distinction of persons. Note *shui³* changes to *shui²* before *huo³*.
貨物	*huo⁴ wu⁴*	Merchandise.

[HSI—HSING.]   PART VII.—THE TONE EXERCISES.   441

111. 西 *hsi*, west.
    東西 *tung¹ hsi¹* . . . . East and west; a thing.
    酒席 *chiu³ hsi²* . . . . A dinner (to guests).
    喜歡 *hsi³ huan¹* . . . . To like; to be pleased with.
    粗細 *ts'u¹ hsi⁴* . . . . Coarse and fine; the quality of anything coarse or fine.

112. 夏 *hsia*, summer.
    瞎子 *hsia¹ tzŭ* . . . . A blind man; personally addressed as *hsien-shêng*.
    雲霞 *yün² hsia²* . . . . Cloud and mist.
    春夏 *ch'un¹ hsia⁴* . . . . Spring and summer.

113. 向 *hsiang*, towards; in the direction of.
    香臭 *hsiang¹ ch'ou⁴* . . . . Fragrance and stench.
    詳細 *hsiang² hsi⁴* . . . . Minutely; detailedly.
    思想 *ssŭ¹ hsiang³* . . . . To think; bethink you!
    方向 *fang¹ hsiang⁴* . . . . Direction taken or to be taken.

114. 小 *hsiao*, small.
    消滅 *hsiao¹ chien³* . . . . To diminish; to fall off.
    學徒 *hsiao² t'u²* . . . . An apprentice.
    大小 *ta⁴ hsiao³* . . . . Great and small; the size of.
    談笑 *t'an² hsiao⁴* . . . . To chat and laugh.

115. 些 *hsieh*, few; little of.
    些微 *hsieh¹ wei¹* . . . . A trifle; in a small degree.
    靴鞋 *hsüeh¹ hsieh²* . . . . Boots and shoes; *hsieh*, commonly written 鞋.
    流血 *liu² hsieh³* . . . . To bleed; bleeding.
    謝恩 *hsieh⁴ ên¹* . . . . To thank for favour shown.

116. 先 *hsien*, before, in time.
    先後 *hsien¹ hou⁴* . . . . Before and after.
    清閒 *ch'ing¹ hsien²* . . . . Tranquil; undisturbed by cares, noise, etc.
    危險 *wei² hsien³* . . . . Dangerous.
    限期 *hsien⁴ ch'i¹* . . . . A given date; a limited period.

117. 心 *hsin*, the heart; also, the mind.
    心性 *hsin¹ hsing⁴* . . . . The nature of the heart or mind; its character, morally.
    尋東西 *hsin² tung¹ hsi¹* . . . . To ask for a thing and give nothing in return.
    書信 *shu¹ hsin⁴* . . . . A note; a letter.

118. 姓 *hsing*, family name; surname.
    星宿 *hsing¹ su⁴* . . . . The stars; *lit.*, star-constellation.
    行爲 *hsing² wei²* . . . . Conduct; actions.
    睡醒 *shui⁴ hsing³* . . . . Asleep or awake; to wake up.
    姓名 *hsing⁴ ming²* . . . . Surname and name.

119. 學 *hsio*, to learn.
    學問 *hsio² wên⁴* . . . . Acquired knowledge; learning; *lit.*, learning and asking.

120. 修 *hsiu*, to repair; to prepare.
    修理 *hsiu¹ li³* . . . . To put in order, *e.g.*, mechanism, roads, etc.
    糟朽 *tsao¹ hsiu³* . . . . Rotten.
    領袖 *ling³ hsiu⁴* . . . . Collar and cuff, or sleeve; also, *fig.* for the best hand, the managing man.

121. 兄 *hsiung*, elder brother.
    兄弟 *hsiung¹ ti⁴* . . . . Elders and juniors in a family.
    狗熊 *kou³ hsiung²* . . . . A dog-bear; a bear said to resemble a dog.

122. 須 *hsü*, necessary; must.
    必須 *pi⁴ hsü¹* . . . . Must; is sure to.
    徐圖 *hsü² t'u²* . . . . To take time in devising; to deliberate.
    應許 *ying¹ hsü³* . . . . To promise.
    接續 *chieh¹ hsü⁴* . . . . In connexion with or continuation of the foregoing; *lit.*, receiving, taking up, and continuing.

123. 喧 *hsüan*, the uproar of a crowd.
    喧嚷 *hsüan¹ jang³* . . . . Clamour of many voices.
    懸掛 *hsüan² kua⁴* . . . . To be suspended; as a hanging lamp, a sign-board.
    揀選 *chien³ hsüan³* . . . . . . To select [officials for promotion]. Note *chien³* changes to *chien²*.
    候選 *hou⁴ hsüan⁴* . . . . [Of officials] awaiting selection.

124. 雪 *hsüeh*, snow.
    靴鞋 *hsüeh¹ hsieh²* . . . . . . Boots and shoes. *See* under 115, *hsieh²*.
    穴道 *hsüeh² tao⁴* . . . . In anatomy, the space between the joints; the points at which, in acupuncture, the needle is introduced; applied in geomancy to the features of ground.
    雨雪 *yü³ hsüeh³* . . . . Rain and snow. Note *yü³* changes to *yü²*.
    鑽穴 *tsuan¹ hsüeh⁴* . . . . . . To excavate, as a mine; of wild beasts, to dig a den to lie in.

125. 巡 *hsün*, to go rounds.
    熏蒸 *hsun¹ chêng¹* . . . . . . Of steamy vapour (after rain, off a fen, etc.).
    巡察 *hsün² ch'a²* . . . . To go rounds, as a watch, a cruiser, etc.
    營汛 *ying² hsün⁴* . . . . A military post; collectively, the military in a particular locality; *lit.*, battalions, or cantonments and minor stations.

126. 學 *hsüo* (also, as in 119, *hsio*; also, *hsüeh*), to learn.
    學生 *hsüo² shêng¹* . . . . . . A pupil; a student.

127. 衣 *i*, *yi*, clothes.
    衣裳 *i¹ shang¹* . . . . Clothes in general; originally, *i*, of the upper clothing, *shang*, of the lower.
    一個 *i² ko⁴* . . . . One. *See* "The Numeratives," Part III, p. 4.
    尾巴 *i³ pa¹* . . . . The tail of beasts, fish, etc. Note *i³* properly *wei³*.
    容易 *yung² i⁴* . . . . Easy; *yung* also read *jung*.

[JAN–JU.] PART VII.—THE TONE EXERCISES. 443

128. 染 *jan*, to dye.
　　然否 *jan² fou³* . . . . Is it thus or not? also, Whether it be so or not [is uncertain].
　　沾染 *chan¹ jan³* . . . . Thoroughly saturated with; deep dyed in; used literally, but also *fig.* of vicious habits.

129. 嚷 *jang*, to talk too loud; to be noisy.
　　嚷嚷 *jang¹ jang¹* . . . . To blab; to let out secrets.
　　瓤子 *jang² tzŭ* . . . . The inside of a melon, pulp, seeds, and juice; also, the works of a watch, etc.
　　嚷鬧 *jang³ nao⁴* . . . . To quarrel; to have altercation with a man; to make a row, as one man or many.
　　謙讓 *ch'ien¹ jang⁴* . . . . . . To decline anything offered one; to decline praise as unworthy of it.

130. 繞 *jao*, to wind round (*act.* and *neut.*).
　　饒裕 *jao² yü⁴* . . . . Affluence; *lit.*, plenty to eat and more.
　　圍繞 *wei² jao³* . . . . To enwreath; to wrap round; also, *fig.* of a siege.
　　繞住 *jao⁴ chu⁴* . . . . To deprive of the power of movement by tying; also, *fig.* of affairs. Cf. complication; hand-tied.

131. 熱 *jê*, *jo*, hot.
　　惹事 *jê³ shih⁴* . . . . To make or provoke trouble.
　　冷熱 *lêng³ jê⁴* . . . . Cold and hot; cold and heat; temperature. *See* Part III, 227.

132. 人 *jên*, man.
　　人物 *jên² wu⁴* . . . . Men and all other created things; also, a "man," in a good sense.
　　容忍 *jung² jên³* . . . . Forbearing; tolerant; *jung* also read *yung*.
　　責任 *tsê² jên⁴* . . . . Responsibility; *lit.*, the blame-bearing, the blame-trust.

133. 扔 *jêng*, to throw from one.
　　扔棄 *jêng¹ ch'i⁴* . . . . To fling away as useless; *jêng¹* also read *jêng³* in other combinations.

134. 日 *jih*, the sun; the day.
　　日月 *jih⁴ yüeh⁴* . . . . Sun and moon; also, days and months.

135. 若 *jo*, if.
　　若論 *jo⁴ lun⁴* . . . . If it be argued; also, if one is speaking of a subject, as regards, with reference to.

136. 肉 *jou*, meat; flesh.
　　揉的一聲 *jou¹ ti¹ i⁴ shêng¹* . . . There was a sudden whir, or any like sound, not loud; *jou*, properly, to rub between the hands.
　　剛柔 *kang¹ jou²* . . . . Hard and soft; morally, firm and yielding.
　　骨肉 *ku³ jou⁴* . . . . Bone and flesh; also, *fig.* of near relationship, but then *ku²*.

137. 如 *ju*, if; like as; also, in accordance with.
　　如貼 *ju¹ t'ieh¹* . . . . Of management of private affairs, satisfactory; also, of health, good.
　　如若 *ju² jo⁴* . . . . If.
　　強入 *ch'iang³ ju³* . . . . To force wares on a buyer; to force one's things into a house; to force an object into a hole that is too small for it. Note *ch'iang³* becomes *ch'iang²* before *ju³*.
　　出入 *ch'u¹ ju⁴* . . . . To go out and come in; hence, expenditure and revenue; also, in judicial sentences, *ch'u*, lenient, *ju*, severe.

138. 輭 *juan*, soft.
    輭弱 *juan³ jo⁴* . . . . . . Soft and weakly; feeble.

139. 瑞 *jui*, blessings; prosperity.
    花蕊 *hua¹ jui³* . . . . . . The stamens and pistil of a flower.
    祥瑞 *hsiang² jui⁴* . . . . . . Prosperous condition, sc., of a State.

140. 潤 *jun*, moistened.
    潤澤 *jun⁴ tsê²* . . . . . . [Of weather] soft, slightly damp; *tsê²* also *tsê⁴*.

141. 榮 *jung*, anciently, the beauty of flowers, plants, etc., as distinguished from that of trees.
    榮耀 *jung² yao⁴* . . . . . . Brilliant, *e.g.*, as a *cortège*, etc.; oftener used of externals, but also of virtue, ability, etc.; *yao⁴* also read *yo⁴*.
    毧毛 *jung³ mao²* . . . . . . Down of birds' feathers; the shorter hair of camels, etc.

142. 嘎 *ka*, the *ca* in cachinnation.
    嘎嘎的笑 *ka¹ ka¹ ti¹ hsiao⁴* . . A roar of laughter.
    打嘎兒 *ta³ ka² 'rh* . . . . . To play at ball; *ka-'rh* is a wooden ball struck with a stick.
    嘎雜子 *ka³ tsa² tzŭ* . . . . . A cross-grained fellow; not sympathetic; a strong term of abuse.
    雞嘎嘎蛋兒 *chi¹ ka⁴ ka⁴ tan⁴ 'rh* . Cry of a hen laying.

143. 卡 *k'a, ch'ia*, a post in a pass.
    卡倫 *k'a¹ lun²* . . . . . . An inland Customs station or frontier guard house; also read *ch'ia³* or *k'a³*.

144. 改 *kai*, to change.
    該當 *kai¹ tang¹* . . . . . . Ought rightly to be.
    改變 *kai³ pien⁴* . . . . . . To change, sc., laws, fashions, etc., for good or evil.
    大概 *ta⁴ kai⁴* . . . . . . A general outline; generally; probably.

145. 開 *k'ai*, to open.
    開閉 *k'ai¹ pi⁴* . . . . . . Open or closed; sc., a gate, a shop, etc.
    慷慨 *k'ang³ k'ai³* . . . . . Liberal; large-hearted. Note *k'ang³* nearly *k'ang¹* before *k'ai³*.

146. 甘 *kan*, sweet.
    甘苦 *kan¹ k'u³* . . . . . . Sweet and bitter.
    追趕 *chui¹ kan³* . . . . . . To go after; to pursue.
    才幹 *ts'ai² kan⁴* . . . . . . Abilities.

147. 看 *k'an*, to see; to look at.
    看守 *k'an¹ shou³* . . . . . To keep guard over.
    刀砍 *tao¹ k'an³* . . . . . . To strike with a sword.
    看見 *k'an⁴ chien⁴* . . . . . To see.

148. 剛 *kang*, hard; hardness; also, firm.
    剛纔 *kang¹ ts'ai²* . . . . . Just now; just then. It is thought by some that this character is corruptly used for 將 (*chiang¹*).
    剛剛兒 *kang¹ kang² êrh* . . . Only just; exactly.
    土堈子 *t'u³ kang³ tzŭ* . . . . A rise in the level of ground. Note *t'u³* becomes *t'u²* before *kang³*.
    檯杠 *t'ai² kang⁴* . . . . . . To carry a bier; vulgarly, to dispute, to argue angrily.

149. 炕 *k'ang*, a stove-bed.

 康健 *k'ang¹ chien⁴* . . . . At ease in mind and in vigorous health.
 扛擡 *k'ang² t'ai²* . . . . To carry, as luggage on the shoulder, *k'ang*; with poles between two men, *t'ai*; or, generally, of porterage.
 慷慨 *k'ang³ k'ai³*. *See* under 145.
 火炕 *huo³ k'ang⁴* . . . . The stove-bed of brick used in the north of China.

150. 告 *kao*, to tell to.

 高低 *kao¹ ti¹* . . . . High and low; the height of; also, of persons, difference of degree or ability.
 稿案 *kao³ an⁴* . . . . Official papers; the correspondence, archives, of an office.
 告訴 *kao⁴ su⁴* . . . . To inform; to tell to; *su* alone is, properly, to complain.

151. 考 *k'ao*, to examine, as candidates for degree, for employment in clerkships, etc.

 尻骨 *k'ao¹ ku³* . . . . The *os coxendicis*.
 考察 *k'ao³ ch'a²* . . . . To examine; to search.
 倚靠 *i¹ k'ao⁴* . . . . To depend on, as a friend on a friend, or a subordinate on a superior authority.

152. 給 *kei*, properly *chi*, to give; hence, *to* and *for*.

 放給 *fang⁴ kei³* . . . . To issue, as grain, money, clothes, etc., to the poor, pay to troops, etc.

153. 刻 *k'ei*, properly *k'ê*, to engrave; only pronounced as here in *k'ei sou*.

 刻搜 *k'ei¹ sou¹* . . . . To annoy; to act vexatiously to.

154. 根 *kên*, root.

 根本 *kên¹ pên³* . . . . The very beginning, *fons et origo*; the cradle of a race; the family of a man; the origin of a case: *kên*, properly, the root of a tree below, *pên*, above, the soil.
 鬭哏 *tou¹ kên²* . . . . The "chaff" of mountebanks, strolling story-tellers, etc.
 艮卦 *kên⁴ kua⁴* . . . . The symbol or diagram *kên*; the seventh of the *pa kua*, eight diagrams, which may be called the categorical indices of Chinese philosophy: *kên*, generally indicative of immobility; stable.

155. 肯 *k'ên*, to wish; to choose.

 肯不肯 *k'ên³ pu⁴ k'ên³* . . . . Will you . . . . ? *lit.*, will you or won't you? but, in effect, not so strong.
 一揹子 *i² k'ên⁴ tzŭ* . . . . A bundle of anything that one requires both hands to encircle.

156. 更 *kêng*, more; to change.

 更改 *kêng¹ kai³* . . . . To change; to alter.
 道埂子 *tao⁴ kêng³ tzŭ* . . . . . Any raised footpath left by the side of a field.
 更多 *kêng⁴ to¹* . . . . More; a greater number or quantity.

157. 坑 *k'êng*, a hollow; a ditch; a pit.

 坑坎 *k'êng¹ k'an³* . . . . A dip in a road.

158. 各 *ko, kê*, each; every.
 哥 哥 *ko¹ ko¹* . . . . Elder brother.
 影 格 *ying³ ko²* . . . . Copy-slips: *ying*, a shadow; hence, an appearance; *ko*, here in the sense of lines laid down for guidance. The Chinese copy-slip is in columns of characters separated by lines, and the student traces the characters through a sheet of paper laid over the copy-slip.
 各 自 各 兒 *ko² tzu⁴ ko³ 'rh* . . . . By oneself.
 幾 個 *chi³ ko⁴* . . . . Some; a certain number; how many?

159. 可 *k'o, k'ê*, to be right; to be able; with adjectives and in attributive constructions, much what the termination *bilis* is in Latin.
 磕 頭 *k'o¹ t'ou²* . . . . To *kotow*.
 瞌 睡 *k'o² shui⁴* . . . . To nod with sleep.
 饑 渴 *chi¹ k'o³* . . . . Hunger and thirst.
 賓 客 *pin¹ k'o⁴* . . . . A guest.

160. 狗 *kou*, a dog.
 溝 渠 *kou¹ ch'ü²* . . . . Ditches: *kou*, large and artificial; *ch'ü*, small waterways; generally, the drains of a city.
 小 狗 兒 的 *hsiao³ kou² 'rh ti¹* . . (To a child) You young dog! (not abusive).
 豬 狗 *chu¹ kou³* . . . . Pigs and dogs, said of dirty people; also, *lit.*=domestic animals in general.
 足 彀 *tsu² kou⁴* . . . . Sufficient.

161. 口 *k'ou*, the mouth.
 摳 破 了 *k'ou¹ p'o⁴ liao³* . . . . To work a hole through with the finger. Note *liao* enclitic, nearly *lo⁴*.
 口 舌 *k'ou³ shê²* . . . . Altercation.
 叩 頭 *k'ou⁴ t'ou²* . . . . To knock the head on the ground; to *kotow*.

162. 古 *ku*, ancient.
 料 估 *liao⁴ ku¹* . . . . To estimate, as cost, amount of materials.
 骨 頭 *ku² t'ou⁴* . . . . A bone; one's bones. Observe *ku*, properly *ku³*, here *ku²*; *t'ou* properly *t'ou²*, here *t'ou⁴*.
 古 今 *ku³ chin¹* . . . . Ancient and modern; in past times and at present.
 堅 固 *chien¹ ku⁴* . . . . Stable, sound, strong, as a city wall, a ship, etc.

163. 苦 *k'u*, bitter.
 窟 窿 *k'u¹ lung¹* . . . . A hole.
 甜 苦 *t'ien² k'u³* . . . . Sweet and bitter; also, *fig.* of one's lot in life.
 褲 子 *k'u⁴ tzŭ* . . . . Trowsers.

164. 瓜 *kua*, gourd.
 瓜 果 *kua¹ kuo³* . . . . Gourds and fruit; collective of such productions.
 多 寡 *to¹ kua³* . . . . Many and few; how many? the number of.
 懸 掛 *hsüan² kua⁴* . . . . . . To suspend, be suspended, in space.

165. 跨 *k'ua*, to bestride.
   - 誇獎 *k'ua¹ chiang¹* . . . . To praise, oneself or another. Note *ch'iang¹* properly *ch'iang³*.
   - 傍子 *k'ua³ tzŭ* . . . . A person remarkable for country accent, unfashionable dress, etc.
   - 跨馬 *k'ua⁴ ma³* . . . . To ride with both legs on the same side.

166. 怪 *kuai*, singular; strange; monstrous.
   - 乖張 *kuai¹ chang¹* . . . . . . Of a person with ways of his own; one who does not get on well with others.
   - 拐騙 *kuai³ p'ien⁴* . . . . . . To do one out of anything; to beguile (as kidnappers) children, slaves, etc.
   - 怪道 *kuai⁴ tao⁴* . . . . Not strange! No wonder! The sentence is elliptical.

167. 快 *k'uai*, quick.
   - 搔癢癢 *k'uai² yang³ yang* . . . To scratch an itching. Note that *k'uai*, properly *k'uai³*, becomes *k'uai²* before *yang³*, and that the second *yang* is atonic.
   - 快慢 *k'uai⁴ man⁴* . . . . . . Quick and slow; the speed of.

168. 官 *kuan*, an official.
   - 官員 *kuan¹ yüan²* . . . . . . An official; *yüan* meaning the same thing as *kuan*.
   - 管理 *kuan³ li³* . . . . To manage; to take care of. Note *kuan³* becomes *kuan²* before *li³*.
   - 習慣 *hsi² kuan⁴* . . . . . . To be practised in; to be expert at; to be well used to.

169. 寬 *k'uan*, wide; roomy.
   - 寬窄 *k'uan¹ chai³* . . . . . . Wide and narrow; the breadth of.
   - 款項 *k'uan³ hsiang⁴* . . . . . Larger and smaller items; expenditure.

170. 光 *kuang*, lustre; brightness.
   - 光明 *kuang¹ ming²* . . . . . Bright; intelligent.
   - 廣大 *kuang³ ta⁴* . . . . . . Extensive.
   - 遊逛 *yu² kuang⁴* . . . . . . To stroll; to exercise; to travel, as a tourist.

171. 況 *k'uang*, moreover.
   - 誆騙 *k'uang¹ p'ien⁴* . . . . . To humbug; to cheat; to swindle.
   - 狂妄 *k'uang² wang⁴* . . . . . Arrogant and wrong-doing; said of persons in high station.
   - 況且 *k'uang⁴ ch'ieh³* . . . . . Moreover; in addition.

172. 規 *kuei*, a pair of compasses.
   - 規矩 *kuei¹ chü⁴* . . . . . . Proper custom or conduct; *lit.*, compasses and rule, but then *chü³*.
   - 詭詐 *kuei³ cha⁴* . . . . . . Artful; deceitful.
   - 富貴 *fu⁴ kuei⁴* . . . . . . Rich; *lit.*, rich and honourable.

173. 愧 *k'uei*, to be ashamed.
   - 虧欠 *k'uei¹ ch'ien⁴* . . . . . To be in debt.
   - 葵花 *k'uei² hua¹* . . . . . . The sunflower.
   - 傀儡 *k'uei³ lei³* . . . . . . A marionette; *lit.*, an ugly doll. Note *k'uei³* becomes *k'uei²* before *lei³*.
   - 慚愧 *ts'an² k'uei⁴* . . . . . Shame.

174. 棍 *kuên, kun,* a staff.
 翻 滾 *fan¹ kuên³* . . . . Topsy-turvy, like things in a pot of boiling water.
 棍子棒子 *kuên⁴ tzŭ pang⁴ tzŭ* . . Sticks and staves, such as children might use in play, or ruffians in a fray.

175. 困 *k'uên, k'un,* one of the eight *kua.* See under **154,** *kên.*
 坤 道 *k'uên¹ tao⁴* . . . . Earth, or terrestrial matter; the female principle, as distinct from the male.
 閨 閫 *kuei¹ k'uên³* . . . . . . Whatever belongs to woman; used often like our phrase *the sex*; also, as feminineness.
 乏 困 *fa² k'uên⁴* . . . . Tired and sleepy.

176. 工 *kung,* labour.
 工 夫 *kung¹ fu¹* . . . . Labour; also, the time it occupies; hence, leisure.
 金 礦 *chin¹ kung³* . . . . . . Gold mines.
 通 共 *t'ung¹ kung⁴* . . . . . . The whole of any thing or number.

177. 孔 *k'ung,* hollow.
 空 虛 *k'ung¹ hsü¹* . . . . . . Cleaned out; empty.
 面 孔 *mien⁴ k'ung³* . . . . . . The cavities of the face, eyes, ears, nostrils, etc.; the face generally.
 閒 空 *hsien² k'ung⁴* . . . . . . With nothing to do; leisure.

178. 果 *kuo,* fruit.
 飯 鍋 *fan⁴ kuo¹* . . . . A pan to cook rice in.
 國 家 *kuo² chia¹* . . . . The State; *lit.,* State-family.
 結 果 *chieh² kuo³* . . . . The fruit is formed; also, *fig.* of a result; also, *ne plus ultra.*
 過 去 *kuo⁴ ch'ü⁴* . . . . To pass by.

179. 闊 *k'uo,* wide.
 寬 闊 *k'uan¹ k'uo⁴* . . . . . . Extensive; *e.g.,* as a country.

180. 拉 *la,* to draw; to drag.
 拉 扯 *la¹ ch'ê³* . . . . To drag, *sc.,* a person; also, *fig.,* to implicate; also, of the relationship of someone with one's relation; *q.d.,* such a person dragged into relationship.
 邋 遢 *la² t'a⁴* . . . . Slovenly in dress; in business, the opposite of 俐 羅 (*li⁴ lo¹*), prompt, decided.
 喇 叭 *la³ pa¹* . . . . A trumpet.
 蠟 燭 *la⁴ chu²* . . . . Properly, a wax candle; but used of all candles.

181. 來 *lai,* to come.
 來 去 *lai² ch'ü⁴* . . . . To come and go.
 倚 賴 *i³ lai⁴* . . . . To rely on.

182. 懶 *lan,* idle.
 鬅 鬆 *lan¹ san¹* . . . . Dawdling; *lit.,* of hair dishevelled.
 貪 婪 *t'an¹ lan²* . . . . Covetous.
 懶 惰 *lan³ to⁴* . . . . Idle.
 燦 爛 *ts'an³ lan⁴* . . . . Properly, bright, as fire-light; variegated in colour.

183. 浪 *lang*, a wave.

    檳榔 *ping¹ lang¹* . . . . The betel or areca nut.
    狼虎 *lang² hu³* . . . . Wolves and tigers; when *fig.* of ravenous appetite or gluttony, *hu* is atonic; also, *fig.* of temerity.
    光朗 *kuang¹ lang³* . . . . . . Bright; unblemished; *e.g.*, as fine jeweller's work.
    波浪 *po¹ lang⁴* . . . . Waves.

184. 老 *lao*, old.

    打撈 *ta³ lao¹* . . . . To fish up, or try to fish up, out of water, whether person or thing, visible or invisible.
    勞苦 *lao² k'u³* . . . . Fatigue, bodily rather than mental.
    老幼 *lao³ yu⁴* . . . . Old and young.
    旱澇 *han⁴ lao⁴* . . . . Drought and inundation.

185. 勒 *lé* (also *lei*, see under 186), originally, a bit; it has other meanings, but is not used colloquially except in combination with a verb, as here.

    勒索 *lé¹ so³* . . . . To "squeeze;" to extort anything from; *lé¹* more commonly *lé²*.
    歡樂 *huan¹ lé⁴* . . . . To rejoice, to make merry, as a large party together.

186. 累 *léi, lei*, to entangle; to embarrass.

    勒死 *lei¹ ssŭ³* . . . . To strangle.
    雷電 *lei² tien⁴* . . . . Thunder and lightning.
    累次 *lei³ tz'ŭ⁴* . . . . Time after time.
    族類 *tsu² lei⁴* . . . . One's relatives; *q.d.*, the whole tribe.

187. 冷 *léng*, cold.

    稜角 *léng² chio² ⁴* . . . . . . *Lit.*, edge and corner; *fig.* for extremity, *q.d.*, nothing to lay hold of; *chio* also *chiao³*.
    冷熱 *léng³ jo⁴* . . . . Cold and hot; temperature.
    發愣 *fa¹ léng⁴* . . . . To be absent; to stare idiot-like; to be taken aback.

188. 立 *li*, to stand upright.

    玻璃 *po¹ li¹* . . . . Glass; *li¹* properly *li²*.
    分離 *fên¹ li²* . . . . Separated, as members of a family dispersed.
    禮貌 *li³ mao⁴* . . . . Politeness; manners.
    站立 *chan⁴ li⁴* . . . . To stand up, as persons.

189. 倆 *lia*, vulgar for *liang*, two.

    倆三 *lia³ sa¹* . . . . Two or three.

190. 兩 *liang*, the Chinese ounce.

    商量 *shang¹ liang¹* . . . . . . To consult together.
    涼熱 *liang² jo⁴* . . . . Cool and hot.
    斤兩 *chin¹ liang³* . . . . . . Catties and ounces.
    原諒 *yüan² liang⁴* . . . . . . To pardon.

191. 了 *liao*, to end; to complete.
    無聊 $wu^2\ liao^2$ . . . . In despair; *lit.*, without resource.
    了斷 $liao^3\ tuan^4$ . . . . To decide definitely, as a case in court; the decision of a case.
    材料 $ts'ai^2\ liao^4$ . . . . Materials; *e.g.*, building materials.

192. 裂 *lieh*, arrayed in order.
    罷咧 $pa^4\ lieh^1$ . . . . An interjection, common at the end of a sentence, = that's all about it.
    瞎咧咧 $hsia^1\ lieh^2\ lieh^2$ . . . . . Whining of small children; in grown-up people, maudlin, as of the speech of a drunken man; also, to talk nonsense. *N.B.*—Emphasise the first *lieh*.
    咧嘴 $lieh^3\ tsui^3$ . . . . To draw down the corners of the mouth in a way indicative of contempt or hostility. Note *lieh* nearly *lieh²*.
    擺列 $pai^3\ lieh^4$ . . . . To array at given distances; *e.g.*, a rank of soldiers.

193. 連 *lien*, to unite.
    連上 $lien^1\ shang$ . . . . . . United; coupled; to couple.
    憐恤 $lien^2\ hsü^4$ . . . . To compassionate.
    臉面 $lien^3\ mien^4$ . . . . . . The face.
    練習 $lien^4\ hsi^2$ . . . . To practise; practised in.

194. 林 *lin*, a forest; a grove.
    淋拉起來 $lin^1\ la^1\ ch'i^3\ lai^2$ . . . Began to drizzle.
    樹林子 $shu^4\ lin^2\ tzŭ$ . . . . . A forest.
    房檁 $fang^2\ lin^3$ . . . . The cross-beams of a roof.
    租賃 $tsu^1\ lin^4$ . . . . To hire [a room or house].

195. 另 *ling*, additional.
    零碎 $ling^2\ sui^4$ . . . . Fragments; odds and ends.
    領袖 $ling^3\ hsiu^4$. *See* under **120**, *hsiu*.
    另外 $ling^4\ wai^4$ . . . . Separately; additionally.

196. 略 *lio*, originally, to lay out ground, *e.g.*, in fields. See *lüeh* (**202**), *lüo* (**204**).
    謀略 $mou^2\ lio^4$ . . . . Strategical combinations; plan of a campaign.

197. 留 *liu*, to detain; to keep.
    遛打 $liu^1\ ta$ . . . . To stroll; *ta* atonic.
    收留 $shou^1\ liu^2$ . . . . To take in, to give hospitality to, a person for a certain length of time.
    楊柳 $yang^2\ liu^3$ . . . . The willow.
    五六 $wu^3\ liu^4$ . . . . Five or six.

198. 騾 *lo*, a mule.
    捋起袖子 $lo^1\ ch'i^3\ hsiu^4\ tzŭ$ . . To tuck up the sleeves.
    騾馬 $lo^2\ ma^3$ . . . . Mules and horses.
    裸身 $lo^3\ shên^1$ . . . . Stark naked.
    駱駝 $lo^4\ t'o^2$ . . . . A camel.

[LOU–LUN.] PART VII.—THE TONE EXERCISES. 451

199. 陋 *lou*, mean, in spirit or appearance; used only in combination.

 摟衣裳 *lou¹ i¹ shang¹* . . . . . To hold up the skirts of one's long dress.
 樓房 *lou² fang²* . . . . A house with an upper story.
 酒簍 *chiu³ lou³* . . . . Wine baskets; large wicker bottles lined with oiled paper. Note *chiu³* does not here become *chiu²*.
 鄙陋 *pi⁴ lou⁴* . . . . Mean-spirited; vulgar-minded; ungentlemanlike in conduct.

200. 律 *lü*, a statute.

 驢馬 *lü² ma³* . . . . Asses and horses.
 屢次 *lü³ tz'ŭ⁴* . . . . Several times; repeatedly.
 律例 *lü⁴ li⁴* . . . . Statutes and minor enactments.

201. 戀 *lüan*, affection for one's family, birthplace, etc.

 依戀 *i¹ lian⁴ or lüan⁴* . . . . . To cling affectionately to family, home, friends, etc.

202. 略 *lüeh*. See *lio* (196). It is hard to say when this character is pronounced *lüeh* and when *lio*.

 忽略 *hu¹ lüeh⁴* . . . . From carelessness, from indifference . . . .

203. 掄 *lün*, to whirl round.

 混掄 *huên⁴ lün¹* . . . . Whirling madly round, sc., a staff or the like.
 淋溼 *lün² shih¹* . . . . Soaked with rain. See under 194, *lin*.
  lün³ tzŭ . . . . A characterless word meaning a weal.

204. 略 *lio*. See *lio* (196) and *lüeh* (202).

 大略 *ta⁴ lio⁴* . . . . General outline.

205. 路 *lu*, a road.

 嘟嚕 *tu¹ lu¹* . . . . A bunch of grapes, cash, fish, etc.; a sound like *turrh*, of common occurrence in Mongolian; hence, applied to thick guttural speech of any man.
 爐灶 *lu² tsao⁴* . . . . A kitchen fire.
 船櫓 *ch'uan² lu³* . . . . The stern paddle of a junk, commonly called a "yuloh."
 道路 *tao⁴ lu⁴* . . . . Roads and ways.

206. 亂 *luan*, confused; disorderly.

 雜亂 *tsa² luan⁴* . . . . Of things jumbled together.

207. 論 *lun*, to speak of; to discuss a matter.

 車輪 *ch'ê¹ lun²* . . . . The wheel of a cart.
 囫圇 *hu² lun³* . . . . In the gross, without distinction of quality; of bolting down a fruit *whole*; commonly *hu² lun*.
 無論 *wu² lun⁴* . . . . Not to speak of=setting apart something already spoken of.

208. 龍 *lung*, the dragon.

窟窿 *k'u¹ lung¹* . . . . A hole.
龍虎榜 *lung² hu³ pang³* . . . . The published list of passed graduates; *lit.*, the roll, or placard, of dragons and tigers. *See* note on *hu³* (102).
瓦隴 *wa³ lung³* . . . . The lines or furrows between the tiles of a roof. Note *wa³* nearly *wa²*.
胡弄局 *hu⁴ lung⁴ chü²* . . . . . Of any thing or affair which *seems* all right, but has been so made or managed as to be worthless: *hu⁴ lung*, to take in by words or deeds; *chü*, properly, a chess-board.

209. 馬 *ma*, the horse.

爹媽 *tieh¹ ma¹* . . . . Daddy and mammy.
麻木 *ma² mu⁴* . . . . Numb, as a foot asleep, a paralytic limb.
馬鞍 *ma³ ngan¹* . . . . A saddle.
打罵 *ta³ ma⁴* . . . . Blows and curses; abuse.

210. 買 *mai*, to buy.

葬埋 *tsang⁴ mai²* . . . . . . To bury.
收買 *shou¹ mai³* . . . . . . To buy things brought to one for sale.
發賣 *fa¹ mai⁴* . . . . For sale; to sell or expose to sale.

211. 慢 *man*, slow.

顢頇 *man¹ han¹* . . . . . . Dilatory; the opposite of 簡決 (*chien chüeh*), to decide promptly, summarily.
隱瞞 *yin³ man²* . . . . . . Close, as the opposite of talkative, outspoken.
豐滿 *fêng¹ man³* . . . . . . Abundant, *sc.*, as a dinner; *fêng tsu*, plentiful, as a year.
快慢 *k'uai⁴ man⁴* . . . . . . Quick and slow; the speed of.

212. 忙 *mang*, hurried; hasty.

白茫茫 *pai² mang¹ mang¹* . . . The brightness of a large sheet of water. Cf. *hao hao*, Part V, Lesson XCI, Note 4.
急忙 *chi² mang²* . . . . . . Haste (not hurry); without loss of time.
鹵莽 *lu³ mang³* . . . . In a rough-and-tumble style; applied by an ancient philosopher to his own carelessness as a farmer. Observe *lu³* nearly *lu²* before *mang³*.

213. 毛 *mao*, hair.

貓狗 *mao¹ kou³* . . . . . . Cats and dogs; in such phrases as what a noise they make, etc.
羽毛 *yü³ mao²* . . . . Feathers; *lit.*, feathers and hair.
卯刻 *mao³ k'ê⁴* . . . . The fourth of the 12 two-hour periods of the Chinese day; say, 5 to 7 A.M.
相貌 *hsiang⁴ mao⁴* . . . . . . Appearance of the face; the countenance.

214. 美 *mei*, beautiful (of woman's beauty).

煤炭 *mei² t'an⁴* . . . . Coal and charcoal.
美貌 *mei³ mao⁴* . . . . Handsome countenance (of a woman).
愚昧 *yü² mei⁴* . . . . Stupid; used of one's own humble opinion.

[MÊN–MIU.]   PART VII.—THE TONE EXERCISES.   453

215. 門 *mên*, a gate; a door.

     捫挲 *mên¹ sun¹* . . . . Groping, as in the dark: *mên*, to press the hand on; *sun*, to move it, smoothing or patting the object.

     門扇 *mên² shan⁴* . . . . . . The leaf of a door.

     憂悶 *yu¹ mên⁴* . . . . Sad: *yu*, grief; *mên*, joylessness.

216. 夢 *mêng*, a dream.

     蒙了去 *mêng¹ liao ch'ü* . . . . . To make away with; to swindle out of.

     結盟 *chieh² mêng²* . . . . . . To bind oneself by an oath, to Heaven or to man.

     勇猛 *yung³ mêng³* . . . . . . Ardour in fight, in study, etc. Note *yung³* nearly *yung²* before *mêng³*.

     睡夢 *shui⁴ mêng⁴* . . . . . . To dream.

217. 米 *mi*, rice with the husk off.

     眯瞇眼 *mi¹ fêng² yen³* . . . . . Eyes nearly closed by nature.

     迷惑 *mi² huo⁴* . . . . Blindness of a vicious mind; all abroad, as a person who has lost his way.

     米糧 *mi³ liang²* . . . . Food in general; as we say, bread.

     機密 *chi¹ mi⁴* . . . . Close, in word or deed.

218. 苗 *miao*, the young blade of corn, etc.

     喵喵的貓叫 *miao¹ miao¹ ti mao¹ chiao⁴* The mewing of cats.

     禾苗 *ho² miao²* . . . . The young blade of corn.

     藐小 *miao³ hsiao³* . . . . . . Small; of insignificant dimension; used contemptuously or not. Observe *miao³* nearly *miao²* before *hsiao³*.

     廟宇 *miao⁴ yü¹* . . . . Temples in general; *yü¹* properly *yü³*.

219. 滅 *mieh*, to extinguish.

     咩咩的羊叫 *mieh¹ mieh¹ ti yang² chiao⁴* The baa-ing of sheep.

     滅火 *mieh⁴ huo³* . . . . . . To extinguish a light or a fire.

220. 面 *mien*, the face.

     綿花 *mien² hua¹* . . . . . . Cotton.

     勉力 *mien³ li⁴* . . . . To exert oneself.

     臉面 *lien³ mien⁴* . . . . . . The face.

221. 民 *min*, the people, as distinct from the Government.

     民人 *min² jên²* . . . . The people; one of the people, as distinct from the Bannermen.

     憐憫 *lien² min³* . . . . To feel pity; *lien hsü* (see *lien²*, under 193) is to show pity.

222. 名 *ming*, a name.

     姓名 *hsing⁴ ming²* . . . . . . Name and surname.

     性命 *hsing⁴ ming⁴* . . . . . . Life; as in the phrase, cases of life and death, etc.

223. 謬 *miu*, perverse.

     謬妄 *miu⁴ wang⁴* . . . . . . Atrocious and wrong; *e.g.*, aspirations or actions.

224. 末 *mo*, the end or tip.
    摩不著 *mo¹ pu⁴ chao²* . . . . . To fail to find or discover (*mo²*, to grope for).
    蘑菇 *mo² ku¹* . . . . A mushroom.
    塗抹 *t'u² mo³* . . . . To blot out a character.
    始末 *shih³ mo⁴* . . . . From beginning to end (of a story).

225. 謀 *mou*, to plot; a plan.
    圖謀 *t'u² mou²* . . . . To lay plans, for good or for evil.
    某人 *mou³ jên²* . . . . A certain man; So-and-so.

226. 木 *mu*, a tree.
    模樣 *mu² yang⁴* . . . . . . Style, appearance, of men or things; *mu²* alone, a mould.
    父母 *fu⁴ mu³* . . . . Father and mother.
    草木 *ts'ao³ mu⁴* . . . . . . Plants and trees; the vegetable kingdom.

227. 那 *na*, the demonstrative pronoun *that*.
    在這兒那 *tsai⁴ chê⁴ 'rh na¹* . . Here; in this place. Note *na*, simply an expletive.
    拏賊 *na² tsei²* . . . . To seize a thief.
    那個 *na³ ko⁴* . . . . Which one? Which?
    那裏 *na⁴ li* . . . . That place; there. Note *li³* in *li-t'ou*; but in *na⁴-li*, there, nearly *li⁴*; also in *na³-li*, where? the latter *na* consequently remaining *na³*.

228. 奶 *nai*, milk.
    牛奶 *niu² nai³* . . . . Cow's milk.
    耐時 *nai⁴ shih²* . . . . Putting up with the fortunes of the hour.

229. 男 *nan*, the male; man.
    喃喃囈語 *nan¹ nan¹ i⁴ yü³* . . The babbling of a person in a dream.
    男婦 *nan² fu⁴* . . . . Men and women; politely said of persons of both sexes suffering by any general calamity.
    災難 *tsai¹ nan⁴* . . . . Calamity. Note *nan*, difficult, read *nan²*.

230. 囊 *nang*, a bag; a purse.
    啁囔 *tu¹ nang¹* . . . . To mumble; to talk indistinctly; to babble, as a baby.
    囊袋 *nang² tai⁴* . . . . A money bag or purse hung from the waist.
    攮了一刀子 *nang³ liao i⁴ tao¹ tzŭ* . To have run a knife into [a man]. Note *liao* enclitic.
    齉鼻子 *nang⁴ pi² tzŭ* . . . . Applied to the sound of a voice, a nasal twang, or voice impeded by a cold.

231. 鬧 *nao*, properly, noise of voices; very commonly, to be angry; also, of things that should not happen, to happen; as we say, war, plague, or less matters, *broke out*.
    撓著 *nao¹ cho* . . . . Fingering; fiddling with.
    鐃鈸 *nao² po²* . . . . Cymbals, great and small.
    煩惱 *fan² nao³* . . . . In great trouble.
    熱鬧 *jo⁴ nao⁴* . . . . Noisy, bustling, as a fair, a street, etc.

232. 内 *nei*, inside.
　　内外 *nei⁴ wai⁴* . . . . Within and without; inner and outer; native and foreigner.
　　凍餒 *tung⁴ nei³* . . . . Cold and hunger (approaching starvation).

233. 嫩 **nên**, tender, as meat, young sprouts; the bones and flesh of a young child are **nên**.
　　老嫩 *lao³ nên⁴* . . . . Tough and tender, of meat, young plants.

234. 能 *nêng*, to be able.
　　才能 *ts'ai² nêng²* . . . . . Capacity; ability.
　　道兒濘 *tao⁴ êrh nêng⁴* . . . . The roads are sticky.

235. 你 *ni*, thou.
　　泥土 *ni² t'u³* . . . . Dirt, as on a travel-soiled dress, in an unclean room, etc.
　　擬議 *ni³ i⁴* . . . . To suggest; to propose for, or after, deliberation.
　　藏匿 *ts'ang² ni⁴* . . . . . . To hide (*act.* and *neut.*) with evil intent.

236. 娘 *niang*, a mother; in the plural, women.
　　爹娘 *tieh¹ niang²* . . . . . Daddy and mammy.
　　蘊釀 *yün⁴ niang⁴* . . . . . Brewing up, as for a storm; fermenting, as liquor.

237. 鳥 *niao*, a bird.
　　嘵嘵的貓叫 *niao¹ niao¹ ti mao¹ chiao⁴* . Cats' mewing.
　　鳥獸 *niao³ shou⁴* . . . . . . Birds and beasts.
　　屎尿 *shih³ niao⁴* . . . . . . Filth; *lit.*, dung and urine.

238. 揑 *nieh*, to work with the fingers.
　　揑弄 *nieh¹ nung⁴* . . . . . . To mould, as clay; to knead, as dough.
　　呆獃 *nieh² tai¹* . . . . . . Loutish; stupid in appearance.
　　罪孽 *tsui⁴ nieh⁴* . . . . . . The retribution of sin done in a previous existence=ill-fortune.

239. 念 *nien*, to think of; to remember; also, to read.
　　拈花 *nien¹ hua¹* . . . . . . To pick flowers.
　　年月 *nien² yüeh⁴* . . . . . . Years and months.
　　捻匪 *nien³ fei³* . . . . . . The Nien-fei, *lit.* Filchers, a banditti who infested the borders of Shantung and Honan. Observe the *nien³* nearly *nien²* because followed by *fei³*.
　　念誦 *nien⁴ sung⁴* . . . . . . To recite, as the Buddhist priest his books.

240. 您 *nin*, in Peking a polite form of the second person.
　　您納 *nin² na⁴* . . . . The same as *nin*.

241. 寗 *ning*, tranquility. This character was properly written 寧, but being the second in Mien Ning, the name of the Emperor the style of whose reign was Tao Kuang, was altered as the law requires. The form below is also admissible.
　　安寗 *an¹ ning²* . . . . . . In a state of peace.
　　擰壞 *ning³ huai⁴* . . . . . . To spoil by fiddling with or wrenching.
　　佞口 *ning⁴ k'ou³* . . . . . . A specious, glib talker; *lit.*, an eloquent mouth,=a smooth tongue.

242. 虐 nio, tyrannical.
 暴虐 pao⁴ nio⁴ . . . . Passionate and tyrannical; tyranny.
243. 牛 niu, the ox.
 妞兒 niu¹ 'rh . . . . One's little girl.
 牛馬 niu² ma³ . . . . Oxen and horses; one's cattle.
 鈕扣 niu³ k'ou⁴ . . . . Buttons of a Chinese dress; k'ou-tzŭ are, strictly, flat buttons; niu-tzŭ, round.
 拗不過來 niu⁴ pu kuo⁴ lai² . . There is no bringing him round or over.
244. 挪 no, to move from one place to another.
 挪移 no² i² . . . . To shift one's residence; of officials, to misapply public money.
 懦弱 no⁴ jo⁴ . . . . Imbecile; of no ability.
245. 耨 nou, to weed.
 耕耨 kêng¹ nou⁴ . . . . To till and to weed; agricultural operations.
246. 女 nü, woman.
 男女 nan² nü³ . . . . Male and female; man and woman; husband and wife.
247. 虐 nüeh. See nio (242).
248. 虐 nüo. See nio (242).
249. 奴 nu, a slave; when alone, not applied to women.
 奴僕 nu² p'u² . . . . A slave; one's slaves in general; also, one's servants.
 努力 nu³ li⁴ . . . . To exert oneself.
 喜怒 hsi³ nu⁴ . . . . Temper 不常 (pu ch'ang) uneven.
250. 暖 nuan (also nan), warm, as weather, clothes, room, etc.
 暖和 nuan³ ho² . . . . Warm; also read nang³ huo⁴.
251. 嫩 nun. See nên (233).
 老嫩 lao³ nun⁴. See nên⁴, under 233.
252. 濃 nung, of liquids, thick; especially with reference to colours.
 濃淡 nung² tan⁴ . . . . (Of colours) deep and faint.
 擺弄 pai³ nung⁴ . . . . To busy oneself about, as one's garden, etc.; also, to meddle with, to fiddle with.
253. 訛 o, ⁿgo, to deceive [people].
 哦一聲 o¹ i shêng¹ . . . . To give an o of assent.
 訛錯 o² ts'o⁴ . . . . Error, in reporting, copying, etc.
 善惡 shan⁴ o⁴ . . . . Virtue and vice; the virtuous and the vicious.
254. 偶 ou, ⁿgou, properly, an image; hence, of times concurring; accidentally.
 毆打 ou¹ ta³ . . . . To beat.
 偶然 ou³ jan² . . . . Accidentally; q.d., it occurred thus.
 嘔氣 ou⁴ ch'i⁴ . . . . To provoke a man to anger by one's words; lit., to spit [that which causes] wrath.

[PA–PANG.]   PART VII.—THE TONE EXERCISES.   457

255. 罷 *pa*, to cause to cease.
    八九 *pa¹ chiu³* . . . . Eight or nine.
    提拔 *t'i² pa²* . . . . To prefer, or give a chance to, one man before another.
    把持 *pa³ ch'ih²* . . . . To engross power, business. There is another expression for usurpation of high authority.
    罷了 *pa⁴ liao* . . . . It is ended; or, that is all about it.

256. 怕 *p'a*, to fear.
    趴下 *p'a¹ hsia* . . . . To crouch, as a dog; to go down on one's hands and knees.
    扒桿兒 *p'a² kan¹ 'rh* . . . . . To climb up a mast or pole.
    恐怕 *k'ung³ p'a⁴* . . . . To fear.

257. 拜 *pai*, to salute; hence, to visit.
    擗開 *pai¹ k'ai¹* . . . . To break open with the two hands, as an apple, etc.
    黑白 *hei¹ pai²* . . . . Black and white. *See* under 97.
    擺列 *pai³ lieh⁴* . . . . *See* under 192.
    拜客 *pai⁴ k'o⁴* . . . . To visit a person; the paying of visits.

258. 派 *p'ai*, to distribute; hence, very commonly, to send on a mission or errand.
    拍打 *p'ai¹ ta* . . . . To tap with the hand, somewhat hard; *e.g.*, a box, to see whether it is full or empty; a dress, to shake the dust out of it; *ta* atonic.
    木牌 *mu⁴ p'ai²* . . . . A wooden board or tablet, such as is carried in processions.
    一屁股瓞下 *i² p'i⁴ ku³ p'ai³ hsia* . Popped himself down; said of an ill-bred person who takes a seat uninvited.
    分派 *fên¹ p'ai⁴* . . . . To send in different directions; to apportion duties to different persons.

259. 半 *pan*, the half.
    輪班 *lun² pan¹* . . . . To serve in turn. See *pan*, Part III, 414.
    板片 *pan³ p'ien⁴* . . . . Small boards or pieces of wood; *e.g.*, the blocks cut for Chinese printing.
    整半 *chêng³ pan⁴* . . . . The whole and the half.

260. 盼 *p'an*, to look for anxiously.
    高攀 *kao¹ p'an¹* . . . . (Modestly) I have the honour of his acquaintance; *p'an*, in the sense of drawing towards one, *e.g.*, a branch one wants to break off: *kao p'an*, I draw to me the lofty [branch].
    盤查 *p'an² ch'a²* . . . . To search, as the guard at a gate, Customs barrier, etc.; *p'an²*, a bowl, a bath, a receptacle. *See* Part III, Exercise XV, 7, Obs. 4.
    盼望 *p'an⁴ wang⁴* . . . . To look for; to hope for; *sc.*, the coming of a person, a better state of things, etc.

261. 幫 *pang*, to help.
    幫助 *pang¹ chu⁴* . . . . To help.
    細綁 *k'uên³ pang³* . . . . To bind with cords—men, animals, boxes, etc. Note *k'uên³* nearly *k'un²* before *pang³*.
    毀謗 *hui³ pang⁴* . . . . To backbite; to ruin by censure, deserved or undeserved.

262. 旁 *p'ang*, the side of the person, a house, etc.

 胖腫 *p'ang¹ chung³* . . . . . . Swollen, as the body, a limb, a finger.
 旁邊 *p'ang² pien¹* . . . . . . The side; by the side of.
 吹唪 *ch'ui¹ p'ang³* . . . . . . To brag of one's talents, fortune, etc.
 胖瘦 *p'ang⁴ shou⁴* . . . . . . Fat and lean; *p'ang-tzŭ*, a corpulent person.

263. 包 *pao*, to wrap up; to envelop; hence, to enclose, enclosed.

 包裹 *pao¹ kuo³* . . . . . . To wrap up: *pao* singly, to wrap, as in paper, in a cloth, etc.; *kuo*, to tie round, as the head with a handkerchief; the dissyllable *pao kuo* might be used of the former act, but of the latter, *kuo* alone.
 厚薄 *hou⁴ pao²* . . . . . . Thick and thin; morally, of feelings, of intimacy.
 保護 *pao³ hu⁴* . . . . . . To succour; to take care of person or property, one's own or another's.
 懷抱 *huai² pao⁴* . . . . . . To carry in the bosom, as a child, an article.

264. 跑 *p'ao*, to run.

 拋棄 *p'ao¹ ch'i⁴* . . . . . . To fling away anything that is worn out, useless; also, money, goods.
 袍褂 *p'ao² kua⁴* . . . . . . P'ao, the long under-garments, *kua*, the long outer garment.
 跑脫 *p'ao³ t'o¹* . . . . . . To run off, as a prisoner, a dog, etc.
 槍礮 *ch'iang¹ p'ao⁴* . . . . . . Small arms and artillery.

265. 北 *pei*, the north.

 背負 *pei¹ fu⁴* . . . . . . To carry on the back, as a child, a bundle.
 南北 *nan² pei³* . . . . . . South and north.
 向背 *hsiang⁴ pei⁴* . . . . . . Front and rear, of the person, a house; of things, where we speak of *face*, such as a clock, etc.

266. 陪 *p'ei*, to bear company; to be mate to.

 披衣 *p'ei¹ i¹* . . . . . . To throw one's clothes on or over one, not buttoning, tying, etc.
 陪伴 *p'ei² pan⁴* . . . . . . To be a comrade to; to bear one company.
 配偶 *p'ei⁴ ou³* . . . . . . To be mate to; well-mated; said of a well-matched married couple.

267. 本 *pên*, the root of a tree above the ground. See *kên* (154).

 奔忙 *pên¹ mang²* . . . . . . Running about in haste, as a man much occupied.
 根本 *kên¹ pên³*. See under 154.
 投奔 *t'ou² pên⁴* . . . . . . To fly to a person or place for refuge; also, to put up at, as the house of a friend.

268. 盆 *p'ên*, a bowl; a basin.

 噴水 *p'ên¹ shui³* . . . . . . To spurt water out of the mouth, as over a floor to lay the dust, over materials in certain tailoring operations, etc.; *p'ên¹ hu²*, a watering pot.
 盆罐 *p'ên² kuan⁴* . . . . . . Earthenware; *lit.*, bowls and jars; *kuan* also, when of wood, meaning bucket.
 噴香 *p'ên⁴ hsiang¹* . . . . . . To smell agreeably, as flowers, savoury dishes.

[PÊNG–PIEH.]   PART VII.—THE TONE EXERCISES.   459

269. 迸 *pêng*, to jump; to leap.

    绷 緊 *pêng*¹ *chin*³ . . . . . . To fasten tight, as the head of a drum; *pêng* used of any similar tightening with cords, thongs, etc.
    老 蚌 生 珠 *lao*³ *pêng*³ *shêng*¹ *chu*¹ . To have a child in one's old age; *pêng*³, in Peking *pang*³, a clam.
    迸 跳 *pêng*⁴ *t'iao*⁴ . . . . . . To jump about, as a flea, a dog, etc.

270. 朋 *p'êng*, a friend; properly, from circumstances.

    割 烹 *ko*¹ *p'êng*¹ . . . . . . Cookery; *lit.*, *ko*, to cut up the meat; *p'êng*, to fry it.
    朋 友 *p'êng*² *yu*³ . . . . . . Friends. *See* Part III, 636, 637.
    手 捧 *shou*³ *p'êng*³ . . . . . . To hold up in the palms of the two hands joined together. Note *shou*³ nearly *shou*².
    碰 破 *p'êng*⁴ *p'o*⁴ . . . . . . To break by violent contact with; collision.

271. 必 *pi*, necessary; must.

    逼 迫 *pi*¹ *p'o*⁴ . . . . . . To press hard, duly or unduly; oftener, the latter.
    口 鼻 *k'ou*³ *pi*² . . . . . . Features, face; *lit.*, mouth and nose (well or ill looking).
    筆 墨 *pi*³ *mo*⁴ . . . . . . Pencils and ink; also, *fig.*, composition, literary merit.
    務 必 *wu*⁴ *pi*⁴ . . . . . . Must positively; is sure to. Often *wu pi*².

272. 皮 *p'i*, skin; hide.

    批 評 *p'i*¹ *p'ing* . . . . . . To criticise, to canvass the merits of, character, composition, etc.
    皮 毛 *p'i*² *mao*² . . . . . . The hair or fur of an animal.
    癖 好 *p'i*³ *hao*⁴ . . . . . . A hobby.
    屁 股 *p'i*⁴ *ku* . . . . . . The buttocks; the breech.

273. 表 *piao*, the outside; hence, to make manifest; hence, a watch.

    標 文 書 *piao*¹ *wên*² *shu*¹ . . . . To date and punctuate an official document (with red ink).
    表 裏 *piao*³ *li*³ . . . . . . Outside and inside; outer garment and its lining. Note *piao*³ nearly *piao*² before *li*³.
    鰾 膠 *piao*⁴ *chiao*¹ . . . . . . Glue made from fishes' entrails and hides respectively. *See* Part VI, Chapter 30, Note 8.

274. 票 *p'iao*, originally, a gleam of fire.

    漂 沒 *p'iao*¹ *mo*⁴ . . . . . . Of a ship or anything tossing about in water; *q.d.*, now floating, now unseen.
    嫖 賭 *p'iao*² *tu*³ . . . . . . Addicted to women and play; profligacy in general.
    漂 布 *p'iao*³ *pu*⁴ . . . . . . To bleach linen.
    錢 票 子 *ch'ien*² *p'iao*⁴ *tzŭ* . . . A cash note.

275. 別 *pieh*, to separate; different.

    憋 悶 *pieh*¹ *mên*⁴ . . . . . . Sad, as a person under restraint of mind or body; *pieh* is indicative of matter in a condition of repression; *e.g.*, as water in a hose, pus in an abscess, etc.
    分 別 *fên*¹ *pieh*² . . . . . . To distinguish, the distinction of, one from another.
    癟 嘴 子 *pieh*³ *tsui*³ *tzŭ* . . . A toothless person. Note *pieh*³ nearly *pieh*² before *tsui*³.
    彆 拗 *pieh*⁴ *niu* . . . . . . Stiff-necked; not to be brought round.

276. 撇 *p'ieh*, to sweep or brush aside with the hand; *fig.* of changing the subject in conversation.

 擎開 *p'ieh¹ k'ai¹* . . . . (See the line above.) This character is only another form of that in the example of *p'ieh³*.

 撇了 *p'ieh³ liao* . . . . To have rejected, put away, a friend, anything. Note *liao³* enclitic, and read as *la* or *lo*; *p'ieh³* consequently still *p'ieh³*.

277. 扁 *pien*, flat.

 邊沿 *pien¹ yen²* . . . . The edge; along the edge.
 圓扁 *yüan² pien³* . . . . Round and flat.
 方便 *fang¹ pien⁴* . . . . Convenient.

278. 片 *p'ien*, a piece, as of wood, paper, etc.; a clause, as distinct from a sentence.

 偏正 *p'ien¹ chêng⁴* . . . . Slanting and upright; *fig.*, partial and impartial.
 便宜 *p'ien² i⁴* . . . . Cheap. Note *i⁴* properly *i²*.
 愛諞 *ai⁴ p'ien³* . . . . Given to bragging; to parade one's talents, feats, wealth, position, etc.
 片段 *p'ien⁴ tuan⁴* . . . . *Lit.*, clauses and sentences, but=phraseology or composition which is connected and complete. See Part V, Lesson II, 2.

279. 賓 *pin*, a guest.

 賓主 *pin¹ chu³* . . . . Guest and host.
 殯葬 *pin⁴ tsang⁴* . . . . To bury; a funeral: *pin*, to carry and escort the coffin; *tsang*, to inter it.

280. 貧 *p'in*, poor.

 拚命 *p'in¹ ming⁴* . . . . To expose one's life recklessly; to stake one's existence against that of another person; *lit.*, to fling it away; *p'in* also read *p'an⁴*.
 貧窮 *p'in² ch'iung²*. See under 47.
 品級 *p'in³ chi²* . . . . Official grade; *lit.*, class and step.
 牝牡 *p'in⁴ mu³* . . . . (Politely) the male and female of animals: *mu ma*, a stallion; *p'in niu*, a cow.

281. 兵 *ping*, a soldier.

 兵丁 *ping¹ ting¹* . . . . A soldier; *ting*, properly, an adult male, a male aged sixteen.
 稟報 *ping³ pao⁴* . . . . To report or state to a superior; *ping*, ordinarily rendered petition; *pao*, to announce, to give notice of.
 疾病 *chi² ping⁴* . . . . In a bad way; in very bad health.

282. 憑 *p'ing*, to lean against; to rely on; hence, at the pleasure of.

 砰磅 *p'ing¹ p'ang¹* . . . . Of a crashing noise of any sort; *e.g.*, of a man in a rage, a house falling, etc.
 憑據 *p'ing² chü⁴* . . . . Proof; *q.d.*, what one leans on and takes hold of.
 聘嫁 *p'ing⁴ chia⁴* . . . . To marry one's daughter; *lit.*, betrothal and [woman's] marriage; *p'ing* in Peking, *p'in⁴*.

283. 波 *po*, a wave of sea water or fresh.
    水波 *shui³ po¹* . . . . The ripple of water.
    准駁 *chun³ po²* . . . . To authorise or disapprove a transaction or proposition officially.
    播米 *po³ mi³* . . . . To winnow or cleanse rice, as in a *po⁴-chi*. Note *po³* nearly *po²*.
    簸箕 *po⁴ chi¹* . . . . A shallow wicker scoop in which dust or dirt may be gathered, grain winnowed, etc.; it is some three inches high at the back, with sides sloping down to the front.

284. 破 *p'o*, to break by collision, by letting fall.
    土坡 *t'u³ p'o¹* . . . . A mound or hillock of earth, natural or artificial.
    老婆子 *lao³ p'o² tzŭ* . . . . . An old woman.
    筐籮 *p'o³ lo¹* . . . . A shallow wicker basket; *e.g.*, such as in the North carters feed their teams out of.
    破碎 *p'o⁴ sui⁴* . . . . Smashed to pieces.

285. 不 *pou*; this pronunciation of *pu¹*, not, is only used in poetry.

286. 剖 *p'ou*, to rip open.
    掊剋 *p'ou¹ k'o⁴* . . . . Only colloquial in the quotation 掊剋在位 (*p'ou k'o tsai wei*), he is a grasping official. (Mencius.)
    剖開 *p'ou³ k'ai¹* . . . . To rip open a melon or any large fruit.

287. 不 *pu*, not; no.
    我不 *wo³ pu¹* . . . . I say no!
    不是 *pu² shih⁴* . . . . Not to be so; not to be right; hence, a fault.
    補缺 *pu³ ch'üeh¹* . . . . . . To fill a vacancy.
    不可 *pu⁴ k'o³* . . . . It is not admissible; [I, you, he] ought not.

288. 普 *p'u*, universal.
    鋪蓋 *p'u¹ kai⁴* . . . . One's bedding.
    葡萄 *p'u² t'ao* . . . . Grapes; *t'ao* atonic.
    普遍 *p'u³ pien⁴* . . . . In all parts or all sides.
    鋪子 *p'u⁴ tzŭ* . . . . A shop; very commonly written 舖.

289. 灑, 洒 *sa*, to sprinkle.
    撒手 *sa¹ shou³* . . . . To loosen the hand; to let go; also, *fig.* of relaxing efforts.
    一眼瞰著 *i⁴ yen³ sa² chao* . . The eye suddenly lit on.
    洒掃 *sa³ sao³* . . . . To sprinkle with water and sweep (a floor, etc.). Note *sa³* nearly *sa²* before *sao³*.
    姓薩 *hsing⁴ sa⁴* . . . . He is called SA (a Manchu surname.)

290. 賽 *sai*, to rival; to pit oneself or another against.
    顋頰 *sai⁴ chia* . . . . The cheeks; *chia* atonic.
    賭賽 *tu³ sai⁴* . . . . To compete with; to bet.

291. 散 *san*, to disperse.

三四 *san¹ ssŭ⁴* . . . . To distribute, as alms, food to the poor or to prisoners, pay to troops, small employés, etc.
雨傘 *yü³ san³* . . . . An umbrella.
散放 *san⁴ fang⁴* . . . . To distribute, as alms, food to the poor or to prisoners, pay to troops, small employés, etc.

292. 桑 *sang*, the mulberry tree.

桑梓 *sang¹ tzŭ³* . . . . The mulberry and the *tzŭ* (a sort of cedar? WILLIAMS); the trees planted where a village was founded; hence, the home of one's fathers.
嗓子 *sang³ tzŭ* . . . . The throat.
喪氣 *sang⁴ ch'i* . . . . Ill-omened; *ch'i* atonic.

293. 掃 *sao*, to sweep.

騷擾 *sao¹ jao³* . . . . To harass, as an oppressor the people, troops a country; in Peking, *tsao¹ jao³*, to give trouble (*see* Part V, Lesson LXXI, Note 4).
掃地 *sao³ ti⁴* . . . . To sweep the ground.
掃興 *sao⁴ hsing⁴* . . . . . . *Lit.*, swept away pleasure, happiness; a reverse of fortune; also, dejected.

294. 嗇 *sê*, to love inordinately; to covet.

吝嗇 *lin⁴ sê⁴* . . . . Niggardly.

295. 森 *sên*, properly, dense, as foliage; hence used intensively.

森嚴 *sên¹ yen²* . . . . Very severe.

296. 僧 *sêng*, a Buddhist priest.

僧道 *sêng¹ tao⁴* . . . . Priests, Buddhist and Taoist.

297. 索 *so*, originally, a rope.

蓑衣 *so¹ i¹* . . . . A straw rain coat.
鎖上 *so³ shang* . . . . To lock, as a door, a box, etc.
縮手 *so⁴ shou³* . . . . To desist; *lit.*, to draw back the hand.

298. 搜 *sou*, to search, as a guard, police, etc.

搜察 *sou¹ ch'a²* . . . . To search and examine.
老叟 *lao³ sou³* . . . . Reverend Sir (classical). Note *lao³* nearly *lao²*.
咳嗽 *k'ê² sou⁴* . . . . To cough.

299. 素 *su*, properly, simple, unadorned.

蘇州 *su¹ chou¹* . . . . Su-chou (Soochow), the prefecture of that name, in which stands the eastern capital of the province of Kiangsu.
迅速 *hsün⁴ su²* . . . . In great haste; as fast as possible.
平素 *p'ing² su⁴* . . . . Heretofore; *lit.*, even and blank; here applied to past time uninterrupted.

[SUAN-SHANG.]   PART VII.—THE TONE EXERCISES.   463

300. 算 suan, to reckon.
     酸的鹹的 $suan^1$ ti $hsien^2$ ti . . . Sour and salt; suan hsien used fig. in speaking of ability or inability to distinguish between good and evil, etc. Cf. our word taste.
     算計 $suan^4$ chi^4 . . . . To reckon up; also, to calculate an issue, etc.

301. 碎 sui, broken in fragments.
     雖然 sui^1 jan^2 . . . . Although.
     跟隨 $k\hat{e}n^1$ sui^2 . . . . . . Following [a person].
     骨髓 ku^3 sui^3 . . . . The marrow of the bones. Note ku^3 nearly ku^2 before sui^3.
     零碎 $ling^2$ sui^4 . . . . . . Fragmentary; miscellaneous; odds and ends.

302. 孫 sun, a grandson.
     子孫 $tz\breve{u}^3$ sun^1 . . . . Sons and grandsons; also, posterity in general.
     損益 sun^3 yi^4 . . . . Injury and advantage; the relative advantages of; also, modification, as of laws, usages, etc.

303. 送 sung, to accompany, as a visitor to the door.
     松樹 $sung^1$ shu^4 . . . . . . The fir tree.
     毛骨竦然 mao^2 ku^3 $sung^3$ jan^2 . . Horror-struck; lit., hair and bones shuddering. Note that the tone of ku^3 is hardly modified, if at all, though followed by $sung^3$.
     迎送 $ying^2$ $sung^4$ . . . . . . To welcome [the coming] and to speed [the parting guest].

304. 殺 sha, to kill.
     殺死 sha^1 $ss\breve{u}^3$ . . . . To kill, sc., human beings.
     癡傻 $ch'ih^1$ sha^3 . . . . . . A stupid, loutish-looking person. See Part V, Lesson XCIX, Note 7.
     拏剪子剎一點 na^2 $chien^3$ $tz\breve{u}$ sha^4 i^4 $tien^3$ Snip a small piece off.

305. 曬 shai, the action of the sun's rays.
     篩子 $shai^1$ $tz\breve{u}$ . . . . A sieve.
     骰子 $shai^3$ $tz\breve{u}$ . . . . Dice; shai properly read $t'ou^2$.
     曬乾 $shai^4$ kan^1 . . . . . . To dry, or be dried, by exposure to the sun.

306. 山 shan, a mountain.
     山川 $shan^1$ $ch'uan^1$ . . . . . Hills and streams.
     雷閃 lei^2 $shan^3$ . . . . Thunder and lightning.
     善惡 $shan^4$ o^4. See under 79, 253.

307. 賞 shang, to bestow.
     商量 $shang^1$ $liang^1$ . . . . . To consult with a person.
     晌午 $shang^2$ wu^3 . . . . . . Noon. Note shang properly $shang^3$, but $shang^2$ before wu^3; see Part III, 246.
     賞賜 $shang^3$ $tz'\breve{u}^4$ . . . . . . To confer on; to bestow on.
     上下 $shang^4$ $hsia^4$ . . . . . . Above and below; also, nearly, thereabouts.

308. 少 shao, few.
　　火燒 huo³ shao¹ . . . . Burned by fire; also, the name of a bun or cake.
　　刀勺 tao¹ shao² . . . . Knives and spoons; kitchen hardware in general.
　　多少 to¹ shao³ . . . . How many? also, to¹ shao⁴, a good number, or, what a number?
　　老少 lao³ shao⁴ . . . . Old and young.

309. 舌 shê, the tongue.
　　賒欠 shê¹ ch'ien⁴ . . . . To owe; debt.
　　脣舌 ch'un² shê² . . . . Lips and tongue; after fei, to expend,=much discussion.
　　棄捨 ch'i⁴ shê³ . . . . To abandon, a house, a thing; to discard an acquaintance.
　　射箭 shê⁴ chien⁴ . . . . To shoot arrows.

310. 身 shên, the body.
　　身體 shên¹ t'i³ . . . . The body; used in certain phrases only as more polite than shên-tzŭ.
　　神仙 shên² hsien¹ . . . . Spirits and fairies; the latter being shên of a lower order.
　　審問 shên³ wên⁴ . . . . To examine, as parties, witnesses, in a case civil or criminal.
　　甚是 shên⁴ shih⁴ . . . . Very true; quite correct.

311. 生 shêng, to bear, as children; to be born.
　　生長 shêng¹ chang³ . . . . Born and bred.
　　繩子 shêng² tzŭ . . . . A cord.
　　各省 ko⁴ shêng³ . . . . Every province.
　　賸下 shêng⁴ hsia⁴ . . . . There remains [a balance, a surplus, a remnant, etc.].

312. 事 shih, affairs; an affair.
　　失落 shih¹ lo⁴ . . . . Lost, of a thing, not a person.
　　九十 chiu³ shih² . . . . Ninety; also, nine or ten.
　　使喚 shih³ huan⁴ . . . . To employ a servant; to be employed as a servant.
　　事情 shih⁴ ch'ing² . . . . Affairs; an affair. Note ch'ing properly ch'ing², but modified almost to ch'ing¹.

313. 手 shou, the hand.
　　收拾 shou¹ shih . . . . To mend; to put to rights; also, referring to a person, to serve him out: shou, to put away; shih, to pick up, atonic.
　　生熟 shêng¹ shou² . . . . Raw and ripe, as fruits, etc.; of wild tribes, savage and reclaimed.
　　手足 shou³ tsu² . . . . Hand and foot=united as brothers.
　　禽獸 ch'in² shou⁴ . . . . Wild birds and wild beasts.

314. 書 shu, a book; a writing.
　　詩書 shih¹ shu¹ . . . . The "Shu Ching," Canon of History, and the "Shih Ching," Canon of Poetry (commonly known as the Book of Odes); of persons, educated.
　　贖罪 shu² tsui⁴ . . . . To redeem, to pay ransom for, a crime.
　　數錢 shu³ ch'ien² . . . . To count cash.
　　數目 shu⁴ mu⁴ . . . . The numbers; the number of.

[SHUA–T'A.]   PART VII.—THE TONE EXERCISES.   465

315. 刷 *shua*, to brush.
    刷洗 *shua¹ hsi³* . . . . To brush and wash.
    耍笑 *shua³ hsiao⁴* . . . . . . To banter.

316. 衰 *shuai*, to wear out; to decay.
    衰敗 *shuai¹ pai⁴* . . . . . . Downcome; to be ruined, decayed.
    摔東西 *shuai³ tung¹ hsi¹* . . . To switch or flip away a thing.
    草率 *ts'ao³ shuai⁴* . . . . . . Carelessly [executed].

317. 拴 *shuan*, to tie up.
    拴捆 *shuan¹ k'uên³* . . . . . To bind: *shuan*, to make fast; *k'uên*, to bind.
    涮涮 *shuan⁴ shuan⁴* . . . . . To rinse.

318. 雙 *shuang*, a pair.
    成雙 *ch'êng² shuang¹* . . . . To make pairs, or a pair.
    爽快 *shuang³ k'uai⁴* . . . . . Brisk; frank.
    雙生 *shuang⁴ shêng¹* . . . . . Twins.

319. 水 *shui*, water.
    誰的 *shui² ti* . . . . Whose?
    山水 *shan¹ shui³* . . . . . . Scenery.
    睡覺 *shui⁴ chiao⁴* . . . . . . To sleep.

320. 順 *shun*, obedient; that which follows the stream.
    鷹隼 *ying¹ shun³* . . . . . . A species of falcon.
    順當 *shun⁴ tang* . . . . Right, as rule requires; *tang* atonic.

321. 說 *shuo*, to speak.
    說話 *shuo¹ hua⁴* . . . . . . To speak.
    朔望 *shuo⁴ wang⁴ (shuo⁴ or so⁴)* . . The first and the fifteenth of the Chinese moon.

322. 絲 *ssŭ*, silk.
    絲線 *ssŭ¹ hsien⁴* . . . . . . A silken thread; threads of silk.
    死生 *ssŭ³ shêng¹* . . . . . . Dead or live; *e.g.*, is he dead or alive? Life and death [are as Heaven decrees].
    四五 *ssŭ⁴ wu³* . . . . Four or five.

323. 大 *ta*, great.
    答應 *ta¹ ying⁴* . . . . To reply in the affirmative; to assent. Emphasise *ta*.
    搭救 *ta² chiu⁴* . . . . To help; *ta* in the sense of hooking arm to arm.
    毆打 *ou³ ta³* . . . . To assault, to beat violently, with the hand or with weapons. Note *ou³* nearly *ou²*.
    大小 *ta⁴ hsiao³* . . . . Great and small; hence, size, extent, degree of.

324. 他 *t'a*, he.
    他人 *t'a¹ jên²* . . . . A third person.
    佛塔 *fo² t'a³* . . . . A Buddhist pagoda.
    牀榻 *ch'uang² t'a⁴* . . . . . A bedstead; *t'a* used politely in the same sense, alone, as we use *couch* for bed.

325. 歹 tai, bad.
 歹呆 tai¹ nieh². *See* under 238.
 好歹 hao³ tai³ . . . . Good and bad; the quality of. Note hao³ nearly hao².
 交代 chiao¹ tai⁴. *See* under 30.

326. 太 t'ai, too much.
 懷胎 huai² t'ai¹ . . . . To be pregnant; t'ai, the fetus.
 扛擡 k'ang² t'ai². *See* under 149.
 太甚 t'ai⁴ shên⁴ . . . . To too great an extent.

327. 單 tan, single; odd, as distinct from even.
 單雙 tan¹ shuang¹ . . . . . Single and in pairs; odd and even.
 膽子大 tan³ tzŭ ta⁴ . . . . Courageous; *lit.*, large of liver.
 雞蛋 chi¹ tan⁴ . . . . A hen's egg.

328. 炭 t'an, charcoal.
 貪臧 t'an¹ tsang¹ . . . . . . Grasping (said of officials).
 談論 t'an² lun⁴ . . . . To converse; to chat.
 平坦 p'ing² t'an³ . . . . . . Level, as a road or way.
 柴炭 ch'ai² t'an⁴ . . . . . . Fuel (wood, grass, etc.) and charcoal.

329. 當 tang, right.
 應當 ying¹ tang¹ . . . . . . Is properly; ought to [be or do].
 攩住 tang³ chu⁴ . . . . . . To stop by barring the way.
 典當 tien³ tang⁴ . . . . . . To pawn or pledge: tien, in this combination, to mortgage; tang, to pawn.

330. 湯 t'ang, broth; soup.
 喝湯 ho¹ t'ang¹ . . . . To drink soup.
 白糖 pai² t'ang² . . . . . . White sugar.
 躺臥 t'ang³ wo⁴ . . . . . . To lie down: t'ang, to lie on the back; wo, to lie on the side.
 燙手 t'ang⁴ shou³ . . . . . . To scald the hand.

331. 道 tao, a way; the right way.
 刀槍 tao¹ ch'iang¹ . . . . . Swords and muskets (matchlocks).
 搯線 tao² hsien⁴ . . . . . . To reel silk.
 顛倒 tien¹ tao³ . . . . Hind part before; upside down.
 道理 tao⁴ li³ . . . . Right principles; the *rationale* of; also, a system of religion or philosophy. Note li alone, li³, but here nearly li⁴; in other compounds, clearly li³.

332. 逃 t'ao, to flee.
 叨恩 t'ao¹ ngên¹ . . . . . . To receive bounty or a favour; *lit.*, eat bounty.
 逃跑 t'ao² p'ao³ . . . . . . To fly, as a slave, a prisoner, etc.
 討要 t'ao³ yao⁴ . . . . . . To demand, to press for, whether with a claim or without.
 圈套 ch'üan¹ t'ao⁴ . . . . . A snare; a trap; also used figuratively.

333. 得 *tê*, to obtain; to succeed in.
 話叨叨 *hua⁴ tê¹ tê* . . . . . . Prosy talk. Note the first *tê* is heavily accented.
 得失 *tê² shih¹* . . . . To gain and to lose; success and ill-success; the possible out-turn of.

334. 特 *t'ê*, special.
 忐忑 *t'an³ t'ê¹* . . . . Infirm of purpose; little used, and said to be corrupt for 憚愯 (*t'an t'u*).
 特意 *t'ê⁴ i⁴* . . . . A special purpose; on purpose; intentionally.

335. 得' *tei* (corrupt for *tê yao*), must be; must have.
 小鑼兒鏑鏑的聲兒 *hsiao³ lo² 'rh tei¹ tei¹ ti shêng¹ 'rh*, The sound emitted by a small gong when struck.
 必得' *pi⁴ tei³* . . . . Must positively.

336. 等 *têng*, a class; a place in a series; to wait.
 燈燭 *têng¹ chu²* . . . . . . The lights; *lit.*, lanterns and candles, or the candle or light in the lantern.
 等候 *têng³ hou⁴* . . . . . . To wait awhile; to await.
 馬鐙 *ma³ têng⁴* . . . . . . Stirrups.

337. 疼 *t'êng*, sore; painful; also, tender.
 鼕鼕的鼓聲兒 *t'êng¹ t'êng¹ ti ku³ shêng¹ 'rh* The sound of a tom-tom.
 疼痛 *t'êng² t'ung⁴* . . . . . . In pain.
 板櫈 *pan³ t'êng⁴* . . . . . . A wooden bench (long and low); *t'êng* properly *têng*.

338. 低 *ti*, to hang or bend down.
 低頭 *ti¹ t'ou²* . . . . To hang the head.
 仇敵 *ch'ou² ti²* . . . . An enemy: *ch'ou*, feud; *ti*, to stand before, as a rival, antagonist, etc.
 到底 *tao⁴ ti³* . . . . To the bottom; at last; also, objectively, after all.
 天地 *t'ien¹ ti⁴* . . . . Heaven and Earth; as we say, Nature.

339. 替 *t'i*, to take the place of; instead of.
 樓梯 *lou² t'i¹* . . . . A staircase to an upper story.
 提拔 *t'i² pa²* . . . . To select a person by preference.
 體量 *t'i³ liang⁴* . . . . To show consideration to.
 替工 *t'i⁴ kung¹* . . . . To do another's work for him.

340. 弔 *tiao*, to hang.
 貂皮 *tiao¹ p'i²* . . . . Sable; marten's fur.
 弔死 *tiao⁴ ssŭ³* . . . . Death by hanging, oneself or another person.

341. 挑 *t'iao*, to pick out.
 挑選 *t'iao¹ hsüan³* . . . . . . To select; to pick and choose.
 條陳 *t'iao² ch'ên²* . . . . . . To present a memorial or report in sections to the Throne.
 挑着 *t'iao³ cho* . . . . Holding up on the point of anything.
 跳躍 *t'iao⁴ yao⁴* (or *yo⁴*) . . . . To frisk about, as a dog, a horse, etc.; used of great physical activity in a man.

342. 疊 *tieh*, a fold; to fold.

 爹娘 *tieh¹ niang²* . . . . Father and mother.
 重疊 *ch'ung² tieh²* . . . . Repeatedly. Note *ch'ung²*; but *chung⁴*, heavy.

343. 貼 *t'ieh*, properly, to stick, as a placard on a wall; the thing so stuck.

 體貼 *t'i³ t'ieh¹* . . . . To humour; to accommodate; also, to sympathise.
 銅鐵 *t'ung² t'ieh³* . . . . Copper and iron.
 牙帖 *ya² t'ieh⁴* . . . . Licenses to firms being members of a guild; *ya*, properly, a tooth; *q.d.*, one of a set.

344. 店 *tien*, a shop; an inn.

 掂量 *tien¹ liang⁴* . . . . To weigh; of things or matters.
 圈點 *ch'üan¹ tien³*. *See* under **55**.
 客店 *k'o⁴ tien⁴* . . . . An inn.

345. 天 *t'ien*, heaven.

 天地 *t'ien¹ ti⁴*. *See* under **338**.
 莊田 *chuang¹ t'ien²* . . . . . . Farmhouse and land; farms.
 拏舌頭舔 *na² shê² t'ou² t'ien³* . To touch with the tip of the tongue.
 舔筆 *t'ien⁴ pi³* . . . . To work the pencil [on the ink-slab] when about to write.

346. 定 *ting*, to fix; to make stationary; to establish.

 釘子 *ting¹ tzŭ* . . . . A nail.
 頂戴 *ting³ tai⁴* . . . . The button on the official hat distinguishing the rank of the wearer.
 定規 *ting⁴ kuei¹* . . . . To lay down rules; to settle an order of proceeding; *lit.*, to plant [a leg of the] compasses.

347. 聽 *t'ing*, to hear.

 聽見 *t'ing¹ chien⁴* . . . . To hear; *q.d.*, hearing to perceive.
 停止 *t'ing² chih³* . . . . To cease; to cause to cease.
 樹梃 *shu⁴ t'ing³* . . . . The bough of a tree, larger than a *shu chih*, bough or twig.
 聽其自然 *t'ing⁴ ch'i² tzŭ⁴ jan²* . Let [him, it] have [his, its] own way.

348. 丟 *tiu*, to lose.

 丟失 *tiu¹ shih¹* . . . . To lose, as a child stolen or strayed, an animal, or anything inanimate.
 呀吀 *ya⁴ tiu³* . . . . A derisive exclamation addressed to a person who has failed in something; *q.d.*, oh! you clever fellow; you're a nice fellow, you are!

349. 多 *to*, many.

 多少 *to¹ shao³*. *See* under **308**.
 搶奪 *ch'iang³ to²*. *See* under **29**.
 花朶兒 *hua¹ to³ 'rh* . . . . . . A bud.
 懶惰 *lan³ to⁴*. *See* under **182**.

[T'O–TUI.] PART VII.—THE TONE EXERCISES. 469

350. 安 *t'o*, secure; sound.
　　託情 *t'o¹ ch'ing²* . . . . To ask for the patronage of a person, or seek the aid of his influence.
　　駝鳥 *t'o² niao³* . . . . The ostrich. Also written 鴕.
　　妥當 *t'o³ tang⁴* . . . . (Of proceedings) satisfactory, secure.
　　唾沫 *t'o⁴ mo⁴* . . . . To spit: *mo*, spittle; *t'o*, also *t'u⁴*, to spit (saliva only).

351. 豆 *tou*, pulse in general.
　　兜底子 *tou¹ ti³ tzŭ* . . . . . Fig., from beginning to end [of an affair]; the *tou-tzŭ* is specially the receptacle of sacking in which a Chinese mason carries mortar; a similar receptacle may be formed of the flap of a garment or the like; *tou-ti-tzŭ*, from the bottom of such a receptacle.
　　升斗 *shêng¹ tou³* . . . . . *Shêng*, the Chinese pint, dry measure; *tou* = 10 *shêng* (WILLIAMS).
　　綠豆 *lü⁴ tou⁴* . . . . Green beans, as distinguished from black.

352. 頭 *t'ou*, the head.
　　偷盜 *t'ou¹ tao⁴* . . . . To steal; theft.
　　頭臉 *t'ou² lien³* . . . . The head; *lit.*, the head and face.
　　透澈 *t'ou⁴ ch'ê⁴* . . . . To penetrate thoroughly, as having thorough knowledge of any subject; also, to be very intelligent.

353. 妒 *tu*, jealous.
　　督撫 *tu¹ fu³* . . . . *Tu* for *tsung-tu*, governor-general; *fu* for *hsün-fu*, governor of a province.
　　毒害 *tu² hai⁴* . . . . To poison.
　　賭博 *tu³ po²* . . . . To gamble.
　　嫉妒 *chi⁴ tu⁴* . . . . Jealous; envious; also, transitively, to envy.

354. 土 *t'u*, earth; clay.
　　禿子 *t'u¹ tzŭ* . . . . A bald man.
　　塗抹 *t'u² mo³* . . . . To efface, as writing.
　　塵土 *ch'ên² t'u³* . . . . . . Dust.
　　唾沫 *t'u⁴ mo⁴*. *See* under 350.

355. 短 *tuan*, short.
　　端正 *tuan¹ chêng⁴* . . . . . Upright, as things duly placed; also, moral rectitude.
　　長短 *ch'ang² tuan³* . . . . . Long and short; the length of; also, a man's merits and defects, but especially his defects.
　　斷絕 *tuan⁴ chüeh²* . . . . . To cut off, as with a knife; also used figuratively.

356. 團 *t'uan*, a ball; a lump.
　　團圓 *t'uan² yüan²* . . . . . Round as a ball; united, all in a body, as a family.

357. 對 *tui*, opposite to.
　　堆積 *tui¹ chi²* . . . . To pile together; to accumulate.
　　對面 *tui⁴ mien⁴* . . . . . . Opposite to; the opposite of.

358. 退 *t'ui*, to retire.

 推諉 *t'ui¹ wei³* . . . . To put one's work on another; to lay one's fault to another's charge.
 𣤎快 *t'ui³ k'uai⁴* . . . . Fast legs; a good walker.
 進退 *chin⁴ t'ui⁴* . . . . To advance and retire [equally difficult; a dilemma].

359. 敦 *tun*, properly, substantial.

 敦厚 *tun¹ hou⁴* . . . . Honest; sincere; staunch.
 打盹兒 *ta³ tun³ 'rh* . . . . . . To nod from sleepiness; to take a nap. Note *ta* nearly *ta²* before *tun³*; *êrh* absorbed in *tu-rh*.
 遲鈍 *ch'ih² tun⁴* . . . . Slow in thought or action; *tun*, properly, blunt, as a knife.

360. 吞 *t'un*, to swallow; to bolt.

 吞吞吐吐 *t'un¹ t'un¹ t'u³ t'u³* . . Of a man who will tell but half his story; *t'u* being to spit out (anything). Note the first *t'u* nearly *t'u²*.
 屯田 *t'un² t'ien²* . . . . Lands granted to soldiers; military colonies.
 褪手 *t'un⁴ shou³* . . . . To draw the hands into the sleeves, as the Chinese do for warmth's sake.

361. 冬 *tung*, winter.

 冬夏 *tung¹ hsia⁴* . . . . Winter and summer.
 懂得 *tung³ tê* . . . . To understand.
 動靜 *tung⁴ ching⁴* . . . . . . To be stirring; a movement; *lit.*, motion and rest.

362. 同 *t'ung*, the same; together with.

 通達 *t'ung¹ ta²* . . . . To permeate, as the power of Nature; to penetrate, as the will or intelligence of the Sovereign; also, of great intelligence in general.
 會同 *hui⁴ t'ung²* . . . . United with; in association with.
 統帥 *t'ung³ shuai⁴* . . . . . . A generalissimo; in modern times, one holding unusually large military power.
 疼痛 *t'êng² t'ung⁴* . . . . . . In great pain.

363. 雜 *tsa*, miscellaneous.

 腌臢 *a¹ tsa¹* . . . . Dirty; also read *ang¹ tsang¹*.
 雜亂 *tsa² luan⁴* . . . . An omnium-gatherum; confusion.
 咱的 *tsa³ ti* . . . . Why? Why so?

364. 擦 *ts'a*, to rub clean.

 擦抹 *ts'a¹ mo³* . . . . To rub and wipe, as with a cloth.

365. 在 *tsai*, to be; to be in or at.

 栽種 *tsai¹ chung⁴* . . . . . . To plant. Note *chung⁴*, to plant; *chung³*, a sort.
 宰殺 *tsai³ sha¹* . . . . To kill animals.
 在家 *tsai⁴ chia¹* . . . . To be at home.

[TS'AI—TS'Ê.]   PART VII.—THE TONE EXERCISES.   471

366. 才 ts'ai, ability.
 猜想 ts'ai¹ hsiang³ . . . . To imagine; to conjecture.
 才幹 ts'ai² kan⁴ . . . . Ability.
 五彩 wu³ ts'ai³ . . . . The five colours.
 菜飯 ts'ai⁴ fan⁴ . . . . Victuals; lit., the rice and other viands.

367. 贊 tsan, properly, to aid with counsel.
 簪子 tsan¹ tzŭ . . . . Women's head-gear.
 偺們 tsan² mên¹ . . . . We; more commonly pronounced tsa²-mên.
 攢錢 tsan³ ch'ien² . . . . . . To put by money.
 參贊 ts'an¹ tsan⁴ . . . . An official title. See Part III, 494.

368. 慚 ts'an, properly, shame, as from being disgraced.
 參考 ts'an¹ k'ao³ . . . . To compare authorities.
 慚愧 ts'an² k'uei⁴ . . . . . . Shame, felt at one's own wrong-doing.
 悽慘 ch'i¹ ts'an³ . . . . Misery.
 儳頭 ts'an⁴ t'ou . . . . Blockhead; ninny; properly, a man without confidence in himself; applied also to animals and objects, as ts'an t'ou ma, a "screw."

369. 葬 tsang, to bury.
 貪贓 t'an¹ tsang¹ . . . . To covet, as a grasping official; tsang, in the sense of presents.
 葬埋 tsang⁴ mai² . . . . To bury [a corpse].

370. 倉 ts'ang, a granary.
 倉庫 ts'ang¹ k'u⁴ . . . . Granaries and money vaults.
 瞞藏 man² ts'ang² . . . . . . Dishonest concealment [of person or thing].

371. 早 tsao, early.
 週遭 chou¹ tsao¹ . . . . All round; q.d., at every point encountering or encountered.
 穿鑿 ch'uan¹ tsao² . . . . . . Lit., to bore [as through stone] and to cut with a chisel; fig., to start questions in the course of an inquiry.
 來得早 lai² tê tsao³ . . . . . To have come early.
 造化 tsao⁴ hua⁴ . . . . To create, as the Deity; tsao⁴ hua, substantively, the luck born with a man.

372. 草 ts'ao, plants; specially, grass.
 操練 ts'ao¹ lien⁴ . . . . To drill; to be drilled.
 馬槽 ma³ ts'ao² . . . . A manger, either made of wood and movable, or of brick or stone.
 草木 ts'ao³ mu⁴. See under 226.

373. 則 tsê, then; consequently.
 則例 tsê² li⁴ . . . . Laws; regulations; tsê here meaning rule, law.

374. 策 ts'ê, a plan; a means.
 計策 chi⁴ ts'ê⁴ . . . . Ordinarily, any plan; in military matters, strategy.

375. 賊 *tsei*, a thief; a robber; anyone in arms against the Government.
  賊匪 *tsei² fei³* . . . . Brigands; outlaws; rebels.
376. 怎 *tsên*, an interrogative particle.
  怎麽 *tsên³ mo* . . . . How? Why? What?
377. 參 *ts'ên*, uneven, irregular.
  參差 *ts'ên¹ tz'ŭ¹* . . . . Uneven; *e.g.*, as foliage, herbage, etc.; used of inconsequence in action.
378. 增 *tsêng*, to add to.
  增減 *tsêng¹ chien³* . . . . To increase and diminish; modification.
  餽贈 *k'uei⁴ tsêng⁴* . . . . To present, as food or anything, to friends.
379. 層 *ts'êng*, a layer; a story of a house; a step in a series.
  蹭一聲上了房 *ts'êng¹ i⁴ shêng¹ shang⁴ liao fang²* One jump (lit., the sound of one jump) and he was up on the house.
  層次 *ts'êng² tz'ŭ⁴* . . . . Regular order.
  蹭蹬 *ts'êng⁴ têng⁴* . . . . Said in pity for a person who is unlucky, always failing through no fault of his own: *ts'êng*, of feet that drag in walking; *têng*, of inability to move; *q.d.*, one that can never get on.
380. 作 *tso*, to make; to do; in which senses it is always *tso⁴*, whether singly or compounded.
  作房 *tso¹ fang* . . . . The workshop or manufactory; the shop where things are *made*, not *sold*.
  昨日 *tso² jih⁴* . . . . Yesterday.
  左右 *tso³ yu⁴* . . . . Right and left; in the neighbourhood of a place; in the company of a superior.
  坐臥 *tso⁴ wo⁴* . . . . *Lit.*, sitting and lying down,=in all positions; not generally used except when followed by *pu an*, uncomfortable.
381. 錯 *ts'o*, error.
  揉搓 *jou² ts'o¹* . . . . To rub between two hands; to irritate; to annoy.
  矬子 *ts'o² tzŭ* . . . . A dwarf.
  錯失 *ts'o⁴ shih¹* . . . . Error, mistake, in business, copying, etc.; *shih* here meaning to fail or miss.
382. 走 *tsou*, to move; to walk.
  行走 *hsing² tsou³* . . . . Of the subordinates, *to be employed in* a public department.
  奏事 *tsou⁴ shih⁴* . . . . To represent a matter to the Throne.
383. 湊 *ts'ou*, to collect; to be collected together.
  湊合 *ts'ou⁴ ho* . . . . Of persons assembled in one place or enterprise; of funds contributed by a number.
384. 祖 *tsu*, a grandfather.
  租賃 *tsu¹ lin⁴*. *See under* 194.
  手足 *shou³ tsu²*. *See under* 313.
  祖宗 *tsu³ tsung¹* . . . . One's ancestors.

[TSʻU–TSUNG.] PART VII.—THE TONE EXERCISES. 473

385. 粗 *tsʻu*, coarse.

    粗 細 *tsʻu¹ hsi⁴*. See under 111.

    喫 醋 *chʻih¹ tsʻu⁴* . . . . Jealousy; specially, jealousy of the affections; *lit.*, to eat vinegar.

386. 揝 *tsuan*, to grip in the hand.

    鑽 幹 *tsuan¹ kan* . . . . To strive hard after an object; *tsuan*, to bore, to perforate; often, in a bad sense, to strive to compass by intrigue.

    纂 修 *tsuan³ hsiu¹* . . . . To revise, to recompile, a work, a code; *tsuan*, properly, to collect together; specially, materials available.

    揝 住 *tsuan⁴ chu* . . . . To grasp in the hand, *sc.*, anything that is movable and that the fingers can nearly close round.

387. 竄 *tsʻuan*, to burrow, as rats, mice, etc.

    馬 驥 *ma³ tsʻuan¹* . . . . The bound or leap of a horse.

    攢 湊 *tsʻuan² tsʻou⁴* . . . . To make up a set of things, or a sum of money, by picking here and borrowing there.

    逃 竄 *tʻao² tsʻuan⁴* . . . . (Said pompously of rebels or any enemy) flying from one place and finding their way to another.

388. 嘴 *tsui*, the lips.

    一 堆 *i⁴ tsui¹* . . . . A pile [of any objects]; a group [of men].

    嘴 唇 *tsui³ chʻun²* . . . . The lips; the mouth.

    犯 罪 *fan⁴ tsui⁴* . . . . To transgress; *lit.*, to run foul of punishment.

389. 催 *tsʻui*, to urge.

    催 逼 *tsʻui¹ pi¹* . . . . To press with great earnestness (whether justly or not).

    隨 他 去 *tsʻui² tʻa¹ chʻü⁴* . . . . Let him go if, or as, he likes; *tsʻui²* elsewhere *sui²*.

    萃 集 *tsʻui⁴ chi²* . . . . A large assemblage of able or virtuous persons, or of good things.

390. 尊 *tsun*, honoured.

    尊 重 *tsun¹ chung⁴* . . . . To esteem; to show esteem for.

    撙 節 *tsun³ chieh²* . . . . To economise; originally, a classical expression; *lit.*, to walk in (= to practise) moderation.

391. 寸 *tsʻun*, an inch.

    村 莊 *tsʻun¹ chuang¹* . . . . A village.

    存 亡 *tsʻun² wang²* . . . . Dead and living; *e.g.*, father *tsʻun*, mother *wang*, etc.

    忖 量 *tsʻun³ liang* . . . . To think over; to reflect on.

    尺 寸 *chʻih² tsʻun⁴*. See under 37.

392. 宗 *tsung*, a kind; a sort; also, a collective.

    大 宗 *ta⁴ tsung¹* . . . . The larger proportion.

    總 名 *tsung³ ming²* . . . . A general designation.

    縱 容 *tsung⁴ yung* or *jung* . . . . To leave too free; to tolerate license.

393. 葱 ts'ung, onions.
 葱蒜 ts'ung¹ suan⁴ . . . . Onions and garlic.
 依從 i¹ ts'ung² . . . . According to, sc., a man's own view, his advice, etc.

394. 子 tzŭ, a son.
 資格 tzŭ¹ ko² . . . . Length of service; official standing: tzŭ, goods, means; here, pay; ko, the columns of a register; q.d., the time one has been borne on the books.
 子孫 tzŭ³ sun¹ . . . . Sons and grandsons.
 寫字 hsieh³ tzŭ⁴ . . . . To write.

395. 次 tz'ŭ, a time; a turn.
 齜著牙兒笑 tz'ŭ¹ cho ya² 'rh hsiao⁴ . To grin; to show the teeth as one laughs.
 瓷器 tz'ŭ² ch'i . . . . Porcelain; finer earthenware, as distinct from wa³.
 彼此 pi³ tz'ŭ³ . . . . This and that; you and I; mutually. Note pi³ nearly pi².
 次序 tz'ŭ⁴ hsü⁴ . . . . Regular order.

396. 瓦 wa, a tile; pottery.
 刨挖 p'ao² wa¹ . . . . To dig up or out.
 娃娃 wa² wa² . . . . Dolls or effigies of babies in earthenware.
 甎瓦 chuan¹ wa³ . . . . Bricks and tiles.
 鞋襪 hsieh² wa⁴ . . . . Shoes and stockings.

397. 外 wai, outside.
 歪正 wai¹ chêng⁴ . . . . Slanting and perpendicular.
 酯水 wai³ shui³ . . . . To bale water. Note wai³ nearly wai²; properly yao³.
 內外 nei⁴ wai⁴ . . . . Within and without; also, native and foreign.

398. 完 wan, terminated.
 水灣兒 shui³ wan¹ 'rh . . . . . A bay.
 完全 wan² ch'üan² . . . . . . Completed; in a state of completeness.
 早晚 tsao³ wan³ . . . . Early and late; sooner or later. Note tsao³ nearly tsao².
 千萬 ch'ien¹ wan⁴ . . . . . . Thousand myriad; ten millions; fig., any number.

399. 往 wang, to go; hence, towards, to.
 汪洋 wang¹ yang² . . . . . . Vast expanse of water.
 王公 wang² kung¹ . . . . . . Princes and dukes.
 來往 lai² wang³ . . . . To come and to go; intercourse.
 忘記 wang⁴ chi⁴ . . . . To forget.

400. 為 wei (read wei²), to do; to be; but read wei⁴, because of.
 微弱 wei¹ jo⁴ . . . . Sickly, feeble, as men, plants, etc.
 行為 hsing² wei² . . . . . . Actions; conduct.
 委員 wei³ yüan² . . . . . . To depute an officer; the officer deputed.
 爵位 chiio² wei⁴. See under 60.

401. 文 *wén*, ornament; literary culture.
    溫和 *wén¹ huo* or *ho* . . . . . . Warm.
    文武 *wén² wu³* . . . . Civil and military; *wén*=educated.
    安穩 *an¹ wén³* . . . . Steady, as things that stand firm; sound, of recovered health.
    問答 *wén⁴ ta²* . . . . Question and answer; *ta²* elsewhere *ta¹*.

402. 翁 *wéng*, an aged man.
    老翁 *lao³ wéng¹* . . . . The old man; used respectfully of the father of the person addressed.
    水甕 *shui³ wéng⁴* . . . . A large water ewer.

403. 我 *wo*, the pronoun I.
    窩巢 *wo¹ ch'ao²*. See under 15.
    你我 *ni³ wo³* . . . . You and I. Note *ni³* nearly *ni²*.
    坐臥 *tso⁴ wo⁴*. See under 380.

404. 武 *wu*, military.
    房屋 *fang² wu¹* . . . . Buildings; tenements.
    有無 *yu³ wu²* . . . . Possessing or not; existing or not.
    文武 *wén² wu³*. See under 401.
    萬物 *wan⁴ wu⁴* . . . . The myriad things; all things in creation.

405. 牙 *ya*, a tooth.
    丫頭 *ya¹ t'ou²* . . . . A servant girl; *ya*, properly, of the knot of hair on either side of an unmarried girl's head.
    牙齒 *ya² ch'ih³* . . . . The teeth.
    文雅 *wén² ya³* . . . . Polite; well-bred.
    壓倒 *ya⁴ tao³* . . . . To keep pressed down as with a weight.

406. 涯 *yai*, properly, the edge of water.
    天涯 *t'ien¹ yai²* . . . . The horizon.

407. 羊 *yang*, sheep.
    央求 *yang¹ ch'iu²* . . . . To apply to for help; *lit.*, to invitingly beg.
    牛羊 *niu² yang²* . . . . Sheep and oxen.
    養活 *yang³ huo* . . . . To support persons; to rear, as animals, fish, plants, etc.
    各樣 *ko⁴ yang⁴* . . . . Every kind.

408. 要 *yao*, to want; to will; to be about to.
    腰腿 *yao¹ t'ui³* . . . . The back; *lit.*, the loins and the legs; *t'ui* more commonly written 腿.
    遙遠 *yao² yüan³* . . . . Very distant.
    咬一口 *yao³ i k'ou³* . . . . To give a bite to.
    討要 *t'ao³ yao⁴* . . . . To demand.

409. 夜 *yeh*, the night.
 噎住 *yeh¹ chu* . . . . To stick fast, to have something so stuck fast, in the throat.
 老爺 *lao³ yeh²* . . . . Sir; a gentleman, *lit.*, old gentleman; *lao-yeh-'rh*, a popular name for the sun.
 野地 *yeh³ ti⁴* . . . . Uncultivated or uninhabited ground.
 半夜 *pan⁴ yeh⁴* . . . . Midnight; half the night.

410. 言 *yen*, words.
 喫煙 *ch'ih¹ yen¹* . . . . To smoke.
 言語 *yen² yu³* . . . . Words; sayings; oral language.
 眼睛 *yen³ ching*. See under 40.
 河沿兒 *ho² yen⁴ 'rh* . . . . The bank of a river; along the bank.

411. 益 *yi*, advantage; addition to.
 作揖 *tso¹ yi¹* . . . . To make a certain Chinese salutation.
 益處 *yi² ch'u* . . . . Advantage. Note *yi²*; elsewhere, always *yi⁴*.
 易經 *yi⁴ ching¹* . . . . The "Yi Ching," Book of Permutations; said to be the oldest of Chinese classical works.

412. 音 *yin*, sound.
 聲音 *shêng¹ yin¹* . . . . Sounds of any kind.
 金銀 *chin¹ yin²* . . . . Gold and silver.
 勾引 *kou¹ yin³* . . . . To inveigle; to entice into any evil.
 用印 *yung⁴ yin⁴* . . . . To use the seal; to seal officially.

413. 迎 *ying*, to welcome.
 應該 *ying¹ kai¹* . . . . Ought to.
 迎接 *ying² chieh¹* . . . . To receive, as a guest.
 沒影兒 *mei² ying³ 'rh* . . . . There is no sign, *lit.*, no shadow, of such or such a thing.
 報應 *pao⁴ ying⁴* . . . . To recompense, as Heaven.

414. 約 *yo*, to engage; an engagement, a treaty, etc.
 約會 *yo¹ hui⁴* . . . . To make an appointment with.
 音樂 *yin¹ yo⁴* . . . . Musical instruments in general.

415. 魚 *yü*, fish.
 愚濁 *yü¹ cho²* or *chuo²* . . . . Muddled; stupid; *cho*, turbid.
 魚蝦 *yü² hsia¹* . . . . Fish in general; *lit.*, fish and shell-fish.
 風雨 *fêng¹ yu³*. See under 88.
 預備 *yü⁴ pei⁴* . . . . Ready; to make ready.

416. 原 *yüan*, properly, in the beginning.
 冤屈 *yüan¹ ch'ü* . . . . To be wronged, by unjust deed or word.
 原來 *yüan² lai²* . . . . In the first instance; in fact.
 遠近 *yüan³ chin⁴*. See under 38.
 願意 *yüan⁴ i⁴* . . . . To wish.

417. 月 *yüeh*, the moon.

    子曰 *tzŭ³ yüeh¹* . . . . "The philosopher said." These words precede the sayings of Confucius, recorded in the classics of China.

    嚼嚼 *yüeh² yüeh²* . . . . To munch.

    年月 *nien² yüeh⁴* . . . . Years and moons; lapse of time.

418. 雲 *yün*, cloud.

    頭暈 *t'ou² yün¹* . . . . The head giddy; *yun¹* elsewhere *yün⁴*.

    雲彩 *yün² ts'ai* . . . . Clouds.

    應允 *ying¹ yün³* . . . . To consent to.

    氣運 *ch'i⁴ yün⁴* . . . . Luck; of the State's prosperity; *yün ch'i*, of a person's luck.

419. 有 *yu*, to be; to have; possession; existence.

    憂愁 *yu¹ ch'ou²* . . . . Sad (in heart and countenance).

    香油 *hsiang¹ yu²* . . . . Oil made of sesamum seed.

    有無 *yu³ wu²*. *See* under 404.

    左右 *tso³ yu⁴*. *See* under 380.

420. 用 *yung*, to use.

    平庸 *p'ing² yung¹* . . . . Commonplace: *p'ing*, even,=not above the level; *yung*, here, unintelligent.

    容易 *yung² i⁴*. *See* under 127.

    永遠 *yung³ yüan³* . . . . For ever. Note *yung³* nearly *yung°*.

    使用 *shih³ yung⁴* . . . . To employ.

PART VIII.

THE PARTS OF SPEECH.

This Part is divided into the following Sections :—
  I. Introductory Observations.
  II. The Noun and the Article.
  III. The Chinese Numerative Noun.
  IV. Number, Singular and Plural.
  V. Case.
  VI. Gender.
  VII. The Adjective and its Degrees of Comparison.
  VIII. The Pronoun (Personal, Relative, Possessive, Demonstrative, Distributive, Indefinite).
  IX. The Verb as modified by Tense, Mood, and Voice.
  X. The Adverb, of Time, Place, Number, Degree, etc.
  XI. The Preposition.
  XII. The Conjunction.
  XIII. The Interjection.

PART VIII.
THE PARTS OF SPEECH.

SECTION I.
[INTRODUCTORY OBSERVATIONS.]

1.—It seems to give your countrymen a good deal of trouble to acquire our language, sir; what is the difficulty?

2.—There are several difficulties: difficulties of pronunciation, difficulties with the individual words, and, greater still, difficulties of composition.

3.—Yet all foreigners seem to learn each other's languages with tolerable facility; it can't be that Chinese is so entirely different from all foreign languages?

4.—No language in the world is absolutely without something in common with its fellow languages of course. The character of the expressions[1] by which any man gives utterance to his thought will be sure to vary greatly according to circumstances. A phrase may be directly affirmative of existence or non-existence, or it may be interrogative, imperative, optative, or interjectional.[2] When we say, for instance, This man is dead, That man is not dead, there is a direct affirmation of existence or non-existence. Is that man dead? is interrogative. Cut that man's head off, is imperative. Would that that man were well! is optative. Alas! that man is dead, is interjectional. Do you understand my meaning,[3] sir?

5.—Perfectly. The law you are speaking of may be regarded as a general law which affects all language, written or spoken, one to which Chinese and foreigners from natural community of sentiment[4] conform.

6.—Just so; now to come to the difficulty with single words,—it is one peculiar[5] to the Chinese written language. For the formation of words in writing, every other nation that possesses a literature has a given number of characters (*lit.*, pen-strokes), each with a sound of its own; and the combination of a certain number of these not only produces a word in form, but also serves the purpose of establishing its sound.

7.—There is a strong resemblance between this and the Manchu method of writing; but in Chinese, although the language is otherwise written, the words are formed of eight particular strokes; will not these be the same as your letters, sir?

---

[1] Character of expression: *shên ch'i*, gait, air, attitude.
[2] Interjectional: *ching ya*, properly, to start with fright and astonishment.
[3] My meaning: *pi i*, humble, lowly, meaning.
[4] Community of sentiment: more literally, it is *li*, the reasonable consequence, of *tzŭ jan hsiang t'ung*, the natural identity, of man's feelings in every nation.
[5] Peculiar: *tu i*, isolated strangeness. Note its enforcement by the addition of *wei*, only, before *han wên*.

8.—The application of the two differs widely. Chinese words, it is true, are written with eight particular strokes; but though each of these has a sound of its own, the sound of any word they may go to form has no reference whatever to the sounds of the strokes. We will write, for instance, the word *shih* (ten), one of the numerals; this is formed of one horizontal and one perpendicular stroke; the horizontal stroke is properly called *yi*, the perpendicular stroke, *kuén*; the two combined in writing produce the word *shih*. It will be at once apparent that their business is exclusively with its form, and that they have nothing whatever to do with its sound. This [the impossibility of learning the sound of a word from the strokes employed to write it] is regarded by foreigners as a very great difficulty in the study of written Chinese.

9.—How do foreigners succeed[1] in establishing the sound of one of their words in writing?

10.—In this way: foreign nations have for the purpose some twenty odd characters, the principle of combining which so as to form words it does not take very long to understand, and this once learnt, the sound of any word one meets with can be determined;[2] whereas[3] in a Chinese written word there is no positive criterion[4] of its sound. If it has not been met with in reading, its sound cannot be known; the word must be looked out, and when it has been found, there is nothing to guarantee the reader against forgetting its sound when he sees it again.

11.—That is true enough; but we Chinese are in no fear of forgetting the words, because we learn them as single words when we are young children.[5]

12.—Exactly; but we foreigners, not having committed Chinese books to memory, cannot of course fail to encounter the difficulty I describe with single words when we read Chinese, and our difficulties are immeasurably greater when we come to combine[6] words in composition.

13.—I have understood that foreign composition is a somewhat simpler matter than ours.

14.—Yes; because in foreign languages, considered with reference to composition in them, the single words are each referred to a particular category, and for the formation of these into sentences and clauses[7] there are special works which set forth the rules of construction so clearly that they may be comprehended by the student at a glance. There are no works of this sort in Chinese for the positive definition of the laws of composition. A writer constructs his sentences according to his recollection of the manner in which words are combined in the texts he has read,[8] and his sentence constructed, he is enabled to link his sentences together in longer pieces

---

[1] Succeed: *lit.*, *what good method have they?*

[2] Can be determined: *ting-tê chun*, fixing attain, = fix *with*, accuracy. Note that the combination makes the verb to define, to determine, etc., and that although it contains the potential auxiliary *tê* within it, it is reinforced by *nêng*.

[3] Whereas, on the other hand: *chih*, to come to [another question, namely], *jo*, if.

[4] No criterion: *lit.*, there is not a place [at which a person] can *chun*, decide as by standard, [that such a sound] is the assured sound.

[5] Learn them when young: *tsung*, from = at, the time when we are little fellows, we *hsien*, first, = before we go any further, *jên-tê ti*, that which is recognised, read, are single characters.

[6] Combine: *chui*⁴, to connect, to sew together.

[7] Sentences and clauses: *tou*⁴ (note, not *tu*²), a clause in a sentence.

[8] Texts he has read: he remembers the *tzŭ yang*, phraseology, *chi tsai*, recorded and inserted, in books. Note *chi*, to remember, and *chi*, to record.

PART VIII.—THE PARTS OF SPEECH. 483

of composition. The single words in Chinese are classified generally in two grand categories, as *hsü tzŭ* (empty or unsubstantial words) and *shih tzŭ* (solid or substantial words); but I have never arrived at a thorough understanding of the distinction, though I have looked carefully into the question over and over again.

15.—The denomination *shih tzŭ* (substantial words) is generic of all words that have a regular (or *bonâ fide*) signification; and these are subdivided again according as they may be employed into *ssŭ tzŭ* (dead words) and *huo tzŭ* (live words).

It is not so easy to define the precise characteristics of the *hsü tzŭ*. For example, in the sentence *ni pu yao ch'ien mo* (Don't you want money? or, Won't you have money?) the word *mo* has no regular [say, translatable] meaning; it is used simply to show that the sentence is interrogative;[1] it is a *hsü tzŭ* (an unsubstantial word). Of the remaining words[2] in the sentence, *pu* (not) has a substantive meaning, and yet in Chinese it is accounted a *hsü tzŭ*. The words *ni* (thou), *yao* (to want), and *ch'ien* (money) are all *shih tzŭ* (substantial words). Distinguished as *ssŭ tzŭ* (dead words) and *huo tzŭ* (live words), *ni* and *ch'ien* are dead words, and *yao* is a live word.

The word *yao*, again,[3] which we have just spoken of as a live word, and which, in the passage before us, *is* a live word,[4] may be used as a dead word elsewhere; for instance, in the phrase *ch'i yao tsai su* (The essential is despatch), the words *yao* and *su* are unquestionably dead words. Is there no live word then, you will say, in the sentence? yes, to be sure; the word *tsai* (is, or is in) is a live word. If you go farther and ask which words are substantial and which unsubstantial, the answer is that the two words *ch'i* and *tsai*, though each possesses a regular meaning, are in this phrase accounted unsubstantial words.

16.—It is evident, then, that the denominations *hsü tzŭ* and *shih tzŭ* are quite capable[5] of being interchanged, one for the other, as circumstances may require.

17.—Perfectly capable; to such an extent[6] that some people go the length of saying that every word is half a dead word and half a live word.

18.—The limitations[7] of our language are somewhat more inflexible; the terms in it have not the convertibility of terms in Chinese. But now, to come to the English language, let us for the moment separate [its grammar into] two grand divisions, the single words of the language and the laws of sentences. In the one division the single words are referred each to one of

---

[1] Interrogative: *lit.*, that the *k'ou chi*, the air or tone of the sentence, is *ting-wên ti*, interrogating. The verb *ting*, properly, to fix, here implying that the speaker knows what answer he must receive; *q.d.*, You want money, don't you?

[2] Of the remaining words: note the construction:—the remain-ing someones among.

[3] The word *yao*, again: *jan-'rh*, but; *jan*, thus, this is so, *êrh*, and yet . . . .

[4] *Is* a live word: *ku jan*, certainly, positively; very commonly used where an admission is made on the one part to emphasise an objection on the other; *q.d.*, it *is* so here, no doubt, but, etc.

[5] Quite capable: note the construction:—*ta yu*, they possess in a great degree *li*, a principle, qualified by all that intervenes between *yu* and *li*, viz., the according-to-time-and-circumstance-able-to-interchange principle. The verb *t'ung* in *pien t'ung* has the force of both *per* and *trans* in similar Latin compounds.

[6] To such an extent: *shên*, in extreme degree, to such a degree as *chih*, to arrive at this, that there are people, etc.

[7] Limitations: *hsien*, to mark bounds; *chih*, originally, to cut; laws; to govern; *hsien chih*, the laws limiting are somewhat *ssŭ*, dead, inflexible.

nine categories (the Parts of Speech); the other gives the rules by which single words are made into sentences, and sentences into longer sections of composition.

19.—Is the distinction that we observe in Chinese essays[1] between the *ku* (pairs of sentences even in length)[2] and *tuan* (odd sentences)[3] at all the same as the *chü fa* (laws of sentences) of which you have been speaking?

20.—Not the same; in Chinese composition it is the *chü fa* that is important, and it is to the relative proportions of sentences only that attention has to be paid: our theory is this, it is essential to the constitution of any sentence that it contain *kang* (a subject) and *mu* (a predicate).[4] The person, thing, transaction, condition, spoken of, is the subject; the qualifications of the subject, as that it is right or wrong, existent or non-existent, active or passive, form its predicate. It is hence evident that that in which there are nothing but *ssŭ tzŭ*, without any *huo tzŭ*, cannot well be regarded as a sentence; if, for instance, we were merely to say "man," "rain," "horse," without adding a *huo tzŭ* to these three words, we should have the head of a sentence without the tail, neither more nor less; words so spoken could not be considered as being language with a meaning; and the same, it is self-evident,[5] holds good of the exclusive employment in any case of *huo tzŭ* without *ssŭ tzŭ*. The sentences, The man is good, It rains, The horse is fast, are sentences because their intelligibility is complete.[6]

Then as to subject and predicate, in the first of these sentences the word *jên* (man) is the subject, and the words which treat of his qualities are the predicate. In the second sentence, Rain is falling (*Anglicè*, It rains), *yü* (rain) is the subject, and the word that treats of its falling or not falling is the predicate. In the third, *ma* (horse) is the subject, and the words treating of the horse's rate of speed are the predicate.

SECTION II.

[THE NOUN AND THE ARTICLE.]

21.—The distinction of the *kang* from the *mu* is not wholly ignored in Chinese composition, but I have never heard before of the distribution of words into nine categories that you speak of.

22.—Naturally not, sir; in Chinese the words are not assigned in this way to particular categories. In English, all such denominations as person, thing, transaction, circumstances, are

---

[1] Essays: *wên chang* is used generically of all elegant composition, ancient or modern, but specially of the essays required at modern examinations for degree.

[2] The *ku* are the members (*lit.*, the thighs) of a *p'ien* of *wên chang*, a piece of elegant composition; they must be in pairs and of equal length.

[3] The *tuan* are single paragraphs of from 60 to 120 words. An essay may be all of *tuan*, or may have *tuan* between any two pairs of *ku*, or at longer intervals.

[4] Subject and predicate: *kang*, properly, the drag-rope of a net; the chief consideration with reference to the relations of life, subjects of writing, as we say, *the worthier*; *mu*, the eye; used in the sense of subdivision or section. Cf. *chang-mu*, accounts, *mu-lu*, an index.

[5] Self-evident: *pu tai yen i*, one does not wait for words to tell one; *i*, a classical expletive found only at the end of sentences.

[6] Intelligibility is complete: *lit.*, the words have no meaning over and above [what is expressed].

referred to the categorical classification of the language entitled nouns[1] *(ming-mu)*. The words "man," "book," "illness," "year," for example, are all *ming-mu* (nouns).

When a noun occurs in English, whether written or spoken, there is often prefixed to it another word to show whether it has been the subject of a former proposition or not. In Chinese no words are specifically distinguished as performing this function; still, when occasion demands, there is a method of discriminating between definiteness and indefiniteness.

When we hear it said, for instance, *yu ko jên lai, yu i ko jên lai* (A person is come), we know that the person spoken of has not been spoken of before, and that in the mind of the speaker there is an indefiniteness[2] as to the individuality of the person in question. But if a speaker[3] were to say, *na ko jên lai liao* (The person, that person, is come), the hearer would know that the person come was the person who had been earlier mentioned By means of the limitation thus clearly laid down by the speaker, there is a positive indication [of the fact].

23.—Our words[4] *na* and *ché*, properly speaking, are employed to distinguish between *this* and *that*.

24.—That is perfectly true;[5] I shall return[6] to that use of them by-and-by; but in the phrase *na ko jên*, given in paragraph **22**, the *na* employed[7] is not *that* as distinguished from *this* [not the demonstrative pronoun], but serves, in short, to show that the proposition is not indefinite [in other words, it is the definite article].

25.—The Chinese word *ch'i* would seem on some occasions, but not as a rule, to correspond to the English definite article.

26.—You are right; in the phrase *ch'i yü ti* (The remaining ones), the word *ch'i* shows definitively that all besides certain [things or persons] already excluded are included [in the proposition of the speaker]. The *ch'i* in the phrase *ch'i yao tsai tz'ŭ* (The essential is this), again, serves specially to indicate *the* important point [in a proposition]. But take the following :— *hsiang t'a na ko jên ch'i hsin pu k'o wên* (With a man like that there is no telling what is passing in his mind) (*lit.*, no questioning his heart), the *ch'i* is simply to be construed as *t'a* (he, his).

Nouns may be used both in English and Chinese[8] without any prepositive word; *e.g.*, Man is the most intelligent of all created beings; Gold is heavier than silver; in these two sentences,

---

[1] Nouns: *ming*, name; *mu*, still in the sense of subordinate divisions; *q.d.*, name and index. It is scarcely necessary to observe that although no violence is done to the real meaning of the combination *ming-mu* by translating it *nomina*, the Chinese do not apply the term to any word as a grammatical distinction.

[2] An indefiniteness: *mang*, a waste of waters, *wu ting hsiang*, no certain direction.

[3] But if a speaker: *shê*, to place, *ponere*; *jo*, if. Cf. the Portuguese *posto que* and our *sup-pose*.

[4] Our words: note the *hsieh* acting as a plural affix to *ché*, which, however, so far as Chinese grammar is concerned, might with equal propriety stand either alone or be followed by *ko*.

[5] Perfectly true: *tzŭ jan*, self-existent=a matter of course; *k'o*, properly or permissibly; something as in our phrase, It *may* be stated as an axiom that, etc. *See* **26**, *na k'o pu ts'o*.

[6] I shall return: the *ch'ieh*, elliptical for *chan ch'ieh*, for the present; *lit.*, that for the present wait, [until] hereafter again I speak.

[7] The *na* employed: *chuan*, special, particular,=*the* word employed. Note *ch'üeh*, on the contrary, at the head of the last clause of the sentence, rendered in English by the disjunctive *but* at the beginning of the first.

[8] English and Chinese: *lit.*, in the language of both nations there are places=instances [in which the words described] *k'o shê*, may be dispensed with.

"man," "gold," "silver" are generic denominations, and as such can be used without any article; and so with proper names.

SECTION III.

[THE CHINESE NUMERATIVE NOUN.]

27.—Chinese nouns, on the other hand, have the following peculiarity:[1] whenever a noun, person, or thing occurs in Chinese, there may be prefixed to it an associate[2] (or attendant) noun. In the sentences *i ko jên, i wei kuan, i p'i ma, i chih ch'uan*, the words *ko, wei, p'i*, and *chih* are the nouns attendant on *jên* (man) *kuan* (officer), *ma* (horse), and *ch'uan* (ship). These attendant nouns are not exclusively prefixes of the nouns they accompany; they sometimes follow them. In speaking, for instance, of horses or ships collectively, we may say *ma-p'i* (horses), *ch'uan-chih* (shipping).

28.—And where a noun has just occurred, the attendant noun may be used as a substitute for it, as in the following case:—Suppose a person to have been buying cattle and to say to me, *mai liao niu* (I was buying cattle) yesterday; I ask him, *to-shao chih* (how many head) did you buy? he answers, I bought *shih chi chih* (some ten head). In this instance *niu* (cattle) is the noun proper, and *chih*, the attendant noun; the attendant noun being substituted for the noun proper, the repetition of the latter becomes unnecessary.

29.—The attendant noun is also occasionally substituted for the noun proper in the written as well as in the oral language.

30.—To conclude: the true function of the attendant noun is, apparently, to distinguish the generic from the specific (or the general from the particular). The nouns *t'ien*, being *huang t'ien* (Heaven), or *t'u*, being *hou t'u* (Earth),[3] are general designations incapable of subdivision into minor denominations; they have consequently no attendant nouns associated with them. Where the general designation [applies to what] is capable of subdivision into parts or items, the attendant noun is of use in numeration in that it represents the item as distinguished from the total.

31.—[These attendant nouns, therefore, will be spoken of henceforth as Numeratives,] and a list is now given for the use of the student of all the numeratives in connexion with the nouns to which they are attached.

[*The Numeratives arranged in alphabetical order.*]

盞 *chan* [numerative of lamps; *e.g.*,] Bring a lamp; I want to read. The word *chan* is also synonymous with the word *wan* (a cup); you may say *yi chan ch'a* for a cup of tea, or *yi wan ch'a*, with equal propriety; it is not, however, applied to hand lanterns *(têng lung)*, the numerative of which is *ko*.

---

[1] Peculiarity: *chuan shu*, specially belonging to, a particular property.
[2] Associate: *ch'ên*; lit., the backing of cloth, etc., added to a flimsy material. See also 98, 15, Note [7].
[3] Heaven, Earth: *huang t'ien*, sovereign heaven; *hou t'u*, queen, or empress, earth; the twin powers of nature. Cf. Cœlus, father of Saturn, and Tellus; also, *ge anassa*, queen earth. See Sir JOHN DAVIS on Funeral Rites, in "The Chinese," Chapter VIII.

PART VIII.—THE PARTS OF SPEECH. 487

張 *chang* acts as the numerative of all such words[1] as table, chair, bed, stool, bow, paper, loom, net, as being things which show a certain broadness.[2]

陣 *chên* [numerative of showers, gales, outbreaks, etc.; *e.g.*,] a heavy fall of rain, a gale of wind, an uproar, uproarious discussion, of a certain duration. The word *chên* means, properly, to fight an action, and is used as a numerative with reference to the suddenness which is the condition [of the occurrences in question]; it implies, say, such eagerness to arrive that [the person or event] cannot wait.

乘 *ch'êng* is, properly, to board, as a ship, to get on, as a cart, or to mount, as a horse. It is occasionally the numerative of *chiao* (sedan-chair), but *ting* is also used.[3]

劑 *chi* (a dose). A *chi* of medicine is a draught[4] composed of a number of drugs. When a number of drugs are made up into pills, the composition is spoken of as *yi liao yo*.

架 *chia* [literally, a frame; you say,] a piece of ordnance, a single hawk or falcon, a clock, a single tie-beam (wall-plate). Of the tie-beam, you say, speaking of two, *liang chia*; but you may also say *i tui* (a pair).

間 *chien* is the space between four wooden pillars; it is consequently the numerative of house, room, etc.; but we must be careful how we use it. For instance, when a person says, I have bought a *fang-tzŭ*, he means that he has bought a whole *so*, or a whole *ch'u* (a set of premises), comprising *hao hsieh chien fang-tzŭ* (several buildings). Were he to say, *na ko fang-tzŭ hao* (that is a good house), the expression would be understood to apply to all premises[5] inside the outer (*lit.*, the great) gate.[6] If you asked a man, How many *chien* are there in that house *(na ko fang-tzŭ)*, and he were to reply, Some thirty *chien*, he would be speaking of all the apartments[7] into which the house is capable of being subdivided [all the spaces defined by four wooden pillars], without reference to their dimensions. In the palaces of Chinese princes and dukes,[8] there is generally on the north side a building with an upper and lower story, each of which is subdivided into five or seven *chien*. Referring to its divisions, when you are outside you say it is a *fang-tzŭ* of five or seven *chien*; if you are inside the house you say there are *wu ch'i chien wu-tzŭ* (five or seven rooms) [as the case may be]. In the following, We two live in *i ko wu*, the speaker means that there are a number of *chien* in communication

---

[1] All such words: note the *fan* supported by *chi hsieh tzŭ* at the end of the clause.

[2] Which show a certain broadness: note the literal meaning:—it is because its form slightly possesses a width-fashion. Cf. our vulgar *wide-like*.

[3] *Ch'êng* is generally applied to chairs to which bearers are attached; *ting*, to chairs without the bearers.

[4] A draught: *lit.*, made into a broth to be drunk.

[5] All premises: note *t'ung* supported by *tou*, all.

[6] The great gate: *i ko ta mên*, the one great gate; *q.d.*, the sole great entrance.

[7] All the apartments: construe, He does not distinguish great from small; *an ko chien*, he lays the hand on, *sc.*, counts, each apartment, *êrh*, and, speaks. Observe that *an*, amongst other meanings, = *chü*, to hold in the hand; both *an* and *chü* being commonly rendered according to; *q.d.*, by what I have hold of I infer. Note a similar construction of *êrh shuo* under the next numerative; also of *êrh lun*, under *li*.

[8] Princes and dukes: the *wang*, princes, are the two highest classes of Manchu and Mongolian nobles; the *kung*, dukes, the fifth and sixth; the *beilê* and *beitsê*, third and fourth classes, are also included in the generic term *wang kung*. The latter term, *kung*, has also been from ancient times the first of five orders of rank, to a certain extent hereditary, conferred for distinguished service; but the *fu*, palace, is distinctively the residence of the *wang kung*.

with one another, and that there is but one door for ingress or egress. If he were to say, We two live in *i chien wu-tzŭ,* he would mean, We occupy the same apartment, comprised in the space between four pillars. When you ask, How many *chien* are there in this *liu* of *fang-tzŭ,* you are asking the number of houses in the row.

件 *chien* [originally, to divide; to enumerate] is the only numerative of articles of clothing. With such nouns as affairs, utensils, despatches, etc., to which it acts as numerative, it may be exchanged for other numeratives, as *chuang, yang,* and *t'ao.*

隻 *chih* [properly, half a pair] is the numerative of fowl, duck, goose, ox, sheep, tiger, ship, box, and like words; also, of shoe, boot, stocking, arm, hand, foot, eye, all of which being things that make pairs (雙 *shuang*), *chih* is employed to show that a half pair is meant. Of a *shuang* of shoes, for instance, you say that one *chih* has been lost.

枝 *chih* [a branch or twig]; *i chih la* (a candle); *i chih hua* (a stalk of flowers) is used where a number of flower-blossoms are growing on the same stem. You may use *chih* with *pi* (a pencil) and *ti* (a flute), but *kuan* (a tube) is more common. Observe that there is a difference between *chih* and *chih-tzŭ*: you may say a *chih-tzŭ* (column) of troops or irregulars.

軸 *chou* [properly, the nave of a wheel]. The expression *i chou hua-'rh* signifies a scroll mounted; the word *chou* is used with reference[1] to the two knobs of the roller which show themselves at the lower end of the scroll. For the same reason the *kao-fêng* (patents according rank to the parents or ancestors of an official, be they living or dead) are spoken of as being so many *chou* in number.

句 *chü* is the numerative of language, oral or written.

卷 *chüan* [a numerative of book, document, etc.]; you may use it with *ts'ê-tzŭ* (a roll or return),[2] or with *shu* (a book); but *pên* is more common with both.

炷 *chu* [properly, the wick of a lamp]; the numerative of joss-stick; a number of *chu* (sticks or rods of joss-stick) held together by a paper band are called a *ku* (a limb), and five *ku* a *fêng* (say, packet).

處 *ch'u* (place) is synonymous with *ti-fang* (a certain extent of space). When you say that you have bought *i ch'u fang-tzŭ* (a house), you include all premises within the boundary walls; you might say the same of a single building which has no boundary walls.

串 *ch'uan* [a string of things strung together, as] pearls, priests' beads, court beads,[3] cash A string of priests' beads or court beads may also be spoken of as a *kua* of beads. The numerative of bead, as a single bead, is *k'o.*

[1] Is used with reference: note the construction:—*ku tz'ŭ ts'ai shuo,* because of this therefore [do men] say it, being placed at the end of the clause. The *kao-fêng* are, literally, mandates conferring rank: *kao,* intimation of superior to inferior; *fêng,* properly, fief, hence rank. Note that *kao-fêng* is more properly to confer such rank; the patent is *kao-ming.*

[2] *Ts'ê-tzŭ,* roll or return, *sc.,* of persons, such as a muster roll, a census return, etc.; *ts'ê* also read *ch'ai* (see Part VII, 9).

[3] Court beads: the necklace worn in full dress by civilians of the fifth and higher grades; by military men of the fourth and higher grades; *ch'uan* is the numerative of necklace, etc.

PART VIII.—THE PARTS OF SPEECH.

椿 *chuang* (piles),[1] wooden stakes driven into the ground. It is used in the spoken language with *shih-ch'ing* (an affair), where the object of the speaker is to speak specially of one matter amongst a number. The numerative *chien* is much more common with *shih-ch'ing*.

牀 *ch'uang* (a bed) is used with coverlid, mattress, carpet.

方 *fang* (square), numerative of broken brick and stone [in regular heaps],[2] also of excavation [work].

封 *fêng* [originally, a fief; later, a seal; hence, to seal up]. It acts as the numerative of letter and like words. It means, properly, to keep concealed;[3] this is why it is used with *shu-tzŭ*, *shu-hsin* (letters).

幅 *fu²* [properly *fu⁴*, also *fu³* (*see* below) a strip, numerative of paper] is not the same as *chang*; it rather approaches *t'iao*; still, the difference of width [respectively indicated by the two words] is not so very great.[4] A *fu* (sheet) of note-paper is a *chang* of note-paper. Speaking of *pu* (cloth) you may say a *fu³* (length of cloth), or you may number lengths of silk by the *fu³*.

副 *fu* [a numerative of certain things in pairs; originally, to divide in two; hence] used always with reference to sets in pairs, as a pair of *tui-tzŭ* (scrolls with verses, mottoes, upon them), a set of ear-rings; but a set of buttons consists of five.

桿 *kan* [a bough, numerative of] *ch'iang*, [whether translated as] musket or single-pointed spear; of *ch'êng*, steel-yard; of *ch'a*, three-pointed spear. If the *ch'iang* be a *ch'ang-ch'iang* (*sc.*, spear, not musket), it is equally correct to use *t'iao* as the numerative; but *t'iao* cannot be used [with *ch'iang* as musket, or] with the other nouns mentioned.

根 *kên* [properly, a root below the ground] is the numerative of mast, flagstaff, staff or pole, bamboo pole, lamp-wick, felled timber, hair of the head [or body], hair of the beard, and similar nouns; always having reference to form. With *kuên-tzŭ*, a staff or porter's pole, it is as correct to use *t'iao* as *kên*.

個 *ko* [anciently, besides other meanings, an individual], used in a great many different positions, but more constantly in such phrases as *chê ko jên* (this man), *chê ko li* (this sense, principle, theory), *chê ko tung-hsi* (this thing). With other nouns it may or may not[5] be employed.

棵 *k'o* is never employed but as the numerative of tree.

顆 *k'o* [originally, a small head; hence the unit of small round things], used with pearl, head decapitated; in both cases with reference to form. Any round thing can in general be numbered by *k'o*.

---

[1] Note *chüeh²-tzŭ*, a peg; *e.g.*, a tent peg.

[2] See also *to*, below. The numerative of single bricks, etc., is *k'uai*, a piece.

[3] To keep concealed: note the construction:—*lit.*, because this word properly has the meaning of to wrap up [so that there shall be] non-appearance. Note the polysyllable *pao-tsang-pu-lao-ti*, formed by *ti* into an attributive of *li*.

[4] Not so very great: note the construction *k'uan chai*, the width of.

[5] May or may not: *lit.*, when elsewhere using the word *ko*, all [such use of it] is *huo yung*, conditional use.

口 *k'ou* (the mouth); you may use it with cooking-pan, bell, sword, water-jar; of so many persons. But though it does act as numerative to all these nouns, there is a distinction to be observed regarding its use with persons. Males and females spoken of collectively are *k'ou*; females spoken of separately are also *k'ou*; of men, you say so many *ming* (names) or so many *ko* (individuals). The word *tao* with *k'ou* means weapon (sc., a sword); you may also say *i pa tao* for a sword; also, for the pork-butcher's knife.[1] The bell described as *i k'ou chung* is that hung in temples; it has no tongue,[2] and has to be struck to make it sound.

股 *ku* [properly, the under part of the thigh; one of the numeratives of road]; with *tao* (a road or way), *ku = t'iao*; in more polished conversation *ku* is found with *lu* (road).

塊 *k'uai* (a bit, a piece); you may use it with dollar, ink-cake, brick, door-slab *(pien)*; but it is very comprehensive; *e.g.*, take *a* dollar and buy *a* carpet (or, [someone] bought *a* carpet with *a* dollar).

管 *kuan* (a tube), numerative of things that are hollow within and present a certain length [to the grasp]; for instance, pencil, flute, clarionet; in all which cases, however, it may be exchanged for *chih* (numerative of branch, stalk, etc.).

綑 *k'uén* [properly, to bind in a bundle],[3] used with firewood, as faggot; straw, etc., as bundle; onions, as bunch; meaning always that some of the article spoken of is bound up.

粒 *li* [properly, a grain of rice], used, as having reference to the form of the article, with rice or with pill.

領 *ling* [properly, the neck], used only with *hsi-tzŭ* (mat) and *wei pao* (rush screen).[4]

面 *mien* (a face) is numerative of gong, drum, flag or banner, mirror [of glass or metal].

把 *pa* [properly, to grasp in the hand]. All articles that have a *pa*⁴-*'rh* (handle that the hand can lay hold of) are enumerated as so many *pa*³. All such nouns, for instance, as tea-pot, knife, slice[5] (kitchen utensil), fork, fan, lock, take *pa*. With *i-tzŭ* (chair) you may use *pa* or *chang*.

包 *pao* [properly, to wrap] is numerative of all articles that can be made into packages;[6] such, for instance, as sugar, opium.[7]

本 *pén* [properly, the lower trunk of a tree] is used with *shu* (book), *chang* (accounts). With *shu* you may use *chüan* (chapter), but not with *chang*.

---

[1] Butcher's knife: *t'u*², originally, to flay; to kill; *hu*, a person; *t'u hu*, the slayer, sc., of pigs.

[2] Tongue: *to*⁴, clapper of a bell; described in an ancient commentary as the *mu shê*, wooden tongue, of *chin k'ou*, the metal mouth.

[3] *K'un* is properly written with the 64th Radical.

[4] Rush screen: *wei*, the bulrush; *pao*², a coarse screen made of the bulrush.

[5] Slice: the *ch'an*³ is a flat plate of tin or iron with a long handle, used to take things fried out of the pan.

[6] Packages: note the construction:—Whatsoever be things that [man] can wrap up out of sight, [speaking of these] all, can [one] use *pao* to act as the attendant word. Observe that the subject of both verbs, *shou-kuo* and *yung*, is in reality *jên* understood. In Latin *fan = cumque* in *quæcumque*, the *quæ* being represented by *ti*, which stands for *things*; *shou = in* in *involvo*; the words *ch'i lai* = the inflexion of the passive participle in *dus*, or the verbal adjective termination in *bilis*. Coin a word and the sentence would run *Quæcumque sint involubilia*.

[7] Opium: *yen t'u*, smoke-clay, so called from the colour and form of the balls in which the drug is imported.

匹 *p'i* [anciently, amongst other meanings, the unit of horses], the only numerative of *ma* (horse); with ass and mule you may also use *t'ou* (head), and under certain conditions *ko*, which is the invariable numerative of camel.

疋 *p'i* [originally written as *p'i* (numerative of horse), forty Chinese feet], sole numerative of silk piece goods, satin, damask, lawn, gauze, cotton fabrics; it is properly applied only where nothing has been cut off [as we say, *the* piece].

篇 *p'ien* [originally, before the invention of paper, a bamboo writing tablet], numerative of *wên chang* (the essay in measured prose), *fu* (the essay in rhyming prose), and *lun* (the essay in four paragraphs); each of these terms signifying a piece of composition. The question, How many *p'ien* are there in this book? has reference to the number of sheets (= leaves); the *p'ien* here has a different sense from the *p'ien* used of a piece of composition.

鋪 *p'u* (to spread out) is used with no noun but *k'ang* (stove-bed); with *ch'uang* (bed), you always use *chang*. The *p'u*⁴ in *p'u-tien* (shop), though syllabically the same, has a different tone.

所 *so* (a place); *i so fang-tzŭ* (a house) is the same as *i ch'u fang-tzŭ*, both referring to the whole range of buildings within the entrance gate.

扇 *shan* is, properly, an article used to drive away the heat¹ and give oneself air [a fan], on account of its resemblance to which a door is called *shan*. That house has not got all its doors and windows yet; there are four or five still wanting.

首 *shou* [originally, the head; hence, a beginning; here, a stanza] is only used with poetry; *q.d.*, as a word marking the beginning and ending of the lines [*lit.*, sentences, *sc.*, that make a stanza]. The writer makes any number of stanzas according to the subject of his verse,² and the number of lines in each stanza varies; it may be four, eight, twelve, or at the most sixteen. The stanzas are not necessarily of an even number; one may with equal propriety make a poem of four or five stanzas, or of some score.

檯 *t'ai* is, properly, to carry, as two or more persons lifting an object by united action. At a funeral the bier may have as many as sixty-four *t'ai* (bearers) [hence, applied to the thing borne, the numerative of presents sent]. The smallest wedding trousseau consists of eight *t'ai*; if the family be wealthy, there may be as many as a hundred or more. Whenever presents are sent to anyone, the *t'ai* are in pairs.

擔 *tan* is a load³ such as one man carries over his shoulder on a porter's pole. The phrase *t'a t'iao-cho i tan ch'ai-huo* (he is carrying a load of fuel) means that the person spoken of bears the *pien tan* (the flat pole) on his shoulder, and that fuel is borne at the two ends of the pole. If the fuel borne be but a single faggot or parcel, it would be borne (*tiao*) on a *kun-tzŭ* (a staff or stake) [not on a *pien tan*, and the said staff] would be *k'ang* [not *t'iao*] on the shoulder.

[1] Drive away heat: *ch'ui*¹, properly, to drive away wild animals; to drive away *shu*, heat, and *chao fêng*, invite air.

[2] The writer, *shih chia*, the verse man, the poet, *k'an t'i*, looking to what is propounded, = *t'i mu*, his subject, *sui tso*, proceeds to make, verse stanzas many or few.

[3] *Tan*⁴, the load carried; *tan*¹, to carry a load.

刀 *tao* (a knife), only used with paper, a *tao* of paper being a quantity of sheets laid flat one upon the other; employed with reference to the effort required to cut through a quantity of paper so placed.

道 *tao* (a road) is used always in the sense of *t'iao* (a strip), with river, bridge, wall, wound or breach, Imperial Decree. The bridge outside the front gate of the capital is a *san tao ch'iao* (a triple bridge).[1]

套 *t'ao* [properly, an outer casing, a wrapper; now, among other senses, a book wrapper]; *i t'ao shu* means a number of books in one wrapper. One *t'ao* may be the whole of a work, or a work may be divided into several *t'ao*. *I t'ao i-shang* (a suit of clothes) is a *p'ao* (the long inner garment) and a *kua* (the somewhat shorter outer garment); you *ch'uan* (put on) the *p'ao* first, and you *t'ao* (slip over it) the *kua*. *I t'ao chiu pei* is a set of twelve wine cups of graduating sizes which fit one into the other.

條 *t'iao* [properly, a twig]; it is common with silk (as a single thread), cord (as a single string), sash, girdle, chain, dog, rainbow, sense (*q.d.*, the sense or principle of a thing), street, road. You may use *t'iao* with *ho* (a river), but also *tao*.

貼 *t'ieh* [properly, to stick on] is not used as a numerative except with plaster (*sc.*, cataplasm). A *t'ieh* of gold-leaf consists of ten sheets.

頂 *ting* (the crown of the head) is the numerative of chair, cap.

朵 *to* (a bud); as a numerative, only used with flower. The common word for the bud[2] of the unopened flower is *ku-to*.

垛 *to* [anciently, an ante-chamber; also, a target; here, as a stack], like *to*, the numerative of wood, bricks, or earth; but *to* is a regular heap, *tui* an irregular one.

頭 *t'ou* (the head), used with ox, mule, ass; it is equally correct to use *ko* with these nouns. Sheep are numbered by *chih*, not by *t'ou*. [The word *t'ou* is the numerative to many other nouns, such as garlic, head ornaments, cap plumes, etc.]

堵 *tu* [anciently, a wall of fifty feet long] is numerative of wall; *tu* or *tao*.

堆 *tui* is like *to* (a heap); but *to* applies to things regularly stacked, *tui*, to what is piled in confusion. Like *to* it is used with wood, brick; also with earth and like things.[4]

頓 *tun* [originally, to bow the head to the ground; subsequently, a turn or time; hence, a meal], numerative of meal, flogging, as though implying a certain fulness or completeness.

座 *tso* [properly, the standing part of a bed; any seat; a stand for vases, etc.], used with mountain, tomb, temple, pagoda, walled town.

---

[1] Triple bridge: a bridge of three roads side by side.

[2] Bud: the *ku*[1] in *ku-to* has no meaning.

[3] Regular order: note the construction:—one *to* wood, one *to* bricks, [men] saying effect [this proposition, that] there is *pai*, an array, *tê*, effecting, *ch'i*, in regular order, *chêng*, composing;=the two expressions mean wood and bricks placed in regular order.

[4] Like things: *têng lei*, fellow-class kinds, things homogeneous.

PART VIII.—THE PARTS OF SPEECH. 493

尊 *tsun* [properly, that which is respected,[1] specially as ruler or father]; you use it with *p'ao* (cannon), but you also use *wei* and *chia*.

尾 *wei* (a tail), numerative of fish; *t'iao* may also be used with fish.

位 *wei* means the proper position of any person or thing, whether standing up or seated: three officials[2] of the rank of *ta-jên*; a single cannon; some visitors.

文 *wên* [originally, streaks of any kind; later, writing, composition] is numerative of nothing but copper cash. A single cash is commonly spoken of as *i ko ta ch'ien*. Were you to ask,[3] How many cash *(chi wên ch'ien)* does such a thing cost? the answer would be *to shao ta ch'ien* (so many cash). The use of the word in this capacity is found to date from the Chou dynasty,[4] when cash were coined[5] with an inscription upon them.

眼 *yen* (the eye) is used as numerative of well.

SECTION IV.

[NUMBER, SINGULAR AND PLURAL.]

32.—Proceeding next to the consideration of the numbers of nouns, the difference between the Singular and the Plural, we find that the Chinese language has a large variety of forms by which the one number is distinguished from the other: in some cases the noun itself, without the addition of a numeral, will act as a noun of number; in some, plurality is represented by the reduplication of the noun; in some, such words as the following are employed:—

chung (all, a multitude);
to (many);
to¹ shao³ (how many)?
to¹ shao⁴ (a large number);
hao hsieh ko (a good many);
tou (all);

chün (all; specially, both);
ch'üan (the whole, entire);
ta chia (all the persons);
chu (all);
fan (all whatever);
têng (a class, a sort).

Lastly, where the number of a noun has to be stated numerically, the numeral may precede or it may follow the noun.

[1] Respected: cannon are had in special respect, and under certain circumstances are sacrificed to. See note ², below.

[2] Three officials: in German, French, Italian, and other languages, indeed, though more rarely, in English, the appellative of respect is tacked somewhat in this way to certain nouns, but appositively, not numeratively; *e.g.*, their lord-ships the commissioners, *messieurs les députés*, etc. The French might translate *chê i wei p'ao* by *monsieur le dit canon*.

[3] Were you to ask, etc.,=Did you use *wên* in your question, *ko* would be used in the answer, were the cash three, four, or any number.

[4] Chou dynasty: the last of the three long dynasties which preceded our era, overthrown about B.C. 200 by the prince who suppressed his brother feudatories and made himself Emperor of all China.

[5] First coined: construe thus:—the origin of the use of the word *wên* [in this connexion] had its cause in the Chou dynasty, when, in coining cash, *wên tzŭ*, written words, were added thereon.

33.—Take the following examples:—I hear *chung jên* (all men, everyone) say that *hên to* (very many, a great number of) people are come.

34.—How many are there? There are *hao hsieh ko* (a good number).

35.—What kind of people are they¹ *(tou)*? They are *chün* (all) people of perfectly good character.²

36.—Why have they *ch'üan* (all) come, or come in a body? They have *ta chia* (all) public business, which they beg *chu wei* (you gentlemen)³ to manage for them?

37.—There is a clue [to be found in] *fan shih* (all affairs).⁴ These men *(jên têng)* of course returned at once.

38.—In the phrase, A number of people⁵ are come, *to shao* may be used in the sense *hsü to* [that is, if *shao* be read with the 4th tone].

39.—In the phrase *yu jên lai*, you cannot be sure whether one person is come or more; it may be employed where two people are come, or three; of more than three, the common phrase would be *yu chi ko jên*.

40.—When you say *hao hsieh ko jên* (a good few) you mean that the number of persons is tolerably large,⁶ such that you cannot tell⁷ at a glance how many there are.

41.—The people *(na hsieh jên-mên)* in that house (the members of that family) are on very bad terms⁸ with each other.

42.—Unless the speaker is alluding to persons, the word *mên* is not employed.⁹

43.—The words *niu yang* in the phrase *t'a lai ti shih mai niu yang* (He is come to sell oxen and sheep) must not be construed as meaning a single *niu* or a single *yang*. Were a person to say *t'a yao mai chih niu* or *mai p'i ma*, he would certainly mean that he was going to sell one ox or one horse.

44.—In *chê chien fang-tzŭ*, one *chien* only is meant, but *chê fang-tzŭ* means that there is a number of *chien* (apartments), greater or less, in the house. [*See* the numerative *chien*, p. 487.]

---

¹ They: *tou* evidently pluralising the subject, otherwise untranslatable.

² Good character: *liang shan*, virtuous, good citizens, the opposite of *hsiung ngo*, violent and vicious.

³ You gentlemen: *chu wei*, all [your] worships.

⁴ All affairs: *see* farther on the compound relative *fan*; these men, *jên têng*, man class,=more than one.

⁵ Number of people: *hsü*, originally, to listen to, to permit; in ancient texts also found with *chi*, as *chi hsü*, how many?

⁶ Tolerably large: *chiao*, to compare; here, and often,=rather.

⁷ Tell: *lit.*, as if at one glance you cannot reckon clearly.

⁸ Bad terms: observe *pu* before *ho mu*=un in unfriendly, *dis* in disagreeable; so *t'ai pu ya*, very ill-bred or discourteous.

⁹ It should be noted that *mên* may make the plural of most personal nouns and all personal pronouns. You may say *na hsieh jên-mên*, those people, *ta-jên-mên*, their excellencies; *k'ê-shang-mên*, the merchants; but it is used generally, if not always, where the noun is preceded by a demonstrative pronoun or the definite article. The nouns *yeh-mên* and *niang-'rh-mên* are used both as singular and plural: *ni-mên-ti yeh-mên tou san-liao mo?* have all your gentlemen left the office! *yu ko niang-'rh-mên lai*, there is a woman come. The syllable *mên* becomes *mê* or *mo* in *chê-mo-cho, na-mo-cho*, the *cho* being probably corrupt for *chê*, the classical relative.

PART VIII.—THE PARTS OF SPEECH. 495

45.—[The following examples illustrate a variety of plural formations.] There are some people come. How many? Four. What are they come about, those people? They have brought some horses here. Who is going to buy the horses? They are not all going to be sold;[1] one may be possibly bought. I don't much care to buy horses.

SECTION V.

[CASE.]

46.—The English noun has three distinct modes[2] of use assigned it, which are variously applied, according to circumstances.[3] As no such distinctions exist in Chinese, we shall here make shift[4] with a series of three places, the order of which the reader will find illustrated in the four paragraphs following, if he will have the goodness[5] to look at them.

[*The Nominative, as answering the question Who, What, Which.*]

47.—Who smashed[6] (or, Who is it that has smashed) the tea-cup? That small child smashed it.

48.—Who was it that wrote these words? That man CHANG[7] wrote them.

49.—Which is the most intelligent of animals?[8] The dog.

[*The Objective, as answering the question Whom, What, Which.*]

50.—Whom is that small boy beating? He is beating the little girl.

51.—What is that woodman[9] doing there? He is cutting boughs off trees.

---

[1] Going to be sold: construe:—it is not [the case that] all must sell; buy one head [someone] indeed may.

[2] Three distinct modes: *lit.*, the English in the use of nouns define three forms.

[3] Variously applied, according to circumstances: employed interchangeably.

[4] Make shift: *ch'üan-ch'ieh*, provisionally, we shall *fên ch'u*, make or invent a division into, *san têng*, three classes or gradations. The reader will bear in mind the history of our word *case*. The nominative of the noun being the perpendicular, the cases were the divergences, the *fallings* away from it; thus, properly speaking, the nominative is not a case at all; but as it is in all inflected languages the first of the series of forms so styled, it has here been made the first of the three classes between which and the cases an analogy has been attempted.

[5] Have the goodness: *lit.*, please look at the four paragraphs below; *chiu shih*, in that case [you will find them] to be *pang-yang*, examples, of the division into three *têng*, places in a series.

[6] Who smashed: *tsa*², to smash by throwing down or letting fall. Note the construction, which might be transposed, as *tsa-tê na ch'a wan shih shui*. The *tê* in speech would as often as not be *ti*; it is best to treat it as a verb auxiliary of the verb immediately preceding it, and so with *tê* in *hsieh-tê* in the two following examples, whether you construe thus, Who is it that wrote these words? or, Whose writing are these words? the latter idiom giving force to *shih* as the verb substantive, the subject of which is then the word *tzŭ*, which in the former we treat as the object.

[7] That man CHANG: note the *na ko jên* following *hsing Chang ti*, the surnamed CHANG one. Were the sentence to begin *shih na ko hsing Chang ti*, it would still end as in the text.

[8] Animals: *ch'u*⁴ *shêng*, the brute; also used, as with us, of people, as a term of abuse; *ch'u*, read *hsü*, to rear; *liu ch'u*, the six *ch'u*, are horses, oxen, sheep, poultry, dogs, and pigs.

[9] Woodman: *ch'iao fu*, the man who *ch'iao*², collects fuel, is *k'an shu chi-tzŭ*, cutting tree boughs.

[*The Possessive, as answering the question Whose, or of What.*]

52.—Whose was that book¹ that he has lost? It was that book of mine.

53.—Had you not made him a present² of that book of yours? No; it was only lent³ him.

54.—Well, then, ask him for that book of his to replace yours. His is not the same as mine.

55.—What day did you lend it him? I lent it him the day before yesterday.

56.—Why did you lend it him? He met me in the street carrying the book, and asked me to lend it him, but I refused.

57.—If you refused, how came he by it?⁴ When I said I wouldn't let him have it, he snatched it⁵ out of my hand, and said he would return it in a couple of days.

58.—Oh! this was abominable, really; you had better not associate⁶ with him any more.

[*The following show the three Cases.*]

59.—According to English grammar,⁸ in the sentence The outlaws have burned my parent's⁷ house, the word *tsei-fei* (outlaws) is the first place in the series (the nominative case), *fang-tzŭ* (house) is the second (the objective case), and *lao jên chia* (parent's) the third (the possessive case).

60.—This is shown⁹ if you put the following questions:—Who set fire to anything? The outlaws. What did they burn? A house. Whose house was it? My parent's house.

61.—In a word, in every case the noun representing the agent¹⁰ is in the first place of this series, the noun representing that which is acted on is in the second, and the noun representing the possessor, in the third.

---

¹ Whose was that book: *tê* would be generally pronounced *ti* = one, or that which; *q.d.*, the lost one is whose book? The correct analysis of the construction is probably this: *tiu*, to lose, *tiu-tê*, loss achieved, lost; [someone] *tiu-tê*, has lost [a book; that book] is whose book. The *ti* in *shui ti*, clearly = *tê*, to obtain, to possess; the who possessed, possessed by whom, whose, book. Compare the answer, It was that I-possessed book, that book belonging to me, = of mine.

² Made a present: *ni* before *na pên shu* acts as the possessive pronoun, not as the subject of *sung*, before which it would be quite correct to introduce another *ni*.

³ Only lent: so translated to give due emphasis to the denial. Note two *ti*, both = *tê*, and both acting as our participial inflexions in *given* from *give*, *lent* from *lend*.

⁴ Came he by it: how achieved, the having taken it away. Treat *na liao ch'ü* as = *abstraho*, and *tê* as giving the force of the inflexion *abstraxi*; compare the use of the auxiliaries *avoir* and *avere* in parallel constructions.

⁵ Snatched it: *ta*, from; he from my hand within, violently, *lit.*, unyieldingly, tore it away.

⁶ Associate: *ch'uan*, to go through, as a string through things strung; *huan*, to exchange; *ch'uan huan*, intimate relations.

⁷ My parent's: note the use of *wo-mên* instead of the singular; *wo lao jên chia* would not be wrong, but it also means, vulgarly, I myself.

⁸ Grammar: *shuo fa* is commonly rendered phrase, mode of expression.

⁹ Shown: *lit.*, how can [one] see it? one question and one answer you will then perceive it.

¹⁰ Agent: *hsing ti*, the one that acts; acted on, subjected, *shou ti*, the one that receives; possessor, *kuei wei ti*, the one to whom [the property] belongs; *kuei*, to return; compare *re*-vert.

PART VIII.—THE PARTS OF SPEECH.

SECTION VI.

[GENDER.]

62.—The sexes of the human race are distinguished as *nan* (man) and *nü* (woman); those of the brute creation, as *kung* (male) and *mu* (mother). No inanimate thing has gender.[1] Mountain, water, wood, and stone are all considered inanimate things.

63.—[Sex is distinguished sometimes by particular designations, sometimes not; *e.g.*,] Are that man and that woman sitting there husband and wife? No; a brother, and a sister younger than he is.

64.—I have bought seven chickens, of which two are cocks, and five, hens.

65.—The male of horses is *êrh ma* (stallion); the female, *k'o ma* (mare).

66.—The bull[2] is [colloquially] *kung niu*; the cow, *mu niu*.

SECTION VII.

[THE ADJECTIVE AND ITS DEGREES OF COMPARISON.]

67.—For the qualifying[3] and classifying [in the order of their qualities] such of the *ming-mu* as are *shih-tzŭ* (nouns substantive), other words must be added to them. The substantive is as it were the principal; the word added to qualify and describe its degree, the auxiliary[4] (its adjective).

68.—The word "good," for instance, means nothing by itself; it leaves you nowhere;[5] you must add "person" or "thing" to it, and then it will serve the purpose of qualification.

69.—For instance, in the phrases This is a good man, This man is good, the word "good" serves to characterise[6] (or describe) the man.

70.—In This paper is white, That paper is red, the words "white" and "red" specify different kinds of paper.

71.—In the phrases Coarse paper and fine paper, This paper is coarse, That paper is fine, the words "coarse" and "fine" distinguish the [one paper from the other as differing in] degree [of fineness or coarseness].

72.—**[Degrees of Comparison.]**—There is, farther, a gradation[7] of increase and decrease to be observed in the employment of the adjective, which the following section will explain.

---

[1] Has gender: *yin*, the female principle of nature; *yang*, the male. Note the term *ssŭ wu*.

[2] The bull: *mang¹*, properly, a piebald ox or cow; not used colloquially.

[3] Qualifying: *fên hsiang*, dividing into sorts; *ting têng*, determining ranks.

[4] Auxiliary: *fu chu*, to stand by and assist, as a minister his Sovereign; *fu³*, properly, the jaw or cheek; hence the wood which keeps the wheel in its place.

[5] Nowhere: *cho lo*, bottom found in sounding, definite whereabouts of anything. You say that an affair has *cho lo* when it is satisfactorily disposed of.

[6] Characterise: *lit.*, does the service of distinguishing the sort or quality.

[7] Gradation: *ts'êng tz'u*; *lit.*, succession of layers.

73.—He is intelligent. You are more intelligent. You are more intelligent than he. He is the most intelligent of all these people. He is more intelligent than those people. He is more intelligent than anyone. He is the most intelligent man in the world.[1]

74.—That is impracticable. That is more impracticable.[2] That is more impracticable still. Of [all] these methods the most impracticable is that.

75.—The highest roof in Peking is that of the Emperor's palace.

76.—He has more money than I (or, His fortune is larger than mine).

77.—My abilities are not to be compared[3] to his.

78.—He is taller[4] than I (or, I am shorter than he).

79.—Which of those two speaks the better mandarin? LI is rather the better speaker of the two.

80.—Who is the most learned[5] of these three? Also LI.

SECTION VIII.
[THE PRONOUN.]

81.—[**Personal Pronouns.**]—The word by which a man designates himself when he is talking is *wo* (I, me); the word by which I designate anyone that I am addressing[6] in conversation is *ni* (thou, thee). Any person besides you and myself is *p'ang jên* (a third party), and if you and I allude to him in conversation with each other, we designate him *t'a*.

82.—The plural of the personal pronoun is *wo-mên* (we); *tsa-mên* (we two, or, all of us concerned); *ni-mên* (ye); *t'a-mên* (they).

83.—The word *t'a* may be used in speaking of birds and brutes in Chinese, but it is not often applied to inanimate things.

84.—Speaking of a dog, you can say, *t'a* (he) is a good watch-dog.[7] If you were to ask, Is that table taken away, the person addressed would reply, *na liao ch'ü liao;* he could not say, *na kuo T'A ch'ü liao.*

---

[1] In the world: *lit.*, under heaven.

[2] More impracticable: you might transpose *kêng* and *shih*, or introduce *shih* before *tsai*.

[3] Not to be compared: *pi pu ch'i*, cannot rise to a level with his abilities on comparison.

[4] Taller, shorter: his *shên liang*⁴, his body-measure, stature.

[5] Most learned: construe thus:—[*jo lun*, if we consider] these three men's *hsio-wên*, learning, which is strong? Note the adjective *ch'iang* here *strongest*, because the comparison is of more than two; in the foregoing sentence, *stronger*, because two only are compared.

[6] Addressing: note the construction:—I to *shui*, whom, whomsoever,=anyone, am speaking; [my] *ch'êng shui*, designation of anyone is *ni*. Observe that the relation of these indefinite relatives to their antecedents, as also that of the correlative conjunctions, is constantly represented in Chinese, as here, by reduplication, especially of verbs or pronouns; *e.g.*, *ni yao to-shao*, *k'o i na to-shao*, you can take whatever number you want, or, as many as you want; the strict analysis being, you want many or few, you can take many or few; *shih jên shih wu*, be it person, be it thing =whether person or thing, *sui chao sui yung*, as you come upon them so make use of them; *sui*, to follow, here and commonly, according to. Cf. *sequor, secundum*.

[7] Good watch-dog: note *lai*, auxiliary, following *kou*, the object of *t'i ch'i*.

PART VIII.—THE PARTS OF SPEECH. 499

85.—[Relative Pronouns.]
1. The man whom I went to see was not at home.
2. Whom did you go to see?
3. He is a teacher who used [1] to teach me mandarin.[2]
4. What is his name?
5. CHANG.
6. Is it the CHANG who lives in Tiger-skin Lane?
7. What lane [3] did you say?
8. I said Tiger-skin Lane; the lane fourth from the south end [4] of Great East Street, on the west side.
9. That is not the lane in which CHANG lives; he lives outside the walls.
10. Whom is he teaching at present?
11. He is teaching two people, both of them my relations.
12. What is he teaching them? [5]
13. He is instructing the elder in official correspondence,[6] the younger in the Four Books.[7]
14. Which of the two has made the more way? [8]
15. I think the younger is abler than the elder.
16. What are you reading now yourself, sir?
17. I am still at the book that you gave me last year.

86.—You use [9] the pronoun *shui* (who) only of persons; *shên-mo* and *na ko*, whether speaking of persons or things; [*e.g.*,]

87.—Who (*shui*) was it that [10] told you to come? *shên-mo jên* (what person was it, etc.); *na ko jên* (what person was it, etc.).

88.—What are you come for? I am come for the tea-cup. What are you doing here? I am putting the room to rights.

89.—You may say *ni ai hsi shih na yi ko* (which do you like) either of persons or things.

    [1] Who used: note the position of the numerative, which with *yi*, one, = the article *a*, not before, but after, the words which are formed by *ti = tê* into an attributive of the noun; *lit.*, [the man] is formerly-teach-me-mandarin-ing one teacher.

    [2] *Kuan hua*: the spoken language of government.

    [3] What lane: *lit.*, say again what lane it was.

    [4] Fourth from the south end: *lit.*, it is that lane [described by all the words between *tsai*, to be, or, to be in or at, and *ti* or *tê*, which, as we should say, inflects *tsai*. Construe: It] is the-*be*-great-east-street-south-end-road-west-side-number-four-lane-*ing*, that lane.

    [5] What is he teaching them? *lit.*, he teaches them what *kung k'o*, tasks? *kung*, labour; *k'o*, originally, examination.

    [6] Correspondence: *wên shu*, official documentary style, as distinguished from *wên chang*, elegant composition.

    [7] The Four Books: viz., "Ta Hsio," the Study for Adults; "Chung Yung," the Mean; "Lun Yü," the Dicta of Confucius; "Mêng Tzŭ," [the Doctrines of] Mencius.

    [8] Made the more way: *chien chang*, perceptible improvement; *q.d.*, [men] *chien*, see, [him] *chang*, growing.

    [9] You use: remember that *na* when interrogative is *na*³, when demonstrative, *na*⁴.

    [10] Who was it that: note that in these three sentences *ti* is as often used as *tê*.

90.—What is it that he is engaged upon over there? He has not told me what it is.

91.—What he really wants is this.

92.—[Compound Relative Pronouns.]
   1. Whosoever breaks the law[1] must be tried and punished.
   2. Any persons breaking the law, be they who they may,[2] must be tried and punished.
   3. Whosoever is deserving of reward I shall be sure to reward.

93.—1. Those brigands are very ferocious; they kill everyone they fall in with.[3]
   2. Whoever goes into the interior must take out a passport.[4]
   3. That story is false; it is not to be believed, be the teller[5] who he may.
   4. Whoever is recommended[6] by him is promoted and rewarded.
   5. Whatever he desires me to take in hand, I must take in hand.
   6. Did I not tell you to bring over whatever books there were there?
   7. Certainly; and are there any[7] that I have not brought over?
   8. There is a volume in the press that you have left behind.

94.—[Possessive Pronouns.]
   1. Is he not your father?
   2. No; he is my elder brother.
   3. Indeed! what is his age?
   4. He is upwards of twenty years older than I (or, His age is greater than mine by more than twenty years).
   5. Is that book yours, or did you borrow it?
   6. It is my own.
   7. Ah! it is the one you commissioned CHANG to buy for you,[8] is it not?
   8. No; it is one that I bought myself.[9]
   9. You are going[10] to take a walk in the Tung-hua Yüan to-day, aren't you?
   10. No, I can't;[11] I am on duty to-day.

[1] Whosoever breaks the law: *so yu*, whosoever or whatsoever there be; *so*, originally, place, position; *q.d.* the position is this, *yu*, there are law transgress-ing [persons]; *tsung*, all, *tei*, [man] must, try and punish.

[2] Be they who they may: *wu lun* [the agent, here government], does not discuss who it is that has broken the law; [the person who has broken the law, having broken it,] *chiu*, in consequence, must [the government] try and punish.

[3] Fall in with: [let them] meet whom [they will], all they slay.

[4] Passport: *chih*, to grasp in the hand, *chao*, that which shows, a testimony; *chih-chao* is generic of various documents of the kind which are *ling*, taken out. Understand *ti jên* after *nei ti*, the interior, all persons that enter, etc. Note that *nei ti* is also one expression for China as distinguished from *wai kuo*, foreign countries.

[5] Be the teller: *p'ing*, as before, at the option of; let who will tell it, all ought [man] not to believe.

[6] Recommended: construe:—leave it to him to recommend [persons; those persons] are *shui*, any persons; all obtain promotion and reward.

[7] Are there any: *lit.*, still are there I-have-not-brought-over ones?

[8] Buy for you: note *kei ni*=what we call the dative case; *ti*, relative, representing *jên*, man, and *shu*, book. Is it *the-one-that* you commissioned *him-that-is* surnamed CHANG to buy for you?

[9] Myself: *wo pên jên*, and above with *ti*, as my own.

[10] You are going, etc., may also be translated, won't you go? or, you had better go.

[11] I can't: *pu hsing*, elliptical for *wo pu nêng hsing*.

11. Wouldn't it do if I were to take your duty[1] for you?
12. I am much obliged[2] to you, but I must do the thing myself.
13. What is the difference[3] between your doing it and anyone else's doing it?
14. In the first place, I am the responsible person (or, it is my duty), and besides, if I did not see to it myself I should be sure to lay myself open[4] to being found fault with by my superiors.
15. Who would tell them?
16. They wouldn't need to be told; they would find it out themselves.

95.—[Demonstrative Pronouns.]

1. Which of these two horses is the better?
2. In my opinion this is a good horse and that is a bad one.
3. Which is the better bank of that river?
4. There is some scenery on that side; this side is somewhat barren.[5]
5. Have you bought all these oxen?
6. I have bought those three dun cows; these black ones are his purchase.
7. What do you want to do with these things of mine?[6]
8. They are not all yours.
9. Which of them is not mine?
10. This is not yours.
11. Very good; then I can do without[7] that one; leave those.

96.—[Distributive Pronouns.]

1. Every[8] member of the official establishment of the State has got his own duties.
2. Those two men have each[8] his own way of going to work.
3. In gambling, every player puts up his own stake.[9]
4. Neither of those propositions is a good one.
5. Two people gave him advice[10] that day, and had he attended to either[11] he might have saved his life; unfortunately, he attended to neither.

[1] Take your duty: construe:—[If you] commit to me instead of you to *tang*, bear, would it be well or not?

[2] Much obliged: *fei hsin*, as before. Note *tei=tê yao*, it becomes, or is become, necessary; it is certainly necessary that I myself *pan*, should despatch, *ti*, that which [is the business of my *ch'ai shih*]. You might construe: The business is such that I must, etc.

[3] What difference: *i yang*, one and the same fashion; cf. uni-form. *Lit.*, you individually=you yourself, transact, your own transacting, *hai*, compared with, another man's transacting, there is what non-uniformity?

[4] Lay myself open: *lit.*, I should certainly invite my superiors' *t'iao-ch'ih*, reproof; *t'iao*, to pick out, *sc.*, one's fault; *ch'ih*[4], to blame. Note *ko-tzŭ-ko*[3]-*'rh* and *tzŭ-chi-ko*[3]-*'rh*=self.

[5] Barren: *huang*, either without wood or uncultivated.

[6] Things of mine: note *wo* without *ti*, yet, by position,=the possessive.

[7] Do without: the *k'o* before *pu yao* diminishes the directness of the affirmation; *q.d.*, those, be it, I do not claim.

[8] Every, each: note *ko*[2] *jên*, not *ko*[4] *jên*.

[9] His stake: *chu*, the direction of the fancy; in gambling, the stake by which one backs what one fancies; *hsia chu*, to put down one's stake.

[10] Gave him advice: for him, or to him, put forth a *chu-i*, opinion.

[11] Attended to either: *t'ing*, had he listened to *shui ti*, that which was the opinion of whichever he would, *tou*, both ways, could he, etc.

6. He asked me whether I wanted to take the house on a long lease or a short one; I told him either would do.
7. It does not signify which of you two copies this paper; either will do.
8. They two go home three times a month, one being allowed to go on each occasion.
9. There will probably be something to do to-morrow, and so one of you two must remain here; it doesn't signify which; either will do.
10. The other day he got drunk and struck everyone[1] he met.
11. You say that these banditti all wear red turbans,[2] don't you?
12. Whether they all wear them or not I can't say, but every one[3] that I saw had a red turban on.
13. Which of these two people do you like the better?
14. I do not like either of them.
15. When you come in here, you men, you must every one of you have on a belt ticket.[4]
16. Which do you think the better of these two?
17. Either is as good as the other.
18. Which of these two jade things[5] will you have?
19. They are both good; if I am to choose one,[6] the one is as good as the other.

97.—[Indefinite Pronouns.]

1. Which of those porcelain things does he want to buy?
2. He wants to buy them all.
3. Which article is it that you want to buy?
4. I do not want to buy any.
5. Are you in the right, or is he?
6. Everybody says that I am.
7. The disorder[7] has broken out very seriously in his family; they have all died of it but himself.
8. Anyone could understand that.
9. Why doesn't he get someone to give him an opinion about that?
10. There is no one competent.[8]
11. What? in an affair of this kind anyone could; but they say that he is a self-willed[9] man, and will not take anyone's advice but his own.

---

[1] Struck everyone: *yü chien jên*, [when] he happened to meet persons, *chiu*, thereupon, he struck. Cf. the Latin *cunque*, or *cumque*, originally *quumque*, our *ever*, generalising time, and hence, events.

[2] Red turbans: note that *tou* pluralises *tsei*; did you not say that those brigands all are round the head swathing red cloth?

[3] Note *ko⁴ ko⁴*, every one, each one; those that I saw were each swathing red cloth ones.

[4] Belt ticket: *yao p'ai*, the badge hung in the girdle; *tai*, specially, to wear as a girdle, but freely used as to carry, to lead.

[5] Two jade things: jade things of two kinds, differing in form, quality, or otherwise.

[6] Choose one: *t'iao i ko*, if it be [a question of] choosing one, *na³ i ko*, any one, *shih tê*, is good, will do.

[7] The disorder: note *na⁴ ko*, that disorder spoken of before, therefore translated *the* disorder.

[8] No one competent: there is no one able *t'i*, vicariously, *ta suan*, to make calculation.

[9] Self-willed: *chih*, holding tenaciously; *niu*, twisting.

PART VIII.—THE PARTS OF SPEECH. 503

12. He is greatly to be pitied; nobody takes an interest in[1] him, and it isn't only that people in general don't take an interest in him, but there are some people who hate him very much.
13. Could you say how many?
14. How many do you suppose?
15. I make out five.
16. I believe that there are a great many more.
17. Did anyone tell you?
18. Yes; someone did tell me that in a certain family there are several people who dislike him much.

98.—1. Here, I say, how much coal have you bought here?[2]
2. Eight piculs altogether.
3. Why did you buy so much?
4. You said that I was to buy a large quantity.
5. I said a large quantity, but I did not want as much as this.
6. If you don't want so much, you can sell some of it to somebody else.
7. How many cash did you pay?[3]
8. I paid four *tiao*[4] a picul for it.
9. What a price! what shop did you buy it at?
10. At the T'ai Hsing in P'ing-an Street.
11. If it was so dear there, why didn't you go somewhere else?
12. There is no other coal-store in this neighbourhood.[5]
13. What? why, the other day, when I was in P'ing-an Street, I saw ever so many coal-stores.
14. There are some some way off, but they have all an understanding[6] with each other.
15. But even if they have, you might beat them down; they don't all mean to patronise[7] each other to such an extent as each to stand out for exactly what the other takes. And the coal doesn't look very good either; it's all nonsense asking four *tiao* a picul for such coal as this.

[1] Take an interest in: *kuan*, to look after.
[2] Bought here: *chê ko mei*; how much of this coal have you been buying?
[3] Did you pay: note the construction:—*shih*, to be, untranslatable in our idiom; *q.d.*, you are in the position of having bought it for how much?
[4] Four *tiao*: originally, a *liang*, tael, ounce of silver, = 1,000 copper cash Peking currency; 1 *tiao* = 500 such cash; now the tael is worth 13 *tiao* and upwards. The proper cash has not been coined for some years, and its place is taken by a very base 10-cash piece, really worth about two cash.
[5] In this neighbourhood: *lit.*, [if you go] from this to *tso chin*, what is on the left side and near; *tso* elliptical for *tso yu*, right and left.
[6] Understanding: *t'ung ch'i*, intercommunicating, co-operating, spirit; used also of a third party's mediating or communicating between two persons.
[7] Patronise: *ch'ên*[4], properly, that which is worn next the skin; used as, to deal with, the custom of a customer. Construe:—they cannot here-[a-man]-wanting-so-much-there-[a-man]-must-also-want-so-much [wise], all be of a mutually patronising intention. The two clauses beginning *chê-'rh* and *na-'rh* together make a long adverbial construction; *q.d.*, on the you don't sell I don't sell principle. Note *shih* where we should expect *yu*, to have; you may say *wo shih chê ko i-ssŭ*, I am of this opinion.

16. If I recollect right,[1] last year this kind of coal was something dearer.
17. Anyhow, I don't want such a quantity as this; I can't take the whole of it; you just put out[2] so much of it and sell it to someone else.
18. If you don't want the whole of it, how much do you want?
19. It will do if you keep three or four piculs.
20. And will you pay that price for it?
21. Yes, I will give you the money another day.

SECTION IX.

[THE VERB AS MODIFIED BY MOOD, TENSE, AND VOICE.]

99.—Words that predicate[3] being, doing, suffering, whether of person or thing, are in English referred to one of the nine categories before mentioned [that of the Verb, to wit]. No such line being drawn in Chinese, and the invention of an equivalent[4] [for the word verb] presenting some difficulty, we shall take on us to employ the term *huo tzŭ* (live words), which, though incomplete,[5] is unobjectionable, and we shall endeavour, with the reader's permission, to show by examples the analogies and contrasts of the *huo tzŭ* as employed under different conditions[6] in both languages.

100.—Were a Chinese to say *ma p'ao, niao fei, ch'ung p'a, yü yu*, these sentences, uttered thus consecutively, must be taken to signify that, as a species, the horse gallops, the bird flies, the reptile creeps, the fish swims.

101.—Should you happen to hear a man say *ma p'ao*, you would in that case infer that he was speaking of some particular horse as being in the act of galloping; it is much more usual, however, under these circumstances, to say *na ko ma p'ao*.

102.—The sentences *t'a nien shu, wo hsieh tzŭ* (He studies, I write) may mean either that we two are at this moment respectively engaged in studying and writing, or that these are habitually our respective tasks.

103.—To the question, Are you two men both asleep there, the answer being, I am awake, but he is asleep, it is equally correct to reply in any one of the following forms:—

t'a shui, wo hsing-cho;
t'a shui-chiao, wo hsing-cho;
t'a shih shui-chiao, wo hsing-cho, or *wo shih hsing-cho.*

---

[1] Recollect right: I seem to remember.
[2] Put out: *po*, set aside, very common of extraordinary application of Government funds; *chi ch'êng*, properly, some tenths.
[3] Predicate: *i*, to put forward as a proposition; *chi*, reaching to, touching. Construe:—In English, whether in the case of person or thing, *so yu; tzŭ yang*, whatever words there be of the kind that *i chi*, treat of, *wei*, being, *tso*, doing, *shou*, receiving, etc.
[4] Equivalent: *lit.*, it is comparatively hard *ch'uang ch'u*, to invent, a special term.
[5] Incomplete: *lit.*, though you cannot regard it as one altogether corresponding, the provisional employment of it is still in no way improper.
[6] Different conditions: *jung wo*, allow me; *mien ch'iang*, to make an effort; also used modestly of what one can do; *tso ko pang-yang*, to give an example of the *hsiang-tui*, corresponding, and *hsiang-fan*, contrasting, places in the verb as the two notions *sui yung*, according to circumstances employ it.

PART VIII.—THE PARTS OF SPEECH. 505

104.—These are mainly examples of the verb as predicating being [the **verb substantive**]. We shall postpone consideration of the verb as active and passive until we have said something about the six modes (Moods) in which the English verb may be used.

105.—[**The Indicative Mood.**]—For instance, in the sentences *wo ai t'a* (I like him), *ni k'ên pu k'ên* (will you not?) the words *ai* and *k'ên* respectively show that what is meant is a direct unconditional[1] assertion and a direct unconditional question.

106.—[**The Conditional Mood.**]—Were I to say, If he comes I shall be sure to see him, my words would imply an uncertainty whether he was really coming.

107.—[**The Potential Mood.**]—The sentence, He may (or can) act as a teacher, may mean either that he is competent to be a teacher or that he can be a teacher if he pleases.

108.—[**The Imperative Mood.**]—When you use the single word *lai* (come) to anyone, you command him to come; so, *tsou pa* (go!) *p'ao a* (be off!)

109.—[**The Infinitive Mood.**]—In the sentence *t'a ai k'an shu* (he likes to study), *ai* (like) and *k'an* (behold) are both verbs; but *ai* being governed[2] by *t'a* (he) is according to English grammar in the indicative mood, while *k'an*, which has no word in particular to govern it, is regarded as general or indefinite. There is a manifest difference,[3] for instance, between the [construction of] the *k'an* in *k'an shu hao* (it is good to study), *k'an shu shih ko hao shih* (it is a good thing to study), where it applies generally to all persons whatsoever, and that of the *k'an* in *t'a k'an shu* (he studies), where a particular person is indicated as the student.

110.—[**The Participle.**]—Besides the five modifications more or less explained[4] above, to which the English verb is liable, there remains a sixth which it is rather more troublesome to deal with. In the following:—

CHANG's best beloved child *was* sick;[5]

The minister most favoured by this Emperor[6] of the Han conspired[7] against him;

When the shell[8] exploded the soldiers standing up were wounded, those lying down escaped;

---

[1] Direct unconditional : *lit.*, the words *ai* and *k'ên* respectively *tang*, represent, the *i-ssŭ*, purpose, of plainly indicating and definitively establishing direct assertion and direct interrogation. Strictly, they do not; it is shown by the context.

[2] *Ai* being governed: *chi*, since, *shu*, is T'A *tzŭ so chu*, that which the word *t'a* governs; but *shu* very commonly means belonging to, subordinate to, in the jurisdiction of.

[3] Manifest difference : note the construction :—[in the] first and last of these two modes of expression the points of non-identity can at one sight be comprehended; *liao*, to comprehend, *jan*, the true-ness or accuracy.

[4] More or less explained : although the five *pien-huan*, transformations, have been *lio*, in outline, summarily, *shuo ming*, explained, *hai*, yet, there is one kind comparatively difficult to illustrate.

[5] *Was* sick: *tang shih*, at the time [referred to].

[6] This Emperor, *na*, that = the. Most favoured: *ch'ung*[3], to love, to favour, as Heaven the Emperor, as the Emperor a subject. The Han Ti, Emperor of the Han, referred to, is Hsien Ti, about A.D. 220.

[7] Conspired: *mou*, planned, *p'an*[4], rebellion.

[8] Shell: *cha*[4], a character unauthorised by the dictionaries, made up of *huo*, fire, and *cha*, suddenly; *cha p'ao*, a shell; *cha k'ai*, to explode.

My rheumatism¹ is so bad that I am never comfortable standing, sitting, or lying down;

A State in disorder resembles a tottering² wall;

the forms *t'êng-ai-ti* (tenderly loved), *ch'ung-ti* (favoured), *chan-cho* (standing up), *t'ang-cho* (lying down), *tso-cho* (sitting or seated), *yao t'an-t'a* (about to collapse), when translated into English, will all be ranged under the sixth mood or modification of the verb. The use of the words *ti* and *cho* appears to be this: the addition of them to the verb, whether of being or doing, helps it to bring out a secondary meaning³ in support of that primarily indicated by it; they are intended to show that the condition of whatever is, or is done, is one either of now being, of having been, or of being about to be.

111.—[The Tenses.]—Whether it regard existence or action, there are in all but three places in the order of time, viz., the past,⁴ the future,⁵ and the present;⁶ these are its three grand divisions, in which, at the same time, there are subordinate distinctions⁷ to be observed.

112.—The grand divisions are exemplified generally in the following:—I went to the yamên yesterday; I am reading to-day; to-morrow I shall rest.

113.—The following are illustrations of the subordinate distinctions:—

1. Have you written that despatch? I am writing it.
2. Have you bought that book? I have bought it.
3. When he came in the morning I was eating my breakfast; when he returned in the evening I had gone out.

---

¹ Rheumatism: *lit.*, bones sore; construe: my bones *na-mo*, being thus, as they are, are truly of a soreness; recumbent, standing, sitting, all ways am I not at ease.

² Tottering: *lit.*, a wall about to collapse. Note that in these examples wherever *ti* has been made to represent participial inflexion, it might in English, with equal if not greater propriety, be construed as the relative: the child that CHANG most loved; the minister that the Han Ti most favoured, etc.

³ Secondary meaning: *lit.*, if we carefully examine into the true use of *ti* and *cho*, it appears that the [sense] that the verb, whether it treat of action or existence, indicates when standing by itself, is the *chêng i*, proper or primary sense; add *ti* or *cho*, and they *p'ei ch'u*, by their alliance bring out, *p'ang i*, a by-standing, = secondary, sense; they are for the purpose of *pu tsu*, complementing, matter originally demonstrated by the *huo tzŭ*, whether it is in the condition of actually being, actually having been, or actually about to be. The term *chêng i* often means the plain, proper, sense of a particular word or passage; with *p'ang i* it is used with reference to Chinese composition much as we use subject and predicate. Say, A ship carries passengers, says a Chinese; ship is the *kang* (see above, 20), what is here said of her is the *mu*; that the ship is a ship is the *chêng i*; that she carries passengers is the *p'ang i*.

⁴ Past: *i*, to end, to cease; *ching*, to pass through.

⁵ Future: *lit.*, that which is not yet; *wei* is also used as a simple negative; as in *wei pi*, it does not follow, it is not certain.

⁶ Present: that which is under the eye.

⁷ Subordinate distinctions: the simple English grammar which I have more or less followed describes the tenses illustrated in paragraph 112 as the main tenses, and subdivides these in the order of the examples given in 130, viz.:—

1. "Am writing," present incomplete.
2. "Have bought," present complete.
3. "Was eating," past incomplete; "had gone," past complete.
4. "Shall be going," future incomplete; "shall have settled," future complete.
5. "Have been writing," progressive form of present complete.
6. "Shall have been studying," progressive form of future complete.
7. "Do apply," present emphatic; "did look out," past emphatic.

PART VIII.—THE PARTS OF SPEECH. 507

4. When will you come to me? Shall I come to-morrow at noon? No; at noon I shall be going to the yamên; but don't be uneasy; I shall have settled that affair for you before we meet again.
5. I am writing (or, I have written) to Peking to tell them to ship all my books for this place. I have been writing, too, all the morning.
6. The day after to-morrow I shall have been studying that book three months, and I shall have finished the eighth volume this evening.
7. You must apply, you know. But I do apply. When you were buying a horse, why didn't you look out for a good one? I did look out for a good one, but I couldn't find one.

114.—[Dialogue showing the construction of the **Active Verb** in most of its **Moods and Tenses**.]

1. What are you sitting looking at upstairs there?
2. At a man that there is over there.
3. What is he doing?
4. Beating something.
5. Do you know the man?
6. No; I never saw him before.
7. How long have you been sitting up there looking at him?
8. Not very long.
9. I think you are mistaken; nobody is beating anything.
10. No, I am not mistaken; I am still looking at him.
11. I think you are mistaken though, and that there is no one there at all.
12. What do you mean by no one at all? I was looking at him (or, I saw him) when I first said I was, and I am still looking at him (or, I see him still).[1]
13. Had you seen him before I put my first question to you?
14. Yes, long before.[2]
15. You said just now that you had not been sitting here long.
16. And what I said was the truth.
17. I shall go and see if there is any man that you are looking at.
18. Very good; when you get to the spot you will be able to tell whether there is or not.
19. Can you wait till I come back?
20. If you are back soon I shall be still sitting here.
21. Have you got nothing to do?
22. Yes, I have; but I shall be sure to have done it all by the time you return.[3]
23. If there is a man there when I get there, I'll apologise when I come back again.

[1] Construe:—At the time I first spoke, seeing was seeing; now still is it the fact that there is seeing.
[2] Long before: note *chiu* isolating and emphasising *tsao*.
[3] By the time you return: *tao pu liao*, [time] will not have reached your return; I then shall have for certain concluded my business.

24. I shall have been laughing at you for at least three days before you find out the truth.¹
25. How do you mean laughing at me three days before I find it out?
26. I say that it will be at least three days before you can satisfy yourself.²
27. How can I possibly have to wait three days if I go to look immediately?
28. If you were to go to look this instant, you would be too late all the same.
29. How is that possible if you can still see the man?
30. If I were to say³ that he was still there, I shouldn't be speaking the truth.
31. Haven't you been saying all this time that you were looking at him?⁴
32. I might have⁵ been looking at him when I said so, but it doesn't follow that you could overtake him now.
33. You mean that he is gone, don't you?
34. If I do, can you contradict me?
35. It doesn't matter whether I can or not; when you saw him moving you might have told me.
36. If you had come upstairs, you might have seen him yourself.
37. You would not let me come up then; will you let me now?
38. You can either come up or go after the man, as you please.⁶
39. What would be the good of my going after him; I might be chasing him all the morning without finding him?
40. There, there; don't be angry.
41. I am not angry, but I don't believe what you say.
42. Now, don't go on in that way; supposing that I was trying to take you in when I spoke before, I am speaking the truth now.
43. You have been taking me in all this time.
44. And supposing I have, what harm?
45. Well, in one word, do you think I could catch him up now?
46. You could easily have caught him up had you gone when I first told you to go.
47. If I had gone then, it's not so certain that I should have taken the same road as he.
48. Well, don't go at all, if you're so full of objections.⁷

¹ To prevent any confusion, the reader should understand that the person seen by the speaker sitting upstairs has moved from where he was when the conversation began, but is still in sight. Shall have been laughing: *chih pu chi*, see Part V, Lesson XXXIV, Note 4. Construe: I await your *k'an ming*, seeing clearly, completely; at the least I, before [you do], have three days laughter not ended, = shall have been laughing and shall still be laughing.

² Satisfy yourself: *wên ming*, inquire so as to ascertain; *ming*, as in *ch'a ming*, *k'an ming*, completing the act implied.

³ *Chiao*: compare Part V, Lesson II, Note 4; *q.d.*, were any cause to make me say he is still at that place, etc.

⁴ Looking at him: construe:—all this time have you not been holding *chêng-tsai-k'an-cho-ti* language, the language of one who was actually beholding.

⁵ I might have: *tang shih*, at the time, *chêng k'an cho*, [though I were] actually behold-ing, *wei pi*, it does not follow that now [you] are still able to overtake [him].

⁶ As you please: *lit.*, you follow your liking to come up, your liking to look for the man, both are admissible.

⁷ Full of objections: *chiao ch'ing*, of a self-willed nature that takes a line of its own.

PART VIII.—THE PARTS OF SPEECH.   509

49. Am I to go?
50. No; you couldn't find the man, for you don't know him; I shall go home.
51. Well, before you go, now I'm up here, show me what direction he took.
52. It doesn't signify whether I show you or not; he can't be back again for the next three days.
53. Where will he be for the next three days?
54. He is gone to superintend[1] something they are doing at the family cemetery.
55. You said you didn't know the man; how do you know that he is repairing his cemetery?
56. I did not recognise him at first, but I saw afterwards that it was WANG LI.
57. What was WANG LI doing here beating anyone?
58. I didn't say that he was beating anyone.
59. Was he beating a horse then?[2]
60. No, he was beating a mule.
61. How could I have caught him up if he was on a mule.
62. He was not riding the mule; he was leading it.
63. You do nothing but make a fool of me; I sha'n't ask you any more questions.
64. I like that; it is you who are suspicious;[3] but don't ask any more if you don't like.

115.—[Examples of the Passive Verb.]—The foregoing dialogue was intended to illustrate the use of the verb in English, but as it contains comparatively but few instances of the Passive Verb, it is proposed to make good this deficiency[4] in the following examples.

116.—The sentence, Parents bring up children, predicates of "parents" that they are the agents of an act. In Children are brought up by parents, "children" are the object of an act.

117.—The words *ni ta wo* (you beat me) distinguish you as the agent; in *wo pei ni ta* (I am beaten by you; *lit.*, suffer your beating), I am the object or recipient. And in Chinese there are various ways of producing the latter construction.[5]

---

[1] Superintend: *chien*, to inquire into, to assume direction of.
[2] Beating a horse then: *hun*, a strong disjunctive; *q.d.*, as he was not beating a man, was he then beating a horse? Note the addition of *lai-cho* and *cho* in examples 59, 61, and 62, and their omission in 57, 58, and 60, although the inflexion of our verb is nearly uniform.
[3] Suspicious: you *ko-tzŭ-ko-'rh*, your own self, raise doubts.
[4] Deficiency: *lit.*, we now *ta-suan*, contemplate, adding a few phrases, *pu tsu*, to supply a *ko chü*, form illustrative of, *shou ti*, the passive [as opposed to *hsing ti*, the active].
[5] Latter construction: *lit.*, the *li*, sense, being that of receiving something, when this is treated of in Chinese the *tzŭ-yen*, phrases, are not only one. The grammarian described such constructions as *is building*, or *is being* built, as the passive incomplete. It will be seen in the following examples that the Chinese passive, except where it is rendered by *chiao*, to cause, the precise operation of which is obscure, is produced by the employment of certain verbs signifying to receive, to perceive, or to suffer; all of them active verbs to which that which we regard as the verb changing to the passive voice, in reality, becomes the object.

118.—1. *E.g.*, That man is certainly to be pitied; he used to be WANG *ta-jên's* gate-keeper some time ago, and in that capacity he was falsely accused of taking presents and saying nothing about it; for which he was severely beaten and discharged.¹

2. As he was returning to his native place he fell in with some robbers, was carried off into the mountains, and not only stripped of everything, but so terribly injured that he must have died had he not been picked up by a cart that was passing that way.²

3. When he got to his own village he found that the whole country had been recently overrun by banditti, that his father had been burnt out, and everything belonging to him destroyed.³

4. His wife, who had come from a well-to-do family, had been deserted by her sons when the troubles broke out, and when he applied to her friends to see what they could do for him, although they had money he was told that trade had been bad and that they had lost too much to be able to assist him in any way.⁴

5. Now just imagine what a case it was; he began with being falsely accused; was abused and beaten; then, besides being robbed and wounded, he finds his house utterly cleaned out; and, to wind up, after being victimised to this extent, he is made fun of by his wife's relations: was there ever such a case of misery?⁵

---

¹ *Lit.*, That man certainly may [men] pity; formerly, at WANG *ta-jên's* acting as gate-keeper, *pei*, he was the subject of, men's wrong; [they] said [he] privily took money; because of this, he suffered beating very severely; then [his master] taking him discharged [him].

² *Lit.*, He returning to his village went; on the road, again, fell foul of robbers; [they] taking him carry [him] into the mountains; not only everything did they steal away clean; also received he wounds very serious; was it not that a cart by that place passed, that there were people who taking him lifted him up, he with complete certainty must have died.

³ *Lit.*, He returning to his own village, then knew that the locality inhabited by him recently all had been the subject of robber's disturbance; his father's house [they] had also burned; all property whatsoever [they] had also destroyed.

⁴ *Lit.*, His wife was originally a virgin in a family, the proprietors of wealth; at the time the robbers appeared, [she] *chiao*, was the subject of, her sons' abandoning [her] and running away; the man seeking found out his father-in-law's family; asked them on his behalf to calculate a little; they, although they had money, answering said, our trade has of late been very bad; in everything have we suffered (*lit.*, eaten) loss; it is ten thousand times (=infinitely) difficult to help you.

⁵ *Lit.*, Bethink you; in the first instance, *chiao*, he suffered, men's false accusation; endured beating, endured reviling; afterwards he suffered robbery, robbed and received wounds; in addition, utterly was there not one *so yu*, that which is (=anything) in his house; he in his single person having received all this hardship, still *chien hsiao*, feels the laughter, is ridiculed, *chiao*, by his wife's family: resembling this kind of misery, heretofore has there been a man's receiving?

Note *chiao*⁴, which is not to be explained except in one of two ways: either it is corruptly used for *chiao*, otherwise *chio*, to perceive, which, however, is only read *chiao*⁴ in *shui-chiao*, to sleep; or it is *to cause*, and must be governed by an impersonal agent understood. This last construction might stand in *chiao êrh-tzŭ jêng hsia*, was abandoned by her sons (*q.d.*, something made her sons abandon her), but will not explain the *chiao* in *chiao t'a nü-jên chia li chien hsiao*; for the subject of *chien*, to see, to perceive, to be sensible of, is at once pronounced by Chinese to be *t'a* understood. Practically, it is in general simplest to ignore the etymological claims of *chiao*, and to translate it as *by*. It is noteworthy that *shou*, to receive, originally meant to give; *ai*, to endure, originally, to strike; *pei*, to suffer, to be the subject of, originally, a coverlid, thence, to cover, to affect.

PART VIII.—THE PARTS OF SPEECH. 511

SECTION X.

[THE ADVERB, OF TIME, PLACE, NUMBER, DEGREE, ETC.]

119.—[Adverbs of Time.]

1. Will that man be here to-day, do you think? I don't think he will; he may come to-morrow.
2. Why didn't he come yesterday? He did come yesterday, but he was late.
3. Why should he have been later than you? My business at the yamên is over [1] sooner than his.
4. Did he come before I went out? No, sir; after you had gone out.
5. You tell him to come to-morrow the moment his business at the office is over. I don't think [2] I can; I sha'n't see him before he is here to-morrow.
6. How do you mean? wouldn't you see him if you were to go to the yamên directly? No, I should be sure to miss him; he would certainly have left the yamên before I arrived.
7. Where does he live now? In the lane that I used to live in.
8. When do you mean you used to live there? At the time of your first visit to Peking, sir.
9. That is a long time back. Yes, it's ten years ago, isn't it? Indeed,[3] it soon will be ten years.
10. Didn't you come to Peking the first time in the suite of WANG ta-jên? No; that was the third time I came.
11. How many [4] times have you been to Peking altogether? Five times in all; the first time I came with my father, who was then alive.[5]
12. When was it that your father [6] came to Peking? In the 23rd year of Tao Kuang.
13. And when did he go home again? After three or four months' stay.
14. And your second visit? That was two years later; I was sent up here by [7] my father on business.

---

[1] Business over: note *san*, properly, the dispersion of a number, thence, as below in example 5, applied to the individual in a number, of employés. Is over: that is, habitually; *ch'ang shih chê-mo-cho*, always it is thus.

[2] Don't think: I fear it is not to be done.

[3] Indeed: *yüan shih*, it is certainly the fact that indeed quickly [will be] 10 years ended.

[4] How many: note the *chi tz'ŭ*, how many times, between the verb *chin-kuo*, have entered, and *ching*, the capital, its object.

[5] Then alive: *hsien fu*, my late father, a phrase we seldom use; note that the speaker so designates his father throughout.

[6] *Ling hsien chün*, your late father: had his father been alive he would have been spoken of as *ling tsun*.

[7] Sent up by: note the construction:—*shih*, [it, the occasion you ask about] was—all that follows. Notice the position of *yu shih* after *wo*, me, and the *lai* at the close, which shows that the speaker is speaking in the place to which he had been sent.

15. I remember the occasion very well; you didn't stay very long that time. No; I had been in Peking but a few days when I was recalled by a pressing letter from home.
16. Yes? it was to tell you that your father was very ill, I think? No; my younger brother had been so badly hurt that he was not expected to live.
17. Your brother is still alive? Oh yes; he recovered after a while.
18. If my memory serves me, your father was ill at the time?[1] Yes, he was; I heard of his illness on my way down, and he died a few days after I got home.
19. And that was the reason why you were so long[2] without coming to Peking again? Of course; I couldn't leave home while I was in mourning[3] for him; I came up after my mourning was over,[4] and it was then that I accompanied WANG ta-jên.
20. Is WANG ta-jên still in Peking? He is away on duty at present, but he will be back in a few days.
21. I hear that you purpose leaving Peking yourself, sir, shortly?[5] Yes, I shall be off presently; I expect to go home as soon as my term of service here is over.

120.—[Adverbs of Place.]

1. Where is that man from? From T'ung Chou.
2. Which is farthest from Peking, T'ung Chou or Chang-chia Wan? Reckoning from the Ch'i-hua Mên,[6] T'ung Chou is somewhat the nearer.
3. Have you been there? Where do you mean?
4. I meant to T'ung Chou. I have never been to T'ung Chou; I have been once at Chang-chia Wan.
5. How come you to have been at Chang-chia Wan and not at T'ung Chou? I was coming from T'ien-ching (Tientsin) by cart, and that was what brought me to Chang-chia Wan.
6. Oh, then you are not a Peking man? No, I am not.
7. And what is your country, sir? I am a Chiangsu (Kiangsu) man.
8. And from which prefecture? My native place[7] is Su-chou (Soochow).
9. Do you know the SUNGS who live inside the east gate of Su-chou? I suspect you mean outside the east gate.

---

[1] Ill at the time: note *lai-cho* showing continuance in the state specified, not its commencement.

[2] So long: [this] *shih*, was, *so i*, the reason why, *hsü chiu*, very long, etc.

[3] In mourning: *ting yu*, specially, the mourning of an official for his parents; *ting*, solitary, q.d., orphan; *yu*, sorrow.

[4] Mourning over: *man fu*, having completed my *fu*; the *fu* in *i-fu*, clothes, here mourning apparel.

[5] *Pu jih*, shortly: short for *pu to ti jih-tzŭ*.

[6] The *Ch'i-hua Mên*: popular name for the *Ch'ao-yang Mên*, the great east gate of Peking.

[7] Native place: *chi*², originally, a tablet; hence, a record, specially of registration; *pên chi*, the place to which I am registered as belonging.

PART VIII.—THE PARTS OF SPEECH.

10. I am not quite sure whether they live inside or outside; the SUNG I mean used to be in the Censorate.¹ To be sure; I have been at his house often enough.²
11. Wasn't it the year before last that he returned home? I don't remember exactly; he has been back and forward³ so often.
12. What time was it that he came to such grief on the road? Oh, that time! that was the year before last; a relative of mine was with him.
13. He fell in with some robbers in Ta-ming Fu, didn't he? Not robbers; they were braves⁴ that had mutinied.⁵
14. Did he meet them, or was he pursued by them?⁶ Neither; he heard that there was trouble on the high road, so he turned off by a branch road⁷ in a southerly direction.
15. Well, then, how was it that he didn't contrive to keep out of their way? So far from⁸ keeping out of their way, he went right in amongst them.
16. Was he in a cart or riding? In a cart; and when he got to a certain spot he found the mutineers in his front and in his rear, so that he could neither advance nor retreat.
17. I was told that they fired upon him too? No, they didn't fire.
18. How came he to be hurt then? Well, in this way: he and my relative were both in the same cart, my relative sitting on the left side, and the Censor⁹ SUNG on the right; the braves came to rifle the cart, and, crowding in¹⁰ upon it from the left, threw it over¹¹ on its side; the two passengers went with it, and my relative being above and the Censor below, the Censor got badly bruised.¹²
19. Dear me! how was it that after going so far the braves didn't take their lives?¹³ It was all luck¹⁴ that they escaped.

¹ Censorate: *yü shih*; *lit.*, imperial historiographer; an ancient title now given to the members of the *Tu-ch'a Yüan*, all-examining court, which we style the Censorate.
² Often enough: *hao hsieh t'ang*; the word *t'ang*⁴, otherwise *tang*⁴, here = times.
³ Back and forward: treat *shih-ch'ang-ti* as the adverb continually, constantly, etc.
⁴ Braves: *hsiang yung*, village or country braves.
⁵ Mutinied: *pien*, to turn, to change.
⁶ Pursued by them: note *chiao*; did [something] cause them to overtake him.
⁷ Branch road: *lit.*, he going by a *ch'a tao*, forked road, slanting south went.
⁸ So far from: *fan tao*, on the reverse, he went into their midst.
⁹ The Censor: SUNG *tu lao-yeh*, the *tu* representing *Tu-ch'a Yüan*.
¹⁰ Crowding in: *yung*³, originally, to carry in the bosom; to surround, to follow as a crowd, to hustle; from the left side crowding came.
¹¹ Threw it over: *ch'i*³, to press on, to push; *chi tê* pushed it so that the result effected was that it *hêng t'ang hsia*, crosswise lay down.
¹² Badly bruised: *shuai*¹, to give a shock to, as a blow or a fall; the hurts of the Censor, by reason of the *shuai*, shock, were *hên chung*, very heavy.
¹³ The braves *pu yao*, did not insist, on their lives.
¹⁴ All luck: *chiao hsing*; see Part IV, Dialogue IX, 41.

20. What kind providence[1] came to their rescue? Well, as the braves were dragging their baggage out of the cart, their servants, who were all mounted, came up from behind,[2] and the braves, not knowing what to make of the sound of the horses' feet, were panic-struck, and fled in all directions.[3]

121.—[Adverbs of Number.]

1. How many times have you been to the temple of Kuan Ti?[4] I have been thrice to the door, but I have only gone in once.
2. Why didn't you go in the second time after having been in the first? Before I got in the first time I paid the priests' fee.[5]
3. And wouldn't they take their fee the second time? They wanted it, but I said that I had paid the time before because it was my first time of coming, and that this time I should not pay.
4. But when they wouldn't let[6] you in the second time, why should you have gone a third?[7] Someone said that the priests and I had misunderstood each other the second time, and recommended me to try again.
5. And what said the priests on this third occasion? Why, they were even more impracticable[8] than the time before; they said in so many words that it was quite impossible I should come in.
6. On what grounds? In the first place, because it was a Government temple; in the second, because the superior[9] was not at home; and thirdly, because, said they, you didn't give anything the last time you came, sir.
7. But when they took this line didn't you say anything about feeing them? I did, but they said that even if I were to give three times as much as I did on the first occasion, they could not undertake to let me in.

122.—[Adverbs of Degree.]

1. This is very good; that is very much the reverse.
2. He does not write well; his brother writes very well.
3. He praises[10] you very highly.

---

[1] Kind providence: what *chiu hsing*, star of rescue, divine intervention.

[2] Came up from behind: *lit.*, those followers of theirs, riding beasts overtaking came.

[3] *Lit.*, the braves heard the sound of horses galloping; knew not what it was; all in the four directions in dismay dispersed.

[4] Kuan Ti, a hero of the Han dynasty, since deified and worshipped as the God of War.

[5] Priests' fee: *hsiang ch'ien*, money to buy incense.

[6] Wouldn't let: *pu chiao*, not to cause; often, as here, to refuse permission; also, to prohibit.

[7] Gone a third: note the *yu* before *ch'ü*; why must you a third time again go?

[8] More impracticable: they still more liked not to consider the question; they plainly said [that I] *tuan*, positively, could not go in.

[9] Superior: *tang-chia-ti*, the manager; in a family or a religious house, what the *chang-kuei-ti* is in a shop; *tang*[1] in the sense of filling a post.

[10] Praises: *tsan*[4], to speak of, to speak well of, to note; *tsan mei*, to note the goodness of.

PART VIII.—THE PARTS OF SPEECH.

4. He was highly flattered[1] by your invitation to dinner the other day.
5. That affair to the north of Peking incensed the Emperor extremely.[2]
6. You were excessively angry about a thing of no importance, and then you said what was very discourteous.[3]
7. That man's stupidity is beyond everything; he understands nothing that's said to him.
8. When will [the tailor] bring me that thing? It was nearly finished[4] last night, and I think they will be sure[5] to have quite done it by this time.
9. That house was nearly finished last month, and now it is quite ready.
10. I have been such a time without studying that I have almost forgotten the "T'ung Chien;" the "Han Shu" I have quite forgotten.[6]
11. As for those two men, CHANG and LI, that I met to-day, I hardly know CHANG, and I don't know LI at all.
12. Those hills used to be covered thick with wood, but the people have taken so little care[7] of it that there is now hardly any.
13. Those are all good men, and LI is the best of them.
14. He doesn't want to have to do with[8] any of those people, and least of all with LIU.
15. He punished them all severely, but WANG more severely[9] than any of them.
16. He called on me to-day, principally[10] for the purpose of presenting his son to me.
17. Did not you say so yesterday? I did.
18. Wasn't this what you said yesterday? Yes, to be sure;[11] that was what I said.
19. Isn't this a good plan? No. Isn't it your plan? Not at all. Well, which of these two is the better? We can have a talk about this one; the other is utterly impracticable.
20. Have you found those two men? I found out LI's house, but he was not at home; as for CHANG, there is no such person.
21. It is blowing terribly.

[1] Highly flattered: *lit.*, he much *chio*, felt, *t'i mien*, the respectability, the honour, *sc.*, that your invitation conferred on him.

[2] Incensed extremely: *lit.*, the Emperor's wrath *chi-liao*, culminated.

[3] Very discourteous: *t'ai pu ya liao*, extremely, or too greatly, not *ya*, good breeding.

[4] Nearly finished: *tê liao*, so used of anything that is in hand.

[5] Think they will be sure: *liao*, in the sense of *to calculate*; *liao ku*, to conjecture. Except it be used in what we call the imperative mood, *liao ku* seems always to have *cho* affixed to it. Treat it here adverbially: probably [by] this time *chun*, for certain, it is finished.

[6] Quite forgotten: *so* must here be taken as an intensive of *ch'üan*, all, altogether all; the expression is peculiar to Peking, and would probably not be understood elsewhere.

[7] So little care: *t'ai*, too much, *pu chao ying*, not attend to.

[8] Have to do with: *sc.*, as employés; *yao*, in the sense of to require the services of; hence, *pu yao*, to discharge, a servant or subordinate.

[9] More severely: *p'ien*¹, leaning to a side; hence, partial, special; *p'ien chung*, special gravity or severity.

[10] Principally: *chung ti*, the weighty matter; by position=weightiest.

[11] To be sure: *yüan shih*, in very truth it was.

22. The stars are beautifully bright[1] this evening.
23. The snow is excessively deep.
24. That tea *is* spoiled, but not all spoiled; there is some of it that it will do to use.
25. That teacher does not teach well.
26. He sings very well.
27. I am a little tired.

123.—[Miscellaneous Adverbial Constructions.]

1. Where is the child? He's nowhere but[2] in the house; he can't be anywhere else.
2. I know all about the thing; when he did it, where he did it, why he did it, and how he did it.
3. The moment he heard about the thing he went off.
4. He has been a long time ailing, and he is not well yet.
5. He is quite cured of his old complaint (or, of the complaint he used to suffer from).
6. He has only been here a few days this time.
7. He has been over here once in the last few days.
8. The tiles were blown clean off the roof just as he left the house.
9. The morning was clear, but all of a sudden the sky clouded over.
10. I get up most mornings[3] at daybreak.
11. I couldn't bring the boxes, because it was impossible to get them packed in time.[4]
12. Those gentlemen started too late[5] to get out of the city.
13. His wages are five taels a month.
14. He had a narrow escape of being cashiered.[6]
15. That servant was pretty near being discharged.
16. I go out for a walk every day.
17. He is always very glad to see us when we go to call on him.
18. In his action with the outlaws he got the worst of it.
19. He took a good deal of pains in the matter, but without any result.
20. That place was once very thickly peopled; it is sadly bare[7] now.
21. It's a long way, but at the pace I go I shall soon be there.

---

[1] Beautifully bright: are bright [so that man] *k‘o*, may properly, *hsi*, rejoice.

[2] Nowhere but: note *tso yu*; q.d., [seek him] to the right, [seek him] to the left; *tsung*, in sum, *pu kuo*, he is not beyond, *shih tsai chia*, being in the house.

[3] Most mornings: *huang*³, properly, a hanging curtain; here used as implying uncertainty (swinging to and fro?); q.d., as a rule I get up, but sometimes I do not, etc.

[4] Packed in time: note *pu liao*, could not, inserted between *tai* and *lai*, the whole clause being the subject of the verb *shih*; [the cause of] my inability to bring the boxes was [that the person or persons packing them] *i shih*, in the one moment, *shou-shih*, packed, *pu chi*, not arriving, did not complete; sc., at the *same* moment that I departed.

[5] Too late: *kan*, [though] hastening, could not get out of the city.

[6] Cashiered: *huai kuan*; q.d., to ruin one's official position; he *ch‘a i tien*, wanted but little, = a little more and he would.

[7] Sadly bare: *hsiao*¹, properly, a plant (according to Dr. WILLIAMS, rue); applied descriptively to mournful sights or sounds; *hsiao-t‘iao*, forlorn, desolate.

SECTION XI.

[THE PREPOSITION.]

124.—1. A man appeared above (or over) the wall.
2. He is leaning against the wall.
3. I saw that knot of men at the time, and CHANG was not among them.
4. The intimacy[1] between them is of very long standing.
5. I went to see him but he was not at home, so I left word that I would come again before sunset.
6. They put a log across the path and I caught my foot[2] in it and came down.
7. He met with a very serious risk[3] on his journey.
8. Is there a garden behind the house?
9. There is a temple on the hill, and some houses in a hollow[4] at the back of the hill.
10. We went past the Tung-hua Mên.
11. Did you go into the garden?
12. We went right through[5] it.
13. Yesterday it was very hot throughout the whole day.
14. I have heard nothing about the matter we discussed that day, since we parted.
15. The boats going up stream are tracked against the current.
16. He brought his horse out of the stable, jumped upon him,[6] and rode off.
17. I walked round the Huang Ch'êng[7] yesterday.
18. He was going away from me when first I saw him, and then he faced about[8] and came towards where I was.
19. The man ran across the field and by the footpath towards the road.[9]
20. CHANG *lao-yeh* is off to Hankow.
21. Is he going by land or by water?

[1] Intimacy: *chiao ch'ing*, reciprocation of [friendly] sentiments; the days of this state of things are *shên*, deep, many. The passage is translated in this way merely to bring in the position *between*; various other English idioms would of course be equally correct.

[2] Caught my foot: *pan*, properly, to wrap round and so to embarrass; *lit.*, they taking a log of wood, *hêng*, put it crosswise, on the road; [it] caught me, [and by catching caused me] a fall.

[3] Serious risk: *hsien*, dangerous. Note the curious idiom: he encountered *hên li hai ti*, or *tê*, that which was so *li hai* that it became, *i ko hsien*, a danger. See *li hai* above in many places.

[4] A hollow: *tung*[4].

[5] Right through: *ta* giving activity to *ch'uan*, to pierce through, as to many other verbs; *q.d.*, by way of the interior we penetrated through.

[6] Jumped upon him: *p'ien*, to get on a horse; also written with the radical on the other side; in the form here used, often meaning to cheat.

[7] The Huang Ch'êng: the Imperial Enclosure, a wall some six miles long surrounding the Emperor's palace at Peking.

[8] Faced about: then he turned his face and I saw him = he seemed to, come towards my part.

[9] Towards the road: *pên*[1], to run; here read *pên*[4], towards. The latter is a use of the word not authorised by the dictionaries.

22. He goes up the river in a steamer.
23. How long will he take?
24. Seven days.
25. I thought a steamer could run from Shanghai to Hankow in four days?
26. So she can; but this one has cargo to deliver and take in at all the ports along the line.[1]

SECTION XII.
[THE CONJUNCTION.]

125.—1. He came to the yamên although it was raining so hard.
2. The winter this year is not very cold nor yet very damp.
3. Not only the boys went to see what was going on that day, but the girls too.
4. His idea is that people can make out what he writes whether he has written it carefully or otherwise.
5. I shall go at any rate, whether you go[2] or not.
6. Both he and I were wounded.
7. I feel pretty sure that you'll like it when you have tried it.
8. Do it[3] either way; either will answer.
9. Say quick, east or west; which is it to be?
10. This is not merely pleasant[4] but useful as well.

SECTION XIII.
[THE INTERJECTION.]

126.—Sudden sensations[5] may find utterance in expressions which differ according as the feeling expressed is one of admiration, delight, pity, dislike, astonishment, or desire.

1. [For instance,] Indeed! before you have been learning three months, to speak so correctly.
2. Ah! is it possible that after so many years of suffering you should have no feeling for the suffering of others?
3. Odious man! he has not only wasted time[6] doing nothing, but what he has done is done so badly.

---

[1] Along the line: *yen*, properly, down the tide; used as along, a road, an edge, etc.
[2] Whether you go: *pu kuan*, I regard not, it matters not to me.
[3] Do it: the *ch'u* is not to be taken as *go*, but simply as auxiliary of *pan*.
[4] Merely pleasant: *ching*, only, *k'ung*, emptily, *hsi-huan*, [that which people] delight in.
[5] Sudden sensations: the subject of the whole sentence is *shên ch'i*; the two first clauses are made pendent by *chiu*. Construe thus:—language proceeding from the lips, when in the heart suddenly there is that which is encountered, *chiu*, in such case, [the *shên ch'i*, spirit of the expression] *shih*, will be, *ko têng shên ch'i pu t'ung*, different kinds of spirit. Observe that *ko têng* pluralises *shên ch'i* at the same time that *ko*, each, is preferentially used as it were to disjoin the several feelings specified, q.d., whether of admiration or delight, etc. Note admiration, *t'an*[4], properly, to sigh; dislike, *tsêng*[1] *wu*[4], to hate; astonishment, *hsiang pu tao*, unexpected, *ching*, to be startled.
[6] Wasted time: *pai*, vainly, *tan wu*, to delay and mismanage; not only this, but there have *nao*, presented themselves, several faults.

4. Poor fellow! to be so near¹ his promotion, and to be cashiered for a thing of so little importance.
5. Ah! your foreign contrivances² are really most ingenious.³
6. WANG *lao-yeh* greatly admired⁴ those verses you wrote the other day; he kept on exclaiming,⁵ Beautiful!
7. Astonishing! that a man should prefer⁶ a bad thing when he might have a good thing; it's utterly unreasonable.
8. May CHANG *lao-yeh* soon be well of his wound, and he will come to our rescue.
9. I hear that he is well again. Indeed? that's good.⁷ And what is more, they say that he may be here the day after to-morrow. The day after to-morrow? May it be so!⁸

¹ So near: note the force of *tou;* also that *t'a* is the subject of *shêng;* that of *ko*, to cashier (*lit.,* to strip), is Emperor, or Government, understood.
² Contrivances: *chi*, a spring, *chi ch'i*, things moving by springs.
³ Ingenious: *ch'iao*, cunning; *miao*, abstruse, minute, fine.
⁴ Greatly admired: *tsan miao* praised as fine.
⁵ Kept on exclaiming: *lien hu¹*, repeatedly cried out.
⁶ Prefer: *lit.,* he *fang-cho*, putting down, *q.d.,* not touching, the good thing, *pu yao*, rejects or declines it, *p'ien yao*, preferentially demands, the bad thing; is there such a principle, such reasoning, as this?
⁷ That's good: *hao chi*, the height of good.
⁸ May it be so: *pa pu tê*, one can't lay hold of it, it is too good to be true.

ERRATA AND ADDENDA.

ERRATA AND ADDENDA.

PART III.	Page	15.	11. For "insect (or reptile)" read "snake"
"	"	18.	1. Col. 1. For 拿東西 read 拿了東西
"	"	21.	55. For "[I] do not." read "I do not."
"	"	23.	Line 4. After "ground." repeat "A person (or persons) stretched on the ground."
"	"	23.	72. For $ting^2$ read $ting^3$
"	"	23.	76. " $p'i^{1\ 2\ 3}$ read $p'i^{1\ 3}$
"	"	23.	76. " $p'i^2$ read $p'i^1$
"	"	23.	78. " $p'i^2$ (76) read $t'ou^2$ (48)
"	"	23.	78. " $liang^3\ p'i^2\ l\ddot{u}^2$ read $liang^3\ t'ou^2\ l\ddot{u}^2$
"	"	27.	93. " $p'i^3$ read $p'i^1$
"	"	28.	98. Col. 3. For pu^4 read pu^2
"	"	29.	113. Obs. For $ta^3\ h\hat{e}n^3$ read $ta^4\ h\hat{e}n^3$
"	"	34.	140. Last line but one. After "other words" insert "in the 4th tone"
"	"	38.	153. Col. 2. For yi^1 read yi^4
"	"	41.	8 (two places). For $yi^2\ pa^3$ read $yi^4\ pa^3$
"	"	50.	3. For $yi^1\ hsia^4\ chung^1$ read $yi^2\ hsia^4\ chung^1$
"	"	50.	3. " $yi^1\ tien^3\ chung^1$ read $yi^4\ tien^3\ chung^1$
"	"	51.	6 and Obs. 1. For "regular" read "equable"
"	"	59.	289. Note that $ch\hat{e}n^1\ yen^3\text{-}'rh$ is not used in Peking, but $ch\hat{e}n^1\ pi^2\text{-}'rh$.
"	"	63.	311. For hua^4 read hua^1
"	"	66.	324. Col. 3. For i^1 read i^4
"	"	67.	328. Obs. For $yao^4\ i\ yao^4$ (32) read $yao^4\ i\ yao^1$ (566)
"	"	72.	360. Col. 2 and 4. For $m\hat{e}n^2$ read $m\hat{e}n^1$
"	"	72.	360. $Ma^2\ hsien^4$ is cobbler's thread; $ma^2\ sh\hat{e}ng^2\text{-}'rh$ is twine.
"	"	73.	365. For $mien^4\text{-}pao^4$ read $mien^4\text{-}pao^1$
"	"	73.	369. Last line. For $shui\ kuo\text{-}tz\check{u}$ read $shui\ kuo$
"	"	80.	7. Obs. 4. For $p'an^4\ fei^1$ read $p'an\ fei^4$
"	"	87.	5. For "they" read "these loads"
"	"	90.	3. Obs. 3 (two places). For huo^4 read huo
"	"	93.	Line 2. Note that $sai^1\ chieh^4$ is the inside of the cheeks, the outside of which is called $lien^3\ tan^4\text{-}tz\check{u}$; the gills of a fish are $sai\ chieh$.
"	"	95.	4. For $t'i^4\text{-}t'ou^2\text{-}tao^4$ read $t'i^4\text{-}t'ou^2\text{-}tao^1$
"	"	102.	8. Obs. For han^2 read han^4
"	"	108.	555. Col. 5. For pu^2 read pu^4
"	"	115.	10. Obs. 2. " $tz\check{u}$ read $tz'\check{u}$
"	"	116.	5. " 2. " "converse" read "reverse"
"	"	116.	595. Col. 3. " pu^4 read pu^2
"	"	117.	599. " 4. " han^2 read han^4
"	"	117.	599. " 5. " kai^4 read kai^1
"	"	118.	617. " 7. " $chien^1$ read $chien^4$
"	"	123.	646. For "characters" read "words"
"	"	131.	681. Col. 2. For $ch'ang^2\ ch'ang^2$ read $ch'ang^2\ ch'ang^1$

ERRATA AND ADDENDA.

PART III. Page 133. 702. Col. 7. For i^4 read i
" " 136. 708. " 5. " $fên^4$ read $fên^1$
" " 143. 755. " 1. " i^1 read i^4
" " 147. 765. $Mei^2\ lao^4$-'rh would be better rendered by "penniless," or "on his beam ends."
" " 150. 3. Note that 落 is read la^4.
" " 154. 792. After last sentence, insert "Against the current."
" " 174. 4. For Lao^3-yeh^1 read Lao^3-yeh
" " 175. 8 (four places). For $chiao^1$ read $chiao^4$
" " 177. 900. Col. 6. For 五 read 三
" " 183. 939. For "started in practice" the more common expression is $kua\ liao\ p'ai^2\ liao$.
" " 188. 965. Col. 7. For $jung^2\ jung^2$ read $jung^1\ jung^1$
" " 204. 1058. For "can pick up" read "is good at"

PART IV. Page 241. 73. Obs. For $chiao\ ch'ê$ read $chiao\ ch'ê$-'rh or $chiao\ ch'ê$-$tzŭ$

PART V. Page 284. Note 9. Omit " or $ch'iao^3$ "
" " 289. " 2. For " 捻 $nieh^1$, also read $nien^4$, to nip in the fingers" read " 蹑 $nieh^4$, to tread"
" " 291. " 6. " 陶 read 淘
" " 306. " 1. " "the same as $ts'ao$" read "should be $ts'ao$"
" " 341. " 8. " "not i^3" read "but i^3 is permissible"

PART VI. Page 362. Note 6. For 骨 read 咕
" " 391. Chapter XXVI, 3. For "Where may have you been" read "Where may you have been"
" " 395. Note 8. For 权 some read 橽
" " 398. 9. For "fever" read "influenza"
" " 412. Chapter XXXVII, 3. For "And so no more" read "But no more"

PART VII. Page 437. 88. For yu^3 read $yü^3$
" " 447. 165. " $ch'iang^1$ read $chiang^1$
" " 457. 257. " 撇 read 掰
" " 463. 301. After "before sui^3" insert "Colloquially, $ku^2\ sui^4$."

PART VIII. Page 489. Note 3. Cancel the last sentence.
" " 491. Last line but two of text. For $tiao$ read $t'iao$
" " 492. Cancel Note 3.
" " 493. 32. For $to^1\ shao^4$ read $to^1\ shao$
" " 494. 38. " "read with the 4th tone" read "not intonated"
" " 495. Note 4. For " $ch'üan$-$chieh$, provisionally" read " $tui\ fu\ cho$, as a makeshift."
" " 504. " 6. " "notions" read "nations"

北京大学中国语言学研究中心

早期北京话珍稀文献集成

主编 刘云

——西人北京话教科书汇编

分卷主编　翟赟　郭利霞　陈颖

国家出版基金项目
NATIONAL PUBLICATION FOUNDATION

语言自迩集

（第二版）

［英］威妥玛　编著

卷一

北京大学出版社
PEKING UNIVERSITY PRESS

图书在版编目(CIP)数据

语言自迩集：第二版：全三册 /（英）威妥玛编著. — 影印本. —北京：北京大学出版社，2017.9
（早期北京话珍本典籍校释与研究）
ISBN 978-7-301-28675-3

Ⅰ.①语… Ⅱ.①威… Ⅲ.①北京话—汉语史—史料 ②北京话—对外汉语教学—研究资料 Ⅳ.①H172.1

中国版本图书馆CIP数据核字（2017）第214842号

书　　名	语言自迩集（第二版）（卷一至卷三）（影印本）
	YUYAN ZI ER JI (DI-ER BAN)
著作责任者	[英]威妥玛　编著
责任编辑	王铁军　孙娴
标准书号	ISBN 978-7-301-28675-3
出版发行	北京大学出版社
地　　址	北京市海淀区成府路205号　100871
网　　址	http://www.pup.cn　新浪微博：@北京大学出版社
电子信箱	zpup@pup.cn
电　　话	邮购部 62752015　发行部 62750672　编辑部 62753334
印刷者	北京京华虎彩印刷有限公司
经销者	新华书店
	720毫米×1020毫米　16开本　74.75印张　505千字
	2017年9月第1版　2017年9月第1次印刷
定　　价	298.00元（全三册）

未经许可，不得以任何方式复制或抄袭本书之部分或全部内容。
版权所有，侵权必究
举报电话：010-62752024　电子信箱：fd@pup.pku.edu.cn
图书如有印装质量问题，请与出版部联系，电话：010-62756370

总　序

语言是文化的重要组成部分，也是文化的载体。语言中有历史。

多元一体的中华文化，体现在我国丰富的民族文化和地域文化及其语言和方言之中。

北京是辽金元明清五代国都（辽时为陪都），千余年来，逐渐成为中华民族所公认的政治中心。北方多个少数民族文化与汉文化在这里碰撞、融合，产生出以汉文化为主体的、带有民族文化风味的特色文化。

现今的北京话是我国汉语方言和地域文化中极具特色的一支，它与辽金元明四代的北京话是否有直接继承关系还不是十分清楚。但可以肯定的是，它与清代以来旗人语言文化与汉人语言文化的彼此交融有直接关系。再往前追溯，旗人与汉人语言文化的接触与交融在入关前已经十分深刻。本丛书收集整理的这些语料直接反映了清代以来北京话、京味文化的发展变化。

早期北京话有独特的历史传承和文化底蕴，于中华文化、历史有特别的意义。

一者，这一时期的北京历经满汉双语共存、双语互协而新生出的汉语方言——北京话，她最终成为我国民族共同语（普通话）的基础方言。这一过程是中华多元一体文化自然形成的诸过程之一，对于了解形成中华文化多元一体关系的具体进程有重要的价值。

二者，清代以来，北京曾历经数次重要的社会变动：清王朝的逐渐孱弱、八国联军的入侵、帝制覆灭和民国建立及其伴随的满汉关系变化、各路军阀的来来往往、日本侵略者的占领，等等。在这些不同的社会环境下，北京人的构成有无重要变化？北京话和京味文化是否有变化？进一步地，地域方言和文化与自身的传承性或发展性有着什么样的关系？与社会变迁有着什么样的关系？清代以至民国时期早期北京话的语料为研究语言文化自身传承性与社会的关系提供了很好的素材。

　　了解历史才能更好地把握未来。新中国成立后，北京不仅是全国的政治中心，而且是全国的文化和科研中心，新的北京话和京味文化或正在形成。什么是老北京京味文化的精华？如何传承这些精华？为把握新的地域文化形成的规律，为传承地域文化的精华，必须对过去的地域文化的特色及其形成过程进行细致的研究和理性的分析。而近几十年来，各种新的传媒形式不断涌现，外来西方文化和国内其他地域文化的冲击越来越强烈，北京地区人口流动日趋频繁，老北京人逐渐分散，老北京话已几近消失。清代以来各个重要历史时期早期北京话语料的保护整理和研究迫在眉睫。

　　"早期北京话珍本典籍校释与研究（暨早期北京话文献数字化工程）"是北京大学中国语言学研究中心研究成果，由"早期北京话珍稀文献集成""早期北京话数据库"和"早期北京话研究书系"三部分组成。"集成"收录从清中叶到民国末年反映早期北京话面貌的珍稀文献并对内容加以整理，"数据库"为研究者分析语料提供便利，"研究书系"是在上述文献和数据库基础上对早期北京话的集中研究，反映了当前相关研究的最新进展。

　　本丛书可以为语言学、历史学、社会学、民俗学、文化学等多方面的研究提供素材。

　　愿本丛书的出版为中华优秀文化的传承做出贡献！

王洪君、郭锐、刘云
2016年10月

"早期北京话珍稀文献集成"序

清民两代是北京话走向成熟的关键阶段。从汉语史的角度看,这是一个承前启后的重要时期,而成熟后的北京话又开始为当代汉民族共同语——普通话源源不断地提供着养分。蒋绍愚先生对此有着深刻的认识:"特别是清初到19世纪末这一段的汉语,虽然按分期来说是属于现代汉语而不属于近代汉语,但这一段的语言(语法,尤其是词汇)和'五四'以后的语言(通常所说的'现代汉语'就是指'五四'以后的语言)还有若干不同,研究这一段语言对于研究近代汉语是如何发展到'五四'以后的语言是很有价值的。"(《近代汉语研究概要》,北京大学出版社,2005年)然而国内的早期北京话研究并不尽如人意,在重视程度和材料发掘力度上都要落后于日本同行。自1876年至1945年间,日本汉语教学的目的语转向当时的北京话,因此留下了大批的北京话教材,这为其早期北京话研究提供了材料支撑。作为日本北京话研究的奠基者,太田辰夫先生非常重视新语料的发掘,很早就利用了《小额》《北京》等京味儿小说材料。这种治学理念得到了很好的传承,之后,日本陆续影印出版了《中国语学资料丛刊》《中国语教本类集成》《清民语料》等资料汇编,给研究带来了便利。

新材料的发掘是学术研究的源头活水。陈寅恪《〈敦煌劫余录〉序》有云:"一时代之学术,必有其新材料与新问题。取用此材料,以研求问题,则为此时代学术之新潮流。"我们的研究要想取得突破,必须打破材料桎梏。在具体思路上,一方面要拓展视野,关注"异族之故书",深度利用好朝鲜、日本、泰西诸国作者所主导编纂的早期北京话教本;另一方面,更要利用本土优势,在"吾国之旧籍"中深入挖掘,官话正音教本、满汉合璧教本、京味儿小说、曲艺剧本等新类型语料大有文章可做。在明确了思路之后,我们从2004年开始了前期的准备工作,在北京大学中国语言学研究中心的大力支持下，早期北京话的挖掘整理工作于2007年正式启动。本次推出的"早期北京话珍稀文献集成"是阶段性成果之一，总体设计上"取异族之故书与吾国之旧籍互相补正"，共分"日本北京话教科书汇编""朝鲜日据时期汉语会话书汇编""西人北京话教科书汇编""清代满汉合璧文献萃编""清代官话正音文献""十全福""清末民初京味儿小说书系""清末民初京味儿时评书系"八个系列，胪列如下：

"日本北京话教科书汇编"于日本早期北京话会话书、综合教科书、改编读物和风俗纪闻读物中精选出《燕京妇语》《四声联珠》《华语跬步》《官话指南》《改订官话指南》《亚细亚言语集》《京华事略》《北京纪闻》《北京风土编》《北京风俗问答》《北京事情》《伊苏普喻言》《搜奇新编》《今古奇观》等二十余部作品。这些教材是日本早期北京话教学活动的缩影，也是研究早期北京方言、民俗、史地问题的宝贵资料。本系列的编纂得到了日本学界的大力帮助。冰野善宽、内田庆市、太田斋、鳟泽彰夫诸先生在书影拍摄方面给予了诸多帮助。书中日语例言、日语小引的翻译得到了竹越孝先生的悉心指导，在此深表谢忱。

"朝鲜日据时期汉语会话书汇编"由韩国著名汉学家朴在渊教授和金雅瑛博士校注，收入《改正增补汉语独学》《修正独习汉语指南》《高等官话华语精选》《官话华语教范》《速修汉语自通》《速修汉语大成》《无先生速修中国语自通》《官话标准：短期速修中国语自通》《中语大全》《"内鲜满"最速成中国语自通》等十余部日据时期（1910年至1945年）朝鲜教材。这批教材既是对《老乞大》《朴通事》的传承，又深受日本早期北京话教学活动的影响。在中韩语言史、文化史研究中，日据时期是近现代过渡的重要时期，这些资料具有多方面的研究价值。

"西人北京话教科书汇编"收录了《语言自迩集》《官话类编》等十余部西人主编教材。这些西方作者多受过语言学训练，他们用印欧语的眼光考量汉语，解释汉语语法现象，设计记音符号系统，对早期北京话语音、词汇、语法面貌的描写要比本土文献更为精准。感谢郭锐老师提供了《官话类编》《北京话语音读本》和《汉语口语初级读本》的底本，《寻津录》、《语言自迩集》（第一版、第二版）、《汉英北京官话词汇》、《华语入门》等底本由北京大学图书馆特藏部提供,谨致谢忱。《华英文义津逮》《言语声片》为笔者从海外购回,其中最为珍贵的是老舍先生在伦敦东方学院执教期间,与英国学者共同编写的教材——《言语声片》。教材共分两卷:第一卷为英文卷,用英语讲授汉语,用音标标注课文的读音;第二卷为汉字卷。《言语声片》采用先用英语导入,再学习汉字的教学方法讲授汉语口语,是世界上第一部有声汉语教材。书中汉字均由老舍先生亲笔书写,全书由老舍先生录音,共十六张唱片,京韵十足,殊为珍贵。

上述三类"异族之故书"经江蓝生、张卫东、汪维辉、张美兰、李无未、王顺洪、张西平、鲁健骥、王澧华诸先生介绍,已经进入学界视野,对北京话研究和对外汉语教学史研究产生了很大的推动作用。我们希望将更多的域外经典北京话教本引入进来,考虑到日本卷和朝鲜卷中很多抄本字迹潦草,难以辨认,而刻本、印本中也存在着大量的异体字和俗字,重排点校注释的出版形式更利于研究者利用,这也是前文"深度利用"的含义所在。

对"吾国之旧籍"挖掘整理的成果,则体现在下面五个系列中:

"清代满汉合璧文献萃编"收入《清文启蒙》《清话问答四十条》《清文指要》《续编兼汉清文指要》《庸言知旨》《满汉成语对待》《清文接字》《重刻清文虚字指南编》等十余部经典满汉合璧文献。入关以后,在汉语这一强势语言的影响下,熟习满语的满人越来越少,故雍正以降,出现了一批用当时的北京话注释翻译的满语会话书和语法书。这批教科书的目的本是教授旗人学习满语,却无意中成为了早期北京话的珍贵记录。"清代满汉合璧文献萃编"首次对这批文献进行了大规模整理,不仅对北京话溯源和满汉语言接触研究具有重要意义,也将为满语研究和满语教学创造极大便利。由于底本多为善本古籍,研究者不易见到,在北京大学图书馆古籍部和日本神户外国语大学竹越孝教授的大力协助下,"萃编"将以重排点校加影印的形式出版。

"清代官话正音文献"收入《正音撮要》(高静亭著)和《正音咀华》(莎彝尊著)两种代表著作。雍正六年(1728),雍正谕令福建、广东两省推行官话,福建为此还专门设立了正音书馆。这一"正音"运动的直接影响就是以《正音撮要》和《正音咀华》为代表的一批官话正音教材的问世。这些书的作者或为旗人,或寓居京城多年,书中保留着大量北京话词汇和口语材料,具有极高的研究价值。沈国威先生和侯兴泉先生对底本搜集助力良多,特此致谢。

《十全福》是北京大学图书馆藏《程砚秋玉霜簃戏曲珍本》之一种,为同治元年陈金雀抄本。陈晓博士发现该传奇虽为昆腔戏,念白却多为京话,较为罕见。

以上三个系列均为古籍,且不乏善本,研究者不容易接触到,因此我们提供了影印全文。

总体来说,由于言文不一,清代的本土北京话语料数量较少。而到了清末民初,风气渐开,情况有了很大变化。彭翼仲、文实权、蔡友梅等一批北京爱国知识分子通过开办白话报来"开启民智""改良社会"。著名爱国报人彭翼仲在《京话日报》的发刊词中这样写道:"本报为输进文明、改良风俗,以开通社会多数人之智识为宗旨。故通幅概用京话,以浅显之笔,达朴实之理,纪紧要之事,务令雅俗共赏,妇稚咸宜。"在当时北京白话报刊的诸多栏目中,最受市民欢迎的当属京味儿小说连载和《益世余谭》之类的评论栏目,语言极为地道。

"清末民初京味儿小说书系"首次对以蔡友梅、冷佛、徐剑胆、儒丐、勋锐为代表的晚清民国京味儿作家群及作品进行系统挖掘和整理,从千余部京味儿小说中萃取代表作家的代表作品,并加以点校注释。该作家群活跃于清末民初,以报纸为阵地,以小说为工具,开展了一场轰轰烈烈的底层启蒙运动,为新文化运动的兴起打下了一定的群众基础,他们的作品对老舍等京味儿小说大家的创作产生了积极影响。本系列的问世亦将为文学史和思想史研究提供议题。于润琦、方梅、陈清茹、雷晓彤诸先生为本系列提供了部分底本或馆藏线索,首都图书馆历史文献阅览室、天津图书馆、国家图书馆提供了极大便利,谨致谢意!

"清末民初京味儿时评书系"则收入《益世余谭》和《益世余墨》,均系著名京味儿小说家蔡友梅在民初报章上发表的专栏时评,由日本岐阜圣德学园大学刘一之教授、矢野贺子教授校注。

这一时期存世的报载北京话语料口语化程度高,且总量庞大,但发掘和整理却殊为不易,称得上"珍稀"二字。一方面,由于报载小说等栏目的流行,外地作者也加入了京味儿小说创作行列,五花八门的笔名背后还需考证作者是否为京籍,以蔡友梅为例,其真名为蔡松龄,查明的笔名还有损、损公、退化、亦我、梅蒐、老梅、今睿等。另一方面，这些作者的作品多为急就章，文字错讹很多，并且鲜有单行本存世，老报纸残损老化的情况日益严重，整理的难度可想而知。

上述八个系列在某种程度上填补了相关领域的空白。由于各个系列在内容、体例、出版年代和出版形式上都存在较大的差异，我们在整理时借鉴《朝鲜时代汉语教科书丛刊续编》《〈清文指要〉汇校与语言研究》等语言类古籍的整理体例，结合各个系列自身特点和读者需求，灵活制定体例。"清末民初京味儿小说书系"和"清末民初京味儿时评书系"年代较近，读者群体更为广泛，经过多方调研和反复讨论，我们决定在整理时使用简体横排的形式，尽可能同时满足专业研究者和普通读者的需求。"清代满汉合璧文献萃编""清代官话正音文献"等系列整理时则采用繁体。"早期北京话珍稀文献集成"总计六十余册，总字数近千万字，称得上是工程浩大，由于我们能力有限，体例和校注中难免会有疏漏，加之受客观条件所限，一些拟定的重要书目本次无法收入，还望读者多多谅解。

"早期北京话珍稀文献集成"可以说是中日韩三国学者通力合作的结晶，得到了方方面面的帮助，我们还要感谢陆俭明、马真、蒋绍愚、江蓝生、崔希亮、方梅、张美兰、陈前瑞、赵日新、陈跃红、徐大军、张世方、李明、邓如冰、王强、陈保新诸先生的大力支持，感谢北京大学图书馆的协助以及萧群书记的热心协调。"集成"的编纂队伍以青年学者为主，经验不足，两位丛书总主编倾注了大量心血。王洪君老师不仅在经费和资料上提供保障，还积极扶掖新进，"我们搭台，你们年轻人唱戏"的话语令人倍感温暖和鼓舞。郭锐老师在经费和人员上也予以了大力支持，不仅对体例制定、底本选定等具体工作进行了细致指导，还无私地将自己发现的新材料和新课题与大家分享，令人钦佩。"集成"能够顺利出版还要特别感谢国家出版基金规划管理办公室的支持以及北京大学出版社王明舟社长、张凤珠副总编的精心策划，感谢汉语编辑室杜若明、邓晓霞、张弘泓、宋立文等老师所付出的辛劳。需要感谢的师友还有很多，在此一并致以诚挚的谢意。

"上穷碧落下黄泉，动手动脚找东西"，我们不奢望引领"时代学术之新潮流",惟愿能给研究者带来一些便利,免去一些奔波之苦,这也是我们向所有关心帮助过"早期北京话珍稀文献集成"的人士致以的最诚挚的谢意。

刘　云

2015年6月23日

于对外经贸大学求索楼

2016年4月19日

改定于润泽公馆

导 读

张卫东

一、威妥玛与《语言自迩集》及其版本

威妥玛（Thomas Francis Wade，1818—1895），曾就读剑桥大学。1841年随英军来华，学习北京话和粤语。1843年任香港英国殖民当局中文翻译、香港最高法院粤语翻译。1847年退伍，任英国驻华商务监督署汉文副使。1853年任英国驻上海副领事。1854年被委任为上海海关第一任外国税务司。1855年任驻华公使馆汉文正使。1861年任英国驻华使馆参赞、中文秘书，负责海外雇员的汉语教学，期间研发了威妥玛式拼音，编著了汉语口语课本《寻津录》《语言自迩集》等。1871年升任驻华公使。1882年卸任回国，将他的四千多册中文藏书捐予剑桥大学。1888年成为剑桥大学首任汉学教授。威妥玛23岁来中国，64岁卸任回国。1852年曾因疟疾回国治疗，次年返回上海。除去这一年，他在中国生活了整整40年。

《寻津录》（*Hsin Ching Lu*，1859），是威妥玛在香港编著出版的第一部汉语教材，对北京话口语语音、词汇以及语法特点进行了一次试验性探索，因而被他反复强调这是一部"试验手册"（*Book of Experiments*）。第一册为课本，第二册是一份84页的《北京话字音表》。全书两册共170页。第一次推出了威妥玛制订的拉丁字母表音法及其拼音方案。该方案精准记录了北京官话声韵调特点：27个声母，39个韵母，4个声调，共397个音节，反映了北京话见、精组细音声母腭化，尖团合流，疑微两母消失并入零声母，四

呼俱全，入声调和入声韵消失等时代特征。到《语言自迩集》，音节数量由397个增加到420个。此后，这个方案被普遍用来拼写中国的人名、地名等专有词语，一般称为威妥玛式拼音。清末至1958年汉语拼音方案公布前，中国和国际上流行的就是这个中文拼音方案。

《语言自迩集》（以下简称《自迩集》）先后出了三个版本：1867年第一版，1886年第二版，1903年节略版。

1867年第一版《序言》中，威妥玛这样表明其编著宗旨：

> 笔者的一项职责，就是指导英国驻中国领事馆招募人员学习汉语；……它的基本功能是帮助领事馆的学员打好自己的基础，用最少的时间学会这个国家的官话口语，并且还要学会这种官话的书面语，不论它是书本上的、公文信件上的，抑或具有公众性质的文献资料中的官话。

威妥玛进一步介绍其编著体例与内容安排：

> 本书主要分为两大部分，分别称为"口语（Colloquial）系列"和"公文（Documentary）系列"。书名所用的"自迩集"（TZǓ ÊRH CHI），也许译成"循序渐进的课程"（Progressive Course）更妥。中国经典云"行远必自迩"，千里之行，始于足下。两部分课程称为"集"，其一属于资料汇编，冠以"语言"二字以示区别，所收的词汇与短语都是口语的；而另一集收的是"公文"，属书面语、公文课程。
> ……
> 本系列的第一章讲"发音"（Pronunciation）；第二章讲"部首"（The Radicals），即常用汉字的书写构件；第三、四、五、六章是

练习，有些是这一种类型，有些是另一种类型，是通行于各大都市衙门的口语（the oral language），直接称之为"北京话"（the Peking Dialect）；第七章是一套练习，用以举例说明北京话里声调的影响；第八章及最后的"勘误与补遗"，称之为"词类章"（Chapter on the Parts of Speech），讨论汉语口语在某些条件下——即便不是全部——类似我们用语法术语所描述的同类现象。

第一版《自迩集》（不含书面语教材《文件自迩集》），一共四卷。第一卷即"口语系列"，共分八章。第二卷是口语系列的答案（Key）。第三卷是《平仄编》（新版《北京音节总表》，威妥玛对他的表音方案做了修订，包括增加iai韵和uo韵，增加了23个音节，令《北京音节总表》中的音节数达至420个）。第四卷是《汉字习写法》，为汉字书写练习配套教程。

19年之后，即1886年，《自迩集》出了第二版。此时威妥玛已经68岁，卸任回国4年了。这一版分三卷。第一卷仍是"口语系列"的八章。第二卷是第三、四、五、六、七、八章中文课文的标音、英译和注释，并随课文进程相应附加了1080条字词释义和用法示例，相当于一部小型辞典。第三卷是四个附录：

附录一"（英文）词语汇编（第二卷第三、四、五、六章）"；

附录二"汉字引得（第二卷第二、三、四、五、六、七章，以部首为序）"；

附录三"北京话音节表、北京话字音表、异读字表"；

附录四"汉字书写练习"。

跟第一版比较，主要的改动是，在中文课文旁边都加了英文译文，每一个汉译英练习之后都附加了英译汉练习，并呈上了英文答案。由"北京话声调方面的高级权威"禧在明（Walter Hillier）先生"细心地校正了新版前七章里每个词的声调符号";将"问答章之十"即"一段关于语言的句法结构的对话"删除了,换上了"他自己写的一段对话",因为"不止一个认真的初学者抱怨说,原来的那段让人吃不消"。"原来的那段",话题从汉字部首、汉字结构、口音、反切、"音母"记音、"京话字音的定数"(不论声调"共总四百一十多"),直到《清文指要》《清汉合璧》和"我们这儿说话的神气、层次、句法呀",共77条,2200多字,确实"让人吃不消"。另一个较大的改动,就是原来的第五章即"续散语(十八章)"全部删除,将原来的第六章"谈论篇"提为第五章,增加了"践约传"为第六章。这些是《第二版序言》提到的改动,而大量的未曾提及的改动,是在中文课文里数不胜数的细微修改、加注、标音和润色等。例如第一版"散语章四十之七":

12—17条:这屋里很黑,拏一盏灯来。有人拏了那盏灯去。桌子上的那腊灯谁拏了去了?是我给厨子拏过去了。厨房里没有火。饭锅是煮饭的,锅盖就是饭锅的盖儿。茶碗、茶盅都可以有盖儿。酒杯、酒盅子这两个东西不大很分。

第二版"散语章·练习七"(Exercise VII)相应的话条就有不少改动:

7.4 这屋里黑了,快拿灯来。桌子上的那腊灯是谁拏了去了?是我给厨子拏过去了。厨房的火弄①上还没著②呢。

注:①弄 lung^2,参见163。

②著 chao^2,在这里不是助动词,跟练习5.1中的不同,而是一个独立的动词,表示燃烧。

7.5 饭锅 fan^4-kuo^1 是煮饭的,锅盖 kuo^1-kai^4 就是饭锅的盖儿。茶碗

ch'a² wan³ 茶盌 ch'a² chung¹ 也有有盖儿 kai–'rh 的。

注：也有 yeh yu，也可以有；有盖儿的 yu kai–'rh ti，有盖子的东西。

7.6 酒杯 chiu³ pei¹ 酒盅子 chiu³ chung¹–tzǔ 这两个东西不大很分，可也分得出来①，本是酒杯比酒盅儿大②。

注：①分得出来 fên tê ch'u lai，可以用"区别"（distinguished）或"能区分"（distinguishable）替代；动词的语气和时态完全由上下文决定。回答问题时，"你分得出来分不出来？"（Can（or do）you distinguish or not?）"分得出来。"（I can（or do）distinguish）跟我们说的话一样，用陈述语气现在时态。

②本 pên³，实际上，参见120；是 shih⁴，事实上。在这个意义上，"本 pên³"是各种副词性结构中的一个成分。

第二版此类修改几乎遍布全书，但目标只是一个，就是从语音、词汇和语法各方面努力记好当时的北京话，记好说话时的语境、神气、语态，向学生准确地介绍当时的北京话，让学生学到真正地道的北京话。这一努力，使得第二版"口语系列"的篇幅大增，是第一版的两倍多。

1903年出版的第三版，是《自迩集》的节略版。这年，威妥玛已去世8年。《第三（节略）版出版者序言》（Publishers' Preface to Third（Abridged）Edition）交代：

以节略的方式再版威妥玛的伟大著作，是采纳了禧在明（Walter Hillier）先生的建议。他是1886年第二版的合作者，也是威妥玛先生的遗嘱执行人。

这篇1903年4月写于上海的《序言》，执笔者应该是禧在明本人。他在《序言》中介绍说：1886年以来，又出了许多汉语口语的新课本。英国公使馆里译员学生课程中，《自迩集》的许多课文已被替换。《谈论篇》和《秀才求婚》多年前就放弃了。而《自迩集》的初衷，是用来教领事馆学生的——至少眼下还是如此——只印出那些章节来继续做他们的课本。现在重版所包含的只是第一章到第四章，即：关于发音和部首的介绍，以及随后的散语章和问答章。在主管当局看来，学习北京话口语的学生以这四部分为入门，即可成功。

《序言》强调："对于威妥玛的表音系统，赞成的，反对的，都已经说了许多，写了许多。对于这场旷日持久的争论，我们已经不想再多说什么了，除非有初学者请求。就是说，要记住，这是唯一的拉丁字系统，它传播流布甚广，并获得持久的成功。"

以上三个版本，都是正版。历史上还曾出现过"盗版"。锺少华先生曾寄来一封短信："近日翻出家中一本（仅一本）《自迩集》，发现与你书上的个别翻译不同，故复印两页寄上，请核对。"从复印件看，是木刻版，小开本，每页竖排9行，每行24字。共30页，全是"问答十章"的。其中一页，是"问答章之七"的第63条至80条。经核对，是1867年第一版的"盗版"，而且是一"精致盗版"，因为从这一页看，除了未标条目，竟未错一字：

你这个人竟是打听！小儿原是在户部。他不是单住么？他这会儿单搬出去了。请问他住在甚么地方儿？他是在交民巷，西头儿路北里。他是在交民巷住么？真是！你疑惑作甚么？我估摸是城外头住的。离衙门那们远，不行，你怎么估摸着是城外头呢？昨儿日头落，碰见他的车，在琉璃厂。那有这个话？他昨儿晚上在我这儿来着。车是他的，他却没在车上。他没在车上，你怎么知道车是他的？车上坐着个老婆子，他说是孟大爷的车。老婆子抱着个孩子么？不错，是个七八岁的小孩子。必是我那小孙子。嗳？那早晚儿那儿去？老爷放心，有点儿事情。

这一节，第二、三两版的文字完全相同，跟第一版的不同之处有（第一版//第二、三版）：

1. 他是在交民巷，西头儿路北里。//他在交民巷，西头儿路北。
2. 真是！你疑惑作甚么？//真的阿！你疑惑作甚么？
3. 我估摸是城外头住的。//我估摸是在城外头住的。
4. 离衙门那们远，……//离衙门那么远，……
5. 那有这个话？//那'儿有这个话？
6. 嗳？那早晚儿那儿去？//嗳？那早晚儿那'儿去？

共有六七处的变动。从5和6两条追到第一版（正版）可知："那'儿"（哪儿）的这种写法，威妥玛编第一版的时候，确实还没发明出来。这个"那'儿"（哪儿）可以看作《自迩集》第一版跟二、三版版本辨识的标志之一。

从这种"盗版"的出现还可以推知：一、《自迩集》第一版刊出不久，中国民间便有人盗印了它的中文课文用以教外国人学汉语；二、民间对这种汉语教材的认可；三、民间的这种对外汉语教学，当时规模应该已经不小，方使这种教材有了相当的市场，否则，书商是不会下本儿冒险刊印的。

以前，我们只知道《自迩集》是那个时代英美人学汉语普遍使用的课本，是日本人改学北京话时的唯一依托，也曾引起朝鲜人和俄国人的注意和转抄、模仿，却未见有中国人翻印与使用这套课本的报道。现在，这一"盗版"的发现，让我们可以确信：这套课本在清末民初中国民间的对外汉语教学中曾扮演过重要角色，发挥过积极作用。

《自迩集》之所以能够获得如此成功，取决于威妥玛非凡的努力，取决于跟威妥玛同心同德、长期合作的中外学者团队。

威妥玛1841年来华，当年便投身汉语的学习，以近乎神奇的速度学会了粤语并应聘出任了香港最高法院的粤语翻译。与此同时，他一刻不停地开始学习北京话，不久便成为观察与研究汉语、对中国官话特别是北京话有独到见地的一流汉语语言学家。他的身边逐渐形成了一个高水平的中外学者团队。团队中的中国学者，为首的是生于北京的一位学者，威妥玛尊称为"老师"："我的老师应龙田（Ying Lung-t'ien）"，"一位受过良好教育的北京人，一位令人钦佩的发音人"。从他们在香港相遇，直到1861年应龙田去世，他们没有分开过，包括1852年威妥玛因疟疾回国治疗一年，1853年调任上海，应龙田都跟威妥玛在一起，参与《寻津录》和《自迩集》的编撰工作。威妥玛先后请过数十位中国老师和中国朋友帮忙（有资料显示他曾"从北京引进大量老师到香港"），其中还有一位留下姓名的，叫于子彬（Yü Tzǔ-pin），一位满族学者。威氏非常尊重中国老师，并作为自己的一条为人原则："我的为人是，我不能让自己相信我对汉语的认识会跟我的中国老师一样好。"他对于中国老师和中国朋友提供的帮助，绝不贪天功为己有，只要一有机会就真诚地表示敬意与谢意：

> 正如我在《寻津录》（*Hsin Ching Lu*）或称"试验手册"（*Book of Experiments*）中——我的字母表1859年第一次在那里发表——解释的，在北京话的口语中，这个声调（按，第五声即入声）已不复存在（the non-existence any longer），而第一次唤起我注意的是应龙田（Ying Lung-t'ien），一位受过良好教育的北京人，一位令人钦佩的发音人，

他已为我自行重新整理了一份词汇表,其中的调类是实际使用的。他的表中,所有第五声都并入第二声,而一年之后我住进北京的时候,我发现应龙田是对的。我听过一位非常有资格的鉴定专家表态说,他的声调分类"无懈可击"。

凡他认为对于学习口语并非必不可少的词语,全部删去,将剩余的部分重新归类,保留原来的声母和韵母,作为检索音节的类目,但是,对于大量词语的语音做了订正,有些是改变了发音或者声调,有些则是二者都改了,并且彻底清除了第五声即所谓入声(re-entering tone)。我发现,他对声韵和声调两方面的判断,在整个七年中经受住了考验,被认为大体正确。对于一个人讲话所需词语数量,他的限制比较严格,这是很了不起的,因为他自己的用语,跟他选定的语汇一样丰富讲究。他1861年去世。为了弥补他所提供的字表之不足,从一个比他分析过的大得多的词汇表里进行独立的选择,从那时起已由另一些本地助手为我做起来了。

二、《语言自迩集》是现代汉语普通话零公里里程碑

《自迩集》问世后,在汉学界引发了一场不小的论争。论争涉及两个方面,一方面涉及表音法方案或某些章节内容的编排,另一方面的争论是关乎官话标准音、关乎北京话历史地位的。

表音法方案方面,威妥玛说:"我认为,它被反对的主要有三项。"即浊擦音j(日母)、ang韵中的主要元音a和"儿"êrh音的描写。用拉丁文字母描写北京话的这几个音确非易事,对于那些熟悉西语西文而略知北京话的汉学家们,更各有不同的体验和自以为是的表音方案。威妥玛在这方面遭遇的反对,多数是学术范围的,即使争论不休,也算是正常的。这方面的一些

争论旷日持久，莫衷一是，再争亦无益，所以，威妥玛在《第二版序言》作了最后申述后便宣布："此后，我要跟这个讨论告别了。"

而另一方面涉及的，却是一个大问题——关乎北京话历史地位的论争。《自迩集》问世之前，汉语官话史上刚刚经历了一场大变革，这场大变革催生了《自迩集》，而《自迩集》的面世，又引发了一场大论战。

《寻津录》《自迩集》以北京话作为教学目标语言，这在西人编著的汉语教科书中是第一次。此事曾轰动一时，与其说是引发一场大论战，还不如说是旷日持久的讥讽、责难与围攻。威妥玛曾回顾说："……1859年我出版的初级读物《寻津录》一书……这个系统并没有被普遍接受，然而对它表示异议的，通常来自那些在本书出版之前开始研究的人；任何初学者，只要他采用这个系统并得到帮助，这种异议与声讨就会出现。"

"那些在本书出版之前开始研究的人"是些什么人呢？他们研究的是什么？他们是早先抵达中国的西方人，将南京官话作为研究对象并成为"颇负盛名的汉学家"，"因有这种特殊造诣而十分骄傲""独占鳌头"的权威。他们认定南京官话才是"帝国官话"（kuan hua of the Empire），并为它付出了毕生时间与精力。他们看不到或不承认"帝国官话"已经由南京官话转为北京官话。于是他们将《自迩集》采用的这个系统讥讽为"公使馆汉语"（Legation Chinese），对于《自迩集》承认第五声即入声在北京话所代表的"帝国官话"里已经消失（the disappearance），汉学权威卫三畏博士"最近已断然提出抗议"。

"这种异议与声讨"即起因于"帝国官话"代表点的转变。以研究南京官话起家的汉学权威们看不到或者说是不愿意承认这种转变，有些人更恼羞成怒。他们不像日本学界那样平静地顺应了这种转变。专攻日本汉语教育史的六角恒广教授说：

那时候可以说,不仅在北京,即使在世界上,北京官话的教科书,除威妥玛的这本《语言自迩集》以外,再也没有了。明治九年(1876)9月,日本的汉语教学,从官方到民间,同时由南京话转向北京话。威妥玛的《语言自迩集》第一版便成了此时日本汉语教育唯一可用的教材。1879年日本出版的北京官话课本《亚细亚言语集》,即以《语言自迩集》为蓝本。

威妥玛这样介绍当时的"官话"和"帝国官话":

"官话"作为口语媒介,不只是属于官吏和知识阶层,而且属于近五分之四的帝国民众。在如此辽阔的地域,伴随它的必是多种多样的方言(dialects)。艾约瑟先生,谁也不如他那么勤奋地去探究过这些不同方言的规则与界线。他把官话划分为三个主要系统:南方官话(the southern mandarin)、北方官话(the northern mandarin)和西部官话(the western mandarin),他以南京、北京和成都——四川省省会,分别代表各个官话系统的标准。他认为南京官话(Nanking mandarin)在更大的范围被理解,尽管后者更为时髦;可是他又承认那些想说帝国官廷语言的人一定要学习北京话,而净化了它的土音的北京话,就是公认的"帝国官话"。

"官话""分为三个主要系统","南京、北京和成都""分别代表各个官话系统的标准"。在官话全国通语形成之前,它们就是官话的三个"准通语",皆属一方之"权威方言"。

通过自己的学习与独立研究,威妥玛较早地认识到这一点:

选择并确定一种话（a dialect），这大约是20年前的事，其次就是建立表音法。那时没人把北京话作为写作对象，而各种表音法都声称描写的是南方官话——诸如马礼逊博士（Dr. Morrison）（即第一部汉英辞典的编纂者）、麦都思博士（Dr. Medhurst）和卫三畏博士（Dr. Wells Williams）等人——他们对于本地话系统的描写，远不是无懈可击的。对于马礼逊表音法，有人主张把它看作官话表音法，艾约瑟先生根本否定任何这类主张。他说："马礼逊正在编撰他的很有实用价值的音节辞典（syllabic dictionary），却没有意识到他所列的音根本不是官话音，而是已经废弃不用的发音。"麦都思博士作了一些修订以求完善的表音法，几乎是马礼逊博士表音法的翻版；他辩解说，我没把它当作最好的，却因为它是最知名的。我相信，卫三畏博士正跟辞典编纂者的儿子、很有造诣的马儒翰先生（Mr. John Robert Morrison）合作，重订《音节辞典》（the Syllabic Dictionary）的语音系统，但是迄今只涉及了拼写方式。因而，这种表音法最后虽说更匀称整齐，但在我看来，似乎并不比第一种更臻精确。

这场论争意味着，大约是1850年前后，北京音才获得官话正音的地位，成为"帝国官话"的代表。北京音获得官话全国通语地位，意味着历史已步入"以北京音为标准音"的现代汉语普通话阶段。正是在这个意义上说：《自迩集》是现代汉语普通话零公里里程碑。

而看不到这种变化的还有另一种表现：1950年代，权威学者就坚持说："至少六百年来北京音一直是官话正音。"（张卫东，1998）真的"至少六百年来北京音一直是官话正音"吗？这是近现代汉语史理论架构上的一个基本问题。《自迩集》的问世，标志着北京音成为"官话正音"即现代普通话标准音（"净化了它的土音的北京话"），自1850年至今不过160多年。

对于中国语言学界承认北京音成为官话正音"至今不过160多年"这一点的难度，看来一点儿也不亚于160年前那些汉学权威们承认南京音已经让位于北京音的难度。

三、《语言自迩集》是19世纪中期北京话的描写语言学巨著

《自迩集》的初衷，是为学生编一部学习"帝国官话"即清末北京官话的课本，不期然成了北京话描写语言学的经典巨著。2001年版《语言自迩集：19世纪中期的北京话》的《译序》说："本译稿采用的是1886年的第二版。这是目前能见到的唯一的本子，从二版序言推知，也是最好的本子。这部三卷本的汉语课本，共一千一百余页，容量极大。百余年前的这部北京话描写语言学巨著，在中国现代语言学史上，可能拥有多项'第一'。"商务印书馆前副总编辑李思敬先生曾说："这部书可列为语言学经典。"今天，我们仍然认为，这种评价，殊不过分。

《自迩集》采用描写语言学的视角、方法和手段，全方位地精确考察、记录北京话的语音、词汇、语法，力图"拥有本地人说话的自然气质"，"符合语言习惯"。不仅有共时平面的描写，还有历时的比较和历史的探讨。如此一来，《自迩集》就成了迄今所能见到的19世纪中期北京话最为珍贵富饶的语料库。《自迩集》作为汉语教材，有许多值得今日借鉴的地方。而作为百余年前的北京话描写语言学巨著、一个半世纪前的北京话大型语料库，已往的研究只能算初步，未来尚需我们从语音、词汇、语法各方面进行更系统深入的研究与讨论。

（一）语音

有了《自迩集》记录在案的大量可靠的记音资料，我们就可以把北京话元、明、清、民国至今诸如《蒙古字韵》《老乞大谚解》《朴通事谚解》《自迩集》《国音字典》《现代汉语词典》等标音文献系联成一条长链，将北京

话六七百年的语音演变史，形成一个可以目睹其演变过程的历史。这一求证过程与结果，又逆向证明了《自迩集》所提供的北京话资料之可信与可靠。

近代官话语音演变是一个相当长的历史过程，各方言区的演变也往往是不同步的，先后发生格局性音变，通过交际实践而互动，诸如轻重唇分化、全浊清化、重韵合流、浊上变去、入声舒化等，相继普遍发生，并被吸纳、集中。这种吸纳与集中发生在哪里，跟各权威方言的表现相关。例如"入声舒化"在北系官话区和南系官话北缘普遍发生，南京音则"顽强地"保留入声，就失去了做全国通语的一个砝码。近代官话史上最后一波格局性音变，即从《中原音韵》时代先后发生的三组入声韵和一组阳声韵为代表的文白异读的消变，被谁拒绝，为谁吸纳，便是关键：

第一组，宕江二摄铎药觉三韵萧豪歌戈两韵并收。北系变萧豪，南系变歌戈，属北系官话的北京音形成部分字萧豪歌戈两韵并收，而以南京音为代表的南系官话坚持歌戈而拒绝萧豪。这组两韵并收经过一系列持续变化，终于在《伍伦全备谚解》（1709）之后、《自迩集》（1867）之前，萧豪韵优势和文读音地位让位于歌戈韵。这一音变结果，被北京音吸纳，被南京音和大部分南方官话拒绝（其北缘受北京音影响接纳了少数萧豪韵异读）（张卫东，2010）。

第二组，通摄屋浊二韵鱼模尤侯两韵并收。南、北同变鱼模，以武汉为代表的西部官话（含上江官话和西南、西北官话）变尤侯，北系官话吸纳了部分字的尤侯读法，属北系官话的北京音形成部分字鱼模尤侯两韵并收，赖南北合力鱼模韵读法始终保持着正音地位，部分字尤侯韵读法虽然"反客为主"获得正音地位，但始终维持在不足一成的低水平。而以南京音为代表的南系官话坚持鱼模而拒绝尤侯。北京音再获晋级全国通语的又一筹码（张卫东，2012）。

第三组，《中原音韵》之后出现的曾梗二摄德陌麦三韵洪音皆来歌戈两韵并收。这些字《中原音韵》归皆来、《蒙古字韵》归佳韵（与皆来同），《西儒耳目资》归第二摄e"入声甚"，相当于歌戈。从明代中叶《翻译老乞大》（1517）可知，这种"两韵并收"已经出现：脉（左韵-aiω，右韵-e），北德色濇克黑伯百栢珀帛白窄核（左韵-ŭiω，右韵-e），客隔（左韵-ŭiω，右韵-ie），国或（左韵-uiω，右韵-ue）；少数字左右音都是皆来韵：摘（左韵-ŭiω，右韵-ai），得特肋尅剋（左右皆-ŭiω），忒（左韵-ŭiω，开口；右韵-ui，合口）。德陌麦三韵洪音，从今方言现状看，北系官话变皆来（洪-ai），南系官话变歌戈，北京音在北系官话变皆来的基础上吸纳南系官话歌戈韵读法，形成皆来歌戈两韵并收。南系官话的北缘（济南、西安等）多变为-ei韵，这可能是北系官话皆来韵影响所致，也可能是其自身机制所致，无论怎样，是给北系官话变皆来增加了砝码。南系官话的大部分坚持歌戈读法至今。在争当通语的"较量"中这一波的"输"与"赢"亦无需赘言。（张卫东，2016）

第四组，曾梗通三摄阳声韵重组形成[əŋ、iŋ、uŋ、yŋ]一套韵母。《中原音韵》东钟庚青两韵并收，实际上就是中古曾梗通三摄阳声韵重新组合全过程的发端，300年之后，通过《西儒耳目资》可见这种"重组运动"在南方官话已有表现。在《老》《朴》等朝鲜谚解文献中，这种运动持续着，通摄"风缝蜂"等轻唇字直到《老七》（1745）方有松动："缝蜂"二字右音变"庚青"（-ㅜㅇ，即-uŋ），左音不变（-ㅡㅇ，即-uŋ），而"风"到《老A》（1795）仍不变（左右音皆-ㅜㅇ，即-uŋ）。威妥玛也一直关注着这个情况。在《语言自迩集》第一章《发音》中，他不无兴奋地报告说：

ên，êng两个韵母是被用来替代声母f，m，p音节中的un，ung的。这种情况最先见于在广东出版的教广东人学官话的本地课本。人们发现，这种演变已被北京人完全认可了。上个世纪满洲人的发音还是

fung，mung，不过也经常是fên，mên，pên。

按，最后一句原文疑有阙，全文应该是"上个世纪满洲人的发音还是fun，mun，pun；fung，mung，pung，不过也经常是fên，mên，pên；fêng，mêng，pêng"。就是说，上个世纪满洲人（北京内城人口主体）发音已是-un/-ên，-ung/-êng"两韵并收"。"风、梦"等字，通摄帮组最后几个仍读合口-ung韵的字终于有了开口-êng韵异读，由fung，mung，pung变为fêng，mêng，pêng！他异常兴奋，是因为早在编写《寻津录》（1859）时，他已注意到的"这种演变"，终于被广东出版的官话课本证实了，表明"被北京人完全认可了"，涉及现代汉民族共同语的最后一个格局性的音变终于完成了。（张卫东，2013）

这四组音变，皆属格局性音系变化，是近代官话史上南、北、西各大区域权威方言相互激荡、叠加、约定俗成的结果，不是任何主观意志的"认定"与"取舍"。这四组音系变化的历史是客观的、物质的，可知，可察，可量化分析，量变到质变，行迹可循，规则可现，绝不是"没有规范的"，更不"可能因人而异"。这一波格局性音系变化，具有区别不同质的阶段的标志性，跟"入派三声""浊音清化"等普遍的历史音变意义完全不同。而北京音系吸纳了近代发生的各项重要的音系变化，特别是这最后一波格局性音系变化，体现了最大的包容性，从而成为区别于其他各区域权威方言的特点之一。

至此，一个"现代汉民族共同语形成之层级模式"浮现在眼前：近代官话的长期演变发展，逐渐形成了南、北、西三大区系，并在各自区域形成了权威方言——南京话、北京话、成都话三个"准通语"。以金尼阁《西儒耳目资》、马礼逊《华英字典》为代表的明清来华传教士所记，是以南京音为标准音的南部准通语；而朝鲜谚解《老》《朴》系列所记，是以北京音为标准音的北部准通语。明代南部准通语影响大些，入清以后北部准通语地位持续上升，在新的政治、经济、文化条件下的社会交流交往，促使近代官话进一步演变发展，并产生了形成全国通语的需要与可能。北京话，以其得天独厚的社会条件、语言条件，加上它的包容性，终于获得了全国通语的地位。

现代汉语的标准音是北京音。当我们这么说的时候，"北京音"指的是有着上述形成史的19世纪中后期的北京音，是已晋级为现代汉民族共同语标准音的北京音；它已不只是北系官话的代表，它的基础方言已扩展为广义的"北方官话"（北系官话+南系官话+西部官话）。这是"现代汉语"题中应有之义，反映现代北京音跟各官话方言的新型关系，是北京音能够成为现代汉民族共同语标准音的语言学基础。据我们目前的考察，这一切，最早地、全面地、如实地反映在应运而生的威妥玛《自迩集》中。威妥玛《自迩集》无可争议地、当之无愧地成为近代官话史终结、现代汉语史开启的标志性文献，实乃历史必然。

（二）词汇

《自迩集》的词汇量极大，借以进行那个时代北京话词汇的共时研究是很方便的。细心的读者会发现，书中还有许多材料可以引导人们拓展新的研究领域。例如，《自迩集》里常见一种说法：某字"不见于字典"，某字"不被字典所承认""未被字典所承认""本地字典不承认它"，或者某音、某义、某个用法"不见于本地字典""本地字典不认可"，等等。

这里所说的"字典""本地字典"，看来就是《康熙字典》。所说"不见于字典"的各字，确为《康熙字典》未收的字。有的字收了，或音、义有所不同，甚至相反。例如：

（1）傻sha^3，本指精明的家伙，但口语所指却正好相反。

《康熙字典》：傻，《广韵》沙瓦切，《集韵》《韵会》数瓦切，并沙上声。轻慧貌。《韵笺逸字》傻音洒。《韵会》傻俏不仁。

（2）懵懂 $mêng^2$-$tung^3$，失去了知觉，失礼了，不合时宜；懵

mêng，健忘的，愚笨的；懂tung，亦有大体相同的意思；"懂tung"的第二个义项的意思是"理解、明白"，但不被本地字典所承认。

《康熙字典》：懂，《正韵》多动切，音董，懵懂，心乱也。

（3）抿著嘴儿min³ cho tsui，合拢嘴唇；各字典不承认"抿"的这个意思。

《康熙字典》：抿，《集韵》眉贫切，揩字省文。《说文》抚也。一曰摹也。

（4）篮lan²，一般比"筐子"小点儿，虽然字典上说得正相反。

《康熙字典》：篮，《正韵》卢监切，并音蓝，大笼筐也。

从一些小注还能看到某些字词定形的曲折过程，例如今"崭新"一词，就几经周折：斩新chan³ hsin¹，新制的，刚刚切下来的湛chan⁴，本书第一版用了这个字，卫三畏的字典（Williams's Dictionary）也收了这个字，但中国字典给的是前一个读音chan³。

《自迩集》对这方面的观察是很敏感的，并且不厌其烦地记录下来，这是在引导学生学会观察、认识和把握活的动态，因而是地道的北京话。而客观上就给我们留下了词汇及其相关用字新陈代谢的实录。让我们再看一些例子（"不见于本地字典"仍指《康熙字典》）：

（1）傢chia¹，这个字不见于本地字典。

（2）伙huo³，也不见于本地字典；二字合成"傢伙chia¹-huo³"一词，指各种各样的厨具。随便儿说，小型武器也可以叫"傢伙chia¹-huo³"；如梭标，步枪，或任何随身用具。

（3）噗嗤p'u¹ ch'ih¹，发笑的声音；前一个字不见于字典。

（4）惦tien⁴，想念着；惦记tien chi，出于好意地记挂着某人。字典里没有"惦tien"字。

（5）嘟哝tu¹ nang¹，轻声低语……"嘟tu"字不见于字典。

《国音字典》嘟、哝二字单立：嘟ㄉㄨ都阴，状声字。哝ㄋㄨㄥ农阳，哝哝，多言而声细，如"群司兮哝哝"，见《楚辞》。《现汉》【嘟囔】dū·nang，【嘟哝】dū·nong，音近义同。

（6）账chang⁴，账单；账目。这个字是"帐chang⁴"的讹体；本地字典不承认它；然而，却用得非常普遍，已经取代了正体"帐"。

（7）愣lêng⁴，发呆；这个字，字典不承认。

《国音字典》：愣㊀ㄌㄥ冷去 ①呆貌。②卤莽貌。③率意而行……㊁ㄌㄥ棱阴，愣儿，犹言呆子……。《现汉》单音lèng，义同㊀。

（8）圪蚤ko⁴-tsao³，或读tsao¹，蚤目昆虫：圪ko，字典不承认的字；蚤tsao，书面语单用。

《国音字典》：圪ㄍㄜ各去（入），圪蚤，虫名，即蚤。语音似ㄍㄜ·ㄗㄠ。

（9）镣铐liao⁴ k'ao⁴，脚镣……铐k'ao，铐在脚上的，通常叫"脚镣"；"铐"字，未被字典所承认。

《国音字典》：铐，考去，手铐，械手之刑具。

（10）炸cha⁴，是未被本地字典认可的字，由火huo（火烛）乍cha（突然）构成；炸炮cha p'ao，炸弹；炸开，爆炸。

《国音字典》：炸㊀ㄓㄚ乍去 ①谓火力爆发。②激怒，如"他听了登时炸了"。③喧噪哄散。㊁ㄓㄚ札阳（入）谓以油煎食物。

《自迩集》也"参与"了造字。它自创了两个"字"：那'（na³）、得'（tei³）。当时表what、where、anywhere的新词na³，表must的tei³，一时都找不到合适的汉字，只得借用旧有的、音义有些关联的"那"和"得"加修饰符号，创造出"中西合璧"的"那'"与"得'"。其实，这不能算严格意义上的"汉字"。后来，假借了音义都不同的"哪"取代了"那'"，假借了音义确有关联的"得"取代了"得'"。得，曾摄德韵字，在入声消失过程中变化出 te 和 tei 二音，即"两韵并收"，是合乎历史音变规律的，以"得"取代"得'"，实为回归原点。

这类情况，正与现代汉语新语素、复音词大量涌现相关。

《康熙字典》，据中华书局影印本出版说明，"依据明代《字汇》《正字通》两书加以增订"，成书于1717年。其所"增"者，在很大程度上反映了明中至清中二百年间官话语用情况的发展变化。例如心部五画"怎"字下将"始见"于《五音集韵》对"怎"的解释全文录入后，加"按"曰：

此字《广韵》《集韵》皆未收，唯韩孝彦《五音集韵》收之。今时扬州人读"争"上声，吴人读"尊"上声，金陵人读"津"上声，河南人读如"楂"，各从乡音而分也。

《自迩集》异读字表：怎 tsên^3 | tsêng^3。

练习十六介绍说：怎 tsên^3，如何，什么，在北京口语里总是随个"么 mo^1"（23）说"怎么"，而且韵母里的 n 听不到了，双音节的发音变成了 tsêm^3-mo，重音在第一个音节。

这是北京音。而异读"怎 tsêng^3"可能是语流音变的结果，也可能是"扬州人读'争'上声"叠加于北京话的。

再如近指代词"这"。《康熙字典》辵部七画"這"：

《广韵》鱼变切，《集韵》牛堰切，并音彦。《玉篇》迎也。《正字通》周礼有"掌訝"主迎。訝，古作"這"。毛晃曰：凡称"此箇"为"者箇"。俗多改用"這"字。這，乃迎也。

《康熙字典》简要回顾"這"的音韵训诂史，正确地指出：近代汉语近指代词"这"是假借古字而音"者"。《自迩集》异读字表列出6个异读音：这chai⁴｜chê⁴, chei⁴, tsê⁴, tsên⁴, tsêng⁴, 完全不睬其"迎這"之古音古义。《国音字典》近指代词"这"的两个音，跟其中chê⁴、chei⁴二音相同。（《国音字典》㊀ㄓㄜ 宅去（入），此，如"三十六峰犹不见，况伊如燕這身材"……按古用"者"作"此"字义，唐以后用"這"者始多。㊁ㄓㄟ 近指，盖"这一"之合。㊂ㄧㄢ 雁去，迎也，见《玉篇》。）而余下的4个异读除了chai⁴，另外3个：tsê⁴，可能来自没有卷舌音的方言区，叠加于北京话；tsên⁴、tsêng⁴，则见于语流音变。

从1717年到1867年，即从《康熙字典》到《自迩集》的150年，正是北京话从近代演进到现代的最后关键阶段。入声的阴声化，全浊声母的清化，尖团音的混一，异读的大量出现，量词、代词、助词、介词、叹词等各系统的成长与完善化，表述方式的改变与词法、句法结构的适应性变化等等，呈现出语音、词汇、语法、文字全面的大变化或细小微调并存的更新大局面。文字是语言的书写工具。语言与文字，于社会平稳发展时期，一般是大体平衡的。文字一般会随语言的演进发生适应性的新陈代谢。第一性的"语"，第二性的"文"，二者同步互动发展，达至大体平衡，这是最理想的。然而，文字的创新往往滞后，跟不上语音、词汇的发展变化。特别是语言剧烈变动期间，"语"与"文"的平衡不仅会被打破，甚至会严重失衡。这种时候，在"新词"面前，读书人往往会自认"不会写"。然而从总体上说，民间却不会那么消极。言语交际的需要往往促成新字新词率先于民间诞生。民间造字自古亦然。但是，教习语文的课本，能像《自迩集》这样不存芥蒂地大胆、自然地启用民间造字与新词，却是极少见的。这样做，丝毫不存猎奇与哗众取宠之意，完全是为了让学生能学到地道的、即时鲜活的北京话。这样的教学取向，使得《自迩集》在成为当时最好的汉语课本的同时，也成为那个时代北京话语用状况的敏锐观察与忠实记录。

（三）语法

威妥玛多次声明，《自迩集》是作为教材编纂的，没把它当作一本语法书来写。然而，这并非意味着《自迩集》只讲语音、词汇而不讲语法。在1867年《第一版序言》里，威妥玛用了相当的篇幅讨论和比较中西语文、语法的同与不同，克服重重困难（"没有一套共同的语法术语"）陈述其汉语语法观。威妥玛的汉语语法观极具学术价值。

在语法方面，对于汉语跟英语的同异，威妥玛的表述清晰明确、一语中的，表现得冷静而客观，请看《第一版序言》中的几段话（下画线为笔者所加）：

> 外国语言学家告诉我们，语法（Grammar），作为言语科学（the Science of Words），<u>可分为语源学（Etymology）和句法（Syntax）两部分</u>；而语源学规律又再分为屈折的和派生的（the laws of Inflexion and of Derivation）。<u>汉语服从这个规定，但只是有限度地服从</u>。在派生规律（derivation）方面，它的语源学有些地方跟其他语言有某些共同点；而在屈折规律（inflexion）方面，它没有语源学。

他注意到汉语"字""词"的关系：

> 至于派生规律，汉语所有单个词（single words）的词源在很大程度上是可知的，因为在书面语中它们每一个都有其典型（representative），罕有例外；而这些典型形态被不太准确地称为"汉字"。

他敏锐地发现：汉语语法的核心就在于"汉语词的多功能性"：

> 至于语源学的另一分支，即屈折变化方面，我再重复一遍，

汉语语法完全不允许它占有一席之地；汉语词的多功能性（the versatility）——如果可以这样称呼的话，即汉语中对于这么多的词语（尤其是我们倾向于称之为名词和动词的词）有共通性，在有广泛差别的语法功能的可容性方面达到如此程度：任何把语言权威性地划分到像我们语言中"词性"的范畴里去的努力，都将枉费心机。而且，我们语言中的词类分析当然得有它们相对应的汉语说法，且不管能否对它们作词类分析；在所有别的语言中用屈折变化生效而产生的大部分结果所需的那些方法，汉语自身也拥有，否则汉语就不成其为一种语言。汉语并不打乱它的词语系统，也不是要把它的各部分——不论是现存的还是过时的——都合并到词语系统中去，从而实现我们用格、数、语气、时态、语态等术语或诸如此类的东西所表述的情况。汉语通过词语的句法处理，几乎达到了这些现存的限定所能实现的一切，几乎全部保持了词语在别处整体或独立运用的能力。

他敏锐地察觉到"汉语词的多功能性"，没有跌进"词无定类"的泥淖；他科学地论断"在所有别的语言中用屈折变化生效而产生的大部分结果所需的那些方法，汉语自身也拥有"，"汉语通过词语的句法处理，几乎达到了这些现存的限定所能实现的一切"，从而深刻地揭示了汉语的内在机制和语法特征。这些话说得何等好啊！一百多年前，一个接受欧洲语言学严格训练的西方人，来到东方研究汉语，竟无一丝"生搬硬套"的味道。这跟早期留洋的不少中国人对自己母语所作的"生吞活剥"式的分析，形成鲜明对照。

原书第二卷之第八章"词类章"与第一卷之第八章"言语例略"内容大体相同。后者为中文课文，分13段，无段名；前者为英语译文和注释，亦分13段，各有段名，借用西方语言学的概念，讨论当时北京话口语的语法。威妥玛强调"该章不是讲语法，也没当语法来写"。这13节没有以西语语法的框框套汉语,没有机械地"对照"与"类比";所得汉语词类10种,跟我们今天的词类分析十分接近,而其中的某些成果,例如对量词的认识与表述,中国学者直到20世纪50年代初才达到同一水平。(何九盈,2008)

第八章"绪论"(Introductory Observations)首先肯定:"天下各国的话,没有全不相同的地方儿。是人心里的意思发出来,随势自然分好些神气(character of expression: 神气 shên ch'i, gait, air, attitude)。"这是"文字语言的总例(a general law which affects all language, written or spoken),是中外各国人情自然相同之理"。随后,威妥玛借用中国传统的"死字""活字""实字""虚字"之说,揭示"汉语词的多功能性"的存在:

> 至于那个"死字""活字"不同,就是"你""钱"这两个字是"死"的,那"要"字一个字是"活"的。然而那"要"字,才说是"活字",在此处固然是"活"的,别处也能够当"死"的用。比如"其要在速ch'i yao tsai su(要点是从速)"这一句,那"要yao"字、"速su"字可不是"死字"么?再问这一句里头,"活字"没有么?就是那"在tsai"字必算是"活字"。又考这些字里"虚""实"之分,就是那"其ch'i""在tsai"这俩字,虽然各有正义,在这儿仍算是"虚字"。

中国有些学者已经通过自己独立研究走上同一条路,可谓殊途同归。范晓接替胡裕树主持修订的《现代汉语》1995年重订本已改弦易辙,距离"汉语词的多功能性"仅一步之遥了。而北京大学早在20世纪60年代已经迈出这一步。朱德熙先生1985年的《语法答问》抓住"汉语自己的特点",在中国第一次推出"汉语词的多功能性"的概念,并强调"这件事不但影响我们对整个词类问题的看法,而且还关系到对句法结构的看法":

有的汉语语法书所以会走上这条路（按，指"词无定类"），根本的原因是受了印欧语法观念的束缚，看不见汉语自己的特点，不知道汉语的名词、动词、形容词都是"多功能"的，不像印欧语那样，一种词类只跟一种语法成分对应。（7页）

汉语词类没有这种形态标记，不管放在什么语法位置上，形式都一样，这就造成词类多功能的现象。另外一方面，由于汉语动词没有限定形式与非限定形式（不定形式和分词形式）的对立，这就造成了词组和句子构造上的一致性。（9页）

在印欧语里，词类和句法成分之间有一种简单的一一对应关系。大致说来，动词跟谓语对应，名词跟主宾语对应，形容词跟定语对应，副词跟状语对应……（而就汉语而言）动词和形容词既能做谓语，又能做主宾语。做主宾语的时候，还是动词、形容词，并没有改变性质。这是汉语区别于印欧语的一个非常重要的特点。说它重要，因为这件事不但影响我们对整个词类问题的看法，而且还关系到对句法结构的看法。（5—6页）

在这方面，启功先生的《汉语现象论丛》、王宁先生的《汉语现象和汉语语言学》在20世纪90年代初也都迈出了这一步，如王宁（1996:39—40）用"不干胶""多面体"来形容"汉语词的多功能性"，十分形象：

像英语、俄语这些种语言，一个词像一根小铁钩，一边有环，一边带钩，这个钩钩进那个环，连成一条就是一句话。钩和环得对合适了，大钩穿不进小环，大环挂不牢小钩，词的自由结合度很小，错了一点就被判为语法错误。可汉语的词像一个多面体，每面抹的都是不干胶，面面都能接，而且用点心都可以接得严丝合缝。比如回文诗，干脆结成一个圈儿，从哪儿都能念。这虽是文字游戏，可难道不启发人去想汉语的特点吗？

参考文献

何九盈（2008）《中国现代语言学史》，商务印书馆，北京。

启　功（1997）《汉语现象论丛》，中华书局，北京。

王　宁（1996）汉语现象和汉语语言学，载于《汉语现象问题讨论论文集》，文物出版社，北京。

张卫东（1998）北京音系何时成为汉语官话标准音，《深圳大学学报（人文社科版）》第4期。

张卫东（2010）论《中原音韵》的萧豪歌戈"两韵并收"，《语言学论丛》第四十一辑，商务印书馆，北京。

张卫东（2012）论《中原音韵》的鱼模尤侯"两韵并收"，载于早稻田大学文学部《中国语学研究·开篇》VOL.31。

张卫东（2013）论《中原音韵》东钟庚青之"两韵并收"，《语言学论丛》第四十八辑，商务印书馆，北京。

张卫东（2016）曾梗二摄德职陌麦韵入声洪音字的"两韵并收"——基于《老朴》等标音文献的考察，《语言学论丛》第五十三辑，商务印书馆，北京。

朱德熙（1985）《语法答问》，商务印书馆，北京。

TZŬ ÊRH CHI.

語言自邇集

(YÜ YEN TZŬ ÊRH CHI).

A

PROGRESSIVE COURSE

DESIGNED TO ASSIST THE STUDENT OF

COLLOQUIAL CHINESE

AS SPOKEN IN THE CAPITAL AND THE METROPOLITAN DEPARTMENT.

IN THREE VOLUMES.

SECOND EDITION.

PREPARED BY

THOMAS FRANCIS WADE,
Sometime H.B.M.'s Minister in China.

AND

WALTER CAINE HILLIER,
Chinese Secretary to H.B.M.'s Legation, Peking.

VOL. I.

SHANGHAI:
PUBLISHED AT THE STATISTICAL DEPARTMENT OF THE INSPECTORATE GENERAL OF CUSTOMS,
AND SOLD BY
KELLY & WALSH, LIMITED, SHANGHAI, YOKOHAMA, AND HONGKONG.
LONDON: W. H. ALLEN & Co., WATERLOO PLACE.

1886.

PREFACE TO SECOND EDITION.

The nature of the work entitled the "Tzŭ Êrh Chi," and the reason for adopting these words as its title, will be found explained in the Preface to the First Edition, published in 1867, and now (of course at the instance of my friends) reprinted with this. Seriously, that Preface may be found of some use to the beginner, and I do not object to being spared the trouble of re-casting it.

The principal changes introduced in the present edition are the following. Part III—the Forty Exercises—of the earlier edition was adversely criticised on two grounds. Elder scholars declared that the idioms were in many instances forced, and they stigmatised the phrases collected in it as Legation Chinese. I was Secretary of Legation at Peking, as well as Chinese Secretary, when I compiled the work. The phraseology, although frequently retouched, was no doubt open in some degree to this objection. The younger scholars, who took up the book as their primer, complained, on the other hand, that the method of the Exercises, each of which demanded an acquaintance with from 20 to 25 fresh words, new in form, in sound, and in meaning, laid too severe a tax upon ordinary memories.

I fear that my novices, at all events, were right, and, as a brief inspection of the revised Part III will show, the path of their successors has been compassionately smoothed. They will advance at the rate of from five to ten new words or characters a stage; they will be practised in very brief sentences before they come to the more ambitious exercises; and they will find relief in the more convenient typographical arrangement by which the Chinese and English texts are printed side by side. Lastly, they will derive, I trust, considerable advantage from the English-Chinese exercise that follows every exercise in Chinese-English, the Chinese text of which is given in the key, in Volume I.

Of this last I cannot boast that alone I did it. The idea was mine and I had begun to work it out; but my return to England in 1882, had I been physically and mentally equal to labour of the kind required, would have seriously postponed the completion of my task, for I am one of those who have *not* persuaded myself that I know the language as well as my native instructor, and I would not undertake to put forth Chinese of my own composing without a competent referee by my side. But I had the good fortune to possess some valuable English auxiliaries. Mr. WALTER HILLIER, then Assistant Chinese Secretary, but now deservedly filling the higher post of Chinese Secretary, carried back with him in 1883 the whole of the new text, completed or uncompleted. I think that the English-Chinese Exercises are entirely his work. There was also much to be done in the short sentences in small type, intended to illustrate the new vocabulary, the shorter sections of which have superseded the long column that so distressed the student of the old Forty Exercises. All that was wanting Mr. HILLIER has supplied, and it is to his proficiency as a speaker, in which capacity no Englishman to my knowledge surpasses him, that the removal of the reproach of sin against idiom may be chiefly ascribed. Errors, no doubt, remain to be denounced; but I am not without hope that this Part of the Colloquial Series will be held to have been greatly improved.

I was also indebted to Mr. DONALD SPENCE for his assistance on the voyage home in the completion of these short sentences, of which I had prepared little more than a fourth part; but his contribution, from the circumstances of time and place, was necessarily less significant than Mr. HILLIER'S. Mr. HILLIER, who is a high authority upon the tones of the Peking dialect, has also carefully corrected the tone-marks of every word in the first seven Parts of the new edition.

Part IV—the Ten Dialogues—remains as it was, except that Mr. HILLIER, as my plenipotentiary, has seen good to suppress the tenth dialogue, a conversation about the construction of the language. He has substituted for it a dialogue of his own composition. This, as it purports to take place between two friends at a restaurant, is no doubt a more palatable subject than that of the dialogue suppressed, against which more than one earnest beginner has been heard to protest as over-trying to digestion.

Part V—the Hundred Lessons—is the old Part VI, for an account of which the reader is referred to the old Preface. Mr. HILLIER has added the tone-marks to the words explained in the notes, but has not, to the best of my belief, disturbed the older translation.

Part VI—the Graduate's Wooing—is a redistribution of the matter of the old Part V, with many amendments and additions. It has a history of its own, which I had proposed to tell, in Chinese, in a brief preface to the text of the Part, but which I find, from the proofs forwarded me, has been left out. I reproduce my translation of it here, in honour of the native scholar to whom the credit of re-arranging the Chinese text is primarily due. I say primarily due, for, with the aid of another scholar, I added largely to the Chinese text.

"After some 20 odd years' desultory study of Chinese, written and spoken, the writer (myself) had compiled and published two elementary works on the language—the one being a collection of words and phrases, the other a collection of official documents. It became subsequently apparent that the want of all relation between the sentences given in two Parts of the Colloquial Course would make reference troublesome, and to obviate the difficulty which was being constantly brought before him, he had been thinking of throwing them together in a connected form, when, before effect could be given to his intention, YÜ TZŬ-PIN, a scholar of Manchuria, of his own motion took the "Hsi Hsiang Chi," or Story of the Western Wing, as a framework, and filled it up with the phrases of the Third and Fifth Parts of the Course, stringing them together consecutively—to the undoubted convenience of all future students. The idea was most excellent, and the writer has not been guiltless of presumption in taking upon him, with the help of some Chinese friends whose services he has enlisted, to abridge and modify certain passages in the story so constructed, and to amplify others.

"To the scholar YÜ TZŬ-PIN belongs indisputably the exclusive credit of the original conception. The merit of an improvement is not to be named in the same day with that of an invention. The writer does hope, nevertheless, that, thanks to the great care bestowed upon its revision by the native gentlemen who have taken part in it, the composition in its present shape will for certain be found an assistance to the student of colloquial Chinese as spoken at Peking."

The translation of the story of the Graduate's Wooing, or, more closely to follow the Chinese title I selected for it, the "Promise That Was Kept," is mine. When completed it was laid before certain of our students then passing their two years' novitiate in the Legation in 1881, in order that they might point out the passages requiring explanation. The copious notes which satisfy this requirement are one and all from the pen of Mr. HILLIER. As a story, I may observe, it pretends to no merit whatever, though it sufficiently represents the Chinese idea of what a love-tale should be. It is little more than a mechanical contrivance, as its closing chapter explains, for the bringing of certain phrases together so as to relieve the weariness of studying them detached. By an oversight, in the first line the epoch assigned it is that of the T'ang dynasty, A.D. 600–900, at which date treaties with the nations of the West were unknown, and foreign sportsmen did not, as related in Chapter XXXVI, shoot deer in the neighbourhood of a Chinese port.

There remain Parts VII and VIII. In the former—the Tone Exercises—I think that I see here and there traces of Mr. HILLIER's revising hand. The latter, entitled the Parts of Speech, he has left almost untouched. I have not revised it. To the best of my belief, its correctness, so far as it goes, has not been challenged. But it does not go far enough by a great deal, and it had been my intention to enlarge its limits considerably. It is difficult to teach Chinese grammar otherwise than, so to speak, incidentally. One has to multiply precedents, and the Part in question is, in my judgment, so framed as to furnish advantageous opportunity for illustration. Whether it will ever be my privilege to realise the hope entertained regarding its development, I am concerned to admit is now somewhat doubtful. Failing myself, may some younger workman be found willing to build upon the foundation I have laid, or, warned by its defects, to lay another.

I do not think it necessary to combat in detail all the differences of opinion regarding the orthography of the "TZŬ ÊRH CHI." The majority of Englishmen who have used the Course, now nearly twenty years on its trial, and a fair proportion of Americans, are in the main satisfied with it. Some experts in the organism of speech would prefer in certain syllables a modification of my system, but the changes they recommend appear to me to be on the side of complication rather than simplicity. One or two writers of mark, from the pains bestowed upon the question and the confidence with which they speak, might have been supposed to possess authority; but, in one case at least, my critic, I am justified in affirming, had positively no ear for any language, his own included; and the dialectic peculiarities of one or two others of those who have sat in judgment on the Syllabary have disinclined me to put full faith in their appreciation of Sound or Tone. My Syllabary is not absolutely unassailable, but, from debates upon the subject at which I have assisted, I doubt

PREFACE TO SECOND EDITION.

that any will ever be invented over the orthography of which there will not be the same kind of fight that there has been over mine and the systems of sinologues older than myself. The rendering of Chinese sounds by foreign alphabets—their transliteration, as it is called—is at the best but approximately successful. And so I leave the case to the charity of the rising generation, to assist whom in their progress *tzŭ érh chih yüan*, from what is near to what is far off, the course was devised.

On second thoughts, I shall allow myself a brief rejoinder to one or two of the objections raised against the Syllabary's prescriptions. The late Dr. WILLIAMS has emphatically protested against the disappearance of the 5th or re-entering tone. As I explained in the "Hsin Ching Lu," or Book of Experiments, in which the first edition of my Syllabary was published in 1859, the non-existence any longer of this tone in the *colloquial* language of Peking was first brought to my notice by YING LUNG-T'IEN, a fairly educated Pekingese and an admirable speaker, who of his own motion had re-arranged a complete vocabulary for me, under the tone categories practically in use. In his tables the whole of the 5th tone was merged in the 2nd, and when a year later I took up my abode in Peking, I found that YING LUNG-T'IEN was right. I have heard a very competent judge pronounce his distribution of the tones "invulnerable."

In the written language the 5th tone is, academically, recognised, and Dr. WILLIAMS when compiling a dictionary did nothing but what was right in retaining it. But he never could be made to understand that in reading aloud a lettered Chinese will utter a word with a different tone from that which may distinguish it when he is uttering it colloquially. The five-tone law is especially binding on the native, no matter what dialect he speaks,—in Cantonese there are eight tones, in Amoy, I believe, fifteen,—the law, I say, is especially binding on him in the verse or verse prose, which is one of his proudest accomplishments. Even in English poetry we have some experience of what we may be obliged to do by rhyme or other metrical condition. A better instance of the accommodation arrived at between two systems is supplied by the usage of the modern Greeks, whose pronunciation of a language much less far removed from its ancient form than Italian from Latin is—

when they speak—entirely under the sway of accent, but who would not be free when imitating the Homeric line in ancient Greek to ignore the prosodiacal rights of dactyl and spondee.

My scheme of orthography has been demurred to chiefly, I think, in three particulars. Syllables which to my ear commence with a soft *j*, such as I write *jan, jo, ju*, it appears to some of my friends should be written *ran, ro, ru*. I will not deny that students with a very fine ear have voted for the latter system. I cannot allow that they are right. It is noteworthy that in 1793, when LORD MACARTNEY visited Peking, the sound which I endeavour to represent by a soft *j* appeared to BARROW to be best represented by *zh*, the equivalent of the consonantal sound beginning the last syllable of contu*s*ion. It is true that in the century we have almost proof that various sounds, vowel and consonant, have changed; but BARROW's transliteration is worth observing. I shall add that whenever I have tried to make a Pekingese say after me *ran, ro, ru*, he has invariably pronounced the syllables *lan, lo, lu*. The tongue, in my belief, poises itself differently in the two efforts,—in the effort to bring out the soft *j*, and the effort to bring out *r*.

Two very good speakers contend that the syllable I write *kuang* is pronounced more like *kwong*. I shall here quote BARROW against myself. According to my system, I should write *K'ang-hsi* for the style of the second reign of this dynasty. BARROW writes it *Kaung-shee*. This, again, is valuable as indicating the impression of an uninitiated ear, and I shall admit that, although I have set down *a* as the *a* in *father*, it does in many cases approach the sound *awe*. But I cannot represent it by *o* as in *long* without infringing on the functions I have assigned that vowel elsewhere. In Cantonese the word I write *kuang* is indisputably *kwong*.

Lastly, there is the sound *êrh*, which has cost one of the two speakers above referred to no small amount of dissertation. If he reads the *ê* as the *e* in *merry*, he is right; but my rule prescribes that it must be read as in *merchant*. I cannot write *urh*, as Dr. MORRISON and others have written, because the vowel *u* is in my system the Italian *u*, and the syllable in question would then have to be pronounced *oorh*. And so I take leave of the discussion.

I must not close without an expression of sincere gratitude to SIR ROBERT HART, Inspector General of Customs in China, and indeed to the Customs Service in general. By SIR ROBERT HART's permission, the new edition has been printed at the press of the Customs establishment at Shanghai, and without one farthing of charge to myself. His Commissioner, Mr. DREW, as the head of the Statistical Department of the Customs Service, has supervised the impression, and to him and to Messrs. PALAMOUNTAIN and BRIGHT, members of his staff, as able as willing, for their nursing care of the new production during the last two years, I am bound to acknowledge a debt of obligation which it will be impossible for me to repay.

ATHENÆUM CLUB, LONDON,
    4th July 1886.

PREFACE TO FIRST EDITION.

"What Chinese is it that you want to learn, sir?" asked the first sinologue of established reputation that I consulted; "there is the language of the ancient classics, and the language of more modern books, and the language of official documents, and the epistolary language, and the spoken language, of which there are numerous dialects; now which Chinese is it that you wish to begin with?" The learned gentleman was one of a very small number who, at the time the Treaty of Nanking was signed, monopolised the credit of an acquaintance with the language, and, in the pride of this exceptional eminence, he was by no means averse to mystification of the uninitiated. Still, without doubt, the question with which he began and ended is the first that must be answered by anyone who aspires to learn Chinese, or professes to teach it; what does either mean by Chinese, divided as it is into written and spoken, and subdivided as the written and spoken languages are, the former by its variety of styles, the latter by more dialectic differences than the most advanced scholar is as yet in a position to define.

The answer must depend upon the vocation of the inquirer. Is he a philologist pure and simple, or a merchant who wishes for direct intercourse, orally or in writing, with his native constituents, or a missionary whose object is the propagation of spiritual truth, or an official interpreter whose duties, as an international agent, will continue, until such time as the Chinese become competent to interpret and translate for themselves, scarcely inferior to the duties of the missionary in importance?

The business of the writer is with aspirants of the last-mentioned class. It is one of his duties to direct the studies of the gentlemen destined to recruit the ranks of Her Majesty's Consular Service in China; and although the work now submitted to the public will not perhaps be esteemed valueless by either the missionary or the merchant who may use it, its primary object is to assist the Consular Student in grounding himself with the least possible loss of time in the spoken government language of this country, and in the written government language as it is read, either in books, or in official correspondence, or in documents in any sense of a public character.

The work is in two principal divisions, respectively denominated Colloquial and Documentary Series. The words TZŬ ÊRH CHI which recur in the title of both may be fairly translated Progressive Course. To go far, says a Chinese classic,* we must start *tzŭ êrh*, from what is near. The two courses are *chi*, collections of matter, of which that distinguished by

---

* The "Chung Yung," Rule of the Mean, or avoidance of extremes, the second of the Four Books known as Confucian, the bible of Chinese morality, contains the following passage:—

自 *tzŭ* 高 *kao* 如 *ju* 邇 *êrh* 必 *pi* 行 *hsing* 辟 *pi* 之 *chih* 君 *Chün*
卑。*pi* 必 *pi* 登 *têng* 辟 *pi* 自 *tzŭ* 遠 *yüan* 如 *ju* 道 *tao* 子 *tzŭ*

"The way [in wisdom] of the *chün-tzŭ* (model man) is as that of the traveller, who to go far must start from what is near; or of him that climbs, who to go high must start from what is low." Whoever would be a proficient must begin with what is elementary.

the prefix *yü yen*, words and phrases, is the colloquial; the other, being a collection of *wén chien*, written papers, the documentary course. The first, that contained in the present volume, is the only one of the two that is legitimately denominated progressive. This does lead the scholar *tzŭ êrh*, from what is near, to no inconsiderable distance in the spoken language, and if he have the patience thoroughly to master the text of it before venturing on the Documentary Series, he will have so familiarised himself with the form and meaning of written words as greatly to lessen his difficulties as a translator. Beyond this the Colloquial is not an introduction to the Documentary Series, nor can any one of the 16 parts of the latter be said to be an introduction to any other part; the term Series, therefore, as applied to the volume of documents, is in some sort a misnomer. But this is unimportant. That collection of papers fairly answers the end proposed, which is to set before the student, in bold type and properly punctuated, a number of specimens of Chinese documentary composition. A Key or Commentary, now in course of preparation, will accompany the course, and may possibly be followed by a translation of the whole of the papers contained in it.

Our immediate affair is the Colloquial Series, which occupies the volume before us. In the Appendices are repeated all the words that have been met with in the Chinese text, in the order in which they first occur. The Key forms an additional volume; the Syllabary,* of which more will be said by-and-by, another; and the Writing Course, another. The student is recommended to keep these four volumes separate.

The first Part of the Series is devoted to Pronunciation; the second, headed "The Radicals," to the construction of the written words ordinarily known as Chinese characters; the third, fourth, fifth, and sixth, are exercises, some in one shape, some in another, in the oral language of the metropolitan department, styled for brevity the Peking Dialect; the seventh is a set of exercises designed to illustrate the influence of the tones upon the dialect in question; the eighth and last, entitled a "Chapter on the Parts of Speech," is a talk in colloquial Chinese upon certain, though by no means upon the whole, of those conditions that are the equivalents in Chinese of such as we describe by the term grammatical. Something farther will be said regarding this last Part elsewhere, which will explain to the reader the occasion of this cautious periphrasis.

The order of the Colloquial Series has been dictated by the following considerations. The persons whose requirements it is the primary object of its compilation to satisfy are, as I have said above, Consular Students, to whom the knowledge of the written is not less indispensable than that of the oral language. They have to learn not only to talk, but to translate from and into written Chinese. Their foremost duty is beyond doubt application to the spoken language; not because there devolves upon the interpreter a heavier responsibility as a speaker than as a translator; on the contrary, an error in the *litera scripta* may be unquestionably of the greater significance; but because it is established by experience that while the difficulties of the written language give way perceptibly before a sustained effort to surmount them, even comparative proficiency in speaking is not to be achieved by adults of average aptitude unless the dialect to be spoken is specially and diligently laboured at while the ear is fresh. On the

---

* The Second Edition of the Syllabary will appear in the third volume.

other hand, it has been admitted by some of the very few foreigners who have limited themselves to the acquisition of a dialect phonetically, and some of the best speakers have so limited themselves, that the difficulties of the written language, when they did at last turn to it, appeared doubly disheartening. Why this should be so, it is needless here to inquire; the data on which either of the above conclusions is based are not abundant; but they suffice, in my opinion, to justify the recommendation that while, for a given time, he accept improvement in speaking as his chief obligation, the student should nevertheless allow himself to consider no word or phrase added to his vocabulary, of the written form of which he is not assured. He is not at all engaged by this injunction to the study of Chinese composition, between the idiom of which, no matter in which of its departments, and that of the colloquial language, no matter in which of its dialects, there are notable diversities; but he is called upon to examine with his eyes the constitution of every word or phrase that he is committing to memory. This conceded, that the eye is so far to assist the ear, it follows that his first step must be to acquaint himself with the construction of written words. He cannot do this until he is familiar with the Radicals, and accordingly a list of these, with translation, illustrations, and test tables, is supplied him in Part II. These are the indices under which all words are classed by modern Chinese lexicographers: many of them are themselves independent words used both in speech and writing; some are used in writing alone; some are obsolete symbols; but whether words or symbols, they must of course be retained each by name or sound, and as every sound has to be represented by a combination of the letters of foreign alphabets, a consideration of the orthographic system employed to this end must of necessity precede the study of the Radicals, and the system here employed is therefore assigned a place under the head of Pronunciation in Part I.

The question of Pronunciation, it will there be seen, is divided into Sound, Tone, and Rhythm. The two last are all-important, and have been farther treated of with some detail in the prefatory pages of the Key to Part VII. The first, which should rather have been described as Orthography, is of less consequence by much. No orthography that professes to reproduce the syllabic sound of a Chinese dialect is at the best more than an approximation. Neither vowels nor consonants, even when their defectiveness has been relieved by diacritic marks, are equal to the whole duty imposed upon them. Still, the learner, having made choice of a dialect, would soon find himself embarrassed if he tried to make way without any orthographic system at all, and his confusion of both sounds and tones would certainly be augmented if, while still in his apprenticeship, he attempted the fabrication of a system, in preference to adopting the work of an older hand. Students using the present work are of course left no option as to dialect or orthographic system. The system it provides, except that, to include certain occasional varieties, the number of syllables in it has been raised from 397 to 420, is almost the same as that contained in the "Hsin Ching Lu," an elementary work published by me in 1859. This system has been by no means universally approved, and although the objections taken to it have come generally from those who had commenced their studies before its appearance, it will be to the advantage of any beginner who may use it that these objections should be declared and combated *in limine*. But before going farther into this question, it may be as well to explain why the particular dialect here set before him has been selected.

Some standard was necessary. Scarcely any stranger can have heard the spoken language of China mentioned without observing that one form of it is alluded to as the Mandarin Dialect. This is the *kuan hua*; properly translated, the oral language of Government. The word *kuan*, an official, has been europeanised through the Portuguese as *mandarin*, and this term has become, as Mr. EDKINS remarks,* too convenient an equivalent for *kuan* to be lightly abandoned; but the word *dialect* is misleading, for the *kuan hua* is the colloquial medium not only of the official and educated classes, but of nearly four-fifths of the people of the Empire. In so vast an area, however, it follows that there must be a vast variety of dialects. Mr. EDKINS, than whom no one has more diligently explored the laws and limits of these differences, divides the *kuan hua* into three principal systems, the southern, the northern, and the western, of which he makes Nanking, Peking, and Ch'êng-tu, the capital of the province of Szechwan, respectively the standards. The Nanking mandarin, he observes, is more widely understood than that of Peking, although the latter is more fashionable; but he admits that "the Peking dialect must be studied by those who would speak the language of the Imperial Court, and what is, when purified of its localisms, the accredited *kuan hua* of the Empire."

The opinion here cited but confirms a conclusion long since arrived at by myself, to wit, that Pekingese is the dialect an official interpreter ought to learn. Since the establishment of foreign legations with their corps of students at Peking, it has become next to impossible that any other should take precedence. When, in due time, the beginner's services are required at the Yamên of Foreign Affairs, he finds that the language he has been learning is that spoken by the chief officers of the Imperial Government. Meanwhile, his teachers, servants, and nine-tenths of the people he comes in contact with, naturally speak nothing else. Lastly, whether it be the fact or not that the peculiarities of Pekingese are, as it is alleged, by degrees invading all other dialects of the mandarin, the student may rest assured that if he speak Pekingese *well*, he will have no difficulty in understanding or being understood by any mandarin-speaking native whose dialect is not a flagrant divergence from the standard under which it would be enrolled by the geographer or the philologist. I have seen one interpreter who was really a proficient in Pekingese as intelligible at Hankow as in the capital; I have known another, who was reputed to speak a local dialect of mandarin with fluency, unable to communicate with any mandarin but one whom circumstances had made familiar with the particular dialect he spoke.

This point, the selection of a dialect, decided, now some 20 years ago, the next step was the construction of an orthography. No one at the time had written on Pekingese, and the orthographies professing to represent the southern mandarin—those of Dr. MORRISON, compiler of the first dictionary in Chinese and English, Dr. MEDHURST, and Dr. WELLS WILLIAMS— were far from unassailable representatives of the native system they professed to reproduce. To the first, Mr. EDKINS goes so far as to deny all claim to be regarded as a mandarin orthography. "MORRISON," says he, "in preparing his very useful syllabic dictionary, was not aware that the sounds he followed were not mandarin at all, but an obsolete pronunciation." Dr. MEDHURST, with some modifications for the better, nearly copied Dr. MORRISON's orthography; not, he says, as being the best, but because it was the best known. Dr. WILLIAMS, working, I believe, in

* "Grammar of the Chinese Colloquial Language, commonly called the Mandarin Dialect," by the Rev. JOSEPH EDKINS. Shanghai, 1864. 2nd Edition, page 7.

concert with the lexicographer's accomplished son, Mr. JOHN ROBERT MORRISON, recast the system of the Syllabic Dictionary, but only so far as the mode of spelling is concerned. The last orthography, consequently, though more symmetrical, is, in my opinion, hardly nearer accuracy than the first.* The only sinologue of standing who spoke the Peking mandarin was Mr. ROBERT THOM. By his advice that dialect had been studied, and with great success, by Mr. THOMAS MEADOWS, and to the latter gentleman I was indebted not only for a right direction at starting, but for much assistance which there was at the time no one else within reach to afford. His "Desultory Notes" appeared shortly after, and to the chapters in that work relating to the language and administration of China, I am bound to acknowledge my obligations. These Notes contain, I believe, the first published scheme of a Pekingese orthography, but while admitting in general the justice of the author's appreciation of the characteristics of the dialect, I did not as a rule subscribe to his method of representing those characteristics; and although it was in the main due to Mr. MEADOWS's suggestions that I got upon the right track, I am not, on reflection, aware of having adopted anything from his system but the initial *hs*, of which more in the proper place.

My difficulty when I first tried to form a list of syllables was this, that no native work contained a syllabic system at all to be relied on. If you want to speak Cantonese as it is spoken in Canton, you can buy a vocabulary that will keep you perfectly straight so far as sound is concerned. The Chinese have a rude expedient which it is an abuse of terms to call spelling, by which a native who is more or less lettered can divine the sound of a new written word once he has found it. The written word *p'ao*, for instance, tells him the initial sound of a certain word; the written word *t'ien*, below *p'ao*, supplies the final; and amalgamation of *p'ao* and *t'ien* gives him *p'ien*. The Canton vocabulary is divided into chapters according to the tones, and the initials being arranged after a predetermined order, and the terminals, also in a fixed order, under every initial, the word sought is looked for under its terminal. The process of course involves some preliminary acquaintance with the Chinese written language. Other dialects besides Cantonese have similar standard vocabularies: there are some for various shades of the mandarin; there are also phrase books with elaborate orthographic systems for instructing outsiders, at all events Cantonese, in mandarin pronunciation; but the latter I found to possess, almost all, two serious defects, the mandarin they attempted to reproduce was both in idiom and sound an antiquated dialect, and the initial and final sounds combined in them to effect an imitation of the mandarin syllable, still presenting themselves to the provincial student as unmutilated syllables of the dialect he had been accustomed to speak, neither adequately informed the eye nor confirmed the ear.

It was not till 1855, when I had been making and re-making orthographies for some eight years, that a native author brought out a fair approximation to a Peking sound table. This was published at Canton; but my teacher, YING LUNG-T'IEN, had already of his own motion

---

* I should be sorry were it to appear that I spoke without sufficient respect for the labours of Dr. MORRISON. It is impossible, as Mr. MEADOWS has remarked, not to feel a sort of gratitude to one who has so abridged the toil of the student. Dr. WELLS WILLIAMS, the most industrious of sinologues, has nearly ready for the press a dictionary, which, as it will be an improvement upon his very useful work published some 10 years ago, will be a notable addition to the materials for an education in Chinese.

compiled for me an index of words, which, after reducing the syllables to alphabetic order, I eventually appended to the "Hsin Ching Lu" as the Peking Syllabary. His base was an old edition of the "Wu Fang Yüan Yin," Sounds in the general Language of the Empire according to their Rhymes,—a vocabulary with a most limited exegesis, but comprising some 10,000 authorised characters, that is, written words, arranged in five tone divisions (*see* Part I, page 6), the words in each division being classed with reference to 12 initials and 20 finals in a prescribed order. Having struck out of this all words that he thought unavailable for colloquial purposes, he re-classed the remainder, retaining the primitive initials and finals as indices of syllabic categories, but changing either the sound or tone, or both, of a large number of words, and entirely suppressing the 5th or re-entering tone. His judgments both on sound and tone I have found, during the seven years his table has been on trial, to be generally held correct. His measure of the number of words that should suffice a speaker has proved somewhat restricted, and this is remarkable, for his own stock of phraseology was as copious as it was elegant. He died in 1861, and to supply what was defective in his list, an independent selection has since been made for me by other native assistants, from a much larger vocabulary than that which he had dissected. The revised collection being then incorporated in the original Syllabary, a fresh copy of this and its Appendix was carefully prepared for the press under the superintendence of Mr. CHARLES BISMARCK, Chinese Secretary of the Prussian Legation, a scholar of much promise, whether as a speaker or translator. The new Appendix is entirely the work of his hand.

The value of the Syllabary, practically, is this. The eye and the ear, it will be borne in mind, are so to work together that no word is to be considered in the student's possession until he shall have assured himself of its written form. The written form, or character (*see* Part II, page 13), consists of two parts: the Radical, which vaguely indicates the sense of the word; the Phonetic, which vaguely indicates its sound. When his teacher uses a word unknown to the student, the latter, by referring to the Syllabary (and after a very short acquaintance with the orthography his ear will guide him to the right syllable), will find under that syllable not only the word he seeks in its proper tone class, and printed in its authorised form, but grouped as near as may be on the same line with it all words of the same sound which have also the same phonetic. His comparison of these, his observations of the difference between their radicals and the difference or identity of their tones, will do much to impress the word sought, with all its incidents—form, sound, and tone—upon the memory. In the absence of his teacher, again, he will find his recollection of the characters he ought to know, in general strengthened, and, particularly, his knowledge of the tones confirmed, by reference to the Syllabary, while the distinction between sounds and tones common to the same words is taught or recalled to him by the Appendix.

The method of spelling resorted to in this work, I have said above, has been more or less attacked. Accuracy being impossible, I have inclined to the combinations that seemed to me to reproduce most simply the syllabic sounds without indifference to the exigencies of the tone scale; and for the sake both of printer and student, I have always, where I could, employed alphabetic symbols in preference to diacritic marks. Thus the *i* as in *ship* is shortened in *chih*, *shih*, by the *h* which succeeds it, instead of being written *ĭ*. Neither *ch'ĭ* nor *chih* will be pronounced correctly without the information that must accompany any orthographic system, but it appears to me that the alphabetic method has the advantage of simplicity. The vowel *u* in the various diphthongs in which it figures is preferred to *w*, because, as the Tone Exercises in Part VII will show, the emphasis falls, under some tones, on the *u*, under others, on the vowel or vowels coming after it. The syllable *yu*, under some tones, reads like *yo* in *yore*, but it is elsewhere incontestably *yu*, and we want *yo* as a distinct sound for the syllable *yo* as in *yonder*. So with *iu* in the syllables *liu, miu, niu*. These, under some tones, are nearly *leyeu, meyeu, neyeu*, but under the 2nd tone the student will find that he requires, if I may call it so, the more monosyllabic sound of *liu*. For like reasons I prefer *ui* to *uei*. The sound which is, to my ear, *er* in *perch*, or *ur* in *murrain*, Mr. EDKINS writes *ri*; I have preferred *êrh*. The initial *j* is intended to approach the sound of *s* in *fusion*, *z* in *brazier*, the French *j* in *jaune*. If the organs exercised in the pronunciation of this consonant be closely watched, it will no doubt appear that it is preceded by something like *r* or *er*; but not so markedly as to call for special indication. A speaker softening the *j* as in French will be as surely understood when he says *ju jo* as if he strives to utter a modification of *ru ro*; indeed, with greater certainty than if he makes this latter effort. Lastly, there is the initial *hs*, which some complain is liable to confusion with *sh*. The aspirate precedes the sibilant; if the first *i* in *hissing* be dropped, you retain very exactly the Chinese syllable *hsing*. Rules cannot go far in such matters. The ear must advise itself by practice.*

On the sounds which I write *ssŭ, tzŭ*, and *tz'ŭ*, it is scarcely necessary to discourse. The vowels in these syllables defy a European alphabet more obstinately than any we have to deal with. Dr. MORRISON's *sze* was changed by Dr. WILLIAMS to *sz'*. I used this for many years, but a tendency I noticed in some speakers to pronounce the syllable *sizz*, determined me to restore the vowel. Mr. EDKINS writes *si*, which is neither better nor worse than *ssŭ*, or, as it

---

* This initial *hs*, as the Sound Table will show, is only met with before the vowel sounds of the Italian *i* or the French *u*, and the syllables beginning with it have a history of their own which claims a passing remark. Many of the words now pronounced *hsi* were some years ago *hi*, many others *si*; similarly, words now pronounced *hsü* were some of them *hü* and some *sü*. In very modern mandarin vocabularies these syllabic distinctions are preserved. The fusion of them is variously accounted for. While the Peking Syllabary was undergoing revision, I was urged by my friend Mr. EDKINS to admit into my orthography some change that might serve as an index of the original sound in the case of words differing as above, and had the work been of a lexicographic character, I would have adopted the suggestion. Nothing could be easier than to mark all words that have been HI, as H^sI, and all that have been SI, as ^HSI; so with *hsü* and *sü*; and to the philologist this recognition of pedigree might be of a certain value; but the syllable to be learned by the student of the colloquial language in this dialect, whether he express it by *hsi*, *hsü*, or otherwise, is still a sound common to all the words classed under it by the native speakers who compiled the syllabaries. The change would have involved a double tabular arrangement under all the syllables concerned, and it is to be doubted whether the beginner would not have been rather confused than advantaged by having what is now become, practically, but one category of sound, subdivided into two. If I live to publish a vocabulary (not of Pekingese, but of mandarin in general), for which I have been for some years collecting materials, the peculiarity will not be left unnoticed.

The initial *ch* is common before all the vowels, but wherever it precedes the above vowel sounds, *i* or *ü*, it has been, and in other dialects still is, either *k* or *ts*. Thus *kiang* and *tsiang* are now both pronounced by a Pekingese, *chiang*; *kin* and *tsin* have both become *chin*. With some speakers the articulation will sometimes vacillate between *ch* and *ts* in these sounds, but the *ch* as a rule predominates, and you never hear the *k* hard. It is an instance of the caprice of these dialectic peculiarities that in the adjoining department of Tientsin, *ch* is *ts* even before *a*; the word *ch'a*, tea, is *ts'a*. At Shanghai, it is something like *dzó*; at Foochow, *t'a*; at Amoy *t'i* (our *tea*); and at Canton, again *ch'a*.

read in the old Syllabary, *szŭ*. The vowel that *ĭ* or *ŭ* is supposed to stand for does not exist in our system, and, represent it by what letter we will, some diacritic mark is indispensable.

For practical purposes the beginner, having at his side of course a native instructor,—no orthography, however scientific, will teach him to pronounce without one,—will find, I believe, the illustrations that accompany the orthography in Part I, with the farther observations prefixed to the Key of Part VII, amply sufficient to regulate his ear. Until some more ambitious dictionary than any as yet published by a foreigner, overbears the distinctions taken by existing controversialists, controversy on the subject of syllabification will continue. The notes attached to the different parts of this course will enable the beginner to dispense almost entirely with a dictionary, and I would advise him, for the time being, to take what they tell him upon trust, and until he shall have reached a point considerably beyond their limits, to refrain from theorising in the matter either of sense or of sound.

The notice on the third page of the Key will enable anyone to proceed with Part III who has fairly worked up the Test Tables in Part II, and then onward to the end of Part VI. The principle of instruction in all these, especially in Part III, is, to a certain extent, that which the methods of AHN and OLLENDORFF have popularised in Europe. To a certain extent only. All specimens of these methods that I have examined, it is true, at once introduce the pupil to a certain stock of words and sentences; but the order of their lessons is regulated by that of the divisions of ordinary European grammars. They begin with the Article, decline the Noun, conjugate the Verb, and so on. I shall have to refer again to the absence of inflexional mechanism in Chinese, and the consequent impossibility of legislating as in other tongues for its etymology. Suffice it here to say, that preliminary investigation of etymological laws aids us less in this than perhaps in any language; the sooner we plunge into phraseology the better. The Forty Exercises of Part III were prepared two years ago, at first with 50 characters in the vocabulary column placed on the right of each. A gentleman of above average proficiency in certain European languages, whom chance made the *corpus vile* of the experiment, remonstrated against the magnitude of this task as excessive for a tyro. The vocabulary was accordingly reduced, and after four revisions, the Exercises were left as they now are. The progress of the Consular Students who have used them in manuscript is fair guarantee of their utility as elementary lessons.

The Ten Dialogues of Part IV, which come next, were dictated by me to a remarkably good teacher of the spoken language, who of course corrected my idiom as he took them down. The matter of most of them is trivial enough, but they give the interpreter some idea of a very troublesome portion of his duties, namely, the cross-examination of an unwilling witness. It was with this object that they were composed.

The Dialogues are followed by the Eighteen Sections,* the term section being chosen for no reason but to distinguish the divisions of this Part V from those of the foregoing parts and of the next succeeding one. The phrases contained in each of its 18 pages are a portion of a larger collection written out years ago by YING LUNG-T'IEN. I printed the Chinese text of this, with a few additions of my own, in 1860. Finding them in some favour with those

* Incorporated in Part VI, Second Edition.

who have used them, I have retained all but my own contributions to the original stock, or such phrases in the latter as are explained in other parts of this work, and now republish them as a sort of continuation of Part III. The contents of that Part are in Chinese styled *San Yü*, detached phrases; those of the fifth Part are *Hsü San Yü*, a supplement to those phrases. The intermediate Dialogues are *Wên Ta Chang*, question and answer chapters, and the papers which follow in Part VI are *T'an Lun P'ien*, or chapters of chat, for distinction's sake entitled The Hundred Lessons. These last are nearly the whole of a native work compiled some two centuries since to teach the Manchus Chinese, and the Chinese Manchu, a copy of which was brought southward in 1851 by the Abbé Huc. Its phraseology, which was here and there too bookish, having been thoroughly revised by YING LUNG-T'IEN, I printed it with what is now reduced to the *Hsü San Yü*; but it has since been carefully retouched more than once by competent natives.

The Sections and Lessons of the two last Parts possess the advantage of being the spontaneous composition of native speakers. As such they are of course more incontestably idiomatic than the Exercises and Dialogues of Parts III and IV.

The words *Lien Hsi Yen Shan P'ing Tsê Pien*, which form the Chinese title of Part VII, will translate freely as Exercises in the Tone System of Peking, and the prefecture in which it stands. Of the Exercises themselves it is unnecessary to say much more than that, from the very commencement, the student will do well to have a portion of them read over and over again to him daily by his teacher, whom he should try to follow *vivâ voce*. This will be to many a very irksome operation, and the Exercises are all translated in order that the learner may be spared the dulness of attending to the sound of words in complete ignorance of their sense; but their chief end is to drill him thoroughly in the nature and law of the tones, and although, if he retain their meanings, he will find a large share of these a useful addition to his vocabulary, he should be more anxious to acquire from them a just notion of the rules and practice of accentuation, which they are intended to illustrate. His command of speech will be every day receiving accessions from the earlier portions of the Series, on which he will naturally bestow the greater share of his attention. The Key to this Part will inform him of the plan of these Tone Exercises, which are in the order of the syllables alphabetically arrayed in the Sound Table appended to Part I.

He is at the same time specially invited to observe the principle on which the Chinese notes appended to the characters that act as syllabic indices in this Part are constructed.

The *tzŭ*, written words of the Chinese language, as observed in Part I, are some thousands, while the *yin*, sounds, by which the *tzŭ* are called, are but a few hundreds, in number. Many of the *tzŭ* will never be met with in the oral language, but whether the student be engaged on the oral language or the written, his instructor will be constantly making reference, by its *yin*, to such or such a *tzŭ*; and inasmuch as, under many of the sounds, a number of *tzŭ* are known not only by one *yin*, syllabic sound, but often by the same *shêng*, intonation, of that sound, the confusion between the *tzŭ* alluded to and other homophonous *tzŭ*, unless the written form of the first be before the hearer's eye, may be imagined. The difficulty is fairly met by the Chinese practice of recalling the dissyllabic or polysyllabic combination in which the *tzŭ* spoken of most commonly plays a part. Just as in English, if it be necessary to particularise whether by a certain sound we mean *wright*, *write*, *right*, or *rite*, we make our meaning clear by a context that shows whether the syllable uttered is that in ship*wright*, to *write* letters, *right* and left, or *rite* of baptism, so a Chinese will explain that the *ai* he is speaking of is the *ai* in *ai-ch'iu*, to implore, in *ch'ên-ai*, dust, in *kao ai*, tall and short, or in *ai-hsi*, to love; but homophony being in his language as much the rule as in ours it is the exception, he is very constantly obliged to fall back on this expedient.

The moral of this digression is that when studying Chinese, oral or written, the student should always endeavour to connect a newly discovered monosyllable with its best known associate; if his teacher be worth anything he will always be ready with this when called upon; and then, never forgetting that in a large majority of instances the *tzŭ*, no matter with what others they may combine, preserve their capability of employment as independent monosyllables or in distinct alliances, he will find the difficulties presented by the acquisition of a *primâ facie* monosyllabic language considerably diminished. The dialogue which closes the Supplement of Part VIII is an illustration of the difficulty in question, and the expedient proposed to remove it.

And now to come to the eighth and last Part of this Series. After what has been said above on the subject of grammatical analysis, the introduction of a chapter purporting to treat of the Parts of Speech in Chinese may be thought an inconsistency. The reader is requested to bear in mind that the chapter is not, and does not assume to be, a grammar. It is no more than the result of an experiment which there has not been time to elaborate, of an attempt to set before the student some of the chief contrasts and analogies in the grammatical conditions of inflected English and uninflected Chinese.

The foreign linguist tells us that Grammar, as the Science of Words, is divisible into Etymology and Syntax, and that etymology again subdivides itself into the laws of Inflexion and of Derivation. The Chinese language yields but a qualified submission to this decree. In the sense of *derivation* its etymology has something in common with that of other tongues; in the sense of *inflexion* it has no etymology.

As to derivation, the pedigree of all single words in Chinese is to a certain point accessible, for the single words have, with rare exceptions, each one its representative in the written language, and these representative forms, called with some confusion Chinese characters, are invariably made up of two elements known to foreign sinologues as the Radical and the Phonetic. The radical indicates the category of *sense*, the phonetic the category of *sound*, to which any word belongs. Neither radical nor phonetic, it is true, is in all cases such an index of sense or sound as to ensure prompt recognition of either; for although there has never been in Chinese that fusion of parts that has so obliterated the primitive features of other languages, the monosyllabic sound has been in many instances modified in the course of time, and both radicals and phonetics, but especially the latter, there is reason to believe, have on occasion been corruptly exchanged. Still, the native dictionaries supply us with information fairly satisfying as regards the hereditary descent of some thousands of the single words constantly met with. In what we may call polysyllabic combinations, the work is apparently easier, because each syllable is a word in its original integrity, and we are at first sight led to infer that explaining the separate parts we can explain the whole. But it is far from being always evident how, its ancient or its more modern signification considered, the word claiming attention has come to play the part it does as the confederate of the word or words to which we now see it allied. The sense in which the compound is used, both colloquially and in writing, is frequently to be arrived at only by referring to the text of the classical work in which it first appears, or of the historian or other later writer who has applied the classical quotation after a fashion of his own; and interpretation of the polysyllabic compound by, as it were, a sub-translation of its component parts will often be as utterly misleading as an explanation of the epithet Shakesperian based on the hypothesis that the words *shake* and *spear* contain the secret of its meaning.

It is essential, therefore, that while examining each member of a compound apart, for without this examination the single word will not be retained in his memory, the student should be on the watch against temptation too eagerly to adopt what may seem the self-evident conclusion deducible from his analysis. This caution is not wholly valueless with reference to any of the polysyllabic languages, where it is but seldom that the compound retains its parts so unmodified as to force upon us the recollection of their independent significations; but it is doubly necessary in Chinese because, from the relation of the spoken and written languages, no one syllable of a compound ever presents itself in any other form than what belongs to it when it is employed as an independent monosyllable. Experience of the danger to which a vicious process of etymological investigation exposes the translator must be my excuse for occupying so much space with the subject.

As to the other branch of etymology, namely, inflexion, it cannot, I repeat, be allowed to have a place in Chinese grammar at all; and the versatility, if it be lawful to call it so, of the Chinese word, the capacity common to so many words (especially to those that we are wont to call nouns and verbs), for grammatical services so widely differing, is such that any attempt to divide the language authoritatively into the categories known to us as Parts of Speech would be futile. Still, our parts of speech must of course have their equivalents in Chinese, whether we are able to categorise them as parts of speech or not; nor could Chinese be a language unless it possessed within itself the means of producing most of the results effected in all other tongues by inflexion. It does not break off portions of its words or incorporate in them fragments of words, extant or obsolete, for the purpose of indicating the conditions we describe by the terms Case, Number, Mood, Tense, Voice, or the like; but it achieves nearly as much as these modifications can effect by a syntactic disposition of words, all extant, and almost all universally retaining their power to employ themselves integrally and independently elsewhere.

Now, for speculative purposes there are various treatises on mandarin grammar which may be perused with profit by the more advanced student—in particular, those by M. BAZIN and Mr. EDKINS; but I have no faith in these, or in any grammar that I have examined, as helps, *in the beginning*, towards acquisition of the spoken language. It occurred to me, nevertheless, shortly after I had put my hand to the elementary course now published, that if this were accompanied by a collection of examples that should give some notion, as I have said above, of the contrasts and analogies of the two languages, it might avail to remove some of the stumbling-blocks common to beginners in either, without committing them to the bondage of rules fashioned too strictly after our European pattern; and taking the simplest school grammar I could find, I went through its etymology with the able teacher before mentioned, translating the examples to him *vivâ voce*, and expounding to the best of my ability the rules and definitions these examples were intended to illustrate. Our embarrassment was a grammatical nomenclature, for as China does not as yet possess the science of grammar, she is of course very ill found in its terminology; and the reader will see to what straits the would-be grammarian is reduced in describing, for instance, the Case of the noun. The teacher, thus inoculated, suggested sundry amplifications and curtailments as we read on, and the text finally approved being submitted to another learned native, he pronounced it to be a *Yen Yü Li Lüo*, or Summary of the Laws of Phraseology, by which somewhat pretentious designation it is accordingly distinguished in the "Tzŭ Êrh Chi." The experiment was pursued so desultorily, and the Chapter on the Parts of Speech, as I prefer to call it, is so crude and incomplete a production, that I am scarcely willing to expose it to the criticism of the majority, who, notwithstanding the modesty of this title, can scarce fail to be as little pleased with it as its author. To the beginner, for all that, and it is for the beginner that the colloquial course is intended, its text and notes will prove of a certain value; not the least this, that its matter and method will together provide both his Chinese teacher and himself with a means of adding largely to the kind of information which the chapter does not profess more than partially to supply. The Memorandum before mentioned will show how I think he will best turn its contents to account.

The whole Colloquial Series has been either written or re-written in the last two years, and it has been printed, with the Documentary Series, at Shanghai in the last few months. The fact that five presses, scarce any of them accustomed or adapted to the execution of printing on a grand scale, have been employed at the same time upon the volumes now issued, must be my excuse for the long list of errata appended to some of them. The errors noticed would have been more numerous but for the friendly offices of Messrs. Mowat and Jamieson, Consular Assistants stationed at Shanghai. The former gentleman bids fair to become an authority upon the tone system. I am indebted to him for calling my attention to a grave oversight in the construction of the 3rd Tone Exercises in Part VII, and it is to his accuracy and diligence that the present correctness of the Key to that Part is mainly to be ascribed.

If I do not wind up, as is the wont of diffident writers, with a depreciation of the merits of my work, it is not because I am blind to its imperfections. Still, these admitted, a campaign extending over about a quarter of a century encourages me to believe that the Series will be of no small assistance to the interpretorial wants which it is more particularly designed to relieve. The collection of elementary matter it contains will put any student of ordinary aptitude and application in possession of a very respectable acquaintance with the oral language in one twelvemonth from the day he arrives at Peking. The course is far from exhaustive, but the speaker who can pass in it will find himself in a position of which he need not be ashamed. Let him give it a fair chance for at least his first 18 months, and above all let him abstain during that period from exploration of any shorter path to perfection that he may imagine he has discovered; from all original attempts at systematisation. There is much about the written language to lure a novice from what he may not unnaturally regard as the less serious, because it appears the less formidable, undertaking. A man with a quick ear may fancy that, working at written texts with a native instructor, the verbal explanations of the latter will bring him the habit of speech without any special consecration of his powers to its acquirement, and his progress in reading is so much more evident, and as such so flattering to his self-love, that he may easily persuade himself to prefer the labour that seems to promise the more immediate remuneration of his pains. There can be no greater error. If he yield to the temptation, if he neglect the spoken language for the written during his novitiate, he will repent his mistake throughout the whole of his career. Even when his acquaintance with the colloquial course before him shall have satisfied a competent examiner, he must not by any means look upon the oral language as a thing that will now take care of itself. All that the course professes to give him is a respectable foundation. To fit himself for the higher duties of his calling, he must considerably enlarge his range. For this purpose he can draw on no better source than popular fictions of the country. The dialogue and descriptions, under proper guidance, will enrich his vocabulary, and he will gather from both a knowledge of Chinese thought and character, which, restricted as difference of habits makes our intercourse with this people, is nowhere else more pleasantly or usefully supplied. In Chinese, of all languages, it is an economy of time to consult a good translation; and the student may safely trust to Sir JOHN DAVIS's version of "The Fortunate Union," or to those of "Les deux Cousines" and "Les jeunes Filles lettrées," recently published by M. STANISLAS JULIEN, the greatest of living sinologues. But, translated or untranslated, the novel should be read with a native sufficiently learned to explain the allusions in it, and to guard his pupil against too ready adoption of its phrases as colloquial. A fair proportion of them, of course, are colloquial, but deeply as the vulgar tongue of China is rooted in her literature, there is much in such works as we are speaking of that is far too classical for everyday use, and the random employment of quasi-Johnsonian phraseology would be to a native hearer as astounding as Sir WALTER SCOTT's visitors are stated to have thought his resuscitation of FROISSART. This rock avoided, the future interpreter should remember that improvement in its form is scarcely less a duty than augmentation of his vocabulary.

It is in no spirit of academical purism that I make this observation. It is justified by the peculiar circumstances which render the relations of the foreign and Chinese official so far from satisfactory. The latter, rising from the educated class, which is in reality the governing class of this Empire, is a man thoroughly conversant with the philosophy, history, law, and polite literature of his own country, and there is nothing that more confirms him in the stubborn immobility which so baffles the foreign agent than his conviction that it is impossible for that barbarian to rise to the level of Chinese education. The discussion of affairs may often be conducted, I grant, in Chinese little better than the French of ARTHUR PENDENNIS, without any perceptible prejudice to the interests immediately at stake; but I hold that the foreign agent is responsible for something more than a mere hand-to-mouth despatch of his daily business. It is essential to the interests of China and of foreign nations alike that the governing class should be brought to amend its erroneous estimate of foreign men and foreign things. His opportunities of influencing it are not numerous, but with the exception of the foreign agent, there is no one who possesses any opportunity of influencing the governing class at all.

Beginning as late as most of us begin, it would be hardly possible, were it desirable, that we should traverse the enormous field in which a lettered Chinese is so at home, but it is by no means an extravagant ambition that our speech should become sufficiently polished to disabuse the learned man of his belief that we are incapable of cultivation; and it lies, I say, almost exclusively with the foreign official to commence the removal of this impression. I had hoped to bring out this year a short history of China, which might have served to introduce the student interpreter to that higher style of language to which I conceive it incumbent upon him to strive to advance; but this, with some other enterprises projected on his behalf, must wait. Pending their maturity, I commend to his patient attention the humbler phraseology of this elementary course.

SHANGHAI, 16th *May* 1867.

CONTENTS.

	PAGE.
MEMORANDUM FOR THE GUIDANCE OF THE STUDENT	xxvii

PART I.—PRONUNCIATION:—

    Sound or Orthography... 3

    Tone 7

    Rhythm... 9

    Sound Table 10

PART II.—THE RADICALS:—

    Explanatory Remarks 20

    General Table 22

    Modifications 30

    Test Table I 31

    Test Table II 32

    Test Table III 33

    Exercises in the Colloquial Radicals 35, 34

    Key to the Exercises in the Colloquial Radicals 36

PART III.—*San Yü Chang*, THE FORTY EXERCISES (Chinese Text) 45

PART IV.—*Wên Ta Chang*, THE TEN DIALOGUES (Chinese Text) 156–127

PART V.—*T'an Lun P'ien*, THE HUNDRED LESSONS (Chinese Text) 230–157

PART VI.—*Chien Yo Chuan*, THE GRADUATE'S WOOING, or THE STORY OF A PROMISE THAT WAS KEPT (Chinese Text) 284–231

PART VII.—*Lien Hsi Yen Shan P'ing Tsê Pien*, THE TONE EXERCISES (Chinese Text) 285

PART VIII.—*Yen Yü Li Lüo*, THE PARTS OF SPEECH (Chinese Text)... 350–314

ERRATA 351

MEMORANDUM FOR THE GUIDANCE OF THE STUDENT.

1. The Tables of Errata will be found at page 351 of Volume I and page 521 of Volume II, and the student's first care should be to amend the text throughout.

2. Having secured a teacher, he should have the Sound Table given on page 10 read over to him, carefully noting the value of the vowels and consonants employed in the orthography, as explained on pages 3–7.

3. There is nothing to prevent him at the same time studying the Radicals. He will find on page 20 sufficient information as to the course he is to pursue with these.

4. To retain them he should write them out, and, to avoid a false direction, he had better copy them as he finds them in the Writing Exercises (Volume III), of which they form the first part. His teacher will show him how they must be traced, and while he forms his hand by the practice, the interval that he devotes to it will relieve both eye and ear.

5. As soon as he is fairly familiar with the Tables and Exercises on pages 31–43, he will proceed to Part III.

6. From the moment he has read Part I, he should, for at least an hour a day, have read to him a portion of the Tone Exercises in Part VII. He will see that Volume II supplies him with a full translation of these; but, as I have observed in the Preface, he need not at first regard the Tone Exercises as a contribution to his vocabulary. In the orthography there given, the tone of every syllable is marked in the manner explained in Part I, page 8; these tone marks will assist his ear, and he must patiently repeat what his teacher will read aloud to him, till the latter pronounces his intonation correct. When he comes to Part III, he should not only watch his teacher's intonation of the single words, combined words, and short sentences, but he should continually invite his criticism as well as that of other teachers. His attention is at the same time particularly called to the observations on page 421 of Volume II, regarding the rhythm of short sentences or other polysyllabic combinations. Until he has finished Part III, he need not trouble himself with the Syllabary (in Volume III), but thenceforth it should be frequently consulted, and the difference in breathing should be as carefully noted as that in tone. *See* remarks on page 7 of Part I.

7. I should recommend that the English version of Part VIII be read through as soon as the student is ready to go on with Part III. The translation which accompanies this in Volume II and the Notes will tell him almost all he can require to know about the Exercises in this Part; but he will soon begin to apply what he learns from these in conversation with his teacher, and the text of Part VIII (Volume II), especially from page 486 to the end, will often stand him in the stead of a vocabulary. More careful examination of the Chinese text of Part VIII may be deferred until he has accomplished the Ten Dialogues. He will then find himself able to read all the short dialogues illustrative of the verb, adverb, etc.

8. As to general directions. I have insisted much in the Preface to the First Edition upon the danger of being seduced from the spoken by the attractions of the written language. The student must equally guard against a temptation to abandon the more fatiguing for the easier parts of the Colloquial Series. A man of average aptitude and power of work should be able to pass in the Forty Exercises in a few months. He will then know by sight the written forms of some 1,200 words, the Radicals included. There are not 300 new words in Part IV—the Ten Dialogues,—and he will fly through these consequently in a few days; but I should urge him to read them some eight or ten times before he goes farther. Part V—the Hundred Lessons—contains several dialogues, and these, and of course, similarly, the dialogues of Part IV, will be best turned to account by having them read aloud by two teachers. As the student goes through either of these Parts with notes and translation, he should engage one of his colleagues to combine with him in this *vivâ voce* exercise. The value of listening is scarcely enough appreciated in any language. The learner is generally too anxious to begin to talk. Part VI—the Graduate's Wooing—calls for no remark that does not apply to the two foregoing.

Finally, let the more eager beware of over-zeal at starting, and let all, as far as in them lies, have fixed hours for the different sections of their work. They are proposing to themselves, primarily, the acquisition of the oral language, and, subsidiarily, such acquaintance with its written forms as will enable them to recognise those they have met in reading, and to reproduce them in writing. For the time being the last object is of the less consequence. The more important is the first; but if the student is to use this course, the first is scarcely separable from the second. The relative quickness of the eye and ear is so different in different persons that proportions of work to be assigned to either must be left to the individual. He should early decide which it is incumbent on him to use the more—learning by his teacher's repetition of the text, if his ear is slow; re-perusing the text, if he finds that the characters slip from his memory. Under any circumstances, let him as soon as possible lay down a rule for the division of his time—so much for reading, so much for writing, so much for exercise of the ear, whether listening or conversing; and for some months to come let him be slow to disturb his rule. There is no language of which the acquirement is so forwarded by method as the Chinese, be the memory quick or slow.

PART I.

PRONUNCIATION.

PART I.
PRONUNCIATION.

1. In order to correctness of pronunciation in Chinese, three conditions must be satisfied; there must be accuracy of Sound, of Tone, and of Rhythm.

Of these three conditions, accuracy of sound, as considered with reference to the expression of it, syllabically or alphabetically, is the least important. We run less chance of being misunderstood if we say *lan* for *nan*, for instance, provided that we preserve the correct tone, than if we were to say *nan*[2] when we should have said *nan*[1].

Still, we must have a distinct idea of the syllable we are to pronounce, and as Chinese furnishes, in comparison with our alphabets, nothing but the most imperfect aid to the end in view, we are forced to supply the deficiency by combinations of our own alphabetic symbols, sometimes at the rate of their prescriptive values, sometimes reinforcing them by diacritic marks, or arbitrarily constraining them to do a duty for which there is little precedent.

2. Sound.—The values assigned to the letters of the alphabet employed in the spelling of the syllables given below are here considered independently of *tone*; but the syllable has been spelt generally in the form that appeared to approach nearest to an adequate representation of the spoken *sound*, and at the same time to admit, without change of the letters composing it, of an application to it of the inflections proper to a change of *tone*.

Vowels and Diphthongal Sounds.

a. The *a* in *father*; when pronounced singly, in particular after words terminating in vowel-sounds, slightly nasalised, as though preceded by '*ng*.

ai. Nearly our sound *aye*, but better represented by the Italian *ai*, in *hái, amái*.

ao. The Italian *ao* in *Aosta, Aorno*; but not unfrequently inclining to *á-oo*, the Italian *au* in *cauto*.

e. In *eh, en*, as in *yet, lens*.

ei. Nearly *ey* in *grey, whey*, but with greater distinctness of the vowels, as in the Italian *lei, contei*.

é. Nearest approached in English by the vowel-sound in *earth*, in *perch*, or in any word where *e* is followed by *r*, and a consonant not *r*; as in *lurk*. Singly, or as an initial, it has the nasal prefix '*ng* stronger than the syllable *a*.

éi. The foregoing *é* followed enclitically by *y*. Strike out the *n* from the word *money*, and you have the syllable *méi*. If the syllable *néi* exist at all (which some Chinese, who pronounce it *nui*, dispute), the *éi* is most apparent in *néi*.

érh. The *urr*, in *burr, purr*.

i. As a single syllable, or as a final, the vowel-sound in *ease, tree*; in *ih, in, ing*, shortened as in *chick, chin, thing*.

ia. With the vowels distinct; not *ya*, but as in the Italian *piazza, Maria.* In some syllables terminating in *ia, iang, iao,* the *ia* is in certain tones almost *éa* or *eyah.* This is oftener observable where the initial is *l, m,* or *n ;* but even with these the usage is capricious.

iai. The *iaj* in the Italian *vecchiaja.*

iao. The vowels as in *ia* and *ao,* with the terminal peculiarity of the latter. This sound is also modified by the *tone.*

ie. With the vowels distinct, as in the Italian *siesta, niente.* The *i* is modified, as in the case of *ia,* under similar circumstances; that is, in certain tones *ie* inclines to become *éé,* or *eyeh,* often making *lien, nien* almost *leyen, neyen.*

io. Shorter than the Italian *io ;* more nearly the French *io* in *pioche.*

iu. As a final, nearly *eeyew* or *eeoo,* at all times longer than our *ew.* Thus *chiu* is not *chew,* but rather *chyew,* and the tone may make the vowel sounds even more distinct. In the syllables *liu, niu,* the *i* is affected as in *ia, ie ;* they become almost *leyew, neyew.* In *chiung, hsiung* (the only syllables ending in consonants into which I have introduced *iu*), it must be admitted that in most instances, though not in all, the *iung* is rather *eeyōng* than *eeyoong,* the *ō* representing *o* in *roll.*

o. Something between the vowel-sound in *awe, paw* and that in *roll, toll.* When single, it commences with a slight consonantal sound, part nasal and guttural, which the *'ng* inadequately expresses, and is inflected at the close as if an *a* or *ah* were appended to it. The tones seriously modify this syllable. As a final the power of the vowel remains the same, with the same terminal inflection, and not altogether divested of the guttural peculiarity which it is not within the compass of our alphabet to reproduce. Let the reader, as an experiment, try to pronounce *lo* as *law,* prolonging the *aw* in his throat.

ou. In reality *éō ;* the vowel-sounds in *burrow* when all the consonants are withdrawn; in English, nearest the *ou* in *round, loud.*

ü. When uttered alone, as it is at times for *yü,* or when a final, nearest the vowel-sound in the French *eût, tu.* In *ün* it is not so long as in the French *une ;* but nearer the *ün* in the German *München.*

üa. Occurs only in the final *üan,* which in some tones is *üen ;* the *ü* as above, but the *a* much flatter than in the final *an ;* nearer the *an* in *antic.*

üe. The *ü* as above, the *e* as in *eh ;* the vowel-sounds in the French *tu es* represent this combination perfectly.

üo. A disputed sound, used, if at all, interchangeably with *io* in certain syllables.

u. When single (as at times instead of *wu*), and when a final, the *oo* in *too ;* in *un* and *ung* it is shorter, as in the Italian *punto, lungo.* In the latter final it vacillates between *ung* and *ōng,* being nasalised at the close so as to produce a sound between the French *long* and *longue.*

ua. As we pronounce it in Juan; nearly *ooa,* which in many instances contracts to *wa.* In the finals *uan, uang* it is also sometimes *óa* or *oá,* as the tones may rule.

uai. As in the Italian *guai ;* the above sound *ua,* with the *i* in *ai* appended to it ; the *u* subject to the same changes as in *ua.*

PART I.—PRONUNCIATION. 5

uei. The *u* as in *ua, uai*, often in value *w;* the *ei* as in *ei* final; the vowel-sounds in the French *jouer* answer fairly to *uei.*

ué. The *u* as in *ua;* the *é* as explained before. It is found only in the final *uén*, which sounds as if written *ú-ŭn*, frequently *wén* or *wun*. It is in many cases difficult to distinguish *uén* from *un;* for instance, *kun* from *kuén*.

ui. The *u* as above, followed enclitically by *i*, as if *oo-y;* the vowel-sounds in *screwy;* more enclitic than in the French *Louis* or the Italian *lui.* It is in some tones *uei.*

uo. The *u* as above; the *o* as in *lone;* the Italian *uo* in *fuori;* often *wo*, and, at times, nearly *ŏō.*

ŭ. Between the *i* in *bit* and the *u* in *shut;* only found with the initials *ss*, *tz*, *tz'*, which it follows from the throat, almost as if the speaker were guilty of a slight eructation. We have no vowel-sound that fairly represents it.

Consonantal Sounds.

ch. Before any of the above finals except *ih*, simply as in *chair, chip;* before *ih* it is softened to *dj;* *chih* being in many cases pronounced *djih.*

ch'. A strong breathing intervening between the initial *ch* and the vowel-sound, but without reduplicating the latter. Drop the first vowel in *cháhá*, or the italicised letters in *much-harm*, and the *ch-ha* remaining will give a fair idea of the syllable *ch'a*. This may also be obtained if we contrast the smooth syllable *cha* with *tcha*, the breathing becoming apparent in the greater effort needed to utter the latter syllable. The *ch'* does sometimes soften like the unaspirated *ch* before *ih*, but much more rarely.

f. As in *farm.*

h. As the *ch* in the Scotch *loch;* the *ch* of the Welch and Gaelic.

hs. A slight aspirate preceding and modifying the sibilant, which is, however, the stronger of the two consonants. To pronounce *hsing* let the reader try to drop the first *i* in *hissing*. He will exaggerate both the aspirate and the sibilant, but the experiment will give him a clear idea of the process. The aspiration is effected by closing the middle of the tongue upon the back of the palate before the tip of the tongue is raised for the sibilation. It differs from *sh*, although this difference is less observable before the diphthongs *ia, ie.*

j. Most nearly the French *j* in *jaune;* our *s* in *fusion*, or *z* in *brazier*, are the nearest imitation of which our alphabet admits. Some foreigners read *j* as *r*, but this I hold to be entirely wrong.

k. As *c* in *car*, *k* in *king;* but when following other sounds, often softened to *g* in *go, gate.* In the word *ko*, for instance, the Numerative proper to many nouns, when this is preceded by *na*, that, or *ché*, this, the *k* is softened, the two syllables being pronounced almost *nago, chégo.*

k'. The aspirate as in *ch'*. Drop the italicised letters in *kick-hard* and you will have *k'a;* in *kick-her*, and you have *k'é.*

l. As in English.

m. As in English.

n. As in English.

ng. A consonantal sound of partly nasal and partly guttural influence upon the vowels it precedes. To produce *nga*, take the italicised consonants in the French mo*n gal*ant; for *ngai*, in mo*n gail*lard; for *ngo*, in so*n gos*ier. It is never so evident in a syllable pronounced by itself as when following another syllable that terminates in a vowel or in *n*.

p. As in English.

p'. The aspirate as in *ch', k'*. Observe the manner in which an Irishman pronounces *p*arty, *p*arliament; or drop the italicised letters in *s*l*a*p-har*d*, and you will retain *p'a*.

s. As in English.

sh. As in English.

ss. *ssŭ* is the only syllable in which this initial is found. The object of employing *ss* is to fix attention on the peculiar vowel sound *ŭ*, which, as stated above, it is so hard to reproduce.

t. As in English.

t'. As in *k', p'*, etc. Observe an Irishman's pronunciation of *t* in *t*error, *t*orment; or drop the italics in *h*i*t-har*d, and you have *t'a*.

ts. As in *jetsam, catsup*; after another word, often softened to *ds* in *gladsome*.

ts'. The aspirate intervening as in *ch* and other initials. Let the reader drop the italicised letters in *b*ets-har*d*, and he will retain *ts'a*.

tz. Is employed to mark the peculiarity of the final *ŭ*, but is hardly of greater power than *ts*.

tz'. Like *ts'* above. This and the preceding initial are, like *ss*, only used before the *ŭ*.

w. As in English, but very faint before *u*, if indeed it exist at all.

y. As in English, but very faint before *i* or *ü*.

In the final *ao* I have followed the Manchu spelling, against MORRISON and WILLIAMS, who write *aou, áu*. This, as I have admitted, is the approximate sound in certain tones.

The final *eh*, used only in *yeh*, may seem unnecessarily separated from *ieh*. In my opinion the consonant *y* is sufficiently plain to authorise it, and the tone-inflection is not less practicable in the syllable *yeh* than in *ieh*. So with the final *ên*.

In the final *é* some confusion with *o* is unavoidable. I have endeavoured to guide myself by the Manchu, but find that although native teachers consign them to different finals, it is next to impossible in many words to say whether *é* (or *ngé*), *ché, jé, ké, mé, té*, or *o, cho, jo, ko, lo, mo, to*, be the correct orthography. The same is true with the aspirated *ch, k, t*; but I think that after the aspirate, in general, the *o* prevails, also that while none of these syllables, sometimes sounded as ending in *é*, is exempt from the changes to *o*, there are many in *o* which never change to *é*. It will be found that some natives incline more to the one and some more to the other.

The final *éi* is of doubtful existence even in *néi*, which certainly ends in a sound somewhat different from the terminal of *lei, mei*. These have taken the place of *lui, mui*, the old orthography of the Mandarin as spoken in the South.

The finals *ên* and *êng* were originally substituted for *un* and *ung* in syllables beginning with *f, m, p*, after the latest native works published at Canton to teach the Cantonese to talk

PART I.—PRONUNCIATION. 7

Mandarin, and the modification has been found to be fully authorised by the Pekingese. The Manchu orthography of last century was *fung, mung,* but always *fén, mén, pén.*

The *u* in *iung, ung,* and in *ua, uai* and other combinations, in which it figures both as *o* and *w,* has been retained nevertheless as the vowel most certainly to be recognised in the simplest form of the *sound,* and as the most convenient for exhibiting the variation of the *tone* without change of *syllable,* to which end, moreover, it was expedient to avoid using the initials *hw, kw.*

Breathings.

The aspirate which intervenes between the initials *ch, k, p, t, ts, tz,* and the vowels following them, is indicated, as will have been seen above, by an inverted comma in preference to an *h,* lest the English reader, following his own laws of spelling, should be led to pronounce *ph* as in *triumph, th* as in *month,* and so on, which would be a serious error. The full recognition of the aspirate's value is of the last importance; the *tones* themselves are not of more. A speaker who says *kan* when he ought to say *khan* might as well speak of Loudon for London.

3. Tone.—There is no subject on which it is more important to write, and none on which it is harder to avoid repeating what has been said by others.

The ideas of a Chinese are capable of expression in writing in some thousands of characters that may be used singly or in combination with each other. The sound of each of these is such that without much violence to fact we call it a monosyllable. The Chinese term this monosyllable *yin.* In no dialect known to us does the number of the *yin* exceed a few hundreds; hence great confusion to the ear, and distress to the memory when it would distinguish between sounds, characters, or ideas which it can only recall by an alphabetic denomination common to many. Under the *yin* or sound *i* in MORRISON's Dictionary there are 1,165 characters, differing in form and meaning. Of this *yin* there are, however, subordinate divisions, the *shéng,* which we translate tones, keys in which the voice is pitched, and by which a variety of distinctions is effected, so delicate as to be retained only after long and anxious watching by the foreign ear, but so essential an acquisition that, until by practice his intonation be accurate, the foreign speaker is in hourly danger of making very laughable mistakes. A good deal that he says will no doubt be understood, but, whether he theorise or not on the matter, until his speech be *tonically* correct, no missionary or interpreter need imagine himself secure of being intelligible.

The term *tone* has been so long accepted as the equivalent of the Chinese *shéng* that it may be hardly worth while attempting to disturb the usage. It might be notwithstanding rendered with greater propriety *note,* in a musical sense, although no musical instrument to my knowledge is capable of exhibiting more than an approximation to the *shéng.* Dr. HAGER, in his folio on the Elementary Characters of the Chinese Language (1801), has tried to give an idea of the *shéng* as musical notes. The attempt has been repeated, I believe, more recently by the late Dr. DYER, the celebrated sinologue.

The number of the *shêng* differs in different dialects. Books recognise five. In the Peking dialect there are now four: 1st, the *shang-p'ing*, or upper-even tone; 2nd, the *hsia-p'ing*, or lower-even tone; 3rd, the *shang*, or ascending tone; 4th, the *ch'ü*, receding or departing tone.

In the 1st tone, the *upper-even*, it may be enough to observe, the vowel-sound, whether the word be pronounced quickly or slowly, proceeds without elevation or depression. One of our sinologues has not incorrectly styled it the *affirmative* tone.

In the 2nd tone, the *lower-even*, the voice is jerked, much as when in English we utter words expressive of doubt and astonishment.

In the 3rd tone, the *ascending*, the sound becomes nearly as abrupt, but more resembling what with us would indicate indignation and denial.

In the 4th tone, the *receding*, the vowel-sound is prolonged, as it were, regretfully.

The *ju*, or *entering*, an abrupt tone still recognised in studying the written language— that is to say, in committing Chinese books to memory—is now ignored in the practice of the spoken language of Peking; in this most of the words or characters ranged under it in the vocabularies having been transferred to the 2nd tone. But the *ju shêng* is not extinct in some other dialects.

It is simplest, as Mr. MEADOWS suggests, to distinguish the four tones of Pekingese by numbers. I write the *shêng* of the syllable *pa*, accordingly, as follows:—

pa^1, pa^2, pa^3, pa^4.

The sounds of the syllables repeated in the above order form a sort of a *chime*, which can only be learned by the ear, but which it is not difficult to learn. When he has caught it the student should never hear a new phrase without taking it to pieces and satisfying himself and his teacher, word by word, of the proper tone or note of each. So long as his teacher declines to pass his notation as correct, so long should he carefully repeat the word or words disputed.* When absent from the teacher he will be able to fortify his ear by recurrence to the Syllabary.

There is some danger of misleading a student who has *not* caught the chime, and once he has he will dispense with all illustration. We will hazard but one parallel, for better or for worse. Let A, B, C, D be four persons engaged in conversation, and a question be put by B regarding the fate of someone known to them all. In the four lines below I have supposed A to assert his death in the 1st tone; B to express his apprehension that he has

---

* To give an instance of the scrapes into which inaccuracy in the tones may betray the speaker, a gentleman who really speaks the language well was asking, in 1858, where yen^1, the salt for the supply of Peking, was obtained, and was told first, to his astonishment, that it was all imported by foreigners; objecting to this, and explaining that he meant fresh salt, or the salt consumed in daily food, he was yet more astonished to hear that it was yen^2, brought from the inland province of Honan; nor was it until after some minutes' cross-examination that the Chinese addressed, detecting his error and correctly intoning the syllable, replied, "from the salines of the province of course." The foreigner had been intoning yen^2, the sound for, amongst others, the word *salt*, as though it were yen^1, the sound for, amongst others, the word *smoke*; and the Chinese had believed the first question to refer to opium, commonly called smoke, and the second, in which some qualifications had been added, to refer to native tobacco.

been killed, in the 2nd; C to scout this suspicion, in the 3rd; and D to confirm it sorrowfully, in the 4th.

1. *shang-p'ing,*   A.   Dead.
2. *hsia-p'ing,*   B.   Killed?
3. *shang,*   C.   No!
4. *ch'ü,*   D.   Yes!

Now in this short dialogue, or tetralogue, English speakers would ordinarily so pitch the voice as to make the whole a tolerable approximation to the chime the student has to acquire; but the analogy would entirely mislead him were he not to qualify it by remembering that in the four words instanced the voice rises and falls according to the emotion of the speaker, whereas the pitch of *pa*^{3}, *pa*^{4}, or any other syllables, is independent of any such motive. The tone of the syllable has as little relation to its sense as the note allotted to any word in most of our songs has to its meaning. The distinction next to be observed is this, that while there is nothing to prevent the same word being allotted in different songs to any note in the scale, it is only by exception that in Chinese speech the place of a word in the tone-scale is ever exchanged for another. So *p'a*, to fear, is always *p'a*^{4}; *chiao*, to teach, is at times *chiao*^{1}, at times *chiao*^{4}; for with a new meaning a word will change its tone, sometimes even its sound.

As the student has been told above, however, the correct application of the tones will only come to him by the practice of the ear, and in order to discipline his ear a set of Tone Exercises has been prepared in another Part of this Colloquial Series. To these his attention is earnestly recommended.

4. Rhythm.—What tone is to the individual sound, rhythm is to the sentence. Like the tone, it can only be acquired from a native. The student must take careful note of the proper place of the emphasis. He must not be surprised to find the rhythm in apparent antagonism to the tone in some cases, especially when an adjective or adverb is formed by reduplication of a word, with the enclitic particle *ti* appended, as in *sung-sung-ti, hsieh-hsieh-ti,* where his teacher will refuse to recognise any difference between the tones of the two *hsieh,* although to our ear the accent of the second differs widely from that of the first, resting in some of these polysyllabic combinations on the one and in some on the other syllable.

5. And now for the sake of securing an accurate idea of the pronunciation of each syllable, let the student carefully follow a Pekingese through the Sound Table which occupies the next pages.

SOUND TABLE,

Or List of Syllables distinguished as belonging to the 1st, 2nd, 3rd, and 4th Tone Classes.

NOTE.—The following sounds, *a, ai, an, ang, ao, é, én, éng, o, ou,* are as often pronounced ⁿᵍ*a*, ⁿᵍ*ai*, ⁿᵍ*an*, and so on. *See* the remarks on the subject on page 6, under the initial *ng*.

		1	2	3	4			1	2	3	4
1.	a, ⁿᵍa	阿	…	阿	阿	21.	chêng	正	…	整	正
2.	ai, ⁿᵍai	哀	埃	矮	愛	22.	ch'êng	稱	成	懲	秤
3.	an, ⁿᵍan	安	…	俺	岸	23.	chi	雞	吉	己	記
4.	ang, ⁿᵍang	昂	昂	…	…	24.	ch'i	七	奇	起	氣
5.	ao, ⁿᵍao	熬	熬	襖	傲	25.	chia	家	夾	甲	價
						26.	ch'ia	掐	…	卡	恰
						27.	ch'iai	…	…	楷	…
6.	cha	渣	劄	拃	乍	28.	chiang	江	…	講	匠
7.	ch'a	叉	茶	扠	杈	29.	ch'iang	腔	牆	搶	戧
8.	chai	齋	宅	窄	債	30.	chiao	交	嚼	脚	叫
9.	ch'ai	拆	柴	冊	…	31.	ch'iao	敲	橋	巧	俏
10.	chan	沾	…	盞	站	32.	chieh	街	結	解	借
11.	ch'an	攙	饞	產	懺	33.	ch'ieh	切	茄	且	妾
12.	chang	章	…	長	賬	34.	chien	奸	…	減	見
13.	ch'ang	娼	長	廠	唱	35.	ch'ien	千	錢	淺	欠
14.	chao	招	著	找	兆	36.	chih	知	值	指	志
15.	ch'ao	炒	巢	炒	鈔	37.	ch'ih	赤	遲	尺	翅
16.	chê	遮	…	者	這	38.	chin	斤	…	錦	近
17.	ch'ê	車	…	扯	撤	39.	ch'in	親	勤	寢	唚
18.	chei	…	…	…	這	40.	ching	睛	…	井	靜
19.	chên	眞	…	枕	震	41.	ch'ing	輕	晴	請	慶
20.	ch'ên	嗔	臣	磣	趁	42.	chio	…	角	…	…

PART I.—SOUND TABLE.

	1	2	3	4			1	2	3	4
43. ch'io	...	...	...	却敉	72. chui	追	...	...	墜
44. chiu	究	...	酒糗	敉	73. ch'ui	吹	垂	...	...
45. ch'iu	秋	求	...	...	74. chun	...	...	准蠢	...
46. chiung	...	...	窘	...	75. ch'un	春	純	蠢腫	重銃
47. ch'iung	...	窮	...	...	76. chung	中	...	腫籠	...
48. cho	卓	濁	...	...	77. ch'ung	充	虫	籠	重銃
49. ch'o	擉	...	...	...	78. ch'uo	擉	...	...	...
50. chou	週	軸綢	肘	綽畫						
51. ch'ou	抽	綢局	醜舉	臭句	79. ê, ᵑê	阿	我	額	惡搵
52. chü	居	局	舉取	去眷	80. ên, ᵑên	恩	...	...	...
53. ch'ü	屈	渠	取捲	眷勸	81. êng, ᵑêng	哼	...	...	...
54. chüan	捐	...	捲犬	勸倔	82. êrh	...	兒	耳	二
55. ch'üan	圈	全絶	犬蹇	倔確俊						
56. chüeh	厥	絶癩	蹇	確俊	83. fa	發	法	髮反	法
57. ch'üeh	...	缺	蹇菌	...	84. fan	翻	煩	反訪	飯放
58. chün	君	...	菌	...	85. fang	方	房	訪匪	放分
59. ch'ün	...	羣	...	...	86. fei	非	肥	匪粉	費分
60. chüo	...	爵	...	...	87. fên	分	墳	粉	分奉
61. ch'üo	...	...	却	住	88. fêng	風	縫	...	奉
62. chu	猪	竹	主	住	89. fo	...	佛	...	...
63. ch'u	出	厨	處	處	90. fou	...	浮	否	卑
64. chua	抓	爪	...	...	91. fu	夫	扶	斧	父
65. ch'ua	欻	...	...	...						
66. chuai	拽	...	跩	拽	92. ha	...	蝦	哈	哈
67. ch'uai	揣	...	揣	踹	93. hai	哈	孩	海	害
68. chuan	專	...	轉	傳串	94. han	頂	寒	喊	漢項
69. ch'uan	穿	船	喘	串壯	95. hang	砕	行	...	好
70. chuang	裝	...	奬	壯創	96. hao	蒿	毫	好	好
71. ch'uang	瘡	牀	闖	創						

#		1	2	3	4
97.	hê, hei	黑	…	黑	…
98.	hên	…	…	很	恨
99.	hêng	哼	恆	…	橫
100.	ho	喝	河	…	賀
101.	hou	齁	侯	吼	後
102.	hu	忽	壺	虎	戶
103.	hua	花	滑	話	話
104.	huai	…	懷	…	壞
105.	huan	歡	環	緩	換
106.	huang	荒	黃	謊	晃
107.	huei, hui	灰	回	悔	賄
108.	huên, hun	昏	魂	渾	混
109.	hung	烘	紅	哄	汞
110.	huo	劐	活	火	貨
111.	hsi	西	席	喜	細
112.	hsia	瞎	霞	…	夏
113.	hsiang	香	詳	想	向
114.	hsiao	消	學	小	笑
115.	hsieh	些	鞋	血	謝
116.	hsien	先	閒	險	限
117.	hsin	心	尋	…	信
118.	hsing	星	行	醒	姓
119.	hsio	…	學	…	…
120.	hsiu	修	…	朽	袖
121.	hsiung	兄	熊	…	續
122.	hsü	須	徐	許	續
123.	hsüan, hsüen	喧	懸	選	選
124.	hsüeh	靴	穴	雪	穴
125.	hsün	熏	巡	…	汛

#		1	2	3	4
126.	hsüo	…	學	…	…
127.	i, yi	衣	一	尾	易
128.	jan	…	然	染	…
129.	jang	嚷	瓤	嚷	讓
130.	jao	…	饒	繞	繞
131.	jê	…	…	…	熱
132.	jên	…	人	忍	任
133.	jêng	扔	…	…	日
134.	jih	…	…	…	若
135.	jo	…	…	…	肉
136.	jou	揉	柔	…	入
137.	ju	如	如	入	軟
138.	juan	…	…	軟	靯
139.	jui	…	…	蕊	瑞
140.	jun	…	…	…	潤
141.	jung	…	榮	…	…
142.	ka	嘎	…	嘎	嘎
143.	k'a	卡	…	卡	…
144.	kai	該	…	改	槩
145.	k'ai	開	…	慨	幹
146.	kan	甘	…	趕	看
147.	k'an	看	…	斫	杠
148.	kang	剛	…	…	炕
149.	k'ang	康	…	扛	抗

PART I.—SOUND TABLE.

		1	2	3	4			1	2	3	4
150.	kao	高	…	稿	告	178.	kuo	鍋	國	果	過
151.	kʻao	尻	…	考	靠	179.	kʻuo	…	…	…	闊
	kê, kʻê; *see* ko, kʻo.										
152.	kei	…	…	給	…	180.	la	拉	邋	蝲	蠟
153.	kʻei	刻	…	…	…	181.	lai	…	來	…	賴
154.	kên	根	哏	…	艮	182.	lan	鬎	婪	懶	爛
155.	kʻên	…	…	肯	掯	183.	lang	榔	狼	朗	浪
156.	kêng	更	…	埂	更	184.	lao	撈	勞	老	澇
157.	kʻêng	坑	…	…	…	185.	lê	勒	…	…	樂
158.	ko, kê	哥	格	各	個	186.	lêi, lei	累	雷	累	類
159.	kʻo, kʻê	可	可	渴	客	187.	lêng	…	稜	冷	愣
160.	kou	溝	狗	狗	彀	188.	li	璃	離	禮	立
161.	kʻou	摳	…	口	叩	189.	lia	…	…	倆	…
162.	ku	估	骨	古	固	190.	liang	量	凉	兩	諒
163.	kʻu	窟	…	苦	褲	191.	liao	…	聊	了	料
164.	kua	瓜	…	寡	掛	192.	lieh	咧	咧	咧	列
165.	kʻua	誇	…	侉	跨	193.	lien	連	憐	臉	練
166.	kuai	乖	…	拐	怪	194.	lin	…	林	懍	另
167.	kʻuai	…	…	擓	快	195.	ling	…	零	領	另
168.	kuan	官	…	管	慣	196.	lio	…	…	…	略
169.	kʻuan	寬	…	款	…	197.	liu	遛	留	柳	六
170.	kuang	光	…	廣	逛	198.	lo	擄	騾	裸	駱
171.	kʻuang	誆	狂	詭	況	199.	lou	樓	樓	簍	陋
172.	kuei	規	…	詭	貴	200.	lü	…	驢	屢	律
173.	kʻuei	虧	揆	傀	愧	201.	lüan	…	…	…	戀
174.	kuên, kun	…	…	滾	棍	202.	lüeh	…	…	…	略
175.	kʻuên, kʻun	坤	…	閫	困	203.	lün	掄	倫	圇	論
176.	kung	工	…	礦	共	204.	lüo	…	…	…	略
177.	kʻung	空	…	孔	空	205.	lu	嚕	爐	櫓	路

	1	2	3	4		1	2	3	4
206. luan	…	…	…	亂	232. nei	…	…	…	內嫩
207. lun	…	輪	圇	論弄	233. nên	…	…	…	…
208. lung	窿	龍	隴	弄	234. nêng	…	能	…	…
					235. ni	…	泥	擬	匿釀
209. ma	媽	麻	馬	罵	236. niang	…	娘	…	尿孽念
210. mai	…	埋	買	賣	237. niao	嫋	…	鳥	…
211. man	顢	瞞	滿	慢	238. nieh	捏	…	奀	佞虐拗懦
212. mang	茫	忙	莽	…	239. nien	拈	年	捻	…
213. mao	貓	毛	卯	貌	240. nin	…	您	擰	…
214. mei	…	煤	美	昧	241. ning	…	甯	…	…
215. mên	捫	門	…	悶	242. nio	…	…	…	…
216. mêng	懜	盟	猛	夢	243. niu	妞	牛	鈕	…
217. mi	眯	迷	米	密	244. no	…	挪	…	虐拗懦糯
218. miao	喵	苗	藐	廟	245. nou	…	…	…	…
219. mieh	咩	…	…	滅	246. nü	…	…	女	虐
220. mien	…	綿	勉	面	247. nüeh	…	…	…	虐
221. min	…	民	憫	…	248. nüo	…	…	…	怒
222. ming	…	名	…	命	249. nu	…	奴	努	…
223. miu	…	…	…	謬末	250. nuan	…	…	暖	嫩
224. mo	摩	麼	抹	木	251. nun	…	…	…	…
225. mou	…	謀	某		252. nung	…	濃	…	弄
226. mu	…	模	母						
					253. o, ⁿgo	哦	訛	…	惡
227. na	那	拏	那	那	254. ou, ⁿou	毆	…	偶	嘔
228. nai	…	…	奶	耐					
229. nan	喃	男	…	難	255. pa	八	拔	把	罷怕拜
230. nang	囔	囊	攮	齉	256. p'a	葩	扒	…	百
231. nao	撓	鐃	惱	閙	257. pai		白	擘	

PART I.—SOUND TABLE.

		1	2	3	4			1	2	3	4
258.	p'ai	拍	牌	瓝	派	287.	pu	不	不	補	不
259.	pan	班	...	板	半	288.	p'u	鋪	葡	普	鋪
260.	p'an	攀	盤	...	盼						
261.	pang	幫	...	綁	謗						
262.	p'ang	胖	旁	髈	胖	289.	sa	撒	𠥯	洒	薩
263.	pao	包	薄	保	抱	290.	sai	顋	...	...	賽
264.	p'ao	拋	袍	跑	礮	291.	san	三	...	傘	散
265.	pei	背	...	北	背	292.	sang	桑	...	嗓	喪
266.	p'ei	披	陪	...	配	293.	sao	騷	...	...	掃
267.	pên	奔	...	本	奔	294.	sê	嘶	...	...	嗇
268.	p'ên	噴	盆	...	噴	295.	sên	森	...	...	...
269.	pêng	繃	...	...	迸	296.	sêng	僧	...	...	...
270.	p'êng	烹	朋	棒	碰	297.	so	唆	...	鎖	溯
271.	pi	逼	鼻	筆	必	298.	sou	搜	...	叟	嗽
272.	p'i	批	皮	鄙	屁	299.	su	蘇	...	速	素
273.	piao	標	...	表	鰾	300.	suan	酸	...	...	算
274.	p'iao	漂	嫖	漂	票	301.	sui	雖	隨	髓	碎
275.	pieh	憋	別	撇	彆	302.	sun	孫	...	損	...
276.	p'ieh	撆	...	撇	...	303.	sung	松	...	竦	送
277.	pien	邊	便	扁	便	304.	sha	殺	...	傻	曬
278.	p'ien	偏	便	諞	片	305.	shai	篩	...	色	煞
279.	pin	賓	貧	品	殯	306.	shan	山	...	閃	善
280.	p'in	拼	貧	品	牝	307.	shang	商	...	賞	上
281.	ping	兵	...	稟	病	308.	shao	燒	杓	少	少
282.	p'ing	砰	憑	...	聘	309.	shê	賒	舌	捨	射
283.	po	波	婆	駁	簸	310.	shên	身	神	審	慎
284.	p'o	坡	婆	笸	破	311.	shêng	生	繩	省	賸
285.	pou*	不	...	...	...	312.	shih	失	十	使	事
286.	p'ou	掊	...	...	剖	313.	shou	收	熟	手	獸

* Pronounced *pou* in poetry only.

		1	2	3	4			1	2	3	4
314.	shu	書	贖	數	數	342.	tieh	…	…	…	帖
315.	shua	刷	…	耍	…	343.	t'ieh	貼	…	鐵	店
316.	shuai	衰	…	摔	率	344.	tien	掂	…	點	掂
317.	shuan	拴	…	…	涮	345.	t'ien	天	田	忝	定
318.	shuang	雙	…	爽	雙睡	346.	ting	釘	…	頂	聽
319.	shui	…	誰	水	睡	347.	t'ing	聽	停	梃	…
320.	shun	…	…	…	順朔	348.	tiu	丟	…	唗	惰唾
321.	shuo	說	…	…	朔四	349.	to	多	奪	朶	豆
322.	ssŭ	絲	…	死	四	350.	t'o	託	駝	妥	透
						351.	tou	兜	頭	斗	妒
323.	ta	答	搭	打	大	352.	t'ou	偸	頭	…	唾
324.	t'a	他	…	塔	榻	353.	tu	督	毒	賭	斷
325.	tai	獃	…	歹	代	354.	t'u	禿	塗	土	…
326.	t'ai	胎	擡	…	太	355.	tuan	端	…	短	對
327.	tan	單	…	膽坦	蛋炭	356.	t'uan	…	團	…	…
328.	t'an	貪	談	攤	當	357.	tui	堆	…	…	退
329.	tang	當	…	黨	燙	358.	t'ui	推	…	骽	鈍
330.	t'ang	湯	糖	儻	倒	359.	tun	敦	…	盹	褪
331.	tao	刀	…	搗	道	360.	t'un	吞	屯	懂	動
332.	t'ao	叨	逃	討	套	361.	tung	冬	同	統	痛
333.	tê	叨	得	…	特	362.	t'ung	通	雜	咱	…
334.	t'ê	…	…	…	…	363.	tsa	贊	擦	…	在
335.	tei	鏑	…	得	鐙	364.	ts'a	栽	…	宰	茱
336.	têng	燈	疼	等	櫈	365.	tsai	猜	才	彩	贊
337.	t'êng	鏊	敵	…	地	366.	ts'ai	簪	偺	攢	儳
338.	ti	的	提	底	替	367.	tsan	參	慚	慘	葬
339.	t'i	梯	貂	體	弔	368.	ts'an	參	…	昝	…
340.	tiao	挑	條	挑	跳	369.	tsang	鹹	…	臧	…
341.	t'iao					370.	ts'ang	倉			

		1	2	3	4			1	2	3	4
371.	tsao	遭	鑿	早	造	396.	wa	挖	娃	瓦	襪外
372.	ts'ao	操	槽	草	…	397.	wai	歪	…	昏	萬忘
373.	tsê	…	則	…	…	398.	wan	灣	完	晚	位
374.	ts'ê	…	…	…	策	399.	wang	汪	王	往	間
375.	tsei	…	賊	…	…	400.	wei	微	為	委	甕
376.	tsên	…	…	怎	…	401.	wên	溫	文	穩	臥
377.	ts'ên	參	…	…	…	402.	wêng	翁	…	…	物
378.	tsêng	增	…	怎	贈	403.	wo	窩	…	我	…
379.	ts'êng	蹭	…	層	蹭	404.	wu	屋	無	武	…
380.	tso	作	昨	左	作						
381.	ts'o	搓	矬	…	錯	405.	ya	丫	牙	雅	壓
382.	tsou	…	…	走	奏	406.	yai	…	涯	…	…
383.	ts'ou	…	…	…	湊	407.	yang	央	羊	養	樣要
384.	tsu	租	足	祖	…	408.	yao	腰	遙	咬	夜
385.	ts'u	粗	…	…	醋	409.	yeh	噎	爺	野	沿
386.	tsuan	鑽	…	纂	揝	410.	yen	煙	言	㲼	易
387.	ts'uan	驟	攢	…	竄	411.	yi	揖	益	銀	印
388.	tsui	堆	…	嘴	罪	412.	yin	音	迎	引	應
389.	ts'ui	催	隨	…	萃	413.	ying	應	…	影	樂
390.	tsun	尊	…	樽	寸	414.	yo	約	魚	雨	預
391.	ts'un	村	存	忖	縱	415.	yü	愚	原	…	願
392.	tsung	宗	…	總	…	416.	yüan	冤	嵌	遠	月
393.	ts'ung	蔥	從	…	字	417.	yüeh	日	銀	允	運
394.	tzŭ	貲	…	子	字	418.	yün	暈	雲	油	右
395.	tz'ŭ	齜	磁	此	次	419.	yu	憂	油	有	用
						420.	yung	庸	容	永	用

u; see wu.

PART II.

THE RADICALS.

PART II.

THE RADICALS.

6.—We now come to the written character, which the student must for the time be pleased to accept as made up of two parts, its Radical, and that part which is not its Radical. The latter part various sinologues have for fairly sufficient reasons agreed to term its Phonetic. In a large majority of words the phonetic indicates the sounds, that is to a certain extent. The radical, with a like limitation, indicates the category of the sense.

The radicals are 214 in number. Some of them are subject to modifications which entirely change their figure. The following General Table shows them arranged in 17 classes, according to the number of pencil strokes in each radical; that is, the radicals of one stroke in the first class, those of two in the second, and so on. Many radicals in the latter classes will be seen to be made up of radicals of fewer strokes, e.g., 109, 180, 209.

Before each radical is a number marking its place in the general series, the name of the character so numbered, and its tone; after the character, its meaning, and then a number of characters, never exceeding three, which have been selected as illustrating the part that the radical after which they stand generally plays in the composition of characters, whether in its full or its modified form. The radicals that undergo modification are marked with an asterisk (*), and their modified forms are collected at the end of the General Table. This list of modified forms should be consulted as the radicals are being acquired.

The character, it has been said above, consists of its radical and its phonetic. Let the student turn to Radical 3 and he will see in the character given to illustrate its part in the composition that the radical *chu*, a point, stands on the top of it. The remainder, three horizontal strokes and a vertical one, are its phonetic. Let him turn to the 12th Radical, *pa*, eight, and he will see that it is placed under the phonetic in the characters given as examples. In the examples opposite the 64th Radical, *shou*, the hand, the radical stands in the first example, in full form, on the left of the phonetic; in the second, in modified form, also on the left; in the third, in full form, underneath the phonetic.

To look out a character in the dictionaries arranged according to radicals, it is essential, of course, in the first place to decide correctly under what radical it is classed. This point assured,—and the knowledge necessary to this end is sooner attained by practice than might be supposed,—the number of strokes in the phonetic must be accurately counted, because in the dictionaries in question the characters under each radical are subdivided into classes, according to the number of strokes in the phonetic. The counting of these, even where they are numerous, will not be found so formidable a task once the student becomes familiar with the radicals, for he will observe that the phonetic is either resolvable into other radical characters, or, in some instances, is simply a single radical character added to the radical;

PART II.—THE RADICALS. 21

and once he knows, as he soon will, the place of any radical in the General Table, he will recall the number of strokes composing it without the trouble of counting them.

Take the third example opposite the 85th Radical, *shui*, water. The radical itself is the abbreviated form of *shui*: the phonetic resolves itself into four radicals; the centre of the upper part is the 149th, of seven strokes; this is flanked on both sides by the 120th, of six strokes; and below is the 59th, of three strokes; making in all twenty-two strokes. In the second example of the 29th Radical, the phonetic is simply the 128th Radical; in the second example of the 75th Radical, the phonetic is that same radical repeated. The rule regarding the composition of the phonetic is not strictly universal, but by the beginner it may be accepted as very generally obtaining.

To assist the student in acquiring a working knowledge of the radicals, three test tables are subjoined.

The first contains all the characters chosen to illustrate the use of the radicals in the General Table, arranged in order of the number of their strokes collectively. When the student shall have examined the first 30, or 20, or even 10, of the radicals in the General Table, let him run down the right-hand column of the Test Table, and try to identify the radicals of the characters therein placed, turning to the General Table for assistance whenever his memory fails him. This will speedily acquaint him with the radicals and the part they most commonly play.

The second Test Table contains all the radicals redistributed in categories of subjects, according to the meaning of each. Some are in consequence repeated. At the top of the right-hand column, for instance, we have the 72nd, as the sun, followed by the 73rd, the moon; then the 72nd again, as day, followed by the 36th, as night. It is hoped that this will at the same time aid and exercise the memory; but it will not be of as great service to him as the following table, the third.

The third table exhibits the radicals in three classes, distinguished for brevity's sake as colloquial, classical, and obsolete. The colloquial are those which represent words used, many of them frequently, in conversation; the classical, those not met with in conversation but found in books and writing; the obsolete, those which, although the dictionaries allot them a signification, are no longer employed except as radical indices. The colloquial radicals are 142 in number, the classical 25, the obsolete 47.

The student is recommended, when he shall have examined the General Table sufficiently to have formed a definite idea of the nature and functions of the radical characters arranged in it, to betake himself to the Exercises in the Colloquial Radicals which immediately follow this third Test Table. In these he will find a number of short combinations of words, all of them, with the exception of one or two, which are separately explained, radical characters, arranged more or less in categories of subjects. If he will keep to these exercises till he really knows every character in them, he will be master of 138 of the 214 radicals, and he will have easy victory over the remaining 76.

The explanations set opposite the radicals in the General Table might often be expanded or modified, but will be found for the present sufficient.

GENERAL TABLE.

1 Stroke.

1. yi¹²⁴   一   one; unity.
2. kun³   丨   a stroke connecting the top with the bottom.
3. chu³   丶   a point; a period.
4. p'ieh³   丿   a line running obliquely to the left.
5. yi¹⁴   乙   a character in the time cycle of China; also used as *yi*, one.
6. chüeh²   亅   a hooked end.

2 Strokes.

7. êrh⁴   二   two.
8. t'ou²   亠   above.
9. jên²   人*   man.
10. jên²   儿   man.
11. ju³⁴   入   in, into; to enter.
12. pa¹²   八   eight.
13. chiung³   冂   border waste-land.
14. mi⁴   冖   to cover over.
15. ping¹   冫   an icicle.
16. chi¹³   几   a stool.
17. k'an³   凵   able to contain.
18. tao¹   刀*   a knife; a sword.
19. li⁴   力   strength.
20. pao¹   勹   to wrap round.
21. pi³   匕   a spoon or scoop; a weapon.
22. fang¹   匚   a chest.
23. hsi³   匸   able to contain or conceal.
24. shih²   十   ten.
25. pu³   卜   to divine.
26. chieh²   卩*   a joint.
27. han⁴   厂   a ledge that shelters.

且 不 七
典 乍 中
乏 也 主
亂 九 丸
  事 了

亮 井 五
你 京 交
兒 來 今
兩 兆 允
典 全 內
  兵 六
  冕 冒
    冠
湊 准 冬
出 憑 凡
則 凹 凸
勒 別 分
  勁 助
  包 勻
  匙 北
  匪 匠
南 半 匹
原 卡 千
  却 占
  厚 危
    底

PART II.—THE RADICALS. 23

28.	ssŭ¹; mou³	厶	private; selfish.
29.	yu⁴	叉	again.

3 Strokes.

30.	k'ou³	口	the mouth.
31.	wei²	囗	able to enclose.
32.	t'u³	土	earth.
33.	shih⁴	士	a scholar.
34.	chih³	夂	to step onwards.
35.	ts'ui¹	夊	to step slowly.
36.	hsi¹ ²	夕	evening.
37.	ta⁴	大	great.
38.	nü³	女	a female.
39.	tzŭ³	子	a son.
40.	mien²	宀	roof of a cave.
41.	ts'un⁴	寸	an inch.
42.	hsiao³	小	little.
43.	wang¹	尢*	bent, as an ailing leg.
44.	shih¹	尸	a corpse.
45.	ch'ê⁴	屮	sprouting; vegetation.
46.	shan¹	山	a hill.
47.	ch'uan¹	巛*	streams.
48.	kung¹	工	labour.
49.	chi³	己	self.
50.	chin¹	巾	a napkin; head gear.
51.	kan¹	干	a shield; to concern.
52.	yao¹	幺	small.
53.	yen³	广	roof of a house.
54.	yin³	廴	continued motion.
55.	kung³	廾	the hands folded, as in salutation.

去 參 疊
反 取 　
　 　 　
可 嚙 嚷
回 困 團 壞
在 墓 壺 壽
壯 夆 　 　
夏 　 　 　
外 夜 夢 　
太 天 奇 姓 學 寒 對
奶 好 孫 家 尊 尖 　
孔 官 專 少 就 　 　
尺 屋 　 　 　 層
屯 嶺 巡 　 　 　
峯 　 巧 　 　 　
州 　 　 　 　 　
左 巷 　 　 差 　
布 帳 　 幫 　 　
平 年 　 幹 幾 廚
幻 店 建 　 　 廚
床 　 　 　 　 　
廷 弄

56.	yi⁴	弋	to shoot with the bow.
57.	kung¹	弓	a bow (arcus).
58.	ch'i⁴	彐*	pointed like a pig's head.
59.	shan¹	彡	streaky, like hair.
60.	ch'ih⁴	彳	to step short.

式 弔 彙 彩 往　弟 後　張 得

4 Strokes.

61.	hsin¹	心*	heart; mind.
62.	ko¹	戈	a lance; a spear.
63.	hu⁴	戶	a house door.
64.	shou³	手*	the hand.
65.	chih¹	支	a prop; to issue money.
66.	p'u¹	攴*	to tap lightly.
67.	wên²	文	{ stripes or streaks; ornament, as opposed to plainness; literature; unit of Chinese copper cash currency. }
68.	tou³	斗	Chinese measure = about 20 chin. (See 69.)
69.	chin¹	斤	{ Chinese pound = about 1⅓ lb. English; usually spoken of as a catty; chin also an axe. }
70.	fang¹	方	square.
71.	wu²	无*	not.
72.	jih⁴	日	the sun; the day.
73.	yüeh¹⁴	曰	to speak.
74.	yüeh⁴	月	the moon.
75.	mu⁴	木	wood; trees.
76.	ch'ien⁴	欠	to owe; to be deficient.
77.	chih³	止	to stop (neuter).
78.	tai³	歹*	decayed bones of a murdered man; bad.
79.	shu¹	殳	a quarter-staff.
80.	wu²⁴	毋	wu, do not!
81.	pi³	比	to compare; lay side by side.
82.	mao²	毛	hair, fur.
83.	ch'i⁴	气	vapour.

必 愛 慢
成 我 或
房 扁 掌
拜 換
改 散 敦
斌 斑
料 斟
斧 斬 新
旁 旗
旣
昂 春 晝
更 書 替
有 朋 朝
本 林 柴
次 欷
正 步
死 武
殺
每
毯
氣

PART II.—THE RADICALS.

84.	*shih*⁴	氏	family; one's house from past time till now.	民
85.	*shui*³	水*	water.	永 河 灣
86.	*huo*³	火*	fire.	炕 炭 然
87.	*chao*³	爪*	claws.	為 爵
88.	*fu*⁴	父	father.	爺
89.	*yao*²	爻	crosswise.	爽
90.	*ch'iang*²	爿	the Radical 91 reversed.	牀 牆
91.	*p'ien*⁴	片	a slab of wood; a slice or piece.	牖
92.	*ya*²	牙	the back teeth.	
93.	*niu*²	牛*	oxen; kine.	牲 特 牽
94.	*ch'üan*³	犬*	the dog.	狗 獸 獻

5 Strokes.

95.	*yüan*²	玄	black; originally *hsüan*², but not so read now.	兹 率
96.	*yü*⁴	玉*	precious stones.	玻 瑞 璃
97.	*kua*¹	瓜	the gourd.	瓢 瓣
98.	*wa*³	瓦	tiles.	瓶
99.	*kan*¹	甘	sweet.	甚 甜
100.	*shêng*¹	生	to live; to produce.	產
101.	*yung*⁴	用	to use.	甫
102.	*t'ien*²	田	fields; arable land.	男 畱 略
103.	*p'i*³	疋	the bale or piece of cloth, silk, etc.	疑
104.	*ni*¹⁴	疒	disease.	疼 病
105.	*po*¹⁴	癶	back to back.	發
106.	*pai*²; *po*¹²	白	white.	百 的 皇
107.	*p'i*²	皮	skins; bark.	皺 盆 盡
108.	*min*³	皿	covered dishes.	盡 盼 直
109.	*mu*⁴	目	the eye.	看 矜 矩 短
110.	*mou*²; *mao*²	矛	a long lance.	矜
111.	*shih*³	矢	arrows.	知

112.	shih²	石	stone.	
113.	ch'i²; shih⁴	示	spiritual power; revelation.	
114.	jou³	肉	the print of a fox's foot.	
115.	ho²	禾	any kind of grain.	
116.	hsüeh²·⁴	穴	a cave in the side of a hill.	
117.	li⁴	立	to stand up or still.	

6 Strokes.

118.	chu²	竹*	the bamboo.	
119.	mi³	米	rice uncooked.	
120.	mi⁴; ssŭ¹	糸	raw silk as spun by the worm.	
121.	fou³	缶	earthenware.	
122.	wang³	网*	a fishing net.	
123.	yang²	羊	sheep.	
124.	yü³	羽	feathers.	
125.	lao³	老	old.	
126.	êrh²	而	and; but yet.	
127.	lei³	耒	the plough.	
128.	êrh³	耳	the ear.	
129.	yü⁴	聿	a pencil.	
130.	jou⁴; ju⁴	肉*	flesh; meat.	
131.	ch'ên²	臣	minister; servant of the sovereign.	
132.	tzŭ⁴	自	self; from.	
133.	chih⁴	至	to come or to go; arrive at.	
134.	chiu⁴	臼	a stone mortar.	
135.	shé²	舌	the tongue.	
136.	ch'uan³	舛	at issue; in error.	
137.	chou¹	舟	ships; boats.	
138.	kên⁴	艮	limitation; also character in the time cycle.	
139.	sê⁴; shai³	色	colour.	

140.	ts'ao³	艸*	plants; herbs.
141.	hu¹	虍	the tiger's streaks.
142.	ch'ung²; hui⁴	虫	reptiles having feet.
143.	hsieh³; hsüeh³⁴	血	blood.
144.	hang²; hsing²	行	hang, a row, as of buildings; hsing, to go, to do.
145.	yi¹	衣	clothes.
146.	ya⁴	襾*	to cover; commonly mistaken for 西 (hsi¹), west, which is, strictly speaking, not a radical.

7 Strokes.

147.	chien⁴	見	to perceive, with the eye, nose, ear, or mind; sometimes the sign of passive or reflective verbs.
148.	chio²³; chiao³	角	horns; a corner.
149.	yen²	言	words.
150.	ku¹³	谷	a valley.
151.	tou⁴	豆	beans; a sacrificial bowl of wood.
152.	shih³	豕	the pig.
153.	chai⁴; ti³	豸	reptiles without feet.
154.	pei⁴	貝	the tortoise; his shell; hence, precious.
155.	ch'ih³⁴	赤	flesh colour.
156.	tsou³	走	to walk or run.
157.	tsu²	足	the foot; enough.
158.	shên¹	身	the body.
159.	ch'ê¹; chü¹	車	vehicles; sedans.
160.	hsin¹	辛	bitter.
161.	ch'ên²	辰	the 5th horary period of the Chinese day. 7 to 9 A.M.; also a character in the time cycle.
162.	ch'o⁴	辵*	moving and pausing.
163.	yi⁴	邑*	any centre of population.
164.	yu³	酉	the 10th horary period, 5 to 7 P.M.; also a character in the time cycle.
165.	pien⁴	釆	to part and distinguish; not to be confused with 采 (ts'ai³), colour.
166.	li³	里	a hamlet of 25 families; the Chinese measure = about one-third of an English mile.

8 Strokes.

167.	chin¹	金	the metals; gold.	針　錯　鑿
168.	chang³; ch'ang²	長*	to grow; long, length.	
169.	mên²	門	a gate; a door.	開　間　關
170.	fu⁴; fou⁴	阜*	a mound of earth.	阿　陋　陪
171.	li⁴; tai⁴	隶	to reach to; to arrive at.	隸
172.	chui¹	隹	short-tailed birds.	隻　雙　雞
173.	yü³	雨	rain.	雪　雲
174.	ch'ing¹	青	sky-blue.	靖　靜
175.	fei¹	非	negative; wrong.	靠
176.	mien⁴	面	the face; the outside.	

9 Strokes.

177.	ké²; ko²	革	a hide stripped of hair; to strip the hide; to flay.	靴　鞋
178.	wei²	韋	tanned hide.	韓
179.	chiu³	韭	leeks.	韮
180.	yin¹	音	sound.	韻　響
181.	yeh⁴	頁	the head; leaf or page of a book.	頂　頭　類
182.	fêng¹	風	wind.	颳　飄
183.	fei¹	飛	to fly, as birds.	
184.	shih²	食	to eat.	飲　養　餓
185.	shou³	首	the head.	馘
186.	hsiang¹	香	fragrance.	馨　馥

10 Strokes.

187.	ma³	馬	the horse.	騎　騾　驚
188.	ku³	骨	the bones.	體　髓
189.	kao¹	高	high.	
190.	piao¹	髟	shaggy.	髮　髫　鬢

191.	tou⁴	鬥 to fight; to emulate.	鬧	鬪
192.	ch'ang⁴	鬯 { a sacrificial bowl of porcelain; luxuriant vegetation; contentment. }	鬱	
193.	ko²; li⁴	鬲 a sacrificial vase on crooked feet.	鬴	鬻
194.	kuei³	鬼 spirits of the dead.	魁	魂 魔

11 Strokes.

195.	yü²	魚 fish.	魯	鮮 鰲
196.	niao³	鳥 birds.	鳳	鴨 鷹
197.	lu³	鹵 natural salts.	鹹	鹽
198.	lu⁴	鹿 the deer species.	麒	麗 麟
199.	mai⁴; mo⁴	麥 wheat.	麵	
200.	ma²	麻 hemp.	麼	

12 Strokes.

201.	huang²	黃 yellow; clay colour.	黇	黌 黌
202.	shu³	黍 millet.	黎	黏
203.	hei¹³; hê⁴	黑 black.	點	黨
204.	chih⁴	黹 embroidery.	黻	黼

13 Strokes.

205.	mêng³; min²	黽 of the frog or toad kind; to exert oneself.	黿	鼇
206.	ting³	鼎 a two-eared tripod used in sacrifice.	鼐	
207.	ku³	鼓 the drum, etc.	鼕	鼗
208.	shu³	鼠 the rat kind.		

14 Strokes.

209.	pi²	鼻 the nose.	鼽	
210.	ch'i²	齊 arranged in order.	齋	齎

15 Strokes.

211.	ch'ih³	齒 front teeth.	齡	齧

16 Strokes.

212.	lung²	龍	the dragon tribe.	龑 龕
213.	kuei¹	龜	the tortoise, turtle, etc.	鼀

17 Strokes.

214.	yo⁴	龠	flutes, pipes, etc.	龣

The characters in the foregoing table marked with an asterisk (*) are, some generally, some always, modified when employed as radicals of other characters. In the following are given the modifications recognised in the great Chinese lexicon of K'ANG HSI. There are a few others allowed in manuscript, which will be acquired without great difficulty.

人 亻 兀 爪 艹 閃
刀 刂 且 牛 爿 卄
刂 巳 小 犬 丬
尢 尢 玉 牜
巛 川 丑 竹 攵
彐 卜 才 网 月
心 手 攵 肉 廿
支 旡 夕 艸 西
无 夕 冫 襾 辵
歹 水 氺 辵 阝
水 火 川 邑 長
            長 阝
            阜

PART II.—THE RADICALS.

RADICAL TEST TABLE I.

辯騾魔鰲齋韜聽龔龕龢驚體髓鬪麟豔鬢鷹灣鹽釁豐鱉鬱

馥騎鼇壞獸齋臨關韻鬍魯麒麗繡巤飀顱顴嚷辮覺辭釋響飄馨鹹麴嶺黨齒蠹

靜頭鴨氽嶺幫爵瓢糞艱韓馨舉舞罷髓靴餮鞋髓養髮鬧黎學耨親錯說

貌賓躲輕辭魁魂麼璃窗疑鳳亂黿團壽墓夢旗獄豎算聞臺與蜜肇

聖葬號解象梁絲畫跨路載靖韭鳳亂黿團壽墓夢旗狀豎算聞臺與蜜肇

禽等策梁絲舒泉街衢輩量開閒雲飲豐歕斜新瑞盞碎禁犛

欲貪赦這野雪頂晃壺寒尊就幾換掌散敦斌斑替朝欤毯然為爺牽發短碎

送湊勒匙參專巢帳彩得斬既畫爽率瓶甜產略票章粗累羽習船規訛

旁書柴殺氣特茲疼病矩破祖秦窖缺翁耕能草匍起赳辱酒針陪隻

牲玟甚皇盅看盼秎秋紅美耍臭站翁耕能草匍起赳辱酒針陪隻

牀狗的直知冏者服肯花虎虱衫表迎兒兩典取夜奇姓官店或房斧昂朋林武河炕

更步甬男罕艮却阿事服肯花表迎京來兒兩典取夜奇姓官店或房斧昂朋林武河炕

奶好尖州年式成有次死每百考那你兵別助却底困壯巡廷弄我歧

冬凸凹出包北半占卡去可外左巧布平幼必全本正民永交兆回在矛

七九了久也凡勺千不中乏五井今六分匹反太天孔少尺屯甲且主乍允內

RADICAL TEST TABLE II.

1 日月日夕　2 風雨气冫水　3 鬼示卜豐豆鼎鬲　4 金鼓龠音　5 干

支乙辛子酉辰艮爻　6 金木水火土　7 山川谷穴阜田門　8 玉石鹵水

9 色青黃赤白黑玄　10 人儿氏自己爻子女士臣　11 身心廾手足首頁而

影耳鼻面目見面　12 言曰口舌牙齒皮肉骨血气　13 力用工　14 尸首骨

卩尢疒　15 入夂夊廴行走辵彳止立食　16 厶卯鬥攴　17 生長大小長

幺　18 厂宀广襾口里門戶邑阜　19 衣巾襾　20 舟車皿几匕斗白瓦缶

21 魚网牛耒糸皮革韋　22 刀匕干戈弋弓矢矛殳斤　23 匚勹匸　24 艸

木竹瓜鬯屮禾米豆韭麥麻黍　25 辛甘香　26 牛羊犬豕馬鹿鼠　27 鳥隹

虫豸龍魚龜黽角貝　28 羽飛爪肉釆文彡虍髟　29 疋斗斤寸方長　30 一

二八十　31 片比爿　32 旡欠足齊　33 亠亼高彑聿　34 毌又癶舛非

35 丨丶丿亅

RADICAL TEST TABLE III.

1. Colloquial.

一二人入八刀力十卜又口土士大女子小寸尸山川工己巾干弓心戈戶
手支文斗斤方日月木欠止歹比毛氏水火爪爻片牙牛犬玉瓜瓦甘生
用田疋白皮目矛矢石禾穴立竹米缶羊羽老而耳肉臣自至臼舌舛舟色
虫血行衣見覺言谷豆貝赤走足身車辛辰酉里金長門雨青非面草韭音
頁風飛食首香馬骨高鬥鬼魚鳥鹿麥麻黃黍黑鼎鼓鼠鼻齊齒龍

2. Classical.

乙几匕夕弋无殳毋爻皿耒聿艮豕豸邑阜韋鬯鬲鹵黹黽龜

3. Obsolete.

丶丿亅亠儿冂冖冫凵勹匚匸卩厂厶囗夂夂宀尢屮广廴廾彐彡彳
彳气爿疒癶禸糸网艸虍襾釆隶隹髟龠

生牛肉老米[25]白米[26]小米子[27]老玉米[28]黃米[29]

蟲[8]羽毛[9]羊毛[10]皮毛[11]飛鳥[12]高飛[13]大鹿[14]鹿角[15]金魚[16]魚子[17]比目魚[18]石首魚[19]走馬[20]老馬[21]

9. 牛[1]羊[2]牛馬[3]魚蟲[4]草蟲[5]牙蟲[6]蟲牙[7]毛毛

小川[22]馬竹[23]馬口[24]齒青[25]牛白馬[26]土牛木馬[27]西口馬[28]龍[29]龍門[30]門龍舟[31]黃羊子[32]小山羊

10. 金[1]木水火土[2]田大田[3]瓜田[4]十羊[5]

羊[33]皮香牛皮[34]老鼠[35]小犬[36]犬子[37]金龜[38]土龜[39]卜長[40]蟲

田禾黍[6]山水山川[7]草木[8]西山山谷[9]谷口[10]西方[11]大雨[12]雨西[13]風風水[14]風言[15]羊角[16]風香[17]田[18]

里[18]土音[19]水音[20]山音水色[21]一色[22]大雨[23]欠雨[24]雨水[25]十日[26]一雨[27]土山子黃土[28]黑土[29]鬼風[30]火金[31]

鼓金[32]瓜木瓜[33]木耳木魚子[34][35]

11. 長一寸[1]八寸[2]二八斗[3]豆子十斤米[4]一二疋[5]一二頁[6]

八十二里[7]非止[8]一人止欠[9]一文[10]一方[11]一[12]自辰至酉日[13]用斗[14]

月[2]月一日[3]一見山高月小月[4]月色[5]月夕[6]自辰至酉日[7][8][9]

14. 火石[1]山子石[2]石白子石門[3][4]

13. 青黃赤白黑青[1][2]

白[3]黑白青黃赤[4]黃而黑香色[5]月白色[6]玉色[7]月白色玉色女色[8][9][10]

石[5]人石[6]馬白玉[7]金口玉言[8]瓦缶[9]金玉瓦面瓦片[10][11]

EXERCISES IN THE COLLOQUIAL RADICALS.

1. 人¹ 氏² 人³ 口⁴ 戶⁵ 自己 子⁶ 女⁷ 女⁸ 子 父⁹ 子¹⁰ 貝 子¹² 臣¹³ 士¹⁴ 子

白¹⁵ 衣 大 士 文¹⁶ 士¹⁷ 文 人 鬼¹⁸ 子

2. 人 身¹ 己 身 人² 心³ 口⁴ 手 足 耳⁵ 方 面⁶ 大 耳⁷ 牙⁸ 齒

鼻²² 子 骨²³ 尸²⁴ 手²⁵ 面²⁶ 目 見²⁷ 面²⁸ 見²⁹ 面³⁰ 面子 生³¹

門⁹ 口¹⁰ 舌¹¹ 齒 口¹² 音¹³ 力 骨¹⁴ 尸¹⁵ 首 骨¹⁶ 血¹⁷ 心 黑¹⁸ 一¹⁹ 生 心 血²⁰ 赤²¹ 二 一 心

3. 入¹ 門 干² 支 支³ 用⁴ 力

用⁵ 人⁶ 心⁷ 足 用⁸ 手⁹ 長¹⁰ 工 工¹¹ 瓦 木 工¹² 木 工 大¹³ 小¹⁴ 工 工¹⁵ 人¹⁶ 工 火 食 女¹⁷ 工

手¹⁸ 工 水¹⁹ 手 鼓²⁰ 手 老²¹ 手 生²² 立²³ 自²⁴ 立 行²⁵ 行²⁶ 走²⁷ 香²⁸ 香²⁹ 片 甘³⁰ 心 鼎³¹ 力人³²

4. 大¹ 小 子² 比 父³ 高⁴ 老

一³³ 齊 比 齊 食³⁵ 言 比³⁶ 方 小³⁷ 齊 心 見³⁹ 長 見⁴⁰ 小 心⁴¹ 高 高⁴²

5. 手¹ 巾

6. 舟¹ 車 車² 馬³ 車⁴ 車 門 水⁵ 車 小⁶ 車 子⁷ 門 戶⁸ 大 門⁹ 小 門° 門¹⁰ 二 門

子¹ 小² 老 小³ 心⁴ 衣⁵ 歹⁶ 人⁷ 高⁸ 大 身⁹ 高 力 大 叉¹⁰ 高 叉 大 人¹¹ 老 叉 曰 二 毛

雨² 衣³ 皮 面⁴ 女 衣

7. 刀¹ 子² 干 戈 矢 石 弓⁴ 矢⁵ 弓 刀 石 一⁶ 力⁷ 弓

8. 西¹ 瓜 黃² 瓜 香³ 瓜⁴ 皮 瓜⁵ 子⁶ 禾 黍⁷ 黍 子 米 麥⁸ 麥⁹ 大¹⁰ 小¹¹ 麥

門¹¹ 口 門¹² 面 土¹³ 門 土 戶 車¹⁴ 戶 走¹⁵ 馬 大 門

十⁷ 力 弓 牛⁸ 角 弓

豆¹² 角 黃¹³ 豆 黑¹⁴ 豆 小¹⁵ 麻 子 竹¹⁶ 子 韭¹⁷ 黃 肉¹⁸ 片 用¹⁹ 刀 片 肉 牛²⁰ 肉 羊²¹ 肉 鹿²² 肉 一²³ 方 肉 一²⁴ 斤

EXERCISES IN THE COLLOQUIAL RADICALS. KEY.

1.

1. *jên² shih⁴*, a person from such or such a place; e.g., What is he? He is a Canton *jên² shih⁴*.
2. *mên² shih⁴*, husband and wife's family name. The phrase is used to or of a married woman. Who are her husband's family (*mên²*), and who her own (*shih⁴*)?
3. *jên² k'ou³*, men and women; males and females in a family.
4. *hu⁴ k'ou³*, families; *lit.*, doors and mouths; used in speaking of the population of a street, village, town.
5. *tzŭ⁴ chi³*, self, oneself.
6. *tzŭ³ nü³*, sons and daughters.
7. *nü³ tzŭ³*, a daughter.
8. *nü³ jên²*, a wife.
9. *fu⁴ tzŭ³*, father and son.
10. *lao³ tzŭ³*, a father. Proper name of an ancient philosopher.
11. *pei⁴ tzŭ³*, Chinese for *bei tsé*, a Manchu title of nobility.
12. *ch'ên² tzŭ³*, public servants.
13. *ta⁴ ch'ên²*, minister of state; also the designation of certain particular officials of high rank.
14. *shih⁴ tzŭ³*, a hard student; a reading man.
15. *pai² i¹ ta⁴ shih⁴*, common designation of the goddess Kuan-yin.
16. *wên² shih⁴*, a learned scholar.
17. *wên² jên²* (stronger than *shih⁴ tzŭ³*); a scholar.
18. *kuei³ tzŭ³*, devil; only so used when applied to foreigners.

2.

1. *jên² shên¹*, a man's person.
2. *chi³ shên¹*, one's own; as of affairs, property, etc.
3. *jên² hsin¹*, the heart or mind.
4. *hsin¹ k'ou³*, the breast; *lit.*, heart's mouth.
5. *shou³ tsu²*, hand and foot (not literally, but figuratively); of the relationship of brothers.
6. *êrh³ mu⁴*, the sight and hearing, when spoken of as quick or not; *fig.*, a police detective; a spy, whether officially employed or otherwise.
7. *fang¹ mien⁴ ta⁴ êrh³*, with square face and large ears; characteristics of manly beauty; at the same time, signs of a distinguished career.
8. *ya² ch'ih³*, a tooth; the teeth.
9. *mên² ya²*, the upper front teeth.
10. *k'ou³ shê²*, altercation; *lit.*, mouth and tongue.
11. *k'ou³ ch'ih³*, mouth and teeth; used specially with reference to the pronunciation, accurate or inaccurate, of the dental sounds. See also below, 9, 24.
12. *k'ou³ yin¹*, mouth sounds; pronunciation.
13. *mu⁴ li⁴*, strength of sight.
14. *ku³ jou⁴*, bone and flesh (not literally, but figuratively); of intimate relationship.
15. *shih¹ shou³*, a corpse; *lit.*, corpse and head.
16. *ku³ hsüeh³*, bone and blood; *fig.*, of intimate relationship.
17. *hsüeh³ hsin¹*, blood, heart; the quality of a staunch friend, faithful, adherent.
18. *hei¹ hsin¹*, black heart; the opposite of *hsüeh³ hsin¹*.
19. *yi⁴ shêng¹ hsin¹ hsüeh⁴*, whole life's heart blood; said of long-sustained application to a good purpose.

PART II.—THE RADICALS.

20. *ch'ih⁴ hsin¹*, red heart; said of ministerial fidelity.
21. *êrh⁴ jên² yi¹ hsin¹*, two persons of one mind; agreement; a union conducive to success.
22. *pi² tzŭ³*, the nose.
23. *ku³ shih¹*, a skeleton; *lit.*, bone and corpse.
24. *shou³ hsin¹*, the palm of the hand; *lit.*, hand's heart.
25. *shou³ mien⁴*, inside of hand and fingers; applied figuratively to affairs that are easy to understand.
26. *mien⁴ mu⁴*, the face; *lit.*, face and eyes.
27. *chien⁴ mien⁴*, to see the face; to have a personal interview.
28. *mien⁴ chien⁴*, to see with one's own eyes; certainly a person; doubtfully a thing.
29. *yi⁴ mien⁴*, simultaneously; *lit.*, one and the same face; used of two acts done at the same time by the same agent.
30. *mien⁴ tzŭ³*, the outer face or outside, as opposed to the lining or inside, of clothes; applied also to the surface of affairs.
31. *mien⁴ shêng¹*, a face such as one has not seen before; *lit.*, face raw or new; but used disapprovingly.

3.

1. *ju⁴ mên²*, to enter the doors; used figuratively of commencing a study. There is another phrase for entering a door literally.
2. *kan¹ chih¹*, the stems and branches, *sc.* of the cyclic system by which time is reckoned in China.
3. *chih¹ yung⁴*, expenditure; *lit.*, what is issued and used.
4. *yung⁴ li⁴*, to exert oneself; use strength.
5. *yung² jên²*, to employ people with discrimination.
6. *yung¹ hsin²*, to apply oneself; use the mind.
7. *tsu² yung⁴*, enough to use; most commonly of revenue or income.
8. *yung⁴ kung¹*, of application; to use labour.
9. *ch'ang² kung¹*, long labour; service on long engagement, as opposed to service described as *yüeh⁴ kung¹*. (See 10.)
10. *yüeh⁴ kung¹*, service by the month.
11. *wa³ mu⁴ kung¹*, the service employed on building; *lit.*, labour of tile and wood, *sc.* of tiler and carpenter.
12. *t'u³ mu⁴ kung¹*, labour employed on earth and wood, *sc.* in laying foundations.
13. *ta⁴ kung¹*, in building, of the more skilled labour; employed.
14. *hsiao³ kung¹*, of the less skilled labour, hodmen, etc.
15. *kung¹ jên²*, house servants; also farm labourers.
16. *jên² kung¹ huo³ shih²*, expense of living; *lit.*, labour and subsistence.
17. *nü³ kung¹*, needlework; *lit.*, women's work.
18. *shou³ kung¹*, handiwork, specially that of tailors, joiners, carvers, etc.
19. *shui³ shou³*, sailor; boatman.
20. *ku³ shou³*, drummer.
21. *lao³ shou³*, old hand; experienced.
22. *shêng¹ chang³*, bred and born; *lit.*, born and grown up.
23. *li⁴ chih³*, to come to a standstill.
24. *tzŭ⁴ li⁴*, able to stand alone; independent by reason of character or abilities.
25. *hsing² chih³*, conduct, goings on (*q.d.* whether moving or still, out of doors or at home); used also of an affair: will it go on or not?
26. *hsing² tsou³*, to move; be employed in a public office.

27. *hsing² hsiang¹*, the burning of incense in temples by officials. There is another term for the same sacrifice when performed by the people.
28. *kao¹ hsiang¹*, the tall sticks of incense.
29. *hsiang¹ p'ien⁴*, slices of fragrance; of scented tea.
30. *kan¹ hsin¹*, willing; *lit.*, with pleasant heart.
31. *ting³ li⁴*, strong, as a sacrificial tripod; complimentarily used to a person on whose superior influence the speaker relies.
32. *jên² li⁴*, produced by men's ability; *lit.*, strength, as opposed to spontaneous growth; used mostly of flowers, etc.
33. *yi⁴ ch'i²*, all at the same time or together.
34. *pi³ ch'i²*, to equalise the length or height of cords, poles, etc.: *pi³*, laying side by side; *ch'i²*, to make even.
35. *shih² yen²*, to eat words; break faith.
36. *pi³ fang¹*, for instance; by comparison; also used substantively as a parallel case.
37. *hsiao³ hsin¹*, careful; beware!
38. *ch'i² hsin¹*, unanimous.
39. *chien⁴ chang³*, to grow; *q.d.* to feel, or be the subject of growth; used of animals or vegetables; of man, morally or physically. *Chien⁴ ch'ang²*, used of eminence of a particular quality or attainment; it is hardly colloquial.
40. *chien¹ hsiao³*, view small; of a niggardly disposition.
41. *hsin¹ kao¹*, of lofty aims; noble ambition.
42. *kao¹ chien⁴*, far-seeing, as in politics, family affairs, etc. Complimentarily, another person's opinion; *lit.*, [your] lofty view or idea.

4.

1. *ta⁴ hsiao³*, large and small; hence, size.
2. *tzŭ³ pi² fu⁴ kao¹*, the son taller than the father.
3. *fu⁴ lao³ tzŭ³ hsiao³*, the father old, the son young; used where the father is very old to have so young a son.
4. *lao³ hsiao³*, old and young.
5. *hsin¹ tai³*, of evil disposition.
6. *tai³ jên²*, villains, such as thieves, murderers.
7. *hsiao³ jên²*, the man morally small, as opposed to the *chün¹ tzŭ³* (君子), the man morally and intellectually perfect.
8. *kao¹ ta⁴*, tall; lofty.
9. *shên¹ kao¹ li⁴ ta⁴*, tall of stature and of great strength.
10. *yu⁴ kao¹ yu⁴ ta⁴*, both tall (or high) and large.
11. *jên² lao³ yu⁴ yüeh¹ êrh⁴ mao²*, when a man is old he is also said to be *êrh⁴ mao²*, two-haired, *sc.* to have hair white and black.

Obs.—Colloquially, *yüeh¹* is only used, as here, in proverbs, quotations, etc.

5.

1. *shou³ chin¹*, a handkerchief.
2. *yü³ i¹*, rain clothes; a waterproof dress.
3. *p'i² i¹*, clothes of fur, or lined with fur.
4. *nü³ i¹*, women's apparel.

PART II.—THE RADICALS.   39

6.

1. *chou¹ chü¹*, (politely) junk or cart, land or water carriage.
2. *ch‘ê¹ ma³*, carts and horses.
3. *êrh⁴ ma³ ch‘ê¹*, a cart with two horses; *êrh⁴ ma³ chü¹*, a name for the water tobacco pipe, more commonly spoken of as *shui³ yen¹ tai⁴*.
4. *ch‘ê¹ mên²*, the *porte cochère*; entrance by which carts, etc., are admitted.
5. *shui³ ch‘ê¹*, water-cart.
6. *hsiao³ ch‘ê¹ tzŭ³*, the small or single-wheeled cart or wheelbarrow.
7. *mên² hu⁴*, entrance gate or gates of a house.
8. *ta⁴ mên²*, the greater gate; specially, an entrance gate.
9. *hsiao³ mên²*, smaller entrance gate.
10. *êrh⁴ mên²*, the gate you come to in Chinese premises after passing the *ta⁴ mên²*, chief entrance gate.
11. *mên² k‘ou³*, gateway, doorway.
12. *mên² mien⁴*, the front of a shop; *q.d.* its doorway face.
13. *t‘u³ mên² t‘u³ hu⁴*, mud buildings, as in villages, poor suburbs; *lit.*, doorways and window-spaces of earth.
14. *ch‘ê¹ hu⁴*, carters in general; not used in Peking of one man.
15. *tsou³ ma³ ta⁴ mên²*, any large gate of a house court through which there is room for horses to ride.

7.

1. *tao¹ tzŭ³*, a knife.
2. *kan¹ ko¹*, shield and spear; *fig.*, for war.
3. *shih³ shih²*, the arrow and the stone; archery and slinging.
4. *kung¹ shih³*, bow and arrow; archery.
5. *kung¹, tao¹, shih³*, bow, sword, and stone.
   Obs.—Military graduates have to prove their strength by drawing the bow, exercise with the sword, and raising the stone.
6. *yi¹ li⁴ kung¹*, a bow that requires power equal to 1 catty weight to draw it; the bow easiest drawn.
7. *shih² li⁴ kung¹*, a bow of 10 catty power; really the stiffest bow an archer attempts to draw, though there are bows nominally of 16 catty power.
8. *niu² chiao³ kung¹*, cow-horn bow. All bows are stiffened with cow horn or iron, the latter, however, being for show.

8.

1. *hsi¹ kua¹*, water melon; *lit.*, Western melon.
2. *huang² kua¹*, cucumber; *lit.*, yellow melon.
3. *hsiang¹ kua¹*, the melon generally eaten as fruit; *lit.*, scented melon.
4. *kua¹ p‘i²*, rind of any gourd.
5. *kua¹ tzŭ³*, seeds of any gourd.
6. *ho² shu³*, rice and millet uncut.
7. *shu³ tzŭ³*, millet.
8. *mi³ mai⁴*, rice and wheat cut; as we say corn or grain.
9. *mai⁴ tzŭ³*, wheat.
10. *ta⁴ mai⁴*, barley.

11. *hsiao³ mai⁴*, wheat.
12. *tou⁴ chiao³*, a bean-pod; *lit.*, bean-horn.
13. *huang² tou⁴*, the bean commonly eaten.
14. *hei¹ tou⁴*, black pulse.
15. *hsiao³ ma² tzŭ³*, cumin.
16. *chu² tzŭ³*, bamboo tree.
17. *chiu³ huang²*, leeks; *lit.*, leeks yellow.
18. *jou⁴ p'ien⁴*, slices of meat; *p'ien⁴* here a substantive.
19. *yung⁴ tao¹ p'ien⁴ jou⁴*, using knife slice meat; to slice meat with a knife; *p'ien⁴* here a verb.
20. *niu² jou⁴*, beef.
21. *yang² jou⁴*, mutton.
22. *lu⁴ jou⁴*, venison.
23. *yi⁴ fang¹ jou⁴*, a lump or hunch (*lit.*, square) of meat.
24. *yi⁴ chin¹ shêng¹ niu² jou⁴*, 1 catty of fresh (or raw) beef.
25. *lao³ mi³*, old rice; rice that has been some time in store.
26. *pai² mi³*, new (*lit.*, white) rice; also rice of better quality than the *huang² mi³*. (See 29.)
27. *hsiao³ mi³ tzŭ³*, oats.
28. *lao³ yü⁴ mi³*, Indian corn of a certain age.
29. *huang² mi³*, a coarse rice; not brought up to Peking.

9.

1. *niu² yang²*, sheep and cattle.
2. *niu² ma³*, cattle and horses.
3. *yü² ch'ung²*, insects that fish eat; larvæ of gnats, etc.
4. *ts'ao³ ch'ung²*, plants and insects, *q.d.* botany and entomology; also any insects found in grass or plants.
5. *ya² ch'ung²*, teeth insects. The Chinese believe toothache to be their work.
6. *ch'ung² ya²*, a tooth, or teeth, suffering from insects; aching.
7. *mao² mao² ch'ung²*, hairy insect; caterpillar.
8. *yü³ mao²*, camlet; also feathers and hair; plumage of a bird.
9. *yang² mao²*, wool.
10. *p'i² mao²*, hair of fur; also *fig.* of maladies not serious; *q.d.* affecting the surface only.
11. *mao² nü³*, spinster; a girl whose hair is still unparted on the forehead; applied rather to young girls not of nubile years.
12. *fei¹ niao³*, birds; *lit.*, flying birds.
13. *kao¹ fei¹*, flying high.
14. *ta⁴ lu⁴*, the red deer; *lit.*, great deer.
15. *lu⁴ chio²*, deer's horn.
16. *chin¹ yü²*, gold fish.
17. *yü² tzŭ³*, fish eggs; spawn.
18. *pi³ mu⁴ yü²*, pair-fish, supposed to be inseparable; *fig.*, of the married state.
19. *shih² shou³ yü²*, a kind of sciæna; commonly called the *huang² hua¹ yü²*, yellow-flower fish, yellow marked or spotted fish.
20. *tsou³ ma³*, a horse that ambles along quietly; such a horse as Chinese officials prefer to ride.
21. *lao³ ma³*, an old horse.
22. *hsiao³ Ch'uan¹ ma³*, a Szechwan pony.
23. *chu² ma³*, horse made of bamboo.
24. *k'ou³ ch'ih³*, mouth's teeth; *sc.* a horse's teeth, by which his age is known.
25. *ch'ing¹ niu² pai² ma³*, grey cow, white horse; used literally; but also figuratively, of marriages of which the conditions are astrologically objectionable.
26. *t'u³ niu² mu⁴ ma³*, ox of clay, horse of wood; *fig.*, of stupid people.
27. *hsi¹ k'ou³ ma³*, a horse from the western frontier; *lit.*, western mouths, *sc.* frontier passes.

PART II.—THE RADICALS.

28. *lung² chao³*, dragon's claws; as in embroidery, painting, etc.
29. *lung² mên²*, the dragon's gate, through which candidates for degrees enter the examination hall.
30. *tou⁴ lung² chou¹*, contending dragon boats; the boats in which men race at the fête of the fifth moon.
31. *huang² yang² tzŭ³*, a kind of antelope.
32. *hsiao³ shan¹ yang²*, a goat's kid.
33. *yang² p'i²*, a sheepskin.
34. *hsiang¹ niu² p'i²*, Russia leather, *sc.* scented cow-hide.
35. *lao³ shu³*, a rat, *sc.* an old rat.
36. *hsiao³ ch'üan³* (of one's own son), a little dog.
37. *ch'üan³ tzŭ³*, dog, as in 36.
38. *chin¹ kuei¹*, a small kind of land tortoise.
39. *kuei¹ pu³*, divination; *lit.*, that practised with reference to the marks on a tortoise's back.
40. *ch'ang² ch'ung²*, a serpent; *lit.*, the long reptile.

10.

1. *chin¹, mu⁴, shui³, huo³, t'u³*, metal, wood, water, fire, earth; the five elements of the Chinese system.
2. *t'ien² t'u³*, lands; fields.
3. *ta⁴ t'ien²*, the autumn crops, which are many and of large value as compared with those of spring.
4. *kua¹ t'ien²*, lands growing gourds, melons, etc.
5. *yi⁴ t'ien² ho² shu³*, a field all rice or millet; a well-filled field.
6. *shan¹ shui³*, scenery; *lit.*, hills and water; also, the water on the hills; torrents.
7. *shan¹, ch'uan¹, ts'ao³, mu⁴*, scenery; landscape; *lit.*, hills, streams, herbage (or plants), and trees. *Shan¹ ch'uan¹*, the water system of a country.
8. *hsi¹ shan¹*, the hills to the west.
9. *shan¹ ku³*, hill and valley; valleys in the hills.
10. *ku³ k'ou³*, a gorge, narrow pass; *lit.*, valley's mouth.
11. *hsi¹ fang¹*, the western region; western country; often, specially, Thibet, the land of Buddha.
12. *ta⁴ fêng¹*, high wind; a gale.
13. *hsi¹ fêng¹*, west wind.
14. *fêng¹ shui³*, air and water; the influence superstitiously attributed to certain aspects of buildings, localities, etc.
15. *fêng¹ yen²*, words borne on the wind; rumour.
16. *yang² chiao³ fêng¹*, ram's horn wind; a whirlwind; name given to a child's convulsions.
17. *hsiang¹ fêng¹ shih² li³*, fragrance blown 10 *li*.
18. *t'u³ yin¹*, sounds of the locality; a local dialect.
19. *shui³ yin¹*, water sounds; *lit.*, the murmur of flowing water; *fig.*, affection of one's proper accent caused by residence away from home, *q.d.* by drinking the water of the strange place.
20. *shan¹ yin¹*, sounds in hills; an echo.
21. *shui³ sê⁴*, tint of water; its pleasant tint, as in spring or autumn; used also of the complexion of a handsome woman.
22. *yi⁴ sê⁴*, of uniform colour.
23. *ta⁴ yü³*, heavy rain.
24. *ch'ien² yü³*, there is a want of rain.
25. *yü³ shui³*, rain water; also the name of one of the 24 periods into which the Chinese year is divided.
26. *shih² jih⁴ yi⁴ yü³*, rain once in 10 days; preceded by another sentence, wind once in five days; weather to please farmers.

27. t'u³ shan¹ tzŭ³, an artificial mound in a garden, etc.; t'u³ shan¹, a hill or mound of earth, as distinguished from one of rock.
28. huang² t'u³, clay.
29. hei¹ t'u³, black loam; specially of the dirty soil of Peking.
30. kuei³ huo³, devil fire, will-o'-the-wisp.
31. chin¹ ku³, gong; lit., metal and drum; fig., sounds of war; the gong properly gives the signal to retire, the drum to advance.
32. chin¹ kua¹, a red gourd not eatable; one of the insignia borne on a pole at funerals and at certain state ceremonies.
33. mu⁴ kua¹, papaya, BRIDGMAN (?). In the North a scented melon, not eaten, but used in medicine.
34. mu⁴ ĕrh³, a tree's ear; an edible lichen.
35. mu⁴ yü² tzŭ³, a hollow wooden vessel on which the Buddhist priest taps when chanting or begging.

11.

1. ch'ang² yi² ts'un⁴, 1 inch long.
2. pa² ts'un⁴ ĕrh⁴, 8 inches 2 [tenths].
3. pa¹ tou⁴ tou⁴ tzŭ³, 8 measures of pulse. The addition of tzŭ³ to other nouns is common.
4. shih² chin¹ mi³, 10 catties of rice.
5. yi¹ ĕrh⁴ p'i³, one or two bales of cloth, drapery, etc.
6. yi¹ ĕrh⁴ yeh⁴, one or two leaves of a book.
7. pa¹ shih² ĕrh⁴ li³, 82 li = some 27 miles.
8. fei¹ chih³ yi⁴ jĕn², not only one person.
9. chih³ ch'ien⁴ yi¹ wĕn², only one cash short.
10. pa¹ k'ou³ jĕn² eight persons; q.d. such or such a family consisting of. The expression is no more to be taken literally than "half a dozen" with us.
11. yi¹ fang¹, a whole neighbourhood.
12. yi² ts'un⁴ chien⁴ fang¹, to be an inch square. The verb chien⁴ is here reflective.
13. tou³ fang¹, literally, bushel-square; the square or oblong space left often in the trellis-work of a Chinese window, to admit the light; said to derive its name from the size, not the form, of the space so reserved.
14. jih⁴ yung⁴ tou³ chin¹, daily expend a measure of gold; expenditure of a wealthy man. Cf. our pot of money.

12.

1. jih⁴ jih⁴, every day.
2. yüeh⁴ yüeh⁴, every month.
3. yi⁴ jih² yi² chien⁴, to see or visit once every day.
4. shan¹ kao¹ yüeh⁴ hsiao³, mountains lofty, moon small; the moon rising behind lofty mountains; phrase used of the picturesque effect of such a scene.
5. yüeh⁴ sĕ⁴, moonlight; rather used of a moon old and bright.
6. yüeh⁴ hsi¹, moonlit night; part of rather a high-flown phrase applied to the beauties of spring.
7. tzŭ⁴ ch'ĕn² chih⁴ yu³, from about 8 A.M. to about 5 P.M. The Chinese day and night are divided into 12 two-hourly periods. The ch'ĕn² is the fourth before midnight; yu³, the third from noon.
8. jih⁴ tzŭ³, a day.
9. ch'ang² chih⁴ jih⁴, of days lengthening after the winter solstice.

13.

1. *ch'ing*¹, *huang*², *ch'ih*⁴, *pé*², *hé*⁴ (or, in Peking, *po*², *ho*⁴); sky-blue or deep-green, yellow, blood-red, white, black.
2. *ch'ing*¹ *pai*², blue-white=pale blue.
3. *hei*¹ *pai*² (so pronounced in Peking colloquial), black and white, as of a chessboard's squares; also used when speaking of intense stupidity that cannot tell white from black.
4. *ch'ing*¹ *huang*², green and yellow. Unripe grain is said not to have reached the age when these colours mingle. The phrase is also applied to a sickly countenance.
5. *ch'ih*⁴ *sé*⁴, bright scarlet, such as is used on temples, etc.; also ruddy, as a person's complexion. In the latter sense it is pronounced in Peking *ch'ih*⁴ *shai*³.
6. *huang*² *érh*² *hei*¹, yellow and yet black; said of the countenance in certain sickness.
7. *hsiang*¹ *sé*⁴, the colour of *hsiang*¹, Chinese incense sticks, which we call joss-sticks; a pale yellow dye seen in silks, cloth, etc.
8. *yüeh* ⁴*pai*² *sé*⁴, moon-white(=pale blue) colour.
9. *yü*⁴ *sé*⁴, colour of jade; much the same as *yüeh*⁴ *pai*² *sé*⁴.
10. *nü*³ *sé*⁴, lust after women.

14.

1. *huo*³ *shih*²; a flint.
2. *shan*¹ *tzŭ*³ *shih*², a rockery; the stones used to make one.
3. *shih*² *chiu*⁴ *tzŭ*³, a stone mortar.
4. *shih*² *mén*², a gate or doorway of stone; passage through a rockery; rock pass between hills.
5. *shih*² *jén*², human figure of stone.
6. *shih*² *ma*³, stone horse.
7. *pai*² *yü*⁴, white jade.
8. *chin*¹ *k'ou*³ *yü*⁴ *yen*², mouth of gold words of jade; such as the Emperor speaks; Imperial affirmations or predictions. Used with negatives in rejecting what is said to you by another, as *not* infallible. What you say, or he says, is *not* mouth of gold, etc.
9. *wa*³, *fou*³, *chin*¹, *yü*⁴, tile, earthenware, gold, jade (or jewels). The first two are better to buy than the last; thrift is better than profusion.
10. *wa*³ *mien*⁴, tile face=the roof of a house.
11. *wa*³ *p'ien*⁴, a bit of tile.

PART III.

THE FORTY EXERCISES.
(CHINESE TEXT.)

EXERCISE I.

1. 十六。二十九。三十。四十五。六十七。八十。

2. 第十七。二十三個。百二十三個。千三百三十個。千三百五十六個。五個人。

3. 第一。第二。十七。千八百。百六。十五。

4. 第一百。萬零三。百個五。十七萬。零六百。一十七。二十。

5. 一百萬。三十五萬。五百萬。萬零零一。六萬零零。五百零零。七十萬。

6. 七萬零一。百一九。十零一。千萬。四十。六萬。一千。

7. 五萬零八十。八九萬八千。四百零二一。千零五。零七十二八。千一三百六十。一百零三。

8. 一百二十一。八十五。百五百九。四九百。萬三千。

9. 有幾個。十幾個。有人來。來人。有些個。有好些個人。有人。多少人。個來人。多少人。來三萬。多人。

10. 數十幾個。幾個。幾十個不止兩。十幾個八九個。十來個。十個二百多。五千多。

11. 長三寸。一口。四口人。幾口人。一身有。五斤牛肉。六斤肉。羊肉幾斤。斤魚。

12. 七斗麥子。九斗米。一斗黍。斗子。

13. 幾個牙。長幾萬。里至多。四萬里。有山足。高二百。里三百五。斤有零。

PART III.—THE FORTY EXERCISES.

EXERCISE I. KEY.

1
十二十。
四九十。
七十三。
四十五。
一百九。
十九。

2
四萬零一。
百六十八。
三百萬零。
一千二百。
二十四。
八。
二百二十九。
十。

3
第二十。
一第三。
二第八。
百四十。
十七。
有八九個人來。

4
第九百九。
十九第七。
百萬零六。
千五百四。
十三。第三。
千五百六。
百萬零四。
十七。

5
五百萬零。
二百零一。
三百萬零。
二十七。
四十六。
九千九萬。
九十九。

6
有好些個。
馬多少。
牛有。
馬有。
五十。
六十。

7
有幾斤魚。
有七斤零。
幾兩。
小米子有。
六斗。
十八斗米。
馬十四斗豆。
子。

8
有十幾個人來。
有五十個人來。
有一百多個人。
來多一身。
一口。

9
有十來斤。
魚十九斤。
牛肉十七。
斤鹿肉十。
四斗米十。
八斗豆子。
十斗小米子。

10
長多少。
里長好。
些里足。
一千七。
百里足。
九百里。
有山足。
高八里。

EXERCISE II.

1. 我們倆甚麼人。
2. 那個人是誰。
3. 那個人是個好人。俗這人是個好人。他是個賣甚麼的。他是賣好人的。
4. 我要好的有沒有。這個很好那個不好。這個好那個不好。這個好來有人來。有人來。有些個人來。他是那兒的人。
5. 他來了沒有。他沒來了。他們來了好幾個人。這個東西是你的。這個東西是我們的。
6. 他們來了多少。他們有多少人。有多少。有多少個人。這個東西是你的。那個東西是我們的。
7. 這個是我們的那個是他們的。這個是誰的人。那兒有十幾個人。那兒有幾個人。不多的。那兒有幾個人。
   那麼大。那麼小。
   那麼東西。那麼些個東西。
   俗這人。是個好人。有很好。那個人很好不好。
   那兒的人不是這兒的人。

8. 我不要這個他們要這個他們的不大好。你們那兒有好的沒有。沒有好的。你有好的沒有。
9. 這個東西很好得。那個東西很好得。那個馬很好得。那個馬很好的。你要買那個馬。長得很長。你們是幾口人。我們
10.
11. 你要買那竹子長得高八寸多。
12. 那個人比我的兒子
13. 我們有這個東西沒有。好的我們不要了。你們那兒有好的沒有。我們不要這個東西。我買不了那麼些個。

好的。好得。好。
好得。長得不走。你得
很。好得好。長得不毛。來了口人我們是十來口人。

PART III.—THE FORTY EXERCISES.

EXERCISE II. KEY.

1. 你的馬。我的羊。他的車。你們的東西。我們的米。我們的好東西。他們的手巾。這兒賣很好的刀子。

2. 你們買、我們賣。他們要買甚麽東西。他們要買這個東西。我們要買這個米。我們要買好東西。

3. 你有好馬這麽、小那沒有。誰的是、我的。你有多少馬、我有三個馬。這兒馬不少。

4. 這個馬是那個人的。那個人是那兒的人。他不是這兒的人。他賣的東西好不好、不很好。

5. 你是那兒的人、我是這兒的人。那個買賣人沒有很好的東西。我們倆買賣人賣好東西。

6. 我要買東西、這兒有賣東西的。五個兒子他五個兒子在這兒。三個月、你用的是黃土的。他鼻長、有三寸多長。

7. 我要買東西、這兒有賣東西的。五個兒子他五個兒子在這兒。

8. 他有多少兒女。他有四個女兒、三個兒子。

9. 你要得多少、我要得那麽的。長得很、不是金的。

10. 那個東西是金的麽、不是金的。那個長得很長、不是金的。

11. 那個人長得很長、不是金的。

7. 好東西。要甚麽東西、要一斗麥子。西、你賣不賣、你里他是賣瓦的。黑豆這兒魚的山水很好。他。

EXERCISE III.

1 有人拿東西來了。有拿不得進屋子裏來的。那人是屋裏住房子這有多少房甚麽他沒在家裏做你在那兒住。

2 那人是進屋來。拿不著這個人來要拿那人是裏來。一個房子有三十家。上那兒去住。是東城住。

3 那東西去。拿不著這個房子比五間房子了。上街去了。著好他那東西很多的那人你住的房街上走着街住着好。他那

4 那東西沒有一個房子好住的人很多。人開的舖子在那兒開的是做

5 多了一個人是拿不了的。人住。子大小我上的人很多。在那兒是甚麽買賣的。

6 拿不了去。外頭土大。間小屋子。

7 你們那兒他在家裏做你在那兒住。

8 他那舖子東城有。他來了沒有三個西城有。他來了得去麽。過不四個我們這兒他沒進來。去你上那兒去。我不上那兒去。

9 沒有那麽大的過去了。他上

10 這個道兒過你做甚麽要下雨下過他那麽大雨這門開

11 沒買賣那個舖子街買東西兒上來了。那個人得起了這麽大雨住了這開不

12 是我的那舖子去過。他來我沒去過。來。風起來大得住了。你小心拿不住了。

13 裏買東西的人過沒有。

EXERCISE III. KEY.

1. 你住在城裏頭我在城外頭住我住的房子有六間。你在那兒開鋪子那兒住家。

2. 這個房子比那個房子大多了。這個房子有十間那個房子有四間。大街上住的人不很多鋪子不少。

3. 他住家在那兒他在西城一個小小兒的房子裏住。他在那兒開鋪子是不是。他不是買賣人。

4. 進屋裏來街上有土那屋門兒開了。他開着幾個鋪子。他開着三四個鋪子。他的買賣在東城。他的鋪子不很大。

5. 他在家裏做甚麼。他沒有甚麼做的。他出城去了往那兒去了他往西去了。他要做甚麼。他要買車買馬。

6. 我要買他的東西的那個買賣人往那兒去了。我住的房子他知道不知道。他沒進過你的屋子他是不知道。

7. 他那個人的房子比你我的房子好多了。他那房子有多少間。有八間我的房子有六間你的房子有四間。那房子的口面大。

EXERCISE IV.

1 有人說這是誰家外頭大人進你愛你快些把門開他在那個地的房子誰來了來你們這個兒走,城開門開道兒方兒住知道我做五六都得站不門一關了,關上上躺不得是不出來,他不愛我不你回不叫他起是我說不出來是甚個人在樓上大愛你胸戶把著叫誰說的他做過多麼人坐著他了家了胸戶關他起的你那少回我不是地下我身子來把了,你說一回知道大愛。上胸戶門關了。乏走不關上。上。

2 ...

3 ...

4 ...

5 ...

6 ...

7 ...

8 ...

9 走著來的步下他那個人回來了是這兒的騾走著他走了來沒有他子好是那兒馬的,我是坐車來上那'兒去了上衙的騾子好麼不是來的是騎的他是步行門去了他去是坐那騾子沒有馬來的我的,我在前頭來兒兒騾子沒多少買是騎馬他在後頭走,小轎子是坐那兒的好了,我那匹他不大兒轎子比那了三頭馬跑得很我快走了慢愛坐車是他那頂兒的慢。騾子七個快慢兒的走。轎子好。騾子驢都騾快。

EXERCISE IV. KEY.

1

他在樓上坐著叫他快往這兒來他不快來的很慢我在頭裏坐車他在後頭坐轎子。

2

叫他買兩輛車四匹馬他說這兒沒有馬他說騾子比馬好他買了騾子沒買了他買了多少騾子買了四頭他買了驢沒有他沒買你沒叫他買驢。

3

他上衙門去是坐轎子是坐車他說是坐車坐轎子都不愛他是步行去的他不愛坐轎子的不快他回來的不快他在地下躺著起不來。

4

那匹馬比這匹快馬比騾子快騾子比驢快他到了沒到沒有他做甚麼他慢慢兒的走著叫他快來。

5

你有幾頂轎子有兩頂你的騾馬有多少有四匹馬三頭騾子五個驢你有車沒有沒有我的車都賣了你站著做甚麼不做甚麼你愛坐著我愛站著。

EXERCISE V.

1. 我要請先生教書你給我找了先生沒有找著了他不來他說學生那麼多不肯來先生請坐。請教這是甚麼字。

2. 叫人把那字典拿來請先生找出那個字來。字甚麼要找呢。要找熊字。

3. 請問這個字你認得不認得這個字我還沒看見過呢。這個字你看見過你還沒有。那個字眞沒有看見過。

4. 你告訴我他那個人的口音有你的好音不大甚麼沒有我的口音不大甚麼好他認得的字麼那兒沒有呢。的字比我認得的多。

5. 這個字你見過沒見過。見過了。你告訴我是甚麼字。我不記得那個字了。還有不記得的字麼。還有沒有呢。記得的少不記得的多。

EXERCISE V. KEY.

1. 我請了先生來教我說話。你還要學寫字不要。請先生告訴我的字還不多。我的口音正不正。不很正你認得的字還不多。真。

2. 那字典在那兒。在先生的屋裏他那兒找字呢他找的馬那馬跑的很快。你請他給抄下來先生不肯來他告訴我你的口音很不好說話又不真。

3. 我的先生你見過沒有。我見他騎著馬那馬跑的很快。我找字典記字你認得不認得那個字。著了那個字你認得不認得那個字我還沒瞧見過。

4. 這幾個學生學甚麼學寫字學認字他們的先生是誰。我不知道是誰你見過沒有見過。還在這兒教學生那個馬好不好。好不很好。他跑得慢。

5. 你愛騎馬不愛馬跑得快我不愛騎他這個馬好不好。在這兒教學生那個字你抄了沒有。還沒抄哪。要快抄。騎住了。

EXERCISE VI.

1. 他說的官話還可以，可是沒有你的好。他說的官話還有土音。聽見說你得了幾本書都看完了沒有？得是得，看了不過一兩本。

2. 我聽見說你學著官話呢，學得很好。那四聲你分得出分不出？聲你分得出分不出，都還可以分得開。

3. 那一本書你看完了沒有？

4. 你念了多少日子的書？我念了十個月的書。那書上的字都記得那麼多，忘了好些個了，還有記錯了幾個字不認得了的。

5. 他那個人懂得官話不懂？我聽見人說他不懂。得他認得字不認得？還認得，認過四五千字。你那兒知道呢？上月我們在一塊兒看書。我叫他抄寫，他行不行？甚麼不行的。

6. 你告訴我，他的話聽得出聽不出來？聽不出來。

7. 你念過的書千不萬不可忘了。錯了，可你說得很是。

8. 你會用這兒的字典麼？會用。是會用，找字可得慢些兒。

PART III.—THE FORTY EXERCISES.

EXERCISE VI. KEY.

1
拿那一管筆給我這個筆不好還有好的沒有了沒有好的還有兩三管。

2
拿一張紙、一塊墨一管筆寫字。你要我寫甚麼字。這書上不認得的字都寫。

3
我聽見說你學官話呢,你懂得不懂得我不大懂念的日子不多。

4
四聲你會分不會都會不肯字是那一聲是上聲不錯你拿這張紙寫那個字你寫錯了。

5
那一本書你看完了沒有。看完了也很明白的不認得的字沒有那兒沒有呢,不認得的多,認得的少。

6
我的話你懂不懂懂你口音這麼正我很懂得。

7
你給我買一張紙,一管筆,可以不可以。可以。你還要墨不要。還要五張紙兩管筆,明白不明白。都明白了。

EXERCISE VII.

1. 廚房。一把刀子。一把鏟子。一個炒勺。一個飯鍋。一個鍋蓋。一個茶壺。一個茶盅。一個酒杯。一個酒盅子。

2. 他要上炕躺著。我在炕上躺著。你快把鋪蓋鋪上。那個人快上牀了。

3. 那牀上有帳子。沒有他。在牀上躺著。我在椅子上坐著呢。

4. 這屋裏黑了。快拿燈來。桌子上的那蠟燈子是誰擎了去了。是我擎過去了。弄廚房的火上還沒著的。

5. 飯鍋是煮飯的。鍋蓋是飯鍋的蓋兒。茶壺是沏茶的東西。很分得出來。可也有蓋兒。

6. 酒杯酒盅。本是酒杯。分別得出來。比酒盅兒大。

7. 那屋裏桌子椅子都壞了。說桌椅分是兩張。兩張八張椅子。

8. 那個勺子比本大。勺子比勺子小。匙子比勺子還小。說的是一把勺子一把匙子。這都是京話。這麼用。

9. 你們屋裏有蓆沒有。裏有蓆子我們沒有。炕上都有蓆子。

10. 你們兒用蠟燈那麼些蠟是作甚麼用。是家裏都用。我們黑下也用。是用蠟燈。

11. 你買了那麼些蠟是作甚麼用。是廚房裏用。都是黑下用。也是用蠟燈。看書用的。

EXERCISE VII. KEY.

1. 炕上的蓆子他給拏了去了。叫他給我拏來，這床上的鋪蓋那兒他也賣了。

2. 蠟燈在那兒。椅子上把那蠟燈拿了去，你找個燈來。那燈拏了去，這屋裏著了沒有。這麼黑看不見。這麼黑我找不著。我見那蠟燈在那兒，我找去。

3. 酒盅子比酒杯小，茶盅茶碗都可以說。有小的飯鍋的蓋兒。鍋的蓋比茶碗的蓋兒大。

4. 那屋裏蓆子帳子都壞了。你快買帳子去。了，子買帳去。把鋪蓋。把鋪蓋，鋪好了。

5. 給我一把刀子一把刀子一把勺子，桌子上有刀子沒有勺子。你叫廚子給你拏把勺子。

6. 廚子煮飯用的飯鍋他那個人拏了去了，廚子說那飯他煮不了。我問那個人是誰拏了飯鍋，他說不知道是誰。

7. 你那話說錯了。我沒說，我看見他做的，我說是你告訴我是他做的。你沒明白不明白，你不用說你明白不明白你做甚麼，誰找你的錯兒，你做你的，我做我的。

8. 我要分這塊紙給那五個人，他的可得比那四個人的分兒大。你去請他把拏了去的我那兩本書還給我。

EXERCISE VIII.

1. 一條橈子是長的。一個撓子是方的。說條子的多，說撓子的多，都是個說話用的話。學話的用。

2. 花瓶。酒瓶。酒壺。茶壺。盤子。碟子。

3. 點燈。吹燈。倒酒了。他倒下茶水來。這東西站不住倒下來了。火燒了。火滅了。

4. 倒水。你把水給他倒了。這個水倒滿了。手也說得壺是滿了。那是酒壺。酒壺滿了。那是酒壺。空的是空的。

5. 空是沒有東西在裏頭空壺的那是空酒壺。

6. 那花瓶是甚麼人弄破了的。那是我弄破的。可沒有壞還可以使收拾收拾。那傢伙弄壞使不得。

7. 那刀子。鋪子。盤子。勺子。碟子飯盤子。碗酒杯。這些個。都是喫飯的傢伙。

8. 花瓶。是算花瓶麼。也算。以可算。是傢伙。

9. 爐子有大小不同。房裏做飯用的是爐子，炕裏燒爐子，屋裏燒的是爐子。也是爐子。

10. 叫人倒茶。叫人把茶拿來在茶碗裏頭沒有。你點了我自己點上了。他自己滅火。

11. 吹燈。人把燈吹滅了。燈吹滅了。是燈滅了。火滅了。

12. 那個壺裏有水沒有。個是空一個是滿的。你把那的倒。空的倒滿了水。

PART III.—THE FORTY EXERCISES.

EXERCISE VIII. KEY.

1. 我真不知道你要那麼些椅子做甚麼。

2. 你還算算請了二十五個人來吃飯想我們用的那幾張椅子二十五個人還坐得下麼。

3. 二十五個人不坐在吃飯的屋子裏的廚房很使得。

4. 有了撬子可坐開了請問撬子還好看不好看。還有碟子飯碗得找幾個可不知道往那兒找去。

5. 我們這兒有三十個飯碗。

6. 那飯碗使不得碗有叉六個破的。

7. 我不管破不破叫人來收拾就得了。

8. 我買了他一桌傢伙還有廚房用的些個零碎東西同燒火使的他開的帳給算一算錯不錯。

9. 我不會算帳這是那兒的話那先生還沒教給你認數目字麼。

10. 那小寫的數目字我認得了這寫的大字我還不懂。

EXERCISE IX.

1
前兒就是前天昨兒是天冷昨天今兒明兒後兒明天後天都是那麼著。

2
天氣分得暖和颱風熱天涼天晴天下雨下雪這些都在裏頭

3
一點半鐘就是一點兩刻。一點鐘就下鐘是一點

4
他那個人念過二十多年的書不過做了五六個月的先生這個人白日愛騎馬黑下回家看書。

5
我今兒走下月可以回來。你這個人今兒八下鐘還沒起來麼.

6
前年後年說得前月後月不大說。這兒很說。後月天熱的時候兒下雨。天冷就下雪。天晴了。

7
前四天颱北風第二天天氣很冷昨兒夜下雨今兒天晴了。

8
今年天氣暖和得很沒有去年那麼冷。今年的時令不正這幾年不見過四月裡還下雪呢。

9
我們倆到這兒好些年了。他是上月到的他們倆去年來過了。

PART III.—THE FORTY EXERCISES.

EXERCISE IX. KEY.

1. 你那一年到京裏來的。

2. 我是今年到的。日子不多,不過有半年。

3. 你的京話說的很到不錯。

4. 那都是我在南方學過的。

5. 那就是你看這兒水土好。好不

6. 這水土不好,和這兒甚麼不很熱,甚麼時候熱,在這兒過不過,年不知道冷怎麼樣。

7. 在屋裏很暖和,可是這麼說,要在外頭走幾可,天可不得了。

8. 聽見說這兒的雪很大。

9. 不是下雪,一年下不過二寸。我說的是颱風吹的冷。

10. 你天天甚麼都做甚麼。

11. 我天天七點鐘起來,就喫半點鐘的飯,先生來,回頭點請念書,就喫半點鐘的書,咯回來,馬出去騎。

12. 那們今兒喫完了飯,和我來騎馬,去不行。

13. 你瞧天氣涼了,要下雨,晴不了。

14. 可不是那們明個去好,定甚麼時候兒。

15. 定一就走,到甚麼涼涼快點兒,跑得了。

EXERCISE X.

1 工夫。年年是每年不是每年就那麽。每月每月還是這麽樣。每天每天躺著天天上炕就是他那房子就是他各兒住著。

2 他是早起起來响午上街晚响回家看書到夜裏三更天就在炕兒去那各自各兒去那各自

3 各自各兒就是自已一個這個事情得你各自各兒就是他各自各兒住著。

4 上半天下了雨下半天晴了前打更的打更一夜頭一更就是冷三更天更就是定更。

5 夜裏那打更的打更一夜有五更一夜

6 天長做事的工夫多天夫沒有空兒短事沒有那兒情得擱在屋裏桌子上了。

7 他多喒回來他明兒罷那是陰天今兒早起下的霧很大那麽大的霧去罷。

8 天上的雲彩滿了就那兒站著沒得一會子做甚麽呢那麽快偺們還一走罷。

9 你在那飯得了罷還

10 上街走

EXERCISE X. KEY.

1 昨兒晚上我聽見街門口上有好些個聲兒你聽見是甚麼樣兒的聲兒。

2 就在那就是更夫打更的聲兒。每夜分作五更頭一更是定更第三更就是半夜。這打更的白日裏沒事到夜裏就一點空兒也沒有他就在那小房子裏各自各兒住著也沒女人也沒兒子不管晴天陰天都得'出來'不能說今兒我攔著不罷。一年到頭都是一樣。

4 今兒個滿天都是雲彩陰的什麼都看不見了。

5 可不陰了麼。早起下大霧來著到晌午可就晴了一會子到黑上來還不定晴不晴呢。

6 這時候一天比一天短夫先擱著罷我們的夜書了，俗打算過幾天再念起。說。

7 這會子不得工夫先擱著罷我打算過幾天再念起。說。

EXERCISE XI.

1 腌臢乾淨。衣裳靴子。鞋襪子。把衣裳穿上。把靴子脫下來。一雙靴子。

2 那一雙靴子得補上一點兒皮子他買了十雙襪子那一條手巾那衣裳穿一條手巾那也不算多洗靴子溫和水使不得。

3 這盆水腌臢了換乾淨的拏來我洗臉那衣裳腌臢罷不用補衣裳躺著那一件衣裳他穿了好些日子沒換呢。

4 這件衣裳破了叫人給補補罷他脫了衣裳躺著那一件衣裳他穿了好些日子沒換呢。

5 你快起來罷穿上衣裳他脫了衣裳躺著那一件衣裳他穿了好些日子沒換呢。

6 今兒個天冷你得多穿一件衣裳你見他衣裳是鞋那都看我是做甚麼在家裏沒事我就穿鞋他是穿靴的時候兒子是穿鞋呢。

7 這條手巾不乾淨擱在臉盆裏洗一洗罷你愛穿的是靴子是鞋那都看我是做甚麼在家裏沒事我就穿鞋上衙門的時候可得穿靴子。

8 你那一雙皮靴子這麼些日子兒都不好罷那火要擱著得不刷一刷罷不太熱最好的溫了半天老開不了。

9 你洗手是愛使涼水是愛使開水兩樣兒都不好涼水太涼減了這水太熱最好的溫了半天老開不了。

10 你快把這水倒在鍋裏溫一溫就是溫和水呢。

PART III.—THE FORTY EXERCISES.

EXERCISE XI. KEY.

1
老太太告訴我說今兒起的大早。

2
不錯,昨兒晚上在外頭喫飯回來晚了,道兒真不好走,不用說靴子衣裳都弄臟了,就是臉也都臟的看不得,回家時就叫人拏溫和洗臉水兒來把衣裳靴子都脫了一看襪子也破咯得補咯。叫人拏雙鞋來擱在炕爐子那兒換了一身乾淨衣裳。哎呀這靴子著了雨不好脫,在我說還是穿好,喫了碗茶心裏就好點兒,可是夜裏的雨下的很可怕,你也出門來著嗎。

3
我是穿了一身好衣裳來著不肯弄壞了,沒出門兒。

4
請喝茶。這茶話都不用說了。

5
這茶水開不開的嗎。

6
水在火上擱了半天可不是開開。

EXERCISE XII.

1 女人們小的時候兒學針線,他們多一半不認得字。帽子是說一頂。縫裁衣裳都說一件。裁縫衣裳也叫裁衣裳。

2 你洗澡的時候兒不要把頭髮擱在水裏,有裏兒的衣裳是有裏兒的,頭髮一着水老乾不了。

3 單衣裳是就有一面兒沒有裏兒的夾衣裳是夾的。那一件衣裳中間有棉花的。

4 砍肩兒是有前後沒外頭穿的衣裳短的就叫馬褂子。這一條褲子是棉的單衣裳。

5 褂子是儘裏頭穿的儘汗衫子。那一件衣裳長的是夾的。

6 帽子有小帽兒官帽兒兩樣兒,官帽兒一個裁縫補了。帽子也分涼帽暖帽。

7 你會做針線不會。我兒裁了還沒縫呢。那一件破馬褂子得擎擎子是一身都洗。

8 那一件砍肩那一把木梳是誰梳頭也就沒有不少可是我有五十多了,年那麼沒有去洗澡很好。

9 你老先生頭髮短得很,頂兒上不多少是花多不少。

10 今年棉花多不少。

11 補了。一件汗衫上的土。天兒洗澡的時候兒頭髮的多。

PART III.—THE FORTY EXERCISES.

EXERCISE XII. KEY.

1 裁縫叫他進來了。

2 您要做什麼衣裳。

3 您說要褂子還是小袄好幾件汗衫兒棉的夾的單的都要做。

4 您要做的褲子砍肩兒都是要在儱裏頭的那個甚麽。

5 要做的是肩兒小裀不在儱裏是。

6 不錯那個褂子都不要天氣太熱了。你做個單的就得的。

7 那個褂子都不要是做什麽樣兒的。

8 兩樣兒都是做什麽樣兒的。

9 袖子

10 我比這個要長點兒。

11 你小心點兒這衣裳都比著身子裁到晚上天天兒裳得幾天針線不多兒老不用胰子的樣木有沒他是那

12 您要是天天兒裳得幾天針線不多就得

13 這衣裳得幾天就得

14 我很會做得他有點臟的看不得老不用胰子的樣

15 這個裁縫臟的看不得他有點兒老不用胰子的樣

16 那他沒有木梳罷

穿著就有樣把衣裳撣乾淨了就老了。
新你不要一就壞了。
兒穿就壞了。
了就不壞了。
兒頭髮也不梳。

EXERCISE XIII.

1 賬目。花錢花費，四吊錢的票子。不知道那個東西的兩銀子還不了那輕重得拏秤稱一稱。

2 他欠人的賬目不少。他該的賬的錢拏來給我使。我借花錢好'花錢都說得他那把我的錢拏給人使。

3 我借錢是天兒的花費不很多。他愛宜。那個花瓶不值錢。個人過於花錢他的本錢快完了罷。

4 我們家裡天天兒的花費不貴這一件皮掛子價值很便宜。今年的棉花很賤他家裏花一個大錢都沒有。

5 那個房子價錢

6 那當十的大錢裏頭有七分有三銅的有西同銀子錢分是鐵的。一個樣兒那黃金比銀子重鐵比銀子輕。

7 票子是一張紙上頭寫着錢數兒買東西誰怕花個一二兩定賣你要可得'賣花倆這個人一開口就是十兩八兩的話。

8 那花瓶兒該當花錢的時候兒他賣不賣。

9 袟子他當了錢兒他不開口就是十兩八兩的話。

EXERCISE XIII. KEY.

1 我打算上口外去聽見說票子不好使、還是用銀子方便、還有那小銅錢兒也得要點兒。

2 要是一定要可錢是一個當十個的大錢這銀子到口外換著用的那個錢不很費事不用說銀子的價錢不同就是平的大小也不一樣。

3 不錯京裏使的錢是一個當十個的大錢這銀子到口外換著用的那個錢不很費事不用說銀子的價錢不同就是平的大小也不一樣。

4 聽見說出了關錢房錢算起來花費可也不少呢、你回來的時候怕要該下些賬。

5 火食是賤要是把這個車錢房錢算起來花費可也不少呢、你回來的時候怕要該下些賬。

6 要該賬是一定得還的。還不了、請你借給我點兒錢就是了。

7 你還打算借呢、先頭裏你短我好幾兩銀子老沒還我還借這子、換多少錢。

8 那就罷了。今兒銀子換多少錢。

9 今兒銀子換十七吊多錢。

10 那麼你給我平罷。你平二十兩銀子罷。

11 平得了、拏了去罷。你這一道兒上太太平平的。

EXERCISE XIV.

1 雞子兒牛奶燈油香油這菜弄得吃不得快撤了去罷。燈油是豆子做的香油是芝蔴做的火油出在地裏。

2 我昨兒買了三百斤煤五十斤柴火八十斤炭火四石米二百斤麵。天冷的時候煤炭用的多。

3 炕爐子是燒煤的多。火盆是用炭火盆是屋裏用的、不是做飯做水的。

4 菜有生的有熟的在火上做的都是熟菜。生菜在地下長出來就可以吃得。

5 你去給我買一個小雞子三四個雞子兒還要牛奶要牛奶便宜我就要幾斤。我們這兒買牛奶不論斤數兒都是論碗論瓶。

6 買果子是論箇的多。你快弄飯去、飯得了就端上來。

7 你愛吃饅頭愛吃飯。兩樣兒都不愛、我愛喝湯愛喝什麼湯呢。肉湯雞湯都好。

8 我明天要請人吃飯給他們什麼菜好。不論甚麼菜都可以、他們都是俗們本家的人。

EXERCISE XIV. KEY.

1
我今年的煤錢花的不少那煤的價兒一天比一天貴柴火又出的不多每月花的至少也得十三塊。

2
那是你燒那頂好的煤都是口外來的我賤多着呢廚房裏也好使。

3
聽見說你很好吃你今兒吃的廚子做的廚房飯罷好不好。來。告訴廚子做那個生菜小雞兒用雞子做那個香油和細鹽不塊兒粗鹽還要各樣兒的果子叫他小心點兒買熟分的。

4
是他做的湯和那奶油點心錯。

5
這個飯倒是不錯我那個廚子不行一點兒弄茶的本事都沒有。

6
那是他學的不好請你喝點兒黃酒我記得你不愛喝水。

7
今兒這個飯喫的很好酒也喝得很足這火也燒的頂暖和的咱們倆還要甚麼咯。

EXERCISE XV.

1 算計道路的遠近、直走近繞着走遠。東西南北坐船。過河那船上的客不少。

2 我們明天一早開船兒在那兒住著呢。往南邊去。客店裏住。我聽見說河裏的水淺沒有海水深。他是南邊人。

3 你去年進京的時候愛坐船、那是看地方兒南邊沒有車走道兒的。城外頭客店有不大好住的。那都看掌櫃的好不好在我說人乏了那兒都好。到店裏不過歇着罷了。

4 你走路愛坐車愛坐船那是看地方兒南邊沒有車走道兒的。客人都是坐船走河路走海的船兒大。

5 你老前年坐海船不是受了累了麼不錯是颶大風船在山東海邊兒上擱了淺我們那些人辛苦的了不得。

6 船上吃飯是甚麼人管。也是船家管船上的頭兒叫船管兒的管船兒的南邊就叫老大。

7 你算計是坐船貴是坐車貴坐車比坐船花的錢多。沒有的話、那兒有車價比船價還貴呢。你不知道北邊的你要坐車那掌櫃的也要使幾個錢還有天天兒住店的盤費沒算。

EXERCISE XV. KEY.

1
刻下京城是目下說的南京。
在北邊兒的是直道他京城就叫北京。
就叫北京。
幾百年前他京城就是
南邊也有個京城就是
個京城就是
是目下說的就很
的南京。

2
我和他進城去我走的是直道繞着道兒走的就很遠

3
河有大小
大河的水
的不是說河海
同。
比河邊兒上的
大河邊兒上的
地。海中間的水
沒有海深的水可
海深。都很深。

4
河邊兒海
邊兒那都
路得坐
是說河海
船海面
上的
船的
水淺
中
間的水可
大河
的都
走的都
是小船
兒。

5
人走水
路得坐
船海面
上的
船的
大河
走的都
是小船
兒。

6
坐船不用住
店坐車可得
天天兒住店
花的錢多箕
計盤費還是
坐船花的錢
少。價值也比
車價兒便宜。

7
掌櫃的
是舖子
裏管事
的人客
店裏也
有掌櫃
的。

8
在我說坐船坐車都好。坐
船就是怕颮大風坐車怕
下大雨那可都要受累。有
一年我們坐車道兒上下
起雨來一路連個賣吃兒
的都沒有很苦乏的了不
得。後來到店裏歇了一夜
就好了。

EXERCISE XVI.

1. 那馱子太重了、一個牲口馱不了這些東西不好帶、這些東西是甚麼話裝在箱子裏就好帶了。

2. 行李是走道兒的客人帶的東西用甚麼包起來他是皮子做的有木頭做的甚麼都裝得。

3. 包上包兒是把東西帶了來做甚麼是裝零碎東西擎氈子把的道兒上那小箱子到店裏就兒起身怕走、要不快點子都齊了就走不了城了。

4. 那口袋你駝外來的你小心着行李馱子都齊了就走、要不快點兒起身怕走不了城了。

5. 駱駝都是口得餧牲口。

6. 跟班的是使喚的人。他叫跟班的把箱子裝在車上、他趕不上了。

7. 牲口身上馱着的東西就叫馱子驢馱子、騾馱子都說得、馬馱子可不大說。

8. 我出門去、他的跟班的在後頭追我、了半天也沒趕上、我老遠的看見他跑的、可不論趕得上趕不上、你快跑着追他就是了。

9. 那個人在那兒呢、他出去了、你快跑可以趕上、他他早走了、怕趕不上罷無論趕得上趕不上、你快跑着追他就是了。子可不知道我呢。是道我呢。

EXERCISE XVI. KEY.

1. 無論甚麼人都出外'帶得行李。

2. 車快來了,你先打點行李箱子。衣包和口袋還得'收拾收拾。

3. 這屋裏的地毯有了土了,得拿出去打一打,桌子上鋪的布也很腌臢'得洗了。

4. 叫馬夫把牲口餧上一會兒我要出門,不用人跟着,告訴我帶的東西給裝好了。

5. 北邊地方帶東西都是用牲口,叫牲口,有驢馱子、駱駝馱子,也叫駞馱子,駞轎是騾子,駞的轎子。

6. 你走這樣的快,我跟不上。

7. 他出去兒工夫不大你快追着,告訴他,快給借那兒錢兒,他說是無論如何'借點兒來,我還有東西給他帶呢。

8. 我有點兒事使喚你,你到他那兒給借倆錢兒,他說是無論如何'一定得'借點兒來。

9. 那個人好利害利害。

10. 夏天熱的利害,冬天冷的很,熱那都是利害的,話頭兒,不熱的時候兒就是春秋天兒。

EXERCISE XVII.

1 人的頭裏頭有腦子就叫腦袋你這個辮子得梳了。我老了耳朶聽不眞眼睛看不眞。

2 那個人鼻子眼睛長得很奇怪。我心疼這個馬不肯叫他走乏了。

3 這個人很結實那個人輭弱得不過是身子很本地的事結實這個坐兒很輭和。

4 你的身子有病麽沒有病買他罷看着是老實你矮他幾不了我怎麽管得了那麽騎着怕拉不住。

5 這一匹馬很老實你買他罷看着是老實你矮他幾天兒賺不住。

6 偺們這五六年沒有見你的鬍子都白了。是我這幾年病得利害連家裏的人都不認得我。

7 道兒上躺着的那個人兩腿都有病麽不是是人老了腰長有病直不起來。我的指頭疼。

8 你這麽慢走是是身上有病連嘴唇子都破了那女人的指甲麽長把他的胳臂抓破了。

9 他的舌頭我是有甚麽事麽要沒事麽這麽拉拉拽拽是甚麽樣子呢有話直說就是了。

10 你這麽拽着

PART III.—THE FORTY EXERCISES.

EXERCISE XVII. KEY.

1. 這事叫人怎麼去和他說。

2. 人到老來的時候兒樣樣兒都不行耳朵聽不明眼也看不真嘴唇說話連嘴唇都不中用了

3. 春天的時候兒頭髮就要打辮子我乾我的辮子看還沒有人的鬍子長呢。

4. 這麼點兒的小孩子還有人的鬍子長麼。

5. 你看他也不好好抓你的指甲長了我的胳臂也不好。

6. 你不要那麼拉拽着我你的指甲弄壞了我的胳臂也不好。

7. 他腿上有病兒走道兒拉着很疼。

8. 我看他正在有力氣的時候兒身子怎麼這麼軟弱。

9. 這樣兒軟弱人你連拉帶拽還怕不把他拉躺下

10. 今兒我看見一個人面目長的很奇怪。

EXERCISE XVIII.

1 年輕的人多愛刮臉人到了四十多就有鬍子了。叫頭髮前些個剃頭的來。我要打辮子。女人們梳頭。

2 剃頭剃的是那辮子以外的短頭髮。前些個剃頭的年不剃頭的那賊就叫長髮賊。

3 說人體面是說他是個好人說體面也說得剃面是說他長得體面頭刮臉了我背你都是用剃頭鋪。

4 他那屋子蓋得和水兒也不用胰子。你乏說得剃頭刮臉了我背你罷。他肚子裏有學問他上了剃頭刀。

5 我們本地人剃頭不使溫水兒也不用胰子。你乏說得剃頭刮臉了我背你罷。他肚子裏有學問他上了吊了。

6 明天那地方官要斬幾個賊聽見說斬賊黃的那一把刀不很快刀不過重就是了。

7 你鼻梁兒上怎麼這麽四個楞兒有四個角兒我昨兒叫人家刀楞兒打了一下兒可不說。

8 四方的東西有四個楞兒有四個角兒。

EXERCISE XVIII. KEY.

1. 李家那個小千金長得多麼好瞧,你看見沒有。

2. 我瞧見了。重眉毛大眼睛,高鼻梁兒,倆鬢角兒,頭髮又黑又亮,顋頰的肉皮兒也很細,小下巴頦兒長脖細腰兒,脚兒也不大,身體也不粗,果眞不錯。

3. 他滿身骨頭疼,都'是身子有病麼。不是,是他老了。氣血不足了。

4. 刮臉剃頭也得'找剃頭的。

5. 人的胸前背後也說前心後心。

6. 口袋裝很重的東西,得'背在脊梁背兒上,也可以擱在肩髂兒上。

7. 你怎麼了,臉上氣色不好。是肚子疼麼。

8. 不是肚子疼,是我這隻脚的踝子骨叫個小人兒拿石頭打了一下兒,連波稜蓋兒都疼的了不得。

9. 城門外頭吊着好些個人腦袋,有人告訴我說都是斬下來的賊首級。

EXERCISE XIX.

1. 這一匹馬走的慢這麼全是你買的底下人生的兒女。

2. 君上是百官萬民的主家生子兒子的是算不了的是沒有爵位。

3. 爵位尊是說人做的官文官帶兵分不過分不大好是他們是他們月底要點名兒多的時候就找些個人充數兒。

4. 管民的是文官帶兵的是武官。

5. 文武官的衣裳一定的不過帶的補子不同。

6. 各地方的官兵額數是有的兵額數不足的時候兒多到月底要點名兒就找些個人充數兒。

7. 山東那塊兒出了個好官那知道是誰該誰得着補就是誰。

8. 拿銀錢買官那就叫捐官他那捐官是捐的麼不是的是出兵缺不知道是誰得的。

9. 那帶兵的大官一點兒本事沒有前些日子那賊都跑到山裏頭去了他要當時追他們很可以把他們殺退了。

10. 貴姓賤姓馬。

PART III.—THE FORTY EXERCISES.

EXERCISE XIX. KEY.

1 天下最大的就是君上最多的就是民人君上又叫那樣兒的爵位很尊貴。

2 我的一個他很同學的在懂得做官是官有定額的官事還打當額有缺就得補額以來着請你給找個門路。

3 他很懂得做官是官有定額的官事還打當額有缺就得補額以來着請你給找個門路。

4 贊聽見說用你做參贊兵起就有缺無外的有人就是參贊官。

5 人就是參贊官。

6 額外我打算找點兒事沒找着請你給找個門路。

7 你給我一隻小雞子。

8 不管有錢沒錢要好些個弄好的擱在裏頭充數兒的擱兒了。底下我再告訴你話都有麼。

9 我定東西的時候兒說住了都中間兒怎麼給擱在一邊兒了。底下我再告訴你話都有麼。

10 叫你把桌子擱在屋子當中間兒怎麼給擱在一邊兒了。

11 百家姓兒全有不過是聽熟了的那些姓那兒就是了。

12 那兒能全有不過是聽熟了的那些姓那兒就是了。

13 你給我一隻小雞子。

和人家要一定弄好的擱兒弄好些個擱在裏頭充數兒的你要不換好的我全退回去。是勒。

家裏的我全退換好的可得記着罷。麼。

EXERCISE XX.

1 城門上的官兵是盤查出入的。

2 國家定的律例是治民的本分，人人夏天收的麥子夏天收，就叫夏收，春天種的麥春天收，就叫春麥。

3 種地是小民的本分，夏天種的麥子夏天收，就叫夏收，春天種的麥春天收，就叫春麥。

4 秋天種的麥子夏天收，就叫秋收，春麥和秋麥是一樣的，一樣的麥子，怎麼不能算一樣，秋麥總不好，普天下百姓都知道。

5 那麼着，春麥和秋麥是一樣的，一樣的麥子，怎麼不能算一樣，秋麥總不好，普天下百姓都知道。

6 近年天下大亂，是官長治理的不好，普天下百姓都知道。

7 你那個兒子太不說理，告訴他甚麼話總不理會，甚麼事不論甚麼事，全愛說嘴。

8 去年來了一羣賊把那一片房子都燒了，那住着的人怎麼樣，呢。他們早都跑了。

9 好些個人在一塊兒，那兒告訴他我叫一羣馬牛羊數兒多本人兒晚半晌兒去見他過也說了一羣。

10 你把我的名片拿到他那兒去，告訴他我本人兒晚半晌兒過去見他有話說。

EXERCISE XX. KEY.

1. 普天下都有中國人。各國都有律例律例是國家定出來治理百姓的章程是各官立的。

2. 昨兒有人把一羣羊趕到我地裏頭把我種的麥子都給喫了。

3. 看街的就是巡察各地面亂了你給理罷。

4. 我那些個書不知是誰的子都給拉害你理他做甚麼。

5. 那個人性暴的利

6. 萬里長城是普天下的第一奇。七大奇裏的第一奇。聽見說是一位君上勒令百姓做的。

7. 不錯那君上無道之至治理百姓做完了苦城沒有幾年天下就大亂了。

8. 會生客之時先得穿官衣。

EXERCISE XXI.

1. 你的主意怎麼樣，是去好，還是不去好呢。自然是去好。

2. 把我那一個小棍兒拏來，我要出門，把我那一桿槍裝上，我要打鳥兒，可不定打的着打不着。

3. 我昨兒把那桿槍拏起來，不知道是裝得了的，偶然放了一下，四面兒都有人，恰巧沒打着誰，要是打着了，可了不得了。

4. 背地裏拏東西不叫人知道就沒有理，那算是偷把人家的東西硬拏了去，是好些個賊，夜裏明火拏着槍刀到人家硬拏東西，就是搶。

5. 說話混說。

6. 我的洗澡水怎麼這麼混，打了於懶惰，學生過不大的工夫兒，過一會兒就好了。

7. 我那個不愛用功打他兩下兒看罷。

8. 那一天有倆賊，一個拏着一條長槍，一個拏着一根大棍子，四下裏混打了那倆賊混打起着裝上槍就打，那拏棍子的拐下槍就跑了咯，那拏槍的那個人是特意來的，還是偶然來的，怕是偶然來的，可也不定。

EXERCISE XXI. KEY.

1　去年有十幾個賊拿着槍刀進城來了，把我鋪子裏的東西搶的乾乾淨淨的了。一點鐘前我那懶惰的底下人囘家去了，他走的時候兒沒把門關上怕也是特意做的。

2　那些賊裏頭有一個把我砍了一下兒我就請了個外國大夫給治好了。還有一個賊拿着我裝好了的鳥槍偶然給放了。

3　看街的聽見那槍的聲兒就來瞧一瞧是甚麼事他看見賊害了怕一直的跑了。在道兒上看見個做官的也不知同那個官混說些甚麼話。

4　那做官的說你不用說這些個我就帶我的兵去拿那些賊去。那賊聽說快有兵來都四散了。

5　這時候兒我那個底下人囘來了，說他的事做完了。那做官的和他說怕你和他們是一氣兒罷他囘的話都不真，就叫人拿棍子把他打了幾下兒。

6　你年輕的時候兒要這麼懶惰不愛念書趁到長大了的時候那兒還成得了人麼不成人就沒有過日子的路兒昨兒個你把書扔下同那客人們放槍去。他們散了以後你還不念書。

EXERCISE XXII.

1
那人幹的事總不叫人知道。大約不是甚麼好事，不然他怎麼背人。可不是麼，人家常說好話不背人，背人沒好話。

2
那一件事還沒辦妥當了，章程得'敢可不知道李大人准不准。大約沒甚麼更敢的。

3
要幹甚麼事先得'在事上，規定個准主意。

4
幹事的時候兒心不攔在事上，那就叫失神。

5
定妥辦事的法子總在他身上。

6
那個人有一件要事，得趕着辦，他一點兒不忙，同人催他快着，是喝酒些兒他不肯聽。

7
他在那兒擎倆胳臂混掄是幹什麼，怕什麼裏往下定。

8
條約是各國和中國立的章程。

9
這樣兒菜是廚子專給你麼開，你弄的全是參差不齊。

10
大凡帳目都是一條一條的那麼寫的你倒不吃。

PART III.—THE FORTY EXERCISES.

EXERCISE XXII. KEY.

1. 凡念書的時候兒偶然有不懂得的話若是用心揣摩大約那意思就明白了。

2. 昨兒我約他上西山去他說先回家去問一問准否怕是不准他往遠處去。

3. 寫信寫文書有寫錯了的地方兒得拿一塊紙補在那錯字上這就叫打補子。

4. 你這麼失神甚麼事都辦不來不妥當。

5. 那花盆是我專意給你帶來的你不要這是瞧不起我罷。

6. 這話說的真胡鬧我不要是我不好意思白要你的東西。

7. 這屋裏的傢伙甚麼都參差不齊給理一會子罷。

8. 你忙甚麼去了我一錯眼兒你就跑了又得我拿棍子掄你幾下兒了。

9. 你幹甚麼去。

10. 他們向來定規的辦法是不好更改的。

EXERCISE XXIII.

1. 城門口兒方的地兒窄的來往的車馬多。

2. 外頭是甚麼人嚷底下人兩個小兒一個人兒和趕車的那人兒吵呢你出去告訴他們不要嚷嚷看鬧出事來。

3. 你看那長的真醜。

4. 那好看的笑話那長的醜的那醜的生了氣把茶碗摔碎了有人說了他兩句他害起怕來了躺在地下把胳臂掆了。

5. 搯住他的辮子要拉他去他就說茶碗是掉下去的。

6. 晚飯吃多了夜裏愛做夢他叫馬摔了。

7. 我告訴你一個笑話兒昨兒我困的利害在椅子上坐着就同人把墨水兒倒在我嘴裏我都不知道。

8. 街道那麼窄那麼大的車拉不過去。

EXERCISE XXIII. KEY.

1 昨兒個有兩個人在城上那個窰的地方兒吵嚷一個長得好看一個很醜的那好看的和那醜的說沒二句話這件事你倒底做不做。

2 那醜的說我就說你這話說錯了一則怕言語說不得。你自己怎麼罷。我不做若是去做罷若是你不做我怎麼能做呢。

3 那一個大笑起來了就說你這話說錯了怕言語怕是做不了罷。還不快去呢這明明兒的是叫我把你摔下去說完那醜的就跑下去了。

4 你准是做夢罷昨兒城上沒有人。

5 我前兒個在前門大街那兒騎着馬不知道甚麼人在後頭吵嚷叫我那個馬開腿跑了去不大會兒我就掉下去了把踝子骨擱了一下兒還好擱的不大重歇了一歇兒可就好了那馬不知道跑到那兒去了這會兒還沒找着呢。

6 我今兒走了一天困極了沒法子最好是歇一夜明兒就歇過兒來了。

EXERCISE XXIV.

1 昨兒晚上那兒有人來之先看見甚麼能知道日後的祥瑞的就那就叫吉兆。

2 事情沒有用的錢子行兒手挐住了後來怕是要道日後太少過的錢不叫產業。

3 家裏日子有就找進這些年的相好你幫我們個錢肯不肯他說沒有甚麼不肯眞是不能我們底道的現在產業也沒了連弄一個大錢都很費事。

4 過日子有就准進個錢肯不肯那就不能我們底根本有幾個錢你是知道的現在產業也沒了連弄一個大錢都很費事。

5 那時候兒我甚麼都沒了正法來怕是要正法的就地正法。

6 你們這車要是當天兒今兒就走趕進城這三五天可就去我多要動身那麼着多兒我多賞你們的酒錢。了一路平安罷。

7 你多嗒起身我要沒丟那銀子麼就鋪子了。我們節正去年就好賞兒個完不了。月。

8 你們那鋪子怎麼不開中秋不然這件事今分手了。

9 八月十五、個忙兒

10 請你幫

EXERCISE XXIV. KEY.

1. 他那底根兒他有產業,過日子是他一個人子還很寬綽,有一年連個人兒的事月的不下雨,種的地全丟了錢情真不收成他家裏的事情麼不順當了。本錢慢慢了,還是不吉兒的都花完了,現在窮人家了得很。他相好的朋友們連累了祥。偶然還幫他幾個錢。呢。

2. 那些種地的人,多一半也丢了錢了,近來那個地方就很不安窘着。我倒沒受甚麼累,怎麼是這在我說事情不論吉凶都麼先兆兒。有一天我做了有個夢。夢見有一個人來,把我裏的麥子都給燒了,這麼着我就把麥子都生賣了,後來雨,我的錢倒是早已先得了。

3. 大人說的不錯後來我丟了錢了,現在我就是個要飯兒的人了。

4. 你不是姓張麼,怎麼窘成這個樣兒前我記得你還有產業,日子還過得下去呢。

5. 請大人把這個瓶留下罷。我窮的很。朋友們不肯幫把家裏的傢伙不是當就是賣,現在就有這一個了。

EXERCISE XXV.

1. 稱人家祖就是令祖您是我父親的老兒尊人旁人問人家的父親重人的父親就稱人家老翁。的意思。

2. 令祖好阿令尊好阿是問人家的祖父是說令尊還是說令翁多。

3. 向人說自己的弟兄是舍弟。有不是買的買的是家兒舍弟。人家的弟兄是說令弟。

4. 奴才就是使喚的人回來我得去迎接。他們老翁下葬我得去幫幫他們去。

5. 今兒家祖回來我得去迎接。

6. [continuing]

7. 生絲不是你們這兒的土貨麼。可不是土貨請您替我挑一點兒好的。

8. 我兄弟給大人請安他說他明兒怕不能來找了個兒替他幾天。

9. 我挑出來的那瓦盆總得挑着攔在車上不行。

10. 他把紙弄成團兒往的人肩膀兒上挑我臉上扔。

11. 牲口駝的東西叫駄子那上挑的東西叫挑子人背背子。上的東西叫

PART III.—THE FORTY EXERCISES.

EXERCISE XXV. KEY.

1 大前兒個我們家兄回家來了、帶着有二百多團綠五十疋絨、我父親叫我接着他去、就手兒幫着他把貨拏進來。

2 那麼令家父跟先祖從前也是做那樣布的買賣的、您這個話問的有甚麼高見呢。

3 可不是麼。

4 我們舍弟要買些個細絲、請您令兄挑、是有一樣、他挑點兒好的、怕價錢長了、現在很貴呢。

5 那有甚麼不行的、挑罷、是一定給令弟挑就是、有一樣、他挑點兒好的、怕價錢長了、現在很貴呢。行不行。

6 您請罷、回來見。

7 昨兒個他們令祖下葬、我叫我們的底下人去幫幫他們、這奴才們不肯聽我的話、到了兒沒去。旁人說那兒有鬼、他們害了怕了、說不去。後來他的孫子叫了他們一個來、他喳的一聲、慢慢兒的走過來、我那孫子就拏棍子把他打了幾下兒。

8 您的底下人說的話、有一點兒真呢。那一天夜裏我打那兒過、看見一個鬼、混跑、頭髮是紅的、臉是黃的、我一瞧見、怕的我了不得。

9 這是那兒的話、准是你又喝多了。

EXERCISE XXVI.

1 我們明兒上西山去罷、到那兒、就找個樹林子、在青草地裏坐着、又涼快又沒土。你說好不好。

2 去倒沒有甚麼不能去的、我却想着還是在太陽地裏曬暖兒好、樹林子坐着長、怕跑不過、時候兒還不對呢。

3 俗們倆人賽着跑罷。正對我的很、都是過於當刻不肯花錢他們的錢一天比一天增的多。

4 他那倆兄弟利害、兩天貴、不分老嫩都是二百錢一斤。

5 那葱這

6 草木是苗子花草樹木的總名、麥子南的、川東林子。那桑樹林、頭地裏曬得鋪在日人家好些個銀子。天有八下鐘了、小人兒們該睡覺了。

7 苗子叫樹人分子綠了、一曬、曬乾了就壘起來。

8 樹多要把溼衣裳弄乾了、

9

10 聽見說對過兒住的那個人壘次吞了

說得。苗兒也出了苗兒火熟的。森森

EXERCISE XXVI. KEY.

1

那一天我們兩個人在樹林子裏賽着拉弓來着。天氣很好日頭曬的還暖和那一帶樹林子綠森森得好看。拉完了弓我告訴他一個笑話兒。

2

我就說從前有一個姓馬的是個賣葱的。有一天他在桑樹林子裏頭地上睡覺他起來的時候兒看見有一個人在他跟前站着大聲的笑。

3

他生了氣說這兒有甚麼笑頭兒啊。那個人對他說這個地方很溼你的衣裳都弄溼了'得鋪在太陽地裏曬一曬而且你帶的貨也丟了。

4

那老頭兒瞧了一瞧,眞是口袋都空了,就說不是你吃了我的嫩葱却是誰他說我沒白吃給着的價錢在那兒說着就把幾個大錢扔在草裏。

5

那姓馬的想着眞是錢向前拿去,一錯眼兒那個人就沒了錢也找不着了,這姓馬的知道不是人却是個鬼。

6

那個人嗇刻的利害。他是打雲南那地方兒來的。我想他本是一個苗子,前幾年他做乾草的生意。他的銀錢一個月比一個月增的多了,他盡次吞人家的錢,自己却不愛花。

EXERCISE XXVII.

1 我們倆人起初很親熱後來他待我傲慢這麼着我就和他絕了交了。

2 我昨兒到你那兒去拜會怎麼不見你這話有點兒不可憑罷怕是你留下名片就走了。

3 你待我這麼傲慢回來告訴你父親憑你愛告訴誰就告訴誰我都不怕。

4 某人告訴我說見的時候你那一筆賬的銀子還沒交出來你不慚愧麼。

5 那倆瓶乍見的時候好相是一對兒細細兒的一瞧尺寸就不一樣。

6 有人嫉妒我這個好兒然而這也是件平常的事而且也是我應當得的。

7 應當倆字的意思怎麼分別沒有別的法子總得看上下文就知道了。

8 會客的時候主人在東邊兒坐賓客在西邊兒坐陪著的人在下邊兒坐對不對那總是看屋子的方向。

9 我素常不愛拜客冬天得穿厚衣裳夏天穿薄兒。

10 寬厚是刻薄的對面兒

PART III.—THE FORTY EXERCISES.

EXERCISE XXVII. KEY.

1
某人你們見過面麼。我們沒見過。我們也是今兒初次見。人很好卒見就和他很熟。

2
聽見別人說他原是厚道人素日待人行事也不刻薄。

3
要是和我認得的那個人比起來我認得的那人可不是這麼樣。

4
憑他是誰都待的傲慢。看見人有好事他就嫉妒拿人的東西他要他也不慚這樣兒的人怎麼能不和他絕交呢。

5
我實在沒工夫兒辦憑你辦去罷。

6
請客是請人吃飯。客應坐在上面。主人旁邊兒陪著。

7
你那個小鳥兒要他幹甚麼交給我罷。得了。得了。你怎麼見人家的東西就要。

8
你一個人去我陪着你去好不好。

EXERCISE XXVIII.

1 那桌面兒上的東西不很是當初是外國光潤把他們這兒也會做料貨和玻璃有點兒分別。

2 玻璃是外國來的瓶子怎麼破了不是碰破了不是碰破了是燒的時候兒破了一塊兒是裱。

3 那玻璃瓶子怎麼破了不是碰破了紙糊在什麼上頭是糊雙張兒紙糊得一塊兒說。

4 膓戶紙裂了叫裱糊匠來糊上單張兒叫木匠做的多木紗是紗做的紗是絲做的。

5 各行的手工人棉花做的布是棉花做的。

6 布是棉花做的。

7 那一塊紗顏色兒淡了必須染別的顏色兒舊的顏色兒是紅的還可以染別的您要別的顏色兒也可以染藍的。

8 你瞧那一疋紅紗顏色兒光潤不光潤怎麼是光潤呢那紗原來是新的染的顏色又是好看這紗光潤說別的也行。

9 我拿那個玻璃瓶來要擦一擦兒必是當廚子碰破了你行幾上頭碰破了收拾不收拾不必收拾了。

10 他是甚麼行當廚子你行幾我們弟兄五個我行二。

PART III.—THE FORTY EXERCISES.

EXERCISE XXVIII. KEY.

1 這屋裏糊的紙腌臢叫個裱糊匠來給糊新的。

2 這一張畫兒你找個人給裱一裱裱的紙上可別太厚了。

3 膧戶破了拿張紙給糊上。進風兒。你染藍的麼你倒給染出紅的來了顏色兒又淡又不光潤。

4 這紗你怎麼給染成這個顏色兒。我不是告訴

5 我這掛子太舊了，穿不得了。

6 膧戶上的玻璃有了土了必得拿布擦一擦兒在那擦屋裏就不這麼黑了。

7 染東西的顏色在那兒買。顏料鋪裏就賣。

8 你小心拿著那玻璃盃別給碰了。

9 總沒下雨天乾的利害。你瞧這桌面子都乾裂了。

10 買賣都分行。京城裏各行最大的就是銀酒茶布四行。

EXERCISE XXIX.

1 剛纔我們在這兒商量這件事情再三舊書套送給的喊他過來我他總不答應末末了兒還是我買了個新的。

2 再三再四的請他把那個舊書套送給買賣後來落下我他總不答應末末了兒還是我買了個新的。

3 我們十個人從前定得湊錢做那個箱子叫你一個單把本錢取回去的我瞧這個兒怎麼也不肯再往裏挪那麼了。

4 我兄弟送我量了不殼五石一個單套兒車兒怎麼足拉的挪那麼了。

5 這米我量了不殼五石入錢了。遠。

6 在我說、這麼些個不止過車我們一到五石不是二套車怕拉不了罷。

7 我是從南邊兒來的向來沒坐到他那兒了這是怎麼他你看他把門碰壞了那倒沒甚麼叫道兒上連丟帶碰趕到了山上就沒甚麼了。

8 我永遠不那馬還不好兒的拴上子兒送上山來誰想他們個木匠來收拾收拾就得理叫他等一等兒再來罷。

9 那馬還不好兒的拴上子兒送上山來誰想他們

10 昨兒我叫他們買一百雞

PART III.—THE FORTY EXERCISES.

EXERCISE XXIX. KEY.

1. 我纔出門剛要走的時候兒有人來找我說你不在家等一會兒再來。

2. 借人家的傢伙到用完了不給送回去還這麼見東西落不殼我用罷。

3. 從我到這裏來我各處去湊總湊不殼挪東湊西湊不殼花的。

4. 這個錢缺少的利害日子永遠上不殼是東挪西就要套車。

5. 他過日子口捵錢不殼和你商量要是身上有一點兒行不行。

6. 把性套車。

7. 我買了一套書帶的錢不殼和你商量要是身上有借給我一點兒不行。

8. 我疑惑他說的話不實你到那兒給打聽打聽。

9. 你背著我做事不叫我知道可小心著日後要是叫我打聽出來我可不答應。

10. 外頭有人喊你答應一聲兒出去看看說那天我以後他總不巧。

11. 阿，原來又是他從那天我在家你說巧不巧。

12. 他來了兩末兒都趕上想出個辦法來請你給斟酌好。

13. 我們辦這件事想出兩個辦法來請你給斟酌使那個好。

EXERCISE XXX.

1 臺灣是中國東南海裏的地方兒南北兩頭兒山嶺兒又多又大那山峯長得也很好看。

2 江河湖海是天下大江的江面有的地方兒寬下裏和湖相同。水的總名兒。

3 咱們這兒的小河兒很窄有浮橋就可以過去那長江西去一路都是順流了江西那兒的山水也可以。

4 那長江之流打西到東湖北來的船到江西去一路峰是高而尖的山嶺也高就是沒有那尖的樣子。

5 那山峯的尖兒是個個不同。山

6 尖兒那個字眼兒甚麼有甚麼河喝水麼小巷住家兒的都是筆尖兒刀尖兒都說得。是井水。多。

7 京城裏沒賣大半在大街上開鋪子衙衞兒的地方就叫那墳地很大必是闊人家兒的。

8 京城京城外頭城沒有甚麼人家的野地連野地有墳墓的也算。

9 他是個鄉村兒會是會很遠了可不行這道河浮的過去浮不過去。

10 你會浮水麼河浮不過去去浮不過河面兒太寬浮不過去。

11

EXERCISE XXX. KEY.

1 臺灣是中國的地方有二百多年了。南北下裏有峰嶺裏頭有幾個頂高的山嶺地方不很寬闊却有幾道小河兒河邊兩面的田地出產的東西很多鄉村和城都有裏頭住的人同民人一樣我聽見說有幾個地方兒住著野人也有人說那些野人吃人那都是散著住不成鄉村也有人說那些野人吃人那兒做買賣的大半和民人做近來却有太西各國的船來往外國人也有在那兒住著做買賣的。

2 中國有幾道江也大也深,很可以走得大船長水的時候兒流得很快往上走的船覺著很慢往下流的水在船上看着覺得更快了。那小河兒又窄又灣,都是河船來往的走道兒的人可以打浮橋上過去。

3 那一國有幾個大湖,湖面很寬闊,大裏下和海一樣。湖裏頭也有山峰,大小船都可以走得一那土有大風那浪眞利害。

4 有地方兒要做一個小巷裏頭。那一天我去找他,我進錯了衚衕兒,沒找着他的家。

5 我有一位朋友,他住在一

EXERCISE XXXI.

1. 我們倆人剛纔鬧著玩兒他把棍子在我腦袋上打了一下兒安靜點兒罷別太粗了總得'想着你兄弟年幼那麽重的手脚他耐不得。

2. 聽見說老爺欠褂子怕耐不得長那甚麽不可難說要過身上穿着常冒雨自然壞有點兒的快獸一不舒服。獸兒。

3. 我這件新

4. 他那羞辱人的娘兒們。樣子眞討人嫌。

5. 男女就是爺們。賊把男女老少都殺了。

6. 他一家子老幼一輩兒和祖父一輩兒和兒孫一輩兒眞是討人嫌我錯了，你錯了，都不分。是長輩兒的是年高年的全輕的不舒服。晚輩。

7. 和祖父一輩兒一輩兒的是

8. 你怎麽這麽冒失。碰着了我了，罷管我呢快些兒辦的利害。爽你這麽獸頭獸腦的在是沒留神。

9. 你過於笨的利害。爽快些兒辦罷管我呢你這麽獸頭獸腦的還要說人。

10. 我們過日子眞艱難耐着些兒罷你這麽能耐人，難道一輩子不出頭麽。

EXERCISE XXXI. KEY.

1
街上那兒有一個要玩意兒的。男女老幼好些個人在那兒看。你聽見說麼。

2
你還說呢。我纔剛上街的時候兒看見好些個爺們娘兒們在那兒站着,我想着必是有甚麼玩意兒不然那些人在那兒獃着臉兒看甚麼呢。我正要去看恰巧有個人冒冒失失的問了我一句話,說你不舒服,大好了。我一看不是別人是一家兒的一個平輩長得又蠢又笨,也不知道說的都是那'兒的事。實在是討人嫌。

3
你說的不是某人麼。他父親我認得人很安靜,說話行事也極爽快,前幾年他不大寬綽,近來看他那個樣兒倒很舒服,想是日子比原先好過一點兒咯。

4
你受人家的羞辱就是耐着點兒也不難爲甚麼生氣呢。

EXERCISE XXXII.

1. 他臨死的時候、他的兒他的兒孫們都爭起來家產來略。

2. 良民不是犯國法的人。

3. 大臣上朝的時候兒不是進皇宮麼。不是進皇宮皇宮是皇上住的地方兒就是禁地向例連大臣們都不准到的。

4. 你把這幾件文書給號、禁止底下人上打儘頭裏的、日子號起。

5. 我們大人出了號令、禁止底下人要錢、要是犯了禁必要治罪的。

6. 幹這沒良心的事難免犯法、做就是別打良民比為匪、倒不強麼、反倒不愛做、眞是怪事。

7. 隨你們倆人鬭嘴兒、打起來、要是罪名總出於皇上的恩典。

8. 大赦天下、寬免犯人的罪、免得受熱、他那個病隨你怎麼治、早晚總是要死的。

9. 你別在太陽地裏走、酌情建立地方官為臨民的官、地方官治理的好、自然就能安靖了。

10. 朝廷隨地

EXERCISE XXXII. KEY.

1 好些年前,有一個人姓林,要做皇上。沒反以前他先把他的死黨布散的各處都有,連皇宮禁地也有他的人。後來事情破了,他自已也叫人拿住了,他的死黨還在山東河南反了好幾個月。

2 百姓反了,皇上就令大臣平定那不安靖的地方兒。那大臣臨走的時候兒,得上朝去見皇上。

3 那文書是第幾號。還號。沒號。皇上住的地方就說得是京,那城就叫南京。

4 北京城建立的年分不遠。從前朝廷建立在南邊兒那方城就叫南京。

5 鬥雞是良民不要的玩意兒。那必是定死罪了。也是然而那應該的人要是明火,的誰還能免不了死罪,那樣兒面的事,也是最不體的人若不殺他,良民是應該例的。怎麼能穀過安靖日子呢。禁的。

6 我聽見說那姓李的這話是不錯的,見我罷我雖然不是的,是叫人家費的事,你若是真這個姓李有錢的總。

7 你隨時來那就是我朋友了,我最怕的

8 的好

9 樣兒叫我來見你,你瞧我還常來不常來呢。麼碗飯吃一杯茶喝。

EXERCISE XXXIII.

1 那座廟門口兒牆上貼着告示和尚去禁止娘念經兒們上廟燒香。

2 他們令祖死了今兒個今日飯明天有事明天辦剛剛爺關夫子是不行。墨又得'濃。

3 俗語兒說、老爺廟是和尚廟麼不錯、得寫楷書書行書草字都不行。

4 這文書上廟關的房裏頭夫子俗叫老爺關夫子是文話俗話就是老爺。

5 那山上廟子一層比一層高。

6 那山上廟子一層比一層高。

7 你抽空兒給我畫一張畫兒行不行早已過去的時候兒就是往古。

8 古來有位聖人姓孔他的教後世叫做聖教為中國最尊重的同時還有老子的教叫做道教。佛教是西方僧家傳來的尊佛爺出家的是僧家俗說就叫和尚尊老子出家的是道士聖教又名儒教儒教的人叫俗家教的總名就叫僧道儒。

9 京城的廟多、有的是和尚廟上掛的那張古畫兒今兒拿新紙裱上一層。

10 我屋裏牆上掛的那張古畫兒今兒拿新紙裱上一層。

EXERCISE XXXIII. KEY.

1 古來二千四百三十多年前的時候中國有一位姓孔的人人人都稱他爲聖人他平日說的話成了一本書人看這個書就知道學好怎麼學呢是這麼着做官呢替君上辦事好怎麼學呢是這麼着做官呢替君上辦事總得用心在家呢還得尊重爺娘待弟兄該當疼愛就是自己的女人也要和和氣氣兒的交朋友的心必須實在能發照著這麼行,就是儒教中的好人了。

2 寫字有眞字草字之分眞字也叫楷書。寫楷書的時候和草字一樣,就叫草字,這話可不知道對不對。

3 怎麼叫草字有人說是字寫出來和草一樣就叫草字寫楷書的時候墨要濃纔好看草字也不知道對不對。

4 念書寫字都得專心不可空念和唱曲兒一樣。

5 佛是西方的聖人傳他的教的書就叫佛經佛經的道理不過叫人靜心們的別名又說僧人。

6 和尚是念佛經的人他字筆畫看不眞貼着上邊兒的下邊兒又有擦壞了的地方兒也不知道是甚麼事。

7 前兒我見了一張告示在牆上貼着上邊兒的字筆畫看不眞下邊兒又有擦壞了的地方兒也不知道是甚麼事。

EXERCISE XXXIV.

1 這麼些日子沒來,渴想渴想。彼此彼此。

2 打這塊兒往東一直到天邊兒上都是水。

3 衆人都說皇上新近專派了一位大官察考倉庫裏頭銀米的數兒對不對或銀或米若有短少列位怕要得處分依我說他來不來碍不着咱們的事。

4 這一個打雜兒的有甚麼好處你這麼戀戀不捨的。

5 你們中進的錢甚麼的是大宗兒就是祖宗留下的產業阿。

6 老不下雨,鄉下人盼望的利害。昨兒剛長點兒雲彩偏偏兒的又叫風颳散了。

7 另找一輛車罷若是跨着轅兒必要弄一身土。

8 京城是五方雜處的地方兒。

EXERCISE XXXIV. KEY.

1. 中國各城裏頭都有倉有庫。倉是裝米的,庫是擱銀子的,這倉庫都有官人管理,銀子米若丟了,都爲官人是問。倉庫裏頭收着的銀子和米年年總得查一回。那一年我有一個朋友是管銀庫的,夜裡查了些個賊,打開庫門,把裏頭的銀子數兒補還我那朋友那兒有那麼些個現銀子呢,斟酌些日子沒有法子就跑了。

2. 那有甚麼用處。就是跑到天邊兒上去那官人還能拿不到麼,就是拿不到也不能回家,就是不能回家也不能常住阿。

3. 依我看,還是等着聽處分倒比滿地方兒跑強多了。

4. 趕車的,你瞧阿,有個人坐在車後頭了,如今你要送我偏不要咯。

5. 去年我和你要那毛氈子你搶不得給我,如今你要送我我偏不要咯。

EXERCISE XXXV.

1 我那個時辰表給鐘表鋪裏送去、叫他們給修理修理。就手兒問他們我那個風雨表收什得了沒有。

2 他手裏捏着管筆、彷彿要寫甚麽。瓦盆兒是盆兒匠捏的。

3 那、賊捏造告示、作爲官出的。

4 他帶的貨物捏報是行李、叫關上查出來、全都入了官了。

5 先灑水後掃地、不然、那土就飛起來咯。

6 你那個小狗兒眞好看。毛兒也長、腿兒也短、耳朶也不小、就是嘴頭兒有點兒尖。

7 他們那兒打碎、別就是要蓋房子罷。

8 若論圓扁的不同、西瓜是圓的、扁豆就是扁的、錢是又圓又扁的。

9 我沒犯法、人告我做賊、那不是我的寃枉麽。

10 他近來的事情不好、那都是他的報應。我實在想不出甚麽法子來報答他待我的恩典。

EXERCISE XXXV. KEY.

1

我看你那兒使喚的那個打雞兒的很好做事很快當屋子裏灑掃的很乾淨我去了永遠見他拿着笤帚在那兒掃地我那個底下人野的利害那麼大身量兒走道兒老是前逩後跳的成天家不是打雞就是鬭狗彷彿小人兒的樣子。

他揑報是狗跳在桌子上往下一逩碰下來的。還說要是說他弄壞的那可寃枉了他了這樣兒的人我還怎麼用呢。

2

還有一樣兒沒開過眼。有一天我的時辰表壞了打算着要找人修理擱在桌兒上了他看見了拿在手裏說這是個甚麼呢又圓又扁的沒揑住一失手掉的地下了。我問他表怎麼了。

3

我看你用的那個人也不錯本來是鄉下的人粗率點兒也是有的那樣兒人一定有力氣往後要是砌牆叫他幫著打碎做小工兒倒也罷了。

EXERCISE XXXVI.

1 這櫃子裏的抽屜拉不出來。使勁一抽就拉出來了。

2 那一件事耽悞了是甚麼緣故。那緣故太多不容易說。

3 您這位少爺今年多大歲數兒。小兒今年十八歲了。他的生日是六月初八過年就要給他辦事咯。趕到您那兒辦喜事的日子我必要去道喜去。

4 你別打算欺哄我。我告訴你那不是件容易事。我很對兒。你的硬若論誆騙人，你可不是個兒。

5 可惜那個人過於糊塗，說不明白就耽悞了我半天的工夫。

6 我們倆彼此很對勁。可惜他那個兄弟很會欺哄人，去年還誆騙了我幾兩銀子呢。

7 我最不喜歡他待有年紀兒人的那樣子。我告訴你，那都是小的時候兒老家兒不管他的緣故。

8 他是個安靜人，不論甚麼事都是從從容容兒的辦。

PART III.—THE FORTY EXERCISES.

EXERCISE XXXVI. KEY.

1 過了新年又長了一歲了。

2 你們老人家今年多大年紀家父現在八十二歲了。這樣兒年紀也算得是有壽數兒的人了。

3 昨兒我等了你一天你為甚麼不找我去。有個緣故我正要走恰巧有個遠親來了，我沒法子陪他坐着說話兒就悞住了。過了半天他纔走了，天也不早了，我就沒找你去。

4 你們住的那地方兒上大街很近買甚麼東西實在是便當。我們住的這小衚衕兒很不方便，買點兒甚麼真不容易。

5 他那個人一點勁兒沒有，還想要學武。有，可惜心裏沒了。多麼糊塗。

6 你喜歡吃這茶不是剛見了那抽屜裏頭還有些個呢。

7 你別欺哄我，纔剛我看見了那抽屜裏頭還有多不好，的東西誆騙人銀錢的。

8 在鋪子裏買東西不欺哄人，街上買東西可得留神，東西不好多，有賣不好的東西誆騙人銀錢的。

EXERCISE XXXVII.

1. 您公事忙不忙。也不算很忙天天兒總有閒着的時候兒。

2. 我有一件事情奉求。李老爺該我的那一筆賬我屢次上他那兒去要他們的人總說沒空兒不見我您多偺閒着託您替我要一要纔好。

3. 昨兒我一個相好的因為孩子病心裏煩悶急要發信到鄉下問一問託我替他雇一個人送信。我雇了一個人打發他去了到後半天他囘來說沒有找着。我知道他是撒謊所以不肯給他錢。

4. 小價錢買來的大價兒賣那就是賺錢。貨是一兩銀子一斤買的還是一兩銀子賣的所以不能賺錢。

5. 他帶着一車子私貨進城門上的官人過來查問他慌慌忙忙的說是行李。官人不信把箱子打開一看果然裝的都是私貨所以全入了官了。

6. 天上的星星雖多掃帚星可不常見。

7. 我鄉下買了個所在趕到夏天在那兒住着小孩子們必是樂極了。

EXERCISE XXXVII.　KEY.

1　你平常做甚麽怎麽我屢次的上你那兒去你家裏的人老答應說是你不在家你想我那兒有工夫呢不是公事就是私事家務又多那一樣兒不得'我辦所以永遠沒閒空兒。

2　人若是悶得慌到街上走一走最好。看見點兒可樂的事心裏自然就不煩了要是碰不下雨的日子不能出去可叫人急得慌。

3　有一件急事得煩個人給他送個信兒去你閒着沒事就奉求你給他個信兒不行我沒閒空兒請另託別位罷。我想不論打發誰去都行。

4　那孩子愛撒謊。我打發他雇車去他囘來告訴我街上沒車我不信打發別人去雇了不大的工夫兒就雇來了。總知道是那孩子要賺錢趕車的不肯跟着他撒謊所以沒雇成。

5　他的買賣很賺錢所有各樣兒零碎貨物都賣所以雖然是個雜貨鋪兒買賣到不錯。

EXERCISE XXXVIII.

1 小兒得了在工部裏帖寫的差使都是承您的情。

2 現任的官出了缺上司就派員署理趕到新派實任官到衙門候補的差使就完了。

3 六部的上司都稱堂官堂官以下就是司官新到衙門官員戴的書班當差的書班和書班一樣。

4 京城的衙門辦稿不是司官就是書班。供事是有頂的差使可就和書班一樣。

5 文書發了之後存起來的稿子就叫陳案。

6 他偷了我們墳上的樹我寫了一個稟帖上衙門去告他那衙役們不給送進去說先得給他們多少錢你還不知道那衙門人的習氣麼就是他老子去打官司也是一樣兒的要錢。

7 新來的那位官員是做甚麼的是上司派來的委員間那明火案兒的口供。

EXERCISE XXXVIII. KEY.

1. 人要是無論差使大小當官就得'學習行走候補的官先最大的衙門是六

2. 事有了都得給差使是當那就是堂官又說上部裡最大的官

3. 不是得'國家出差使。衙門的時候就是堂官又說上部裡最大的官

4. 承當力寶任兒學著當差。管各司的官兒叫司官又說司員稿

5. 件事是署任事不有缺就可以司官又說司員稿子都是他們辦的。

6. 甚麼人能說派着署。有交給書班辦的。

7. 承辦。是一樣。差使。

6. 書班是書吏的俗名兒。事情辦妥了稿子寫好了給堂官看。叫回堂畫稿。

7. 凡各衙門有外差得'差委派去的官員。

8. 衙役皂隸是各衙門裡使喚作零碎事的官人。

9. 供事是考來的中了就有頂戴。比書班尊貴些。

10. 辦過了的官事文件收存起來叫存稿。稿裡有准辦過的有不准的。可都是陳案。

EXERCISE XXXIX.

1. 他那一件事情成了,是他的命運好,在我說不關運氣都是他有志氣肯用功的好處。

2. 作善得福,作惡得禍,這的命運這都是天命所定本兒都不是天命所定自然之理。

3. 他打直隸運來的米沒的賺錢連氣不行任憑待他怎麽好總是抱怨。

4. 可惜那個人雖然聰明,到底脾氣不行,幾不吃虧,不然就有了病,趕後悔不來了。

5. 天氣寒冷的時候兒人得'活動活動身子幾不吃虧,不然就有了病,趕後悔不來了。

6. 你專在這不相干的事情上用功有甚麼益處,你們老人家花了若干的銀子給你捐了官,你不正經當差使這不是辜負老家兒的恩典嗎,眞叫人家寒心阿疼的要命。

7. 這個學生極靈又願意用功其餘那些個孩子眞是不中用。

8. 你臉上發了福舊年這個時候兒看戶不那個聰明,你那個樣兒就活不了,的開。

9. 把臉戶開罷。戶不開。

EXERCISE XXXIX. KEY.

1. 他的性情很好,一點兒脾氣都沒有,怎麼能得禍況且長得也是很有福氣的樣兒。

2. 人生來的命有好有歹,就是運氣也不能一個樣兒。

3. 無論做甚麼事總得有志氣,自然成得了事,若一點兒志氣都沒有一輩子也不用想有進益。

4. 他那個人你別瞧了,說話行事倒很活動,一點兒也不死樣。人也極聰明,很有志氣,老在家裏,那兒也不願意去,最愛用功。

5. 你借別人的錢,他怕你出利錢吃虧,替你還上,這是你的益處,你倒抱怨他多事,這不是辜負人家的好意麼,叫人寒心不寒心。日後他知道和你要錢,准是要後悔的。

6. 行善做惡那都在人作,惡的人悔改了,一樣也是善人。

7. 這幾樣兒很好,給我留下其餘的拿了去,我不要。

8. 這小狗兒很有靈性,我說甚麼,他都懂得。

EXERCISE XL.

1. 你天天來不兒來不若要緊急的事情橫豎得叫你去。

2. 可惜他蓋的那房子不像房子的式樣好像馬棚似的住着很不像樣兒。

3. 那一所兒房子通共有多少間。通共有一百多間除了人住的下賸還有四五十間。

4. 我合算起來有一萬兩銀子的外欠除了還賬之外下賸還有二千兩銀子的盈餘。

5. 我月月兒進的錢總不敷沒有盈餘反倒賸下些個賬目不能還過這種樣兒的日子真叫我傷心。

6. 有人放槍把他那小孩子打着的頭是橫的。

7. 門旁邊兒的木頭是豎的門上的木頭是橫的。

8. 在地下平擱的東西說橫說豎那都是隨勢酌情的活動話若是在面前直着的爲豎在旁面橫的人就以爲是橫。

PART III.—THE FORTY EXERCISES.

EXERCISE XL. KEY.

1

我纔剛告訴你有件緊急的事預先把馬備好了等着、到這時候兒你還沒預備呢我不說你罷你眞叫我着急、說你倒像我脾氣不好似的。

2

俗們這賬得通長了算一算我借過你幾次合在一塊兒通共有多少錢除去我還你的下剩我算計着還有一點兒盈餘。

3

你借的錢多還的錢少那兒還有盈餘呢。

4

我瞧你外面倒像很明白你怎麼連橫竪都不知道叫你把畫兒掛上竪的是在門兩旁掛的橫的是在門上頭掛的你都給掛錯了。

5

這件事你交給我辦。我給你橫竪我給你辦好了。

6

你不要說了那一件事你辦的好叫我傷心。上次我打算搭個天棚託你給買蓆誰想你一點兒準沒有東西也沒買來連你的面兒都見不着了。

請酒大家先乾一杯。 15 請,請。 16 請茶,我可不布、都沒外人、自取罷。 17 那最好大家讓起來倒顯着拘泥還是隨便的好您瞧剛說是不讓怎麽又讓起來了。我們也得回敬總是。 18 不是那麽着這幾樣兒茶是我前兩天就打發人到櫃上告訴了託他們竈上用心給做一做,似乎比現弄的好點兒。我看諸公都不動筷兒,我不能不布一布,您何妨嘗一嘗。 19 諸位別住筷兒,總得吃飽呀。 20 我們都吃得飽了,酒也喝醉了,這樣兒的盛設叫您費心。 21 今兒沒甚麽可吃的酒也不好叫諸位屈量。 22 您那兒的話呢今兒個也不說甚麽了,車來了,天也不早了,得回去了。過一天再到您府上道謝去。 23 豈敢,豈敢,您請便罷,我也不敢奉留了。 24 諸公還坐會兒,我先失陪請了,別送,留步,主人也不必送、請回去陪別位客罷。 25 我就到這兒候乘。 26 磕頭,磕頭。 27 再見,再見。

太早咯不但別位客不能到齊碰巧了連主人還未必能發到呢。 5 我還要請教您我若是領他這個情似乎還得寫個回字兒罷 6 那倒不用，您既是把帖子留下了，那就是您一準要去的憑據帖子不是。 8 不錯這規矩是這麼着您明兒去的時候兒到了庄子的門口兒先叫您的管家遞了您的名片那門口兒伺候的人接過片子來就頭裡帶道兒讓您進去主人在那'屋裡就讓您到那'屋裡，不用說先作個揖回來把那個請帖兒雙手遞給他嘴裡說我又來討擾的了不得尊帖上下的字眼兒實在不敢當主人一面接帖兒一面也說兩句謙虛話大家就坐下喝茶等別的客都來齊了，那纔讓坐擺飯。 9 有時候兒客不能都到若只短一半位就不儘等着了，趕到來了，就讓在那空座兒上坐。為甚麼呢，那座位都是主人早已算計定了的，到了入座的時候兒雖然應該謙讓，主人萬不肯叫你們隨便坐所以後來的有給他留下的空座兒他來了也不用很讓就坐下了。 10 哎呀閣下來了，失迎的很，您恕我。 11 那'兒的話，我來晚了罷叫諸公受等。 12 不晚也都剛到咱們入席罷。 13 這個座兒實在有僭的很。 14 理當理當諸位

問答章之十

1 今兒早起有個朋友送了個帖兒來、是要請我在飯庄子上吃飯、我心裏有點兒猶豫、是為甚麼呢、我想貴國的一切見面兒應酬的禮節、我都不大很熟、倘若落了過節兒倒教人家笑話。 2 您別那麼想阿、等我把那個俗套子告訴您、您就明白了。您把那個帖兒給我瞧瞧。阿原來是張大老爺請您在慶會堂吃飯阿、這個庄子好、地方又寬綽、屋子很涼快、我常去、他那個茶做的講究像樣兒、都得味兒、誰家也沒有他那麼好、您去罷、樂得的大家談談散散悶兒呢。 3 我聽說貴國請客、那帖子上定的時刻不能算準成、彷彿罷、寫的是午刻必得未刻去纔好。 4 那看帖子是怎麼寫的、如果有個準字、就得到了那時候兒就得去、張大老爺這帖子上沒有那準字、就寫的是四點鐘、您就是六點鐘去、也不晚去的

我倒有一個法子、今兒個忙些兒沒空兒細說、請先生明兒過來嗒們再商量行不行。 53 可以沒有甚麼不行的、我就遵命了、明兒個幾點鐘見們申初見罷。 55 那們我失陪了。 56 您請。 57 請。

實在有甚麼益處兒呢。29 三字經是三個字一句、爲的是小孩子容易念、那千字文因爲沒有重字、小孩子念了、就可以認得一千字麼呢。31 常念的都是先念四書、後來念五經、有幾年的工夫呢。32 您從念四書起、到念完了五經、就是先生十四歲那一年。33 兩頭兒算起來有六七年的工夫。34 阿、那五經念完了、就是先生十四歲那一年。35 不錯、還沒到十四歲呢。36 先生從多大歲數兒上開講。37 我從十二歲上纔開講、38 開講的時候兒、還是自已看註子還是聽先生的解說。39 我一開講的時候兒是聽先生的解說講過一年多、就自已看註子後來作了二年多的詩合文章、纔進學、早阿、是先生的天分高。41 那兒的話呢、那也是微倖後來鄉試下了多少場、八年纔中了舉人。42 先生今年貴庚。43 我今年三十歲。44 先生中舉人之後這六年裡頭有甚麼公幹。45 沒有甚麼事情、前二年在家裡教書、後幾年在外頭作幕幫朋友、46 請問令友榮任是甚麼官。47 是山東的知縣、他去年不在了、我纔回來的。48 先生作過幕那更好了。49 怎麼更好呢。50 好處是這麼樣、我那朋友學話之後還要學文書。51 可惜就是這個教話沒頭緒。52 那

問答章之九

1 有先生來要見老爺。
2 請進來。
3 進來了。
4 先生請坐。
5 請坐。
6 先生貴姓。
7 賤姓蘇。
8 先生到這兒來貴幹。
9 昨兒聽見一個相好的說起閣下要請先生。
10 阿必是那張先生說的。
11 不錯是張先生說的。
12 張先生他告訴您是我要找先生是我替別人找先生。
13 他沒告訴我詳細可不是閣下要請麼。
14 不是我要請是一個相好的託我請。
15 令友還是貴國的人麼。
16 是本國的人到貴處日子不多。
17 既是新來的我們的話恐怕不懂罷。
18 不錯漢話一句都不懂漢字一個也不認得。
19 這麼着我怎麼能教給他說呢。
20 先生先得教他說話能說些兒那看書再說。
21 他一字不懂我從那兒教起。
22 先生是老手了在貴國教過多少門生怎麼不能教他說話是不學而會的至於念書是從小兒背念熟的恐怕令友不能照着我們這兒的小孩子那麼費事罷。
23 我們的教學那是另有一個法子先生從多大念書。
24 那是自然的也可以商量一個法子先生從多大念書。
25 我從七歲念起。
26 先生一念是先念三字經千字文麼。
27 不錯先念的是那個。
28 貴國人都先念這兩個小書兒

爺那些個鋪盖甚麽的，可以僱一輛小車兒裝上合老爺一塊兒走，其餘上船，打通州那們走。 72 按照那麽着我就坐裝行李的那輛車麽。 73 老爺另僱一輛車兒坐好罷。 74 那車是單套，是二套呢。 75 老爺要快，必得用二套的，現在雨水大，道兒不好走，三套的也不妨。 76 哎道兒不好走，坐車不大對我的勁兒，在這兒雇馬行不行。 77 驟子馬都可以雇，只怕我們的鞍子老爺騎着不合式。 78 我們那兒馬身上的傢伙我都帶着呢，可以備，那嚼帽子怕不肯戴。 79 也怕不行，那馬鞍子我們的馬還可以安，嚼子拴扯手的那傢伙恐怕我們的馬戴不慣，要鬧性子不如買匹外國馬倒好。 82 外國馬在天津這兒那'兒可以買。 83 行了，我們行裡有匹馬，是我們行中夥計的，他要賣那馬很好，又老實又快，來往進京有三四回了。 84 那麽着我就到行裡商量商量還有那些個大箱子運到通州的時候兒，雇甚麽人送進京去。 85 老爺就雇小的，好不好。 86 好，倒沒甚麽不好的，只怕這麽些日子你們行裡離不開你，不容你去。 87 行了，離得開，今兒打發我來不是聽老爺的吩咐來了麽。

合我要多少錢。55那倒難說老爺會說我們的話,可以先合他商量看他要的價兒若多不妨駁他再還他個價兒。56那都行了,就是第二天進京,還得打那麼走。57早起離了河西務,還是往西北去,有二十多里是到安平,還有二十多里是馬頭,從馬頭還算有二十里地到張家灣那個老是先有個小河兒麼。59不是那城是南北下裡騎着河面兒的老爺進了南順着大街過了河,就出北門外頭有兩股岔道兒往北的是上通州去往西偏着點兒的那就是進京的了。60接那兒到京還有多遠呢。61看老爺進那個門,若是城裡頭進沙窩門兒還算有五十多里路,若是到城外店裡住,進沙窩門兒還算有五十多里路,若是到城裡頭走東便門那是往北點兒多個二三里地也不算很遠。62上外國公館是進那個門好。63那外國公館都是在海岱門裡頭御河橋一帶,在我說是進東便門方便些兒。64很好,如今我明白了還有一件事我走的這麼快我的行李怎麼樣呢。65老爺的行李有多少子也是老爺的麼。66就是門外頭擱着的那些東西。67甚麼那些大箱子也是老爺的麼。68原是啊。69老爺想兩天進京,恐怕不能都帶罷,不但用好些個大車費錢還不能很快。70那麼你說還有甚麼好法子。71依我說老

好。河西務那兒還是那個店好。35那兒有一個富與、一個順來、兩個都是大店、一個在街南頭兒、一個在街北頭兒。36這兩個是那個方便呢。37若論房子吃食都差不多兒、南頭兒方便北頭兒方便、那是隨老爺的意。38南的北的有甚麼不同相離的很遠麼。39離的却不甚遠河西務沒有這兒府城那麼大地方不過是個鎮店一條長街兩邊兒有些個鋪子甚麼的。40這麼說起來南的北的有甚麼不一樣的。41沒有甚麼不一樣的、是我向來給老爺們帶道總是一進街就住下的時候兒多。42你說的那是打天津去的、在南頭兒住、打京裡來的、在北頭兒住、是不是。43不錯老爺明白。44就是了我到了店裡叫他們弄甚麼茶好呢。45老爺怕沒吃過我們的茶罷。46沒吃過呢。47阿老爺還沒吃過不如從天津做一點兒好拿的茶帶着。48甚麼自已帶着、到了店裡吃他們的飯他們願意麼。49那倒沒甚麽店裡還得他們的房錢有一定的價兒麼。50這房錢51我們人住店差不多有一定的價兒、若是外國客人怕那掌櫃的他多要幾個錢。52那掌櫃的就是店東麼。53那都不定、有是店東做掌櫃的、有是店東外請別人替他照應買賣做掌櫃的。54就是這個房錢大概

一道橋、到熱鬧街兒那兒、再打聽第二道橋、過了第二道橋、往西北就是進京的大道。16 聽見說還有過河的地方兒有沒有。17 那是擺渡罷、擺渡是有。18 擺渡是有、那車馬怎麼樣呢。19 車馬沒甚麼、那都可以擺過去。20 往後怎麼樣呢。21 往後是這麼着、離了擺渡口兒還是順著大道走、到離天津三十多里的那個鎮店、叫浦口、就是頭段兒。22 那'兒呢、頭一段兒不是河西務麼。23 河西務遠多了、那算是一天的道兒、過了浦口之後、先到楊村後到南蔡村挨晚兒的時候兒可以到河西務、這些地方兒相隔大約都是三十多里地。24 按道兒說這河西務離京還有多遠呢。25 按道兒說、就算是中間兒了。在那兒住一夜、明兒個就進得了京咯。26 住一夜是在那'兒呢。27 貴國的人向來有住店的有住廟的。28 是店裡好、是廟裡好呢。29 依我說、是店裡方便些兒、廟裡留客是格外的事情、一來不定有房子沒有、二來如果趕車的多、和尚不願意再者、丟了東西為誰是問呢。30 阿店裡丟東西是店主人應管麼。31 原是那麼着、還有一說、吃的喝的店裡都能預備、廟裡連廚房都沒有。32 沒廚房、廟裡在那'兒弄飯呢。33 他們弄的都是素菜葷的他們不能弄。34 阿、那們不如店裡

問答章之八

來著,是不是。96 可不是拏着呢,剛纔從我們那兒買的。97 是小孫子跟他要來着麼。98 不是令孫哭了,他說你別哭,我送給你點兒玩意兒。畫兒算玩意兒,為甚麼不送到小兒那兒去呢。100 那張大爺的姪兒今兒早起到我們鋪子裡來打聽令郎的住處。我們說知道您納不知道他,他叫我們把畫兒送到府上就是了,過兩天他還要親自來呢。

1 請老爺安。 2 好阿。你是甚麼人。 3 我是英順行打發來給老爺帶路進京的。老爺定規多喒走。 4 明兒就要走。 5 老爺要走的是水路是旱路呢。 6 是旱路好,是水路好。 7 水路呢,這兩天雨大河水長了,上水的船拉着費事,再遇着北風怕五六天到不了通州。 8 哎,這麼着那水路就不行。走旱路怎麼樣呢。 9 若是老爺明兒一早動身趕着走,第二天晚上就可以到京,慢着點兒,第三天足行了。 10 這旱路你熟罷。 11 哎,這十幾年常來往,怎麼不熟呢。 12 我不用人帶道,你細細兒告訴我都是打那麼走,行的。老爺出了城東邊兒那個浮橋知道不知道。 14 那個知道。 15 您過了這

PART IV.—THE TEN DIALOGUES.

住麽。65 他這會兒單搬出去了。66 請問他住在甚麽地方兒。67 他在交民巷西頭兒路北。68 他是在交民巷住麽。69 真的呵你疑惑作甚麽。70 我估摸是在城外頭住的。71 離衙門那麽遠不行你怎麽估摸着是城外頭兒來着。72 昨兒日頭落碰見他的車在琉璃廠。73 那'兒有這個話他昨晚上在我這兒來着。74 車上坐着個老婆子他說是孟大爺的車。75 車是他的他却沒在車上。76 他沒在車上你怎麽知道車是他的。77 老婆子抱着個孩子麽。78 不錯是個七八歲的小孩子。79 必是我那小孫子噯那早晚兒那'兒去。80 老爺放心有點兒事情。81 有點兒甚麽事情呢車驚了麽。82 不是本來道兒不好走。83 那是車翻了麽。84 也不然是合對頭兒車碰了。85 碰了老爺沒說開麽。86 倒不是沒說開。87 是小孩子受了傷了麽。88 却沒甚麽那早晚兒他從車上跳下來的時候兒把腿扭了一下兒。89 可惡知道那個車是誰的不知道。90 就是那張爺他姪兒的。91 還是他呀那麽送畫兒是作甚麽呢。92 這畫兒是給您納令孫的。93 特意買畫兒壓驚是甚麽意思呢。94 畫兒是先買的並不是特意買的。95 碰車的時候兒他手裡就擎着

30 那堂子衖衕住的張爺您納認識不認識。
31 張爺我認識就是他買的麼。
32 還不是他。
33 不是他,提他作甚麼不說呢。
34 我提他有個原故。
35 有原故爲甚麼不說呢。
36 您納太急,回來就明白了。
37 你這是要戲我的話,我不依。
38 那'兒敢耍戲您納,你不能說我進去了,你去罷。
39 有正經話爲甚麼不說。
40 提起來話兒長。
41 就是沒空兒。
42 噯,別忙別忙,還有話說呢。
43 有話就快說,我認得不認得。
44 那張爺您納說是認得。
45 那我先告訴你了。
46 他們令姪您納認得,他多嗻晚兒回來的。
47 見過一次,不很熟。
48 叫送這個畫兒的就是他。
49 他叫送來的。
50 甚麼回來呢,他出外來着麼。
51 他從前不是跟官出去麼。
52 那個我不知道,是那年出去的。
53 我記得是前年往江西去了。
54 前年出去的,我從去年還見他在城裡頭呢。
55 那都不論,他給我送畫兒是作甚麼。
56 本不是給您買的。
57 不是給我買的,你拏來作甚麼,我決不買這個。
58 說甚麼買呀,錢是他給過了。
59 你這個來回話兒我始終不明白。
60 等我再告訴您幾句話。
61 就快說,別儘着耽悞工夫兒。
62 您納的少爺不是在戶部有差使麼。
63 你這個人竟是打聽,小兒原是在戶部。
64 他不是單

問答章之七

1 是你叫門麼。 2 是我叫門。 3 你是那兒的。 4 我是城外頭來的。 5 你找誰。 6 找姓孟的。 7 我就姓孟。 8 阿您納就是孟爺。 9 不錯我姓孟找我作甚麼。 10 廣文齋打發我來的。 11 廣文齋不是書舖麼。 12 不錯是書舖。 13 叫你送甚麼書來麼。 14 不是送書來了。 15 怎麼手裡拏的不是書麼。 16 不是書竟是個書套。 17 沒有書竟送個空書套作甚麼。 18 這書套不是空的。 19 不是空的還裝着甚麼。 20 裝着幾張畫兒。 21 畫兒怕不是送這兒來的罷。 22 沒錯是給這兒送來的。 23 為甚麼我沒有買畫兒。 24 我知道不是您納買的。 25 那麼為甚麼給我送了來。 26 有別人給您納這兒買的。 27 給您納買的罷。 28 買的意思您納倒不用打聽。 29 到底是誰給買的。我買畫是甚麼意思

54 我是說着玩兒呢來的是刻字匠要錢來了。 55 叫他月底再來罷。 56 他先來過兩回了。 57 不錯是有的我應許了還錢是得給的。 58 大人不必費事了我替您開發了罷。是決不見他了。

33 體面有甚麼體面呢、那天穿的那褂子也不怎麼樣。34 怎麼樣不怎麼樣也算是值錢的、他騎的那騾子也是很好的。35 我估摸他是坐車來的。36 不是坐車騎着騾子來的、那騾子十分的膽壯。37 旣然是這麼着你旣知道他這麼靠不住又愛花錢你還這麼護着他是個甚麼道理。38 人家從前很享福、如今沒有路兒了、我見了他心裡怎麼能不憐恤。39 噯、怎麼憐恤他是憑你竟是有一句話可不用託我給他找甚麼事情。40 可惜了兒的眼看着他這個人是要要飯的。41 等他要飯的時候兒、給他頓飯吃到可以叫我保他作甚麼我萬也不能。42 按那天定的約了他後兒來。43 後兒他來了、你可以把我起先說的那話告訴他。44 告訴他是大人一定不肯幫他麼。45 不是那個話、是告訴我出了城了。46 他若是問大人多喒回來。47 你就說不知道多喒回來。48 他若是天天兒來打聽呢。49 憑他來多少囘總不許他進來。50 我想不如簡直的告訴他、你轉託別人、不用倚靠大人咯、好不好。51 那却不行、若是簡直的告訴他不肯相幫、必得把所以然的話細說明白了、那更不必了。52 哼、院子裡說話不是徐永的聲兒麼。53 若是他、隨你用甚麼話推辭、我

16 怎麼那個走私是叫官場中查着了。 17 哎您想一想那官役勒索的錢多官場中有不知道的理麼。 18 勒索了不過三百兩銀子也不算很多。 19 你說是不多這數兒也是應當合他們同事的那巡船上的人不但沒按着分兒分給同事的他們自己留的也是彼此相爭。 20 大家爲錢爭鬧後來有個報了官的是不是。 21 就是了官旣知道這件事便細究個水落石出把老徐從重的罰了連他的功名也革了。 22 老徐像這麼丟臉也難怪徐永遮掩是該遮掩的誰敎他張揚來着也不用編造他父親因朋友受累的這些假話呀。 24 那可也過逾虛詐咯。 25 他說這個話的時候兒我就有一半兒不信我記得那李永城合他父親很熟和我心裡打着合他打聽這個人。 26 大概那姓李的說他沒有甚麼好話罷。 27 一句好話也沒有那徐永他是很認得徐永頭裡求他給找一個事情他心軟了依了沒考過就保舉了。 28 是個甚麼差使。 29 是個貼寫的事情沒有一個月就不要他了。 30 不要他是因爲他行止不好是因爲他沒本事呢。 31 兩樣兒都不好楷書所不能寫怎麼能做貼寫呢而且說的話一句也靠不住。 32 那個人奇怪呀沒有錢穿的怎麼那麼體面呢。

問答章之六

78 那巡喩船早躲開了,徐永他經過那樣兒的事就長了一個見識,不照前次從豐,只給十兩銀子罷了。 79 他們依不依。 80 那兒不依呢,他們都喝的半醉了,要搜他的船也不能了,他給的不論怎麼少都可以依得。

1 那旁忿話兒算結了,他那年辦洋薬是甚麼人託他的,他告訴了你沒有。 2 我不記得。 3 他不是說是他父親叫他去的麼。 4 那我實在是不記得咯。 5 不論你記得不記得,實在是他父親叫他買的,後來他父親關閉買賣的緣故,就是因為這個。 6 那兒呢,是他打算的不好麼。 7 打算的不好那一句話也有的,那洋薬出口是往天津去的。 8 阿,在天津叫人搜出來了麼。 9 那船始終沒到天津,走到山東海面兒上,叫海賊把船扣住了。 10 這麼着老徐的資本全丟了罷。 11 不錯,不但丟了資本,連項戴也丟了。 12 他原來有個功名麼,那我却不知道。 13 是,他就是頭年捐的。 14 是捐過阿,然而海賊那一案怎麼會干涉着他的功名呢,難道說他與海賊通了麼。 15 那却不因為海賊,是因為走

給一百兩銀子、是沒有的事、說是若不給三百兩、是要全封了。57 這三百兩他給不給呢。58 他沒有這麼些個錢。59 他還有甚麼法子辦呢。60 他寫了個字兒叫他們跟上海洋行裡取錢。61 奇怪他們也肯要這個字兒麼、62 他出了這個虎口是個便宜。63 怎麼呢、那巡役們要了這個字兒又有甚麼反悔呢。64 不是那麼樣、他們大家沒商量安的時候兒、柴船和巡船一塊兒往下走、撞了人家灣着的兩隻船、65 又是兩隻巡哨的船麼。66 不是關上的船、是欽差劉大人的船、一隻是預備他自己坐的、一隻是他下人坐的。67 可笑還是半夜的時候兒麼。68 不到半夜二更多天。69 二更多天劉大人合底下人必都睡了罷。70 劉大人怕是在**城裡**頭公館裡底下人們還在船上樂呀、唱阿、鬧呢。71 就是那些個底下人們到底與海關上無干。72 原是呀、竟是徐永那個柴船撞了他們的船、先是一驚後來心定了一定兒就合他們要賠補的錢。73 要賠補甚麼呢。74 賠補他們受驚賠補官船的損壞、隨便甚麼都算應賠補的。75 他甘心受他們這個我不明白。76 一則是寡不敵衆、二則是他的膽虛。77 膽虛、是應該膽虛、到了兒怎麼樣呢。

起來辦洋藥的那一層他還些微的有點兒難處。33別是那洋藥短了罷。34短是不短價錢天天兒長東西還是足夠買的。35賣的還是公然賣麼。36也不算公然都是躉船棧房裡藏的。徐永常去的是在窰衚衕兒裡頭一個小舖兒的後頭。37吃的時候兒還是在洋行裡麼。38不是館麼眞是有甚麼老子有甚麼兒子。39阿這徐永也常上烟盡是替人家辦的罷可是他那個難是甚麼呢。40吃的也不大很利害。41阿自已不吃了要出還誑慊了好些日子。42那時候兒烟禁沒開他辦得把烟下在裡頭偸着出口。43底下怎麽出的口呢。44有裝柴火的船他去呢。45我以為上海的柴火都是進口的出口是往那兒出事來了。46去的地方兒大概不遠那船裝的實在是柴火少洋藥多。47所以鬧抓住了。48鬧出事來是這麼著那柴火船順着水放下去抽冷子有巡船來抓住了就把這貨封了麼。49抓住了就把這貨封了麼。50還沒有封那些巡役們說你若不多兒給我們錢可就要搜你的船了。51巡役們跟他要多少錢呢。52他們沒說數兒盡是叫他從豐。53這徐永他要給多少兒。54他那人糊塗說要給一百兩。55一百兩那寔在從豐了巡役們也不覺多麽。56那兒不覺多看柴火船兩。

PART IV.—THE TEN DIALOGUES.

親賠本兒不是真的麼。

7 賠本兒原是賠本兒、可不像他說的那麼賠本兒。

8 不是像他說的賠本兒還是怎麼着呢。

9 他賠本兒全是他自己糊塗、自己拋費了、沒別的。

10 到底家裡養活的人口多、11 他養活家口倒沒有那件事、不用提別的、那徐福慶早就不在了。

12 早去了世了麼他那些個兒女却是誰養活呢。

13 他女兒在他沒去世之前就都死了、兒子單生了一個、就是這個撒謊的。

14 那怕大人是聽錯了罷。

15 一點兒也沒聽錯、我細細兒的考查過了。

16 不錯、我說過。

17 這四五年來你都沒見過他們罷。

18 不止四五年、有九年十年的光景沒見了。

19 就是了。那老徐在布舖作買賣、他的名聲怎麼樣。

20 那一時人就說他狂傲沒有甚麼別的不好。

21 他不是很愛吃烟麼。

22 吃烟是有的、也有一點兒貪酒。

23 却原來就是你在上海遇見那徐永他在那兒作甚麼。

24 他說是有人托他辦土貨呢、是茶葉是湖絲。

25 甚麼土貨呢、是茶葉是湖絲。

26 有茶葉有湖絲有藥材。

27 這些土貨是要運到那兒去呢。

28 他說是往北往南、我不記得。

29 他沒提辦洋貨麼。

30 他巧來提過、我不記得咯。

31 沒提過辦洋藥麼。

32 辦洋藥原有的、大人提到、我纔想

問答章之五

67 那倒是歲數還小呢常愛病。68 常愛病麼是甚麼病。69 打我母親死了他缺奶後來不很足壯。70 這實在可憐還有你們弟兄們量必可以幫着過日子。71 我却很願意可惜沒個道路大哥作甚麼呢。72 你是長房的不是。73 我排二。74 可是你得還有你的兄弟可怎麼樣呢。75 他腿脚兒有殘疾,甚麼都不能幹。76 嗳,這個光景可了不得栽培他們念書他們學的還算不錯。77 我父親收買賣的時候兒他們還小呢,不能個事情對不對。78 說來說去你的意思是要託我給你找今兒個來意實在是因爲這個不是。79 大人肯這麼疼愛我我感激的心一言難盡了。80 就是你口。82 也罷等我給你打算打算,請你過了十天前後兒來,再說。81 不是大人先提起來,我實在是不敢開人的提拔,我過幾天再來請安。84 偺們過兩天見請。85 大人請坐。83 眞是承大

1 龍田那徐永再來的時候兒你告訴他我出城去了。2 嗳,可惜叫他白喜歡了,他怎麼得罪了大人了。3 甚麼得罪呢他那些個話通身都是假的。4 怎麼呢他不是徐福慶的兒子麼。5 這徐福慶的兒子那却是呵。6 他說他父

好了沒有。41 年紀這麼大眼睛還算可以。42 那兒說到年紀歲數兒合我差不多兒。43 家父今年六十九,比他大兩歲。44 我七十一,45 我父親要能彀像大人這麼硬朗那是求之不得的了。46 怎麼不能呢,他沒有我受的累多。47 大人是為國家當重任辦事受的累多,我老子為家業心裡也有他的辛苦。48 那是從前做買賣時候兒累的,如今是回家歇着了。49 囘家,是囘家,也是無可奈何。50 怎麼呢,買賣不好麼。51 也不盡是那麼樣。52 怎麼呢,莫不是銀錢被了竊。53 比丟了還可惡,所掙的錢差不多兒叫人家都騙凈了。54 可惜了兒的,是怎麼呢,欠主兒賴了麼。55 大人不是那麼樣,我父親保的那個朋友跑了,可惡令尊的精神就是因為這個受傷,是不是。57 自然是家裡人口多,沒力量養活,不免着急。58 你父親跟前你們幾個姐妹。60 這麼多呢,未必都在家裡罷。61 個個兒都在家裡。62 我想那姑娘都是出嫁的。63 本有兩個出了門子,給的都是武官,上回西路出兵都陣亡了。64 阿,他們倆孀婦就回家來麼。65 是,都回家來了,一個帶着兩個孩子,一個帶着六個孩子。66 噯,那人口真真的不少,還有一個姑娘沒出門子麼。

問答章之四

1 龍田。 2 大人叫我作甚麼。 3 院子裡那個人是誰。 4 那個人是姓徐的。 5 阿是你認識的麼。 6 是我陳認識的。 7 你們倆是在那兒遇見的。 8 是在上海會過的。 9 是多喒呢。 10 好些年了。 11 你合他很有交情麼。 12 可以我們本是個遠親。 13 你們是親戚麼他作甚麼來了你知道不知道。 14 不知道大人要我問他麼。 15 問問他也好。 16 他說是他父親打發他來給大人請安的。 17 來見我作甚麼。 18 他說是他父親打發他來給大人請安的。 19 他父親是作甚麼的呢。 20 從前是作買賣現在閒着呢。 21 這人我所不記得是個作甚麼買賣的呢。 22 西城那個大布鋪大人那兒不記得他兒子麼。 23 阿那徐福慶阿他我還記得來的是他兒子麼。 24 不錯是他的兒子。 25 讓他進來。 26 大人讓你哪。 27 大人好。 28 請坐請坐。 29 大人請坐。 30 請坐請坐來。 31 喳。 32 沏茶來貴姓是徐麼。 33 賤姓徐。 34 徐福慶是你父親麼。 35 不錯家父的名字是徐福慶。 36 前幾年我們就認識他好阿。 37 托大人的福打發我來給大人請安。 38 叫他惦記着着寒勞你的駕咯。 39 該當的。 40 我模模糊糊的記得他眼睛不大好如今

104 是道兒上茶館兒裡的人。

105 離城門有多遠兒。

106 不遠兒。

107 是來順兒在那兒喝茶來著麽。

108 不是喝茶，是喝酒，那兒的人呢。

109 你合他一塊兒吃麽。

110 沒有，我出去拴鞭子去了。

111 拴好了鞭子就回茶館兒了麽。

112 趕我囘來，他們先跑了。

113 跑了，就是坑你的車錢麽。

114 不但車錢連茶館兒的飯錢都沒給。

115 阿，他們跑了，茶館兒就是合你要這個錢麽。

116 可不是麽，我不肯給，他們就打了我了。

117 茶館兒打你這一層我有甚麽法子。

118 打不打沒甚麽要緊，請老爺找補我的車錢我就走了。

119 車錢還容易，把他的工錢折給你就是了。

120 老爺可以這就賞罷叫小的囘去。

121 車錢你放心罷，這個茶館兒裡的事情你合他沒話麽。

122 沒話，沒話，請老爺給了錢，小的就囘去。

123 你實在是個忠厚人哪，肯擔待人家的，不是，可是你回村兒裡，要告訴來順他老子，他兩個兒子沒有一個是材料兒的，這宗檬兒的人我決不要他們咯。

來順一個坐兒麼。 72還有他一個同伴兒。 73要快是那'個的主意。 74來順僱車來的時候兒說若快可以多加幾個錢 75你們說明白了是多少錢 76說定了的是五吊錢。 77連他要給加的錢都在裏頭麼。 78都說在一塊兒 80總沒合他打架。 79車價還罷了，是因為這個打架來着麼。 80[略] 81怎麼了，你不是纔說挨了打了麼。 82小的說挨打可不是他打的。 83不是他，是誰。 84有好些個人小的不認得都是誰。 85都是來順帶了來的伴兒麼。 86不是一個也不是來順帶來的。 87他們是搶東西的麼。 88也不然嗳呦說起來話長。 89就是話長你也得說了。 90請老爺補還我的錢我就走了。 91別忙別忙這件事我還得分晰明白。 92不值得駾惧老爺的工夫。 93那你不用管只要我問你甚麼你說甚麼。 94老爺還問甚麼呢。 95這個張來順是馬駒橋的人麼。 96他父親在村兒外頭種個茶園子 97這麼著這來順兒必是你素來認得的。 98他小時候兒在街上玩兒我常看見他。 99他小時候兒是老實阿是琉璃呢。 100小的不肯說人的短處。 101不要你偏說短處他有好處你不能殼說麼。 102請老爺補還我的車錢我就走了。 103就是毆打你的是處

們是誰、要的是甚麼錢。38那天替老爺買的桌子、鋪子裡要錢。39那鋪子不是在西城麼。40不是、鋪子是在城外頭。41城外麼、離那'個門近。42阿、小的想起來了、在安定門外。43這鋪子在北邊兒在南邊兒還不知道麼。44阿、小的外的道兒不大熟。45這裡頭我有點兒不大明白的地方兒。46老爺不明白甚麼。47你這個人總得說實話。48小的不敢撒謊。49阿院子裏甚麼人吵嚷呢。50小的出去看一看罷。51不用去放窗戶罷。52咳、有個人闖進來是甚麼事情。53你不是趕車的麼闖進來幹甚麼。54嗳哎小的給老爺磕頭求老爺作主。55作甚麼主呢。56嗳哎丟了錢挨打求老爺伸冤。57你丟錢挨打、與我何干。58不關老爺的事、却關老爺的底下人。59我那個底下人丟錢麼。60阿不錯、就是他、我頭裏沒理會他。可是那個來順麼。61他合你怎麼了。62我的車錢他那'兒給了麼。63是北城來的那個車麼。64甚麼北城阿、我是馬駒橋店裏的。65咳、這個還得說詳細你可小心細說罷。66小的若有一句謊、老爺要了我的腿都使得。67你們今兒是甚麼時候兒起的身。68雞叫的時候兒糊套車。69是單套是二套。70是二套車、為走的快。71車上就是這

問答章之三

1 來。 2 隨進來問 老爺要甚麼。 3 你是甚麼人。 4 小的叫來福。 5 你姓甚麼。 6 小的姓張。 7 你在這兒幹甚麼。 8 小的是替哥哥來替工。 9 你哥哥是誰。 10 小的的哥哥叫來順。 11 阿,就是給我看書房的那個來順兒麼。 12 不錯,就是那個來順。 13 他沒告假,怎麼走了呢。 14 因為老爺欠安他不便告假。 15 怎麼不等我好了呢。 16 家裡有件很要緊的事。 17 有甚麼要緊的事情呢。 18 小的母親病的利害。 19 既這麼着怎麼他走了,你來了呢。 20 他回去是小的的父親叫他小的來是怕躭悮老爺這兒的工夫。 21 阿,別的先勿論底下人出門到底應當告假。 22 請老爺饒他罷小的哥哥也快來了。 23 你家裡離這兒遠近。 24 不算很遠。 25 怎麼不很遠。 26 至多有四里地,還是在東城呢。 27 是了,你這個人先回去罷。 28 小的哥哥就得回來麼。 29 到晚晌來也可以。 30 阿那不是來順來了麼。 31 阿叫他進來。你去罷。 32 老爺沒有甚麼別的事使喚小的。 33 沒事,你去罷。來順。 34 小的糊塗,請老爺寬恕。 35 你真糊塗,出去為甚麼不言語。 36 老爺欠安他們是急於合我要錢。 37 他

33 那是我們本家。34 更好了,他新近不是放了巡撫了麼。35 是阿,放的是河南巡撫你納還有什麽高見。36 我想你若還當着差使那老大人必肯提拔你。37 這是錯想了,你不知道,他向來不喜歡我。38 你不過這麽想甚麽,是個對證兒。39 他上次出外我求他帶我來着。40 他怎麽回答你的。41 他說的就是天底下沒有人我也不要你。42 阿,他說的這麽言重,有甚麽緣故麽。43 他恨我年輕的時候兒不勤儉。44 唉,你放心罷,旣往不咎老大人那兒還那麽恨你。45 你不知道,他還有別的話呢。46 那兒有總不肯寛宥的話麽。47 他說過,我無論到甚麽分兒上再不能照應你。48 可惜,有這個好機會,你得不着益處兒。49 沒法子,誰教我底根兒沒出息呢。50 令尊留下的家產,專歸你一個人兒了,是還分給一家兒了呢。51 還有我們家兄舍弟這一個人分了一分兒。52 分的還是令兄的多呀。53 不是,是三個人均分的。54 留下的是銀錢哪,是產業呀。55 有現銀子,也有房子買賣。56 身底下住房,你又不是長子,爲甚麽歸你。57 從前先父在的時候兒家兄就管買賣。58 阿,就是你在家裡伺候令堂。59 原是阿,因爲舍弟也是在外頭作幕。

問答章之二

1 您納騎的不是我們這兒的馬麼。
2 不錯是在貴處買的馬。
3 是誰替你買的。
4 店裡那些人替我挑的。
5 他們合你要了多少錢。
6 他們要了三十兩銀子。
7 你給了沒給呢。
8 我看着價錢多一點兒沒給。
9 你到底給了多少銀子。
10 我跟他們定規是二十二兩銀子。
11 這匹馬從前是我的。
12 阿你為甚麼賣了。
13 因為家裡沒錢纔賣了。
14 不是因為有甚麼毛病阿。
15 一點兒毛病都沒有。
16 你底跟兒多少錢買的。
17 那時候兒有錢買的貴。
18 你那時候兒是有差使不是。
19 我頭裡是當舖門到先父去世的時候兒攔下了回去料理家務。
20 哎呀令尊病的日子久麼。
21 可不是麼病了十來年。
22 他納這些年的病誰照應家裡呢。
23 我父親雖不能出門還可以管裡的事呢。
24 令尊若是在世你的差使還可以當不可以當呢。
25 可以當不可以當還說不定。
26 怎麼說不定呢。
27 差使的得項若是多些兒纔寬綽。
28 你從前當着還得賠墊麼。
29 倒沒那個總得能多點兒纔寬綽。
30 你別怪我說你擱下的不當。
31 那麼依你納主意當時叫我怎麼辦呢。
32 那王大人不是你們親的不當

問答章之一

1 您貴處是那兒。 2 敝處是天津,沒領教。 3 我也是直隸人。 4 阿,原來是同鄉。 5 他那一位是那兒的人。 6 他是外國人。 7 到這兒來做甚麼您知道不知道。 8 我不知道您問他本人兒就知道了。 9 請問尊駕到我們這兒做甚麼。 10 我是個做買賣的。 11 您帶了來的都是甚麼貨。 12 都是東洋的油漆碎貨。 13 阿,您貴國是日本國麼。 14 不錯,是日本國。 15 怎麼呢,我聽見說過貴處出入很難。 16 頭裡却難,近來開了禁咯就好些兒咯。 17 我們的商民也有上那兒去的沒有。 18 貴國的商民也有。 19 我們的人在那兒是那一省的人多。 20 他們多一半兒是打廣東福建去的。 21 他們的買賣大小呢。 22 只怕沒甚麼很大的罷。 23 為甚麼呢,沒有本錢麼。 24 他們的本錢大概不很多。 25 沒錢往東洋去幹甚麼。 26 他們多一半兒是跟太西各國的人去的。 27 太西國的人帶他們去有甚麼益處兒。 28 是用他們管行作經手的。 29 他們合日本國的人對勁兒不對勁兒。 30 彼此怕都有點兒不相信罷。

PART IV.

THE TEN DIALOGUES.
(CHINESE TEXT.)

出這個賤貨兒來噯完了、福分都叫他老子享盡了、這就是他的結果了、再想要陞騰、如何能呢。

談論篇百章之一百

1 你這是怎麼說呢天天兒喫得飽飽兒的、竟抱着琵琶絃子彈、有甚麼益處兒呢、要從此成名啊、還是要靠着這個過日子呢。2 咱們幸而是滿洲、喫的是官米月間有的是錢糧。一家子頭頂着脚趾着都是主子的並不學正經本事差使上也不巴結、只是在這上頭鑽着心兒學真是玷辱了滿洲咯。與其把有用的心思費在這沒用的地方兒何不讀書呢。3 人往高處兒走、水往底處兒流、琵琶絃子上任憑你學到怎麼樣兒的好、卑汚下賤的名兒總不能免。正經官場中能彀把彈琵琶絃子算得本事麼。4 若說我的話不可信、大人們官員們裡頭、那一個是從彈琵琶絃子上出身的呀、你如今能指出來麽。

談論篇百章之九十九

1 人是比萬物最尊貴的，若不懂好歹不明道理與那畜生何異啊。 2 就是朋友們裡頭，你我彼此恭恭敬敬的豈不好麼。 3 他如今來了的時候兒動不動兒的就發豪橫信着嘴兒混罵人算是自己的本事啊，還是怎麼樣呢你們瞧瞧長得那個嘴巴骨子臊着個大肚子，直是個傻子，還自充懂文墨的好叫人肉麻啊。再那說話的聲兒像狗叫啊似的，人家都厭煩得不聽咯。 4 這個人若有一點兒人心的也該知覺咯，還腆着臉不知恥，倒像是誰喜歡他呢，越發興頭起來咯。是怎麼說呢。 5 他老子一輩子也是漢子來着，不知道怎麼作了孽咯，養

也怕是這麼樣都散了。 2 我剛到了家就颳起來了實在是大樹稍兒叫風摔得那個聲兒真可怕直颳到三更天纔略住了些兒。 3 今兒早起往這麼來的時候兒看見道兒上的人們都是站不住個個兒是吸吸哈哈的跑。 4 我先是順着風兒走，還好些兒後來迎着風兒走的時候兒那臉啊顋啊就像是針兒扎的似的凍得疼手指頭拘攣了連鞭子都拏不住，吐的唾沫沒到地兒也就凍成冰一截兒一截兒的摔碎咯。 5 嗳呀有生以來誰經過這個樣兒的冷呢。

談論篇百章之九十七

1 前兒黑下好冷啊睡夢中把我凍醒了天一亮我急忙起來開開房門一瞧原來是白亮亮的下了一地的雪。2 喫了早飯小晌午的時候兒那雪飄飄颺颺的越發下起大片兒的來咯我心裡想着沒有事怎麼能彀得一個朋友來說說話兒也好啊。3 可巧家下人們進來說有客來咯我心裡很喜歡一面兒就叫收拾下酒茶兒一面兒又叫爐了一盆子炭火趕着請了弟兄們來把預備齊了的酒茶端上來慢慢兒的喝着酒把簾子高高兒的捲起來一瞧那雪景兒比甚麼都清雅紛紛的下着山川樹木都是雪白看着更高了興。擎過棋來下了兩盤。喫了晚飯點上鐙纔散了。

談論篇百章之九十八

1 昨兒個在衙門的時候兒一點風兒都沒有很晴的好天來着忽然變了日頭都慘淡了這麼着麼我就說天氣不安要颳大風趁着沒有颳咱們快走罷各人

談論篇百章之九十五

1 這許多日子的連陰雨下得我心裡都熟咯、這兒也漏了、那兒也溼了、連個睡覺的地方兒都沒有。2 而且又是蚊子臭虫蛇蚤叮得實在難受翻來覆去的過了亮鐘並沒有困把眼睛強閉着又忍了一會兒剛剛兒的恍恍惚惚的困上來咯正似睡不睡的忽然從西北上就像山崩地裂的是一個樣、响了一聲把我陡然間嚇醒了、過了好一會子身上還是打戰兒、心裏還是突突的跳睜開眼一瞧屋裡所有的東西都沒有損壞一點兒叫人出去一看說是街坊家的山牆叫雨淋透了倒咯。3 噯呀睡夢之中、那兒經得起那麼大的响聲兒震哪。

談論篇百章之九十六

1 昨兒清早兒起來屋裡很黑我疑惑是太陽還沒出來。到院子裡一瞧、原來天是亮了可陰的漆黑我洗了臉纔要上衙門、那天一星子半點兒的下起雨來了略等了一會兒涮涮的下响了、又坐了一坐兒喝了盅茶忽然打了個霹雷這雨就傾盆似的下來了、我想着這不過是一陣兒暴雨罷咧、等過了再走那兒知道直下了一天一夜總沒有住、到了今兒早飯後纔恍恍惚惚的看見日頭

談論篇百章之九十四

1 哎呀,這個樣兒的大雨,你往那'兒去來着快進來罷。 2 我的一個朋友不在咯,送殯去來着今兒早起,天陰陰兒的雖然有要下雨的光景,到了晌午又是響晴的天往回裏走着的時候兒忽然一片一片的鋪開了稠雲了,我就和家裏人們說這天氣不安當快走罷不然咱們一定要着雨咯。正說着就涮涮的下起來咯兒台,你說在漫荒野地裏可往那'兒去躲呢雨衣氈褂子還沒穿送當渾身都濕透咯。 3 無妨我有衣裳拏出來你先換上,天也晚了,明兒再進城罷。我們這個僻地方兒雖然沒有甚麼好東西家裏養的小猪兒,雞宰一兩隻給你喫。 4 噯喫還說甚麼但得這個好地方兒棲身,就是便宜了。不然還怕不冒着雨兒走麼又有甚麼法子呢。

錢兒度命。若像我這個樣兒的喫現成兒的,從從容容的寫字,他能彀麼况且冬冷夏熱是自古至今不易之理,索性靜靜兒的耐着,或者倒有爽快的時候兒俗語兒說得心定自然凉若竟着會子急,還能脫了麼。

談論篇百章之九十三

1 今兒好利害呀、自從立夏之後、可以說得起、是頭一天兒的熱咯、一點兒風絲兒也沒有、所有的傢伙都是燙手兒的、熱越喝涼水越渴、沒了法兒咯、我洗了個澡、在樹底下乘了會涼兒、心裏纔略好了些兒、嗐這樣兒的燥熱天、別人兒都是光着脊梁坐着、還怕中暑呢、你怎麼只是低着頭寫字、是甚麼罪孽啊、不要命了麼。2 你這都是沒官差、白閒着安閒慣了的話、譬如小買賣人兒們、挑着很重的擔子、壓着肩膀兒、伸着脖子、各處兒跑着吆喝、汗流如雨的、纔能賺得百數

上船彼此說着話兒、喝着酒、到了東花園兒、又趕回閘上來、早已就日平西了。2 纔喫完了飯、我就說衆位僟們走罷、跟的人都是步行兒、家又離得很遠、他們還說說笑笑的、儘自坐着動也不動、後來看見日頭快落了、這纔上了馬、忙着往回來趕。3 到了關裏的時候兒、恍恍惚惚的月亮都出來了、從城裏頭出去的人們都叫快走、說掩了一扇門咯。心裏更着了急、緊加鞭子催着馬趕到了跟前兒、末尾兒的、還是關在城外頭了。4 實在是乘興而往掃興而回。

談論篇百章之九十一

1 前兒我們往西山裏逛去、那個樂、可說得是盡了興了。白日裏游玩的樂啊、那是不必說的了、到了黑下的時候兒更暢快。2 我們幾個人喫了晚飯、坐上船、不大的工夫兒月亮就上來了、照得如同白日一樣、慢慢兒的撐着船、順着水兒往下走、轉過了山嘴兒一瞧、那水和天的顏色兒上下一樣、浩浩如銀、竟無所分別、實在是水清山靜。3 趕撐到蘆葦深的去處兒忽然聽見廟裏的鐘聲兒順着風兒悠悠楊楊的來了、那時候心裏頭萬慮皆空、好像水洗了似的、那麼乾淨、就是出了世的神仙、也不過是這麼樣兒樂罷咧、我們幾個人更高了興咯、直喝到天亮、也不覺醉、也不覺乏。4 人生在世、像這個樣兒的風清月朗的景致、能彀遇着幾回、若是徒然虛度了、豈不可惜了兒的麽。

談論篇百章之九十二

1 前兒我們幾個人、甚麼是逛來着、竟是受了罪咧。出了城兒、放着正經道兒不走、不知道繞到那兒去了。沿着路兒間着找着、剛剛兒的到了閘口的跟前兒坐

談論篇百章之九十

1 這春天的時候兒、一點兒事沒有、白閒着、竟在家裡坐着、很覺悶得謊呵。2 可不是麽、昨兒我兄弟來了、往城外頭游玩去、約會我出城到了曠野的地方兒、遠遠的一瞧、春景兒真令人可愛、河沿兒上的桃花兒是鮮紅、柳枝兒是碧綠、而且樹枝兒各樣的雀鳥兒在那兒叫喚的實在好聽、一陣兒一陣兒的春風兒、颳得草香撲鼻、水上的小船兒、也是來來往往的不斷、兩岸上的游人、都是三五成羣兒的逛、我們倆、從小道兒上曲曲灣灣的走到了樹林子多的地方兒、一看、也有彈的、也有唱的、也有賣茶賣酒的、而且賣活魚活蝦的、都很賤、故此我們倆足足的游玩了一天、兒台可別怪我沒有來約、不是瞞着你納、只怕遇見和你納有不對勁兒的人、哪所以沒找你納來。

談論篇百章之八十八

1 昨兒喫了祭神的肉、就是了、又叫送背鐙的肉作甚麼。2 甚麼話呢、老兄台咯、是該當送的、方纔還要叫人請您去來着、你納是知道的、就是這幾個奴才們、宰豬的宰豬、收拾雜碎的收拾雜碎、那個都不費手呢、因爲這個纔沒有能彀打發人去請。3 你的事情沒有人替手兒、我是知道的、還等着你請麼、沒有這個規矩、別叫主人分心、咱們就序着齒一溜兒坐下喫。4 兄台們請喫肉、泡上湯喫。衆位會着朋友們來喫大肉來了、我還恐怕趕不上呢、誰想來的正是時候兒。5 哎呀、這是甚麼話呢、錯了、咱們當初有這個樣兒的規矩來着麼、這個肉啊、是祖宗的克食、有強讓的理麼、況且親友們來去還不迎不送呢、像這樣兒讓起來、使得麼。

談論篇百章之八十九

1 我們在關東的時候兒天天兒打圍來着、這天我們打圍去、在草裡跑出個麅子來、我趕緊的打馬拉開弓一射、略落了點兒、後回手拔箭的空兒、只見麅子的尾巴動啊動的、一轉眼就跑過了山梁兒、奔山前往上去、疾忙我緊跟着趕了去、

談論篇百章之八十七

1 兄台、你這位令郎是第幾個的。 2 這是個老生兒子。 3 出了花兒了沒有。 4 去年出得花兒。 5 這些個都是挨肩兒的麼。 6 都是挨肩的生了九個存了九個。 7 哎真是難得的兄台、這不是我說句玩兒話、大嫂子真能幹哪久慣會養兒子、可以算得是個子孫娘娘了實在是有福的人哪。 8 甚麼福啊、前生造的罪罷咧、大些兒的還好點兒、這幾個小的兒每天吱兒喳的、吵得我腦袋都疼了。 9 世上的人都是這麼樣、富的人們又嫌多了抱怨像我們子孫稀少的人們、想有一個在那兒呢、叫老天爺也難了有十幾歲了。 11 七歲上沒得若有今年十歲了。 12 那繞真是個好孩子到如今提起他來我都替你傷心那個相貌兒言語兒的安安詳詳兒的上前問好可憐見兒的那個小嘴兒甚麼話兒都會說若問他一件事情倒像誰教給他的一個樣兒從頭至尾的告訴、一句兒也落不下、像那個樣兒的孩子、一個頂十個養這許多沒用的作甚麼。

談論篇百章之八十六

1 這不是給女婿做的衣裳麼。2 是啊。3 這些人是做甚麼的。4 他們是僱了來的裁縫們。5 哎呀咱們家裏的舊規矩你們都忘了麼老時候的孩子們都會做衣裳來着就以做棉襖論罷鋪上棉花合上裏兒都是大家動手翻過來的時候兒這個縫大襟那個打盪子這個煞胳肢窩那個上領條兒綠袖口兒的綠袖口兒釘鈕襻兒的釘鈕襻兒不過一兩天的空兒就做完了。況且連帽子都是家裏做來着。或是買着穿人家都從鼻子裡見笑啊。6 兒台的話說的雖然有理。但你只知其一不知其二。那個老時候兒和如今一個樣兒比得麼況且娶的日子眼看着就到了，招着指頭兒算，剛剛兒的賸了十天的工夫，如今這麼不留空兒的叫裁縫連着夜兒做趕得上趕不上還不定呢。若是死守着舊規矩那可是在旂杆底下誤了操了。大睜着眼兒就誤了，那成甚麼事呢。

通知裏頭太太們，把小兒帶進去，給太太們瞧瞧。彼此都合了意的時候兒，再磕頭也不遲啊。

談論篇百章之八十五

1 吾兒今兒來有甚麼見教。 2 因為有緣我們特來求親來咯我這個孩子雖然沒有超羣的才貌奇特的本事但只是不喫酒不賭錢就是那些迷惑人的去處兒胡游亂走的地方兒一概也沒到過若不棄嫌老爺們就賞賜句疼愛的話兒你往前些兒咱們叩求。 3 老爺們別大家坐下聽我說一句話咱們都是老親一個樣兒的是骨肉誰不知道呢但只是作夫妻這件事都是前世裏造定的緣分由不得人的為父母的自已眼瞇着孩子們原不過盼着能彀配個好對兒纔把苦拔苦掖的心腸也就完了話雖是這麼說我還有長輩兒沒有瞧見郎呢再者來的太太們把我們女孩兒也瞧瞧。 4 是啊老爺說的很有理就請

1 事麼容讓他些兒又費了我甚麼了呢。 沒有哼全都忍了又坐了好一會子看着他的光景順着他的氣兒慢慢兒的哀求他剛剛兒的他纔點了頭咯。 5 你想一想我的性子若是略急一點兒你的事情就不妥了

4 任憑他儘着量兒數落我一聲兒也

談論篇百章之八十四

1 我原想你這件事情和他說去很容易來着誰想這種可惡的東西竟這麽樣兒的口緊不依倒鬧得很費了事咯。2 我把咱們商量的話告訴了他一遍他倒沉下臉來說我說的話是胡說我一聽這話氣就到了脖頸子上了心裡說要怎麼樣就怎麼樣罷滿心裡要惹他一惹。3 後來我想了一想自己問着自己說你錯了這來不是為自己的事為的是朋友們若是鬧起來不耽誤了人家的

實在在的仗着你疼他一定替他說說在屁股後頭跟着總不放我。2 我起根兒臉輭你是深知道的人家這麽樣兒的着急跪着哀求怎麼好意思叫他沒趣兒回去呢因為推脫不開所以我纔應承了白兒的告訴了那個朋友咯不承望不是他一個人兒的事說是人多掣肘沒肯應承我還要看光景再說來後來想了一想說罷呀看事情的樣子是不能挽回了必定強壓派着叫人家應允使得麽。4 故此我回來告訴了他個信兒倒說我壞了他的事咯望着我擦臉子好叫人傷心哪早知道這麽樣我何必說來着這是圖甚麽呢。

談論篇百章之八十二

1 我有一件事要託吾兄,只是怪難開口的,甚麼緣故呢,實在求的事情太多了,但只是不求你納除你納之外,再也沒有能成全我這件事的人,因此我又煩瑣你納來咯。2 你不是為找姓張的那件事情來了麽。3 是啊,你納怎麼知道了。4 今兒早起你們令郎就和我說了,喫早飯的時候兒,我就去了一次,偏偏兒的遇見他不在家,纔交响午我又去了,剛一進院子,就聽見上房裡頭,說啊笑的聲兒,我上了台階兒悄悄的把窗戶紙兒舔破了,從窗戶眼兒裡往裡一瞧,看見這個給那個斟酒,那個給這個回敬,正攪在一處兒喫喝熱鬧呢,我原想進去,來着因為有好些個不認識的朋友,冲散了人家喝酒的趣兒,怪不得人意兒的,我就抽身出來了,他們家下人看見要告訴去,我急忙擺手兒攔住了,你可別忙,明兒我起個黑早,和他說妥當了,就完咯。

談論篇百章之八十三

1 誰情愿去管他的事情來着麽,我是好好兒的在家裡坐着的人啊,不知道他在那塊兒打聽得說我認識那個人,一連來了好幾次,和我說兄台,我這件事實

天天在裏頭靜靜兒的持齋念經,不出來化緣,要喫沒有得喫,要穿沒有得穿,叫誰養活他呢。他竟喝風過日子麼。

談論篇百章之八十一

1 我有一件事特來求吾兄指教來咯。若要行,似乎略有點兒關係的地方兒。若是中止了不行,又很可惜了兒的現成兒的到了嘴裡的東西不喫,平白的讓人,有這個理麼行又不是,止又不是,實在是叫我進退兩難了,怎麼能殼得一箇萬全之計纔好啊。 2 這個事情,是顯而易見的。有甚麼不得主意的地方兒呢。你若是不行,是你的造化。若是行了,你能殼堵得住誰的嘴啊。趕到吵嚷開了,人人都知道了,你那纔到了難處兒了呢。這點兒些微的小便宜兒算甚麼。那正是日後的禍苗呢。有利必定有害,喫了虧的時候兒,後悔就晚了。若照着我的主意,別猶豫不決的,拏定主意不動,再遲疑不斷的拉扯住了,那就打不成米,連口袋都丟了。要出個不像事的大醜呢。

談論篇百章之七十九

1 古語兒說的、幼不學老何為、這個話、是特意叫人勤學不可懶惰的意思啊、說是不拘甚麼樣兒的人、學會了米粒兒大的一點兒能幹、就算得完全了一輩子的事情了、何況是好好兒的肯學、還有甚麼不能幹的、何怕不作官呢。2 而且又是旗人、喫的不愁穿的不愁、不用種地、不用挑擔子、不用作手藝、坐着喫國家的糧米、有這些個便宜、自幼兒若不努力勤學、以着甚麼本事、給主子出力呢、拏着甚麼報答上天生養的恩呢。

談論篇百章之八十

1 作好事、是說人應該行孝悌忠信的道理、並不是竟會供神佛齋僧道、就算作好事了、比方作惡的人們、任憑怎麼樣兒的修橋補路、焉能解了他的罪惡呢、是神佛也不能設降福給他啊。2 那喫齋的上天堂、喫肉的下地獄、這種樣兒的話、都是和尚道士們、借端餬口的、豈可深信得麼、他們若不拏着這麼長那麼短的利害話、嚇唬人、怎麼詐騙人的錢財呢、若叫他們盡遵着佛教、關着廟門兒

談論篇百章之七十八

1 這是個甚麼意思呢甚麼稀罕東西每逢看見就和人家尋也不覺絮煩麼實在太不體面了罷人家臉上過不去也給過你好些次了你心裡還不知足麼必定叫人家盡其所有的都給了你能彀麼。2 況且給是人情不給是本分你反倒使性子摔搭人那兒有這個情理呢比方是你的東西人家愛惜你自已倒不愛惜麼若是不由你作主澈底兒都拏了去你心裡頭怎麼樣呢。3 昨兒因為是我肯忍你那行子罷咧若除了我不拘是誰也不肯讓你麼好兒的記着我這話快快兒的改罷。4 你若是個沒有一點兒能爲的那還又是一說現在還是有喫有穿的只是要占個小便宜是個甚麼緣故呢也不怕人家背地裡說你眼皮子淺麼。

有一樣可惡的每逢他來不拘甚麼好啊歹啊的還得先藏起來叫他瞧見不得儻若叫他看見了連問也不問摟摸着拏着就走。甚麼說頭兒了像這種樣兒的雜碎都壞盡了就是你這麼愛便宜能彀獨自得麼。3 實在他這一輩子也沒有甚麼說頭兒了像這種樣兒的雜碎都壞盡了就是你這麼愛便宜能彀獨自得麼。

8 離我們家的墳地很近。 9 噯若是這麼着道兒很遠哪至少說着也有四五十里地如果你再去見了他先替我道惱啊等下了班兒再同着你去看看他給他道煩惱出殯之前還請你千萬給我個信兒就不能送到他墳上去也必送到城外頭了平素間我們雖沒有甚麼大來往每逢遇見的時候兒說起話兒來就很親熱況且人生在世那個不是朋友呢他這樣兒的喪事我盡個人情想來也沒有人說我趕着他走動的話罷。

談論篇百章之七十七

1 他來的時候兒我在家裡正睡覺呢猛然驚醒了一聽上房裡來了客了在那兒說話兒呢想是誰來了呢說話這麼大嗓子必是那個討厭的來了罷走進去一瞧果然是他。直挺挺的坐着議論不斷的自來了總沒有住嘴兒這樣兒那樣兒的直說了兩頓飯的工夫兒到了黃昏的時候兒他纔走了。 2 漢子家又沒有甚麼事情,就在人家家裡整天家坐着說話這也受得麼他那個東西不但把些個陳穀子爛芝麻人家講究餒了的事情儘自說聽得人家的腦袋都疼了還

PART V.—THE HUNDRED LESSONS.

談論篇百章之七十六

1 他們家裡誰不在了。大前兒我從那兒過看見他家裡的人們都穿着孝呢。因為忙着來該班兒也沒得間一間剛纔聽見說是他叔叔不在了。是他親叔叔麼。

2 不錯是他親叔叔。

3 你弔喪去沒有。

4 昨兒念經我在那兒坐了一整天呢。

5 多喒出殯啊知道不知道。

6 說是月底呢。

7 他們的塋地在那兒.

方亮兒就起身往回裡走、道兒上除了打尖也總沒有敢歇着剛剛兒的趕掩城門兒的時候兒總進來了。

5 在遠地方兒立墳難說是好、若是到了子孫們、沒有力量兒就難按着時候兒上墳了。

6 可不是麼舊塋地裡倒離得很近、因為沒有地方兒葬埋人口、請了看風水的人瞧他們說是那一塊地好、故此在那兒立了墳咯。遠是遠些兒總而言之、咱們有有的道理、沒有是沒有的道理、無論是怎麼樣兒的窖、不能殼坐車連步行兒去、也要到墳上奠一鍾酒啊若到了子孫們就難定了、只看他們有出息兒沒出息兒就是咯、若是個沒有出息兒不惦念上墳的子孫、就是他們住得離着墳地很近還未必能殼燒一張紙錢呢。

談論篇百章之七十四

1 昨兒往誰家去來着回來的那麼晚。 2 我是瞧咱們朋友去來着他家住得太遠在西城根兒底下呢又搭着留我喫了一頓飯故此回來的略遲些兒。 3 我有一件要事和你納商量打發了幾次人去請去你納那兒家下人們說坐了車出去了也沒留下話我算計着你納去的地方兒很少不過是咱們圈兒內的這幾個朋友們罷咧瞧完了一定到我家裡來誰知道等到日平西也不見來算是白等了一天哪。 4 兄台打發找我的人沒到以前我已經早出了門了回家的時候兒小子們告訴說老兄這兒打發了兩三次人來叫我彼時就要來着因為太晚了又恐怕關了柵欄兒所以今兒纔來。

談論篇百章之七十五

1 你前兒往莊子上上墳去來着麼。 2 是啊。 3 怎麼今兒纔回來。 4 我們墳地離得很遠所以當天去不能回來又在那兒歇了兩夜。前兒個頂城門兒就起了身直走到晚上纔到了墳上。昨兒個供了飯奠了酒又歇了一夜今兒東

談論篇百章之七十三

1 你納往那兒去來着。 2 我往那邊兒一個親戚家去來着閣下順便兒到我們家裡坐坐兒罷。 3 兄台你納在這左近住麼。 4 是啊新近纔搬在這房子來的。 5 若是這麼着咱們住的離着卻不甚遠啊我若是知道府上在這兒就早過來瞧來了老兄先走。 6 豈有此理這是我家啊你納請上坐 7 我這兒坐着舒服。 8 你納這麼坐了叫我怎麼坐呢。 9 我已經坐下了這兒有個靠頭兒。 10 來掌火來。 11 老兄我不喫煙嘴裡長了口瘡了。 12 若是這麼着快倒茶來。 13 兄台請喫茶 14 老弟請看飯去把現成兒的先掌了來。 15 兄台別費心我還要往別處兒去呢。 16 怎麼了現成兒的東西又不是為你納預備的隨便兒將就着喫點兒罷。 17 兄台我還是外人嗎已經認得府上了改日再來咱們坐着說一天的話兒今兒實在沒空兒告假了。

是一點兒心也沒有甚麼好東西啊諸位就着喫些兒太盛設了我們自家喫呢若不喫飽也不肯放下筷子啊有甚麼說得呢那就是愛惜我兄弟了。 6 你這就不必過讓了、 7 若是那麼着我還

天的話兒現成兒的飯喫了去，我也不另弄別的喫的咯。4 但只往這兒來了，無緣無故的就這麼樣騷擾啊，我心裡也不安哪，因其這個我就不敢常來。5 你怎麼這麼外道呢，咱們從幾兒分過彼此來着，若再隔幾天你不來我還要預備點兒東西，特請你去呢，這一頓現成兒的空飯又何足掛齒況且你的甚麼東西我沒喫過啊，你若這樣兒的不實誠竟是明明兒的叫我再別往你家去的意思啊。

談論篇百章之七十二

1 老兄你怎麼纔來我等了這麼半天了，差一點兒沒有睡着了。2 我告訴你說我們纔要動身往這兒來，想不到遇見個討人嫌的死肉刺刺不休又不要緊這麼長那麼短的只是說不完。我若沒有事絮叨些兒何妨呢只管由他說罷咧但只怕你等急了，沒法兒我說我們有事明兒再說罷這纔把他的話攔住了不然早來都坐煩了。3 別說太遲了，來的正是時候兒。誰在這兒呢快放桌子想必爺們都餓了，飯哪甚麼的都簡決些兒。4 嗳兄弟你這是怎麼說呢。有副的白肉就得了又要這麼許多的菜蔬作甚麼。把我們當客待麼。5 我這不過

的伴的沒褲子這話是當眞哪旣如此就該當回過味兒來咯還有甚麼心腸說這兒的酒好那兒的茶好和富貴人們一般一配的各處兒游玩那時候兒我就說等着到了上冬的時候兒看他怎麼樣再瞧罷咧如今果然應了我的話了。 3 老兄話雖是這樣兒說現在他旣落到這步田地上可當眞的瞧着叫他死麼。我心裡想着咱們大家畧攢湊攢湊弄點兒銀子幫幫他纔好。兒幫他銀子還不是主意。怎麼說呢他的脾氣你還不知道麼一到了手就完連一點兒浮餘也不留全花了倒不如買一套衣裳給他還有點兒益處。 4 若像這樣

談論篇百章之七十一

1 這一向你又往那兒奔去了。遇見有空兒何不到我這兒走走呢怎麼總不見你的面兒咯。 2 我早就要瞧您來着不想叫一件旁不相干兒的事情絆住了竟受了累了整天家忙那兒有點兒空兒呢。我若不想法子連今兒還不能彀脫身兒呢今兒個摘脫是說我有件要緊的事情撒了個謊剛剛兒的纔放我出來了。 3 你來的很好我正悶得慌呢。想來你也可以抽點空兒麼咱們坐着說一

談論篇百章之六十九

1 兄台你納這麼固辭我的東西不肯留下我十分不明白你的心意還是因為我來遲了故此纔這麼樣兒待我還是因為別的呢。2 素常我尙且長長兒的來老家兒的好日子倒不來那怎麼是朋友呢實在是知道晚了若是先知道應當早來纔是。3 雖說是有我不多沒我不少替你納待客也好啊若論你納高親貴友送來的禮物還少麼想來是喫不了的我這點子微物兒又何足掛齒呢然而也是我一點兒孝心。4 那兒敢必定請老人家喫呢但只略嚐點兒就是愛惜我了使我的意思總完了但是決意不收下我還是在這兒坐着啊還是囘去呢實在叫我倒爲了難了。

談論篇百章之七十

1 大哥你聽見了麼咱們那個饞嘴的東西說是破敗得很困住了襤褸成個花子樣兒戰抖抖的披着一塊破被。2 那趁愿該死的去年甚麼罪兒他沒受過甚麼苦兒他沒喫過但凡有一點兒志氣也改悔過來了俗語兒說的窮的伴富

PART V.—THE HUNDRED LESSONS.

談論篇百章之六十八

1 好人再沒有過於你的了。還不住口兒的稱讚你那個朋友太過於老實了。那混帳行子有甚麼大講究頭兒啊、斷不可提他。2 他若有求煩人的事情、別人說甚麼話、他就照樣兒依着行、他的事情一完把頭一轉是人全不認得。3 他去年窄住的時候兒求到我跟前、誰問他有甚麼來着他自己說他有好書你納要看我送來。4 像這麼樣兒的應許我後來事情完了書連提也不提了日子久沒信兒那一天我遇見他說你許給我那部書怎麽樣了、誰知當面兒一間、他臉上一紅一白的、只是支吾說不出甚麼緣故來咯。5 這一部書有甚麼稀罕啊給我不給我也不要緊、竟是無故的哄人、未免太討人嫌了。

心啊保不定這是害我罷。我很信服這原是我一生的毛病兒我豈不知道麼就是遇見這樣兒的事情不由的嘴就癢癢說出來古人原有不可與言而與之言謂之失言的話啊從今兒起我痛改前非罷日後再要這麼樣兒多說話縱使兄台往我臉上啐唾沫我也甘心領受。2 兄台你說的這些話實在是給我治病的艮藥啊、

談論篇百章之六十六

1 嗳世上沒有記性的人再沒有比你過逾的了前兒我怎麼囑咐你來着這件事情任憑他是誰總不可叫人知道了你到底兒洩漏了咱們倆悄悄兒商量的話如今吵嚷的處處兒沒有人沒聽見過了他們這些人儻若羞惱變成怒望了咱們不依動起手腳兒來咱們得了甚麼便宜了麼把好好兒的事情倒弄壞了全都是你呀 2 老兄像你這麼樣兒怪我我真委屈現在事情已經這樣兒了我縱然分辨個牙清口白的你肯信麼我的心就是老天爺看得眞是我說來着不是我說來着久而自明依我的主意你先不必抱怨索性粧個不知道看他們的動靜依呢就依了如果不依的時候兒再作道理預備也不遲啊

談論篇百章之六十七

1 你啊是個很好的人心裡沒有一點渣兒就是嘴太直知道了人家的是非一點分兒也不肯留必要直言奉上雖然交朋友有規過的道理也當看他的爲人可勸再勸罷咧若不這樣兒只說是個朋友並不分親疏就勸那如何使得呢方纔說的這些話那不是好心麼他倒心裡很不舒服瞪着眼疑惑着說嗳呀要小

談論篇百章之六十五

1 方纔我上衙門回來從老遠的轟得一羣人騎着馬往這邊來了到了跟前兒細認了一認原是咱們舊街坊某人穿的騎的都很體面真是肥馬輕裘的面貌兒也大胖了他看見我連理也沒理把臉往那們一扭望着天就過去了彼時我就要叫住他很很的羞辱他來着後來我想了一想說罷啊做甚麼他理我我就體面了麽誰住那們那大工夫和他計較這些個。2 噯老兄你納不記得麽三年以前在咱們那兒住着的時候兒那是甚麼樣兒來着很窮啊喫了早起巴結晚上的天天兒游魂似的忍着餓各處兒張羅拾着一根草都是希罕的一天至不濟也到我家兩三次不是尋這個就是要那個我的甚麼他沒喫過筷子都咂明了如今是求不着人了一旦之間就變了性咯忘了舊時候兒的景况了也不是咱們自已擡舉自已這種小人乍富的脾氣偺們很可以不理他罷了。

3 ... 是他的便宜了是沒德行咯。

4 噯他父母生下這種樣兒的賤貨兒來討人家的厭也實在是沒德行咯。

說罷咧、我若說出根子來、未免又說我揭短了。2 你的家鄉我的住處誰不知道誰呢、你不受人家的揉挫、纔有幾天兒啊、如今賤貨兒這就和我作起足來了、是甚麼意思呢、索性說失了言兒咯、那個還可以恕得過去偏死扭着說你的話是了、一口咬定了、不肯認錯、能不叫人更生氣麼。3 你太把我看輕咯、實在不知道你仗着甚麼能彀有這個樣兒的舉動兒、誰也不能殺了誰、誰還怕誰麼、若果然要見個高低兒、很合我的式、若略打一個磴兒、也不是好漢子。

談論篇百章之六十四

1 那是個沒出息兒的東西、你怎麼瞧上他來着呢、雖是個人身子、却是牲口腸子、總是躲着他些纔好呢。2 你把我這句話、擱在心上、他原是個無事生事的混帳行子啊、又黑、常是聽見風兒就是雨兒的、人家略有點兒細故叫他聽見他就滿處兒混嚼說張揚個不堪啊、把這兒的事情傳在那兒、把那兒的信兒告訴這兒、兩下裏成了釁兒的時候兒、他可從中作好人兒。3 你若看我說的話信不得、你瞧、不但沒有一個人兒和他相好、若不指着他的脊梁駡他、那就

談論篇百章之六十二

1 誰和他說長道短了麼本是他的話，逼着叫我說啊瞞得住別人兒，瞞得住你麼自從過年以來他還走了甚麼差使麼今兒是在那兒喝了酒了，剛一進門兒來就是噯呀，我怎麼瞧見你啊若照他那麼說，我不脫空兒的，整月家替他當差使反倒不是了麼真使我的氣就到了脖頸子上了今兒且不必論明兒再說罷。 2 老兄不用望他較量這個和他一般一配的爭競做甚麼他一味好跟人要個嘴皮子，你有甚麼不知道的想來又是喝醉了你只當是沒看見沒有聽見就結了何必理他呢。 3 老弟你不知道這樣兒輕了欺硬的怕的東西跟前若給他留點分兒他更長了價兒了他索性說我是閙著玩兒不知不覺的話說冒失了人家或者可以原諒罷咧，反倒滿臉的怒氣誰還怕他不成。 4 兄台你別生氣我把這個酒鬼帶在僻靜的地方兒指着臉兒罵他一頓給你出出氣。

談論篇百章之六十三

1 壞了腸子咯把我輕慢得了不得我和你說話，都不配麼動不動兒的就拏巧話兒譏誚我把自已當成甚麼咯。每日裡鼻子臉子的常在一塊兒混混，我只不

談論篇百章之六十一

1 你們很相好啊如今怎麼了總不登你的門檻兒了麼。 2 我不知道他。想是有誰得罪了他略罷。不然還有一說從前我們還好好端端的來往着來着就是因為一半句話上也不犯記在心裏惱了就不往我這兒來了。不來也沒甚麼要緊怎麼背地裡還只說我這樣兒不好那樣兒利害所有遇見我認識的朋友們當作話把兒蹧塌我這是甚麼心意呢。新近給我們孩子娶媳婦兒我還臉上下不來請他去來着連一個狗也沒打發來我所遇見的朋友都是這個薄情的可叫我怎麼再往後結交呢。 3 那個人說話行事很假信不得我沒說過麼那個時候兒你還理論麼倒很有點兒不舒服我來着。 4 原是俗語兒說的知人知面不知心他心裏頭的好歹如何能彀知道得透澈呢將來只得小心。 5 那就是了。不分好歹一概都說是很相好的使得麼。

談論篇百章之六十

1 你太沒有經過事怯極了。有話為甚麼放在心裏直去和他講明說開就完了。他也是個人罷咧能彀不按着道理行麼說出緣故來你就從頭至尾的一一的分解開了怕他能彀把你怎麼樣麼怕殺呀還是怕喫了你呢。2 況且別人都沒動靜兒你來不來的先這麼怕他這樣兒那樣兒的防備着還有個漢子的味兒麼。3 依我勸你也放寬了心罷他果然不依你若和你見個高低兒還給你留

的樣兒是有甚麼緣故呢。2 不知道他素來沒一天不在街上下雨下雪的日子他總在家裏除此以外是地方兒他就去逛叫他在家得住呢這一向因沒出大門兒竟在家裡呢昨兒我去瞧他 3 啊臉面兒還像先麼。4 很瘦了竟是坐不安睡不寗似的我瞧着很疑惑總要問他可巧又來了一個親戚把話打住了。5 嗳呀若依你這麼說大約是叫那件事絆住心亂了雖是那麼說然而有經過大難不怕小煩的話啊他那個人從前甚麼樣兒的難事都清清楚楚兒的辦完了這些細故又算甚麼要緊的呢也值得那麼憂愁麼

談論篇百章之五十八

1 你這麼寃他是甚麼道理人家恭恭敬敬的在你跟前討個主意知道就說知道不知道就說不知道罷了撒謊作甚麼儻若把人家的事情耽誤了倒像你有心害他似的他若是個可惡的人也就不怪你這麼樣兒待他我看他那個人很老實一瞧就知道是個慢性子別人若是這麼欺負他咱們還當攔勸惡之你反倒這樣兒的刻薄了眞眞的我心裏過不去。2 兄台你原來不知道可要叫他誆哄了啊那種東西外面皮兒雖像愚蠢心裏却不得他那性情險惡之極你沒試過就不知道他的壞處兒了法子多圈套兒大慣會和人討憑據不論甚麼事預先拏話勾引你把你的主意套了去然後遠遠兒的觀望着聽你的空子稍微有點兒破綻跟進去就給你一個觖屁股將兒台你想這個事情原有關礙我的地方兒啊若是把徹底子的主意告訴他如何使得呢你這麼怪我我不委屈麼。

談論篇百章之五十九

1 咱們那個朋友遭了甚麼為難的事麼這幾天看他那個愁容滿面無聊無賴

談論篇 百章之五十七

脊梁來倒退着走我說兄台小心門檻子話沒說完絆住脚了身子往後一歪仰着面兒跌了去咯我急忙趕上扶住幾幾乎沒跌倒我還長長兒的勸他呢後來知道他的脾氣不能敂了不是有出息兒的東西何必白勞骨乏舌的勸他呢

1 兄台你聽見了麼話頭話尾的都是刻薄我穿的膧舊還算是小孩子呢能彀懂得甚麼這也不是他們知道的事情啊新衣裳是偶然有事情穿的罷咧我這不過家常穿的舊些兒何妨呢漢子家沒有本事該當羞罷咧穿的有甚麼關係呢卽如我雖不穿好的心裏頭却比那穿好的還寬綽。 2 不是我誇口他呀甚麼緣故呢不求告人不欠債這就沒有可恥的地方兒。若像他們這種年輕的人兒們我眼角兒裡也沒有他只知道穿鮮明衣裳搖搖擺擺的竟充體面能知道學漢子的本事麼若像他們這個樣兒的就是叫綢緞裹到底兒又有甚麼奇處兒呢。 4 最下賤沒眼珠兒的人們混說他體面巴結他們罷咧若是我說他們不過是個掛衣裳的架子

談論篇百章之五十六

1 他那個動作兒是個甚麼樣兒呢。在人家跟前兒說話結結巴巴的怎麼問怎麼答都不知道畏首畏尾的怎麼進怎麼退也不懂得醒着倒像人家睡着了一樣的白充個人數兒糊裡糊塗的怎麼長來着呢。你們相好啊略指教指教他也就好了。 2 這個人你納沒在一塊兒長來還不深知比這個可笑的事還多呢。和他一處兒坐下說起話來正說着這個忽然想起別的來就說那個不然呢搭拉着嘴骨不錯眼珠兒瞪着你猛然間又說出一句無頭無尾的獃話來叫人笑斷了肚腸子啊前兒瞧我去來着後來臨走的時候兒不往前直走轉過

多嗆遇見一個利害人喫了虧的時候兒你繞知道有關係呢。 2 老弟你令兄的話實在是不錯玩笑是辯嘴的由頭久而久之生出甚麼好事來呀若是傍不相干兒的人肯這麼說得關切麼你雖長了身量歲數兒還早呢務必要留心改了啊。 3 咱們沒有從那個時候過麼正是貪玩兒的時候呀我的意見不如趁這個空兒趕緊請一位名師教他念書漸漸兒的知識開了明白了世務的時候兒自然而然的就改好了又愁甚麼沒出息呢。

談論篇百章之五十四

1 看起你來只就是嘴能幹外面兒雖像明白心裏却不燎亮不尋嗔你來就是你的便宜你可惹他作甚麼好話總不聽倒像神鬼指使的一個樣強拘着去了到底碰了釘子回來咯。 2 那該死的你說他是誰了不得有名兒的利害人啊從不給人留分兒與他不相干的事還可以略有一點兒妨碍他的地方兒不拘是誰壓着勁兒必要站住理得了便宜纔歇手。 3 這不是咯到底把臥着的老虎哄起來了自找喫虧這有甚麼趣兒呢俗語兒說的有拐棍兒不跌跤有商量兒不失着光你一個人兒的見識能彀到那兒任憑怎麼樣我總比你長幾歲這一層若果然是該行的就是你心裏不願意去我還該提撥着你催着你叫你去呢豈有倒攔着你的情理麼。

談論篇百章之五十五

1 你怎麼這麼樣兒不穩重若是體體面面兒坐着誰說你是木雕泥塑的廢物麼你若不言不語的誰說你是啞吧麼倒像在人跟前兒故意兒鬪笑兒似的惹了這個又招那個有甚麼樂處兒呢你自己不覺罷咯傍邊兒的人都受不了了。

談論篇百章之五十三

1 別人說他與你何干呢。怎麼我這麼勸你越勸越生氣咬太急躁了罷等客散了、再說罷、必定此刻要分辨明白麼。 2 兄台你說得這個話我心裏竟聽不進去。咱們是一個船兒上的人哪這個事也與你有點兒牽連難道沒有一點兒罣礙麼他們議論他連咱們也稍上了、你不攔着反倒隨着他們的口氣兒說這是甚麼意思我心裏真有點兒不服。 3 不是那麼着若有話、從從容容兒的說你這麼急繃繃的難道就算完了事咯麼你看這兒在座的人都是為你的事情來的你只管這麼怒氣冲冲的倒像要把誰攆出去的似的這些人怎麼好意思坐着呢要走罷又恐怕你臉上下不來若在這兒多坐會兒你又山嚷怪叫的叫喊這就叫人進退兩難了啊以後朋友們還怎麼和你來往呢。

談論篇百章之五十一

1 人若是不該死自然而然的有救星兒他那一夜病得很沉重，昏過去了，等了好一會子，纔甦醒過來，我嘴裏雖然是安慰老人家說請放心無妨無妨心裏實在是沒指望兒了。2 誰想那老人家的福氣大病人的造化好到了第二天，另請了一個大夫治了治眼看着一天比一天的好了。3 前兒我去看他見他的身子雖然沒有還元兒，臉上的氣色兒可轉過來了，也略長了點兒肉了。在那兒靠着枕頭喫東西呢我說好啊，大喜咯。這一塲病可不輕雖然沒死也脫了一層皮呀。4 他和我笑嘻嘻的說托着大家的福如今出了災略可大好了。

談論篇百章之五十二

1 你勸我喫藥何嘗不是好話但只是我另有一個心思若果然該當服藥我又不是看財奴有愛惜銀錢不愛惜身子的理麽都因爲前年我喫錯了藥幾幾乎沒有喪了命到今兒想起來心裏還跳呢。2 如今的醫生好的雖有，百裏也不過挑一其餘的只知道擇銀子錢他那兒管人家的性命死活呢。3 你若不信請一個來試一試藥性他還不定懂得了沒有，就大着膽子給人家治病慌慌張

談論篇百章之五十

1 夏天的時候兒他還可以札掙着走來着近來這些日子添了病竟躺下了閙家子亂亂烘烘的沒主意老家兒們愁得都瘦了。2 那一天我去瞧他見他瘦得不成樣兒了,在炕上倒氣兒呢,我慢慢兒的走到他跟前兒說你如今好了些兒麼。3 他睜開眼瞧見我把我的手緊緊的揢住說哎我的兄台這是我的罪呀病到這個分兒上大料是不能好了我不知道甚麼樣兒的藥沒喫過纔好了一好兒又重落了這是我命該如此我並不委屈。但只惦記父母上了年紀兄弟又小再者親戚骨肉都在這兒我能撂得下誰呢。4 話沒說完眼淚直流下來好傷心哪就是鐵石的人聽了他的那個話也沒有不慘得慌的

惦記我麼我也沒有甚麼說的只是記在心裏等着病好了,再磕頭道謝罷。3 他嘴裏雖然是這麼說身子可露出扎掙不住的樣兒來了。4 我們就說,老弟你是個很聰明的人不用我們多說好好兒的養着身子,快好了罷我們得空兒再來瞧你說完就囬來了

談論篇百章之四十八

1 我這幾天有事，一連熬了兩夜渾身很乏，沒有勁兒。2 昨兒晚上，要早睡來着。只因親戚們，普裏普兒的，都在這兒會齊兒，我怎麼擰下去睡呢。身子雖然強扎掙着還在那兒陪着坐哎，眼睛却十分受不得了，眼皮子也搭拉了心裏也糊塗了，沒法子等到客一散，就抓了個枕頭穿着渾身的衣裳睡着了，直到四更天纔醒，不知道是怎麼着了點兒涼，覺着腹中膨悶渾身發燒就像火烤的一樣，又搭上害耳朵底子疼得連顋頰都腫了，飲食無味坐臥不安。3 我想是停住食了，就服了一劑打藥，把內裏所有好啊歹的東西都打下來了，這心裏纔覺着鬆快些兒。

談論篇百章之四十九

1 他本是個弱身子又不知道保養，過貪酒色，所以氣血虧損了。2 如今的病很延纏，昨兒我們去瞧的時候兒，他還扎掙着來到上房，和我們說，這樣兒的熱天氣，常勞動兄台們來瞧，太勞乏了，我實在不敢當又不住的送東西過於費心，我十分感情不盡總還是親戚們，關心想着我。若是傍不相干兒的人，能彀這麼

談論篇百章之四十七

1 我看你酒上很親一時也離不開貪得過逾了每逢喝酒必要喝得很醉到站不住脚兒的時候兒纔算了這不是好事啊少喝點兒不好麼。2 若是赴席有喜事呢多喝點兒還無妨若不論有事沒事只管擎著盅子不離嘴的喝生出甚麼好事來呀不過是討女人兒子厭煩在長輩兒們跟前得不是輕着耽誤了要緊的事情重着要惹出大禍來咯若說是藉着酒學了本事長了才幹成了正經事情的叫人家敬重那個可少啊。3 總而言之酒就是亂性傷身子的毒藥任着意兒喝萬萬使不得你若不信照着鏡子瞧一瞧鼻子臉都叫酒糟透了你又不是平常的人兒不分晝夜的這麼喝這不是自已害了自已麼。

麼捆兒若是陷進去了那是個底兒就是不犯王法也是連一個大錢賸不下都是家業弄個精光的纔撂開手這樣兒的事情我眼裏見的耳朶裏聽的雖不多也有了百數個咯咱們是知已的朋友既知道了若是不勸要相好的作甚麼是不賭錢纔好我必定打聽作甚麼呢。

談論篇百章之四十六

1 哎呀老弟你怎麼咯。咱們纔隔了幾天哪、這麼快鬍子都白咯、露出老樣兒來了。你別怪我嘴直聽見說、你如今上了要錢場兒了、還該下許多的賬。若果然是那麼着、不是玩兒的呀、得略收收兒纔好哪。你納若不信、請細細兒的打聽打聽、就知道了。 2 這都是沒影兒的話、胡編造的、你自己不知道麼、看起朋友們、都議論你來、想必你是有點兒罷咧。這要錢、有甚

不能保養身子前兒喫早飯的時候兒就很涼來着、一會兒的時候兒又熱起來了、人人都受不得、我炮燥的出了一身透汗、脫了袍子要涼快涼快又喝了碗涼茶、立刻就頭疼起來了、鼻子也流清鼻涕、傷了風咯、嗓子也瘂了、身子像坐在雲彩上的一樣、暈暈忽忽的不舒服。 3 不獨你是那樣兒、我的身子也不爽快懶急動、幸而昨兒把所喫所喝的全吐了、不然今兒也就扎挣不住了。 4 我教給你法子、但只餓着肚子少少兒的喫東西。若是那麼着、就是些微的着點兒涼、也就無妨了。

談論篇百章之四十四

1 老弟你瞧他今兒又醉了喝得成了泥咯,站都站不住了,我問他那個事情,你告訴人家沒有,他前仰兒後合的直瞪着倆眼睛一聲兒不言語又不是聾子啞吧,為甚麼不答言兒,今兒若不把這個該殺的痛痛快快的責罰他一頓,我就起個誓。 2 兄台罷喲,他想是忘了,沒有去他的不是,他不知道麼因為這個心裏害怕不敢答言兒今兒既然是我在這兒看着我的面上饒過這一次罷從今以後叫他很很心戒了酒罷俗語說的主子管奴才靴子裏摸襪子他能躲到那兒去啊,他不改呢仍舊還是這麼往醉裏喝那時候兄台重重的責罰他,我就是再遇見也不管求情了。 3 老弟你不知道他是生來不成器的東西,若說喝酒就捨了命比他老子的血還親今兒饒了他,我保他不能改,至多一兩天不喝罷咧過了後兒必定還是照着樣兒喝。

談論篇百章之四十五

1 兄台你怎麼咯臉上刷白的冷孤丁的就瘦成這個樣兒了。 2 老弟你不知道。因為這幾天澗溝的味兒很不好又搭着天氣乍涼乍熱的沒準兒故此人都

談論篇百章之四十三

1 昨兒個我往別處兒去的時候兒這賤奴才們就任着意兒辯嘴吵鬧趕到我囘來那猴兒們正吵嚷呢我咳嗽了一聲走進來咯賊眉鼠眼的使眼色兒一個個的躲避着走咯。2 今兒早起剛起來該殺的們都來咯直橛兒的跪着說奴才們該死求的求磕頭的磕頭這樣兒我的氣纔略平了些兒我說你們怎麽略不好好兒的肉癢癢了罷必定叫我打一頓有甚麽便宜呢從今兒以後再要這麽着小心你們那皮肉若不結結實實的打你們也不知道怕呀。3 說完都喳的一聲答應着出去了。

4 我若是氣上來真得把他打死了纔解恨過了氣兒又一想可怎麽樣呢當眞的打殺他罷又怪不忍得而且是家生子兒火棍兒短強如手撥咯遇着我有一點兒得項或是有點兒喫喝兒的地方兒倒偏疼他些兒撂下這個拏起那個猴兒似的一樣兒唧叮咕咚的不安靜。

談論篇百章之四十一

1 兄台、你納瞧這種樣兒的壞孩子可有麼。別人這樣兒那樣兒的勸他、不過是要他好、恐怕他學壞了的意思、人都是這樣兒、往正經本事上學很難、若往壞處兒學就很容易。2 到如今我就是說破了嘴、他也不肯聽、反倒無精打彩的噘着嘴撆着臉子剛纔我心裏實在受不得、動了氣很很的打了他一頓。3 他臉上一紅、和我說只是找我的錯縫子作甚麼、眼淚汪汪的走了、真是個糊塗沒造化的人哪。4 俗語兒說的、良藥苦口忠言逆耳、若不是一家兒我巴不得兒的哄着叫他喜歡呢、必定討他的厭煩作甚麼。

談論篇百章之四十二

1 你看這種賤貨、竟不是個人哪、長得活脫兒的像他老子一個樣、越瞧越討人嫌。2 不論是到那兒、兩隻眼睛、撐顧撐顧的任甚麼兒看不見、混撞嘴裏磕磕巴巴的、實在是湎人。3 正經事情上絲毫不中用、若是陶氣很能、一點兒空兒不給、常叫他在跟前兒服侍、還好些兒、若不然就陶氣的了不得、真是個鬧事精

的官件件兒都算得正對、絲毫也不錯的、我想過去的事情雖然都應了、但只未來的事怕未必能應他的話罷。3 雖然話是這麼說、咱們那兒花不了這幾百錢呢、與其在家裏白坐着不如去逛一逛只當解個悶兒又有何不可呢。

談論篇百章之四十

1 我告訴你個笑話兒剛纔我一個人兒這兒坐着看見窗戶檔兒上落着一個雀兒、老爺兒照着他的影兒一跳一跳的。2 我慢慢兒的捻手捻腳兒的走到跟前兒、隔着窗戶紙兒一抓把窗戶抓了個大窟窿、恰好抓住了一看是個家雀兒。3 纔一到手嚓嚕的一聲飛咯、我趕緊關上門、剛拏住又掙脫了滿屋子裏正趕着拏的時候兒、小孩子們聽見拏住雀兒了、一齊都來咯趕的趕、有一個小孩子、使帽子扣住了。4 後來我說、哎、人家還買雀兒放生呢、你拏他作甚麼放了罷。他一定不肯、打着墜毂轆兒的要沒法兒給了他咯他纔跳跳鑽鑽的喜歡着去了。

談論篇百章之三十九

1 兄台你可聽見麼新近城外頭來了一個算命的都說是很靈就像神仙轉世的一個樣兒把咱們過去的事倒像誰告訴他的筭得極真說得準對咱們的人們去的很多整天家接連不斷的命棚裏都擠滿了有這樣兒的高明人咱們何不也叫他瞧瞧去。 2 我早已知道了我的朋友這幾天都去過前兒我也到了那兒把我的八字兒叫他瞧了瞧父母屬甚麼兄弟有幾個女人姓甚麼多偺得着我今兒特來見你告訴了我好拏了去你要甚麼東西合着你的意思來補你的情就是鋪子裏沒有賣的我也必定想着法子各處兒尋了來給你心下如何 4 索性你頭裏拏了去倒好了。 5 怎麼咯。 6 丟咯。 7 嗐可惜了兒的菩提誦珠兒雖多像那個樣兒的却很少啊天天的拏來拏去汗漚透了很光滑了不拏的時候兒該收在櫃子裏就好了子裏去在排牐兒上掛着忘了沒收回來一找那兒還有呢連踪影兒都不見了 8 哎也是該丟上月我往園不知道叫誰偷了去咯。

談論篇百章之三十七

1 你們對過兒的那所房子如何。 2 你問他作甚麼。 3 我有個朋友要買 4 那個房子住不得很凶底根兒是我們家兄住着來着地勢很好門面房七間、到底兒五層住着很合樣又乾淨後來到了我姪兒的手裏說廂房剻爛了從新蓋了蓋忽然鬼啊怪的作起祟來了起初鬧的還好些兒久而久之的白日裏出了聲兒咯後來就顯了形兒了家裏的女人們動不動兒的就撞磕着嚇的傷了性命兒的都有。跳神也枉然送祟也沒用沒法兒賤賤的價兒就賣了。 5 兄台你知道麼這都是運氣不好的緣故。若是時運旺的時候兒就有邪祟他也躲避着不能害人。但是我那個朋友膽兒很小我把這個打聽的實話告訴他就完了買不買由他罷。

談論篇百章之三十八

1 兄台你那盤誦珠兒我說要拏去、到底沒有拏了去。 2 甚麼緣故呢。 3 我遭遭兒來了、你都沒在家沒見你、舍糊着拏你的東西去有這個理麼。因爲這麼

談論篇百章之三十六

1 台們提起話兒來就說鬼我也告訴你們一件怪事你們說的都是在古兒詞上看下來的我這個是我親自經過的。2 那一年我們出城閒逛囘來的時候看見道傍邊兒有座大墳院房屋牆垣都破爛了歪的歪倒的倒那裏頭各樣兒的樹木長得可是很深密。3 我們說這個地方兒很涼快咱們進去歇一歇兒把帶着的果子菜放下就在墳前坐着喫喝起來了。4 衆人看見都嚇愣了剛要躲着走子裏所斟的酒忽然自己熻熻的都着了我一個叔叔忙擺手兒說住你們別怕頭裏的時候兒有給鄂博留謝儀的話啊今兒降在這兒了忙斟了一鍾酒禱告着祭奠了祭奠那所着的酒立刻都滅了。5 這是我親見的事情你們說怪不怪

時候兒那個該殺的又進來了我那朋友就猛然起來拏着把腰刀把他斫了一下兒那個東西哎呀了一聲倒在地下了。5 叫了家下人來點上鐙一照很可笑原來是個賊爲偸東西故意兒的粧成鬼來嚇唬人來咯。

甚麼白有個袱子的名兒就是咯、毛稍兒也壞了、顏色兒也變了、反穿不得了。

10 若是那們關了俸的時候兒再買件好的就是了。你們是年輕的人兒們、正在往上巴結的時候兒遇着朝會的日子穿件好的打扮打扮是該當的、我若是穿了好的、不但不得樣兒、而且不舒服況且我們武職差使上也用不着好衣裳索性穿舊的破的、倒和我們很對勁兒。

11 哎我是過了時的人了、還講究甚麼樣兒呢、但只煖和就是了。

談論篇百章之三十五

1 我有個朋友膽子很大夏天的時候兒黑下撐着窗戶睡正睡着、覺着耳朶裏聽見有響聲兒。睜開眼一瞧大月亮底下、有一個怪物臉似黃紙眼睛裏流血、渾身雪白頭髮蓬鬆着一跳一跳的前來。

2 我那朋友在睡夢中驚醒忽然看見嚇了一大跳。心裏說哎呀這就是鬼罷、悄悄兒的瞧着看他怎麼樣。

3 那鬼跳了不久的工夫兒就開開了立櫃擎出許多衣裳來挾在胳肢窩裏從窗戶裏跳出去了。

4 我那朋友心裏暗想着、若果然是鬼、有擎衣裳的理麼正想着的

談論篇百章之三十四

1 這件貂鼠褂子是在舖子裏買的麼。 2 不是舖子裏的,是廟上買的。 3 多少銀子買的。 4 你猜一猜。 5 這件至不濟也值三百兩銀子。 6 我從二百兩上添起,添到二百五十兩他就賣了。 7 怎麼這麼賤哪,我想從前像這樣兒的,至平常也得五百兩銀子,你看這一件,顏色兒黑,毛道兒厚又平正,而且風毛出得齊截,面子的緞子又厚,花樣兒也新鮮又合如今的時樣兒,就是比着你的身子做也不過這麼樣罷咧。 8 我記得你納也有一件來着。 9 哎我那個算

跑得又快射馬箭一點兒張裏的毛病兒都沒有又隨手又妥當。 3 看起這個來你原來不認得馬若是好馬骹子必定結實耐得勞苦,圍場上又熟,樣兒好又靈便,那種好的就是英雄少年們,繫上撒袋騎着像飛鷹一般,真可觀,你這馬是甚麼口也老了,下巴都搭拉了,腿也頓肯打前失,況且你的身子又笨,與你不大相宜呀。 4 哎可怎麼樣呢,如今已經買定了,只得將就着養活罷咧,我並沒有緊差使,又沒有甚麼遠差使,但是老實就和我對勁兒,究竟比步行兒強啊。

PART V.—THE HUNDRED LESSONS.

談論篇百章之三十二

1 老弟是幾兒打屯裏來的。2 我到了有些日子了。3 老弟來了、我總沒聽見說、若是聽見、也早來贐你來了。4 咱們住的地方兒離又是官身子、那裏聽得見呢。5 我問你、你們的地在那兒。6 在霸州所屬的地方兒。7 挨着琉璃河麼。8 不是是渾河那塊兒。9 今年那兒的莊稼好不好。10 好得很、十分收成了。11 這奇怪咯、他們不是先說潦了、又說旱了麼。12 那都是謠言、信不得的、別說別的、黑豆的價兒就十分便宜、十來個錢一升、這有許多年沒有這麼賤了。13 真麼。14 可不是真麼。15 若是這麼着、你再打發人去的時候兒、請替我買幾石來、用多少銀子、算明白了告訴我、我照着原買的價兒給你。16 是啊、我看見你納槽上拴着好幾匹馬、買豆子餧是該當的、與其在咱們這兒買的價兒貴、不如在那兒帶了來、有減半兒的便宜呢。

談論篇百章之三十三

1 若買、就買匹好馬、拴着看、也有趣兒、費草費料的、拴着這麼匹儍頭馬、作甚麼。
2 兄台不知道、這匹馬昨兒牽了來、我就拉到城外頭試過了、可以騎得顚得穩、

談論篇百章之三十一

1 你還沒起身麼。 2 早晚兒就要起身了、馱子行李都整理安當了、只是盤纏銀子還短點兒。俗語兒說上山擒虎易開口告人難的話、我今兒纔信了、捨着臉兒各處兒借、總沒借着沒法兒找兄台來了、或銀子、或當頭、求你納借給我點兒。等我回來的時候兒本利一倂奉還。 3 幸虧你來得早、若略遲些兒就趕不上了。方纔屯裏擎了幾兩銀子來還沒用呢、你擎一半兒去使、等喝了茶、我再平給你、我問你這不是初次出門麼。 4 可不是麼。 5 我告訴你些個話、出遠門兒的道理、處朋友們、以和爲貴、待底下的官人們、不必分內外都是一樣兒的疼愛、就有可以弄銀子錢的地方兒也該想着臉面、要緊別手長了、若是亂來於聲名上大有關係呀。 6 兄台說的都是金玉良言、兄弟永遠記着就是咯。

7 那個胖子、我知道了、這一個可是誰呢。 8 我間他們的姓來着每人都留下了個職名、等我擎來給你納看。從那'兒來、你們別把他看輕了相貌雖然長得歪歪扭扭的、筆底下很好、心裏也有韜略兒、是早已出了名的人了、提起他來誰不知道呢。 9 哎呀、這猴兒差一點兒、沒有噴嚏的笑了。

談論篇百章之三十

1 今兒有誰來過麼。2 你納出去之後，有倆人來，說是你納陞了官，道喜來了。

3 誰出去答應的。4 我在門口兒站着來着，說你納沒在家，老爺們請到裏頭坐罷，他們不肯進來，回去了。

5 都是甚麼樣兒呢。6 一個是胖子，比你納略高些兒，四方臉兒，連鬢鬍子，豹子眼兒，紫棠色兒，那一個眞可笑，臟得看不得，一隻眼還是斜着，又是糙稠麻子，滿下巴的捲毛兒鬍子，咬着舌兒望我一說話，我點兒穿點兒。若到了筋骨硬的時候兒穿呢，也不得味兒瞇着孩子們的下巴頦兒過日子，有甚麼趣兒啊。只是別過逾了，就是略算計着所得的分兒樂一樂，也很使得呀。2 這個話你是知道我的事情說的呀。還是揣摸着說的呢。我果然是銀錢富富餘餘的樂，也是應當的，只是不像別人有銀錢有產業，叫我拏甚麼樂呢。叫我借了債穿哪，還是賣了房子喫呢。若是依你這個話行錢財兒花盡了的時候兒嘆口氣就死了纔好，萬一不死還有氣兒活着，可怎麼樣兒過呢。到那時候兒就是我求你，你還理我麼。

談論篇百章之二十八

1 哎你太奢侈了各樣兒的東西上必得愛惜儉省纔是過日子的道理呀我若不說你我又忍不住若是把喫不了的飯給家下人們喫那不好麼你竟任着意兒倒在溝眼裏是為甚麼呢心裏也安麼。米的艱難種地的拉縴的受的都是甚麼樣兒的辛苦纔到得這兒就是一個米粒兒也不是容易得的啊。3 況且咱們不能像那些個財主人家兒喫着這個想着那個。有的是現成的銀子錢嘴有甚麼捆兒呢喫有甚麼盡頭兒呢若是這麼慣了不但折福而且要破家呀。4 有年紀兒的人們常說惜衣得衣惜食得食你的福田能有多大呢若是這麼樣兒的不會過隄防着日子久了自已捱上了餓那時候兒纔後悔也就遲了啊。

談論篇百章之二十九

1 人生百歲不過一眨眼兒的光景把銀子錢結結實實的收着作甚麼我想這個浮生如夢的身子能殼樂幾天兒呢一晃兒就不中用了不如趁着沒有老喫

談論篇百章之二十七

1 你不知道這種好強都是年輕血氣旺的緣故等着喫過幾次虧自然而然的就心灰了。2 我這個人從前最好打把勢天天兒演習後來不了他跟前兒這樣兒的本事。3 這一日在我舅舅家還遇見了一個人是從屯裏來了一個瘌子會耍刀他們倆說要試一試本事各自拏了各自的兵器兒有他呢拏起鎗來直往他心口上就是一扎那個瘌子一點兒也不忙從容的使刀一搪我們家兄的鎗尖兒齊各楂兒的折了一節兒去了。趕着就抽鎗沒抽迭瘌子的刀早已放在脖子上了我們家兄要躲叫他夾着脖子一摔摺出好遠的去了。5 因為這麼着他很沒趣兒我也再不學了看起這個來天下的能人還少麼。

說了使得麼。3 我生來的性兒就是難纏若是事情沒得實兒強壓着頭叫我行我斷不肯若信我的話就叫他等着儻若不信叫他求別人兒去辦罷咧誰攔着他呢。

嘴裏雖然跟你好背地裏害得你很不輕人若是落在他的圈套兒裏就是一個仰面的觔斗在他手裏坑害的人可不少了屈着指頭兒算不清啊友們提起他來都說是可怕沒有不頭疼的 4 這就是俗語兒說的人心隔肚皮知人知面不知心的話兒是特為這種人們說的咯。 5 我還算是僥倖若不留心遠着他必定也受了他的籠絡。

談論篇百章之二十五

1 哎你的性子也太疲了若是不能的事情就罷了既然應承了又不趕緊的辦只是給人家躭擱着是甚麼意思呢若像這樣兒的行事朋友們還怎麼信你的話呢。 2 想來你是自己不覺罷咧我實在替你害羞與其這麼顢頇着索性把實在的光景告訴人家他也好歇了心另外打算哪。

談論篇百章之二十六

1 這是甚麼話呢論事情還沒有影兒呢就略遲些兒也不要緊正經事情的主兒尚且不着急你先這麼催逼着是個甚麼道理啊。 2 不論甚麼事情總要詳細了又詳細得了正經主意纔可以告訴人若像你們糊裏麻裏的不得准兒就

談論篇百章之二十三

1 兄台請騎着我失躲避了啊乏乏兒的又下來作甚麼。2 甚麼話呢若沒有看見就罷了我在老遠的就看見了有騎着的理麼。3 兄台不到家裏坐麼。4 是啊咱們許久沒見了我進去略坐一坐兒哎呀栽了許多的花兒了麼又養着許多金魚兒。山子石兒堆得也好心思用得很巧層層都有樣兒這個書房寶在乾淨怎麼雅怎麼入眼正是咱們念書的地方兒。5 好離是好啊但只恨是我自己沒有甚麼朋友一個人兒念書很冷清。6 這有何難呢你若不厭煩我給你作伴兒來何如。7 若是那們着真是我的造化了我請還恐怕不來呢若果真來真是我的萬幸咯,那兒還有厭煩的理呢。

談論篇百章之二十四

1 起初我見他的時候兒待人兒很親熱又很爽快相貌又體面漢仗兒又魁偉俐牙俐齒的真會說話兒我看着很羨慕他心裏說怎麼能和他相與相與總好不住口兒的誇獎他。2 後來交上了一塊兒常混混細細兒考較他所行所爲的事情原來不是個正經人虛架子弄空的而且心裏又陰險不給人好道兒走

談論篇百章之二十二

一件事來把臉放在那兒啊。3因為這上頭惱就由他們惱罷,我到底沒去告訴家裡的人們,不拘誰來找我,答應不在家,想不到你來了,糊塗奴才們也照着樣兒答應不在家,打發了去咯,纔進來告訴我,我急忙差人去趕他回來說沒趕上叫我心裏很過意不去。實在我是不知道你納千萬別計較。

1我們倆底根兒相好,而且又連了幾層親,如今許多年沒得見面兒了,我打出兵回來,就要找了他去,叙談叙談不想叫事情絆住,竟沒空兒去,到昨兒順便兒到他家一間那兒的人說他搬了好久咯,現在小街兒西頭兒枴灣兒住着呢。

2我照着告訴的話,找了去走到儘溜頭兒嚼拉兒裏頭,纔看見他的房子門兒關着呢,我敲着門兒大聲兒叫了好一會子,纔出來了一個走不動的老媽兒,他說主人沒在家別處兒去了,我說等你們老爺回來告訴他,說我來瞧來了。

3這個老媽兒的耳朶又很聾,總聽不見我沒法兒就在他們隔壁兒小鋪兒裏借了個筆硯,把我瞧他去的話,寫了個字兒留下了。

談論篇百章之二十

1 那個人哪、是咱們舊街坊啊、眼看着長大的孩子、隔了能有幾天兒、如今聽見說、很出息了、做了官了、起初我還半信半疑的、來着後來在朋友們跟前打聽果然是真的、看起這個來是有志者事竟成和有志不在年高這兩句話眞是不假啊。 2 兄台你的話雖然是這麼說、也是他老家兒有陰功纔生出這樣兒成人的孩子來呢、很樸實又良善、除了學馬步箭的工夫素常在家就是看書、荒唐的道兒一步兒也不肯走、況且公事上又很小心、很勤謹、至於有便宜有得項的地方兒、他總不沾染、這正是合了積善之家必有餘慶的那句話了。

談論篇百章之二十一

1 咱們這些人裏頭、你還是外人兒麼、要瞧我、就一直進來、又何必先通報呢、旣到了門口兒、怎麼又回去了呢、想必是我們家裡的人們說我沒在家、你惱咯、是這個緣故不是啊、我若不說出緣故來、你怎麼知道呢。 2 這一向咱們那羣孩子們合着夥兒開了要錢塲兒、方纔來起誓發願的、必定叫我去、我不得空兒、你是深知道的、一會兒一會兒的差使、如何能定呢、而且王法又很緊、儻若鬧出

談論篇百章之十九

1 你打聽的不是那位老弟麼。 2 是啊。 3 他是個囊中之錐不久就要出頭咯。 4 甚麼緣故呢。 5 他生來得安靜學問淵博行動兒漢仗兒都出衆差使上又勤居家過日子是一撲納心兒的勤儉父母跟前又孝順弟兄們跟前又親熱眞是沒有一點兒毛病兒況且待朋友們又很護衆不拘誰托他一件事他不應就罷了他若是點了頭必定替你盡力的辦不成不肯歇手因此誰不敬他誰不親近他。 6 是啊他這樣兒的人豈有窒過一生的理麼俗語兒說吉人天相天必降福啊。

7 他們倆不信回去一看仍舊是金子只是砍成兩半兒咯。 8 管仲鮑叔每人摯了一半兒走咯那個莊稼漢還是窒着手兒囘去咯。 9 古時候兒的人們相與的道理是這個樣兒啊這話雖是小說兒上的實在可以給如今見利忘義的人們作個榜樣兒。

你們有甚麼雛啊把一條兩頭兒蛇告訴我說是金元寶差點兒沒要了我的命。

談論篇百章之十八

1 若說相與朋友應該學古時候兒的管仲鮑叔。 2 他們倆有一天在荒郊野外的地方兒迸看見道傍邊兒有一個金元寶。 3 他們彼此對讓誰也不肯揀仍擺下走咯。 4 遇見一個莊稼漢就告訴他說那兒有個金元寶你去揀去罷。 5 那個莊稼漢聽了這話趕忙着去到那兒一找並不見金子只見有一條兩頭兒蛇。 6 嚇了一大跳連忙使鋤把蛇砍成兩截兒就趕趕他們倆嚷着說我和姜的桃唆就爭家產或是聽了傍人離間的話各自各兒懷着異心的很多。 2 就是天天兒聽了這些讒言耳濡目染到心裏都裝滿了一時間不能忍以致於打架辯嘴就成了讎咯。 3 也該想一想產業沒了還可以再置女人死了也可以再娶弟兄們若是傷一個就像手脚折了一隻的一個樣爲能再得呢。 4 比方偶然閙出一件禍事來那還得骨肉相關的弟兄們拚命巴結着搭救啊。若是傍人恐怕連累着躲還躲不迭呢還肯替你出力麽。 5 看起這個來再沒有如同弟兄們親的咯人爲甚麽不細細兒的想想這些個呢。

談論篇百章之十六

1 養兒原爲防備老爲人子的應該想着父母的勞苦養活的恩就趁着父母在着拏好穿的好喫的孝敬他和顏悅色的叫老家兒喜歡。 2 若是喫穿不管饑寒不問的像外人兒似的看待叫兩個老人家傷心到了百年之後任憑你怎麼慟哭中甚麼用啊就算是你出於誠心誰信呢不過因爲怕人家笑話假罷咧就是供甚麼樣兒的珍饈美味誰見靈魂兒來受享了麽也還是活人兒饞揉罷咧死的人有甚麼益處啊。 3 還有一種更不好的人說父母上了年紀兒了老輩晦了吵鬧着強要分家的說到這個場處不由的叫人生氣傷心這種樣兒的人天地不容神鬼都是恨的焉能善終呢。 4 你只靜靜兒的看着一眨眼兒的工夫兒他們的子孫也就照着他們的樣兒學了。

談論篇百章之十七

1 弟兄們是一個母親肚子裏生的小的時候兒在一塊兒喫一塊兒玩兒不分彼此何等樣兒親熱來着後來長大了漸漸兒的生分的緣故大約都是聽了妻

談論篇百章之十五

1 啊眾位弟兄們可要小心這位老大人的才情敏捷，有決斷，無論甚麼事情，到手就有條有理兒辦結咯。而且心裏明白，認得人好歹瞞不過他的眼睛去。又最憐愛凡有勤謹體面少年的子弟們，到了挑缺應陞的時候兒肯提拔保舉。但是遇着差使上滑的面子上要獻勤兒討好，占便宜的，這種人，可要小心着，免叫他拏住若是叫他楞着了，斷沒有輕放過去的。2 你們的話雖是這麼說，弟兄們，天天兒眼巴巴兒的盼着要仗着我成人，我若是應保舉的不保舉，應約束的不約束，怎麼還能賞功罰罪呢。我是生成的心直口快，想來說話行事還正派，故此人家都服我，願意給我出力啊。

就像是他自己的一個樣兒，很着急必定儘着力兒搭救，眞是一位厚道積福的老人家，故此我若是隔久了，不去看一看，心裏頭只是不過意。4 俗語兒說的，一人有福托帶滿屋。現在那家業充足子孫與旺，都是他老人家行為好的報應啊。

談論篇百章之十三

1 當差行走的、只看各自的機會、時運若平常樣樣兒總不着、不論甚麼事、眼看着要成偏會生出岔兒來、有一種彩頭好、走好運的人、真是沒有不照着他所思所算的、爽爽利利兒隨了心的眼瞜着、就是優等高陞、裏却不然、只論巴結不巴結、若是素餐尸位的、整年家不行走、還該當革退呢、再指望陞官能彀麼、當差的人第一要勤謹、朋友們裏頭要和氣、別各別另樣的、別不隨羣兒、有事不攀人、不論甚麼差使、一撲納心兒的辦、勇往向前行了去、必定是在高等兒上有不得的道理麼。2 你納是這麼說、我心裏却不然、只論巴結……

談論篇百章之十四

1 這姓張的、待人很冷淡、我認得一個有了年紀兒的人、却不是這樣兒、見了人很親熱、若是坐在一處兒、論起學問來、很喜歡講今比古、接連不斷、整天家說也不乏。2 若是遇見年輕的人兒們了、他和顏悅色的、往好處兒引誘、該指撥的地方兒指撥、該教導的地方兒教導。3 最仁愛又最護衆、見了人家有苦處、

談論篇百章之十二

1 兄台恭喜咯說放章京揀選上了。 2 是啊、昨兒揀選的把我擬了正了。 3 擬陪的是誰啊。 4 你不認得是一個前鋒校有圍。 7 我替你納算計熟咯一定要戴孔雀翎子咯。 5 他有兵麼。 6 沒有兵寔奇處兒比我好的多着的呢。 8 別過獎咧我有甚麼奇處兒也定不得。 9 這是太謙了你納是甚麼時候兒的人年久咯若論起來和你納一塊兒行走的朋友都作了大人咯在你納後頭年輕的人兒們也都陞了。若論你納的差使出過兵受過傷現在又是十五善射你納說旗下強過你納的是誰我知道了想是怕我來喝喜酒啊 10 喝酒有甚麼呢果然若得了別說是酒合着你納的意思我請你納。

11 真的呀、在你納家我還作客麼不敢撒謊。 12 那們就沏茶來。 13 我不喝。 14 怎麼。 15 我還要到別處兒去呢該去的地方兒多太去晚了人都犯思量兄台請喫罷別送看帶了味兒去。 16 那兒有這個理不出房門兒使得麼哎來了空空的連茶也沒喝請呀、改日再見到家裡都替我問好罷。

是粧假罷。

談論篇百章之十

1 射步箭是咱們滿洲人最要緊的事看着容易做着難就是黑下白日的長拉抱着弓睡的都有若拉到出類拔萃的好能出了名的有幾個呢。3 身子要正髂子要平一身要很自然沒有毛病兒還又搭着弓硬箭出去的有勁兒再箭兒中纔算得是好呢。若有不是的地方兒請撥正撥正。要仗着大拇指頭戴翎子略樣兒又好又很熟撒得又乾淨人若都能像你還說甚麼呢但只是弓還略輕些兒前手略有一點兒定不住把這幾處兒毛病兒若改了不拘到那兒去射一定出眾有誰能壓得下你去呢。2 難處在那兒呢。4 兄台你納看我射箭比從前出息了沒有。5 你射的步箭有甚麼說得呢。早晚兒

談論篇百章之十一

1 兄台新喜啊。2 好說大家同喜啊。3 兄台請坐。4 做甚麼拜年哪。6 甚麼話呢。7 老兄長啊是該當磕頭的。8 請起請起陞官哪得子啊過富貴的日子啊請起請上坐這現成兒的葷餃子請喫幾個罷。9 我在家裡喫了出來的。10 喫得那麼飽麼年輕的人兒纔喫了就餓啊若不喫想必

着臉兒念給人家聽呢從前那一國誰和誰打過幾次仗這個拏刀砍那個使斧架這個又拏鎗札那個又使棍搪若說是敗了來的都是雲裏來霧裏去的神仙剪草爲馬撒豆兒成兵的。4 明明兒的是謊話那糊塗人們當成眞事還獸頭獸腦有滋有味兒的聽呢有見識的人看見不但笑話而且懶怠瞧你往這上頭用心做甚麼。

談論篇百章之九

1 那個書取了來咯沒有。2 取去了還沒拏來呢。3 使喚誰去的至今還沒來麼。4 打發那小孩子取去了我們先叫他去他肯聽我們的話麼有要沒緊兒的就擱時候兒後來我說有兄台的話他纔忙着去了那一部書不是四套麼他只拏了三套來我們說他你爲甚麼漏下了一套若不趕着取去等着主人回來必不依你呀他反倒說我們告訴得糊塗不明白抱怨着去了，5 這種樣兒的滑東西也有麼若差人迎他去罷又恐怕走岔了道兒是往那個熱鬧地方兒玩去咯若不嚴嚴兒的管教斷斷使不得等他回來的時候兒把他捆上重重兒的打一頓纔好不然慣了他就更不堪了。

談論篇百章之七

1 你是明白漢字的人哪要學繙譯很容易只是專心別隔斷了挨着次兒的學兩三年的工夫兒自然就有頭緒兒了若是三日打魚兩日曬網的就念到二十年也是枉然。 2 兄台瞧瞧我的繙譯求你納罩改一改。 3 你學得大有長進了句句兒順當字字兒清楚沒有一點兒肬星兒若是考可以操必勝之權。這一次考筆帖式遞了名字沒有。 4 若是考得很好只怕秀才未必准考罷。是那兒的話呢像你這樣兒的八旗都許考獨不准你考的理有麼況且義學生還准考呢秀才倒不准咧因為准考你姪兒這個空兒纔趕着學滿洲書呢你快補名字罷別錯過了機會啊。

談論篇百章之八

1 你別看小說兒這種書若是看書看通鑑可以長學問記得古來的事情以好的爲法以不好的爲戒於身心大有益處啊。 2 至於看小說兒古兒詞都是人編的沒影兒的瞎話就是整千本兒的看了有甚麼益處呢。 3 有一種人還皮

談論篇百章之六

1 今兒早起背他們的書,一個比一個的生哼啊哼的張着嘴瞪着眼只是站着。

2 看他們這麼着我說且住了聽我的話你們旣然是念滿洲書就該一樸納心兒的學、像這麼樣兒的充數兒沽虛名多儚是個了手啊、不但你們是虛度日月、連我也是白費了勁兒咯、這是你們自已悞了自已咯、還是我悞了你們呢。

3 已經長成了大漢子的、說着也是這個樣耳朶雖然聽了並不放在心上太皮臉了罷把我說的苦口良言全當成了耳傍風咯。

4 別說我找你們的錯縫子。

5 我如今也沒法兒譬如我當了差使回來、滕下的空兒、歇歇兒那不好麼。為甚麼呢、不過因為是骨肉叫你們出息成人的意思啊。了、只好盡心的教導完我的責任就是了。聽不聽隨你們罷咧、叫我可怎麼樣兒呢。

空兒教我們、若不是這麼着、兄台要念書、也是好事罷咧、替你說說又費了我甚麼呢。

談論篇百章之五

1 老弟你天天從這兒過、都是往那兒去啊。 2 念書去。 3 不是念滿洲書麽。 4 是。 5 現在念的都是甚麽書。 6 沒有新樣兒的書、都是眼面前兒的零碎話和清話指要這兩樣兒。 7 還教你們寫清字楷書不啊。 8 如今天短沒寫字的空兒等着天長了、不但教寫字還教學繙譯呢。 9 老弟我為這念書的事、真是鑽頭覓縫兒的那兒沒有找到啊、可惜我們左近沒有念清書的學房我想着你們念書的這學房就可以到多唠我也去念去請你替我先說說罷。 10 兄台你打量教我們的是誰啊是師傅麽不是呀是我的一個族兄所有教的都是我們一家兒的子弟再者就是親戚們並沒有外人可怎麽說呢我們族兄又要我們天天兒上衙門不得閒兒是因為我們過懶不肯自已用功他萬不得已兒勻着

連老子孃都叫人家咒罵啊。 5 老弟你白想一想父母的恩情為人子的能彀報得萬一麽旣不能彀光宗耀祖的罷咧反倒叫父母受人家的咒罵沒出息兒到甚麽分兒上了。 6 細想起這個來人若是不念書不修品使得麽

談論篇百章之四

1 人生在世頭一件要緊的是學念書呢特為的是明白道理學得道理明白了在家呢孝順父母做官呢給國家出力不論甚麼事可自然都會成就。 2 人若是學得果然有了本事無論到那塊兒不但別人尊重你就是你自己也覺着體面。 3 還有一種不念書不修品的全靠着鑽幹逢迎作他的本事我不知道他們心裏到底要怎麼樣啊我實在替他害羞。 4 這一種人不但自己辱身壞名

兒漢音很熟練哪不但這個而且記得話兒還多那纔可以算得起是好呢。 3 他比你如何。 4 我怎麼敢比他我可不是他的對兒啊差得天地懸隔呢。 5 甚麼緣故呢。 6 他學得日子深會得多頗好書至今還是不住嘴兒的念不離手兒的拏着看若要趕他實在難哪。 7 弟台你這話只怕有點兒說錯了罷你忘了有志者事竟成這句話了麼他也是學會得罷咧並不是生了來就知道的啊咱們那點兒不如他任憑他是怎麼樣兒的精熟咱們只要拏定主意用心去學雖然到不了他那個地步兒料想也就差不多兒咯。

談論篇百章之二

1 聽見說你的清話、如今學得很有點兒規模兒了麼。 2 那'兒的話呢。人家說的我雖懂得、我自家要說還早呢。不但我說的不能像別人兒說得成片段兒、而且一連四五句話就接不上了。還有個怪處兒、是臨說話的時候、無緣無故的怕錯不敢簡簡决决的說、這麼樣可叫我怎麼說呢。我也灰了心咯。想著就是這麼樣兒學來學去、也不過就是這麼個本事兒咯、那兒還能彀有長進呢。 3 這都是你沒熟的緣故。我告訴你無論他是誰、但凡遇見個會說清話的你就趕著和他說。再有那清話精通的師傅們、也要往他們那兒去學、或是和清話熟習的朋友們時常談論。天天兒看書記話、平常說慣了嘴兒。若照着這麼學至多一兩年自然而然的就會順着嘴兒說咯、又愁甚麼不能呢。

談論篇百章之三

1 老弟你的清話、是甚麼空兒學的聲兒說得好、而且又明白。 2 啊承兄台的過獎。我的清話算甚麼呢。我有個朋友、滿洲話說得很好又清楚又快沒有一點

PART V.—THE HUNDRED LESSONS.

談論篇百章之一

1 我聽見說你如今學滿洲書呢麼。很好。滿洲話是咱們頭一宗兒要緊的事情,就像漢人們各處兒各處兒的鄉談一個樣兒不會使得麼。2 可不是麼。我念了十幾年的漢書,至今還摸不着一點兒頭緒呢。若再不念滿洲書,不學繙譯,兩下裏都耽誤咯。因爲這麼着,我一則來瞧瞧兄台,二則還有奉求的事情呢。只是怪難開口的。3 這有甚麼難呢,有話請說。若是我做得來的事情,咱們倆,我還推辭麼。4 我所求的,是你納疼愛我就是勞乏些兒可怎麼樣呢。抽空兒給我編幾個話條子我念,兄弟若能彀成了人,都是兄台所賜的。我再不敢忘了恩哪。必要重報的。5 你怎麼這麼說呢。你是外人嗎。只怕你不肯學,既然要學巴不得教你成人呢。說報恩是甚麼話呢,咱們自己人說得嗎。6 若是這麼着,我就感激不盡了。只好給兄台磕頭咯,還有甚麼說得呢。

PART V.

THE HUNDRED LESSONS.
(CHINESE TEXT.)

如何報喜高中、如何即日授了官職、如何衣錦還鄉的、順道兒回到普救寺來鶯鶯見他臉上發福、十分喜動顏色、崔老太太也很高興、以禮款待、就替他們二人張羅起喜事來、懸燈結彩、鼓樂喧闐的非常熱鬧、張生頂冠束帶的合鶯鶯拜了天地、陪着親友、喝了喜酒、衆賓散去、夫妻入了洞房、這都不消說得。3 眞是錦上添花的一般、要提他們夫婦和氣闔家歡樂、諸事吉祥、這種情節俱是自然而然的、筆下雖不註明、看官必可了然。

過筆硯來看那筆尖兒都禿了換了管新的。10 說姑娘這封信帶着送點兒甚麼精緻的東西比空信強啊。11 鶯鶯說最好我的意思就要送副鈕子。娘說奴婢意見那兒有塊紅綢絹子比鈕子好不好呢。12 紅成對的纔好這兩樣兒都寄了去罷。13 鶯鶯想着禮物成雙娘說這兩樣兒都寄了去罷。14 說着就鋪上紙拏起筆來寫紅娘靠着桌子看鶯鶯覺着那桌子動彈疑惑是他就說你別搖撼快把桌腿子墊穩了罷。接着要再寫抽冷子有個撲燈蛾兒飛來把燈撲滅了又從新點上躭擱了許久的工夫兒纔寫完了連東西一齊封好打了圖書就叫人送到信局子裡去囑咐他就寄到京裡去越快越好。15 可巧信到的那一天正是張生進塲的頭一天,他接着拆開從頭至尾看了一遍又看那兩樣兒東西見絹子雖然落了點兒顏色兒却是因為心上的人一番美意就寶而藏之格外珍重收在箱子裡了。

第四十段

1 這且不提可惜敘到此處那原板自遍集內續散語一篇俱已用完撰成這賤約傳於散語外加增的不少無法再為鋪張。2 第二天張生如何進塲出塲後

第三十九段

1 却說鶯鶯在家這一天叫紅娘拏鏡子來照臉見臉上焦黃的嘆說這都因為這些天沒有見他的面兒呌這麼牽腸掛肚的很難受見天的嘆息不絕。2 現在正是十冬臘月的天氣鶯鶯多穿了件棉襖還不暖和。3 想着心上人在京裏住這天寒火冷的時候兒不知道他怎麽過呢。4 就同紅娘到張生先住的那屋子裏看了看見那屋子關門閉戶的很冷清清簷兒上都搭了蜘蛛網略隔窗一看滿地下盡是塵土鶯鶯盼咐叫人打掃乾淨了還在那兒老站着又是發怔又是憂悶。5 紅娘勸說我們走罷在這冷清清的地方兒做甚麽。6 鶯鶯剛轉身要走看見樹稍兒上落下一個鳥兒就止步一看忽聞左近有女人哭的聲兒就問是什麽人。紅娘說他我們那隔壁兒住的丈夫新近出外有事不定多少日子纔回來。7 鶯鶯嘆了口氣說兔死狐悲物傷其類我跟他真是同病相憐了。8 紅娘跟着說嗐張生這一回走那不都是那小孩子滿嘴裏混說的起禍的根苗就是他啊鶯鶯說罷呀旣往不咎不用再提了。9 大家回屋裏悶坐愁嘆了好久到了晚上鶯鶯忽想要寫封信給張生纔好紅娘拏

哭着跑來喊說、15 我叫螞蜂螫着了胳臂肘兒都腫了疼的很利害。16 那先生就埋怨他說、誰叫你在外頭瘋跑呢、帶你出來常不安頓底下只好留在學房裏罷說完就走了。

第三十八段

1 等他們離門口兒遠了琴童就問主人那老學究是誰。張生嘆了一聲說他那位原是我家鄉的老前輩前半路兒很有名望如今年紀大了衰邁了好些眞是物理循環在所不免。2 那琴童嗯了一聲說衰邁原是衰邁了他說的那個話都是白水煮豆腐一點兒味兒都沒有。3 那孩子這種鹵莽的話若是每常、早挨上說了這會兒張生悶得慌所以都不大理會直到街上走走。4 那街上來來往往做買做賣的熱鬧之極有搖鈴兒是賣綫的也有搖鼓兒的又有攛籃子的各式各樣兒的都有。走到十字街兒見有幾座藥鋪兒忽想起舊病來了進鋪子問這裏有常山沒有、那些人說沒有、左間沒有、右間也沒有、間來間去白費了工夫、張生心裏罵他們不中用的東西、就回廟裏來歇息不提。

師徒二人就過廟裏來。8 琴童通知他主人、張生見了那老知交的進來、就迎接上前、喜說幾年不見了、好呀老先生同說托福、老兄府上都好啊。9 他們彼此謙遜了一番、老先生說昔年曾記得老兄文才茂富多時不見、一定更高了此處可有什麼筆墨賜我看一看。10 恰巧有鶯鶯那天叫紅娘送來的那首詩在桌子上擱著、那老先生瞧見是張字紙一手就挐過來要看、誰知道那些字是蠅頭小楷、他目力不及、就說這屋裏黑一點兒、我眼睛模糊怕看不真、讓我把牕戶開開罷。11 張生替他把牕戶搘上、他把詩看完了、喜笑顏開讚不絕口、看了又看、愛不釋手、那們着好半天、太陽晃得慌眼睛都睜不開了、只得又把牕戶放下來。12 張生想着這詩的名望原是鶯鶯的、如此稱揚我和尚爲妙這種樣兒的話、說別的話、正要開口、那老者顚三倒四的總以出家當做戲應酬朋友罷咧。張生更覺得不投機、只好勉強回答幾句、都不過逢塲做戲應酬朋友罷咧。13 大家又坐了好半天、還是議論不斷的、直叫張生心裏急躁、只怕這人沒時候兒走、末後兒老先生告辭說今天我有一家兒東家那邊兒還有事、我得回去了、改日再來領教罷。14 張生心覺暢快正送他出門、走到院子裏只見那小學生

第三十七段

1 他們正在敘談、梢工喳叫一聲、快看這不是羊角風嗎。忽見河面攪亂、敢情是個大颱風颳起來了。那風吹膨了篷、船歪得利害、危險得很、那些水手、你跑我嚷的、都趕緊鬆繩下篷、幸虧不到半刻的工夫兒、風就過去了、他們大家照常說笑、竟是張生一人暗中嘆惜說、

2 這別是凶兆罷、莫非驚驚死了、魂靈兒跟我來了嗎。

3 琴童揣摩出他的意思來、就想了個巧着兒安慰他說、老爺放心罷、吉人自有天相、俗語兒說的、逢凶化吉、遇難成祥、那陣風還算得了什麼呢、這且不說、

4 那船到了地土、他們主僕二人就捨舟登車、曉行夜宿的過了些天、到了京裡。

5 一進大城、聽見街上亂轟轟吵嚷的、是前門大街走了水了、客店裡怕不便留客、就在城裡找了個廟住下了。

6 那廟隔壁兒有個老教學的、也是從西洛地方兒來的、原合張生是穿房入屋的交情、聽見張生來京、在那廟裡住着、心裡念舊理應前去拜望、就合學生們說、我去拜個朋友就回來、你們的書可得念熟了啊、等我回來、若是背不上來、可隄防着罷。

7 那裏頭有個小學生是先生偏疼的、要跟了去、間先生許我去麼、先生說、可以去、竟管去、可不許淘氣。他們

了一揖用漢話間詢。張生答了禮這人又說貴國的話我是學過幾句可惜文字我不明白這兒有個字帖兒請閣下替我把這意思講出來行不行。9 張生趕緊接過字帖兒來字字句句細細兒的都告訴了他那人謝了他費心談論了一會兒又請問貴國使的銅錢上是甚麼字。10 張生說一面是漢字是國家的年號一面是篆字連我也不大認得。11 二人言來語去的閒談那人又請教。12 他們纔說這邊兒有屠戶那屠戶是幹甚麼的。13 張生說屠戶這兩個字原指的是宰猪宰羊的人常說凡是賣肉的也都叫屠戶。14 說完話那人就拜謝而去不大的工夫兒打發人送了一筐子雞蛋來張生叫琴童都擎出來把筐子還他外給賞錢二百囘去替說道謝。15 那來人走了,船又開了,都是隨事扯篷拉縴。16 快到第二個馬頭又見岸上有幾個外國人肩髈兒上扛着鳥槍好像打圍的樣子張生納罕問他們是要做甚麼的船家說那山上羵𪊨野鹿最多各樣兒都有,這是通商口子洋行開得不少那外國商人每逢不做生意的時候兒就上山打圍這山林子裏人說還有大熊呢虎豹也有。

急腿慢總趕不上你走到半路又是粗風暴雨的天雖然打着把雨傘衣裳都淋透了泥有脚面這麼深實在是難走雨還沒有住我可怎麼好呢 5 張生聽這一番話就跳起來一看果然滿屋裏精濕連他也濺了一身水沒有別的法子只好等了一會子太陽出來正在把鶯鶯那衣裳打開在草上曬着不料有一大羣人來轟轟嚷嚷的張生剛要不依他們猛然驚醒却是南柯一夢他嗐了一聲就站起來到外頭一看原來是大天大亮的了 6 又過了兩天張生正在船上閒望忽然眼前見一座高山船靠了一個熱鬧的馬頭有好些個人抬着大箱子上岸去鬧鬧吵吵的說話呢張生看那箱子彷彿裝的是外國犯禁的貨只因那箱子的皮面兒不像從外國裝來的猜着必是從外省來的私貨張生暗嘆可見走私不止於外國就是我們中國也在所不免這不是盡知責人而不知責已嗎 7 想着這個忽然見岸上遠處有些奇形怪狀的人等來近些兒聽他們的言語張生也不懂得問琴童他們說的是那兒的話真合跑獬馬的打扮無異 8 琴童說他們是外洋的人正在聽他們的時候兒這裏頭有個人過船來向張生作

第三十六段

1 不提鶯鶯在家度日如年,且說張生在船上合琴童看岸上的景致兒。2 就問船家幾時灣船。船家說今兒站船要早些兒,前邊兒河底下有個漩窩,這時候兒風颳得利害,小心些兒。到草橋我們就好灣船了。3 說着到了草橋,把纜拴在木椿子上,下了錨。到了傍晚的時候兒,張生喫了飯後,不大會兒就睡了覺了。4 剛似著不著,昏昏沉沉的時候兒,忽然看見鶯鶯來了說,今兒天氣頂熱,我心

用的,都繫到艙底下。6 他們兩位堂客坐了一會兒,張生問幾時開船,船家說老爺齊畢了就要開船了。鶯鶯聽這句話,就流淚合張生說相公進京,飲食起居常要格外留意,別心懸兩地纔好。7 張生聽這關切的話,回勸說請放心,我自然諸事留神,小姐在家也要保重身體無須我囑咐。鶯就合紅娘跟着老太太下船上岸,坐轎回去了。到了家中伺候老太太安歇,他們主僕二人進了屋子鶯鶯淚流不止說他走了,不由得我惦記着日久天長怎麽好呢。9 紅娘說姑娘別難受,萬事起頭兒難過幾天就好了。

張生要去多少日子。11張生說、我考試一完、立刻就回來、順心的事還能躭擱嗎。12他二人悲歡離合的情腸、眞是萬語千言、多半夜也說不盡正是詩上說的、世上萬般愁苦事、無非死別與生離。

第三十五段

1 到第二天太陽剛出來、琴童他們亂亂轟轟的把行李都搬到車上、張生就上車起身了。崔老太太那邊兒預備着三乘小轎兒帶着鶯鶯同紅娘過來、三個人都坐上轎子、送了幾里地到了河邊兒靠船的地方兒、大家下了車轎、老太太先向張生說、相公路上諸事留心、水陸平安罷。2 話畢就帶着鶯鶯要上船相送、又腿脚軟弱單身走不動、等紅娘先後攙着母女這纔勉强上了跳板、過到船上。3 那些個船有下錨的、有繫纜的、張生僱的是一隻大櫓船、船上三隻桅杆很高。4 他們過來見船家不少、船艄上坐着有柁工、還有好些拉縴的、蹲在船頭上。5 張生就叫船家幫着琴童把那行李一半兒放在客艙裏、好隨便用、一半不常

有言在先、把我女兒許配給你、其所以沒有就辦的緣故、是因為我們家的女壻向來沒有做秀才的、至不濟也是翰林出身、你若能得個翰林、也壯壯我們的門風兒啊。4 張生答說、旣是岳母如此吩咐、子壻自然要爭這一口氣的、事不宜遲、明早就起身上京。說完拜別、彼此各自分散。5 到了晚上、鶯鶯帶着紅娘過來給張生送行。紅娘上前幫着琴童收拾行李、先把衣裳一件一件疊舒展了、裝在箱子裏、見還有個包袱裝不下去、想着必是太鬆了、就告訴琴童壓緊點兒就好了。6 那屋裏籥角兒上有一大瓶酒、紅娘叫琴童倒出一半兒來預備著喝。7 林邊脚撬兒上見有雙新鞋、琴童說小了、恐怕穿着脚疼、紅娘就去叫人拏楦頭楦一楦。還沒回來之先、鶯鶯問張生說、要點心不要、各式各樣的都有、你到那上不爬村兒下不爬店兒的地方兒好、有得喫、比沒有東西總強啊。8 張生謝說很好、實在費心了、就包了些放在點心盒子裏。9 那人拏鞋回來、琴童看那箱子得捆緊些兒、纔好、就叫紅娘姐姐、請幫我繞結實這繩子、繫個活扣兒容易解。10 紅娘幫着他都弄妥當了、張生向紅娘道謝說、辛苦你了。後來行李一切都弄齊了、鶯鶯問

第三十三段

1 原來鄭恆那個東西自從丟米之後仍然兩手空空真是上天無路入地無門。俗語兒說人急上房狗急跳牆到這一天他想除非做賊再沒有活路兒了。

2 當天夜裡出了門順着牆根兒溜走了不遠兒撞見一夥子人看見他雖不認識也就猜着是同道的了拉他合了夥從此畫伏夜行也倒足喫足喝的那兒知道好運不到底世間除了士農工商總可以靠得住那兒有做賊能長遠的呢到這一天他們夥計犯了事連鄭恆也拏到官場去了審問實了定了罪名都一齊刺字充軍各犯都上了鐐銬解去了鄭恆身子本弱不到兩站就拖累死了。

3 崔老太看完了想遭難的人雖是沒出息兒到底是他的內親不由得心酸了一陣後一轉念倒是不幸中之大幸於女兒合張生的親事倒很相宜忙叫人請張相公過來。

第三十四段

1 張生正在屋裏看書聽見崔老太太請不知道什麼事也是懷着鬼胎怕那些天的事情發作了。

2 趕緊過來見面問了好老太太說道,

3 張相公我原本

第三十二段

1 老太太聽了這番話想了半天，如夢方醒，就叫紅娘去請姑娘。2 紅娘回屋裏來請鶯鶯，問老太太叫你什麼事，紅娘說，再別提了，我們私下做的事老太太全知道了。3 鶯鶯問怎麼知道的。4 紅娘說，可是若要人不知除非已莫為，姑娘想偺們家有這個歡郞還愁事不破嗎。5 鶯鶯一聽唬的心驚胆戰急間那麼怎麼好呢。6 紅娘說那道不要緊姑娘竟管去罷老太太頭裏是有氣來着叫我說了半天他那氣都消了，如今都沒有事了。7 鶯鶯纔起身一步兩蹭的挪到老太太這邊兒來本來滿肚子委曲說不出來一見老太太不由得低着頭就哭起來了。8 崔老太太原是心慈面軟的，看這個樣子又是可憐倒和顏悅色的安慰說，我思索必有個章程就是咯。9 孩兒別哭了，這件事是你娘辦錯了，放心罷，容了一聲擦了眼淚辭回繡房去了。10 鶯鶯聽見這一天的雲霧都散了，忙答應裡寔在萬難佈置皆因從前業已許過人家兒那一層躊躇的了不得，11 可是老太太嘴裡雖然這麼安慰女兒心不巧不成書恰到第二天接着娘家哥哥的一封信，打開一看，先不過問些寒暄的話，後頭竟是叙內姪鄭恆的一番結果。12 誰想

大聲說、老太太知道啊、耳聞不如眼見、他小孩子家說話東拉西扯的、萬也聽不得。10 老太太厲色說、這事左不過是你一個人兒幹的、怎麼是小孩子撒謊、他目睹眼見你還敢嘴硬不認帳麼、我告訴你、再要強嘴、那可是往身上找打咯。11 紅娘為人最有權變聽這一番震嚇的話、搪塞不開就知道是不能遮掩的了、隨即陪笑說、12 我有話要說、又不便直言、老太太要惱我的罪可是再要撒謊我一定不饒。13 崔老太太說、你有什麼眞寶的話都可以說我不生氣、老太太要想我的罪恕我的不好起初念經那一天帶了姑娘去、那不是抛頭露面惹禍招災的嗎、這纔叫孫飛虎知道姑娘的標緻了、帶了兵來要搶姑娘、那時候兒老太太說過、有人解了圍、就把姑娘許給他、是不是、後來張生化險為平救了俺們一家子、怎麼又反覆了、改做兄妹、那不成了過河兒拆橋麼、這個爽約之錯在誰身上呢、15 況且雖係私會奴婢敢保毫無劣跡、我又常在跟前兒、倘有甚麼邪情、甘心領罪、16 加之婚嫁原是好事俗語兒說單絲不成線獨木不成林、這就是天意人緣兩相湊合、旣然他們倆人都願意你老人家何苦討人嫌呢、還不分青紅皁白合我生氣、那不是更背晦了嗎、通長算起來、依我大膽勸睜個眼兒閉個眼兒就完了。

第三十一段

1 這且不提,再說崔歡郎原是別人家的兒子,過繼給崔家來的,這孩子太不長進,鑽頭覓縫兒的盡打聽事情,不知道他怎麼瞧出他們的楞縫兒來了,就跑來說長道短的告訴了老太太。 2 老太太聽了詫異的了不得,說怪不得你姐姐他們這些天幹事鬼鬼崇崇的,說話都透含糊,我就猜着是有緣故,你快去叫紅娘來。 3 歡郎去叫紅娘,鶯鶯正合紅娘做活計呢,聽見老太太叫嘍了一跳,鶯鶯遞了個眼色兒,紅娘會意就同歡郎過來。 4 老太太一見就怒容滿面的問紅娘道,你們這陣子背着我做的都是些個什麼事啊,我問你姑娘到張生屋裏去,你怎麼不回我。 5 紅娘回稟說老太太問的是什麼話,我全不懂得這些天連張相公的面兒奴婢都沒有見。 6 老太太更加惱怒說,你們做這樣兒的醜事,你還敢賴嗎,你們黑更半夜的事歡郎都告訴我了,這件事不是你替他們傳話,他們萬不敢做家門的羞恥都不顧了,如今鬧得很不像樣子了,這個罪魁不是你是誰呢。 7 紅娘轉面合歡郎低聲說,你這小少爺纔是三鼻子眼兒多出口氣兒呢,夢見什麼說什麼,盡拉些個老婆舌頭太多嘴了罷。 8 老太太說,你嘴裏合他嘟嚨甚麼,知道我耳朶聾聽不清楚,這不是安心氣我嗎。 9 紅娘

太太叫我們拜爲兄妹可是一樣兒老太太步步兒留心若是知道我過去探病、那時候兒怎麼好紅娘說人不知鬼不覺的怕什麼只要做得機密就是咯。

4 鶯鶯聽了這話很可心到了晚上帶了紅娘過張生這邊兒來了。

5 那紅娘本不是個輕浮人暫留姑娘在外自己先走了兩步免得失禮進了屋裏不好聲張、怕病人心驚見張生自然不便努嘴兒擠眼兒的只好把手一招張生就知道是鶯鶯來了、趕緊迎接出來間好只見鶯鶯進了門滿臉通紅低頭坐下。

6 張生先說愚兄賤恙較重多虧賢妹諸事慇懃又勞賢妹親來看視心中實覺不安。

7 鶯鶯含羞說些須小事何足掛齒日前一家大難臨頭不是我兄獨力救援焉有今日、小妹此來不避嫌疑不過聊盡兄妹之情。

8 二人言來語去更加敬愛紅娘在旁見夜深了怕人知覺說請姑娘回去罷天不早了鶯鶯深知有理勉强起身紅娘纔扶着回去了。

9 張生送到門外直等着鶯鶯去遠了他還在院子裏獃獃的站着心裏總是七上八下的到快天亮纔同屋裏來了。

10 從此時常見面兩下裏眞是如膠似漆的一般、張生的病一回比一回好上來了、漸漸的復了原兒了。

相公的，快請看罷。10張生一聽這個話轉憂爲喜，趕緊伸手接過來拆開一看，就說呀怎麼還是一首詩呢詳細看完了繞然大悟，說光景是今兒晚上來看我的病。11紅娘說是姑娘來看病麼他怎麼沒有合我提呢怕不能罷。12張生說明明白白兒是眞的，我想是老太太先叫我們結爲兄妹可是他盡兄妹的情分也許啊。13說話之間琴童回張生水溫熱了，澡盆也預備好了，紅娘就告別回去了。張生洗了澡覺得身上舒服了好些剛要出來活動活動忽然聽見吻喳喳的響，回頭看見貓拏住一個耗子心裏想這屋裏耗子多，小心鶯鶯來了害怕，就叫人把那些窟窿堵上。到院子裏又見地下坑坑窪窪的也叫琴童拏土填平了。

第三十段

1 不提張生在這兒靜候鶯鶯，且說紅娘囘去告訴鶯鶯張生見天喫藥總不見大好那大夫說他怕是心病呢。2 鶯鶯嘆了一聲說哎我前思後想要親自去看他又覺得很爲難，紅娘說其實也沒有什麼爲難的人家從前怎麼救咱們呢，又有拜兄妹這一層姑娘就是去看看病也是應當盡心的。3 鶯鶯說，雖然老

第二十九段

1 紅娘等大夫去遠了、低聲說、老太太合姑娘爲相公的病憂悶的了不得、許了愿、那一天相公的病好了、就宰牛祭天。 2 張生說宰牛作什麼殺生害命的與我有什麼益處、反倒添了罪了。 3 紅娘本是有情有義的人、他這種氣話饒不理會、倒還煎湯熬藥的伺候他、又叫琴童熬點兒粥兒、勤攪着點兒不要叫他糊了。 4 張生身上覺得不爽快、止不住的蒳撓、想能洗個澡纔舒服、就叫琴童把水温熱了、那院子裏現成的井、井臺兒上有轆轤、琴童就慌手冒腳的跑到井上去打水、幾乎没跌個觔斗、紅娘看他這麼冒失、喊著說、 5 嘻、那井是頂深的小心些兒、失了腳可不是玩兒的、琴童笑嘻嘻的答應着打了水、温在火上。 6 張生等水這個工夫兒、就同紅娘在那兒說閒話兒、問他、你們姑娘此刻在家做甚麼呢、紅娘聽見心裏好笑、 7 假意說、我來的時候姑娘拏着釣魚竿兒釣魚呢、我們花園子裏原本有座小山子、底下都是泉眼、流到池子裏頭、那水就有下巴頦兒這麼深、水裏各種的魚多着呢、等相公病好了可以請去逛逛。 8 張生私下想、難爲鶯鶯倒有心釣魚、我這兒有意、他怎麼反無情呢。 9 紅娘見他沉吟不語、剛轉身要走、忽然一愣說、喲、我差一點兒忘了、姑娘還有個字帖兒叫我給

兒上不便惹他忍氣吞聲的依舊跳墻回來。5 心裏想這個氣真覺得難受又捨不得走竟是深不是淺不是左不做人難這麼一來這病越發利害了第二天法本聽見恩客有病憂悶得很簡直來告訴老太太。老太太聽見也是煩悶就叫人請大夫又盼咐紅娘去看。我從來酸鹹苦辣都沒有受過昨兒冤屈的不得俗語說'黃泉路上無老少怕是好不了咯。7 紅娘來問這時候相公好些張生說嗐至於呢你安心養病罷我帶了劑藥來是姑娘交給我的你喫下去管保就好了。8 紅娘聽了這話心如刀割笑說嗐'那兒是那麼懷肚子有石頭這麼硬嘴裏流涎黏涎子這是夾氣傷寒的來派。9 正說着大夫來了看了病說現在時令不好上吐下瀉的多這位相公倒不是。10 琴童在旁邊兒插口說相公還咳嗽呢今兒喝水喝嗆了更加利害了。11 張生生氣說誰叫你混答言語的等問着你再開口。12 大夫候了脈就拏出個藥包兒來說這兒有兩樣兒藥攪和着喫早晚分兩次用一兩可以見效。13 紅娘把那藥細看了一回間大夫這黑膏子也是藥麼。大夫合他說九散膏丹都是藥這醫學裏深奧得很那兒能容易知道呢。14 隨即辭了張生說明兒後兒再來奉看罷說完就走了。

第二十八段

1 張生又把詩拏出來左思右想、越想越對心裏巴不能彀兒的到了晚上纔好。往外看一看纔晌午錯、等了半天太陽平西了、回頭聽了聽鐘怎麼不響、一看站住了就說了琴童一頓、問他為什麼沒上弦。琴童答應着就趕緊上上了。一會兒見快黑上來了、不大的工夫兒又掌上燈喜歡的張生就從墻上往那邊兒望、那兒有個人影兒呢、只得又回屋裏來、直等到定更似乎纔聽見環珮聲響忙又上墻一看、果然是鶯鶯來了、張生輕手躡腳兒的跳下墻去。 2 鶯鶯一見間錯瞧了、只是因為我想情度理不肯把那扇子給老太太看。就是什麼人子細一看原來是張生就正顏厲色的說、我是光明正大的人相公別拏你有病說罷我這些天叫紅娘常來問候、也是盡我的心還有別的話要叫紅娘傳說、又怕他說話含含糊糊的傳錯了、所以想着是當面奉勸纔妥當我的愚意可是當今的老佛爺最重的是科甲誰不知道嗎俗語說寶劍贈與烈士紅粉贈與佳人、你的文墨精通怎麼不立個獨占鼇頭的志向、將來建功立業、誰不尊重呢、若是這樣兒的老不成材兒日後不過是個白丁兒、人就看得稀鬆平常了。 3 這一片嚴詞說完轉身就回去了。 4 張生纔要說話、想他正在氣頭

的送了去。7紅娘看這個翻來復去的脾氣無法可治不由得失笑說，8哎，姑娘不怕他動心嗎叫他看見又要添病了。9鶯鶯更羞惱變成怒了賭氣子把信摔在地下。10紅娘只得檢起來心裏納著氣兒細想我低三兒下四的伺候他怎麼一動兒兩動兒就生氣我替他們來回的送信辛辛苦苦的圖甚麼。11想了會子也無法藏着一肚子氣直過張生那邊去了。12且說張生盼紅娘不來在屋裏踱來踱去要想個갔兒找他就叫琴童去合紅娘要個針線來釘書，恰巧紅娘正拏着信自言自語的來了。13把信遞給張生張生打開一看，上頭也是一首詩，念了半天纔揣摩出裏頭的意思鶯鶯很有心要合他會面，就喜出望外的告訴紅娘說，14我看他這詩裏頭明露着約我今兒晚上相會你替我想想怎麼去呢若是跳牆過去好不好。15紅娘假怒說嘻，這是什麼話怎麼盡造謠言說瞎話不告訴老太太就便宜了你這可是得一步進一步，貪心不足了。16張生回說我幹什麼撒謊呢的確是真的絲毫不錯。暗想小姐怎麼竟有私約這可是奇怪他知道張生有病彷彿不關心似的誰想又有這番舉動實在是出人意料之外了。想完了辭別張生回去了。17紅娘

娘說、扇子上可別落款、隄防着老太太看見、他疑心太重。23張生想這話有理、就研濃了墨蘸飽了筆、一眨眼兒的工夫就寫完了一首秃頭兒的詩、遞給紅娘、囑付說姑娘看見說甚麼你可來告訴我。

第二十七段

1 紅娘就回去了、把桃送給鶯鶯、心裡想這扇子不好簡直的給他、就搭赸着放在桌子上不言不語的走開了。2 鶯鶯一眼看見拏過來、咳說這把扇子是那兒來的、是誰寫的、我看不出筆跡來、噯必定是那張生寫的、怎麼這麼安心瞧不起我、不用說是你昨兒見面兒的話、你這麼個頭不怕對不光兒來麼、我去告訴老太太、看你怎麼樣。3 紅娘忙說、姑娘千萬別生氣、這個錯兒不在我身上、主意我也不敢出、若是老太太問我、我如何敢說姑娘打發我送東西去呢。4 鬧得鶯鶯是輕不好重不好、就問他、那相公病好了麼。5 紅娘說、沒很好、勸他喫藥那都是白說、問他必定要怎麼纔好呢、他也不言語。6 鶯鶯忖度了半天、心裏有點兒抱慚、強說、那麼我有寫得了的一封信、你趕緊點兒給他送去。12 紅娘答應了，第二天就來告訴張生說事情辦的有點影子了。張生問怎麼見得呢。13 紅娘說昨兒晚上他聽著琴聲兒直發怔，彷彿有什麼心事似的，就叫我買果子送來給您納相公想明人還用細講麼。14 張生說很好，那麼倒叫你費心了。正說著，忽然害起冷來了，渾身發料紅娘唬了一跳，問是怎麼了。15 張生說，我這兩天發瘧子呢。紅娘說，那麼你就喫點兒藥安心靜養罷。16 說著就上廟門口兒去，可巧有人挑著一挑子西瓜賣呢。紅娘間他怎麼賣。他要了一個價兒，紅娘還了個價兒，他嘴裏說不夠本兒，手裏可拏著扁擔不走，等著又添了點兒他纔賣了。17 紅娘把西瓜就給張生送來，問他此刻點兒嗎。18 張生說，好些兒了，這東西送得很巧，看樣子還可以，你不喫點兒嗎。19 紅娘說多謝多謝，張生儘自抓癢癢兒，整夜不能睡，此刻斜靠着炕桌子打盹兒忽然看見琴桌兒上盤子裏有買下的桃，倒很好，就間紅娘你們姑娘愛喫桃不愛喫，煩你拏幾個去回敬他罷。20 原來這屋裏蚊子多張生儘自抓癢癢兒，整夜不能睡，此刻斜靠着炕桌子打盹兒忽然看見琴桌兒上盤子裏有買下的桃，倒很好，就間紅娘你們姑娘愛喫桃不愛喫，煩你拏幾個去回敬他罷。21 紅娘說，我們姑娘倒還愛喫，把好的揀了幾個。剛要走，張生又叫他等一等兒，說，我寫把扇子，你一塊兒帶了去。22 紅

第二十六段

1 紅娘跟倒他屋裡去看他的精神大不高與低聲問道相公爲什麽這麽煩悶。
2 張生說我多喝了兩盅。
3 紅娘抵着嘴兒笑說你那兒喝酒來着沒酒兒三分醉只怕這個話有點兒不對罷不如宣說了纔好呢張生說我盡是白費事落不出好來老太太言不應口在他倒不要緊可是叫我終身怎麽受呢。
4 紅娘說啊我猜得就不錯你何不問我我倒有個法子。
5 張生忙問事已如此你有甚麽着兒。
6 紅娘笑着說各人的巧妙不同我說出來管保叫你喜歡相公不是最講究琴嗎我們姑娘最愛聽的是琴你今兒晚上彈琴看他聽見說甚麽。
7 張生一聽這話就跳起來說是眞的麽這麽說倒對我的心了那麽我晚上就彈一套琴託你在旁邊兒看他的光景再來告訴我。
8 紅娘答應着去了、到晚上鶯鶯猛然聽見琴聲很詫異。
9 用心用意的聽了半天問紅娘這是那兒的琴韻悠揚不知道甚麽人彈呢。
10 紅娘說這多半兒是張相公彈琴解悶在這兒住不常了。
11 鶯鶯一聽喫了一驚如同我看他席散之後很透憂悶怕坐在針氈上一樣勉強說他不能這就走罷你明兒聽着街上有賣好果子的買

9 說着就帶了紅娘過來了。見了張生，拜了一拜，張生還了一揖，大家坐下老太太細看他們二人郎才女貌眞是天生的一對兒佳偶心裏愁思想道若不是女兒有了人家兒叫他們成就婚姻豈不是好如今是無可奈何了只得合鶯鶯說姑娘自今以後別把張相公當外人看待你們倆兄妹相稱彼此友愛我心裏也安了。10 鶯鶯聽了這個話的意思簡直的是好了疤瘌忘了疼心裏說不好咯，媽媽怎麼又變了卦了。於是愁眉不展的坐了一會子告辭了張生就走了。

11 紅娘這事有點兒撓頭人說好事多磨眞眞可惜。河拆橋了，剛要開口自覺著怪難啟齒的老太太猜着他的心意就迎頭說有個緣故相公不知道小女是從小時候兒許了我內姪鄭恒了，相公救我們一家子寔在是難以補報，今生今世怎麼能忘相公的恩義呢。13 俗語兒說眼不見嘴不饞耳不聽心不煩張生雖是個老寔人，在危急之時挺身出力並沒有望謝的心，今兒聽老太太這樣兒的話未免大失所望，一句話也回答不出來，提離提盞的身子都不能自主滿桌子美酒嘉肴白看着他，一點兒也喫不下去，不大的工夫兒悶悶不樂的告辭了老太太就走了。

第二十五段

1 底下人登時擺上飯來,酒席肴饌檨檨兒講究,乾果子鮮果子都有,席上的傢伙都是古窰的瓷器,合紙那麼薄。 2 屋裏四面的書架子直到棚頂兒滿滿兒的堆着都是書擺飯的時候兒張生不住的四下裏看,原來這書都是南邊兒刷來初印的紙板很好。 3 老太太見張生眼光全在書架子上,就間相公所講究的書是什麼檨兒的,張生說這書倒是越舊越好,就是一樣兒,裏頭容易蠹魚子,總不免蛀壞了。 4 老太太說這兒的書經史子集檨檨兒都有,底下相公要看,儘管拏着看就是了。 5 說着說着大茶都上齊了,管家請老太太讓客,老太太拏筷子布了幾檨兒茶,就說相公別客氣,纔好啊,我的牙都活動了,嚼不動這些東西。紅娘你去請姑娘來陪着罷。 6 那鶯鶯平日是睡慣了早覺的,今兒知道請張相公喫飯,所以起來得極早梳洗完了在繡房裡悶坐,等了半天紅娘來說, 7 老太太請姑娘陪張相公喫飯呢,我想這麼辦喜事老太太真是會省錢,從前那麼大手大脚的花慣了,現在又打起算盤來了,眞是大處不算小處算。 8 鶯鶯說,你說話太歛咯,叫老太太聽見怎麼能不打你呢,總得收着點兒纔好。

第二十四段

1 張生轉身進來看見紅娘忙忙忉忉的打二門裏出來。 2 就笑問他,今兒甚麼風吹了你來。紅娘就說因為老太太要請相公搬到書房裏住,先請明兒過去喫早飯。 3 張生說哎何必費事我可不敢當老太太既然叫我我一定去奉擾。 4 到第二天打扮得整整齊齊的。剛要戴帽子琴童說那是老樣兒的帽子不大與時何不換一頂時樣兒的呢。 5 張生換了帽子衣冠齊楚斯斯文文的就過那邊兒去了。 6 底下人趕緊掀起書房的簾子張生進去看牆上掛着一張畫兒就是鶯鶯的行樂圖畫得活脫兒合鶯鶯一個樣兒又精工又細緻。 7 張生飽看了一頓都目瞪口獃了。老太太過來一見忙說了些感激的話張生作揖謙讓說, 8 老太太過獎了,常言道與人方便自己方便,這算得了什麼功勞呢。

去領餉,我只好告辭了。 5 張生一聽是公事在身不敢很留又切實的謝說,這一邊驚師動衆小弟實然是於心不安一邊兒說着一邊兒送將軍出去臨別又再三的說勞駕的很了。 6 將軍謙讓說那兒的話呢後會有期請留步罷說完就彼此拜別。

第二十二段

1 白馬將軍看了信、大喫一驚、嗐說了不得、立時點動人馬、搖旗納喊的直奔普救寺來了。2 張生聽見人馬的聲音彷彿天塌地陷一個樣兒、就知道是救星來了。3 那孫飛虎遙望這個聲勢心就忐忑起來了、只得把刀插在鞘子裏直蹭到將軍馬跟前跪下滿嘴裏告饒兒。4 白馬將軍原知道這個賊是積年漏網的大盜到手不拏豈不錯了機會呢、就傳令把他就地正了法、那賊的手下人准他們改邪歸正聽候安置繞可以寬恕。

第二十三段

1 事情平復之後張生出來見了白馬將軍拜謝他救命之恩。將軍又讚張生的智略、彼此謙虛了幾句、將軍隨把大拇指頭上一個鹿觭角的搬指兒摘下來送給張生說、2 偺們多年不見、把這個作爲見面禮兒罷、老兄可別推却。3 張生雙手接過來道了謝誇讚這搬指兒做的精巧、間這花樣兒是做出來的麽。將軍說這花樣兒是長成的。他們這一席話難以盡述。4 張生留他住了兩天、到第三天白馬將軍說這兩天騷擾得很了、明兒是我們營裏放餉的日子、衆兵都

然想起他來、就對張生說、打發惠明去滿行、可有一樣兒、他的脾氣是軟硬不喫、若是舉薦他、他必不肯去、總要拏話激發他纔行呢。3張生想了一想說、我有法子、就高聲叫說、除了惠明、有敢給白馬將軍送信去的快來見我、那惠明聽見這樣兒話、急忙跑來鬧著偏要去、張生索性再逗他兩句說、那不是玩兒的事啊、別人還不能、何況你若是悞了事、誰擔這個不是呢。4惠明楊楊得意的答說、饅頭沒有餡兒、我喫著怪沒味兒的、等我砍死那賊頭兒做肉餡子喫纔好相公儘管把信交給我、可是那白馬將軍若是不來、爲誰是問呢。5張生說那與你不相干。法本又加一句擠對他說、你再替我帶著辦件別的事罷。惠明急說、那可不行、一身不能當二役。6張生見他志向無敵就說、那麼著你快去罷。7惠明趾高氣揚立刻告別、就單人獨馬的出門去了、一邊兒跑一邊兒嚷著說、你們誰來試試誰的勁兒大儘著力兒試試看看誰強誰弱。8原來這廟在頂高的趄坡子上、那馬出了門下坡兒容易、就撒開腿跑連竄帶跳的彷彿驚了一樣。9那賊就是追步下那兒追得上惠明一氣兒直跑到蒲關打懷裏掏出信來當面呈給白馬將軍、把那情節一五一十都報明白了。

第二十段

1 可是張生雖然這麼勸慰那賊兵還在廟外吶喊不止。張生旣說了大話不能不想個好法子以踐其言。忙出來問道誰能先送封信給孫飛虎去法本說、這姓孫的是個粗魯人不通文理、寫信是不中用的不如傳話倒簡决。麼很好、你能去說一聲兒嗎法本說曖、我不勝其任這個大事誰敢承擔呢。3 張生說不用你做別的、就告訴孫飛虎說、此時姑娘嚇得心驚肉跳呢、把兵退後一箭之地、等兩三天姑娘定一定神兒就送出來、你快去罷別發怯原是膽怯支吾了半天纔答應着出去、把這話傳說了、孫飛虎先還不肯應允、再三的央告他、纔勉強答應說到三天不送出人來、我可是殺個雞犬不留。

第二十一段

1 法本回來把這話告訴了張生。張生一聽、說旣是那麼着可別躭擱工夫了。就嚷着問誰有膽子趕早兒送封信給白馬將軍去、緊催他飛速快來。2 那些和尙裏頭沒有一個人敢言語一聲兒、倒是廟後院兒裏有個燒火的老和尙名叫惠明、雖是個笨漢子、拳脚倒打得好、揝着拳頭打人沒有敢跟他還手的。法本忽

呀,這個禍事可從來沒有經過呀。4 老太太聽了這一番話,喫這一驚非同小可,趕緊的蹀蹀躞躞跑到鶯鶯屋裏告訴他,鶯鶯聽了唬得讓啕慟哭一句話都說不出來了。那老太太年紀過大遇了事說話都很背晦就向和尚說,哎我的親戚本家沒有什麼人可倚靠就有一個娘家的哥哥又陞到蘇州去了,誰能快找他囘來纔好。5 法本說,那話還提他幹什麼只好替老太太問廟裏的那些人或者有退兵的法子,也不定老太太說好巴不能殼兒的呢,你快去問罷。6 就轉臉兒合鶯鶯說,若是把你送出去實在是丟人,不把你送出去我們的性命又不保。我想問廟裏的人有能殺賊救難的,就把你許給他,你肯不肯。7 鶯鶯見這件事太急差口難開的無奈點了點頭。8 法本就出去對衆人說了這番話。只見張生走進院子來說老太太別怕別怕,那賊我倒能降伏他們,但放寬心就是咯。9 老太太聽了這話很喜歡說,你一個書生那兒能用武呢。10 張生說我固然不會動武,我可有個朋友是白馬將軍他駐劄蒲關那賊剛有信兒要來的時候兒我就打發人知會他了,他必有計策來救。11 這個話不過是登時安慰老太太的意思。老太太一聽越發樂的不可支了,真是心悅誠服,就說事情辦妥必當重報鶯鶯心裏也安穩了好些。

第十九段

1 說着就彼此分手,那頭目不敢遲延,立刻回到山上,如此如彼的稟報了孫飛虎。

2 孫飛虎大喜,以爲此去定能得勝,第二天帶著可山的僂儸,嘴裏吹著喇叭蜂擁的來了,把那廟團團圍住,圍的水洩不通,口口聲聲要鶯鶯出來答話。

3 法本知道了,嚇得慌慌張張,就跑到老太太院子裏,喊叫說,老太太聽見了嗎,外頭來了一大股賊,那賊頭兒孫飛虎是個最凶惡的強盜,大不通情理,常是圖財害命,帶了那麼整千整萬的人來,搵鑼擂鼓,大喊,著要鶯鶯姑娘出去答話,哎

緊抱了家去。

6 又走了幾步,瞧見有個人抱著小狗兒,那狗耳朶奉拉著很好看,打算要買,合他講了半天的價兒,總沒有停當,仍舊逛了一會子,又要進廟。

7 那些孩子還在門外貪玩兒,不躱開道兒,張生皆因不高興,惱說,罷讓我過去,把那玩意兒攔開些兒,別佔這麼寬地方兒。

8 嗐,起開罷,讓我過去,把那錢頭目兒不走,就說,今兒您納還不回家嗎。

9 那孩子們嚇得趕緊讓了道兒,張生進了廟,見那頭目兒不走,就說,今兒您納還不回家嗎。

10 原來這人早打聽了鶯鶯的情節,正要去告訴他的寨主,就說,可不是嗎,我正要走呢,驚擾老兄這幾天,實在是過意不去,改天再謝罷。

見了、硯台也常找不着、你管幹什麼的。

14 琴童說、這寔在不是小的錯兒、這些東西使完了都是擱在原地方兒。

第十八段

1 那頭目在旁邊兒看這光景猜着八九分是爲他在這兒的緣故、心裏很見笑、踏趷着問、老兄穿的油鞋很好、不是從廣東帶來的麼。2 張生滿心是氣一語不發、姓錢的又冷笑着問琴童、你跟你們老爺倒不累得慌月月兒可有多少工錢、琴童看主人的眼色兒、也不敢回答、大家怔了一會子、張生轉臉兒合琴童要水烟袋、琴童這纔瞧見了、趕緊拏過來。張生又怒罵說、見。琴童一時找不着張生喫了兩袋烟、扔下那姓錢的太粗魯、有哄狗絞豬了廟門。 3 睜着眼兒的瞎子擺在那兒看不見。4 可巧有好些個孩子在門外頭玩呢、玩兒的有摔跤的、還有看小鷄兒對鬪、賭輸贏的、說這隻鷄鬪不過那隻鷄、又有最小的在那兒分辯說、這些鷄公的母的怎麼分得清呢、年紀長的告訴他們說草鷄是下蛋公鷄是打鳴兒。年幼的偏不服這個話。5 這些熱鬧兒上加着有個最小的孩子在人羣兒裏穿、沒有人管。張生過來看見、恐怕擠了他、很心疼、叫人趕

一聲說啊不在了嗎寔在是好人不長壽真是可惜 4 隔了一會兒又問閣下在此地住是單居呀是搭夥呢 那頭目答應說啊請問有個崔家原在前莊兒住聽說他們搬到這兒來了真的麼 5 張生說倒不是搭夥這廟裏都是同居各爨 6 那頭目答應說啊請問有個崔家原在前莊兒住聽說他們搬到這兒來了真的麼 7 張生聽這話怔了一怔似乎記得那人從前在村兒裏不就說那我倒不知道不關己事不勞神您再問問別位罷 的越想越起疑怕他這一來不懷好意只好閧住這個話意住了兩天不肯動身 8 那姓錢的見一計不成只好另打別的主意燒透一回比一回不濟今兒這些個東西更壞得利害咯 找尋琴童又發作了說這些天的茶越發不好了煮肉也沒有煮透燒肉也沒 9 張生見他不走氣不打一處來喫飯的時候兒借著 做的張生說誰叫你做茶來着必是那廚子又醉了快叫他來 10 琴童說這是小的 邊回來說廚子來了張生面紅耳赤的直問他為什麼盡喝酒不好好兒的做茶 11 琴童出去一 必得罰你的工錢看你以後留神不留神 12 那廚子原是個酒鬼碰著這個勢頭兒心裏想這繧是貼錢買罪受呢不敢辯白忍氣吞聲的出去了 13 張生又把錯兒挪到琴童身上問他我屋裏的東西原是叫你看着的怎麼小刀子也不

第十六段

1 這且不題單說離此不遠有一座山內中有夥強盜佔踞多年寨主名叫孫飛虎帶領著僂儸約有一千多人到處搶奪。2 他那一天也在普救寺看見鶯鶯燒香回到寨裏合他手下人說剛纔廟裏那女子長得十分好看我意欲娶他做個壓寨夫人你們大家夥兒誰能立這個頭功。3 那夥伴兒說那頭有個頭目姓錢的回稟說那到不難可得'依我的主意纔行。4 那孫飛虎原不是言聽計從的脾氣聽著問尊駕能有甚麼好法子嗎。5 那錢頭目明知是瞧不起他的話假作謙恭回說風聞有我們個同鄉姓張的在那廟裏住著呢容我去看看他就可以順便兒打聽打聽。6 孫飛虎聽這話很對路喜歡的受不得就說很好辦成之後重重有賞。7 這錢頭目得了令不敢躭擱就改作平常人的打扮、一直的往普救寺來。

第十七段

1 見了張生彼此道了久違、說了幾句客套話、那錢頭目說、請問尊大人從前的病如今大好了麽。2 張生謝說、承問、承問、家父早已去世了。3 這頭目嘆了

去打個問訊、指着張生告訴老太太說、我這位朋友也要在今兒個給他爻親念經。 4 老太太見張生是個書生的樣兒、就說那也是好事、都在一天念也沒甚麼不可以的說完了、在大殿上就做起佛事來廟裏來看熱鬧兒的那些人也有老頭兒也有小夥子看見鶯鶯都說這個姑娘纔好看呢、大家夥兒你言我語的、鬧的和尚們都是心神不定、幹事也顚三倒四的了法本見他們無心念經、嚷說、嗐你們別草草了事、用點兒心纔好呢。 5 那殿外有個小和尚在那兒獃著法本吩咐他把那果子拏刀子剖了皮兒切碎了、那小和尚答應了、一邊兒切果子一邊兒也只顧着看鶯鶯鬧得他手指頭就叫刀子刺破了法本罵他不中用、好喫懶做的、不是東西。 6 這都是鶯鶯相貌出衆的緣故、不但是小和尚一個人兒失神連廚房裏有個和尚天生的又聾又啞、在院子裏拏斧子劈劈柴、一個不留神把斧子頭兒也摔掉了當時又有個一隻虎也跑來看鶯鶯不料被斧子頭兒絆了個大趴虎兒。 7 這麽亂轟轟的眞可笑、惹得法本又是氣又是急沒有法子只好掐著誦珠兒念咒假粧著看不見。 8 佛事完了鶯鶯跟著老太太回去了張生也磕了頭囘來、換了衣裳、脫了靴子。 9 在那兒悶悶不樂、坐臥不安、趿拉著鞋滿地走。

第十五段

1 誰想第二天還是照舊,到了第三天早起張生忽問今兒不是十五了麼。琴童說不錯,是十五了。張生趕著打了辮子,前邊兒去問法本念經的事預備停當了沒有法本說,還沒有安當呢,也就快了。張生打懷裏掏出一塊銀子來雙手奉上說這是十足紋銀一錠作爲香資,請收下罷。 2 法本謝說相公過於費心了,我應當効勞纔是。 3 張生說那兒的話呢,他們正在這兒開談,崔老太太合鶯鶯在家裏已經齋戒沐浴完了,一齊過廟裏前院兒來往客堂裏走。法本迎上前

5 張生拏過來剝了皮,喫了一點兒說這東西又酸又澁狠不好。 6 琴童見左不好右不好沒有法子又想起廚子買了些嫩豆腐來問主人說您喫不喫。張生說叫廚子竟點兒下剩的煮罷。兒的茶都鹹得利害又沒有往常的香味兒就盼咐琴童告訴他總要留神纔好。 8 琴童答應了,歛了傢伙端上茶來。那茶滾熱的,渴不到嘴,張生等著涼一涼兒的時候兒就伸著一條腿蹺著一條腿,左不過是生氣。琴童只得忍氣吞聲,指望他主人氣頭兒過咯就好了。

7 做了來喫完了,又叨叨廚子說,今

偷著看原來是鶯鶯在樹底下燒香呢。5 樹林子雖密、面貌還露得出一半點兒來看他的模樣兒倒像比從前越發俏皮似的、不由得更加愛慕了。6 鶯鶯燒完了香那紅娘指著那些棵小樹兒說這棵樹上的果子都熟了、那棵樹上纔結可惜樹根子都叫螞蟻蛀了。7 這種剌剌不休的話張生都聽得很清楚、心裏想這些小樹兒不如拔了去省得攬眼、可巧琴童出來見他主人在半懸空裏爬著牆急忙的叫說老爺可別撒手小心摔下來、可不是玩兒的啊。8 張生唶說怎麼這麼大驚小怪的、要叫人都知道麼。

第十四段

1 等了一會子鶯鶯家去了、張生回到屋裏來琴童端過夜飯來誰想張生心裏是七上八下的看什麼都不合式就靠著桌子盡找尋他們。2 說這廚子做東西忒腌臢米裏盡是沙子潤的不淨為什麼不拏篩子過一過酒也這麼涼你怎麼不燙、喝了一口又說這個味兒也苦得很快拏瓶子倒回去。3 琴童答應了端上湯來張生嚐、更不對心思急說這湯怎麼落上土了、快把浮頭兒的撤了去、緊底下的也給倒了。4 琴童說纔買了個石榴不知道甜不甜老爺嚐嚐

第十三段

1 且說那張生還在院子裏一個人兒站著思來想去心裏說這是我自已䇶撞難怪那頭說話不饒人想到這兒眞不耐煩就坐在一塊石頭上納悶兒等到傍晚兒的時候兒琴童打下房兒過來看見他主人臉上發愁嚇了一跳說喲冰涼的石頭老爺坐在那兒不怕冰著麼嘻這兒蠍子多小心螫著罷。

2 張生厭煩說這陰涼兒裏坐著倒涼快你幹什麼來了琴童說請老爺喫飯來了。

3 張生說我嗓子裏嚥不下去你們喫你們的罷仍舊沒動窩兒直坐到半夜月明如畫猛然聽見牆那邊兒有女子的聲兒。

4 張生躡手躡脚兒的爬上牆去嘴多舌的人聽見告訴老太太那還了得咯。

4 張生說哎我拙嘴笨顋的不會說話請你寬恕些兒以後我多加謹愼就是了紅娘說啊原該如此纔好別了張生囘去。

5 告訴鶯鶯說那一天見著的那個秀才姑娘記得嗎敢情是個姓張的纔剛又遇見了就把彼此說的話一五一十的學說了一遍。

6 鶯鶯想了一會兒就猜著張生的心思了眞叫他半驚半喜忙說你可別告訴老太太呀。

7 紅娘說那可自然當言則言我怎麼不知道呢。

第十二段

1 自此之後張生天天兒在院子裏遊玩合紅娘雖然遇見過幾次總是羞口難開。2 這一天寔在是忍耐不住，說有件事奉託姑娘果能成全我就感激不盡了底下遇著姑娘有事我也必然盡心幫助姑娘是知道的只要兩個人齊心努力甚麼事不能成呢。可是你們老太太家法過嚴託你在裏頭周旋別偏著那邊兒總得向著我這邊兒纔好。3 紅娘一聽心裏想著這話怎麼這麼冒失就說相公太懵懂咯好歹都不知道了滿嘴裏胡說八道的若叫多

在十五一齊念經有甚麼不行的嗎。6 張生一聽就喜歡得眉開眼笑那紅娘就問法本這位相公這麼笑是什麼緣故呢。7 那法本原是老江湖什麼事情也瞞不過他那底細他早已看出來了就說倒沒有甚麼別的意思這位不過是聽見十五能彀一齊念經心裏樂極了紅娘聽了這話就進客房裏暑坐一坐兒悄悄兒的間屋裏的和尚說外頭那一位姓什麼那和尚一五一十的都告訴了他紅娘出來要走張生就趁勢問道姑娘是給誰辦事紅娘說我給我們老太太辦說著就扭頭回去了。

兒桌椅也都齊備了。12 張生看了一遍就說、還罷了、這桌腿子鏇的都好、椅子也結實、這沒有什麼說的了、就告訴廟裏的人、這個是該攔在這兒的、這兒是該攔這個的、牆上再掛四幅畫兒叫他們小心些兒別弄破了、這些個收拾完了叫琴童馬上就搬了行李來安排好了。

第十一段

1 主僕二人住下之後過了幾天張生見個小姑娘帶著小孩子出來問法本、給崔大人念經的事定了日子沒有法本說日子是定了本月十五。2 張生看這小姑娘長得很俊、首飾都是鍍金的、頭兒梳的也端正就扯了法本一下兒低聲問道這是崔府上什麼人。3 法本說他自然是崔姑娘的了頭名叫紅娘那鶯鶯小姐本是才貌雙全這紅娘跟著他對雙生兒他姑娘見他能言快語說話做事痛快臉上又很惱憽諸事都靠他、倒是姑娘一個大幫手。4 張生聽這一番話就掉過頭來高聲向法本說、從我父親去了世我早要念經來著、趁這個機會託師傅捎帶捎帶行不行。5 法本還沒得回答、那紅娘本是好心腸兒又看見張生是個斯文人就低聲說這位相公要

人跟著取錢就手兒找個木匠做那些應用的東西又間法本修齊了得多少日子法本說大約十來天的工夫兒就完了說完就分手找工人去了。

第十段

1 琴童在旁邊兒聽他主人這樣兒話心裏想著這個顧前不顧後的脾氣可不行就趕緊說老爺帶的銀子不多在這兒都花了到京裏怎麼樣呢。2 張生怒說這是你該管的麽我甘心情願替老師爻出力與你何干呢。3 琴童心裏暗說俗語有兩句順情說好話耿直惹人嫌由他去罷我也難管了。4 過了些日子張生又到廟裏問法本那房子得了沒有法本說房子到快完了可惜那木匠太笨傢伙做得不合式纔叫他從新另做了。5 張生看這麽躭擱日子心裏著急就親自找那個木匠去。6 告訴他說那桌子椅子得趕緊的做你總要照我的話辦得留點兒神纔好。7 木匠說老爺通共要幾件訴你要兩張桌子五張椅子倆搭五哇不是七個嗎就回頭嘱咐琴童著他們做一時一刻都別躭擱。9 琴童問限他幾天做得了呢。10 張生說這個東西也不多三五天兒總可以完了罷。11 那房子是早已修好了不到五天

第九段

1 到了第二天、張生一早兒起來就到廟裏去見了老和尚法本。

2 彼此通了姓名之後、張生就說要租幾間房子法本先問尊駕府上是那兒。

3 張生說我是外鄉人、來這兒為的是辦點兒事、在店裏住著不方便、火食也太貴、所以要搬開、瞧著寶剎很好、打算搬進來、還要挨著西邊兒那家兒近些兒纔好。

4 這都是張生為人樸實、向來說話不藏私、所以心裏有什麼說什麼。

5 法本說這倒沒有動手呢、張生說大可以慕化重修、可是廚房烟熏火燎得很腌臢、我原要收拾來著、還巧咯那邊兒有兩間西廂房、

6 法本說這是崔家的家廟、他住的房子就在隔壁院牆就是他的住房、家私不是沒有可不知道這項錢他肯出不肯出、不過劃著多花點兒銀子罷咧、就說你儘管修蓋若是不夠、都在我身上、我幫著你好不好。

7 張生想這個事情我

8 法本道謝說、好極了、多承施主美意。

9 張生登時請他就打發

沏碗新的來。5小沙彌趕著換了好茶,喝茶之後彼此在廟裏各處遊玩。張生猛然看見西邊兒有個花園子,門是半掩半開的,裏頭有一位姑娘帶著一個丫頭也在那兒逛。6那姑娘臉皮兒雪白,嘴唇兒鮮紅,頭髮又是漆黑的,梳著個元寶鬢,頭上插著清香的玫瑰花兒,耳朵上帶着碧綠的耳環子,手腕子上還有一對焦黄的金鐲子,身上穿的是翠藍布大衫,加上佩著好些珠寶玉器都是金子鑲成的,是人沒他打扮的那麼齊整。7張生一見心裡驚異的了不得,連身子都不自主了。那姑娘在門裡看見張生唇紅齒白,舉止不凡,真不是個尋常人的樣兒,恰與張生心意相同,張生就問法聰,你知道那姑娘是誰家的。8法聰回答說,那是官宦人家,崔大人的家眷,崔大人不在了之後,崔老太太帶著姑娘寄居在此,手頭兒上寬綽,真是逍遙快樂得很。9張生暗想道,我普天下都走偏了,看見的女子也真不少,那兒還有比這個好的呢,可惜了兒的就是有一樣兒,在這兒多住些日子,未免悞了考期,若是去考試又怕錯了這個機會,真叫我進退兩難,心裏猶豫不決,再一轉念有這樣的好姑娘,我甯可不去考試罷。10就問法聰,這兒有房子沒有,我也要搬到廟裏來住。11法聰說,師傅沒在家,

第八段

帶著兵住在蒲關防守他的武藝超羣調度有法人都稱他爲白馬將軍。6張生惦記著他想著何不抽空兒先去看看那朋友然後再上京於事也無妨就繞了兩步道兒到了蒲關在關廂裏找個客店住下了。因爲勞碌得很要歇息歇息再出去遊逛。7這麼著歇了一會兒就問店裏的夥計這兒有甚麼可去的地方夥計說有個普救寺離這兒不很遠那兒十分有趣兒。8張生說哦是了你先弄點兒東西我喫我餓極了。9那夥計就上街去買了個滷牲口來又端了兩碗滷麪。10張生喫完了就吩咐店裏夥計們餵馬小心照應零碎東西就帶著琴童一齊出了店門。

1這一天本是蒲關的廟會路上的人眞是川流不息的很難走。2琴童大聲說你們起開別攔著道兒那些人就讓開了一條路主僕二人毿過去了一直的奔了普救寺走了幾步兒遠遠的看見這座廟眞是威武得很。3到了廟裏頭曲曲灣灣的走了半天毿出來一個小和尙名叫法聰彼此通了名姓就讓到屋裏去喝茶。4小沙彌端上茶來法聰說嘻這茶忒淡了彷彿白開水似的快

了，不但白活了半輩子，還惹得旁人說長道短的，我不由的很嫌他。先前有人說他好，實在是騙了俺們了。我看姑娘做事這麼沒有心腸想必也爲這個是不是。鶯鶯歎了一聲說嗐，你是怎麼了，大淸早起別混說。紅娘說那麼著依姑娘想是幹甚麼好我奉陪就是咯。鶯鶯說花園子裏那一天你種的那些個樹大槪都發了芽兒了，你跟我去看一看好不好。

第七段

1 不說他們閒逛，單說彼時西洛地方有個秀才姓張，名琪，號叫君瑞。2 他們老人家也做過大官早已告退還鄉謝了世了。這秀才是個小漢仗兒相貌倒很秀氣，爲人謙恭和靄，又是文武全才，眞是沒有人不佩服他。正在懷才欲試恰巧遇着大比之年這秀才决意要來京趕考，就帶了一個底下人名叫琴童走的頭一天張生合那琴童天濛濛亮兒的時候就要起身，你預備的東西都齊截了麼。4 琴童回稟說小的都弄齊截了。第二天一淸早他們主僕二人就起了身走了幾天到了一個地方兒張生想起一個姓杜的來住得離這兒不遠，本同張生是患難朋友情投意合，很像弟兄一樣。5 他如今做了武官，

撬開門把那米都偷了去了。13鄭恒直睡到晌午大錯纔醒就趕緊的先賒米那兒還有一點兒呢又見門也撬開了就翻身下炕說呀怎麼了帶着太陽就鬧賊嗳我眞是越窮越遭跌就連哭帶喊的嚷了半天也是不中用了。14那都是鄭恒的根基本來不好他父親當初在外省做官就知道受賄賂那百姓的困苦他全不憐恤不論鰥寡孤獨的他都是一樣兒的勒揹遇事假公濟私又沒有正經本事到底被人參了朝廷大發雷霆叫他閉門思過後來在家得了個癱瘓病醫治不好就死了。15這鄭恒是他最疼的兒子在小的時候縱他撒野這麼說起來家裏旣是根子先壞了那鄭恒自已怎麼能好呢眞是靛缸裡拉不出白布來。此刻他全家都敗盡了這纔是天理昭彰絲毫不爽呢。

第六段

1現在單提鶯鶯和他的了頭紅娘兩個人名雖主僕情同手足那紅娘原長的俏皮幹事情麻利說話又伶牙俐齒的。2這一天鶯鶯在繡房裏合他說我這幾天頭昏腦悶的很難受不知道是甚麼緣故。3紅娘囘答說姑娘別是有件甚麼心事罷。我白猜一猜不是因爲那鄭恒嗎。可是啊我想他的歲數兒也不小

地裏商量說。6 我早就學會了一樣兒本事今兒何妨試演試演呢可有一樣兒我獨自一個兒可做不來你們幫著我弄了那東西來大家均攤勻散的分好不好。7 那些人嚇他說這種犯法的事萬做不得你別是要作死罷那禿子那兒理會這個就唬嚇他們說你們不肯合夥兒也可以等我犯了事叫官拏住我若不把你們攀出來就叫我不得好死。8 那些人想了一想這話不是玩兒的賊咬一口入骨三分不依著他也是白饒就回過頭來合鄭恆說酒還有這些個呢我們大家儘著力兒的喝較較量可小啊足已彀了那禿子說這是甚麼話拏酒灌他看他喝不喝。9 鄭恆本是欺軟怕硬的脾氣見他們出言不遜怕大家夥兒都跟他鬧糟糕沒法子只好同他們儘量喝。直喝到五更多天濛濛亮兒的時候東倒西歪的站不住了。10 鄭恆倒不至於喝得不過半醉因為他早有點兒疑心看見這樣光景便猜個八九不離十兒。趁他們悄悄兒的拉着驢前仰後合的家去了。11 趕到了家就大天亮了可巧遇見那姓田的打發拉驢的人來把驢拉回去了。12 鄭恆進了門先擱下米後關上門在炕上坐下歇了一會兒就躺下睡着了過了不大的工夫兒正在睡得人事不知的時候兒那禿子遮遮掩掩的來了拏鐵通條

過逾費心了，可就是分量太沉，我提溜不動怎麽好。16 姓田的說，我有匹大騾驢，借給你駞了去底下可別再抛費了。17 鄭恆切切實實的答應了，別了他那朋友走出來。

第五段

1 可惜他那脾氣仍舊不改，一直的還是到那熟要錢場兒上去了。那些個要家兒都是沒見過世面的人，知道鄭恆近來並沒有錢，忽然有這麽一件掛子，真叫他們想不到，就有個人過來問說，這是甚麽做的，我倒是近視眼看不清楚，鄭恆就嗔着他說，這個與你甚麽相干，你倒別說俏皮話兒，我現在餓了，你們替我把這個衣裳出脱了，買些個酒菜兒來大家夥兒吃好不好。2 那些人聽了，正中下懷，很喜歡不大的工夫兒，就把那衣裳賣了，買了好些個東西來。3 就有人把肉燉上燉得稀爛噴香，有忙著攄麪的，又有烙餅的，正預備着還有人要想喫，他一有酒有肉情面立時就掉過來了，都是同他喫喫喝喝，開懷暢飲的。煮餑餑兒真是各人的意見不同。4 你看鄭恆沒有錢的時候兒，這些人都躲著他，他一有酒有肉朋友柴米夫妻，這話真真的不錯啊。5 那要錢的裏頭有個禿子，是平日刁鑽不過的，他看見鄭恆有那些個米，就見財起意，合他們三兩個人在背

說我不過合你借幾個錢罷咧可行則行可止則止何必這樣兒的光景呢趕着站起來要走。3姓田的那個人本是個滾刀筋見他要走就轉過笑臉兒來說剛纔我不過是說玩兒話俗語兒說得好銀錢如糞土臉面值千金偺們倆從前是怎麼樣兒的相好來着要讓你白說了這句話那不是前功盡棄了嗎。4獃了一會兒又說你的這件衣裳歡舊這縫補的事你自已還會麼鄭恒面紅過耳說縫補綻是各人的本分事你別笑話人。5姓田的說那兒的話呢我送你一件新鮮的好不好。6說着就拏出一個半新不舊的包袱來裏頭包着許多衣裳就在炕上打開了問老兄要幾件。7鄭恒說難道你還肯給我多少麼在我是越多越好。8姓田的說我只給你一件你隨手兒拏罷不用挑揀。9鄭恒聽他這刻薄話並沒理會趁這個空兒冷眼看見有件斬新的袖子就拏出來故意兒說這件不很好。10田二嚙的一聲笑說你包含些兒罷若是貪心不足就討人厭了你拏這一件的罷出了門兒可不管換。11鄭恒笑問這會兒要換行不行。12姓田的說依我看你別三心二意的了拏這個去就很好。13鄭恒謝了他說我也囘敬你點兒什麼。14姓田的說留着你的罷我不短什麼可是這口袋裏還有五十斤米你也順便兒帶了去罷。15鄭恒說那可

這麼說恰巧那姓田的愛戴高帽子聽他這樣兒話就很喜歡。6 鄭恒接着又說我最愛體面楊氣你納是知道的、竟是一文錢瘀倒英雄漢這話正是我的景况啊、就剩了您這兒是我一線之路、實然是無可奈何了。今兒個來找閣下幫幫我行不行都可以。7 那姓田的向來是只顧自已佔便宜決不肯喫虧的手兒。一聽說出這樣兒話來、不由得就著急說、你打算要尋甚麼。鄭恒說不拘甚麼都好、隨便兒就是了。8 那姓田的立刻臉上就變了顏色兒說、你來的真不湊巧我那買賣賠了、貨物剩得也不多、甚麼賺錢不賺錢、只好賤賣不賺的都賣了。目下生意也不做了。還有該人家的帳也沒還清楚、又搭著莊稼被大水淹了、銀子雖有一半點兒不過僅彀我自己用的。還有一件、我原打著要捐官又要買地。我自已還週轉不開、你想想怎麼能借給人呢。

第四段

1 鄭恒聽了這個話就說、那個拏銀子捐官盡是上檔、買地倒罷了。請問你納現在種着多少畝地。2 那姓田的猛然說、管我呢、不必狗拏耗子多管閒事了。那鄭恒原是個膽兒小的人、不敢惹事、見他那朋友說著好話兒就翻臉、也就急著

第二段

1 合該也是他命中有救。忽然想起來還有個朋友可以求他幫助這個人姓田行二,盡給人家拉篷扯縴原是白手成家到這個時候兒可就發了大財了。他起初本不是個正經人,如今都收歛了。 2 那鄭恒因為自己沒有本事從前也跟他搭過夥計,兩個人有些個勾搭連環的事情。 3 這一天鄭恒想著要去找這個朋友借點兒錢。忙着就穿上褂子,藍不藍綠不綠的舊得怪難看一瞧,偏偏兒的又掉了倆鈕襻兒,又得拿針釘上,再看他那帽子也沒有帽襻兒,怕耽悞了時候兒沒有工夫收拾就這樣搖頭提腦的去了,到了田二家門口兒就叫門。

第三段

1 那田二出來一抬頭見是鄭恒,就讓進去了說,你打那'兒來。 2 鄭恒說兄弟是從家裏來,現時分文都沒有仗著甚麼餬口呢。我有個親戚是手藝人原是叫我也跟他學。老兄想我做得來麼。 3 那姓田的說不錯,那個手藝行當兒我們這等人是萬做不來的。 4 鄭恒說原是,我是受用慣了的人,那'兒能耍手藝呢,何況尊駕比神仙還舒服,年又高德又大。我十分羡慕得了不得。 5 鄭恒話是

踐約傳

第一段

1 唐朝的時候兒有位退歸林下的大人姓崔名珏曾在蒲州蓋了一座廟名叫普救寺。2 過了幾年去世之後他的夫人崔鄭氏就搬在廟裏西邊兒獨門獨院兒的住着。3 他跟前有一兒一女那兒名叫歡郞女名叫鶯鶯還帶着一個了頭名叫紅娘跟着鶯鶯寸步不離。4 這鶯鶯正在妙齡的時候兒長得眉清目秀又典雅又莊重很有福氣。5 而且是才貌雙全古往今來無所不知眞草隸篆四樣兒的字全都會寫。6 他小時候兒早已許給崔老夫人的內姪鄭恒做媳婦兒。可惜這鄭恒偏是個沒出息兒的人成天家盡是要排子擺架子極會粧模做樣的還有一種習氣見人吃稀罕物兒穿體面些兒的衣裳他總要跟着學真不是個東西。7 他本有萬數兩銀子的家當兒因此全拋費得乾乾淨淨兒的了。竟是一心的滿處兒去搜羅打聽誰有銀子放帳就借來使使永遠也不還積年累月該的利錢倒比本錢還多又搭着他為人很險嘴裏說好話脚底下絆子不知不覺的就害了人了。眼皮子又淺常愛個小便宜兒見人家有錢非骿絆子不就騙實在是奸詐的了不得。8 所以人都瞧不起他漸漸的揞着兩個空拳頭過日子連一點兒進項都沒有了竟苦到這個地步兒上。

PART VI.

THE GRADUATE'S WOOING

OR

THE STORY OF A PROMISE THAT WAS KEPT.

(CHINESE TEXT.)

PART VII.

THE TONE EXERCISES.
(CHINESE TEXT.)

練習燕山平仄編

A		30	交	63	出	**H**		121	兄
1	阿	31	巧	64	抓	92	哈	122	須
2	愛	32	街	65	敍	93	害	123	喧
3	安	33	且	66	拽	94	塞	124	雪
4	昂	34	見	67	搞	95	砰	125	巡
5	傲	35	欠	68	專	96	好	126	學
CH		36	知	69	穿	97	黑	**I**	
6	乍	37	尺	70	壯	98	很	127	衣
7	茶	38	斤	71	牀	99	恆	**J**	
8	窄	39	親	72	追	100	河	128	染
9	柴	40	井	73	吹	101	後	129	嚷
10	斬	41	輕	74	淮	102	戶	130	繞
11	產	42	角	75	春	103	花	131	熱
12	章	43	郤	76	中	104	壞	132	人
13	唱	44	酒	77	充	105	換	133	扔
14	兆	45	秋	78	揣	106	黃	134	日
15	吵	46	窘	**NGÊ**		107	回	135	若
16	遣	47	窮	79	額	108	混	136	肉
17	車	48	卓	80	恩	109	紅	137	如
18	這	49	綽	81	哼	110	火	138	輭
19	眞	50	畫	82	兒			139	瑞
20	臣	51	抽	**F**		**HS**		140	潤
21	正	52	句	83	法	111	西	141	絨
22	成	53	取	84	反	112	夏		
23	吉	54	捐	85	方	113	向	**K**	
24	奇	55	全	86	非	114	小	142	嘎
25	家	56	絕	87	分	115	些	143	卡
26	恰	57	缺	88	風	116	先	144	改
27	楷	58	君	89	佛	117	心	145	開
28	江	59	羣	90	否	118	性	146	甘
29	搶	60	爵	91	夫	119	學		
		61	郡			120	修		
		62	主						

147	看	**L**	
148	剛	180	拉
149	炕	181	來
150	告	182	懶
151	考	183	浪
152	給	184	老
153	刻	185	勒
154	根	186	累
155	肯	187	冷
156	更	188	立
157	坑	189	倆
158	各	190	兩
159	可	191	了
160	狗	192	裂
161	口	193	連
162	古	194	林
163	苦	195	另
164	瓜	196	略
165	跨	197	留
166	怪	198	駱
167	快	199	陋
168	官	200	律
169	寬	201	戀
170	光	202	掠
171	況	203	掄
172	規	204	略
173	愧	205	路
174	棍	206	亂
175	困	207	論
176	工	208	龍
177	孔		
178	果	**M**	
179	閩	209	馬

PART VII.—THE TONE EXERCISES.

210 買	241 寧	270 朋	301 碎	328 炭	361 冬	392 宗
211 慢	242 虐	271 必	302 孫	329 當	362 同	393 蔥
212 忙	243 牛	272 皮	303 送	330 湯	**TS**	**TZ**
213 毛	244 挪	273 表		331 道	363 雜	394 子
214 美	245 穤	274 票	**SH**	332 逃	364 擦	395 次
215 門	246 女	275 別	304 殺	333 得	365 在	**W**
216 夢	247 虐	276 撇	305 曬	334 特	366 才	396 瓦
217 米	248 虐	277 扁	306 山	335 得'	367 贊	397 外
218 苗	249 奴	278 片	307 賞	336 等	368 慚	398 完
219 滅	250 暖	279 賓	308 少	337 疼	369 葬	399 往
220 面	251 嫩	280 貧	309 否	338 低	370 倉	400 爲
221 民	252 濃	281 兵	310 身	339 替	371 早	401 文
222 名		282 憑	311 生	340 吊	372 草	402 翁
223 謬	**NGO**	283 波	312 事	341 挑	373 則	403 我
224 末	253 訛	284 破	313 手	342 疊	374 策	404 武
225 謀	254 偶	285 不	314 書	343 貼	375 賊	
226 木		286 剖	315 刷	344 店	376 怎	**Y**
	P	287 不	316 裹	345 天	377 參	405 牙
N	255 罷	288 普	317 拴	346 定	378 增	406 涯
227 那	256 怕		318 雙	347 聽	379 層	407 羊
228 奶	257 拜	**S**	319 水	348 丟	380 作	408 要
229 男	258 派	289 撒	320 順	349 多	381 錯	409 夜
230 囊	259 半	290 賽	321 說	350 妥	382 走	410 言
231 鬧	260 盼	291 散		351 豆	383 湊	411 盆
232 內	261 幫	292 桑	**SS**	352 頭	384 祖	412 音
233 嫩	262 旁	293 掃	322 絲	353 肚	385 粗	413 迎
234 能	263 包	294 嗇		354 土	386 撺	414 約
235 你	264 跑	295 森	**T**	355 短	387 竄	415 魚
236 娘	265 北	296 僧	323 大	356 團	388 嘴	416 原
237 鳥	266 陪	297 索	324 他	357 對	389 催	417 月
238 揑	267 本	298 搜	325 歹	358 退	390 尊	418 雲
239 念	268 盆	299 素	326 太	359 敦	391 寸	419 有
240 您	269 迸	300 算	327 單	360 吞		420 用

1	2	3	4	5	6	7	8	9	10	11	12	13	14	15	16
阿	愛	安	昂	傲	乍	茶	窄	柴	斬	產	章	唱	兆	吵	這
是阿哥之阿	是愛惜之愛	是平安之安	是低昂之昂	是恠傲之傲	是乍見乍冷乍熱之乍	是茶酒之茶	是寬窄之窄	是柴炭之柴	是斬絞之斬	是產業生產之產	是章程之章	是歌唱之唱	是先兆之兆	是吵嚷之吵	是這個那個之這
阿○阿	哀埃矮愛	安○俺岸	腌昂○○	熬熬襖傲	渣劄拃乍	义茶拃义	齋宅窄債	拆柴冊○	沾○盞站	攙饞產懺	章○長賬	娼長廠唱	招著找兆	吵巢炒鈔	遮摺者這
是阿	哀求	平安	腌臢	熬菜	渣滓	义手	齋戒	拆毀	沾染	攙雜	章程	娼妓	招呼	吵嚷	遮掩
○	塵埃	○	昂貴	熬夜	劄文	茶酒	住宅	柴炭	○	嘴饞	○	長短	著急	窩巢	摺奏
阿甚麼	高矮	俺們	○	綿襖	一拃	扠腰	寬窄	様冊子	一盞燈	產業	生長	木廠	察找	煎炒	再者
阿哥	愛惜	河岸	○	徣傲	乍見	樹杈	欠債	○	驛站	懺悔	帳目	歌唱	先兆	錢鈔	這個

[CHʻÊ-CHʻIEH.] PART VII.—THE TONE EXERCISES. 289

17	18	19	20	21	22	23	24	25	26	27	28	29	30	31	32	33
車	這	眞	臣	正	成	吉	奇	家	恰	楷	江	搶	交	巧	街	且
是車馬之車	是這塊兒之這	是眞假之眞	是君臣之臣	是邪正之正	是成敗之成	是吉凶之吉	是奇怪之奇	是住家之家	是恰巧之恰	是楷書之楷	是大江之江	是搶奪之搶	是交代之交	是巧妙之巧	是街道之街	是況且之且

車〇扯撒	〇〇〇	眞〇枕震	嗔臣磣趁	正〇整正	稱成懲秤	雞吉已記	七奇起氣	家夾甲價	招〇卡恰	〇〇〇	江〇講匠	腔牆搶戧	交嚼腳叫	敲橋巧俏	街結解借	切茄且妾

| 車馬 | 〇 | 眞假 | 嗔怪 | 正月 | 稱呼 | 雞犬 | 七八 | 住家 | 招花 | 〇 | 大江 | 腔調 | 交代 | 敲打 | 街道 | 切肉 |

| 〇 | 〇 | 〇 | 君臣 | 〇 | 成敗 | 吉凶 | 奇怪 | 夾帶 | 〇 | 〇 | 〇 | 牆壁 | 嚼過 | 橋梁 | 完結 | 茄子 |

| 拉扯 | 〇 | 枕頭 | 砢磣 | 整齊 | 懲辦 | 自己 | 起初 | 盔甲 | 卡子 | 楷書 | 講究 | 搶奪 | 手腳 | 巧妙 | 解開 | 況且 |

| 裁撒 | 這塊兒 | 地震 | 趁着 | 邪正 | 斗秤 | 記載 | 氣血 | 價錢 | 恰巧 | 〇 | 匠人 | 戧木 | 叫喊 | 俏皮 | 借貸 | 姬妾 |

34	35	36	37	38	39	40	41	42	43	44	45	46	47	48	49	50
見	欠	知	尺	斤	親	井	輕	角	郤	酒	秋	窘	窮	卓	綽	晝
是見面之見	是該欠之欠	是知道之知	是尺寸之尺	是斤兩之斤	是親戚之親	是井泉之井	是輕重之輕	是角色之角	是推郤之郤	是酒肉之酒	是春秋之秋	是窘迫之窘	是貧窮之窮	是桌櫈之桌	是寬綽之綽	是晝夜之晝

奸○滅	千錢淺欠	知值指志	赤遲尺翅	斤○錦近	親勤寢嗳	睛晴請慶	輕晴靜	○角○郤	○○○○	究○酒救	秋求糗	○○窘○	○○○○	卓濁	擉○○綽	週軸肘晝

奸臣	千萬	知道	紅赤赤	斤兩	親戚	眼睛	輕重			究辦	春秋		桌櫈	擉碴		週圍
○	錢財	值班	遲誤	○	勤儉	陰晴	角色		○	央求		貧窮	清濁			車軸
裁減	深淺	指點	尺寸	錦繡	寢食	井泉	請安	○	酒肉	飯糗了	窘迫	○	○	○	臂肘	
見面	該欠	志向	翅膀	遠近	狗嗳	安靜	慶弔	○	推郤	救護	○	○	○	○	寬綽	晝夜

[CH'OU-CH'UAI.]   PART VII.—THE TONE EXERCISES.

51	52	53	54	55	56	57	58	59	60	61	62	63	64	65	66	67
抽	句	取	捐	全	絕	缺	君	羣	爵	鄰	主	出	抓	欨	拽	揣
是抽查之抽	是句段之句	是取送之取	是捐納之捐	是齊全之全	是斷絕之絕	是補缺之缺	是君王之君	是成羣之羣	是爵位之爵	見上	是賓主之主	是出外之出	是抓住抓破之抓	是欨一聲之欨	是拉拽之拽	是揣摩之揣
抽綢醜臭	居局舉句	屈渠取去	捐○捲眷	圈全犬勸	噘絕蹶倔	缺瘸○確	君○菌俊	羣○○○	爵○○○	○○○○	猪竹主住	出廚處處	抓○爪○	欨○○○	拽跩拽	揣○揣踹
抽查	居處	冤屈	捐納	圈點	噘嘴	補缺	君王	○	○	○	猪羊	出外	抓破	欨一聲	拽泥	懷揣
綢緞	賭局	溝渠	○	齊全	斷絕	瘸駿	○	成羣	爵位	○	竹子	廚房	○	○	○	○
醜俊	保舉	取送	舒捲	犬吠	○	馬撩壓子	○	菌子	○	○	賓主	處分	雞爪子	○	鴨跩	搗摩
香臭	句段	來去	家眷	勸戒	倔喪	確然	懷秀	○○	○	○	住處	住處	○	○	拉拽	蹧踏

68	69	70	71	72	73	74	75	76	77	78	79	80	81	82
專	穿	壯	牀	追	吹	准	春	中	充	搯	額	恩	哼	兒
是專門之專	是穿戴之穿	是壯健之壯	是牀鋪之牀	是追趕之追	是吹打之吹	是准駁之准	是春夏之春	是中外之中	是充當之充	是搯撞之搯	是額數之額	是恩典之恩	是哼阿之哼	是兒女之兒
專	穿	裝	牀	追	吹	○	春	中	充	搯	阿	恩	哼	○
○	船	牀	牀	○	垂	○	純	○	虫	○	額	○	○	兒
轉	喘	奘	閘	○	○	○	蠢	腫	寵	○	我	○	○	耳
傳	串	○	創	墜	准	准	○	重	銃	○	惡	揾	○	二
專門	穿戴	裝載	牀戶	追趕	吹打	○	春夏	中外	充當	搯撞	太阿	恩典	哼阿	○
○	車船	粗奘	牀鋪	○	垂手	○	純厚	○	虫蟻	○	頞數	○	○	兒女
轉移	痰喘	壯健	閘入	○	○	准駁	蠢笨	腫痛	寵愛	○	爾我	○	○	耳朵
經傳	串通	壯健	創始	廢墜	○	○	○	輕重	鐵銃子	○	善惡	○	揾钩	二三

[FA-HÊN.] PART VII.—THE TONE EXERCISES. 293

83	84	85	86	87	88	89	90	91	92	93	94	95	96	97	98
法	反	方	非	分	風	佛	否	夫	哈	害	寒	碎	好	黑	很
是法子之法	是反倒之反	是方圓之方	是是非之非	是分開之分	是風雨之風	是佛老之佛	是然否之否	是夫妻之夫	是哈哈笑之哈	是利害之害	是寒涼之寒	是打碎之碎	是好歹之好	是黑白之黑	是很好之很
發法髮法	翻煩反飯	方房訪放	非肥匪費	分墳粉分	風縫○○	佛○○奉	○浮否埠	夫扶斧父	哈蝦哈哈	咳孩海害	頂寒好項	碎行○項	蒿毫好好	黑○黑○	○痕很恨
發遣	翻騰	方圓	是非	分開	風雨	佛老	○	夫妻	哈哈笑	咳聲	顛頂	打碎	蒿草	黑白	○
法子	煩惱	房屋	肥瘦	墳墓	裁縫	佛老	浮沉	扶持	蝦蟆	孩子	寒涼	各行	絲毫	○	傷痕
頭髮	反倒	訪查	賊匪	脂粉	○	然否	○	斧鉞	哈吧狗	江海	叫喊	○	好不好	黑豆	好得很
法門	噢飯	放肆	使費	職分	供奉	○	埠口	灸母	哈什馬	利害	滿漢	項圈	好喜	○	恨怨

38

99	100	101	102	103	104	105	106	107	108	109	110	111	112	113	114
恆	河	後	戶	花	壞	換	黃	回	混	紅	火	西	夏	向	小
是恆久之恆	是江河之河	是前後之後	是戶口之戶	是花草之花	是損壞之壞	是更換之換	是青黃之黃	是回去回來之回	是混亂之混	是紅綠之紅	是水火之火	是東西之西	是春夏之夏	是方向之向	是大小之小
亭恆○橫	喝河○賀	鮑侯吼後	忽壺虎戶	花滑話話	○懷○壞	歡環緩換	荒黃謊晃	灰回悔賄	昏魂渾混	烘紅哄烘	劉活火貨	西席喜細	瞎霞○夏	香詳想向	消學小笑
哼哈	噢喝	鮑鹹	忽然	花草	○	歡喜	荒亂	石灰	昏暗	烘烤	劉口子	東西	瞎子	香臭	消滅
恆久	江河	公侯	茶壺	泥滑	懷想	連環	青黃	回去	鬼魂	紅綠	死活	酒席	雲霞	詳細	學徒
○	○	牛吼	龍虎榜	話敗人	○	鬆緩	撒謊	後悔	渾厚	欺哄	水火	喜歡	○	○	大小
兜橫	賀喜	前後	戶口	說話	損壞	更換	一晃兒	賄賂	混亂	煉烘	貨物	粗細	春夏	方向	談笑

[HSIEH-JANG.]   PART VII.—THE TONE EXERCISES.   295

115	116	117	118	119	120	121	122	123	124	125	126	127	128	129
些	先	心	姓	學	修	兄	須	喧	雪	巡	學	衣	染	嚷
是些微之些	是先後之先	是心性之心	是姓名之姓	是學問之學	是修理之修	是兄弟之兄	是必須之須	是喧嚷之喧	是雨雪之雪	是巡察之巡	是學生之學	是衣裳之衣	是沾染之染	是嚷鬧之嚷
些㵎血謝	先閒險限	心尋○信	姓○醒姓	○學○姓	修○朽袖	兄熊○○	須徐許續	喧懸選選	雪穴汛	靴穴	熏巡○汛	衣一尾易	○然染○	嚷瓢嚷攘
些微	先後	心性	星宿	○學	修理	兄弟	必須	喧嚷	靴鞋	熏蒸	學生	衣裳	○	嚷嚷
靴鞋	清閒	尋東西	行為	學問	○	狗熊	徐圖	懸掛	穴道	巡察	○	一個	然否	鄭子
洗血	危險.	睡醒	○	糟朽	○	應許	揀選	雨雪	○	○	○	尾巴	沾染	嚷鬧
謝恩	限期	書信	姓名	領袖	○	接續	侯選	鑽穴	營汛	○	○	容易	○	謙讓

130	131	132	133	134	135	136	137	138	139	140	141	142	143	144	145
繞	熱	人	扔	日	若	肉	如	軟	瑞	潤	榮	嘎	卡	改	開
是圍繞之繞	是冷熱之熱	是人物之人	是扔棄之扔	是日月之日	是若論之若	是骨肉之肉	是如若之如	是軟弱之軟	是祥瑞之瑞	是潤澤之潤	是榮耀之榮	是嘎嘎笑的聲兒	是卡倫之卡	是改變之改	是開閉之開
○饒繞繞	○○惹熱	○人忍任	扔○○○	○○○日	揉柔○若	如如入肉	○○○軟	○○蓝瑞	○○○潤	榮瓩○○	嘎嘎嘎嘎	卡○○○	該○改概	開○慨○
○	○	○	扔棄	○	揉的一聲	如貼	○	○	○	○	○	嘎嘎的笑	卡倫	○	開閉
饒裕	○	人物	○	○	揉的剛柔	如若	○	○	○	○	榮耀	打嘎兒	○	○	○
○	惹事	容忍	○	○	○	強入	○	軟弱	花蓝	○	瓩毛	嘎雜子	○	改變	慷慨
繞住	冷熱	責任	○	日月	若論	骨肉	出入	○	祥瑞	潤澤	○	雞嘎嘎蛋兒	○	夭概	○
圍繞															

[KAN-KU.] PART VII.—THE TONE EXERCISES. 297

146	147	148	149	150	151	152	153	154	155	156	157	158	159	160	161	162
甘	看	剛	炕	告	考	給	刻	根	肯	更	坑	各	可	狗	口	古
是甘苦之甘	是看見之看	是剛纔之剛	是火炕之炕	是告訴之告	是考察之考	是放給之給	是刻搜之刻	是根本之根	是肯不肯之肯	是更多更少之更	是坑坎之坑	是各人之各	是可否之可	是猪狗之狗	是口舌之口	是古今之古
甘〇趕幹	看〇砍看	剛剛堈杠	康扛慷炕	高〇稿靠	尻〇考靠	〇〇〇〇〇	刻〇〇〇〇	根哏〇艮	〇〇肯揩	更〇埂更	坑〇〇〇	哥格各個	磕瞌渴客	溝狗彀	摳〇口叩	估骨古固
甘苦	看守	剛纔	康健	高低	尻骨	〇	刻搜	根本	〇	更改	坑坎	哥哥	磕頭	溝渠	摳破了	料估
〇	〇	剛剛兒	扛撞	〇	〇	〇	〇	艮哏	〇	〇	〇	影格	瞌睡	小狗兒的	〇	骨頭
追趕	刀砍	土堈子	慷慨	稿案	考察	放給	〇	〇	肯不肯	道埂子	〇	各自各兒	饑渴	猪狗	口舌	古今
才幹	看見	擋杠	火炕	告訴	依靠	〇	〇	艮卦	一揩子	更多	〇	幾個	賓客	足彀	叩頭	堅固

163	164	165	166	167	168	169	170	171	172	173	174	175	176	177	178	179
苦	瓜	跨	怪	快	官	寬	光	況	規	愧	棍	困	工	孔	果	闊
是苦甜之苦	是瓜果之瓜	是跨馬之跨	是怪道之怪	是快慢之快	是官員之官	是寬窄之寬	是光明之光	是況且之況	是規矩之規	是慚愧之愧	是棍棒之棍	是乏困之困	是工夫之工	是面孔之孔	是結果之果	是寬闊之闊
窟〇苦褲	瓜〇寡掛	誇〇佮跨	乖〇拐怪	〇〇〇擓快	官〇〇管慣	寬〇〇款	光〇〇廣逛	誆狂〇況	規〇〇詭貴	骯葵愧愧	〇〇〇滾棍	坤〇〇闉困	工〇〇礦共	空〇〇孔空	鍋國果過	〇〇〇〇闊
窟窿	瓜果	誇獎	乖張	〇	官員	寬窄	光明	誆騙	規矩	骯欠	〇	坤道	工夫	空虛	飯鍋	〇
〇	〇	〇	〇	〇	〇	〇	〇	狂妄	〇	葵花	〇	〇	〇	〇	國家	〇
甜苦	多寡	佮子	拐騙	擓癰瘙	管理	款項	廣大	〇	詭詐	愧儡	翻滾	闉闍	金礦	面孔	結果	〇
褲子	懸掛	跨馬	怪道	快慢	習慣	〇	遊逛	況且	富貴	慚愧	棍子棒子	乏困	通共	閉空	過去	寬闊

[LA-LIO.] PART VII.—THE TONE EXERCISES. 299

180	181	182	183	184	185	186	187	188	189	190	191	192	193	194	195	196
拉	來	懶	浪	老	勒	累	冷	立	倆	兩	了	列	連	林	另	略
是拉扯之拉	是來去之來	是懶惰之懶	是波浪之浪	是老幼之老	是勒索之勒	是連累之累	是冷熱之冷	是站立之立	是倆三之倆	是斤兩之兩	是了斷之了	是擺列之列	是接連之連	是樹林之林	是另外之另	是謀略之略
拉邋喇	○來○賴	鬖棽懶爛	榔狼朗浪	摎勞老澇	勒○○樂	勒雷累類	○稜禮愣	璃離禮立	○○倆○	量涼兩諒	○○了料	咧咧咧列	連憐臉練	淋林檁吝	○零領另	○○○略
拉扯	○	鬖鬆	檳榔	打撈	勒索	勒死	○	玻璃	○	商量	○	罷咧	連上	淋拉起來	○	○
邋遢	來去	貪婪	狼虎	勞苦	○	雷電	稜角	分離	○	涼熱	無聊	瞎咧咧	憐恤	樹林子	零碎	○
喇叭	○	懶惰	光朗	老幼	○	累次	冷熱	禮貌	倆三	斤兩	了斷	咧嘴	臉面	房檁	領袖	○
蠟燭	倚賴	燦爛	波浪	旱澇	歡樂	族類	發愣	站立	○	原諒	材料	擺列	練習	租賃	另外	謀略

197	198	199	200	201	202	203	204	205	206	207	208	209	210	211	212
留	騾	陋	律	戀	略	搶	咯	路	亂	論	龍	馬	買	慢	忙
是收留之留	是騾馬之騾	是鄙陋之陋	是律例之律	是依戀之戀	是忽略之略	是混搶之搶	是大略之略	是道路之路	是雜亂之亂	是談論之論	是龍虎之龍	是馬匹之馬	是買賣之買	是快慢之慢	是急忙之忙

遛留柳六	捋騾裸駱	樓樓簍陋	驢驢屢律	○○○戀	○○○略	搶淋○搶	○○○略	○○○路	嚕爐櫨路	○○○論	篭龍籠弄	媽麻馬罵	○埋買賣	顢瞞滿慢	茫忙莽○
遛打	捋起袖子	摟衣裳	驢	○	○	混搶	○	○	嘞嚕	○	窟窿	爹媽	○	顢頇	白茫茫
收留	騾馬	樓房	驢馬	○	○	淋溼	○	爐灶	○	車輪	龍虎榜	麻木	葬埋	隱瞞	急忙
楊柳	裸身	酒簍	屢次	○	○	○	○	船櫓	○	圇圇	瓦隴	馬鞍	收買	豐滿	卤莽
五六	駱駝	鄙陋	律例	依戀	忽略	○	大咯	道路	雜亂	無論	胡弄局	打罵	覆賣	快慢	○

[MAO-NAI.] PART VII.—THE TONE EXERCISES.

213	214	215	216	217	218	219	220	221	222	223	224	225	226	227	228
毛	美	門	夢	米	苗	滅	面	民	名	謬	末	謀	木	那	奶
是羽毛之毛	是美貌之美	是門扇之門	是睡夢之夢	是米糧之米	是禾苗之苗	是滅火之滅	是臉面之面	是民人之民	是姓名之名	是謬妄之謬	是始末之末	是圖謀之謀	是草木之木	是問人那個之那	是牛奶之奶

貓毛卯貌	○煤美昧	捫門○悶	蒙盟猛夢	眯迷米密	喵苗藐廟	哔○滅	綿勉面	○民憫命	名○	○○謬	摩蘑抹末	○謀某○	模母木	那拏那那	○奶耐

| ○ | ○ | ○ | ○ | ○ | ○ | ○ | ○ | ○ | ○ | ○ | ○ | ○ | ○ | ○ | ○ |

| 貓狗 | | 捫滕 | 蒙了去 | 眯睜眼 | 喵喵的貓叫 | 哔哔的羊叫 | | | | 摩不著 | | | | 在這兒那 | |

| 羽毛 | 煤炭 | 門扇 | 結盟 | 迷惑 | 禾苗 | ○ | 綿花 | 民人 | 姓名 | ○ | 蘑菇 | 圖謀 | 模樣 | 拏賊 | ○ |

| 卯刻 | 美貌 | ○ | 勇猛 | 米糧 | 藐小 | ○ | 勉力 | 憫憐 | ○ | ○ | 塗抹 | 某人 | 㚟母 | 那個 | 牛奶 |

| 相貌 | 愚昧 | 憂悶 | 睡夢 | 機密 | 廟宇 | 滅火 | 臉面 | ○ | 性命 | 謬妄 | 始末 | ○ | 草木 | 那裏 | 耐時 |

229	230	231	232	233	234	235	236	237	238	239	240	241	242	243	244	245
男	囊	鬧	內	嫩	能	你	娘	鳥	揑	念	您	甯	虐	牛	挪	耨
是男婦之男	是囊袋之囊	是熱鬧之鬧	是內外之內	是老嫩之嫩	是才能之能	是你我之你	是爹娘之娘	是鳥獸之鳥	是揑弄之揑	是想念之念	是京城稱呼人的話	是安甯之甯	是暴虐之虐	是牛馬之牛	是挪移之挪	是耕耨之耨
喃男○難	囔囊欀欀	撓鐃惱鬧	○○○餒內	能○○擬嫩	能○泥擬	娘○釀	嚷○鳥尿	揑呆○挈	拈年揑念	○○○	甯擰伲	妞牛鈕拗	挪○懦	○○○耨		
喃喃囈語	啷噠	撓着			才能	泥土	爹娘	嚷嚷的貓叫	揑弄	年月	您納	安甯	牛馬	挪移		
男婦	囊袋	鐃鈸							呆獃							
○	攘了一刀子	煩惱	凍餒	○	才能	泥土	爹娘	鳥獸	揑匪	捻匪	○	擰壞	鈕扣	○		
災難	鑲鼻子	熱鬧	內外	老嫩	道兒濟	藏匿	蘊釀	尿尿	罪孽	念誦		佞口	暴虐	拗不過來	懦弱	耕耨

246	247	248	249	250	251	252	253	254	255	256	257	258	259	260
女	虐	虐	奴	暖	嫩	濃	訛	偶	罷	怕	拜	派	半	盼
是男女之女	見上	見上	是奴僕之奴	是暖和之暖	是老嫩之嫩	是濃淡之濃	是訛錯之訛	是偶然之偶	是罷了之罷	是恐怕之怕	是拜客之拜	是分派之派	是整半之半	是盼望之盼
○	○	○	奴努怒	○暖嫩	○	○濃弄	哦訛○惡	毆○嘔偶	八扱把罷	趴扒○怕	掰白擺拜	拍牌弒派	班○板半	攀盤○聢
○	○	○	○	○	○	○	○	哦一聲	○	○	○	○	○	高攀
○	○	○	奴僕	○	○	濃淡	訛錯	毆打	八九	趴下	掰開	木牌	輪班	盤查
○	○	○	○	○	○	○	○	○	提拔	扒桿兒	黑白	一屁股𡛷下	○	板片
男女	○	○	努力	暖和	○	濃淡	訛錯	偶然	把持	○	擺列	分派	○	○
○	○	○	喜怒	○	老嫩	擺弄	善惡	嘔氣	罷了	恐怕	拜客	○	整半	盼望

261	262	263	264	265	266	267	268	269	270	271	272	273	274	275	276	277
幫	旁	包	跑	北	陪	本	盆	迸	朋	必	皮	表	票	別	撇	扁
是幫助之幫	是旁邊之旁	是包裹之包	是跑脫之跑	是南北之北	是陪伴之陪	是根本之本	是木盆之盆	是迸跳之迸	是朋友之朋	是務必之必	是皮毛之皮	是表裏之表	是錢票之票	是分別之別	是撇開之撇	是圓扁之扁

| 幫○鄉 | 胖旁謗胖 | 包薄保抱 | 拋袍跑礮 | 背○北背 | 披陪○配 | 奔○本奔 | 噴盆○噴 | 繃○蚌迸 | 烹朋棒碰 | 逼鼻筆屁 | 批皮癖屁 | 標○表鰾 | 漂嫖漂票 | 憋別瘪彆 | 擎○撇○ | 邊○扁便 |

幫助	胖腫	包裹	拋棄	背負	拔衣	奔忙	噴水	繃緊	割烹	逼迫	批評	標文書	漂沒	憋悶	擎開	邊沿
○	旁邊	厚薄	砲襯	○	陪伴	○	盆礤	○	朋友	口鼻	皮毛	標文書	嫖賭	分別	○	○
細綁	吹謗	保護	跑脫	南北	○	根本	○	老蚌生珠	手捧	筆墨	癖好	表裏	漂布	瘪嘴子	撇了	圓扁
毀謗	胖瘦	懷抱	槍礮	向背	配偶	投奔	噴香	迸跳	老蚌生珠	務必	屁股	碰破	鰾膠	錢票子	彆拗	○ 方便

[P'IEN-SAO.] PART VII.—THE TONE EXERCISES. 305

278	279	280	281	282	283	284	285	286	287	288	289	290	291	292	293
片	賓	貧	兵	憑	波	破	不	剖	不	普	洒灑	賽	散	桑	掃
是片段之片	是賓主之賓	是貧窮之貧	是兵丁之兵	是憑據之憑	是水波之波	是破碎之破	不字作詩裏有作上平用的	是剖開之剖	是是不是之不	是普遍之普	是洒掃之洒	是賭賽之賽	是散放之散	是桑梓之桑	是掃地之掃
偏便誚片	賓○殯	摒貧品牝	兵○稟病	砰憑○聘	波駁播簸	坡婆筥破	掊○剖○	不不補不	鋪葡普鋪	撒瞰洒薩	顋○○賽	三○傘散	桑○嗓喪	騷○掃掃
偏正	賓主	摒命	兵丁	砰磅	水波	土坡	掊剋	我不	鋪蓋	撒手	顋頰	三四	桑梓	騷擾
便宜	○	貧窮	○	憑據	准駁	老婆子	○	不是	葡萄	一眼瞰著	○	○	○	○
愛誚	○	品級	稟報	○	播米	管簍	○	補缺	普遍	洒掃	○	雨傘	嗓子	掃地
片段	殯葬	牝牡	疾病	聘嫁	簸箕	破碎	○	不可	鋪子	姓薩	賭賽	散放	喪氣	掃興

294 嗇	295 森	296 僧	297 索	298 搜	299 素	300 算	301 碎	302 孫	303 送	304 殺	305 曬	306 山	307 賞	308 少	309 舌
是客嗇之嗇	是森嚴之森	是僧道之僧	是勒索之索	是搜察之搜	是平素之素	是算計之算	是零碎之碎	是子孫之孫	是迎送之送	是殺死之殺	是曬乾之曬	是山川之山	是賞賜之賞	是多少之少	是脣舌之舌
嗇	森 ○ ○ ○	僧 ○ ○ ○	蔂 ○ 鎖 縮	搜 ○ 叟 嗽	蘇 速 ○ 素	酸 ○ ○ 算	雖 隨 髓 碎	孫 ○ 損	松 竦 ○ 送	殺 ○ 傻 刡	篩 ○ 骰 曬	山 ○ 閃 善	商 晌 賞 上	燒 勺 少 少	賒 舌 捨 射
	森嚴	僧道	蓑衣	搜察	蘇州	酸的鹹的	雖然	子孫	松樹	殺死	篩子	山川	商量	火燒	賒欠
○	○	○	○	迅速	○	○	跟隨	○	○	○	○	○	晌午	刀勺	脣舌
○	○	○	鎖上	老叟	○	○	骨髓	損盆	○	毛骨竦然	○	○	賞賜	多少	棄捨
客嗇	○	○	縮手	嗾嗾	平素	算計	零碎	○	迎送	瘂傻	骰子	雷閃	上下	老少	射箭
										孥剪子刡一點	曬乾	善惡			

[SHÊN-T'A.]   PART VII.—THE TONE EXERCISES.

310	311	312	313	314	315	316	317	318	319	320	321	322	323	324
身	生	事	手	書	刷	衰	拴	雙	水	順	說	絲	大	他
是身體之身	是生長之生	是事情之事	是手足之手	是詩書之書	是刷洗之刷	是衰敗之衰	是拴捆之拴	是成雙之雙	是山水之水	是順當之順	是說話之說	是絲線之絲	是大小之大	是他人之他
身	生	失	收	書	刷	衰	拴	雙	○	○	說	絲	答	他
神	繩	十	熟	贖	○	○	○	○	○	○	○	○	搭	○
審	省	使	手	數	要	摔	○	爽	水	隼	○	死	打	塔
甚	謄	事	獸	數	○	率	涮	雙	睡	順	朔	四	大	榻
身體	生長	失落	收拾	詩書	刷洗	衰敗	拴捆	成雙	○	○	說話	絲線	答應	他人
神仙	繩子	九十	生熟	贖罪	○	○	○	○	誰的	○	○	○	搭救	○
審問	各省	使喚	手足	數錢	耍笑	摔東西	○	爽快	山水	鷹隼	○	死生	毆打	佛塔
甚是	謄下	事情	禽獸	數目	○	草率	涮涮	雙生	睡覺	順當	朔望	四五	大小	牀榻

[TAI-T'IAO.]

No.	字	釋義	同音字	例詞			
341	挑	是挑選之挑	挑條挑跳	挑選	條陳	挑着	跳躍
340	弔	是弔死之弔	貂○弔	貂皮	○	○	弔死
339	替	是替工之替	梯提體替	樓梯	提拔	體量	替工
338	低	是低頭之低	低敵底地	低頭	仇敵	到底	天地
337	疼	是疼痛之疼	鼕疼○鐙	鼕鼕的鼓聲兒	疼痛	○	馬鐙
336	等	是等第等候之等	燈○等鐙	燈燭	○	等候	板撥
335	得'	是必得之得'	鏑得'○	小鑼兒鏑鏑的聲兒	○	必得'	特意
334	特	是特意之特	忒○特	忒忒	○	○	○
333	得	是得失之得	叨得○	話叨叨	得失	○	○
332	逃	是逃跑之逃	叨逃討套	叨恩	逃跑	討要	圈套
331	道	是道理之道	刀擣倒道	刀槍	擣線	顛倒	道理
330	湯	是喝湯之湯	湯糖鑞燙	喝湯	白糖	蠟臥	燙手
329	當	是應當之當	當○擋當	應當	○	擋住	典當
328	炭	是柴炭之炭	貪談坦炭	貪賤	談論	平坦	柴炭
327	單	是單雙之單	單○膽蛋	單雙	○	膽子大	雞蛋
326	太	是太甚之太	胎檯○太	懷胎	○	○	太甚
325	歹	是好歹之歹	獃○歹代	獃呆	○	好歹	交代

[TIEH-T'UI.] PART VII.—THE TONE EXERCISES.

342	343	344	345	346	347	348	349	350	351	352	353	354	355	356	357	358
疊	貼	店	天	定	聽	丟	多	妥	豆	頭	妒	土	短	團	對	退
是重重疊疊之疊	是體貼之貼	是客店之店	是天地之天	是定規之定	是聽見之聽	是丟失之丟	是多少之多	是妥當之妥	是綠豆之豆	是頭臉之頭	是媢妒之妒	是塵土之土	是長短之短	是團圓之團	是對面之對	是進退之退
參疊○	貼○鐵帖	損○點店	天田餂捵	釘○頂定	聽停梃聽	丟○哋○	多奪朶惰	託駝妥唾	兠○斗豆	偷頭○透	督毒賭妒	禿塗土唾	端○短斷	○團○	堆○○對	推○骸退
爹娘	體貼	損量	天地	釘子	聽見	丟失	多少	託情	兠底子	偷盜	督撫	禿子	端正		堆積	推諉
重疊	○	○	○	○	○	○	○	○	○	○	○	○	○	團圓	○	○
○	銅鐵	圓點	莊田	停止		搶奪	駝鳥	頭臉	毒害	塗抹				骸快	
	○	客店	拏舌頭餂	頂戴	樹梃	呀哋	花朶兒	妥當	升斗	賭博	塵土	長短	○	對面	進退
	牙帖	抔筆	定規	聽其自然	○	懶惰	綠豆	透澈	媚妒	唾沫	斷絕				

359	360	361	362	363	364	365	366	367	368	369	370	371	372	373	374
敦	吞	冬	同	雜	擦	在	才	贊	慚	葬	倉	早	草	則	策
是敦厚之敦	是吞吐之吞	是冬夏之冬	是會同之同	是雜亂之雜	是擦抹之擦	是在家在外之在	是才幹之才	是參贊之贊	是慚愧之慚	是葬理之葬	是倉庫之倉	是早晚之早	是草木之草	是則例之則	是計策之策
敦○眈鈍	吞屯○艱	冬○懂動	通同統痛	臢雜咱○	擦○○	栽○宰在	猜才彩茶	簪偺攢贊	慚慘儳	賊○○葬	倉藏○○	遭鏨早造	操槽草○	○則○○	○○○策
敦厚	吞吞吐吐	冬夏	通達	腌臢	擦抹	栽種	猜想	管子	參考	貪賊	倉庫	遭遭	操練	○	○
○	屯田	○	會同	雜亂	○	○	才幹	偺們	慚愧	○	瞞藏	穿鑿	馬槽	則例	○
打眈兒	○	懂得	統帥	咱的	○	宰殺	五彩	攢錢	悽慘	○	○	來得早	草木	○	○
遲鈍	褪淨	動靜	疼痛	○	○	在家	菜飯	參贊	儳頭	葬理	造化	○	○	○	計策

[TSEI-TS'UN.] PART VII.—THE TONE EXERCISES. 311

375	376	377	378	379	380	381	382	383	384	385	386	387	388	389	390	391
賊	怎	參	增	層	作	錯	走	湊	祖	粗	揩	竄	嘴	催	尊	寸
是賊匪之賊	是怎麼之怎	是參差之參	是增減之增	是層次之層	是作為之作	是錯失之錯	是行走之走	是湊合之湊	是祖宗之祖	是粗細之粗	是揩住之揩	是竄寶之竄	是嘴唇之嘴	是催逼之催	是尊重之尊	是尺寸之寸
○賊○	○怎○	參○○	增○○	蹭層○蹭	作昨○左	搓矬○錯	○走○湊	○湊○	祖足○祖醋	粗○○	鑽攢纂揩	驢攢○竄罪	堆○嘴	催隨○萃	尊○樽○	村存忖寸
		參差	增減	蹭一聲上了房	作房	揉搓		租賃	粗細	鑽幹	馬驢	一堆	催逼	尊重	村莊
賊匪				層次	昨日	矬子		手足		攢湊			隨他去		存亡
	怎麼	○	○	左右	行走	○	祖宗	纂修	嘴唇	○	揩節	忖量
○	○	○	饋贈 蹭蹬	坐卧	錯失	奏事	湊合	噢醋	揩住	逃寶 犯罪	萃集	○	尺寸

392	393	394	395	396	397	398	399	400	401	402	403	404	405
宗	葱	子	次	瓦	外	完	往	爲	文	翁	我	武	牙
是大宗之宗	是葱蒜之葱	是子孫之子	是次序之次	是甎瓦之瓦	是內外之外	是完全之完	是來往之往	是行爲之爲	是文武之文	是老翁之翁	是你我之我	是文武之武	是牙齒之牙
宗○總縱	葱從○	資○子字	齜嵾此次	挖娃瓦襪	灣完晚萬	汪王往忘	微爲委位	溫文穩問	翁○○甕	屋無武物	窩○我臥	丫牙雅壓	
大宗	葱蒜	資格	齜著牙兒笑	刨挖	歪正	水灣兒	汪洋	微弱	溫和	老翁	窩巢	房屋	丫頭
	依從		瓷器	娃娃	完全	王公	行爲				有無		牙齒
總名		子孫	彼此	甎瓦	昏水	早晚	來往	委員	安穩		你我	文武	文雅
縱容	○	寫字	次序	鞋襪	內外	千萬	忘記	爵位	問答	水甕	坐臥	萬物	壓倒

[YAI-YUNG.] PART VII.—THE TONE EXERCISES. 313

406	407	408	409	410	411	412	413	414	415	416	417	418	419	420
涯	羊	要	夜	言	盆	音	迎	約	魚	原	月	雲	有	用
是天涯之涯	是牛羊之羊	是討要之要	是半夜之夜	是言語之言	是損盆之盆	是聲音之音	是迎接之迎	是約會之約	是魚蝦之魚	是原來之原	是年月之月	是雲彩之雲	是有無之有	是使用之用
○涯○○	央羊養橡	腰遙咬要	噎爺野夜	煙言眼沿	揖盆○易	音銀引印	應迎影應	約○○樂	愚魚雨預	冤原遠願	日曦○月	暈雲允運	憂油有右	庸容永用
○	央求	腰骸	噎住	噢煙	作揖	聲音	應該	約會	愚濁	冤屈	子曰	頭暈	憂愁	平庸
天涯	牛羊	遙遠	老爺	言語	盆處	金銀	迎接	○	魚蝦	原來	曦曦	雲彩	香油	容易
○	養活	咬一口	野地	眼睛	○	勾引	沒影兒	○	風雨	遠近	○	應允	有無	永遠
○	各樣	討要	半夜	河沿兒	易經	用印	報應	音樂	預備	願意	年月	氣運	左右	使用

那麼順當。哎²呀、你受了這些年的辛苦、還不知道憐恤人麼。可³惡、那個人不但白耽悞工夫、還鬧了許多的錯兒。可惜了兒、他的官都快陞了、因爲不要緊的事把他革了。啊⁵、你們外國的機器、眞是巧妙得很。你那天作的那首詩王老爺瞧過、就讚妙不止一次連呼妙妙。奇⁷怪、他放着好的不要、偏要那個壞的有這個道理麼。情願那張老爺的傷快好了、就可以來救援。我⁹聽見說他好了。他好了、好極了。又聽見說他後天可以來。後天麼、巴不得的。

那[19]個人跑過這塊莊稼地,從小道兒奔大道跑了。張[20]老爺,他如今往漢口去了。是[21]由水路走,是由旱路走。他[22]是搭輪船從長江去。得[23]多少天纔到。七[24]天。我[25]估摸輪船從上海到漢口,不是四天就到麼。四[26]天就到也可以這個船是因為沿江各口又上貨又下貨所以不能那麼快。

第十二段

125 雖[1]然下很大的雨,他也到過衙門。今[2]年冬天也不大冷,也不大潮。那[3]天那個熱鬧不但小童出來看,連小妞兒也看。他[4]寫的字不論粗細他想人都可以看得出來。不[5]管你去不去,我一定去。連[6]他帶我都是受傷。我[7]想等你試過一回就不怕你不喜歡。憑[8]你去辦,兩個法子都好。你[9]快說,或東或西,是怎麼樣。這[10]個事不是竟空喜歡還有實在好處。

第十三段

126 那心裡忽有所遇,嘴裡說出來的話,就有歎美的,有喜歡的,有憐恤的,有憎惡的,有想不到而驚的,有情願的,各等神氣不同。咳[1],你學話不敷三個月,還說的

第十一段

124 牆[1]頭兒上露出一個人來。他[2]倚靠着牆。那羣人我那時都見過,姓張的不在其內。他們倆交情日子深。我[5]瞧他去,他沒在家,我留下話說日落之前我再來。他[6]們把一根木頭橫在道兒上,絆了我一個觔斗。他[7]道兒上遇見了很利害的一個險。房子背後有園子沒有。山[9]上有個廟,山背後洞裡有房子。我[10]們是從東華門外頭過去。你[11]是進園子裡去麼。我[12]們從裡頭打過個穿兒。昨[13]兒個一天都熱。偺[14]們那天論的那個事,從分手後,還沒聽見甚麼消息。那[15]上水的小船兒,都是頂溜拉着。把[16]那馬從馬圈裡拉了來,騙上跑了。我[17]昨兒個圍着皇城走了一遭。先[18]是看他往那邊去,後來轉過臉,見往我這邊來了。

每月受五兩銀子的工錢。他[14]差一點兒壞了官。那[15]底下人差一點兒散了工。我[16]天天兒出去走一走。我[17]們到他那塊兒瞧瞧,他總是很喜歡。他[18]合賊對敵打了個敗仗。他[19]辦那件事,費了很大的力沒成效。那[20]個地方兒頭裡居民甚衆,如今很蕭條。道[21]兒離遠,我可走得快不大工夫就到了。

PART VIII.—THE PARTS OF SPEECH.   317

123[1] 那小孩子在那兒呢，左右是在家裡，總不過是在家。

[2] 他這件事是甚麼時候兒甚麼地方兒甚麼緣故甚麼法子辦的，我都知道。

[3] 他一聽見那件事立刻就走了。

[4] 他早已有病，至今沒好。

[5] 他早已的病如今好了。

[6] 他這一次來的日子不多。

[7] 他這些天裡頭來過一盪。

[8] 他剛出門去，房頂兒上的瓦就叫風全颳下來了。

[9] 早起天晴，忽然雲彩鋪滿了。

[10] 我早起起來常幌是天一亮的時候兒。

[11] 那箱子我帶不了來，是一時收拾不及。

[12] 那客人們動身晚了，趕不出城去。

[13] 他的是姓劉的。

[15] 那些人他都責罰得利害，偏重的是姓王的。

[16] 他今兒來着重的是帶他兒子見我。

[17] 你昨兒個說麼是這麼說的，是這麼着我說的原是這麼着。

[18] 你昨兒個說的不是這麼說的。

[19] 這個不是好法子怎麼呢，不是你納的法子麼，總不是這兩個法子你說那'一個好，這一個還可以商量，那一個萬不可行。

[20] 那兩個人你找着了沒有，找着了姓李的沒在家姓張的並沒有這麼一個人，是壞的，也不是全壞，還有幾分可用。

[21] 風颳得可怕。

[22] 今兒晚上星星亮得可喜。

[23] 那個雪下得過逾深。

[24] 那茶葉實在不好。

[25] 那位先生教得不好。

[26] 他唱得很好聽。

[27] 我身子些微有點兒乏。

41

是他們不肯要錢麽。他們要是我說上回給、是因爲初次來纔給、這一回不給
了。既⁴是這麽第二次不教你進去、怎麽第三次又去呢。有人說、第二次是彼此
沒說明白、不如再試一試。就⁵是那第三次、和尚怎麽樣呢。他們更不愛商量直
說斷不能進去。爲⁶甚麽原故呢。他們說一來是官廟、二來當家的沒在家、三來
那一天、你納沒給香資。他們既有這個話、你還沒提給他錢麽。我倒提了、他們
說就是比初次多到三倍、也不能叫進去。

122 這個很好、那個不好得很。他²寫得字不大很好、他兄弟寫得十分好。他³十
分讚美你。你納那天請他喫飯、他很覺體面。京北那件事鬧出來、皇上氣極
了。你⁶爲一件不要緊的事過於生氣、說話太不雅了。那⁷人過於糊塗、甚麽話
都不懂。那件衣裳多嗻搴了來、昨兒晚上差不多兒得了、料估着這時候准得
不多忘了、那漢書所全忘了。今兒遇見的那倆人、姓張的差不多沒有了、是百姓太
那房子上月差不多就得了、如今全完了。我好些天總沒看書、通鑑是差
那姓李的所不認得了。頭¹²裡那山上樹木很密、如今差不多沒有了、是百姓太
不照應。那¹³些人都好、最好的是姓李的。那¹⁴些人他都不願意要、頂不願意要

PART VIII.—THE PARTS OF SPEECH.

到過他家好些遍。他[11]回了籍、不是前年麼、他時常的來往、我記不很清楚。他[12]
在道兒上受了一回大罪那是那一次呢。哎、就是前年的事情、我一個親戚、同他
一塊兒走來着。不是在大名府那個地方兒遇見賊了麼、不是賊、是鄉勇變了。
是叫他們追上了、是遇見了、都不是他風聞得大道兒上有事、他走岔道兒斜着
往南去。那麼、怎麼躲不開呢、不但沒躲開反倒走到他們當中間兒去了。
是[16]坐着車是騎着牲口。是坐車到某處兒、前後都是勇、進退兩難。聽[17]見說勇還
放槍沒放槍。那麼是受得甚麼傷呢。是這麼着、我的親戚合宋都老爺坐着一
輛車、我的親戚在左邊宋都老爺在右邊勇從左邊擁了來、要搶車把車擠得橫
躺下、倆人都吊下來了、我的親戚在上頭、摔得傷很重。哎呀[19]、
到這個地步兒勇怎麼不要他們的命、唉、他們脫身是個微倖的事。是[20]來了甚
麼救星呢。是這麼着、勇正把車裏的箱子拉出來的時候兒、他們的那些跟人騎
着牲口趕了來了、勇聽見馬跑的聲兒、不知道是甚麼、都四下裏驚散了。
121[1] 你到過那關帝廟是多少回、到過門口兒三回、往裏頭就是一次。頭[2]一次進
去、第二次為甚麼不進去、我頭一次進去、是先給了廟裏點兒香錢。第[3]二次呢

呢。是過了二年先父打發我有事進京來的。我[15]都記得那次你納進京住得日子也不多。我在京幾天家裏有個急信來。啊[16]不是令先君病重啊不是舍弟受傷說是要死。令[17]弟還在罷不錯他受的傷漸漸兒的好了。我[18]彷彿記得那時候兒是令先君病着來着是真的麼不錯我在道兒上的時候兒聽見說病了到了家幾天就不在了。是[19]所以後來你納許久沒進京。可不是麼丁憂不能出門的滿服後就是跟王大人來的那一次。王[20]大人如今還在京麼現在出差了。過些日子就回來了。聽[21]見說你納不日也要出京麼不錯快走了這兒差使的期滿了就打算回去。

120 他[1]是那兒來的人他是通州來的。離[2]京是通州遠是張家灣遠由齊化門論到通州近一點兒。你[3]到過那兒沒有你問得是那兒。我[4]說得是通州沒到過張家灣怎麼沒到過張家灣。到[5]張家灣怎麼沒到通州呢打天津坐車就到了張家灣。啊[6]這麼看起來你不是京城的人麼我不是京城的人。那[7]麼您貴處是那兒呢。我是江蘇人。是[8]江蘇那一府呢本籍是蘇州蘇州東門裏頭那宋家兒[9]呢。你認得不認得怕是東門外罷。內[10]外我不很記得是從前作過御史的原是我

PART VIII.—THE PARTS OF SPEECH.　　321

且家裏一無所有他一身受了這些苦處還叫他女人家裏見笑像這樣兒的苦難從來還有人受得麼。

第十段

119 您[1]想那一個人今兒個來不來怕今日不能來許明兒個來。他[2]昨兒個爲甚麼不來呢他昨兒個是來了來得晚。你[3]來得早他爲甚麼來得晚。我在衙門裏先散的他後散的常是這麼着。他[4]來是我沒出門以前麼他來的時候兒你納先走了。你[5]告訴他明兒個一散衙門趕着來恐怕不行他明兒個來了我繞可以見他。那[6]兒呢你這就到衙門裏不能見他麼一定趕不上我到衙門他必先走了。他[7]如今住的是那兒。住的是我從前住的那個衚衕。你[8]說的從前是甚麼時候兒是你納初次進京的時候兒。那[9]是早已了不錯那就是前十年是不是原是也快十年了。初[10]次進京不是隨王大人一塊兒麼不是那是第三次了。令先君是多喒進京是道你[11]納通共進過幾次京共總五次初次是隨着先父多[13]喒回去的三四個月的工夫兒就回去了。第[14]二次光二十三年的時候兒。

上呢。他[62]不是騎着是拉着。你[63]滿嘴裏的話都是哄我、我不再問了。咳[64]、這是那'兒的話、你各自各兒起疑、不再問也好啊。115上頭剛看的那個問答章原意是作出英話用這活字的榜樣、就是因爲那都是行的多、受的少。現在打算再添幾句補足了那受的格局。116你打我那字眼兒、是分定那打是你行的、我被你打、是那打爲我所受的、就是那受甚麽的理。117父母養兒女那句話所提是父母行的、兒女爲父母所養這一句、是兒女受的。漢話論的不止一樣的字眼兒。118即如那人實在可憐、從前在王大人那兒做門上、被人寃屈說他私受銀錢、因爲這挨打很利害、就把他辭了。他[2]回鄉去道兒上又碰見賊把他擄到山中、不但甚麽都搶乾淨了、還受了很重的傷、不是有車從那兒過有人把他扶起來、他一定要死了。等[3]他回到本村就知道他那住的地方新近都是被賊擾亂、他父親的房子也燒了、所有的產業也都毀壞了。他[4]女人原是財主家裏的姑娘、賊鬧的時候兒叫兒子扔下跑了、那人找到他丈人家、求他們給他打算些兒、他們雖然是有錢回答說、我們近來的買賣很不好、甚麽都喫虧、萬難相幫。你[5]想他起初叫人寃枉、挨駡挨打、後來是被搶受傷、並

PART VIII.—THE PARTS OF SPEECH.

[31]你這半天不是說正在看着的話麼。[32]當時正看着來着、未必此時還能趕上。[33]你說他走了、是不是。[34]我若是說他走了、你還能敢我麼。[35]敢沒要緊、那時候兒你看見他動身也可以告訴我。[36]那時候兒你許我上樓、自已就看得見了。[37]那時候兒你不許我上樓、這時候兒你許我上樓麼。[38]隨你愛上樓、愛找那個人去、都使得。[39]找他幹甚麼大概道他半天也看不見。[40]噯別有氣。[41]我不是有氣就是不信你的話。[42]噯你別這麼着、從前就算是諠你、如今是真的。[43]你諠了我這麼半天了。[44]就算這麼半天是諠你與你何妨。[45]總而言之、你想我這會兒趕得上麼。[46]我頭裏叫你去的時候兒你就走、還容易趕得上。[47]就是那會兒走、也未必准能按着他的道兒去。[48]你真矯情你別去就得了。[49]你到底叫我去不去。[50]不去罷這個人你不認得不能找我回去了。[51]我如今上來了、你先指給我他往那'兒去。[52]指給不指給不要緊還得等三天他纔能回來。[53]他這三天上那'兒去了。[54]他上墳地裏監工去。[55]你說不認得、怎麼知道是修墳地去頭[56]裏我不認得後來我看出來是王立。[57]王立在這兒打人做甚麼。[58]我沒提他打人。[59]他還是打馬來着麼。[60]不是打馬、是打騾子。[61]他騎着騾子我那'兒趕得

114 你[1]在樓上坐着看甚麼呢。我[2]坐着看那個人。看[3]他在那兒作甚麼呢。我[4]看他是打甚麼呢。那個人你認得不認得。我[5]從前沒見過。你[6]在這兒坐着看了有多大工夫兒。不[7]很大的工夫兒。你[8]看錯了罷沒人打甚麼。我[9]還怕是你看錯了，那兒沒有人。那[10]兒沒人頭裡說到這時候我還看着呢。我[11]還看見沒有人。我[12]那時候兒說的是實話。我[13]沒問你的時候兒，你看見過沒有呢。早[14]我[15]剛纔說在這兒坐的工夫不大。很[16]好你到那兒就知道有沒有。你[17]沒[18]有甚麼事辦麼。事[19]還等[20]你快回來行不行。等[21]我回來行不行。有[22]到不了你回來我就准辦結了。看[23]到了那兒果然是有人囘來我認錯。看[24]明白了至不濟我先有三天的笑話不完。怎[25]麼先有三天的笑話呢。我[26]說至不濟你得等三天纔得問明。我[27]就去看怎麼會耽誤三天。你[28]立刻去看，還趕不上呢。那[29]兒你還看着那個人我怎麼趕不上呢。叫[30]我說他還在那兒那

着坐着都是不安。國勢大亂、就彷彿牆要坍塌似的、以上這幾句裡頭、那疼愛的、籠的、站着、躺着、坐着、要坍塌各等字樣繙做英語都算是歸活字第六個式樣兒。細查那的字着字實用彷彿是這麼著那活字單用的時候兒所指的無論是作是為、就是正意、再加上的字着字、那都是陪出個旁意為補足那活字原指之事或在當時或在已往、或在將來。

111 事情是作的、是為的、所有時候不同、總不過分三等、是已經的、就是過去的、是未有的、就是將來的、就是目下的、這是三個大綱、還有得'分的細目。

112 我昨天看書、明天再歇歇、這三句、就是分時候三等的大宗。你買過那本書沒有。

113 那細目的樣式在後。你辦過那個文書沒有我正在辦着。他早起來的時候兒我正喫飯趕到晚上囘來我已經出門去了。

你[1]多嗒可以過來麼我明兒响午來好不好你是响午來我正要上衙門去。

你[4]倒放心罷攺日彼此相見你那一件事必是我給你都辦妥了。我[5]是寫信給京城裡叫他們把我那些書都打船上寄了來。我這半天也是寫信來着。到[6]後天我看的那個書已經看了三個月了、到今天晚上、第八本就看完了。你[7]總

42

醒着他是睡覺我醒着我是醒着這些樣子都無不可。104 以上這幾句裏用活字是作爲的光景多那行的受的暫且不提先把那英文使用活字各有分定六個式樣的例畧說一說。

105 比方我愛他你肯不肯那愛字肯字各當直說直間指明准定的意思。

106 他來我必見他那是包含著未定准來的意思。

107 他可以做先生那句話就是指他能做先生或指他願做與否任其自便。

108 叫人用來一個字那是令人的話走罷跑阿是令人走令人快走的話。

109 他愛看書那句話裡頭有愛字看字都是活字其中那愛字旣屬他字所主按英文定例是歸爲直說的式樣那看字不屬專主就算爲凡論的字。看書好看書是個好事這倆看字是無論看書的是誰他看書是專指某人是看書的先後這兩個說法的地方兒不同一見就可以了然。

110 以上英文活字如何變換五樣畧已說明還有一樣較比着難講些兒當時姓張的那些孩子們他最疼愛的那個病了那漢帝最寵的臣子謀叛了那炸砲炸開的時候兒那些兵站着的打傷了躺着的都沒打着。我的骨頭那麽疼躺着站

在是豈有此理。我彷彿記得去年這宗煤還貴些兒。[16] 別的不別的這斤數兒太多我可不能全買憑你撥出幾成轉賣給別人罷。[17] 你不全要到底要多少。[18] 留下個三四百斤就彀了。[19] 那煤價呢你給不給。[20] 改日再給罷。[21]

第九段

99 英國無論人物所有議及是為的是受的這宗字樣都歸為那九項之一。漢文並沒有這個限制較難創出個專名子來就是那活字這字樣雖不能算是儘對的權用也無不可容我把兩國隨用的那活字有相對有相反的地方兒勉强做個榜樣。100 卽如有漢人說馬跑鳥飛蟲扒魚游這幾句話旣是這麽接連着所說的必是馬類都是跑的鳥類都是飛的蟲類都是扒的魚類都是游的這個意思。101 或是偶爾聽見旁人說馬跑那句話必算他專指有匹馬正在跑着究竟常說的是那馬跑。102 他念書我寫字這兩句所論是現在我們倆正在那兒做這兩件事或是向來各人如此分課的意思。103 有間的你們倆在那兒都是睡覺麽若一人醒着一人睡其答法各有不同如云他睡我醒着他睡覺我

不要買。是[5]你有理,是他有理呢。衆人[6]都說是我有理。他[7]家裏那個病鬧得利害,除了他一個人其餘都死了。那[8]一件事是人都能明白。那[9]件事他爲甚麼不找人打一個主意。沒有人能替他打算。打算大家都說這個人執拗,不肯聽別人的主意。他[12]實在可憐,人人都不管,不但人家都不管,而且還有很恨他的。啊[13]有幾個數得出來麽。你[14]算是幾個。我算着有五個人。我[16]想不止五個人,還多得很呢。有人告訴你麽。[17]不[18]錯,有某人告訴我說,有某家幾個人,就很不喜歡他。98[1]哎呀,你買的這個煤是多少斤。共[2]總八百斤。怎[3]麽買這麽多呢。你[4]說的得買好些個。我[5]說好些個,也不要這麽多。你[6]不要這麽些個還可以轉賣給別人。你[7]是多少錢買得。是[8]平安街泰興煤鋪。[9]他這麽貴,你爲甚麼不到別處去呢。離[10]這兒左近沒有別的煤鋪。往[11]遠些兒看見好幾個煤鋪呢。離[12]是通氣兒還可以還價兒,不能這兒要多少,那兒也是要多少,都是彼此相襯的意思。看煤也不見很好,這宗煤要賣四吊錢一百斤,實在[13]那兒的話呢,我那一天上平安街看見好幾個煤鋪。他[15]們還是彼此通氣兒。四吊錢一百斤買的。哎[9]買得這麽貴,是在那一個鋪子裏買的。

PART VIII.—THE PARTS OF SPEECH.

一邊兒好。那一邊兒有景致，這一邊兒荒些個。這些牛你都買了麽。這三個黃的是我的，那幾個黑的是他買的。你拏我這些東西作甚麽。不都是你的。那'一個不是我的呢。這一樣就不是你的，這一個我可不要那些個你擱下罷。

96 國家的百官各人有各人的差使。他們倆人各人有各人的辦法。賭錢的各自各兒下各自各兒的注。那兩個主意都不好用。那一天有兩個人給他出主意，聽誰的都可以救他的命。可惜那兩個主意他都沒肯聽。他問我賣房子是長住是暫住，我說怎麽着都可以。這個單子你們倆不論誰抄都可以。

他們倆每月三次回家，每次准一個人回去。明兒個怕有事，你們倆總得留下一個人，不論誰都使得。你那一天喝醉了，遇見人就打。你不是說那賊都是一個人，你可不知道，我見的是個個纏着紅布的。他腦袋上纏着紅布麽。全纏不纏，我看這兩個那一個好呢。那一個都好。這兩樣兒你們這些人進來的時候個個兒都得帶腰牌。不論那一個我都不愛喜。你看這兩個那一個好呢。那一個都好。這兩樣兒

玉器你要那一個。兩個都好，要叫我挑一個，那一個都使得。

97 那瓷器他要買那一個呢。通共他都要買。你要買的是那一件兒。我都

子。89你愛喜是那'一個、說人說物都使得。90他在那兒辦的是甚麼事辦的是甚麼事,他還沒告訴我說。91他實在要的是這們着。92所有犯法的總得'究辦。無論是誰犯了法,就得'究辦。無論是誰,該賞,我必得'賞。93那賊很兒遇見誰都殺。凡有進入內地,必得'領執照。憑誰說都不可信。憑他保舉是誰,都得陞賞。那話是假的。我不是叫你把那邊所有的書都拏過來麼。他叫我辦甚麼,我必得'辦甚麼。櫃裡頭還落下了一本。原是還有我沒拏過來的麼。立94他不是你的父親麼。不是,是我的哥哥。哦,他的歲數兒多大呢。比我大二十多。那一本書是你的,是你借來的,是我本人的。哦是你託那姓張的給你買的麼。不是是我本人買的。你今兒上東花園兒逛逛罷。不行,我今兒有差使。交給我替你當好不好。費你納的心,必得'我自己辦的。你各自各兒辦、合別人辦有甚麼不一樣。不但是我本人的責任,而且我自已各兒不辦,必招上司的挑斥。誰告訴上司。不用人告訴他們,他們自己就查得出來。95這兩匹馬那'一個好。依我說這一匹好,那一匹不好。那一道河的兩岸,那

第八段

81 人說話時、稱自己為我、我向誰說話、稱誰為你、我偺們兩個之外為旁人、我提起旁人稱為是他。82 稱的若不止一個人為我們、偺們、你們、他們。83 漢話裡頭提起禽獸來、他字可以說得、論死物那他字不大常用。84 提起狗來可以說他會看家、問人那桌子挐了去了麼、就答挐了去了、不能說挐過他去了。85 我去拜的那個人沒在家。你去拜的是誰。是從前教我說官話的一位先生。他[4]姓甚麼。姓[5]張。是[6]在虎皮術術住的那張家的麼。再[7]說是甚麼術術。我[8]說得是虎皮術術、他住得是城外頭張先生住得術術、他住得是東大街南頭兒路西裡第四條的那個術術。我的親戚。教[12]他們甚麼功課呢。教[13]那個大的辦文書、小的念四書。他[14]們倆那[9]一個見長。我[15]看那小的比大的強。86 說誰字兒就是提人繞用得說甚麼、說那個這倆字眼兒、提人提東西都用得着。87 叫你來得是誰、叫你來得是甚麼人叫你來得是那[17]個人。88 你要甚麼來、我要那茶碗來、你在這兒做甚麼、我在這兒拾到屋你[16]納現在看的是甚麼書。還是你去

第七段

67 那名目的實字若要分項定等必得加字眼兒。實字像是爲主似的分項定等的字眼兒是輔助的。 68 比方單說好一個字是空說沒有着落好字之外必得加上或人或物的名目那好字纔有分項之用。 69 譬如這是個好人那個人好這兩句那好字是品評人的字眼兒。 70 這個紙白那個紙紅這紅白兩個字是分紙項的。 71 粗紙細紙這個紙粗那個紙細這幾句裏頭那粗細兩個字是分等的。

72 至於用那輔助的字眼兒也得分層次看以下這一章就知道了。 73 他聰明你更聰明你比他聰明這人裏最聰明是他他比他們那些人聰明他是天底下最聰明的人。 74 那是做不來的那更是做不來的那越發做不來的這些法子頂做不來的是那個。 75 京城裏頭的房脊頂高的是皇宮。 76 他的錢比我的錢多。 77 我比不起他的能幹。 78 他身量高我的身量矮。 79 他們倆說官話那一個強姓李的強些兒。 80 這三個人的學問那一個強還是姓李的強。

PART VIII.—THE PARTS OF SPEECH.

借給他呢。他在街上遇見我拏着這本書、他合我借我不肯、得拏了去呢。我說不肯、他打我手裡硬搶了去、說後天還我。 57 你不肯、他怎麼以後不可合他穿換。 58 他寶在可惡你

59 那賊匪燒過我們老人家的房子這一句裏按着英話的說法、賊匪是頭等房子是二等、老人家是三等。 60 怎麼見得呢、一問一答就瞧出來了放火的是誰、是那賊匪。燒的是甚麼、是房子。房子是誰的、是老人家的房子。 61 總之、那名目不論甚麼、是行的當為頭等、是受的就當為二等、是歸為的就當為三等。

第六段

62 人分得是男女、禽獸分得是公母、凡死物都不分陰陽、山、水、木、石、都算是死物。

63 那邊兒坐着的一個爺們、一個娘兒們、是夫婦麼不是、是兄妹。

64 我買了七隻小鷄子、有兩隻公的、五隻母的。

65 兒馬是公的、騾馬是母的。

66 牤牛是公牛、母牛是母牛。

子、是個數兒不定。45 有人來了、是幾個人四個人、那些人做甚麼來、他們是拉了幾匹馬來、那幾匹馬是誰要買的、不是都要賣的、買一匹也可以、我不大很要買馬。

第五段

46 英國用名目、限定三個式樣、都是隨勢變用、漢話裏旣是沒有這個分別、只好對付着分出三等、請看以下四段、就是分三等先後的榜樣。
47 那茶碗是誰砸得、是那小孩子砸得。
48 這個字是甚麼人寫得、是姓張的那個人寫得。
49 畜生裏最靈的是甚麼、最靈的是狗。
50 那小小子兒打得是誰、他打的是那妞兒。
51 那樵夫在那兒做甚麼呢、他在那兒砍樹枝子呢。
52 他把那本書丟了、丟得是誰的書、是我的那本書。
53 你那本書不是送給他麼、不是送給他的、是借給他的。
54 你跟他要他的那本、補你的罷咧、他那一本合我的不一樣。
55 你是那一天借給他的、就是前天借給他的。
56 你爲甚麼

第四段

32 所有陪襯字眼兒、既已講畢、今再論名目單數多數之分、就是漢話分單數兒總數兒、有好些個法子、有本名目不加數目字眼兒可以當數目字用的、有重用名目的字、可以當數目用的、有用這衆多多少好些個、都均全大家諸凡等、這些字的。到了要說名目的數目兒又有把數目字加在上頭的、也有先提名目後加上數目字的。33 卽如聽見衆人說來的人很多。34 有多少。有好些個。35 都是甚麼人均屬良善。36 爲甚麼全來了。大家有公事求諸位辦理。37 凡事有個頭緒。這些人等、自然就回去了。38 來了多少人、那句話也可以當來了許多人講。39 有人來、這句話不能定是一個人來、是多少人來、有兩個人來、有三個人來、這都說得三個人以上常說得是幾個人。40 說好些個人、是人數較多些兒似乎一看數不清。41 他們家那些人們狠不和睦。42 話裏不提人用不着們字。43 他來的是賣牛羊、這句話必不是賣一隻牛一隻羊的意思有人說他要賣隻牛、賣匹馬、賣的一定是一隻牛、一匹馬。44 這間房子、是單說一間、這房

頭　一頭牛、一頭騾子、一頭驢、說一個騾子、一個驢、一個牛、也使得、惟獨羊是論隻不論頭。

堵　堵是做牆字的陪襯、用堵字道字、都是一樣。

堆　堆字合垛字彷彿也能說一堆木頭、一堆磚、一堆土等類、但垛是擺得整齊、堆是擺得雜亂。

頓　一頓飯、一頓打、用這個頓字做陪襯、似乎因為有些兒足了的意思。

座　一座山、一座墳、一座廟、一座塔、一座城、都說得。

尊　一尊礟也說一位礟、一架礟。

尾　一尾魚、還說一條魚。

位　位字的本義無論是人是物、或坐或立、各歸其所就是了、三位大人、一位礟、幾位客。

文　那文字除了銅錢之外、不當陪襯字樣、一文錢、常說是一個大錢、或問這東西要幾文錢、答的是多少大錢、用這文字的原由、是出於周朝鑄錢的時候、錢身加上文字的緣故。

眼　就是說井用這個眼字作陪襯。

PART VIII.—THE PARTS OF SPEECH.

擔
擔是一個人拏扁擔挑着的東西。他挑着一擔柴火是他挑着一擔柴火、扁擔兩頭兒挑着柴火。若僅有一綑柴火那是用棍子挑着扛在肩髈兒上。

刀
刀就是一刀紙這一句話裏用的本是幾十張紙擱平了、搭在一塊兒用刀力切得開的意思。

道
一道河、一道橋、一道牆、一道口子、一道上諭都是有條字的意思。京城前門外頭、那橋是個三道橋。

套
一套書是幾本書套在一塊兒許是一部全書、也許是一部書分爲幾套一套衣裳是一袍一褂先穿袍子後套褂子一套酒杯是十二個酒杯一個比一個小能彀套在一塊兒的。

條
一條線、一條繩子、一條帶子、一條鎖練子、一條狗、一條虹、一條理、一條街一條道這都是常說的到了一貼膏藥也說一道河也說一道河。

貼
貼除了一貼膏藥沒別的用處。一貼金箔、是十張搭在一塊兒。

頂
頂這項字、就是做轎子帽子的陪襯。

朶
除了一朶花沒別的用處那花沒開之先俗名叫咕朶兒。

梁
一梁木頭、一梁磚是好些個磚木在一塊兒擺得齊整。

匹　陪襯馬字專用匹字，至於驢騾說頭說匹、都行，說一個也有能用的時候兒，駱駝常說是幾個。

定　定字專做綢緞綾羅紗布等項的陪襯必是兩頭兒不缺纔說得。

篇　一篇文章一篇賦一篇論都是成章的意思所以用篇做陪襯說這書有多少篇兒那是論張數兒合成章有點兒分別。

鋪　除了一鋪炕之外沒有甚麼別的用處牀總得說一張牀那鋪店之鋪是同音不同聲的。

所　一所房子合一處房子相同，都是總論一個大門之內的。

扇　扇本是驅暑招風的東西，因爲彷彿門的樣兒故此說扇那房子門牕不齊還短四五扇。

首　首字單是做詩纔用，彷彿限定首尾的意思詩家做詩看題隨做詩首多寡不定各首句數不同或有四句或有八句最多十二句十六句都是一首。那首數兒不是一定必要雙數兒做三五首做幾十首都行。

擡　擡本是兩個人或是數人共擧一樣兒東西出殯的能有六十四擡。嫁粧至少的八擡富家一百多擡都許用送禮物的擡都是雙數兒。

股　一股道、就是一條道文話一股路也說得。

塊　一塊洋錢、一塊墨、一塊磚、一塊區、都可以說這塊字的用處、也是最廣的、即如拏一塊銀子買一塊氈子。

管　管是中間兒空的橫長東西的陪襯字、即如一管筆、一管笛、一管簫、要說一枝也是一樣。

綑　一綑柴火、一綑葱、這些個都是因爲有束在一塊兒的意思。

粒　一粒米、一粒九藥、都是指那東西的形像而論。

領　除了一領蓆子一領葦箔之外別處不用爲陪襯。

面　這面字就是做鑼鼓旗鏡的陪襯字。

把　是有把兒手裡可以拏的東西、都論幾把比方一把茶壺兩把刀子一把子、一把义子、一把扇子、一把鎖頭等類都是椅子說一把說一張、都使得。

包　凡是收裹起來的、都可以用包字做陪襯、即如一包糖、一包煙土等類。

本　一本書、一本帳、都說得、一本書還可以說一卷書帳却不能說卷字。

副　一副對字、一副環子、都是一對的意思、一副鈕子可是五個。

桿　一桿槍、一桿秤、一桿义、若是長槍說一條也使得其餘的却不能用條。

根　這根字陪襯的就是桅杆、旗杆、棍子、杆子、燈草、木頭、頭髮、鬍子等名目、都是按着形像說的一根棍子說一條棍子也行。

個　這個字的用處最多、惟獨幾個人、這個理、這個東西、更是常說的、別處用個字都是活用。

棵　這棵字就是專做樹的陪襯並沒別的用法。

顆　一顆珠子、一顆首級、都是按那名目形像說的、是圓的東西、多可以分一顆一顆的。

口　一口鍋、一口鐘、一口刀、一口缸、幾口人、都說得雖然這口字是這些名目的陪襯獨論人還有分別總說男女的人數兒、是論口、單說婦女也是論口、至於專論男人就說多少名、多少個。一口刀原是兵器、一把刀也可以說、屠戶用的也是一把刀、那一口鐘的鐘、是廟裡掛的鐘、裡頭沒有舌、有人撞纔有聲兒。

PART VIII.—THE PARTS OF SPEECH. 341

炷 一炷香是單說一枝香、若是好些炷用紙束在一塊兒、那爲一股、五股在一塊兒爲一封。

處 處處就是地方兒的意思說買了一處房子是一個院牆之內所有的那些間房子都在裏頭連單間沒院牆的也可以說。

串 一串珠子、一串誦珠、一串朝珠、一串錢誦珠朝珠也說一掛。一個珠子是帶顆字陪襯。

椿 地裡打下去的大木橛子叫椿話裏說有一椿事情、是在多少事情裏、單指出一樣兒來。常說的可是一件事

牀 一牀被、一牀褥子、一牀毡子、都說得。

方 這方字就是做碎磚碎石的陪襯字。

封 這封字、是做書信等字的陪襯。因爲這個字本有含而不露之意、所以說一封書字一封信。

幅 幅合張不同、與條字近些兒、但是寬窄沒甚分別、一幅箋紙、就是一張箋紙。論布可以說一幅兒布、論綢子也有說一幅兒的。

件　裏住、這句話、是那幾間屋子連到一塊兒、出入都是由一個門走。或說我們俩住一間屋子、那是四根柱子的中間兒一個單間兒。這一溜房子有多少間、是問這橫連著的房子有多少。

隻　這陪襯衣裳的字是專用件字。到了一件事情、幾件徐伙、幾件文書、這宗字樣、要換別的字陪襯也可以比方說一椿事情、幾樣徐伙、幾套文書、都使得。那隻字陪襯的、是雞鴨鵝牛羊虎、船箱等字、又有鞋靴襪胳臂手脚眼睛、都是原來成雙的、要指一半而說、所以纔用這個隻字、卽如那雙鞋丟了一隻。

枝　沒有一管筆、一管笛說的多。枝子合枝不同用論兵說的是一枝子兵、一枝子勇。一枝燭、一枝花兒是好些朶花兒在一塊兒長着、一枝筆一枝笛、可以說也

軸　一軸畫兒、是一張裱了的條幅、因爲底下兩頭兒露出木頭軸兒來、故此纔說。還有話封論幾軸、也是一樣兒的意思。

句　這句字、就是陪襯話字的、不論口說筆寫都行。

卷　一卷冊子、一卷書、還是說一本冊子、一本書的時候兒多。

PART VIII.—THE PARTS OF SPEECH.

張子。凡桌椅牀凳弓紙機羅這些字用張字做陪襯是因為象形稍有寬大的樣

陣。一陣大雨一陣大風一陣吵鬧這個陣字本意原是打仗因就著那忽然的形勢故用為陪襯字彷彿是來的很急不能等著的神氣

乘。那乘字本是乘船乘車乘馬的乘字轎子有說一乘的又有說一頂的。

劑藥。一劑藥是合好些味藥做湯喝的若是把好些味藥配成丸藥那稱為一料

架。一架礮一架鷹一架鐘一架房桄兩架房柁也能說一對。

間。四根柱子的中間兒就為一間故當房子屋子這些名目的陪襯可也得分別著用人若說我買了房子那是買了一所一處必是包括著好些間房子說那個房子好那就是統一個大門裏都算上或問那個房子裏有多少間那人回答有三十多間那都是那所兒房子裏頭不分大小按各間而說王公府裏大約北面都有樓上下兩層各分五七間不等人要是在樓外分其間數說是五七間房子要在樓裏頭就說是五七間屋子我們倆在一個屋

四句裡頭那個字、位字、匹字、隻字、就是陪襯人官馬船這些名目的。這些陪襯的字、不但竟能加之於先也有加在名目以後之時。比方泛說馬船也能說馬匹船隻。28 又有本名目剛己提過接着再說的、就可以把陪襯的字做爲替換之用。設若有人買了牛、他告訴我說、我昨兒買了牛、我問他買了多少隻、他說買了十幾隻。這就是牛字作爲本名目、那隻字就是陪襯的、有陪襯的替換本名目、本名目就不必重複再提了。29 這替換名目的字樣、不止於話裏常用連詩文內也有可用之時。30 總之細察那陪襯字的實用像是把一切能分不能分的名目、明白指出的意思。何謂不能分名目、卽如皇天之天、后土之土、是獨一無二、不能分晰的專項、那兒有陪襯的字樣呢。至於那些有類能分的名目、要分晰時、此陪襯字樣頗爲得用、其用謂何、乃能指出所說的名目爲總類之那一項。31 如今把那些陪襯的字眼兒連正主的各名目一倂開列於左、爲學話的便用。

盞 擎一盞燈來我要看書、燈籠却論個不論盞。那盞字也當碗字用、一盞茶、一碗茶、都可以說。

知道是誰呢。設若說話的人來了聽了的就知道來的是從前提過的那個人。如此分清了界限那就是確然指明了。23我們這些那字這字原是分別彼此之用。24這可自然那個且等後來再說就是這第二十二段裡專用那個人的那字却沒有彼此之分就為指定不是泛論。25漢話裡用那個其字好像合英文裡指定的字眼兒有時相合也不能以為成例。26不錯卽如其餘的那個其字原是指定除了已經開除之外所剩的都在裡頭。還有其要在此那一句是專指最要的地方兒至於像他那個人其心不可間這一句那其字不過是當他字講名目之前加增指定的字樣兩國的話裡均有可舍之處卽如人是萬物裡最靈的金比銀重這兩句裡那人金銀等字都是總名可以直說不必加增某字的還有人姓地名等字樣也是這麼着。

第三段

27漢話裡頭那名目又有個專屬是這麼着話裡凡有提起是人是物在名目之先可加一個同類的名目做為陪襯的字卽如一個人一位官一匹馬一隻船這

第二段

方能成句。何為綱凡句內所云人、物、事等字眼兒、為綱何為目論人、物、事的是非、有無動作、承受這都為目。看起這個來僅有死字、沒有活字、難算成句、較比起來、僅說人、雨、馬這三個字、不添活字、實屬有頭無尾焉能算是話、若是僅有活字、沒有死字、其理亦然、不待言矣。那人是好、下雨、那馬快這三句語無腔義、所以總成句、分其綱目就是這頭一句裡那人字為綱、論人的好不好是目、第二句下雨、雨字是綱、論起下雨不下是目、第三句馬字為綱、論起走得快為目。

21 句段分為綱目一層、中國也不是總沒有此說、但是閣下所說的、單字分有九類、那是從前總沒聽見提過的。 22 那却自然單字分類之說、漢話向無此理。英文裡頭凡有人、物、事、勢等字、樣應歸單字九類中之一類、名曰名目、即如人、書、病、年、這四個字、都是名目、英國不分作文說話、凡有遇用名目之時、常有將某字加於名目之先、以便指出所提名目、是否已經提過的、這種字樣、漢話裡雖然沒有分晰明白、然遇勢亦有分別虛實之法、譬如說有個人來、有一個人來一聽這兩句話就知道所論的人、並不是從前提過的、那說話的人心裡還茫無定向、並不

是實字、其中要看用法、還有死活之分。虛字較難細辨。比方你不要錢麼、那一句、那麼字本無正義、用之不過是因為指明訂間的口氣、就是虛字。其餘的那幾個字裡頭、那個不字雖有實義、漢文裡頭還算是虛字。那你字、要字、錢字、都為實字。至於那個死字活字不同、就是你錢這兩個字、是死的、那要字一個字是活的。然而那要字、纔說是活字、在此處固然是活的、別處也能彀當死的用、著比其要速這一句那要字速字、可不是死字麼。再問這一句裡頭活字沒有麼、就是那在字必算是活字。又考這些字裡虛實之分、就是那其、在這俩字、雖然各有正義在這兒仍算是虛字。 16 看起這個來、就是虛字實字這個名目大有隨時隨勢能彀互相變通的理。 17 變通是全能彀變通的、甚至於有人說、不論甚麼字、都可以做半活半死的用。 18 我們英國話文限制死些兒、沒有漢字那麼活動、且將英文分兩大端論之、一為單字、一為句法。那單字共分九類、是為單字之一端。至於連字成句、連句成文、那就是句法之一端。 19 倣國向來作文章、也有分股分段的規矩、閣下剛說這句法、或者是那麼樣罷。 20 那却不同、貴國作文講究的是句法、專管那個字句的長短、我們成句之理、就是無論何句必須綱目兩分的

與筆畫本音並不相諧。就以那數目裏的十字兒論寫的是橫豎兩筆那橫的本音一豎的本音滾這兩筆合成就是十字。一看就知道是專管字形於聲音毫無干涉。這就是外國人學漢字以爲最難的地方。9外國人定音還有甚麼好法子呢。10是這麼着外國寫字有二十多筆畫把筆畫連成整字的理用不了多大的工夫兒就能了然學會之後遇見甚麼字都能定得準那個音至若漢字並沒有準能定音的地方兒沒念過就不能知道必得察一察察過一次日後再見了還是保不住不忘。11那是不錯的忘記這一層我們漢人們倒不理會是因爲從小兒先認得的是單字。12就是了我們外國人旣是沒念過貴國的書看書的時候兒未免有那單字的難處等到把單字連綴成文那作文的難處就比單字更甚萬分了。13聽見說外國的文較比我們中國的省事些兒。14不錯是省點兒事原來外國作文其單字皆有一定之類若欲將單字連成句讀專有指定句法明文的書那學者一目了然貴國並無這些指定句法的書所以就可以連句成文。至於那單字統分虛實兩大宗這個理是我考察過了多少囘至今總沒能透澈。15本字裡有正義的統謂

言語例畧

第一段

1 看貴國的人學我們的漢話都像是費事得很却是甚麽難處呢。2 唉那難處不止一樣有口音的難處有單字的難處更有文法的難處。3 怎麽呢外國人各國互相學話看着像不用很多的工夫難道我們這漢話合貴國的話全是兩樣的麽。4 那到不必說天下各國的話沒有全不相同的地方兒是人心裏的意思發出來隨勢自然分好些神氣有直說有無問有令有願望有驚訝各詞比方這人死了那人沒死那是直說有無的話。那人死了沒有是間人的話。斬那人罷是令人的話。把不得那人好了是願望的話。可惜了兒那人死了是驚訝的話。這是鄙意先生明白不明白。5 那兒不明白這就算得文字語言的總例是中外各國人情自然相同之理。6 可不是麽就是論及單字的那個難處惟漢文獨異怎麽呢除了中國之外是有文各國寫字各有筆畫的定數這些筆畫各有本音如果把數筆連在一塊兒不但變成整字還有指定聲音的用處。7 那清文頗有幾分相似漢文雖不相同寫的却分八筆合貴國的筆畫還不麽。8 用法大不相同寫漢字原有八個筆畫筆畫雖有本音一作成整字其音

PART VIII.

THE PARTS OF SPEECH.
(CHINESE TEXT.)

ERRATA.

PART II.	Page 37.	3.	6.	For *hsin*² read *hsin*¹		
,,	,, 38.	4.	2.	,, *pi*²	,, *pi*³	
,,	,, 39.	7.	5.	,, *shih*³	,, *shih*²	
PART III.	Page 55.	2.	Col. 4.	For 字	read 字、	
,,	,, 55.	4.	,, 5.	,, 見過他	,, 見過、他	
,,	,, 55.	4.	,, 8.	,, 哪。	,, 哪	
,,	,, 94.	11.	,, 7.	,, 上的	,, 上背的	
,,	,, 97.	2.	,, 4 and 5.	,, 地上睡覺、	,, 就地兒睡、	
,,	,, 98.	5.	,, 3.	,, 相	,, 像	
,,	,, 119.	1.	,, 8.	,, 間	,, 閒	
,,	,, 119.	5.	,, 8.	,, 到	,, 倒	
,,	,, 120.	4.	,, 3, 5. and 7.	,, 班	,, 辦	
PART IV.	Page 132.	75.	Col. 3.	For 得	read 得'	
,,	,, 151.	59.	,, 9.	,, 那	,, 那'	
PART V.	Page 157.	3.	Col. 8.	For 底	read 低	
,,	,, 164.	1.	,, 6.	,, 謊	,, 慌	
,,	,, 175.	6.	,, 3.	Omit 裡		
,,	,, 189.	1.	,, 5.	For 膣	,, 夥	
,,	,, 195.	2.	,, 6.	,, 膨	,, 膨	
,,	,, 200.	3.	,, 12 and 13.	,, 陶	,, 淘	
,,	,, 201.	2.	,, 6 (two places)	,, 捨	,, 躧	
,,	,, 201.	3.	,, 8.	,, 到	,, 倒	
,,	,, 203.	4.	,, 6.	,, 顯	,, 現	
,,	,, 204.	3.	,, 10.	,, 忽	,, 忽	
,,	,, 218.	3.	,, 8.	,, 輩	,, 背	
PART VI.	Page 237.	15.	Col. 9.	For 事	read 勢	
PART VII.	Page 305.	283 (two places).		For 播	read 簸	
PART VIII.	Page 319.	120.	18. Col. 9.	For 吊	read 掉	
,,	,, 331.	88.	Last col.	,, 到	,, 掇	
,,	,, 341.	31.	Col. 12.	,, 字	,, 子	
,,	,, 345.	26.	,, 8.	,, 舍	,, 捨	
,,	,, 348.	10.	,, 6.	,, 得	,, 得'	
,,	,, 349.	4.	,, 9.	,, 把	,, 巴	

北京大学中国语言学研究中心

早期北京话珍稀文献集成

主编 刘云

——西人北京话教科书汇编

分卷主编 翟赟 郭利霞 陈颖

语言自迩集

（第二版）

[英] 威妥玛 编著

卷三

北京大学出版社
PEKING UNIVERSITY PRESS

集邇自言語

(YÜ YEN TZŬ ÊRH CHI).

A

PROGRESSIVE COURSE

DESIGNED TO ASSIST THE STUDENT OF

COLLOQUIAL CHINESE

AS SPOKEN IN THE CAPITAL AND THE METROPOLITAN DEPARTMENT.

IN THREE VOLUMES.

SECOND EDITION.

PREPARED BY

THOMAS FRANCIS WADE,
Sometime H.B.M.'s Minister in China.

AND

WALTER CAINE HILLIER,
Chinese Secretary to H.B.M.'s Legation, Peking.

VOL. III.

SHANGHAI:
PUBLISHED AT THE STATISTICAL DEPARTMENT OF THE INSPECTORATE GENERAL OF CUSTOMS,
AND SOLD BY
KELLY & WALSH, LIMITED, SHANGHAI, YOKOHAMA, AND HONGKONG.
LONDON: W. H. ALLEN & Co., WATERLOO PLACE.

1886.

CONTENTS.

	PAGE.
APPENDIX I.—GLOSSARY OF WORDS AND PHRASES IN PARTS III, IV, V, AND VI OF VOLUME II	1
APPENDIX II.—INDEX OF CHARACTERS IN PARTS III, IV, V, VI, AND VII OF VOLUME II, arranged according to Radicals	51
APPENDIX III.—THE PEKING SYLLABARY:—	
Explanatory Note...	74
Sound Table	75
Peking Syllabary	79
Table of Characters subject to changes of Sound or Tone	175
APPENDIX IV.—WRITING EXERCISES	199
ERRATA AND ADDENDA	245

APPENDIX I.

GLOSSARY OF WORDS AND PHRASES.

APPENDIX I.

GLOSSARY OF WORDS AND PHRASES

IN

PARTS III, IV, V, AND VI OF VOLUME II.

Aback, taken: Part VI, Chapter xvii, Note 4.
Abbreviated (characters): Part III, Exercise viii*, 10.
Abilities: Part V, Lesson xv, Note 1.
Ability: Part III, Exercise xix, 9; Part VI, Chapter xxiii, 1, Note 1.
Ability of a high order: Part IV, Dialogue ix, 40, Obs. 3.
Able (clever): Part III, Exercise xxxi, 10, Obs. 1.
Able, to be: Part III, **391**.
Abominable: Part IV, Dialogue iv, 56.
About it, while you are: Part III, **765**.
About (more or less): Part III, Exercise i*, 9.
About one, to have: Part III, Exercise xxix*, 7.
About, what he is: Part III, Exercise xxii, 1.
Above the other, one: Part III, **891**.
Absent-minded: Part III, **578**; Exercise xxii, 4.
Absolute (fixed): Part IV, Dialogue x, 3.
Absolutely: Part III, **635**.
Absolution from sins: Part V, Lesson lxxx, 1, Note 3.
Abstinence: Part VI, Chapter xv, Note 7.
Abuse behind one's back: Part V, Lesson lxiv, 3.
Accidental: Part III, **562**.
Accommodation (at an inn): Part IV, Dialogue viii, 37.
Accompany: Part III, Exercise xxvii*, 8.
Accompany (see out): Part III, **765**.
Accomplish: Part III, **30**; Part V, Lesson vi, 2, Note 7.
Accomplishment, an: Part III, **1058**.
Accordance with, in: Part III, **1030**.
According to: Part III, **919**.
Accordingly: Part III, **125**; Part V, Lesson xiv, Note 11.
Account, on no: Part III, Exercise vi, 7; Part V, Lesson xxvi, Note 8.
Account, taken into: Part III, Exercise xv, 7.
Account, turn to good: Part V, Lesson xci, 4, Note 13.
Accounts: Part III, Exercise viii*, 9; Exercise xiii, 1.
Accounts, to go into: Part III, Exercise xl*, 2.

Accounts, to pay off: Part IV, Dialogue vi, 58, Obs.
Accurate: Part III, **1078, 1080**.
Ace of, within an: Part V, Lesson xxx, 6.
Achieve, to: Part V, Lesson xvii, Note 19.
Acquaintance, old: Part IV, Dialogue iii, 97.
Acquaintances, a large circle of: Part IV, Dialogue x, 1, Obs. 4.
Acquaintances, make: Part V, Lesson lxi, 2, Note 8.
Act as, to: Part III, **342, 345**.
Acting appointment: Part III, **1009**.
Action at law, to bring an: Part III, **1025**.
Action, mode of: Part III, Exercise xxii*, 10.
Active service (military): Part III, **504**.
Add: Part III, **687, 689**; Part V, Lesson xxxiv, Note 5.
Add to all this, to: Part V, Lesson xlviii, 2, Note 9.
Add up: Part III, Exercise viii*, 8, Obs.
Addition, in: Part V, Lesson x, Note 9.
Address, to: Part III, Exercise xxv, 1.
Administration of: Part III, Exercise xx, 2.
Administrator: Part III, **585**.
Admire: Part V, Lesson xxiv, Note 3; Part VI, Chapter iii, Note 6.
Adopted son: Part VI, Chapter xxxi, 1, Note 1.
Adulation: Part V, Lesson iv, 3, Note 8.
Advantage: Part III, **925, 1043**.
Advantage, let go an: Part V, Lesson lxxxi, 1.
Advantage unduly, to gain: Part V, Lesson xv, Note 5.
Adventure, an: Part V, Lesson xxxvi, 1, Note 1.
Adversity, friends in: Part VI, Chapter vii, 4, Note 11.
Adversity, the only bond in: Part VI, Chapter v, 4.
Advice, ask your: Part IV, Dialogue x, 5; Part V, Lesson lxxxi, 1.
Advice, to give: Part V, Lesson xli, 1, Note 2.
Advice, to give good: Part V, Lesson xiv, 2, Note 6.
Affair, it would be another: Part V, Lesson lxxviii, 4.
Affect: Part IV, Dialogue vi, 14, Obs. 2.

NOTE.—The asterisk after the number of an Exercise (*e.g.*, Exercise viii*) indicates that the word or phrase will be found in the latter portion of the Exercise, that which has to be turned into Chinese.

Affect prejudicially: Part V, Lesson liii, Note 3.
Affectation: Part VI, Chapter i, 6.
Affection: Part VI, Chapter xxv, 9, Note 10.
Affliction, in: Part V, Lesson l, 1.
After all: Part III, Exercise xi, 2, Obs.; Exercise xvii*, 1, Obs. 2; **647**; Exercise xxix, 2, Obs.; Part V, Lesson iii, Note 6; Lesson xxxiii, Note 18.
After, to go: Part III, **425**.
Afternoon: Part III, **249**.
Afterwards: Part III, Exercise ix*, 11, Obs. 2.
Again and again: Part III, Exercise xxix, 1, Obs.
Age: Part III, Exercise xvii, 8.
Age, one's: Part III, **955**; Part V, Lesson xxxix, 2, Note 7.
Age, what is your: Part IV, Dialogue ix, 42, Obs.
Agent, an: Part VI, Chapter ii, Note 4.
Ages, in all: Part III, **871**.
Aggravated (increased) by: Part VI, Chapter xxviii, 9, Note 16.
Aggravating: Part III, **965**.
Agree (arrange), to: Part III, Exercise xxix, 3, Obs. 1.
Agree (consent): Part III, **784**.
Agree to do anything, he will: Part V, Lesson lxviii, 2.
Agrees with (corresponds): Part V, Lesson xx, Note 9.
Agricultural population: Part III, **539**.
Ague, to have the: Part VI, Chapter xxvi, 15, Note 5.
Ahead, don't look (proverb): Part III, Exercise xxxiii, 3.
Aid, to: Part V, Lesson xix, Note 9.
Ailing: Part IV, Dialogue iv, 67.
Air, to play an: Part VI, Chapter xxvi, 7.
Airs to, to show: Part V, Lesson lxiii, 1.
All: Part III, **123**; Exercise xxii, 10, Obs.; **912**; Part IV, Dialogue x, 11, Obs. 1; Part VI, Chapter xix, 2, Note 1.
All (every man): Part V, Lesson lxi, 5, Note 10.
All, at: Part IV, Dialogue iv, 21.
All, is: Part III, Exercise xxix*, 4, Obs. 2.
All over: Part VI, Chapter xix, Note 1.
All that: Part III, Exercise xxxix, 6, Obs. 1.
All that there are: Part III, **1003**, Obs.
All very well, it's: Part V, Lesson lii, 1, Note 1.
Alley: Part III, **800**.
Alley, blind: Part V, Lesson xxii, 2, Note 9.
Allowance for, make: Part VI, Chapter iv, Note 13.
Allowance (money): Part III, **906**.
Almost (nearly the same): Part III, **1009**.
Along, all: Part V, Lesson lxix, Note 2.
Also: Part III, Exercise v*, 2, Obs.
Alteration: Part III, Exercise xxii, 2.
Altercation: Part III, **11**; Part V, Lesson xvii, 2, Note 12.

Although: Part V, Lesson lxvi, Note 5; Lesson lxvii, Note 7.
Altogether: Part III, **1065**.
Amble: Part V, Lesson xxxiii, 2, Note 3.
Amend: Part III, **578**.
Amiable: Part III, Exercise xxxiii*, 1, Obs. 4.
Amnesty: Part III, Exercise xxxii, 8, Obs. 1.
Amours, illicit: Part III, **982**.
Amply sufficient: Part V, Lesson xiv, Note 14.
Amuse: Part III, Exercise xxxvii*, 2.
Amused, was greatly: Part VI, Chapter xviii, 1.
Amusement: Part III, Exercise xxxii*, 5.
Ancestors: Part III, **660**, **900**.
Anchor, at: Part IV, Dialogue v, 64, Obs. 2.
Anchor, to: Part VI, Chapter xxxvi, 2, Note 1.
Anchor (up, and down): Part VI, Chapter xxxv, 3, Note 4.
Anger, subsided: Part III, Exercise xxix, 8, Obs. 3.
Anger, to repress one's: Part VI, Chapter iii, Note 8.
Angry, felt very: Part V, Lesson lxii, 1, Note 5.
Angry, when I am: Part V, Lesson xlii, 4.
Animal, an: Part III, **411**, **412**.
Animal nature, an: Part V, Lesson lxxvii, 3, Note 9.
Ankle: Part III, **487**; Part VI, Chapter viii, Note 8.
Announce arrival: Part V, Lesson xxi, 1, Note 1.
Annoyed (put out): Part V, Lesson xxi, 1.
Another: Part III, Exercise xxxiv, 7.
Answer, to (argue): Part III, **847**.
Answer (reply), to: Part III, **784**; Part V, Lesson xliv, 1.
Answer, to make: Part IV, Dialogue ii, 40.
Ant: Part VI, Chapter xiii, 6, Note 10.
Anticipate (be beforehand): Part VI, Chapter xxv, 12.
Antiquity: Part III, **878**.
Anxieties: Part IV, Dialogue iv, 47.
Anxiety: Part V, Lesson xci, Note 7.
Anxious: Part III, **989**.
Any, hardly: Part III, Exercise xxix, 10, Obs. 2.
Anything: Part III, Exercise xxx, 6, Obs. 2.
Apart, far: Part IV, Dialogue viii, 38.
Apologise: Part V, Lesson lxii, 3, Note 12.
Apology for a man, an: Part V, Lesson lvi, 1.
Apparent: Part IV, Dialogue x, 17, Obs. 1.
Apparitions (of ghosts): Part V, Lesson xxxvii, 4.
Appeal for aid: Part V, Lesson lvii, 3, Note 4.
Appearance: Part III, **1043**; Part V, Lesson xlvi, 1, Note 1.
Appetite, no: Part V, Lesson xlviii, 2, Note 10.
Application, close (devotes himself): Part V, Lesson c, 2, Note 4.

APPENDIX I.—GLOSSARY.

Applied my money to my own hurt: Part VI, Chapter xvii, 12, Note 7.
Appointments, acting and substantive: Part III, 1009.
Apprentice: Part V, Lesson xci, Note 12.
Approach (draw near): Part III, Exercise xxxii, 1.
Approval, qualified: Part VI, Chapter iv, Note 2.
Archery: Part III, Exercise xxvi*, 1, Obs. 1; Part V, Lesson x, 1, Notes 1, 2, 3.
Archives: Part III, Exercise xxxviii*, 10.
Arena: Part IV, Dialogue vi, 16, Obs.
Argue: Part V, Lesson liii, 1, Note 2.
Arm, the: Part III, 443.
Arm, to carry on the (as a basket): Part VI, Chapter xxxviii, 4, Note 7.
Arm, to put under the: Part V, Lesson xxxv, 3, Notes 11, 12.
Armpit: Part V, Lesson xxxv, Note 13; Lesson lxxxvi, Note 5.
Arms, to hang on by the: Part VI, Chapter xiii, Note 9.
Army, the: Part III, Exercise xix, 6.
Arrest, to: Part III, Exercise xxi*, 4.
Arrive: Part III, 44.
Arrogantly: Part III, 719.
Artificial: Part VI, Chapter xxiii, 3.
As if: Part III, 951.
As much as: Part III, 23.
As to (to come to): Part V, Lesson viii, 2, Note 4.
Ascend: Part III, 48.
Ashamed: Part III, 719, 836; Part IV, Dialogue x, 8, Obs. 6.
Ashore, to get: Part III, Exercise xv, 5, Obs. 3.
Ashore, to go: Part V, Lesson xc, Note 7.
Ask for persistently: Part V, Lesson xl, 4, Notes 11, 12.
Ask, may I: Part IV, Dialogue i, 2, Obs. 2.
Ask, to (politely): Part III, Exercise v, 1, Obs. 2.
Asleep: Part III, 681.
Asleep, half: Part VI, Chapter xxxvi, 4.
Assent: Part V, Lesson xix, Note 7.
Assent to: Part V, Lesson lxxxiii, Note 7.
Assiduous: Part VI, Chapter xxx, 6, Note 4.
Assist: Part III, 641; Exercise xix*, 3; Part VI, Chapter ii, 1, Note 2.
Associate, an: Part V, Lesson lxx, Note 10.
Assumption, to be guilty of: Part IV, Dialogue x, 13, Obs.
Astonished: Part VI, Chapter xxxi, 2, Note 3.
At any rate: Part V, Lesson xxxiii, 4, Note 18.
At, to get (approach near): Part V, Lesson xxvii, Note 6.
Attend upon: Part V, Lesson xlii, Note 7.
Attendance on, close: Part VI, Chapter i, 3.
Attention, give whole: Part III, 578.

Attention to a guest, to pay: Part VI, Chapter xii, Note 1.
Attention, to pay: Part III, Exercise xx, 7.
Attention to, pay proper: Part VI, Chapter xvii, 11.
Attentively: Part VI, Chapter xxviii, 2, Note 3.
Attentiveness: Part V, Lesson xiii, 2, Note 9.
Attractiveness (good looks): Part VI, Chapter xxxi, 14, Note 18.
Attribute, to: Part III, Exercise xxxix, 1, Obs. 1.
Au revoir: Part III, Exercise xxv*, 6, Obs. 2; Part IV, Dialogue x, 27.
Authorise: Part III, 569.
Authorities, the: Part III, Exercise xx, 6, Obs. 2; Exercise xxxii, 10, Obs.; Part IV, Dialogue vi, 16, Obs.
Autumn: Part III, 427.
Avail oneself of an invitation: Part VI, Chapter xxiv, 3.
Available: Part III, 126, Obs.
Avert: Part VI, Chapter xxxi, 11, Note 16.
Avoidable: Part III, 865, Obs.
Away, to move: Part III, 257.
Awkward: Part III, Exercise xxxi, 9.
Awl: Part V, Lesson xix, 3, Note 2.
Awning: Part III, 1077.
Axe: Part VI, Chapter xv, 6, Note 11.
Axle-tree: Part V, Lesson xl, Note 12.

Back, behind the: Part III, 478.
Back of a chair: Part III, 478.
Back out: Part V, Lesson i, 3, Note 7.
Back, to carry on the: Part III, 478.
Back to lean against, a: Part V, Lesson lxxiii, 9, Note 4.
Back, to move: Part VI, Chapter xviii, 8.
Backwards, to walk: Part V, Lesson lvi, 2.
Bad as all that, not so: Part VI, Chapter xxviii, 8.
Bad characters: Part III, 855, Obs.
Bad, too: Part IV, Dialogue vi, 24, Obs.
Bag, a: Part III, Exercise xvi, 4; Part V, Lesson xix, 3, Note 1.
Baggage: Part III, 407.
Balance, a: Part III, 328.
Balance (surplus): Part III, 1071.
Balance in hand: Part V, Lesson lxx, 4.
Bald head: Part VI, Chapter v, 5, Note 13.
Ball of silk, etc.: Part III, 671.
Ball, to roll into a: Part III, Exercise xxv, 10, Obs.
Ballads: Part III, 895.
Balustrade: Part V, Lesson lxxiv, Note 3.
Bamboo: Part III, 470, Obs.
Bandits: Part III, 855, Obs.; Part VI, Chapter xvi, 1, Note 1.

Banditti, the rank and file: Part VI, Chapter xvi, 1, Note 4.
Bandy words with: Part V, Lesson lxii, Note 8.
Bank note (silver): Part III, 324, Obs.
Bank note (cash): Part III, 324, Obs.
Bank, river: Part III, Exercise xv*, 4; Part V, Lesson xc, 2, Note 3.
Bankruptcy: Part IV, Dialogue vi, 5, Obs.
Banner Corps, the eight: Part V, Lesson vii, Note 9; Lesson xii, 9, Note 12.
Barber: Part III, Exercise xviii, 1; Exercise xviii*, 4.
Barber's shop: Part III, Exercise xviii, 3.
Bargain, complete a: Part III, Exercise xxxvii*, 4, Obs. 2.
Bargain, to repent of: Part IV, Dialogue v, 63.
Barometer: Part III, Exercise xxxv, 1, Obs. 2.
Barracks: Part VI, Chapter xxiii, Note 8.
Barren: Part V, Lesson xviii, Note 3.
Barrier (at end of street): Part V, Lesson lxxiv, Note 3.
Barrier (Customs, or military station): Part III, 63.
Barrow: Part III, Exercise xxxvii, 5, Obs. 1.
Bashful: Part VI, Chapter xi, Note 4.
Basin: Part III, 284.
Bask: Part III, Exercise xxvi, 2, Obs.
Basket: Part VI, Chapter xxxvi, 14, Note 12; Chapter xxxviii, 4, Note 7.
Bathe: Part III, 284.
Bawl: Part VI, Chapter xx, 1.
Bay: Part III, 792.
Bead: Part V, Lesson xxxviii, Notes 1, 2.
Beancurd: Part VI, Chapter xiv, 6, Note 10.
Beans: Part III, Exercise i*, 7.
Bear, a: Part VI, Chapter xxxvi, 16, Note 16.
Bear, can't (hate): Part IV, Dialogue ii, 43, Obs. 1.
Bear, cannot: Part V, Lesson xvii, Note 11; Lesson xlii, Note 12.
Bear in mind: Part V, Lesson xvii, 5.
Bear, more than one can: Part V, Lesson ix, Note 9.
Bear (trend): Part IV, Dialogue viii, 59, Obs. 3.
Bear upon: Part III, 63.
Bear with: Part III, Exercise xxxi*, 4.
Beard: Part III, Exercise xvii*, 4; Exercise xviii, 1.
Bearer, a chair: Part VI, Chapter iii, Note 1.
Beasts (of the field): Part V, Lesson xcix, 1, Note 1.
Beat down (object to a charge): Part IV, Dialogue viii, 55, Obs. 2.
Beat, made his heart: Part VI, Chapter xxii, 3, Note 2.
Because: Part III, Exercise xviii, 7; Exercise xix, 1; Exercise xxix, 4, Obs.; 961.
Beckon, to: Part VI, Chapter xxx, 5.
Become (suit), to: Part V, Lesson xxix, 1.

Bed, to go to: Part III, Exercise vii, 2, Obs.; Exercise x, 2, Obs.
Bed with one, to take to: Part V, Lesson x, 1.
Bee: Part VI, Chapter xix, Note 3.
Before: Part III, 85.
Before (in time): Part III, Exercise xx, 8.
Beforehand: Part III, 1065.
Beggar: Part III, 836; Exercise xxiv*, 7, Obs.; Part V, Lesson lxx, 1, Note 4.
Beginning to end, from: Part IV, Dialogue v, 3, Obs.
Behaviour: Part V, Lesson lvi, 1, Note 1.
Believe: Part III, 995.
Bell: Part VI, Chapter xxxviii, 4, Note 6.
Belly: Part III, 478.
Below: Part III, 514.
Bend, to: Part III, 792.
Benevolent: Part V, Lesson xiv, Note 7.
Besides: Part III, Exercise v*, 1, Obs.; 617, 878, 906; Part V, Lesson xxvi, 1, Note 3.
Best of, make the (make it suit): Part V, Lesson xxxiii, Note 16.
Best, would it not be: Part IV, Dialogue vi, 50, Obs. 1.
Best, you had: Part IV, Dialogue viii, 47, Obs.
Bet, to: Part V, Lesson xlvi, Note 5.
Better days, to have seen: Part IV, Dialogue vi, 38, Obs. 1.
Better, far: Part III, Exercise xxxiv*, 3, Obs.
Better for you, all the: Part V, Lesson lxxxi, 2.
Better for you, so much the: Part V, Lesson liv, 1.
Better man than, a: Part V, Lesson xii, 9.
Better still: Part III, 238.
Better to: Part VI, Chapter viii, 9, Note 21.
Better to, it would be: Part V, Lesson xxv, 2, Note 4.
Between, in: Part III, Exercise xii, 3.
Between, to place: Part III, 310.
Beware of: Part V, Lesson viii, 1, Note 3; Lesson xliv, 2, Note 10.
Bidding, to do another's: Part V, Lesson xxix, 1, Note 3.
Bigoted: Part IV, Dialogue x, 17, Obs. 2.
Bill: Part III, Exercise xxvii, 4, Obs.
Bind: Part V, Lesson ix, Note 7.
Bind (in tailoring), to: Part V, Lesson lxxxvi, 5, Note 7.
Biography: Part III, 885.
Birthday: Part III, Exercise xxxvi, 3.
Bit (horse's), a: Part IV, Dialogue viii, 81.
Bit, wait a: Part III, 760.
Bite of insects: Part V, Lesson xcv, 2, Note 4.
Bite, to: Part V, Lesson xxx, Note 13; Part VI, Chapter xviii, Note 4.

APPENDIX I.—GLOSSARY.

Blab all over the place: Part V, Lesson lxiv, 2, Note 4.
Black mail, to levy: Part VI, Chapter v, Note 29.
Black, to look: Part V, Lesson xli, 2, Note 5.
Blacksmith: Part III, Exercise xxviii, 5.
Blame, to: Part III, **54**.
Blame unjustly: Part V, Lesson lxvi, 2.
Blast, roaring of the: Part V, Lesson xcviii, 2.
Blemish: Part V, Lesson vii, Note 5.
Blended together: Part V, Lesson xci, 2.
Bless: Part V, Lesson xix, 6, Note 10.
Blessing: Part V, Lesson xxiii, 7, Note 11.
Blind: Part V, Lesson viii, Note 7.
Blind of one eye: Part VI, Chapter xv, 6, Note 13.
Block-cutter: Part IV, Dialogue vi, 54, Obs.
Block up (impede): Part VI, Chapter viii, 2, Note 1.
Blocks (for printing): Part VI, Chapter xxv, Note 4.
Blow. a: Part III, Exercise xviii, 7, Obs.; Exercise xxviii, 3.
Blown off: Part III, 303, Obs.
Blows, to come to: Part IV, Dialogue iii, 79, Obs.
Blue: Part III, **737**.
Blue, pale: Part VI, Chapter viii, 6, Note 11.
Blunt (outspoken): Part V, Lesson lxvii, 1.
Board: Part VI, Chapter xxv, Note 4.
Boards, chiefs and sub-chiefs of: Part III, Exercise xxxviii, 3.
Boards, the Six: Part III, **1019**.
Boast, to: Part V, Lesson xxiv, Note 4; Lesson lvii, 2, Note 2.
Boasting: Part III, Exercise xx, 7, Obs. 2.
Boat, both in the same: Part V, Lesson liii, 2.
Boatman, head: Part III, Exercise xv, 6.
Body, the whole: Part V, Lesson xxxv, 1, Note 5.
Boil, a: Part V, Lesson lxxiii, Note 5.
Boil, to: Part III, **168**; Exercise xi, 10.
Bolt, to (of a horse): Part III, **451**.
Bonâ fide: Part V, Lesson xxxv, 4.
Bond-servants, children of: Part III, Exercise xix, 2.
Booby: Part V, Lesson xlii, Note 5.
Bookworm (figurative): Part III, **821**.
Bookworm: Part VI, Chapter xxv, 3, Note 5.
Booming of a bell: Part V, Lesson xci, 3, Note 6.
Boorish: Part VI, Chapter xxxviii, Note 4.
Booth: Part IV, Dialogue vii, 72, Obs. 2.
Boots: Part III, **296**.
Boot-trees: Part VI, Chapter xxxiv, 7, Note 7.
Bore, a: Part V, Lesson lxxii, 2, Note 1.
Bore, to be a: Part V, Lesson lxxviii, 1, Note 1.
Bore (weary), to: Part V, Lesson xxiii, 6, Note 9.

Bored: Part III, **989**.
Borrow: Part III, **338, 345**.
Both: Part III, **84; 85**, Obs.
Bother, to: Part IV, Dialogue x, 8, Obs. 5.
Bottle, a: Part III, Exercise xxiv*, 5, Obs.
Bottom: Part III, **514**.
Boudoir: Part VI, Chapter vi, Note 5.
Bounds, keep within: Part VI, Chapter xxv, 8.
Bounty: Part III, **865**, Obs.
Bowels, the: Part V, Lesson lxiii, Note 1.
Bowshot, a: Part VI, Chapter xx, 3.
Box, luncheon: Part VI, Chapter xxxiv, 8, Note 8.
Boxer, a: Part VI, Chapter xxi, 2.
Bracelet: Part VI, Chapter viii, 6, Note 10.
Bracing weather: Part III, **830**.
Brains: Part III, Exercise xvii, 1.
Branch of a tree: Part VI, Chapter xxvii, Note 8.
Brand new: Part VI, Chapter iv, 9, Note 12.
Brandish: Part III, **590**.
Brat: Part V, Lesson xli, 1, Note 1.
Brave: Part V, Lesson xiii, Note 11.
Brazen it out: Part V, Lesson xcix, Note 9.
Bread: Part III, **365**.
Breadth: Part III, Exercise xxx, 3, Obs. 2.
Break, to: Part III, Exercise viii, 6.
Break down, to: Part III, Exercise xvii*, 2, Obs.; Part V, Lesson i, 2.
Break off: Part V, Lesson xvii, 3, Note 16.
Break out (ulcerate), to: Part III, Exercise xvii, 9.
Break out (of sickness): Part III, **590**.
Breakfast: Part III, Exercise ix*, 11, Obs. 1.
Breath, to hold the: Part VI, Chapter iii, Note 8.
Breeding, an air of high: Part VI, Chapter i, 4, Note 10.
Bribes, to give and take: Part VI, Chapter v, 14, Note 27.
Bricklayer and his mate: Part III, Exercise xxxv*, 3, Obs. 2.
Bridal chamber: Part VI, Chapter xl, 2, Note 7.
Bridge: Part III, **800**.
Bridge of the nose: Part III, Exercise xviii, 7.
Bright: Part III, Exercise xxviii, 1.
Bright (of the moon): Part V, Lesson xci, Note 10.
Bring down (calamity): Part V, Lesson xlvii, 2, Note 7.
Brocade: Part VI, Chapter xl, Note 3.
Broil, to: Part III, **167**.
Broke up the party: Part V, Lesson xcvii, 3.
Broken (glass): Part III, Exercise xxviii, 3, Obs.
Broker: Part IV, Dialogue i, 28, Obs. 2.
Broom: Part III, **932**.

Brothel: Part VI, Chapter xxv, Note 2.
Brother, elder: Part IV, Dialogue iii, 8, Obs.
Brotherly intimacy: Part VI, Chapter vi, 1, Note 3.
Brothers, elder and younger: Part III, 660; Exercise xxv, 4, 8, Obs. 1.
Brush, a: Part III, 284.
Brush, to: Part III, Exercise xi, 3.
Bubble, a: Part V, Lesson lxxxviii, Note 6.
Buckle, to: Part VI, Chapter xxxiv, Note 10.
Bud, to, or a: Part VI, Chapter vi, 3, Note 6.
Buddha: Part III, 878; Exercise xxxiii, 8; Exercise xxxiii*, 5, 6.
Budged, never: Part VI, Chapter xiii, Note 7.
Bugs: Part V, Lesson xcv, 2, Note 2.
Build: Part III, 143, 750, 932.
Building, to prepare for: Part III, 932.
Bulge out: Part V, Lesson xcix, Note 6.
Bullet: Part III, Exercise xxi, 8, Obs. 3.
Bully, a: Part V, Lesson lxii, 3.
Bully, to: Part V, Lesson lxiii, Note 5; Part VI, Chapter i, 7.
Bullying: Part V, Lesson xcix, 3, Notes 2, 3.
Bump against: Part III, 755.
Bumper, to drink a: Part IV, Dialogue x, 14, Obs.
Bungler: Part VI, Chapter xii, 4, Note 3.
Burglary: Part III, Exercise xxi, 4, Obs. 2.
Burn (in cooking), to: Part VI, Chapter viii, Note 9.
Burst in: Part IV, Dialogue iii, 52, Obs.
Burst (from over-filling): Part V, Lesson xci, Note 3.
Bury: Part III, 671; Exercise xxv, 6, Obs. 1; Part V, Lesson lxxv, Note 7.
Bushel: Part III, Exercise ii*, 8.
Business: Part III, Exercise xxvi*, 6, Obs.
Business, does his: Part III, Exercise xxvii*, 2, Obs.
Business, mind your own: Part III, 249, Obs.; Exercise xxxi, 9, Obs.
Business, official: Part III, 1009, Obs.
Business, proper: Part III, Exercise xx, 3, Obs.
Business, to give up: Part IV, Dialogue iv, 77, Obs. 1.
Business, to start a: Part III, 755.
Bustling manner: Part V, Lesson lii, Note 7.
Busybody: Part VI, Chapter xxxi, Note 10.
But: Part III, 124, 681.
Butcher: Part VI, Chapter xxxvi, 12.
Butler: Part III, 514.
Butter: Part III, Exercise xiv*, 4, Obs. 1.
Buttocks: Part V, Lesson lviii, Note 9.
Button, an official: Part IV, Dialogue vi, 11, Obs.
Button loop: Part V, Lesson lxxxvi, Note 8.
Button, sew on a: Part V, Lesson lxxxvi, 5, Note 8.

Buy: Part IV, Dialogue v, 31, Obs. 1; Part V, Lesson xvii, 3, Note 14.
By (near): Part III, 241.
By-and-by: Part III, Exercise xxix*, 1.
Bygones are bygones: Part IV, Dialogue ii, 44, Obs. 2.
By no means: Part III, Exercise xiv*, 3, Obs.
Bystanders: Part III, 653.

Cabin of a ship: Part VI, Chapter xxxv, 5, Note 11.
Cadence, mournful: Part V, Lesson xci, Note 6.
Cadence (of music): Part VI, Chapter xxvi, 9, Note 4.
Cakes: Part VI, Chapter v, 3, Notes 9, 10.
Calamity: Part III, 1036.
Calf of the leg: Part III, 478.
Call out: Part III, 425.
Call (pay a visit): Part III, 728, Obs.
Callous: Part V, Lesson xxv, Note 1.
Calumny: Part V, Lesson xvii, 2, Note 8.
Came out with (a remark): Part VI, Chapter xii, 2.
Camel: Part III, 412.
Camp, a military: Part VI, Chapter xxiii, Note 8.
Campaign: Part III, 623.
Cannot but: Part III, Exercise xxxvii*, 5.
Cantonment: Part VI, Chapter xxiii, Note 8.
Capacity: Part III, 776, Obs.
Capital (money): Part III, Exercise xiii, 4, Obs. 2; Exercise xxiv*, 2; Part IV, Dialogue vi, 10, Obs.
Capital (laughable): Part IV, Dialogue v, 67.
Capital, the: Part III, 376.
Capriciousness: Part VI, Chapter xxvii, 7.
Captain of a ship: Part III, 496.
Capture, to: Part IV, Dialogue vi, 9, Obs. 2.
Card, to leave a: Part III, Exercise xxvii, 2.
Card, visiting: Part III, Exercise xx, 10, Obs.; 1025, Obs.; Part V, Lesson xxx, 8, Note 15.
Care: Part V, Lesson xci, 3, Note 7.
Care, to take: Part III, 569.
Care of yourself, take: Part VI, Chapter xxxix, Note 16.
Care, without a: Part VI, Chapter viii, 8, Note 18.
Career, to commence a: Part V, Lesson c, Note 8.
Careful, to be more: Part VI, Chapter xii, 4, Note 4.
Careless: Part III, Exercise xxxi, 8; Exercise xxxv*, 3.
Carelessly: Part III, 885, Obs.
Cares: Part IV, Dialogue iv, 47.
Carpet: Part III, 407.
Carry off (went off with): Part III, 548.
Carry with a pole: Part III, 676.
Cart, a passenger: Part IV, Dialogue viii, 73, Obs.
Cart, please get into your: Part IV, Dialogue x, 25, Obs.
Cart, to get ready a: Part III, 770.

APPENDIX I.—GLOSSARY.

Case, in any: Part III, Exercise xl, 1, Obs. 1.
Case, in that: Part III, Exercise xii, 7.
Case, to close a: Part III, **1030**.
Cash, not a single: Part VI, Chapter iii, 2, Note 2.
Cashier: Part III, **390**.
Cast about, to: Part III, Exercise xix*, 7.
Cast (put off): Part III, **412**.
Cat: Part VI, Chapter xxix, 13, Note 14.
Catch (a cold): Part III, **45**.
Catch at home: Part III, Exercise xxix*, 12, Obs. 2.
Catch with a cap or net, to: Part V, Lesson xl, 3, Note 9.
Ceiling: Part VI, Chapter xxv, 2.
Cemetery: Part III, **809**; Part V, Lesson xxxvi, 2, Note 2.
Cent., one per: Part V, Lesson lii, 2.
Ceremoniously, to act: Part V, Lesson lxxi, Note 6.
Certain, a: Part III, **708**.
Certain to: Part III, Exercise xxxix*, 5, Obs. 2.
Chaff, to: Part VI, Chapter v, 1, Note 4.
Chance, have a: Part III, **906**, Obs. 2.
Chance, it may: Part IV, Dialogue x, 4.
Chance on: Part III, Exercise xxxvii*, 2, Obs.
Change, to: Part III, **273**, Obs.
Change (alter), to: Part III, **570**.
Change one's plans: Part VI, Chapter xxv, Note 12.
Chaplet: Part V, Lesson xxxviii, Notes 1, 2.
Character, what was his: Part IV, Dialogue v, 19.
Charcoal: Part III, **351**.
Charge of, to be in: Part VI, Chapter vii, 5, Note 13.
Charge of, to take: Part IV, Dialogue ii, 22, Obs. 2.
Charitable: Part V, Lesson xiv, 3, Note 8.
Charity, Christian: Part V, Lesson xiv, Note 7.
Charming: Part V, Lesson xc, 2, Note 2.
Charming age, of a: Part VI, Chapter i, 4, Note 9.
Charter, to: Part III, **1003**.
Chat, to: Part V, Lesson xxii, 1, Note 3.
Chatter: Part III, **595**.
Chattering of children: Part V, Lesson lxxxvii, 8, Note 5.
Cheap: Part III, **337**.
Cheap again, half as: Part V, Lesson xxxii, 16, Note 10.
Cheap, to hold: Part V, Lesson xxvii, Note 11.
Cheat, a: Part III, Exercise xxxvi, 6, Obs.
Cheat, to: Part III, **977**; Part IV, Dialogue iii, **113**, Obs.; Part VI, Chapter i, 7, Note 22.
Cheated: Part IV, Dialogue iv, 53.
Checkmate, to: Part V, Lesson lviii, 2, Note 9.
Cheeks: Part III, **464**.
Cheer up: Part III, **989**; Part V, Lesson xxxix, 3, Note 10.

Chess-board: Part V, Lesson xcvii, Note 10.
Chess, to play: Part V, Lesson xcvii, Note 10.
Chest: Part III, **478**.
Chicken: Part VI, Chapter vii, 9, Note 18.
Chief of department: Part III, **1019**.
Chief portion: Part III, Exercise xxxiv, 5.
Chignon: Part VI, Chapter viii, Note 5.
Child: Part III, **1003**.
Childhood: Part III, Exercise xii, 1.
Child's play, not: Part III, **821**.
Chinese: Part III, Exercise xx*, 1; Part IV, Dialogue ix, 18, Obs.; 23, 28.
Choke in drinking: Part VI, Chapter xxviii, 10, Note 18.
Choose: Part III, **676**.
Chopsticks: Part IV, Dialogue x, 18, Obs. 3.
Chronic: Part V, Lesson lx, 2.
Chuckle: Part III, **604**; Part V, Lesson li, 4, Note 9; Part VI, Chapter xviii, 2.
Circle (mathematical): Part V, Lesson lxxiv, Note 1.
Circle (of acquaintances): Part V, Lesson lxxiv, 3, Note 1.
Circuit, make a complete: Part VI, Chapter viii, Note 19.
Circumspect: Part III, Exercise xxxiii*, 1.
Circumstances, according to: Part III, **1080**.
Circumstances, guided by: Part III, **865**, Obs.; Exercise xxxii, 10, Obs.
Circumstances, under no: Part V, Lesson xxvi, Note 8.
Circumvent: Part V, Lesson lviii, 2.
Circus riders: Part VI, Chapter xxxvi, 7, Note 10.
City, imperial: Part III, **841**.
Civil officials: Part III, Exercise xix, 4.
Claims, past: Part VI, Chapter iv, 3, Note 7.
Clan: Part V, Lesson v, 10, Note 5.
Classes, humbler: Part III, Exercise xx, 3.
Classics: Part III, **885**.
Clatter of wheels, etc.: Part V, Lesson lxv, Note 1.
Claw, to: Part III, Exercise xvii, 10.
Clay: Part III, Exercise ii*, 10, Obs.
Clean: Part III, **273**.
Clean out (a drain): Part V, Lesson xlv, 2, Note 4.
Clean sweep, to make a: Part III, Exercise xxi*, 1, Obs. 1.
Clean, to keep a room: Part III, Exercise xxxv*, 1, Obs. 2.
Cleaned out of house and land: Part V, Lesson xlvi, 3, Note 4.
Cleanly: Part III, **273**, Obs.
Clear up (of weather), to: Part III, Exercise ix*, 13.
Clear up (make plain): Part IV, Dialogue iii, 91, Obs.
Clear, your course is: Part V, Lesson lxxxi, 2, Note 1.
Clemency: Part III, **995**.
Clerks, government: Part III, **1019**; Exercise xxxviii, 4.

Climate: Part III, Exercise ix*, 5, Obs.
Clip one's words: Part V, Lesson xxx, Note 13.
Clock: Part III, 225.
Close the city gates: Part V, Lesson lxxv, 4.
Closely (hard), to look: Part V, Lesson lxv, 1; Part VI, Chapter xxviii, 2, Note 3.
Cloth, cotton: Part III, 407.
Clothes-horse: Part V, Lesson lvii, 4.
Clothes, laid down in my: Part V, Lesson xlviii, 2.
Cloudy: Part III, 265.
Clumsy: Part III, 821.
Coal: Part III, 351.
Coarse-looking: Part VI, Chapter xviii, Note 3.
Coat (of an animal): Part III, Exercise ii, 11, Obs.
Coat, a: Part III, 316.
Cockfighting: Part III, Exercise xxxii*, 5.
Coiffure (female): Part III, Exercise xviii, 1, Obs.
Coil, to, or a: Part V, Lesson xxxviii, Note 1.
Cold (in behaviour): Part V, Lesson xiv, Note 1.
Cold in the head: Part V, Lesson xlv, 2, Note 8.
Cold (weather): Part III, Exercise xxxix, 5.
Collar, a: Part IV, Dialogue x, 5, Obs. 1.
Collar of a coat: Part V, Lesson lxxxvi, 5, Note 6.
Collectively: Part III, Exercise xxxiii, 8, Obs. 3.
Colloquial: Part III, Exercise xxxiii, 4.
Collusion: Part III, Exercise xxi*, 5, Obs. 1.
Colour: Part III, Exercise xviii*, 7, Obs. 2; 737.
Colour shop: Part III, Exercise xxviii*, 7.
Colour, to take a: Part III, 737, Obs.
Column: Part III, 755.
Comb, a: Part III, 284.
Comb, to: Part III, 284, Obs.
Come, come: Part V, Lesson xliv, 2.
Come to (after a swoon): Part V, Lesson li, 1, Note 4.
Comet: Part III, 1003.
Comfort (bodily): Part III, Exercise xxiv, 3; Part VI, Chapter viii, Note 18.
Comfort (mental): Part VI, Chapter viii, Note 18.
Comfortable: Part III, 830, Obs.; Exercise xvii, 3.
Comforts, accustomed to: Part VI, Chapter iii, 4, Note 4.
Comical story: Part III, Exercise xxiii, 7.
Commanding appearance: Part V, Lesson xxiv, 1, Note 1.
Commencing from: Part III, Exercise xxxii, 4, Obs.
Commentary: Part IV, Dialogue ix, 38, Obs.
Commission, to: Part III, 995.
Commissioner, Imperial: Part IV, Dialogue v, 66, Obs. 2.

Common occurrence, a matter of: Part III, 689.
Communication, an official: Part III, 1030, Obs.
Compact, to break a: Part III, 830.
Companion: Part IV, Dialogue iii, 72, Obs.
Company, to bear a guest: Part III, 728.
Comparatively few: Part III, Exercise xxx, 9.
Compared with, not to be: Part III, 1058, Obs.
Comparison, to institute a: Part III, Exercise xxvii*, 3.
Compensation: Part IV, Dialogue v, 72.
Competent: Part III, 129.
Compile: Part VI, Chapter xl, 1, Note 1.
Complement: Part III, Exercise xix, 6.
Complete: Part III, Exercise xvi, 5, Obs. 1.
Compliment, return a: Part IV, Dialogue x, 17, Obs. 3.
Complimentary remarks: Part VI, Chapter xvii, 1, Note 2.
Complimentary, too: Part V, Lesson iii, 2, Note 1.
Complimented, fond of being: Part VI, Chapter iii, 5.
Comply with: Part III, 131.
Composed (in mind): Part VI, Chapter xx, 3.
Composition, prose and verse: Part IV, Dialogue ix, 39, Obs. 1.
Compromised, to be: Part V, Lesson xvii, 4, Note 18.
Concealed: Part IV, Dialogue v, 36, Obs. 3.
Concealment: Part VI, Chapter xxxi, 11.
Conceived (thought of): Part V, Lesson xxiii, 4, Note 6.
Concern, not: Part III, Exercise xxxix, 6.
Concern, to: Part III, 63; Part V, Lesson liii, 2, Note 3.
Concoct (invent): Part III, Exercise xxxv*, 2.
Concubine: Part V, Lesson xvii, Note 2.
Conditionally: Part III, Exercise xl, 8, Obs. 1.
Condolence, pay a visit of: Part V, Lesson lxxvi, 3, Note 4.
Condolences, to offer: Part V, Lesson lxxvi, 9, Note 6.
Condone: Part III, Exercise xxxii, 8, Obs. 1.
Conduct: Part IV, Dialogue vi, 30, Obs.; Part V, Lesson xv, 2.
Confederates: Part III, Exercise xxxii*, 1, Obs. 1.
Confer (bestow): Part VI, Chapter xl, 2, Note 2.
Confidence in, to have: Part IV, Dialogue i, 30, Obs.; Part VI, Chapter vii, 2, Note 6.
Confidence, to place: Part V, Lesson xxv, 1, Note 3.
Confiscate: Part III, Exercise xxxv, 4, Obs. 2.
Confucius: Part III, 871, Obs.; Exercise xxxiii*, 1.
Confusion, to put in: Part III, Exercise xx*, 4, Obs.
Congratulate you, I: Part III, 971; Part V, Lesson li, 3.
Connected (distantly): Part IV, Dialogue iv, 13.
Conscience: Part III, 847, Obs.
Conscience, an unquiet: Part VI, Chapter xxxiv, 1, Note 1.

APPENDIX I.—GLOSSARY.

Conscience, guilty: Part IV, Dialogue v, 76, Obs. 2.
Consciousness, to lose: Part V, Lesson li, 1, Note 3.
Consecutively: Part III, 399, Obs.; (in succession) Part V, Lesson xlviii, 1.
Consent: Part III, 784, Obs.
Consequence, of no: Part III, Exercise xl, 1.
Consequences, abide the: Part III, Exercise xxxviii*, 1.
Consequently: Part III, 214; Exercise xv*, 2, Obs.
Consider, let me: Part VI, Chapter xxxii, 9, Note 4.
Consider (reflect): Part III, 776.
Consideration, another: Part IV, Dialogue viii, 31.
Consignment, a: Part III, Exercise xxxix, 3, Obs. 1.
Consist in: Part III, Exercise xxxiv, 5.
Console: Part V, Lesson li, 1, Note 5.
Constantly: Part V, Lesson xxxvii, 4, Note 8; Lesson lxix, 2, Note 2.
Constantly (for ever): Part V, Lesson ii, 3.
Constitution, injured: Part V, Lesson xlix, 1, Note 1.
Constitution (physical): Part III, 604.
Contact, in daily: Part V, Lesson lxiii, 1.
Contain herself for joy, could not: Part VI, Chapter xix, 11, Note 13.
Contemplation, in rapt: Part VI, Chapter xxiv, 7.
Contemporaneous: Part III, Exercise xxxiii, 8.
Contempt for, to have: Part V, Lesson lvii, 3, Note 6.
Contentedness: Part V, Lesson xcix, 4, Note 10.
Context: Part III, Exercise xxvii, 7, Obs.
Continually: Part III, 681.
Contraband: Part VI, Chapter xxxvi, 6.
Contradict: Part IV, Dialogue viii, 55, Obs. 2.
Contradictions: Part IV, Dialogue vii, 59.
Contravene: Part VI, Chapter xvii, Note 1.
Contretemps: Part V, Lesson xiii, 1, Note 1.
Control, to: Part V, Lesson xv, Note 7.
Convenience, at your: Part III, 865.
Convenient: Part III, 333.
Conventional: Part IV, Dialogue x, 17, Obs. 2.
Conversation (connected): Part V, Lesson ii, 2.
Conversation, every-day: Part III, Exercise xxxiii*, 1, Obs. 1.
Conversation, fluent in: Part V, Lesson xxiv, 1, Note 2.
Convert (proselytise): Part V, Lesson lxxx, 2, Note 10.
Convey (merchandise): Part III, 1036.
Cooked: Part III, Exercise xiv, 4.
Cooking: Part III, 171.
Cool: Part III, 229.
Cool down (of anger): Part VI, Chapter xxxii, 6, Note 1.
Coolie: Part III, 912, Obs.
Coolie, temple: Part III, 878.
Coolness (want of regard), to treat with: Part V, Lesson lxi, 2.

Copyist, official: Part III, Exercise xxxviii, 1, Obs.; Part IV, Dialogue vi, 29, Obs.
Cord: Part VI, Chapter xxxiv, 9, Note 9.
Cordial: Part V, Lesson xiv, 1, Notes 1, 2.
Corner: Part III, Exercise xviii, 8; Part VI, Chapter xxxiv, 6, Note 6
Correct: Part III, Exercise xxvii, 8, Obs. 1; Exercise xxxiv, 3, Obs. 2.
Correct (proper): Part V, Lesson xv, Note 9.
Correct (punish): Part V, Lesson ix, 5, Note 5.
Correct, to: Part V, Lesson x, 4, Note 10.
Correction, to make a: Part III, Exercise xxii*, 3.
Correctly: Part V, Lesson xxxix, 1, Note 4.
Correctly (in proper fashion): Part V, Lesson ii, 1, Note 1.
Corrupt (depraved): Part III, 1019.
Cost me my life (nearly killed myself): Part V, Lesson lii, 1, Note 4.
Cotton: Part III, 311.
Cough, to: Part V, Lesson xliii, 1, Note 1.
Count: Part III, Exercise viii*, 2.
Countenance: Part III, Exercise xvii, 2, Obs.; Exercise xvii*, 10, Obs.
Counterpart, the very: Part V, Lesson xlii, 1, Note 2.
Countries, different: Part III, 520.
Country, from the: Part V, Lesson xxvii, 3, Note 8.
Country, the: Part V, Lesson lxxv, Note 1.
Country, the open: Part V, Lesson xc, 2, Note 1; Lesson xciv, 2, Note 4.
Countryman (rustic): Part III, 809.
Courageous: Part V, Lesson xxxv, Note 15.
Course, a matter of: Part III, 562.
Course, of: Part III. 562, Obs.; Exercise xi*, 6, Obs.; Part V, Lesson lxix, Note 1.
Course (of a river): Part III, Exercise xxx, 4.
Court dress: Part III, 841.
Court, the: Part III, 841.
Court, to go to: Part III, 841.
Courteously, to treat: Part VI, Chapter xl, 2, Note 4.
Courtesy, to call by: Part V, Lesson xxxiv, 9.
Court-yard: Part IV, Dialogue iii, 49, Obs.
Cousins: Part V, Lesson v, 10, Note 6.
Coûte que coûte: Part V, Lesson lxxxvi, 6; Part VI, Chapter xii, 2.
Cover (or case) of a book: Part III, 770.
Covered with, get: Part III, Exercise xxxiv, 7, Obs.
Coy: Part VI, Chapter xi, Note 4.
Crab apple: Part VI, Chapter vii, Note 10.
Crack, a: Part III, 287; 737, Obs.
Cracked (of glass): Part III, Exercise xxviii, 3, Obs.
Cracked (of paper, etc.): Part III, 755.
Craft (line of business): Part III, Exercise xxviii, 10, Obs. 1.

Crape: Part III, 742.
Crave: Part III, **995**.
Crawl, to: Part VI, Chapter xiii, Note 9.
Create: Part V, Lesson xxiii, Note 11.
Credit of, the: Part VI, Chapter xxxvii, 12.
Credit of the family, add to the: Part VI, Chapter xxxiv, 3, Note 3.
Credit, to buy and sell on: Part VI, Chapter iii, Note 14.
Credit, undeserved: Part V, Lesson vi, 2, Note 6.
Creditor: Part V, Lesson xxix, Note 5.
Creep, makes one's flesh: Part V, Lesson xcix, 3, Note 8.
Creep (walk softly): Part V, Lesson xl, Note 2.
Criminal: Part III, Exercise xxxii, 8, Obs. 2.
Cripple, a: Part IV, Dialogue iv, 75, Obs.
Crooked: Part V, Lesson xxx, 9, Note 17.
Crops: Part V, Lesson xviii, Note 9.
Crops, to gather: Part III, Exercise xx, 4.
Cross-grained: Part VI, Chapter xxi, 2, Note 3.
Crow, to: Part VI, Chapter xviii, 4, Note 8.
Crowd, thread one's way through a: Part VI, Chapter xviii, 5.
Crowd, to: Part V, Lesson xxxix, 1, Note 5; Part VI, Chapter xix, Note 3.
Cruel: Part III, **623**.
Cruise round to find an opening: Part VI, Chapter xii, Note 1.
Cruiser, Customs: Part IV, Dialogue v, 65, Obs.
Cruiser, revenue: Part IV, Dialogue v, 48.
Cry (loud weeping): Part VI, Chapter xix, 4, Note 7.
Cry (weep), to: Part IV, Dialogue vii, 98, Obs.
Cup: Part V, Lesson xxxvi, 3, Note 5.
Cure, to: Part III, Exercise xxi*, 2, Obs. 3.
"Curios": Part III, **871**, Obs.
Curious, wasn't it: Part V, Lesson xxxvi, 5.
Curly: Part V, Lesson xxx, 6, Note 12.
Current: Part III, **792**, Obs.; Part V, Lesson xxii, Note 8.
Curse, to: Part V, Lesson iv, Note 10; Lesson lxii, Note 16; Part VI, Chapter xv, Note 15.
Curtain or screen, to push back or raise a: Part VI, Chapter xxiv, 6, Note 5.
Curve, a: Part III, **792**.
Custom House: Part III, **509**.
Custom, the: Part IV, Dialogue x, 8, Obs. 1.
Customer, a tough: Part VI, Chapter iv, Note 5.
Customs: Part III, **878**, Obs.
Customs, Maritime: Part IV, Dialogue v, 66, Obs. 1.
Cut his finger: Part VI, Chapter xv, 5, Note 10.
Cut out, to: Part III, **316**.
Cut with a knife: Part VI, Chapter xxviii, 8, Note 13.
Cut with a sword, to: Part III, Exercise xxi*, 2, Obs. 1.
Cyclone: Part VI, Chapter xxxvii, 1, Note 1.

Damage: Part IV, Dialogue v, 74, Obs.
Dangerous: Part V, Lesson xxiv, 2, Note 10; Lesson lxiv, 2, Note 3.
Dash down: Part III, **612**.
Dash off (a letter, etc.): Part V, Lesson lii, 3, Note 7.
Date (time): Part III, Exercise xxxii*, 4, Obs.
Daughter: Part III, Exercise xviii*, 1, Obs.; Part IV, Dialogue iv, 62, Obs. 1; Part VI, Chapter i, Note 8.
Dawdle, to: Part V, Lesson xxv, 2, Note 5.
Day, all: Part III, **310**.
Day and night: Part III, **220**.
Day, break of: Part VI, Chapter v. 9, Note 23.
Day, one fine: Part V, Lesson lxv, 2, Note 9.
Day, the same: Part V, Lesson lxxv, 4, Note 2.
Dazed: Part III, **821**.
Dazzle, to: Part V, Lesson xxix, Note 2.
Dead: Part III, **855**, Obs.; Exercise xxix, 8, Obs. 3; Part V, Lesson lxxvi, 1, Note 1.
Dead (an official): Part III, Exercise xxxviii, 2, Obs.
Deaf: Part V, Lesson xxii, 3, Note 12.
Dear (costly): Part III, **337**.
Dear, dear: Part IV, Dialogue iii, 65, Obs. 1.
Dear me: Part IV, Dialogue iii, 52, Obs. 1; Dialogue iv, 54.
Dear, to pay: Part III, Exercise xiii, 8, Obs. 1.
Death (of a child): Part V, Lesson lxxxvii, Note 8.
Death, sentenced to: Part III, Exercise xxxii*, 6.
Death, the penalty of: Part III, **855**.
Death, to put to: Part VI, Chapter xxii, 4, Note 5.
Debt, to run into: Part V, Lesson xxix, 2, Note 5.
Debtor: Part IV, Dialogue iv, 54, Obs.
Debts: Part III, **345**.
Debts, to collect: Part VI, Chapter ii, Note 5.
Decapitate: Part III, **487**.
Decay of old age: Part VI, Chapter xxxviii, Note 2.
Deceive: Part III, **977**; Part V, Lesson lxii, 1, Note 1.
Decency, no sense of: Part V, Lesson viii, 3.
Deception, gratuitous: Part V, Lesson lxviii, 5.
Decided to: Part III, **585**, Obs.
Decidedly: Part V, Lesson ix, Note 6.
Decidedly (summarily): Part V, Lesson ii, Note 3.
Decline, to: Part III, Exercise xxix, 3, Obs. 5.
Decorum: Part V, Lesson lv, Note 1.
Decrees of Heaven: Part III, **1036**.
Deduct (take away): Part III, **1071**.
Deep: Part III, **384**.
Deer: Part V, Lesson lxxxix, 2, Note 4; Part VI, Chapter xxxvi, 16, Note 14.
Defeat: Part VI, Chapter xviii, Note 6.
Defeated: Part V, Lesson viii, 3, Note 14.

APPENDIX I.—GLOSSARY.

Defect: Part III, **713**, Obs.; Part IV, Dialogue ii, 14; Part V, Lesson vii, Note 5.
Definite: Part III, Exercise xxii, 3.
Degree, in no ordinary: Part VI, Chapter xix, 4, Note 5.
Degree, of highest: Part V, Lesson xiii, Note 5.
Degree (of licentiate): Part IV, Dialogue ix, 41, Obs. 2.
Degrees, by: Part V, Lesson lv, 3, Note 8.
Dejected: Part VI, Chapter viii, Note 23.
Delay: Part III, **961, 965.**
Deliberate: Part III, **965.**
Deliberately (intentionally): Part VI, Chapter xxvii, 2.
Delightful: Part V, Lesson xci, 1, Note 2.
Denial, persist in: Part VI, Chapter xxxi, 10.
Denounce: Part VI, Chapter v, 14, Note 31.
Dense (of foliage): Part III, Exercise xxvi, 8.
Deny: Part VI, Chapter xxxi, 6, Note 8.
Depended upon, not to be: Part III, Exercise xl*, 6.
Deposit, to leave on: Part VI, Chapter viii, Note 17.
Depôt: Part VI, Chapter xxxix, Note 13.
Depraved: Part III, **1019**; Part VI, Chapter v, Note 14.
Depreciatory, self: Part IV, Dialogue x, 8, Obs. 8.
Deputy: Part III, **1019.**
Descend (send down), to cause to: Part V, Lesson xix, Note 10.
Deserve: Part III, Exercise xxvii, 6, Obs.
Designedly: Part V, Lesson xxxv, Note 18.
Desire, as you: Part IV, Dialogue ix, 53, Obs.
Desire immoderately: Part IV, Dialogue v, 22, Obs.
Despair, in: Part V, Lesson ii, 2, Note 5.
Despair, to: Part V, Lesson ii, 3, Note 9.
Despatch, a: Part III, Exercise xxxiii, 5.
Despatches: Part III, Exercise xxii*, 3.
Desperate case (of illness): Part V, Lesson li, 1
Destination, to arrive at: Part VI, Chapter xxxvii, 4.
Destiny, it was his: Part VI, Chapter ii, 1, Note 1.
Desultory conversation: Part VI, Chapter xxiii, Note 6.
Detain (keep to dinner): Part III, **647.**
Detain (politely): Part IV, Dialogue x, 23, Obs. 2.
Detained: Part V, Lesson xxii, Note 4.
Detected, being: Part III, Exercise xxxv, 4, Obs. 1.
Determined obstinacy: Part V, Lesson lxiii, Notes 8, 9.
Détour (a roundabout way): Part III, **376.**
Détour, make a: Part VI, Chapter vii, 6.
Die, to: Part VI, Chapter vii, 2, Note 4.
Died: Part IV, Dialogue ii, 19, Obs. 1; Part V, Lesson lxxxvii, 11, Note 9.
Difference, little: Part III, **1009**, Obs.
Difficulties, to be in: Part III, **855.**
Difficulty: Part III, **830.**

Diffident: Part VI, Chapter xviii, Note 1.
Digression (in conversation): Part IV, Dialogue vi, 1, Obs.
Dilemma, in a: Part V, Lesson lxxxi, 1.
Dilemma, places me in a: Part V, Lesson lxix, 4, Note 7.
Diligence: Part V, Lesson xiii, 2, Note 9.
Dim (of the sun's rays): Part V, Lesson xcviii, Note 1.
Dimensions: Part III, Exercise xxvii, 5, Obs.
Dimensions (of a house): Part V, Lesson xxxvii, Note 2.
Diminutive (very small): Part III, Exercise iii*, 3.
Dimly remember: Part IV, Dialogue iv, 40, Obs.
Din (of children's chatter): Part V, Lesson lxxxvii, 8, Note 5.
Dine out: Part III, Exercise xi*, 2.
Dinner, get to: Part IV, Dialogue x, 12, Obs.
Dinner, go to a: Part V, Lesson xlvii, Note 3.
Dinner set: Part III, Exercise viii*, 8.
Dip a pen in the ink: Part VI, Chapter xxvi, Note 12.
Diphtheria: Part III, **590.**
Direct (then and there): Part VI, Chapter xxvii, 1.
Direction: Part III, Exercise xxvii, 8, Obs. 2.
Directions, opposite: Part III, Exercise xxiii, 1.
Directly: Part III, Exercise xxii*, 9; Exercise xxvii, 5, Obs.; Part IV, Dialogue iii, 28, Obs.
Dirty: Part III, **273.**
Disagreeable: Part III, Exercise xxxi*, 2.
Disappointed: Part IV, Dialogue v, 2, Obs. 1.
Disappointed, to feel: Part VI, Chapter xxv, 13.
Discipline, to enforce: Part V, Lesson xv, Note 7.
Discourse, handle of: Part V, Lesson lxi, Note 5.
Discovered, to be: Part VI, Chapter xxvii, 2.
Discredit on, to bring: Part V, Lesson iv, 4.
Discreditable affair: Part V, Lesson lxxxi, 2.
Discreditable transactions, associated in: Part VI, Chapter ii, 2, Note 6.
Discuss: Part III, **776.**
Discuss (wrangle): Part IV, Dialogue vii, 85, Obs.
Discussion (brings us into the): Part V, Lesson liii, 2, Note 4.
Disgrace: Part IV, Dialogue vi, 22, Obs. 1.
Disgrace of, incur the: Part V, Lesson lxxxi, 2, Note 5.
Disgrace to, a: Part V, Lesson c, 2, Note 5.
Disgraced, to be: Part VI, Chapter xix, 6, Note 9.
Disgraceful: Part III, **612.**
Disgust, to excite: Part V, Lesson xlvii, 2.
Dish: Part III, Exercise xxii, 9.
Dishes (viands): Part V, Lesson lxxii, 4, Note 10.
Dishevelled: Part V, Lesson xxxv, Note 6.
Dishonest: Part IV, Dialogue iii, 99, Obs.
Dishonourable: Part VI, Chapter xxxi, 15, Note 19.

Disinterested: Part VI, Chapter xxv, 13.
Dislike, to provoke: Part III, 836.
Dismissed from office: Part V, Lesson xiii, 2, Note 8.
Disorder: Part III, 533.
Disorder, in: Part III, Exercise xxii*, 7, Obs. 1.
Disorderly: Part III, 533, 590.
Disparage: Part V, Lesson lxi, 2, Note 5.
Display (empty): Part V, Lesson xxiv, 2, Note 9.
Display of viands (politely): Part V, Lesson lxxii, 6, Note 14.
Displeased with: Part V, Lesson ix, 4, Note 3.
Dispose of (sell or pawn): Part VI, Chapter v, 1, Note 5.
Disposed of: Part III, Exercise xxii, 2.
Disposition (temperament): Part III, 623.
Disregard a prohibition: Part III, Exercise xxxii, 5, Obs.
Disregard exhortation (wind in ears): Part V, Lesson vi, 3, Note 10.
Disrepair, in: Part V, Lesson xxxvii, 4, Note 5.
Disreputable: Part III, Exercise xxxii*, 5.
Dissatisfied: Part III, 830, 836; Part V, Lesson xiv, 3, Note 12; Lesson ix, Note 3.
Dissolute: Part V, Lesson xx, 2, Note 7.
Dissuade: Part V, Lesson xlvi, 3.
Distant from (separated): Part IV, Dialogue viii, 23, Obs. 3.
Distaste for, to have a: Part V, Lesson viii, 4, Note 21; Lesson xxvii, 5, Note 16.
Distended (of the stomach): Part V, Lesson xlviii, Note 6.
Distinction, without: Part III, 925, Obs.
Distinctly: Part III, Exercise xvii, 1; Part V, Lesson iii, Note 2.
Distinguish: Part III, Exercise vii, 6, Obs. 1, 2; 708.
Distinguish oneself: Part V, Lesson x, 1, Note 6.
Distinguished appearance: Part VI, Chapter viii, 7, Note 13.
Distress of mind: Part V, Lesson lix, 5, Note 5.
Distressed in mind: Part III, 1077.
Distressed, to feel: Part VI, Chapter xxxiii, 3.
Distressing (painful): Part V, Lesson l, 4.
Distribute: Part III, Exercise xxxii*, 1, Obs. 2.
Disturb: Part VI, Chapter xxiii, Note 10.
Disturb yourself, don't: Part IV, Dialogue iii, 121.
Disturbed, his equilibrium was: Part VI, Chapter xiv, 1, Note 1.
Divan, an opium: Part IV, Dialogue v, 38.
Divide: Part III, Exercise vii*, 8, Obs.
Divided, equally: Part IV, Dialogue ii, 53, Obs.
Divine (guess), to: Part VI, Chapter xviii, 1.
Dizzy: Part V, Lesson xlv, 2, Note 7.
Do out of: Part III, 977.

Do, that will: Part III, Exercise xxv*, 6, Obs. 2; Part VI, Chapter iv, Note 2.
Dock wages, to: Part VI, Chapter xvii, 11.
Doctor, a: Part III, Exercise xxi*, 2, Obs. 2; Part V, Lesson lii, 2, Note 5.
Doctrine: Part III, 871.
Dodge, to: Part V, Lesson xxvii, 4.
Dog, a: Part III, 939.
Dolefully: Part V, Lesson xliii, 2, Note 6.
Domineering: Part V, Lesson xxxii, Note 3.
Don't: Part III, 708.
Door, knock at the: Part V, Lesson xxii, 2, Note 10.
Door, next: Part V, Lesson xxii, 3, Note 13.
Door-sill: Part V, Lesson lvi, 2, Note 6.
Dose, a: Part V, Lesson xlviii, Note 13.
Dotage: Part V, Lesson xvi, Note 14.
Double up the leg, to: Part VI, Chapter xiv, 8, Note 14.
Doubt, to: Part III, Exercise xxix*, 8, Obs. 1.
Doubts, to have: Part III, 784.
Downstairs: Part III, 514.
Draft, prepare a: Part III, 1025.
Drag off: Part III, Exercise xxiii, 5.
Drag, to: Part III, 451.
Drag you in for it: Part VI, Chapter v, 7, Note 17.
Drain, a: Part V, Lesson xxviii, Note 3.
Draper: Part III, Exercise xxv*, 2.
Draw on: Part V, Lesson xiv, Note 4.
Draw pay: Part IV, Dialogue x, 5, Obs. 1.
Draw up (regulations): Part III, Exercise xx*, 1, Obs.
Draw water: Part III, Exercise xxi, 6.
Drawer, pull out and shut to: Part III, 977.
Drawing-room: Part V, Lesson xlix, 2.
Dream, to, or a: Part III, 604.
Dregs: Part V, Lesson lxvii, Note 1.
Dress well: Part IV, Dialogue vi, 32.
Dressed, nicely: Part VI, Chapter xxiv, Note 3.
Drink hard: Part V, Lesson xlvii, 1.
Drink, have too much to: Part III, Exercise xxii, 7.
Drive on (to a carter): Part V, Lesson xciii, Note 9.
Drive out: Part III, 509, Obs.
Drive, to: Part III, 539.
Drooped, eyelids: Part V, Lesson xlviii, 2.
Drooping: Part V, Lesson xxxiii, 3, Note 12; Part VI, Chapter xviii, 6, Note 9.
Drown: Part VI, Chapter iii, Note 16.
Drum, to beat a: Part VI, Chapter xix, 3, Note 4.
Drunk: Part IV, Dialogue v, 80, Obs. 2; Part V, Lesson xlvii, 1.
Drunk, dead: Part V, Lesson xliv, 1, Note 1.
Dry in the sun: Part III, 702.

APPENDIX I.—GLOSSARY.

Dry, to: Part III, Exercise xxvi, 9, Obs. 1.
Due to, all: Part III, **Exercise** xxxix, 1, Obs. 2.
Due to oneself and to others (of money): Part III, Exercise xl, 4, **Obs.** 1.
Due to you (your work): **Part V, Lesson i, 4, Note 9.**
Dull (bored): Part III, **989.**
Dull (tame work): Part V, Lesson xxiii, 5, Note 8.
Dumb: Part V, Lesson xliv, 1, Note 3.
Dummy: Part V, Lesson lv, 1, Notes 2, 3, 4.
Dumplings: Part V, Lesson xi, 8, Note 4; Part VI, Chapter v, 3, Note 10.
Dun, to: Part III, **836.**
Dung: Part VI, Chapter iv, Note 6.
Dust: Part VI, Chapter xxxix, 4, Note 4.
Dust, to: Part III, **303.**
Duster, a: Part III, **303.**
Duty, my: Part IV, Dialogue iv, 39.
Duty, off: Part V, Lesson lxxvi, 9.
Dwell amongst: Part V, Lesson xxxi, 5, Note 10.
Dwell (live): Part V, Lesson xix, Note 6.
Dyer: Part III, **737.**
Dying: Part III, Exercise vii, 2, Obs.
Dynasty: Part III, **841.**

Each the other: Part III, **925.**
Ear: Part III, **436.**
Ear, grate on the: Part V, Lesson xli, 4, Note 9.
Earnest, to be in: Part VI, Chapter i, Note 5.
Ears, to set by the: Part V, Lesson lxiv, 2.
Earthenware: Part III, Exercise ii*, 8.
Ease, at (in body or mind): Part V, Lesson xlviii, 3, Note 15.
Easy: Part III, Exercise xi*, 2; Exercise xxxvi, 2, 4; Exercise xxxvi*, 4, Obs.
Easy circumstances: Part III, **629.**
Easy (in mind), be: Part IV, Dialogue ii, 44.
Easy, to make one's mind: Part V, Lesson lx, 3.
Easy, to take things: Part V, Lesson xxv, 1, Note 1.
Eat into (of insects): Part VI, Chapter xiii, 6, Note 10.
Eaves: Part VI, Chapter xxxix, 4, Note 2.
Eccentricity: Part III, **1036.**
Economy: Part V, Lesson xxviii, 1, Note 2.
Edge (of a cube, etc.): Part III, Exercise xviii, 8; Part V, Lesson xxxiv, 7, Note 7.
Edition, first (of a book): Part VI, Chapter xxv, 2.
Educated, imperfectly: Part IV, Dialogue iv, 77, Obs. 3.
Educated, well: Part V, Lesson xix, 5, Note 4.
Education, a man of: Part V, Lesson xcix, 3.
Effort made by a sick person to keep up: Part V, Lesson xlv, Note 11; Lesson xlviii, 2.
Effort, make an: Part V, Lesson xxv, Note 6.

Effort, speak without: Part V, Lesson ii, 3.
Egg on: Part V, Lesson xvii, 1, Note 3.
Eggs: Part III, Exercise xiv, 1.
Eggs, hard and soft boiled: Part III, **696.**
Eggs, to lay: Part VI, Chapter xviii, 4, Note 7.
Either: Part III, **84.**
Elders: Part III, Exercise xxxvi, 7, Obs. 2.
Element of future trouble: Part V, Lesson lxxxi, 2.
Embarrass: Part VI, Chapter xxvii, 4.
Emergency: Part VI, Chapter xxxiii, 1.
Emperor, the: Part III, **955.**
Emperor, the reigning: Part VI, Chapter xxviii, 2, Note 5.
Emphatically; Part VI, Chapter iv, 17, Note 16.
Empire, the: Part III, Exercise xix*, 1, Obs.
Employé: Part IV, Dialogue viii, 83, Obs. 1.
Empty handed: Part III, Exercise viii, 5; Part VI, Chapter i, 8, Note 23.
Encroach upon capital; Part III, **1049.**
End, a peaceable (death): Part V, Lesson xvi, Note 19.
End on: Part III, Exercise xl, 8, Obs. 2.
End, the farthest: Part V, Lesson xxii, 2, Note 8.
End, to: Part III, **31.**
End to end: Part III, Exercise xl*, 2, Obs.
Ended, this: Part VI, Chapter xxxv, 2, Note 2.
Ends meet, can't make both: Part VI, Chapter iii, 8, Note 19.
Endure patiently: Part V, Lesson xvii, Note 11.
Enemy, your own (your own harm): Part V, Lesson vi, 2.
Enjoin upon: Part V, Lesson lxvi, Note 1.
Enjoy: Part V. Lesson xvi, 2, Note 12.
Enjoyment, perfect: Part V, Lesson xci, 1, Note 1.
Enough: Part III, **776.**
Enough and to spare: Part V, Lesson xxix, 2.
Enough, not: Part III, Exercise xxix*, 4, Obs. 3.
Enough, only just: Part VI, Chapter iii, 8, Note 17.
Enough, to have: Part V, Lesson xlvii, 1, Note 2.
Enterprise, a glorious: Part VI, Chapter xvi, 2, Note 6.
Entertain: Part III, Exercise xxvii, 8.
Entirely: Part IV, Dialogue v, 62, Obs.
Entrails of pigs, etc.: Part V, Lesson lxxvii, Note 9; Lesson lxxxviii, 2.
Epicure: Part V, Lesson lxx, Note 1.
Equal to (competent): Part V, Lesson vii, Note 6.
Equal to (up to): Part V, Lesson ix, Note 9.
Equal to ten, one: Part V, Lesson lxxxvii, 12, Note 12.
Equally divided: Part IV, Dialogue ii, 53, Obs.
Errand, to send on an: Part III, **1009.**
Escape: Part V, Lesson xciii, 2.
Escape, a narrow: Part V, Lesson li, 3, Note 8.
Essential: Part III, **855.**

Essential, foremost: Part V, Lesson i, 1.
Establish: Part III, 847.
Establishment, a separate: Part IV, Dialogue vii, 65, Obs.
Estrange: Part III, Exercise xxxix, 6, Obs. 3.
Estrangement: Part V, Lesson xvii, 1, Notes 5, 7.
Estrangement (less intimate): Part V, Lesson xvii, 1.
Etiquette: Part IV, Dialogue x, 1, Obs. 4.
Even: Part III, 399; Exercise xxxiv*, 2.
Even paces (a horse): Part V, Lesson xxxiii, 2, Note 3.
Even (regular): Part V, Lesson xxxiv, 7, Note 7.
Evening: Part III, 246.
Eventually: Part III, Exercise xv*, 8; 647; 784, Obs. 3.
Ever: Part III, Exercise iii, 9.
Ever, just as: Part V, Lesson xliv, 3.
Ever since: Part V, Lesson lxii, 1, Note 2.
Every: Part VI, Chapter xix, Note 1.
Everybody: Part III, Exercise xxxiv, 3.
Every way, in: Part III, Exercise xvii*, 2, Obs. 1.
Everywhere: Part III, 925.
Everywhere, have looked: Part VI, Chapter viii, Note 19.
Evidence: Part IV, Dialogue ii, 38, Obs.
Evidence, oral: Part III, 1025.
Evidence, to take: Part III, Exercise xxxviii, 7.
Evident that, it was: Part V, Lesson xlix, 3, Note 8.
Exactly: Part III, 760.
Examination, to pass an: Part III, 302; Exercise xxxviii*, 9, Obs.
Examine: Part III, 900.
Example, follow an: Part VI, Chapter i, 6.
Exceedingly: Part III, Exercise xxxvi, 5, Obs.
Excel: Part V, Lesson x, Notes 4, 5.
Excellent: Part III, 604; Part VI, Chapter xxv, 13, Note 17.
Except: Part V, Lesson lix, 2.
Except (unless): Part III, 1071.
Exceptional: Part IV, Dialogue viii, 29, Obs.
Exchange, the: Part III, Exercise xiii*, 8, Obs. 2.
Excite: Part VI, Chapter xxi, 3, Note 6.
Excited, to get: Part III, 533, 989.
Exculpate oneself: Part VI, Chapter xvii, 12.
Excursion, make an: Part V, Lesson xci, 1.
Excuse, invent an: Part VI, Chapter xxvii, 12, Note 8.
Excuses, to put forward: Part IV, Dialogue vi, 53, Obs. 1.
Excuses, to put off with: Part V, Lesson lxviii, 4, Note 2.
Execrate: Part V, Lesson iv, 4, Note 10.
Executed (put to death): Part III, Exercise xxiv, 1, Obs. 3.
Exercises, manly: Part VI, Chapter vii, 2.
Exert oneself: Part III, 1043; Part V, Lesson xiii, 2, Note 6; Lesson lxxix, 2, Note 2.

Exorcists: Part V, Lesson xxxvii, 4, Notes 10, 11.
Expect, I: Part III, Exercise xxxv, 7, Obs.
Expectant official: Part III, Exercise xxxviii, 3, Obs. 1.
Expectation, contrary to: Part V, Lesson lxxxiii, Note 3.
Expected it, when one least: Part VI, Chapter i, 7.
Expects, as one: Part V, Lesson xiii, 1.
Expedient, an: Part VI, Chapter xix, Note 12; Chapter xxxi, Note 15.
Expenditure: Part III, Exercise xiii, 1, Obs.
Expenses, to cover: Part IV, Dialogue ii, 28.
Expenses, travelling: Part V, Lesson xxxi, 2, Note 3.
Experience: Part IV, Dialogue ix, 22, Obs. 1.
Experience, men of: Part V, Lesson viii, 4, Note 19.
Experience of, have had no: Part V, Lesson lviii, 2.
Experience, taught by: Part IV, Dialogue v, 78, Obs. 2.
Experience, to profit by: Part V, Lesson lxx, Note 11.
Expert, an: Part III, 755, Obs.
Expires, term of office: Part III, 1009.
Explain (expound): Part IV, Dialogue ix, 36, Obs.
Explanation: Part IV, Dialogue iii, 65, Obs. 2.
Explanations, enter into: Part IV, Dialogue vi, 51, Obs. 2.
Export: Part III, 676.
Expression: Part III, Exercise xvi*, 10, Obs.
Extra, to pay: Part IV, Dialogue iii, 74, Obs.
Extraordinary (exceptional): Part IV, Dialogue viii, 29, Obs.
Extravagance: Part IV, Dialogue v, 9, Obs.
Extravagant: Part IV, Dialogue ii, 43, Obs. 2; Part V, Lesson xxviii, 1, Note 1.
Extremely: Part III, 604.
Extremity (end): Part III, Exercise xxx, 1.
Eye, in the twinkling of an: Part V, Lesson xiii, 1, Note 4; Lesson xvi, 3, Note 21; Lesson xxix, 1.
Eye, pupil of the: Part V, Lesson lvi, 2, Note 5.
Eyebrows: Part III, 464.
Eye-service: Part V, Lesson xv, 1, Note 4.
Eyes bunged up: Part V, Lesson xlii, 2, Note 3.
Eyes off, to take the: Part III, Exercise xxii*, 9, Obs. 1; Exercise xxvi*, 5.
Eyes, prominent: Part V, Lesson xxx, 6, Note 6.
Eyes, saw with his own: Part VI, Chapter xxxi, 10.
Eyes, to close the: Part V, Lesson xcv, 2, Notes 6, 7.
Eyes, to open the: Part V, Lesson xxxv, 1, Note 3.

Face, a slap on the: Part V, Lesson xcix, Note 5.
Face fell, his: Part V, Lesson lxxxiv, 2.
Face, filled out in the: Part V, Lesson lxv, 1.
Face, the: Part V, Lesson xcix, Note 5.
Face upwards: Part V, Lesson xxiv, Note 13.
Fact, as a matter of: Part VI, Chapter xviii, 10.

APPENDIX I.—GLOSSARY.

Faculty, develop a: Part V, Lesson xlvii, 2.
Faded (of colour): Part III, **742**; **Part VI, Chapter xxxix,** 15.
Fair: Part IV, Dialogue iii, 79.
Fair, a: Part V, Lesson xxxiv, 2, Note 2.
Fair, speak: Part III, **436**.
Fair, speak one: Part VI, Chapter i, 7.
Fairies: Part V, Lesson viii, 3, Note 15.
Faith in, have: Part V, Lesson lxvii, 2.
Falcon: Part V, Lesson xxxiii, Note 9.
Fall down: Part III, **612**, Obs.
Fall into: Part III, **612**, Obs.
Fall off a horse: Part III, Exercise xxiii*, 5.
Fall, try a: Part V, Lesson lx, 3, Note 4.
Falsehood: Part V, Lesson viii, Note 7.
Falsehood, tell a: Part III, **1003**.
Familiar with, be: Part III, Exercise xix*, 12, Obs.
Family credit, add to the: Part VI, Chapter xxxiv, 3, Note 3.
Family (one's own): Part III, Exercise xiv, 8, Obs.
Family repute: Part VI, Chapter xxxi, 6.
Family, support a: Part IV, Dialogue v, 10.
Family, whole: Part V, Lesson l, 1, Note 1.
Famous, become: Part V, Lesson x, Note 6.
Fan, to, or a: Part V, Lesson xcii, Note 6.
Fancy, one's: Part V, Lesson xxiii, Note 6.
Fancy to, take a: Part V, Lesson lxiv, 1.
Far, how: Part III, **376**, Obs.
Far off: Part V, Lesson xxxii, 4, Note 2.
Far, so (up to now): Part V, Lesson lx, 3, Note 5.
Fare, dainty: Part V, Lesson xvi, 2, Note 10.
Fare (food): Part IV, Dialogue viii, 37, Obs.
Fare (hire): Part IV, Dialogue iii, 62.
Farm labourer: Part III, **526**; Part V, Lesson xviii, 4, Note 9.
Farmer: Part III, **526**.
Farming: Part III, Exercise xx, 3.
Farthest, at the: Part V, Lesson ii, 3.
Fashion: Part III, **1030**.
Fashion, in the: Part VI, Chapter xxiv, 4, Note 2.
Fashion, latest: Part V, Lesson xxxiv, 7.
Fasting: Part VI, Chapter xv, 3, Note 7.
Fat (corpulent): Part V, Lesson xxx, 6, Note 3.
Fat in the face: Part III, Exercise xxxix, 8, Obs. 1.
Father: Part III, **653**.
Father (of a third person): Part III, Exercise xxv, 2, Obs. 1.
Father-in-law: Part VI, Chapter xxxiv, Note 4.
Fatigue, died from: Part VI, Chapter xxxiii, 2, Note 6.
Fatigue, get over: Part III, Exercise xxiii*, 6, Obs.

Fatigued: Part VI, Chapter vii, 6, Note 16.
Fault: Part III, **29**.
Fault, find: Part III, Exercise vii*, 7, Obs. 2; Exercise xxiii, 4, Obs. 2; Part V, Lesson x, 4; Lesson xlvii, 2, Note 5; Lesson lxii, 1; Lesson lxxxiv, 4, Note 5; Part VI, Chapter xiv, Note 2; Chapter xiv, 7, Note 11.
Faults of another, correct the: Part V, Lesson lxvii, 1, Note 2.
Favour, ask a: Part III, **995**; Part V, Lesson lxviii, 2.
Favour, matter of: Part V, Lesson lxxviii, 2.
Favour, repay a: Part VI, Chapter xxv, 12.
Favour, show: Part IV, Dialogue ii, 47.
Feasting his eyes on: Part VI, Chapter xxiv, 7.
Feather, a: Part V, Lesson x, 5, Note 12.
Fee, doctor's: Part V, Lesson lii, 3, Note 9.
Feed a horse: Part III, Exercise xvii, 5.
Feel for you, I: Part V, Lesson lxxxvii, 12.
Feel, to: Part III, **681**.
Feet: Part III, **487**.
Feet (length): Part III, **671**.
Fellow, fine: Part V, Lesson xix, Note 5; Lesson xxxiii, 3, Note 6.
Fellow, good: Part IV, Dialogue iii, 123, Obs. 1.
Felt (fabric): Part III, **407**; Part V, Lesson xciv, 2, Note 5.
Ferry: Part IV, Dialogue viii, 17, Obs.; 18, 19, 20.
Fetch: Part III, **765**.
Fettered (hampered): Part V, Lesson xxvi, 3, Note 6.
Fetters: Part VI, Chapter xxxiii, 2, Note 3.
Feud: Part V, Lesson xvii, 2, Note 13.
Few, comparatively: Part III, Exercise xxx, 9.
Fictions: Part V, Lesson viii, 2, Note 7.
Fidget, a: Part V, Lesson xlii, 3, Note 8.
Fidget, to: Part VI, Chapter xxv, 13, Note 16.
Fight, to: Part III, **860**.
Figure (body): Part III, Exercise xviii*, 2, Obs. 2.
Filial piety: Part V, Lesson iv, Note 2.
Final: Part III, Exercise xxii, 5.
Finally: Part III, **784**, Obs. 3.
Fine (of scenery, etc.): Part V, Lesson xcvii, Note 8.
Fine (of weather): Part III, **220**.
Fine, to: Part IV, Dialogue vi, 21, Obs. 3.
Fine weather, perfectly: Part V, Lesson xciv, 2, Note 1.
Finger, a: Part III, **443**; Part V, Lesson x, Note 11.
Finger, tip of the: Part III, **478**.
Fingers, count on the: Part V, Lesson xxiv, 2, Note 15.
Fingers, hold in the: Part III, **932**.
Finish, to: Part VI, Chapter xxxv, Note 2.
Fire a gun: Part III, Exercise xxi, 2, Obs.; Exercise xxi, 8.

Fire (conflagration): Part VI, Chapter xxxvii, 5, Note 2.
Fire, flame of: Part III, Exercise xxvi, 6.
Fire, sound of: Part V, Lesson xxxvi, 3, Note 6.
Fire, stir the: Part V, Lesson xlii, 4, Note 14.
Firewood: Part VI, Chapter xv, 6, Note 12.
Firm, stand: Part III, 48.
First place, in the: Part III, 617.
First thing: Part III, Exercise xv, 2, Obs. 2.
First time: Part III, 235.
Fish, to: Part VI, Chapter xxix, 7, Note 8.
Fishing-rod: Part VI, Chapter xxix, 7, Note 8.
Fist: Part VI, Chapter i, Note 23.
Fit company, not: Part V, Lesson lxii, Note 6; Lesson lxiii, 1.
Fit (cut to the shape of): Part III, Exercise xii*, 11, Obs. 1.
Fit, to: Part VI, Chapter xxx, Note 1.
Fix on: Part III, Exercise xix*, 9, Obs. 1.
Fixture: Part III, Exercise xxxix, 9, Obs.
Flag, a: Part V, Lesson vii, Note 9.
Flagstaff: Part V, Lesson lxxxvi, Note 11.
Flame: Part III, Exercise xxvi, 6.
Flash of light, in the space of a: Part V, Lesson xxix, 1, Note 2.
Flashed upon him (its meaning): Part VI, Chapter xxix, 10, Note 11.
Flat: Part III, 939.
Flatter me, you (too complimentary): Part V, Lesson iii, 1, Note 1.
Flaw: Part III, 713, Obs.; Part V, Lesson vii, Note 5.
Flay: Part VI, Chapter xiv, Note 8.
Flea in your ear, come back with a: Part V, Lesson liv, Note 7.
Fleas: Part V, Lesson xcv, 2, Note 3.
Flew off, head of the axe: Part VI, Chapter xv, 6.
Float, to: Part III, 792, 800.
Flock, a: Part III, 539.
Floods: Part V, Lesson xxxii, 11, Note 6.
Flour: Part III, 360.
Flourishing: Part V, Lesson xiv, Note 15.
Flow, to: Part III, 792.
Flower-bed: Part VI, Chapter xxix, Note 9.
Flower-pot: Part III, 641.
Flowers, wild: Part III, 809.
Fluent in speech: Part V, Lesson xxiv, Note 2.
Flurried: Part III, 989.
Fluttering down, came (of snow): Part V, Lesson xcvii, 2, Notes 3, 4.
Fly, a: Part VI, Chapter xxxvii, 10, Note 7.
Fly about (of dust): Part III, Exercise xxxv, 5.
Foal, a: Part IV, Dialogue iii, 64, Obs.

Fold, to: Part VI, Chapter xxxiv, 5, Note 5.
Fold up: Part III, 689.
Folly: Part IV, Dialogue v, 9.
Fond of (a bad habit): Part V, Lesson xlvii, 1.
Fond of, be: Part III, 345; Exercise xvii, 2; 971.
Fond of (desire immoderately): Part IV, Dialogue v, 22, Obs.
Fool, a: Part V, Lesson xcix, Note 7.
Fool, blundering: Part III, 830.
Fool, to: Part III, 821.
Foolish: Part III, Exercise xxxvi*, 5, Obs.
Foot, go on: Part III, 69; Exercise iv, 9.
Foot, treading under: Part V, Lesson c, Note 3.
Footprint: Part V, Lesson xxxviii, Note 13.
Footstool: Part VI, Chapter xxxiv, 7.
Forage: Part V, Lesson xxxiii, 1.
Forage for supplies, to: Part VI, Chapter i, 7, Note 17.
Forbearance, show: Part V, Lesson lxii, 3.
Forced me to speak: Part V, Lesson lxii, 1.
Foreign: Part IV, Dialogue v, 31, Obs. 2.
Foreign (European) countries: Part III, Exercise xxx*, 1, Obs. 8.
Foreigners: Part III, 539; Exercise xxx*, 1.
Forethought: Part V, Lesson xci, Note 7.
Forge, to: Part III, 951.
Forget: Part V, Lesson xviii, Note 14.
Forgive: Part IV, Dialogue ii, 46, Obs.; Dialogue iii, 34, Obs.; Part V, Lesson lxii, 3, Note 13; Lesson lxiii, 2, Note 7.
Forked road: Part IV, Dialogue viii, 59, Obs. 2.
Form, not up to my: Part III, Exercise xxxvi, 4, Obs.
Form, to: Part III, Exercise xxx*, 1, Obs. 7.
Formal: Part IV, Dialogue x, 17, Obs. 2.
Formalities: Part IV, Dialogue x, 1, Obs. 7; 2, Obs. 1.
Formality: Part IV, Dialogue x, 9, Obs.
Formerly: Part III, 784.
Fortunate, most: Part V, Lesson xxiii, 7, Note 12.
Fortune: Part III, Exercise xxxix*, 2.
Fortune, good: Part III, 1036, Obs.
Fortune, private: Part VI, Chapter i, 7, Note 15.
Forward a letter: Part VI, Chapter xxxix, 14, Note 14.
Forward, put oneself: Part VI, Chapter xxv, 13.
Fowling-piece: Part III, Exercise xxi*, 2.
Fox: Part VI, Chapter xxxix, Note 6.
Fragrant odour, gave forth a: Part VI, Chapter v, 3, Note 8.
Frame, a: Part V, Lesson viii, Note 11.
Frame, to (set): Part VI, Chapter viii, 6, Note 12.
Fraternal duty: Part V, Lesson lxxx, Note 1.
Freeze: Part V, Lesson xcvii, Note 1; Lesson xcviii, 4.

APPENDIX I.—GLOSSARY.

Frequent, to: Part III, Exercise xxx*, 1, Obs. 8.
Fresh (new): Part V, Lesson lvii, 3, Note 7.
Friend: Part III, 636, 637, 641.
Friend, stand my: Part IV, Dialogue iii, 54, Obs. 3.
Friendless (nobody to care for him): Part V, Lesson lix, 1, Notes 2, 3.
Friendly demeanour: Part VI, Chapter v, 4, Note 11.
Friends, good: Part III, 641.
Friends, hot: Part III, 713.
Friendship: Part III, Exercise xxxiii*, 1, Obs. 5; Part V, Lesson xviii, 1.
Friendship, close and distant: Part V, Lesson lxvii, Note 3.
Fright, gave me a: Part III, 945, Obs.
Fright, take (of a horse): Part IV, Dialogue vii, 81.
Frighten, enough to: Part III, Exercise xi*, 2.
Frightened: Part III, Exercise xxi*, 3, Obs. 2; Exercise xxv*, 8, Obs. 2; Part IV, Dialogue v, 72, Obs.
From (in time): Part V, Lesson lxii, Note 2.
From —— to ——: Part IV, Dialogue viii, 60, Obs.
Front, come to the: Part III, Exercise xxxi, 10, Obs. 2.
Front, in: Part III, 85, Obs. 2; Exercise iv*, 1, Obs.; 689.
Front of a house: Part V, Lesson xxxvii, 4, Note 3.
Front, push to the: Part V, Lesson xiii, 2.
Frontage: Part III, Exercise iii*, 7.
Fruit: Part III, 369, Obs.
Fry, to: Part III, 166, 167.
Fuel: Part III, 351.
Full (complete): Part V, Lesson lviii, 2, Note 10.
Full (repletion): Part IV, Dialogue x, 19, Obs.
Full speed: Part III, Exercise xxiii*, 5, Obs. 1.
Fully: Part III, Exercise i*, 10.
Fun of, make: Part III, Exercise xxiii, 4.
Funeral: Part V, Lesson lxxvi, Note 5.
Funeral, attend a: Part V, Lesson lxxvi, Note 5.
Fur edging: Part V, Lesson xxxiv, 7, Note 7.
Fur on a skin: Part V, Lesson xxxiv, 7, Note 6.
Future trouble, first growth of: Part V, Lesson lxxxi, 2.

Gable wall: Part V, Lesson xcv, Note 12.
Gad about: Part V, Lesson lxx, 2, Note 13.
Gains, dishonest (underhand): Part V, Lesson xx, 2.
Gallantly: Part V, Lesson xiii, 2, Note 11.
Gamble: Part III, 821; Part V, Lesson xlvi, 3, Note 5.
Gambling: Part III, 847.
Gang-board: Part VI, Chapter xxxv, 2.
Gape at, to: Part III, Exercise xxxi*, 2, Obs. 3.
Gardener, market: Part IV, Dialogue iii, 96, Obs.
Gasp for breath: Part V, Lesson l, 2, Note 3.

Gates of a yamên: Part III, 919.
Gates, save the: Part III, Exercise xvi, 5, Obs. 3.
Gates were open, moment the: Part V, Lesson lxxv, 4, Note 3.
Gazette, Peking: Part III, 951.
Gear: Part IV, Dialogue viii, 81.
General, a: Part VI, Chapter vii, Note 15.
Generation, a: Part III, 815.
Generations, future: Part III, 871.
Generations, senior, junior, and contemporary: Part III, Exercise xxxi, 7.
Generic: Part III, Exercise xxvi, 6, Obs.
Generous: Part III, Exercise xxvii, 10.
Gentleman: Part III, 496.
Gentleman, old: Part III, 660.
Gentlemanlike: Part VI, Chapter xxiv, 5, Note 4.
Gentlemen: Part III, 912; Part IV, Dialogue x, 11, Obs. 1.
Gently: Part III, Exercise iv, 9.
Genuine: Part III, Exercise xxxiii*, 1, Obs. 5.
Geomancer: Part V, Lesson lxxv, 6, Note 8.
Geomancy: Part V, Lesson lxxv, Note 8.
Get away: Part III, 895.
Get away (from business, etc.): Part V, Lesson lxxi, 2, Note 2.
Get on together: Part III, 971, Obs.
Get out of it, I could not: Part V, Lesson lxxxiii, Note 2.
Get over (a trouble): Part VI, Chapter xxvi, 3.
Get over (pass through): Part III, 836.
Get up: Part VI, Chapter xviii, 8.
Getting through (the winter): Part VI, Chapter xxxix, 3.
Ghost: Part III, Exercise xxv*, 7, Obs. 2.
Gild: Part VI, Chapter xi, 2, Note 2.
Gird (tie) on: Part V, Lesson xxxiii, Note 7.
Girl: Part III, Exercise xviii*, 1, Obs.; Part V, Lesson lxxxvii, 10, Note 7.
Give in, not: Part V, Lesson lxiii, 2, Notes 8, 9.
Give in to a person: Part V, Lesson lxxxiv, 3, Note 4.
Give up (abandon): Part V, Lesson xxvii, 2, Note 4.
Give up (surrender): Part IV, Dialogue x, 7, Obs.
Glad to, only too: Part IV, Dialogue x, 2, Obs. 5; Part V, Lesson i, 5, Note 10.
Glass: Part III, 750.
Glass, look in the: Part V, Lesson xlvii, 3, Note 11.
Glide, to: Part III, 792.
Glimmer: Part V, Lesson xcii, 3, Note 5.
Glittering white: Part V, Lesson xcvii, 1, Note 2.
Glorify: Part V, Lesson iv, 5, Note 14.
Glory to, bring: Part V, Lesson iv, 5, Note 14.
Glossy: Part III, 750.

Glue: Part VI, Chapter xxx, Note 8.
Gluttonise: Part V, Lesson lxx, Note 1.
"Go" (lively): Part III, Exercise xxxix*, 4, Obs. 2.
Go out (of fire): Part III, 196; Exercise viii, 11.
Gobble up: Part V, Lesson xvi, 2, Note 13.
Going to, am: Part III, Exercise xxxvi, 3, Obs.
Going, where are you: Part V, Lesson lxxi, Note 1.
Gong, beat a: Part VI, Chapter xix, 3, Note 4.
Good and bad: Part III, 1054.
Good-bye: Part III, Exercise xxiv, 7, Obs.; Exercise xxv*, 6, Obs. 1; Part IV, Dialogue x, 24.
Good-bye, I'll say (take leave): Part IV, Dialogue ix, 55, Obs.
Good character: Part III, Exercise xviii, 3.
Good-for-nothing: Part V, Lesson iv, 5, Note 15.
Good-for-nothing, a: Part V, Lesson ix, 5, Note 9.
Good-looking: Part III, Exercise xviii, 3.
Good, make: Part III, Exercise xxxiv*, 1, Obs. 3.
Good, make his words: Part VI, Chapter xx, 1, Note 1.
Good, no (of individuals): Part IV, Dialogue iii, 123, Obs. 4.
Good of you, very: Part IV, Dialogue iv, 38.
Good offices: Part III, Exercise xxxviii, 1.
Good to expect, too: Part IV, Dialogue iv, 45, Obs. 2.
Good, what, can come of it: Part V, Lesson xlvii, 2.
Good word for, can't say a: Part V, Lesson lxxvii, 3, Note 8.
Gospel, receive as: Part V, Lesson viii, 4.
Gossip: Part V, Lesson xxxii, Note 7.
Gourmand: Part V, Lesson lxx, 1, Note 1.
Governor of a province: Part IV, Dialogue ii, 34, Obs.
Grab, to: Part V, Lesson xl, 2, Note 4.
Gradually: Part V, Lesson lv, 3, Note 8.
Graduate, to: Part IV, Dialogue ix, 39, Obs. 2.
Grain of rice: Part V, Lesson xxviii, 2, Note 5.
Granary: Part III, 900.
Granddaughter: Part III, 660.
Grandfather: Part III, 660; Exercise xxv, 7; Exercise xxxi, 7, Obs. 2.
Grandmother: Part III, 660.
Grandson: Part III, 660.
Grasp by the hand: Part III, 451.
Grasp tightly: Part III, 612.
Grasping (hand too long): Part V, Lesson xxxi, Note 11.
Grass: Part III, Exercise xxvi, 1.
Grate on the ear: Part V, Lesson xli, 4, Note 9.
Grateful: Part IV, Dialogue iv, 79, Obs. 2.
Grave, a: Part III, 809; Part V, Lesson lxxv, 6.
Grave (of affairs): Part V, Lesson li, Note 2.
Grave, road to the: Part VI, Chapter xxviii, 7, Note 12.
Gravely (sternly): Part VI, Chapter xxviii, 2, Note 4.

Grave-yard: Part V, Lesson lxxv, Note 6.
Great Wall: Part III, Exercise xx*, 6.
Greedy (grasping): Part VI, Chapter i, 7, Note 21.
Green: Part III, 702; Exercise xxvi, 1, Obs.; Part V, Lesson xc, 2, Note 6.
Grey: Part III, 689.
Grief, came to: Part V, Lesson xcii, Note 1.
Grieve: Part V, Lesson ii, Note 9.
Grimed (with smoke): Part VI, Chapter ix, 5, Note 4.
Grind: Part VI, Chapter xxv, Note 15.
Grip, get in his: Part V, Lesson xxiv, 5, Note 16.
Grocer's shop: Part III, 906.
Ground, space of: Part III, 809, Obs. 1.
Grove: Part III, 696.
Grow (cultivate): Part III, 526.
Grow up: Part III, Exercise xxi*, 6.
Grudging consent, give a: Part VI, Chapter xx, 4.
Gruel: Part VI, Chapter xxix, 3, Note 4.
Grumble: Part III, Exercise xxxix, 4.
Guarantee: Part IV, Dialogue vi, 41, Obs. 2.
Guarantee, I'll: Part V, Lesson lx, Note 7.
Guard a blow: Part V, Lesson vii, 3, Note 11.
Guard against: Part V, Lesson xvi, Note 1.
Guard, be on your: Part V, Lesson xxviii, Note 12.
Guard, hold on: Part VI, Chapter vii, 5, Note 13.
Guardian angel: Part V, Lesson li, Note 1.
Guards of the city: Part III, Exercise xx, 1.
Guess, give a: Part VI, Chapter vi, 3.
Guess, to: Part III, 569; Part V, Lesson xxxiv, 4, Note 3.
Guide, a: Part IV, Dialogue viii, 12.
Guide, to: Part V, Lesson xiv, Note 4.
Guided by circumstances: Part III, Exercise xxxii, 10, Obs.
Guileless: Part V, Lesson xx, Note 6.
Guitar: Part V, Lesson c, 1, Note 1.
Gulp down: Part VI, Chapter xiii, Note 6.
Gum: Part VI, Chapter xxx, Note 8.
Gun, let off a: Part III, Exercise xxi, 3; Exercise xl, 6.
Gusto, with: Part V, Lesson viii, 4, Note 18.
Gymnastics: Part V, Lesson xxvii, 2, Note 5.

Habit: Part III, Exercise ix, 4, Obs. 1.
Habit, give up a: Part V, Lesson xlvi, 1.
Habit of, in the: Part V, Lesson xxxiii, Note 13.
Hair, do the: Part III, 436.
Half way: Part IV, Dialogue viii, 25, Obs.
Hall or main building: Part VI, Chapter xv, Note 9.
Halloo, to: Part III, 784.
Hand, carry in the: Part VI, Chapter iv, Note 14.

APPENDIX I.—GLOSSARY.

Hand, lend a: Part III, Exercise xxiv, 10, Obs.
Hand over: Part III, 723.
Hand, stay the: Part V, Lesson liv, 2.
Hand, wave the: Part V, Lesson xxxvi, Note 9.
Handicraftsmen: Part III, Exercise xxviii, 5.
Handkerchief: Part III, 273; Part VI, Chapter xxxix, 12, Note 8.
Handle of discourse: Part V, Lesson lxi, Note 5.
Hands, with both: Part IV, Dialogue x, 8.
Handsome (good-looking): Part III, 612.
Handwriting: Part VI, Chapter xxvii, 2, Note 2.
Handy: Part III, 333; Part VI, Chapter vi, 1, Note 4.
Hang fire: Part V, Lesson lxiii, 3, Note 11.
Hang oneself: Part III, Exercise xviii, 5, Obs. 2.
Hang up: Part III, 891.
Hanging: Part III, Exercise xviii*, 9, Obs.
Happen: Part III, Exercise xxii*, 1.
Happen what might: Part V, Lesson xxi, 3, Note 6.
Happens again, if this: Part V, Lesson xliii, 2, Note 8.
Happy: Part III, Exercise xxxvii, 7.
Harbour (carry in the breast): Part V, Lesson xvii, Note 6.
Hard on, don't be: Part IV, Dialogue iii, 22, Obs.
Hard up: Part V, Lesson lxviii, 3.
Hardly: Part III, 865.
Hardship: Part III, 399.
Hare: Part VI, Chapter xxxix, Note 6.
Harm, do no: Part V, Lesson xlv, 4, Note 12.
Harm done, no: Part III, 919.
Harm, no: Part IV, Dialogue viii, 55, Obs. 1.
Harm, your own doing: Part V, Lesson vi, 2.
Harmless, mode of action that will preserve me: Part V, Lesson lxxxi, 1.
Harness, to: Part III, 770.
Harpsichord: Part VI, Chapter vii, Note 8.
Harvest: Part V, Lesson xxxii, 10, Note 5.
Hasty: Part VI, Chapter xxxvii, Note 11.
Hate: Part IV, Dialogue ii, 43, Obs. 1; Part V, Lesson xvii, Note 13.
Hats (winter and summer): Part III, Exercise xii, 6.
Haul, to: Part III, 451.
Hauled off: Part IV, Dialogue v, 78, Obs. 1.
Haunted house: Part V, Lesson xxxvii, 4.
Have (must): Part III, 539.
Hawk, a: Part V, Lesson xxxiii, 3, Note 9.
Hawser: Part VI, Chapter xxxv, 3, Note 5.
Head: Part III, 436.
Head (of a criminal): Part III, 487.
Head, crown of the: Part III, Exercise xii, 10, Obs. 2.
Head down to the table: Part V, Lesson xciii, 1.
Headlong: Part V, Lesson xxvi, 2, Note 5; Part VI, Chapter xiii, 1, Note 1.

Headlong haste: Part VI, Chapter xxix, 4.
Head-stall: Part IV, Dialogue viii, 79, Obs. 2.
Health: Part IV, Dialogue iv, 56, Obs.
Health, brisk: Part III, 830.
Health suffer: Part III, Exercise xxxix, 5.
Heart beat, makes my: Part V, Lesson lii, 1.
Heart beating: Part V, Lesson xcv, 2, Note 11.
Heart, cut to the: Part VI, Chapter xxviii, 8, Note 13.
Heart, harden the: Part V, Lesson xliv, Note 9.
Heart, learn by: Part IV, Dialogue ix, 23, Obs. 2.
Heart to, had no: Part V, Lesson lxx, Note 12.
Hearty (vigorous): Part IV, Dialogue iv, 45, Obs. 1.
Heaven: Part V, Lesson lxxx, 2, Note 5.
Heaven, unerring justice of: Part VI, Chapter v, 15, Note 38.
Heaviest: Part IV, Dialogue vi, 21, Obs. 2.
Heavy: Part III, 337; Part V, Lesson li, Note 2.
Heel over: Part VI, Chapter xxxvii, 1.
Heel, shoes down at: Part VI, Chapter xv, 9, Note 16.
Heel, turn on one's: Part V, Lesson lxviii, 2.
Held to be: Part III, Exercise xl, 8, Obs. 3.
Hell: Part V, Lesson lxxx, 2, Note 5.
Helm: Part VI, Chapter xxxv, Note 9.
Help along: Part VI, Chapter xxxv, 2, Note 3.
Help it, could not: Part IV, Dialogue iv, 49, Obs.
Help those in distress: Part V, Lesson xiv, 3, Note 9.
Help (to dishes): Part IV, Dialogue x, 16, Obs.
Help up (of a fallen person): Part V, Lesson lvi, 2, Note 7.
Hen: Part VI, Chapter xviii, 4, Note 7.
Heretofore: Part III, 708.
Heretofore, as: Part V, Lesson xviii, Note 7.
Hesitatingly: Part V, Lesson ii, 2.
Heyday: Part V, Lesson xxvii, 1, Note 1.
High (of water): Part IV, Dialogue viii, 7.
Highest posts: Part V, Lesson xii, 1, Note 5.
Hill, crest of a: Part V, Lesson lxxix, 1, Note 3.
Hill, shoulder of a: Part VI, Chapter xxi, 8, Note 11.
Himself (in person): Part IV, Dialogue vii, 100, Obs. 4.
Hinder: Part V, Lesson xxvi, Note 10.
Hindrance, without: Part V, Lesson xiii, 1, Note 3.
Hire, to: Part III, 1003.
Hit: Part III, 555.
Hit it off: Part III, 971, Obs.
Hitherto: Part III, 585, Obs.
Hoarse: Part V, Lesson xliv, Note 3.
Hoe, a: Part V, Lesson xviii, 6, Note 12.
Hold (carry) a baby: Part III, 1049.
Hold (contain): Part III, 418, Obs.
Hold in a horse: Part III, 451; Exercise xvii, 5; 509.

Hold of a ship: Part VI, Chapter xxxv, 5, Note 11.
Hold of, take: Part III, Exercise xxiii, 5.
Hold tightly: Part III, Exercise xxxv*, 2, Obs. 2.
Hold up by the arm: Part VI, Chapter xxxv, 2, Note 3.
Hole: Part III, 800; Part V, Lesson xl, 2, Note 3.
Hole and corner, look in every: Part V, Lesson v, 9, Note 2.
Holes, pick: Part V, Lesson xli, 3.
Home, catch at: Part III, Exercise xxix*, 12, Obs. 2.
Honest: Part III, 977; Part IV, Dialogue iii, 99.
Honest advice: Part V, Lesson xli, 4, Note 8.
Honest (law-abiding): Part III, 847.
Honour, to: Part III, 871.
Honour, you do me too much: Part V, Lesson xlix, 2, Note 4.
Honourable: Part III, 496.
Hoodwink: Part V, Lesson xv, Note 3.
Hop, to: Part V, Lesson xxxv, 1, 3; Lesson xl, 4, Note 13.
Hope, no: Part III, 912, Obs.
Hope (wish): Part III, 912.
Horde: Part III, Exercise xx, 8.
Horizon: Part III, Exercise xxxiv, 2, Obs.
Horizontal: Part III, Exercise xl, 7.
Horn: Part VI, Chapter xxiii, 1, Note 3.
Horn, music: Part VI, Chapter xix, 2, Note 2.
Horse, saddle the: Part III, 1065.
Horse, thrown from a: Part III, Exercise xxiii, 6.
Hospitality, accept: Part IV, Dialogue x, 5, Obs. 1.
House, a: Part III, Exercise xl, 3, Obs. 1, 2; Part V, Lesson xxxvii, 1, Note 1.
House, your: Part IV, Dialogue vii, 100, Obs. 3.
Household, all the: Part V, Lesson l, Note 1.
Householder: Part III, 49.
How: Part III, 457; Part V, Lesson xvi, 3, Note 18; Lesson xix, Note 8.
However: Part III, Exercise xxiv*, 4, Obs. 2.
Huff, go off in a: Part V, Lesson ix, 4.
Hulk, receiving: Part IV, Dialogue v, 36, Obs. 1.
Humbug, to: Part III, 830; Part V, Lesson xv, 1, Note 3; Lesson xli, Note 10.
Humility, affected: Part VI, Chapter xvi, 5.
Humming and hawing: Part V, Lesson vi, 1.
Humour, to: Part V, Lesson lxxxiv, 4.
Hunger: Part V, Lesson xvi, Note 5.
Hunting: Part V, Lesson xii, 6, Note 6.
Hurry after: Part III, Exercise xvi*, 7.
Hurry, in a: Part VI, Chapter xxiv, 1, Note 1.
Hurry, to: Part VI, Chapter xxxvii, Note 11.
Hurry, what's your: Part III, 585.

Husband: Part III, 815; Part VI, Chapter xxxix, 6, Note 5.
Hustle: Part VI, Chapter xviii, 5.

Ice, became: Part V, Lesson xcviii, 4.
Idea of my own, I have an: Part V, Lesson lii, 1.
Ideas, just suited their: Part VI, Chapter v, 2, Note 6.
Ideas, marched with his own: Part VI, Chapter xvi, 6.
Identical: Part III, Exercise xix, 5.
Idiot: Part III, Exercise xxxi, 9.
Idle: Part IV, Dialogue ii, 43, Obs. 2.
Idler: Part V, Lesson xiii, Note 7.
If: Part III, Exercise ix*, 7, Obs. 2; 906; Part IV, Dialogue x, 1, Obs. 5.
Ill: Part III, 457; Exercise xvii, 4.
Ill-conducted: Part IV, Dialogue vi, 30, Obs.
Ill-natured (remarks): Part V, Lesson lvii, 1.
Ill-ordered: Part VI, Chapter xvii, 7.
Ill, seriously: Part V, Lesson li, 1, Note 2.
Ill-spoken of, get oneself: Part VI, Chapter vi, 3.
Illwill, bear: Part IV, Dialogue ii, 44.
Illegal manner, act in an: Part III, Exercise xxxii, 6, Obs.
Ills of life, lesser: Part V, Lesson lix, 5.
Illustrious, make: Part V, Lesson iv, 5, Note 14.
Image, very: Part V, Lesson xlii, 1, Note 2.
Imagination, all: Part IV, Dialogue ii, 38.
Imagine (think): Part V, Lesson v, 10, Note 4.
Imitate: Part III, 96; Part V, Lesson xvi, Note 22.
Immeasurably (as far as heaven from earth): Part V, Lesson iii, 4, Note 4.
Immediately (at once): Part VI, Chapter ix, 9, Note 7.
Imp, an: Part V, Lesson xlii, Note 8.
Impatient: Part III, 989; Part VI, Chapter xxxvii, 13, Note 11.
Impertinence, treat with: Part V, Lesson lxiii, 3.
Impervious: Part VI, Chapter xix, 3.
Impetuous: Part V, Lesson liii, Note 1; Part VI, Chapter xxxvii, Note 11.
Impetuously: Part III, 533.
Impish: Part V, Lesson xlii, Note 8.
Implement: Part V, Lesson xxvii, Note 10.
Implore: Part V, Lesson xliii, Note 6.
Imply: Part IV, Dialogue ii, 35, Obs.
Importance, matter of: Part III, Exercise xxii, 6, Obs. 1.
Importance, of pressing: Part III, xl, 1.
Importance to, attach: Part VI, Chapter i, Note 5.
Important, not: Part III, 1065.
Imposing: Part III, 1080, Obs.; Part VI, Chapter viii, 2, Note 2.
Impossible: Part III, 31.

APPENDIX I.—GLOSSARY. 23

Impostor: Part IV, Dialogue v, 13; Part V, Lesson xxiv, Note 9.
Impracticable: Part III, 585.
Impracticable (of a person): Part V, Lesson lxxxiv, 1.
Improper: Part VI, Chapter xxxi, Note 19; Chapter xxxi, 15.
Impropriety, no: Part V, Lesson xxxix, 3, Note 11.
Improvement: Part V, Lesson x, 4.
Impulsive: Part VI, Chapter xiii, 1, Note 1.
In: Part III, 28.
In the act of: Part III, 28.
Inadvertently, as if: Part VI, Chapter xxvii, 1, Note 1.
Incantations, mutter: Part VI, Chapter xv, 7, Note 15.
Incessant: Part V, Lesson lxxii, Note 3.
Inch, give an, and take an ell: Part VI, Chapter xxvii, 15.
Inclination, follow one's: Part III, 995, Obs.
Including: Part IV, Dialogue iii, 77.
Incompetent: Part IV, Dialogue vi, 30.
Incomplete: Part III, Exercise xxii, 10, Obs. 2.
Inconvenient: Part III, Exercise xxxvi*, 4.
Increase, to: Part III, Exercise xxvi, 4.
Incredible: Part III, 995.
Incumbent of a post: Part III, Exercise xxxviii, 2.
Indebted (under obligation): Part III, Exercise xxxviii, 1; Part IV, Dialogue iv, 83.
Indeed: Part III, 124.
Independent, become: Part V, Lesson lxv, Note 8.
Indifferent (bad): Part III, 689, Obs.
Indigenous: Part III, 407, Obs.
Indigo: Part VI, Chapter v, 15, Note 36.
Indisposed: Part III, Exercise xxxi, 2, Obs. 1.
Individual, private: Part VI, Chapter xxviii, 2, Note 9.
Industry: Part III, Exercise xxxix, 1.
Inefficiency: Part III, 514.
Inevitably: Part V, Lesson lxiii, Note 3.
Inexperienced: Part III, Exercise xxxv*, 2, Obs. 1; Part VI, Chapter iv, Note 13.
Inexpressibly: Part IV, Dialogue iv, 79, Obs. 3.
Inferior, immeasurably: Part V, Lesson iii, 4, Note 4.
Infirmities: Part V, Lesson xxii, 3.
Inflamed (swollen): Part V, Lesson xlviii, 2, Note 9.
Influenza: Part VI, Chapter xxviii, 9, Note 16.
Information, obtain privately: Part V, Lesson lx, 3, Note 6.
Infringe: Part VI, Chapter xvii, Note 1.
Ingenious: Part III, 562.
Ingeniously: Part V, Lesson xxiii, 4, Note 6.
Ingenuous: Part VI, Chapter ix, 4, Note 3.
Ingot: Part V, Lesson xviii, 2, 4, 6, Note 5; Part VI, Chapter xv, Note 4.
Ingratiate oneself: Part V, Lesson iv, Note 8.

Ingratitude: Part III, Exercise xxxix*, 5.
Injure: Part V, Lesson xxiv, Note 14; Lesson xlix, Note 1.
Injury, suffer: Part III, 1077.
Injustice: Part III, Exercise xxxv, 9.
Injustice, do an: Part III, 945.
Injustice, do oneself an: Part V, Lesson l, 3, Note 8.
Injustice, do or suffer: Part VI, Chapter xxxii, 7, Note 2.
Ink, rub: Part VI, Chapter xxvi, 23, Note 11.
Ink-stone: Part V, Lesson xxii, Note 14; Part VI, Chapter xxvi, Note 11.
Inlay: Part VI, Chapter viii, Note 12.
Innermost: Part III, 303.
Inquire: Part III, Exercise xxix*, 8, Obs. 2.
Inquire into: Part III, 617.
Inquiries after health, make: Part VI, Chapter xxviii, 2.
Inquiries, make careful: Part IV, Dialogue v, 15, Obs.
Inquiries, make private: Part V, Lesson lx, 3, Note 6.
Inquiries, thanks for kind: Part III, 1009.
Insect: Part III, Exercise ii*, 11.
Insignia (*pu-tzŭ*): Part III, Exercise xix, 5, Obs.
Insipid: Part VI, Chapter xxxviii, 2.
Insist upon: Part III, 599; Exercise xix*, 8, Obs.; 9, Obs. 2; Part V, Lesson lxxxiii, 3, Note 6.
Inspect: Part III, Exercise xxxiv*, 1.
Installed themselves, had forcibly: Part VI, Chapter xvi, 1, Note 2.
Instance, for: Part IV, Dialogue x, 3; Part V, Lesson vi, Note 12; Lesson lvii, 2, Note 3.
Instance, in the first: Part III, Exercise xxviii, 2, Obs.; Part IV, Dialogue ii, 16.
Instead: Part III, 906.
Instead of: Part VI, Chapter xxix, 3, Note 2.
Instead of (alternative propositions): Part V, Lesson lii, 4, Notes 10, 11.
Insult, to: Part III, 836.
Insulting manner: Part III, Exercise xxxi, 4.
Intellectual brightness: Part V, Lesson liv, 1, Note 2.
Intelligent: Part III, 1043, 1058.
Intelligible: Part V, Lesson iii, 2, Note 2.
Intent upon (taken up with): Part VI, Chapter xviii, 7.
Intent, with: Part V, Lesson xxxv, 5, Note 18.
Intentionally: Part III, 562.
Intentions, good: Part III, 1049.
Interchange of feelings: Part III, 723, Obs.
Intercourse: Part III, Exercise xxii, 8, Obs.
Interest in me, take an: Part V, Lesson i, 4; Lesson xlix, 2.
Interest in, take a kindly: Part V, Lesson xlix, 2, Note 7; Lesson lv, 2, Note 7.
Interest in, take no: Part V, Lesson viii, Note 21.

Interest (on capital): Part III, Exercise xxxix*, 5; Part V, Lesson xxxi, 2, Note 6.
Interfere with (interrupt): Part V, Lesson vii, 1, Note 1.
Interference: Part III, Exercise xxxix*, 5, Obs. 1.
Intermarriages: Part V, Lesson xxii, 1.
Interposition, by: Part V, Lesson vii, Note 1.
Interpreter (official): Part V, Lesson i, Notes 3, 4.
Interrupt (of friendship): Part III, 723.
Interrupt progress of: Part V, Lesson vii, Note 1.
Intimacy, degrees of: Part V, Lesson lxvii, 1, Note 3.
Intimate: Part IV, Dialogue iv, 11; Dialogue vi, 25, Obs. 1; Part V, Lesson xlvi, 3.
Intimate terms, on: Part VI, Chapter xxxvii, 6.
Intolerable: Part V, Lesson lxiv, 2, Note 5; Part VI, Chapter xiii, 1.
Intoxicated: Part IV, Dialogue v, 80, Obs. 2.
Intrigue: Part V, Lesson iv, 3, Note 7.
Introduce: Part VI, Chapter xxi, Note 4.
Introduction, letter of: Part VI, Chapter xxi, Note 4.
Intuition, come by: Part V, Lesson iii, 7.
Inuendo, slander by: Part V, Lesson lxiii, Note 2.
Invent (fabricate): Part IV, Dialogue vi, 23, Obs. 2.
Invest (put in money): Part III, Exercise xxix, 3, Obs. 2.
Invested capital: Part IV, Dialogue vi, 10, Obs.
Invitation, written: Part IV, Dialogue x, 1, Obs. 1.
Invite, to: Part III, 569.
Involuntarily: Part V, Lesson lxvii, 2, Note 4; Part VI, Chapter iii, Note 11.
Involve: Part III, Exercise xxiv*, 3, Obs.
Ironical remarks: Part VI, Chapter xvi, 5.
Irregular: Part III, Exercise xxii, 10, Obs. 2.
Irregularity: Part III, 578.
Irritate: Part V, Lesson lv, 1, Note 6; Part VI, Chapter xxi, Note 6.
Issue on, join: Part V, Lesson lxii, 2.
Itch, to: Part V, Lesson xliii, Note 7; Part VI, Chapter xxvi, Note 8.
Item by item: Part III, Exercise xxii, 10.

Jacket: Part V, Lesson lxxxvi, Note 2.
Jam: Part III, 369.
Jar, a: Part III, Exercise xxiv*, 5, Obs.
Jealous: Part III, 719, Obs.
Jeopardise: Part VI, Chapter xix, 6.
Jerk to a distance: Part V, Lesson xxvii, 4, Note 15.
Jetty: Part VI, Chapter xxxvi, Note 8.
Job, a: Part III, Exercise xix*, 7.
Jobs for other people, do: Part VI, Chapter ii, 1, Note 4.
Join (accompany): Part III, 728.
Join in, let me: Part VI, Chapter xi, Note 6.
Joints: Part III, 470.

Joke (comical story), a: Part III, Exercise xxiii, 7.
Joke, no: Part III, 821.
Joking: Part III, 821; Part IV, Dialogue vi, 54.
Joking, practical: Part III, 821.
Jostle: Part V, Lesson xxxix, Note 5.
Journey, long: Part V, Lesson xxxi, Note 9.
Journey, make a long: Part III, 585.
Judge from: Part III, Exercise xxxi*, 3, Obs. 2.
Jumbled together: Part III, 548.
Jump into: Part III, 945.
Jump, make me: Part III, 945.
Jump up: Part III, 945.
Jumping about: Part III, Exercise xxxv*, 1, Obs. 4.
Jurisdiction: Part V, Lesson xxxii, 6, Note 3.
Just (fair): Part III, 982.
Just now: Part III, 760, Obs.; Part V, Lesson xxxi, 3, Note 8.
Just (only), it was: Part VI, Chapter xiv, 8, Note 15.
Justice, do: Part IV, Dialogue iii, 56, Obs. 2.
Justice (equity): Part III, 1030.
Justice to, not done: Part IV, Dialogue x, 21, Obs.

Keep (detain): Part III, 647.
Kennel (gutter): Part V, Lesson xxviii, 1, Note 3.
Kill: Part III, 509; Exercise xix*, 13; Part V, Lesson xlii, 4, Note 11.
Kill for food: Part V, Lesson lxxxviii, 2, Note 2.
Kiln: Part VI, Chapter xxv, Note 2.
Kind-hearted: Part V, Lesson xiv, 3, Note 7; Lesson xv, 1.
Kindling: Part III, Exercise xiv*, 1.
Kindly disposition: Part VI, Chapter vii, 2, Note 5.
Kindly of, think: Part V, Lesson xlix, Note 7.
Kindness, show special: Part V, Lesson xlii, Note 15.
King (in chess): Part V, Lesson lviii, Note 9.
King, tributary: Part V, Lesson xxi, Note 4.
Kingfisher: Part VI, Chapter viii, Note 11.
Kitchen (a large): Part IV, Dialogue x, 18, Obs. 2.
Knead: Part VI, Chapter v, 3, Note 9.
Knee-cap: Part III, 487.
Kneel: Part V, Lesson xliii, Note 5; Lesson lxxxiii, Note 1.
Knock at the door, to: Part IV, Dialogue vii, 1, Obs.
Knot, tie a slip: Part VI, Chapter xxxiv, 9, Note 10.
Knot (two kinds of): Part VI, Chapter xxxiv, Note 10.
Know how to refuse, not: Part V, Lesson lxxviii, 1.

Labour, gratuitous: Part VI, Chapter xv, Note 6.
Labour, matter of: Part III, Exercise xxx*, 4, Obs.
Lacquerware: Part IV, Dialogue i, 12, Obs. 2.
Lady (young): Part IV, Dialogue iv, 66.

APPENDIX I.—GLOSSARY.

Lady, your good: Part V, Lesson lxxxvii, 7, Note 4.
Lag: Part III, Exercise xxxvi, 2.
Lame: Part V, Lesson xxvii, 3, Note 9.
Land, by: Part IV, Dialogue viii, 5, Obs.; Part VI, Chapter xxxv, 1, Note 1.
Lane: Part III, **800**.
Language: Part III, **595**.
Language, use strong: Part VI, Chapter v, 9, Note 21.
Last, boot: Part VI, Chapter xxxiv, 7, Note 7.
Last (endure): Part III, **836**.
Last year: Part III, Exercise xxxix, 8, Obs. 2.
Late: Part V, Lesson xxvi, Note 2.
Late, of: Part III, Exercise xxiv*, 4, Obs. 1.
Late years, of: Part III, Exercise xx, 6, Obs. 1.
Lately: Part V, Lesson xxxix, Note 1.
Lathe, turn in a: Part VI, Chapter x, 12, Note 3.
Lattice-work, interstices of: Part V, Lesson xl, Note 1.
Laugh against, raise a: Part V, Lesson lv, 1, Note 5.
Laugh at my expense, raise a: Part IV, Dialogue x, 1.
Laugh at, to: Part III, **599**; Exercise xxvi*, 3, Obs. 1; Part V, Lesson viii, 4, Note 20.
Laugh, to: Part III, **989**.
Laughing, burst out: Part III, Exercise xxiii*, 3; Part V, Lesson xxx, 6, Note 14.
Laughing, split one's sides with: Part V, Lesson lvi, 2.
Laughter, roar with: Part III, **830**; Part III, Exercise xxvi*, 2, Obs. 2.
Law, get foul of the: Part V, Lesson xlvi, 3.
Law, give him no: Part V, Lesson lxvii, 1.
Law, go to: Part III, Exercise xxxviii, 6, Obs. 2.
Laws: Part III, **520**; Part V, Lesson xxi, 2, Note 4.
Lay about (beat): Part III, Exercise xxii*, 9, Obs. 2.
Layers: Part III, **891**.
Layman: Part III, **878**.
Lazy: Part III, **555**.
Lead an animal: Part V, Lesson xxxiii, Note 2.
Lead on (induce to talk): Part V, Lesson lviii, 2, Note 7.
Lead, take the: Part III, Exercise xxxi, 10, Obs. 2.
Lead, to: Part V, Lesson xiv, Note 4.
Leads to (is the cause of): Part V, Lesson lv, 2.
Leaf: Part IV, Dialogue v, 25, Obs.
Leaf of a door: Part V, Lesson xcii, 3, Note 6.
Leaf, turn over a new: Part V, Lesson lxx, 2.
League with, in: Part IV, Dialogue vi, 14, Obs. 4.
Leak out (figuratively): Part V, Lesson lxvi, Note 2.
Leak, to: Part V, Lesson ix, Note 2.
Learning, deep: Part V, Lesson xix, Note 4.
Learning, man of: Part III, Exercise xviii, 5, Obs. 1.
Least, at the very: Part V, Lesson xxxiv, 5, Note 4.
Leave, ask: Part IV, Exercise iii, 13, Obs.

Leave behind (or out): Part V, Lesson ix, 4, Note 2.
Leave of, take: Part VI, Chapter ix, 9.
Leave off (take his hand off): Part V, Lesson xix, 5.
Leave, take my: Part IV, Dialogue ix, 55, Obs.
Left hand: Part V, Lesson v, Note 3.
Leg irons (fetters): Part VI, Chapter xxxiii, Note 3.
Legs: Part III, **443**.
Legs of horse, table, etc.: Part V, Lesson xxxiii, 3, Note 5.
Leisure: Part III, **204, 989**.
Leisurely: Part III, **965**.
Lend: Part III, **345**.
Length: Part III, **257, 671**; Exercise xxx, 3, Obs. 1.
Leopard: Part V, Lesson xxx, Note 6.
Lesson to, read a: Part V, Lesson xviii, 9, Note 15.
Lessons, hear: Part V, Lesson vi, 1, Note 1.
Lest: Part V, Lesson xi, Note 8.
Let (allow): Part III, **723**.
Let down (sc., a screen): Part V, Lesson lxxxiii, Note 8.
Let go: Part III, **555**; Part VI, Chapter xxxvii, 11, Note 8.
Let in: Part III, Exercise xxviii*, 3, Obs.
Let out a secret: Part V, Lesson lxvi, 1, Note 2.
Letter, send a: Part III, **995**.
Letters, man of: Part VI, Chapter xxxviii, 1, Note 1.
Levée: Part V, Lesson xxxiv, 11, Note 12.
Level, put oneself on the same: Part V, Lesson lxii, Note 6.
Level, to: Part VI, Chapter xxix, 13, Note 16.
Levity (of manner): Part V, Lesson lv, Note 1.
Liable: Part III, Exercise xvii*, 3, Obs. 2.
Libation, pour out a: Part V, Lesson xxxvi, 4, Note 16.
Liberal: Part IV, Dialogue v, 50; 52, Obs.
Liberal-minded: Part III, **713**.
Liberality, in return for your: Part V, Lesson xxxviii, 3.
Liberty, give a caged bird, etc., its: Part V, Lesson xl, Note 10.
Liberty of observing, take the: Part VI, Chapter xxviii, 2.
Liberty to, feel at: Part III, Exercise xxii*, 6.
Lick, to: Part V, Lesson lxxxii, Note 4.
Lies, tell: Part III, **1003**.
Life for, give his: Part V, Lesson xliv, 3.
Life, never in one's: Part V, Lesson xcviii, 5.
Life, risk: Part V, Lesson xvii, 4, Note 17.
Lifetime, meet with seldom in one's: Part V, Lesson xci, 4.
Lift, give one a: Part IV, Dialogue ii, 36, Obs.
Lift, to: Part VI, Chapter iv, 15, Note 14.
Light (of weight): Part III, **337**.
Light a fire: Part III, **163**; Exercise vii, 4; **198, 204**.

Light (a lamp): Part III, Exercise viii, 10, Obs. 1.
Light (settle) upon: Part III, 765.
Light shone on him: Part V, Lesson xxxv, Note 17.
Like: Part III, 906, 1071; Exercise xl, 2, Obs.; Part IV, Dialogue v, 39; Part V, Lesson xxxiii, 3, Note 10.
Like, just what I should: Part III, Exercise xxvi, 3, Obs.
Like, to: Part III, 971.
Likely: Part IV, Dialogue viii, 54.
Liking, to one's: Part III, 1065.
Limit, extreme: Part V, Lesson xxviii, 3, Note 7.
Limit (restriction): Part V, Lesson xxviii, 3, Note 6.
Limp, feel: Part III, 971.
Line, both ends of the: Part V, Lesson i, 2.
Line, chalk a (on a coat for sewing): Part V, Lesson lxxxvi, 5, Note 4.
Line of action: Part III, Exercise xxii, 3.
Lined: Part III, 316.
Lip: Part III, 436.
List, make a: Part III, 310.
Lit upon, his eye: Part VI, Chapter iv, 9, Note 11.
Litter (mule): Part III, Exercise xvi*, 5.
Little, some: Part IV, Dialogue v, 32, Obs.
Live, to: Part III, 1043.
Lived, if the child had: Part V, Lesson lxxxvii, 10, Note 8.
Livelihood, means of: Part III, Exercise xxi*, 6, Obs. 2.
Living (cost of): Part III, Exercise xiii*, 4, Obs. 2; Part VI, Chapter ix, 3.
Living, get a (keep them alive): Part V, Lesson xciii, 2.
Living image: Part VI, Chapter xxiv, 6.
Load a gun: Part III, Exercise xxi, 8.
Load (a ship): Part III, 418.
Load (beast's): Part III, Exercise xvi, 7.
Load (carried on a pole): Part III, Exercise xxv, 11.
Load (carried on the back): Part III, Exercise xxv, 11.
Load, carry a: Part III, 412.
Loaded (gun): Part III, Exercise xxi, 3.
Lock (sluice): Part V, Lesson xcii, 1, Note 3.
Lodge, to: Part VI, Chapter viii, Note 17.
Lodgers, take in: Part IV, Dialogue viii, 29, Obs.
Loins: Part III, 441.
Loiter: Part VI, Chapter xxi, Note 6.
Long and short of it: Part IV, Dialogue iv, 78.
Long, before: Part IV, Dialogue vi, 40, Obs. 2.
Long, ever so: Part III, 784; Exercise xxxiv, 6.
Long (in duration): Part V, Lesson xix, 3, Note 3.
Long (protracted): Part III, Exercise xxx, 3, Obs. 1; Part V, Lesson xlix, 2, Note 2.
Long sight: Part VI, Chapter v, 1, Note 2.
Long time: Part III, Exercise xvi*, 7, Obs.
Long time, take a: Part III, Exercise xii, 2.

Long, to: Part III, Exercise xxxiv, 6.
Long, too: Part III, 671.
Longer, no: Part III, 760.
Longing to see you: Part III, Exercise xxxiv, 1, Obs.
Look after: Part III, Exercise xvii, 4.
Look (appear): Part VI, Chapter xxvi, 10.
Look down upon (despise): Part III, Exercise xxii*, 5, Obs. 2.
Look out (take care): Part V, Lesson xxviii, 4, Note 12.
Look you up: Part III, 912, Obs.
Looks like: Part IV, Dialogue x, 17, Obs. 1.
Loop, make a: Part III, 891.
Loop, to, or a: Part VI, Chapter xxxiv, Note 10.
Lose: Part III, 647.
Lose a bet: Part VI, Chapter xviii, 4, Note 6.
Loss (by death): Part V, Lesson lxxvi, 9.
Loss, suffer: Part III, 1049, Obs.
Lot (strip, block), a: Part III, Exercise xx, 8.
Lot, whole: Part V, Lesson xlviii, 2, Note 2.
Loud, speak: Part III, 470.
Lout, a: Part V, Lesson xlii, 2, Note 5; Lesson lvii, 4.
Loutish: Part III, 821.
Low caste: Part V, Lesson c, 3, Note 7.
Low fellows: Part V, Lesson lvii, 4.
Lower, to: Part VI, Chapter xxxv, 5, Note 12.
Loyal: Part V, Lesson xli, Note 8.
Luck: Part V, Lesson xxviii, 4, Note 10.
Luck, be in: Part III, Exercise xxvii*, 4.
Luck, have: Part IV, Dialogue ii, 47, Obs.
Luck, he's in: Part V, Lesson lxiv, 3.
Luck, it was: Part IV, Dialogue ix, 41, Obs. 1.
Luck, run of: Part V, Lesson xiii, 1, Note 2.
Luck, spoil one's: Part V, Lesson xxviii, Note 8.
Luck would have it, as: Part III, Exercise xxxvi*, 3; Part V, Lesson lxxxii, 4.
Luckily: Part III, Exercise xxi, 3; Exercise xxiii*, 5, Obs. 2; Part V, Lesson xxxi, Note 9.
Lucky escape: Part IV, Dialogue v, 61.
Lunatic: Part VI, Chapter xxxvii, 16, Note 13.
Lurching (of a drunkard): Part V, Lesson xliv, 1, Note 2.
Lute: Part V, Lesson c, 1, Note 2.

Made for one (clothes): Part V, Lesson xxxiv, 7.
Mahomedan: Part III, 878, Obs.
Maid, serving: Part VI, Chapter i, 3, Note 8.
Maiden name: Part VI, Chapter i, 2, Note 6.
Maigre: Part III, Exercise xxxiii, 2; Part IV, Dialogue viii, 33, Obs.
Main chance, eye to the: Part VI, Chapter iii, 7, Note 10.
Majority: Part III, Exercise xii, 1, Obs.

APPENDIX I.—GLOSSARY. 27

Make money out of: Part IV, Dialogue ii, 27, Obs.
Make off with: Part IV, Dialogue iv, 54, Obs.
Make up to (toady): Part V, Lesson lvii, 4.
Malevolence: Part V, Lesson lviii, Note 5.
Manacles: Part VI, Chapter xxxiii, Note 3.
Manager (of an inn): Part III, **390**.
Manager's office: Part IV, Dialogue x, 18, Obs. 1.
Manchu: Part V, Lesson i, 1, Note 1; Lesson ii, 1, 3; Lesson iii, 1, 2; Lesson v, 3, 6, 9, 10; Lesson vi, 2; Lesson vii, 1, 5.
Manchuria: Part V, Lesson lxxxix, 1, Note 1.
Manchus: Part V, Lesson x, 1.
Manifest: Part IV, Dialogue x, 17, Obs. 1.
Manifest, become: Part V, Lesson xlvi, Note 1.
Manifestation: Part VI, Chapter v, 15, Note 38.
Manly: Part V, Lesson lx, 2, Note 3.
Manner towards: Part III, Exercise xxxvi, 7.
Manufactory: Part VI, Chapter xxxix, Note 13.
Many for, too: Part IV, Dialogue v, 76, Obs. 1.
Market-gardener: Part IV, Dialogue iii, 96, Obs.
Market town: Part IV, Dialogue viii, 39, Obs. 1.
Marriage, contract a: Part VI, Chapter xxv, 9, Note 9.
Marriage, proposal of: Part V, Lesson lxxxv, 2, Note 4.
Marriage, promise in: Part VI, Chapter xix, 6.
Marriage, promised in: Part VI, Chapter i, 6.
Marriage, relations by: Part V, Lesson v, 10.
Married (of women): Part IV, Dialogue iv, 62, Obs. 2.
Married to: Part IV, Dialogue iv, 63, Obs. 1.
Marry: Part III, Exercise xxxvi, 3, Obs.
Marry a wife: Part V, Lesson xvii, 3, Note 15.
Martial exercises: Part V, Lesson xxvii, 2, Note 2.
Mason: Part III, Exercise xxxv*, 3, Obs. 2.
Mast: Part VI, Chapter xxxv, 3, Note 7.
Master, a: Part III, **755**, Obs.
Match for: Part III, Exercise xxxvi, 4.
Match, good: Part VI, Chapter xxv, Note 8.
Match, have a: Part III, Exercise xxvi*, 1.
Match, his: Part V, Lesson iii, 4.
Materials (as timber): Part III, **750**; Part IV, Dialogue v, 26, Obs. 2.
Matter, doesn't: Part III, **919, 1065**.
Matter how, it doesn't: Part III, Exercise xxxii, 9, Obs. 2.
Matter how, no: Part III, Exercise xxxix, 4, Obs. 1.
Matter, it won't: Part III, Exercise xxxiv, 3, Obs. 3.
Matter, no: Part III, **351**.
Matter, what does it: Part V, Lesson lvii, 2.
Matter, what was the: Part III, Exercise xxi*, 3.
Matter with, have anything the: Part III, Exercise xvii, 4.
Mature years: Part III, **955**.

May, be that as it: Part IV, Dialogue iii, 21, Obs.
Meal, a: Part IV, Dialogue vi, 41, Obs. 1; Part V, Lesson ix, Note 8.
Meal, make a good: Part IV, Dialogue x, 19, Obs.
Means, by no: Part III, Exercise xxvii*, 3, Obs.
Means of, make a: Part V, Lesson xlvii, 2, Note 8.
Measure, foot: Part III, **939**, Obs.
Measure (of capacity): Part III, Exercise i, 12; Exercise 1*, 7, 9.
Measure, to: Part III, **776**.
Measurement: Part III, Exercise xxix, 5.
Meddle with what does not concern one: Part VI, Chapter iv, 2, Note 4.
Mediator, act as: Part V, Lesson lxiv, 2, Note 6.
Medicine, administer: Part VI, Chapter v, Note 20.
Medicines: Part IV, Dialogue v, 26, Obs. 2.
Mediocre: Part VI, Chapter xxviii, 2, Note 10.
Meet, to: Part III, **665**.
Meet with: Part III, **45**.
Melancholy, be absorbed in: Part VI, Chapter xiii, 1, Note 2.
Melancholy, fixed air of: Part VI, Chapter xxv, Note 13.
Melancholy (sorrowful): Part V, Lesson xcii, 4, Note 9.
Memorandum: Part IV, Dialogue v, 60, Obs. 1.
Memory, bad: Part V, Lesson lxvi, 1.
Men and women: Part III, **815**.
Mend: Part III, **939**, Obs.
Mend (a whip): Part IV, Dialogue iii, 110, Obs.
Mend clothes: Part III, **289**, Obs.
Mention, not worth: Part V, Lesson lxix, 3, Note 4.
Mention, to: Part III, Exercise xxiii*, 2, Obs.; Part IV, Dialogue vii, 33, 34.
Mentioning, not worth: Part VI, Chapter xxx, 7, Note 5.
Mercy, shows no: Part V, Lesson liv, 2, Note 9.
Merit, hidden: Part V, Lesson xx, 2, Note 4.
Merry: Part V, Lesson xcii, 4, Note 9.
Merry, made: Part VI, Chapter v, 4, Note 12.
Mess apart, to: Part VI, Chapter xvii, 5, Note 3.
Mess, here's a: Part VI, Chapter v, Note 22.
Mess, in a (confusion): Part III, **906**.
Message, convey a: Part III, **885**.
Message, give a: Part III, **989**.
Message, send a: Part III, **995**, Obs.
Messenger, office: Part III, **1009**.
Met, it is long since we: Part VI, Chapter xvii, Note 1.
Meteor: Part III, **1003**.
Method of proceeding: Part V, Lesson lxvi, Note 6.
Methodical: Part III, Exercise xxxvi, 8.
Metropolitan examination: Part VI, Chapter vii, 2, Note 7.
Mice: Part VI, Chapter iv, 2, Note 4.

Middle, in the: Part III, 303; Exercise xix*, 10.
Might be: Part V, Lesson lxxxi, 1.
Mild (of weather): Part III, Exercise ix, 8.
Military service, active: Part III, Exercise xix, 8.
Military service, have seen: Part V, Lesson xii, 5, Note 5.
Milk: Part III, Exercise xiv, 1.
Millionaires: Part V, Lesson xxviii, 3.
Mimic, to: Part VI, Chapter xii, 5, Note 6.
Mincingly, creep: Part V, Lesson xl, Note 2.
Mind, change one's: Part III, Exercise xxix, 8.
Mind, make up one's (fulfil a disagreeable task): Part V, Lesson xliv, 2, Note 9.
Mind, something on one's: Part VI, Chapter vi, 3.
Mind to, give the whole: Part V, Lesson vi, 2, Note 5.
Mind, turn the matter over in one's: Part VI, Chapter xiii, 1.
Mind up, make one's: Part V, Lesson lxxxi, 2.
Mine, coal: Part VI, Chapter xxv, Note 2.
Minutest particular: Part V, Lesson xxxix, 2, Note 8.
Mirror: Part V, Lesson xlvii, 3, Note 11.
Miscellaneous: Part III, Exercise xxxiv, 8.
Mischief: Part V, Lesson xlii, Note 6.
Mischief-maker: Part V, Lesson lxiv, 2, Note 1.
Mischievous: Part VI, Chapter xxxvii, Note 3.
Misdeeds, reward of: Part III, Exercise xxxv, 10, Obs.
Misery: Part III, 399.
Misfortune, meet with a: Part III, 590; Part VI, Chapter v, 13, Note 25.
Misinformed: Part IV, Dialogue v, 14.
Missionaries: Part III, 885.
Mist: Part III, 265.
Mistake, a: Part III, 562.
Mistake, made a: Part IV, Dialogue iii, 34.
Mistake, to: Part III, 965.
Misty: Part VI, Chapter v, Note 23.
Mix (with water): Part III, 210.
Mixed together: Part VI, Chapter xxviii, 12, Note 20.
Mixture: Part III, Exercise xiv*, 4, Obs. 2.
Modest: Part VI, Chapter v, Note 21; Chapter xi, 3, Note 4.
Moisten the pencil before writing: Part VI, Chapter xxvi, 23, Note 12.
Moment ago: Part III, 760.
Moment, for the: Part III, 617; Part VI, Chapter xix, 11.
Moment, in a: Part V, Lesson xxix, Note 2.
Moment, present: Part III, Exercise xv*, 1, Obs. 1.
Moment, the: Part III, Exercise xxix, 7, Obs. 1.
Money: Part III, 443; Exercise xxxiv*, 1; Part IV, Dialogue ii, 54.
Money, invest: Part III, Exercise xxix, 3, Obs. 2.

Money, lose: Part III, 1049.
Money, make: Part III, Exercise xxxvii, 4, Obs.
Money, paper: Part V, Lesson lxxv, 6, Note 9.
Money, ready: Part III, Exercise xxxiv*, 1, Obs. 4; Part IV, Dialogue ii, 55.
Monkey: Part V, Lesson xxx, 9, Note 16.
Month, last: Part III, Exercise vi, 5, Obs. 2.
Month, what day of the: Part V, Lesson xxxii, Note 1.
Moral conduct, regulate: Part V, Lesson iv, 6.
Moral nature, take care of one's: Part V, Lesson iv, Note 6.
Moral sense: Part III, 847, Obs.
Morality: Part III, 878.
More than ever: Part V, Lesson xcvii, Note 5.
More, the: Part V, Lesson xciii, 1, Note 5.
Moreover: Part III, 617, 878.
Morrow, taking no thought for the: Part VI, Chapter x, 1.
Mosquitoes: Part V, Lesson xcv, 2, Note 2.
Most: Part III, Exercise xxii, 10, Obs. 1.
Moth: Part VI, Chapter xxxix, 14, Note 11.
Mother: Part III, 653; Exercise xi*, 1, Obs. 1; Part IV, Dialogue ii, 58, Obs. 2.
Mother-in-law: Part VI, Chapter xxxiv, 4, Note 4.
Mother, your: Part III, Exercise xi*, 1, Obs. 1; Part IV, Dialogue ii, 58, Obs. 2.
Motive: Part IV, Dialogue vii, 28.
Mould, a: Part V, Lesson ii, 1, Note 1.
Mould, to: Part III, 932.
Mount (as a ladder, etc.): Part V, Lesson lxi, Note 1.
Mount (as a picture): Part III, 737.
Mountain pass: Part III, 809.
Mountain scenery: Part III, Exercise xxx, 1.
Mountainous: Part III, Exercise xxx, 1, Obs.
Mourning, be in: Part V, Lesson lxxvi, 1, Note 2.
Mouse: Part VI, Chapter iv, Note 4.
Moustache: Part III, 436.
Mouth full, speak with: Part III, 436.
Mouth open (gaping): Part V, Lesson lvi, 2.
Mouth, purse up the: Part VI, Chapter xxvi, Note 1.
Movable: Part III, Exercise xxxix, 9, Obs.
Move about: Part III, Exercise xxxix, 5.
Move house: Part IV, Dialogue vii, 65, Obs.; Part V, Lesson xxii, 1, Note 6.
Move in chess, false: Part V, Lesson liv, Note 15.
Moved (touched in heart): Part V, Lesson l, 4, Note 9.
Movements, keep your eye on their: Part V, Lesson lxvi, 2.
Muddy water: Part III, 548.
Mulberry tree: Part III, 696.
Murder, commit a: Part III, Exercise xxiv, 1, Obs. 1.
Murderer: Part III, Exercise xxiv, 1, Obs. 2.

APPENDIX I.—GLOSSARY. 29

Muscle: Part III, Exercise xxxvi*, 5.
Mussulman: Part III, 878, Obs.
Must: Part III, 32.
Must be: Part III, Exercise xxxv, 7, Obs.
Muster, call the: Part III, Exercise xix, 6, Obs. 2.
Muttering: Part VI, Chapter xxix, 9, Note 10; Chapter xxxi, 8, Note 12.
Mutual: Part III, Exercise xxxiv, 1, Obs.
Muzzle (face of a dog): Part III, Exercise xxxv, 6.
Myself: Part III, 653, Obs.
Mysterious: Part VI, Chapter xxviii, Note 22; Chapter xxxi, 2, Note 4.

Nails (finger): Part III, 443.
Name, a: Part III, 514.
Name (of a place): Part III, 514.
Name, what is your: Part III, 514.
Names, call one: Part V, Lesson lxii, 4, Note 16.
Narrow: Part III, 617.
Native: Part III, 407, Obs.
Nativity, cast a: Part V, Lesson xxxix, 2, Note 6.
Natural: Part III, Exercise xxxix, 2; Part VI, Chapter xxiii, 3.
Natural products: Part III, 635.
Natural state: Part III, Exercise xiv, 4, Obs.
Nature, beast by: Part V, Lesson lxiv, 1.
Navigable: Part III, Exercise xxx*, 2, Obs. 1.
Near: Part III, Exercise i, 10, Obs. 2.
Nearly, very: Part V, Lesson lii, 1, Note 3.
Necessity, no: Part III, Exercise xv*, 6.
Neck: Part III, 470.
Needle: Part III, 289.
Needle, eye of: Part III, 289, Obs.
Needlework, do: Part VI, Chapter xxxi, 3, Note 5.
Negative, to: Part III, 569.
Neighbour: Part V, Lesson xx, 1, Note 1.
Neighbourhood, in our: Part V, Lesson v, 9, Note 3.
Neither: Part III, 925.
Neophyte: Part V, Lesson xci, Note 12.
Nephew: Part IV, Dialogue vii, 46, Obs.; Part VI, Chapter i, 6, Note 13.
Nervous: Part V, Lesson lvi, 1, Note 3; Lesson lx, 1, Note 1; Part VI, Chapter xv, 4.
Net, a: Part V, Lesson vii, 1, Note 3.
Never: Part III, 539; 585, Obs.; Exercise xxv*, 7, Obs. 1; 765, Obs.; Exercise xxix, 7; Exercise xxix*, 11, Obs. 2; Part IV, Dialogue iv, 51, Obs.; Dialogue vi, 9, Obs. 1; Part V, Lesson xlvii, 1.
Nevertheless: Part III, 689.
New: Part III, 742; Part V, Lesson lvii, 3, Note 7.

New Year's day: Part V, Lesson lxii, 1.
Next (month and year): Part III, Exercise ix, 6.
Nice, look: Part V, Lesson xxiii, 4, Note 7.
Nice-looking: Part VI, Chapter xi, 2, Note 1.
Nice to eat: Part III, 162.
Niggardly: Part III, 689.
Night, at: Part III, Exercise vii, 11, Obs. 4.
Night, pass the: Part IV, Dialogue viii, 26.
Night, sit up at: Part V, Lesson xlviii, 1, Note 1.
Nightfall: Part IV, Dialogue viii, 23.
Nip between the finger and thumb: Part V, Lesson lxxxvi, Note 10.
Nobody else: Part III, 708.
Noise: Part V, Lesson xxxv, 1, Note 2.
Noise, make a: Part III, 595.
Noise (of music): Part VI, Chapter xl, 2, Note 6.
Nonchalantly: Part VI, Chapter xxxvii, 10, Note 6.
None to speak of: Part III, Exercise xxx, 7.
Nonsense: Part III, Exercise xv, 7, Obs. 2; Exercise xxii*, 6, Obs. 1.
Noon: Part IV, Dialogue x, 3, Obs. 2.
North: Part III, 393.
Nose, bridge of the: Part III, Exercise xviii, 7.
Nose, running at the: Part V, Lesson xlv, 2, Note 8.
Note (letter): Part IV, Dialogue v, 60, Obs. 1; Part V, Lesson xxii, 3, Note 15.
Nothing at all: Part III, Exercise xxii*, 6, Obs. 2.
Nothing but, can see: Part III, Exercise xxxiv, 2.
Nothing, come to: Part V, Lesson vii, 1, Note 4.
Nothing, for: Part III, Exercise xxvi*, 4; Part VI, Chapter v, 8, Note 18.
Nothing, it's: Part III, 919.
Nothing to do: Part III, Exercise xi, 7.
Nothing, work for: Part VI, Chapter xv, Note 6.
Notice, give: Part III, 951.
Notice (refer to), to: Part VI, Chapter xv, Note 17.
Notice, to: Part IV, Dialogue iii, 60.
Novels: Part V, Lesson viii, 1, Note 1.
Novitiate: Part III, 1009.
Now: Part III, Exercise xv*, 1, Obs. 2; 906.
Now and again: Part III, Exercise xxiv*, 2.
Now, just: Part III, 760, Obs.
Number, distinguishing: Part III, 860, Obs.
Number, given: Part III, 504.
Number, good: Part III, 7.
Number, make up a: Part III, Exercise xix, 6.
Number, to: Part III, Exercise xxxii, 4.
Numerals: Part III, Exercise viii*, 9, 10.
Nurse, a: Part V, Lesson xxii, Note 11.

Oar, stern: Part VI, Chapter xxxv, 3, Note 6.
Oath: Part V, Lesson xxi, Note 3.
Oath, make: Part V, Lesson xliv, 1, Note 6.
Oats, sown his wild: Part VI, Chapter ii, Note 5.
Object had I, what: Part V, Lesson lxxxiii, 4, Note 9.
Object (intention): Part IV, Dialogue iv, 80.
Object, to: Part IV, Dialogue viii, 55, Obs. 2.
Object to (dislike): Part III, 836.
Object, what is your: Part III, Exercise xxv*, 3, Obs.
Objection, no: Part IV, Dialogue iv, 15; Dialogue viii, 55, Obs. 1.
Objections, make: Part III, Exercise xxix*, 9, Obs.
Obligation, be under: Part V, Lesson iv, 5.
Obliged, extremely: Part V, Lesson i, 6.
Obliged, feels: Part V, Lesson v, 10, Note 8.
Obliged, much: Part III, 345, 647, 855.
Obliged to you, I am: Part III, 1009.
Oblivious: Part VI, Chapter xii, Note 2.
Obscurity, in: Part III, Exercise xxxi, 10, Obs. 2.
Observances, ceremonial: Part IV, Dialogue x, 1, Obs. 4, 7.
Observe (compare): Part V, Lesson xxiv, 2, Note 7.
Obstruct: Part VI, Chapter viii, Note 1.
Occasion (time): Part III, 57.
Occasion, took: Part VI, Chapter xi, 7, Note 9.
Occasions, extraordinary: Part V, Lesson lvii, 2.
Occupants: Part III, Exercise xx, 8.
Occupation, no: Part IV, Dialogue iv, 20.
Occupied: Part III, 895.
Occurrence, of common: Part III, 689.
O'clock: Part III, 225; Exercise ix, 5.
Odd: Part III, 5.
Odd, don't think it: Part IV, Dialogue ii, 30, Obs. 1.
Odd jobs, do: Part VI, Chapter ii, 1, Note 4.
Odd-looking: Part III, Exercise xvii, 2, Obs.
Odds and ends: Part III, Exercise xvi, 4.
Off, be: Part III, Exercise x, 9.
Off on a journey, be: Part V, Lesson xxxi, Note 1.
Off to, where are you: Part V, Lesson lxxi, Note 1.
Offend: Part IV, Dialogue v, 2, Obs. 2.
Offend against: Part III, Exercise xxxii, 2.
Offender, chief: Part VI, Chapter xxxi, 6, Note 9.
Offering to a spirit: Part V, Lesson xxxvi, Note 16.
Offering to a superior: Part V, Lesson xvi, Note 4.
Offerings to idols, make: Part III, 1025.
Office, go to the: Part V, Lesson lxii, 1, Note 3.
Office, in a public: Part IV, Dialogue ii, 19.
Office, remove from: Part III, 504.
Office, term of: Part III, 1009.
Office, turn at the: Part V, Lesson lxxvi, 1, Note 3.

Offices, good: Part III, 1009.
Official duty: Part III, 1009, Obs.; Part V, Lesson lxii, Note 3.
Official family: Part VI, Chapter viii, 8, Notes 15, 16.
Official penalties: Part III, 925.
Official underlings: Part III, Exercise xxxiv*, 1, Obs. 1.
Officials: Part III, 1019.
Officials, high: Part III, Exercise xxxiv, 3; Exercise xxxiv*, 1.
Officials, local: Part III, 641.
Officials, military and civil: Part III, Exercise xix, 4.
Officious: Part VI, Chapter xxxi, Note 10.
Oil, lamp: Part III, Exercise xiv, 1.
Oil, mineral: Part III, Exercise xiv, 1.
Oil, sweet: Part III, Exercise xiv, 1.
Old: Part III, 742, 1030.
Old, become: Part III, Exercise xvii*, 2.
Old, how: Part III, 955.
Old man: Part III, Exercise xxvi*, 4, Obs. 1.
Omen: Part III, 623.
Omit: Part III, 765.
Once: Part VI, Chapter xi, Note 5.
Once for all: Part III, 595.
Once upon a time: Part III, Exercise xxvi*, 2, Obs. 1; Part VI, Chapter i, 1, Note 3.
Once (with verbs of motion): Part VI, Chapter xvii, Note 6.
One after the other, come: Part V, Lesson lxxxvii, 5, Note 2.
One by one: Part III, 548.
One thing, the: Part III, Exercise xv*, 8, Obs.
Oneself: Part III, Exercise x, 3.
Onions: Part III, 696.
Only: Part V, Lesson vii, Note 10; Part VI, Chapter vi, Note 1.
Only, not: Part III, Exercise xxviii, 8, Obs. 2.
Open-mouthed (gaping): Part V, Lesson vi, 1.
Open, to (as a letter): Part VI, Chapter xxxix, 15, Note 15.
Open, will not: Part III, Exercise iii, 13, Obs.
Opening, an: Part III, Exercise xix*, 7, Obs. 2.
Opening (for inquiry): Part V, Lesson lviii, 2, Note 8.
Operations against, commence: Part V, Lesson lxvi, 1, Note 4.
Opinion: Part III, 54; Exercise xxi, 1, Obs.
Opinion, ask for an: Part V, Lesson lviii, 1.
Opinion, offer an: Part III, Exercise xx, 7.
Opinionated: Part IV, Dialogue x, 17, Obs. 2.
Opium: Part IV, Dialogue v, 31, Obs. 2.
Opportune, and the converse: Part VI, Chapter iii, 8, Note 13.

APPENDIX I.—GLOSSARY. 31

Opportunely: Part III, 562.
Opportunity: Part IV, Dialogue ii, 48, Obs.
Opportunity, avail oneself of: Part V, Lesson xvi, Note 3.
Opportunity, take the: Part III, Exercise xxv*, 1, Obs. 2; Part VI, Chapter xvi, 5.
Opportunity, throw away the: Part V, Lesson vii, 5, Note 14.
Opportunity, took the: Part V, Lesson xxii, 1, Note 5.
Opposite: Part III, 689.
Oppressive (tyrannical): Part III, Exercise xx*, 7, Obs. 2.
Ordained (fixed): Part III, Exercise xxxix, 2.
Order: Part III, 533.
Order, arrange in: Part IV, Dialogue iv, 73, Obs.
Order, consecutive: Part V, Lesson lxxxvii, Note 2.
Order, everything in: Part VI, Chapter xv, 1, Note 1.
Order (family precedence): Part III, Exercise xxviii, 10.
Order, issue an: Part III, Exercise xxxii, 5.
Order, keep in: Part III, 533.
Order on, give an: Part IV, Dialogue v, 60, Obs. 1.
Order, put in: Part III, 539.
Orders, take: Part IV, Dialogue viii, 87, Obs.
Ordinary: Part VI, Chapter viii, Note 14.
Ordinary occasion, on an: Part VI, Chapter xxxviii, 3.
Original: Part III, 120, 713; Exercise xxviii, 7, Obs.
Originally: Part III, 647.
Oriole: Part VI, Chapter i, Note 7.
Ornaments, head: Part VI, Chapter xi, 2, Note 2.
Ornaments, lady's: Part VI, Chapter xi, 2, Note 2; Chapter xxviii, 1, Note 2.
Ostentation: Part VI, Chapter i, Note 14.
Others: Part III, 1058, Obs.
Otherwise: Part III, Exercise xxii, 1, Obs. 1; Exercise xxxi*, 2, Obs. 2.
Ought: Part III, 345.
Out (wrong), be: Part III, 1080.
Out he came with (a remark): Part VI, Chapter xii, 2.
Out-of-the-way place: Part V, Lesson xciv, 3.
Outbreak: Part III, 590, Obs.
Outermost: Part III, 303.
Outside: Part III, Exercise xviii, 2, Obs.
Outsider: Part V, Lesson xlix, 2, Note 6.
Outspoken (say out what I feel): Part V, Lesson xv, 2.
Outspokenness: Part VI, Chapter x, Note 1.
Over, all (throughout): Part III, Exercise xxxiv*, 3, Obs.
Over and above: Part III, Exercise xl, 3, Obs. 3.
Over and over again: Part III, Exercise xxvi, 10, Obs. 2.
Over, go: Part III, 41.
Over-bearing: Part V, Lesson xcix, 3, Notes 2, 3.
Overcast: Part III, 265.
Overcast, sky was: Part V, Lesson xciv, 2, Note 2.

Overlap (of a coat): Part V, Lesson lxxxvi, 5, Note 3.
Overtake: Part III, Exercise xvi, 8.
Owe: Part III, 345.
Owing to (thanks to): Part III, 1049, Obs.
Owner (proprietor): Part III, 755, Obs.

Pacify: Part III, Exercise xxxii*, 2, Obs.; Part IV, Dialogue vii, 93, Obs.
Pack, to: Part III, Exercise xvi, 1; Part VI, Chapter xxxiv, 6.
Packed up (of baggage): Part V, Lesson xxxi, 2, Note 2.
Page, turn over a: Part VI, Chapter xxiv, Note 5.
Pain, be in: Part III, 457.
Pair, a: Part III, Exercise xxvii, 5.
Pairs, in: Part VI, Chapter xxxix, 13.
Palace (prince's, etc.): Part IV, Dialogue vii, 100, Obs.
Palace, the Imperial: Part III, 841; Exercise xxxii, 3.
Palatable: Part IV, Dialogue x, 2, Obs. 4.
Pale (of the face): Part V, Lesson xlv, 1.
Palm (of the hand): Part III, 390.
Paper-hanger: Part III, 737.
Paralysis: Part VI, Chapter v, 14, Note 33.
Pardon, I beg your: Part III, Exercise xxxi, 8, Obs.
Pardon, to: Part III, 865.
Parents, duty to: Part V, Lesson iv, 1, Note 2.
Parry a thrust: Part V, Lesson viii, 3, Note 13.
Part (fraction): Part III, Exercise i, 11, Obs. 1.
Part, take his: Part IV, Dialogue vi, 37, Obs.
Part with: Part III, 919.
Particular, be: Part IV, Dialogue x, 2, Obs. 3.
Particular, report every: Part VI, Chapter xix, 1.
Particularly: Part III, Exercise xxxii*, 9.
Parties, both: Part III, 925.
Parties of four or five: Part V, Lesson xc, 2.
Partner: Part IV, Dialogue viii, 83, Obs. 1.
Partner (in a firm): Part III, 755, Obs.
Partnership, dissolve: Part III, Exercise xxiv, 8.
Parts, equal: Part IV, Dialogue vi, 19, Obs.
Pass as: Part III, Exercise xxxv, 3, Obs. 1.
Pass from one hand to the other: Part V, Lesson xl, 3, Note 6.
Passage, take a: Part III, 1077.
Passion, fly into a: Part V, Lesson liii, 3, Note 5; Part VI, Chapter xxvii, 9, Note 4.
Passionate: Part III, 533.
Password: Part III, 860.
Past, for some time: Part V, Lesson lix, 2.
Paste: Part V, Lesson xxx, Note 9.
Pastime: Part III, Exercise xxxii*, 5.
Patch, civil and military: Part III, Exercise xix, 5, Obs.

Patch, to: Part III, Exercise xi, 2.
Patience, lose: Part V, Lesson xvii, 2, Note 11.
Patron: Part VI, Chapter viii, Note 22.
Patronage, intrigue for: Part V, Lesson xiii, Note 6.
Pattern, make your: Part V, Lesson viii, 1.
Pause, after a: Part VI, Chapter iv, 4, Note 8.
Pause, to: Part VI, Chapter xvii, Note 4.
Pawn, article to: Part V, Lesson xxxi, 2, Note 5.
Pawnshop: Part III, 345.
Pawn-ticket: Part III, 345.
Pay, draw: Part IV, Dialogue x, 5, Obs. 1.
Pay (repay): Part III, Exercise xl, 4, Obs. 2.
Pay (settle up): Part IV, Dialogue vi, 58, Obs.
Pay, soldier's: Part VI, Chapter xxiii, Note 9.
Pay (succeed): Part III, Exercise xxxvii*, 5.
Pay-day: Part V, Lesson xxxiv, 10, Note 10; Part VI, Chapter xxiii, 4, Note 9.
Peace: Part III, 629.
Peach tree: Part V, Lesson xc, 2, Note 4.
Peacock: Part V, Lesson xii, 7, Note 7.
Peak (of a mountain): Part III, 809.
Pearl: Part V, Lesson xxxviii, Note 2.
Peccadillo: Part VI, Chapter xxxi, Note 2.
Peel, to (of fruit): Part VI, Chapter xiv, 5, Note 8; Chapter xv, 5.
Pen, able with the: Part V, Lesson xxx, 9.
Penal code: Part III, 520.
Penal servitude: Part VI, Chapter xxxiii, 2, Note 2.
Penalties, official: Part III, 925.
Penalty: Part III, 855.
Pencil, worn-out: Part VI, Chapter v, Note 13.
Pendulous: Part VI, Chapter xviii, Note 9.
People, the: Part III, 496.
Perdu, lie: Part VI, Chapter xxxiii, 2, Note 1.
Perfectly: Part III, Exercise vi*, 7.
Perfectly well: Part III, Exercise xix, 9; Exercise xxix, 5, Obs. 2.
Performance: Part III, Exercise xxxi*, 1, Obs.
Permit, to: Part IV, Dialogue vi, 49, Obs.
Perpendicular: Part III, Exercise xl, 7.
Perplexed: Part VI, Chapter xxxii, 11, Note 7.
Perplexing: Part VI, Chapter xxv, 11, Note 14.
Persistently: Part V, Lesson xl, Notes 11, 12.
Person, in: Part IV, Dialogue vii, 100, Obs. 4.
Person, throw over the (as a cloak, etc.): Part V, Lesson lxx, Note 7.
Perspiration, violent: Part V, Lesson xlv, 2, Note 5.
Perspire: Part III, 310.
Petition, a: Part VI, Chapter xxi, Note 13.
Petition, to, or a: Part III, 1025.

Pheasant: Part III, 809.
Philanthropic: Part V, Lesson xiv, Note 8.
Photograph, to: Part III, 1071.
Physician: Part V, Lesson l, 3, Note 6.
Pick up: Part V, Lesson xviii, 3, Note 6.
Pick up, or out of: Part V, Lesson xii, Note 2.
Pickings: Part IV, Dialogue ii, 27, Obs.
Picture, a: Part III, Exercise xxxiii, 10, Obs. 1.
Picture, draw a: Part III, Exercise xxxiii, 7.
Picul: Part III, 351.
Pieces, in two: Part V, Lesson xviii, 6, Note 13.
Pig, a: Part V, Lesson xciv, 3, Note 6.
Pigtail, plait a: Part III, 436.
Pile, a: Part V, Lesson xxiii, Note 5.
Pillow: Part V, Lesson xlviii, 2, Note 4.
Pills: Part VI, Chapter xxviii, 13, Note 21.
Pimple: Part V, Lesson vii, Note 5.
Pipe, a: Part VI, Chapter xviii, 2, Note 2.
Pique, to: Part VI, Chapter xxi, 2, Note 5.
Pirates: Part IV, Dialogue vi, 9, Obs. 2.
Pit, fall into a: Part V, Lesson xlvi, 3, Note 3.
Pitch down: Part III, Exercise xxiii*, 3, Obs. 2.
Pitted with small-pox: Part V, Lesson xxx, 6, Notes 9, 10, 11.
Pity, to: Part III, 971.
Place, aspire to the highest: Part VI, Chapter xxviii, 2, Note 8.
Place (employment), find a: Part IV, Dialogue iv, 78.
Place, put back in its proper: Part VI, Chapter xvii, 14.
Place (residence, property): Part III, 841; Exercise xxxii, 3; Exercise xxxvii, 7, Obs.
Plain by explanation, make: Part V, Lesson lxvi, 2, Note 5.
Plain (evident): Part III, Exercise xxiii*, 3, Obs. 1.
Plain (guileless): Part V, Lesson xx, 2, Note 6.
Plain speaking: Part VI, Chapter x, 3, Note 1.
Plan: Part III, 585; Part V, Lesson liv, Note 15; Part VI, Chapter xxvi, 5, Note 3.
Plans: Part III, Exercise xxix*, 13.
Plans, organise other: Part V, Lesson lxvi, 2, Note 6.
Plasters: Part VI, Chapter xxviii, Note 21.
Play on a stringed instrument: Part V, Lesson xc, 2, Note 8.
Play (theatrical): Part VI, Chapter xxxvii, Note 10.
Play, to: Part III, 821.
Plea for: Part V, Lesson lxxx, Note 6.
Please, as much as you: Part III, Exercise xxxii, 7, Obs.
Please, as they: Part V, Lesson xxi, 3.
Please, as you: Part III, 865; Exercise xxvii*, 5.
Please, if you: Part VI, Chapter viii, 11.
Please, whom you: Part III, Exercise xxvii, 3, Obs.

APPENDIX I.—GLOSSARY.

Please yourself: Part IV, Dialogue x, 23.
Plough, to: Part III, **539**.
Pluck (of fruit): Part III, **369**.
Pluck up (of plants, etc.): Part VI, Chapter xiii, 7.
Plums: Part III, **369**, Obs.; **407**.
Plunging (of a horse): Part VI, Chapter xxi, 8, Note 12.
Pock-marked: Part V, Lesson xxx, 6, Note 11.
Pocket, to: Part III, **689**.
Pocket, took from his: Part VI, Chapter xv, 1, Note 2.
Poet: Part V, Lesson lxxi, Note 4.
Poetry: Part IV, Dialogue ix, 39, Obs. 1.
Point, man who speaks to the: Part III, **830**.
Point of, on the: Part III, **847**; Exercise xxix*, 1.
Point out a fault: Part V, Lesson lvi, Note 4.
Point out, to: Part III, **443**.
Point, stretch a: Part V, Lesson xxv, Note 6.
Point (tip): Part III, Exercise xxx, 6.
Pointed: Part III, **809**.
Points, good: Part III, **925**; Exercise xxxiv, 4.
Poison: Part V, Lesson xlvii, 3, Note 10.
Poker: Part V, Lesson xlii, 4, Note 14; Part VI, Chapter v, 12, Note 24.
Pole, carrying: Part VI, Chapter xxvi, 16, Note 6.
Politeness, falsehood of: Part V, Lesson lxxi, Note 6.
Pomegranate: Part VI, Chapter xiv, 4, Note 6.
Pond: Part VI, Chapter xxix, 7, Note 9.
Ponder: Part VI, Chapter xxvii, 6, Note 3.
Pool: Part VI, Chapter xxix, Note 9.
Poor: Part III, **635**.
Population: Part III, **539**.
Porcelain: Part VI, Chapter xxv, 1, Notes 2, 3.
Port, a "Treaty": Part VI, Chapter xxxvi, 16, Note 15.
Port, sea or river: Part III, **676**; Part IV, Dialogue viii, 21, Obs. 1.
Portmanteau: Part III, **407**.
Portrait: Part VI, Chapter xxiv, 6, Note 6.
Position, official: Part III, **496**; Exercise xix, 3.
Positively: Part III, Exercise xvi*, 8; Part IV, Dialogue vi, 53, Obs. 2; Part V, Lesson ix, Note 6; Lesson lxix, 1, Note 1.
Possessed (by a demon): Part V, Lesson liv, 1, Note 5.
Possibly, may: Part IV, Dialogue v, 30, Obs.
Post, a: Part V, Lesson xliii, Note 4.
Post, as stiff as a: Part V, Lesson xliii, 2, Note 4.
Post haste, go: Part V, Lesson ix, 4.
Post office: Part VI, Chapter xxxix, 14, Note 13.
Post (pillar): Part VI, Chapter xxxvi, 3, Note 3.
Post, to: Part III, **891**.
Post, your official: Part IV, Dialogue ix, 46, Obs.
Posterity: Part III, **871**.

Pot-luck dinner: Part V, Lesson lxxi, 3.
Potter, a: Part III, Exercise xxxv, 2.
Pour (broth over meat): Part V, Lesson lxxxviii, 4, Note 6.
Pour out: Part III, **189**.
Pour-boire: Part III, Exercise xxiv, 6.
Pout: Part V, Lesson xli, 2, Note 4.
Poverty, bitter: Part III, **1054**.
Power: Part V, Lesson vii, Note 6.
Practice, to start in (of a doctor): Part III, **939**.
Practice, want of: Part V, Lesson ii, 3.
Practise, to: Part V, Lesson xxvii, 2, Note 3.
Praise, to: Part V, Lesson xxiv, 1, Note 4; Lesson lxviii, 1, Note 1.
Prancing: Part VI, Chapter xxi, 8.
Pranks (of goblins): Part V, Lesson xxxvii, Note 6.
Pray: Part V, Lesson xxxvi, 4, Note 15.
Precautions, take: Part V, Lesson lx, 2.
Precedent: Part III, **1030**.
Precious: Part V, Lesson xviii, Note 5.
Precisely: Part IV, Dialogue x, 4.
Prediction, fulfilled: Part V, Lesson xxxix, 2; Lesson lxx, 2.
Prediction, fulfilment of a: Part VI, Chapter xx, Note 1.
Prefer: Part III, Exercise xi, 9.
Preference, show: Part IV, Dialogue iv, 83, Obs.
Prematurely, act: Part V, Lesson xxvi, 3, Note 7.
Preparations, make: Part VI, Chapter xl, 2, Note 5.
Prepare: Part III, **1065**.
Prepared, not (of lessons): Part V, Lesson vi, 1, Note 2.
Presage: Part III, Exercise xxiv*, 4, Obs. 3.
Prescription (medical): Part V, Lesson lii, 3, Note 8.
Present, at: Part III, **647**, Obs.
Present of, make a: Part III, Exercise xxix, 2; Exercise xxxiv*, 5.
Present (offer), to: Part IV, Dialogue x, 8.
Present to a superior, to: Part VI, Chapter xxi, 9, Note 13.
Presently: Part IV, Dialogue vii, 36, Obs.
Press down: Part IV, Dialogue vii, 93, Obs.; Part V, Lesson x, Note 14.
Press to eat: Part V, Lesson lxxii, 6, Notes 13, 14.
Press (urge): Part V, Lesson xxvi, 1, Note 4.
Pressing (urgent): Part III, Exercise xxxvii*, 3.
Pressure upon, put: Part VI, Chapter xxi, 5, Note 8.
Presume (dare): Part IV, Dialogue iv, 81.
Presumption, we may say without; Part V, Lesson lxv, 2, Note 11.
Pretend: Part V, Lesson xi, 10, Note 5.
Pretext for: Part V, Lesson lxxx, Note 6.
Prevent: Part V, Lesson xxvi, 3, Note 10.

Prevented, I was: Part V, Lesson xxii, 1, Note 4.
Price, rising, or high: Part III, 676.
Pride: Part VI, Chapter iii, 6, Note 7.
Pride (self-respect): Part VI, Chapter iii, Note 7.
Priests (Buddhist and Taoist): Part III, 878; Exercise xxxiii, 2, 8, 9; Exercise xxxiii*, 6.
Prime, in one's: Part V, Lesson xxvii, Note 1.
Prince: Part V, Lesson xxi, Note 4.
Principal (capital): Part V, Lesson xxxi, 2, Note 6.
Principle: Part III, 533, Obs.
Private: Part III, 982.
Private ends, turn public opportunities to: Part VI, Chapter v, 14, Note 30.
Private house: Part III, 496, Obs.
Private individual: Part III, 496, Obs.; Exercise xxii*, 6, Obs. 2.
Private life, retire into: Part VI, Chapter i, 1, Note 1.
Privately concerting: Part V, Lesson lxvi, 1.
Prize open, to: Part VI, Chapter v, 12, Note 24.
Probabilities are, the: Part VI, Chapter xxix, 10, Note 12.
Probability, in all: Part IV, Dialogue vi, 26, Obs. 1.
Probably: Part III, Exercise x, 7.
Probably, most: Part III, 569; Part V, Lesson l, 3, Note 4.
Proclamation: Part III, 891, Obs.
Proclamation, issue a: Part III, Exercise xxxv, 3, Obs. 2.
Produce: Part IV, Dialogue v, 24, Obs.
Products: Part III, 635.
Professor: Part V, Lesson ii, 3, Note 7.
Proficient: Part V, Lesson iii, 2, Note 3.
Proficient (make progress): Part V, Lesson ii, 2.
Profound (as a science): Part VI, Chapter xxviii, 13, Note 22.
Progress: Part III, Exercise xxxix*, 3, Obs.
Progress (be proficient): Part V, Lesson ii, 2.
Progressive: Part V, Lesson vii, 1, Note 2.
Prohibit: Part III, 847.
Prolong (a story): Part VI, Chapter xl, 1.
Promise, fulfil a: Part VI, Chapter xx, Note 1.
Promise, man of: Part VI, Chapter xxxviii, 1.
Promise, to: Part V, Lesson lxviii, 4.
Promotion (official): Part V, Lesson xi, 8, Note 2.
Promotion, rapid: Part V, Lesson xii, Note 5.
Promptly: Part III, Exercise xxii, 6; Exercise xxxv*, 1, Obs. 1.
Pronunciation: Part III, Exercise v, 4; Exercise v*, 1, 2; Part V, Lesson iii, 1.
Proof (evidence): Part IV, Dialogue x, 6, Obs.; Part V, Lesson lviii, Note 6.
Prop open: Part VI, Chapter xxxvii, 11.
Prop up: Part V, Lesson xxxv, 1, Note 1.

Properly: Part III, Exercise xxxix, 6, Obs. 2.
Property: Part III, 635; Exercise xxxii, 1.
Property, Government: Part III, 496, Obs.
Propose: Part III, Exercise x*, 7, Obs.
Proprietor: Part III, 755, Obs.
Propriety's sake, for: Part VI, Chapter xxx, 5.
Prospect, the: Part V, Lesson xc, 2.
Prosperity: Part III, 623.
Prosperous: Part III, 1036.
Prosperous journey: Part III, Exercise xiii*, 11, Obs.
Prosperous look: Part III, Exercise xxxix*, 1, Obs.
Prostrate oneself: Part VI, Chapter xxxiii, Note 1.
Proverb: Part III, Exercise xxxiii, 3.
Providence: Part V, Lesson lxxxvii, Note 6.
Province: Part IV, Dialogue i, 19, Obs.
Provinces, in the: Part III, 784, Obs. 2.
Provincials, fellow: Part IV, Dialogue i, 4, Obs.
Provoke: Part VI, Chapter xxxi, 8.
Provoke by censure: Part V, Lesson liv, 1, Note 3.
Provokingly, most: Part III, Exercise xxxiv, 6, Obs.
Public: Part III, 982.
Public duties: Part III, Exercise xxxvii, 1.
Public man: Part IV, Dialogue iv, 47.
Publicly: Part IV, Dialogue v, 35.
Publish abroad: Part IV, Dialogue vi, 23, Obs. 1.
Puddings: Part III, Exercise xiv*, 4, Obs. 1.
Puffed out (of the stomach): Part V, Lesson xlviii, 2, Note 6.
Pull, give a hard: Part III, Exercise xxxvi, 1, Obs.
Pull up (a horse): Part III, 509, Obs.
Pull up (reprimand): Part VI, Chapter xxxviii, 3, Note 5.
Pulley: Part V, Lesson xl, Note 12.
Pulse, feel the: Part V, Lesson lii, 3, Note 6; Part VI, Chapter xxviii, 12, Note 19.
Punctuate: Part III, 192.
Punish: Part III, 855; Part V, Lesson xliv, Note 5.
Punt a boat: Part V, Lesson xci, 2, Note 3.
Pupils: Part IV, Dialogue ix, 22, Obs. 2.
Purging and vomiting: Part VI, Chapter xxviii, 9, Note 14.
Purifications (for religious ceremony): Part VI, Chapter xv, Note 7.
Purple: Part V, Lesson xxx, Note 7.
Purpose, as if on: Part VI, Chapter ii, 3, Note 7.
Purpose, to: Part III, Exercise xiv, 8.
Purpose, to no: Part V, Lesson xci, Note 12.
Purposely: Part III, 562; Exercise xxii*, 5, Obs. 1.
Purse: Part III, 443, Obs.
Pursue a line of action: Part III, Exercise xxxii, 6.
Push on (go fast): Part IV, Dialogue viii, 9.

APPENDIX I.—GLOSSARY. 35

Put a stop to the conversation (said no more): Part V, Lesson lix, 4.
Put aside: Part III, Exercise x, 6, Obs. 2.
Put in (bad with good): Part III, Exercise xix*, 9.
Put off: Part IV, Dialogue vi, 53, Obs. 1.
Put on: Part III, 296.
Put out (a light): Part III, 196.
Put out (displeased), they would be: Part V, Lesson lxxxii, 4, Note 7.
Put out (provoked): Part V, Lesson xxi, 1.
Put up with: Part IV, Dialogue iii, 123, Obs. 2.
Put up with, can't: Part V, Lesson lviii, 1, Note 3.
Put up with it, try and: Part VI, Chapter iv, 10, Note 13.

Qualified, not: Part VI, Chapter xx, Note 2.
Quantity: Part III, Exercise xxix, 6, Obs.
Quarrel: Part III, 595, Obs.
Quarter, give no law or: Part V, Lesson lx, 3.
Question, beside the: Part VI, Chapter xxxvii, Note 9.
Question with, go into the: Part V, Lesson lxv, 1.
Questions, ask: Part IV, Dialogue vii, 63.
Quick: Part III, 1058.
Quick in intelligence and action: Part V, Lesson xv, 1, Note 1.
Quicker: Part III, 425.
Quickly: Part III, 425; Part VI, Chapter xxi, Note 1.
Quickly as possible: Part III, 1065.
Quiet about, keep: Part IV, Dialogue vi, 22, Obs. 2.
Quiet (behaviour): Part III, 830.
Quiet (in manner): Part V, Lesson lxxxvii, 12, Note 10.
Quiet, keep: Part VI, Chapter xxxvii, 16.
Quiet (of a horse): Part III, Exercise xvii, 5, Obs.; Part V, Lesson xxxiii, Note 17.
Quiet (of places and individuals): Part III, Exercise xxxii, 10, Obs.
Quiet spot: Part V, Lesson lxii, 4, Note 15.
Quietly: Part V, Lesson xxxv, 2, Note 9.
Quiver (archery): Part V, Lesson xxxiii, 3, Note 8.
Quiz, to: Part IV, Dialogue vii, 37, Obs.

Race, have a: Part III, Exercise xxvi, 3.
Races, horse: Part III, 776.
Rage, boiling over with: Part V, Lesson liii, 3, Notes 7, 8.
Rage, get into a: Part III, Exercise xxiii, 4, Obs. 1; Part VI, Chapter xxvii, 9, Note 4.
Rage, in a: Part III, Exercise xxvi*, 3, Obs. 1.
Rags, in: Part V, Lesson lxx, 1, Note 3.
Railing: Part V, Lesson lxxiv, Note 3.
Rain, steady: Part V, Lesson xciv, 2, Note 3.
Rain, to walk in the: Part III, 830.

Rain, violent: Part V, Lesson xcvi, 1.
Raise money: Part III, Exercise xxiv, 5.
Ran on, the interest: Part VI, Chapter i, 7, Note 18.
Random, abuse at: Part V, Lesson xcix, Note 4.
Random, at: Part V, Lesson xxvi, 2, Note 5.
Rank: Part III, 496; Part IV, Dialogue vi, 12, Obs.
Rank, hereditary: Part III, 496, Obs.
Rank, purchase: Part III, 504.
Rank, to strip of: Part IV, Dialogue vi, 21, Obs. 4.
Ranks, rise from the: Part III, Exercise xix*, 4, Obs.
Rarity: Part V, Lesson lxv, Note 5.
Rascally: Part III, 665; Part V, Lesson xliii, 1.
Rather than (better): Part V, Lesson xxv, 2, Note 4.
Rattle on (of conversation): Part VI, Chapter xiii, 7.
Raw: Part III, Exercise xiv, 4.
Raw (uncouth): Part III, Exercise xxx, 10.
Razor: Part III, Exercise xviii, 4, Obs.
Readiness, in a state of: Part V, Lesson xxxiv, Note 7.
Ready, all: Part VI, Chapter vii, 3, Note 9.
Ready, get: Part III. Exercise xvi*, 2, Obs.
Ready, have: Part III, 1065.
Ready (of food): Part III, 369.
Really: Part III, Exercise xvii, 8.
Rear (of a company): Part V, Lesson xcii, 3, Note 8.
Rear, take in the: Part V, Lesson lviii, Note 9.
Reason (cause): Part III, 961.
Reason, for no: Part III, Exercise iv*, 5; Exercise xvii, 10, Obs.
Reason, the: Part III, Exercise xix, 1.
Reason, what is the: Part III, 961.
Reasonable being, act like a: Part V, Lesson lx, 1.
Reasoned with myself: Part V, Lesson lxxxiv, 3.
Reasoning: Part III, 533, Obs.
Rebel, to: Part III, 855.
Rebels: Part III, 487; 855, Obs.; Part VI, Chapter xvi, 1, Note 1.
Rebuff, risk a: Part VI, Chapter ix, Note 6.
Rebuke, to: Part VI, Chapter xxxvii, 16, Note 12.
Receipt, a: Part III, 310.
Receive: Part III, 665.
Recently: Part III, Exercise xxxiv, 3, Obs. 1.
Recherché repast: Part VI, Chapter xxv, 1, Note 1.
Recipient of, be the: Part III, 1009.
Reckless: Part III, 548.
Reclaimed (of savages): Part III, Exercise xxvi, 7, Obs.
Recommend: Part VI, Chapter xxi, 2, Note 4.
Recommend for a place: Part IV, Dialogue vi, 27, Obs.
Recommendation, submit a: Part VI, Chapter xxviii, 2.
Record, on: Part III, 1030.
Record, to: Part III, 111.

Recover: Part III, 8.
Recovery, complete: Part V, Lesson li, 3, Note 6.
Red: Part III, 737.
Reeds: Part V, Lesson xci, 3, Note 5.
Reflect: Part VI, Chapter xxvii, 6, Note 3; Chapter xxxii, Note 4.
Reform in earnest: Part V, Lesson lxvii, 2, Note 6.
Reformed character, a: Part VI, Chapter ii, 1, Note 5.
Refuse a present: Part V, Lesson lxix, 1, Note 1.
Refuse, not know how to: Part V, Lesson lxxviii, 1.
Refuse, to: Part III, Exercise xxix, 3, Obs.; Part VI, Chapter xxiii, 2, Note 5.
Regard (consider): Part III, Exercise xl, 8, Obs. 4.
Regret: Part III, 1054, Obs.
Regular: Part III, Exercise ix*, 6, Obs. 1.
Regular establishment: Part III, Exercise xix*, 6, Obs. 2.
Regulations: Part III, 520.
Reins: Part IV, Dialogue viii, 81, Obs. 1.
Rejoinder: Part III, Exercise xxi*, 5, Obs. 2.
Relapse, have a: Part V, Lesson l, 3, Note 7.
Relations, blood: Part III, Exercise xiv, 8, Obs.; Part IV, Dialogue ii, 33.
Relations, husband's and wife's: Part VI, Chapter i, Note 13.
Relations, in direct: Part III, 847.
Relations, private: Part III, 982.
Relieved in mind: Part VI, Chapter xxxvii, 14.
Relish for, have no: Part V, Lesson xxix, 1.
Remaining (left): Part III, Exercise ii, 4, Obs.
Remedy, no: Part IV, Dialogue iv, 49, Obs.
Remember, dimly: Part IV, Dialogue iv, 40, Obs.
Remind: Part V, Lesson liv, 3, Note 17.
Remiss: Part IV, Dialogue x, 10, Obs.
Remove: Part III, 770.
Rendezvous: Part V, Lesson xlviii, 2, Note 3.
Rent to or from: Part VI, Chapter ix, Note 1.
Repair: Part III, 189, 939.
Repair, out of: Part V, Lesson xxxvii, 4, Note 5.
Repeat aloud: Part III, 122.
Repeated, twice: Part IV, Dialogue ix, 29, Obs.
Repent: Part III, Exercise xxxix, 5, Obs. 2; Part IV, Dialogue v, 63.
Repletion, eat to: Part IV, Dialogue x, 19, Obs.
Report (noise): Part III, Exercise xxi*, 3.
Report (rumour): Part V, Lesson xxxii, 12, Note 7.
Reports, spread: Part V, Lesson lxiv, Note 7.
Reprimand, get a: Part VI, Chapter xxxviii, Note 5.
Reproach, to: Part VI, Chapter xxxvii, 16, Note 12.
Reproduce a conversation: Part VI, Chapter xii, 5, Note 6.

Reprove: Part V, Lesson xiv, 2, Note 5.
Repudiate: Part VI, Chapter xxxi, Note 8.
Repulse, to: Part III, 509.
Reputation (character): Part V, Lesson xxxi, 5; Part VI, Chapter xxxi, 6.
Requite (make return): Part V, Lesson lxxix, 2.
Rescue, come to the: Part V, Lesson xiv, Note 9.
Resent: Part III, Exercise xxxix*, 5.
Resentment, feel: Part III, 1049.
Reserve, speak without: Part VI, Chapter ix, 4.
Resolution: Part III, 1043; Part V, Lesson iii, 7, Note 6; Lesson lxx, Note 9.
Respect (admire): Part VI, Chapter iii, 4, Note 6.
Respect, filial: Part V, Lesson xvi, 1, Note 4.
Respect for, have: Part VI, Chapter vii, Note 6.
Respect, to: Part V, Lesson xlvii, 2, Note 9; Lesson iv, 2.
Respectable: Part III, 487.
Respectful: Part V, Lesson lviii, 1, Note 1.
Respective: Part III, Exercise xxii, 8.
Respects, to present: Part III, Exercise xxv, 8, Obs. 2.
Responsibility, acquit oneself of: Part V, Lesson vi, Note 14.
Responsible: Part III, Exercise xxxiv*, 1, Obs. 2; Part IV, Dialogue viii, 29.
Responsible, I'll be: Part VI, Chapter ix, 7.
Rest, the: Part V, Lesson v, Note 7.
Rest, to: Part III, 399, Obs.
Restaurant: Part IV, Dialogue x, 1, Obs. 2; 2.
Restive (of a horse): Part IV, Dialogue viii, 81, Obs. 3.
Restrictions: Part IV, Dialogue i, 16, Obs. 2.
Rests with: Part III, Exercise xxii, 5, Obs.
Result, favourable: Part V, Lesson lii, Note 10.
Reticent: Part V, Lesson xxxviii, Note 4.
Retire: Part III, 506.
Retire from business: Part IV, Dialogue iv, 48.
Retire from office: Part III, 784, Obs. 1; Part VI, Chapter vii, 2.
Retribution: Part III, Exercise xxxv, 10, Obs.
Retribution for sins: Part III, Exercise xxxiii*, 5, Obs. 2.
Retribution for sins in a previous existence: Part V, Lesson lxxxvii, 8.
Retrieve a false step: Part V, Lesson lxxxiii, Note 5.
Return (report), to: Part III, Exercise xxxv, 4.
Reverent behaviour: Part V, Lesson xiii, Note 9.
Reverse, on the: Part III, 182.
Reverse, the: Part III, 689.
Revile: Part V, Lesson iv, Note 10.
Revolution of time: Part VI, Chapter xxxviii, Note 3.
Reward, to: Part III, 641.
Reward of merit: Part V, Lesson xiv, 4, Note 16.

APPENDIX I.—GLOSSARY. 37

Rice, wash: Part VI, Chapter xiv, 2, Note 3.
Right: Part III, 29.
Right angles, at: Part III, Exercise xl, 8, Obs. 4.
Right (exactly): Part III, 303.
Right, is that: Part III, Exercise xxix*, 2, Obs.
Right, set: Part V, Lesson x, Note 10.
Rights of things: Part V, Lesson iv, 1.
Riot, allowed to run: Part VI, Chapter v, 15, Note 35.
Ripe: Part III, 369; Exercise xiv*, 4, Obs. 3.
Rise (in official career): Part V, Lesson xcix, 5, Note 13.
Risk, run the: Part VI, Chapter ix, Note 6.
Risk you run: Part V, Lesson lv, 1.
River: Part III, 384.
River, town built on a: Part IV, Dialogue viii, 59, Obs. 1.
Road: Part III, 520, Obs.
Roast, to: Part III, 169.
Robbed: Part IV, Dialogue iv, 52, Obs. 2.
Robber: Part VI, Chapter xvi, 1, Note 1.
Robe, under: Part V, Lesson xlv, Note 6.
Rockery: Part V, Lesson xxiii, 4, Note 5.
Roebuck: Part V, Lesson lxxxix, 1, Note 2.
Roll, a: Part VI, Chapter x, Note 4.
Roll up: Part V, Lesson xxx, Note 12.
Roller: Part V, Lesson xl, Note 12.
Roof: Part VI, Chapter xxxix, 4, Note 2.
Room full of people: Part V, Lesson lxxxii, 4.
Room, no: Part III, 965.
Roomy: Part IV, Dialogue x, 2.
Roost, to: Part V, Lesson xciv, 4, Note 7.
Rope: Part VI, Chapter xxxiv, 9, Note 9.
Rosary: Part V, Lesson xxxviii, Note 2.
Rose, a: Part VI, Chapter viii, 6, Note 7.
Rough play: Part VI, Chapter xviii, 4, Note 3.
Rough (to the taste): Part VI, Chapter xiv, 5, Note 9.
Rough treatment: Part III, Exercise xxxi, 1, Obs.
Round: Part III, 939.
Round, all: Part III. Exercise xxi, 3, Obs.; Part VI, Chapter viii, 9, Note 19.
Round, get (take in): Part V, Lesson lviii, 2.
Round hand: Part III, 885.
Roundabout (détour): Part III, 376.
Rouse, to: Part V, Lesson liv, 3, Note 12.
Row, a: Part III, 755.
Row, a general: Part VI, Chapter v, 9, Note 22.
Row, make a: Part III, Exercise xxiii, 2, Obs. 1; Part V, Lesson xliii, 1.
Rowdies: Part III, 860.
Rowdy: Part III, 548.
Rub, to: Part III, 755.

Rudder: Part VI, Chapter xxxv, Note 9.
Ruddy: Part V, Lesson xxx, 6, Note 7.
Rude (clumsy): Part III, 821.
Ruin: Part VI, Chapter v, 15, Note 37.
Ruin (injure), to: Part V, Lesson xxiv, 2, Note 14.
Ruined: Part V, Lesson lxx, 1, Note 2; Part VI, Chapter iii, 6, Note 8.
Ruins, fall in: Part VI, Chapter xxii, Note 1.
Rule, foot: Part III, 939, Obs.
Rule, as a general: Part III, Exercise xxvii, 9.
Rule, exception to: Part IV, Dialogue viii, 29, Obs.
Rule, the: Part III, Exercise xxix, 7, Obs. 2.
Ruler (for drawing lines): Part III, 939.
Run after (toady): Part V, Lesson lxxvi, 9, Note 8.
Run away: Part III, 548.
Run down (decayed): Part VI, Chapter xxxviii, 1, Note 2.
Run on (finding fault): Part V, Lesson lxxxiv, 4, Note 5.
Run up against: Part V, Lesson xxxvii, Note 9.
Rung of a ladder: Part V, Lesson xl, Note 1.
Runner, yamên: Part III, 1009; Exercise 1019, Obs.
Running hand: Part III, Exercise xxxiii, 5.
Rush in: Part IV, Dialogue iii, 52, Obs. 2.
Rushes: Part V, Lesson xci, Note 5.
Rustling sound: Part VI, Chapter xxix, 13, Note 13.

Sable: Part V, Lesson xxxiv, 1, Note 1.
Sacrifice, morning and evening: Part V, Lesson lxxxviii, 1, Note 1.
Sacrifices: Part V, Lesson xvi, 2, Note 9.
Sacrificial offering, make: Part V, Lesson lxxv, 4, Note 4.
Sad: Part IV, Dialogue iv, 70, Obs. 1.
Sail, hoist a: Part VI, Chapter ii, Note 4.
Sail, set: Part III, Exercise xv, 2, Obs. 1.
Sails, filled the: Part VI, Chapter xxxvii, 1.
Salad oil: Part III, 360.
Salary, official: Part V, Lesson xxxiv, Note 10.
Saliva of a sick person: Part VI, Chapter xxviii, 9, Note 15.
Sallow complexion: Part VI, Chapter xxxix, 1.
Salt: Part III, 360.
Salt (in taste): Part VI, Chapter xiv, 7, Note 12.
Salutation (of priests or laymen): Part VI, Chapter xv, 3, Note 8.
Salute (in Chinese fashion): Part IV, Dialogue x, 8, Obs. 4.
Same, all the: Part III, Exercise ix*, 7, Obs. 1; Part V, Lesson xxxiv, 11, Note 14.
Same day: Part III, 345.
Sanction, give: Part III, 569.
Sat on (continued to sit): Part V, Lesson xcii, 2, Note 4.

Satin: Part V, Lesson xxxiv, 7, Note 8.
Satisfactorily: Part III, Exercise xxii, 2.
Satisfied, eat till: Part IV, Dialogue x, 19, Obs.
Satisfied, well: Part IV, Dialogue iv, 45, Obs. 2.
Saturated, be: Part V, Lesson xxxviii, 7, Note 10.
Saturated (impregnated): Part V, Lesson xvii, Note 9.
Savages: Part III, Exercise xxx*, 1, Obs. 6.
Save (dispense with): Part III, 865.
Savour, pleasant: Part V, Lesson xxvii, Note 16.
Say: Part III, 48.
Say, might: Part V, Lesson xciii, Note 2.
Say out: Part III, Exercise xvii, 10.
Say, what do you: Part V, Lesson xxiii, 6, Note 10; Lesson xxxviii, 3.
Say, you don't mean to: Part III, 830.
Scabbard: Part VI, Chapter xxii, Note 3.
Scales: Part III, 326.
Scandalous: Part III, 612.
Scar: Part VI, Chapter xxv, 10, Note 11.
Scatter, to: Part V, Lesson viii, 3, Note 17.
Scenery: Part III, Exercise ii*, 10; Exercise xxx, 1; Part V, Lesson xci, Note 11.
Schemer, crafty: Part VI, Chapter v, 5, Note 14.
Scholar, fine: Part VI, Chapter xxviii, 2.
School, free: Part V, Lesson vii, Note 11.
Schoolfellow: Part III, Exercise xix*, 2, Obs. 1.
Scissors: Part V, Lesson viii, 3, Note 16.
Scorched: Part VI, Chapter ix, Note 4.
Scorching hot: Part V, Lesson xciii, 1, Note 4.
Score: Part III, Exercise i, 10, Obs. 1.
Scorpion: Part VI, Chapter xiii, 1, Note 5.
Scot free, get off: Part V, Lesson lx, 3.
Scoundrel: Part V, Lesson lxiv, 2, Notes 2, 3.
Scowl at: Part V, Lesson lxxxiii, 4, Note 8.
Scrape, get into a: Part IV, Dialogue v, 47.
Scratch oneself: Part VI, Chapter xxvi, 20, Note 8.
Screen or curtain: Part V, Lesson xcvii, 3, Note 7; Part VI, Chapter xxiv, 6.
Screen, to: Part IV, Dialogue vi, 22, Obs. 2.
Screw, a (horse): Part V, Lesson xxxiii, 1, Note 1.
Scrolls: Part VI, Chapter x, 12, Note 4.
Sea, go to: Part III, 399.
Sea, on the: Part III, 384.
Seal, official: Part VI, Chapter xxxix, Note 12.
Seal, private: Part VI, Chapter xxxix, Note 12.
Seal, put under: Part IV, Dialogue v, 49, Obs.
Seal, to: Part VI, Chapter xxxix, 14, Note 12.
Seam, close a: Part V, Lesson lxxxvi, 5, Note 5.
Seam, opened: Part VI, Chapter iv, Note 9.
Seam, stitch a: Part VI, Chapter iv, Note 9.

Search, to: Part III, 526.
Seasonable (rain, etc.): Part V, Lesson xcvi, 1.
Seasonable (weather): Part III, Exercise ix, 8, Obs.
Seat, a: Part III, Exercise xvii, 3, Obs. 2.
Seat, take the upper: Part V, Lesson lxxiii, 6, Note 3.
Seat, to: Part III, Exercise viii*, 4, Obs.
Second place, in the: Part III, 617.
Secret: Part V, Lesson xxxvi, Note 4.
Secret, in: Part III, Exercise xxii, 1, Obs. 2.
Secret, tell a: Part III, 595.
Secretary, diplomatic: Part III, 496.
Secretary, private: Part IV, Dialogue ii, 59, Obs.; Dialogue ix, 45, 48.
Secretly: Part V, Lesson xxxv, Note 14.
Security for, go: Part IV, Dialogue iv, 55, Obs.
See (meet): Part III, Exercise xxvii*, 1, Obs.
Seeds: Part III, 526, Obs.
Seeing, sight worth: Part V, Lesson xxxiii, 3, Note 11.
Seemly: Part III, Exercise xvii, 10; Exercise xl, 2, Obs. 3.
Seems to me, it: Part IV, Dialogue x, 5, Obs. 2.
Seen, fit to be: Part III, Exercise xi*, 7.
Select, to: Part V, Lesson xii, 2, Note 2.
Self (oneself), in spite of: Part V, Lesson xvi, 3, Note 16.
Self-sufficiency: Part V, Lesson lxiii, Note 6.
Send: Part III, 765; Exercise xxxv, 1.
Send (despatch): Part III, 906.
Senility, lapse into: Part VI, Chapter xxxviii, Note 2.
Senior, a: Part VI, Chapter xxxviii, 1.
Seniores priores: Part V, Lesson lxxxviii, 3, Note 4.
Sense, men of: Part V, Lesson viii, 4, Note 19.
Sense of, have a: Part V, Lesson iv, 2, Note 4.
Senses, come to one's (after fainting): Part V, Lesson li, 1, Note 4.
Senses, have you lost your: Part VI, Chapter xii, 3, Note 2.
Sentence (grammatical): Part III, 595.
Separated: Part IV, Dialogue viii, 23, Obs. 3.
Seriatim: Part V, Lesson vii, Note 2.
Serpent: Part V, Lesson xviii, Note 10.
Servant: Part III, 414; Part VI, Chapter vi, 1, Note 2.
Servant, office: Part III, 1009.
Servants: Part III, 514, 665; Exercise xxv, 5; Part V, Lesson lxxiv, 4, Note 2.
Serve up (of food): Part III, 369.
Service, hold a: Part III, Exercise xxxiii, 2.
Service to you, my humble: Part IV, Dialogue iii, 54, Obs. 2.
Sesame: Part III, 360.
Set, a: Part III, 153, 770; Part VI, Chapter xxxix, 11, Note 7.

APPENDIX I.—GLOSSARY.

Set on (a dog): Part VI, Chapter xviii, 4.
Setting (jewellery): Part VI, Chapter viii, 6, Note 12.
Severe thrashing, give a: Part V, Lesson xli, 2; Lesson xliv, 1, Notes 4, 5.
Severely: Part V, Lesson ix, 5, Note 5.
Sew: Part III, Exercise xii, 7.
Shadow: Part V, Lesson viii, 2, Note 6.
Shafts, sit on the: Part III, 919.
Shake (the table, etc.): Part VI, Chapter xxxix, 14.
Shake, to: Part V, Lesson lxx, Note 6.
Shallow: Part III, 384.
Shame, feel: Part V, Lesson lvii, 3, Note 5.
Shame, want of: Part V, Lesson vi, 3, Note 9.
Shape, assume: Part V, Lesson xxvi, 1, Note 1.
Share and share alike: Part VI, Chapter v, 6, Note 15.
Share, have a: Part IV, Dialogue ii, 51.
Sharp, look: Part V, Lesson lxxii, 3.
Sharp (of a knife): Part III, Exercise xviii, 6.
Sharp pointed: Part III, 809.
Sharp, say something: Part V, Lesson lxxxiv, 2, Note 2.
Shave, to: Part III, 470.
She-ass: Part VI, Chapter iv, 16, Note 15.
Sheath: Part VI, Chapter xxii, 3, Note 3.
Sheepish: Part VI, Chapter xviii, 1, Note 1.
Sheet of, broad: Part V, Lesson xci, 2, Note 4.
Shift round: Part VI, Chapter xxv, 10, Note 12.
Shine on (light of a lamp): Part V, Lesson xxxv, Note 17.
Ship: Part III, 384.
Ship, receiving: Part IV, Dialogue v, 36, Obs. 1.
Shipshape: Part V, Lesson xv, 1, Note 2.
Shirk duty: Part V, Lesson xv, 1.
Shirt: Part III, 310.
Shiver from cold: Part V, Lesson lxx, 1, Note 5.
Shiver from fear: Part V, Lesson lxx, Note 5.
Shock (noise): Part V, Lesson xcv, Note 14.
Shock, the: Part III, Exercise xxiii*, 5.
Shock to, give a: Part III, 612.
Shoes: Part III, 296.
Shoot at: Part III, Exercise xxi, 2, Obs.
Shooting, go: Part V, Lesson xii, Note 6.
Shore: Part III, 384; Part V, Lesson xc, Note 7.
Short (insufficient): Part III, Exercise xxix*, 4, Obs. 1.
Short sight: Part VI, Chapter v, 1, Note 2.
Shot, fire a: Part III, 555.
Shoulder, carry on the: Part VI, Chapter xxxvi, 16, Note 13.
Shoulders: Part III, 478.
Shout, to: Part III, 425.
Shout to: Part III, 784.
Show you up: Part V, Lesson lxiii, 1, Note 4.

Shred, cooked to a: Part VI, Chapter v, 3, Note 7.
Shrimps: Part V, Lesson xc, 2, Note 9.
Shuffle (in walking), to: Part VI, Chapter xxii, Note 4.
Shut: Part V, Lesson xcv, 2, Note 6.
Side: Part III, 653.
Side (in argument), take the same: Part V, Lesson liii, 2.
Side, put yourself on my: Part VI, Chapter xii, 2.
Side rooms: Part V, Lesson xxxvii, 4, Note 4.
Sieve: Part VI, Chapter xiv, 2, Note 4.
Sift: Part VI, Chapter xiv, Note 4.
Sigh, heave a: Part V, Lesson xxix, Note 6.
Sight, long and short: Part VI, Chapter v, 1, Note 2.
Sight, never let me out of his: Part V, Lesson lxxxiv, 1.
Sign of a shop: Part III, 939.
Sign of, not a: Part V, Lesson xxxviii, 8, Note 13.
Signature, write one's: Part VI, Chapter xxvi, 22, Note 10.
Signify, doesn't: Part III, Exercise xxix, 9, Obs. 2.
Signs, make: Part V, Lesson xliii, Note 3.
Silk: Part V, Lesson lvii, 3, Note 8.
Silk thread: Part III, 671.
Silly: Part III, 821.
Silver, pure: Part VI, Chapter xv, Note 3.
Simple (foolish): Part V, Lesson lxviii, 1.
Since (as): Part V, Lesson xliv, 2, Note 7.
Since, ever: Part V, Lesson l, 3, Note 5.
Since (from the time that): Part III, Exercise xxix*, 3.
Sincere: Part V, Lesson xvi, 2, Note 8.
Sing: Part III, 895.
Singular looking: Part VI, Chapter xxxvi, 7.
Sink, kitchen: Part V, Lesson xxviii, Note 3.
Sir: Part IV, Dialogue ix, 9, Obs.
Size: Part III, Exercise xv*, 3; Exercise xxx*, 3, Obs.
Skim, to (in cooking): Part VI, Chapter xiv, 3, Note 5.
Skip (jump), to: Part V, Lesson xl, 4, Note 13.
Skittish: Part VI, Chapter xxxvii, Note 3.
Skulk off: Part III, 548.
Skylarking: Part III, Exercise xxxi, 1; Part VI, Chapter xxxvii, 7, Note 3.
Slanting: Part V, Lesson xxx, Note 8.
Slave away for: Part VI, Chapter xxvii, 10, Note 6.
Slaves: Part III, 665; Exercise xxv, 5.
Slavish adulation: Part VI, Chapter xxvii, Note 6.
Sleek: Part IV, Dialogue vi, 36, Obs.
Sleep, fall into a: Part III, Exercise xxiii, 7, Obs.
Sleep, nod with: Part VI, Chapter xxvi, Note 9.
Sleep, startled out of: Part V, Lesson xxxv, 2, Note 7.
Sleep, to: Part III, 681, Obs.
Sleeping tiger lie, let a: Part V, Lesson liv, 3.
Sleepy: Part III, 604.

Sleeve, laugh at in one's: Part V, Lesson lxiii, 1, Note 2.
Sleeves: Part III, 316.
Slice, to, or a: Part V, Lesson lxxii, 4, Note 9.
Slightly: Part V, Lesson x, 5, Note 13.
Slip, to: Part V, Lesson ix, Note 4; Lesson liv, Note 14.
Slipped from his hand: Part III, Exercise xxxv*, 2, Obs. 3.
Slippery: Part V, Lesson ix, 5, Note 4.
Slippery (dishonest): Part IV, Dialogue iii, 99, Obs.
Slow (easy-going): Part V, Lesson lviii, 1, Note 2.
Sluice: Part V, Lesson xcii, Note 3.
Smallest degree, in the: Part V, Lesson iv, 5, Note 13.
Small-pox: Part V, Lesson lxxxvii, 3, Note 1.
Smart (energetic): Part III, 830.
Smart in dress, be: Part V, Lesson xxxiv, 11, Note 13.
Smell: Part IV, Dialogue x, 2, Obs. 4.
Smoke tobacco or opium: Part IV, Dialogue v, 21, Obs.
Smooth: Part III, 792, Obs.
Smoothly (easily): Part III, 629.
Smuggle: Part III, 982.
Snake: Part V, Lesson xviii, 5, Note 10.
Snap across: Part V, Lesson xxvii, 4, Notes 12, 13.
Snap off: Part V, Lesson xvii, Note 16.
Snap up: Part V, Lesson lxxvii, 2, Note 7.
Snatch away: Part III, 548.
Sneak away: Part V, Lesson xliii, 1, Note 2.
Sneak (under the cover of a wall), to: Part VI, Chapter xxxiii, 2.
Sneer, to: Part V, Lesson lxxxvi, 5, Note 9.
So: Part III, Exercise xvi*, 6, Obs. 1.
So, and: Part III, Exercise xxix*, 11, Obs. 1.
So it is: Part III, Exercise ix*, 14.
So (therefore): Part III, 1003.
Soaked: Part V, Lesson xcv, Note 13.
Soap: Part III, 284.
Social amenities: Part IV, Dialogue x, 1, Obs. 4.
Soft: Part III, Exercise xvii, 3.
Soldier, be a: Part III, 504.
Somersault: Part V, Lesson xxiv, Note 13.
Son: Part III, 660, 815.
Son, eldest: Part IV, Dialogue ii, 56, Obs. 2.
Son-in-law: Part V, Lesson lxxxvi, Note 1.
Song, sing a: Part III, 895.
Soon as, as: Part III, Exercise xvi, 4, Obs.
Sorts, out of: Part III, Exercise xxxi, 2, Obs. 2; Part V, Lesson xlv, 3.
Sound at heart: Part V, Lesson lxvii, 1, Note 1.
Sound (constitution): Part III, Exercise xvii, 3.
Soundly, will thrash you: Part V, Lesson xliii, 2.
Sounds like: Part III, Exercise xxxiii, 9, Obs.

Soup: Part III, 369.
Sour: Part VI, Chapter xiv, 5, Note 9.
South: Part III, 392; Exercise xv, 2.
Southerner: Part III, Exercise xv, 2.
Sovereign, the: Part III, 496; Exercise xix, 2; Exercise xix*, 1; Exercise xxxii, 10.
Sow, to: Part III, 526.
Space: Part III, 617.
Space for, no: Part III, 965.
Spare (let go): Part IV, Dialogue viii, 86.
Spare time: Part III, Exercise xxxvii*, 1, Obs. 1.
Sparrow: Part V, Lesson xl, 2, Note 5.
Speak of (allude to): Part III, Exercise xxv, 2, Obs. 2.
Speak out (say disagreeable truths): Part V, Lesson xlvi, 1.
Special object: Part V, Lesson iv, 1, Note 1.
Specially: Part III, 578; Exercise xxxiv, 3.
Spectator, observe as a: Part VI, Chapter xviii, 1.
Speculation: Part IV, Dialogue vi, 6.
Speculation (guessing): Part V, Lesson xxix, 2.
Speech, ready of: Part V, Lesson xxiv, Note 2; Part VI, Chapter vi, 1.
Speed, at full (of a horse): Part III, Exercise xxiii*, 5, Obs. 1.
Spell, take a: Part III, Exercise xxxi, 3, Obs.
Spend: Part III, 184, 345.
Spider: Part VI, Chapter xxxix, 4, Note 3.
Spill (upset): Part III, 932.
Spine: Part III, 478.
Spinster: Part IV, Dialogue iv, 62, Obs. 1.
Spirit (of departed souls): Part V, Lesson xvi, 2, Note 11.
Spirits, animal: Part IV, Dialogue iv, 56, Obs.
Spirits, evil: Part V, Lesson xxxvii, 5, Note 12.
Spirits (genii): Part V, Lesson viii, 3, Note 15.
Spirits, high: Part V, Lesson xlii, Note 6.
Spirits, out of: Part III, Exercise xxxvii*, 2; Part VI, Chapter xxvi, 1.
Spit in my face: Part V, Lesson lxvii, 2, Notes 8, 9.
Spittle: Part V, Lesson lxvii, Note 9.
Splashed, be: Part VI, Chapter xxxvi, 5, Note 6.
Split wood, to: Part VI, Chapter xv, 6, Note 12.
Spoil your luck: Part V, Lesson xxviii, 3, Note 8.
Spoiled: Part III, Exercise viii, 6.
Spoon: Part III, Exercise vii, 8.
Spotless (morally): Part V, Lesson xx, 2, Note 8.
Sprain, to: Part IV, Dialogue vii, 88, Obs.
Sprawling on his face, fell: Part VI, Chapter xv, 6, Note 14.
Spread, to: Part III, 407.
Sprightly: Part VI, Chapter vi, Note 4.
Spring: Part III, 427.

APPENDIX I.—GLOSSARY.

Spring, a (of water): Part VI, Chapter xxviii, Note 12.
Sprinkle, to: Part III, 932.
Sprout, to, or a: Part III, 696.
Squabble, to: Part III, Exercise xxxii, 7.
Squander: Part III, 184; Part VI, Chapter i, 7, Note 16.
Square: Part III, Exercise xviii, 8.
Squat on the heels: Part VI, Chapter xxxv, 4, Note 10.
"Squeeze," a: Part III, Exercise xv, 7, Obs. 3.
Squeeze, make a (make money): Part III, Exercise xxxvii*, 4.
Squeeze, to (extort money): Part III, 509.
Squint, a: Part V, Lesson xxx, 6, Note 8.
Stable: Part III, Exercise xl, 2, Obs. 2.
Stables: Part V, Lesson xxxii, 16, Note 9.
Stage in a journey: Part IV, Dialogue viii, 21, Obs. 3.
Staging, a: Part V, Lesson viii, Note 11.
Stained: Part V, Lesson xlvii, 3, Note 12.
Stale news or conversation: Part V, Lesson lxxvii, 2, Note 4.
Stale news, that's: Part III, Exercise xxxi*, 2, Obs. 1.
Stammer, to: Part V, Lesson xlii, 2, Note 4; Lesson lvi, 1, Note 2.
Stand aside: Part VI, Chapter xviii, 8.
Stand (bear), to: Part III, Exercise xxxi, 1.
Stand for, to: Part III, 342.
Stand (frame): Part V, Lesson viii, Note 11.
Stand, I won't: Part IV, Dialogue vii, 37.
Stand, I won't (such language from you): Part V, Lesson liii, 2.
Stand off: Part V, Lesson lviii, 2.
Stand still: Part V, Lesson xxxvi, 4, Note 10.
Staring: Part V, Lesson vi, 1, Note 3.
Start (get off): Part III, Exercise xvi, 5, Obs. 2.
Start (set out): Part III, 526.
Startle: Part V, Lesson xviii, 6, Note 11.
Startled, was: Part VI, Chapter xvii, 7, Note 4.
State, the: Part III, 520.
Stationed at, be: Part VI, Chapter xix, 10, Note 11.
Stature: Part III, Exercise xxxv*, 1, Obs. 3.
Stature, fine: Part V, Lesson xxiv, 1, Note 1.
Staunch: Part III, 713.
Steadily, come down (of rain): Part V, Lesson xciv, 2, Note 3.
Steady (behaviour): Part III, 830.
Steady (respectable): Part VI, Chapter xxx, 5.
Steady, to (by inserting a wedge): Part VI, Chapter xxxix, 14, Note 9.
Steal: Part III, 548.
Steal (creep along): Part V, Lesson xl, 2, Note 2.

Stealthily: Part III, 548; Part IV, Dialogue v, 44, Obs.
Steersman: Part VI, Chapter xxxv, 4, Note 9.
Steps, flight of: Part V, Lesson lxxxii, 4, Note 3.
Stern of a ship: Part VI, Chapter xxxv, 4, Note 8.
Sternness: Part IV, Dialogue ii, 42.
Stew, to: Part V, Lesson xlviii, Note 1; Part VI, Chapter v, 3, Note 7.
Stick, a: Part III, Exercise xxi, 2.
Stick in, to: Part VI, Chapter viii, Note 6.
"Stick" (stupid): Part III, Exercise xxxix*, 4, Obs. 2.
Stiff as a post: Part V, Lesson lxxvii, 1, Note 1.
Stiff with cold, fingers: Part V, Lesson xcviii, 4, Note 3.
Still (as ever): Part V, Lesson xviii, Note 7.
Still (more): Part III, 578.
Still (yet): Part III, 105.
Sting of insects: Part V, Lesson xcv, Note 4.
Sting, to (of scorpions, wasps, etc.): Part VI, Chapter xiii, 1, Note 5.
Stingy: Part III, Exercise xxvi*, 6; Part V, Lesson lii, 1, Note 2.
Stirrup: Part V, Lesson lxxxviii, Note 1.
Stock (origin): Part VI, Chapter v, 14, Note 26.
Stockade, a: Part VI, Chapter xvi, Note 3.
Stockings: Part III, 296.
Stomach-ache: Part III, Exercise xviii*, 8.
Stop a bit: Part V, Lesson vi, 2, Note 4.
Stop (deduct): Part IV, Dialogue iii, 119.
Stop (of rain): Part III, Exercise iii, 12.
Stop people's mouths: Part V, Lesson lxxxi, 2, Note 2.
Stop to the conversation, put a: Part VI, Chapter xvii, 7, Note 5.
Store by, set special: Part VI, Chapter xxxix, 15, Note 16.
Stored: Part IV, Dialogue v, 36, Obs. 3.
Storm, a: Part VI, Chapter xxxvi, 4.
Storm brewing, a: Part V, Lesson lxiv, 2.
Storming and raving with passion: Part V, Lesson liii, 3, Note 10.
Story, know only one part of the: Part V, Lesson lxxxvi, 6.
Stout: Part V, Lesson xxx, 6, Note 3.
Stoves: Part III, Exercise xiv, 3.
Stowed away: Part IV, Dialogue v, 36, Obs. 3.
Straight: Part III, 376.
Straight off, run: Part III, Exercise xxi*, 3.
Straighten the body: Part III, Exercise xvii, 7.
Straightforward: Part VI, Chapter xxviii, 2.
Strain (mental): Part VI, Chapter xxxix, 1.
Straitened (poor): Part III, 635.

Strange, think: Part III, 457.
Stranger: Part III, 390; Exercise xx*, 8, Obs.
Stranger, make yourself a: Part V, Lesson lxxi, 5, Note 5.
Stranger, treat as a: Part V, Lesson lxxii, 4, Note 11.
Strangle: Part III, 855.
Stratagems (in war): Part V, Lesson xxx, Note 18.
Straw: Part III, 702; Exercise xxvi*, 6.
Stream, go with the: Part III, 792, Obs.
Stream, up: Part IV, Dialogue viii, 7.
Strength (bodily): Part III, 971.
Strength (numerical): Part III, Exercise xix, 6.
Strength of mind: Part V, Lesson lxx, 2, Note 9.
Stretch (reach): Part III, Exercise xxvi*, 1, Obs. 2.
String of beads: Part V, Lesson xxxviii, 1, Notes 1, 2.
String together: Part V, Lesson ii, Note 2.
Stringent (severe): Part V, Lesson xxi, 2.
Strip of rank, to: Part IV, Dialogue vi, 21.
Stroll, take a: Part V, Lesson xviii, Note 4.
Stroll, to: Part VI, Chapter vii, 6, Note 17.
Strong: Part III, Exercise xvii, 3, Obs. 1.
Strong (physically): Part III, Exercise xvii*, 8, Obs.
Stronghold: Part VI, Chapter xvi, 1, Note 4.
Study, to: Part V, Lesson c, 2, Note 6.
Stuffing (in a dumpling): Part VI, Chapter xxi, Note 7.
Stumble (of a horse): Part V, Lesson xxxiii, Note 13.
Stupefied: Part V, Lesson xxxvi, Note 7.
Stupidity: Part V, Lesson lviii, Note 4.
Stye (in the eye): Part III, 289, Obs.
Style: Part III, 1030.
Style (fashion): Part III, Exercise xii*, 9, 11.
Style (name): Part III, 860; Part VI, Chapter vii, 1, Note 3.
Style, to: Part III, 871.
Subject, open the: Part V, Lesson i, 2.
Subjection, bring into: Part VI, Chapter xix, 8, Note 10.
Subjects: Part III, Exercise xix, 2.
Submit to: Part III, Exercise xxxiv*, 3, Obs.
Subscribe: Part III, 770.
Subscription for, raise a: Part V, Lesson lxx, 3, Note 16.
Subscriptions for a temple, beg: Part VI, Chapter ix, Note 5.
Substantive appointment: Part III, 1009.
Substitute, a: Part III, Exercise xxv, 8, Obs. 3.
Suburb: Part V, Lesson xcii, 3.
Succeed: Part V, Lesson iv, 1, Note 3.
Succeed, could not fail to: Part VI, Chapter xix, 2.
Succeed (favourable result): Part V, Lesson lii, 4, Note 10.
Succeed in life: Part III, Exercise xxi*, 6.
Success: Part III, Exercise xxxix, 1.

Success is in your hands: Part V, Lesson vii, 3, Note 6.
Successful: Part III, 623.
Succession, in: Part V, Lesson xlviii, 1.
Sudden, all of a: Part V, Lesson xlv, Note 2; Part VI, Chapter xxxix, 14, Note 10.
Suddenly: Part V, Lesson xxxv, 2, Note 8; Lesson xcv, Note 10.
Suffer: Part III, 399.
Suffer (sign of passive): Part IV, Dialogue iv, 52, Obs. 2.
Suffering, went through every form of: Part V, Lesson lxx, 2.
Sugar: Part III, 360.
Suggest: Part V, Lesson xii, Note 3.
Suggestion, not a good: Part V, Lesson lxx, 4.
Suicide, act of: Part V, Lesson xlvii, 3.
Suicide by hanging: Part III, Exercise xviii, 5, Obs. 2.
Suit each other: Part III, 971, Obs.
Suit, follow: Part III, Exercise xxxvii*, 4.
Suit of clothes: Part III, Exercise xi*, 3; Part IV, Dialogue x, 2, Obs. 1; Part V, Lesson lxx, 4, Note 17.
Suitable: Part III, 342.
Suitable, not: Part V, Lesson xxxiii, 3, Note 15.
Suited each other: Part VI, Chapter vii, 4, Note 12.
Suited to: Part V, Lesson xxxiii, Note 15.
Suits, it just: Part III, 1065.
Sullen: Part V, Lesson xli, 2, Note 3.
Summarily: Part V, Lesson ii, Note 3.
Summer: Part III, 427.
Sun: Part III, 265.
Sun, bask in the: Part III, Exercise xxvi, 2, Obs.
Sun, dry in the: Part III, 702.
Sun, suffer from the effects of the: Part III, Exercise xxxii, 9, Obs. 1.
Sunlight: Part III, 750.
Sunny: Part III, Exercise xxvi, 9, Obs. 2.
Sun's disc: Part III, 750.
Sun's rays: Part III, 750.
Sunset: Part III, 265; Part IV, Dialogue vii, 72, Obs. 1.
Sunstroke: Part III, Exercise xxxii, 9, Obs. 1.
Superior in mind, person, etc.: Part V, Lesson lxxxv, 2, Note 5.
Superior to: Part III, 847.
Supernumerary: Part III, Exercise xix*, 6, Obs. 1.
Support a family: Part IV, Dialogue v, 10.
Support, must not count on: Part IV, Dialogue vi, 50, Obs. 3, 4.
Support, to: Part VI, Chapter xxxv, Note 3.
Suppose: Part III, 376, Obs.

APPENDIX I.—GLOSSARY. 43

Suppose, do you: Part V, Lesson vi, Note 12.
Suppose, I: Part IV, Dialogue vi, 26, Obs. 1.
Supposing that: Part III, Exercise xxxiv*, 2.
Sure, be: Part III, Exercise xxv, 7, Obs.; Exercise xxxvii, 7.
Sure enough: Part III, Exercise xxxvii, 5, Obs. 2.
Sure, not: Part III, Exercise xxi, 8.
Surely not: Part IV, Dialogue vi, 14.
Surface (of a river, etc.): Part III, Exercise xxx, 3, Obs. 1.
Surplus: Part III, 1071.
Surprise, with: Part VI, Chapter xxxvi, 16.
Suspect: Part III, Exercise xxix, 7.
Suspect (opine): Part V, Lesson iii, 7, Note 8.
Swagger, to: Part V, Lesson lvii, 3.
Swaggering walk: Part VI, Chapter ii, 3, Note 8.
Swallow, to: Part VI, Chapter xiii, 3, Note 6.
Swamp, to: Part VI, Chapter iii, 8, Note 16.
Swarm, to: Part VI, Chapter xix, 2, Note 3.
Swathed from head to foot: Part V, Lesson lvii, 3, Note 9.
Swear (take an oath): Part V, Lesson xxi, Note 3.
Sweep, to: Part III, 932.
Sweet: Part VI, Chapter xiv, Note 7.
Sweetheart: Part VI, Chapter xxxix, 3.
Swell, to: Part V, Lesson xlviii, Note 9.
Swerve (of a horse in archery trench): Part V, Lesson xxxiii, Note 4.
Swim, to: Part III, Exercise xxx, 11, Obs.
Swindle, to: Part III, 796; Part IV, Dialogue iii, 113.
Swing the arms about: Part III, Exercise xxii, 7.
Sword: Part V, Lesson xxxv, 4, Note 16.
Sword, two-edged: Part VI, Chapter xxviii, 2, Note 7.
Syllable escape me, did not let a: Part V, Lesson lxxxiv, 4.
Sympathetic: Part VI, Chapter xxix, 3; Chapter xxxv, 7, Note 13.
Sympathise with, I can: Part VI, Chapter xxxix, 7, Note 6.
Sympathy: Part VI, Chapter xxxv, Note 13.
Symptoms (medical): Part VI, Chapter xxviii, 9, Note 17.

Table, clear the: Part VI, Chapter xiv, 8, Note 13.
Tail: Part V, Lesson lvi, Note 3.
Tailor: Part III, 316.
Take away: Part III, 369.
Take in (deceive): Part IV, Dialogue iii, 78.

Take off: Part III, 296.
Take on (fret): Part VI, Chapter xxxv, 9.
Take out (capital): Part III, Exercise xxix, 3, Obs. 4.
Tales, old: Part V, Lesson viii, 2, Note 5.
Tales, tell: Part IV, Dialogue iii, 100, Obs.
Talk at: Part V, Lesson lxii, 2, Note 8.
Talk, incessant: Part V, Lesson lxxii, 2, Notes 2, 3.
Talk of the town: Part V, Lesson lxvi, 1.
Talk over (discuss): Part III, 776.
Talked about (noised abroad): Part V, Lesson lxxxi, 2.
Tall: Part III, Exercise ii*, 11.
Tally, to: Part VI, Chapter xxvi, 3.
Task, hard: Part III, Exercise xxxi, 10.
Task, take to: Part V, Lesson lvi, 1, Note 4.
Taste: Part IV, Dialogue x, 2, Obs. 4.
Taste, bitter to the: Part V, Lesson xli, 4.
Taste, to: Part IV, Dialogue x, 18, Obs. 4; Part V, Lesson lxix, 4, Note 5.
Tattered: Part III, 289.
Tattered and torn: Part V, Lesson lxx, Note 3.
Tea in the leaf: Part IV, Dialogue v, 25, Obs.
Tea-house: Part IV, Dialogue iii, 104, Obs.
Tea-shop: Part III, 390.
Tear oneself away from: Part V, Lesson l, 3.
Tear, to: Part III, 451.
Tears, eyes full of: Part V, Lesson xli, 3, Notes 6, 7.
Tell (blab): Part III, 595; Exercise xxiii*, 2, Obs.
Temper: Part III, 1036; Exercise xxxix, 4, Obs. 2.
Temper, get over the worst of his: Part VI, Chapter xiv, 8.
Temper, give vent to: Part V, Lesson lxxviii, 2, Note 3.
Temper, lose one's: Part V, Lesson xli, 2.
Temperament, quick: Part III, 1036.
Tempestuous: Part VI, Chapter xxxvi, 4, Note 4.
Temple (Buddhist): Part III, 878; Part VI, Chapter ix, 3, Note 2.
Temple (Confucian): Part III, 878.
Temple (Taoist): Part V, Lesson xxxiii, Note 11.
Temples, hair on the: Part III, 464.
Temporarily: Part III, 617; Part V, Lesson vi, Note 4.
Tender one's name as a candidate: Part V, Lesson vii, Note 8.
Tender years: Part III, Exercise xxxi, 1.
Tender (young): Part III, 696.
Tender-hearted: Part VI, Chapter xxxii, 8, Note 3.
Term, a: Part III, Exercise xxx, 6, Obs. 1.
Terminus, the god: Part V, Lesson xxxvi, Note 11.
Terms, on good: Part III, 595.
Terms with, on good: Part V, Lesson lxi, Note 2.

Tether, come to the end of one's: Part V, Lesson xcix, 5, Note 12.
Thank you: Part IV, Dialogue iv, 38, Obs. 3.
Thank you enough, can't: Part V, Lesson xlix, 2, Note 5.
Thank-offering: Part V, Lesson xxxvi, 4, Notes 12, 13.
Thanks: Part III, 1009.
Thanks, many: Part IV, Dialogue x, 26, Obs.
Thanks, offer my: Part IV, Dialogue x, 22, Obs.
Theatre: Part VI, Chapter xxxvii, Note 10.
Then and there (at once): Part VI, Chapter ix, Note 7.
Therefore: Part III, 125.
Thermometer: Part III, Exercise xxxv, 1, Obs. 2.
Thick: Part III, 443, 713.
Thick (close together): Part V, Lesson xxxvi, 2, Note 4.
Thick (glutinous): Part III, 885; Part V, Lesson lxviii, Note 3.
Thief: Part III, 487.
Thief, be a: Part III, Exercise xxxv, 9, Obs.
Thieves: Part IV, Dialogue iii, 87.
Thigh: Part III, 478, Obs.
Thin: Part III, 713.
Thin (fallen away): Part V, Lesson xlv, 1, Note 3.
Thing: Part V, Lesson xxxv, 1, Note 4.
Thing, chief: Part V, Lesson iv, 1, Note 1.
Thing, very: Part VI, Chapter xxxiii, 3.
Things, no great: Part IV, Dialogue vi, 33, Obs.
Think: Part III, 681.
Think (imagine): Part V, Lesson v, 10, Note 4.
Think of, couldn't: Part IV, Dialogue x, 23, Obs. 1.
Third person: Part III, Exercise xxv, 2, Obs. 1.
Thirsty: Part III, 912.
Thoroughfare: Part III, Exercise iii, 10.
Thoroughfare, no: Part III, 1065.
Thoroughly: Part V, Lesson lxi, Note 9.
Thought he to himself: Part V, Lesson xxxv, 4, Note 14.
Thought, I: Part IV, Dialogue vi, 35, Obs.
Thrashing, give a: Part III, Exercise xxi, 7; Part V, Lesson ix, 5.
Thread: Part III, 289.
Thread one's way through: Part VI, Chapter xviii, 5.
Thrive (of a child): Part IV, Dialogue iv, 69, Obs. 3.
Throat, pour down the: Part VI, Chapter v, Note 20.
Throat, sore: Part III, 470.
Throng, to: Part VI, Chapter xix, Note 3.
Through, go (experience): Part III, 885.
Through, look (the window): Part VI, Chapter xxxix, 4.
Throw aside: Part III, 555.
Throw away: Part III, 750.
Throw back on: Part III, Exercise xix*, 9, Obs. 3.

Throw down: Part V, Lesson xviii, Note 8.
Throw in (in a bargain): Part VI, Chapter v, Note 18.
Thrown together: Part V, Lesson xxiv, 2, Note 6.
Thrust at, to: Part V, Lesson viii, 3, Note 12.
Thumb, the: Part V, Lesson x, 5, Note 11.
Thumb-ring: Part VI, Chapter xxiii, 1, Note 4.
Thunder, clap of: Part V, Lesson xcvi, Notes 1, 2.
Tickling sensation: Part VI, Chapter xxix, 4, Note 5.
Tide, drop down with: Part IV, Dialogue v, 48.
Tide, fair: Part III, 629.
Tidewaiter: Part IV, Dialogue v, 50, Obs.
Tie to: Part IV, Dialogue iii, 110, Obs.
Tie up: Part III, 770; Part V, Lesson ix, 5, Note 7; Lesson xxviii, Note 6.
Tier: Part III, Exercise xxxiii, 6.
Tiger: Part V, Lesson xxxi, 2, Note 4.
Tight, grasp the hand: Part V, Lesson l, 3.
Tight, sit: Part III, Exercise v*, 5, Obs.
Till, a: Part III, 390.
Time after time: Part III, 982.
Time, all this: Part VI, Chapter xxxi, 4, Note 6.
Time, at the same: Part III, 765, Obs.
Time, by this: Part III, Exercise xxi*, 5.
Time, every: Part V, Lesson xxxviii, Note 3.
Time, find or make: Part III, Exercise xxxiii, 7, Obs.; Part V, Lesson v, 10, Note 9.
Time, in: Part III, 665.
Time, make good use of: Part IV, Dialogue ii, 49, Obs.
Time, nick of: Part III, 562.
Time, once upon a: Part III, Exercise xxvi*, 2, Obs. 1; Part VI, Chapter i, 1, Note 3.
Time past, for some: Part V, Lesson xxi, 2, Note 2.
Time (season or period): Part VI, Chapter viii, Note 20.
Time, take up: Part III, Exercise xxxvi, 5.
Time to time: Part III, 865.
Time, what a: Part III, Exercise xxxiv, 1.
Time will show: Part V, Lesson lxvi, 2.
Times, easy: Part III, Exercise xxxi*, 3, Obs. 3.
Times. many: Part III, 982.
Timidly, walk: Part VI, Chapter xxii, 3, Note 4.
Tingling sensation: Part VI, Chapter xxix, 4, Note 5.
Tip, the: Part V, Lesson xxxiv, Note 9.
Tippler: Part VI, Chapter xvii, 12.
Tiptoe, move on: Part VI, Chapter xiii, 4, Note 8.
Tired: Part III, 58.
Tittle-tattle: Part VI, Chapter xxxi, Note 11.
To (towards, in the presence of): Part V, Lesson xix, 5.
Toady (make up to): Part V, Lesson lvii, 4.
Toddled: Part VI, Chapter xix, 4, Note 6.

APPENDIX I.—GLOSSARY.   45

Together: Part V, Lesson xxxi, Note 6.
Together, be constantly thrown: Part V, Lesson xxiv, 2, Note 6.
Tokio: Part III, 376.
Tolerate: Part III, 965.
Tomfoolery: Part V, Lesson xlii, 3, Note 6.
Tongue: Part III, Exercise xvii, 9.
Tongue, free with the: Part III, 995.
Tongue, be too free with the: Part VI, Chapter xxv, 8, Note 7.
Too: Part III, Exercise xi, 9; Part VI, Chapter viii, 4, Note 4.
Too much: Part III, Exercise xiii*, 7, Obs. 2.
Torn: Part III, Exercise xi, 4; Part V, Lesson lxx, Note 3.
Torrents, came down in: Part V, Lesson xcvi, 1, Note 3.
Toss about (in bed): Part V, Lesson xcv, 2, Note 5.
Total: Part III, Exercise xl, 4.
Tottered: Part VI, Chapter xix, Note 6.
Touch of silver: Part VI, Chapter xv, 1, Note 3.
Touch, to: Part III, 526.
Touched one to see: Part V, Lesson lxxxvii, 12, Note 11.
Tow rope, drag a: Part V, Lesson xxviii, Note 4; Part VI, Chapter ii, Note 4.
Towards: Part III. 48.
Towel: Part III, 273.
Trace of, not a: Part V, Lesson xxxviii, 8, Note 13.
Traced to its source: Part IV, Dialogue vi, 21, Obs. 1.
Track (boats), to: Part IV, Dialogue viii, 7; Part V, Lesson xxviii, 2, Note 4.
Trade, centre of: Part VI, Chapter xxxvi, 6, Note 8.
Tradition: Part III, 885.
Tranquil: Part III, 629.
Translate: Part V, Lesson i, Notes 3, 4.
Transmitted (handed down): Part III, 885.
Transpire (get known): Part III, Exercise xxxii*, 1; Part V, Lesson lxvi, Note 2.
Trap, fall into a: Part V, Lesson xxiv, 2, Note 12.
Treacherous: Part V, Lesson xxiv, Note 10; Lesson lviii, Note 5.
Tread, to: Part VI, Chapter xiii, Note 8.
Treasury: Part III, 900.
Treat (behave): Part III, 713.
Treat medically: Part III, 855, Obs.
Treaties: Part III, Exercise xxii, 8.
Treatment, rough: Part III, Exercise xxxi, 1, Obs.
Tree, a: Part III, 696.
Trees (boot), stretch on the: Part VI, Chapter xxxiv, 7, Note 7.

Tremble with fear: Part V, Lesson lxx, Note 5.
Trepidation, state of: Part V, Lesson lvi, 1, Note 3.
Trials, go through: Part V, Lesson lix, 5.
Trice up, to: Part V, Lesson lxxxiii, Note 8.
Tricky: Part IV, Dialogue iii, 99, Obs.
Trifle, a: Part V, Lesson lix, 5.
Trifles (presents): Part V, Lesson lxix, 3.
Trifles, talk about: Part V, Lesson lxxvii, 2, Note 3.
Trip up, to: Part VI, Chapter i, 7, Note 20.
Troops, move: Part VI, Chapter vii, 5, Note 14.
Trotted: Part VI, Chapter xix, Note 6.
Trouble (ask a favour of), to: Part V, Lesson lxxxii, 1, Note 1.
Trouble, get into: Part III, Exercise xxiii, 2, Obs. 2; Part VI, Chapter v, 7, Note 16.
Trouble, give: Part III, Exercise xxxii*, 9; Part IV, Dialogue x, 8, Obs. 5.
Trouble, go through: Part III, 885; Part IV, Dialogue iv, 46.
Trouble, not any: Part V, Lesson v, 10.
Trouble oneself about, need not: Part V, Lesson lxxix, 2.
Trouble (pains): Part V, Lesson xvi, 1, Note 2.
Trouble, put to: Part V, Lesson lxxi, Note 4.
Trouble, put yourself to: Part V, Lesson i, 4; Lesson xlix, 2, Note 3.
Trouble, take: Part IV, Dialogue iv, 38, Obs. 3.
Trouble you, may I: Part III, 855, Obs.; 989.
Troubled you, sorry to have: Part III, 855.
Trough: Part V, Lesson xxxii, Note 9.
Trousers: Part III, 316; Exercise xii*, 4.
True enough: Part III, Exercise xxvi*, 4.
Trumpet: Part VI, Chapter xix, Note 2.
Trunk: Part III, Exercise xvi, 2.
Truth, in strict: Part VI, Chapter xxvii, 16, Note 9.
Truth, not a shadow of: Part V, Lesson xlvi, 2.
Try (match): Part III, 689.
Try to, don't: Part III, Exercise xxxvi, 4.
Tumble flat on one's back: Part V, Lesson lvi, 2.
Turbulent: Part III, 533.
Turn (bend), a: Part III, 792.
Turn for, a: Part III, Exercise xiv*, 5, Obs.
Turn, it was my: Part III, Exercise xxvii, 6, Obs.
Turn out of doors: Part V, Lesson liii, 3, Note 9.
Turn (time): Part III, Exercise xix, 7, Obs.; Part V, Lesson ix, Note 8; Part VI, Chapter xvii, Note 6.
Turned out to be, it: Part VI, Chapter xii, 5, Note 5.
Twice: Part III, Exercise xxix*, 12, Obs. 1.
Twilight (evening): Part V, Lesson lxxvii, Note 2.

Twine: Part III, 360.
Twist, to: Part IV, Dialogue vii, 88, Obs.
Two, cut in: Part V, Lesson xviii, 6, Note 13.
Two places at once, one's thoughts in: Part VI, Chapter xxxv, 6.
Two-fold: Part III, 891.
Type (printing): Part VI, Chapter xxv, 2, Note 4.

Ugly: Part III, 612.
Ulcer: Part V, Lesson lxxiii, Note 5.
Umbrella: Part VI, Chapter xxxvi, 4, Note 5.
Unchangeable rule: Part V, Lesson xciii, 2.
Uncle (father's younger brother): Part V, Lesson xviii, Note 2.
Uncle (maternal): Part V, Lesson xxvii, 3, Note 7.
Uncommon: Part VI, Chapter viii, Note 13.
Unconcerned (at ease): Part V, Lesson lx, 2, Note 2.
Unconstrained attitude: Part V, Lesson x, 3, Note 7.
Undecided: Part VI, Chapter xiv, Note 1.
Under, keep: Part V, Lesson x, 5, Note 14.
Underlings, official: Part III, Exercise xxxiv*, 1, Obs. 1.
Undermined (by water): Part V, Lesson xcv, 2, Note 13.
Underneath: Part III, 514.
Under-shirt: Part III, Exercise xii*, 5, Obs.
Understanding (collusion): Part III, Exercise xxi*, 5, Obs. 1.
Understanding, private: Part III, 982.
Undertake: Part III, 1009.
Undertake a commission: Part V, Lesson xxv, 1, Note 2; Lesson lxxxiii, 2; Part VI, Chapter xx, 2, Note 3.
Undertakings: Part III, Exercise xxxix, 6.
Undivided attention: Part III, Exercise xxxiii*, 4.
Unendurable (of pain): Part III, Exercise xxxix, 6.
Uneven: Part III, Exercise xxii, 10, Obs. 2; Part VI, Chapter xxix, 13, Note 15.
Unexpected (beat anything one fancied): Part VI, Chapter xxvii, 17.
Unfamiliar with: Part III, 755, Obs.
Unfettered: Part V, Lesson xxvi, 3, Note 6.
Unfortunately: Part III, Exercise xxxvi*, 6.
Ungrateful: Part III, 1049, Obs.
Unhandsome (in conduct): Part III, Exercise xxvii, 10.
Uniform, soldier's: Part III, 860.
Unintentional: Part III, 425.
Unintentionally: Part V, Lesson lxii, 3.
Unless (except): Part III, 1071.
Unlucky: Part III, Exercise xxix*, 12, Obs. 3.
Unmannerly: Part VI, Chapter xxxviii, 3, Note 4.

Unmarried: Part IV, Dialogue iv, 66.
Unnecessary: Part VI, Chapter xl, 2, Note 8.
Unobserved: Part III, Exercise xxi, 4, Obs. 1.
Unprejudiced eye, look upon with an: Part VI, Chapter iv, Note 11.
Unreasonable: Part III, Exercise xx, 7, Obs. 1.
Unreclaimed: Part III, Exercise xxvi, 7, Obs.
Unsteady hand: Part V, Lesson x, 5.
Unsteady (libertinism): Part V, Lesson lxxxv, 2, Note 6.
Unsuited: Part V, Lesson xxxiii, 3, Note 15.
Unwieldy: Part V, Lesson xxxiii, 3, Note 14.
Unwilling: Part III, 1049.
Unworthy, if you don't consider him: Part V, Lesson lxxxv, 2, Note 7.
Up to, right: Part III, Exercise xxxiv, 2.
Upright, set: Part III, 1077.
Upset: Part III, 189.
Upset (in feelings): Part V, Lesson l, 4, Note 9.
Upset (mentally): Part VI, Chapter xxvii, 8.
Upset (overturn): Part IV, Dialogue vii, 83, Obs.
Urge: Part III, 590; Part V, Lesson xxvi, Note 4.
Use for, have no: Part III, 555.
Use, of no: Part III, Exercise xvii*, 2, Obs. 2.
Use, ready for: Part VI, Chapter ix, 9, Note 8.
Used to be: Part V, Lesson lix, 2.
Used to, not: Part IV, Dialogue viii, 81, Obs. 2.
Useful accomplishments: Part V, Lesson lvii, 3.
Useless (in vain): Part V, Lesson vii, Note 4.
Utensils: Part III, 177, 178.
Utterly: Part III, 971.
Utterly without: Part III, Exercise xx*, 7, Obs. 1.

Vacancy, fill a: Part III, 504.
Vacancy occurs: Part III, Exercise xix, 7.
Vain, in: Part V, Lesson vii, Note 4; Lesson xci, Note 12.
Valueless: Part III, 337.
Vanguard (Manchu army): Part V, Lesson xii, 4, Note 4.
Variable (temperature): Part V, Lesson xlv, 2.
Vat: Part VI, Chapter v, 15, Note 36.
Vegetables: Part III, 526.
Velvet: Part III, 671.
Verse: Part IV, Dialogue ix, 39, Obs. 1.
Very: Part III, 8, 35; Part V, Lesson iii, 6, Note 5.
Veteran: Part VI, Chapter xi, 7, Note 8.
Vex: Part V, Lesson xvi, 2.
Vicissitudes: Part VI, Chapter xxviii, 7, Note 11.
Victory: Part VI, Chapter xviii, Note 6.

APPENDIX I.—GLOSSARY. 47

View, to: Part III, Exercise xxiv, 9.
Vigorous: Part IV, Dialogue iv, 69, Obs. 3.
Village: Part III, 809; Part V, Lesson xxvii, Note 8; Lesson lxxv, Note 1.
Villain, you: Part V, Lesson lxiii, 1, Note 1.
Violent: Part III, 847.
Visit places of interest: Part V, Lesson xviii, Note 4.
Visit, to what am I indebted for this: Part V, Lesson lxxxv, 1, Note 2.
Visitor: Part III, Exercise xx*, 8; 728.
Visitors, deny oneself to: Part VI, Chapter vii, Note 10.
Vitality: Part III, Exercise xviii*, 3, Obs. 2.
Vitreous: Part III, 750.
Volley, fire a: Part VI, Chapter ii, Note 6.
Vomit, to: Part V, Lesson xlv, 3, Note 10.
Vow, to: Part V, Lesson xxi, 2, Note 3; Lesson xliv, 1, Note 6.
Vow, make a: Part VI, Chapter xxix, 1, Note 1.

Wadded: Part III, 316; Exercise xii, 3; Exercise xii*, 7.
Wages, cut: Part IV, Dialogue iii, 119, Obs.; Part VI, Chapter xvii, 11.
Wail and weep: Part V, Lesson xvi, 2, Note 7.
Wainscoting: Part V, Lesson xxxviii, 8, Note 12.
Waist, stripped to the: Part V, Lesson xciii, 1, Note 6.
Waistcoat: Part III, 310; Exercise xii, 4, 8; Exercise xii*, 4.
Wait, to: Part III, Exercise xxxviii, 3, Obs. 1.
Wait upon: Part IV, Dialogue ii, 58, Obs. 1; Part V, Lesson xlii, 3, Note 7.
Waiting, kept you: Part IV, Dialogue x, 11, Obs. 2.
Wake: Part V, Lesson xxxv, Note 7.
Walk backwards and forwards, to: Part VI, Chapter xxvii, 12, Note 7.
Walk, to: Part III, 800.
Wall: Part III, 891.
Wall (of enclosure): Part V, Lesson xxxvi, 2, Note 3.
Want (privation): Part V, Lesson xvi, 2, Note 5.
War, go to: Part V, Lesson viii, 3, Note 9.
War, God of: Part III, Exercise xxxiii, 4.
Wardrobe: Part III, 390.
Warehouses: Part IV, Dialogue v, 36, Obs. 2.
Wares, cry: Part V, Lesson xciii, 2, Note 9.
Warning by, take: Part V, Lesson viii, 1, Note 3.
Warrant, I'll: Part V, Lesson lx, 3, Note 7.
Wasp: Part VI, Chapter xix, Note 3.
Waste ground: Part III, 809.
Waste not want not: Part V, Lesson xxviii, 4, Note 9.
Waste time, to: Part V, Lesson vi, 2, Note 8.

Watch, a: Part III, 225; Exercise xxxv, 1, Obs. 1.
Watch for an opportunity: Part V, Lesson lviii, 2.
Watch, to: Part III, 91; Part V, Lesson xv, 2, Note 6.
Water: Part III, 800.
Water, by: Part IV, Dialogue viii, 5.
Watery (thin): Part III, 885; Part V, Lesson lxviii, Note 3.
Waves: Part III, 792.
Wax: Part III, 152.
Way and that, this: Part VI, Chapter xxviii, 1.
Way, be in the: Part III, 919.
Way for, make: Part VI, Chapter viii, 2; Chapter xviii, 9.
Way, get out of the: Part V, Lesson xxiii, 1, Note 1.
Way, give: Part IV, Dialogue x, 9, Obs.
Way, have one's: Part V, Lesson xiii, 1.
Way, over the: Part III, Exercise xxvi, 10, Obs. 1.
Way, see one's: Part IV, Dialogue ix, 51, Obs.; Part V, Lesson i, 2.
Way, show the: Part IV, Dialogue viii, 3.
Ways (habits): Part III, Exercise xxxviii, 6, Obs. 1.
Weak (in health): Part III, 451.
Weak (in purpose): Part IV, Dialogue vi, 27, Obs.
Wealthy: Part III, Exercise xxx, 10.
Weapon: Part V, Lesson xxvii, 3, Note 10.
Wear (last), to: Part III, 836.
Wear out: Part III, Exercise xii*, 11.
Wearied: Part V, Lesson xxv, Note 1.
Weather: Part III, 223.
Web, spider's: Part VI, Chapter xxxix, 4, Note 3.
Wedding: Part III, 971; Part V, Lesson xlvii, 2, Note 4.
Weep: Part V, Lesson xli, Note 6.
Weep bitterly: Part V, Lesson xvi, 2, Note 7.
Weigh: Part III, 327, 328.
Weight: Part III, 776, Obs.
Weight for keeping things in place: Part V, Lesson xl, Note 12.
Weight, keep in place by a: Part V, Lesson xl, Note 11.
Weight off one's mind: Part V, Lesson xci, Note 2.
Well-being: Part III, Exercise xxv, 3.
Well conducted, be: Part V, Lesson iv, 3, Note 6.
Well, do as: Part III, Exercise xi, 4.
Well water: Part III, 800.
Wet (damp): Part III, 702.
Wet, get: Part III, Exercise xi*, 2, Obs. 1.
Wharf: Part VI, Chapter xxxvi, Note 8.
What-do-you-call-'ems: Part III, Exercise xii*, 4, Obs.
What ...... for: Part III, 585.
Wheat, autumn: Part III, Exercise xx, 4.

Wheat, spring: Part III, Exercise xx, 4.
When: Part III, Exercise x*, 6; Exercise xix, 6, Obs. 1; Exercise xxxix, 5, Obs. 1; Part IV, Dialogue x, 8, Obs. 2.
Whenever: Part III, Exercise xxii*, 1; Part V, Lesson ii, 3, Note 6; Lesson xlvii, Note 1.
Whetstone: Part VI, Chapter xxviii, Note 4.
While, good: Part III, Exercise xvi, 8, Obs. 1.
While (period of time): Part III, 129.
Whip, a: Part IV, Dialogue iii, 110, Obs.
Whip behind: Part III, Exercise xxxiv*, 4, Obs.
Whip, laid on with the: Part V, Lesson xcii, 3, Note 7.
Whirlpool: Part VI, Chapter xxxvi, 2, Obs.
Whirlwind: Part VI, Chapter xxxvii, Note 1.
Whole, the: Part III, 809, Obs. 1; Exercise xv*, 8; Part VI, Chapter xix, Note 1.
Wholesale business: Part III, 755.
Why: Part III, 961.
Why won't you: Part III, Exercise xxix, 9, Obs. 1.
Wide: Part III, 671, 792.
Widow: Part IV, Dialogue iv, 64, Obs.
Width: Part III, 671.
Wife: Part III, 815; Part IV, Dialogue iv, 64, Obs.; Part V, Lesson xvii, 1, Note 2.
Wife, elder brother's: Part V, Lesson lxxxvii, Note 4.
Wife, marry a: Part V, Lesson lxi, 2, Note 6.
Wife, your: Part V, Lesson lxxxvii, 7, Note 4.
Wife's family: Part III, 815.
Wild: Part III, Exercise xxvi, 7, Obs.
Wild flowers or grasses: Part III, 809.
Wildly, talk: Part III, 548.
Will (future): Part III, 34.
Willing, I'm perfectly (ready): Part V, Lesson lxiii, 3.
Willow: Part V, Lesson xc, 2, Note 5.
Win to good ways: Part V, Lesson xiv, 2, Note 4.
Win, to (in gambling, etc.): Part VI, Chapter xviii, 4, Note 6.
Wind: Part III, 800.
Wind, fair: Part III, 629.
Wind in the ears, treat as: Part V, Lesson vi, 3.
Wind, not a breath of: Part V, Lesson xciii, 1.
Wind up (a clock or watch): Part VI, Chapter xxviii, 1, Note 1.
Winding: Part III, 895; Exercise xxx*, 2.
Windlass: Part VI, Chapter xxix, 4, Note 6.
Window-bars: Part V, Lesson xl, Note 1.
Window-frame: Part V, Lesson xl, 1, Note 1.
Wine: Part III, Exercise xiv*, 6, Obs.
Wing of a house: Part VI, Chapter ix, 5.

Wink, tip a: Part V, Lesson xliii, Note 3.
Winter: Part III, 427.
Winter, beginning of: Part V, Lesson lxx, 2, Note 14.
Wish, get one's (way): Part V, Lesson xiii, 1.
Wishes, suited her (her view of the question): Part VI, Chapter xxx, 4. Note 1.
With: Part III, 204; Exercise xvi*, 4, Obs. 2.
Withdraw: Part III, Exercise xxix, 3, Obs. 3; Part V, Lesson lxii, Note 4.
Wits about him, has his: Part V, Lesson xxx, 9, Note 18.
Woeful face: Part V, Lesson lix, 1, Note 1.
Woman: Part III, 815.
Woman, married: Part IV, Dialogue vii, 76, Obs.
Woman, old: Part IV, Dialogue vii, 76; Part V, Lesson xxii, 2, Note 11.
Wonder, no: Part III, 457, Obs.
Wonder, people will: Part V, Lesson xi, 15, Note 6.
Wonderful (remarkable): Part V, Lesson lxviii, 1.
Wonders of the world: Part III, Exercise xx*, 6.
Wood, a: Part III, 696.
Word for, say a: Part V, Lesson xliv, 2.
Word for word: Part VI, Chapter xii, 5.
Word, hold to one's: Part VI, Chapter xxvi, 3.
Word, in a: Part III, 539; Part V, Lesson xlvii, 3.
Words, few: Part V, Lesson lxi, 2, Note 3.
Words, in other: Part V, Lesson lxii, 1.
Words thrown away: Part V, Lesson lxvii, 2, Note 5.
Worked, hard: Part VI, Chapter vii, 6, Note 16.
Working out of hours: Part V, Lesson lxii, Note 4.
World, all in the: Part V, Lesson lxvi, 1.
World, all over the: Part III, Exercise xx*, 1.
World, come back from the other: Part V, Lesson xxxix, 1, Note 2.
World, know something of the: Part V, Lesson lv, 3.
World, the: Part III, 539.
World, thrown upon the: Part III, 765.
Worm out of (an opinion): Part V, Lesson lviii, 2.
Worn out: Part V, Lesson xxxvii, Note 5.
Worn out (constitution): Part III, 604.
Worse: Part III, 578.
Worship, to: Part III, 878.
Worship, your: Part III, 815.
Worst of it, get the: Part III, 1049; Part V, Lesson liv, 1, Note 7.
Worst, the: Part V, Lesson lxvi, 1.
Worth, be: Part III, 337.
Worth the trouble, not: Part V, Lesson lxi, Note 4.
Worthless character: Part V, Lesson xliv, Note 11.
Worthless (of no use): Part V, Lesson lv, 1, Notes 2, 3, 4.

APPENDIX I.—GLOSSARY.

Worthy, not: Part IV, Dialogue x, 8, Obs. 7; Part V, Lesson lxvii, 2.
Would you: Part III, 995.
Wound, to: Part III, 1077.
Wrangle: Part III, Exercise xxiii, 2; Exercise xxxii, 1; Part V, Lesson xliii, 1; Lesson lxii, Note 7.
Wrap round: Part V, Lesson xxxiii, Note 4; Lesson lvii, Note 9.
Wrap up: Part III, 407.
Wrapper: Part VI, Chapter iv, 6, Note 10.
Wrath, cool: Part V, Lesson xliii, 2.
Wrestle, to: Part VI, Chapter xviii, 4, Note 5.
Wretch, you miserable: Part V, Lesson lxiii, 2.
Wrist: Part VI, Chapter viii, 6, Note 8.
Writing, four kinds of: Part VI, Chapter i, 5, Note 12.
Writing (the three hands): Part III, Exercise xxxiii, 5.
Wrong, put people in the: Part VI, Chapter xiv, 1, Note 2.

Wrong, think over a: Part V, Lesson xxi, Note 7.
Wrong to, you were: Part IV, Dialogue ii, 30, Obs. 2.

Yarn, spin a: Part V, Lesson lxxii, 2, Notes 4, 5.
Year, happy new: Part V, Lesson xi, 1, Note 1.
Year, last quarter of the: Part VI, Chapter xxxix, 2, Note 1.
Years ago: Part VI, Chapter xxxvii, 9, Note 4.
Years, for: Part VI, Chapter xxii, 4.
Years, of mature: Part III, 955.
Yet, and: Part III, 836.
Yet (up till now): Part III, Exercise xxiii*, 5, Obs. 3.
Yield (of crops): Part III, Exercise xx, 5.
Yield, to: Part IV, Dialogue x, 9, Obs.
Yokel: Part III, Exercise xxx, 10.
Young (of vegetables): Part III, Exercise xxvi, 5.
Youth: Part III, Exercise xxi*, 6; Part V, Lesson lv, 3.

Zeal, serve with: Part III, Exercise xxxviii*, 2, Obs.

APPENDIX II.

INDEX OF CHARACTERS.

APPENDIX II.

INDEX OF CHARACTERS

IN

PARTS III, IV, V, VI, AND VII OF VOLUME II,

ARRANGED ACCORDING TO RADICALS.

一

一 Part III, 1.
三 Part III, 1.
七 Part III, 1.
不 Part III, 8.
上 Part III, 48.
下 Part III, 48.
且 Part III, 616.
丟 Part III, 643.
世 Part III, 867.
並 Part IV, Dialogue vii, 94.
丈 Part V, Lesson xix, Note 5.
丁 Part VI, Chapter xxviii, Note 9.

丨

中 Part III, 302; Part IV, Dialogue ix, 40.
丫 Part VI, Chapter i, Note 8.
串 Part VII, 69.

丶

主 Part III, 490.
凡 Part III, 563.
丸 Part VI, Chapter xxviii, Note 21.
丹 Part VI, Chapter xxviii, Note 21.

丿

乏 Part III, 58.
之 Part III, 538.
乍 Part III, 704.
久 Part IV, Dialogue ii, 20.
乎 Part IV, Dialogue x, 5.
乘 Part IV, Dialogue x, 25.

乙

九 Part III, 1.
也 Part III, 134.
乾 Part III, 271.
亂 Part III, 530.

亅

了 Part III, 31.
事 Part III, 252.

二

二 Part III, 1.
五 Part III, 1.
些 Part III, 7.
况 Part III, 615.
井 Part III, 795.

亠

亮 Part III, 219.
京 Part III, 370.
交 Part III, 721.
享 Part IV, Dialogue vi, 38; Part V, Lesson xvi, Note 12.
亡 Part IV, Dialogue iv, 63.

人

倆 Part III, 1.
來 Part III, 8.
個 Part III, 8.
們 Part III, 13.
他 Part III, 15.
你 Part III, 15.

倦 Part III, 17.
什 Part III, 23; Part VII, 92.
住 Part III, 48.
做 Part III, 50.
以 Part III, 125.
像 Part III, 177.
伙 Part III, 178.
倒 Part III, 182.
使 Part III, 195.
今 Part III, 205.
令 Part III, 208.
候 Part III, 224.
件 Part III, 250.
儘 Part III, 297.
價 Part III, 329.
值 Part III, 330.
便 Part III, 333.
借 Part III, 338.
位 Part III, 492.
例 Part III, 518.
偷 Part III, 542.
偶 Part III, 560; Part VI, Chapter xxv, Note 8.
催 Part III, 589.
舍 Part III, 658.
傲 Part III, 714.
儒 Part III, 870.
佛 Part III, 872.
僧 Part III, 875.
俗 Part III, 876.
傳 Part III, 879.
倉 Part III, 896.
依 Part III, 913; Part IV, Dialogue ii, 31.
偏 Part III, 923.
修 Part III, 934.

信 Part III, 994.	伯 Part VI, Chapter i, Note 13.		
任 Part III, 1006.	合 Part VI, Chapter ii, Note 1.	⼍	
供 Part III, 1020.	估 Part VI, Chapter iii, Note 10.	冠 Part VI, Chapter xxiv, Note 3.	
備 Part III, 1061.	僅 Part VI, Chapter iii, Note 17.		
像 Part III, 1069.	僕 Part VI, Chapter vi, Note 2.	冫	
似 Part III, 1070.	佩 Part VI, Chapter vii, Note 6.	冷 Part III, 226.	
傷 Part III, 1074.	俊 Part VI, Chapter xi, Note 1.	次 Part III, 235.	
作 Part IV, Dialogue i, 28.	傍 Part VI, Chapter xiii, Note 3.	冬 Part III, 426.	
儉 Part IV, Dialogue ii, 43.	僂 Part VI, Chapter xvi, Note 4.	准 Part III, 567.	
伺 Part IV, Dialogue ii, 58.	儸 Part VI, Chapter xvi, Note 4.	決 Part IV, Dialogue iii, 123.	
假 Part IV, Dialogue iii, 13; Part V, Lesson xi, Note 5.	佳 Part VI, Chapter xxv, Note 8.	冲 Part V, Lesson liii, Note 8.	
伸 Part IV, Dialogue iii, 56.	仔 Part VI, Chapter xxviii, Note 3.	凍 Part V, Lesson xcvii, Note 1.	
何 Part IV, Dialogue iii, 57.	佈 Part VI, Chapter xxxii, Note 5.	冰 Part VI, Chapter xiii, Note 4.	
伴 Part IV, Dialogue iii, 72.	伏 Part VI, Chapter xxxiii, Note 1.		
但 Part IV, Dialogue iii, 114; Part V, Lesson ii, Note 6.	傘 Part VI, Chapter xxxvi, Note 5.	⼐	
保 Part IV, Dialogue iv, 55.	倜 Part VII, 56.	出 Part III, 40.	
佑 Part IV, Dialogue vi, 35.		凶 Part III, 620.	
倚 Part IV, Dialogue vi, 50.	儿		
倖 Part IV, Dialogue ix, 41.	兒 Part III, 11.	刀	
倘 Part IV, Dialogue x, 1; Part V, Lesson xxi, Note 5.	先 Part III, 99.	到 Part III, 44.	
僧 Part IV, Dialogue x, 13.	充 Part III, 503.	前 Part III, 82.	
傅 Part V, Lesson ii, Note 7.	兆 Part III, 618.	分 Part III, 130.	
仗 Part V, Lesson viii, Note 9.	兄 Part III, 656.	刀 Part III, 173.	
仙 Part V, Lesson viii, Note 15.	光 Part III, 745.	刻 Part III, 223.	
優 Part V, Lesson xiii, Note 5.	免 Part III, 863.	刮 Part III, 230, 469.	
仁 Part V, Lesson xiv, Note 7.	元 Part V, Lesson xviii, Note 5.	刷 Part III, 274.	
仲 Part V, Lesson xviii, Note 1.	兜 Part V, Lesson lviii, Note 9.	利 Part III, 423.	
仍 Part V, Lesson xviii, Note 7.	允 Part V, Lesson lxxxiii, Note 7.	剃 Part III, 468.	
儻 Part V, Lesson xxi, Note 5.	克 Part V, Lesson lxxxviii, Note 7.	則 Part III, 614.	
偉 Part V, Lesson xxiv, Note 1.	兎 Part VI, Chapter xxxix, Note 6.	別 Part III, 646, 706.	
伶 Part V, Lesson xxiv, Note 2.		剛 Part III, 756.	
俐 Part V, Lesson xxiv, Note 2.	入	列 Part III, 909.	
仰 Part V, Lesson xxiv, Note 13.	全 Part III, 511.	剩 } Part III, 1067.	
侈 Part V, Lesson xxviii, Note 1.	內 Part V, Lesson xlviii, Note 14.	賸 }	
償 Part V, Lesson xxix, Note 5.		劉 Part IV, Dialogue v, 66.	
併 Part V, Lesson xxxi, Note 6.	八	剪 Part V, Lesson viii, Note 16.	
係 Part V, Lesson xxxi, Note 12.	六 Part III, 1.	剃 Part V, Lesson xlviii, Note 13.	
儱 Part V, Lesson xxxiii, Note 1.	八 Part III, 1.	切 Part V, Lesson lv, Note 7.	
倖 Part V, Lesson xxxiv, Note 10.	典 Part III, 95.	刺 Part V, Lesson lxxii, Note 2.	
儹 Part V, Lesson xxxvi, Note 13.	兵 Part III, 499.	刮 Part V, Lesson lxxii, Note 9.	
停 Part V, Lesson xlviii, Note 12.	公 Part III, 979.	刁 Part VI, Chapter v, Note 14.	
佻 Part V, Lesson lv, Note 1.	其 Part III, 1055.	刹 Part VI, Chapter ix, Note 2.	
低 Part V, Lesson lx, Note 4.	共 Part III, 1063.	劃 Part VI, Chapter ix, Note 6.	
僻 Part V, Lesson lxii, Note 15.		剿 Part VI, Chapter xiv, Note 8.	
休 Part V, Lesson lxxii, Note 3.	冂	劈 Part VI, Chapter xv, Note 12.	
傾 Part V, Lesson xcvi, Note 3.	再 Part III, 758.	劄 Part VI, Chapter xix, Note 11.	
傻 Part V, Lesson xcix, Note 7.	册 Part VII, 9.	劍 Part VI, Chapter xxviii, Note 7.	

APPENDIX II.—INDEX OF CHARACTERS.

割 Part VI, Chapter xxviii, Note 13.
副 Part VI, Chapter xxxix, Note 7.
創 Part VII, 71.
刨 Part VII, 396.

力

勒 Part III, 507.
動 Part III, 524.
幼 Part III, 813.
勁 Part III, 966.
務 Part III, 981.
功 Part III, 1042; Part V, Lesson xx, Note 4.
勢 Part III, 1079.
勤 Part IV, Dialogue ii, 43; Part V, Lesson xiii, Note 9.
加 Part IV, Dialogue iii, 74.
勞 Part IV, Dialogue iv, 38; Part V, Lesson xvi, Note 2.
勝 Part V, Lesson vii, Note 6.
勇 Part V, Lesson xiii, Note 11.
勸 Part V, Lesson xli, Note 2.
努 Part V, Lesson lxxix, Note 2.
助 Part VI, Chapter ii, Note 2.
募 Part VI, Chapter ix, Note 5.
效 Part VI, Chapter xv, Note 6.
劣 Part VI, Chapter xxxi, Note 19.

勹

勻 Part III, 175.
包 Part III, 402.
勿 Part IV, Dialogue iii, 21.
勻 Part V, Lesson v, Note 9.
勾 Part V, Lesson lviii, Note 7.

匕

匙 Part III, 176.
北 Part III, 393.
化 Part V, Lesson xxiii, Note 11.

匚

匹 Part III, 76.

匸

匠 Part III, 731.
匪 Part III, 849.

十

十 Part III, 1.
千 Part III, 4.
本 Part III, 120.
卓 Part III, 148.
半 Part III, 236.
午 Part III, 247.
南 Part III, 392.
博 Part V, Lesson xix, Note 4.
升 Part V, Lesson xxxii, Note 8.
卑 Part V, Lesson c, Note 7.

卜

占 Part V, Lesson xv, Note 5.
卦 Part VI, Chapter xxv, Note 12.

卩

却 Part III, 678.
卽 Part V, Lesson lvii, Note 3.
卯 Part VII, 213.

厂

原 Part III, 709.
厚 Part III, 711.
厭 Part V, Lesson xxiii, Note 9.
厲 Part VI, Chapter xxviii, Note 4.

厶

去 Part III, 37.
參 Part III, 493, 576; Part VI, Chapter v, Note 31.

又

受 Part III, 394.
友 Part III, 637.
取 Part III, 761.
反 Part III, 850.
叔 Part V, Lesson xviii, Note 2.
叟 Part VII, 298.

口

咱 Part III, 17.
嗎 Part III, 23.
咯 Part III, 31.

知 Part III, 51.
叫 } Part III, 56.
呌
告 Part III, 108.
呢 Part III, 112.
可 Part III, 124; Part VI, Chapter xix, Notes 1, 5.
噢 } Part III, 160.
吃
喝 Part III, 161.
吹 Part III, 193.
同 Part III, 201.
嗜 Part III, 248.
各 Part III, 254.
單 Part III, 308.
吊 Part III, 322.
喚 Part III, 421.
嘴 Part III, 433.
嗓 Part III, 466.
君 Part III, 488.
名 Part III, 513.
否 Part III, 568.
向 Part III, 580.
句 Part III, 592.
吵 Part III, 593.
嚷 Part III, 594.
吉 Part III, 619.
喧 Part III, 649; Part VI, Chapter xxix, Note 13.
嗇 Part III, 684.
吞 Part III, 685.
和 Part III, 705.
商 Part III, 771.
喊 Part III, 779.
哈 Part III, 829.
古 Part III, 866.
唱 Part III, 892.
另 Part III, 904.
嚇 Part III, 944; Part V, Lesson xviii, Note 11.
喜 Part III, 968; Part V, Lesson xi, Note 1.
哄 Part III, 973; Part V, Lesson liv, Note 12.
司 Part III, 1012.
員 Part III, 1014.
吏 Part III, 1015.
命 Part III, 1034.
善 Part III, 1052.
合 Part III, 1064.
只 Part IV, Dialogue i, 22.

56 TZŬ ÊRH CHI.—COLLOQUIAL SERIES.

哎 Part IV, Dialogue ii, 20.
呀 Part IV, Dialogue ii, 20.
唉 Part IV, Dialogue ii, 44.
咨 Part IV, Dialogue ii, 44.
哪 Part IV, Dialogue ii, 54.
哥 Part IV, Dialogue iii, 8.
噯 Part IV, Dialogue iii, 54.
咳 Part IV, Dialogue iii, 65; Part V, Lesson xliii, Note 1.
喇 Part IV, Dialogue iii, 88.
哨 Part IV, Dialogue v, 65.
哼 Part IV, Dialogue vi, 52.
哭 Part IV, Dialogue vii, 98; Part V, Lesson xvi, Note 7.
嚼 Part IV, Dialogue viii, 79; Part VII, 30.
吩 Part IV, Dialogue viii, 87.
咐 Part IV, Dialogue viii, 87.
味 Part IV, Dialogue x, 2.
噔 Part IV, Dialogue x, 18.
台 Part V, Lesson i, Note 5.
咧 Part V, Lesson iii, Note 7.
品 Part V, Lesson iv, Note 6.
咒 Part V, Lesson iv, Note 10; Part VI, Chapter xv, Note 15.
嚴 Part V, Lesson ix, Note 5.
嗳 Part V, Lesson xvii, Note 3.
囊 Part V, Lesson xix, Note 1.
唐 Part V, Lesson xx, Note 7.
噶 Part V, Lesson xxii, Note 9.
器 Part V, Lesson xxvii, Note 10.
嘆 Part V, Lesson xxix, Note 9.
咬 Part V, Lesson xxx, Note 13.
嘆 Part V, Lesson xxx, Note 14.
嚧 Part V, Lesson xxx, Note 14.
唬 Part V, Lesson xxxv, Note 19.
合 Part V, Lesson xxxviii, Note 4.
嗜 Part V, Lesson xxxviii, Note 6.
嗜 Part V, Lesson xl, Note 7.
嚕 Part V, Lesson xl, Note 7; Part VII, 205.
嗽 Part V, Lesson xli, Note 4; Part VII, 56.
唧 Part V, Lesson xlii, Note 9.
叮 Part V, Lesson xlii, Note 9.
咕 Part V, Lesson xlii, Note 9.
咚 Part V, Lesson xlii, Note 9.
嗽 Part V, Lesson xliii, Note 1.
哀 Part V, Lesson xliii, Note 6.
啞 Part V, Lesson xliv, Note 3.
吧 Part V, Lesson xliv, Note 3.

吐 Part V, Lesson xlv, Note 10.
嘻 Part V, Lesson li, Note 9.
喪 Part V, Lesson lii, Note 4.
哩 Part V, Lesson lii, Note 7.
嗔 Part V, Lesson liv, Note 3.
咂 Part V, Lesson lxv, Note 7.
囑 Part V, Lesson lxvi, Note 1.
啐 Part V, Lesson lxvii, Note 8.
吾 Part V, Lesson lxviii, Note 2.
叨 Part V, Lesson lxxii, Note 5.
叩 Part V, Lesson lxxxv, Note 8.
吱 Part V, Lesson lxxxvii, Note 5.
呒 Part V, Lesson xciii, Note 9.
响 Part V, Lesson xcv, Note 9.
吸 Part V, Lesson xcviii, Note 2.
噴 Part VI, Chapter v, Note 8.
哇 Part VI, Chapter x, Note 2.
周 Part VI, Chapter xii, Note 1.
嚥 Part VI, Chapter xiii, Note 6.
喇 Part VI, Chapter xix, Note 2.
叭 Part VI, Chapter xix, Note 2.
嗡 Part VI, Chapter xix, Note 7.
呈 Part VI, Chapter xxi, Note 13.
史 Part VI, Chapter xxv, Note 6.
嘉 Part VI, Chapter xxv, Note 17.
嗆 Part VI, Chapter xxviii, Note 18.
哈 Part VI, Chapter xxix, Note 10.
呦 Part VI, Chapter xxix, Note 13.
鄉 Part VI, Chapter xxxi, Note 12.
嘰 Part VI, Chapter xxxi, Note 12.
喧 Part VI, Chapter xl, Note 6.
唉 Part VII, 39.
哄 Part VII, 55.
喘 Part VII, 69.
吼 Part VII, 101.
哏 Part VII, 154.
喵 Part VII, 218.
哞 Part VII, 219.
哺 Part VII, 229.
嚷 Part VII, 229.
嚷 Part VII, 230.
嗚 Part VII, 237.
嗒 Part VII, 262.
喧 Part VII, 409.
嘁 Part VII, 417.

口

四 Part III, 1.
回 Part III, 57.

國 Part III, 515.
困 Part III, 601.
團 Part III, 668.
圓 Part III, 935.
因 Part III, 956.
圖 Part IV, Dialogue iii, 96.
圍 Part V, Lesson xii, Note 6.
圈 Part V, Lesson xxiv, Note 12.
固 Part V, Lesson lxix, Note 1.
圖 Part V, Lesson lxxxiii, Note 9.
囫 Part VII, 207.
囵 Part VII, 207.

土

在 Part III, 28.
城 Part III, 48.
坐 Part III, 61.
地 Part III, 67.
塊 Part III, 119.
壞 Part III, 170.
葬 } Part III, 666.
甕
增 Part III, 687.
坑 Part III, 796.
墳 Part III, 804.
墓 Part III, 805.
塗 Part III, 967.
堂 Part III, 1011.
塾 Part IV, Dialogue ii, 28; Part VI, Chapter xxxix, Note 9.
均 Part IV, Dialogue ii, 53.
培 Part IV, Dialogue iv, 77.
塲 Part IV, Dialogue vi, 16; Part V, Lesson xvi, Note 15.
壓 Part IV, Dialogue vii, 93; Part V, Lesson x, Note 14.
堪 Part V, Lesson ix, Note 9; Part V, Lesson lxiv, Note 5.
坊 Part V, Lesson xx, Note 1.
壁 Part V, Lesson xxii, Note 13.
堆 Part V, Lesson xxiii, Note 5.
垣 Part V, Lesson xxxvi, Note 3.
墜 Part V, Lesson xl, Note 11; Part VII, 72.
塑 Part V, Lesson lv, Note 3.
塲 Part V, Lesson lxi, Note 5; Part VI, Chapter xxii, Note 5.
瑩 Part V, Lesson lxxv, Note 6.
埋 Part V, Lesson lxxv, Note 7; Part VI, Chapter xxxvii, Note 12.

APPENDIX II.—INDEX OF CHARACTERS. 57

堵 Part V, Lesson lxxxi, Note 2.
基 Part VI, Chapter v, Note 26.
坡 Part VI, Chapter xxi, Note 11.
壩 Part VI, Chapter xxix, Note 16.
塞 Part VI, Chapter xxxi, Note 16.
塵 Part VI, Chapter xxxix, Note 4.
埠 Part VII, 90.
垌 Part VII, 148.
埂 Part VII, 156.
坜 Part VII, 258.

士

壹 Part III, 183.
壽 Part III, 954.
墦 Part V, Lesson lxxxvi, Note 1.

夂

夏 Part III, 426.

夕

多 Part III, 7.
外 Part III, 48.
夜 Part III, 217.
夢 Part III, 603.
夠 Part III, 773.
夥 Part IV, Dialogue viii, 83.

大

天 Part III, 212.
夫 Part III, 239.
太 Part III, 264.
夾 Part III, 309.
奇 Part III, 454.
失 Part III, 574.
奪 Part III, 541.
套 Part III, 769.
奭 Part III, 823.
奲 } Part III, 931.
夯 }
報 Part III, 947.
奉 Part III, 990.
奈 Part IV, Dialogue iv, 49.
奬 Part V, Lesson iii, Note 1.
奢 Part V, Lesson xxviii, Note 1.
奠 Part V, Lesson xxxvi, Note 16.

奔 Part V, Lesson lxxi, Note 1.
奪 Part VI, Chapter xviii, Note 9.
奧 Part VI, Chapter xxviii, Note 22.
奘 Part VII, 70.

女

好 Part III, 8, 344.
奶 Part III, 363.
姓 Part III, 512.
妥 Part III, 572.
奴 Part III, 661.
嫌 Part III, 692.
媒 Part III, 715.
妒 Part III, 716.
娘 Part III, 812.
耍 Part III, 817.
嬈 Part III, 835.
如 Part III, 901.
委 Part III, 1013.
姐 Part IV, Dialogue iv, 59.
妹 Part IV, Dialogue iv, 59.
姑 Part IV, Dialogue iv, 62.
嫁 Part IV, Dialogue iv, 62.
孀 Part IV, Dialogue iv, 64.
婦 Part IV, Dialogue iv, 64.
始 Part IV, Dialogue vi, 9.
姪 Part IV, Dialogue vii, 46.
婆 Part IV, Dialogue vii, 76.
妨 Part IV, Dialogue viii, 55.
妻 Part V, Lesson xvii, Note 2.
妾 Part V, Lesson xvii, Note 2.
娶 Part V, Lesson xvii, Note 15.
媽 Part V, Lesson xxii, Note 11.
媳 Part V, Lesson lxi, Note 6.
婿 Part V, Lesson lxxxvi, Note 1.
嫂 Part V, Lesson lxxxvii, Note 4.
妞 Part V, Lesson lxxxvii, Note 7.
妙 Part VI, Chapter i, Note 9.
姨 Part VI, Chapter i, Note 13.
婚 Part VI, Chapter xxv, Note 9.
姻 Part VI, Chapter xxv, Note 9.
婢 Part VI, Chapter xxxi, Note 7.
娼 Part VII, 13.
妓 Part VII, 13.
姬 Part VII, 33.
奸 Part VII, 34.
嬰 Part VII, 182.
娃 Part VII, 396.

子

學 Part III, 96.
孫 Part III, 657.
孔 Part III, 868.
孩 Part III, 997.
存 Part III, 1023.
孟 Part IV, Dialogue vii, 6.
孝 Part V, Lesson iv, Note 2.
孤 Part V, Lesson xlv, Note 2.
孽 Part V, Lesson xciii, Note 8.

宀

家 Part III, 48.
字 Part III, 94.
寫 Part III, 101.
完 Part III, 123.
官 Part III, 127.
定 Part III, 215.
宜 Part III, 334.
客 Part III, 385.
害 Part III, 424.
實 Part III, 445.
察 Part III, 522.
安 Part III, 624.
寧 寗 } Part III, 625.
寬 Part III, 627.
寨 Part III, 683.
賓 Part III, 724.
宮 Part III, 838.
宗 Part III, 898.
寃 Part III, 940.
容 Part III, 963.
塞 Part III, 1050.
宥 Part IV, Dialogue ii, 46.
寡 Part IV, Dialogue v, 76.
究 Part IV, Dialogue vi, 21.
富 Part IV, Dialogue viii, 35; Part V, Lesson xi, Note 3.
寶 Part V, Lesson xviii, Note 5.
密 Part V, Lesson xxxvi, Note 4.
宰 Part V, Lesson lxxxviii, Note 2.
守 Part VI, Chapter vii, Note 13.
宦 Part VI, Chapter viii, Note 15.
寄 Part VI, Chapter viii, Note 17; Chapter xxxix, Note 14.
寨 Part VI, Chapter xvi, Note 5.

8

寸

尊 Part III, 495.
專 Part III, 573.
對 Part III, 682.
耐 Part III, 831.
封 Part IV, Dialogue v, 49.
射 Part V, Lesson x, Note 1.
導 Part V, Lesson xiv, Note 6.
尋 Part V, Lesson lxv, Note 6.

小

少 Part III, 7.
尖 Part III, 808.
尙 Part III, 877.
尠 Part V, Lesson xxxvii, Note 5.

尢

就 Part III, 214; Part V, Lesson iv, Note 3.

尸

屋 Part III, 46.
尺 Part III, 670.
層 Part III, 888.
屈 Part III, 976.
屢 Part III, 978.
屆 Part IV, Dialogue x, 21; Part V, Lesson xxiv, Note 15.
居 Part V, Lesson xix, Note 6.
屬 Part V, Lesson xxxii, Note 3.
尾 Part V, Lesson lvi, Note 3.
屁 Part V, Lesson lviii, Note 9.
展 Part VI, Chapter xxv, Note 13.
屠 Part VI, Chapter xxxvi, Note 11.
局 Part VI, Chapter xxxix, Note 13.
尻 Part VII, 151.
尿 Part VII, 237.
尿 Part VII, 237.

屮

屯 Part V, Lesson xxvii, Note 8.

山

峯 Part III, 806.
嶺 Part III, 807.
岔 Part IV, Dialogue vi, 1.
岱 Part IV, Dialogue viii, 63.
岸 Part V, Lesson xc, Note 7.
崩 Part V, Lesson xcv, Note 8.
崔 Part VI, Chapter i, Note 2.
岳 Part VI, Chapter xxxiv, Note 4.

巛

巡 Part III, 521.
州 Part IV, Dialogue viii, 9.

工

巧 Part III, 557.
差 Part III, 577, 1005.
左 Part V, Lesson v, Note 3.

己

巴 Part III, 462; Part V, Lesson i, Note 10.
巷 Part III, 799.

巾

帳 Part III, 146.
帽 Part III, 301.
賬 }
帳 } Part III, 339.
布 Part III, 406.
帶 Part III, 416.
幫 Part III, 640.
常 Part III, 688.
帚 Part III, 929.
幌 Part III, 937.
帖 Part III, 1022; Part V, Lesson vii, Note 7.
幕 Part IV, Dialogue ii, 59.
席 Part IV, Dialogue x, 12.
師 Part V, Lesson ii, Note 7.
希 Part V, Lesson lxv, Note 5.
幅 Part VI, Chapter x, Note 4.

干

平 Part III, 137.
年 Part III, 206.
幹 Part III, 582.
幸 Part V, Lesson xxiii, Note 12.

幺

幾 Part III, 7; Part V, Lesson lii, Note 3.

广

廚 Part III, 165.
店 Part III, 386.
底 Part III, 510.
廟 Part III, 873.
座 Part III, 874.
庫 Part III, 897.
廣 Part IV, Dialogue i, 20.
廠 Part IV, Dialogue vii, 72.
府 Part IV, Dialogue vii, 100.
庚 Part IV, Dialogue ix, 42.
度 Part V, Lesson vi, Note 8.
廂 Part V, Lesson xxxvii, Note 4.
廢 Part V, Lesson lv, Note 4.
庠 Part V, Lesson lxxxviii, Note 4.

廴

廷 Part III, 840.
建 Part III, 842.
延 Part V, Lesson xlix, Note 2.

廾

弄 Part III, 163.

弋

式 Part III, 1029.

弓

張 Part III, 115.
弱 Part III, 447.
弟 Part III, 659.
彀 Part III, 773.
強 Part III, 844.

APPENDIX II.—INDEX OF CHARACTERS. 59

引 Part V, Lesson xiv, Note 4.
彈 Part V, Lesson xc, Note 8.
弶 Part VI, Chapter i, Note 22.
彌 Part VI, Chapter viii, Note 3.
弦 Part VI, Chapter xxviii, Note 1.

彡

彩 Part III, 259; Part V, Lesson xiii, Note 2.
影 Part V, Lesson viii, Note 6.
形 Part V, Lesson xxxvii, Note 7.
彰 Part VI, Chapter v, Note 38.

彳

得 Part III, 30.
很 Part III, 35.
往 Part III, 40.
後 Part III, 83.
律 Part III, 517.
待 Part III, 710.
從 Part III, 782.
彼 Part III, 920.
彷 Part III, 948.
彿 Part III, 949.
役 Part III, 1016.
徐 Part IV, Dialogue iv, 4.
微 Part IV, Dialogue v, 32.
御 Part IV, Dialogue viii, 63.
徹 Part IV, Dialogue ix, 41.
徽 Part V, Lesson lviii, Note 10.
德 Part V, Lesson lxiv, Note 8.
徒 Part V, Lesson xci, Note 12.
徧 Part VI, Chapter viii, Note 19.
循 Part VI, Chapter xxxviii, Note 3.

心

愛 Part III, 52.
快 Part III, 80.
慢 Part III, 81.
念 Part III, 122.
懂 Part III, 135.
忘 Part III, 138.
情 Part III, 251.
怕 Part III, 263.
怪 Part III, 455.
怎 Part III, 456.
急 Part III, 531, 988.

性 Part III, 532.
懶 Part III, 549.
惰 Part III, 550.
恰 Part III, 556.
意 Part III, 559.
忙 Part III, 579.
您 Part III, 648.
想 Part III, 677.
慚 Part III, 717.
愧 Part III, 718.
憑 Part III, 722.
應 Part III, 726, 781.
必 Part III, 743.
感 Part III, 778.
恩 Part III, 861.
戀 Part III, 914.
悞 } Part III, 962.
誤
惜 Part III, 970.
悶 Part III, 984.
慌 Part III, 985.
志 Part III, 1037.
怨 Part III, 1048.
悔 Part III, 1051.
惡 Part III, 1053; Part IV, Dialogue iv, 53.
恨 Part IV, Dialogue ii, 43.
息 Part IV, Dialogue ii, 49.
恕 Part IV, Dialogue iii, 34.
忠 Part IV, Dialogue iii, 123.
慶 Part IV, Dialogue iv, 23.
恬 Part IV, Dialogue iv, 38; Part V, Lesson xlix, Note 7.
憐 Part IV, Dialogue iv, 70.
感 Part IV, Dialogue iv, 79.
恤 Part IV, Dialogue vi, 38.
恐 Part IV, Dialogue viii, 69.
慣 Part IV, Dialogue viii, 81.
愁 Part V, Lesson ii, Note 9.
懸 Part V, Lesson iii, Note 4.
念 Part V, Lesson viii, Note 21.
悅 Part V, Lesson xiv, Note 3.
慟 Part V, Lesson xvi, Note 7.
懷 Part V, Lesson xvii, Note 6.
忍 Part V, Lesson xvii, Note 11.
慕 Part V, Lesson xxiv, Note 3.
忽 Part V, Lesson xxxv, Note 8; Lesson xlv, Note 9.
悄 Part V, Lesson xxxv, Note 9.
愣 Part V, Lesson xxxvi, Note 7.

懇 Part V, Lesson xlvii, Note 7.
慘 Part V, Lesson l, Note 9.
慰 Part V, Lesson li, Note 5.
怒 Part V, Lesson liii, Note 7.
恥 Part V, Lesson lvii, Note 5.
恭 Part V, Lesson lviii, Note 1.
憂 Part V, Lesson lix, Note 5.
怯 Part V, Lesson lx, Note 1.
愿 Part V, Lesson lxx, Note 8.
悌 Part V, Lesson lxxx, Note 1.
悠 Part V, Lesson xci, Note 6.
慮 Part V, Lesson xci, Note 7.
恍 Part V, Lesson xcii, Note 5.
惚 Part V, Lesson xcii, Note 5.
恆 Part VI, Chapter i, Note 13.
患 Part VI, Chapter vii, Note 11.
忒 Part VI, Chapter viii, Note 4.
恬 Part VI, Chapter xi, Note 4.
慎 Part VI, Chapter xi, Note 4.
懷 Part VI, Chapter xii, Note 2.
慎 Part VI, Chapter xii, Note 4.
怔 Part VI, Chapter xvii, Note 4.
惠 Part VI, Chapter xxi, Note 2.
志 Part VI, Chapter xxii, Note 2; Part VII, 334.
誌 Part VI, Chapter xxii, Note 2; Part VII, 334.
忉 Part VI, Chapter xxiv, Note 1.
忖 Part VI, Chapter xxvii, Note 3; Part VII, 391.
悟 Part VI, Chapter xxix, Note 11.
恙 Part VI, Chapter xxx, Note 2.
慇 Part VI, Chapter xxx, Note 4.
懃 Part VI, Chapter xxx, Note 4.
慈 Part VI, Chapter xxxii, Note 3.
悲 Part VI, Chapter xxxiv, Note 11.

戈

我 Part III, 15.
戴 Part III, 299.
或 Part III, 924.
戚 Part IV, Dialogue ii, 32.
戒 Part V, Lesson viii, Note 3.
截 Part V, Lesson xviii, Note 13.
戰 Part V, Lesson lxx, Note 5.
威 Part VI, Chapter viii, Note 2.
戲 Part VI, Chapter xxxvii, Note 10.
戳 Part VII, 29.

戶

房 Part III, 46.
扁 Part III, 936.
所 Part III, 1002.
扇 Part V, Lesson xcii, Note 6.

手

拿 Part III, 36.
把 Part III, 86.
找 Part III, 93.
抄 Part III, 100.
拾 Part III, 188.
打 Part III, 241.
搁 Part III, 253.
換 Part III, 270.
摘 Part III, 298.
揮 Part III, 300.
撒 Part III, 368.
掌 Part III, 387.
指 Part III, 439.
抓 Part III, 448.
拉 Part III, 449.
拽 Part III, 450.
捐 Part III, 502.
搜 Part III, 523.
搶 Part III, 540.
扔 Part III, 552.
揩 Part III, 564.
摩 Part III, 565.
掄 Part III, 588.
捧 Part III, 608.
掉 Part III, 609.
擠 Part III, 610.
搭 Part III, 611.
接 Part III, 664.
挑 Part III, 675; Part V, Lesson xvii, Note 3.
拜 Part III, 725.
擦 Part III, 751.
挪 Part III, 767.
拴 Part III, 768.
掛 Part III, 889.
抽 Part III, 894.
拾 Part III, 917; Part V, Lesson xvii, Note 17.
擔 Part III, 926.
掃 Part III, 928.
撒 Part III, 998.

承 Part III, 1004.
抱 Part III, 1047.
搭 Part III, 1076.
撫 Part IV, Dialogue ii, 34.
提 Part IV, Dialogue ii, 36; Part VI, Chapter iv, 14.
拔 Part IV, Dialogue ii, 36.
挨 Part IV, Dialogue iii, 56.
折 Part IV, Dialogue iii, 119; Part V, Lesson xvii, Note 16.
擔 Part IV, Dialogue iii, 123.
托 Part IV, Dialogue iv, 37.
掙 Part IV, Dialogue iv, 53.
排 Part IV, Dialogue iv, 73.
抛 Part IV, Dialogue v, 9.
撞 Part IV, Dialogue v, 64.
損 Part IV, Dialogue v, 74.
扣 Part IV, Dialogue vi, 9.
掩 Part IV, Dialogue vi, 22.
揚 Part IV, Dialogue vi, 23; Part VI, Chapter iii, Note 7.
摸 Part IV, Dialogue vi, 35.
推 Part IV, Dialogue vi, 53.
搬 Part IV, Dialogue vii, 65; Part V, Lesson xxii, Note 6.
扭 Part IV, Dialogue vii, 88.
擺 Part IV, Dialogue viii, 17.
扯 Part IV, Dialogue viii, 81.
據 Part IV, Dialogue x, 6.
揖 Part IV, Dialogue x, 8.
擾 Part IV, Dialogue x, 8.
拘 Part IV, Dialogue x, 17.
撲 Part V, Lesson vi, Note 5.
操 Part V, Lesson vii, Note 6.
扎 Part V, Lesson viii, Note 12.
搪 Part V, Lesson viii, Note 13.
捆 Part V, Lesson ix, Note 7.
撥 Part V, Lesson x, Note 10.
拇 Part V, Lesson x, Note 11.
撩 Part V, Lesson xii, Note 2.
擬 Part V, Lesson xii, Note 3.
撈 Part V, Lesson xii, Note 10.
擬 Part V, Lesson xiii, Note 1.
攀 Part V, Lesson xiii, Note 10.
揑 Part V, Lesson xv, Note 1.
搡 Part V, Lesson xvi, Note 13.
擗 Part V, Lesson xviii, Note 8.
拐 Part V, Lesson xxii, Note 7.
攔 Part V, Lesson xxvi, Note 10.
挓 Part V, Lesson xxviii, Note 13.

捲 Part V, Lesson xxx, Note 12.
擒 Part V, Lesson xxxi, Note 4.
扮 Part V, Lesson xxxiv, Note 13.
揩 Part V, Lesson xxxv, Note 1.
擠 Part V, Lesson xxxix, Note 5.
捻 Part V, Lesson xl, Note 2. See also Errata, p. 523.
攀 Part V, Lesson liii, Note 9.
拘 Part V, Lesson liv, Note 6.
招 Part V, Lesson lv, Note 6.
扶 Part V, Lesson lvi, Note 7.
探 Part V, Lesson lx, Note 6.
揭 Part V, Lesson lxiii, Note 4.
揉 Part V, Lesson lxiii, Note 5.
挫 Part V, Lesson lxiii, Note 5.
擡 Part V, Lesson lxv, Note 11.
抖 Part V, Lesson lxx, Note 6.
披 Part V, Lesson lxx, Note 7.
攢 Part V, Lesson lxx, Note 16.
挺 Part V, Lesson lxxvii, 1.
持 Part V, Lesson lxxx, Note 9.
攪 Part V, Lesson lxxxii, Note 5.
擎 Part V, Lesson lxxxiii, Note 4.
挽 Part V, Lesson lxxxiii, Note 5.
撩 Part V, Lesson lxxxiii, Note 8; Part VII, 56.
按 Part V, Lesson lxxxv, Note 9.
招 Part V, Lesson lxxxvi, Note 10.
撑 Part V, Lesson xci, Note 3.
攣 Part V, Lesson xcviii, Note 3.
拳 Part VI, Chapter i, Note 23.
搖 Part VI, Chapter ii, Note 8.
提 Part VI, Chapter ii, Note 8.
抬 Part VI, Chapter iii, Note 1.
摑 Part VI, Chapter v, Note 9.
攤 Part VI, Chapter v, Note 15.
搖 Part VI, Chapter v, Note 24.
揹 Part VI, Chapter v, Note 29; Part VII, 155.
投 Part VI, Chapter vii, Note 12.
擋 Part VI, Chapter viii, Note 1.
插 Part VI, Chapter viii, Note 6.
捎 Part VI, Chapter xi, Note 6.
抽 Part VI, Chapter xii, Note 3.
撇 Part VI, Chapter xiv, Note 5.
掏 Part VI, Chapter xv, Note 2.
拱 Part VI, Chapter xv, Note 8.
攤 Part VI, Chapter xix, Note 3.
擋 Part VI, Chapter xix, Note 4.
播 Part VI, Chapter xix, Note 4.

APPENDIX II.—INDEX OF CHARACTERS.

掀 Part VI, Chapter xxiv, Note 5.	斗	早 Part IV, Dialogue viii, 5.
攪 Part VI, Chapter xxv, Note 14.	斝 Part III, 774.	旺 Part V, Lesson xiv, Note 15.
抵 Part VI, Chapter xxvi, Note 1.	斜 Part V, Lesson xxx, Note 8.	晦 Part V, Lesson xvi, Note 14.
擾 Part VI, Chapter xxviii, Note 20; Chapter xxxv, Note 3.		晃 Part V, Lesson xxix, Note 2.
援 Part VI, Chapter xxx, Note 6.	斤	暗 Part V, Lesson xxxv, Note 14.
拖 Part VI, Chapter xxxiii, Note 6.	斬 Part III, 484.	暈 Part V, Lesson xlv, Note 7.
扛 Part VI, Chapter xxxvi, Note 13.	薪 Part III, 739.	昏 Part V, Lesson li, Note 3.
摧 Part VI, Chapter xxxviii, Note 7.	斷 Part V, Lesson vii, Note 1.	旦 Part V, Lesson lxv, Note 9.
拆 Part VI, Chapter xxxix, Note 15.	斧 Part V, Lesson viii, Note 10; Part VI, Chapter xv, Note 11.	曠 Part V, Lesson xc, Note 1.
撰 Part VI, Chapter xl, Note 1.	斯 Part VI, Chapter xxiv, Note 4.	暑 Part V, Lesson xciii, Note 7.
授 Part VI, Chapter xl, Note 2.		昭 Part VI, Chapter v, Note 38.
搵 Part VII, 80.	方	喧 Part VI, Chapter xxxii, Note 8.
摳 Part VII, 161.	於 Part III, 343.	昔 Part VI, Chapter xxxvii, Note 4.
摟 Part VII, 199.	旁 Part III, 651.	
捫 Part VII, 215.	族 Part V, Lesson v, Note 5.	曰
搛 Part VII, 215.	旗 Part V, Lesson vii, Note 9.	書 Part III, 92.
擾 Part VII, 230.	旅 Part V, Lesson lxxxvi, Note 11.	會 Part III, 129.
捌 Part VII, 257. See also Errata, p. 523.	施 Part VI, Chapter viii, Note 22.	更 Part III, 238, 570, 883.
搞 Part VII, 331.	旋 Part VI, Chapter xii, Note 1.	最 Part III, 280.
揉 Part VII, 345.		曲 Part III, 893.
掰 Errata, p. 523.	无	曾 Part V, Lesson lii, Note 1.
	既 Part IV, Dialogue ii, 44.	
戈		月
敷 Part III, 7.	日	有 Part III, 8.
歛 Part III, 90.	是 Part III, 29.	胡 Part III, 586.
收 Part III, 187.	明 Part III, 132.	朋 Part III, 636.
散 Part III, 546.	時 Part III, 207.	服 Part III, 826.
放 Part III, 553.	暖 Part III, 209.	朝 Part III, 839.
改 Part III, 571; Part V, Lesson xi, Note 10.	昨 Part III, 211.	望 Part III, 908.
赦 Part III, 862.	晝 Part III, 216.	朝 Part V, Lesson xci, Note 10.
故 Part III, 959.	晴 Part III, 218.	期 Part VI, Chapter viii, Note 20.
敞 Part IV, Dialogue i, 2.	早 Part III, 244.	
敢 Part IV, Dialogue iii, 48.	晚 Part III, 245.	木
敎 Part IV, Dialogue v, 76; Part VII, 338.	晌 Part III, 246.	東 Part III, 35.
敬 Part IV, Dialogue x, 17; Part V, Lesson xvi, Note 4.	春 Part III, 426.	樓 Part III, 65.
整 Part V, Lesson viii, Note 8.	暴 Part III, 529.	桌 Part III, 148.
敗 Part V, Lesson viii, Note 14.	普 Part III, 534.	椅 Part III, 149.
救 Part V, Lesson xiv, Note 9.	曇 Part III, 686.	欖 Part III, 180.
敏 Part V, Lesson xv, Note 1.	曬晒 } Part III, 701.	條 Part III, 181.
敘 Part V, Lesson xxii, Note 3.	易 Part III, 964.	樣 Part III, 255.
敲 Part V, Lesson xxii, Note 10.	星 Part III, 1001.	梳 Part III, 282.
效 Part V, Lesson lii, Note 10.	晰 Part IV, Dialogue iii, 91.	棉 Part III, 311.
敵 Part VI, Chapter xxv, Note 7.	景 Part IV, Dialogue iv, 76.	桿 Part III, 325.
		柴 Part III, 348.
文		果 Part III, 364.
		櫃 Part III, 388.
文 Part III, 497.		李 Part III, 400.

梁 Part III, 430.
梁 Part III, 475.
棱楞 } Part III, 480.
棍 Part III, 551.
槍 Part III, 554.
極 Part III, 602.
業 Part III, 634.
根 Part III, 644.
桑 Part III, 693.
樹 Part III, 694.
林 Part III, 695.
森 Part III, 697.
某 Part III, 703.
染 Part III, 732.
末 Part III, 783.
橋 Part III, 794.
村 Part III, 803.
禁 Part III, 846.
楷 Part III, 881.
柱 Part III, 941; Part V, Lesson vii, Note 4.
樂 Part III, 986.
隸 Part III, 1018.
案 Part III, 1027.
橫 Part III, 1072.
棚 Part III, 1075.
機 Part IV, Dialogue ii, 48.
架 Part IV, Dialogue iii, 79; Part V, Lesson viii, Note 11.
材 Part IV, Dialogue iii, 123; Dialogue v, 26.
未 Part IV, Dialogue iv, 60; Dialogue x, 3.
栽 Part IV, Dialogue iv, 77.
查 Part IV, Dialogue v, 15.
葉 Part IV, Dialogue v, 25.
檯 Part IV, Dialogue v, 36.
概 Part IV, Dialogue vi, 25.
楊 Part IV, Dialogue viii, 23.
格 Part IV, Dialogue viii, 29.
榮 Part IV, Dialogue ix, 46.
模 Part V, Lesson ii, Note 1.
楚 Part V, Lesson iii, Note 2.
耀 Part V, Lesson vii, Note 6.
校 Part V, Lesson xii, Note 4.
束 Part V, Lesson xv, Note 7.
榜 Part V, Lesson xviii, Note 15.
棠 Part V, Lesson xxx, Note 7.
槽 Part V, Lesson xxxii, Note 9.

檔 Part V, Lesson xl, Note 1.
槭 Part V, Lesson xliii, Note 4.
枕 Part V, Lesson xlviii, Note 4.
檻 Part V, Lesson lvi, Note 6.
枝 Part V, Lesson lxviii, Note 2.
梧 Part V, Lesson lxviii, Note 2.
柵 Part V, Lesson lxxiv, Note 3.
欄 Part V, Lesson lxxiv, Note 3.
杆 Part V, Lesson lxxiv, Note 3.
棄 Part V, Lesson lxxxv, Note 7; Part VI, Chapter iv, Note 7.
桃 Part V, Lesson xc, Note 4.
柳 Part V, Lesson xc, Note 5.
棲 Part V, Lesson xciv, Note 7.
棋 Part V, Lesson xcvii, Note 10.
杜 Part VI, Chapter vii, Note 10.
樸 Part VI, Chapter ix, Note 3.
榴 Part VI, Chapter xiv, Note 6.
板 Part VI, Chapter xxv, Note 4.
檢 Part VI, Chapter xxvii, Note 5.
权 Part VI, Chapter xxvii, Note 8.
標 Part VI, Chapter xxxi, Note 18.
檀 Part VI, Chapter xxxiv, Note 7.
樱 Part VI, Chapter xxxv, Note 6.
桅 Part VI, Chapter xxxv, Note 7.
柁 Part VI, Chapter xxxv, Note 9.
椿 Part VI, Chapter xxxvi, Note 3.
柯 Part VI, Chapter xxxvi, Note 7.
杠 Part VII, 148.
檁 Part VII, 194.
梯 Part VII, 339.

欠

歇 Part III, 397.
歉 Part III, 969.
欺 Part III, 972.
欽 Part IV, Dialogue v, 66.
飲 Part IV, Dialogue ii, Note 5.
欷 Part VI, Chapter xxvi, Note 10.
歌 Part VII, 13.

止

步 Part III, 69.
正 Part III, 103.
武 Part III, 498.
此 Part III, 921.
歲 Part III, 952.
歸 Part IV, Dialogue ii, 50.
歪 Part V, Lesson xxx, Note 17.

歹

殘 Part IV, Dialogue iv, 75.
殯 Part V, Lesson lxxvi, Note 5.
殃 Part VI, Chapter v, Note 25.

殳

殺 Part III, 505.
毆 Part IV, Dialogue iii, 103.
段 Part IV, Dialogue viii, 21.
殿 Part VI, Chapter xv, Note 9.

毋

每 Part III, 240.
母 Part III, 652.
毒 Part V, Lesson xlvii, Note 10.

毛

氈毡 } Part III, 404.
毯 Part III, 405.
毫 Part V, Lesson xxxix, Note 8.

气

氣 Part III, 232.

氏

民 Part III, 128.

水

沒 Part III, 33.
滅 Part III, 194.
滿 Part III, 200.
涼 Part III, 229.
淨 Part III, 272.
洗 Part III, 275.
澡 Part III, 276.
温 Part III, 281.
汗 Part III, 306.
油 Part III, 353.
湯 Part III, 361.
河 Part III, 377.
海 Part III, 378.
深 Part III, 380.
淺 Part III, 381.

APPENDIX II.—INDEX OF CHARACTERS. 63

波	Part III, 479.	
治	Part III, 527.	
混	Part III, 547; Part V, Lesson xxiv, Note 6.	
法	Part III, 584.	
濕涇 }	Part III, 700.	
淡	Part III, 738.	
潤	Part III, 746.	
永	Part III, 764.	
湊	Part III, 766.	
灣	Part III, 786.	
江	Part III, 787.	
湖	Part III, 788; Part IV, Dialogue v, 26.	
洸	Part III, 789.	
泯	Part III, 790.	
瀾	Part III, 791.	
浮	Part III, 793.	
濃	Part III, 884.	
派	Part III, 905.	
渴	Part III, 911.	
灑洒 }	Part III, 927.	
求	Part III, 991.	
活	Part III, 1039.	
準	Part III, 1078.	
津	Part IV, Dialogue i, 2.	
洋	Part IV, Dialogue i, 12.	
漆	Part IV, Dialogue i, 12.	
沙	Part IV, Dialogue iii, 106.	
洌	Part IV, Dialogue iv, 32.	
激	Part IV, Dialogue iv, 79; Part VI, Chapter xxi, 5.	
涉	Part IV, Dialogue vi, 14.	
渡	Part IV, Dialogue viii, 17.	
浦	Part IV, Dialogue viii, 21.	
漢	Part IV, Dialogue ix, 18; Part V, Lesson xviii, Note 9.	
泥	Part IV, Dialogue x, 17.	
洲	Part V, Lesson i, Note 1.	
清	Part V, Lesson iii, Note 2.	
沽	Part V, Lesson vi, Note 6.	
滋	Part V, Lesson viii, Note 18.	
漏	Part V, Lesson ix, Note 2.	
滑	Part V, Lesson ix, Note 4.	
潘	Part V, Lesson xvii, Note 9.	
淵	Part V, Lesson xix, Note 4.	
沾	Part V, Lesson xx, Note 8.	
溜	Part V, Lesson xxii, Note 8.	

演	Part V, Lesson xxvii, Note 3.	
渾	Part V, Lesson xxxii, Note 4.	
潦	Part V, Lesson xxxii, Note 6.	
滅	Part V, Lesson xxxii, Note 10.	
濟	Part V, Lesson xxxiv, Note 4.	
添	Part V, Lesson xxxiv, Note 5.	
漚	Part V, Lesson xxxviii, Note 10.	
淚	Part V, Lesson xli, Note 6.	
汪	Part V, Lesson xli, Note 7.	
淘	Part V, Lesson xlv, Note 4; Part VI, Chapter xxxvii, Note 3.	
涕	Part V, Lesson xlv, Note 8.	
沉	Part V, Lesson li, Note 2.	
漸	Part V, Lesson lv, Note 8.	
游	Part V, Lesson lxv, Note 4.	
洩	Part V, Lesson lxvi, Note 2.	
渣	Part V, Lesson lxvii, Note 1.	
沫	Part V, Lesson lxvii, Note 9.	
決	Part V, Lesson lxix, Note 6.	
泡	Part V, Lesson lxxxviii, Note 6.	
沿	Part V, Lesson xc, Note 3.	
浩	Part V, Lesson xci, Note 4.	
澜	Part V, Lesson xciv, Note 3.	
漫	Part V, Lesson xciv, Note 4.	
淋	Part V, Lesson xcv, Note 13.	
污	Part V, Lesson c, Note 7.	
淹	Part VI, Chapter iii, Note 16.	
滾	Part VI, Chapter iv, Note 5.	
湛	Part VI, Chapter iv, Note 12.	
灌	Part VI, Chapter v, Note 20.	
濛	Part VI, Chapter v, Note 23.	
洛	Part VI, Chapter vii, Note 1.	
涵	Part VI, Chapter vii, Note 18.	
澁	Part VI, Chapter xiv, Note 9.	
沐	Part VI, Chapter xv, Note 7.	
浴	Part VI, Chapter xv, Note 7.	
泉	Part VI, Chapter xxviii, Note 12.	
瀉	Part VI, Chapter xxviii, Note 14.	
涎	Part VI, Chapter xxviii, Note 15.	
池	Part VI, Chapter xxix, Note 9.	
消	Part VI, Chapter xxxii, Note 1.	
漩	Part VI, Chapter xxxv, Note 2.	
濺	Part VI, Chapter xxxvi, Note 6.	
洞	Part VI, Chapter xl, Note 7.	
泮	Part VII, 6.	
渠	Part VII, 53.	
永	Part VII, 109.	
汎	Part VII, 125.	
沿	Part VII, 410.	

火

燋	Part III, 107.	
炕	Part III, 141.	
燈	Part III, 150.	
煎	Part III, 166; Part VII, 15.	
炒	Part III, 167.	
煮	Part III, 168.	
燒	Part III, 169.	
點	Part III, 192.	
爐	Part III, 197.	
熱	Part III, 227.	
煤	Part III, 346.	
炭	Part III, 347.	
蒸	Part III, 366.	
無	Part III, 422.	
然	Part III, 561.	
煩	Part III, 987.	
照	Part III, 1028.	
烟	Part IV, Dialogue v, 21.	
灰	Part V, Lesson ii, Note 5.	
焉	Part V, Lesson xvi, Note 18.	
烙	Part V, Lesson xxxvi, Note 6.	
爛	Part V, Lesson xxxvi, Note 5.	
炮	Part V, Lesson xlv, Note 5.	
燥	Part V, Lesson xlv, Note 5.	
熬	Part V, Lesson xlviii, Note 1.	
烤	Part V, Lesson xlviii, Note 8.	
烘	Part V, Lesson l, Note 2.	
災	Part V, Lesson li, Note 10.	
燎	Part V, Lesson liv, Note 2; Part VI, Chapter ix, Note 4.	
煞	Part V, Lesson lxxxvi, Note 5.	
燙	Part V, Lesson xciii, Note 4.	
爐	Part V, Lesson xcvii, Note 6.	
燉	Part VI, Chapter v, Note 7.	
烙	Part VI, Chapter v, Note 9.	
焦	Part VI, Chapter viii, Note 9.	
煳	Part VI, Chapter viii, Note 9.	
薰	Part VI, Chapter ix, Note 4; Part VII, 125.	
耿	Part VI, Chapter x, Note 1.	
爨	Part VI, Chapter xvii, Note 3.	
營	Part VI, Chapter xxiii, Note 8.	
烈	Part VI, Chapter xxviii, Note 7.	
熊	Part VI, Chapter xxxvi, Note 16.	

爪
- 爵 Part III, 491.
- 爲 Part III, 848, 957.
- 爭 Part III, 856.
- 爬 Part VI, Chapter xiii, Note 9.

父
- 爺 Part III, 811.
- 爹 Part VII, 209.

爿
- 牀 Part III, 145.
- 牆 Part III, 887.
- 壯 Part IV, Dialogue vi, 36.

片
- 牕 Part III, 64.
- 牖 Part V, Lesson xxxviii, Note 12.

牛
- 牲 Part III, 411.
- 特 Part III, 558.
- 牽 Part V, Lesson xxxiii, Note 2.
- 物 Part V, Lesson xxxv, Note 4.

犬
- 獸 Part III, 820.
- 犯 Part III, 851.
- 狗 Part III, 933.
- 狂 Part IV, Dialogue v, 20.
- 猶 Part IV, Dialogue x, 1.
- 獨 Part V, Lesson vii, Note 10.
- 獻 Part V, Lesson xv, Note 4.
- 猴 Part V, Lesson xxx, Note 16.
- 猜 Part V, Lesson xxxiv, Note 3.
- 猛 Part V, Lesson xxxv, Note 15.
- 獄 Part V, Lesson lxxx, Note 5.
- 猪 Part V, Lesson xciv, Note 6.
- 獅 Part VI, Chapter xxxvi, Note 10.
- 狐 Part VI, Chapter xxxix, Note 6.
- 狸 Part VI, Chapter xxxix, Note 6.
- 猫 Part VI, Chapter xxxix, Note 6.

玄
- 率 Part III, 882.

玉
- 班 Part III, 414.
- 理 Part III, 528.
- 瑞 Part III, 622.
- 現 Part III, 645.
- 玻 Part III, 747.
- 璃 Part III, 748.
- 玩 Part III, 816.
- 王 Part IV, Dialogue ii, 32; Part V, Lesson xxi, Note 4.
- 琉 Part IV, Dialogue vii, 72.
- 珍 Part V, Lesson xvi, Note 10.
- 珠 Part V, Lesson xxxviii, Note 2.
- 瑣 Part V, Lesson lxxxii, Note 1.
- 琴 Part V, Lesson c, Note 1.
- 琶 Part V, Lesson c, Note 1.
- 玷 Part V, Lesson c, Note 5.
- 珏 Part VI, Chapter i, Note 2.
- 環 Part VI, Chapter ii, Note 6.
- 珙 Part VI, Chapter vii, Note 2.
- 琴 Part VI, Chapter vii, Note 8.
- 玫 Part VI, Chapter viii, Note 7.
- 瑰 Part VI, Chapter viii, Note 7.
- 珮 Part VI, Chapter xxviii, Note 2.

瓜
- 瓢 Part VII, 129.

瓦
- 瓶 Part III, 185.
- 瓷 Part VI, Chapter xxv, Note 3.
- 甕 Part VII, 402.

甘
- 甚 Part III, 23.
- 甜 Part VI, Chapter xiv, Note 7.

生
- 生 Part III, 96.
- 產 Part III, 633.
- 甦 Part V, Lesson li, Note 4.
- 甥 Part VI, Chapter i, Note 13.

田
- 當 Part III, 342.
- 甲 Part III, 440.
- 留 Part III, 642.
- 畫 Part III, 736.
- 男 Part III, 810.
- 異 Part IV, Dialogue i, 30; Part V, Lesson xvii, Note 7.
- 申 Part IV, Dialogue ix, 54.
- 畧 Part V, Lesson x, Note 13.
- 由 Part V, Lesson xvi, Note 16.
- 畏 Part V, Lesson lvi, Note 3.
- 暢 Part V, Lesson xci, Note 2; Part VI, Chapter v, Note 12.
- 畜 Part V, Lesson xcix, Note 1.
- 畝 Part VI, Chapter iv, Note 3.
- 番 Part VI, Chapter xi, Note 5.
- 畢 Part VI, Chapter xxxv, Note 2.

疋
- 疑 Part III, 777.
- 疏 Part V, Lesson lxvii, Note 3.

疒
- 病 Part III, 452.
- 疼 Part III, 453; Part VI, Chapter v, Note 34.
- 疾 Part IV, Dialogue iv, 75.
- 疲 Part V, Lesson xxv, Note 1.
- 癇 Part V, Lesson xxvii, Note 9; Part VII, 57.
- 癰 Part V, Lesson xliii, Note 7.
- 痘 Part V, Lesson xliv, Note 3.
- 瘦 Part V, Lesson xlv, Note 3.
- 痛 Part V, Lesson lxvii, Note 6.
- 瘠 Part V, Lesson lxxiii, Note 5.
- 疤 Part V, Lesson lxxiii, Note 5.
- 癆 Part V, Lesson lxxiii, Note 5.
- 癥 Part VI, Chapter iii, Note 8.
- 癰 Part VI, Chapter v, Note 33.
- 瘓 Part VI, Chapter v, Note 33.
- 疤 Part VI, Chapter xxv, Note 11.
- 瘌 Part VI, Chapter xxv, Note 11.
- 癢 Part VI, Chapter xxvi, Note 5.
- 瘋 Part VI, Chapter xxxvii, Note 13.
- 痰 Part VII, 69.

APPENDIX II.—INDEX OF CHARACTERS.

癶

發 Part III, 993.
登 Part V, Lesson lxi, Note 1.

白

百 Part III, 4.
的 Part III, 19.
皇 Part III, 837.
皂 Part III, 1017.
督 Part V, Lesson xci, Note 8.

皿

盞 Part III, 151.
盃 Part III, 155.
盅 Part III, 156.
盤 Part III, 190.
盆 Part III, 278.
鹽 Part III, 357.
盔 Part III, 1038.
盈 Part III, 1068.
壺 Part IV, Dialogue iv, 79.
盛 Part IV, Dialogue x, 20; Part V, Lesson lxxii, Note 13.
溢 Part V, Lesson lxxxvi, Note 4.
盜 Part VI, Chapter xvi, Note 1.
盒 Part VI, Chapter xxxiv, Note 8.
盃 Part VII, 25.
盟 Part VII, 216.

目

看 Part III, 91.
瞿 Part III, 102.
直 Part III, 374.
眼 Part III, 431.
睛 Part III, 432.
眉 Part III, 458.
相 Part III, 606, 639; Part V, Lesson xix, Note 9.
睡 Part III, 679.
冒 Part III, 822.
盼 Part III, 907.
眾 Part III, 910.
省 Part IV, Dialogue i, 19.
瞪 Part V, Lesson vi, Note 3.
瞎 Part V, Lesson viii, Note 7.
瞵 Part V, Lesson xiii, Note 4.
瞞 Part V, Lesson xv, Note 3.

眨 Part V, Lesson xvi, Note 21.
瞬 Part V, Lesson xxxv, Note 3.
睿 Part VI, Chapter viii, Note 16; Part VII, 54.
眦 Part VI, Chapter xxvi, Note 9; Part VII, 359.
睹 Part VI, Chapter xxxi, Note 14.
眛 Part VII, 217.
瞳 Part VII, 217.
瞰 Part VII, 289.

矢

短 Part III, 256.
矩 Part IV, Dialogue x, 8.
矬 Part VII, 381.

石

碗 Part III, 158.
破 Part III, 186.
碟 Part III, 191.
碎 Part III, 203.
砍 Part III, 304.
石 Part III, 350.
碓礙礑 } Part III, 918.
砌 Part III, 930.
磋 Part IV, Dialogue iii, 54.
硯 Part V, Lesson xxii, Note 14.
磴 Part V, Lesson lxiii, Note 11.
碧 Part V, Lesson xc, Note 6.
碌 Part VI, Chapter vii, Note 16.
碌 Part VI, Chapter xi, Note 3.
磨 Part VI, Chapter xxv, Note 15.
碓 Part VI, Chapter xxvii, Note 9.
砢 Part VII, 20.
磣 Part VII, 20.
礦 Part VII, 176.
砰 Part VII, 282.
磅 Part VII, 282.

示

票 Part III, 323.
神 Part III, 575; Part V, Lesson viii, Note 15.
祥 Part III, 621.
祖 Part III, 654.
示 Part III, 890.
禍 Part III, 1032.

福 Part III, 1033.
禮 Part IV, Dialogue x, 1.
禱 Part V, Lesson xxxvi, Note 15.
祭 Part V, Lesson xxxvi, Note 16.
祟 Part V, Lesson xxxvii, Note 6.

禾

和 Part III, 210.
秤 Part III, 326.
稱 Part III, 327.
秋 Part III, 426.
程 Part III, 519.
種 Part III, 525.
耕 Part III, 536.
私 Part III, 980.
稟 Part III, 1021.
稿 Part III, 1024.
秀 Part IV, Dialogue ix, 40.
穯 Part V, Lesson xiv, Note 10.
稼 Part V, Lesson xviii, Note 9.
稠 Part V, Lesson xxx, Note 10.
穩 Part V, Lesson xxxiii, Note 3.
稍 Part V, Lesson xxxiv, Note 9.
稀 Part V, Lesson lxviii, Note 3.
穀 Part V, Lesson lxxvii, Note 3.
禿 Part VI, Chapter v, Note 13.
租 Part VI, Chapter ix, Note 1.
科 Part VI, Chapter xxviii, Note 6.
稜 Part VII, 187.

穴

空 Part III, 199.
穿 Part III, 290.
竄 Part III, 545.
窄 Part III, 613.
窮 Part III, 631.
窘 Part III, 632.
窩 Part IV, Dialogue iii, 106; Part V, Lesson xxxv, Note 13.
竊 Part IV, Dialogue iv, 52.
究 Part IV, Dialogue x, 2.
竈 Part IV, Dialogue x, 18.
寫 Part V, Lesson xxxii, Note 2.
窟 Part V, Lesson xl, Note 3.
窿 Part V, Lesson xl, Note 3.
突 Part V, Lesson xcv, Note 11.
窟 Part VI, Chapter xxv, Note 2.
窪 Part VI, Chapter xxix, Note 15.

立

站 Part III, 59; Part VI, Chapter xxxiii, Note 5.
端 Part III, 367.
竳 Part III, 516.
竞 Part IV, Dialogue iv, 51; Part V, Lesson iii, Note 6.
競 Part V, Lesson lxii, Note 7.
童 Part VI, Chapter vii, Note 8.

竹

第 Part III, 6.
箇 Part III, 8.
筆 Part III, 116.
管 Part III, 117.
籠 Part III, 198; Part V, Lesson xxiv, Note 16.
算 Part III, 202.
箱 Part III, 401.
節 Part III, 467.
笑 Part III, 598.
等 Part III, 759.
答 Part III, 780.
笨 Part III, 819.
簧 Part III, 950.
簡 Part IV, Dialogue vi, 50; Part V, Lesson ii, Note 3.
筷 Part IV, Dialogue x, 18.
箭 Part V, Lesson x, Note 2.
簾 Part V, Lesson xcvii, Note 7.
篆 Part VI, Chapter i, Note 12.
篷 Part VI, Chapter ii, Note 4.
筋 Part VI, Chapter iv, Note 5.
篩 Part VI, Chapter xiv, Note 4.
策 Part VI, Chapter xix, Note 12.
竿 Part VI, Chapter xxix, Note 8.
筐 Part VI, Chapter xxxvi, Note 12.
籃 Part VI, Chapter xxxviii, Note 7.
簷 Part VI, Chapter xxxix, Note 2.
簧 Part VII, 199.
筱 Part VII, 283.
笑 Part VII, 283.
筐 Part VII, 284.
籮 Part VII, 284.

米

糖 Part III, 356.
粗 Part III, 358.
糊 Part III, 730.
料 Part III, 749.
糢 Part IV, Dialogue iv, 40.
精 Part IV, Dialogue iv, 56.
粧 Part V, Lesson xi, Note 5.
粒 Part V, Lesson xxviii, Note 5.
糠 Part V, Lesson xxx, Note 9.
糟 Part V, Lesson xlvii, Note 12.
糞 Part VI, Chapter iv, Note 6.
糕 Part VI, Chapter v, Note 22.
粉 Part VI, Chapter xxviii, Note 7.
粥 Part VI, Chapter xxix, Note 4.
糢 Part VII, 45.

糸

給 Part III, 87.
紙 Part III, 114.
線 Part III, 286.
縫 Part III, 287; Part V, Lesson v, Note 2.
細 Part III, 359.
繞 Part III, 375.
累 Part III, 395; Part V, Lesson xvii, Note 18.
辮 Part III, 429.
結 Part III, 444.
級 Part III, 486.
索 Part III, 508.
總 Part III, 537.
約 Part III, 566.
綽 Part III, 628.
絲 Part III, 667.
絨 Part III, 669.
綠 Part III, 698.
素 Part III, 707.
絕 Part III, 720.
紅 Part III, 734.
紗 Part III, 741.
繩 Part III, 757.
經 Part III, 880.
紀 Part III, 953.
綠 Part III, 958.
緊 Part III, 1059.
納 Part IV, Dialogue ii, 1; Part VI, Chapter xiii, Note 2.
繃 Part IV, Dialogue iv, 54.
終 Part IV, Dialogue vi, 9; Part V, Lesson xvi, Note 19.
編 Part IV, Dialogue vi, 23.
縣 Part IV, Dialogue ix, 47.
緒 Part IV, Dialogue ix, 51.
繳 Part IV, Dialogue x, 7.
繙 Part V, Lesson i, Note 3.
練 Part V, Lesson iii, Note 3.
網 Part V, Lesson vii, Note 3.
絆 Part V, Lesson xxii, Note 4.
絡 Part V, Lesson xxiv, Note 16.
纏 Part V, Lesson xxvi, Note 6.
繹 Part V, Lesson xxviii, Note 4.
紫 Part V, Lesson xxx, Note 7.
繫 Part V, Lesson xxxiii, Note 7; Part VI, Chapter xxxv, Note 12.
緞 Part V, Lesson xxxiv, Note 8.
綢 Part V, Lesson liii, Note 5.
綱 Part V, Lesson lvii, Note 8.
綻 Part V, Lesson lviii, Note 8; Part VI, Chapter iv, Note 9.
縱 Part V, Lesson lxvi, Note 5; Part VI, Chapter v, Note 35.
絮 Part V, Lesson lxxii, Note 4.
紛 Part V, Lesson xcvii, Note 9.
絃 Part V, Lesson c, Note 2.
縑 Part VI, Chapter iv, Note 9.
繡 Part VI, Chapter vi, Note 5.
紋 Part VI, Chapter xv, Note 3.
繼 Part VI, Chapter xxxi, Note 1.
緻 Part VI, Chapter xxxi, Note 18.
繩 Part VI, Chapter xxxiv, Note 9.
纜 Part VI, Chapter xxxv, Note 5.
絹 Part VI, Chapter xxxix, Note 8.

缶

缺 Part III, 500.
罇 Part V, Lesson xxvii, Note 12.
缸 Part VI, Chapter v, Note 36.
罐 Part VI, Chapter xiv, Note 1.

网

罷 Part III, 242.
署 Part III, 1007.
罰 Part IV, Dialogue vi, 21.
罵 Part V, Lesson iv, Note 10.
置 Part V, Lesson xvii, Note 14.
罣 Part V, Lesson liii, Note 3.
罕 Part V, Lesson lxv, Note 5.
羅 Part VI, Chapter i, Note 17.

APPENDIX II.—INDEX OF CHARACTERS.

羊
羣 Part III, 535.
羞 Part III, 832.
義 Part V, Lesson vii, Note 11.
美 Part V, Lesson xvi, Note 10.
羨 Part V, Lesson xxiv, Note 3.

羽
翁 Part III, 655.
習 Part III, 1008.
翻 Part IV, Dialogue vii, 83.
耀 Part V, Lesson iv, Note 14.
翎 Part V, Lesson x, Note 12.
翠 Part VI, Chapter viii, Note 11.
翰 Part VI, Chapter xxxiv, Note 2.
翅 Part VII, 37.

老
考 Part III, 899.

耒
耗 Part VI, Chapter iv, Note 4.

耳
聽 Part III, 131.
聲 Part III, 136.
聖 Part III, 869.
耽 Part III, 960.
聰 Part III, 1040.
聾 Part V, Lesson xxii, Note 12.
耻 Part V, Lesson lvii, Note 5.
聊 Part V, Lesson lix, Note 2.

肉
肯 Part III, 104.
腕 Part III, 268.
臟 Part III, 269.
臉 Part III, 277.
胰 Part III, 279.
脫 Part III, 292.
肩 Part III, 305.
能 Part III, 391.
膡 Part III, 428.
肓 Part III, 434.
胳 Part III, 437.
臂 Part III, 438.
腰 Part III, 441.
腿 Part III, 442.
脖 Part III, 465.
胸 Part III, 471.
脯 Part III, 472.
背 Part III, 473.
脊 Part III, 474.
勝 Part III, 476.
肚 Part III, 477.
脚} Part III, 481.
腳}
股 Part III, 543.
脾 Part III, 1031.
膽 Part IV, Dialogue v, 76.
膿 Part IV, Dialogue vi, 36.
肛 Part V, Lesson vii, Note 5.
胖 Part V, Lesson xxx, Note 3.
肌 Part V, Lesson xxxv, Note 12.
腹 Part V, Lesson xlviii, Note 5.
膝 Part V, Lesson xlviii, Note 6.
腫 Part V, Lesson xlviii, Note 9.
脈 Part V, Lesson lii, Note 6.
臀 Part V, Lesson lvii, Note 1.
腸 Part V, Lesson lxiii, Note 1.
肘 Part V, Lesson lxxxiii, Note 4.
腋 Part V, Lesson xcix, Note 6.
膲 Part V, Lesson xcix, Note 9.
腕 Part VI, Chapter viii, Note 8.
腐 Part VI, Chapter xiv, Note 10.
肴 Part VI, Chapter xxv, Note 1.
膏 Part VI, Chapter xxviii, Note 21.
膠 Part VI, Chapter xxx, Note 8.
胎 Part VI, Chapter xxxiv, Note 1.
臘 Part VI, Chapter xxxix, Note 1.
腔 Part VII, 29.
胖 Part VII, 262.

臣
臨 Part III, 843.
臥}
卧} Part V, Lesson xlviii, Note 11.

至
臺 Part III, 785.
致 Part V, Lesson xci, Note 11.

白
舊 Part III, 740.
與 Part IV, Dialogue iii, 57.
舉 Part IV, Dialogue vi, 27.
與 Part IV, Dialogue viii, 35.
舅 Part V, Lesson xxvii, Note 7.
舀 Part VII, 397.

舌
舖 Part III, 46.
舒 Part III, 825.
舘 Part IV, Dialogue iii, 104.
舔 Part V, Lesson lxxxii, Note 4.

舟
船 Part III, 383.
般 Part V, Lesson xxxiii, Note 10.
艄 Part VI, Chapter xxxv, Note 8.
艙 Part VI, Chapter xxxv, Note 11.

艮
艱 Part III, 827.
艮 Part III, 845.

艸
萬 Part III, 4.
著}
着} Part III, 45.
蓋 Part III, 143.
蕭 Part III, 144.
茶 Part III, 157.
菜 Part III, 164.
花 Part III, 184.
芝 Part III, 354.
苦 Part III, 396.
葱 Part III, 690.
苗 Part III, 691.
草 Part III, 699.
薄 Part III, 712.
藍 Part III, 735.
落 Part III, 763.

若 Part III, 902.
莫 Part IV, Dialogue iv, 52.
藥 Part IV, Dialogue v, 26.
藏 Part IV, Dialogue v, 36.
英 Part IV, Dialogue viii, 3.
菜 Part IV, Dialogue viii, 23.
葦 Part IV, Dialogue viii, 33.
蘇 Part IV, Dialogue ix, 7.
莊 Part IV, Dialogue x, 1; Part V, Lesson xviii, Note 9.
萃 Part V, Lesson x, Note 5.
蔭 Part V, Lesson xii, Note 9.
荒 Part V, Lesson xviii, Note 3.
蓬 Part V, Lesson xxxv, Note 6.
菩 Part V, Lesson xxxviii, Note 7.
藉 Part V, Lesson xlvii, Note 8.
藝 Part V, Lesson lxxix, Note 1.
蘆 Part V, Lesson xci, Note 5.
葦 Part V, Lesson xci, Note 5.
蒲 Part VI, Chapter i, Note 4.
芽 Part VI, Chapter vi, Note 6.
莽 Part VI, Chapter xiii, Note 1.
薦 Part VI, Chapter xxi, Note 4.
薰 Part VI, Chapter xxvi, Note 12.
蒴 Part VI, Chapter xxix, Note 5.
茂 Part VI, Chapter xxxvii, Note 5.
蒼 Part VI, Chapter xxxvii, Note 7.
茄 Part VII, 33.
菌 Part VII, 58.
蒿 Part VII, 96.
葡 Part VII, 288.
萄 Part VII, 288.

虍

號 Part III, 858.
處 Part III, 922.
虧 Part III, 1044.
虎 Part IV, Dialogue v, 61; Part V, Lesson xxxi, Note 4.
虛 Part IV, Dialogue v, 76.
戲 Part IV, Dialogue vii, 37.

虫

蠟 Part III, 152.
蠱 Part III, 818.
蛇 Part V, Lesson xviii, Note 10.
蝦 Part V, Lesson xc, Note 9.

蚊 Part V, Lesson xcv, Note 2.
虼 Part V, Lesson xcv, Note 3.
蚤 Part V, Lesson xcv, Note 3.
蠍 Part VI, Chapter xiii, Note 5.
蟄 Part VI, Chapter xiii, Note 5.
螞 Part VI, Chapter xiii, Note 10.
蟻 Part VI, Chapter xiii, Note 10.
蛀 Part VI, Chapter xiii, Note 10.
蛋 Part VI, Chapter xviii, Note 7.
蜂 Part VI, Chapter xix, Note 3.
蠹 Part VI, Chapter xxv, Note 5.
蠅 Part VI, Chapter xxxvii, Note 7.
蜘 Part VI, Chapter xxxix, Note 3.
蛛 Part VI, Chapter xxxix, Note 3.
蟆 Part VII, 92.

行

街 Part III, 48.
衕 Part III, 66.
行 Part III, 754.
衚 Part III, 797.
衖 Part III, 798.

衣

裏 Part III, 48.
表 Part III, 222.
初 Part III, 234.
衣 Part III, 266.
裳 Part III, 267.
補 Part III, 288.
襪 Part III, 295.
衫 Part III, 307.
褲 Part III, 312.
裁 Part III, 313.
袖 Part III, 314.
袖 Part III, 315.
袋 Part III, 403.
裝 Part III, 415.
裹 Part III, 600.
裱 Part III, 729.
裂 Part III, 753.
被 Part IV, Dialogue iv, 52.
裹 Part V, Lesson xxxiii, Note 4.
袍 Part V, Lesson xlv, Note 6.
裘 Part V, Lesson lxv, Note 2.
襁 Part V, Lesson lxx, Note 3.

褸 Part V, Lesson lxx, Note 3.
襖 Part V, Lesson lxxxvi, Note 2.
襟 Part V, Lesson lxxxvi, Note 3.
襲 Part V, Lesson lxxxvi, Note 8.
袱 Part VI, Chapter iv, Note 10.
裸 Part VII, 198.
褪 Part VII, 360.

西

要 Part III, 32.
西 Part III, 35.
覆 Part V, Lesson xcv, Note 5.

見

見 Part III, 91.
規 Part III, 581.
親 Part III, 650.
覺 Part III, 680.
覔 Part V, Lesson v, Note 2.
觀 Part V, Lesson xxxiii, Note 11.
視 Part VI, Chapter v, Note 2.

角

觔 Part V, Lesson xxiv, Note 13.
觭 Part VI, Chapter xxiii, Note 3.
解 Part VI, Chapter xxxiii, Note 4.

言

誰 Part III, 23.
話 Part III, 53.
說 Part III, 54.
請 Part III, 89.
認 Part III, 97.
訴 Part III, 109.
記 Part III, 111.
該 Part III, 340.
論 Part III, 349.
計 Part III, 389.
語 Part III, 591.
詑 Part III, 597.
討 Part III, 834.
誑 } Part III, 974.
誆 }
訛 Part III, 992.
謊 Part III, 999.

APPENDIX II.—INDEX OF CHARACTERS.

證 Part IV, Dialogue ii, 38.
詳 Part IV, Dialogue iii, 65.
讓 Part IV, Dialogue iv, 6; Part V, Lesson viii, Note 19.
讓 Part IV, Dialogue iv, 25.
詐 Part IV, Dialogue vi, 24.
護 Part IV, Dialogue vi, 37; Part V, Lesson xiv, Note 8.
許 Part IV, Dialogue vi, 49; Part V, Lesson xxiii, Note 3.
講 Part IV, Dialogue ix, 36.
註 Part IV, Dialogue ix, 38.
詩 Part IV, Dialogue ix, 39.
試 Part IV, Dialogue ix, 41.
謙 Part IV, Dialogue x, 8.
諸 Part IV, Dialogue x, 11.
謝 Part IV, Dialogue x, 22; Part VI, Chapter vii, Note 4.
談 Part V, Lesson i, Note 2.
譯 Part V, Lesson i, Note 4.
誓 Part V, Lesson vi, Note 12.
詞 Part V, Lesson viii, Note 5.
謹 Part V, Lesson xiii, Note 9.
誘 Part V, Lesson xiv, Note 4.
讓 Part V, Lesson xvii, Note 8.
誓 Part V, Lesson xxi, Note 3.
誇 Part V, Lesson xxiv, Note 4.
謠 Part V, Lesson xxxii, Note 7.
誦 Part V, Lesson xxxviii, Note 2.
議 Part V, Lesson xlvi, Note 2.
診 Part V, Lesson lii, Note 6.
誅 Part V, Lesson lxii, Note 13.
譏 Part V, Lesson lxiii, Note 2.
誚 Part V, Lesson lxiii, Note 2.
讀 Part V, Lesson lxviii, Note 1.
設 Part V, Lesson lxxii, Note 14.
誌 Part V, Lesson lxxx, Note 8.
讓 Part V, Lesson c, Note 6.
調 Part VI, Chapter vii, Note 14.
訊 Part VI, Chapter xv, Note 8.
訕 Part VI, Chapter xviii, Note 1.
譲 Part VI, Chapter xix, Note 7.
詫 Part VI, Chapter xxxi, Note 3.
諞 Part VII, 278.

豆

豎 Part III, 1073.
豐 Part IV, Dialogue v, 52.
豈 Part IV, Dialogue x, 23; Part V, Lesson xix, Note 8.

豕

豫 Part IV, Dialogue x, 1.
豬 Part V, Lesson xciv, Note 6.
豪 Part V, Lesson xcix, Note 2.

豸

貌 Part III, 605.
豹 Part V, Lesson xxx, Note 6.
貂 Part V, Lesson xxxiv, Note 1.
貓 Part VI, Chapter xxix, Note 14; Part VII, 213.

貝

買 Part III, 35.
賣 Part III, 35.
貴 Part III, 331.
賤 Part III, 332.
費 Part III, 341.
賊 Part III, 485.
貲 Part III, 494.
貧 Part III, 630.
賞 Part III, 638.
貼 Part III, 886.
賺 Part III, 1000.
負 Part III, 1046.
賠 Part IV, Dialogue ii, 28.
貪 Part IV, Dialogue v, 22.
貧 Part IV, Dialogue vi, 10.
賜 Part V, Lesson i, Note 9.
責 Part V, Lesson vi, Note 14.
賭 Part V, Lesson xlvi, Note 5.
賴 Part V, Lesson lix, Note 3.
顀 Part V, Lesson lxx, Note 5.
賒 Part VI, Chapter iii, Note 14.
賄 Part VI, Chapter v, Note 27.
賂 Part VI, Chapter v, Note 27.
贖 Part VI, Chapter xv, Note 6.
贏 Part VI, Chapter xviii, Note 6.
贈 Part VI, Chapter xxviii, Note 7.
貰 Part VI, Chapter xxx, Note 3.
貸 Part VII, 32.

走

起 Part III, 43.
趕 Part III, 420.
趁 Part V, Lesson xvi, Note 3.
趣 Part V, Lesson xxvii, Note 16.
赴 Part V, Lesson xlvii, Note 3.

超 Part V, Lesson lxxxv, Note 5.
越 Part V, Lesson xciii, Note 5.
趨 Part VI, Chapter xviii, Note 1.
趄 Part VI, Chapter xxi, Note 11.

足

跑 Part III, 88.
路 Part III, 373.
跟 Part III, 413.
踝 Part III, 482.
跨 Part III, 915.
跳 Part III, 943.
蹇 Part IV, Dialogue v, 36.
踪 Part V, Lesson xxxviii, Note 13.
跪 Part V, Lesson xliii, Note 5.
踐 Part V, Lesson liv, Note 14; Part VI, Chapter xviii, Note 5.
跌 Part V, Lesson liv, Note 14.
蹲 Part V, Lesson lxi, Note 5.
跐 Part V, Lesson c, Note 3.
蹋 Part VI, Chapter xiii, Note 7.
蹉 Part VI, Chapter xiv, Note 14.
趴 Part VI, Chapter xv, Note 14.
跋 Part VI, Chapter xv, Note 16.
蹄 Part VI, Chapter xvi, Note 2.
踏 Part VI, Chapter xviii, Note 1.
蹀 Part VI, Chapter xix, Note 6.
蹊 Part VI, Chapter xix, Note 6.
踐 Part VI, Chapter xx, Note 1.
趾 Part VI, Chapter xxi, Note 10.
蹭 Part VI, Chapter xxii, Note 4; Part VII, 379.
跡 Part VI, Chapter xxvii, Note 2.
蹟 Part VI, Chapter xxvii, Note 2.
踱 Part VI, Chapter xxxii, Note 7.
躊 Part VI, Chapter xxxii, Note 7.
躇 Part VI, Chapter xxxii, Note 7.
蹲 Part VI, Chapter xxxv, Note 10.
躁 Part VI, Chapter xxxvii, Note 11.
蹙 Part VII, 56.
踐 Part VII, 66.
蹬 Part VII, 67.
蹭 Part VII, 67.

身

躺 Part III, 60.
躴 Part IV, Dialogue iv, 45.
躲 Part IV, Dialogue v, 78; Part V, Lesson xxiii, Note 1.

車

輧	Part III, 71.
車	Part III, 73.
輞	Part III, 74.
輕	Part III, 335.
頓	Part III, 446.
轟	Part III, 814.
轎	Part III, 916.
轉	Part IV, Dialogue vi, 50.
較	Part V, Lesson xxi, Note 7.
轂	Part V, Lesson xl, Note 12.
轆	Part V, Lesson xl, Note 12; Part VI, Chapter xxix, Note 6.
轟	Part V, Lesson lxv, Note 1.
軍	Part VI, Chapter vii, Note 15; Chapter xxxiii, Note 2.
輸	Part VI, Chapter xviii, Note 6.
轤	Part VI, Chapter xxix, Note 6.
軸	Part VII, 50.

辛

辦	Part III, 583.
辜	Part III, 1045.
辭	Part IV, Dialogue vi, 53; Part V, Lesson i, Note 7.
辯	Part V, Lesson xvii, Note 12.
辨	Part V, Lesson liii, Note 2.
辣	Part VI, Chapter xxviii, Note 11.

辰

辱	Part III, 833.

辵

這	Part III, 10.
進	Part III, 40.
過	Part III, 42.
道	Part III, 48.
還	Part III, 105.
遠	Part III, 371.
近	Part III, 372.
邊	Part III, 379.
連	Part III, 398.
追	Part III, 419.
退	Part III, 506.
逃	Part III, 544.
迎	Part III, 663.
送	Part III, 762.
迸	Part III, 942.
造	Part III, 946; Part V, Lesson xxiii, Note 11.
運	Part III, 1035.
通	Part III, 1062.
過	Part IV, Dialogue iv, 7.
遞	Part IV, Dialogue vi, 22.
逾	Part IV, Dialogue vi, 24.
遵	Part IV, Dialogue ix, 53.
遐	Part IV, Dialogue x, 8; Part V, Lesson vii, Note 8.
逢	Part V, Lesson iv, Note 8.
選	Part V, Lesson xii, Note 2.
迭	Part V, Lesson xvii, Note 19.
逛	Part V, Lesson xviii, Note 4.
避	Part V, Lesson xxiii, Note 1.
遲	Part V, Lesson xxvi, Note 2.
逼	Part V, Lesson xxvi, Note 4.
遭	Part V, Lesson xxxviii, Note 3.
透	Part V, Lesson xxxviii, Note 10.
逗	Part V, Lesson lv, Note 5.
迷	Part V, Lesson lxxxv, Note 6.
週	Part VI, Chapter iii, Note 19.
遜	Part VI, Chapter v, Note 21.
遊	Part VI, Chapter vii, Note 17.
逍	Part VI, Chapter viii, Note 18.
遙	Part VI, Chapter viii, Note 18.
違	Part VI, Chapter xvii, Note 1.
遏	Part VI, Chapter xvii, Note 6.
速	Part VI, Chapter xxi, Note 1.
逃	Part VI, Chapter xxiii, Note 7.
迹	Part VI, Chapter xxvii, Note 2.
邁	Part VI, Chapter xxxviii, Note 2.
遛	Part VII, 197.

邑

那	Part III, 10, 23.
都	Part III, 84.
鄉	Part III, 802.
部	Part III, 1010.
郎	Part IV, Dialogue vii, 100.
郊	Part V, Lesson xviii, Note 3.
鄂	Part V, Lesson xxxvi, Note 11.
邪	Part V, Lesson xxxvii, Note 12.
鄭	Part VI, Chapter i, Note 5.

酉

酒	Part III, 154.
醜	Part III, 607.
酌	Part III, 775.
醉	Part IV, Dialogue v, 80.
酬	Part IV, Dialogue x, 1.
醒	Part V, Lesson xxxv, Note 7.
醫	Part V, Lesson lii, Note 5.
配	Part V, Lesson lxii, Note 6.
酸	Part VI, Chapter xiv, Note 9.

釆

釋	Part VI, Chapter xxxvii, Note 8.

里

重	Part III, 336.
量	Part III, 772.
野	Part III, 801.

金

錯	Part III, 139.
鋪	Part III, 142.
鍋	Part III, 172.
銼	Part III, 174.
鐘	Part III, 221.
針	Part III, 285.
金	Part III, 317.
銀	Part III, 318.
銅	Part III, 319.
鐵	Part III, 320.
錢	Part III, 321.
鎮	Part IV, Dialogue viii, 39.
鑽	Part V, Lesson iv, Note 7.
鑑	Part V, Lesson viii, Note 2.
鋒	Part V, Lesson xii, Note 4.
鋤	Part V, Lesson xviii, Note 12.
錐	Part V, Lesson xix, Note 2.
鍾	Part V, Lesson xxxvi, Note 5.
鏡	Part V, Lesson xlvii, Note 11.
釘	Part V, Lesson liv, Note 7.
鈕	Part V, Lesson lxxvi, Note 8.
鐙	Part V, Lesson lxxxviii, Note 1; Part VII, 336.
鋼	Part VI, Chapter viii, Note 10.
鑲	Part VI, Chapter viii, Note 12.
鎚	Part VI, Chapter x, Note 3.

APPENDIX II.—INDEX OF CHARACTERS.

鍍 Part VI, Chapter xi, Note 2.
錠 Part VI, Chapter xv, Note 4.
鑼 Part VI, Chapter xix, Note 4.
釣 Part VI, Chapter xxix, Note 8.
鐐 Part VI, Chapter xxxiii, Note 3.
銬 Part VI, Chapter xxxiii, Note 3.
鐲 Part VI, Chapter xxxv, Note 4.
鈐 Part VI, Chapter xxxviii, Note 6.
鐺 Part VI, Chapter xxxviii, Note 6.
錦 Part VI, Chapter xl, Note 3.
鈔 Part VII, 15.
銃 Part VII, 77.
錢 Part VII, 91.
鏺 Part VII, 231.
鑿 Part VII, 371.

門

間 Part III, 47; Part V, Lesson xvii, Note 5.
開 Part III, 50.
關 Part III, 63.
問 Part III, 110.
閉 Part III, 983.
閩 Part IV, Dialogue iii, 52; Part VII, 71.
閣 Part IV, Dialogue ix, 9.
閭 Part V, Lesson l, Note 1.
閘 Part V, Lesson xcii, Note 3; Part VI, Chapter xvii, Note 5.
閉 Part V, Lesson xcv, Note 6.
閑 Part VI, Chapter iv, Note 4.
閌 Part VI, Chapter xl, Note 6.
閃 Part VII, 306.

阜

陰 Part III, 260.
陽 Part III, 261.
阿 Part III, 596.
陪 Part III, 727.
隨 Part III, 864.
陳 Part III, 1026.
除 Part III, 1066.
院 Part IV, Dialogue iii, 49.
陣 Part IV, Dialogue iv, 63.
隔 Part IV, Dialogue viii, 23; Part V, Lesson iii, Note 4.
陛 Part V, Lesson xi, Note 2.
防 Part V, Lesson xvi, Note 1.

降 Part V, Lesson xix, Note 10; Part VI, Chapter xix, Note 10.
險 Part V, Lesson xxiv, Note 10.
隧 Part V, Lesson xxviii, Note 12.
陷 Part V, Lesson xlvi, Note 3.
階 Part V, Lesson lxxxii, Note 3.
陡 Part V, Lesson xcv, Note 10.
陸 Part VI, Chapter xxxv, Note 1.
隴 Part VII, 208.

隶

隸 Part VI, Chapter i, Note 12.

隹

雙 Part III, 294.
雞 Part III, 362.
隻 Part III, 382.
難 Part III, 828.
雜 Part III, 903.
雇 Part III, 996.
離 Part IV, Dialogue iii, 23.
雀 Part V, Lesson xii, Note 7.
雛 Part V, Lesson xvii, Note 13.
雄 Part V, Lesson xxxiii, Note 6.
雕 Part V, Lesson lv, Note 2.
雅 Part V, Lesson xcvii, Note 8.

雨

零 Part III, 5.
雪 Part III, 228.
雲 Part III, 258.
霧 Part III, 262.
靈 Part III, 1057.
霸 Part V, Lesson xxxii, Note 3.
露 Part V, Lesson xlvi, Note 1.
震 Part V, Lesson xcv, Note 14.
霹 Part V, Lesson xcvi, Note 1.
雷 Part V, Lesson xcvi, Note 2.
靄 Part VI, Chapter vii, Note 5.

青

靜 Part III, 824; Part V, Lesson xvi, Note 20.
靖 Part III, 859.
靛 Part VI, Chapter v, Note 36.

非

罪 Part III, 852.
靠 Part IV, Dialogue vi, 31.

革

鞋 Part III, 291.
靴 Part III, 293.
韉 Part III, 295.
鞭 Part IV, Dialogue iii, 110.
鞘 Part VI, Chapter xxii, Note 3.

韋

韜 Part V, Lesson xxx, Note 18.

音

響 Part V, Lesson xxxv, Note 2.
韻 Part VI, Chapter xxvi, Note 4.

頁

頭 Part III, 48.
頂 Part III, 72.
顋 Part III, 460.
頰 Part III, 461.
頦 Part III, 463.
額 Part III, 501.
順 Part III, 626.
顏 Part III, 733.
須 Part III, 744.
願 Part III, 1041.
預 Part III, 1060.
領 Part IV, Dialogue i, 2; Dialogue x, 5.
項 Part IV, Dialogue ii, 27.
頓 Part IV, Dialogue vi, 41; Part V, Lesson ix, Note 8.
顯 Part IV, Dialogue x, 17.
頗 Part V, Lesson iii, Note 5.
類 Part V, Lesson x, Note 4.
顛 Part V, Lesson xxv, Note 5.
頂 Part V, Lesson xxv, Note 5.
頷 Part V, Lesson xxxiii, Note 3.
顧 Part V, Lesson xlii, Note 3.
頸 Part V, Lesson lxii, Note 5.
題 Part VI, Chapter xv, Note 17.

風

颱 Part III, 231.
飄 Part V, Lesson xcvii, Note 3.
飆 Part V, Lesson xcvii, Note 4.
颶 Part VI, Chapter xxxvii, Note 1.

食

飯 Part III, 159.
饅 Part III, 365.
饈 Part III, 408.
餒 Part III, 1056.
饞 Part IV, Dialogue iii, 22 ; Part VI, Chapter v, Note 18.
館 (or 舘) Part IV, Dialogue iii, 104.
養 Part IV, Dialogue iv, 57.
飽 Part IV, Dialogue x, 19.
餃 Part V, Lesson xi, Note 4.
餈 Part V, Lesson xiii, Note 7.
饈 Part V, Lesson xvi, Note 10.
饐 Part V, Lesson xvi, Note 13.
飲 Part V, Lesson xlviii, Note 10.
饒 Part V, Lesson lxx, Note 1.
餿 Part V, Lesson lxxvii, Note 4.
餬 Part V, Lesson lxxx, Note 7.
餅 Part VI, Chapter v, Note 9.
餑 Part VI, Chapter v, Note 10.
飾 Part VI, Chapter xi, Note 2.
餂 Part VI, Chapter xxi, Note 7.
餉 Part VI, Chapter xxiii, Note 9.
饌 Part VI, Chapter xxv, Note 1.

馬

騎 Part III, 70.
馬 Part III, 75.
騾 Part III, 77.
驢 Part III, 78.
駱 Part III, 409.
駝 Part III, 410.
馱 Part III, 417.
驅 Part III, 975.
駕 Part IV, Dialogue i, 9.
駒 Part IV, Dialogue iii, 64.
驚 Part IV, Dialogue v, 72.
駁 Part IV, Dialogue viii, 55.
騷 Part V, Lesson lxxi, Note 4.
騰 Part V, Lesson xcix, Note 13.
騁 Part VI, Chapter iv, Note 15.
駐 Part VI, Chapter xix, Note 11.
驪 Part VII, 387.

骨

體 Part III, 483.
骰 Part V, Lesson xxxiii, Note 5.
骶 Part V, Lesson lxi, Note 5.

髟

髮 Part III, 283.
髯 Part III, 435.
鬢 Part III, 459.
鬆 Part V, Lesson xxxv, Note 6.
鬘 Part VI, Chapter viii, Note 5.
鬘 Part VII, 182.
鬣 Part VII, 182.

鬥

鬧 Part III, 587.
鬮 Part III, 857 ; Part V, Lesson lv, Note 5.

鬼

魂 Part V, Lesson xvi, Note 11.
魁 Part V, Lesson xxiv, Note 1.

魚

鮑 Part V, Lesson xviii, Note 2.
鮮 Part V, Lesson lvii, Note 7.
鯉 Part VI, Chapter v, Note 28.
鮡 Part VI, Chapter xviii, Note 3.
鰾 Part VI, Chapter xxx, Note 8 ; Part VII, 273.

鳥

鷹 Part V, Lesson xxxiii, Note 9.
鴛 Part VI, Chapter i, Note 7.
鴦 Part VI, Chapter i, Note 7.
鳴 Part VI, Chapter xviii, Note 8.
鴨 Part VII, 66.

鹵

鹹 Part VI, Chapter xiv, Note 12.

鹿

麤 Part V, Lesson lxxxix, Note 2.
麈 Part VI, Chapter xxxvi, Note 14.

麥

麪 Part III, 352.

麻

麼 Part III, 23.
麻 Part III, 355.

黍

黏 Part VI, Chapter xxviii, Note 15.

黑

墨 Part III, 118.
黨 Part III, 854.

黽

鼈 Part VI, Chapter xxviii, Note 8.

鼓

鼕 Part VII, 337.

鼻

齉 Part VII, 230.

齊

齋 Part IV, Dialogue vii, 10.

齒

齡 Part VI, Chapter i, Note 9.
齩 Part VI, Chapter xviii, Note 4.
齜 Part VII, 395.

APPENDIX III.

THE PEKING SYLLABARY.

EXPLANATORY NOTE.

The *P'ing Tsê Pien*, literally, Book of the Tones, smooth and otherwise, is a new edition of the Peking Syllabary appended to the "Hsin Ching Lu," or Book of Experiments, published in 1859.

The history and purpose of the Syllabary are explained in the Preface to the First Edition of the "Tzŭ Ĕrh Chi" (*see* Volume I). To use it the student must be acquainted with the Sound Table immediately following, which prescribes the Syllabic differences recognised in the Dialect. In the Second Table he will find, under each Syllable, the characters held by speakers of the Dialect to belong to the same Sound, distributed in four columns (numbered respectively 1, 2, 3, 4). Of these, Column 1 contains the characters in the first, or *shang-p'ing*, Tone; Column 2, those in the *hsia-p'ing*; Column 3, those in the *shang*; and Column 4, those in the *ch'ü*. Characters that have more than one Sound or Tone are pointed with a small circle on their right; and the Third Table repeats the whole of those so pointed in such form that the student referring to it will see at a glance to what changes any word in it is either syllabically or tonically liable. Throughout the Second Table the aspirated stand side by side with the unaspirated Syllables, and the characters under either or both having a common phonetic are, so far as circumstances will admit of it, aligned with each other, either singly or in groups. By examination of these groups, the student will refresh his memory, not more in the matter of Tone than as regards the signification of the words he may have met with.

I.—SOUND TABLE.

#	A		#			#			#	H	
1	a	阿	31	ch'iao	巧	64	chua	抓	92	ha	哈
2	ai	愛	32	chieh	街	65	ch'ua	欻	93	hai	害
3	an	安	33	ch'ieh	且	66	chuai	拽	94	han	寒
4	ang	昂	34	chien	見	67	ch'uai	揣	95	hang	行
5	ao	傲	35	ch'ien	欠	68	chuan	專	96	hao	好
	CH		36	chih	知	69	ch'uan	穿	97	hê, hei	黑
6	cha	乍	37	ch'ih	尺	70	chuang	壯	98	hên	很
7	ch'a	茶	38	chin	斤	71	ch'uang	牀	99	hêng	恆
8	chai	窄	39	ch'in	親	72	chui	追	100	ho	河
9	ch'ai	柴	40	ching	井	73	ch'ui	吹	101	hou	後
10	chan	斬	41	ch'ing	輕	74	chun	准	102	hu	戶
11	ch'an	產	42	chio	角	75	ch'un	春	103	hua	花
12	chang	章	43	ch'io	郤	76	chung	中	104	huai	壞
13	ch'ang	唱	44	chiu	酒	77	ch'ung	充	105	huan	換
14	chao	兆	45	ch'iu	秋	78	ch'uo	擉	106	huang	黃
15	ch'ao	吵	46	chiung	窘				107	huei, hui	回
16	chê	這	47	ch'iung	窮		Ê		108	huên, hun	混
17	ch'ê	車	48	cho	卓	79	ê	額	109	hung	紅
18	chei	這	49	ch'o	綽	80	ên	恩	110	huo	火
19	chên	真	50	chou	晝	81	êng	哼			
20	ch'ên	臣	51	ch'ou	抽	82	êrh	兒		HS	
21	chêng	正	52	chü	句				111	hsi	西
22	ch'êng	成	53	ch'ü	取		F		112	hsia	夏
23	chi	吉	54	chüan	捐	83	fa	法	113	hsiang	向
24	ch'i	奇	55	ch'üan	全	84	fan	反	114	hsiao	小
25	chia	家	56	chüeh	絕	85	fang	方	115	hsieh	些
26	ch'ia	恰	57	ch'üeh	缺	86	fei	非	116	hsien	先
27	ch'iai	楷	58	chün	君	87	fên	分	117	hsin	心
28	chiang	江	59	ch'ün	羣	88	fêng	風	118	hsing	性
29	ch'iang	槍	60	chüo	爵	89	fo	佛	119	hsio	學
30	chiao	交	61	ch'üo	却	90	fou	否	120	hsiu	修
			62	chu	主	91	fu	夫	121	hsiung	兄
			63	ch'u	出						

122	hsü	須	150	kao	告考	184	lao	老
123	hsüan,hsüen	喧	151	k'ao		185	lê	勒
124	hsüeh	雪	152	kei	給	186	lêi, lei	累
125	hsün	巡	153	k'ei	刻	187	lêng	冷
126	hsüo	學	154	kên	根	188	li	立
			155	k'ên	肯	189	lia	俩
	I		156	kêng	更	190	liang	兩
			157	k'êng	坑	191	liao	了
127	i, yi	衣	158	ko, kê	各	192	lieh	裂
			159	k'o, k'ê	可	193	lien	連
	J		160	kou	狗	194	lin	林
			161	k'ou	口	195	ling	另
128	jan	染	162	ku	古苦	196	lio	略
129	jang	嚷	163	k'u		197	liu	留
130	jao	繞	164	kua	瓜	198	lo	駱
131	jê, jo	熱	165	k'ua	跨	199	lou	陋
132	jên	人	166	kuai	怪快	200	lü	律
133	jêng	扔	167	k'uai		201	lüan	戀
134	jih	日	168	kuan	官	202	lüeh	略
135	jo	若	169	k'uan	寬	203	lün	掄
136	jou	肉	170	kuang	光	204	lüo	略
137	ju	如	171	k'uang	況	205	lu	路
138	juan	輭	172	kuei	規	206	luan	亂
139	jui	瑞	173	k'uei	愧	207	lun	論
140	jun	潤	174	kuên, kun	棍	208	lung	龍
141	jung	絨	175	k'uên, k'un	困			
			176	kung	工		**M**	
	K		177	k'ung	孔			
			178	kuo	果	209	ma	馬
142	ka	嘎	179	k'uo	闊	210	mai	買
143	k'a	卡				211	man	慢
144	kai	改		**L**		212	mang	忙
145	k'ai	開				213	mao	毛
146	kan	甘	180	la	拉	214	mei	美
147	k'an	看	181	lai	來	215	mên	門
148	kang	剛	182	lan	懶	216	mêng	夢
149	k'ang	炕	183	lang	浪	217	mi	米

218	miao	苗
219	mieh	滅
220	mien	面
221	min	民
222	ming	名
223	miu	謬
224	mo	末
225	mou	謀
226	mu	木

N

227	na	那
228	nai	奶
229	nan	男
230	nang	囊
231	nao	鬧
232	nei	內
233	nên	嫩
234	nêng	能
235	ni	你
236	niang	孃
237	niao	鳥
238	nieh	揑
239	nien	念
240	nin	您
241	ning	甯
242	nio	虐
243	niu	牛
244	no	梛
245	nou	耨
246	nü	女
247	nüeh	虐
248	nüo	虐
249	nu	奴
250	nuan	暖
251	nun	嫩
252	nung	濃

[O–TSO.] APPENDIX III.—THE PEKING SYLLABARY. 77

O

| 253 | o | 訛 |
| 254 | ou | 偶 |

P

255	pa	罷
256	p'a	怕
257	pai	拜
258	p'ai	派
259	pan	半
260	p'an	盼
261	pang	幫
262	p'ang	旁
263	pao	包
264	p'ao	跑
265	pei	北
266	p'ei	陪
267	pên	本
268	p'ên	盆
269	pêng	迸
270	p'êng	朋
271	pi	必
272	p'i	皮
273	piao	表
274	p'iao	票
275	pieh	別
276	p'ieh	撇
277	pien	扁
278	p'ien	片
279	pin	賓
280	p'in	貧
281	ping	兵
282	p'ing	憑
283	po	波
284	p'o	破
285	pou	不
286	p'ou	剖
287	pu	不
288	p'u	普

S

289	sa	撒
290	sai	賽
291	san	散
292	sang	桑
293	sao	掃
294	sê	嗇
295	sên	森
296	sêng	僧
297	so	索
298	sou	搜
299	su	素
300	suan	算
301	sui	碎
302	sun	孫
303	sung	送

SH

304	sha	殺
305	shai	曬
306	shan	山
307	shang	賞
308	shao	少
309	shê	舌
310	shên	身
311	shêng	生
312	shih	事
313	shou	手
314	shu	書
315	shua	刷
316	shuai	衰
317	shuan	拴
318	shuang	雙
319	shui	水
320	shun	順
321	shuo	說

SS

| 322 | ssŭ | 絲 |

T

323	ta	大
324	t'a	他
325	tai	歹
326	t'ai	太
327	tan	單
328	t'an	炭
329	tang	當
330	t'ang	湯
331	tao	道
332	t'ao	逃
333	tê	得
334	t'ê	特
335	tei	得
336	têng	等
337	t'êng	疼
338	ti	的
339	t'i	替
340	tiao	弔
341	t'iao	挑
342	tieh	疊
343	t'ieh	貼
344	tien	店
345	t'ien	天
346	ting	定
347	t'ing	聽
348	tiu	丢
349	to	多
350	t'o	妥
351	tou	豆
352	t'ou	頭
353	tu	肚
354	t'u	土
355	tuan	短
356	t'uan	團
357	tui	對
358	t'ui	退
359	tun	敦
360	t'un	吞
361	tung	冬
362	t'ung	同

TS

363	tsa	雜
364	ts'a	擦
365	tsai	在
366	ts'ai	才
367	tsan	贊
368	ts'an	慚
369	tsang	葬
370	ts'ang	倉
371	tsao	早
372	ts'ao	草
373	tsê	則
374	ts'ê	策
375	tsei	賊
376	tsên	怎
377	ts'ên	參
378	tsêng	增
379	ts'êng	層
380	tso	作

381	ts'o	錯		TZ		403	wo	我	
382	tsou	走	394	tzǔ	子	404	wu	武	
383	ts'ou	湊	395	tz'ǔ	次				
384	tsu	祖					Y		
385	ts'u	粗		W		405	ya	牙	
386	tsuan	揝				406	yai	涯	
387	ts'uan	竄	396	wa	瓦	407	yang	羊	
388	tsui	嘴	397	wai	外	408	yao	要	
389	ts'ui	催	398	wan	完	409	yeh	夜	
390	tsun	尊	399	wang	往	410	yen	言	
391	ts'un	寸	400	wei	爲	411	yi	益	
392	tsung	宗	401	wên	文	412	yin	音	
393	ts'ung	蔥	402	wêng	翁	413	ying	迎	
						414	yo	約	
						415	yü	魚	
						416	yüan	原	
						417	yüeh	月	
						418	yün	雲	
						419	yu	有	
						420	yung	用	

II.—PEKING SYLLABARY.

	1	2	3	4
阿 1 A	阿啊脬嗄	一呀	阿	阿
愛 2 AI	挨˚唉˚京呆矮 一噯	挨˚埃崖涯獃˚	騃˚唉˚譪薆 噯靉	哎艾呃˚睚得隘˚餲礙愛膉
安 3 AN	安˚挨˚鞍唵˚庵鵪		蝻 俺˚唵˚	案按暗闇岸諺˚
昂 4 ANG	昂脬	昂˚		
傲 5 AO	嗷˚熬˚咬麞	厫熬˚螯鰲凹囂翱 璈鼇獒	襖熅拗˚	傲鄂奧懊燠澳

[CHA–CH'AN.]

乍 6 CHA
1. 扎紮喳苴咱痂蛰
2. 扎札楂苗劄閘柵
3. 扎拃詐鮓眨
4. 乍炸蚱詐

茶 7 CH'A
1. 叉釵喳差察擦桶詁
2. 查碴槎察眷茶搽
3. 扠一岔
4. 权汊岔刹咤詫榰

窄 8 CHAI
側摘謫—齋
—責擇澤齋宅翟
側仄窄
—債這豸寨瘵

柴 9 CH'AI
差拆釵儕
柴豺
冊跳蠆
瘥

斬 10 CHAN
占氈苫沾霑詹瞻譫梅擔旃氈鸇章
展搌輾眨—盞
占站綻綻—棧港戰瓚蘸—顫暫
—剷歲懺諓—擔闖—顫

產 11 CH'AN
儳劖鑱攙毚—
巉饞厘灛躔纏蟾禪蟬—瞕—嶄
剷鏟產躔鏟驏
劖鑱—産躔鏟—詔

[CHANG–CHEI.] APPENDIX III.—THE PEKING SYLLABARY.

	1	2	3	4		1	2	3	4
章 12 CHANG	章彰樟鄣璋漳韹 憧璋嫜鑾張—賬 彰樟漳鞟—賑掌	— — — — — — —	鞝 — — — 長° — 掌°	嶂障瘴丈仗杖長帳賑漲脹悵	唱 13 CH'ANG	昌倡娼閶 倡猖閭 — — — —	嫦嚐 常嘗償 — 長場腸場	昶惝敞氅 廠檠氅 — 暢° — 場	唱倡鬯 — — — — 悵° 韔暢
兆 14 CHAO	召昭酌招 — 釗朝嘲	着著 — — —	沼爪帊抓找 — —	召詔照帊笊兆旋棹趙肇	吵 15 CH'AO	超吵抄鈔 — 焯綽	— 巢晁鼂朝潮	— 吵炒謿—投° 扯吵	鈔 耀 — —
這 16 CHÊ	蔗鷓嗻遮著酌蟄	轍°折°哲摺—蟄 —	— 者 蹟 —	這浙柘輒懾 — 這°	車 17 CH'Ê	車砗 —	— —	扯吵 —	徹澈 轍澈僝瘈 —
這 18 CHEI	—	—	—	這°					

TZŬ ÊRH CHI.—COLLOQUIAL SERIES. [CHÊN–CH'ÊNG.]

眞 19 CHÊN	1 眞珍診貞禎蓁箴針怔砧椹斟簪	2 —	3 賮袗診畛—枕————斟°	4 鎭朕振震賑陳鵀—————譖°	臣 20 CH'ÊN	1 嗔瞋琛	2 臣沉辰宸陳塵橙	3 —磣輾蜃紛	4 狁趁稱趂—闐榇襯°
正 21 CHÊNG	正怔征貞楨爭掙崢琤眰蒸徵瞠	正怔鉦偵禎禎猙琤諍錚臧膯	—	正整—政—朕鄭掙證倀—拯拯°	正怔証症証——	成 22 CH'ÊNG	稱撜—偵蟶鐺崢鎯°	呈程极丞承成誠礽乘棖橙湞澂懲脝	逞騁———————————懲°	稱掌秤——————乘—————

[CHI-CH'I.] APPENDIX III.—THE PEKING SYLLABARY. 83

| | 吉 23 CHI | 1 幾機磯譏饑一奇一剞掎一隮齋一一勦積勣肌汲萁箕基朞一極一擊吃鶻姬乩啷喞 | 2 一一一一一急一一一一瘠一積及伋級笈一藉籍亟一極一一一一即 | 3 幾蟣一已紀一一一一擠濟一脊一几机一給一一一藉籍疷極殛一一一一訖 | 4 一一一忌紀記跽寄騎一劑濟霽一踖寂勣一績蹟岌級給祭際藉籍亟一殛擊繫技伎芰屐塈鯽載 | 奇 24 CH'I | 1 妻凄悽棲萋一崎踦谿七柒圻頎戚漆一一一一其淇萁箕期欺喫一一洲吃 | 2 歔凄悽棲杞奇琦騎齊擠蠐倅耆蚔棊一一一其淇萁箕期棋麒綦耆一乞岐歧 | 3 一屺杞起一一一一一一一一豈啟企一一一一其淇萁箕期棋麒綦耆一乞岐跂 | 4 妻一一一杞起一一一一一一一戚刺棄卻泣炁氣隙憩器一一一一一一一契一一切砌乞技一一 |

84 TZŬ ÊRH CHI.—COLLOQUIAL SERIES. [CHI-CH'IA.]

吉 23 CHI [cont.]

1 稽 ― ― ― 激笄 ― ― 迹跡 ― ―

2 稷 ― ― ― 激劇集 ― 吉桔髻 ― ― 疾蒺 ―

3 ― ― ― ― 激劇 ― 迹髻棘 ― ―

4 計稷輯悸洎 曁漑激劇鯽覬薊迹髻棘旨褶嫉繼偈 鯚

奇 24 CH'I [cont.]

1 稽茸緝 ― ― ― ― ― ― ― 詰

2 ― ― ― ― ― ― ―

3 ― ― ― ― ― ― ―

4 昃茸緝戢 ― ―

家 25 CHIA

夾挾 ― 鋏家傢稼嘉葭加袈枷迦甲稽嘎佳

26 CH'IA

却 刧挾頰 ― ― ― 茄 ―

裕 ― ― ― ― 賈假毠 ― 舉甲

芙梜頰鋏 ― 傢嫁價假架袈駕掔 ― 叞 ―

恰 26 CH'IA

夾卡 ― 咭挵搯

― ― ― ― ― ―

― 卡 ― ― ―

恰跲洽 ―

[CH'IAI-CH'IAO.] APPENDIX III.—THE PEKING SYLLABARY. 85

	1	2	3	4		1	2	3	4
					楷 27 CH'IAI	—	—	楷 揩	—
江 28 CHIANG	江 扛 將° 漿 僵 殭 繮 薑 姜	—	—	槳 蔣 獎 穮	虹° 將° 醬 匠° 強 降 絳 糨	搶 29 CH'IANG	戕 槍 戧° 蹌 諡 鎗 羌 唴 羥 腔 蜣 鏘 錚	檣 嬙 薔 — — 強 — 鯨 — — —	— — 謚 強 — 蹌 — —	搶 戧° — — — — — —
交 30 CHIAO	交 郊 蛟 鮫 焦 蕉 樵 雛 僬 澆 嬌 驕 膠 艽 椒 教° 角	咬° — — — — — — 嚼° — 覺° —	咬° 皎 餃 較 姣 勦 — 僥 腳° 嬌° 攪 — —	挍° 餃 較 叫 僬 醮 嚼° 窖 酵 嬌 嗷 覺 教° 角	巧 31 CH'IAO	雀 鵲 敲 — — 鴜 樵 瞧 磽 蹺 — —	雀 鵲 — — — 樵 翹 喬 蹻 轎 僑 蕎 橋	雀 鵲 — — 巧 — 愀 曉 悄 — — —	— — — — 竅 — — 俏 峭 鞘 誚 哨°

86 TZŬ ÊRH CHI.—COLLOQUIAL SERIES. [CHIEH-CH'IEH.]

	1	2	3	4		1	2	3	4
街 32 CHIEH	街 且° 皆 啃 堦 鋏° 揭 歇 界° — 嗟° 結 — — — — — — — 癤 — 接 綾°	捷° 媗 媞 偕 — — 俠 偈 竭 絜 潔 桔 結 頡 桀 傑 檞 — 隔 杰 刦 叶° 協° 垓 截° 許 節 — —	— 姐 — — — — — — — — — — — — 櫟 解 — — — — — — — 節 — — —	捷 睫 介 价 伷 鋏 洨 界° 絜 — — — — 頁° 解 廨 隔 呷 藉 戒 誡 — — 截 楫 禊 借 屆 傑 綾°	且 33 CH'IEH	切° 趄° —	— — 伽 茄 瘸 —	— 且° — — — — — — 挈 —	切° 趄° 怯 — — 愜 篋° 匧° 竊 慊 — — — — — — — — — — — — — — — — — — — 妾 唼

[CHIEN–CH'IH.] APPENDIX III.—THE PEKING SYLLABARY. 87

見 34 CHIEN

1
磯 菱 韉 間° 芇 緘° 煎 堅 肩 菅 尖 奸 漸 兼 搛 鶼 艱 監° 甄° 鰜°

2
—

3
塞 簀 戩 — 簡 鐗 減 揃 — 儉° 檢 — 鱺° 繭 吮 柬° 揀 諫

4
見 踐 餞 健 閒° 鐧 澗 箭 僭 件 — 劍 漸 歎 — 監 檻° 艦 雋 薦 諫

欠 35 CH'IEN

1
搴 塞 賽 騫° — 籖 鈐 牽 縴 — 嵌° 驪 僉 愆 歉 謙 — 千 芊 阡 — 鉛°

2
錢 鈐 黔 — 前 潛 涎 — 騴 籤 — 乾 虔 — — 鉗 — — —

3
— 淺 — — 前 — — — 慊 — — — — — 遣 —

4
欠 茜 蒨 倩 — 搏 縴° 荐 茜 嵌 — — 塹 — — — — 縴 — 斥 叱

知 36 CHIH

知 蜘 之 芝 汁 脂 — 贄 淄 蓄 緇 鎚 織 識

2
知° — 侄 姪 — — — — — — 執 蟄 — — 職 —

3
— — 止 址 扯 祉 趾 芷 — — 旨 指 — — 治 —

尺 37 CH'IH

4
智 至 侄 桎 郅 綏 — — 摯 贄 鷙 熱 — 識

1
— 痴° — 差 蹉 侈° 飭 勅 喫 吃 蚩 嗤

2
— 痴° 踟° 匙 — 篪 — — 治 答° — 嗤

3
— 祉 恥 侈° 褫 — — — 嗤

4
— 飭 勅 敕° 笞 — 熾

	知 36 CHIH [cont.]	1 熾°値厄櫛隻支枝 秩° 袛	2 直値質緇徵只 袛	3 陟値質躓只咫 秩 一徵 砥	4 一値置擲踌滯忮跖寘彘秩 稚制製撫豸志 痣誌	尺 37 CH'IH [cont.]	1 熾癡赤陝 絺 摛螭 鴟	2 癡 恃馳埤持池遲	3 敁齒 一尺	4 熾赤厕荝 翅 掣 親 沁 浸 嗯
	斤 38 CHIN	斤斸筋肋筋金今津浸寢 禁襟 荊巾		僅 瑾謹	近勁晉搢 始浸盡 禁 噤 進	親 39 CH'IN	親 欽 侵	芹秦勤懃 禽芩 衾琴	一寢 衾

[CHING-CH'IU.] APPENDIX III.—THE PEKING SYLLABARY. 89

	1	2	3	4		1	2	3	4
井 40 CHING	經°涇菁睛京驚晶旌耕荊更矜津兢	—	一到頸請耿景儆警	經°徑勁清靜敬竟鏡弳°—盡飢淨	輕 41 CH'ING	輕青情清頃傾卿	一情晴鯨榮擎	一請一	脛°倩清磬慶一親°
角 42 CHIO	—	角°覺爵—脚	角覺爵嚼脚腳	催°嚤	郤 43 CH'IO	—	一爵嚼	一雀鵲—却°	雀°鵲碏却°郤°穀橋壆
酒 44 CHIU	湫啾啾酋—究鳩糺赳繆樞	—	一酒韭九一糺久玖	救—鷲究俯白舅—麀咎欳	秋 45 CH'IU	秋°鶖鰍坵丘	鰍°坵—爵嚤	求球毬賕述録裘仇°囚虬	糗

	1	2	3	4		1	2	3	4
窮 46 CHIUNG	一 一 一	窮° 一	窘° 一 迥°	一 一 一	窮 47 CH'IUNG	傾° 一 一 一 一	穹窮筇蛩瓊	頃° 烱絅迥° 恐 一	一 一 一 一
卓 48 CHO	棹° 一 一 着° 一 汆 捉	卓濁櫂着著酌折啄斷榷	一 一 一 一 一 一 一	倬啜憨輟濯苗° 一 一 一	綽 49 CH'O	一 掉 一	一 一 一	一 戳 一	綽° 襪觸齪齱
晝 50 CHOU	州洲舟一周週啁粥謅	妯軸° 一 肘 一 一	柷° 帚 一 肘 一	晝咒說宙紂繇縐皺	抽 51 CH'OU	抽一瘳一一一一一搊	紬儔疇愁惆稠	丑扭° 一 瞅醜稠稠酬讐仇°	臭 一 一 一 一 一 一

[CHÜ-CH'ÜEH.] APPENDIX III.—THE PEKING SYLLABARY. 91

	1	2	3	4		1	2	3	4
句 52 CHÜ	菊苴趄拘居 ー ー 虛戲矩雎跔車俱	菊掬 ー ー ー ー ー 局	踘咀舉 ー ー 寋莒笸矩秬 ー ー	遽 一舉句鋸聚屢懼戲 ー 巨詎跙具俱 炬拒鉅	取 53 CH'Ü	曲麯蛆 陸趨屈 ー ー 衢墟嶇區軀	麴麯劬 ー 醵 ー ー 衢癯渠蕖 嶇驅圄	曲 ー ー 取娶 ー ー ー 鉅	漆 ー 去趣 ー ー ー 覷覰 ー ー
捐 54 CHÜAN	捐涓娟鵑鐲	ー ー ー ー	一卷捲錈	狷絹 卷倦 菤眷養 圈	全 55 CH'UAN	一鐫圈擐	攢捲拳 捲拳全 筌泉悛 權顴 癢蹶	犬畎 ー ー ー ー	綣券 圈 寋驉 ー ー 勸
絕 56 CHÜEH	一蹶撅 ー ー 嗟	絕厥蹶謫 決 玦 倔 角 覺 爵	橛鐝 譎 抉 訣 觖 掘 角 覺 爵	歴 ー ー ー	缺 57 CH'ÜEH	ー ー ー 缺	ー ー ー ー	ー ー ー ー	ー 闋却御関 碏卻雀確

	1	2	3	4		1	2	3	4
君 58 CHÜN	君軍竣° 踆均 逡鈞麏		窘° 菌	郡菌竣俊 畯餕駿°	羣 59 CH'ÜN		羣群 帬		
爵 60 CHÜO		爵°			却 61 CH'ÜO				却°
主 62 CHU	主° ── 朱侏 株珠 猪諸 豬蛛 誅粥°	主° ── 竺築 ── 尗── 嘱嚸 矚燭 蛛舳 逐篴	主° 拄 阻 ── ── 助── 囑囑 渚煮 ── ── ── ── 祝°	主° 麈詛 ── ── ── 助箸 ── ── 翥	注住柱駐佇貯 註蛀咮── 宁竚── ── 助筯蹢著── 妯° ── 礿杼澍鑄柷祝	出 63 CH'U	出° 樞初姝 駒樗	── ── ── ──	佇° 苧杵處楚 俎岨儲除 芻鶵鋤 ── 儲	齭畜 ── 處° 怵悚蠹 齭觸 鉏褚

[CHUA–CH'UI.] APPENDIX III.—THE PEKING SYLLABARY. 93

	1	2	3	4		1	2	3	4
抓 64 CHUA	撾°抓髽	—	爪仄	大苴	欻 65 CH'UA	欻	—	—	—
拽 66 CHUAI	搲°	—	跩輚轉	拽°	揣 67 CH'UAI	揣°	膗	揣惴	踹膪膪
專 68 CHUAN	專甎鱄 磚膞顓 耑	—	囀°轉	傳°囀°轉 撰饌賺°篆	穿 69 CH'UAN	川°拴栓 遄孱櫋 穿	川°傳船 — 椽	舛°喘 —	釧篡°串 —
壯 70 CHUANG	莊粧 裝庄妝 椿春	—	奘	壯狀撞	牀 71 CH'UANG	創瘡窗囪	床牀淙°	創闖 礃	創愴憧
追 72 CHUI	堇騅 隹錐追鎚觜°	棰	—	惴錘縋贅 惙綴墜對	吹 73 CH'UI	推°確 吹°炊 倭	椎垂陲 槌	揣 —	吹毳

	1	2	3	4		1	2	3	4
准 74 CHUN	惇°諄°屯 窀°	—	隼准準	—	春 75 CH'UN	春椿鶞°	純渲諄唇	蠢 — 唇°	—
中 76 CHUNG	中°盅鍾 忠 衷 鍾 鐘 終°	夷 —	冢塚 — 種 腫	中°仲重種種眾 踵	充 77 CH'UNG	中°冲忡沖翀 衝 — 春°艟充	崇重 — 虫蟲	寵 — — —	— 仲° — — 銃°
					擉 78 CH'UO	擉睉戳	擉眰戳	—	觸 焯 綽°

[Ê-ÊRH.] APPENDIX III.—THE PEKING SYLLABARY. 95

	1	2	3	4
額 79 Ê	哦˚阿˚ — — —	娥˚ 鵝˚ 蛾˚ 訛˚ 額 —	我˚ — — —	餓˚ 諤 鶚 額 惡˚ 鱷
恩 80 ÊN	恩 —	—	—	摁˚ 按˚
哼 81 ÊNG	哼 —	—	—	—
兒 82 ÊRH	兒˚ — —	兒˚ 洱 而	耳 珥 餌 而˚ 爾 邇 余	眲 二 貳 入 䶊 駬˚

	1	2	3	4
法 83 FA	法°伐髮發	法°伐筏閥罰	法°一髮一	法°乏一鏺
反 84 FAN	番°幡擱翻一藩繙帆一	番°幡蕃燔藩一繁凡°樊礬煩	反°坂返一一一凡°	販飯泛氾范一一汎梵範犯一
方 85 FANG	方妨坊肪芳	防°魴防房一	做仿仿舫訪紡髣	放一一
非 86 FEI	非菲°蜚扉霏緋妃飛一	肥淝一一一一	一菲°翡悱斐誹匪篚一一	痱一翡癈廢費沸肺蒂°柿吠縛

	1	2	3	4
分 87 FÊN	分° 芬 棼 紛 氛 焚° 一	汾 濆 鼖 燓 坟 黂 墳	粉 一 一 一	分° 忿 僨 憤 奮 糞
風 88 FÊNG	風 楓 峯 瘋 烽 鋒 蜂 丰 封 豐 酆 灃	一 逢 縫° 馮 一 一 一	諷° 一 一 一 捧 一 一 一	諷° 鳳 縫° 奉 俸 一 一 一
佛 89 FO	佛°	佛°	一	婦°
否 90 FOU	不° 一 一	罙 桴 芣 浮 枹	否° 缶° 一	阜 埠° 覆

夫
91
FU

1
夫芙°
鈇麩
咘
―
―
敷°
―
―
―
枹°
俘浮°
郛莩
―
―
―
―
―
―
―
膚
―
―
―
―
―
―

2
扶芙°
蚨髴°
弗佛°
佛°
敷°縛
符苻
枹孚浮°
桴伏
袱茯
福幅°
蝠復°
腹
―覆°
袚
―
―
―
―
―
―凫
―服

3
―
甫
脯簠
輔黼
―
―
―
―
拊府
俯腑腐
―俛°
―頫腊
撫
―
―
―
―
―
―
―腹°
―
咉斧釜
―紱
―
―
―
―
―

4
咈拂
―
―
髯°
怫沸
佛°
傅賻
―付駙
咐附訃
仆赴
―
―
―
―
―
袱
―
富幅
副輻
復°腹
覆°
馥父
―
負芾
絥賦
―婦
―臕

[HA–HANG.] APPENDIX III.—THE PEKING SYLLABARY. 99

	1	2	3	4
哈 92 HA	哈°	蝦	哈°	哈°
害 93 HAI	咳 — —	咳°頦孩還	一頦醢海	亥一害°和
寒 94 HAN	邯°一頇酣憨 犴 旰	邯°開函°涵函舍寒還翰°韓 —	罕 齒一頷喊° — — —	汗開悍銲旱捍一憾撼一翰°瀚漢和
硜 95 HANG	硜 — — —	亢°航頏行桁杭衡	吭° — — —	吭°沆巷°項 —

	1	2	3	4
好 96 HAO	哮°―蒿橈°――――	毫豪°壕濠°耗―號°嗥昊鶴°	好°――――――	好°浩皓鎬耗°涸號°皞顥―
黑 97 HÊ, HEI	黑°	―	―	―
很 98 HÊN	哏°――	哏°很°狠°痕	―很°狠―	恨°――
恆 99 HÊNG	亨°哼°――――	亨°珩衡°桁蘅恆姮莖	――――	―荇°―橫―

[HO-HOU.] APPENDIX III.—THE PEKING SYLLABARY.

河 100 HO

1
劃°
ー
ー
ー
ー
ー
ー
ー
ー
喝°
呵°
苛°
ー
荷°
訶
ー
ー
ー
ー

2
禾龢合盒
ー
ー
曷 斜°
褐 活 何
ー 荷
ー 和
盍 闔 劾
胢 核°
ー
ー
ー
ー
ー
覈°

3
火夥°
ー
哈
ー
ー
ー
ー
呵
ー
ー
ー
ー
ー
黑°
ー
ー
ー

4
鑊° 獲 嚇°
赫 貉 郃 劃° 攉 瘧°
畫 霍 喝° 害
蠚 暑 紇 惑
或° 荷 賀 和 黑 禍 郝 貨 涸 壑 豁 鶴 翯 呝

後 101 HOU

駒°
ー
ー
ー
ー

侯°
喉 猴
瘊 糇 餱
ー
ー

吼
ー
ー
ー
ー

候° 壎
厚 後 鱟
后 逅

102　　　　TZŬ ĚRH CHI.—COLLOQUIAL SERIES.　　　[HU-HUAI.]

	4	3	2	1
戶 102 HU	戶屝屭簢一一惚颹糊岵怙祜洹護鵠鸌侮欷縠	虎唬琥一一一一一一一一滸	摢乎呼囫一一胡瑚葫餬㶇糊㪱髻壺弧核斛狐	滹乎呼忽惚颹葫餬一薨一縠
花 103 HUA	化話華樺一攫一畫樺	話一一一一一	滑猾磆華譁鏵驊划劃踝	化花華譁一找一
壞 104 HUAI	壞一一	踝一一	懷槐淮獲	

[HUAN-HUEI.] APPENDIX III.—THE PEKING SYLLABARY. 103

	1	2	3	4
換 105 HUAN	儇° — — — 歡欢獾讙貛鸛驩	儇° 壈 圜 寰 環 還° 鐶 闤 饔 — 完 芄 汍 桓 萑 宛°	— — — — — 浣 莞 皖 — 綰 睆 —	奐 換 唤 渙 煥 瘓° — 睆 宦 幻 豢 懽 — 患
黃 106 HUANG	荒 慌 逭° 肓° — —	皇 隍 徨° 凰 煌 篁 蝗 鰉 黃 殰 簧	慌° 謊 恍 幌 怳 熀 悅 況 —	— — — — — — — — 況° 貺 攩
回 107 HUEI, HUI	揮 煇 暉 輝 翬 灰 恢° 撝 隳 徽 闞 豨 麾 —	回 徊 迴 囬 佪° — — — — — 旭°	悔° — 誨 會 — 賄° 匯° 旭°	悔° 晦 誨° 會 繪 檜 賄 匯° 濊 蕙 蟪° 惠 噦 彗 聵 殨 瞶 翽 濆 隳°

	1	2	3	4
回 107 HUEI, HUI [cont.]	— — — — —	— — — — —	毇 燬 — — —	卉 彙 恚 喙 諱
混 108 HUÊN, HUN	昏 婚 惛 葷° 閽	餛 魂 渾°	混° 焜 渾°	混° 掍 圂 溷
紅 109 HUNG	烘 — 吽° — — — — — — — 轟	洪 橫 璜 鬨° 虹 紅 葒 弘 泓 靈 鴻 嶸 宏 閎	哄 — — — — — — —	誤 橫° 鬨 吽 — 汞 — — — — —
火 110 HUO	和° 劐° 穫° 豁 霍 —	和° 惑 活 — —	火° 伙 夥 — —	或° 惑 獲 禍° 貨 攉

西
111
HSI

1
西栖
恓息熄
息熄
一晳
希郤
歔稀
奚傒
溪蹊
僖嘻
嬉
禧
肸
習
羲曦
嘶戲
撕
系
係
昔
惜
夕
醯
熙
錫
攜
徙
吸
隰
樓
犀

2
席蓆
息熄
熄
——
——
——
——
龠
——
——
——
——
習悉
膝
——
昔磶
一夕
——
——
錫攜
嘘襲

3
璽
——
——
熄晳
晰唏
——
——
喜嘻
嬉禧
——
——
葸洗
——
——
迄
——
——
——
徙屣

4
愾繶
——
——
析淅
晰蚸
舄歙
塈
——
盻
——
蟋戲
壻系
係臘
咥
——
汐麥
鬩繫
禊檄
細裼
——
——

14

	1	2	3	4
夏 112 HSIA	蝦鰕呀瞎ーーー	蝦瑕遐柙轄峽狹匧詰斜	ー	夏廈下洽祫陜嚇鞊劫
向 113 HSIANG	相湘箱香鄉襄瓖肛䃨 緗絎鄉鑲䮒	庠祥翔降ーーーーー	想响享嚮響鮝餉ーーー	相向象 像繈頊鄉巷 椽
小 114 HSIAO	宵逍魈消硝綃曉澆蕭簫唠 䬤鮹蛸霄嘵驍瀟蠨鴞楞 㚈梟嚻	爻肴崤哮學ーーーーー	小篠ーーー曉ーーーー	肖誚魈孝敎効效 綃哮笑校傲嘯ーーー

APPENDIX III.—THE PEKING SYLLABARY.

些 115 HSIEH

1
歇° 蝎°
些° 一
一
一
一
一
一
楔 挈°
一 揳
薛

2
斜° 鋏°
挾 絜°
鞋 駭
挈 械
骸 脅
恊 邪
一 袤 攜
一 諧 躞
一 叶°

3
一
寫 血°
一
一
一
一
一
一
一
一
一

4
羯° 楔°
瀉 屧°
泄 渫°
蝶 洩°
一 絏
楔 契°
一 揳
屑 挾
一 躞
爕
解 懈 蠏 瀉 謝
邂 薤 榭 褻 卸 械

先 116 HSIEN

先 秈 弦 痃 挸 洗°
仙 掀 絃 癎 毯 銑
忺 憸 舷 嫺 佃 險 闞 喊
僊 躚 閑 鷴 涵° 鮮
攑 鶱 函 絨 鹹 薛 癬
鮮 緘 一 爔
蘞 軒 咸 嫌 一 轞 玁 顯 燹 獼
纖 嫣 一 檻 喻
袨° 銜 涎 鈷 賢
攕 暹 一

陷° 餡°
霰 獻
獻 線 愆
見 現 縣 羨 憲 檻° 艦 限
一 一

荁

	1	2	3	4
心 117 HSIN	沁° 莘° 心 辛 忻 愍° 欣 薪 新 歆 馨°	覃° 尋 ー ー ー ー	隼° ー ー ー ー ー	汛° 訊° 迅° 信 牪 卂 ー
性 118 HSING	騂 星 惺 猩° 醒 煋 腥 ー ー ー 與° 蜻 餳° 馨	邢 型 形 ー 行° ー 陘 ー ー 餳	悻 㨲 醒° 省 ー ー ー ー	倖 姓 幸 性 顐 行° 荇 脛 杏 與° ー ー
學 119 HSIO	ー	學° ー	ー	俎° 謔°
修 120 HSIU	咻 貅 休 髹 羞 儵° 脩 修	囚° 泗 酋 遒 蝤 ー ー ー	宿° 朽 ー ー ー	宿° 鵂 莠 綉 秀 繡 銹 袖 鏽 岫 嗅

	1	2	3	4
兄 121 HSIUNG	兄 凶 洶° 胷 胸 芎	雄 熊 — — — —	迥° — 洶° — — —	敻 — — — — —
須 122 HSÜ	胥 虛 嫩 須 吁 戌 勗 畜 粟 欻 戌	糈 噓 歔 鬍 盨 恤° 卹 宿 需 訏 紆°	徐 俗 醑 — — — — — — — —	詡 煦 旭 項 許 嶼 聚 — — — —	壻 敍 旭° — 恤° 卹° 緒 續 絮 — 勗 畜 蓄	婿 渝 序 — — — — — — — —
喧 123 HSÜAN, HSÜEN	旋° 漩 璇 儇 嬛 — 宣 喧 萱 諠	旋° 漩° 璇 眩° — 瑄 揎 諠 璇° 軒 朘°	旋° 漩° 璇 玄 眩° 絃 宣 懸 璇 — — 劉°	癬 — 泫 — 選° — — — — — —	颮 — 炫 眩° 衒 選 楦 袀° 現 陷° 一 劉	拘 — — — — — — 絢° — — —

	1	2	3	4
雪 124 HSÜEH	削°靴 —	學°㩦 澰°— 䨮 — 穴 —	雪°削°血°岤 薛 —	雪 — 血 — 穴 —
巡 125 HSÜN	熏 勳 曛 蕙 獯 纁 蕈° —	循 洵 岣 旬 恂 荀 珣 諤 馴 巡 蕁° —	筍 笋 隼 —	汛° 迅 狥 — 誨 峻 巽 訓 濬 濬 —
學 126 HSÜO		學°		
衣 127 I, YI	伊 咿° 一° — 宜° — 黟 — — 猗 欹 漪 —	亦° 奕° — 壹° 夷 姨 痍 胰 宜 誼 貽 怡 飴 移 頤 疑 擬 嶷 猗° —	亦° — 以 苡 — 螘° — 擬 已 倚 椅 —	亦° 奕° — 壹° — 懿 宜° 馴 弋 曳 洩 — 邑 浥° 悒 挹 益 盆 溢 艗 隘

衣
127
I, YI
[cont.]

1
噫 — — 癔 繄 翳 醫 — — — 衣 依 — 乙 揖 — — — — — — — — — — — — — — — — — — —

2
倪 猊 鯢 輗 霓 沂 涯 遺 蛾 鮨 — — — — — 迤 — — 儀 — — — — — — — — — — — — — — —

3
— — — — — — — — — — — — 苢 — 尾 — 矣 艤 蟻 — 倚 扆 — — — — — — — — — — — —

4
鎰 鎰 鎰 瞌 晩 意 億 慧 憶 臆 癔 懌 懌 譯 場 剔 翊 易 蜴 羿 翌 義 熠 蟻 衣 裔 扆 乙 揖 翼 議 液 被 噫 疫 掖 腋 藝 毅 泄 乂 柂 刈 抑 佚 異 佾 逆 逸 詣 射 語 肆 劓

	1	2	3	4
染 128 JAN	一 一	然 燃 髯	染 冉 苒	一 一
嚷 129 JANG	瀼 一 一	壤° 攘 獽 禳	壤° 攘 讓 一	一 讓 禳 釀
繞 130 JAO	橈 燒 蕘	饒 一	遶° 繞 擾	遶° 繞° 弱
熱 131 JÊ, JO	一	一	若° 惹	爇 若° 日°
人 132 JÊN	一 一 一 紉°	壬 任° 妊 人 仁 仍° 紉°	一 衽° 恁 飪 仍° 忍 橪 一	荏 任° 衽° 刃 仞 一 紉° 認 孕° 椹 稔

[JÊNG–JU.] APPENDIX III.—THE PEKING SYLLABARY. 113

	1	2	3	4
扔 133 JÊNG	扔°扨°	仍°	扔°仍°	—
日 134 JIH	—	—	—	日°
若 135 JO	—	—	惹°	若°箬°熱°弱°
肉 136 JOU	揉°	柔揉踩猱°	揉°	肉°
如 137 JU	如°	如°茹°儒嚅薷°	茹°入擩汝乳辱°	入儒擩廿褥乳肉辱溽蓐褥°

15

	1	2	3	4
輭 138 JUAN	— — — —	— — — —	輭蠕軟阮	— — — —
瑞 139 JUI	— — — — —	— — — — —	汭芮䭃蕊𦽏	瑞銳䭃睿
			蚋藥	
潤 140 JUN	— — —	— — —	允	閏潤
絨 141 JUNG	— — — — — —	茸榮縈戎猱容蓉	揖冗氄	— — — — — —
		𤣪 狨絨榕鎔慵融		

[KA-K'AO.] APPENDIX III.—THE PEKING SYLLABARY. 115

	1	2	3	4		1	2	3	4
嘎 142 KA	嘎°	嘎°	嘎°	嘎° 噶	卡 143 K'A	卡°	—	卡°	—
改 144 KAI	陔 垓 荄 勾 咳 街° 剴	陔 該 勾 呃 街° 剴	— — — — — —	欸 — — — — —	蓋 丐 漑° 槩 槩	開 145 K'AI	開	—	凱 愷 垍 鎧 咳 慨 — 愾 楷	—
甘 146 KAN	乾° 干 杆 玕 肝 竿 秆 甘 泔 柑 疳	— — — — — — — — — — —	— 扦 — 秆 — — — — — — —	擀 鼾 桿 趕 敢 橄 感 — — — —	幹 旰 — — — 紺 — — — — —	看 147 K'AN	看 — 堪 戡 刊 龕	— — — — — —	吹° 砍 侃 刊 檻	看° 勘 倪° 瞰 闞 喊
剛 148 KANG	亢° 扛 肛 缸 江 岡 剛 堈 綱 鋼 將°	— — — — — — — — — — —	— — — — 尚 堈° — —	— — — — 杠 虹° 槓 — — — —	炕 149 K'ANG	康 糠	— 扛°	忧 慷 沆	亢° 抗 伉 炕
告 150 KAO	高 篙 羔 糕 餻 咎° 櫜 皐 糕	膏 — — — — — — — —	— — — — — — — —	槁 稿 毫 杲 鎬° 鎬 薹 — — —	告 詰 — — — — — — —	考 151 K'AO	敲° 尻	— —	烤 薹 考 拷 烤	烤° 犒 靠 拷 —

	1	2	3	4		1	2	3	4
給 152 KEI	—	—	給°	—	刻 153 K'EI	刻°	—	—	—
根 154 KÊN	根跟觔°	哏 —	梗° —	艮°亘	肯 155 K'ÊN	—	—	肯°齦懇	掯° —
更 156 KÊNG	秔更°稉庚賡脛耕羹	—	哽埂梗骾	更°	坑 157 K'ÊNG	坑傾鏗誙	—	肯	掯°
各 158 KO, KÉ	咯柯哥擱胳割鴿	各°格閣擱鬲槅蛤閤葛呃革	各°一屙咢——忆合恰閤攪個箇	各°硌硌—————葛	可 159 K'O, K'É	可°坷珂嗑科蝌箜稞髁刻頟壳磕剋	可° — 軻 — — — — 咳欬槛瞌 —	可°坷—————渴刻 瞌	疴恪客廓科擴—稞課錁刻去——克剋閬°

[KOU–K'UA.] APPENDIX III.—THE PEKING SYLLABARY. 117

	1	2	3	4		1	2	3	4
狗 160 KOU	勾 鉤 拘 篝 溝 緱 °	狗 ° —	狗 枸 苟 耇	詬 姤 垢 彀 構 遘 媾 覯 購	口 161 K'OU	圓 摳 膒 ° 芤 摀	—	口 扣 °	叩 扣 釦 ° 寇 蔻
古 162 KU	古 估 ° 咕 蛄 菇 呱 孤 沽 姑 鴣 罛 觚 苽 茹 — 瀔 穀 蔛 骨 辜 谷	— — — — — 骨 ° —	古 估 罟 鼓 臌 牯 汩 賈 盬 蠱 股 瑴 殳 — 骨 滑 谷 峪	估 故 酤 涸 錮 痼 雇 顧 僱 — — — — — — 滑 —		枯 哭 砣 圣 涸 酷 嚳 刳 堀 窟 °	—	苦	庫 褲 — — — — 袴 ° —
瓜 164 KUA	瓜 呱 ° 孤 刮 聒 驢 鴰 媧 蝸 騧	— — — — — 骨 —	呱 — — — — 骨 —	— 括 适 聒 ° 鴰 卦 挂 掛 罣 寡 — 副 寡	跨 165 K'UA	夸 姱 誇 °	—	— 誇 °	胯 袴 跨 — —

	1	2	3	4		1	2	3	4
怪 166 KUAI	乖唝	—	夬拐	怪壞	快 167 K'UAI	—	—	擓擙劊	快筷駃塊噲
官 168 KUAN	官棺權觀鸛關瘝鰥綸冠莞	—	—	捾管舘 — — — — — — 筦斡	寬 169 K'UAN	寬	—	欸	貫慣灌觀鸛罐 — 冠裸盥卯
光 170 KUANG	光胱誆	—	—	洸逛廣	況 171 K'UANG	匡筐誆	狂誑	—	框眶況壙曠纊
規 172 KUEI	嬀歸龜規瑰圭珪晷撅鱖	—	—	宄軌癸簋鬼 — — 晷 — 垝詭	愧 173 K'UEI	盔詼巋	恢揆葵窺魁奎逵尷夔	—	匱簣愧塊饋噌 — 餽 — 跬

[KUÊN–K'UO.] APPENDIX III.—THE PEKING SYLLABARY. 119

	1	2	3	4		1	2	3	4
棍 174 KUÊN, KUN	昆°崐° 鯤鵾 䰐	— — — —	袞滾 鯀 —	棍° — — —	困 175 K'UÊN, K'UN	昆°崐° 坤髡 閫°壼	— — — —	捆悃 稇綑° 閫°壼	困悃° — —

	1	2	3	4		1	2	3	4
工 176 KUNG	工攻 功紅° 弓躬蚣 公供龔恭宮肱肩	— — — — — —	駉 獷憬卅 — — —	— — 共供°貢 — — —	孔 177 K'UNG	空°崆 — — — —	— — — — —	孔恐 — — — —	空°控 — — — —

	1	2	3	4		1	2	3	4
果 178 KUO	一幗°蟈°郭鍋戈°聒一過°	國°幗°馘馘椰° — — — 虢	猓蜾 果菓椁郭椰° — — — 裹	啯°蟈 — — — 聒°攪過°	闊 179 K'UO	— — — — — —	— — — — — —	— — — — — —	闊°濶° 擴犞廓 — — —

	1	2	3	4
拉 180 LA	喇° — — 糯° 拉	剌° — — — —	喇° — — — —	剌° 辣 臈 蠟 糯° 落°
來 181 LAI	— — — — —	來 郲 萊 騋 — — —	— — — — —	徠 睞 賚 瀨 賴 籟 癩 糯° 檒
懶 182 LAN	— — — — 鹽° —	闌 攔 欄 瀾 蘭 藍 爁° 籃 襤 盩 棼° 巒° 鸞 占 嵐	— — 濫° 爁 壁 覽 攬 棼° 懶 — —	爛 亂° — 濫 — 纜 — — — —
浪 183 LANG	— — 跟 哴°	琅 稂 狼 郎 廊 榔 螂	悢 — 朗° 閬 榔° —	浪 — 朗° 閬°

	1	2	3	4
老 184 LAO	一一一橑一一一	老栳勞嘮楞癆醪躼牢	老栳姥一一潦一一	一一勞澇一癆潦獠烙絡 落酪
勒 185 LÊ	扐一			肋勒洛樂
累 186 LÊI, LEI	一縲勒一一一	累雷擂一纍擂礧贏	累縲儡壘耒磊蕾一	累肋脇儡擂攂類淚酹
冷 187 LÊNG	崚倰稜陵楞	凌稜一楞	冷一一一	棱一睖愣

立 188 LI

1 哩娌貍――李―莉漓―璃篱―――――――麗鸝

2 貍―貍邐婺梨犂――漓―璃綡離籬罹鸘犂黎―――――驪鸝

3 里娌俚理―鯉醴――裡裏禮禮李履―――――――邐鑫

4 哩歷曆瀝攊利唎噁瀝靈俐唎莉痢立笠茌颯厲癘糲栗力戾 噁瀝礫勵慄粒蒞瀝礪勵慄溧泪礫麗儷嚚吏隸例

倆 189 LIA

倆

	1	2	3	4
兩 190 LIANG	兩°　量　―　跟°　粱°　―	―　魉°　量　糧　艮　蜋　梁　粱°　樑　涼　涼	兩°　魉　―	俩°　輛°　量　―　―　―　―　掠°　晾　諒　亮
了 191 LIAO	撩　―　―　―　―	僚°　遼　―　寮　潦　―　寥　―　料°　聊　嘹	燎°　―　暸°　了　蓼　―	燎°　瞭　暸°　―　廖　罿　署　―　料°　掉°
裂 192 LIEH	―　咧°　―　―	乜°　咧　―　―	捋°　咧　―　―	列　冽　咧　裂　翃　劣　沥　勒°　獵　躐　鬣

	1	2	3	4
連° 193 LIEN	連° 漣° — — — — — — —	連° 璉° 漣° 蓮 褳 縺 槤 鎌 廉 濂 臁 簾 鎌 帘 聯 奩 憐	輦° — — 斂° 臉 — — — — —	璉° 楝°煉 楝 練 鍊 斂°歛 殮 瀲 戀° — — — —
林° 194 LIN	— — — — —	林 淋 琳 霖 臨 鄰 粼 嶙 鱗 麟	— — 凜 廩 懍 檁 —	淋° 藺°躪 臨° 燐 吝 悋 賃°
另° 195 LING	— — — — — — —	令° 伶 泠 囹 玲 翎 蛉 羚 鈴 零 舲 櫺 靈 齡 凌 陵 菱 綾	— 領 嶺 — — 凜°廩 —	令° — — — — — — 另

	1	2	3	4
略 196 LIO	—	—	畧°	—
留 197 LIU	鎏°餾溜遛—	流旒鎏鎦榴遛飀 琉硫瘤遛鶹騮劉瀏	柳—留綹——	六°陸—溜°餾鎦磟—瀏° 雷
駱 198 LO	擄°————	—摞螺羅儸蘿钃蠃 驟羅玀邏钃贏膈覷	擄°瘰—擺砢抒裸贏氀	樂摞勒攞咯烙絡洛°落酪駱雒擧—
陋 199 LOU	摟°—	婁°樓鏤— 蔞縷髏藪	嶁°摟鏤—	陋漏瘺露—

	1	2	3	4
律 200 LÜ	— — — — — — — —	婁° 屢° 鏤 一 間 廬 驢 一	掠° 屨° 褸 縷 呂 僂 攄 膂 旅 祓 陸° 履	一 一 褸° 一 慮 蔉 綠° 鋦 一 律
戀 201 LÜAN	— —	攣 癵	孿 孿	戀° 一
略 202 LÜEH	—	—	畧°	畧°
掄 203 LÜN	一 一 掄° 一 輪° 一	倫 崙° 圇 掄 淪 綸° 論° 輪° 淋	一 圇° 一 一 一 一	一 一 一 一 論° 一
略 204 LÜO	一 一	一 一	畧° 一	畧° 掠

	1	2	3	4
路 205 LU	落° ⸺ ⸺ ⸺ ⸺ 䘘 ⸺ ⸺ 嚕 ⸺	路° 盧° 瀘 臚 艫 轤 驢	盧° 爐° 廬 顱 鑪 鱸	鹵 滷 ⸺ ⸺ 擄 ⸺ ⸺ 魯 櫓	路° 賂 輅 潞 露 鷺 六° 陸° ⸺ ⸺ ⸺ 菉 祿 轆 碌° 綠 錄 簏 ⸺ 磟 鹿 樚 漉 簬 麓 勠 僇 謬 戮
亂 206 LUAN	⸺	欒 灤 臠° 鑾	戀° ⸺	卵 ⸺	亂° ⸺
論 207 LUN	⸺ ⸺ ⸺	倫° 圇 掄	崙° 圇 綸 論 輪 稜	⸺ 圇 ⸺ ⸺	⸺ ⸺ ⸺ 論 ⸺
龍 208 LUNG	隴 ⸺ ⸺ ⸺ 窿	龍° 爐 瓏 䶬 龓 聾 籠 隆 窿	襱° 攏 隴 ⸺ ⸺ 籠° ⸺	弄° ⸺ ⸺ ⸺ ⸺

	1	2	3	4
馬 209 MA	沫°抹 媽 嗎° 摸 模° 麽	麻 蔴 瀮 一 瑪° 蟆 一	馬 嗎° 碼 禡° 瑪° 螞 麽	榪 禡 一 螞° 罵 媽 一
買 210 MAI	一 麥° 一 一 一 一 一	埋° 霾 一 一 一 一 一	買 一 一 一 一 一 一	賣° 麥 陌 貊 脉° 脈 邁 貉 靆 霢°
慢 211 MAN	顢 一 一 一 一	瞞 一 漫° 蔓° 謾 饅 埋° 蠻	滿 一 一 一 一	慢 慢 慢° 墁 漫° 蔓° 一
忙 212 MANG	一 一 一 芒° 一	忙 邙 芒 肓 尨 沁 悙 茫° 鋩 厖	莽 漭 蟒 一 一 一 一	一 一 一 一 一

	1	2	3	4
毛 213 MAO	摸°一貓°一	毛旄一矛°髦貓錨茅蝥	卯昴一一	芼眊貌茂冒°髦貌°帽貿媢媚
美 214 MEI	—	梅没眉帽枚媒莓郿楣玫煤蘪湄	每美浼一	妹昧魅媚墨妹寐媚墨袂
門 215 MÊN	們°捫悶—	門捫°璊	們°懑悗	們悶懣—
夢 216 MÊNG	一濛°矇懵	蒙濛矇甍虻盟萌氓䖟龜	蠓猛懵懵	一孟夢一

	1	2	3	4
米 217 MI	一 眯°彌°筬 一	迷 愫 謎° 彌° 獼 瀰 麋 麇 麛 一	米 眯° 乜 一 饢 弭 一	覓 甍 謎° 宓° 密 蜜 謐 汨 系 袟
苗 218 MIAO	喵 一 一	苗 描 猫 一	眇 秒 緲 渺 淼 藐	妙 廟 庙 一
滅 219 MIEH	咩 一	乜° 明°	一	滅 搣 筬°
面 220 MIEN	一 一 一 一 一	眠 棉 綿 一 一 一 一	緬 眄 俛° 娩 黽 瞑 澠	面 麵 丏 麪 一 一 一 一
民 221 MIN	一 一 一 一 一 一	民 岷 珉 緡 旻 閩 黽° 瞑 脗	泯 抿 愍 一 一 閔 憫 皿 黽° 敏 脗	一 一 一 一 一 一

[MING—MO.] APPENDIX III.—THE PEKING SYLLABARY. 131

	1	2	3	4
名 222 MING	— — — — — —	名 茗 明° 銘 盟° 冥 溟 蜢 鳴 酩	皿° — 瞑 溟 眠	命 — — — — —
謬 223 MIU.	— —	矛° 眸	— —	謬° 繆
末 224 MO	— 麼° 摩 — — — — 摸° —	— 麼° 摩° 磨° 魔 饃 — 模 謨 —	邈 抹° — — — — —	末 沫° 抹 秣 磨 脈° 沒 陌 墨° 嘿 默 万 麥 螞 霡 莫 慔 漠 寞 膜° 幕° 慕 墓

	1	2	3	4
謀 225 MOU	— — — — —	謀 拇 模 牟 眸° 伴 鍪 犙	某° 拇° 牡° 畝° — —	茂° 貿 袤 瞀 懋 —
木 226 MU	— — — — — — — —	沒° 歿° 模 — — — — —	母 拇 牡° 姥 媽° 畝 — —	沒° 歿 莫° 暮 幕 墓 慕 木 沐 目 穆 繆 鶩 牧 睦 霂 苜
那 227 NA	那° 哪° — —	拿 呐° 挐	那° — —	那° 内° 衲 枘 納 捺
奶 228 NAI	— — —	— — —	那° 乃 奶 氖° 妳 妳	那° 奈 氖 耐 褦 奈 —

	1	2	3	4
男 229 NAN	一一喃°一一	難°南喃°楠男俺°一	一揇暖°煖一唵°赧	難°攤一一一一
囊 230 NANG	嚷噥一	囊一	攮壤°曩暖°煖	儾齉一
鬧 231 NAO	撓°一一	撓°鐃啘°猱猫°	惱瑙腦臑一	鬧淖一一
內 232 NEI	一	一	餒那一	內°那°
嫩 233 NÊN	一	一	那°一	那°嫩°
能 234 NÊNG	能°儂°一	能濃獰膿農	那°一一	那°弄拰濘淳寧

	1	2	3	4
你 235 NI	呢°	尼 怩° 呢° 泥 妮	旎 你 擬° 薿	昵 嬺° 禰 溺° 匿 惄° 睨° 逆 暱° 嶭 膩
孃 236 NIANG	—	娘 孃 釀°	—	釀
鳥 237 NIAO	裊	—	鳥° 蔦 裊 嫋 杳° 嬲°	尿° 謔 嬲 溺 虐 瘧°
揑 238 NIEH	揑 捻°	呆°	—	涅 捻° 錜 甚 躡 惁 臬 孽

	1	2	3	4
念 239 NIEN	拈° 粘 鮎 年 言	拈° 黏 鮎 年 言 涎	捻° 輦 碾 撚 趁 一	念 ° 艦 諗 一 一 一
您 240 NIN	一	您	恁	賃°
甯 241 NING	一 一 一	寧° 嚀 擰 凝	擰 擰 一	寧° 濘 甯 佞 虐 虐° 瘧 謔
虐 242 NIO	一 一	一 一	一 一	虐° 瘧 謔
牛 243 NIU	妞 一 一	牛° 一	忸 扭 柠° 紐 鈕	衄 拗 謬° 謬
挪 244 NO	哪 一 喏	那° 挪 娜 踻 儺 一	一 一 娜° 諾	懦 糯 一 諾 訥 掇

	1	2	3	4
耨 245 NOU	—	—	—	弄° 耨
女 246 NÜ	籹	—	女°	絮°
虐 247 NÜEH	—	—	—	虐° 瘧 謔°
虐 248 NÜO	—	—	—	虐° 瘧° 謔°
奴 249 NU	—	奴 孥 駑	努 弩 哅	怒 —
暖 250 NUAN	—	—	餪 暖° 煖°	—
嫩 251 NUN	—	—	—	嫩°

[NUNG–OU.] APPENDIX III.—THE PEKING SYLLABARY. 137

	1	2	3	4
濃 252 NUNG	一 儂° 濃° 一	農 儂° 濃° 膿	一 一 一 一	擃 弄° 一
訛 253 O	一 哦° 阿 疴	峨 俄 哦° 娥 鵝° 蛾° 訛° 閦 額	我° 一 一 一 一	餓° 堊 鄂° 惡 諤 鶚° 萼 呃° 厄 一 額 搕 過 鱷° 罷 嶪
偶 254 OU	漚° 嫗° 歐 毆 謳° 膒° 謳 鷗 緱 一	一 一 一 一 一 一 藕°	一 嘔° 熰 毆 謳 毆 偶 耦 藕	漚° 嘔° 慪 一 一 一 一 一 一

	1	2	3	4		1	2	3	4
罷 255 PA	八 叭 巴 把° 芭 疤 笆 捌 鏺	扒 吧 把° 芭 犯	八° — — — 拔 魃	一 — 把° — —	怕 256 P'A	趴 一 怕 — 琶 葩	趴 扒 — — 杷 爬 耙		一 怕 帕
拜 257 PAI	擺掔	白° 帛	伯 柏 百 栢 擺	稗 帛 敗 拜 偙	派 258 P'AI	揰° 拍	揰° 牌 俳 杯 菩		抓 派 湃
半 259 PAN	班° 般 搬 頒	斑 扳 瘢 蟹 頒°	斑° 瘢 蟹 頒°	板 版	半 捽 叛 伴 絆 畔 扮 辦 瓣 辯°	盼 260 P'AN	扳° 癬 番 拚 攀	磻 蟠 繙 磐 盤 瓣		判° 泮 盼°	叛° 盼°
幇 261 PANG	帮 梆 哪 幇 幇	那 哪		綁 榜 膀 膀°	一 傍 判 泮 蚌 盼 拼 棒 謗° 叛	旁 262 P'ANG	磅 滂 胖	旁 傍 滂 膀 徬	憉 螃 逄 仿 龐	謗° 膀 — 仿	胖

[PAO-P'ÊN.] APPENDIX III.—THE PEKING SYLLABARY. 139

	1	2	3	4		1	2	3	4
包 263 PAO	包苞褒剝 胞褒剝	雹雹 — — — 薄°	鮑保堡裸葆寶 — 鴇 —	抱鮑° 刨° — 瀑°爆 曝報豹	跑 264 P'AO	泡胞 — — — 拋	刨咆庖炮袍跑匏麅 廡燻	— — — 跑 —	泡°砲°炮°礮囊 — 暴°摻

北 265 PEI	卑碑 — — 陂背悲 — 杯盃桮	羆° — — — — — —	俾 — — — 彼北 — 悒	佩琲 婢禪俉 焙臂被背 邶貝 秕狽狒 — 備倄悖藼	陪 266 P'EI	— — — — — 酷 — 披 — — 坏坯怀	— 陪 培賠 — 俳襲 — 坏° 呸 胚	— — — — — — — 丕	佩珮沛霈 — 配轡岥 披 — — — 噴°

| 本 267 PÊN | 賁 — 奔犇 錛 — 犇 | — — — — — — | — — — 本畚 — — | — 笨犇洴奔犇 | 盆 268 P'ÊN | 噴° — — 盆湓 | 盆湓 | — — — — 噴° 体 |

迸 269 PÊNG	1 抨崩痭 弸繃	2 — — —	3 — 琫蚌	4 迸捧埲	朋 270 P'ÊNG	1 烹漰硼 — — 澎怦	2 朋棚硼痭鵬 膨彭蓬芃 砰	3 — 捧 — — — —	4 摚碰䈽 — — — —

| 必 271 PI | — — — — — — — — — 逼 | — — 挈鼻羆 — 必 — — — 觱篦 — | — — 壁 一鄙 — — — — 鼙比妣匕 — 否 — 筆 | 辟壁薜嬖避鄙婢睥髀必芯閟愎畢躃敝蔽斃鼙比庳箆幅閉費賁贔碧弼 | 皮 272 P'I | — — 僻劈霹闢 — — 匹披 — 批 一砒 — 胚坯 | — — — 羆睥脾 — — 匹皮疲 — 比枇砒貔 | 辟擗癖劈鄙 — — 圮疟 匹披 — 缶批庀狴 — 否痞 | 辟僻 屁甓霹闢譬 — — — 愎 — — 屁 — — — |

APPENDIX III.—THE PEKING SYLLABARY.

	1	2	3	4		1	2	3	4
表 273 PIAO	摽標飈杓廔髟彪	—	—	鰾—表俵婊裱	票 274 P'IAO	漂飄鰾	嫖瓢	漂膘	票漂勲 殍
別 275 PIEH	出°—憋鼈蟞虌	別	粃—憋	—憋—蟞虌	撇 276 P'IEH	撇氅潎瞥	撇氅瞥	—	潎瞥蟞虌
扁 277 PIEN	蝙編鯿—鞭邊籩	—	扁匾—縹貶	遍忭汴便弁辯變辦辮耕	片 278 P'IEN	偏篇翩	— 便	扁諞—耕	騙騗片
賓 279 PIN	嬪繽濱鑌頻蘋檳彬斌	—	—	擯儐臏殯髩—稟	貧 280 P'IN	嬪繽	—頻蘋—貧	顰嚬—品	嬪牝聘

	兵 281 PING	1 兵梹氷冰－－－并° －	2 －－－凭° －－－	3 丙柄炳－禀秉－屏餅	4 －病－－井併並	憑 282 P'ING	1 平坪枰萍評屏°瓶－娉	2 －－傰凭拚凴餠蘋°	3 －－－－－－－－	4 －－－－－－娉聘
	波 283 PO	波玻°菠白－－－－－不剝鉢蔔餑撥－－幡	－－菠°白伯泊－鉑百博搏膊薄°－－－幡°	跛簸－－－白伯泊－鉑百博膊－－鈬駮－	－簸－帛伯泊舶栢箔迫鉑百博膊餺鯊跋鈸魃擘北臬電播	破 284 P'O	坡玻°頗婆撲朴珀－－拾－－渤潑－－－	－婆°撲朴－－－－－踣°－－－膰°	破－－－－－－－－－僕璞匐勃淳－匣管－吭－－	破－嫛撲朴拍珀粕魄－僕模匐浮葧－－－－－

[POU-SA.] APPENDIX III.—THE PEKING SYLLABARY. 143

	1	2	3	4		1	2	3	4
不 285 POU	不	—	—	—	剖 286 P'OU	裒	—	剖°	—

	1	2	3	4		1	2	3	4
不 287 PU	不晡—勃撥°—	不—逋—脖—僕°濮	捕補鋪卜—北°譜—堡°	不晡步悖布怖簿埠部瀑	普 288 P'U	—鋪—噗樸°	葡蒲—菩—匍蔔	浦—扑°—普潽樸	舖鋪堡——————

	1	2	3	4
撒 289 SA	撒°靸°颯°三薩	撒臢	撒洒灑°——	卅趿°靸°颯°—薩

	1	2	3	4
賽 290 SAI	一攙°偲°搋°腮 鰓 篩	一搋°	一一一一一	塞°攙°賽一一
散 291 SAN	三°叁一鬅珊	一一一一	一散°饊糝傘	三°散°一一
桑 292 SANG	喪°桑一	一一一	一磉顙 搡顙	喪°一一
掃 293 SAO	慅騷搔艘臊繅一	一一一一	掃°一嫂一一	掃°一噪臊°燥譟彗颾

	1	2	3	4
嗇 294 SÊ	嘶°	嘶°	索°	色°
	說°	瑟°	—	瑟°
	—	—	—	嗇
	—	—	—	穡 濇°
	—	—	—	澁°
	虱°	—	—	塞°
	蝨° 蝨°	—	—	—
森 295 SÊN	森°	—	—	—
僧 296 SÊNG	僧	—	—	—
索 297 SO	索°	—	索°	—
	𢹂°	—	𢹂°	𢹂°
	蹜 縮	—	縤 鎍	朔° 槊
	莎 挲 娑	—	瑣 鎖	素°
	唆° 梭	—	—	嗦
	蓑	頣°	率	蟀
	些°	—	所°	數°
搜 298 SOU	嗖 𣙰	—	叟-	瘦°
	溲 艘	—	嗾	—
	餿 颼	—	擻 籔	藪
	蒐	—	—	嗽 漱
	摗	—	—	—

	1	2	3	4
素 299 SU	俗°酥擻°蔬甦蘇	束°速°疎俗°宿一粟肅	—	束°速疎°素宿蓿粟慄肅驌訴所夙窣愬遡術°溯續謖塑述
算 300 SUAN	狻酸	—	—	算蒜
碎 301 SUI	歲雖雎尿°荽綏遂	隋°隨°遂	髓	碎誶啐粹荽喙°隧彗穗燧篲繐祟

[SUN-SHAI.] APPENDIX III.—THE PEKING SYLLABARY. 147

	1	2	3	4
孫 302 SUN	孫猻飱 蓀	— —	笋°筍°損	巺°巽噀
送 303 SUNG	松菘 淞鬆 — 誦°慫嵩	— — —	悚°竦聳	訟頌宋誦送訴
殺 304 SHA	沙裟 砂紗殺 鯊 — 歃煞杉	— — —	傻耍洒灑	刹厦 嗄 — 灑罄歃煞 — 唼
曬 305 SHAI	篩攦 釃	— — —	色°—骰灑°	洒°晒殺°曬

	1	2	3	4
山 306 SHAN	山 埏 羴 ― ― ― ― 煽 諤 揚 鳣 蟮 衫 衫 摻° 刪 姍 潸	― 單° ― 禪° 蟬° ― 苫° ― ― ― 澶 ― ― ― ― ―	疝° 閃 陝 ― ― ― ― ― ― ― ― ― ― ― ― ―	疝° 訕 單 墠° 禪° 鱓 善 膳 苫° 扇 諤 騙 擅 瞻° 瞻 掞 ― 柵 ―
賞 307 SHANG	商 ― ― 裳° 傷 愓 殤 觴	尚° 晌° 常 嫦 裳 甚 ― ―	― 肩 晌° 飽 賞 ― ― ―	尚° 上 ― ― ― ― 愓° ―
少 308 SHAO	弰 梢 稍 筲 ― 颸 鞘 燒	― ― ― ― 勺° 芍° 釣° 灼° 杓° 韶	少° ― 鞘° ― ― ― ― ―	少° ― ― 紹 ― ― 劭 邵 哨°

舌
309
SHÊ

1
瑟°賒°奢°涉°

2
舌折佘蛇闍歙°

3
捨°

4
舍捨色°
射麝
葉設涉赦社澁賷濇輒攝

身
310
SHÊN

身申°紳
伸呻深參°蔘蓡詵駪娠莘森瘁

一申°神甚忱蜃

審瀋嬸沈哂

審瀋嬸甚黮沈諗滲哂矧愼朕蜃腎

	1	2	3	4
生 311 SHÊNG	生牲 笙猩勝升 甥陞森聲	澠繩	眚省	盛剩乘聖勝騰
事 312 SHIH	史尸屍師飾蠅 鷈獅鰤詩虱施濕螫匙笓噬一失———視——著	十拾什時塒薛鰣弛石世匙寔實食蝕矢掖射室植視釋——識—	史使屎豕始—弛———————矢———諡	式弒試軾寺恃涖薛勢事妬碩世貰湜笓噬是市士逝—室殖視釋氏識嗜嚞 禔 仕誓

	1	2	3	4
事 **312** SHIH [cont.]	一一一一一一一	一一一一一一一	一一一一一一一	似°日°示°豉°適°聞°諡諡奭°
手 **313** SHOU	收一一一一	熟°一一一一	手一守°首°	受綬°授狩首壽售瘦°獸°
書 **314** SHU	書梳疏蔬鯠一疎殊叔紓舒殳一	孰熟°墊°一一一尤束荣叔淑屬属忝贖銃°一	署暑薯蜀所黍鼠數薮一屬°	署°一疏恕洫°述°術°束°數嫩庶豎縮戍倏樹嘍墅

	1	2	3	4
刷 315 SHUA	刷°唰°霎	—	耍°	唰°
衰 316 SHUAI	衰°摔	—	摔°	帥率
拴 317 SHUAN	拴°栓橉	—	—	涮
雙 318 SHUANG	雙°霜孀驦	—	爽	雙
水 319 SHUI	雖衰°	誰	水	帨稅說°瑞睡
順 320 SHUN	—	醇犉唇蒓純	盾楯	順舜蕣瞬

[SHUO–SSǓ.] APPENDIX III.—THE PEKING SYLLABARY. 153

	1	2	3	4
說 321 SHUO	說° — — —	勺°杓° 芍°酌° 妁 灼°着° —	所° — — —	鑠 鑠° 朔° 槊° 嗍 溯 槊 敕° 數°
絲 322 SSǓ	司 絲 鷥 茲 厮 澌 斯 嘶 撕 — 思 緦 罳 私 蛳°	祠 詞 辭 — — — — — —	死 — 涘 — — — — —	伺° 笥 嗣 飼 俟 涘 竢 巳 祀 思° 姒 似° 駟 四 泗 食 寺 咒 肆 耜 賜

20

大 323 TA	1 達噠橽縫答—劀嗒	2 達———答搭—劀 㡎	3 ——撻———答搭劀妲—	4 大撻—縫—搭塔 杳 踏 遝	他 324 T'A	1 塌踢他——搭—	2 ——獺——搭	3 —獺——塔	4 榻獺傝撻—闥—
歹 325 TAI	愾獃呆	—	歹—	玳黛獬戴殆迨戴待瑇	太 326 T'AI	臺擡台抬苔駘	—紿	太汰貸忒泰態
單 327 TAN	單鄲彈禪眈虳丹擔—蕁石蛋噉	—	—	—擔胆亶—揮擔蕁石蛋噉	炭 328 T'AN	揮探貪攤—坍	揮彈罈—壇痰潭淡墨	忐坦—菼禫—啗	—探—嘆炭揮—沓

[TANG—TEI.] APPENDIX III.—THE PEKING SYLLABARY. 155

	1	2	3	4		1	2	3	4
當 329 TANG	當璫襠鐺° — — 盪	— — — —	黨攩讜党 — —	當檔宕蕩盪 礑	湯 330 T'ANG	堂螳鏜湯盪踢°	堂螳棠膛錫唐塘 塘糖	儻倘倘帑 — — 踢°	一宕燙盪踢錫

道 331 TAO	叨朷汆 刀忉	叨 — — — —	擣 一倒 — — 擣	擣島倒 — — 擣	蹈到倒悼道幬盜纛	逃 332 T'AO	滔掏韜叨 陶淘	逃桃淘萄 一檮 — —	討 — — — —	套 — — — —

得 333 TÊ	叨° —	得° 德悥	— 一	得° 德	特 334 T'Ê	— —	— —	— —	忒° 忑特慝

得 335 TEI	鏑 一	— —	得° —	— —	

等 336 TÊNG	1 登燈簦	2 —	3 等戥	4 澄°鄧 凳 磴 瞪°蹬 鐙 膛	疼 337 T'ÊNG	1 騰°	2 騰 謄 縢 疼	3 —	4 橙 藤
的 338 TI	低 氐 隄°堤° 隄 敵 滴 的 一 礋	嫡 適 敵 鏑 抵 狄 翟 糴 覿 篴 迪 笛 滌	坻 底 抵 邸 抵° 詆 蒂 覿	嚁° 適 一 鏑 — 禘 帝 諦 締 殢 弟 悌 娣 第 睇°地 杕 逮 遞	替 339 T'I	— 剔 倜	— 堤° 禔 踶 題 醍 啼 蹄 替 薁 稊 綈 鵜	— 梯° 睇°	体° 體	嚏 — 惕 薙 屈 逖 替 殢 剃 悌 俤 涕 第
弔 340 TIAO	刁 叼 貂 凋 啁 雕	— 刖 彫 鵰 —	—	鳥° —	釣 錦 弔 窎 佻 調 掉 弔	挑 341 T'IAO	桃° 跳° 佻 桃°	苕 笤 迢 髫 條 調 蜩	桃° 朓 — 掉°	眺 跳° 糶 — 掉°

[TIEH–T'ING.] APPENDIX III.—THE PEKING SYLLABARY. 157

	1	2	3	4		1	2	3	4
丟 348 TIU	丟	—	铥°	铥°					
多 349 TO	多° — — — — — — —	多° 度° — — — — — 鐸	— — — — — 桗° — — — 奪	— 桗 度 揆 惰 駄 掇 — 柮 跺 躱	妥 350 TʻO	佗 斥 扥	挖 託 脫° 他 拖	佗° 柁 陀 — 堶 駄 — 錘 — 毳	妥 廆 脫 堶 隋 — — — — —
			枀 垜 踩 躱 —	裰 剟 跥 澤 大 唑					佗 柝 蛻 拓 哪 唾 魄 彙 撐
豆 351 TOU	都° 兜 挽 — — —	— — — — — —	斗° 抖 蚪 陡 — —	斗 蚪 陡 — — —	頭 352 TʻOU	斗° 頭° 偷	投 頭 —	骰 — —	透 — —
				豆 荳 痘 逗 餖 登 鬥 竇 讀					

[TU–T'UN.] APPENDIX III.—THE PEKING SYLLABARY. 159

肚 353 TU	1 都°嘟凸塗毐—°督°—	2 —°—毒讀憤°—獨°	3 堵賭睹—肚瀆匵憒犢—	4 —°突°杜°肚毒磓妬蠹督獨咄渡啄斁度	土 354 T'U	1 禿瘏突°脫塗正兔菟—	2 —°圖茶塗—駼菟徒屠	3 —土°吐—	4 唾°—吐°—
短 355 TUAN	耑°端—	—	短—	叚°煅緞斷	團 356 T'UAN	湍—	團漙摶糰	痠°—	彖—
對 357 TUI	堆°—	—	—	碓對懟兌°銳隊	退 358 T'UI	推忒太頹	魋忒太癩	腿—	退—蛻
敦 359 TUN	敦惇墩撴蹲—	—°—°—鈍	躉—盹	燉°遁囤鈍頓	吞 360 T'UN	暾吞—	燉屯—鈍豚臀	氽°——	—裩—鈍遯

	冬 361 TUNG	1 東棟 ― ― ― 冬	2 ― ― ― ―	3 董懂 ― ― ―	4 棟涷 衕㇀ 㑁 洞 勳° 爧	同 362 T'UNG	1 仝 ― 痌 通 捅 ― ― 鼕 ― ―	2 仝桐 同桐 恫筒 痌銅 通 ― ― 佟 童 僮 瞳 曈	3 ― ― ― 筒 捅 桶 統 ― ― 潼 犝 艟 彤	4 ― ― ― 衕 勳° 痛
	雜 363 TSA	匝咋 紮 臢 ―	市 砸 偺° 攃 雜	咱° ― ― ― ―	匝 ― ― ― ―	擦 364 TS'A	擦 礤	―	―	―
	在 365 TSAI	― 栽 哉 災 跌°	宰 ― 載 仔 ―	在 再 載	才 366 TS'AI	― 猜 ― ― ―	才 材 財 裁 纔 ―	彩 綵 採 猜° 跐 踹	菜蔡 ― ― ― ―
	贊 367 TSAN	簪° ― ― ― ―	咱° ― ― 偺°	― 攢 趲 ― ―	贊 儹 瓚 揝 賺 暫 鏨	慚 368 TS'AN	參 叅 驂 飱 餐	蠶 䜽° ― 殘 慚	惨 黲 ― 燦° ― 慚	諺 儳° 粲 燦 棧° 識

[TSANG—TS‘Ê.] APPENDIX III.—THE PEKING SYLLABARY. 161

	1	2	3	4		1	2	3	4
葬 369 TSANG	臧臟臓牂 臧°臟°	傖啌咱 —	— — — 牂	藏臓葬牂°	倉 370 TS'ANG	滄艙蒼鎗 倉傖蒼°	藏° —	— —	— —
早 371 TSAO	魕蹧 遭糟	鑿 —	早澡蚤棗°	皂燥躁譟造灶竈 早懆譟°	草 372 TS‘AO	嘈槽° 漕螬 曹槽	早°草驔	— —	操°糙 造°懆
則 373 TSÊ	— — — — —	責擇 擢澤 宅則° 賊磔	— — — — —	責幘 嘖—側廁賊蠌戟 摘°謫 嘖蚱胙 仄昃 拙轍這 桚翟櫛	策 374 TS‘Ê	欣° —銼	— —	圿拆° 策冊° 側°惻測 笧

21

	1	2	3	4		1	2	3	4
賊 375 TSEI	—	賊°		—					
怎 376 TSÊN	參° —	—	怎° —	這° 譖 —	參 377 TS'ÊN	參° 蔘 —	岑 涔 —	頸° 磣 —	櫬° 覷° 貾° 齔 識
增 378 TSÊNG	曾° 憎 增 甑 罾 矰 繒	—	怎° —	—憎 — 甑° 贈 這 綜	層 379 TS'ÊNG	噲° —	曾° 層 嶒 叢°		噲° —
作 380 TSO	醝° 作 咋 — 撮	— 作° 昨 鑿° —	—左 佐 桫 繓 —	—作 咋 作° 柞 坐 座 繓 做 啜 歠 攦	錯 381 TS'O	搓 磋 蹉 — 撮	嵯 鹺 齹 痤 矬 —撮°	—	厝 措° 錯 剉 挫 脞 胜 撮

	1	2	3	4		1	2	3	4
走 382 TSOU	陬諏鄹謅 緅鯫租騶掫騶	足°卒°族	走°阻°祖°	奏°做°甑°驟°皺°縐°	湊 383 TS'OU	驫°粗	—	—	湊輳醋簇°
祖 384 TSU	租°趄	卒°足°—族°	岨°阻°組	啐°瘁°做°胙°昨°蹴°蹙°簇°跛°	粗 385 TS'U	粗胍麤°	—	—	晬萃悴°醋錯°蹴°鍊族
攢 386 TSUAN	鑽°	—	鑽纘鐏髻纂爥	鑽攢——	竄 387 TS'UAN	攛驢炊°	攢°積°	—	竄驢厝篡曩
嘴 388 TSUI	堆°	—	觜嘴	最蕞罪醉	催 389 TS'UI	崔催瘁°縗	隨	璀	脆悴°啐°悴烨瘁翠

	1	2	3	4		1	2	3	4
尊 390 TSUN	尊樽遵僎 鐏	—	樽 —	唆°竣餕雋 唆°駿儁	寸 391 TS'UN	村邮籢	存蹲	忖 —	寸刌
宗 392 TSUNG	宗棕緵 踪鬃縱蹤櫻 踪°縱°蹤°驄 種°	—	一終徸縱總 —	粽從聳縱蹤 從驟	蔥 393 TS'UNG	琮從瑽怱聰	淙從一叢 蔥驄	— 徔°	—
子 394 TZŬ	子°孜肯鮆咨姿紥滋孳 耔貲髭訾恣貲諮孳鎡則° 紫觜酏訾	—	子°仔紫觜 — — — — — 梓泲姊 —	字 — — — — 自 — — 漬	次 395 TZ'Ŭ	一差疵	祠詞 疵雌 茨茨 餈 兹°慈	— 此跐 —	伺束刺 差刺此 — 此賜 — 瓷 — 磁

	1	2	3	4
瓦 396 WA	哇 注 娃° 娃 蛙° 跬° 蛙 鼃 窪 凹° 挖	劃 娃° — — — —	瓦 — — — — —	斡 襪 韈 — — —
外 397 WAI	歪° 喎 蛙°	— —	歪° 昏	外 —
完 398 WAN	— 剜° 豌 — 彎 灣	刓 園 完 頑 岏 —	— 椀 宛° 婉° 盌 輓 輓 晚 綰	翫 玩 腕 腕 萬 薨 —
往 399 WANG	尫 汪 亡 — —	王 芒° 忘 硭 —	枉 往° 岡 惘 網 輞 魍	旺 往° 忘 望 妄 —

| 爲 400 WEI | 1 偉違—隈煨—猥—逶嵬巍僞——蜩—葳———微。 | 2 韋違幃闈—圍—危桅—嵬巍—爲——謂—濰惟—帷——微薇 | 3 偉葦緯—猥危—萎諉—僞—壘——唯尾媙—鮪 | 4 偉衛緯 味喂穢 未畏濊—矮餧魏位爲 胃渭 蜩謂彙遺磑銳睿慰洧 尉 蔚 |
| 文 401 WÊN | —溫煴瘟— | 文紋蚊—雯—聞— | 抆—搵。 刎吻穩諢 胭 | 汶紊搵—慍蘊—問縕 |

[WÊNG—WU.] APPENDIX III.—THE PEKING SYLLABARY. 167

	1	2	3	4
翁 402 WÊNG	翁 嗡	—	蓊	雍 甕
我 403 WO	倭 蹉 阿 呵 渦 萵 窩	訛	我	臥 齷 握 沃
武 404 WU	吾 汙 圬 浛 弧 溫 — — 烏 嗚 — 午 巫 誣 屋 喔 渥	吾 捂 圄 鵂 梧 吳 蜈 — 無 蕪 毋	五 伍 武 鵡 — — 舞 憮 嫵 廡 侮 午 仵 忤 — 握	悟 晤 寤 物 牾 誤 惡 勿 愭 杌 溫 兀 鶩 舞 務 毋 侮 霧 鄔 塢 戊 沅 沃 誣 嫗 喔

	1	2	3	4
牙° 405 YA	呀°枒°鴉婭扎押鴨了壓魘	牙枒芽涯啀耶——	雅亞啞瘂——押°——	迓訝亞°—婭軋椏——壓°
涯 406 YAI		涯°挨°		隘°
羊 407 YANG	——央°䄃訣鞅°	羊佯徉洋陽—煬楊瘍颺	痒°養癢———仰	恙漾樣怏—煬軮—

[YAO-YEH.] APPENDIX III.—THE PEKING SYLLABARY.

	4	3	2	1	
要 408 YAO	要獄鷂曜耀約葯樂若岳佻溺瘧鑰	鹼咬杳昏拗 — 殀 — — — —	搖瑤遙謠 䍃窑猺颻 — — 殀堯殺姚爻 — 餚 —	腰吆凹邀約嗷夭妖 — — — —	
夜 409 YEH					
	業酈葉讞邑咽腋夜碣臬孽仒泄拽射頁擛馦曄	也野冶 — — — — — — — — — —	爺耶邪呆 — — — — — — — —	爺擷噎 — 咽掖 — — — — — — —	

言 410 YEN.

1
咽
烟 胭
厭° 慊
焉 鄢
嫣 蔫
奄 腌
醃 淹
— 閹
— 煙
— 菸
— 湮
— 炎°
—
—
—
—
—

2
一
沿 逌°
鉛
埏 涎
蜒 筵
嚴 巖
喦 崟
檐 檣
研 妍
—
—
—
—
炎°
緣 閆
眼 顏
言
盐 鹽
— 閻

3
一
沿 逌°
魘
—
儼 衍
兖
掩 脧
—
—
—
—
剡
偃 蝘
眼 演
齴
— 験
— 二

4
咽
沿 厭°
厭 嚥
— 一
燕° 諺°
彥 讞
釅
—
—
—
啖° 緣
晏 宴
一 唁
雁 鴈
焰 焰
— 験°
艶 灩
硯

益 411 YI See I.

[YIN-YO.] APPENDIX III.—THE PEKING SYLLABARY. 171

		1	2	3	4
音 412 YIN		姻茵喑陰湮闉慇媜京 因氤音堙禋殷	淫婬寅銀崟吟听蟬狺 霪霒齦崟	蚓尹飲隱	滕°—廕蔭°孕恁°印—
迎 413 YING		盈°應膺鶯鶯英一蠅°嬰嚶櫻	盈°楹瑩瑩營瀛贏蠅°迎凝— 螢° 熒 贏 籇°	郢甬穎影———瘿—	———應————映硬媵—
約 414 YO		約°——————————————	————————————————	————————————————	蒴樂°幄°握°龠°籥°虐°耀 藥°喔°渥°躍°籥°鑰°獄°瘧°躍°若°岳

魚
415
YÜ

1
ㄧ
ㄧ
ㄧ
ㄧ
ㄧ
ㄧ
ㄧ
於°
瘀
淤
ㄧ
ㄧ
ㄧ
ㄧ
譽°
ㄧ
ㄧ
ㄧ
ㄧ
ㄧ
ㄧ
ㄧ
ㄧ
吁
迂
紆
傴
ㄧ
愚
ㄧ
ㄧ
ㄧ

2
愉 榆 瑜
愈 瑜 覦
揄 媮
ㄧ 逾 覦 於
ㄧ ㄧ
予 好
與° 旟
璵 譽° 漁
ㄧ 與°
臾 庾
ㄨ 黃 諛
腴 娛 驢 汙
虞 于 竽
孟 餘
畬 禺 愚
嵎 舁 雩
ㄧ ㄧ

3
羽 禹
ㄧ ㄧ
ㄧ ㄧ
ㄧ ㄧ
於 雨
ㄧ ㄧ
與° 嶼
ㄧ 圄°
語ㄧ
女 庾
ㄧ ㄧ
ㄧ ㄧ
宇 圉

4
喻 愈
ㄧ ㄧ
逾 諭
踰 玉 獄°
獄 預 豫
ㄧ ㄧ
譽 鋊 聿 女
語 欲 裕 煜 芋
浴 鷸
峪 禦 禦 煜
慾 澳 嫗° 蔚
尉 慰 熨 遇
寓 育 蔚
域 棫° 蟻
遹 馭 疫°
飫 菀
毓 鬱
鷸

	1	2	3	4
原 416 YÜAN	— — — — 鳶淵 — — — 宛° 鴛鵷宛	京°原 源 員°圓 捐° 緣°檽 鳶淵° 袁圜 猿轅 元阮 沅芫楥° 受°垣	— — — — — 遠 — 阮惋° 宛° 婉琬 菀°畹鵷	愿願 — 眩 — — — — 院 — — 怨苑
月 417 YÜEH	曰° 噦 —	噦° —	—	曰°月悅閱 樂°藥°越燿躍 鉞燿°躍° 曜獄°蒳 耀約岳粵軏 瀹°掄° 籥鑰° 逾°

	1	2	3	4
雲 418 YÜN	暈 氳 —	員° 芸 耘 篔 云 紜 勻 雲 —	殞 隕 允° 犹 —	韻 運 鄆 暈° 熅 縕 緼 蘊 醞 孕° 熨
有 419 YU	憂 耰 悠 優 攸 幽 麀 鰌 呦 —	猶 獸 輶 蕕 蜎 由 油 疣 牛 尤 遊 蝣 游 鯈 郵 —	酉 — 有 允 友° 莠 — 懮	煩 祐 佑 宥 囿 右 侑 柚 琇 莠 誘 幼 又 羑 牖
	雍° 壅 饔 傭 塘 啀 庸 鄘 邕 癰 —	瑩° 嶸 榮 螢 熒 縈 濚 縈 容 榕 蓉 鎔 融 喁	擁° 雍 甬 壅 俑 涌 惥 勇 踊 衕 湧 永	瑩° — 用 — — 泳 詠
用 420 YUNG				

III.—TABLE OF CHARACTERS SUBJECT TO CHANGES OF SOUND OR TONE.

A	阿[1]	a[3], a[4], ê[1], o[1], wo[1].	CH'A	喳[1]	cha[1].	CH'AN	蟾[2]	shan[2].
	腌[1]	ang[1].		差[1]	ch'ai[1], ch'ih[1], ch'ih[2], tz'ŭ[2].		賺[2]	chuan[4], tsan[4].
	呀[2]	hsia[1], ya[1].		岔[3]	ch'a[4].		顫[4]	chan[4].
				扠[3]	ch'ao[3].		讖[4]	ts'an[4], ch'ien[1], ts'ên[4].
AI	呆[1]	tai[1].	CHAI	側[1]	chai[3], tsê[4], ts'ê[4].	CHANG	賬[1]	chang[4].
	挨[1]	ai[2], yai[2].		摘[1]	tsê[4].		掌[1]	chang[3].
	噯[1]	ai[3].		齋[1]	chai[2].		章[1]	chan[1].
	唉[1]	ai[3].		讁[1]	tsê[4].		長[3]	chang[4], ch'ang[2].
	獃[2]	tai[1].		宅[2]	tsê[2].		帳[4]	ch'ang[4].
	呃[4]	o[4].		責[2]	tsê[2], tsê[4].			
	隘[4]	yai[4], yi[4].		擇[2]	tsê[2].	CH'ANG	倡[1]	ch'ang[4].
				澤[2]	tsê[2].		長[2]	chang[3], chang[4].
AN	按[1]	an[4], ên[4].		翟[2]	ti[2].		常[2]	shang[2].
	俺[1]	nan[3].		仄[3]	chua[3], tsê[4].		場[2]	ch'ang[3].
	俺[3]	nan[2].		窄[3]	tsê[4].		暢[3]	ch'ang[4].
	諺[4]	yen[4].		這[4]	chê[4], chei[4], tsê[4], tsên[4], tsêng[4].		悵[4]	chang[4].
ANG	昂[1]	ang[2].	CH'AI	拆[1]	ts'ê[4].	CHAO	召[1]	chao[4].
	腌[1]	a[1].		差[1]	ch'a[1], ch'ih[1], ch'ih[2], tz'ŭ[2].		酌[1]	chê[4], cho[2], shuo[2], chê[2].
AO	咬[1]	chiao[2], chiao[3].		豺[2]	ts'ai[2].		朝[1]	ch'ao[2].
	熬[1]	ao[2].		冊[3]	ts'ê[4].		著[2]	chê[4], cho[2], chu[4], chê[2].
	凹[2]	wa[1], yao[1], yeh[4].		跐[3]	ts'ai[3], tz'ŭ[3].		着[2]	chê[4], cho[1], cho[2], shuo[2], chê[2].
	嚻[3]	hsiao[1].					爪[3]	chua[3].
	拗[3]	yao[3].	CHAN	占[1]	chan[4].		抓[3]	chua[1].
	澳[4]	yü[4].		章[1]	chang[1].		找[3]	hua[1].
	燠[4]	yü[4].		瞻[1]	shan[4].		棹[4]	cho[1].
				貶[3]	cha[3].			
CHA	扎[1]	cha[2], cha[3], ya[1].		輾[3]	ch'ên[3], nien[3].	CH'AO	吵[1]	ch'ao[3].
	咱[1]	tsa[2], tsan[2], tsang[2].		橏[3]	ts'an[4].		鈔[1]	ch'ao[1].
	痄[1]	chia[1].		暫[3]	tsan[1].		綽[1]	ch'o[4], ch'uo[4].
	喳[1]	ch'a[1].		瓉[3]	tsan[4].		朝[2]	chao[1].
	苴[2]	cho[4], chü[2], chua[4].		囋[3]	ch'an[4].		扠[3]	ch'a[3].
	劄[2]	ta[1], ta[2].						
	詐[3]	cha[4].	CH'AN	儳[1]	ts'an[4].	CHÊ	著[1]	chao[2], cho[1], chu[4], chê[2].
	眨[3]	chan[3].		讒[1]	ts'an[2].		着[1]	chao[2], cho[1], cho[2], shuo[2], chê[2].
	蚱[3]	tsê[4], cha[4].		禪[2]	shan[2], shan[4], tan[1].		蟄[1]	shih[1].
	炸[4]	tso[4].		蟬[2]	shan[2].		酌[1]	chao[1], cho[2], shuo[2], chê[2].

CHÊ	折²	cho², shê².	CHÊNG	正¹	chêng³, chêng⁴.	CHI	給³	chi⁴, kei³.
	蜇²	chih².		怔¹	chêng⁴, chên¹.		鯽³	chi⁴.
	轍²	ch'ê⁴.		徵¹	chih³.		濟⁴	chi⁴.
	柘⁴	shih².		極³	ch'êng².		騎⁴	ch'i².
	這⁴	chai⁴, chei⁴, tsê⁴, tsên⁴, tsêng⁴.		朕⁴	chên⁴, shên⁴.		技⁴	ch'i².
							溉⁴	kai⁴.
CH'Ê	車¹	chü¹.					繋⁴	hsi⁴.
	掣⁴	ch'ih⁴.	CH'ÊNG	偵¹	chêng¹.			
	轍⁴	chê².		崢¹	chêng¹.	CH'I	吃¹	chi¹, ch'ih¹.
				錚¹	chêng¹, ch'iang¹.		崎¹	ch'i².
CHEI	這⁴	chai⁴, chê⁴, tsê⁴, tsên⁴, tsêng⁴.		稱¹	ch'êng⁴, ch'ên⁴.		期¹	ch'i², chi¹.
				鐺¹	tang¹.		葺¹	ch'i¹.
				澄²	têng⁴.		緝¹	ch'i¹.
CHÊN	怔¹	chêng¹, chêng⁴.		橙²	ch'ên².		妻¹	ch'i¹.
	診¹	chên³.		乘²	ch'êng⁴, shêng⁴.		凄¹	ch'i¹.
	貞¹	chêng¹.		盛²	shêng⁴.		悽¹	ch'i¹.
	楨¹	chêng¹.		懲²	ch'êng².		棲¹	hsi¹.
	禎¹	chêng¹.		極²	chêng³.		戚¹	ch'i⁴.
	甄¹	chien¹.					溪¹	ch'i¹.
	斟¹	chên³.	CHI	几¹	chi³.		漆¹	ch'ü⁴.
	簪¹	tsan¹.		奇¹	ch'i².		稽¹	chi¹.
	朕⁴	chêng⁴, shên⁴.		吃¹	ch'i¹, ch'ih¹.		圻¹	ts'ê⁴.
	譖⁴	tsên⁴.		期¹	ch'i¹, ch'i².		乞²	ch'i³, ch'i⁴.
				極¹	chi².		奇²	chi¹.
				激¹	chi², chi⁴.		騎²	chi⁴.
CH'ÊN	橙²	ch'êng².		幾¹	chi³.		豈²	chi³.
	輾³	chan³, nien³.		擊¹	chi¹.		擠²	ch'i¹, chi³.
	磣³	ts'ên³.		績¹	chi¹.		萁²	chi¹.
	稱⁴	ch'êng¹, ch'êng⁴.		擠¹	chi³, ch'i².		箕²	chi¹.
	趁⁴	nien³.		勣¹	chi⁴.		杞²	ch'i³.
	闖⁴	ch'uang³.		積¹	chi¹.		刺²	tz'ŭ⁴.
	櫬⁴	ts'ên⁴.		迹¹	chi¹.		禦²	ch'io⁴, ch'üeh⁴.
	讖⁴	ts'ên⁴.		萁¹	ch'i².		技²	chi⁴.
				箕¹	ch'i².		契⁴	hsieh⁴.
				稽¹	ch'i¹.			
CHÊNG	貞¹	chên¹.		亟²	chi⁴.	CHIA	夾¹	ch'ia¹.
	偵¹	ch'êng¹.		殛²	chi⁴.		挾¹	chia², chieh², hsieh².
	楨¹	chên¹.		級²	chi¹, chieh⁴.		鋏¹	chia⁴, chieh¹, chieh⁴, hsieh².
	瞪¹	têng⁴.		藉²	chi⁴.		甲¹	chia³.
	瞪²	têng⁴.		籍²	chi².		痂¹	cha¹.
	禎²	chên¹.		劇²	chi⁴.		袈¹	chia⁴.
	拯³	chêng⁴.		髻²	chi⁴.		傢¹	chia⁴.
	崢¹	ch'êng¹.		稷²	chi⁴.		嘎¹	ka¹, ka², ka³, ka⁴.
	錚¹	ch'êng¹, ch'iang¹.		紀³	chi⁴.			

[CHIA-CHIH.] APPENDIX III.—THE PEKING SYLLABARY. 177

CHIA	稽¹	ch'iai³, chieh¹.
	頰²	chia⁴.
	假³	chia⁴.
	賈³	ku³.

CH'IA	卡¹	ch'ia³, k'a¹, k‘a³.
	夾¹	chia¹.
	洽⁴	hsia⁴.

| CH'IAI | 楷³ | k'ai³. |
| | 稭³ | chia¹, chieh¹. |

CHIANG	將¹	chiang⁴, kang¹.
	槳¹	chiang³.
	虹⁴	hung², kang⁴.
	降⁴	hsiang².
	強⁴	ch'iang², ch'iang³.

CH'IANG	戧¹	ch'iang⁴.
	鎗¹	ch'iang³.
	鏘¹	ch'êng¹, ch'êng¹.
	蹡¹	ts'ang¹.
	強²	ch'iang³, chiang⁴.
	鯨²	ch'ing².

CHIAO	角¹	chiao³, chio³, chio³, chüeh³.
	僥¹	chiao³.
	澆¹	hsiao¹.
	敎¹	chiao⁴.
	嬌¹	chiao³.
	燋¹	chiao⁴.
	醮¹	chiao⁴.
	咬²	chiao³, ao¹.
	爵²	chio², chio³, ch'io², chüeh², chüo².
	嚼²	chiao¹, chio², ch'io².
	覺²	chiao⁴, chio², chio³, chüeh².
	較³	hsiao⁴.
	餃³	hsiao⁴.
	腳	} chio², chio³.
	脚	
	校⁴	hsiao⁴.
	敎⁴	ho¹, ho⁴.

CH'IAO	雀¹	ch'iao³, ch'io³, ch'io⁴, ch'üeh².
	敲¹	k'ao¹.
	鵲¹	ch'iao³, ch'io³, ch'io⁴, ch'üeh².
	鞽²	ch'iao².
	轎²	ch'iao².
	誚⁴	hsiao⁴.
	哨⁴	shao⁴.

CHIEH	且¹	ch'ieh³, chü¹.
	鋏¹	chieh⁴, chia¹, chia⁴, hsieh².
	界¹	chieh⁴.
	結¹	chieh².
	街¹	kai¹.
	嗟¹	chüeh¹.
	綏¹	chieh⁴.
	歇¹	hsieh¹.
	楷¹	chia¹, ch'iai³.
	隔¹	chieh⁴, ko².
	狹¹	chia¹, chia², hsieh².
	節²	chieh³.
	脅²	hsieh², lei¹.
	捷²	chieh⁴.
	蜇²	tieh², t'ieh³.
	截²	chieh⁴.
	恊²	hsieh².
	絜²	hsieh⁴.
	繫²	chieh⁴, hsieh².
	叶²	hsieh².
	解³	chieh⁴, hsieh⁴.
	浹³	hsieh².
	藉⁴	chi², chi⁴.
	頁⁴	yeh⁴.

CH'IEH	切¹	ch'ieh⁴, chü¹, tsu¹.
	趄²	ch'üeh².
	且³	chieh¹, chü¹.
	笡⁴	ts'ê¹.
	箧⁴	hsia².

CHIEN	間¹	chien⁴.
	監¹	chien¹.
	鐫¹	ch'üan¹.

CHIEN	甄¹	chên¹.
	縅²	hsien².
	漸³	chien⁴.
	鋼³	chien⁴.
	儉³	chien⁴.
	搴¹	ch'ien¹, hsien¹.
	蹇¹	ch'ien¹.
	揀¹	lien⁴.
	諫³	chien⁴.
	見⁴	hsien⁴.
	檻¹	hsien⁴, hsien⁴, k'an³.
	閒¹	hsien².
	艦⁴	hsien⁴.
	建¹	chin⁴.
	雋¹	tsun⁴.

CH'IEN	繟¹	ch'ien⁴.
	鈐¹	ch'ien².
	鉛¹	yen².
	黔¹	ch'ien².
	嵌¹	ch'ien⁴.
	識¹	ts'ên¹, ts'an⁴, ch'an⁴.
	搴¹	chien³, hsien¹.
	塞¹	chien³.
	蹇²	hsien¹.
	前²	ch'ien³.
	乾²	kan¹.
	倩²	ch'ing⁴.

CHIH	知¹	chih².
	炙¹	chih⁴.
	值¹	chih², chih⁴.
	識¹	chih⁴, shih².
	贄¹	chih⁴.
	擲¹	chih⁴, jêng¹.
	鷙¹	chih⁴.
	熾¹	ch'ih².
	只¹	chih³, chih⁴.
	秩¹	chih⁴.
	質¹	chih³, chih⁴.
	植²	chih⁴.
	塾²	chê².
	任²	chih⁴.

CHIH	徵²	chih³, chêng¹.	CHING	鯨¹	ch'ing², ch'iang².	CH'IU	楸¹	yu¹.
	祉³	ch'ih³.		莖¹	hêng².		仇²	ch'ou².
	治³	ch'ih².		經¹	ching⁴.		囚²	hsiu².
				京¹	yüan², yin¹.			
CH'IH	吃¹	chi¹, ch'i¹.		津¹	chin¹.	CHIUNG	窮²	ch'iung².
	笞¹	ch'ih¹, ch'ih³.		窀¹	ching⁴.		迥³	ch'iung³, hsiung³.
	赤¹	ch'ih⁴.		耿³	kêng³.		窘³	chün³.
	侈¹	ch'ih³.		請³	ch'ing³.			
	差¹	ch'ih¹, ch'a¹, ch'ai¹, tz'ŭ¹.		頸³	kêng³.	CH'IUNG	傾¹	ch'ing¹, k'êng¹.
	嵯¹	tso¹, ts'o².		勁³	chin⁴.		窮²	chiung².
	嚏¹	ch'ih³.		盡⁴	chin⁴.		頃³	ch'ing¹, ch'ing³.
	痴¹	ch'ih².		甑⁴	tsêng⁴.		恐³	k'ung³.
	瓻¹	ch'ih².					迥³	chiung³, hsiung³.
	勅¹	ch'ih⁴.	CH'ING	情¹	ch'ing².			
	飭¹	ch'ih⁴.		頃¹	ch'ing³, ch'iung³.	CHO	拙¹	tsê⁴.
	治²	chih⁴.		傾¹	ch'iung¹, k'êng¹.		棹¹	chao⁴.
	特²	shih⁴.		鯨²	ch'iang², ching¹.		著¹	cho², chao², chê¹, shuo², chê².
	匙²	shih¹, shih².		請³	ching³.		折¹	chê², shê².
	祉³	chih³.		倩⁴	ch'ien⁴.		柮¹	tsê⁴.
	敕⁴	shuo⁴.		親⁴	ch'in¹, ch'in⁴.		著¹	chao², chê¹, chu⁴, chê².
	掣⁴	ch'ê⁴.					酌¹	chao¹, chê¹, shuo², chê².
	斥⁴	t'o¹.	CHIO	角²	chio², chiao¹, chiao³, chüeh².		苴¹	cha¹, chü¹, chua⁴.
	熾⁴	chih¹.		脚²	chio³, chiao³.		綴³	chui⁴.
				爵²	chio³, chiao², ch'io², chüeh², chüo²		綴⁴	tsê⁴.
CHIN	劤¹	kên¹.		覺²	chio³, chiao³, chiao³, chüeh².			
	肋¹	lê⁴, lei⁴.		腳³	chiao³.	CH'O	襏⁴	chui⁴, to⁴.
	津¹	ching¹.		嚼³	chiao², chiao⁴, ch'io².		觸¹	ch'u⁴, ch'uo⁴.
	浸¹	chin⁴, ch'in⁴.		催³	ch'io⁴.		綽¹	ch'ao⁴, ch'uo⁴.
	荊¹	ching¹.					黜¹	ch'u¹, ch'u⁴.
	禁¹	chin⁴.	CH'IO	却¹	ch'io⁴, ch'üeh⁴, ch'üo⁴.			
	狷³	yin².		爵²	chiao², chio³, chio³, chüeh⁴, chüo²	CHOU	粥¹	chu¹.
	勁⁴	ching⁴.		嚼²	chiao², chiao⁴, chio³.		妯²	chu⁴.
	建⁴	chien⁴.		雀²	ch'io⁴, ch'iao¹, ch'iao², ch'üeh⁴.		軸²	chu⁴.
	盡⁴	ching⁴.		鵲²	ch'io⁴, ch'iao¹, ch'iao², ch'üeh⁴.		杻³	ch'ou², niu³.
				卻¹	ch'i¹, ch'üeh⁴.			
CH'IN	親¹	ch'in⁴, ch'ing⁴.		碏¹	ch'üeh⁴, hsi¹.	CH'OU	仇²	ch'iu².
	衾²	ch'in³.		催¹	chio⁴.		杻³	chou³.
	浸⁴	chin¹, chin⁴.					扭³	niu³.
	沁⁴	hsin¹.	CHIU	咎²	chiu⁴, kao¹.			
				究¹	chiu⁴.	CHÜ	且¹	chieh¹, ch'ieh³.
CHING	更²	kêng², kêng⁴.		赳¹	chiu⁴.		趄¹	ch'ieh¹, ch'ieh⁴, tsu¹.
	耕¹	kêng¹.		科¹	chiu².			
	荊¹	chin¹.						

APPENDIX III.—THE PEKING SYLLABARY.

CHÜ	車[1]	ch'ê[1].	CH'ÜEH	瘸[2]	ch'ieh[2].	CH'U	出[1]	pieh[1].
	跙[1]	chü[4].		卻[4]	ch'i[4], ch'io[4].		貙[1]	ch'o[4], ch'u[4].
	狙[1]	chü[2].		却[4]	ch'io[1], ch'io[4], ch'üo[4].		伫[3]	chu[4].
	矩[1]	chü[3].		碏[4]	ch'io[4], hsi[2].		處[3]	ch'u[4].
	俱[1]	chü[4].		雀[4]	ch'iao[1], ch'iao[3], ch'io[3], ch'io[4].		竚[4]	chu[4].
	虛[1]	hsü[1].		鵲[4]	ch'iao[1], ch'iao[3], ch'io[3], ch'io[4].		悚[4]	sung[3].
	戯[1]	chü[2], ch'ü[4].		絡[4]	lo[4], lao[1].		畜[4]	hsü[1], hsü[4].
	足[2]	tsu[2].					觸[4]	ch'uo[4], ch'o[4].
	苴[2]	cha[2], cho[4], chua[4].	CHÜN	竣[1]	chün[4], tsun[4].			
	舉[3]	chü[4].		菌[3]	chün[4].	CHUA	抓[1]	chao[3].
	鉅[4]	ch'ü[3].		窘[3]	chiung[3].		仄[3]	chai[1], tsê[4].
	屨[4]	lü[2], lü[3].		俊[4]	tsun[4].		爪[3]	chao[3].
	聚[4]	hsü[3].		畯[4]	tsun[4].		大[4]	ta[4], tai[1], to[4].
				餕[4]	tsun[4].		苴[4]	cha[2], cho[4], chü[2].
CH'Ü	曲[1]	ch'ü[3].		駿[4]	tsun[4].			
	麴[1]	ch'ü[2].				CH'UA	—	—
	衢[1]	ch'ü[2].	CH'ÜN	—	—			
	鉅[3]	chü[4].				CHUAI	拽[4]	chuai[4], hsieh[2], hsieh[4], yeh[4].
	去[4]	k'o[4].	CHÜO	爵[2]	chiao[2], chio[2], ch'io[2], chüeh[2].		轉[3]	chuan[3], chuan[4].
	漆[4]	ch'i[1].						
	戲[4]	chü[1], chü[4].	CH'ÜO	却[4]	ch'io[1], ch'io[4], ch'üeh[4].	CH'UAI	搨[2]	ch'uai[3].
							膗[2]	ch'uai[2].
CHÜAN	捐[1]	yüan[2].	CHU	主[1]	chu[2], chu[3].			
	卷[3]	chüan[4].		咪[1]	chu[4].	CHUAN	耑[1]	tuan[1].
	捲[3]	ch'üan[2].		茱[1]	shu[2].		轉[3]	chuan[4], chuai[3].
	圈[4]	ch'üan[4], ch'üan[4].		蛛[1]	chu[2].		囀[3]	chuan[4].
				粥[1]	chou[1].		傳[2]	ch'uan[2].
CH'ÜAN	圈[1]	ch'üan[2], chüan[4].		祝[2]	chu[4].		賺[4]	ch'an[2], tsan[4].
	鐫[1]	chien[1].		遂[2]	ti[2].			
	攥[1]	ts'uan[1].		屬[2]	shu[2], shu[3].	CH'UAN	樞[1]	shuan[1].
	捲[3]	chüan[3].		囑[2]	chu[3].		川[1]	ch'uan[2].
	攢[2]	ts'uan[2].		矚[2]	chu[3].		拴[1]	shuan[1].
	竄[4]	ts'uan[4].		阻[3]	tsu[3], tsu[4], tsou[3].		栓[1]	shuan[1].
	驫[4]	ts'uan[1], ts'uan[4].		助[3]	chu[4].		傳[2]	chuan[4].
	爨[4]	ts'uan[4].		詛[3]	tsu[3].		篡[2]	ts'uan[4].
				佇[4]	ch'u[3].			
CHÜEH	嗟[1]	chieh[1].		著[4]	chao[2], chê[1], cho[2].	CHUANG	舂[1]	ch'ung[1].
	角[1]	chiao[1], chiao[3], chio[2], chio[3].		妯[4]	chou[2].			
	爵[1]	chiao[2], chio[2], chio[3], ch'io[2], chüo[2].		竚[4]	ch'u[3].	CH'UANG	創[1]	ch'uang[1], ch'uang[3].
	覺[1]	chiao[2], chiao[4], chio[2], chio[3].		軸[4]	chou[2].		淙[2]	ts'ung[2].
				碡[4]	tu[4].	CHUI	觜[1]	tzŭ[1], tsui[3].
							祓[2]	ch'o[4], to[4].
							綴[4]	cho[4].

CH'UI	吹¹	ch'ui⁴, k'an³.	ÊN	摁⁴	wên³, wên⁴.	FOU	不¹	pu¹, pu², pu⁴, po¹, pou¹.
	炊¹	ts'uan¹.		按⁴	an¹, an⁴.		浮²	fu¹, fu².
	推¹	t'ui¹.					否³	pi³, p'i³.
			ÊNG	哼¹	hêng².		缶³	p'i³.
CHUN	屯¹	tun².					覆⁴	fu², fu⁴.
	惇¹	tun¹.	ÊRH	兒¹	êrh².		埠⁴	pu⁴.
	諄¹	ch'un².		而²	êrh³.			
	隼³	hsin³, hsün³.		余³	yü².	FU	浮¹	fu², fou².
				入⁴	ju³, ju⁴.		枹¹	fu².
CH'UN	鶉¹	shun².		馴⁴	i⁴.		芙¹	fu².
	唇²	ch'un³, shun².					敷¹	fu².
	諄²	chun¹.	FA	伐¹	fa².		佛²	fo¹, fo².
				法¹	fa², fa³, fa⁴.		彿²	fu⁴.
CHUNG	中¹	chung⁴, ch'ung¹.		髮¹	fa³.		髯²	fu⁴.
	衆⁴	chung⁴.		乏²	fa⁴.		復⁴	fu⁴.
	終³	tsung³.					覆⁴	fu⁴, fou⁴.
	種³	chung⁴, tsung¹.	FAN	番¹	fan¹, p'an¹.		腹⁴	fu⁴, fu³.
	仲⁴	ch'ung⁴.		幡¹	fan².		宓⁴	mi⁴.
	重⁴	ch'ung².		藩¹	fan².		祓²	fu⁴.
				繙¹	pan².		幅²	fu⁴.
CH'UNG	中¹	chung¹, chung⁴.		凡²	fan³.		俛³	mien³.
	春¹	chuang¹.					芾⁴	fei⁴.
	重²	chung⁴.	FANG	仿³	p'ang².		婦⁴	fo⁴.
	仲⁴	chung⁴.		彷³	p'ang³.		絆⁴	fei⁴.
	銃⁴	shu².						
			FEI	菲¹	fei³.	HA	哈¹	ha³, ha⁴, ho³.
CH'UO	綽⁴	ch'ao⁴, ch'o⁴.		翡¹	fei¹.		蝦²	hsia¹, hsia².
	觸⁴	ch'u⁴, ch'o⁴.		蒂¹	fu¹.			
				費⁴	pi¹.	HAI	咳¹	hai².
Ê	阿¹	a¹, a³, a⁴, o¹, wo¹.		紼⁴	fu¹.		還²	han², huan².
	哦¹	o¹.					孩²	hai³, k'ê¹.
	娥²	o².	FÊN	分¹	fên⁴.		和⁴	han⁴, ho², ho⁴, huo¹, huo².
	蛾²	o².		棼¹	fên².		害⁴	ho¹.
	鵝²	o².						
	訛²	o², wo².	FÊNG	逢²	p'ang².	HAN	邯¹	han².
	額²	ê¹, o², o⁴.		縫²	fêng⁴.		函²	hsien².
	我³	o³, wo³.		捧³	p'êng³.		涵²	hsien².
	餓⁴	o⁴.		諷³	fêng⁴.		還²	hai², huan².
	惡⁴	o⁴, wu⁴.					閑²	han².
	諤⁴	o⁴.	FO	佛¹	fo², fu².		翰²	han⁴.
	鴉⁴	o⁴.		婦⁴	fu².		喊³	hsien³, k'an⁴.
	鱷⁴	o⁴.					和⁴	hai⁴, ho², ho⁴, huo¹, huo².

[HANG–HSI.] APPENDIX III.—THE PEKING SYLLABARY.

HANG	行²	hsing², hsing⁴.
	亢²	kang¹, k'ang⁴.
	吭³	hang⁴.
	項⁴	hsiang⁴.
	巷⁴	hsiang⁴.

HAO	撓¹	nao¹, nao².
	哮¹	hsiao⁴.
	耗²	hao⁴.
	號²	hao⁴.
	鶴²	ho⁴.
	好³	hao⁴.
	涸⁴	ho⁴, ku⁴, k'u⁴.

| HÊ, HEI 黑¹ | hei³, ho⁴. |

HÊN	哏¹	hên².
	很²	hên³.
	狠²	hên³.

HÊNG	亨¹	hêng¹.
	哼¹	êng¹.
	莖²	ching¹.
	橫²	hêng⁴, hung², hung⁴.
	荇⁴	hsing⁴.

HO	苛¹	k'o¹.
	呵¹	ho³, wo¹.
	劉¹	huo¹.
	荷¹	ho², ho⁴.
	喝¹	ho⁴.
	合²	ko⁴.
	活²	huo².
	和²	ho⁴, hai⁴, han⁴, huo¹, huo².
	核²	hu².
	褻²	ho⁴, chiao⁴.
	哈³	ha¹, ha³, ha⁴.
	火³	huo³.
	夥³	huo³, i¹.
	或⁴	huo⁴.
	嚇⁴	huo², huo⁴, hu¹.
	嚇⁴	hsia⁴.
	涸⁴	hao⁴, ku⁴, ku⁴.
	禍⁴	huo⁴.
	貨⁴	huo⁴.

HO	獲⁴	huai², huo⁴.
	黑⁴	hei¹, hê³.
	鶴⁴	hao².
	畫⁴	hua².
	劃⁴	hua².
	穫⁴	ho¹.
	藿⁴	hu¹.
	害⁴	hai¹.

| HOU | 候² | hou⁴. |

HU	乎¹	hu².
	呼¹	hu².
	笏¹	hu⁴.
	惚¹	hu¹.
	惑¹	ho², huo², huo⁴.
	葫¹	hu².
	餬¹	hu².
	霍¹	ho⁴.
	核¹	ho².
	弧⁴	wu².
	俙⁴	wu³, wu⁴.

HUA	化¹	hua⁴.
	華¹	hua².
	譁¹	hua².
	找²	chao³.
	滑²	ku⁴.
	劃²	ho⁴.
	踝⁴	huai³.
	話⁴	hua⁴.
	畫⁴	ho⁴.

HUAI	獲¹	ho⁴, huo⁴.
	踝¹	hua².
	壞⁴	kuai⁴.

HUAN	儇¹	huan².
	鸛¹	kuan¹, kuan⁴.
	完²	wan².
	宛²	wan³, yüan³.
	還²	hai⁴, han².
	莞⁴	kuan¹.
	瘓⁴	tuan³.

HUANG	肓¹	mang², mêng².
	遑¹	huang².
	慌¹	huang³.
	況⁴	k'uang⁴.

HUEI, HUI	恢¹	k'uei¹.
	虺²	hui³.
	悔³	hui⁴.
	海³	hui⁴.
	匯³	hui⁴.
	賄³	hui¹.
	會⁴	hui¹, kuei⁴.
	喙⁴	sui⁴.
	彗⁴	sao⁴, sui¹.
	蕙⁴	lei³, wei⁴.
	噦⁴	yüeh¹, yüeh².

HUÊN, HUN	葷¹	hsün¹.
	渾²	hun³.
	混³	hun⁴.

HUNG	吽¹	hung¹.
	虹²	chiang⁴, kang⁴.
	橫²	hung⁴, hêng², hêng⁴.

HUO	和¹	huo², hai⁴, han⁴, ho², ho⁴.
	窩¹	wo¹.
	劉¹	ho¹.
	穫¹	ho⁴.
	惑¹	huo², ho⁴, hu¹.
	活²	ho².
	火²	ho³.
	夥²	ho³, i¹.
	或⁴	ho⁴.
	貨⁴	ho⁴.
	禍⁴	ho⁴.
	獲⁴	huai², ho⁴.

HSI	息¹	hsi².
	熄¹	hsi².
	系¹	hsi⁴.
	係¹	hsi⁴.
	夕¹	hsi².
	昔¹	hsi².

HSI	晰¹	hsi³.	HSIEH	揳¹	hsieh⁴.	HSIN	馨¹	hsing¹.
	嘻¹	hsi³.		些¹	so¹.		莘¹	shên¹.
	禧¹	hsi³.		歇¹	chieh¹.		尋²	hsün².
	兕¹	ssŭ⁴.		薛¹	hsüeh³.		覃²	t'an².
	唏¹	hsi³.		浹²	chieh⁴.		隼³	chun³, hsün³.
	徙¹	hsi³.		脅²	lei⁴, chieh².		汛⁴	hsün⁴.
	錫¹	hsi².		挾²	chia¹, chia², chieh².		迅⁴	hsün⁴.
	攜¹	hsi², hsieh².		鋏²	chia¹, chia², chieh¹, chieh⁴.		訊⁴	hsün⁴.
	棲¹	ch'i¹.		拽²	hsieh⁴, chuai¹, chuai⁴, yeh⁴.			
	溪¹	ch'i¹.		協²	chieh².	HSING	猩¹	shêng¹.
	習²	hsi².		絜²	chieh², chieh⁴.		醒¹	hsing³.
	媳²	hsi³.		叶²	chieh².		馨¹	hsin¹.
	碏²	ch'io⁴, ch'üeh¹.		擷²	hsi¹, hsi².		興¹	hsing¹.
	唏³	hsi⁴.		斜²	hsia².		錫¹	hsing², t'ang².
	洗³	hsien³.		躞⁴	hsieh⁴.		行¹	hsing¹, hang².
	繫⁴	chi⁴.		血⁴	hsüeh³, hsüeh⁴.		省³	shêng³.
	歙⁴	shê¹.		洩⁴	i¹.		荇⁴	hêng⁴.
	壻⁴	hsü¹.		契⁴	ch'i¹.			
				泄⁴	i⁴, yeh⁴.	HSIO	學¹	hsiao², hsüeh², hsüo².
HSIA	呀¹	a², ya¹.		絜⁴	chieh².		削¹	hsiao¹, hsüeh¹, hsüeh³.
	蝦¹	ha², hsia².		解⁴	chieh³, chieh⁴.		謔⁴	niao⁴, nio⁴, nüeh⁴, nüo⁴.
	斜²	hsieh².						
	峽²	hsia⁴.	HSIEN	摻¹	shan¹.	HSIU	囚²	ch'iu².
	筴²	ch'ieh⁴.		鮮¹	hsien³.		宿³	hsiu⁴, hsü¹, su², su⁴.
	詰²	hsia⁴.		搴¹	chien³, ch'ien¹.			
	嚇⁴	ho⁴.		褰¹	ch'ien¹.	HSIUNG	洶¹	hsiung³.
	厦⁴	sha⁴.		軒¹	hsüan¹.		迥³	chiung³, ch'iung³.
	洽⁴	ch'ia⁴.		嫣¹	yen¹.			
				函²	han².	HSÜ	恤¹	hsü⁴.
HSIANG	相¹	hsiang⁴.		涎²	yen².		卹¹	hsü¹, hsüeh³.
	降²	chiang⁴.		涵²	han².		夙¹	su⁴.
	嚮³	hsiang⁴.		緘²	chien¹.		宿³	hsiu³, hsiu⁴, su², su⁴.
	苍⁴	hang⁴.		閒²	chien².		紆¹	yü¹.
	項⁴	hang⁴.		絃²	hsüan².		謳¹	ou³, ou¹.
				檻²	hsien⁴, chien⁴, k'an³.		昫¹	hsü⁴.
HSIAO	削¹	hsio⁴, hsüeh¹, hsüeh³.		喊³	han³, k'an⁴.		畜¹	hsü⁴, ch'u⁴.
	魈¹	hsiao⁴.		洗³	hsi³.		虛¹	chü⁴.
	澆¹	chiao¹.		見⁴	chien⁴.		粟⁴	su², su⁴.
	囂²	ao².		現⁴	hsüan⁴.		俗²	su¹, su².
	炙²	yao².		艦⁴	chien⁴.		醒²	t'i².
	肴²	yao².		陷⁴	hsüan¹.		旭³	hsü⁴.
	學²	hsio², hsüeh², hsüo².					聚³	chü¹.
	哮⁴	hao¹.	HSIN	欣¹	ts'ê¹.			
	校⁴	chiao⁴.		沁⁴	ch'in⁴.			
	誚⁴	ch'iao⁴.						

APPENDIX III.—THE PEKING SYLLABARY.

HSÜ	峸³	yü³.	I, YI	一¹	i², i⁴.	JÊ, JO	日⁴	jih⁴, shih⁴.
	壻⁴	hsi⁴.		乙¹	i⁴.		熱⁴	jo⁴.
	絮⁴	nü⁴.		衣¹	i⁴.			
	續⁴	su⁴.		依¹	i³.	JÊN	紉¹	jên¹, jên⁴.
				夥¹	ho³, huo³.		仍²	jên³, jêng², jêng³.
HSÜAN, HSÜEN	軒¹	hsien¹.		宜¹	i², i⁴.		任²	jên⁴.
	劗¹	hsüan⁴.		壹¹	i², i⁴.		恁³	yin⁴.
	眩¹	hsüan², hsüan³.		瘞¹	i⁴.		衽³	jên⁴.
	宣¹	hsüan².		揖¹	i⁴, jung³.		孕⁴	yin⁴, yün⁴.
	旋¹	hsüan².		亦¹	i³, i⁴.			
	潆²	hsüan², hsüeh².		奕¹	i⁴.	JÊNG	扔¹	jêng³.
	璇¹	hsüan².		蛾²	ê², o².		擲¹	chih¹, chih⁴.
	璿¹	hsüan².		盆²	i⁴.		仍²	jêng³, jên², jên³.
	擓²	hsüeh².		涯²	ya², yai².			
	絃²	hsien².		擬²	i³, ni³.	JIH	日⁴	jê⁴, shih⁴.
	選³	hsüan⁴.		遺²	wei⁴.			
	現⁴	hsien⁴.		頤²	so².	JO	惹³	jê³.
	陷⁴	hsien⁴.		展³	i⁴.		若³	jê³, yao⁴, yo⁴, jê⁴.
				尾³	wei³.		弱⁴	jao⁴, ni⁴, niao⁴.
HSÜEH	削¹	hsüeh³, hsiao¹, hsio⁴.		蟻³	i⁴.		熱⁴	jê⁴.
	穴²	hsüeh⁴.		泄⁴	hsieh⁴, yeh⁴.			
	擦²	hsüan².		射⁴	shih⁴, shê⁴, yeh⁴.	JOU	揉¹	jou², jou³.
	學²	hsiao², hsio², hsüo².		液⁴	shih².		猱²	nao².
	漩²	hsüan¹, hsüan².		掖⁴	yeh⁴.		肉⁴	ju⁴.
	血³	hsüeh⁴, hsieh³.		浥⁴	yeh⁴.			
	岬³	hsü², hsü⁴.		疫⁴	yü².	JU	如¹	ju².
	雪³	hsüeh⁴.		語⁴	yü³, yü⁴.		茹²	ju³, ku¹.
	薛³	hsieh¹.		馹⁴	êrh⁴.		辱²	ju⁴.
				洩⁴	hsieh⁴.		儒²	ju⁴.
HSÜN	葷¹	hun¹.		隘⁴	yai⁴, ai⁴.		入³	ju⁴, êrh⁴.
	尋²	hsin².		逆⁴	ni⁴.		乳³	ju⁴.
	詢²	hsün⁴.					擩⁴	ju⁴.
	筍³	sun³.	JAN	—	—		肉⁴	jou⁴.
	笋³	sun³.						
	隼³	chun³.	JANG	壤²	jang³, nang³.	JUAN	阮³	yüan², yüan³.
	汛⁴	hsin⁴.		禳²	jang⁴.			
	迅⁴	hsin⁴.		讓⁴	jang⁴.	JUI	蕤³	jui¹.
	訊⁴	hsin⁴.					瑞⁴	shui⁴.
	巽⁴	sun⁴.	JAO	遶³	jao⁴.		銳⁴	tui⁴, wei⁴.
	遙⁴	sun⁴.		繞³	jao⁴.		睿⁴	wei⁴.
				弱⁴	ni⁴, niao⁴, jo⁴.			
ÜO	學¹	hsiao², hsio², hsüeh².	JÊ, JO	若³	jo⁴, yao⁴, yo⁴, jê⁴.			
				惹³	jo³.			

[HSÜ–JUI.]   183

JUN	允³	yün³, yu³.	KAO	各¹	chiu¹, chiu⁴.	K'O, K'Ê	科¹	k'o⁴.
							剋¹	k'o⁴.
JUNG	容²	yung².	K'AO	敲¹	chiao¹.		稞¹	k'o⁴.
	溶²	yung².		烤³	k'ao⁴.		瞌²	k'o³.
	榕²	yung².		拷³	k'ao⁴.		咳²	k'ai³.
	蓉²	yung².					去⁴	ch'ü⁴.
	鎔²	yung².	KEI	給³	chi³, chi⁴.		闊⁴	k'uo⁴.
	榮²	yung².					濶⁴	k'uo⁴.
	熒²	yung².	K'EI	刻¹	k'o¹, k'o³, k'o⁴.			
	縈²	yung².				KOU	緱¹	ou¹.
	融²	yung².	KÊN	勍¹	chin¹.		狗²	kou³.
	慵²	yung².		梗³	kêng³.			
	揖³	i¹, i⁴.				K'OU	嘔¹	ou¹.
			K'ÊN	肯³	k'êng³.		扣³	k'ou⁴.
KA	嘎¹	ka², ka³, ka⁴, chia¹.		掯⁴	k'êng⁴.			
						KU	古¹	ku³.
K'A	卡¹	k'a³, ch'ia¹, ch'ia³.	KÊNG	更¹	kêng⁴, ching¹.		佑¹	ku⁴.
				耕¹	ching¹.		呱¹	kua¹, kua³.
KAI	街¹	chieh¹.		耿³	ching³.		谷¹	ku³.
	溉⁴	chi⁴.		梗³	kên³.		骨¹	ku², ku³.
				頸³	ching³.		茹¹	ju², ju³.
K'AI	楷³	ch'iai³.					穀¹	ku³.
	咳³	k'o².	K'ÊNG	傾¹	ch'ing¹, ch'iung¹.		穀¹	ku³.
				肯³	k'ên³.		汨³	mi⁴.
KAN	乾¹	ch'ien².		掯⁴	k'ên⁴.		滑⁴	ku⁴, hua², k'u¹.
	捍¹	kan².					賈⁴	chia³.
			KO, KÊ	戈¹	kuo¹.		涸⁴	hao⁴, ho⁴.
K'AN	刊¹	k'an³.		擱¹	ko².			
	看¹	k'an⁴.		各²	ko³, ko⁴.	K'U	袴¹	k'u⁴, k'ua⁴.
	吹³	ch'ui¹, ch'ui⁴.		閣⁴	ko⁴.		涸¹	ku⁴, hao⁴, ho⁴.
	侃³	k'an¹.		隔⁴	chieh², chieh⁴.			
	槛⁴	chien⁴, hsien², hsien⁴.		葛⁴	ko³.	KUA	呱¹	kua³, ku¹.
	喊⁴	han³, hsien³.		哥¹	k'o¹.		聒¹	kua⁴, kuo¹, kuo⁴.
				合⁴	ho².		鴰¹	kua⁴.
KANG	亢¹	hang², k'ang⁴.						
	扛¹	k'ang².	K'O, K'Ê	可¹	k'o², k'o³.	K'UA	誇¹	k'ua³.
	將¹	chiang¹, chiang⁴.		奇¹	ho¹.		胯³	k'u¹, k'u⁴.
	摃¹	kang¹.		頦²	hai², hai³.			
	虹⁴	chiang⁴, hung².		坷³	k'o³.	KUAI	壞⁴	huai⁴.
				嗑³	ko³.			
K'ANG	扛²	kang¹.		刻⁴	k'o³, k'o⁴, k'ei¹.	K'UAI	瑰¹	k'uei⁴.
	亢⁴	hang², kang¹.						

KUAN	莞¹	huan³.	KUO	戈¹	ko¹.	LÊ	洛⁴	lo⁴.
	冠¹	kuan⁴.		郭¹	kuo³.		勒¹	lei¹, lieh⁴, lo⁴.
	觀¹	kuan⁴.		堝¹	kuo².		樂⁴	lo⁴, yao⁴, yo⁴, yüeh⁴.
	綸¹	lün², lun².		蟈¹	kuo⁴.		肋⁴	chin¹, lei⁴.
	鸛⁴	kuan⁴, huan¹.		聒¹	kuo⁴, kua⁴, kua⁴.			
	斡³	wa⁴.		過²	kuo⁴.	LÊI, LEI	勒¹	lê¹, lieh⁴, lo⁴.
	盥³	kuan⁴.		椁²	kuo³.		縲¹	lei¹.
							累²	lei¹, lei⁴.
K'UAN	—	—	K'UO	闊⁴	k'o⁴.		攂²	lei¹.
				濶⁴	k'o⁴.		礧³	hui⁴, wei⁴.
KUANG	誆¹	k'uang².					儡³	lei¹.
			LA	喇¹	la³.		脇⁴	hsieh², chieh².
K'UANG	誆²	kuang¹.		瘌¹	la⁴.		淚⁴	li⁴.
	況⁴	huang⁴.		剌²	la⁴.		肋⁴	chin¹, lê⁴.
				落⁴	lao⁴, lo⁴, lu¹.			
KUEI	瑰¹	kuei⁴.				LÊNG	楞¹	lêng².
	晷¹	kuei³.	LAI	攋⁴	li⁴.		稜¹	lêng².
	鱖¹	kuei⁴.					睖¹	lêng⁴.
	愧⁴	k'uei⁴.	LAN	籃¹	lan².			
	會⁴	hui³, hui⁴.		婪²	lan³.	LI	李¹	li³.
				爁²	lan³.		哩¹	li⁴.
K'UEI	恢²	hui¹.		孌²	luan².		鯉¹	li².
	跬³	wa¹.		鸞²	luan².		莉¹	li⁴.
	塊⁴	k'uai⁴.		濫⁴	lan⁴.		漓¹	li².
	愧⁴	kuei⁴.		臠	luan⁴.		璃¹	li².
							籬¹	li².
KUÊN, KUN	昆¹	k'un¹.	LANG	踉¹	lang².		麗	li².
	崑¹	k'un¹.		榔¹	lang², lang³.		鸝¹	li².
				朗³	lang².		澧²	li⁴.
K'UÊN, K'UN	昆¹	kun¹.		閬³	lang⁴.		履⁴	lü³.
	崑¹	kun¹.					淚⁴	lei⁴.
	閩²	k'un³.	LAO	撈¹	lao².		颯⁴	sa¹, sa⁴.
	壼¹	k'un³.		老²	lao³.		攋⁴	lai⁴.
	悃³	k'un⁴.		栳²	lao³.			
				勞²	lao⁴.	LIA	倆³	liang⁴.
KUNG	紅¹	hung².		癆²	lao⁴.			
	供¹	kung⁴.		潦³	lao⁴, liao².	LIANG	兩¹	liang³.
				姥³	mu³.		踉¹	liang³.
K'UNG	空¹	k'ung³.		烙⁴	lo⁴.		梁¹	liang².
	恐³	ch'iung⁴.		落⁴	la⁴, lo⁴, lu¹.		量¹	liang², liang⁴.
				酪⁴	lo⁴.		梁²	niang².
				絡⁴	ch'üeh⁴, lo⁴.		魎²	liang³.
							倆⁴	lia³.
							掠⁴	lüo⁴, lu³.

LIAO	料⁴	liao⁴.	LO	攎¹	lo³.	LUO	搻³	lüo⁴, liao⁴, lio³, lüeh³, lüeh⁴.
	潦²	lao³, lao⁴.		摞²	lo⁴.		掠⁴	liang⁴, lü³.
	燎³	liao⁴.		捋³	lieh³.			
	瞭³	liao⁴.		攞³	lo⁴.	LU	落¹	la⁴, lao⁴, lo⁴.
	掉⁴	tiao⁴, t'iao³.		洛³	lê⁴.		路²	lu⁴.
	搻⁴	lio³, lüeh³, lüeh⁴, lüo³, lüo⁴.		落³	la⁴, lao⁴, lu¹.		盧²	lü².
				烙³	lao⁴.		驢²	lü².
LIEH	咧¹	lieh², lieh³, lieh⁴.		絡³	ch'üeh⁴, lao⁴.		轆²	lu⁴.
	乜²	mieh².		酪³	lao⁴.		六⁴	liu⁴.
	捋³	lo³.		勒³	lê⁴, lei¹, lieh⁴.		碌⁴	lü⁴.
	勒⁴	lê⁴, lei¹, lo⁴.		樂³	lê⁴, yao⁴, yo⁴, yüeh⁴.		綠⁴	lou⁴.
							露⁴	niu⁴, miu⁴.
LIEN	連¹	lien².	LOU	摟¹	lou³.		謬⁴	liu⁴, lü³.
	漣¹	lien².		簍²	lü².		陸⁴	
	璉²	lien⁴.		褸²	lü³.			
	斂³	lien⁴.		鏤²	lü².	LUAN	欒²	lun².
	輦³	nien³.		露⁴	lu⁴.		鸞²	lun².
	揀⁴	chien³.					亂⁴	lan⁴.
	戀⁴	lüan⁴.	LÜ	婁²	lou².			
				履²	lü³, chü⁴.	LUN	棱²	lêng⁴.
LIN	淋²	lin⁴, lün².		鏤²	lou².		倫²	lün².
	臨²	lin⁴.		盧²	lu².		崙²	lün².
	凜³	ling³.		驢²	lu².		掄²	lün².
	廩³	ling³.		陸³	liu⁴, lu⁴.		圇²	lun³, lün², lün³.
	貧⁴	nin⁴.		褸³	lü⁴.		論²	lun⁴, lün², lün⁴.
				掠³	liang⁴, lüo⁴.		綸²	kuan¹, lün².
LING	令²	ling⁴.		縷³	lou².		輪⁴	lün¹, lün².
	凜³	lin³.		履³	li³.			
	廩³	lin³.		綠⁴	lu⁴.	LUNG	窿¹	lung².
							籠³	lung³.
LIO	搻³	liao⁴, lüeh³, lüeh⁴, lüo³, lüo⁴.	LÜAN	戀⁴	lien⁴.		弄⁴	nêng⁴, nung⁴, nou⁴.
			LÜEH	搻³	lüeh⁴, liao⁴, lio³, lüo³, lüo⁴.			
LIU	溜¹	liu⁴.				MA	沬¹	mo⁴.
	遛¹	liu⁴.	LÜN	掄¹	lün².		摸¹	mao¹, mo¹, mou².
	鎏²	lin².		輪¹	lün², lun².		嗎¹	ma³.
	瀏²	liu⁴.		淋²	lin², lin⁴.		蟆²	ma².
	六⁴	lu⁴.		倫²	lun².		媽²	mu³, ma⁴.
	碌⁴	lu⁴.		崙²	lun².		麽²	ma³, mo¹, mo².
	陸⁴	lü³, lu⁴.		圇²	lün³, lun², lun³.		瑪²	ma³.
				論²	lün⁴, lun², lun⁴.		螞³	ma⁴.
				綸²	lun², kuan¹.			

APPENDIX III.—THE PEKING SYLLABARY.

MAI	麥¹	mai⁴, mo⁴.	MIAO	—	—	MOU	摸¹	ma¹, mao¹, nuo¹.
	埋²	man².					矛²	mao², miu².
	脉⁴	mo⁴.	MIEH	乜²	lieh².		拇³	mou³, mu³.
	鷔⁴	mo⁴.		明²	ming².		眸²	miu².
				篾⁴	mi⁴.		牡³	mu³.
MAN	埋²	mai².					某³	mu³.
	漫⁴	man⁴.	MIEN	俛³	fu³.		畝³	mu³.
	蔓²	man⁴.		湎³	shêng².		茂⁴	mao⁴.
				娩³	wan³.		貿⁴	mao⁴.
MANG	茫¹	mang².						
	育	huang¹, mêng².	MIN	黽²	mêng², min³.	MU	沒²	mu⁴, mei², mo⁴.
	芒²	wang².		賠³	min³.		歿²	mu⁴.
				皿³	ming³.		牡³	mou³.
MAO	摸¹	ma¹, mo¹, mou².					某³	mou³.
	貓¹	mao².	MING	明²	mieh².		畝³	mou³.
	貌⁴	mao⁴.		盟²	mêng².		媽³	ma¹, ma⁴.
	矛²	miao², mou².		溟²	ming³.		姥³	lao³.
	茂⁴	mou⁴.		皿³	min³.		拇³	mou³, mou³.
	貿⁴	mou⁴.					莫⁴	mo⁴.
			MIU	矛²	mao², mou².		幕⁴	mo⁴.
MEI	沒²	mo⁴, mu², mu⁴.		眸²	mou².		暮⁴	mo⁴.
	袂⁴	mi⁴.		謬⁴	lu⁴, niu⁴.		慕⁴	mo⁴.
	墨⁴	mo⁴.		繆⁴	mu⁴, niu⁴.		繆⁴	niu⁴, miu⁴.
MÊN	們¹	mên³, mên⁴.	MO	摸¹	ma¹, mao¹, mou².	NA	那¹	{ na³, na⁴, nai², nai⁴, nei³, nei⁴, nên³, nên⁴, nêng³, nêng⁴, no².
	悶⁴	mên⁴.		麼²	mo², ma¹, ma³.		哪¹	t'o⁴.
	捫²	mên².		摩²	mo².		哪²	nao².
	懣⁴	mên⁴.		磨²	mo⁴.		內⁴	nei⁴.
				抹³	mo⁴.			
MÊNG	濛¹	mêng².		沒⁴	mei², mu², mu⁴.	NAI	那³	{ nai⁴, na¹, na³, na⁴, nei³, nei⁴, nên³, nên⁴, nêng³, nêng⁴, no².
	矇²	mêng².		沫⁴	ma¹.		䴉³	nai⁴.
	懵³	mêng³.		墨⁴	mei⁴.			
	肓	mang², huang¹.		脉⁴	mai⁴.	NAN	喃	nan².
	盟²	ming².		螞⁴	ma¹, ma³.		俺³	an³.
	黽²	min², min³.		麥⁴	mai¹, mai⁴.		難²	nan².
				莫⁴	mu⁴.		喃⁴	an¹, an³.
MI	眯¹	mi³.		幕⁴	mu⁴.		煖³	nang³, nuan³.
	篾¹	mieh⁴.		慕⁴	mu⁴.		暖³	nang³, nuan³.
	彌²	mi².		鷔⁴	mai⁴.		攤⁴	t'an¹.
	謎⁴	mi⁴.						
	汨⁴	ku³.						
	宓⁴	fu².						
	袂⁴	mei⁴.						

NANG	馕³	nan³, nuan³.	NIEH	捏¹	nieh⁴, nien³.	NÜO	虐⁴	niao⁴, ning⁴, nio⁴, nüeh⁴, yo⁴.
	曩³	nan³, nuan³.		呆²	yeh⁴, ai¹, tai¹.		謔⁴	niao⁴, nio⁴, nüeh⁴, hsio⁴.
	壤³	jang², jang³.		臬⁴	yeh⁴.		瘧⁴	niao⁴, nio⁴, nüeh⁴, yao⁴, yo⁴.
				孼⁴	yeh⁴.			
NAO	撓¹	nao², hao¹.				NU	—	—
	猫²	jou².	NIEN	拈¹	nien².			
	呶²	na².		言²	yen², yüan².	NUAN	煖³	nan³, nang³.
	蹽³	niao³.		捻³	nieh¹, nieh⁴.		暖³	nan³, nang³.
				趁³	ch'ên⁴.			
NEI	那³	{ na¹, na³, na⁴, nai³, nai¹, nei⁴, nên³, nên⁴, nêng³, nêng¹, no².		輾³	chan³, ch'ên³.	NUN	嫩⁴	nên⁴.
	内⁴	na⁴.		輦³	lien³.			
						NUNG	儂¹	nung², nêng³.
NÊN	那³	{ nên⁴, na¹, na³, na⁴, nai³, nai⁴, nei³, nei¹, nêng³, nêng⁴, no².	NIN	賃⁴	lin⁴.		濃²	nung⁴, nêng⁴.
	嫩⁴	nun⁴.	NING	寧²	ning⁴, nêng⁴.		弄⁴	lung⁴, nêng⁴, nou⁴.
				擰²	ning³.			
NÊNG	能¹	nêng².		凝²	ying².	O	阿¹	a¹, a³, a⁴, ê¹, wo¹.
	儂¹	nung¹, nung².		虐⁴	niao⁴, nio⁴, nüeh⁴, nüo⁴, yo⁴.		哦¹	ê¹.
	濃²	nung¹, nung².					訛¹	ê², wo².
	那³	{ nêng¹, na¹, na³, na⁴, nai³, nei³, nei¹, nên³, nên⁴, no².	NIO	虐⁴	niao⁴, ning⁴, nüeh⁴, nüo⁴, yo⁴.		娥¹	ê².
	弄⁴	lung⁴, nou⁴, nung⁴.		謔⁴	niao⁴, nüeh⁴, nüo⁴, hsio⁴.		峨¹	ê², i².
	寧⁴	ning², ning⁴.		瘧⁴	niao⁴, nüeh⁴, nüo⁴, yao⁴, yo⁴.		鵝¹	ê².
							額⁴	o⁴, ê², ê⁴.
NI	呢¹	ni².	NIU	牛²	yu².		我³	ê³, wo³.
	擬³	i², i³.		杻³	chou³, ch'ou³.		呃⁴	ai⁴.
	溺⁴	jao⁴, jo⁴, niao⁴.		扭³	ch'ou³.		餓⁴	ê⁴.
	溺⁴	niao⁴, yao⁴.		謬⁴	lu⁴, miu⁴.		諤⁴	ê⁴.
	瀰⁴	ti⁴, t'i⁴.		繆⁴	mu⁴, miu⁴.		鶚⁴	ê⁴.
	逆⁴	i⁴.					惡⁴	ê⁴, wu⁴.
			NO	那	{ na¹, na³, na⁴, nai³, nai⁴, nei³, nei⁴, nên³, nên⁴, nêng³, nêng⁴.		齷⁴	ê⁴.
NIANG	粱²	liang².		娜²	no³.			
				諾³	no⁴.	OU	漚¹	ou⁴.
NIAO	杳³	yao³.					嫗¹	yü⁴, wu⁴.
	鳥³	tiao³.	NOU	弄⁴	lung⁴, nêng⁴, nung⁴.		嘔¹	k'ou¹.
	蹽³	nao³.					毆³	ou³.
	尿⁴	sui¹.	NÜ	女³	yü³, yü⁴.		甌³	ou³.
	溺⁴	jao⁴, jo⁴, ni⁴.		絮⁴	hsü⁴.		繣⁴	kou¹.
	溺⁴	ni⁴, yao⁴.					藕⁴	ou³.
	虐⁴	ning⁴, nio⁴, nüeh⁴, nüo⁴, yo⁴.	NÜEH	虐⁴	niao⁴, ning⁴, nio⁴, nüo⁴, yo⁴.		嘔⁴	ou⁴, hsü¹.
	謔⁴	nio⁴, nüeh⁴, nüo⁴, hsio⁴.		謔⁴	niao⁴, nio⁴, nüo⁴, hsio⁴.	PA	八¹	pa².
	瘧⁴	nio⁴, nüeh⁴, nüo⁴, yo⁴.		瘧⁴	niao⁴, nio⁴, nüo⁴, yao⁴, yo⁴.		把¹	pa², pa⁴.
							撥¹	po¹, pu¹.
							杷⁴	p'a².

P'A	趴¹	p'a².	P'ANG	滂¹	p'ang².	P'EI	坏¹	p'ei².
	杷²	pa⁴.		仿²	fang³.		披²	p'ei¹.
				傍²	pang⁴.		佩⁴	pei⁴.
PAI	摚¹	p'i³.		逢²	fêng².		珮⁴	pei⁴.
	白²	po¹, po², po⁴.		彷³	fang³.			
	帛²	pai⁴.		謗³	pang⁴.	PÊN	奔¹	pên⁴.
	百³	po², po⁴.		膀³	pang³.		賁¹	pi⁴.
	伯³	po², po⁴.					犇¹	pên⁴.
	柏³	po⁴.						
	栢³	po⁴.	PAO	剖¹	p'ou³.	P'ÊN	噴¹	p'ên⁴.
				剝¹	po¹.		体⁴	t'i³.
P'AI	捭¹	p'ai².		胞²	p'ao¹.			
	菩²	p'u².		鹿²	p'ao².	PÊNG	蚌³	pang⁴.
				薄²	po².		搴⁴	p'êng².
PAN	頒¹	pan².		堡²	p'u⁴, pu³.			
	班¹	pan².		刨²	p'ao².	P'ÊNG	硼¹	p'êng².
	扳¹	p'an¹.		鮑³	p'ao².		捧³	fêng³.
	斑¹	pan².		暴⁴	p'ao⁴.		搴⁴	pêng².
	搬¹	su¹.		瀑⁴	pu⁴.			
	瘢²	p'an².				PI	必²	pi⁴.
	叛⁴	p'an⁴, pang⁴.					箆²	pi⁴.
	辯⁴	pien⁴.	P'AO	泡¹	p'ao⁴.		羆²	pei², p'i².
	瓣⁴	p'an².		胞¹	pao¹.		否³	fou³, p'i³.
				刨²	pao⁴.		比³	p'i², pi⁴.
P'AN	扳¹	pan¹.		炮²	p'ao³.		彼³	pei³.
	番¹	fan¹, fan².		跑²	p'ao³.		壁³	pi⁴.
	瘢¹	pan².		庖²	pao².		鄙³	pi⁴.
	繙²	fan¹.		鮑²	pao⁴.		麀³	pi⁴.
	辮²	pan⁴.		瓢²	piao².		妣³	p'i³.
	判⁴	pang⁴.		熏⁴	pao⁴.		婢⁴	pei².
	泮⁴	pang⁴.					愎⁴	p'i⁴.
	叛⁴	pan⁴, pang⁴.					辟⁴	pi³, p'i³.
	盼⁴	pang⁴.	PEI	背¹	pei⁴.		避⁴	pei⁴.
				羆¹	pi², p'i².		賁⁴	pên⁴.
				北¹	po⁴, pu³.		費⁴	fei⁴.
PANG	謗³	p'ang³.		彼¹	pi³.		髭⁴	pei⁴.
	蚌³	pêng⁴.		俾¹	p'i¹, p'i².		庇⁴	p'i³.
	盼⁴	p'an⁴.		避²	pi⁴.			
	判⁴	p'an⁴.		佩⁴	p'ei⁴.	P'I	批¹	p'i³.
	泮⁴	p'an⁴.		珮⁴	p'ei⁴.		砒¹	p'i².
	叛⁴	pan⁴, p'an⁴.		婢⁴	pi⁴.		匹¹	p'i², p'i³.
	拚⁴	p'ing².		葡⁴	po², p'o⁴.		披¹	p'i³.
	傍⁴	p'ang².		髭⁴	pi⁴.		僻¹	pei⁴, p'i⁴.
	謗³	p'ang³.						

P'I	劈¹	p'i³.	PIN	繽¹	p'in².	PO	鏺²	po⁴.
	霹¹	p'i⁴.		稟³	ping³.		播⁴	po⁴.
	闢¹	p'i⁴.		拼⁴	ping¹, ping⁴.		簸⁴	po⁴.
	比²	pi³, pi⁴.		擯⁴	p'in⁴.		柏⁴	pai³.
	羆²	pei², pi².					栢⁴	pai³.
	否³	pi³, fou³.	P'IN	擯¹	pin⁴.		北⁴	pei³, pu³.
	缶³	fou³.		繽¹	pin¹.		雹⁴	pao².
	辟³	p'i¹, pi⁴.		頻¹	pin¹.			
	鄙³	pi³, pi⁴.		嚬¹	pin¹.	P'O	扑¹	p'o⁴, p'u³.
	庇³	pi⁴.		顰¹	pin¹.		朴¹	p'o⁴.
	妣³	pi³.		蘋¹	pin¹, p'ing².		婆²	p'o².
	愎⁴	pi⁴.		聘⁴	p'ing⁴.		珀⁴	p'o⁴.
				嬪⁴	pin¹.		玻	po¹.
PIAO	杓¹	shao².					皤²	po¹.
	麃¹	p'ao².	PING	并¹	ping⁴, pin¹.		破⁴	p'o⁴.
	俵³	piao⁴.		凭²	p'ing².		葡	pei, po¹.
				屏³	p'ing³.		魄	t'o⁴.
P'IAO	漂	p'iao³, p'iao⁴.		稟³	pin³.		僕⁴	pu².
							撲⁴	p'u⁴.
PIEH	出¹	ch'u¹.	P'ING	娉¹	p'ing⁴.		樸⁴	p'u³.
	憋¹	pieh⁴.		拼²	pang⁴.			
	蟞¹	p'ieh⁴.		屏²	ping³.	POU	不¹	pu¹, pu², pu⁴, fou¹, po¹.
	鱉¹	p'ieh⁴.		凭²	p'ing².			
				蘋²	pin¹, p'in¹.	P'OU	剖³	pao¹.
P'IEH	撇¹	} p'ieh³.		聘	p'in⁴.			
	瞥¹					PU	不¹	pu², pu⁴, fou¹, po¹, pou¹.
	潎	p'ieh⁴.	PO	白¹	pai², po², po⁴.		撥	pa¹, po¹.
	瞥	p'ieh⁴.		皤	p'o².		僕	p'o⁴.
	鱉	pieh¹.		撥	pa¹, pu¹.		北³	pei³, po³.
	鱉	pieh¹.		蔔	pei⁴, p'o⁴.		譜	p'u³.
				餑¹	po⁴.		堡	pao³, p'u⁴.
PIEN	扁³	p'ien³.		菠	po².		鋪	p'u⁴.
	耕³	p'ien².		不¹	pu¹, pu², pu⁴, fou¹, pou¹.		瀑	pao⁴.
	便⁴	p'ien².		剝	pao¹.		埠	fou³.
	辯⁴	pan⁴.		玻	p'o¹.			
				百²	pai³, po⁴.	P'U	撲¹	p'o⁴.
P'IEN	便²	pien⁴.		伯²	pai³, po⁴.		鋪	p'u¹.
	耕²	pien³.		泊²	po⁴.		菩	p'ai².
	扁³	pien³.		鉑²	po⁴.		扑³	p'o⁴, p'o¹.
				博²	po⁴.		樸	p'o⁴.
PIN	頻¹	p'in².		膊²	po⁴.		譜	pu³.
	嚬¹	p'in².		薄²	pao².		堡	pao³, pu³.
	蘋¹	p'in², p'ing².					鋪	pu³.
	嬪⁴	p'in⁴.						

[SA-SHAO.] APPENDIX III.—THE PEKING SYLLABARY. 191

SA	三¹	san¹, san⁴.	SO	些¹	hsieh¹.	SUNG	誦¹	sung⁴.
	趿¹	sa⁴.		索¹	so³, sê³.		聳³	tsung³.
	靸¹	sa⁴.		捼¹	so³, so⁴.		悚³	ch'u⁴.
	颯¹	sa⁴, li⁴.		唆¹	tsun⁴.		訴⁴	su⁴.
	撒²	sa², sa³.		頤²	i².			
	薩⁴	sa⁴.		所⁴	su⁴, shu³, shuo¹.	SHA	杉¹	shan¹.
	灑³	sha³, sha⁴, shai³.		素⁴	su⁴.		殺¹	shai⁴.
	洒³	sha³, shai⁴.		數⁴	shu³, shu⁴, shuo⁴.		猷¹	sha⁴.
				朔⁴	shuo⁴.		煞¹	sha⁴.
SAI	摋¹	sai².					洒³	shai³, sa³.
	攞¹	sai⁴.	SOU	瘦⁴	shou⁴.		灑³	sha⁴, sa³, shai³.
	塞⁴	sê⁴.					耍³	shua³.
			SU	俗¹	su², hsü².		厦⁴	hsia⁴.
				搬¹	pan¹.			
SAN	三¹	san⁴, sa¹.		宿⁴	su⁴, hsiu³, hsiu⁴, hsü¹.	SHAI	色³	sê⁴, shê⁴.
	散³	san⁴.		束⁴	su⁴, shu², shu¹.		灑³	sa³, sha³, shai³.
				速²	su⁴.		洒³	sa³, sha³.
SANG	喪¹	sang⁴.		粟²	hsü¹, su¹.		殺⁴	sha¹.
				蕭²	su⁴.			
SAO	臊¹	sao⁴.		術⁴	shu⁴.	SHAN	杉¹	sha¹.
	掃³	sao⁴.		述⁴	shu⁴.		摻¹	hsien¹.
	燥⁴	tsao⁴.		所⁴	so³, shu³, shuo³.		挻¹	yen².
	譟⁴	tsao⁴.		夙⁴	hsü¹.		訕¹	shan⁴.
	彗⁴	sui⁴, hui⁴.		訴⁴	sung⁴.		蟾¹	ch'an¹.
	颼⁴	shao¹.		素⁴	so⁴.		苫¹	shan⁴.
				績⁴	hsü⁴.		單²	shan¹, tan¹.
SÊ	說¹	shuo¹, shui⁴.					禪²	shan⁴, ch'an², tan¹.
	虱¹	shih¹.	SUAN	—			蟬²	ch'an².
	蝨¹	shih¹.					姍³	shan⁴.
	颯¹	shih¹.	SUI	尿¹	niao³.		瞻³	chan¹.
	嘛¹	sê².		荽¹	sui⁴.			
	瑟²	sê⁴, shê¹.		遂¹	sui².	SHANG	裳¹	shang².
	索³	so¹, so³.		雖²	shui¹.		慯¹	shang⁴.
	色⁴	shai³, shê⁴.		隋²	t'o³.		晌²	shang³.
	溢⁴	shê⁴.		隨²	ts'ui².		尚²	shang⁴.
	塞⁴	sai⁴.		彗²	sao⁴, hui⁴.		常²	ch'ang².
	濇⁴	shê⁴.		崒²	ts'ui².			
				喙⁴	hui⁴.	SHAO	颼¹	sao⁴.
SÊN	森¹	shên¹, shêng¹.					艄¹	shao³.
			SUN	笋³	hsün³.		勺¹	shuo².
SÊNG	—			筍³	hsün³.		灼¹	shuo².
				巽⁴	hsün³.		芍²	piao¹, shuo².
				遜⁴	hsün⁴.			

SHAO	杓²	tiao⁴.	SHIH	盃¹	sê¹.	SHUAI	衰¹	shui¹.
	釣²	tiao⁴.		蝨¹	sê¹.		摔¹	shuai³.
	少³	shao⁴.		筮¹	shih⁴.			
	哨⁴	ch'iao⁴.		噬¹	shih⁴.	SHUAN	拴¹	ch'uan¹.
				螄¹	ssŭ¹.		栓¹	ch'uan¹.
SHÊ	涉¹	shê⁴.		薛¹	shih⁴.		欄¹	chuan¹.
	瑟¹	sê², sê⁴.		弛¹	shih³.			
	折²	chê², cho².		世²	shih⁴.	SHUANG	雙¹	shuang⁴.
	歙³	hsi⁴.		柘²	chê⁴.			
	捨⁴	shê⁴.		射²	i⁴, shê⁴, yeh⁴.	SHUI	衰¹	shuai¹.
	色⁴	sê⁴, shai³.		矢²	shih³.		雖¹	sui¹.
	射⁴	i⁴, shih², yeh⁴.		食²	ssŭ⁴.		瑞⁴	jui⁴.
	涉⁴	sê⁴.		拾²	i⁴.		說⁴	sê¹, shuo¹.
	葉⁴	yeh⁴.		識²	shih⁴, chih¹, chih⁴.			
	濇⁴	sê⁴.		室²	shih⁴.	SHUN	鶉¹	ch'un², ch'un³.
				釋²	shih⁴.		唇¹	ch'un¹.
SHÊN	申¹	shên².		日²	jê⁴, jih⁴.		盾³	tun⁴.
	莘¹	hsin¹.		寺⁴	ssŭ⁴.			
	瘍¹	yang³.		恃⁴	ch'ih².	SHUO	說¹	sê¹, shui¹.
	森¹	sên¹, shêng¹.		似⁴	ssŭ⁴.		勺²	shao².
	參¹	ts'an¹, tsên¹, ts'ên¹.		褆⁴	t'i².		芍²	shao².
	甚²	shên⁴.		適⁴	ti², ti⁴.		杓²	piao¹, shao².
	蜃²	shên⁴.					灼²	shao².
	沈³	shên⁴.	SHOU	熟²	shu².		酌²	chao¹, chê², chê⁴, cho².
	審⁴	shên⁴.		首³	shou⁴.		着²	chao², chê², chê⁴, cho¹, cho².
	哂⁴	shên⁴.		瘦⁴	sou⁴.		所²	so³, su⁴, shu¹.
	瀋⁴	shên⁴.					朔²	so⁴.
	嬸⁴	shên⁴.	SHU	叔¹	shu².		敕²	ch'ih⁴.
	朕⁴	chên⁴, chêng⁴.		疏¹	shu⁴.		數⁴	shu³, shu⁴, so⁴.
				束¹	shu⁴, su², su⁴.			
SHÊNG	森¹	sên¹, shên¹.		菽²	chu¹.	SSŬ	思¹	ssŭ⁴.
	猩¹	hsing¹.		銃²	ch'ung⁴.		螄¹	shih¹.
	勝¹	shêng⁴.		熟²	shou².		祠²	tz'ŭ².
	澠¹	mien³.		屬²	chu², shu³.		詞²	tz'ŭ².
	省³	hsing³.		所²	so³, su⁴, shuo³.		辭²	tz'ŭ².
	乘²	ch'êng², ch'êng⁴.		數²	shu⁴, so⁴, shuo⁴.		似⁴	shih⁴.
	盛²	ch'êng².		署²	shu⁴.		伺⁴	shih⁴.
				述⁴	su⁴.		寺⁴	shih⁴.
SHIH	史¹	shih³.		術⁴	su⁴.		兕⁴	hsi⁴.
	視¹	shih², shih⁴.					食⁴	shih².
	匙¹	shih², ch'ih².	SHUA	唰¹	shua⁴.		賜⁴	tz'ŭ⁴.
	螫¹	chê¹.		耍³	sha³.			
	虱¹	sê¹.						

TA	答¹	ta².	TANG	當¹	tang⁴.	TI	篴²	chu².
	剳¹	ta², cha².		鐺¹	ch'êng¹.		覿²	ti³.
	達¹	ta².		盪⁴	tang⁴, t'ang⁴, t'ang².		糴²	ti³.
	撻¹	ta³, t'a⁴.		宕⁴	t'ang⁴.		殢⁴	t'i⁴, ni⁴.
	縫²	ta⁴.					悌⁴	t'i⁴.
	搭²	ta⁴.	T'ANG	堂¹	t'ang².		睇⁴	t'i¹.
	大⁴	chua⁴, tai⁴, to⁴.		踼¹	t'ang³, t'ang¹.		嚏⁴	t'i⁴.
	踢⁴	t'a¹.		盪⁴	t'ang⁴, tang¹, tang⁴.			
				錫⁴	hsing¹, hsing².	T'I	睇¹	ti⁴.
T'A	踢¹	ta⁴.		宕⁴	tang⁴.		提²	ti¹.
	獺³	t'a⁴.					禔²	shih⁴.
	撻⁴	ta¹, ta³.	TAO	朶¹	to³.		醍²	hsü².
				倒²	tao³, tao⁴.		替²	t'i¹.
TAI	呆¹	ai¹, nieh⁴, yeh⁴.		搗²	tao³.		堤²	ti¹.
	獃¹	ai².		纛⁴	tu¹.		体⁴	p'ên⁴.
	大⁴	chua⁴, ta⁴, to⁴.					殢⁴	ni⁴, ti⁴.
	貸⁴	t'ai⁴.	T'AO	叨¹	tê¹.		悌⁴	ti⁴.
				萄¹	t'ao².		嚏⁴	ti⁴.
T'AI	苔¹	t'ai².						
	太⁴	t'ui⁴.	TÊ	叨¹	t'ao¹.	TIAO	鳥³	niao³.
	忒⁴	t'ê⁴, t'ui¹.		得²	tei³, t'ê⁴.		掉⁴	liao⁴, t'iao³.
	貸⁴	tai⁴.		德⁴	tê⁴.		釣⁴	shao².
							調⁴	t'iao².
TAN	單¹	shan², shan⁴.	T'Ê	忒⁴	t'ai⁴, t'ui¹.		佻⁴	t'iao¹, yao².
	石⁴	tan⁴.		忑⁴	t'u¹.			
	禪¹	ch'an², shan², shan⁴.				T'IAO	佻¹	t'iao¹, yao⁴.
	擔¹	tan³.	TEI	得³	tê², tê⁴.		挑¹	t'iao³.
	苔¹	tan³.					跳⁴	t'iao⁴.
	撣³	t'an¹.	TÊNG	瞪⁴	chêng¹.		調²	tiao⁴.
	彈¹	t'an².		澄⁴	ch'êng².		掉³	liao⁴, tiao⁴.
	撢¹	t'an¹, t'an².		瞠⁴	chéng¹.			
	澹¹	t'an².				TIEH	跌¹	tieh⁴, tsai¹.
	擔¹	yen².	T'ÊNG	騰¹	t'êng².		喋²	tieh⁴, t'ieh⁴.
	箪⁴	tien⁴.					碟²	tieh⁴.
			TI	敵¹	ti².		蝶²	t'ieh³.
T'AN	探¹	t'an⁴.		提¹	t'i².		躞²	tieh³, tieh⁴.
	攤¹	nan⁴.		堤¹	t'i².		蛱²	chieh², t'ieh³.
	彈²	t'an⁴.		抵²	ti³.		凸⁴	tu¹.
	澹²	t'an⁴.		適²	ti⁴, shih⁴.		跕⁴	tien³.
	覃²	hsin².		鏑²	ti⁴.			
	撣⁴	tan³.		翟²	chai².	T'IEH	帖¹	t'ieh³, t'ieh⁴.
							貼¹	t'ieh⁴.

T'IEH	蝶³	tieh²	T'O	佗¹	t'o², t'o⁴	TUAN	耑¹	chuan¹
	蜨³	chieh², tieh²		斥¹	ch'ih⁴			
	鐵³	t'ieh⁴		他¹	t'a¹	T'UAN	瘓³	huan⁴
	喋⁴	tieh², tieh³		脫¹	t'o³, t'u¹			
				堶²	t'o³	TUI	堆¹	tsui¹
TIEN	掂¹	tien⁴		馱⁴	to⁴		銳⁴	jui⁴, wei⁴
	跕³	tieh⁴		柂⁴	to⁴			
	填⁴	t'ien²		隋³	sui²	T'UI	太¹	t'ai⁴
	闐⁴	t'ien²		唾⁴	t'u⁴		忒¹	t'ai⁴, t'ê⁴
	淀⁴	ting⁴		哪⁴	na¹		推¹	ch'ui¹
	鈿⁴	t'ien²		魄⁴	p'o⁴			
	簟⁴	tan⁴				TUN	惇¹	chun¹
			TOU	都¹	tu¹		蹲¹	ts'un²
T'IEN	悿¹	t'ien³		斗³	t'ou¹		盾³	shun³
	塡²	tien⁴		讀⁴	tu²		鈍⁴	t'un⁴
	闐²	tien⁴					燉⁴	t'un²
	鈿²	tien⁴	T'OU	斗¹	tou³			
	諂³	t'ien⁴		頭¹	t'ou²	T'UN	屯²	chun¹
							鈍²	tun⁴
TING	釘¹	ting⁴	TU	凸¹	tieh⁴		燉²	tun⁴
	挺⁴	t'ing³, t'ing⁴		都¹	tou¹			
	淀⁴	tien⁴		塗¹	t'u¹, t'u²	TUNG	崠¹	tung⁴
				督¹	tu⁴		慟¹	t'ung⁴
T'ING	听¹	yin²		蠹¹	tao⁴		衕¹	t'ung⁴
	廷¹	t'ing²		獨²	tu²			
	蜓¹	t'ing²		犢²	tu³	T'UNG	捅¹	t'ung³
	庭¹	t'ing²		讀²	tou⁴		痌¹	t'ung²
	霆¹	t'ing²		毒²	tu²		筒¹	t'ung³
	聽¹	t'ing⁴		肚³	tu⁴		衕⁴	tung⁴
	挺³	t'ing⁴, ting⁴		土⁴	t'u³		慟⁴	tung⁴
				咄⁴	to⁴			
TIU	㖫³	tiu⁴		度⁴	to², to⁴	TSA	臢¹	tsang¹
				礑⁴	chu⁴		咱¹	cha¹, tsan², tsang²
TO	多¹	to²		突⁴	t'u¹		偺¹	tsan², tsang²
	度⁴	to⁴, tu⁴						
	掇³	to⁴	T'U	脫¹	t'o¹, t'o³	TS'A	—	—
	朶³	tao¹		荒¹	t'u¹			
	跥⁴	to⁴		忑¹	t'ê⁴	TSAI	跌¹	tieh¹, tieh²
	大⁴	chua¹, ta⁴, tai¹		塗¹	t'u², tu¹		仔³	tzŭ³
	澤⁴	chai², tsê²		突¹	tu¹		載³	tsai⁴
	襐⁴	ch'o⁴, chui¹		土³	t'u³			
	咄⁴	tu¹		吐⁴	t'u⁴			
	馱⁴	t'o²		唾⁴	t'o⁴			
	柂⁴	t'o²						

TS'AI	猜[1]	ts'ai[3].	TSÊ	宅[2]	chai[2].	TS'ÊNG	蹭[1]	ts'êng[4].
	豺[2]	ch'ai[2].		責[2]	tsê[4], chai[2].		曾[1]	tsêng[1].
	趾[3]	ch'ai[3], tz'ŭ[3].		則[2]	tzŭ[2].		叢[2]	ts'ung[2].
				賊[2]	tsê[4], tsei[2].			
TSAN	簪[1]	chên[1].		澤[2]	chai[2], to[4].	TSO	作[1]	tso[2], tso[4].
	咱[2]	cha[2], tsa[3], tsang[2].		擇[2]	chai[2].		撮[1]	ts'o[1], ts'o[2].
	偺[2]	tsa[2], tsang[2].		仄[4]	chai[3], chua[3].		齹[1]	ch'ih[1], ts'o[2].
	糌[3]	tso[3].		拙[4]	cho[1].		昨[2]	tsu[4].
	攢[3]	tsan[4].		這[4]	chai[4], chê[4], chei[4], tsên[4], tsêng[4].		鑿[2]	tsao[2].
	暫[4]	chan[4].		柮[4]	cho[2].		桚[3]	tsan[3].
	瓉[4]	chan[4].		側[4]	chai[1], chai[3], ts'ê[4].		繓[3]	tso[4].
	賺[4]	chuan[4], ch'an[4].		窄[3]	chai[3].		怍[4]	cha[4].
				蚱[4]	cha[3], cha[4].		阼[4]	tsu[4].
				摘[4]	chai[1].		做[4]	tsou[4], tsu[4].
TS'AN	參[1]	shên[1], tsên[1], ts'ên[1].		謫[4]	chai[1].			
	慚[2]	ts'an[3].		輟[4]	cho[4].	TS'O	挫[4]	ts'o[4].
	讒[2]	ch'an[1].					撮[4]	ts'o[2], ts'o[4], tso[1].
	燦[3]	ts'an[4].	TS'Ê	欣[1]	hsin[1].		齹[4]	ch'ih[1], tso[1].
	棧[4]	chan[4].		拆[1]	ch'ai[1].		厝[4]	ts'u[4], ts'uan[4].
	儳[4]	ch'an[4].		圻[1]	ch'i[1].		措[4]	ts'u[4].
	譏[4]	ch'an[4], ch'ien[1], ts'ên[4].		冊[1]	ch'ai[3].		錯[4]	ts'u[4].
				側[1]	chai[1], chai[3], tsê[4].			
TSANG	臢[1]	tsa[1].		笑[1]	ch'ieh[4].	TSOU	租[1]	tsu[1].
	臟[1]	tsang[4].					騾[1]	tsou[4].
	髒[1]	tsang[3], tsang[4].	TSEI	賊[2]	tsê[2], tsê[4].		足[2]	chü[2], tsu[2].
	咱[2]	cha[1], tsa[3], tsan[2].					卒[2]	tsu[2].
	偺[2]	tsa[2], tsan[2].	TSÊN	參[2]	shên[1], ts'an[1], ts'ên[1].		族[2]	tsu[2].
	藏[1]	ts'ang[2].		怎[3]	tsêng[3].		阻[3]	chu[3], tsu[3], tsu[4].
				這[4]	chai[4], chê[4], chei[4], tsô[4], tsêng[4].		祖[3]	tsu[3].
				譖[4]	chên[4].		做[4]	tso[4], tsu[4].
TS'ANG	蹌[1]	ch'iang[1].						
	藏[2]	tsang[4].	TS'ÊN	參[1]	shên[1], ts'an[1], tsên[1].	TS'OU	粗[1]	ts'u[1].
				磣[3]	ch'ên[3].		麤[1]	ts'u[1].
TSAO	鑿[2]	tso[2].		襯[4]	ch'ên[4].		醋[4]	ts'u[4].
	皁[4]	ts'ao[3].		親[4]	ch'ên[4].		簇[4]	tsu[4].
	造[4]	ts'ao[4].		讖[4]	ch'an[4], ch'ien[1], ts'an[4].			
	燥[4]	sao[4].				TSU	租[1]	tsou[1].
	譟[4]	sao[4].	TSÊNG	曾[1]	ts'êng[2].		趄[1]	chü[1], ch'ieh[1], ch'ieh[4].
				憎[1]	tsêng[4].		足[2]	chü[2], tsou[2].
TS'AO	操[1]	ts'ao[4].		甑[4]	ching[4], tsêng[4].		卒[2]	tsou[2].
	皁[3]	tsao[4].		怎[3]	tsên[3].		族[2]	tsou[2].
	造[4]	tsao[4].		這[4]	chai[4], chê[4], chei[4], tsê[4], tsên[4].		阻[3]	tsou[3], chu[3], tsu[4].
				綜[4]	tsung[1].		祖[3]	tsou[3].

TSU	詛³	chu³.	TS'UN	躉²	tun¹.	WAN	剜¹	wa².
	悴⁴	ts'ui⁴.					完²	yüan¹, yüan³.
	啐⁴	ts'ui¹, ts'ui⁴.	TSUNG	蹤¹	tsung¹.		宛³	huan², yüan³.
	做⁴	tso⁴, tsou⁴.		縱¹	tsung³, tsung⁴.		婉³	mien³.
	阼⁴	tso⁴.		綜⁴	tsêng⁴.			
	昨²	tso².		種³	chung³, chung⁴.	WANG	芒²	mang².
	簇⁴	ts'ou⁴.		慫³	ts'ung³.		忘⁴	wang⁴.
	蹴⁴	ts'u⁴.		終³	chung¹.		往³	wang⁴.
				從⁴	ts'ung¹, ts'ung⁴.			
TS'U	粗¹	ts'ou¹.		聳⁴	sung³.	WEI	爲¹	wei³.
	麤¹	ts'ou¹.					偉³	wei³, wei⁴.
	厝⁴	ts'o⁴, ts'uan⁴.	TS'UNG	從¹	ts'ung¹, tsung¹.		違²	wei⁴.
	措⁴	ts'o⁴.		叢²	ts'êng².		蝟⁴	wei⁴.
	錯⁴	ts'o⁴.		淙³	ch'uang².		倭¹	wo¹.
	醋⁴	ts'ou⁴.		慫³	tsung³.		微²	wei².
	踧⁴	tsu⁴.					嵬¹	wei².
			TZŬ	子¹	tzŭ³.		巍²	wei².
TSUAN	鑽¹	tsuan³, tsuan⁴.		則²	tsê².		危²	wei³.
				兹¹	tz'ŭ².		爲²	wei⁴.
TS'UAN	炊¹	ch'ui¹.		觜¹	chui¹, tsui³.		謂²	wei⁴.
	攛¹	ch'üan¹.		髭¹	tzŭ³.		尾³	i³.
	驟¹	ts'uan⁴, ch'üan⁴.		仔³	tsai³.		緯³	wei⁴.
	攅¹	ch'üan².					尉⁴	yü⁴.
	攛⁴	tso⁴, ts'u⁴.	TZ'Ŭ	差¹	ch'ih¹, ch'ih², ch'a¹, chai¹, tz'ŭ⁴.		蔚⁴	yü⁴.
	竄⁴	ch'üan⁴.		疵¹	tz'ŭ².		慰⁴	yü⁴.
	爨⁴	ch'üan⁴.		祠²	ssŭ².		銳⁴	jui⁴, tui⁴.
	篡⁴	ch'uan⁴.		詞²	ssŭ².		睿⁴	jui⁴.
				玆²	tzŭ¹.		遺⁴	i².
TSUI	堆¹	tui¹.		辭²	ssŭ².		潰⁴	hui⁴, lei³.
	嘴³	chui¹, tzŭ¹.		此³	tz'ŭ³.			
				跐³	ch'ai¹, ts'ai¹.	WÊN	溫¹	wu¹, wu⁴.
TS'UI	啐¹	ts'ui⁴, sui⁴, ts'u⁴.		伺⁴	ssŭ⁴.		搵³	wên², ên⁴.
	隨¹	sui¹.		刺⁴	ch'i⁴.		蘊⁴	yün⁴.
	倅¹	tsu⁴.		賜⁴	ssŭ⁴.			
						WÊNG	雍¹	yung¹, yang¹.
TSUN	俊⁴	chün⁴.	WA	凹¹	ao², yao¹, yeh⁴.			
	唆¹	so¹.		娃¹	wa².	WO	阿¹	a¹, a³, a⁴, ô¹, o¹.
	峻⁴	chün³, chün⁴.		蛙¹	wai¹.		呵¹	ho¹, ho³.
	竣⁴	chün⁴.		跬³	k'uei³.		倭¹	wei¹.
	餕⁴	chün⁴.		剜²	wan¹.		窩¹	huo¹.
	駿⁴	chün⁴.		斡⁴	kuan³.		訛²	ê², o².
	雋⁴	chien⁴.					我³	o³.
			WAI	歪¹	wai³.		沃⁴	wu⁴.
				蛙¹	wa¹.		握⁴	wu³, yo⁴.

[WU-YO.] APPENDIX III.—THE PEKING SYLLABARY. 197

WU	吾¹	wu².	YAO	若⁴	jê³, jo⁴, yo⁴.	YEN	檐²	tan⁴.
	弧¹	hu².		佻⁴	t'iao¹.		驗³	yen⁴.
	渥¹	yo⁴.		岳⁴	yüeh⁴.		諺⁴	an⁴.
	喔¹	wu⁴, yo⁴.		葯⁴	yo⁴, yüeh⁴.		讞⁴	yeh⁴.
	温¹	wên¹, wu⁴.		溺⁴	ni⁴, niao⁴.			
	誣²	wu⁴.		瘧⁴	niao⁴, nio⁴, nüeh⁴, nüo⁴, yo⁴.	YI.	See I.	
	毋²	wu⁴.		曜⁴	yüeh⁴.			
	圄²	yü³.		耀⁴	yüeh⁴.	YIN	京¹	ching¹, yüan².
	鵜²	wu³.		耀⁴	yo⁴, yüeh⁴.		听²	t'ing¹.
	侮³	wu⁴, hu¹.		嶽⁴	yüeh⁴, yü⁴, yo⁴.		狺²	chin³.
	握³	wo⁴, yo⁴.		樂⁴	lê⁴, lo⁴, yo⁴, yüeh⁴.		憖⁴	jên³.
	舞³	wu⁴.		藥⁴	yo⁴, yüeh⁴.		孕⁴	jên⁴, yün⁴.
	沃⁴	wo⁴.		鑰⁴	yo⁴, yüeh⁴.		媵⁴	ying⁴.
	惡⁴	o⁴.						
	嫗⁴	ou¹, yü¹.	YEH	咽¹	yeh⁴, yen¹, yen⁴.	YING	瑩¹	ying².
				掖¹	i⁴.		盈¹	ying².
YA	扎¹	cha¹, cha², cha³.		爺¹	yeh².		應¹	ying⁴.
	呀¹	a², hsia¹.		呆²	nieh³, ai¹, tai¹.		蠅²	ying².
	枒¹	ya².		耶²	ya².		熒²	yung².
	押³	ya³.		臬⁴	nieh⁴.		瑩²	yung², yung⁴.
	婭⁴	ya⁴.		凹⁴	ao², wa¹, yao¹.		瑩²	yung², yung⁴.
	壓⁴	ya⁴.		頁²	hsieh⁴.		凝²	ning².
	耶²	yeh².		泄⁴	hsieh¹, i⁴.		甬³	yung³.
	涯²	i², yai².		洩⁴	i⁴.		媵⁴	yin⁴.
	亞³	ya⁴.		射⁴	i⁴, shê⁴, shih⁴.			
				拽⁴	chuai¹, chuai⁴, hsieh², hsieh⁴.	YO	約⁴	yao¹, yao⁴, yüeh⁴.
YAI	涯²	i², ya².		葉⁴	shê⁴.		若⁴	jê³, jo⁴, yao⁴.
	挨²	ai¹.		孽⁴	nieh⁴.		岳⁴	yao⁴, yüeh⁴.
	隘⁴	ai⁴, i⁴.		讞⁴	yen⁴.		虐⁴	niao⁴, ning⁴, nio⁴, nüeh⁴, nüo⁴.
				咽⁴	yen⁴, yeh⁴, yeh⁴.		瘧⁴	niao⁴, nio⁴, nüeh⁴, nüo⁴, yao⁴.
YANG	軮¹	yang⁴.					葯⁴	yao⁴, yüeh⁴.
	煬²	yang⁴.	YEN	炎¹	yen².		渥⁴	wu¹.
	痒³	shên¹.		咽¹	yen², yeh¹, yeh⁴.		握⁴	wu³.
				嫣¹	hsien¹.		喔⁴	wu¹, wu⁴.
YAO	凹¹	ao², wa¹, yeh⁴.		燕⁴	yen⁴.		耀⁴	yao⁴, yüeh⁴.
	堯²	yao².		厭¹	yen⁴.		躍⁴	yüeh⁴.
	約²	yao⁴, yo¹, yüeh⁴.		言²	nien², yüan².		樂⁴	lê⁴, lo⁴, yao⁴, yüeh⁴.
	爻²	hsiao².		沿²	yen³, yen⁴.		藥⁴	yao⁴, yüeh⁴.
	肴²	hsiao².		鉛²	ch'ien¹.		嶽⁴	yao⁴, yüeh⁴, yü⁴.
	妖²	yao³.		迢²	yen³.		淪⁴	yüeh⁴.
	杳³	niao³.		挺²	shan¹.		禴⁴	yüeh⁴.
	拗³	ao³.		涎²	hsien².		籥⁴	yüeh⁴.
				緣²	yen⁴, yüan².		鑰⁴	yao⁴, yüeh⁴.

28

YÜ	於¹	yü², yü³.	YÜAN	鳶¹	yüan².	YÜN	暈¹	yün⁴.
	愚¹	yü².		言²	nien², yen².		員²	yüan².
	譽¹	yü², yü⁴.		京²	ching¹, yin¹.		允³	jun³, yu³.
	訏¹	hsü¹.		阮²	yüan³, juan³.		孕⁴	jên⁴, yin⁴.
	余²	êrh³.		員²	yün².		熨⁴	yü⁴.
	庾²	yü³.		捐²	chüan¹.		蘊⁴	wên⁴.
	輿²	yü³.		緣²	yen², yen⁴.			
	愈²	yü⁴.		菀³	yü⁴.	YU	楸¹	ch'iu¹.
	逾²	yü⁴, yüeh⁴.		宛³	wan³, huan².		牛²	niu².
	女³	yü⁴, nü³.					允³	jun³, yün³.
	雨³	yü³.	YÜEH	曰¹	yüeh⁴.		蓒³	yu⁴.
	圄³	wu⁰.		噦¹	yüeh², hui⁴.			
	語³	yü⁴, i⁴.		岳⁴	yao⁴, yo⁴.	YUNG	雍¹	yung³, wêng⁴.
	峴³	hsü¹.		逾⁴	yü², yü⁴.		容²	jung².
	尉⁴	wei⁴.		約⁴	yao¹, yao⁴, yo¹.		溶²	jung².
	蔚⁴	wei⁴.		葯⁴	yao⁴, yo⁴.		榕²	jung².
	慰⁴	wei⁴.		曜⁴	yao⁴.		蓉²	jung².
	熨⁴	yün⁴.		燿⁴	yao⁴.		鎔²	jung².
	疫⁴	i⁴.		耀⁴	yao⁴, yo⁴.		甖²	ying².
	宛⁴	yüan¹.		躍⁴	yo⁴.		榮²	jung².
	嫗⁴	ou¹, wu¹.		樂⁴	lê⁴, lo⁴, yao⁴, yo⁴.		瑩⁴	yung⁴, ying².
	澳⁴	ao⁴.		藥⁴	yao⁴, yo⁴.		螢²	ying².
	燠⁴	ao⁴.		嶽⁴	yao⁴, yo⁴, yü⁴.		榮²	jung².
	嶽⁴	yao⁴, yo⁴, yüeh⁴.		淪⁴	yo⁴.		縈²	jung².
				籥⁴	yo⁴.		融²	jung².
YÜAN	宛¹	yüan³, wan¹.		籲⁴	yo⁴.		甬³	ying¹.
	淵¹	yüan¹.		鑰⁴	yao⁴, yo⁴.			

APPENDIX IV

WRITING EXERCISES.

APPENDIX IV.
WRITING EXERCISES.

The Writing Exercises, as the student will see, repeat the Radicals and other characters made known to him in Parts I, II, and III of the Colloquial Series.

Every character in Chinese is assumed to be written with the eight strokes given below. The rules opposite each of these are abridged from the translation of a well-known set of rules contained in the "Chinese Chrestomathy" of Dr. Bridgman. The directions regarding the position of the writer's hand and pencil following them are from the same work. The names of the strokes are those used at Peking.

1. *tien*   This is made by a slant of the pencil, which moving first towards the right is then turned round towards the left.

2. *hêng*   This is made by a leap of the pencil, which, stopping short on a point, is drawn off to the left.

3. *chih*   Here the pencil must not be held perfectly erect, for then the stroke will lack body.

4. *kou*   The pencil brought down is made to diverge a little, and raised upwards with a jerk.

5. *t'i*   This resembles a part of a broken line, with the point thrown upwards.

6. *p'ieh*   The best form of this is made by turning the pencil's point off to the left, with a heavy stroke.

7. *fu*   This is made by a sudden jerk of the pencil, and should be short and slender.

8. *na*   Here the pencil delicately rises, and then spreads off with a full stroke.

Let the thumb be placed with the back towards the body, facing outwards; let the fore and middle fingers, with the back turned outwards, be brought near it, facing the body,—thus holding fast the pencil; let the fourth and little fingers, placed close together, be brought part way in inside the pencil, pointing towards you, with the fist half open and hollow within, and with the fingers close together.

几	入	亅	一
凵	八	二	丨
刀	冂	亠	丶
力	冖	人	丿
勹	冫	儿	乙

APPENDIX IV.—WRITING EXERCISES.

夕	口	卩	匕
大	土	厂	匚
女	士	厶	匸
子	夂	又	十
宀	夊	口	卜

弋	干	山	寸
弓	幺	巛	小
丑	广	工	尢
彡	又	己	尸
彳	廾	巾	少

APPENDIX IV.—WRITING EXERCISES.

欠	无	攴	心
止	日	文	戈
歹	曰	斗	戶
殳	月	斤	手
毋	木	方	支

玉	片	火	比
瓜	牙	爪	毛
瓦	牛	父	气
甘	犬	爻	氏
生	玄	爿	水

穴	矢	白	用
立	石	皮	田
竹	示	皿	疋
米	内	目	疒
糸	禾	矛	火

舛	臣	而	缶
舟	自	耒	网
艮	至	耳	羊
色	臼	聿	羽
艸	舌	肉	老

APPENDIX IV.—WRITING EXERCISES.

走	豆	两	虍
足	豕	見	虫
身	豸	角	血
車	貝	言	行
辛	赤	谷	衣

面	隶	里	辰
革	隹	金	辵
韋	雨	長	邑
韭	青	門	酉
音	非	阜	采

APPENDIX IV.—WRITING EXERCISES.

鳥	鬥	香	頁
鹵	鬯	馬	風
鹿	鬲	骨	飛
麥	鬼	高	食
麻	魚	髟	首

	齒	鼎	黃
	龍	鼓	黍
	龜	鼠	黑
	侖	鼻	黹
		齊	黽

APPENDIX IV.—WRITING EXERCISES.

沒了甚麼買賣得很	偺們倆這在那兒的	少有好些個你我他	幾千數百萬零來多	兩三第四五六七九

站	頭	開	住	誰
起	知	鋪	著	要
躺	道	關	街	不
地	做	膲	上	是
快	過	出	房	東
慢	前	去	間	進
都	後	往	屋	城
愛	叫	外	裏	家

APPENDIX IV.—WRITING EXERCISES.

坐轎樓下回到驢騾	四輛步頂衙說眞正	抄寫教學請瞧拏字	典話找看先認還肯	告訴呢記問騎跑紙

蠟燈盞隻酒杯茶碗	炕蓆床帳鋪蓋卓椅	聽明也懂平聲忘錯	念完可以給官會分	張筆管墨塊把本書

| 碎今年時令暖和昨 | 滅使燒爐空滿同算 | 破收拾盤碟喫黠吹 | 傢伙橈條倒壺花瓶 | 盅廚煮飯鍋錏勺壞 |

樣	晚	更	刻	天
短	晌	夫	氣	就
雲	午	每	候	定
彩	晗	夜	冷	晝
陰	事	得	熱	晴
霧	情	打	雪	亮
空	擱	罷	涼	鐘
怕	各	早	颳	半

夾	戴	脫	刷	裳
躲	撐	靴	洗	件
褲	帽	雙	臉	太
裁	砍	襪	盆	腌
袵	肩	最	縫	臟
袖	汗	溫	補	換
梳	衫	儘	穿	乾
髮	單	摘	鞋	淨

油	費	賤	吊	針
芝	當	便	票	線
糖	於	宜	桿	胰
鹽	好	輕	秤	澡
粗	煤	重	稱	銀
細	炭	借	價	銅
湯	柴	賬	值	鐵
雞	麪	該	貴	錢

苦乏歇連李箱包袋	船客店掌櫃計受累	路直繞河海邊深淺	熟論石京遠近南北	奶果菜饅喝弄端撒

氈布簍駱駝牲跟班	裝帶馱追趕喚無利	害春夏秋冬腦辮柔	眼睛嘴脣鬍胳臂指	甲抓腰腿壯健輭弱

民	棱	剃	顋	拉
主	踝	胸	頰	拽
爵	脚	背	巴	病
位	體	脊	頦	疼
參	斬	梁	脖	奇
贊	賊	髁	嗓	怪
尊	級	肚	節	眉
武	君	波	刮	鬢

謬普羣耕耨囊總謂	搜律例治理暴虐亂	國章程卡倫巡察刻	退勒索中底全姓名	兵缺額捐充謀策殺

APPENDIX IV.—WRITING EXERCISES.

改妥當專失神參差	思凡揣摩約准否更	巧特意偶然成硬按	混懶惰棍扔放槍恰	之搶奪偷股逃竄散

| 則況且兆吉凶祥瑞 | 貌美陋摔掉擱撘窄 | 阿哈嘎訛衰困極夢 | 掄催語句吵喧嚷哼 | 忙向規幹辦法胡鬧 |

APPENDIX IV.—WRITING EXERCISES.

迎	祖	能	恆	安
接	翁	丟	產	寧
葬	兄	根	朋	順
絲	孫	現	友	寬
團	舍	您	賞	綽
絨	弟	喳	相	貧
尺	奴	親	幫	窮
貨	才	旁	留	窘

| 素原待敦厚薄傲嫉 | 濕曬晒某乍初和別 | 苗嫩桑樹林森綠草 | 對賽嗇吞疊次增蔥 | 昂替挑想怎却睡覺 |

APPENDIX IV.—WRITING EXERCISES.

| 裂行剛纔再等取送 | 須光潤玻璃料擦碰 | 紅藍淡新舊紗氊必 | 拜應陪裱糊匠染顏 | 妬慚愧絕交實憑賓 |

野屯墳墓峯嶺尖男	闊浮橋井坑衖衕巷	從末臺灣江湖流浪	彀斟酌疑惑喊答應	落永湊挪拴套商量

匪	廷	耐	獸	爺
反	建	羞	冒	娘
犯	臨	辱	爽	幼
罪	强	討	靜	輩
死	良	嫌	舒	頑
黨	禁	皇	服	耍
爭	舞	宮	艱	蠢
鬭	爲	朝	難	笨

| 庫宗考如若雜另派 | 牆層掛畫唱曲抽倉 | 尚傳經楷率更濃貼 | 孔聖儒佛廟座僧俗 | 號靖恩赦免隨古世 |

逆	欻	揑	捨	盼
跳	修	洒	礙	望
造	表	灑	碍	列
報	圓	掃	彼	眾
彷	扁	帚	此	涯
彿	剖	砌	處	依
答	寬	砕	偏	戀
歲	枉	狗	或	跨

急	私	欺	容	紀
奉	務	哄	易	壽
求	閒	誆	便	因
託	空	騙	勁	為
發	悶	屈	塗	緣
信	慌	常	喜	故
雇	樂	屢	歡	耽
孩	煩	公	惜	悮

APPENDIX IV.—WRITING EXERCISES.

福	稿	吏	任	撒
命	陳	役	署	謊
運	案	皂	習	賺
志	照	隸	部	星
益	式	供	堂	所
活	脾	稟	司	雖
動	性	帖	委	承
聰	禍	存	員	差

似橫竪傷棚著準	備通共合除剩盈像	悔善惡其餘靈緊預	願功虧辜負抱怨寒

APPENDIX IV.—WRITING EXERCISES.

手	骨	口	人	貝	人
心	血	舌	身	子	氏
用	面	口	心	臣	女
力	目	音	口	士	父
用	鼻	目	手	子	子
工	子	力	足	鬼	戶
入	骨	骨	耳	子	口
門	尸	肉	目	鼓	自
支	口	尸	牙	手	已
用	齒	首	齒		

老小心歹高大大臣手巾	心高用人大小子比父高	小心比方齊心見長見小	食肉革面行文食言土音	舛錯人力行走一齊見面	生長立止甘心辛苦鼎革

老	香	麥	弓	瓦	雨
米	瓜	豆	矢	面	衣
白	肉	角	弓	瓦	皮
米	片	小	刀	片	衣
小	牛	麻	石	刀	舟
米	肉	子	西	子	車
子	羊	竹	瓜	干	車
麥	肉	子	禾	戈	馬
子	鹿	韭	黍	矢	門
牛	肉	黃	米	石	戶

西方欠雨土山子黃土黑	田土山水川谷石穴	角金木水火土又風又雨	羊皮羽毛羊毛香牛皮牛	魚長虫西口馬龍爪老鼠	羊牛馬魚虫飛鳥大鹿金

APPENDIX IV.—WRITING EXERCISES.

色黄而黑香色火石白玉	辰至酉青白黑青黄赤	十口人一方日日月月自	十二里非止一人八口人	斗豆子十斤米一二疋八	土雨水長一寸八寸二八

陋	牀	取	更	兵	奶	平	冬	分	七
亮	狗	夜	步	別	好	幼	凸	匹	九
冒	的	奇	甬	助	尖	必	凹	反	了
冠	直	姓	男	却	州	本	出	太	久
則	知	官	罕	底	年	正	包	天	也
勁	岡	店	良	困	式	民	北	孔	凡
南	者	或	却	壯	成	永	半	少	勺
屋	服	房	阿	巡	有	交	占	尺	千
巷	肯	斧	事	床	次	兆	卡	屯	不
建	花	昂	京	廷	死	全	去	弔	中
後	虎	朋	來	弄	每	匠	可	且	乏
扁	虱	林	兒	弟	百	危	外	主	五
拜	衫	武	兩	往	考	回	左	乍	井
春	表	河	典	我	那	在	巧	允	今
炭	迎	炕	卦	改	你	孕	布	内	六

APPENDIX IV.—WRITING EXERCISES.

| 雲飲疊薈幹廚彙愛斟新瑞盞碎禁羣 | 禽等策粱絲書舒眾街衕輩辜量開間 | 散敦斌斑替朝欵毯然為爺牽發短碎 | 欲貧赦這野雪頂冕壺寒尊就幾換掌 | 率瓶甜產略票章粗累羞翎習旣畫規訛 | 送凑勒匙參專巢帳張趕彩得斬船規訛 | 站缺翁耕能草豈起躬辱酒針陪隻 | 旁書柴殺氣特茲罟疼病矩破祖秦窄 | 虐哀要郐重准匪厚原夏孫家峯羞料 | 牲玻甚皇盅盆看盼矜秋紅美要耐臭 |

麟	辯	類	馥	鮮	靜	舞	貌	團	聖
艷	驟	嚷	騎	尠	頭	餓	賓	墓	葬
鬢	魔	瓣	鏊	黏	鴨	衙	躲	壽	號
鷹	鰲	覺	壞	點	鼐	靠	輕	夢	解
灣	齋	辭	獸	黻	嶺	鞋	尷	對	象
鹽	鬭	釋	臨	黿	幫	魁	魂	慢	賊
釁	聽	響	關	齋	爵	養	麼	旗	跨
豐	囊	飄	韻	竄	牆	髮	璃	獸	路
鼇	龔	馨	鬍	舊	瓢	鬧	層	豎	載
鑒	龕	鹹	魯	謬	糞	黎	窗	篡	靖
鬱	龢	麩	麒	豐	鼇	學	疑	聞	靴
	驚	犧	麗	饜	舉	耨	皺	臺	韭
	體	黨	黼	醫	艱	親	窮	與	鳳
	髓	齡	鼗	雙	韓	錯	罷	蜜	亂
	鬭	蠹	駒	雞	馘	隸		說	憑

ERRATA AND ADDENDA.

Appendix II.	Page 54.		Under Radical 入 insert "兩 Part III, 1."
Appendix III.	Page 88.	36. Col. 2.	Omit the circle attached to 直.
,,	,, 101.	101. ,, 2.	For 侯° read 侯°.
,,	,, 123.	190. ,, 2.	After 梁 insert a circle.
,,	,, 138.	259. ,, 2.	,, 瘢 ,, ,,
,,	,, 140.	271. ,, 4.	,, 愎 ,, ,,
,,	,, 159.	358. ,, 1.	Omit the circle attached to 額.
,,	,, 161.	369. ,, 1.	For 臘° read 臢°.
,,	,, 163.	389. ,, 2.	After 隨 insert a circle.

SHANGHAI:
STATISTICAL DEPARTMENT OF THE INSPECTORATE GENERAL OF CUSTOMS.

"早期北京话珍本典籍校释与研究"丛书总目录

早期北京话珍稀文献集成

（一）日本北京话教科书汇编

《燕京妇语》等八种　　　　　　四声联珠
华语跬步　　　　　　　　　　　官话指南·改订官话指南
亚细亚言语集　　　　　　　　　京华事略·北京纪闻
北京风土编·北京事情·北京风俗问答
伊苏普喻言·今古奇观·搜奇新编

（二）朝鲜日据时期汉语会话书汇编

改正增补汉语独学　　　　　　　修正独习汉语指南
高等官话华语精选　　　　　　　官话华语教范
速修汉语自通　　　　　　　　　无先生速修中国语自通
速修汉语大成　　　　　　　　　官话标准：短期速修中国语自通
中语大全　　　　　　　　　　　"内鲜满"最速成中国语自通

（三）西人北京话教科书汇编

寻津录　　　　　　　　　　　　北京话语音读本
语言自迩集　　　　　　　　　　语言自迩集（第二版）
官话类编　　　　　　　　　　　言语声片
华语入门　　　　　　　　　　　华英文义津逮
汉英北京官话词汇　　　　　　　北京官话：汉语初阶
汉语口语初级读本·北京儿歌

（四）清代满汉合璧文献萃编

清文启蒙　　　　　　　　　清话问答四十条
一百条·清语易言　　　　　清文指要
续编兼汉清文指要　　　　　庸言知旨
满汉成语对待　　　　　　　清文接字·字法举一歌
重刻清文虚字指南编

（五）清代官话正音文献

正音撮要　　　　　　　　　正音咀华

（六）十全福

（七）清末民初京味儿小说书系

新鲜滋味　　　　　　　　　过新年
小额　　　　　　　　　　　北京
春阿氏　　　　　　　　　　花鞋成老
评讲聊斋　　　　　　　　　讲演聊斋

（八）清末民初京味儿时评书系

益世余谭——民国初年北京生活百态
益世余墨——民国初年北京生活百态

早期北京话研究书系

早期北京话语法研究
早期北京话语法演变专题研究
早期北京话语气词研究
晚清民国时期南北官话语法差异研究
基于清后期至民国初期北京话文献语料的个案研究
高本汉《北京话语音读本》整理与研究
北京话语音演变研究
文化语言学视域下的北京地名研究
语言自迩集——19世纪中期的北京话（第二版）
清末民初北京话语词汇释